THE CAMBRIDGE

History of the Book in Britain

*

VOLUME I

c. 400–1100

This is the first comprehensive survey of the history of the book in Britain from Roman through Anglo-Saxon to early Norman times. The expert contributions explore the physical form of books, including their codicology, script and decoration, examine the circulation and exchange of manuscripts and texts between England, Ireland, the Celtic realms and the Continent, discuss the production, presentation and use of different classes of texts, ranging from fine service-books to functional schoolbooks, and evaluate the libraries that can be associated with particular individuals and institutions. The result is an authoritative account of the first millennium of the history of books, manuscript-making and literary culture in Britain which, intimately linked to its cultural contexts, sheds vital light on broader patterns of political, ecclesiastical and cultural history, extending from the period of the Vindolanda writing tablets through the age of Bede and Alcuin to the time of the Domesday Book.

RICHARD GAMESON is Professor of the History of the Book at Durham University. He has published over seventy studies of medieval manuscripts, book culture and art history, including *The Early Medieval Bible* (1994), *The Role of Art in the Late Anglo-Saxon Church* (1995), *St Augustine and the Conversion of England* (1999), *The Manuscripts of Early Norman England* (1999), *Codex Aureus: An Eighth-Century Gospel-Book* (2001–2) and *The Earliest Books of Canterbury Cathedral* (2008).

THE CAMBRIDGE

History of the Book in Britain

The history of the book offers a distinctive form of access to the ways in which human beings have sought to give meaning to their own and others' lives. Our knowledge of the past derives mainly from texts. Landscape, architecture, sculpture, painting and the decorative arts have their stories to tell and may themselves be construed as texts; but oral tradition, manuscripts, printed books and those other forms of inscription and incision such as maps, music and graphic images, have a power to report even more directly on human experience and the events and thoughts which shaped it. In principle, any history of the book should help to explain how these particular texts were created, why they took the form they did, their relations with other media, especially in the twentieth century, and what influence they had on the minds and actions of those who heard, read or viewed them. Its range, too – in time, place and the great diversity of the conditions of text production, including reception – challenges any attempt to define its limits and give an account adequate to its complexity. It addresses, whether by period, country, genre or technology, widely disparate fields of enquiry, each of which demands and attracts its own forms of scholarship.

The Cambridge History of the Book in Britain, planned in seven volumes, seeks to represent much of that variety, and to encourage new work, based on knowledge of the creation, material production, dissemination and reception of texts. Inevitably its emphases will differ from volume to volume, partly because the definitions of Britain vary significantly over the centuries, partly because of the varieties of evidence extant for each period, and partly because of the present uneven state of knowledge. Tentative in so many ways as the project necessarily is, it offers the first comprehensive account of the book in Britain over one and a half millennia.

JOHN BARNARD · DAVID MCKITTERICK · I. R. WILLISON
General Editors

Frontispiece: The Durham Gospels: incipit to John's Gospel (DCL, A.II.17, fol. 1r)

THE CAMBRIDGE

History of the Book in Britain

*

VOLUME I

c. 400–1100

*

Edited by

RICHARD GAMESON

CAMBRIDGE
UNIVERSITY PRESS

CAMBRIDGE UNIVERSITY PRESS
Cambridge, New York, Melbourne, Madrid, Cape Town,
Singapore, São Paulo, Delhi, Tokyo, Mexico City

Cambridge University Press
The Edinburgh Building, Cambridge CB2 8RU, UK

Published in the United States of America by Cambridge University Press, New York

www.cambridge.org
Information on this title: www.cambridge.org/9780521583459

First published 2012

Printed in the United Kingdom at the University Press, Cambridge

A catalogue record for this publication is available from the British Library

ISBN 978-0-521-58345-9 Hardback

Contents

PART III TYPES OF BOOKS AND THEIR USES

PART IV COLLECTIONS OF BOOKS

PART V CODA

Plates

Contributors

MICHELLE P. BROWN, Professor of Medieval Manuscript Studies, School of Advanced Studies, University of London

T. M. CHARLES-EDWARDS, Professor of Celtic and Fellow of Jesus College, University of Oxford

JULIA CRICK, Associate Professor, Department of History, University of Exeter

NANCY EDWARDS, Professor in Archaeology, School of History, Welsh History and Archaeology, Bangor University

FIONA GAMESON, Tutor, St Cuthbert's Society, Durham University

RICHARD GAMESON, Professor of the History of the Book, Durham University

DAVID GANZ, olim Professor of Palaeography, King's College, University of London

MARY GARRISON, Lecturer in Medieval History, Department of History, University of York

M. R. GODDEN, Rawlinson and Bosworth Professor of Anglo-Saxon, University of Oxford

MICHAEL GULLICK, Independent Scholar, Walkern, Hertfordshire

SCOTT GWARA, Professor in the Department of English Language and Literature, University of South Carolina

DAVID HOWLETT, Director and Editor, Dictionary of Medieval Latin from British Sources, Oxford

ROHINI JAYATILAKA, Senior Research Fellow, Faculty of English, University of Oxford

SIMON KEYNES, Elrington and Bosworth Professor of Anglo-Saxon, and Fellow of Trinity College, University of Cambridge

MICHAEL LAPIDGE, olim Elrington and Bosworth Professor of Anglo-Saxon, University of Cambridge and Notre Dame Professor of English at the University of Notre Dame, now Fellow Emeritus, Clare College, Cambridge

ROSALIND LOVE, Senior Lecturer in Insular Latin, Department of Anglo-Saxon, Norse and Celtic, and Fellow of Robinson College, University of Cambridge

PATRICK MCGURK, olim Birkbeck College, University of London

HELEN MCKEE, Independent Scholar, Englefield Green, Surrey

ROSAMOND MCKITTERICK, Professor of Medieval History and Fellow of Sidney Sussex College, University of Cambridge

RICHARD MARSDEN, Professor Emeritus, School of English Studies, University of Nottingham

NANCY NETZER, Professor of Art History and Director of the McMullen Museum of Art, Boston College

THOMAS O'LOUGHLIN, Professor of Historical Theology, Department of Theology and Religious Studies, University of Nottingham

ANDY ORCHARD, Provost and Vice-Chancellor, Trinity College, Toronto

RICHARD W. PFAFF, Professor Emeritus of History, University of North Carolina, Chapel Hill

SUSAN RANKIN, Professor of Medieval Music and Fellow of Emmanuel College, Cambridge

BARBARA RAW, Professor Emerita of Anglo-Saxon, University of Keele

REBECCA RUSHFORTH, olim Research Associate in the Department of Anglo-Saxon, Norse and Celtic, and Research Fellow of Corpus Christi College, University of Cambridge

DONALD SCRAGG, Professor Emeritus of Anglo-Saxon Studies, University of Manchester

R. S. O. TOMLIN, University Lecturer in Late Roman History and Fellow of Wolfson College, University of Oxford

M. JANE TOSWELL, Department of English, University of Western Ontario

TERESA WEBBER, Senior Lecturer in Palaeography and Codicology and Fellow of Trinity College, University of Cambridge

PATRICK WORMALD (†), olim Fellow of Wolfson College, Oxford

Acknowledgements

Colophons in medieval manuscripts sometimes allude in more or less explicit terms to the vast amount of labour that the production of the volume has entailed and to the burden that it has represented. Some provide information that permits the reader to deduce how long the volume took to write. Others helpfully outline the respective contributions of co-workers, even occasionally commenting on their application to the task. Like most collaborative volumes of this kind, the present one has taken longer than was once hoped.

Of all those who have been involved, I wish first to thank the general editors of this series, John Barnard, David McKitterick and Ian Willison. They have provided crucial support in guiding this volume towards completion. At Cambridge University Press, Linda Bree and Maartje Scheltens have been of quite exceptional help. Then, Kirsty Bennett provided invaluable assistance with the time-consuming business of processing the indices. Above all, it is to my wife that I owe the continuous support that alone has made a Sisyphean task sustainable. Sisyphus' labour was, of course, unending: the volume that you have in your hands marks an end in itself, though far from an end to the study of the subject. To borrow another topos that runs from ancient author, through medieval scribe, to modern writer, 'scripsi ut potui non ut volui'.

Richard Gameson

Abbreviations

ANS	*[Proceedings of the Battle Conference for] Anglo-Norman Studies*
ASC	*Anglo Saxon Chronicle*
ASE	*Anglo-Saxon England*
BAV	Biblioteca Apostolica Vaticana, Vatican City
BHL	*Bibliotheca Hagiographica Latina Antiquae et Mediae Aetatis*, ed. Socii Bollandiani, 2 vols. (Brussels, 1898–1901), *Supplementi* (Brussels, 1911), *Novum Supplementum* (Brussels, 1986), cited by item number
BL	British Library, London
BM	Bibliothèque municipale
BnF	Bibliothèque nationale de France, Paris
BodL.	Bodleian Library, Oxford
BR	Bibliothèque royale Albert I, Brussels
BSB	Bayerische Staatsbibliothek, Munich
CBMLC	Corpus of British Medieval Library Catalogues
CCCC	Corpus Christi College, Cambridge
CCCM	Corpus Christianorum Continuatio Mediaevalis
CCCO	Corpus Christi College, Oxford
CCSL	Corpus Christianorum Series Latina
CIL	*Corpus Inscriptionum Latinarum*, ed. T. Mommsen *et al.* (Berlin, 1869–), cited by series and entry number
CL	Cathedral Library
CLA	*Codices Latini Antiquiores*, ed. E. A. Lowe, 11 vols., plus Supplement (Oxford, 1934–71); 2nd edn of vol. II (Oxford, 1972)
Colophons	[Bénédictins du Bouveret], *Colophons de manuscrits occidentaux des origines au XVIe siècle*, 6 vols. (Friburg, 1965–82)
CMCS	*Cambridge/Cambrian Medieval Celtic Studies*
CSASE	Cambridge Studies in Anglo-Saxon England
CUL	Cambridge University Library

DCL	Durham Cathedral Library
EEMF	Early English Manuscripts in Facsimile
EETS	Early English Texts Society
EHR	*English Historical Review*
ep.	epistola
ES	*English Studies*
facs.	facsimile
HBS	Henry Bradshaw Society
HE	Bede, *Historia ecclesiastica*, ed. Colgrave and Mynors (Oxford, 1969)
JEH	*Journal of Ecclesiastical History*
JRS	*Journal of Roman Studies*
JTS	*Journal of Theological Studies*
KB	Kongelige Bibliotek; Kungliga Bibliotek
LB	Landesbibliothek
MGH	Monumenta Germaniae Historica
New Pal. Soc.	New Palaeographical Society, *Facsimiles of Ancient Manuscripts*, 1st and 2nd series (London, 1903–30)
NLS	National Library of Scotland, Edinburgh
NLW	National Library of Wales, Aberystwyth
n.s.	new series
ÖNB	Österreichische Nationalbibliothek
ODNB	*Oxford Dictionary of National Biography*
o.s.	old series
O.S. facs.	*Facsimiles of Anglo-Saxon Charters*, 3 vols. (Ordnance Survey, Southampton, 1878–84)
Pal. Soc.	Palaeographical Society, *Facsimiles of Ancient Manuscripts* (London, 1874–94)
PBA	*Proceedings of the British Academy*
PL	*Patrologiae Latinae Cursus Completus*, ed. J.-P. Migne, 221 vols. (Paris, 1844–64)
PML	Pierpont Morgan Library, New York
q., qq.	quire(s)
RB	*Revue bénédictine*
RIA	Royal Irish Academy, Dublin
RIB	*Roman Inscriptions of Britain* (Collingwood and Wright 1990–5, 1995)
RS	Rolls Series
s.a.	sub anno

SB	Staatsbibliothek
SC	Summary Catalogue (BodL.)
Settimane	*Settimane di Studio del Centro Italiano di studi sull'alto medioevo* (Spoleto)
s.n.	no number
s.s.	supplementary series
Tab. Sulis	Tomlin 1988
Tab. Vindol.	Bowman and Thomas 1994
TCBS	*Transactions of the Cambridge Bibliographical Society*
TCC	Trinity College, Cambridge
TCD	Trinity College, Dublin
UB	Universitätsbibliothek; Universiteitsbibliotheek
UL	University Library

Dating conventions and formulae

Few of the books that are the subject matter of this volume are dated or datable on internal grounds; in most cases the dates assigned to them are informed estimates based on their appearance. In the footnotes and certain listings, such estimated dates are generally indicated by the use of a formula consisting of a Roman numeral, which denotes the century, plus a superscript number, fraction or word, which signals the part thereof. Thus 'x' means the tenth century as a whole, 'x^{in}' the beginning of the tenth century, '$\mathrm{x}^{1/4}$' the first quarter of the tenth century, 'x^{1}' the first half of the tenth century, '$\mathrm{x}^{\mathrm{med}}$' the middle of the tenth century, 'x^{2}' the second half of the tenth century, '$\mathrm{x}^{3/3}$' the last third of the tenth century, 'x^{ex}' the end of the tenth century, 'x/xi' the end of the tenth or the beginning of the eleventh century; and so on. The use of two superscript qualifiers indicates that the likely date straddles the periods in question: thus '$\mathrm{xi}^{\mathrm{med}-3/4}$' signifies the middle to the third quarter of the eleventh century. Correspondingly, 'viii–ix' denotes eighth to ninth century. *s.* (= *saeculum*) means 'century'.

1

From Vindolanda to Domesday: the book in Britain from the Romans to the Normans

RICHARD GAMESON

Covering more than a millennium of the history of the book in Britain, the present volume by itself deals with a longer period than do all the rest of this series put together. Extending from Roman Britain to the first generation of the Anglo-Norman realm, it embraces both of the two 'memorable' dates in English history (55 BC and AD 1066); and stretching in bibliographical terms from the Vindolanda Tablets through the Lindisfarne Gospels to the Domesday Book, it includes some of the most famous and fascinating artefacts of written culture ever produced in these isles.

The first millennium is also notable as the period during which Britain was repeatedly invaded – by Romans, Anglo-Saxons, Vikings and Normans – with a consequent ebb, flow and cross-fertilisation of cultural life. A grand narrative of bibliographical history may be constructed around these momentous events. In outline, one sees the arrival of books and Latin literacy with the Romans; their decline in lowland Britain (in contrast to their presumed survival in other regions) following the departure of the legions and the settlement of the Anglo-Saxons; and the reintroduction of (now specifically Christian) literary culture to these areas as an integral part of the missions from Rome and Ireland, leading in turn to masterpieces of book production and decoration from the end of the seventh century into the eighth. Then, during the period of the Viking invasions, there was the demise of book-making and even of clerical literacy. A revival from the end of the ninth century, slow at first, quickened during the second half of the tenth century, and was complemented by a growth in the production of works in Old English, a phenomenon which flourished above all in the eleventh century. The last main development (only the earliest stages of which fall within our period) was a reorientation in perceived library needs in the aftermath of the Norman Conquest, and hence a change in the type of books that were sought and copied.

The many individual chapters that follow, fleshing out this skeleton, deal with specific topics, generally within particular sub-periods. To introduce the field as a whole, providing a context for all this material, it will be useful to highlight here some broad points of comparison and contrast between the world of books in the main periods – Roman, pre-Viking, post-Viking, early Norman – that are treated in this volume.

Although no examples have come down to us, we may reasonably assume that most of the books that were available in Roman Britain will have taken the form of *rotuli* (rolls). There is no reason to doubt that the owners of villas in Britain, like their counterparts elsewhere in the Roman Empire, will have had collections of texts on *rotuli*, which were stored in *capsae* (bucket-like cases) or in deep cupboards whose internal spaces may have been subdivided into 'pigeon holes'. The rise of the codex to a predominant position as the vehicle for literary texts, a phenomenon of the fourth century AD, is likely to have touched Britain as much as elsewhere. Another of the key bibliographical changes of late Antiquity, the adoption of parchment instead of papyrus as the support for formal writing, may indeed have been precocious in Britain owing to the abundance of suitable animals (for parchment) on the one hand and the great distance from the Nile (the source of papyrus) on the other. As the codex had a close association with Christianity, one presumes that the earliest Christians in Britain, too, will have had their scriptures in this form, and that after the edict of Milan (AD 313) it, like the religion, will have prospered. Whatever the truth of this point, the future belonged to the codex, and all the extant books considered in the present volume take this form. We may accordingly list the shape and nature of books among the many points of contrast distinguishing the culture of Britain in the fourth century from the seventh: at the end of the fourth century, while new books may have been made as codices (as was the norm for Christian scriptures), older ones in *rotulus* form were doubtless still in circulation. The books that missionaries brought to Anglo-Saxon England from the end of the sixth century onwards and all those that were then made in Britain were of codex form.

Concerning the status of those who manufactured books, one presumes that in Roman Britain (as elsewhere in the Roman Empire), it was principally the responsibility of appropriately qualified slaves, freedmen and 'secretaries'. By contrast, for much of the Anglo-Saxon period – and in the poorly documented British and Celtic realms no less than in the English regions – the production of books was manifestly the prerogative of ecclesiastics, a few of whom may occasionally have been working for important lay folk. Only at the very end of our period do we begin to encounter evidence of paid professional involvement – and in the context of production that is still firmly linked to ecclesiastical centres.

In terms of their content, the book collections of Roman Britain will have been dominated by the Latin classics – as is implied by the citations that appear on a couple of the writing tablets from Vindolanda and by the subject matter of contemporary mosaics – with, in the fourth century, an increasing number of Christian texts (sufficient, evidently, to educate the infamous late antique heretic, Pelagius (fl. *c.* 380–420)). In early Christian Britain, by contrast, gospel-books and psalters were doubtless the most common and widely distributed texts, along with some liturgica. Pedagogy may have provided some common ground between all our periods – to the extent that the curriculum of Christian schools incorporated texts and grammars of Antiquity and late Antiquity.

A handful of exceptional early Anglo-Saxon centres, such as Wearmouth-Jarrow and York in the north and Canterbury and Malmesbury in the south, accumulated a sufficient quantity and range of books for their holdings to be described as libraries. Very few of the manuscripts in question appear to have survived the period of the Viking invasions, let alone down to the present day. Insight into the nature of these collections is largely dependent on the writings of their most illustrious alumni. Notwithstanding the uncertainties and ambiguities involved in deducing from haphazard citations, allusions and requests what may actually have been in the book cupboards, such libraries would seem to have numbered a couple of hundred volumes at the most. Without placing too much weight on the details of Alcuin's poetic evocation of the holdings of York in the later eighth century, the general impression that he gives of a cross-section of the writings of the Fathers of the church along with some Latin classics and other pedagogical works is likely to be sound.

The collections that were amassed by the major monasteries of late Anglo-Saxon England seem on the whole to have been more restricted in range, with an emphasis on devotional and pastoral texts rather than the writings of the church Fathers, and with multiple copies of the works of a small number of late antique and Anglo-Saxon Christian poets rather than a range of classical ones. On the other hand, this was the period when works in the vernacular, above all homily collections, began to be produced in significant numbers, some destined for wide distribution. While many late Anglo-Saxon volumes continued to see active service in the aftermath of the Norman Conquest, there was then a reorientation towards accumulating runs of patristics. A 'snapshot' of one important monastic book collection at the very end of our period is provided by the overview of Ely's holdings that is embedded within the *Liber Eliensis*: in or around 1093 the foundation possessed some 300 manuscripts, of which nearly 100 were service-books (including twenty-two psalters, nineteen missals and fourteen gospel-books) and just over 200 were other types of texts.

If in Roman Britain books might be used for entertainment as well as for education and religion, the first role was hardly to survive into subsequent centuries. Conversely, in the Anglo-Saxon period (as presumably in poorly documented sub-Roman Britain) books took on enhanced functions as a prerequisite of Christian devotion, some moreover becoming cult objects in their own right. From *c.* 600 the works of Latin classical authors which might previously have been read not only as an essential part of a liberal education but also as a civilised pastime were – if they were used at all – exclusively an adjunct to a more narrowly focused educational curriculum wherein they illustrated good style for students of the language. It was for this purpose, one presumes, that St Dunstan (d. 988) famously had a Celtic copy of Ovid's *Ars amatoria* (Book I) in his so-called 'Classbook', nestling between Eutyches' *Ars de uerbo* on the one hand and computistical and liturgical texts on the other.

Concomitant with their centrality to Christian devotion and ceremony in the early Middle Ages, gospel-books and psalters became foci for calligraphic elaboration and artwork. If there were ornamented copies of classical texts in Roman Britain, their decoration is likely to have taken the form of illustrations to the text, with perhaps a prefatory image of the author shown as a contemplative philosopher-type. Pictorial art in the finest books of Christian Britain (as in early medieval Europe as a whole) was often directed towards stressing the divine inspiration of the authors and hence the sacred status of their texts. Furthermore, some of the lettering of these holy works might be embellished, projecting by means of ornamentation the sacrality of their words and messages. Luxurious treasure bindings completed the transformation of such books from vehicles of written communication to resplendent, sacred objects with great intrinsic as well as symbolic or communicative value. St Boniface (d. 754), the Anglo-Saxon missionary to Germany, advertised the values and purposes of such deluxe volumes when requesting Abbess Eadburh of Minster-in-Thanet to make him a golden copy of the Petrine Epistles, the appearance of which would impress the heathen with its importance; moreover, as he goes on to underline, the making of such a manuscript would itself bring spiritual rewards to those involved.

If the percentage of society that was personally literate will always have been small, it was surely significantly higher in Roman Britain than in early Christian Anglo-Saxon England. A presumed expansion in the numbers of literate clerics in the later seventh to eighth centuries, as oblates benefited from the educational opportunities provided by newly established religious foundations, was followed by a demonstrable contraction in the ninth century – a phenomenon eloquently lamented by Alfred the Great (d. 899). The subsequent growth in the use of the vernacular as a literary language, decisively promoted by the same king, meant that the content of certain types of books was in principle accessible to all hearers at least. Indeed, certain collections of Old English homilies seem to have been multiplied and distributed precisely in order to reach the widest possible audience in this way. In the generation after the Norman Conquest, as the larger ecclesiastical institutions turned their energies towards amassing runs of patristics, the emphasis was upon books for *lectio divina*, even theological study, but for internal use – i.e. there was a wider range of texts and a greater depth of holdings for just one restricted class of audience. Moreover, the relatively pristine condition of certain of these volumes gives rise to a suspicion that they may sometimes have been copied more to complete 'sets' than for active service: they filled a gap in a collection rather than meeting the urgent needs of readers.

Many of the books used in Roman Britain are likely to have been imported from elsewhere in the Roman Empire, arriving via well-organised routes of communication. The possibility of such distribution lies behind the rueful quip of the classical poet Martial (d. AD 101×4) to the effect that his work was even read in Britain (*Epigrammaton libri XII*: XI, 3). Notwithstanding the subsequent demise of a pan-European political authority, the circulation of books between Britain and her neighbours was to remain a major phenomenon throughout our period; moreover, Ireland was added to the places with which there was bibliographical exchange. The Christian missions from Rome (via Francia) and from Ireland defined the earliest channels for the importation of books to Anglo-Saxon England; by the eighth century England was herself exporting manuscripts (including a few that had come from Italy a century earlier) to the new mission fields in Germany. From the end of the ninth century books started to be imported to England from the Carolingian Empire, with some arriving from the Celtic realms; while from the end of the tenth century Anglo-Saxon books were increasingly reaching the Continent, above all nearby Flanders and Normandy. The Norman Conquest, which fostered bibliographical exchange between England and Normandy in particular, was merely refocusing a very long-established tradition.

The phenomenon continued at more local levels. There is plentiful evidence, direct and indirect, for the circulation of books and texts between different regions of Britain as between individual centres within regions. In the eighth century Albinus of Canterbury dispatched material to Bede at Jarrow, and Milret of Worcester's copy of Porfyrius was on loan to a Cuthbert who was almost certainly the archbishop of Canterbury of that name; at the end of the ninth century King Alfred envisaged sending a copy of the Old English *Pastoral Care* to all the bishoprics in his kingdom, where they might in turn be copied for further distribution; from the early eleventh century Ælfric's *Sermones catholici* were being disseminated around southern England; and when at the end of the century St Albans was building up its library by copying exemplars that were supplied by Lanfranc at Canterbury, it typified a trend. Such narratives of bibliographical exchange sometimes correspond to broader patterns of intercourse known from other sources, at other times they complement them, but the fact that books and texts were frequently on the move throughout our period is not in doubt.

The survival rate of books from our four broad sub-periods is most uneven. Younger volumes have of course had fewer centuries and hazards to traverse, and hence a stronger survival is to be expected. In addition, the ravages of the Viking age clearly inflicted particularly severe damage on the great book collections of early Anglo-Saxon England, just as the arrival of the Anglo-Saxons themselves had doubtless been highly destructive to the literary remains of Roman and sub-Roman Britain. Moreover, in this last case (the earliest material) there was the additional vulnerability that some, perhaps many, Roman books were made of papyrus, a far less durable material than parchment, particularly in the cool damp climate of Britain. Thus while we have hundreds of manuscripts from late Anglo-Saxon and early Norman times, and barely a hundred (of which many are fragmentary) from pre-Viking England, there is not a single example from Roman Britain.

There are no less significant imbalances within the body of extant material itself. The survival of books from the British and Celtic realms is very poor in comparison with that from England (and the manuscripts from these regions which have come down to us had often migrated to England or elsewhere at some point prior to the sixteenth century). It is inconceivable that the many learned British (*plures uiri doctissimi*) mentioned by Bede (*Historia ecclesiastica*, II, 2) did not have access to books, possibly in significant quantities, but no trace of one now remains. Again, despite fairly plentiful evidence for the early church in Cornwall and Wales, no manuscripts older than the ninth century survive from these regions. Correspondingly, it is difficult to point to manuscripts of Scottish provenance before the tenth-century Book of Deer (demonstrably at Deer in Aberdeenshire in the twelfth century) and the eleventh-century Anglo-Saxon gospel-lectionary that belonged to Queen Margaret of Scotland

(d. 1093); yet the traces of parchment-making unearthed at the monastery of Portmahomack in Pictland, and Bede's reference to the ecclesiastical writings (*scripturae ecclesiasticae*) read by the Pictish king Nechtan at the beginning of the eighth century (*Historia ecclesiastica*, v, 21), remind us of the presence and manufacture of books there at a much earlier date. Sadly, but inevitably, however, given the dearth of extant material, these regions and their early bibliographical history are doomed to be under-represented in any discussion: we must remain mindful that this is so.

The imbalances continue into the (rather larger) corpus of Anglo-Saxon books. The sample of early Anglo-Saxon manuscripts is misleadingly dominated by fine decorated ones – which doubtless owed their survival to their high grade and treasured status. And even from late Anglo-Saxon and early Norman England, periods when manuscripts are altogether more plentiful, various classes of material are massively under-represented in the sample – school books, for instance, because they were 'used to death', and liturgical books because, if they had not already been superseded and scrapped centuries before, they were outlawed at the Reformation. Furthermore, many individual centres of production and use have misleadingly poor showings. The nature (whether 'secular' or monastic) of a foundation in the sixteenth century and its survival or otherwise at the Dissolution of the Monasteries (1536–40) had an enormous impact on the transmission of its books, as did its geographical location and the existence or otherwise of conveniently placed antiquaries and local collectors. Moreover, in the absence of early medieval catalogues and 'library markings', our ability to localise surviving manuscripts to a particular house often depends on individual library practices during the later Middle Ages – the survival and quality of booklists and catalogues, the existence of identifiable shelf-marks and *ex libris* inscriptions. Indeed, there are only three centres – Worcester and the two Canterbury houses, St Augustine's and Christ Church – for which we have sufficient attributable manuscripts to permit a rounded examination of their book culture during the late Anglo-Saxon period.

Yet, as the previous paragraph hinted, our manuscripts are also part of the story that is told in successive volumes of *The Cambridge History of the Book in Britain*: they were used and shelved in different ways in the later Middle Ages, sometimes being listed in catalogues (where their age or language was occasionally noted as distinctive); they were alienated, dismembered and subsequently 'collected' in the sixteenth century; passing thereafter through various hands into institutional *fonds*, coming to be valued, preserved, studied and exhibited as antiquities in modern times.

As the chapters within this volume tend to focus on evolving trends and innovations, it is worth reminding ourselves at the outset that 'new' collections often included 'old' books. A famous and relatively well-documented example of the phenomenon is the Lindisfarne Gospels (British Library, Cotton Nero D.iv). The oldest record concerning its production and function – an undatable Old English poem preserved within a later prose account – notes that the manuscript was written by Bishop Eadfrith (d. 721) 'for all the *halgum* who are on [Lindisfarne]' and that it was bound by Æthilwald, bishop of Lindisfarne, and adorned with a treasure cover by Billfrith the anchorite. Depending upon how one interprets *halgum* in this context, the verse may imply that the gospel-book had been made for all Lindisfarne's saints (that is: specifically dedicated to Aidan, Cuthbert and Oswald) or for all its holy folk (namely for the use and benefit of all the members of the community, present as well as past). Be that as it may, it manifestly was and remained one of the community's key treasures, carried onwards by the brothers when eventually, in 875, they abandoned Lindisfarne. The community and the gospels came to rest at Chester-le-Street in the 880s. Here, in the third quarter of the tenth century the manuscript was supplied with a full interlinear Old English gloss by the priest Aldred; he appended an elaborate colophon, restating the circumstances of the original production of the volume, weaving his own contribution as glossator into the account of its history: 'Eadfrith, Ethilwald, Bilfrith, Aldred made or, as the case may be, embellished this gospel-book for God and Cuthbert'. Artfully expanding the verses that he had inherited (whether in oral or written form is unknown), Aldred also refocused (or articulated a refocusing of) the function of the book: 'Eadfrith bishop of the Lindisfarne Church originally wrote this book for God and for St Cuthbert and – jointly – for all the saints whose relics were in the island.' By the tenth century, then, the manuscript was explicitly seen as made for a celestial company, above all God and St Cuthbert; indeed Ealdred tells us that his own (new) work as glossator was accomplished 'with the help of God and St Cuthbert'.

In 995, within a generation of Aldred's contribution, the community of St Cuthbert (and its gospels) moved on to Durham, which in the aftermath of the Norman Conquest was reformed into a Benedictine priory (1083). The continuing importance of the venerable Anglo-Saxon gospel-book to this new Benedictine community at the northern extremity of the fledgling Anglo-Norman realm is underlined in the 'house history' that was written at the beginning of the twelfth century by its cantor, Symeon. He it was who recorded how the Lindisfarne Gospels had played a decisive role in the history of the community at one of its darkest hours. During its wanderings, the community had resolved to return to Ireland, and duly set sail; however, when their gospel-book 'ornamented with gold and gems' was washed overboard, they realised the folly of their plan, begged divine forgiveness, and headed back to England. Thanks to a vision of St Cuthbert, who instructed them to search the shoreline, they recovered 'that same holy book of the gospels which retained its enrichment of gems and gold on the outside as on the inside it showed the former beauty of its letters and pages, as if it had not been touched by the water at all'.

Symeon sums up by linking past and present – the creation of the book on Lindisfarne four centuries before and its veneration in Durham in his own day: 'Now the aforementioned book is today preserved in this church which has merited to have the body of that same holy father, and in it ... there is no sign that it has been harmed by the water. This circumstance is believed certainly to be due to the merits of St Cuthbert himself and also of those who had been the makers of the book.' After describing the contributions of Eadfrith, Æthilwald and Billfrith in similar, though not identical, terms to those used by Aldred in the tenth century, he concludes: 'these men ... left in this work something through which all those who come after them may appreciate their devotion towards the saint'.

In like manner, through the rich material examined in the present volume, may be appreciated the devotion to manuscripts, learning and book-crafts, as well as the spirituality, of early Britain as a whole.

PART I THE MAKING OF BOOKS

2

The material fabric of early British books

RICHARD GAMESON

> A certain enemy cut me off from life, robbed me of my mortal strength, then dipped me and dunked me in water, took me out again, and set me in the sun where I utterly lost the hairs that I had. Then the hard edge of a knife cut me, scraped clean of impurities. Fingers folded me, and the bird's joy repeatedly made tracks across me with lucky droppings; across the burnished rim it swallowed dye from the tree, a measure of liquid, then stepped on to me again and journeyed with black tracks. Then a man clad me in protective boards, covered me with hide, adorned me with gold. Thereupon the wondrous work of smiths made me radiant, encased in filigree.

As this famous Riddle from the Exeter Book of Old English poetry teasingly records,[1] medieval books were made from sheets of parchment which were cut to size, folded and gathered into groups to form quires. The sheets were marked with prickings to guide the rulings, which in their turn guided the script. When the sheets had been written, rubricated and (if appropriate) decorated, the quires were finally sewn onto cords which were laced into wooden boards, to form a codex. Each stage of this process was subject to variations according to the time and place of manufacture, and to the nature and grade of the manuscript itself. The volume described in the Riddle was probably a gospel-book (as the text goes on to reveal): accordingly, its functional binding of wooden boards clad in leather was ornamented with a treasure cover of gold and filigree work. The same luxurious process is described in the *Life of St Wilfrid* (d. 709), who 'ordered jewellers to make for [his gold-on-purple gospel-book] a casing fabricated entirely of the purest gold and [adorned] with the most precious gems',[2] and is alluded to in the colophon of the Lindisfarne Gospels: 'Æthelwald … impressed [the book] on the outside and covered it, as he well knew how to do. And Billfrith the anchorite forged the ornaments which are on it on the outside and adorned it with gold and with gems and

1 No. 26: Krapp and Dobbie 1936, pp. 93–4; Muir 1994, I, pp. 306–7.

2 Colgrave 1927, p. 36.

also with gilded-over silver – pure metal.'[3] This, however, was definitely the exception, not the norm.

Notwithstanding such documentary references and the occasional contemporary image, the vast majority of our information about the processes involved in making early British books comes from close inspection of the manuscripts themselves. Now, the most striking fact that emerges from detailed examination of the codicology of the hundreds of manuscripts in question is the range of practices that were used. Even within volumes that generally follow one particular procedure, there may be occasional departures from it – the reasons for which are not always apparent. To add to the complexity of the situation, by no means all our manuscripts preserve the physical evidence necessary for interpreting their manufacture: the prickings, for instance, may have been trimmed away; or it may be impossible to decipher which rulings were 'direct' and which 'transferred'. Moreover, codicological evidence alone is not always sufficient to permit one to reconstruct unambiguously the methods that were followed. In order to chart a coherent path through an almost overwhelming mass of disparate information, some of it more or less equivocal, the account that follows is necessarily simplified; details and discrepancies are ignored or elided. The hand-made book was a flexible artefact, and each exercise in manufacturing one was a unique operation, subject to variables that are now unknowable.

Parchment

The basic material of the medieval book was, as the Riddle advertises, animal skin.[4] While in theory the pelt of almost any reasonable-sized creature could be used to make parchment, in practice the skin of calf, sheep and goats was doubtless the mainstay of production. Apart from the inherent suitability of their pelts, the circumstance that these animals were widely farmed made them an accessible and reasonably manageable source. The most readily available such animal in eleventh-century England was the sheep, as is underlined by a unique Old English farming memorandum.[5] Individual county returns for the Domesday survey give figures that range from 20,000 to 50,000, and these are

3 Kendrick, Brown, Bruce-Mitford *et al.* 1956–60, II, bk 2, pp. 5–11. Most of these phrases also appear in the OE poem that has been shown to lie behind this section of Aldred's colophon: Roberts 2006.

4 The standard modern account remains Reed 1975.

5 BL, Add. 61735; Robertson 1939, appendix 2, no. ix, listing 15 calves, 47 goats and 250 sheep on a farmstead of Ely. For Domesday livestock: Darby 1977, pp. 162–70. *Pergamentum uel membranum* is defined as *bocfel* ('book-skin') in BL, Cotton Julius A.ii: Wülker 1884, I, p. 315.

undoubtedly well below the real totals: Norfolk is estimated actually to have had nearly 100,000 sheep, while in 1125 more than 1,600 are recorded on the estates of Peterborough Abbey alone. Parchment supply was inseparable from animal husbandry, and shared its strengths and limitations. If the damp, temperate climate of the British Isles was ideal for growing the rich fodder that would nourish healthy animals, conversely natural and man-made disasters – of the sort to which the *Anglo-Saxon Chronicle* and other annals bear eloquent witness[6] – undoubtedly took their toll on the herds, which in turn will have had an impact on the availability and quality of parchment. Skins for good parchment had to be 'harvested' in due season, not salvaged from fatalities: when farming was disrupted, reasonable pelts will have been more difficult to obtain. Parchment is likely, then, to have been in short supply when the Viking onslaught was at its height, contributing to the decline of book production in England during the second half of the ninth century. Correspondingly, the thick parchment of the earliest manuscript of King Alfred's translation of Gregory's *Regula pastoralis*[7] – no less than the poor hands of its scribes – attests to a decay of the infrastructure for furnishing the raw material, along with an atrophying of skill in processing it, during the previous generation.

The practical organisation of parchment production in early Britain and Ireland is lost to us, as is tangible indication of its overheads. At the earlier end of our period, monastic communities are likely to have been responsible for making their own parchment: the quantity of cattle remains (including juvenile and neonatal examples) associated with the complex of buildings at Green Shiel, on the north shore of Lindisfarne, raises the possibility that this was where that community manufactured its vellum; and a more extensive range of remains associated with parchment-making has come to light at the Pictish monastery of Portmahomack, Easter Ross.[8] At the later end, professional parchment-makers based in urban centres may have played a more important role in supplying demand; certainly, at the very beginning of the twelfth century Abbot Fabricius of Abingdon (1100–17) could designate certain tithes 'for buying parchment for restoring the books of the church'.[9] However, the great variations in the quality of the membrane used in late Anglo-Saxon books as a

6 E.g. *ASC* A, 894–5 (893–4) refers to a Viking raiding army stealing cattle; 897 (896) records three years of pestilence afflicting cattle.

7 BodL., Hatton 20. 8 O'Sullivan 2001, 42; Carver and Spall 2004.

9 *Historia ecclesie Abbendonensis*, ch. 219: Hudson 2002, p. 216. In the tenth century Winchester had a street of tanners, who could doubtless also have made parchment (Biddle 1976, pp. 235 and 247), and by *s.* xii a parchment-maker is recorded by name: 'Ainulfus parcheminus' (*ibid.*, pp. 118 and 147). The *Magna Vita Sancti Hugonis*, II, p. 12 (Douie and Farmer 1985, I, p. 85) equally implies that parchment could be bought commercially.

whole, and the mediocre parchment of some of the volumes made at even so well-established an urban centre as Canterbury in the later eleventh century, suggest that this should not be exaggerated.[10] Yet what is beyond doubt is that parchment production stood alongside tanning as part of the extensive use of animal resources that was central to our early societies; and that contemporary animal husbandry generated skins as a matter of course. It is likely to have been standard farming practice to reduce stock at the approach of winter, and many calves and other animals were probably killed at this time, if not shortly after birth: ordinary procedures implied a high annual slaughter rate.[11] Nonetheless, ensuring a regular supply of membrane in the right place at the right time undoubtedly required effort and organisation; and the difficulties of maintaining a continuous supply of consistent parchment even in late Anglo-Saxon England are underlined by those volumes of a generally reasonable standard, produced in major scriptoria, whose membrane nevertheless varies in quality and type from page to page.[12]

The basic process of parchment manufacture comprised a preliminary wetting of the flayed skin, followed by a more intense soaking in a solution possibly made with decaying vegetable matter but generally with lime, in order to loosen the hairs and the fatty tissue; a second such soaking might follow the de-hairing, whereafter the skin was stretched on a frame – the tension being essential to produce parchment as opposed to leather – and smoothed with a half-moon shaped knife. The quality of the end-product varied according to the type, age and health of the animal on the one hand, and to the manner and care with which the skin was treated on the other. Beasts with white hair would tend to provide a lighter finished product than those with darker hair. Younger animals offered better, thinner membrane than did older ones, with calf and kidskin giving particularly good material: in addition to the ageing of the skin itself, the hairs in the pelt thicken with maturity, with the result that membrane from older animals has denser and more noticeable follicle-pocking. To make good parchment, the animal had to be bled immediately after stunning, thus preventing its veins from marking the membrane. Whether

10 That this was not simply a side-effect of disruption from the Norman Conquest is indicated by the very variable parchment of, e.g., the *s.* xi$^{1\text{-med}}$ Canterbury hymnal, DCL, B.III.32, fols. 1–55.

11 A significant percentage of the sheep and goats kept by Eynsham Abbey in the eleventh century, for example, were slaughtered at or before the end of their first summer: Hardy *et al.* 2003, p. 398.

12 E.g. the membrane in Lambeth Palace Library, 204 (a Canterbury copy of Gregory, *Dialogi* and Ephraem Syrus, *De compunctione cordis*) varies in numerous ways from page to page: some leaves are much thinner than others, certain surfaces are quite rough, while hair follicles are clearly visible on some hair sides but not on others. Equally, some of the sheets in Exeter's copy of Augustine, *Confessiones*, BodL., Bodley 815, are stout while others are very thin.

the de-hairing bath was fortified with lime, vegetable matter or some other substance will also have affected the nature of the end-product,[13] and further variations resulted from the degree to which the skin was scraped (with a knife) for evenness, then pounced (with pumice, bone or chalk) to create a suitably matt, de-greased working surface.

The nature of the resulting page depended, in addition, on the part of the skin from which it was taken. Thin patches, holes and variations in tone and texture were more likely towards the extremities of the pelt; leaves taken from the perimeter of the skin inevitably have irregular and imperfect edges. In books of large dimensions, such irregularities were sometimes an unavoidable consequence of the size of the sheets required; in small volumes, like an eleventh-century glossary in London, and a collection of Priscian excerpts in Paris,[14] it was a symptom of economy. The nap of the membrane inevitably affected the quality of the writing: even a skilled scribe would be hard pressed to maintain a good, regular hand on an uneven surface; while thick, fuzzy textures and thin papery ones could lead to the ink bleeding or running.[15] The scribal exclamations in the ninth-century Irish Priscian at St Gallen include: 'The parchment is defective and the writing'; and 'new parchment and bad ink to say nothing else'.[16] Equally, thin, weak membrane was more likely to be slit during the process of ruling, as happened, for instance, in a couple of Exeter manuscripts.[17]

Correspondingly, the quality of the membrane provides a clear indication both of the importance of a project and of the standards of the scriptorium responsible. Particularly good parchment – well-prepared, virtually flawless, even in tone and texture – was, as one would expect, the prerogative of exceptionally fine volumes produced in major centres at times of affluence. Outstanding early instances are the Lindisfarne Gospels and the Vespasian Psalter (the task of finding suitable sheets for the Northumbrian book was more demanding, incidentally, since its leaves are roughly twice the size of those of the Southumbrian one).[18] In general, sacred texts and liturgical books were written on finer parchment than reading volumes, with particularly stout membrane sometimes being reserved for illuminated pages in the former.[19]

13 Cains 1990 hypothesises that such a difference in practice may underlie the contrasts between the parchment of Irish as opposed to other early medieval books.
14 BL, Harley 3376; BnF, n.a.l. 586.
15 As in, e.g., CUL, Ii.2.11; TCC, R.15.22; BL, Cotton Faustina B.iii; and CCCO, 279B.
16 St Gallen, Stiftsbibliothek, 904; Plummer 1926, p. 12.
17 CCCC, 191 and 196.
18 BL, Cotton Nero D.iv (85,000 mm²); Cotton Vespasian A.i (42,300 mm²).
19 Thus, e.g., in TCC, B.10.4, and Cambridge, Pembroke College, 301, both gospel-books. Unusually, in the Lindisfarne and Lichfield Gospels, as also the Book of Kells, the parchment was generally

When English copies of such texts appear on inferior parchment it normally implies production outside a major centre or during a low period in scribal activity as a whole; alternatively, it could indicate that they were destined for use in a 'lesser context', such as a parish church.[20] The quality of parchment used for 'library' books at a given scriptorium might be affected by the volume of its output. While desultory copying could mean that parchment was made on an ad hoc basis with a consequent lack of standardisation, conversely vigorous productivity might strain local resources. Late eleventh-century books from Christ Church, Canterbury – where there was an energetic programme of copying texts – are generally written on poorer parchment than coeval manuscripts from nearby St Augustine's Abbey, whose rate of book production was then more leisurely. At contemporary Salisbury, a new foundation scrambling to transcribe a multitude of texts, the ambient quality was even lower.

For much of our period, the general standard of parchment used in England seems to have been higher than that in Ireland.[21] Equally, the average quality of the membrane used for Latin manuscripts in late Anglo-Saxon England was, on the whole, better than that deployed for vernacular ones: particularly poor parchment, such as that in the Herbal, British Library, Harley 585, and the homiliary, Bodleian Library, Junius 85–6, is rare outside Old English manuscripts, while very few books with especially fine parchment have texts which are principally in the vernacular. One substantial Old English homiliary from Worcester, Bodleian Library, Hatton 113+114, is exceptional in this respect. Its manufacture coincided with the apogee of Worcester book production, but this is hardly a sufficient explanation for the phenomenon: the fine quality of the parchment suggests that it was perceived to be an important project, possibly to be associated with St Wulfstan who was prior, then bishop, there during the period in question.

Although rarer in fine volumes, holes are virtually ubiquitous in our manuscripts, even appearing in deluxe ones like the Lindisfarne Gospels, the Book of Kells and the Canterbury Codex Aureus.[22] Some flaws within the area of

deployed with the spine of the animal running horizontally across the middle of the page (rather than vertically up it): Powell 1965; Meehan and Cains 1990; Brown 2003b, pp. 201–2.

20 The parchment of the gospel-book, BodL., Bodley 155, for example, often has very yellow hair sides. The theory that this book was produced in a second-rank scriptorium receives strong support from its idiosyncratic script and display script; it was at Barking by *s.* xii, if not before.

21 Overview of Irish specimens: O'Neill 1984, with comment on p. xiii. That even a well-equipped English centre might fall short of the most demanding requirements is indicated by the fact that in the 1130s the professional artist, Master Hugo, insisted on supplies being acquired *in partibus Scotie* – presumably Scotland (and common sense would then suggest the borderlands or lowlands) – apparently unable to find parchment suitable for his art in the region of Bury St Edmunds, where he was then working: *Gesta sacristarum*: Arnold 1890–6, II, p. 290.

22 BL, Cotton Nero D.iv; TCD, 58; Stockholm, KB, A.135.

the text-block were simply left and then written around;[23] others were sewn up first, thus reducing the area which the scribe had to avoid.[24] Occasionally, membrane patches were applied to the offending spot, and the page was written on as normal: one large example appears in the Durham Gospels and there are several in the Irish Rawlinson Gospels.[25] These patches were attached by means of an adhesive; those in the St Gallen Priscian,[26] by contrast, were sewn into place.

Almost all our extant early British manuscripts are wholly written on virgin parchment: palimpsests are extremely rare. Virtually the only exceptions are a couple of leaves in the eighth- or early ninth-century Hereford Gospels, and a late eleventh-century copy of works by Cicero, Sallust and Pseudo-Atticus which is of Thorney provenance, for whose pages portions of at least five different English manuscripts, ranging in date from the eighth to the early eleventh century, were reused.[27] In both cases it seems more reasonable to assume that the recycled leaves came from volumes which were already damaged, imperfect or had been rendered obsolete than that they were deliberately cannibalised. In relation to the gospel-book, the presence of reused parchment is concordant with other indications that the manuscript was produced in a provincial centre, arguably in Wales, with very limited resources. In the case of the classical compendium the recycled leaves were used for texts that would have been of relatively low status in a Benedictine context. The general dearth of palimpsests otherwise is not difficult to understand. Whereas there were fair numbers of antique books available for reuse on the Continent in the early Middle Ages, the very different course of England's history in the fifth and sixth centuries had doubtless removed this 'resource'. However many books there were in Roman and sub-Roman Britain (and not one has come down to us), by the comparatively late date at which Christianity reached the Anglo-Saxons, little is likely to have been left. With few books to recycle, and

23 E.g. in the *s.* vii gospel fragment, DCL, A.II.10 endleaves etc. (where a large hole appears in the first page of Mark's Gospel), and in the Echternach Gospels, BnF, lat. 9389.

24 E.g. BR, 444–52, fols. 26, 45, 56, 72, 73, 80; TCC, B.3.25, fols. 83, 93 (cord lost); Winchester CL, 1, fol. 63.

25 DCL, A.II.17 (where the single case, fol. 74, was ringed in orange-red dots); BodL., Rawlinson G.167.

26 St Gallen, Stiftsbibliothek, 904.

27 Hereford CL, P.I.2, fols. 93+96 (a bifolium). The underwriting is barely visible and wholly illegible to the naked eye; its size and line-spacing, however, suggests that the sheet was from a rather grander book than that for which it was reused. NLS, Adv. 18.7.8: Ker 1956a (with enhanced photographs). Most of the under-writing has been successfully erased; faint but perceptible vertical rulings remain on 16r–v, 19r–v, 22r–v, 26r–v, 28r–v and 31r–v. The surface of the sheets is sometimes rougher and more fragile than that of the average manuscript, but this does not seem to have affected the over-writing. The reuse of an Anglo-Saxon book or sheets in France *c.* 1000 (Orléans, Médiathèque, 342) and at Trier *c.* 1100 (BAV, Reg. lat. 497) represents a different phenomenon.

a climate that was amenable to the production of parchment, palimpsesting never took root in English scriptoria. There seems to have been no general policy of cleaning and reusing discarded written sheets. Such rejected leaves as do appear were not washed and rewritten: they were simply deployed, as they were, for endleaves.[28]

The number of skins that were required to make a book varied according to the length of the text and the dimensions and grade of the proposed volume on the one hand, and the type and age of the animals on the other. The calf skins that are used for making parchment today range in size from 0.25 to 0.45 m^2 for aborted foetuses up to 0.5–0.7 m^2 for young animals; their width varies between *c.* 500 and 900 mm. Making allowance for the likelihood that early medieval animals were a little smaller than their modern counterparts, we may proceed to some approximate computations. For an exceptionally large volume such as the mighty Bible, British Library, Royal 1 E. vii+viii, whose pages now measure 550 × 330 mm and for which bifolia of more than 550 × 660 mm were therefore required, one would only obtain a single bifolium from a skin of *c.* 700 mm in width. With a more conventional but still large volume of *c.* 350 × 250 mm (the bifolia of which would measure 350 × 500 mm), one could extract two bifolia from each skin. For modest-sized volumes of up to 300 × 175 mm one might get four bifolia, possibly more; and for very small ones, measuring 175 × 150 at most, one might squeeze eight or more – with some imperfect edges. To pursue the point further, let us consider the cases of a series of notional volumes each comprising 100 folios. Such a book which measured 550 × 330 mm presupposed fifty animal skins; one of 350 × 250 required twenty-five; one of 300 × 175 needed no more than thirteen, while our 'pocket' book could be made from seven or fewer. Although it is impossible to translate such figures into a meaningful monetary 'cost', it is quite clear that bigger books required greater resources than smaller ones, and represented a considerable investment of raw materials. Correspondingly, the choice of a larger format than was strictly necessary made a statement about the status of the project and the prosperity of the centre in question; as, too, did reliance on smaller sizes than were really convenient, and the cramming of pages with more text than was comfortable to read. These points should be borne in mind during our discussion of the dimensions of books, below.

How many hides were required for an entire book collection? Once again, we can only answer the question in very general terms. Let us consider the

28 E.g. the *s* xi^{med} collectar fragment that was used as endleaf and rear pastedown in Canterbury CL, Add. 172: Gameson 2008, no. 11.

fifty-five surviving volumes that are associated with Salisbury in the generation after the Norman Conquest. If for convenience we assume that they each had 100 folios, we reach a total of 2,750 bifolia. If we further assume (given the undoubted facts that Salisbury books tend to be on the small side for the period and were economically produced) that all the bifolia were obtained at the rate of four per skin, then we arrive at a grand total of 688 animals. This, needless to say, is a minimum figure, not least because we have undoubtedly lost some of the volumes that were produced at this time (most obviously liturgica). Yet the parchment in question was deployed over a prolonged period; and if we divide the total by twenty-five (i.e. the approximate number of years), we reach an annual figure of twenty-eight skins. Even allowing for lost books, the requirement per year is unlikely to have been much above forty. Salisbury was one of the most energetic centres during the generation in question, and seems to have copied texts with unusual zeal and rapidity: other scriptoria are unlikely to have had a consistently higher consumption. Forty skins a year is not an enormous number, even in view of the disruptions to English agriculture caused by the Conquest. If it had to be met by a limited number of local suppliers, then problems may have arisen; but provided that resources came from a fairly large hinterland with a reasonably organised supply-chain, and assuming that sheep and goats as well as calves might be used, then this is unlikely to have been the case. Nevertheless, if, as seems likely, it was difficult to regulate the arrival of textual exemplars – occasionally they might be obtained in some quantity and might only be retainable for a limited time – then periods of 'crisis' were unavoidable. The fact that the parchment of some of the Salisbury books is very poor while that of others of the same 'grade' of text is not, is suggestive in this connection. Salisbury is an extreme case; nevertheless, as noted above, the variability of eleventh-century British parchment as a whole suggests that supplies were still fairly piecemeal and not the result of a well-developed professional industry.

Dimensions

The first thing that strikes one about a medieval book is its size. This can vary enormously. The page area of the aptly named Codex Gigas is a staggering 750 times that of a Book of Hours in St Petersburg.[29] These manuscripts contain different texts (the Bible plus Isidore, Josephus and Cosmas

29 Stockholm, KB, A.148: 900 × 500 mm. St Petersburg, Russian National Library, Erm. Lat. 17: 30 × 20 mm.

of Prague; and the *Horae* respectively), they were written in different countries (Bohemia and France) more than a century apart, and both were, by any standards, extraordinary. Yet even within a single century and one country the same text could be copied to vastly differing sizes – the page area of the largest eleventh-century English psalter is twenty times that of the smallest one[30] – and the booklists of our period, few in number though they are, occasionally comment on the size of a volume: 'the great psalter', 'the little troper', and, most famously, 'one large book in English about various things, written in verse'.[31]

The factors that controlled the outer limits of the size of a book are fairly obvious: the upper threshold was defined by the dimensions of the sheets of parchment which were readily available, while the lower one was determined by the size of the script that it was possible to read and write comfortably. These, however, were very distant extremes, as the examples mentioned above show. Now it is important to remember that very few of our books preserve their original dimensions: all the manuscripts that are not in their first binding will have been trimmed in subsequent centuries, probably several times, and are likely to have been reduced by centimetres rather than millimetres. Yet so long as we bear in mind that virtually every manuscript will originally have been bigger, and provided we do not place too much weight on individual figures, we are unlikely to be seriously misled. The following discussion is accordingly couched in general terms.

The dimensions and format of volumes varied according to the nature and length of the text, the date of production, the preference of the scriptorium and the projected function. Books that were destined to be carried around, such as the appropriately named, Irish 'pocket gospels'[32] or the Portiforium of St Wulfstan,[33] were almost inevitably going to be of modest to small dimensions. The same is true of some mass-books, such as the 'Red Book of Darley', along with certain manuscripts that were designed for use in personal devotions – prayerbooks, and the gospel-lectionary of Margaret of Scotland.[34] Equally, the exceptionally small size of a little-known eleventh-century psalter in the Bodleian (82 × 58 mm) leaves little doubt that it was prepared for private use by an individual.[35] Conversely, volumes with especially long texts, notably the Bible, Latin homiliaries and some of

30 BnF, lat. 8824; BodL., Laud lat. 81.

31 Lapidge 1985, nos. XII and X.

32 E.g. BL, Add. 40618; RIA, D.II.3, fols. 1–11; TCD, 59; Fulda, Landesbibliothek, Bonifatianus 3.

33 CCCC, 391.

34 CCCC, 422 (190×130 mm). BodL., Lat. liturg. f.5 (173 × 110 mm).

35 BodL., Laud lat. 81: actual-size plate: Rushforth 2007, fig. 47.

the works of the Fathers, were invariably fairly large, and this is the case whatever their date.[36]

Books from the generations on either side of 1100, when many English institutions were labouring to build up semi-coherent libraries, reveal something of a hierarchy of size. The Bible was – doubtless for symbolic as well as practical reasons – the grandest book of all: a generous folio. It was closely followed by certain volumes of paraliturgical material – Latin passionals and homiliaries – whose hagiographical content and use for lections, as well as the length of their texts, likewise militated in favour of large size. These, along with some patristic texts, were imposing quartos. Other reading books, along with 'school books' and vernacular works, were, by and large, octavos. The fact that these basic sizes were determined by the number of times one halved the sheet of parchment is conveniently demonstrated by Brussels, Bibliothèque royale 444–52, a St Augustine's Abbey volume of *c.* 1100. Fols. 18+23 were originally folded and pricked for deployment in another project that was to have been exactly half the size of the present book. At this stage it was decided to put the sheet to its current use: it was turned through 90°, each former bifolium becoming a whole folio, to fit a book measuring 350 × 245 (an appropriate size for a collection of Augustine and other patristic texts) as opposed to the original 245 × 175 mm.[37]

The texts for *lectio divina* copied in the late Anglo-Saxon period were generally smaller than the patristic volumes that were transcribed after the Conquest – the size as well as the number of the latter will have provided a subtle but nonetheless inescapable witness to a new order. Books whose texts are wholly or substantially in Old English are, on average, a little smaller than those whose texts are entirely or primarily in Latin. Though many vernacular volumes were not much, if at all, smaller than Latin ones, the corpus of Old English manuscripts includes few that are genuinely big, and nothing to match the great Latin bibles, service-books and runs of patristics. Seen in this perspective, the rare vernacular volumes which were larger than average – notably Cambridge, Corpus Christi College, 12 (OE *Regula pastoralis*; 409 × 262 mm) and 41 (OE Bede; 347 × 214); British Library, Royal 12 G. xii etc. (Ælfric, *Grammar*; 400 × 280); Bodleian Library, Eng. bib. c. 2

36 E.g. the *s.* x TCC, B.4.27 (Isidore, *Quaestiones*); Oxford, Queen's College, 320 (Isidore, *Etymologiae*); TCO, 54 (Augustine, *In psalmos*).

37 Other examples appear in BL, Royal 5 E.xi (Aldhelm; Christ Church; *s.* x/xi), a manuscript with lots of half-sheets: various of its bifolia appear to have been prepared for use in a volume of twice the size, but were then cut in half, turned sideways, and each former folio was deployed as a bifolium (the bifolium 94+95 is a particularly clear case, preserving across its top margin the multiple prickings that formerly ran down the long side margins of the original page).

(OE gospel-book; 350 × 250) and Exeter Cathedral 3501 (OE poetry; 320 × 225) – are all the more outstanding, and the fact that the size of the last occasioned comment in Leofric's inventory (quoted above) becomes more intelligible. One type of text for which a particular size seems to have been preferred is the Old English homiliaries devoted to, or principally containing material by, Ælfric, most examples of which measure around 280 × 170 mm.[38] The manuscripts of Ælfric's *Grammar and Glossary*, by contrast, show much greater variations in size, ranging from 188 × 135 up to an enormous 400 × 280 mm.[39] Two further points that stand out from the late Anglo-Saxon material are that all the copies of Gregory's *Regula pastoralis* (Latin and Old English alike) are comparatively big, 300 × 200 mm or more;[40] and that no single text was produced in such a diversity of sizes as the psalter – a striking physical advertisement of its varied yet central role in contemporary culture.[41]

The non-liturgical manuscripts of late tenth- to eleventh-century date associated with Christ Church, Canterbury, are remarkably consistent in size. The average dimensions for the group are *c.* 250 × 160 mm, and fewer than one in seven of the volumes stray very far from this. Books written at Exeter during the third quarter of the eleventh century belong to one of two main sizes, 192 × 120 and 290 × 175 mm, with one outlier measuring 330 × 220. The smaller format was used for grammatical and homiletic material, the larger one for liturgical and para-liturgical texts; the isolated bigger book is Gregory's *Regula pastoralis*, which is thus larger than the locally produced gospel-book, psalter and missal. Manuscripts associated with Worcester dating from the later tenth century are characterised by disparities of size (and shape), something which may reflect the piecemeal activity of the scriptorium then. In the earlier eleventh century, as scribal activity quickened, this was replaced by a greater regularity of format with a preferred size of *c.* 290 × 190 mm for Latin and Old English texts alike. By the mid eleventh century, Latin and Old English texts were being quite sharply distinguished, the former produced to *c.* 310 × 210, the latter to *c.* 230 × 155 mm. The first of these two sizes continued to be used at Worcester in the early twelfth century, as a larger format (*c.* 350 × 250 mm) emerged alongside it.

38 The one real exception is the two-part Rochester set, BodL., Bodley 340+342, volumes which measure 312 × 220 and 325 × 210 mm respectively.

39 BL, Royal 12 G.xii, fols. 2–9 + Oxford, All Souls College, 38, fols. 1–12.

40 The largest being the enormous OE copy, CCCC, 12.

41 The smallest (BodL., Laud lat. 81) measures 82 × 58 mm, the largest (BnF, lat. 8824) 530 × 190 mm; NB the 'facsimile' of the latter (Colgrave 1958) actually presents it at two-thirds actual size. A good number of psalters belong to one of three main sizes: *c.* 225 × 140, 275 × 180, 330 × 200 mm.

Although the very poor survival rate of anything apart from *verba sacra* from before the Viking age impedes generalisations about this early material, a few tentative observations may still be made. First, early Anglo-Saxon books seem, on the whole, to have been bigger than Irish ones. Second, 'Insular' gospel-books were – if we discount the 'pocket' copies – rather large by contemporary Continental standards, with three from southern England, along with the Irish MacRegol Gospels, being particularly imposing.[42] Third, early Anglo-Saxon patristic manuscripts could be bulkier than their late Anglo-Saxon equivalents – the result of being written in more space-hungry scripts. The Durham Cassiodorus was, even so, a giant of the genre (420 × 295 mm);[43] its imposing format suggests production in a community that held the author, Cassiodorus, in particular esteem – as we know to have been the case at Wearmouth-Jarrow but may well have been true elsewhere.

Size came to play a determining role in whether long lines or a two-column layout was employed. Both presentations had been used by late antique and early medieval scribes on the Continent, and the layout of some of the formally written volumes produced in early Anglo-Saxon England was probably defined by that of their exemplar; with regard to the Lindisfarne Gospels, the Hatton *Rule of St Benedict*, and the Canterbury Codex Aureus (all set out in two columns), we can be fairly confident that this was the case.[44] At the same time, both formats clearly became part of the 'active' repertoire of early English scriptoria, as is conveniently demonstrated by the circumstance that one of the two earliest copies of Bede's *Historia ecclesiastica* is presented in long lines, while the other is set out in two columns.[45] In this case, unusually, it is the smaller volume that has two columns and the larger one long lines (the fact that the latter seems to have been a hastier and less punctilious piece of work may be the key here). In general, however, the reverse was true; and from the tenth century, certainly, physical size was one of the most important factors in determining the layout of a volume. Although big manuscripts written in long lines are by no means unknown, it was clearly more convenient for the reader to have the text-block on large pages divided into two columns. Even in long-line manuscripts, the length of a line of text rarely exceeded 125 mm – which

42 Avranches, BM, 48 (fols. i–ii), 66 (fols. i–ii), 71 (fols. A–B) + St Petersburg, Russian National Library, O.v.I.1 (fols. 1–2); BnF, lat. 281+298 (Codex Bigotianus); Stockholm, KB, A.135 (Codex Aureus); BodL., Auct. D.2.19.

43 DCL, B.II.30.

44 BL, Cotton Nero D.iv; BodL., Hatton 48; Stockholm, KB, A.135.

45 Respectively, CUL, Kk.5.16 (facsimile: Hunter Blair 1959), and St Peterburg, Russian National Library, Q.v.I.18 (facsimile: Arngart 1952). Of other *s.* viii copies of the work, BL, Cotton Tiberius A.xiv and PML, M 826 are set out in two columns (see Plate 4.4), while Kassel, Gesamthochschulbibliothek, 4° MS. theol. 2 is presented in long lines.

(all things being equal) was evidently perceived to be the upper threshold for the eye to navigate. In point of fact, the individual columns in most of the two-column books have a width of about 80 mm, and this is unquestionably far more comfortable to read than the equivalent continuous length which (including the intercolumnar space) would be at least 180 mm. A two-column format was employed in about one in eight of our eleventh-century manuscripts, almost all of which are of greater than average size.[46] It should be added that more than half of the volumes in question date from after the Conquest, and most contain patristics, often long works. Significantly, a larger volume in two columns need not require more, and could in fact use less, parchment than a smaller long-line copy in the same script type.[47]

Two further factors should also be mentioned. The first is language, for books whose primary text was in Old English were commonly written in long lines whatever their size.[48] Thus of the five large books in Old English mentioned above, four were still set out in long lines; the only exception, the copy of Ælfric's *Grammar*, is the very biggest of the lot.[49] The second consideration is script type and size, for this has a direct bearing on the length of line which the eye can follow. The writing in the tenth- and eleventh-century two-column volumes was almost invariably a moderate size minuscule (be it Caroline or Square); in relation to larger scripts – the grand Uncial or Insular Half-Uncial of earlier manuscripts, the generous Anglo-Saxon minuscule of some later vernacular ones – long lines of 185 mm were quite acceptable:[50] the number of words per line only amounts to about ten, while in the Exeter Book of Old English poetry it is often merely eight. Correspondingly, when a particularly small script was employed, two columns might be preferred even if the volume itself was of modest, even diminutive, proportions. Thus the text of an Irish 'pocket' gospel-book, which measures a mere 132 × 103 mm, is set out in two columns, but then the script is tiny;[51] the same is true of the Books

46 Measuring *c.* 350 × 250 mm and above.

47 Two parts of Gregory's *Moralia*, York Minster Library, XVI.Q.1 and 2, dating from *s.* xi^{ex} and *s.* xii^{in} but probably part of the same set, are a convenient case to consider. The earlier measures 342 × 232 (260 × 150) and is written in long lines, with an average of *c.* 300 words per page, i.e. one word per 265 mm^2. The later, measuring 370 × 255 (290 × 180) is set out in two columns and has *c.* 400 words per page, i.e. one word per 236 mm^2.

48 Explored further by Schipper 2003 who suggests that this reflects the influence of the models disseminated under Alfred's influence, and the wish to distinguish them from works in Latin (the difficulty with the second hypothesis is that the great majority of coeval Latin works were likewise presented in long lines).

49 BL, Royal 12 G.xii, fols. 2–9 + Oxford, All Souls College, 38, fols. I–VI and i–vi.

50 As in the Northumbrian gospel-book, DCL, A.II.17, part 1. On these script types and their characteristics see Chapters 4, 6 and 7 below.

51 BL, Add. 40618.

of Armagh (195 × 145), Mulling (165 × 120) and (for the most part) Dimma (175 × 142).[52] In all these volumes the writing is so small that there are still up to eight words per column line. The inconvenience when such principles were not followed is illustrated by a gospel-book fragment in Dublin that measures around 155x120 mm, whose text is presented in thirty-six or thirty-three long lines of microscopic Insular Minuscule – thereby achieving some fifteen very difficult to read words per line.[53]

Shape

If the shape of a manuscript was subject to certain conventions, a few volumes overstepped them. Although highly unusual, such bizarre late medieval books as the circular *Codex rotundus* of Hildesheim, the heart-shaped Chansonnier of Jean de Montchenu, the oval *Horae* in Paris, and the fleur-de-lys-form one in Amiens dramatically make the point that the shape of a manuscript could be customised to a remarkable degree.[54]

Early British books were, with one exception, more conservative than these curiosities. The vast majority are, as one would expect, modestly oblong with height to width proportions of between 1.4→1 and 1.5→1; a splendid example of this last ratio is the late eleventh-century St Augustine's Abbey copy of the Pauline Epistles with Lanfranc's gloss (Fig. 2.1c).[55] The corpus as a whole, however, ranges from shapes which are much squarer to ones which are altogether more attenuated. At the oblong end of conventional formats are a Julian of Toledo in Oxford and the Wulfstan Collection in Copenhagen[56] which have height to width ratios of 1.67 and 1.68→1 respectively (Fig. 2.1b); while the Grimbald Gospels, whose ratio is 1.32→1, typifies a fairly square book (Fig. 2.1a).[57] Now all the manuscripts we have just cited are still in medieval bindings (two of them probably the 'original' ones, another including one 'original' board) and, as they have not therefore suffered unduly from the binder's knife, their dimensions and proportions are unlikely to have changed much, if at all.

The pages of the earliest codices – emulating the appearance of *rotuli* – tended to be fairly square, with a height to width ratio in the region of 1→1. Thus a fifth-century Italian Sallust measures *c.* 300 × 290 mm with a written

52 TCD, 52, 60 and 59. 53 TCD, 60, fols. 95–8.
54 Respectively: Hildesheim, Dombibliothek, 728 (and cf. BnF, lat. 10526); BnF, Rothschild 2973; BnF, Smith-Lesouëf 36; Amiens, BM, Lescalopier 22 (501).
55 Canterbury CL, Add. 172: 190 × 126 mm; Gameson 2008, no. 15.
56 Oxford, University College, 104: 188 × 122 mm. Copenhagen, KB, GKS. 1595 (4°): 235 × 140 mm.
57 BL, Add. 34890: 320 × 242 mm.

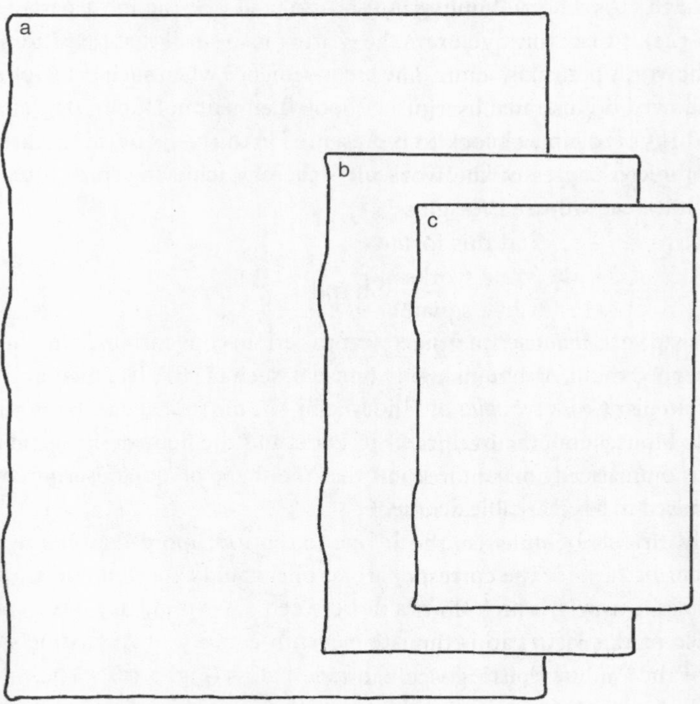

2.1 Dimensions of Books. (a) BL, Add. 34890; (b) Copenhagen, KB, G. K. S. 1595 (4°); (c) Canterbury CL, Add. 172.

area of 180 × 180; an early sixth-century Juvenal and Persius is 295 × 250 (written area 180 × 170); and the famous fifth-century Vergilius Romanus is 325 × 325 (230 × 240).[58] A handful of early Irish and English volumes are at the squarer end of rectilinear, having a height to width ratio in the region of 1.3 or less →1, and this may be a distant echo of such practices.[59] Two volumes that do approach the proportions of the fifth- and sixth-century manuscripts cited above are the eighth-century Codex Aureus and the Harley 603 Psalter of *c.* 1000, both of which have a height to width ratio of approximately 1.2→1, and there is little doubt that this is because they were made directly or (in the latter case) indirectly in imitation of a late antique exemplar (see

58 BAV, Reg. lat. 1283B; Vat. lat. 5750; Vat. lat. 3867, all written in Rustic Capitals.

59 CCCC, 173 (ii); CCCC, 197B; TCC, B.10.5; RIA, D.II.3 (part i); D.II.3 (part ii); DCL, A.II.17; Lichfield CL, 1; BL, Cotton Vespasian A.i; Royal 1 B.vii; BnF, lat. 281+298; BodL., Auct. D.2.19; Selden Supra 30; Douce 140; and St Gallen, Stiftsbibliothek, 51.

Fig. 2.2b).[60] Another volume with similar proportions, whose text makes the influence of a late antique exemplar a possibility, is the Worcester Vergil of *c.* 1000.[61] A potentially more important factor here, however, was the circumstance that the manuscript was prepared with wide margins on both sides of the main text-block to provide space for glosses. Certain other late Anglo-Saxon copies of the works of antique or late antique authors that were likewise prepared for glossing also have proportions in the region of 1.2→1 to 1.3→1,[62] and this format can be traced back to some Carolingian manuscripts of the same works.[63] Yet the planned inclusion of glosses did not invariably result in a squarer book: the fine, glossed copy of Boethius' *De consolatione philosophiae* from St Augustine's Abbey[64] has a height to width ratio of 1.5→1, proportions which are entirely typical of the vast majority of our volumes.

Another class of manuscripts whose members tend to be on the square side is the Latin gospel-book, more than half of which have a height to width ratio lower than 1.4→1 (see Fig. 2.1a). A key factor here was the wish to have broad margins both to emphasise the status of the text and to contain an apparatus (in the form of the correspondences). Revealingly, the Old English copies of the gospels, which do not include the correspondences, are slightly narrower than their Latin counterparts, while the most oblong affiliates of the group are two Latin gospel-lectionaries which likewise lack the marginal apparatus.[65] It was noted above that psalters vary in size more than any other single text, and there is, correspondingly, a fair degree of variation in their shape. Nevertheless, in contrast to gospel-books, they tend towards the oblong end of the spectrum – reflecting the fact that their text was written in verses.

There are a few manuscripts whose attenuation is particularly pronounced, having a height to width ratio of around 1.9→1 or even more (Fig. 2.2a and c).[66] In most of these cases the unusually oblong shape had little practical implication: the book is no more or less easy to handle for its attentuated format. The

60 395 × 314, and 380 × 310 mm respectively.
61 BAV, Reg. lat. 1671. Plates showing the margins: Gameson 1996a, plates 3–4.
62 E.g. TCC, O.3.7 (Boethius; 292 × 222); O.4.10 (Persius; 327 × 257); and O.4.11 (Juvenal; 295 × 242 mm).
63 E.g., BL, Harley 3095 (Boethius; 276 × 218). On the origins of such layouts: Holtz 1984.
64 BodL., Auct. F.1.15 (i): 375 × 250 mm. Plate showing much of the margins: Rogers 1991, ill. 25.
65 Cambridge, Pembroke College, 302 (1.97→1); BodL., Lat. liturg. f.5 (1.6→1).
66 E.g. Cambridge, Pembroke College, 302 (197 × 100); Leiden, Universiteitsbibliotheek, Scaliger 69 (140 × 60); BL, Harley 110 (260 × 115); Harley 5431 (230 × 85); ?Harley 2110, fols 4*–5* (original dimensions uncertain; written area *c.* 212 × 107); Royal 8 B. xi (220 × 110); Madrid, El Escorial, Real Biblioteca, E.II.1 (445 × 180); BodL., Bodley 311 (350 × 180); Laud misc. 482 (240 × 87); BnF, lat. 8824 (526 × 186).

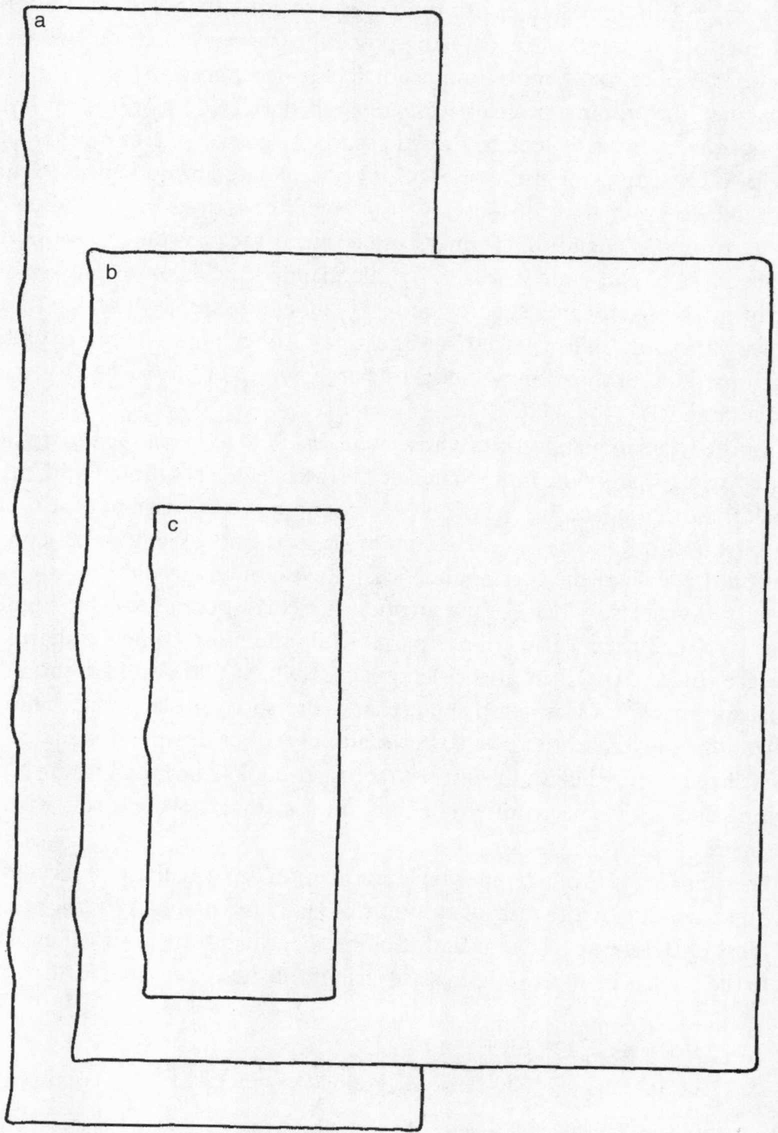

2.2 Dimensions of Books. (a) BnF, lat. 8824; (b) Stockholm, KB, A.135; (c) BL, Harley 5431.

exception is the Paris Psalter which at an amazing 526 × 186 mm (2.83→1) is far from easy to manipulate (Fig. 2.2a).[67] A tenth-century *Regula S. Benedicti* from St Augustine's Abbey, and a mid eleventh-century penitential from Worcester approach its proportions, having height to width ratios of around 2.7→1 (Fig. 2.2c);[68] however, as these are much smaller books (230 × 85 and 240 × 87 mm), they are considerably easier to use. The same is true of virtually the only pre-1200 Continental manuscript which appreciably outstrips the Paris Psalter in terms of attenuation, namely the mid-twelfth-century St Gallen Processional whose pages measure 250–253 × 75–80 mm, giving it a height to width ratio of up to 3.2→1.[69] Yet not only is this a much smaller book than our psalter, it is in fact mounted in two parts into an unusual medieval binding not unlike the surround of a wax-tablet diptych, which gives it effective dimensions of 295 × 112 mm (i.e. 2.63→1). The Paris Psalter, by contrast, has no such compensating 'holder', and it is a very large book; indeed, it is the coupling of attenuated shape with large scale that makes it so unwieldy. Its case is additionally intriguing because the format seems ili-suited to the content and layout – Latin and Old English arranged in parallel columns with, moreover, a broad outer margin. One can adduce later parallels for such dimensions, one can see how pages of such a shape could easily be obtained from ordinary sheets of parchment, and one can even observe how the layout echoes that of glossaries where the words of the different languages are set out in narrow parallel columns;[70] but the reasons behind the design of this extraordinary book still resist easy explanation.

To sum up the practical implications of the material in this and the previous section: by the end of our period, most book collections are likely to have been made up of volumes which were quite disparate in size and shape. If this militated against orderly storage (hardly a major problem when the number of items in most collections was fairly small), it could (prior to the development of systematic catalogues and shelf-marks) have offered the modest advantage that certain classes of books could be readily distinguished, and certain individual items actually identified, by their external form. Indeed, one of the clauses in the *Monasteriales indicia* (the monastic sign language) seems to work on this assumption: 'if you want a book of long dimensions, then stretch out your left hand and wave it, and place your right arm over your left at the length of the book'.[71]

67 BnF, lat. 8824; see n. 41. 68 BL, Harley 5431; BodL., Laud misc. 482.

69 St Gallen, Stiftsbibliothek, 360: Duft and Schnyder 1984, pp. 129–45; Schmucki, Ochsenbein and Dora 1998, no. 67.

70 E.g. that in BR, 1828–30. 71 Banham 1991, ch. 12.

Written area

The aesthetic of the page, not to mention the important practical detail of how much text it could contain, was established by the dimensions of the written area as well as by the size and shape of the volume as a whole. It is most unfortunate that, because of subsequent trimming, it is impossible to study the precise, original disposition of the written area in relation to the page as a whole for more than a handful of manuscripts. Nevertheless, those volumes such as the Grimbald Gospels and the Copenhagen Wulfstan collection[72] which are still in medieval bindings reveal that the text-block was so positioned that the four margins around it were each of a different width: the inner margin was the smallest, the upper one slightly larger, the outer one bigger again, while the lower one was the largest of all. This has an attractive harmony of its own; simultaneously, in relation to whole openings, since the width of the two inner margins taken together approximates to that of the individual outer margins, each block of text has matching lateral borders (Fig.2.3). Now, the two specimens cited above are quite distinct both in status and in shape, showing that these principles applied not only to a deluxe gospel-book of squarer than average dimensions but also to a piecemeal, working compilation of oblong proportions; indeed, in many manuscripts which have been quite drastically trimmed it is still possible to discern that the text-block was positioned and the margins calibrated according to this widely used system. Only one set of written instructions for page design is known to have come down to us from the early Middle Ages and it is surely no coincidence that the principles it enunciates are closely similar.[73]

Might the size of the written area have been influenced by other precepts? It is sometimes stated that in oblong manuscripts the height of the written area was, as a general rule, the same as the width of the page as a whole. An unequivocal example of this phenomenon, still in a very early binding, is the mid-eleventh-century gospel-book, Morgan Library, M 709, whose width (190 mm) is virtually identical to the height of the text-block (192 mm).

72 See nn. 56–7 above.

73 Text added in *s.* x to the lower margin of BnF, lat. 11884, fol. 2v (Saint-Rémi, Reims; *s.* ix[ex]): 'How the appearance of the page should be: with five parts of length to four of width. Give a fifth part to the lower and outer margin; and that same part divide in three and (subtracting one) you will give two to the upper margin. Again divide these two parts into three and (subtracting one) you will give two to the inner margin [i.e. $\frac{4}{9}$ of a unit]. If a middle margin will have been inserted, it will be equal to this [i.e. $\frac{4}{9}$ of a unit]. Assuredly, you divide the [horizontal] lines according to the nature of the script for grander script requires wider-spaced lines, smaller script narrower ones.' Translated from the text printed by Maniaci 1995, p. 26; earlier edition and discussions: Muzerelle 1989, pp. 127–31; Rand 1934, pp. 87–9; see further in general Tschichold 1965.

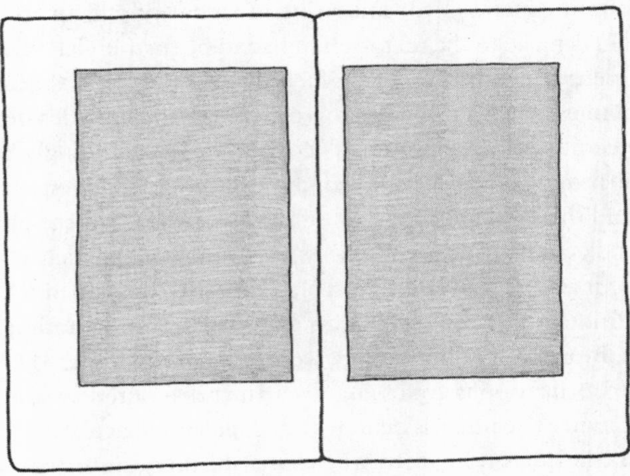

2.3 Relationship of text-block to page.

Few late Anglo-Saxon manuscripts, however, show this feature so clearly. Conversely, it is sometimes evident that this principle cannot have been followed – when the present width of the manuscript still exceeds the height of the text-block (as is true, for instance, of the Bible, British Library, Royal 1 E.vii+viii[74]) or where the width of the book is much smaller than the height of the text-block (as in the penitential, Laud misc. 482[75]). This last book does, however, alert us to another possible relationship between the general size and the written area, for here the ratio of height to width of the text-block is identical to the ratio of height to width of the volume as a whole.[76] The same principle is exemplified by the gospel-book, Morgan Library, M 708, which is still in its original binding: at 295 × 190 mm with a written area of 214 × 130, the respective ratios of height to width are only 0.1 apart[77] with the result that to the naked eye the proportions of the text-block echo those of the manuscript. Yet creating a text-block which echoed the shape of the volume was no more an invariable principle than was the practice of having the height of the text-block match its width. Once allowance has been made for distortion through trimming, a good number of books can still be seen to have a written area which is appreciably more oblong than the volume itself – a side-effect of having wide outer margins.

74 550 × 330 with a written area of 460 × 240.
75 Width: 87 mm. Height of text-block: 179 mm.
76 Respectively 179 × 64 (2.8→1) and 240 × 87 mm (2.8→1).
77 1.55→1 and 1.65→1.

An important general factor militating in favour of wide margins was the wish to avoid damage to the text itself: it had to be surrounded with sufficient space if it were not to be thumbed when the manuscript was handled. Even in small volumes, a reasonably expansive margin was thus a desideratum, and parsimony here is a clear symptom of economy. Correspondingly, particularly expansive margins – prodigal use of parchment – could function as a symbol of opulence, and this was doubtless part of the explanation for the phenomenon in gospel-books and liturgical volumes.[78] As noted above, particularly generous margins might also be supplied if the volume were to be glossed. The works of Boethius, Prudentius, Sedulius, Statius and Vergil were sometimes prepared thus, as too, by the end of our period, were parts of the Bible.[79] Distinct from such planned, primary-phase glossing, broad margins were sometimes filled by subsequent users. The point is demonstrated most spectacularly by a spacious copy of the Old English Bede, to whose inviting margins were soon added a wide variety of texts (including masses, homilies and charms) of no relevance to the *Historia ecclesiastica*.[80]

The arrangement of the parchment

Even with reasonably well-prepared membrane, there remains a contrast in tone and texture between the hair side (H) and flesh side (F) of the sheet; the former tends to be yellower and a little rougher than the latter. To minimise the discrepancy on a given opening, medieval scribes generally arranged the sheets within quires so that hair sides faced hair sides, and flesh sides, flesh.[81] In early Italian manuscripts, such as the sixth-century Gospels of St Augustine, the membrane is consistently arranged so that like faces like, with a flesh side outermost (FH, HF: Fig. 2.4).[82] In early Irish books, by contrast, the disposition of the sheets is altogether less regular. In the Cathach of St Columba, the Stowe Missal and the Book of Mulling,[83] for instance, hair and flesh sides sometimes confront each other within the quires, sometimes not, and either may form the outermost face of the quire. The construction of the

78 E.g. BL, Add. 57337; Rouen, BM, Y.6.

79 E.g. Canterbury CL, Add. 172; Oxford, Keble College, 22.

80 CCCC, 41: Hohler 1980; Grant 1982; Keefer 1996.

81 This is sometimes (rather inaccurately) referred to as 'Gregory's Rule', from C. R. Gregory's observation (1907, p. 324) that quires of Greek biblical manuscripts were so constructed that the first recto, last verso and central opening are all flesh sides, and that like side faces like on all other openings; the reduction of 'Gregory's Rule' to this second point seems to have been initiated by Rand 1929, I, p. 12, in response to the different conventions of Latin manuscripts.

82 CCCC, 286. As also in many Greek books.

83 RIA, s.n.; RIA, D.II.3 (pt ii); TCD, 60.

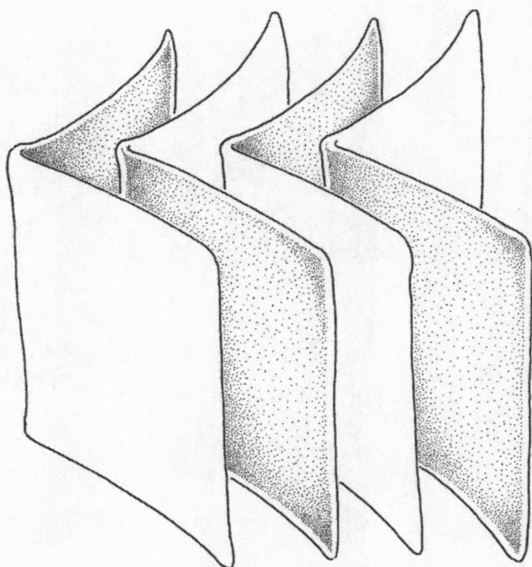

2.4 The typical arrangement of the parchment in the quires of an early Italian manuscript (FH, HF).

Codex Usserianus Primus is more orderly:[84] the skins that make up its quires all face the same way; thus, except at the centre of the gathering and where two quires abut, hair sides face flesh sides (HF, HF: Fig. 2.5). For convenience of reference, this will be termed the 'Insular' arrangement. Such a disposition shows, incidentally, that the quires in question were not constructed by *pliage*, since *that* system – taking a whole, prepared skin, folding it in half three times in succession, and then trimming it on two sides to create four bifolia, one inside the next – inevitably formed gatherings in which hair side faced hair, and flesh, flesh (Fig. 2.6). On the contrary, such Insular quires were probably put together from a pile of individual bifolia which had already been cut to the basic shape required.

The Insular system of arranging parchment was exported to the Continent in the wake of Irish missionary activity – the seventh-century Basilius and Orosius in Irish script that were written at, or brought to, Bobbio, for instance, and the various Irish manuscripts at St Gallen have their parchment arranged

84 TCD, 55.

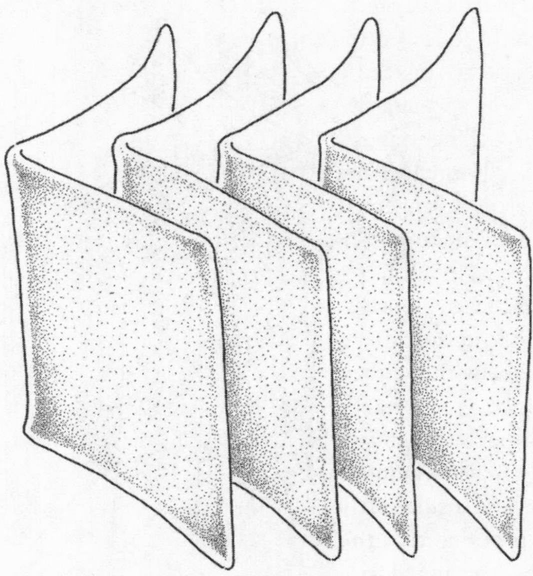

2.5 The typical arrangement of the parchment in the quires of an early Insular manuscript (HF, HF).

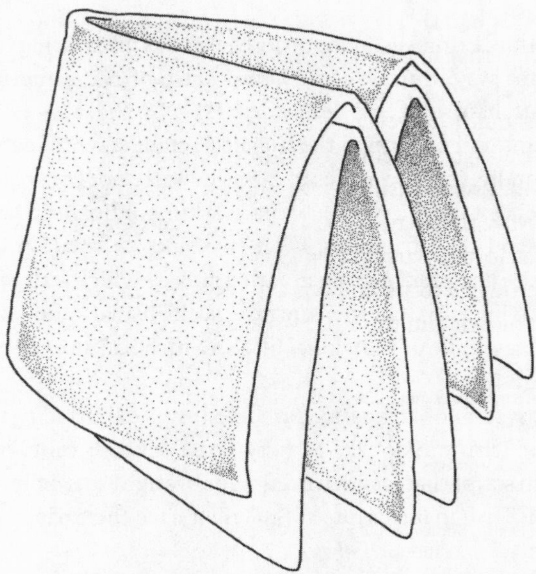

2.6 *Pliage*: forming a quaternion by folding a skin in half three times in succession.

thus.[85] It found particularly fertile ground closer to home, in England, for such was the procedure followed in Anglo-Saxon scriptoria until the later tenth century. Indeed, this was the case not only in Anglo-Saxon centres where Irish influence was particularly pronounced, but also in ones where connections with the Continent and the Mediterranean were strong. Although the Codex Amiatinus normally has a flesh side on the outside of each quire, other irregularities in the arrangement of the parchment betray its Northumbrian origin; the Moore Bede may likewise have flesh sides outside each quire, but the sheets 'within' all face the same way; and if one of the reconstructible quires of the Wearmouth-Jarrow gospel-book at Utrecht seems to have a flesh side outermost, the other sports a hair side, and there was no attempt to make like face like within either of them.[86] Even such superficial relationships with Italian practices were abandoned in later Northumbrian, possibly York or Wearmouth-Jarrow, manuscripts such as the Durham Cassiodorus and the Oxford copy of Bede's Commentary on Proverbs, whose parchment is generally arranged in the Insular manner.[87] Kent presents a similar picture. It seems reasonable to presume that the Roman missionaries who came to southern England will have arranged parchment according to the norms of their homeland. Be that as it may, by the time of the earliest Southumbrian manuscripts that have come down to us – none of which predates the eighth century – these traditions had been superseded. The membrane in the Kentish copy of Acts is generally arranged HF, HF; that of the Codex Bigotianus is either FH, FH or HF, HF; while that in the Vespasian Psalter and the Codex Aureus is fairly random.[88]

The point should, however, be made that whereas Italian parchment is characterised by a strong contrast between the yellower hair side and the whiter flesh side, with Insular membrane the discrepancy is generally less pronounced. Now this may be because of its high quality and even finish (as in the Lindisfarne and Barberini Gospels along with the Vespasian Psalter[89]) or, conversely, owing to its ambient low quality (as in the Book of Dimma, the Hereford Gospels and the Vatican Psalm catena[90]). In either case, since the

85 Milan, Biblioteca Ambrosiana, C.26.sup. and D.23.sup. St Gallen, Stiftsbibliothek, 51 (predominantly), 60 and 904.

86 Florence, Biblioteca Medicea-Laurenziana, Amiatino 1; CUL, Kk.5.16; Utrecht, UB, 32, fols. 94–105. Too little survives of the Wearmouth-Jarrow gospel-book in DCL, A.II.17 (part 2, fols. 103–11) to describe the arrangement of its parchment; however, it was clearly not according to the 'Italian system'.

87 DCL, B.II.30; BodL., Bodley 819.

88 BodL., Selden Supra 30; BnF, lat. 281+298; BL, Cotton Vespasian A.i; Stockholm, KB, A.135.

89 BL, Cotton Nero D.iv; BAV, Barb. lat. 570; BL, Cotton Vespasian A.i.

90 TCD, 59; Hereford CL, P.I.2; BAV, Pal. lat. 68.

2.7 The so-called 'Continental' arrangement of the parchment in a quaternion (HF, FH).

discrepancy between the sides of the membrane was minimal, the niceties of its arrangement were unimportant. That said, it should be stressed that even when there was a more visible contrast – and even in volumes whose appearance mattered, made in centres which undoubtedly had access to manuscripts whose quires were constructed in the Mediterranean way – the Insular arrangement was still preferred.[91]

The parchment of ninth-century Carolingian manuscripts was generally disposed so that like faced like with a hair side outermost (HF, FH) – what we shall, for convenience, term the 'Continental' arrangement (Fig. 2.7). It is possible that the mixed preparation – part Insular, part Continental – found in a couple of Southumbrian volumes dating from the first half of the ninth century was a reflex to this;[92] but if so, they were isolated incidents, and the Insular system remained the norm.[93] Indeed, despite the interruption of Anglo-Saxon scribal traditions during the third quarter of the ninth century, despite the stimulus of the Continental example in its subsequent revivification, and despite the fact that most of the manuscripts imported into England during the ninth

91 E.g. in the canon tables of Stockholm, KB, A.135.
92 BL, Royal 1 E.vi; BnF, lat. 10861.
93 *Teste*, e.g., CUL, Ll.1.10; CCCC, 144.

and tenth centuries had their sheets arranged in the Continental way, English scribes were far from speedy in abandoning the practices of their forebears.[94]

Up until the middle of the tenth century there are merely occasional English volumes whose parchment is wholly or largely arranged in the Continental manner,[95] plus a few scribes who used the Continental system in quires where there was a more pronounced contrast in tone between the sides of the membrane (and not in those where there was not).[96] Only one centre (St Augustine's Abbey, Canterbury) seems to have adopted the Continental practice in any systematic way during this period,[97] and, intriguingly, it abandoned it again in the second half of the century.

The Continental system only really began to make headway in the second half of the tenth century, as part of the closer interaction with the Continent associated with the rise of the Benedictine reform movement; but even then the pace of change was leisurely. Unsurprisingly, just as the fine manuscripts associated with Bishop Æthelwold of Winchester (d. 984) display a vigorous embracing of Continental culture in their minuscule script, display script and decoration, so too their parchment was arranged in the Continental manner: the quires of the New Minster Charter of 966 and Æthelwold's Benedictional of *c*. 971×984, along with those of the closely related Benedictional in Paris, are wholly or predominantly thus.[98] Whether this was previously a feature of the scriptorium of Abingdon, where Æthelwold had been abbot *c*. 954–63, is now unknowable owing to the dearth of surviving manuscripts. Equally, as we have virtually no Winchester 'library' and school books of later tenth-century date, we cannot be certain that it was the universal practice there in Æthelwold's day; the creators of the high-grade volumes that have come down to us may have been pioneers in this respect.

St Dunstan's milieu, from which a larger body of material survives, appears more complicated. Mid-tenth-century Glastonbury (based on the exiguous evidence of a couple of books[99]) had mixed practices, with the Continental arrangement preponderant. The two systems similarly co-existed at Christ Church, Canterbury, in the second half of the tenth century. Symptomatic of this situation is the fact that one of the two manuscripts that have the best claims to be associated with Archbishop Dunstan (the Bosworth Psalter[100]) has

94 Difference in the quality of the parchment may again have been a retarding factor: thus that of the Continental stratum of the northern Frankish Leofric Missal (BodL., Bodley 579) is perceptibly inferior to that of the two additional Anglo-Saxon strata.
95 BL, Add. 47967; Royal 2 B.v; and Royal 12 D.xvii.
96 E.g. in BodL., Junius 27; and Bodley 49. 97 *Teste*, e.g., TCC, B.11.2.
98 BL, Cotton Vespasian A.viii, fols. 1–33; Add. 49598; and BnF, lat. 987.
99 CUL, Ee.2.4; BodL., Hatton 30. 100 BL, Add. 37517.

its parchment entirely arranged in the Insular manner, while that of the other (the Sherborne Pontifical[101]) is wholly disposed in the Continental way. One possible deduction from this is that individual scribes were free to arrange their parchment as they wished. Be that as it may, the Canterbury material shows quite clearly that access to Continental exemplars was not in itself enough to inspire change. The point is underlined by a late tenth-century Christ Church Isidore, which was transcribed page by page from an identifiable Carolingian manuscript:[102] whereas the parchment of the model is consistently HF, FH, that of the copy is equally consistently HF, HF.

St Oswald's milieu is altogether more difficult to evaluate since book production at Worcester – potentially our key source – seems to have remained desultory until well into the eleventh century. That said, it is striking that of the two volumes which have a reasonable claim to have been made there during Oswald's episcopacy and which were, moreover, written by the same scribe, one has its parchment arranged in the Insular manner, the other mainly in the Continental way.[103] One should resist the temptation of deducing that the former necessarily predates the latter – a point underlined by another manuscript that hovers uncertainly in Oswald's circle: the earliest bilingual copy of the *Rule of St Benedict*.[104] The original text of this manuscript is entirely the work of one scribe. The sheets of the first seven quires are consistently arranged in the Insular way; quire VIII is mixed, though predominantly Continental; and the next three gatherings are entirely Continental in disposition. Nevertheless, the last two quires (XII–XIII) revert to the Insular system.

Returning to Canterbury, where we have a fairly large sample of library volumes, we find that both practices continued until *c.* 1000, but thereafter the Continental system was the norm. The parchment of St Gallen, Kantonsbibliothek (Vadiana), 337, a copy of B's *Vita Dunstani* from St Augustine's Abbey, which was probably produced 995×1004, is almost entirely HF, FH, as is that of all the Christ Church manuscripts associated with the scribe Eadwig Basan, whose datable work falls in the second and third decades of the eleventh century.[105] By the early eleventh century most English writing centres followed suit. By and large, the chronology of change

101 BnF, lat. 943. 102 Respectively TCC, B.4.27 and Salisbury CL, 101.

103 BL, Royal 8 B.xi; Worcester CL, F.91. 104 CCCO, 197.

105 Hanover, Kestner-Museum, W.M.XXIa.36; Florence, Biblioteca Medicea-Laurenziana, Plut. XVII.20; BL, Add. 34890; Arundel 155; Cotton Vespasian A.i (supplementary quire); Harley 603, fols. 28–49; York Minster Library, Add. 1. BodL., lat. liturg. D.3, fols. 4–5 is too fragmentary to evaluate.

seems to have been the same in vernacular books as in Latin ones – as one would expect. If more irregularities appear in Old English manuscripts at a slightly later date – as, for instance, in the eleventh-century Old English Bede in Cambridge, many of whose quires are HF, FH, FH, HF[106] – this may be because the (often unprovenanced) volumes in question were made outside the major scriptoria that produced our principal Latin witnesses.

The final stages of the transition from one system to the other may be illustrated statistically. Of the sixty manuscripts dating from the first quarter of the eleventh century about whose structure I have complete information, thirty-nine were entirely made according to the Continental arrangement, eleven were wholly constructed in the old Insular way, while ten contained a mixture of the two systems. By contrast, taking a random cross-section of sixty books dating from the second quarter of the century, we find that only two were consistently Insular, six were mixed, while fifty-two were entirely Continental in the arrangement of their parchment.[107]

Quire structure

The quires of early Irish manuscripts could vary considerably in size and were often quite large. Those of the Cathach of St Columba, the Codex Usserianus Primus, the Book of Durrow and the Rawlinson Gospels are generally composed of ten leaves (10s);[108] the gatherings of St Gallen, Stiftsbibliothek 51 (gospel-book) and 60 (John's Gospel) are 10s or 12s (including many singletons); the three that make up a copy of the Pauline Epistles in Würzburg are all 12s;[109] while those in a gospel-book in London may have as many as 16 and even 20 leaves.[110] The variation that was possible within a single manuscript may be illustrated by the Stowe Missal[111] – whose gatherings seem originally to have been a 10 (one leaf of which was used as a paste-down), two 12s and a 14 – and the Book of Armagh[112] which has quires of 4, 6, 8, 10 and 12 leaves. In the Book of Dimma,[113] radical changes in quire size were linked to

106 CCCC, 41. The arrangment of the parchment is noticeably more variable in the stint of the first scribe (qq. I–XIII) than in that of his colleague (XIV–XXXI) who – judging by the fact that he wrote the first page of the book and effected the join between the two stints – was the senior partner.

107 Occasional divergencies from the norms of Continental preparation in manuscripts of later *s.* x and early *s.* xi date may sometimes have been motivated by the wish to use a particular side of the skin for artwork that was scattered irregularly through the book, as was evidently the case in the Winchester Benedictional, Rouen, BM, Y.7 and the gospel-book TCC, B.10.4.

108 RIA, s.n.; TCD, 55; TCD, 57; BodL., Rawlinson G. 167.

109 Würzburg, UB, M.p.th.f.12.

110 BL, Add. 40618.

111 Dublin, RIA, D.II.3 (pt ii). Warner 1915, pp. x–xi, with diagrammatic reconstruction of the particularly complicated second and third quires.

112 TCD, 52.

113 TCD, 59.

the textual content: Matthew and Mark were written on a single quire each (the first considerably larger than the second, of course), while Luke and John were both divided between two gatherings of more modest proportions. The Book of Mulling and the Cadmug Gospels took this philosophy to its logical conclusion and presented each gospel on a single quire, the results consisting of around 22, 16, 26 (+1) and 12 (+1) leaves in the first, 18, 14, 18 and 15 in the second.[114] The practice of beginning each gospel on a new quire can be traced back to some of the very earliest gospel codices and remained widespread in the early Middle Ages. Large quires and variations in quire size, by contrast, are much rarer, and point to the archaic and informal roots of Irish book-making. Nevertheless, these practices continued in Irish circles to the end of our period: the quires in the Irish Psalter at Rouen, for instance, are composed of 12 leaves, those of that in Edinburgh of 14, while the 'Southampton' Psalter has an 8, three 10s, four 12s, and a 13.[115] Equally, the Book of Deer, of presumed Scottish origin, is composed of six quires of 12, preceded by one of 4 and terminated by one of 10.[116] Seen in this company, the Book of Kells with its quires of 8 and 10 leaves, and the St Gallen Priscian, which is entirely composed of quaternions, appear very disciplined.

The quires of the extant late antique and early medieval continental manuscripts are generally more regular than those of Irish ones, being formed from 10 or, more commonly, 8 leaves; and these were the structures that were widely adopted in Anglo-Saxon England. Most English books from the eighth century – the earliest period for which we have a reasonable sample – are constructed from one or other of these forms, or occasionally (as in the Codex Bigotianus) both.[117] Other structures intermittently appear – the Vespasian Psalter has 6s as well as 8s, the Gregory in the Vatican (if it is an English book), has 2s and 8s,[118] while the Canterbury Codex Aureus is largely composed of 7s (the consequence of its extraordinary design concept) – nevertheless, there is no doubt that by the eighth century, Anglo-Saxon books were composed of more regular quire structures than their Irish equivalents. Moreover, this was just as true north of the Humber (where Irish influence was stronger) as south of it. The greater regularity of the gatherings in Anglo-Saxon books is

114 TCD, 60 (all the leaves are now remounted singletons: this is the reconstruction of the original arrangement proposed in *CLA*, II, no. 276); Fulda, Hessische LB, Bonifatianus 3.

115 Rouen, BM, A.41; Edinburgh UL, 56; Cambridge, St John's College, C.9.

116 CUL, Ii.6.32.

117 8s include: CCCC, 69 and 173 (pt ii); DCL, B.II.30; BL, Cotton Nero D.iv; Royal 1 B.vii; Loan 74; BodL., Bodley 819; Douce 140; Hatton 48; Selden Supra 30; BAV, Barb. lat. 570. 10s include: CUL, Kk.1.14; Kk.5.16; CCCC, 197B; BAV, Pal. lat. 68.

118 BAV, Pal. lat. 259.

presumably a reflection of England's closer relations with the Continent from the seventh century. It may also be because most of the Anglo-Saxon volumes that have come down to us are higher-grade products than their Irish counterparts, for other types of gathering do sometimes appear in small 'personal' books[119] as in particularly 'scrappy' ones.[120]

The Hereford and Lichfield Gospels,[121] two eighth-century manuscripts with a western British provenance, appertain to the Irish rather than to the Anglo-Saxon tradition of book-making in this respect, for the former is entirely constructed from 12s, while the latter include quires of 8, 9, 10, 11 and 13 leaves. Whether this illuminates early western British practices as a whole is a moot point. By the ninth century, insofar as the exiguous evidence allows any generalisations, Welsh scribes seem to have had a penchant for quinions (i.e. 10s).[122]

Quaternions (8s: four sheets giving eight folios, sixteen pages) remained the preferred structure in English books throughout the ninth century[123] and indeed thereafter – exactly as on the Continent (Fig. 2.8; see also figs. 2.4, 2.5 and 2.7). Most departures from this form are confined to isolated quires, and were generally motivated by their position in the volume or the nature of the text they bear.[124]

Self-contained units of text, such as calendars, canon tables or other prefatory material, were regularly given a quire of their own which might consequently be of a different size from those in the rest of the book. One vernacular homiliary from Worcester, for example, is entirely composed of quaternions with the exception of the gathering that contains the calendar, this being a quinion;[125] the calendar in the Sacramentary of Robert of Jumièges[126] occupies a quire of six leaves; while the canon tables in the gospel-book that was given to Saint-Rémi, Reims,[127] exactly fit a quire of five leaves (two bifolia prefaced by a singleton). Such physical separation was eminently sensible since these sections almost invariably had a different ruling pattern from that used in the rest of their respective books. The main body of the Arundel 60 Psalter, for

119 E.g. BL, Cotton Nero A.i; Harley 2965; Royal 2 A.xx.

120 E.g. BodL., Junius 85+86.

121 Hereford CL, P.I.2; Lichfield CL, 1.

122 Appearing in CUL, Ff.4.42; CCCC, 153; BodL., Auct. F.4.32.

123 E.g. CUL, Ll.1.10; CCCC, 144; Royal 1 E.vi (from ix¼); BodL., Hatton 20 (*s.* ix[ex]).

124 A notable exception from *s.* x[1] is the gospel-book, Boulogne, BM 10, all of whose quires are 10s. Then there are two sets of *s.* xi[ex] books with divergent quire sizes, one lot produced at Durham, the other at Christ Church, Canterbury; the fact that other broadly coeval books from these same centres employed quaternions shows that this was not, even temporarily, a scriptorium norm in either case.

125 BodL., Hatton 113. 126 Rouen, BM, Y.6. 127 Reims, BM, 9.

2.8 A regular quaternion (four sheets, giving eight folios, sixteen pages).

instance, is ruled with twenty-four horizontals bounded on either side by double verticals; by contrast, its first quire (mainly comprising the calendar, and composed of twelve not eight leaves) is consistently ruled with thirty-four horizontals and twelve verticals.

Equally, a slightly larger or smaller quire might be deployed at the end of a book – or of a particular text within a multi-work volume – tailored to the quantity of material that remained to be accommodated. A singleton was added for this purpose to the last quire of one Old English gospel-book;[128] the final gathering of a collection of hymns and canticles was enlarged to a quinion;[129] that of a Boethius was expanded to a sextion (twelve);[130] while the ultimate quire of the Royal 1 D.ix Gospels was increased to a generous thirteen leaves (thereby being able to embrace the end of the gospel text plus the table of lections). The mid-eleventh-century gospel-book at Reims shows evidence of more careful forward planning, for instead of expanding only the final quire and having to do so unduly (as in the previous case), here not only the last quire but also the penultimate one were enlarged to quinions.[131] The extension was well calculated for the text ends on the recto of the final leaf. In other volumes, the concluding quire was curtailed for exactly the same reason: the final gathering of the Royal 1 D.iii Gospels was reduced by one leaf, the text having finished on the previous page; that of a penitential in Brussels lost

128 CCCC, 140.
129 BL, Cotton Julius A.vi, fols. 18–90.
130 TCC, O.3.7.
131 Reims, BM, 9.

its closing two folios;[132] while three leaves were 'cancelled' (i.e. deliberately removed) from that of Exeter's copy of Chrodegang's *Regula canonicorum*.[133] Even slenderer is the concluding quire of the gospel-lectionary of Margaret of Scotland,[134] which comprises only four folios, two of which are singletons; while in one copy of Aldhelm's *Carmen de virginitate*,[135] the last gathering is simply a bifolium, the text ending on its final verso.

A comparable procedure was occasionally followed within the body of volumes as a response to major textual subdivisions. The phenomenon is most common, however, in gospel-books, reflecting the fact that their four 'constituent units' were more clearly perceived to be separate than were the subsections of most other texts; moreover, the practice of beginning each gospel on a new quire had the recommendation of tradition, as we have seen.[136] In order to achieve this, it was sometimes necessary to adjust the structure of the preceding quire. In the gospel-book at Besançon, for example, the ends of Matthew, Mark and Luke, plus the preliminary matter for the following gospel, were all contained in quires of six leaves, while the general prefaces and canon tables were written on a single quire of fourteen folios; similarly, the Exeter Gospels was entirely composed of regular quaternions except at the beginnings of Luke and John, which started with quires of two and ten leaves respectively.[137]

Occasionally, variant quires within the body of a text might reflect the circumstance that the volume was written by several scribes working simultaneously. The eighth-century Kentish copy of Acts, Bodleian Library, Selden Supra 30, was the work of two scribes. The first wrote four regular quaternions, but his or her[138] final quire before scribe 2 took over was a greatly reduced oddment comprising two singletons (the first now lost) followed by a bifolium. It is difficult to see why the scribe should have finished the stint thus had the next section not already been written. In one manuscript of Ælfric's *Grammar*, to take another example, the first main hand wrote fols. 7r–52r, the second main hand taking over on 53r.[139] Now fol. 52 is the end of quire VII which,

132 BR, 8558–63, part C (ii). Equally, the final quire of the late eleventh-century part-bible, Hereford, CL, O.IX.2 (a volume otherwise composed of 8s) is a 6, the last two leaves of which are themselves blank.

133 CCCC, 191. Equally, Antwerp, Plantin-Moretus Museum, M.16.8 (Boethius, *De consolatione philosophiae*), quire XII, is a small gathering of five folios (two bifolia and a central singleton), designed to bring Book IV to an end.

134 BodL., Lat. liturg. f.5. 135 CCCC, 285.

136 Late Anglo-Saxon examples include: Besançon, BM, 14; Hanover, Kestner-Museum, W.M.XXIa.36; BnF, lat. 272; lat. 14782; BodL., Bodley 441 (in OE).

137 Besançon, BM, 14; BnF, lat. 14782.

138 The most probable place of origin for the book being the double minster, Minster-in-Thanet.

139 BL, Harley 3271.

most unusually in a manuscript of regular quaternions, is a gathering of six leaves (a quaternion from which leaves 7 and 8 have been cancelled). Again the logical deduction is that the two scribes had been working on their respective portions of the text simultaneously, and that the blanks in this central quire were subsequently cancelled when the finished gatherings were assembled, in order that the stints should dovetail more effectively.

The most impressive example of the phenomenon is the monumental pandect, Codex Amiatinus, almost all of whose 130 quires are regular quaternions. Leaving aside the complicated reworked prefatory gathering, virtually all those that diverge from this form contain the end of a biblical book. More significantly still, they invariably also coincide with the end of a scribal stint.[140] The obvious inference is that most of the seven scribes were, by and large, working simultaneously, a deduction strengthened by the similarity in the total length of their contributions, all but one of which is in the region of twenty quires.

Pairs of half-sheets (singletons) were sometimes substituted for complete bifolia, permitting the use of pieces of parchment that were too small to form whole sheets, or had been salvaged from other contexts. Such half-sheets, being slightly less robust than proper bifolia, were commonly located at 'sheltered' positions within the body of the quire: that is, neither as the outermost nor the innermost leaves but rather one of the pairs in between – sheets 2 and 3 (fols. 2–3 and 6–7) of a quaternion. Four quires in the Exeter Psalter[141] include a pair of singletons, which in each case appear as leaves 3 and 6 (Fig. 2.9a);[142] in quire XXIII of the Winchcombe Psalter, on the other hand, the two singletons were leaves 2 and 7 (Fig. 2.9b).[143]

Singletons were far less common at the inner and outer faces of quires (fols. 1+8 and 4+5); yet the form was not invariably avoided. A singleton stands at the end of quire 67 of the Codex Amiatinus, for instance; in a late eleventh-century Bede manuscript in Oxford, two singletons form the outermost leaves of quire VI (Fig. 2.10a); while in quire II of a Jerome in Cambridge, they are the innermost ones (Fig. 2.10b).[144] An even more radical use of half-sheets appears in the second quire of an Aldhelm in London: this has only two bifolia, and there are two pairs of half-sheets, one of which forms the outermost leaves of the quire.[145] (This last example should be seen in its context, namely

140 Florence, Biblioteca Medicea-Laurenziana, Amiatino 1: Alidori *et al.*, 2003, pp. 3–58, esp. 4–7.

141 BL, Harley 863.

142 Other instances of the same arrangement appear, e.g., in CUL, Ii.2.11 (OE gospels) and BL, Arundel 60 (psalter).

143 CUL, Ff.1.23.

144 Florence, Biblioteca Medicea-Laurenziana, Amiatino 1; Oxford, Trinity College, 28; CUL, Gg.4.28.

145 BL, Royal 5 E.xi.

2.9(a) Quaternion with half-sheets (singletons) for leaves 3 and 6.

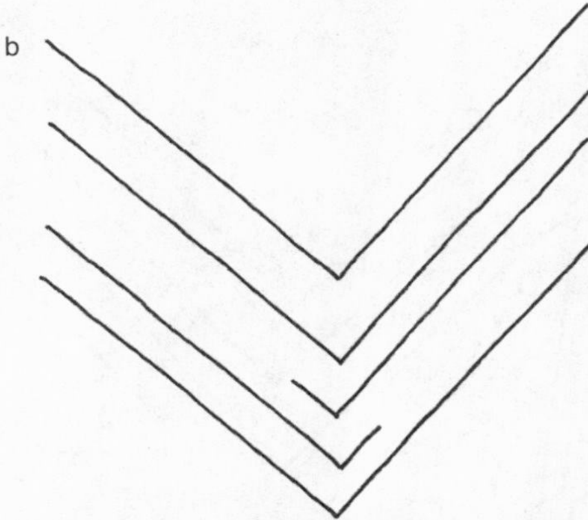

2.9(b) Quaternion with half-sheets (singletons) for leaves 2 and 7.

a manuscript in which a large number of half-sheets were used.[146]) Such structures were presumably viewed as serviceable rather than desirable, and they are correspondingly more likely to have been the result of a scribal error which necessitated the replacement of a page. That such was probably the reason for the one such structure in the Missal of New Minster, Winchester, is underlined

146 The fact that the flyleaves are duplicate copies of the text that appears on fols. 116–17 – presumably first versions that were subsequently rejected – leads one to wonder whether the same phenomenon (cancelling and rewriting leaves) accounts for the unusually disjointed structure of what is externally quite a handsome book.

2.10(a) Quaternion with half-sheets (singletons) for leaves 1 and 8.

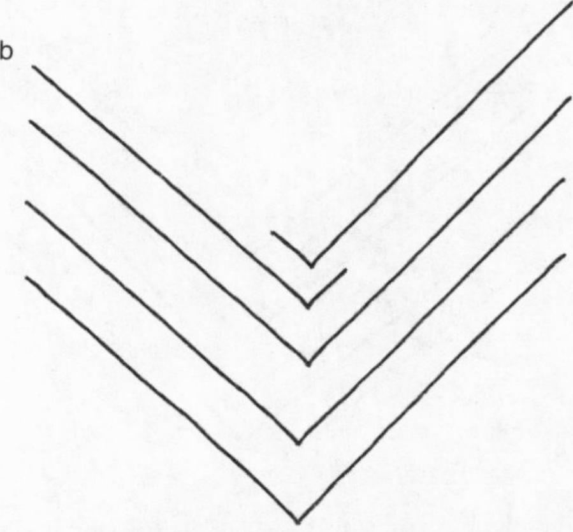

2.10(b) Quaternion with half-sheets (singletons) for leaves 4 and 5.

by the fact that the final leaf of the quire in question was the work of a different near-contemporary hand from that of the main scribe of the book: this folio was very probably an early substitution.[147]

Responses to error apart, the practice of 'cancelling' blank leaves – freeing valuable half-sheets that could be deployed elsewhere – represented a prudent use of membrane, and was widespread. Wholly respectable volumes produced

147 Le Havre, BM, 330, q. VI (fols. 40–7). The same hand also did the whole outer bifolium of q. XXII (163+70).

in major scriptoria have quires featuring pairs of singletons.[148] Yet such structures were undoubtedly more common in manuscripts from outside the 'mainstream' of Anglo-Saxon book production. The circumstance that one or more pairs of half-sheets appear in the middle of four of the twelve quires of the eighth-century Hereford Gospels is consonant with other evidence which suggests that the volume was the product of a minor writing centre;[149] the fact that more than half the quires in an early tenth-century Southumbrian Isidore have them is concordant with its manufacture at a time when English book production was in the doldrums;[150] while in the case of Harley 3826, a manuscript made around the millennium, no fewer than nineteen of whose twenty-one quires include pairs of singletons, the highly economical structure probably reflects the lowly grade of the content (a collection of grammatical texts).

Changes in structure could also, of course, be motivated by the desire to insert or replace material. Thus an extra folio was inserted into quire VII of a collection of texts concerning St Swithun to facilitate the addition of the verse, *Aurea lux patrie uuentana splendet in urbe*.[151] Similarly, two singletons bearing a short letter-collection were added to the end of quire V in the Copenhagen Wulfstan codex.[152] Altogether more dramatically, seventeen extra homilies were intercalated into a copy of Ælfric's first series of Catholic Homilies, involving the introduction of more than fifty leaves scattered through the volume – a process which, furthermore, necessitated the excision of some original leaves and the consequent recopying of certain passages of the original text.[153] Such drastic reworkings aside, these processes are easiest to perceive when the matter in question differs from the main text, as is most obviously the case with artwork. Both the surviving miniatures in the eighth-century Durham Cassiodorus were supplied on singletons, the other face of which remained blank.[154] In the eleventh-century Sacramentary of Robert of Jumièges, the Passion cycle (four full-page miniatures depicting in turn the

148 E.g. TCC, B.1.42 and BL, Harley 5431 from St Augustine's; PML, M 869 from Christ Church.

149 Hereford CL, P.I.2: Gameson 2002c.

150 TCC, B.15.33.

151 BL, Royal 15 C.vii, fols. 49–57 are a unique quire of nine in a book otherwise almost entirely constructed from regular quaternions. The disposition of hair and flesh sides on fols. 49–51 (HF, FH, FH) makes it unlikely that fol. 49 was supplementary to the end of the previous quire (VI), indicating instead that it was the start of q. VII and highlighting fol. 50 as the 'intruder'. Lantfred's *Translatio et miracula* finished on fol. 49v, line 5; while Wulfstan's *Narratio* started on what is now 51r. Soon afterwards it was decided to add the hymn between the two, using the remaining space on 49v and inserting an extra leaf (now fol. 50) to accommodate the rest.

152 Copenhagen, KB, G. K. S. 1595 (4°), fols. 41–2; they are written by a different hand from the rest of this section.

153 BL, Cotton Vitellius C.v; the process is described by Ker 1957, no. 220, and Pope 1967, pp. 26–33.

154 DCL, B.II.30, fols. 81 and 172.

Betrayal, the Crucifixion, the Deposition, and the Resurrection) was painted on a self-contained bifolium that was inserted into the centre of quire XI;[155] all three miniatures in the New Minster Prayerbook appear on parts of self-contained bifolia,[156] as do the portraits of Mark, Luke and John in the Copenhagen Gospels,[157] and that of Luke in the Exeter Gospels.[158]

In a late eleventh-century Cicero and Macrobius, the original scribe inserted a single leaf as the penultimate folio of the first quire as part of a painstaking campaign to make good an omission.[159] Occasionally, if the amount of text wanting was limited, it was supplied by the insertion, not of a whole page, but rather of a small slip of parchment. The phenomenon is common to 'library' texts,[160] saints' lives,[161] liturgica,[162] and even a fine psalter.[163] Though physically obtrusive, the result is much neater than if the scribe had crammed the missing text into the margin, or had effaced and rewritten the page in a smaller hand. Needless to say, the practice was by no means restricted to British books, and as a Continental parallel for its use in high-grade volumes one may cite the case of an exquisite mid-eleventh-century gospel-lectionary made at Echternach.[164]

Quire signatures

The frequency with which early British scribes signed their gatherings – and thus how regular a feature of our books quire signatures were – is irrecoverable, since it is difficult to know which of the many manuscripts that are now without signatures never had them, and which have lost them through subsequent trimming of the leaves. Nevertheless, the number of volumes which preserve fairly wide margins yet bear no trace of any such markings is sufficient to suggest that signatures were not an invariable feature of early British book production: Canterbury Cathedral, Add. 172, an excellently preserved late eleventh-century volume with wide margins still in a contemporary binding, and wholly without them, is a particularly valuable witness in this respect.[165]

155 Rouen, BM, Y.6, fols. 71–2.
156 BL, Cotton Titus D.xxvi, fols. 18+19; Cotton Titus D.xxvii, blank+65; 74+75.
157 Copenhagen, KB, G. K. S. 10 (2°), respectively: excised bifolium between fols. 56 and 57; 82+83; excised leaf after 123+124.
158 BnF, lat. 14782, fols. 73+4.
159 Bodl., Auct. F.2.20 part B: quire I = fols. 17–25 (24 being the insertion).
160 CCCC, 285 (fol. 92); York Minster Library, XVI.q. 2 (after fol. 141).
161 St Gallen, Kantonsbibliothek (Vadiana), 337 (pp. 37–8).
162 BnF, lat. 10575 (pontifical, benedictional).
163 BodL., Douce 296 (fols. 83–4).
164 BR, 9428 (cat. 461). 165 Gameson 2008, no. 15.

With that caveat clearly in view, we may proceed to state that the most common form of signature during our period as a whole was a Roman numeral, and that it is most frequently found at the centre of the lower margin on the final verso of the quire. Splendidly visible examples (in which, moreover, the numeral is preceded by a 'Q' for *quaternio*) appear in eighth-century copies of Apponius, the *Historia ecclesiastica* and the *Rule of St Benedict*, in a copy of Bede *In Proverbia* from the turn of the century, and in a ninth-century Priscian.[166] The diverse origin of these books demonstrates the diffusion of the practice. The use of letters is also found from an early date (as in the seventh-century Durham A.II.10 gospel fragment), but a little less frequently and sometimes in a subsidiary capacity. Thus, illustrating the last point: letters survive beneath some of the numerals in the Codex Amiatinus; the Canterbury Codex Aureus has a continuous sequence of numerals running throughout it, and a series of letters which, though contemporary with the numbers, is confined to Luke's Gospel; while the Durham Cassiodorus has numerals on the final versos of its quires and letters on their first rectos.[167] Conversely, the Durham Gospels of *c*. 700, the eighth-century collection of canons at Cologne, and the ninth-century Book of Cerne provide early instances of manuscripts in which letters alone were employed, majuscules in the first, minuscules in the last two.[168] By the tenth century, in England at least, letters appear to have achieved near parity with numbers.

Other positions for signatures were also used. In the eighth-century Codex Amiatinus and the St Petersburg Bede they are still in the lower margin of the final page but over to the right-hand side. A clutch of manuscripts have them in the centre of the lower margin on the first rectos of the quires,[169] while in a pair of books from Worcester they are in this same margin but over to the left.[170] More unusually, an eighth-century Northumbrian gospel-book, an Æthicus Ister of *c*. 1000 from Worcester, and an eleventh-century grammatical collection of Durham provenance have them in the top margin of the first recto, at the centre, to the left, and in the right-hand corner respectively.[171] Occasionally, more than one place was used: in a *Vita Gregorii* (from Worcester again) the first signature appears on the final verso of quire I,

166 Boulogne, BM, 74; CUL, Kk.5.16; BodL., Hatton 48; Bodley 819; St Gallen, SB, 904.

167 This last usage is paralleled in, e.g., BAV, Pal. lat. 259 (Gregory; viii–ix; England or Anglo-Saxon centre on the Continent).

168 Durham CL, A.II.17; Cologne, Dombibliothek, 213; CUL, Ll.1.10.

169 E.g. Avranches, BM, 81; CCCC, 183 (the only exception is q. I which is signed on the final verso; but the first recto here – whose verso was to receive the pictorial frontispiece – was left entirely blank); BL, Royal 15 B.xxii; Oxford, BodL., Hatton 23; BnF, n.a.l. 586.

170 BodL., Hatton 113+114; Junius 121.

171 DCL, A.II.16; BL, Cotton Vespasian B.x; Oxford, St John's College, 154.

while all the others – continuing the same alphabetical sequence – are on the first rectos.[172] Even more diverse are the practices in a scrappy *Regula S. Benedicti* at Cambridge, wherein the numerals for quires I, II and IV appear on the final verso of their gatherings, that for quire V is on the first recto, while quire III has contemporary 'iii's on both the first recto and the last verso.[173]

A few variant practices deserve mention. In addition to a set of quire signatures comprising a numeral followed by a letter, the ninth-century Mercian *Expositio missae*, Bodleian Library, Hatton 93, bears a contemporary foliation at the bottom of each recto: the scribe started with the alphabet, then moved on to a couple of supplementary sigla followed by some Roman numerals, before returning to letters once again. Correspondingly, across five quires in one eleventh-century vernacular homiliary, the individual leaves are lettered from 'a' to 'o'.[174] Some Salisbury scribes at the very end of our period, by contrast, made precocious, albeit intermittent, use of catchwords instead of quire signatures.[175] Though such practices were to be taken up in future centuries, they appear as isolated innovations in the context of our corpus.

Sometimes, signatures were presented in a more decorative manner. Those in the eighth-century Southumbrian Codex Bigotianus,[176] for instance, appear within simple cartouches (echoing the presentation of the signatures in the 'authorial' Roman manuscript of Gregory's *Regula pastoralis*[177]); those in the late eighth- or early ninth-century Northumbrian Bede *In Proverbia* are framed by four ivy leaves;[178] while plentiful examples from the eleventh century are flanked by divers patterns of dots and dashes. There is little in our corpus, however, to rival some of the more exotic forms that appear elsewhere and at a later date – such as the mid-twelfth-century copy of Augustine *In psalmos* from Marchiennes in Flanders, several of whose signatures incorporate the house's *ex libris*.[179]

Pricking and ruling

To prepare the sheets for ruling, they were pricked with an awl or a knife; both implements were sometimes employed, as, for instance, in the Lichfield Gospels. The exact number of holes was obviously dependent on how many lines were to be ruled, but there were inevitably very many more running down the page (to guide the horizontal lines for the text-block) than across it (to guide the vertical boundaries). One act of pricking often served to mark a whole quire.

172 BL, Royal 6 A.vii. 173 CUL, Ll.1.14.
174 CCCC, 201, pp. 8–160, 167–76. 175 E.g. BodL., Bodley 392 and 756.
176 BnF, lat. 281+298. 177 Troyes, BM, 504.
178 BodL., Bodley 819. 179 Douai, BM, 250.

The placement of the punctures varied with time. In late Antiquity, pricking to guide the horizontal rulings was often done down the centre of the page – such was the case, for instance, in the sixth-century Gospels of St Augustine, made in Italy[180] – and this practice was imitated in the eighth-century Kentish Codex Aureus (Fig. 2.11a). In a seventh-century Italian gospel-book which was also in England at an early date, the holes have moved slightly closer to the edge of the leaf, being positioned amid the outermost of the two columns of writing (Fig. 2.11b).[181] The prickings in most older Irish and Anglo-Saxon manuscripts were located on the outer edge of the text-block. When the manuscript was to be ruled with single vertical boundaries, the punctures literally abutted the text (Fig. 2.11c).[182] Where, however, a double vertical border was envisaged, the prickings were slightly distanced from the writing area itself (Fig. 2.11d).[183] Both practices continued in English scriptoria into the ninth century, as the Book of Cerne and the Royal 1 E. vi Bible fragment show respectively.

The prickings in the eighth-century Kentish copy of Acts,[184] are disposed in two quite different ways which correspond exactly to the stints of the two scribes, suggesting that they prepared their own sheets. The second scribe pricked at the edge of the text-block (Fig. 2.11c), the first well out into the margin (Fig. 2.11e). Pricking in the margins, which is equally a feature of some Italian manuscripts from the sixth century onwards,[185] also appears in the early eighth-century Codex Amiatinus from Wearmouth-Jarrow and the ninth-century Irish Priscian at St Gallen. Both practices – pricking at the outer edge of the text-block, and in the margins – are found in Carolingian books.[186] The late ninth-century copy of Alfred's translation of the *Regula pastoralis* was pricked in the margins;[187] and this was almost invariably the practice in English scriptoria thereafter.

The sheets of many late antique manuscripts were clearly ruled open – as whole bifolia. This is indicated by the fact that there are only two sets of vertical

180 CCCC, 286.

181 BodL., Auct. D.2.14. As also, e.g., in BnF, lat. 17226 (Italy, *s.* vii).

182 E.g. Boulogne, BM, 74; CUL, Kk.5.16; Hereford CL, P.I.2; Milan, Biblioteca Ambrosiana, D.23. sup.; BodL., Rawlinson G.167; St Gallen, Stiftsbibliothek 51; BAV, Pal. lat. 68; Pal. lat. 259.

183 E.g. BL, Cotton Vespasian A.i; Cotton Nero D.iv; BnF, lat. 281+298; Saint-Omer, Bibliothèque de l'agglomération, 257; BAV, Barb. lat. 570.

184 BodL., Selden Supra 30.

185 E.g. Florence, Biblioteca Medicea-Laurenziana, LXV.1 (*s.* vi); BAV, Vat. lat. 5465 (*s.* viii); Vat. lat. 7016 (*s.* viii). In different portions of St Paul in Carinthia, Stifsbibliothek, 1.1 (*s.* v^2) the prickings were placed between the columns, within the outer columns, and in the outer margins.

186 Both appear (along with other variants) in, e.g., BnF, lat. 12283 (Bede, *Expositio Actuum Apostolorum*; Corbie).

187 BodL., Hatton 20.

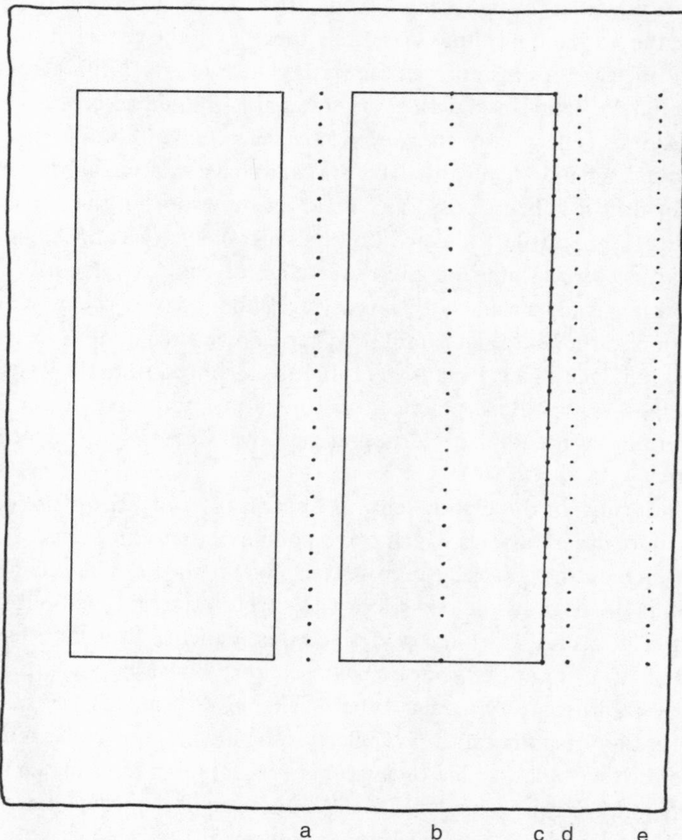

2.11 Page (a recto) showing the range of typical placements for the rows of prickings used to guide horizontal rulings.

prickings to guide the horizontal rulings per bifolium (i.e. one set per folio), and also by the circumstance that some or all of the horizontal lines extend continuously between them (i.e. running without a break across the inner margins of the pages: Fig. 2.12a). In Insular manuscripts, by contrast, pricking and ruling was generally done with the sheets folded, not open. Consequently, there are normally two sets of prickings on each folio; moreover, the ruling does not extend right across the inner margins (Fig. 2.12b).

In this simple form, the phenomenon is well known – as also is the fact that Insular scribes took their practices with them to the Continent. Such

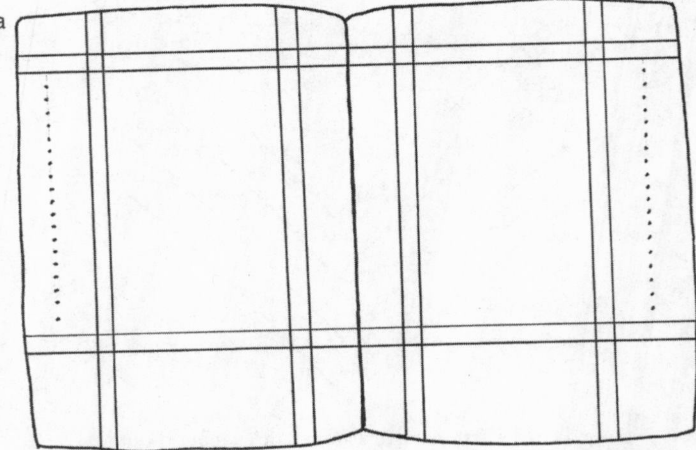

2.12(a) Opening of a manuscript whose sheets were ruled open.

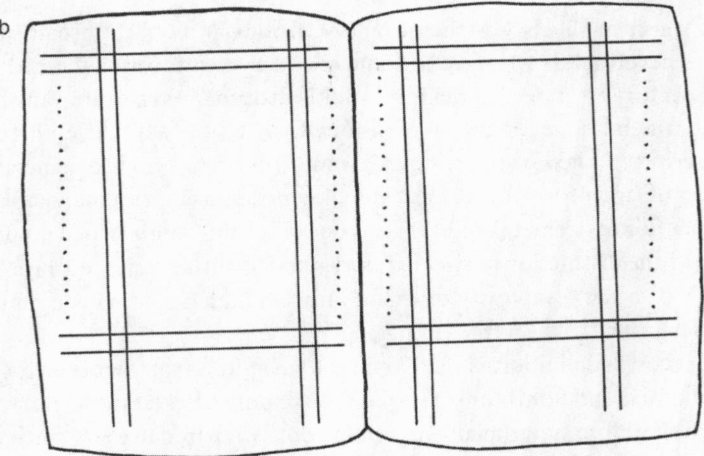

2.12(b) Opening of a manuscript whose sheets were ruled folded.

preparation is, for example, one of the 'Insular' features that appear in certain manuscripts of the 'Court Schools' of Charlemagne.[188] Though pricking and

188 E.g. the Dagulf Psalter (ÖNB, lat. 1861) of the so-called 'Ada' group and the Coronation Gospels (Vienna, Schatzkammer, s.n.) of the 'Coronation' group were pricked in both margins and ruled after folding.

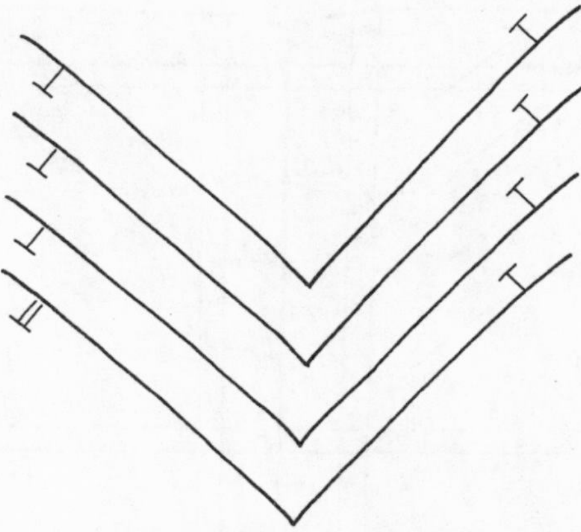

2.13 Direct pricking on to the first recto, transmitted throughout the quire.
(The double-stemmed T-form indicates the primary surface pricked; the single-stemmed T-form indicates the holes made into subsequent leaves.)

ruling on open sheets was the norm in Carolingian books, 'Insular' preparation is nevertheless a feature of some of them, even towards the end of the ninth century.[189] Indeed, pricking in both margins never quite vanishes on the Continent, appearing very occasionally in tenth- and eleventh-century manuscripts,[190] then reappearing in greater force from *c.* 1100, generally for volumes of larger format whose greater dimensions made a second set of guide holes per folio extremely useful. This is one of several points which muddy the waters of the distinction between 'Insular' and 'Continental' preparation, and hence add to the complexity of examining and understanding the transition from the former to the latter in England.

The second such point is that some early Anglo-Saxon manuscripts from Northumbria and Southumbria alike[191] were only pricked in the outer margin, and therefore superficially resemble books prepared in the 'Continental' way: however, close inspection of the punctures and the disposition of direct and indirect ruling shows that the sheets were in fact folded when they were pricked and ruled. The circumstance that the prickings which were applied to the first folio served for the whole quire (Fig. 2.13), and the fact that direct rulings done in the first half of the quire were transmitted to the

189 E.g. Arras, Médiathèque, 699 (Amalarius; *s.* ix$^{3/4}$).
190 E.g. BR, 5573 (gospel-book; Gembloux; *s.* xi$^{2/4}$).
191 Thus respectively BL, Royal 1 B.vii; Cotton Vespasian A.i.

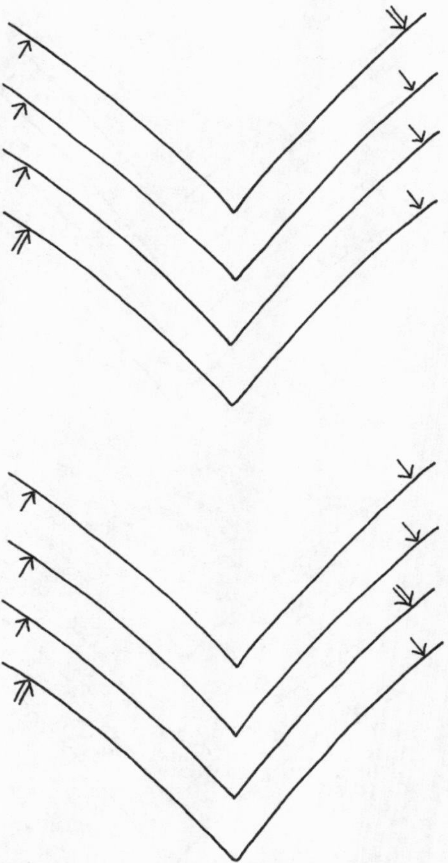

2.14 (a and b) Disposition of direct and transmitted ruling. (The double-stemmed arrows indicate directly applied ruling; the single-stemmed arrows indicate transmitted ruling.)

second half (across the centre: see Fig. 2.14b, c, d) leave no room for doubt on the matter.

Third, it is extremely likely that quires prepared in the Continental way were also generally folded before pricking and ruling began, even if they were then opened again for these processes to be carried out. If they were formed by *pliage*, this was inevitably going to be the case (Fig. 2.6), but even if assembled from a pile of separate bifolia, it remains highly probable: the crucial point was that the ruling grid as a whole had to be correctly aligned with the fold in

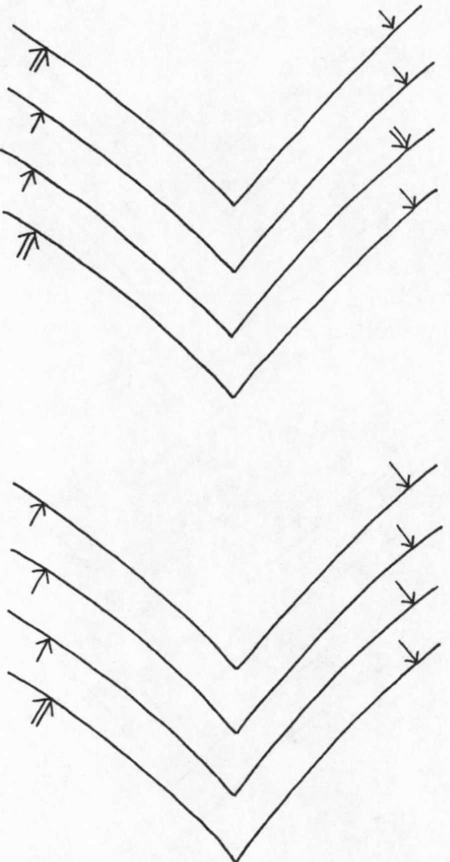

2.14 (c and d) (*Cont.*)

the bifolium (otherwise the text-block might list to a greater or lesser extent when the volume was finally bound).[192] Clearly, this could only be achieved if the sheets had been folded – and so bore the central crease – prior to pricking and ruling. The parchment of the Exeter Book[193] is sometimes arranged in the Insular manner, sometimes in the Continental way; certain bifolia seem to

192 Rare examples of listing text-blocks in our corpus are q. v of the informal compilation, Copenhagen, KB, G. K. S. 1595 (4°); and q. I of Evreux, BM, 43 (Sedulius etc.; *s.* x3/4). Rouen, BM, A.566 (Cat. gén. 275), q. v provides a broadly contemporary example in a low-grade Norman liturgical volume of Rouen Cathedral provenance.

193 Exeter CL, 3501; see n. 1 above.

have been ruled together open, while other quires appear to have been ruled folded. Yet it is clear that the first stage in every case was to make up the quires and fold them, since each gathering bears a set of matching prickings which run through every folio from recto to verso, becoming steadily fainter as one advances through the quire (Fig. 2.13).

Fourth, although the vast majority of ninth- and tenth-century Continental manuscripts were ruled open, there are nevertheless exceptions. Notwithstanding a single set of prickings per page, and horizontal rulings that extend some way into the margins, it is clear from the disposition of direct and transmitted rulings that the sheets of Orléans, Médiathèque 82 (79), for example, a glossed Pauline Epistles made at Flavigny between 894 and 918, were folded when they were ruled.

It is rare in the two centuries after *c.* 900 to find an English book pricked in both margins.[194] Nevertheless, the disposition of direct and transferred ruling, not to mention the transmission through whole quires of single sets of prickings, show that preparation folded continued to be the norm during the first half of the tenth century.[195] Ruling open appears around the middle of the century[196] – though it is clear that the quires were still pricked folded[197] – and both systems (ruling folded and ruling open) were practised during the following generation. Indeed, both are sometimes found in broadly contemporary works from a single scriptorium (the mid-tenth-century Glastonbury Caesarius, for instance, was ruled open, but the coeval Smaragdus from the same centre was prepared closed[198]), and even within the oeuvre of a single scribe.[199] The fact that at Winchester, while the New Minster Charter of 966 was ruled closed, the Benedictional of Æthelwold of 971×84 and the closely related Benedictional that is now in Paris were prepared open is symptomatic of the forward trend;[200] and ruling open steadily gained ground during the second half – and particularly the last third – of the tenth century. Now, it will be noted that this new procedure was being adopted at a slightly earlier date than the change from the 'Insular' to the 'Continental' way of arranging parchment. Consequently, certain books produced in the second half of the tenth century, notably some from Christ Church, Canterbury, were ruled

194 Exceptions include: Copenhagen, KB, G. K. S. 10 (2°); BL, Cotton Faustina C.i, fols. 66–93; BodL., Junius 11; and Winchester CL, 1.

195 *Teste*, e.g., TCC, B.15.33; BL, Add. 47967; Royal 5 F.iii; and BodL., Tanner 10. See Fig. 2.13.

196 E.g. BodL., Hatton 30 (sometimes); BL, Royal 4 A.xiv; and Royal 12 D.xvii.

197 *Teste*, e.g., Oxford, Trinity College, 54.

198 Respectively BodL., Hatton 30; CUL, Ee.2.4.

199 Thus Lambeth Palace Library, 149, is mainly ruled folded; Exeter CL, 3501, variedly; BodL., Bodley 319, mainly open.

200 BL, Cotton Vespasian A.viii; Add. 49598; BnF, lat. 987.

open but still had their parchment disposed in the 'Insular' way. The change from 'Insular' to 'Continental' practices as a whole was a piecemeal process – as the actual ruling procedures underline.[201]

Ruling procedures

Throughout our period, ruling was normally done in hard (or 'dry') point: the lines were scored into the sheets with a tool that had a fine, hard but rounded tip – be it some form of stylus or the back of a knife. From the late tenth century, lead and crayon begin to make occasional appearances. Three of the six quires in a copy of B's *Vita Dunstani* that was made at St Augustine's, Canterbury, at some point between 995 and 1004 were ruled in crayon; the approximately coeval Anglo-Saxon core of a collection of saints' lives now in Boulogne was ruled in crayon; while both lead and red ink or crayon were used intermittently (principally for pages with decoration) in the slightly older Winchester Benedictional at Rouen.[202] In general, as this last case advertises, they were reserved for special circumstances – for instance, if major illumination was planned for the verso,[203] or if a passage had to be re-ruled. The hard-point rulings in the Arenberg Gospels of *c.* 1000 and in a mid-eleventh-century Canterbury hymnal, for example, were rather faint and from time to time were strengthened or supplemented in ink and lead respectively.[204] One folio of the Caligula Troper, a volume made around the time of the Norman Conquest, was originally prepared for a different project and was subsequently re-ruled in lead to adapt it for the present manuscript;[205] on the central sheet of quire II in a late eleventh-entury Cassian and Bede from Worcester the original hard-point ruling went astray and was redone in lead;[206] while on fols. 189–92 of a late eleventh-century copy of Hugh of Langres' Commentary on the Psalms, two discreet lead lines were added above the top of the original

201 As mentioned above, there was on the Continent at the very end of our period a resurgence of pricking in both margins, as a function of the increasing size of books: the pages of giant bibles and grand volumes of patristics (e.g. Douai, BM, 246 and 252; Valenciennes, BM, 9 and 39) were much easier to rule if pricked in both margins. However, since the re-adoption of *this* practice in England was more a phenomenon of *s.* xii than *s.* xi, it falls outside our remit here.

202 St Gallen, Kantonsbibliothek (Vadiana), 337. Boulogne, BM, 106. Rouen, BM, Y.7 in which red ink/crayon was also used for under-drawing. As specimen *s.* ix Continental precedents, one may cite BnF, lat. 9452, where much of the ruling was done in red, and Tours, BM, 22, where both red and brown were used.

203 Eadwig Basan's section in BL, Harley 603, is another case in point.

204 PML, M 869; DCL, B.III.32, part I.

205 BL, Cotton Caligula A.xiv, fols. 1–36: fol. 6.

206 BodL., Hatton 23.

hard-point text-block, thereby raising the number of lines from thirty-eight to forty.[207]

It was not until the late eleventh century that lead or crayon began to be adopted for more extensive use, and then only in a couple of centres. Christ Church, Canterbury, seems to have been the pioneer: more than half of the extant volumes produced at Christ Church between *c.* 1066 and *c.* 1110 were fully or partly ruled in lead, crayon or even ink. St Augustine's Abbey was less radical than its near neighbour in this respect as in many others, and lead and ink were not used there with any regularity until the turn of the century. Most other scriptoria were even more conservative.[208] The newly emerging practice does not represent 'Normanisation', for Norman scriptoria were themselves only just beginning to make the change: all but one of the volumes which were certainly or very probably made in Normandy and acquired for Durham by William Carilef in the late eleventh century are ruled in hard point,[209] and exactly the same is true of the Norman manuscripts that came to Exeter around 1100.[210] Indeed, hard point remained the normal ruling tool in both countries into the early twelfth century; ruling in lead did not really begin to gain ground generally in England until the second quarter of the twelfth century.

In the finest early manuscripts, hard-point ruling appears to have been carried out very lightly on both sides of each sheet, ensuring that it was not only accurate and even but also very discreet.[211] The only late Anglo-Saxon parallel (i.e. where the high status of the volume might have motivated this same practice) is the Copenhagen Gospels.[212] The other tenth- and eleventh-century instances of hard-point ruling on both sides of the sheet have more pragmatic rationales: an elaborate gloss or intercalated illustrations meant that the details of the ruling pattern itself changed from one side of the folio to the other;[213] alternatively, the thickness or stiffness of the parchment prevented ruling applied on one side from being perceptible on the other.[214]

207 BL, Arundel 235.

208 Exceptionally, BL, Cotton Tiberius B.ii (*Vita*, *Miracula S. Edmundi*; Bury St Edmunds; *s.* xi/xii) is mainly ruled in faint red.

209 The exception is DCL, B.II.13 (Augustine, *In Psalmos* 51–100) in which both hard point and lead were used.

210 The one exception, in which hard point and lead were used, is BodL., Bodley 717.

211 E.g., the Lindisfarne Gospels (BL, Cotton Nero D.iv).

212 Copenhagen, KB, G. K. S. 10 (2°).

213 E.g. CUL, Kk.3.21 and BnF, lat. 17814 (both Boethius, *De consolatione philosophiae* with commentary by Remigius); BL, Cotton Claudius B.iv (illustrated OE Hexateuch); Harley 603 (illustrated psalter).

214 E.g. in Oxford, Oriel College, 3 (Prudentius).

More common in early manuscripts was the practice of ruling several sheets together, greater force being applied – a practice with venerable precedents.[215] If the disadvantage was that the surface of the top sheet of the pile might occasionally be slit,[216] the advantage was that the process was greatly expedited. Naturally, the ruled impression became fainter the further one moved into the quire, and re-ruling occurred when and where necessary (see Fig. 2.14). The number of leaves that were done at one time depended on the thickness of the membrane and the force exerted. Most pages of the Irish Psalter at Rouen and the Alfredian Pastoral Care manuscript, whose parchment is quite stout, had to receive direct ruling.[217] In the Northumbrian Royal 1 B.vii Gospels, on the other hand, the impression was regularly transmitted through two or three leaves and sometimes as many as six; in an eighth-century Kentish copy of Acts, it served for between two and four leaves at a time; while in a later tenth-century bilingual *Regula S. Benedicti*, it was generally good for four.[218] The implication of cases like this last one was that, in a regular quaternion, the scribe had to apply ruling to only two pages: 1r, whose impression was transmitted through the first half of the quire, and then 5r which likewise served for the second half (Fig. 2.14a). Such procedures were commonplace in England until the late tenth century.

The normal practice in England in the eleventh century was rather different: ruling was generally done on the hair sides of most sheets while they were open and separated from each other; the bifolia were subsequently put together in quires with hair sides facing hair sides, and flesh, flesh – which also meant that the pages which were furrowed with the impress of ruling faced each other, as did those that were embossed with the projecting ridges (Fig. 2.15). Now clearly the rise of this practice was not going to predate the changeover from the 'Insular' to the 'Continental' way of arranging the parchment within the quire; but neither was it inextricably linked to it. In point of fact, tracing the lineage of the procedure, and identifying the reasons why English scribes adopted it, is by no means straightforward.

The practice – which, for convenience, we shall term 'new standard preparation' – developed on the Continent during the ninth century; a version of it appeared at Tours, for instance, around the middle of the century.[219] Yet,

215 E.g. Bologna, Biblioteca Universitaria, 701 (Lactantius; *s.* v[2]) was ruled after folding, on the first recto of each quire and on succeeding rectos as required.

216 As e.g. in BodL., Tanner 10; equally the Continental Worcester CL, Q.28 (Eusebius).

217 Rouen, BM, A.41 (24); BodL., Hatton 20.

218 BodL., Selden Supra 30; CCCO, 197.

219 Though here, as sheets were sometimes ruled in pairs and then rearranged, the system could be more complicated: Rand 1929, I, pp. 10–18. Fig. 2.16(b).

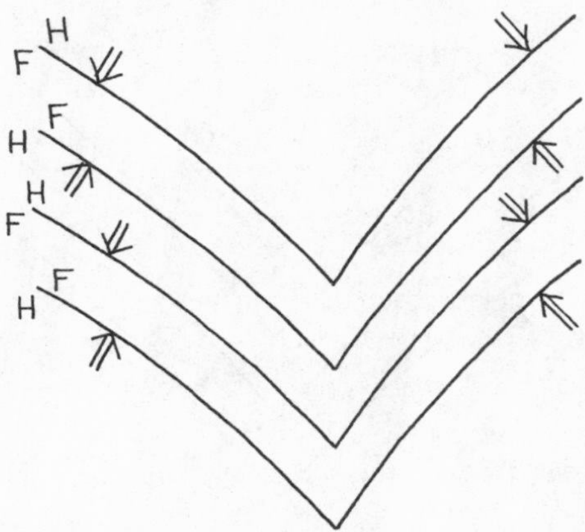

2.15 Quaternion with parchment arranged HF, FH, and with ruling applied directly to each hair side.

although its use spread significantly during the second half of the ninth century, it did not become normative then – if it was fairly common in volumes from northern Francia, for example,[220] it was rarer in certain other centres, and was exceptional in Breton ones.[221] Nor was such preparation universal on the Continent in the tenth century: at Fleury, for instance, it was a regular feature by the second half of the tenth century, but not during the first;[222] and if it was the norm at Saint-Bertin in the later tenth century, it was less so at contemporary Reichenau. Thus the 'living traditions' to which tenth-century Anglo-Saxon scribes may have been exposed were not unified on this point. Furthermore, the majority of the extant ninth-century Continental volumes that certainly or probably came to England at an early date do not, in fact, exhibit 'new standard preparation'. The quires of the Carolingian Julian of Toledo in Cambridge, the Juvencus and Aldhelm in London, and the Proverbs, Ecclesiastes and Cantica Canticorum in Rouen, to cite some cases in point, were generally ruled open with a single direct impression on one of the outer sides, which was transferred through the rest of the quire with diminishing clarity (Fig. 2.16a).[223] Moreover, even access to a model for the new procedure

220 There is no shortage of exceptions even here: e.g. Valenciennes, BM, 69 (gospel-book; *s.* ix/x), whose sheets were through-ruled in one go.

221 The quires of the Breton Gospel-Book, Boulogne, BM, 8, e.g., were made up (HF, FH) and through-ruled in one go, a single impression on an outer bifolium being transmitted through the 'pile' as a whole: Fig. 2.14d. The same is true of most of the quires in Alençon, BM, 84.

222 It is not a feature of, e.g., Orléans, Médiathèque, 82 and 337.

223 CCCC, 399; BL, Royal 15 A.xvi; Rouen, BM, A.292.

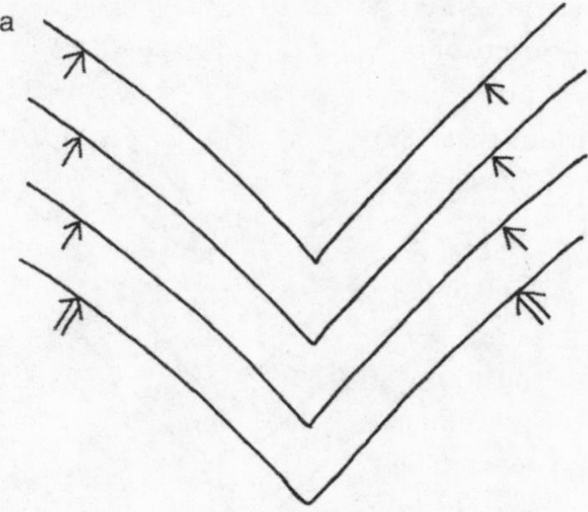

2.16(a) Four sheets ruled together, one impression on an outer side being transmitted throughout.

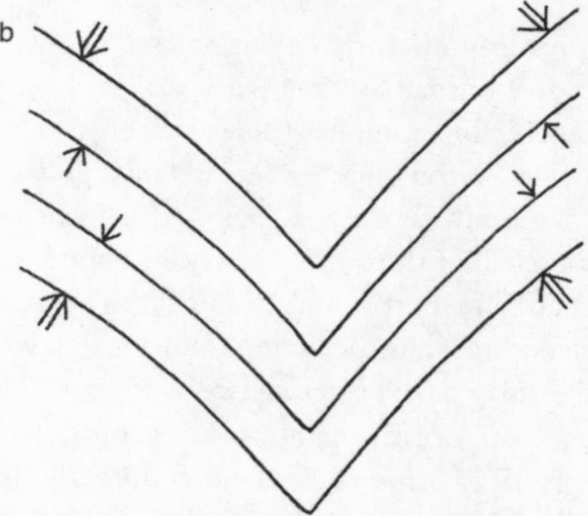

2.16(b) Sheets ruled in pairs then rearranged so that furrowed hair sides face each other, ridged flesh sides likewise.

did not necessarily lead to its being imitated, as the Leofric Missal underlines: the original stratum of this northern French manuscript was mainly prepared in the 'new standard' way, but the quires that were added to it in England in the later tenth century were not.[224]

224 BodL., Bodley 579. Equally, BL, Add. 24193 (Fortunatus; *s.* ix[1]; France): the parchment of the original book was arranged HF, FH and was ruled folded (prickings in outer margin only) with single horizontal line ruling; that in the two quires (fols. 2–16) added by Anglo-Saxons (*s.* x[2]), by

In fact, the preparation of tenth-century English books is characterised by an almost bewildering variety of practices. The case of Christ Church, Canterbury, reveals that different procedures could co-exist even at a fairly advanced date in a major scriptorium that was undoubtedly exposed to Continental influences. The quires of Christ Church manuscripts from the period *c.* 960 – *c.* 1010 display:

1. hard-point ruling on some hair sides, done with the quires made up and folded, the impressions being transmitted to the following leaf or leaves, the parchment being arranged in the old Insular way (HF, HF);
2. the same, with the parchment disposed in the Continental manner (HF, FH);
3. hard-point ruling on each hair side, but with the parchment arranged in the old Insular way (HF, HF);
4. ruling on hair sides, the arrangement of the leaves being mixed;
5. ruling on both sides of the leaves which were arranged in the Continental way; and
6. hard-point ruling on the hair sides, the parchment being arranged HF, FH.

Now, although these different types have been so listed as to culminate in the procedure that was to become the norm, it should be stressed that it is difficult to perceive clear chronological patterns in their use during the period in question. Rather than a logical progression from 'old style' to 'new standard' preparation, it seems that a variety of procedures co-existed until the beginning of the eleventh century.

The wholesale adoption of 'new standard preparation' in England was, like the other changes we have examined, a piecemeal process. 'Bald's Leechbook' of the mid-tenth century provides an exceptional, early example:[225] apart from quire I (which was ruled open in one go: Fig. 2.16a), the gatherings are mainly HF, FH with direct, hard-point ruling on most hair sides (Fig. 2.15). The quires of the New Minster Charter (966) were through-ruled, folded (Fig. 2.14), but those of the Benedictional of Æthelwold and the Paris Benedictional were wholly made in the new way (Fig. 2.15). The witness of one conveniently datable manuscript suggests that 'new standard preparation' was adopted at St Augustine's *c.* 1000,[226] but as this effectively coincides with the end of the drive to build a library there and the production of books then fell off dramatically, it is difficult to be certain. Christ Church was, as we have seen,

contrast, is HF, HF, pricked in both margins, and ruled with double horizontals. The original stratum of BL, Royal 15 A.xvi (Juvencus, Aldhelm, etc.) was pricked in the outer margin only; the Anglo-Saxon addition (fols. 74–84) was pricked in both margins.

225 BL, Royal 12 D.xvii. 226 St Gallen, Kantonsbibliothek (Vadiana), 337.

still just flirting with the new procedure around the millennium, and the same is true of Worcester: in both places the definitive adoption of 'new standard preparation' came in the early eleventh century.

Three further general points should be made about this aspect of the manufacturing of English books. First, the principle of applying ruling to the hair side of the sheets was gaining ground before the definitive shift was made to arranging the parchment in the 'Continental' way. Consequently, once this latter custom had been adopted, 'new standard preparation' inevitably followed. Second, as 'new standard preparation' required that the sheets be open when ruled, it is *this* more than the arrangement of the parchment as such that attests to manufacturing the quires in the 'Continental' way. Correspondingly, the melange of ruling practices that existed in England *c.* 1000 shows that, even when parchment was being arranged HF, FH, the procedures of English scribes were still not really those of many of their Continental counterparts. Third, after the move to 'new standard preparation', most hair sides received direct ruling. It is rare to find the expedient that was used at Tours, for instance, in the ninth century whereby the sheets were actually ruled in pairs arranged HF, HF – so that both hair sides would bear a ruling furrow and both flesh sides a ridge – and were then rearranged so that like faced like (Fig. 2.16b). (One isolated Anglo-Saxon example of the practice is the later tenth-century sacramentary now at Orléans.[227]) The adoption of 'new standard preparation' by English scribes meant that the labour involved in making the quires of ordinary manuscripts increased substantially.

Ruling patterns

In a few manuscripts, such as the ninth-century Juvencus from Wales,[228] the only rulings supplied were those defining the outer boundaries of the text-block – the lines of writing within them were aligned by eye alone. Correspondingly, the evidence of partially completed leaves confirms that on more conventionally prepared sheets, it was the outer bounding grid that was ruled first, and the 'inner' horizontals were supplied subsequently, as one would expect.[229] Normally, one horizontal was ruled for each line of

227 Orléans, Médiathèque, 127 (105). 228 CUL, Ff. 4. 42.

229 E.g. the Lantfred and Wulfstan of Winchester, Rouen, BM, U.107, fols. 28–85: the outer bifolium of q. 1 (28+35) was initially being prepared for a different context with a different pattern and was then re-ruled for the present book: only the double vertical and horizontal bounding lines were supplied in the original ruling.

text. However, following a practice used for certain deluxe manuscripts in late Antiquity, double lines were supplied in some of the finest early British books, notably the Lindisfarne and Lichfield Gospels, the Wearmouth-Jarrow Gospels at Durham, the Book of Kells and the Canterbury Codex Aureus.[230] Such pairs of lines guided not only the feet but also the heads of the letters, thereby ensuring maximum regularity of script. A few volumes – notably the MacRegol and Barberini Gospels[231] – are partly ruled with double horizontal lines, partly with single. In the latter manuscript, the double-line passage is confined within the stint of one particular scribe, raising the possibility that he was responsible for ruling his own sheets. Double horizontal ruling reappears in a few Latin books of later tenth-century date and Old English ones of the first half of the eleventh century.[232] Several of the former set are written in a particularly tall Anglo-Saxon Square Minuscule which obviously benefited from being guided at both head and foot; however, this was not the determining factor per se, for an equal number are written in Caroline Minuscule, while other manuscripts in a comparable or even grander Square Minuscule[233] have but single horizontal lines. The common denominator to most – though admittedly not all – of this first group is production at Christ Church, Canterbury. The majority of the eleventh-century Old English examples are Ælfric homiliaries (though, again, other copies of that work were ruled more conventionally).

In volumes where initials were placed within the text-block (rather than in the margins) single vertical lines sufficed to define the boundaries of the written space;[234] when – as was commonly the case – the margins were to contain initials, double lines were generally used. Further verticals were sometimes supplied to guide marginal texts – the correspondences in gospel-books, for example.[235] If the manuscript was to have a more elaborate layout (including, for instance, interspersed illustrations or a full marginal commentary) the ruling pattern was necessarily more complicated. In a glossed copy of Boethius' *De consolatione philosophiae*, there is an extra horizontal line for an

230 BL, Cotton Nero D.iv; Lichfield CL, 1; DCL, A.II.17, fols. 103–11; TCD, 58; Stockholm, KB, A.135.

231 BodL., Auct. D.2.19; BAV, Barb. lat. 570.

232 Latin: CCCC, 57; Evreux, BM, L.43 (in part); Exeter CL, 3507; BL, Harley 1117 (pt i); Harley 3020 (pt ii); Royal 12 C.xxiii; BodL., Bodley 718; BnF, lat. 943; lat. 17814; and BAV, Reg. lat. 1671 (briefly). Old English: CCCC, 162; BL, Cotton Julius E.vii; Cotton Vitellius C.v (part of original stratum); Cotton Vitellius D.xvii; Harley 5915, fol. 13; and BodL., Bodley 340+342.

233 Most notably, BL, Add. 37517 (the Bosworth Psalter).

234 E.g. Hereford CL, P.I.2.

235 Occasionally an additional vertical was ruled, presumably at an earlier stage, to guide the prickings themselves.

interlinear gloss between each of the rulings for the main text, while columns of narrower rulings to guide the marginal apparatus flank the main text-block.[236]

Such additional complexities aside, the number of general ruling patterns that were used is surprisingly large: drawing only on the corpus of eleventh-century English books whose text is set out in long lines, we find more than thirty different designs. Conversely, the number of them that were actually popular is very small. Many of the patterns are employed in a couple of volumes at most: indeed a few only appear in one part of a single book. The post-Conquest Christ Church copy of Eusebius' *Historia ecclesiastica*, for instance, has three different ruling patterns none of which reappears in any coeval English manuscript.[237] Similarly, a copy of Aldhelm's prose *De virginitate* that was made at Christ Church around the millennium has two main ruling patterns, one of which does not appear elsewhere, while the other is only paralleled in two books, a coeval copy of Aldhelm's *Carmen de virginitate* also from Christ Church and a post-Conquest Isidore from Salisbury, the latter of which has a second pattern which is itself unattested elsewhere.[238] The majority of these idiosyncratic ruling grids are asymmetrical in some respect. The first pattern that was used in the aforementioned Isidore is a typical example: at the top, only the first horizontal ruling is extended, but at the bottom both the last and the penultimate horizontals are carried across the page. The asymmetry could equally apply to the vertical rulings: in part of a gospel-book of Barking provenance, for example, the inner vertical boundary is defined by a pair of lines, whereas the outer one is delineated by a single ruling.[239] The fact that such patterns were maintained from one sheet to the next in their respective manuscripts shows that they were not mistakes as such; nevertheless, they are very much in the minority. Indeed, the most popular non-symmetrical design (in which the bottom one, and the top two horizontals were extended) is found in a mere four volumes.

Most scribes preferred symmetrical designs, with the same number of horizontals extended at the top as at the bottom and with matching vertical rulings on either side of the text-block. Two such patterns were considerably more popular than all the others, each of them being used in approximately a third of the eleventh-century corpus; both were straightforward, as one

236 CUL, Kk.3.21. On the Continental and Irish antecedents of such designs, for which *s.* ix was the crucible: Holtz 1984.

237 CCCC, 187.

238 Respectively BL, Royal 5 E.xi; BodL., Bodley 577 and Bodley 444.

239 BodL., Bodley 155.

2.17 Common ruling patterns.

would expect. One is characterised by double verticals on both sides of the text block, and by the extension of the first and last horizontal (Fig. 2.17a); the other differs from this only in extending the first two and the last two horizontals (Fig. 2.17b). Although their relative simplicity was undoubtedly an important factor in their popularity, it will be noted that neither is the simplest grid possible – i.e. having the first and the last horizontal extended and with only one vertical ruling to either side of the text block (Fig. 2.17c). The reason why this last design, although slightly less complicated, was less popular was undoubtedly that it was not as practical, since it failed to provide as much guidance for initials in the margin.

Aside from the two outstandingly popular designs just mentioned, there are but three others which are attested by twenty witnesses or more. The most frequently occurring of these (i.e. the third most popular overall) is characterised by single extended horizontals at top and bottom, and by a border of double verticals which stop neatly at the aforementioned horizontals (Fig. 2.17d). Because of this last feature, the pattern required a little more care to realise than the others we have considered. It is no surprise, then, to find that it was used in a good number of high-grade manuscripts, including several fine gospel-books, the Tiberius Psalter, the Caligula and Winchester Tropers, and the Sacramentary of Robert of Jumièges.[240] It does appear in various less exalted volumes including an Old English Bede, a couple of vernacular homiliaries, and a copy of Ælfric's *Grammar*, all of which are, however, well produced.[241] Conversely, the simplest pattern of all (described above: Fig. 2.17c) which is also the fourth most popular design, is found in a higher proportion of lower-grade volumes. Though not restricted to such – for its set embraces a fine gradual and gospel-lectionary[242] – they nevertheless comprise the majority of its members.

By contrast with the two groups that we have just discussed, all the adherents to the fifth design (which is characterised by double verticals and by the extension of the first and the third, then the last and the antepenultimate horizontals: Fig. 2.18) do have something in common, namely the fact that they were written after 1066. Concordant with a post-Conquest date, a good number of the manuscripts in question are of known origin – which enables us to see that this particular pattern was used in at least six different scriptoria. The same design also became popular at Mont Saint-Michel in the later eleventh century, but while this might conceivably have encouraged the adoption of the pattern at St Augustine's Abbey, the wide diffusion of the design in England rules out the possibility that it was accepted under the influence of a single Continental centre.

240 E.g. CCCC, 473; Cambridge, Pembroke College, 301; TCC, B.10.4; BL, Loan 11; Mortain, s.n.; BnF, lat. 272; Reims, BM, 9; BL, Cotton Tiberius C.vi; Stowe 2; Cotton Caligula A.xiv, fols. 1–36; BodL., Lat. liturg. f.5; Rouen, BM, Y.6.

241 CUL, Kk.3.18; Ii.4.6; BL, Royal 15 B.xxii; BodL., Hatton 113+114.

242 Durham, UL, Cosin v.v.6; Cambridge, Pembroke College, 302 – both small books it will be noted, measuring 160 × 65 mm (text-block 110 × 65) and 197 × 100 (155 × 67) respectively.

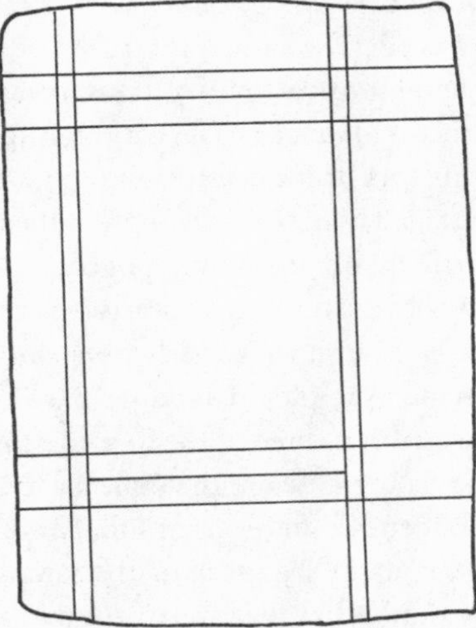

2.18 Ruling pattern.

There is little correlation between ruling patterns and place of production, beyond what was inevitable in view of the general popularity of a small number of designs. Thus the mid- and later eleventh-century Worcester volumes are spread across three of the four main patterns, while some post-Conquest Christ Church books follow each of the main designs. In fact, I am only aware of one case where a very high percentage of broadly coeval manuscripts from a single centre use the same pattern. The books in question are those produced at Exeter in Bishop Leofric's day (1050–72), all but one of which share a ruling grid which is flanked by double verticals and has the first and last pairs of horizontals extended (Fig. 2.17b). The predominance of this pattern did not, however, outlive Leofric, for although a few of the books which were probably made at Exeter in the last quarter of the century still employ it, others do not. The case of St Augustine's in the late eleventh century – the *proxime accessit* in terms of favouring one design over the others – merely underlines how exceptional was Exeter's adherence to a single pattern. For although there is a preponderance in favour of extending the first, the third, the last and the antepenultimate horizontals (Fig. 2.18), the relevant volumes amount to less than half of the abbey's output at the time, and three of them are only partly ruled thus. The first generation of Exeter scribes emerge as having been unusually homogeneous in their treatment of such preliminaries.

The presentation of text in two columns, with a concomitant increase in the number of vertical borders, enlarged the range of possibilities.[243] Hence, despite the fact that the number of two-column manuscripts is very modest in comparison with the long-line ones, the corpus still includes some twenty different patterns of this sort. It is no surprise to find that the most common (which in this case means having four or more adherents) were essentially two-column versions of the outstandingly popular long-line designs. Once again, there is rarely any obvious correlation between choice of grid and place of origin – the relevant late eleventh- to early twelfth-century Christ Church books, to take an extreme example, include no fewer than twelve different pattern types. Thus the fact that three of the four St Augustine's Abbey books that were written in two columns share the same pattern is worthy of note.[244] Given that they are also identical in terms of number of lines per page, are of closely similar size, and contain the work of the same author (Augustine of Hippo), there can be no doubt that they were prepared as a matching set.

The extent to which variety was tolerated is shown by the number of manuscripts which include more than one ruling pattern. In a few cases the adoption of a different grid corresponds with a change in scribe;[245] in others it probably reflects a disjunction in the date of manufacture;[246] while in a handful of cases it may have been the result of divergencies in production method – the circumstance that the upper and lower horizontal rulings in the Prudentius at Boulogne and the Sulpicius Severus in the Vatican, for instance, are sometimes extended and at other times not, could indicate that certain quires were ruled open, others folded.[247] (The date of both these volumes, within sight of the millennium when a variety of preparation procedures flourished, adds to the plausibility of such a scenario.) In many volumes, however, there is no such 'obvious' explanation for the phenomenon, and the implication would seem to be that consistency in these minutiae was unimportant. The point is underlined by manuscripts such as the well-produced, neatly written and visually homogeneous Cassian plus Bede made at Worcester during the heyday of its scribal activities in the later eleventh century, which nevertheless has no fewer than four different ruling patterns; and a relatively orderly late eleventh-century Hugh of Langres, in which the number of horizontal lines varies from page to page.[248]

243 On the choice of two columns as opposed to long lines see pp. 25–7 above.
244 BR, 444–52; Canterbury, CL, Lit. A.8, and U3/162/28/1.
245 E.g. BL, Royal 15 C.x; and BAV, Reg. lat. 1671.
246 E.g. Arras, Médiathèque, 867 (346); CCCC, 190B; and BL, Cotton Vitellius C.v.
247 Boulogne, BM, 189; BAV, Reg. lat. 489.
248 Respectively BodL., Hatton 23, and BL, Arundel 235.

The care with which the ruling was done varied appreciably from one book to the next. While in many manuscripts the horizontals are neatly confined within the vertical rulings, in a good number of others they overrun them irregularly. Although a higher proportion of high-grade books than of lower-grade ones was carefully ruled, as one would expect, there are plenty of exceptions. Mis-rulings are common in the deluxe Kentish Codex Aureus and the fine Arenberg and Royal 1 D.ix Gospels; conversely, the 'workaday' eleventh-century Winchcombe Psalter is scrupulously neatly ruled. Looking at the work of the Exeter scriptorium in Leofric's day (whose remarkable homogeneity with regard to ruling pattern was noted above) we find that most of the manuscripts were exemplarily prepared, but that a couple were not (both of which, intriguingly, contained important texts).[249] Irrecoverable variables such as the individual responsible or the time available presumably lie behind such apparent anomalies. Moreover, a poor scribe could still pride himself on careful ruling; indeed, given his lesser pen control, it might have been all the more necessary. Ultimately, a lack of finesse in the hard-point ruling should be seen in relation to the fact that the resultant grid, though crucially important, was a largely invisible part of the substructure of the page; and it is sobering to note how many otherwise handsome twelfth-century books were carelessly ruled in the more obtrusive media of lead and crayon.

Ink, pigments, gold and silver

The available data specifically on early British inks and pigments is limited. There are no extant Irish or Anglo-Saxon recipes describing their manufacture,[250] and few of our pre-Conquest manuscripts have undergone the scientific investigation that is necessary for a sound identification of their components. The comments that follow reflect current knowledge about early medieval pigments in general, derived from the handful of surviving treatises on the subject[251] and modern experimentation with their recipes;

249 CUL, Ii.2.11 (OE gospels), esp. qq. X–XI. Also CCCC, 191 (Chrodegang, *Regula canonicorum*), wherein there is irregular over-running, a listing text-block and some slits in the parchment caused by the ruling.

250 The earliest extant probably English example is the fragment from *De coloribus et mixtionibus*: BL, Cotton Nero A.vii, fol. 40, of *s.* xi[ex].

251 Principally: Pliny, *Historia naturalis*, libri 33–7; Leyden Papyrus X: Caley 1926; *Compositiones variae: Compositiones ad tingenda musiva*: Hedfors 1932; Johnson 1939; *Mappae clavicula* [a composite work]: Smith and Hawthorne 1974; Halleux 1990; Heraclius, *De coloribus et artibus Romanorum*: Merrifield 1847, I, 182–257; *De clarea*: Thompson 1932; *De coloribus et mixtionibus*: Smith and Hawthorne 1974, 26–8; Theophilus, *De diversis artibus*: Dodwell 1961; Hawthorne and Smith 1979. For an overview of the field as a whole: Clarke 2001.

this is collated with such detailed investigations of early British books as have been published.[252] Yet this is a restricted and imprecise basis from which to approach a complicated and technical topic. Accordingly, the present section merely surveys the range of pigments that were apparently current, with some consideration of their composition, manufacture and properties.

The practicalities of how, and at what cost, individual centres acquired their pigments are obscure. Ink was easy to make, the materials were readily available, and it would have been intolerable for a writing centre not to control its own supply. By contrast, it is often impossible to divine whether the pigments used in a given book were manufactured locally, regionally, or were imported. The circumstances doubtless varied from pigment to pigment, from place to place, and from one period to another. Some ingredients, such as orpiment, mercury and lapis lazuli, had to be imported, while others *could* have been made or obtained in Britain (though even here we should distinguish between those vegetable sources and minerals like lead and ochres which were fairly widespread, and others, such as copper and silver, whose deposits were confined to particular regions). The dispatch of colours or even ink from one place to another is occasionally documented on the Continent,[253] and the same probably happened in Britain. Organising a reliable colour supply – be it acquiring pigments ready to use, or the materials to make them – required effort and resources; and it is no accident that the periods and locations of most extensive colour use coincide with times and places of relative prosperity and strongest contact with Europe and the Mediterranean.[254] It also required forward planning, even with regard to substances that were made locally, for organic matter had to be garnered in season, and some artificial pigments were slow to form: white lead required a month or more; certain types of verdigris needed up to half a year.

Many of the notes that follow will be concerned with individual colourstuffs; however these did not in themselves form ink or paint. To be made workable and durable, pigment was generally ground in water on a slab to form a paste of the required consistency.[255] Different substances needed different

252 E.g. Fuchs and Oltrogge 1994; Brown, Brown and Jacobs 2003; Brown and Clark 2004; and Clarke 2004. The findings of pioneers, notably Roosen-Runge and Werner 1960 and Roosen-Runge 1967, have been shown to be unreliable in detail. More generally: Thompson 1936; Flieder 1968; Bat-Yehouda 1983; Feller 1986; Guineau 1990; Guineau and Vezin 1992; Roy 1993; and Coupry 1999.

253 E.g. the letter from Bishop Frothar of Toul to Abbot Aglemar (*s.* ix[1]): Scholosser 1892, no. 896.

254 Correspondingly, the limited palette – orange, pink, yellow and black – of the Hereford Gospels (Hereford CL, P.I.2) is one of several factors that point to manufacture away from one of the major centres of book production.

255 As depicted in the *s.* xii[med] Dover Bible, CCCC, 4, fol. 241v: Alexander 1992, ill. 26.

amounts of grinding to achieve their optimum colour, while in some cases several distinct shades could be obtained from a single substance by varying the particle size: malachite, for example, may become lighter when ground more finely, vermilion gets darker. In addition to water, the admixture of an adhesive, such as egg white, glair (whipped egg white, left to stand[256]), tree gum (dried sap) or an animal-derivative glue, was required to provide viscosity and to ensure that the paint adhered satisfactorily to the page. The composition of the medium might influence the appearance and the property of the paint: egg white, for instance, enhanced sheen, but it also gave the paint surface a propensity to crack; egg yolk enriched reds but the result was less adhesive and more prone to smudging. The nature of a given colour and the intensity of its tone were variables that depended on the quality of the raw materials, the care with which the pigment had been obtained from them, and the skill and intentions of whoever turned it into paint, as well as on the relative proportions of the elements in the mixture. Different intensities of the same colour were sometimes juxtaposed for aesthetic effect – and at other times to achieve contrast with economy. Conversely, maintaining constant tones throughout one volume (which may have taken months, even years, to produce) required a consistency of materials, quantities and procedures, along with a scriptorium discipline, that were challenging to achieve.

Inks and pigments could be applied in different ways for divers ends when writing text, distinguishing initials, drawing lines and painting pictures.[257] These included delineating a design with firm ink lines then tinting selected areas with colour (as, for instance, in the Durham Cassiodorus[258]); drawing in brown-black ink then shadowing the contours with coloured lines (a fine example being the frontispiece to the 'Ramsey' Psalter[259]); drawing with colour alone (as in the Harley 603 Psalter and the Arenberg Gospels, contemporary products of Christ Church, Canterbury[260]); using paints individually to colour areas with even tones (the case, for example, in areas of the Lindisfarne Gospels[261]); applying multiple washes of a single colour to achieve translucent but rich varying shades (to be seen in the Douce Psalter[262]); and mixing different colours, overpainting and scumbling to make a modulating highly painted

256 See further *De clarea* (Thompson 1932); also Heraclius, *De coloribus*: Merrifield 1847, I, pp. 232–3.

257 For analysis of the different stages in the preparation of the miniatures in the unfinished BL, Cotton Claudius B.iv, see Dodwell and Clemoes 1974, pp. 61–4.

258 DCL, B.II.30.

259 BL, Harley 2904, fol. 3v (now sadly faded): Wormald 1952, frontispiece.

260 BL, Harley 603; PML, M 869.

261 BL, Cotton Nero D.iv; Roosen-Runge and Werner 1960, superseded by Brown *et al.* 2003.

262 BodL., Douce 296.

surface (as in the Codex Aureus, the 'Athelstan Psalter', and the Caligula Troper[263]). For success with these last techniques, the artist had to know which ingredients could and could not be combined satisfactorily. The tract *De coloribus et mixtionibus* provided guidance on the subject: 'darken brown with black, lighten it with minium ... make flesh-coloured pigment with red lead and white, darken it with vermilion, lighten it with white lead', and so on.[264] The incompatibility of certain substances was essential knowledge if adverse chemical reactions were to be avoided, and the same treatise observed, 'Darken orpiment with vermilion, and there is no lightening for this since it turns all other pigments dung coloured.' It subsequently advised: 'Orpiment is not compatible with folium, green, red lead or white lead. Green is not compatible with folium'; while another such commentator ('Heraclius') warned that if they are combined, 'the quality and beauty of the pigments themselves ... and the work done with them are spoiled and destroyed'.[265]

Colour, no less than different script types, played an important role in the visual articulation of texts. Rubric was distinguished by being written in red; display script highlighting the most important textual divisions might be coloured, as might the initials marking sections within it; sentence capitals were sometimes in-filled or stroked with colour. Between the seventh and the ninth centuries key initials were regularly written in ink and accentuated by an outline of red dots; in the tenth and particularly the eleventh century they were often drawn in colour alone (sometimes in repeating sequences). The presence of preparatory 'colour notes', defining the colour of such letters, shows that by the late eleventh century their provision could be carefully planned.[266]

The materials of the 'artist' and the 'scribe' overlapped. Dark ink was an essential component of drawings and paintings, while pigments could be utilised for writing. A full range of colours was deployed for initials and display scripts, and in special circumstances extensive use could be made of coloured inks. In the Winchcombe Psalter, for instance, the Latin and Old English versions were written on alternate lines, the former in brown ink, the latter in orange;[267] equally, the same pigments were used for the coloured script and display script as for the artwork in the later tenth-century additions to the Leofric Missal.[268] Nor was there an absolute division between painting and

263 Stockholm, KB, A.135; BL, Cotton Galba A.xviii + BodL., Rawlinson B.484, fol. 85 (the added miniatures); BL, Cotton Caligula A.xiv, fols. 1–36.

264 *De coloribus et mixtionibus*, ix–xi (Smith and Hawthorne 1974, pp. 27–8).

265 Heraclius, *De coloribus*: Merrifield 1847, I, pp. 252–4.

266 E.g. in BodL., Hatton 23. See further Petzold 1990; also Gousset and Stirnemann 1990.

267 CUL, Ff.1.23.

268 BodL., Bodley 579, qq. VI–VIII.

drawing. A pen was regularly used to add outlines and details to areas of paint, and certain areas of colour were applied with a pen not a brush.[269]

Certain broad diachronistic patterns can be perceived in the Anglo-Saxons' use of pigments which correspond to general contours of their cultural history. Though some dyestuffs were doubtless employed during the pagan period, we can safely assume that interest in inks and pigments arose as a side-effect of the arrival of the book with Christianity at the end of the sixth century. Knowledge of the raw materials, the sources of supply, and the requisite practical skills were presumably taught by the first missionaries and their Irish and Continental supporters. Like their Irish counterparts, early Anglo-Saxon scribes were particularly fond of the three bright pigments, orpiment yellow, verdigris green and red lead, and these remained a staple of book decoration well into the Viking age. By the eighth century a few exceptional scriptoria had access to a more extensive range of colours, and gold and silver were starting to be used.[270] Around the middle of the eighth century a particularly spectacular feat of chrysography was achieved in Kent.[271]

The same pigments, including the metals, remained current in England into the ninth century; but between the mid ninth and the early tenth century the range of colours in general use declined, corresponding to the reduction in the quality and quantity of book production as a whole. Symptomatic is the fact that a royal commission of the 890s, the Oxford copy of the Old English *Regula pastoralis*, used only three colours (red lead, along with a very dilute, apparently organic, yellow, and a green).[272] Skill in preparing and using pigments appears to have decayed alongside proficiency in writing; moreover, it is likely that all but the most readily available ingredients were difficult to obtain during the Viking onslaught.

The decorator of the Old English *Regula pastoralis* grew more skilful in the preparation and use of his three pigments as work progressed – the colours become more intense and are better applied on the later folios of the book. A few manuscripts dating from the first half of the tenth century show a broadening of the palette;[273] from the mid tenth century a wider selection of pigments

269 Neither of the two late Anglo-Saxon written sources that list the implements needed by a scribe – *Monasteriales indicia* (Banham 1991, pp. 44–6) and the Colloquies of Ælfric Bata (Gwara and Porter 1997, pp. 110–16) – mentions a brush, while the latter specifies 'plenty of pens for writing and decorating'.

270 A luxurious gold-on-purple manuscript was in England by the later seventh century (*Vita Wilfridi*, ch. 17: Colgrave 1927, p. 36; cf. Bede, *HE*, v, 19: Colgrave and Mynors 1969, p. 528) though whether there were any indigenous practitioners of the techniques then is unclear.

271 Stockholm, KB, A.135: Gameson 2001–2.

272 BodL., Hatton 20.

273 BodL., Tanner 10 and Junius 27; BL, Cotton Galba A.xviii; and TCC, B.16.3.

was once again in general use in southern England, and by the eleventh century high-grade books from a major centre like Canterbury could have a rich chromatic range.[274] Correspondingly, we find increasing use of colour for display scripts, and more adventurous deployment of paint in decoration. Whereas yellow had often been favoured for highlighting sentence initials from the seventh to the early ninth century, henceforth some form of red was generally preferred. Gold (and occasionally silver) reappeared in the 960s, and continued to distinguish deluxe volumes for the best part of a century, making the Anglo-Saxon manuscripts in question some of the most lavish books of contemporary Europe. Becoming less common from the mid eleventh century, gold remained scarce in the generations after the Norman Conquest. Around the same time, purples began to feature more prominently, particularly at Worcester and St Augustine's Abbey, Canterbury. If full-page miniatures were rare in English books of the second half of the eleventh century, the rise in the deployment of coloured section initials, bi-coloured embellished initials, and multi-coloured arabesque ones ensured that a good selection of pigments continued to be current; indeed they were more widely used than ever before.

Within these general trends the number, quality and expense of the colours in a given book reflected the nature of the text, the projected function of the volume, and the prosperity, connections and scribal standards of the centre that produced it. The best scriptoria preserved and transmitted technical expertise as well as texts, script styles and artwork, for as *De coloribus et mixtionibus* observed, 'The first of the painters' skills is the preparation of pigments.'[275]

Ink[276]

Two distinct types of ink were known in the early Middle Ages, one based on carbon, the other on gallo-tannic acid ($C_{14}H_{10}O_9$). The latter type was by far the most common.

Carbon-based inks, which seem to have been widely used in Antiquity and feature in early medieval recipe collections, consisted of a black pigment composed of soot or charcoal, mixed with an adhesive and diluted with water. The resulting dark ink was not prone to decay or to adverse chemical reactions. Its demerit was that it adhered to the parchment rather than penetrating it, and could rub off with use.

274 For analysis of the pigments in BL, Arundel 155 from Christ Church see Brown and Clark 2004, pp. 184–6.
275 Preface (Smith and Hawthorne 1974, p. 26).
276 See in general Bat-Yehouda 1983; Winter 1983.

The acid-based inks comprised vegetable extracts containing gallo-tannic acid, combined with iron salt (ferrous sulphate; copperas: $FeSO_4$) or green vitriol (also iron sulphate). The iron reacted with the acid to give a dark precipitate, which blackened with exposure to oxygen. Gum was added to the ink, less as an adhesive than to give the liquid a satisfactory viscosity. The acid could be obtained from oak galls (the vegetable tumour caused by the gall wasp laying its eggs in the bud of the tree) or bark, such as hawthorn and oak. One Old English word for ink, *beamtelg* ('tree die') reflects its vegetable origin.[277] In both cases the material was crushed, then soaked or boiled in water. Iron salt was formed by the evaporation of water from ferrous earths; in Antiquity it was obtained from Spain. If the components of such ink were incorrectly balanced, the acidity could harm the parchment, or the ink might have a tendency to flake off; but if made well, the encaustic substance penetrated and adhered tenaciously to the fabric of the page. The ink of the penitential, Oxford, Bodleian Library, Bodley 718, for instance, is dark and thick and can be seen to have flattened the nap of the membrane where it has been applied. Another Old English word for ink, *blæc*, aptly characterises the rich shiny nature of such substances.[278]

Ink could also be made from vegetable extracts like hawthorn (crataegus) without the addition of iron. The resulting liquid was – or soon became – browner in tone, occasionally almost yellow. Some such difference in material or manufacture lies behind the contrast between the black of Insular inks and the browner shades used by some Continental scribes. The tone of iron gall ink could also vary, owing to the circumstance that the black compound is not properly soluble in water: consequently, if the liquid is left to stand, the black particles gradually sink, leaving a lighter brown fluid at the top of the receptacle, a dark black one at the bottom. Interestingly, when volumes written in brown inks passed into Anglo-Saxon hands, the fainter letters were sometimes retouched in darker Insular ink, as happened, for instance, in a ninth-century 'Flemish' copy of Job and Esdras and in an eleventh-century French copy of Paul the Deacon's Homiliary.[279] Conversely, one little-known result of the Norman Conquest was to increase the amount of brown (or browning) ink used in England for a couple of generations.

A broad-nibbed pen without a reservoir rapidly exhausts its ink supply: thus unless dipped regularly, the density of the strokes soon diminishes. The careful scribe would dip to replenish the ink before this became necessary. Successive fading then refreshing of ink could reflect a spacious ink-hungry script, or

277 Riddle 26: Krapp and Dobbie 1936, p. 193 (translation at the head of this chapter).
278 *Wulfstan's Canons of Edgar*: Fowler 1972, p. 2.
279 BL, Arundel 125; Cambridge, Pembroke College, 23.

alternatively hasty work. The Insular Half-Uncial of the Lichfield Gospels,[280] where the scribe can sometimes be seen to refresh his pen every three to four words, provides an example of the former. As an instance of the latter – hasty writing with insufficient ink – we may cite a copy of Paul the Deacon's Homiliary from the very end of our period: the result looks scratchy.[281]

In addition to being the substance of the main text, black-brown inks were regularly used for display script, initials and artwork. Ink lines were often designed to show through washes of colour, giving them form; equally, they might be applied subsequently to sharpen the boundaries between different colours, or to add detail or pattern to painted areas. While it seems reasonable to presume that iron gallo-tannate blacks will have been used for some such work, carbon-based ones have been positively identified in the artwork of a range of manuscripts scattered across our period.[282]

White

The simplest way to achieve the absence of colour was to leave a blank space and allow the parchment to show through. Bare parchment was regularly used to articulate interlace; numerous ink initials, monochrome and polychrome alike, utilise the gap between two parallel lines or areas of colour to incorporate 'white' into the design;[283] and details in certain miniatures were also rendered thus.[284] More dramatically, both before and after the Viking age, coloured subjects were set against plain parchment within a painted frame. Early instances include the evangelist portraits in the Book of Durrow and the Lindisfarne and Echternach Gospels,[285] late ones the portraits in the Grimbald Gospels and in two of the gospel-books of Judith of Flanders.[286]

White pigment might be made from naturally occurring substances like chalk (calcium carbonate: $CaCO_3$), gypsum, bone and shell. Some such material is suspected to have been the basis of the white used in the Book of Kells, and chalk is known to have been deployed in the Lindisfarne Gospels.[287] Given the

280 Lichfield CL, 1. 281 CUL, Kk.4.13 (provenance: Norwich).

282 Clarke 2004, table 2; Brown and Clark 2004, table 8.

283 Fine early examples appear in the Vespasian Psalter (BL, Cotton Vespasian A.i), good late ones in the Bosworth Psalter (BL, Add. 37517).

284 E.g. in the Sacramentary of Robert of Jumièges (Rouen, BM, Y.6).

285 TCD, 57; BL, Cotton Nero D.iv; BnF lat. 9389.

286 BL, Add. 34890; PML, M 708 and 709. Also, e.g., Cambridge, Pembroke College, 301; TCC, B.10.4; BodL., Douce 296. In the gospel-lectionary of Margaret of Scotland (BodL., Lat. liturg. f.5) the 'whiteness' of the ground behind the evangelists is accentuated by the circumstance that the parchment immediately outside the frame is washed a light red; however, it is debatable whether this was a deliberate device as opposed to a side-effect of the accidental immersion in water that the book is known to have endured.

287 Fuchs and Oltrogge 1994, p. 141; Clarke 2004, p. 239, table 3.

imposing presence of high-quality chalk on the east Kentish coast, it would be logical to expect a higher than average incidence of calcium carbonate white in Canterbury books; in the absence of scientific investigation, however, this can be nothing more than a hypothesis.

The alternative manufactured white pigment was white lead, a compound of lead carbonate and hydrated lead oxide ($2PbCO_3.Pb(OH)_2$) that was well known in Antiquity.[288] Lead (galena) is widespread in Britain, and Bede listed it among the metals in which the country was rich.[289] When lead is exposed to acetic acid vapour and carbon dioxide in a warm environment, a white crust of lead carbonate eventually forms on the metal. The necessary conditions could be achieved by wrapping lead in beer-vat or wine-press refuse and arranging it over vessels of vinegar in a pile of dung. Theophilus recommended placing thin sheets of lead 'in a hollow piece of wood ... and pour[ing] in some warm vinegar or urine to cover them'.[290] A period of four to twelve weeks was required for the carbonate to form. The white crust was removed and washed clean of salts, then ground to form a workable pigment.

White lead is relatively rare in early Anglo-Saxon manuscripts, though it was certainly known in both Northumbria and Southumbria, as is demonstrated by the Lindisfarne Gospels and the Vespasian Psalter respectively.[291] Now, these are particularly sophisticated manuscripts, and this alerts us to the fact that white lead was particularly useful in contexts that were chromatically rich. Permanent, dense and opaque, it could be applied over other colours. (Its strength in this respect is demonstrated in the Kentish Codex Aureus where it was used extensively for writing on purple parchment.) In the late Anglo-Saxon period white lead was widely deployed for adding highlights to, and re-outlining areas of colour: much of the shimmer of later tenth- and eleventh-century English painting derived from its application in these ways. In addition, it could be mixed with other pigments to lighten them or to produce compound colours, such as pink (red lead, vermilion or kermes plus white lead);[292] or it could be worked into selected areas of a given colour on the page to modulate its appearance.

The demerits of white lead were that it was incompatible with verdigris and orpiment, and could itself blacken (to lead sulphide) through exposure to the hydrogen sulphide of the air. More sinister, inhalation of the

288 *De coloribus et mixtionibus*, vii (Smith and Hawthorne 1974, 27; also 42 and 64); Gettens *et al.* 1993.
289 *HE*, I, 1: Colgrave and Mynors 1969, p. 16.
290 *De diversis artibus*, I, 37: Dodwell 1961, p. 33.
291 BL, Cotton Nero D.iv; Cotton Vespasian A.i: Brown and Clark 2004, pp. 182 and 188.
292 See further *De coloribus et mixtionibus*, ix–x (Smith and Hawthorne 1974, p. 27).

substance (inevitable when collecting and grinding it) engendered lead poisoning.

Red

After black-brown ink, red was the most widely used colour. It was regularly employed not only for decoration, but also for rubric and – first in the form of dots, subsequently as a wash – for highlighting capitals. Very occasionally it was used for longer sections of text.[293] In addition, non-opaque reds were used for under-drawing throughout our period. The ubiquity of red is advertised, incidentally, in the many Byzantine portraits which show the evangelist as a scribe equipped with both black and red inkwells – a type echoed within the Anglo-Saxon corpus by the Codex Amiatinus' image of Ezra, whose writing equipment includes a bipartite ink-dish holding red and black ink.[294]

Red lead (minium)[295]

A lead tetroxide (Pb_3O_4), this was manufactured either directly from lead itself, or by roasting white lead while stirring with an iron rod. Through variations in the nature of the initial material and in the method of preparation, it might be accompanied by other oxides in differing proportions, affecting the colour obtained, which could range from red to orange. Whatever the exact tone, minium at its best was bright and opaque. Though prone to discoloration and incompatible with orpiment, it appears to have been more stable than white lead; however it, too, caused lead poisoning, a process exacerbated by the toxic fumes produced during roasting.

Widely used for artwork throughout our period, red lead also seems to have been commonly deployed for rubric – a circumstance reflected in the Old English gloss for *minium*: *bocread* ('book red')[296] – and for the red dots that surround the initials in Insular manuscripts (those in a ninth-century Mercian *Expositio missae*, to take one example, comprise irregular, three-dimensional blobs of paint, added after the other colours[297]). The opacity and viscosity of the pigment, which well suited it for such use, also recommended it where overpainting was required – as, for instance, when red was applied decoratively

293 E.g. CCCC, 265, pp. 228–31 (penitential collection). The Carolingian gospel-book, BL, Harley 2795 is written entirely in red.

294 Florence, Biblioteca Medicea-Laurenziana, Amiatino 1, fol. Vr: Weitzmann 1977, plate 48.

295 *De coloribus et mixtionibus*, vii (Smith and Hawthorne 1974, p. 27); Theophilus, *De diversis artibus*, I, 37: Dodwell 1961, p. 33; Fitzhugh 1986.

296 Bosworth and Toller 1898, p. 114.

297 BodL., Hatton 93. For the presence of red lead in the *s.* viii–ix Mercian prayerbooks, BL, Harley 7653 and Royal 2 A.xx, see Brown and Clark 2004, pp. 182–3 and 188.

to other coloured letters in the Codex Aureus; or was employed for writing on the yellow or white grounds of Hrabanus Maurus' *carmina figurata*.[298]

Vermilion[299]

A manufactured mercuric sulphide (HgS), vermilion was made by combining and heating metallic mercury and sulphur, then allowing the vapour to condense on a colder surface, such as the top of the vessel. The pigment collected as a dark red formation, which could then be ground finely to make a bright pigment. Though sulphur was not available in Britain (the best-known European deposits being in Sicily), it could be synthesised from pyrites, which is common here. The resulting red was pure, powerful and stable. Its chief demerit was toxicity: in the short term, inhalation and skin absorption could cause nausea, vomiting, diarrhoea and migraine, the chronic effect being irreversible damage to the nervous system. Now vermilion has not to date been certainly identified in any British manuscript prior to the twelfth century; however, since the pigment was enthusiastically adopted in Normandy from the mid eleventh century,[300] it is possible that further investigation of books made in England in the aftermath of the Conquest may yet change this picture.

Mineral reds

A bright red could be made from cinnabar (HgS), the naturally occurring form of vermilion.[301] A product of volcanic activity, cinnabar had been mined in Tuscany, near Trieste (Siena), and above all in southern Spain since Antiquity; however, no example has yet been identified in an early British book. Red ochre, by contrast, has been observed in several Anglo-Saxon manuscripts, but then this was an earth colour formed by the weathering of iron ores such as haematite (Fe_2O_3) of which there were abundant deposits in Britain, occurring for instance in Avon, Cornwall, Cumbria, Devon, Furness, Lancashire and Somerset. Current data suggest that it was rather less popular than red lead.

Kermes[302]

A red of a more purple hue, this was obtained from the female *Kermes vermilio*. The insect lived on the kermes oak (*Quercus coccifera*), a Mediterranean tree.

298 CUL, Gg.5.35.
299 The earliest recipe appears in the *s.* viii–ix Lucca *Compositiones variae*: Hedfors 1932. See also *De coloribus et mixtionibus*, i (Smith and Hawthorne 1974, p. 26; also 61); Theophilus, *De diversis artibus*, I, 34: Dodwell 1961, 31–2); Gettens *et al.* 1993.
300 Coupry 1999, pp. 74–6 with fig. 13.
301 Illustrated in colour (along with many other minerals that were used for pigments) in Kirmeier *et al.* 1994, pp. 139–46.
302 Schweppe and Roosen-Runge 1986.

The extract itself was brown, but by the controlled admixture of alum or potash a spectrum of reds and pinks could be obtained: alkali fostered shades of violet to purple; acid encouraged orange tonalities. Kermes has been identified in certain Anglo-Saxon textiles, and given its versatility (it could, for instance, be safely mixed with white lead to form pinks), it is conceivable that it may sometimes have been deployed in manuscripts.

Orange

Orange was available from lead oxide (PbO) and tetroxide (Pb_3O_4), the latter of course being technically 'red lead'. A handsome example is the brilliant thick orange display script in the late tenth-century penitential collection, Bodleian Library, Bodley 718, and various other cases have been positively identified.[303]

Yellow

Along with red and green, yellow was one of the three main colours of Insular illumination. We shall begin with its best-known form.

Orpiment

Orpiment is a trisulphide of arsenic (As_2S_3) which occurs in the oxidised parts of arsenic-bearing veins and in subvolcanic contexts (for instance, as a deposit associated with thermal springs). It is not found in Britain, but there are deposits in France, Germany, Switzerland, Italy, Bosnia, Romania, Macedonia, and above all Kurdistan. Although the source and routes of the supply to the British Isles are unclear, the ubiquity of the pigment in Insular manuscripts suggests that it cannot have been particularly difficult to obtain. Orpiment provided a dramatic yellow whose intensity and opacity recommended it to Insular scribes, not least for display script and sentence capitals. It features in the major decoration of such early Northumbrian manuscripts as the Lindisfarne and Echternach Gospels, as also in that of the Southumbrian Vespasian Psalter; and, though less prominent after the Viking age, it remained in the repertoire of some late Anglo-Saxon artists.

Orpiment had several grave demerits. It was highly toxic: prolonged skin contact caused ulceration, while inhalation in the short term irritated the mucus membranes, in the long term leading to poisoning. The pigment was difficult to modify, and was incompatible with certain other colours: it could sometimes reduce white lead, red lead and verdigris to a dull metallic hue. As

303 Brown and Clarke 2004, tables 1 and 3–5.

these were also bright colours, aesthetically ideal for major decoration, juxtaposition with them was irresistible – the good painter tried to ensure that they did not touch one another.

Early British books contain further yellows whose observable properties (such as translucency and non-aggressivity) or pale faded-looking tones indicate that they were made from substances other than orpiment. Possible candidates include the following.

Yellow ochre

A limonite (like red ochre) which is very common throughout Europe including Britain, yellow ochre provided a serviceable earth colour which was less exotic and intense than orpiment. Unlike orpiment, it could be applied as a transparent glaze over ink lines and letters, leaving them showing through. Moreover, it was not aggressive to its neighbours.

Saffron[304]

The dried stigmas of the *Crocus sativa* provided a golden yellow that was handsome, non-reactive, versatile and easy to prepare – the extract had merely to be infused in glair. Found in much of Europe and the East (though difficult to crop in Britain), saffron was cultivated with particular vigour by the Arabs in Spain. The disadvantages of the pigment were that it was fugitive and, since one ounce presupposed more than 4,000 flowers, costly.

Buckthorn

The dried berries of the common buckthorn (if gathered before they are ripe), also the bark of the common buckthorn, and the bark and leaves of the alder buckthorn could be used as the basis of a yellow dye, which, however, was not light-fast.

Bile

The ground gall of a fish or ox, mixed with chalk and vinegar, created a readily available yellow paint that recipe books recommended for golden writing. Ox gall could also be used in combination with orpiment or indeed gold itself.

Green

Here the early medieval scriptorium faced a dilemma: the finest pigment was an aggressive substance; the safer alternatives were aesthetically less attractive.

304 *De clarea*: Thompson 1932, p. 78.

'Verdigris'[305]

The most brilliant colours came from 'verdigris', a pigment – or more accurately, a range of pigments – based on copper (a metal to whose availability in Britain Bede referred).[306] When thin plates of copper were exposed to vinegar in warm conditions (for instance, by hanging them over warm vinegar, buried in marc), a blue or blue-green crust formed on them.[307] This might simply be dissolved in wine, apple juice or spurge (euphorbia) sap and left to thicken; however, dissolving it in acetic acid had a purifying effect, minimising the propensity to change tone. The nature of the vinegar influenced the shade of pigment obtained; it could be tempered with rue or parsley juice (sap green); and further variations in hue could be engineered by the admixture of stale urine. Moreover, different 'batches' might be combined, and malachite ($CuCO_3.Cu(OH)_2$) – a mineral which occurs in the oxidised areas of copper deposits and which had to be ground and levigated to make a pigment[308] – could also be mixed in. The resulting greens could be brilliant in tone.[309] However, some of them might also be highly corrosive. Copper acetate degrades cellulosic materials, and this range of pigments can generally be seen to have penetrated parchment (as in the Croyland Psalter), and sometimes to have eaten it entirely away (spectacularly, for instance, on a couple of pages in the Book of Durrow[310]). Furthermore, verdigris was incompatible with pigments containing sulphur (ultramarine, orpiment), from which it had to be carefully segregated. Yet despite these physical disadvantages, its rich tones guaranteed wide use, and it has been reliably identified in manuscripts straddling our entire period.

Compound green

A more stable, though muted, green (*vergaut*) could be made by mixing indigo blue (woad) and orpiment yellow; and this, too, seems to be fairly widespread in early medieval illumination. It appears, for instance, alongside verdigris in the Lindisfarne Gospels, and as the only green in the altogether humbler

305 *De coloribus et mixtionibus*, v (Smith and Hawthorne 1974, pp. 27 and 61); Theophilus, *De diversis artibus*, I, 35–6: Dodwell 1961, pp. 32–3; Banik 1990; Kuhn 1993.

306 See n. 289 above.

307 The brief account of Heraclius (Merrifield 1847, I, pp. 238–9) is worth quoting: 'Fill a basin with white wine vinegar and put into it strips of copper, and throwing therein any other copper that you can procure; let it remain there for the space of one, two, or three months, and you will then find an excellent green colour.'

308 Gettens and Fitzhugh 1993.

309 E.g. the Mercian prayerbook, BL, Royal 2 A.xx: Brown and Clark 2004, p. 183; colour plate Webster and Backhouse 1991, p. 209.

310 Respectively, BodL., Douce 296; TCD, 57. Also, e.g., BL, Stowe 2.

Northumbrian gospel-book, Royal 1 B.vii; it has equally been identified in Southumbrian manuscripts both before and after the Viking age.[311]

Mineral and vegetable greens

Other harmless, though less rich or more granular, greens could be obtained from celadonite (*terre verte*), a green clay particularly associated with Verona;[312] and from the closely related glauconite. Then there were vegetable sources such as aquilegia (columbine) flowers, woodbine berries, and elder and mulberry leaves. The dried berries of the common buckthorn (if picked when ripe) and those of the alder buckthorn (gathered when unripe) furnish rich if fugitive greens. All these types of green – copper-based, ochre-based, *vergaut* and sap – have been perceived in the Book of Kells.

Blue

Ultramarine[313]

The finest blue – ultramarine – was obtained from lapis lazuli, a complex rock composed of the sulphur-rich, blue mineral lazurite, along with pyrites and calcite. It is the most chemically complicated mineral pigment: $(Na,Ca)_8(AlSiO_4)_6(SO_4,S,Cl)2$. From Antiquity the source had been mines in the Badakshan district of Afghanistan.[314] A large amount of lapis lazuli yielded only a small quantity of good pigment, and it was time-consuming to extract. Because of this, as well as the distance involved, ultra-marine was extremely expensive. Yet for reasons that are not fully understood, it became more current in north-west Europe as a whole towards the millennium when a purer version of the pigment became available.[315] Accordingly, although it is not present in the Lindisfarne Gospels (contrary to what was once supposed), lazurite has been positively identified in various late Anglo-Saxon manuscripts, and not only the finest but also various more ordinary ones.[316]

Azurite[317]

A carbonate of copper ($2CuCO_3.Cu(OH)_2$), azurite provided a less costly mineral blue with a slightly greenish tinge. Often found in association with

311 E.g. Codex Aureus; BL, Royal 1 E.vi (bible); Add. 49598 (Benedictional of Æthelwold), Add. 34890 (Grimbald Gospels): see Brown and Clark 2004, p. 184. Orléans, Médiathèque, 127 ('Winchcombe Sacramentary'): see Roger and Bosc 2008, p. 42.

312 Grissom 1986. 313 Plesters 1993.

314 *Teste*, e.g., Marco Polo, *The Travels*: Latham 1958, pp. 76 and 106.

315 Fuchs and Oltrogge 1994, pp. 147–8; Coupry 1999, esp. pp. 72–4 and 77.

316 E.g. high-grade: BL, Arundel 155; Add. 34890; CCCC, 44; Orléans, Médiathèque, 127. Less elevated: CCCC, 9, 140, 196, 265, 322. See Brown and Clark 2004, pp. 185–7; Clarke 2004, p. 237 with table 1; and Roger and Bosc 2008, p. 428.

317 Gettens and Fitzhugh 1993.

malachite, it is widespread in Britain but usually only in small quantities; however, it was also available in Italy, Spain and above all France, Germany and Hungary. To be made into pigment, it was pulverised, levigated and sieved; the coarser the powder, the darker the blue obtained. The deepest grades, being particularly granular, sometimes required application in multiple coats.

Egyptian blue[318]

This calcium-copper tetrasilicate ($CaCuSi_4O_{10}$), popular for mural painting in Antiquity, has also been recognised in some Carolingian wall paintings and, more relevant in the present context, on a fragmentary Anglo-Saxon capital from St Augustine's Abbey, Canterbury.[319] More recently, it has been identified in a couple of Anglo-Saxon manuscripts, both of high status and dating from the late tenth century.[320]

Vegetable blues

Inexpensive but less luxurious blues could also be obtained from vegetable matter such as elderberry, mulberry, bilberry and indigo. Indigo proper ($C_{16}H_{10}N_2O_2$) was imported from the East; however, woad provided a locally available substitute.[321] In both cases, the blue was obtained from the decomposition of the glucoside indican. After drying and crushing, the leaf residue was dampened and allowed to ferment. This was the basic component of a blue dyebath; the scum that formed on the surface could be collected, dried and used as a blue pigment. Another stable colour, indigo was widely used from an early date, appearing, for instance, in the Irish Books of Armagh and Mulling, not to mention in the more exalted contexts of the Lindisfarne and Barberini Gospels, the Book of Kells and the Codex Aureus; it reappears in late Anglo-Saxon manuscripts such as the Arundel 155 Psalter and the Grimbald Gospels.

Purple

The substances that could be used as the basis for a purple dye ranged from shellfish through elder (sambucus) berries to folium and lichen; it could also, of course, be obtained from a mixture of red and blue. Folium was prepared from the seeds and flowers of the tournesol plant (*Crozophora tinctoria*), native to

318 Tite *et al.* 1982.
319 Tweddle *et al.*, 1995, p. 131; Howard 2003, pp. 39–40.
320 Orléans, Médiathèque, 127 ('Winchcombe Sacramentary') and BnF, lat. 987 (Benedictional): Roger and Bosc 2008, pp. 422–3 and 436 with colour ill. 7.
321 Advice concerning the cultivation of which is given in the OE text, 'Gerefa': Liebermann 1886. See in general Schweppe 1997.

southern France, which, when crushed, exude a reddish juice. The tone could be varied from blue to red via the controlled addition of alkaline substances such as wood ash, stale urine or quick-lime. The cudbear lichen (*Ochrolechia tartaria L.*), native to England, could give richer colours which might likewise be lightened by the addition of acids or made more purple by alkalis. The merits of the dye obtained from the British whelk (*Nucella lapillus*; the dog whelk) were celebrated by Bede, who noted that it neither 'faded through the heat of the sun nor exposure to rain; indeed the older it is, the more beautiful it becomes'.[322] Purples of various types and tones are scattered through our corpus, and the Canterbury Codex Aureus provides a tantalising witness to the fact that considerable quantities of a purple dye, along with the skill to use it effectively, were available in one Southumbrian centre in the mid eighth century. Unfortunately, scientific investigation has yet to shed much light on the nature of the purples found in British books; to date only one small instance of the use of whelk dye has been positively identified, and it is unclear whether the molluscs in question were of British or foreign origin.[323]

Brown

Ink, with or without a ferrous component, might be used, the tone of which could be further varied by dilution. Some ochres could also be deployed.

Gold[324]

Although gold (Au), occurs in small quantities in many places in Britain and has been mined commercially in Devon and Wales since Roman times, local sources do not seem to have been exploited to meet Anglo-Saxon needs; on the contrary, the evidence of contemporary coinage and jewellery indicates dependence upon imported metal. Gold was applied to books in two ways: it could be laid in leaf form on to areas which had been pre-painted with glair or gum; alternatively, the leaves could be pulverised and turned into an ink with water and glair or gum. The challenging task of grinding gold leaf could be achieved by adding honey or salt which was subsequently rinsed out, or by making the metal brittle via a dose of mercury which would then be evaporated away. Once in place, both forms of gold could be burnished with a hard, smooth agent (such as a stone, a knife blade or, as Heraclius disarmingly

322 *HE*, I, 1: Colgrave and Myors 1969, p. 15. On purple in early Anglo-Saxon England, see Henderson 1999, pp. 122–35 (esp. 127–31 for comment on this passage).
323 BAV, Barberini lat. 570: Clarke 2004, p. 232. The nature of the dye obtained from the British *Nucella lapillus* is investigated by Cooksey and Withnall 2001.
324 *Mappae clavicula*: Smith and Hawthorne 1974, pp. 66; Alexander 1964–5.

recommends, 'the tooth of a savage bear'[325]) to enhance their sheen. As the pressure involved tended to bow the surface of the membrane, it also gave the golden area a slightly rounded cross-section. Less advantageously, the rubbing could scar the surface of the page, encouraging dirt to collect – whence the grubby marks around the gold initials in such fine books as the Ramsey Psalter – or even, as in St Margaret's gospel-lectionary, inflict damage on the neighbouring script.[326] Other pigments might be added to enhance or modulate the appearance of ink gold: orpiment to provide a yellow medium, giving the illusion of a denser coating; verdigris for a green tinge; red lead or vermilion for a redder tone. Such devices, along with variations in the nature of the metal itself, presumably lie behind the reddish hue of the gold ink in the Royal 1 D.ix Gospels and the gospel-lectionary of St Margaret, and the green tint of some of that in the Codex Aureus.

The precious metal first appears in our corpus in the highest-grade Northumbrian books produced around 700: very small amounts of gold ink and gold leaf were used in the Lindisfarne Gospels, while modest quantities of gold leaf were tellingly deployed in the Codex Amiatinus and in a Wearmouth-Jarrow gospel- book.[327] Gold leaf was used in more generous quantities in the eighth-century Kentish Vespasian Psalter; and then altogether more lavishly in the aptly named Codex Aureus: here with supreme luxuriousness substantial passages of the gospel texts were written in gold on purple parchment.[328] While gold ink was used for long stretches of the text, gold leaf was deployed in the miniatures and in some of the initials in Luke's Gospel. As in the closely related Vespasian Psalter, the leaf was left unburnished, thus having a faceted, slightly wrinkly appearance. Gold continued to be part of the repertoire of Anglo-Saxon illuminators into the first half of the ninth century, as the Book of Cerne, the Royal Bible fragment and the Durham (?Lindisfarne) *Liber vitae* reveal;[329] unsurprisingly, it then fell into abeyance until the later tenth century. Gold reappeared in the period of the Benedictine reform, advertising the relative prosperity of the West Saxon regime and its greatest monasteries.[330]

Although burnished, many frame bars and initials in late Anglo-Saxon books retain the lumpy texture characteristic of liquid gold, and the individual

325 Heraclius: Merrifield 1847, I, pp. 190–1.
326 BL, Harley 2904. BodL., Lat. liturg. f.5.
327 Florence, Biblioteca Medicea-Laurenziana, Amiatino 1; Utrecht, UB, 32, fols. 94–105.
328 Stockholm, KB, A.135. facsimile: Gameson 2001–2.
329 BL, Royal 1 E.vi; CUL, Ll.1.10; and BL, Cotton Domitian vii. On the chrysography of the last see Gameson 2007, esp. pp. 62–5.
330 The New Minster Charter (BL, Cotton Vesp. A.viii) is entirely written in gold. A small quantity of continuous gold script appears in the Winchester Benedictional, Rouen, BM, Y.7.

particles are clearly visible under magnification – as is the case, for example, in the New Minister Charter, the Sacramentary of Robert of Jumièges, and the Croyland (Douce 296) Psalter. Where, in this last book, parts of the gold have scaled or rubbed off, one can see that the form of lettering that was to be golden was first delineated in red ink. Correspondingly, white and black were sometimes applied on top of gold, either to give definition – sharpening the contours of the metal-covered area – or to add detail. White lead appears thus in the Croyland Psalter, while dark ink was also used for this purpose in the Arundel 155 Psalter and in the small but exquisite 'Hereford' gospel-lectionary.[331] Gold leaf could be laid on a foundation of gesso to give the impression of greater body; and various recipes recommended mixing gold with silver or tin to bulk it out – some such mixture seems to have been used on the evangelist portraits of the economically conceived late eleventh-century Exeter Gospels.[332] Yellow might be painted under the gold to reinforce its presence, as in the Vespasian Psalter; but yellow and oranges were also used as (poor) substitutes for gold when considerations of expense or availability prohibited the metal itself, as was the case, for instance, in the Tiberius Psalter, a manuscript produced around the time of the Conquest.[333]

Aside from its aesthetic appeal, gold added both intrinsic and symbolic value to a book, conveying the worth of its words and the veneration with which it was regarded – as St Boniface (d. 754) appreciated.[334] The point is also reflected in the use of the metal for key names in texts that were otherwise written in ordinary ink, notably litanies and *vitae sanctorum*.[335] The beauty of the metal was worth protecting: a documentary reference reveals that silk slips were sometimes inserted to shield golden letters.[336]

Silver

Local sources of silver (AG) were more plentiful (as Bede noted[337]), but some supplies were probably also imported. It could be treated and applied like gold. Silver was far less common in books, partly because of its reduced symbolic value, but mainly no doubt owing to its propensity to tarnish. Nevertheless, modest quantities were utilised during the peaks of Anglo-Saxon book

331 BodL., Douce 296; BL, Arundel 155; Cambridge, Pembroke College, 302. The black sits in little 'troughs' lightly impressed into the metal.

332 BnF, lat. 14782: Avril and Stirnemann 1987, colour plate C.

333 BL, Cotton Tiberius C.vi.

334 Boniface's letter to Abbess Eadburh of Minster, Thanet: Tangl 1916, no. 35; Whitelock 1979, no. 172.

335 E.g. BL, Cotton Tiberius B.ii.

336 Turgot, *Vita S. Margaretae*: Hinde 1868, III, p. 33.

337 See n. 322 above. The richest deposits are in Devon, Cornwall and Wales.

production, generally in contexts where gold was also used. The key point is that silver was employed for variation and to create metallic counterpoint, not as an alternative to, or substitute for gold.

Small quantities of silver appear alongside gold in the Codex Amiatinus; and the metal was used more extensively in the Vespasian Psalter and, above all, the Codex Aureus. That it remained in the illuminator's repertoire during the first half of the ninth century both north and south of the Humber is revealed by the Royal Bible fragment and the Durham (?Lindisfarne) *Liber vitae* respectively. Notwithstanding its presence – for metallic counterpoint – in certain manuscripts of the Franco-Saxon school produced in northern Francia in the later ninth century, silver did not find favour in late tenth-century Winchester. On the other hand, it was used to (originally) spectacular effect at Canterbury in the early eleventh century for the decorated pages of the Grimbald Gospels,[338] possibly reflecting the influence of Saint-Bertin (at nearby Saint-Omer), where it had been a regular feature of book decoration around the millennium. Nevertheless, despite significant use elsewhere in Europe from Flanders to Salzburg in the eleventh century,[339] the deployment of silver in English manuscripts remained strictly limited: the Grimbald Gospels apart, its main appearances are in the canon tables of the Copenhagen Gospels and in one of the gospel-books associated with Judith of Flanders.[340] After the Norman Conquest, while gold became rare in books, silver almost vanished.[341]

*

As was stated at the outset, it is impossible in a short compass to do justice to the complexities of manufacturing early medieval books. We have here outlined the nature and qualities of the various materials that were used, sketched the general processes involved, and indicated the major diachronistic changes, with the aim of providing a clear yet reasonably nuanced framework within which individual examples may be situated and understood. It cannot be sufficiently stressed, however, that aside from the evolution of procedures, all writing centres – even well-regulated ones – were subject to forces and variables, internal and external, which may have affected the details of their work at a given time. And the further one moves from the major scriptoria, the less

338 BL. Add. 34890: Backhouse *et al.* 1984, colour plate 16.
339 E.g. BR, II.175 and PML, M 781 respectively.
340 Copenhagen, KB, G. K. S. 10 (2°); PML, M 708.
341 An exception being the sparing use in the evangelist portraits of the Exeter Gospels, BnF lat. 14782.

standardised and resilient supply chains and procedures are likely to have been. Consequently, this survey will have achieved its purpose if it leaves the reader with, on the one hand, a reasonably clear picture of the basic materials and methods that were employed, but on the other, with the sense that the distinctions between techniques – particularly the preparation and ruling of the quires – were less hard and fast than some accounts seem to imply, that the stages of transition were more complicated, and that the likelihood of ad hoc variations was fairly high. The scientific identification of the materials used in our books is in its infancy, while the recognition and interpretation of codicological evidence requires patience, experience and skill, and is a more delicate business than is often realised.

3
Anglo-Saxon scribes and scriptoria

RICHARD GAMESON

Among the members of a Northumbrian monastic house celebrated in verse in the early ninth century by Ædiluulf, *presbiter* of that community, was a certain Ultán:

> He was a saintly priest of the Irish race, and he could adorn books with fair writing, and by this art he thus made the shape of the letters lovely, one after another, such that no contemporary scribe could equal him; and it is no wonder if a worshipper of the Lord could do such things, when the creating Holy Spirit already ruled his fingers and had inspired his dedicated mind to starry-heaven.[1]

From this and the following passages we learn that the expert calligrapher was an expatriate Irishman, working at a monastic community that was dependent upon Lindisfarne, in the time of its founder-abbot Eanmund (so during the first third of the eighth century); we are told that he had a long writing career; in addition, we are informed that his skill was God-given, his work divinely inspired, and accordingly that, after death, the hand with which he had 'merited to embellish the words of the Lord' could work miracles. Given that Ædiluulf was writing approximately a century later and is thus unlikely to have known Ultán personally, it is also apparent that the great scribe's memory had been kept golden within the community, and that his work remained a source of admiration and inspiration.

Ædiluulf's encomium of Ultán provides one set of answers to questions that are central to the study of Anglo-Saxon scribes: who they were and where they were trained; how and why they laboured; and how they and their work were regarded. Unfortunately, however, Ultán was clearly an exceptional individual, and such accounts are extremely rare: very few scribes were the subject of any sort of record, let alone a biographical note.[2] In general, therefore, our

1 Æthelwulf, *De abbatibus*, ch. 8: Campbell 1967, pp. 19–23; comment: Nees 1993.
2 See e.g. n. 7 below.

answers to the above questions must be pieced together from passing references in written sources principally concerned with other matters and, above all, from the witness of the surviving manuscripts themselves.

Only one contemporary image has come to us that would seem to represent an Anglo-Saxon scribe (or illuminator) at work, and it is very small. Tucked into a roundel on the upright to the decorated initial 'B' for Psalm 1 in the mid-eleventh-century Bury St Edmunds Psalter is a small, cowled, halo-less figure, who with his right hand writes in a book or page that is supported on a draped lectern.[3] If the imagery is conventional, its context is highly evocative, for our monastic calligrapher is thus assimilated to the 'blessed man' celebrated at the start of Psalm 1 'who walks not in the counsel of the ungodly' but delights 'in the law of the Lord' and 'whatever he does shall prosper'. This depiction thus arguably sheds more light on the rationale and rewards of scribal labour than on its practicalities.

Various other representations of saintly writing figures, though indebted to inherited visual models and principally designed to project the authority of the texts they accompany, nevertheless enable us to glimpse something of the working world of the Anglo-Saxon scribe. The portraits in the eleventh-century Hereford gospel-lectionary are particularly interesting in this connection, since they show several stages of the writing process: Matthew dips his quill in an ink-well; Mark trims his pen; Luke holds his book open, his pen tucked behind his ear; and John writes in his book, holding down the page with a knife.[4] The tools and activities depicted in such vignettes may be compared with the writing implements that feature in the relevant section of the mid-eleventh-century Canterbury copy of the *Monasteriales indicia* (the monastic sign-language used for non-vocal communication) and with those mentioned in one of the eleventh-century monastic colloquies of Ælfric Bata.[5] The *Indicia* include signs for styli, wax tablets (large and small), a ruler, an ink-well and a quill pen; while Ælfric Bata's chatty monks declare their need for wax tablets, styli, penknives, other knives, awls and rulers, parchment and (?spare or scrap) sheets, ink, razors, whetstones and 'plenty of pens for writing and decorating'. Some such writing implements have been recovered from Anglo-Saxon contexts at various sites, including Barking, Flixborough, Jarrow, Whitby and Winchester.[6]

3 BAV, Reg. Lat. 12, fol. 21r: Millar 1926, plate 19; in colour: Gameson 2000a, ill. 135.
4 Cambridge, Pembroke College 302, fols 9r, 38r, 60v and 88v: Ohlgren 1992, pp. 465, 467, 469 and 471; colour: Rushforth 2007, figs. 18 and 24.
5 Sections 112–17: Banham 1991, pp. 44–6. Colloquium XIV: Gwara and Porter 1997, pp. 110–16.
6 Biddle 1990, II, pp. 729–59; Webster and Backhouse 1991, nos. 65, 66r–t, 67i–k, 69v, 105d and 107c–e.

The scribe

Who, then, were the scribes of our early English books? The overwhelming majority were, of course, ecclesiastics. Some of the handful of scribal colophons found in our manuscripts make this explicit: the Rægenbold and Farmon who added the Old English gloss to the MacRegol Gospels describe themselves as priests; the Edward who added a supply leaf to the end of an Irish gospel-book styles himself as a deacon; the Aldred who glossed the Lindisfarne Gospels and then added prayers to the Durham Collectar (or Ritual) rose from priest to provost between these two occasions; while the Godeman responsible for the Benedictional of Æthelwold, the Eadwig Basan of his eponymous gospel-book, and the Ælfsige (Ælsinus) of the New Minster Prayerbook all recorded themselves as monks.[7] Yet even without such specific information, the ecclesiastical dominance of literacy throughout our period makes this proposition a certainty.

That said, it must immediately be acknowledged that clerics were a protean class. Some of the greatest Anglo-Saxon scriptoria – Lindisfarne, Wearmouth-Jarrow and Canterbury before the Viking age, Winchester and St Augustine's Abbey, Canterbury thereafter – were monastic at the time in question; however, monks by no means had a monopoly of book production. The nature of the community at Christ Church, Canterbury – secular clerics or Benedictine monks – during the initial revival of its scriptorium in the later tenth century is a vexed question. Whatever the truth of this particular case, other clerics certainly wrote books. The community of regular canons whose manuscripts have been most favoured by the vicissitudes of time is Exeter. Alongside the older books that were acquired and donated by their bishop, Leofric (d. 1072), there survives a group of some fifteen volumes linked by common scribal hands, some of which also penned Leofric *ex libris* inscriptions, charters relating to Exeter, or passages in the Leofric Missal:[8] clearly the products of a scriptorium at Exeter active after 1050, these manuscripts were doubtless written by the canons who then comprised the staff of the cathedral. In terms of quality and script type, we may note in passing, these books are indistinguishable from contemporary products of Benedictine scriptoria. Correspondingly, it is highly likely that some of the visually disparate manuscripts that have come

7 Gameson 2002d, nos. 16, 10, 14+15, 17, 29, 30. The last also features in the New Minster *Liber vitae* (BL, Stowe 944, fol. 21v) as 'Ælfsige sacerdos', and is presumably also the 'Ælfsinus sacerdos' whose obit was entered into the New Minster (Ælfwine) prayerbook: it is sobering but typical that such sources make no reference to the fact that the man was a *scriptor*.

8 Listed with refs.: Gameson 1996b, pp. 144–6.

down to us from the first half of the tenth century were produced by the clerics whom the monastic reformers were subsequently to vilify. Be that as it may, the books of Salisbury (Old Sarum), one of the most scribally active centres in the aftermath of the Norman Conquest, were demonstrably written by the canons themselves.[9]

Equally, some ecclesiastics – whatever their exact clerical status – may have been in the service of high-ranking secular individuals when they worked on books. Asser of St David's (d. 908/9) has left us with a vivid description of some of his labours as King Alfred's literary 'secretary'. The Welshman read texts to the king who, from time to time, asked him to transcribe passages into his personal collection of devotional writings. When the 'hand-book' transpired to be full, Asser prepared a new quire for it, 'And on that same day, I wrote at his urging in the same quire no fewer than three other statements that pleased him.'[10] Equally, it was at Alfred's court – however that be defined – that amanuenses produced first copies of the vernacular texts that the king translated or commissioned. How long and in what form a 'court scriptorium' producing books survived thereafter are unclear. 'Royal staff' presumably added some of the donation inscriptions to the older volumes which, having come by various routes into Athelstan's possession, were subsequently presented by that king to religious houses; but whether they also wrote whole books *de novo* is another matter. (One would dearly like to know for certain where the copy of the *Vitae Cuthberti* that he commissioned and presented to Chester-le-Street was written: production at Old Minster, Winchester, is ruled out on the grounds of an error in the Winchester episcopal list, though whether this also excludes the court itself is debatable; be that as it may, Glastonbury Abbey would surely still be regarded as the strongest contender.[11]) From the mid tenth century onwards, it seems likely that West Saxon royalty would turn to the flourishing monastic scriptoria that were literally on their doorstep in Winchester for most of their bibliographical needs, while doubtless receiving gifts from elsewhere (as King Cnut is recorded to have been offered a couple of high-grade books from a scribe of Peterborough[12]). Around the millennium Ealdorman Æthelweard and his son, Æthelmær, obtained at least some of their reading matter from Ælfric the homilist and hence presumably from Cerne and Eynsham. Yet Æthelweard must surely also have had at least one scribe in his retinue

9 Webber 1992. 10 *De rebus gestis Ælfredi*, ch. 88: Stevenson 1904, pp. 73–4.

11 CCCC, 183; for a summary of its Glastonbury connections see Gwara 2001, pp. 130–40. On Athelstan's books in general: Keynes 1985.

12 William of Malmesbury, *Vita Wulfstani*, I, 1: Darlington 1928, p. 5.

responsible for transcribing the Latin version of the *Anglo-Saxon Chronicle* that the ealdorman prepared for his cousin in Essen; and half a century later, one or more Anglo-Saxon scribe-artists appear to have worked in the household of Judith of Flanders, wife of Tostig Godwinson, first in England, then perhaps on the Continent.[13] Thus the possibility that literary items were still sometimes copied *in aula regis* by clerics who were temporarily or permanently in royal employ should not be discounted. From the material that has come down to us, it is legal, genealogical, historical and other 'secular' texts, above all in the vernacular, that seem leading candidates for production in such contexts, especially perhaps if they are written in hands that are difficult to parallel elsewhere – manuscripts precisely like the fragmentary *Waldere* or even indeed the 'Beowulf Codex'.[14] In this connection it is also worth drawing attention to a collection of religious verse, mainly in Latin, written in the first half of the eleventh century, which bears in a crude eleventh-century hand the suggestive gloss: 'domino suo, N., dei gracia Regis capellano' ('to his lord, n[ame], by grace of God chaplain of the king').[15]

That some ecclesiastical scribes were female is clear; what percentage of the 'writing force' they represented at a given time is, however, unknowable – beyond the fact that they will always have been a minority. Documentary and archaeological evidence attests to literary activity and book production at, for instance, the great royal 'nunneries' of Whitby in Northumbria and Minster-in-Thanet in Kent in the seventh and eighth centuries; indeed, the latter would seem to have had a reputation for chrysography, and one extant eighth-century manuscript can reasonably be attributed to it.[16] However, even here it is impossible to isolate an unequivocally female contribution since Thanet was actually a double minster (as, too, was Whitby). Some book production doubtless went on at the more prosperous late Anglo-Saxon nunneries, such as Barking, Romsey, Shaftesbury and Wilton, not to mention Nunnaminster in Winchester. Edith of Wilton (961–84) was famously credited with skill as a scribe by her biographer, Goscelin; however, as this appears amidst a 'purple passage' lauding her many remarkable God-given accomplishments, as the only specific example of her work to be adduced is a devotional compilation, and as Goscelin was writing approximately a century after her death, it is difficult to know what credence, if any, should be given to this claim.[17] On the other

13 Campbell 1962; McGurk and Rosenthal 1995.

14 Copenhagen, KB, N. K. S. 167b (4°) (Zettersten 1979, with facs.); BL, Cotton Vitellius A.xv.

15 BnF, lat. 8092.

16 Tangl 1916: Boniface, ep. 35 (cf. ep. 30); BodL., Selden Supra 30: Gameson 1999b, pp. 327–30.

17 *Vita Edithae* chs. 8 and 11: Wilmart 1938, pp. 55–6 and 68–9; Hollis 2004, pp. 38, 66 and 34.

hand, it is a reasonable presumption that the tenth-century Salisbury Psalter that was designed for a female house in the south-west was made within the community that owned it (possibly Shaftesbury); the same may be true of the slightly younger gospel-book of Barking provenance;[18] and the colophon in an early twelfth-century copy of Smaragdus' *Diadema monachorum* from Nunnaminster, Winchester, specifically identifies its writer as a *scriptrix*.[19] Nevertheless, our corpus of identifiable female scribal work is so small that it is difficult to say very much about it.

Similarly hard to quantify is the contribution of paid professional scribes, since our knowledge of their existence depends entirely on passing references that are exiguous in the extreme. In fact, only two possible pre-Conquest instances are currently known. The circumstance that both are from Worcester reflects the exceptionally full (by Anglo-Saxon standards) literary records of that centre; it may also relate to the fact that, although a major house, Worcester does not seem to have had a flourishing scriptorium of its own until the mid eleventh century. Bishop Oswald (d. 992) granted land to a priest called Goding on condition, Hemming's Cartulary explains, that he worked as a scribe, writing many books. Whether or not this individual was a member of the community (whose nature, monastic or otherwise, at the time in question is, in any case, a matter of debate), he was certainly given 'financial' rewards for his work.[20] Then, in the 1050s Bishop Ealdred granted land to one Wulfgeat, who may possibly be identical with the 'Wulfgeatus scriptor Wigornensis' recorded in a colophon that has been preserved in a slightly younger Worcester manuscript.[21] Only after the Conquest do references to professional scribes become slightly more plentiful and less ambiguous. The first is a remarkable account (written, it must be acknowledged, in the mid thirteenth century on the basis of a lost document compiled in the mid twelfth[22]) of the creation and construction of a separate scriptorium staffed with hired professionals at St Albans in the time of Abbot Paul (1077–93). The imponderable issue here is the extent to which actual circumstances (as opposed to available sources) may have changed with the Conquest and the accompanying emphasis on building up substantial reading collections. Impossible to distinguish visually in the corpus of exant manuscripts, the contribution of paid professional scribes to late Anglo-Saxon book production will always remain elusive.

18 Salisbury CL, 150 (Pal. Soc. I, plates 188–9); BodL., Bodley 155.
19 BodL., Bodley 451: Gameson 2002d, no. 42.
20 Robertson 1939, no. LXI; Sawyer 1968, no. 1369; Hearne 1722, I, p. 265.
21 Sawyer 1968, no. 1409. BodL., Junius 121, fol. 101r: Gameson 2002d, no. 36.
22 Riley 1867, pp. 57–8. For subsequent developments: Gullick 1998b.

What can, by contrast, be recognised in the extant manuscripts is the input of 'foreign' scribes, marked out by their racially distinct handwriting or artwork. This is impossible, not to mention largely meaningless, to pursue in the pre-Viking-age material, when writing was an imported skill, when the earliest practitioners were immigrants – be it from Francia, Italy or Ireland – and when the first 'native' scribes emulated the styles of their foreign exemplars and tutors. Ultán, it will be remembered, was an Irishman, 'plying his trade' in early eighth-century Northumbria, but it is unlikely that his basic letter-forms differed greatly from those used by Anglo-Saxon contemporaries within the extended, ultimately Columban, *familia* of Lindisfarne; for his encomiast, Ædiluulf, it was the quality of his hand, not the form of his script, that distinguished him from 'modern scribes'. After the Viking age, however, the situation was rather different, since Anglo-Saxon scribes persisted in using indigenous forms of writing that were in sharp contrast to the varieties of Caroline Minuscule practised by their Continental contemporaries and, when they finally adopted the Caroline, they developed types of the script which are, on the whole, recognisably 'English'.[23] Thus British Library, Cotton Claudius A.i (fols. 5–36), a copy of the *Breviloquium Vitae Wilfridi* commissioned by Archbishop Oda (941–58) and glossed in English hands of the later tenth century but wholly written in a mid-tenth-century Continental Caroline Minuscule, stands out as the work of a 'foreign' scribe probably at Canterbury – perhaps even of the Frankish author, Frithegod, himself. The fact that the same scribe collaborated with two further Continentals and two Anglo-Saxons on a second copy of the same text would seem to confirm that he (and his expatriate colleagues) were working in England at the time in question.[24]

Of similar cases, it will suffice to cite the main scribe of the York Gospels (written in Canterbury shortly after the millennium) and one of the principal scribes of the Portiforium of St Wulfstan (made at Worcester 1064×9), whose hands would not look out of place in contemporary Flanders or northern France.[25] Intermittent before 1066, such cases unsurprisingly mushroom in the couple of generations after the Conquest, as Norman and other Continental personnel became a more insistent presence in English regular communities. The phenomenon is epitomised by the late eleventh-century

23 See further Ganz and Rushforth, Chapter 7 in this volume.

24 Lapidge 1988a. Second copy: St Petersburg, Russian National Library, O.v.XIV.1.

25 York Minster Library, Add. 1: facs. Barker 1986. CCCC, 391; the scribe in question wrote pp. 373–4/25; 375–[with *s.* xii interruption]580/24: Robinson 1988, II, ill. 31; Budny 1997, II, ills. 602–3.

Canterbury copy of the Pauline Epistles with Lanfranc's gloss, which includes stints by Norman – more particularly Mont Saint-Michel – scribes alongside work in archetypical late standard Caroline Minuscule of St Augustine's Abbey type.[26]

An early eleventh-century copy of Vitruvius' *De architectura*, also of St Augustine's Abbey provenance, which was the product of close collaboration between an English scribe and French or Flemish ones, raises a different point, for it is debatable on which side of the Channel this team was working at the time.[27] Just as distinctive script and illumination can reveal the presence of Continentals in English centres, so too can they show the contribution of Anglo-Saxons to Continental scriptoria. A striking early example is the Trier Gospels, made at Echternach in the first half of the eighth century: this was the product of collaboration between a senior scribe who twice named himself as Thomas and whose script and decoration is wholly Insular, and an unnamed Continental, responsible for the greater part of the book, whose work is entirely Merovingian in its idioms.[28] Then, if one lone English-seeming hand appears in the extant books that were made at Saint-Vaast, Arras, in the eleventh century,[29] the Anglo-Saxon presence at Fleury around the millennium was rather more significant. Among the team of three main hands (or hand-types) and five minor ones that was responsible for an astronomical manuscript that was surely made there then, one of the main and two of the minor scribes have English hands, another shows some English features though is principally Continental, while the rest are unequivocally Continental;[30] the manuscript was decorated by an itinerant Anglo-Saxon artist who, in addition to supplying a drawing in a second Fleury book, also worked at Saint-Bertin as well as in the circle of Bishop Oswald of Worcester.[31] Another Anglo-Saxon scribe who was active at Fleury around the same time, copying the *Mathesis* of Firmicus Maternus and contributing to a rhetorical collection, is actually

26 Canterbury CL, Add. 172: Gameson 2008, cat. 15. Other examples illustrated: Ker 1960, plates 2–3; and Gameson 1999c, plates 6–7.

27 BL, Cotton Cleopatra D.i, part A (fols. 2–82*).

28 Netzer 1994, esp. chs. 4–5. She suggests (p. 117) that, though Thomas's work shows a clear debt to Lindisfarne, he was not actually trained there 'but in a provincial center, like Echternach, by a scribe-artist from [Lindisfarne]'. Whatever the truth, a Northumbrian stands behind part of this manuscript.

29 Arras, Médiathèque, 343: see chapter 14, p. 354 note 39, in this volume.

30 BL, Harley 2506. The substitution of the name 'Berno' for that of 'Abbo' in the reference to how many places Abbo was the abbot in a copy of his *De differentia circuli et sphaerae* therein would only be necessary in a community where Abbo had now become abbot – as was uniquely the case at Fleury after 987.

31 Also appearing in Boulogne, BM, 11; BL, Harley 2904; PML, M 827; and Orléans, Médiathèque, 175.

named by a note in the margin of the latter book; the fact that he was called Leofnoth confirms the racial indications of his handwriting.[32]

A further example of the general phenomenon is a gospel-book in Antwerp which probably dates from the second quarter of the eleventh century.[33] The first fifteen pages of the Gospel of St Matthew were written by an Anglo-Saxon, but all the rest – along with the marginal concordances and the verse initials in the Anglo-Saxon stint – was done by Flemish hands. Similarly, although the two surviving decorated letters (for the incipits of Mark and John), which are conceived in the Anglo-Saxon 'Type II' initial style, were probably drawn by an Englishman, the capitals which accompany the first and the portrait of St John beside the second – along with arches of the canon tables – were done by Flemish hands. The interweaving of the English and the Flemish work implies that the book was the result of genuine collaboration; and given the quantitative preponderance of the Flemish contribution, it is logical to presume that this happened in Flanders. The fact that all the corrections are by Flemish hands supports this hypothesis, as does the early provenance of the volume: subsequent additions to fols. 175v–6 (two prayers, a papal bull of 9 April 1105 and two inventories, one dated 1115[34]) show that at the beginning of the twelfth century the manuscript belonged to Notre-Dame at Bruges (established in 875, then a parish church from 961, this was refounded as a collegiate church in 1091).

The scriptorium

Scriptoria, in the simple sense of places where book-making was carried out, will have varied enormously in size, scope and formality. If major ecclesiastical foundations were, as we have seen, the principal foci of scribal activity, one must not forget alternative circumstances such as the royal court and noble households, noted above, or even the tent of an itinerant bishop – as Aldred's colophon to his contribution to the 'Durham Collectar' happens to record: 'Aldred the Provost wrote these four collects at Oakley to the south of Woodyates, among the West Saxons on [10 August 970] before Tierce for Ælfsige the bishop, in his tent.'[35] It would not be at all surprising if a scrappy, composite codex like the Copenhagen Wulfstan manuscript, made for and

32 BnF, lat. 7311 and 7696 (responsible for 127v, col. ii, bottom – 148, col. ii, line 7; name written in green on 147r): Vezin 1977.

33 Antwerp, Plantin-Moretus Museum, M.16.15 (194).

34 Bischoff 1967, no. 14; Derolez and Victor 1997, no. 8.

35 DCL, A.IV.19. Facs.: Brown *et al.* 1969.

used by an ecclesiastic whose responsibilities were split between Worcester, York and the court, was likewise put together in different locations and, perhaps, partly written 'on the hoof'.[36]

Nevertheless, given the complexity and expense of book production, it makes best sense on the whole to imagine a smaller number of major centres supplying the needs of most other places than to envisage every minster, manor or parish church, not to mention noble household, attempting to make its own manuscripts. Even if such churches and chapels could have mustered the material resources, the dim view of tenth-century clerical literacy taken by Ælfric suggests that few would have had personnel with the ability to take advantage of them.[37] This general model of provision from major centres can be documented in the case of Wearmouth-Jarrow: Bede saw at least some of his writings as useful for contemporaries who did not have access to the exceptional library resources of his own twin community (or the strength to read it all), and both epistolary and documentary evidence reveals that its scriptorium laboured to supply copies of his work to even the darkest corners of Continental Europe.[38] Wearmouth-Jarrow was an exceptionally large twin community, but the example makes the additional point that size alone was not the key factor: the presence of a prolific house author also played an important part here. Indeed, a bibliophile superior, talented calligraphers and house authors were ultimately more important than sheer size in determining scriptorium activity. Thus Ælfric at Cerne, then Eynsham, envisaging the distribution of his *Sermones catholici*, was necessarily committing to ambitious 'publishing' operations centres which were unlikely otherwise to have undertaken them. The surviving manuscripts of the 'First Series' and the different versions they represent have been taken to reflect some twenty-one manuscripts of the work produced in Ælfric's own scriptorium, first at Cerne, then at Eynsham.[39]

If we set the bar higher and define a scriptorium as an organised group of scribes, decorators and binders, we are dealing with a costly and complicated organism that required considerable institutional commitment. The creation and maintenance of such an operation presupposed the means, the manpower and motive. The first of these conditions meant, in effect, sufficient resources to organise an adequate supply of parchment, ink and pigment, along with

36 Copenhagen, KB, G. K. S. 1595 (4°). Facs.: Cross and Tunberg 1993. See also chapter 37 below.

37 *Grammar*, Preface: Zupitza 1880, p. 3.

38 *Libri quatuor in principium Genesis*, Preface: Jones 1967, p. 1. Tangle 1916, nos. 75, 76, 116, 125.

39 Clemoes 1997, pp. 1–168, esp. 160–2. Thirty-four manuscripts produced outside Ælfric's scriptorium survive in whole or in part; they are believed to imply the existence of some fifty others (*ibid.*, p. 162).

the connections and opportunity to obtain exemplars. The second implied the capacity to educate potential scribes in the relevant literary skills – reading and writing in both Latin and Old English – to train them as calligraphers, and to 'budget' the considerable man-hours that scribal labour implied. As for the third, while the ubiquitous need for key texts provided a general motive (particularly at times of acute need such as the early generations of the conversion period or the aftermath of the Viking ravages), all the indications are that a thriving scriptorium presupposed something more. The implications of this are best appreciated with reference to the handful of examples for which we have both attributable manuscripts and a reasonable amount of contextual information.

The particular circumstances of Wearmouth-Jarrow, with its initial connections to Rome, its early bibliophile abbots who imported numerous books from the Continent, and then the presence among the community of the greatest scholar of Christendom, a prolific author whose works were much in demand, explains the singular dynamic of its scriptorium, whose first products were labour-intensive high-grade church books that imitated Mediterranean styles, and which then moved on to more expeditiously produced 'reading' books.[40] With regard to Lindisfarne, its unique situation in the aftermath of the Synod of Whitby, trying to reclaim lost spiritual status and continue the best of its Insular heritage within a now officially 'Roman' church, arguably lay behind the efflorescence of its scriptorium at the end of the seventh and the start of the eighth century, whose finest volume was a particularly masterly synthesis of Irish and Roman styles.[41] When in the late tenth century Winchester flourished as a centre of deluxe book production it was manifestly thanks to an energetic and colourful Maecenas in the person of Bishop Æthelwold, and while it continued to produce volumes, some fine, thereafter, the acme of its achievement was closely connected to his regime. The profiles of Christ Church, Canterbury, and Worcester can equally be linked to their known historical circumstances – and over longer periods of time. The scriptorium of Christ Church seems to have been revitalised during the long archiepiscopacy of the reformer, Dunstan; if the momentum for making high-grade library texts carried on into the early eleventh century, the sack of Canterbury by the Vikings in 1011 delivered the *coup de grâce* to this phase of work. Rapidly revived, the scriptorium seems subsequently to have focused its energies on high-status gospel-books and liturgica, some for export, its output slowly declining towards the middle of the eleventh century. The Norman

40 Parkes 1982. 41 Gameson 2001; Brown 2003b.

Conquest and the arrival of Lanfranc, along with a devastating fire in 1067, brought the imperative to copy patristic texts, a phase characterised by rapidly written books of quite divergent appearance – from which a new 'house style' for such works gradually emerged in the late eleventh century.[42] At Worcester, notwithstanding the presence of such major figures as St Oswald (d. 992) and Wulfstan the Homilist (d. 1023), book production remained slack throughout the tenth century and for the first half of the eleventh. Only from the mid-eleventh century, effectively the time of St Wulfstan (prior by *c.* 1055, bishop from 1062), did a Worcester scriptorium develop a regular rhythm and, concomitantly, a house style. The Norman Conquest notwithstanding, it then continued to work in much the same ways and idioms, albeit copying some newly fashionable patristic texts with modest concessions to 'modern' styles of initial decoration, until the end of the eleventh century – but then St Wulfstan's episcopacy lasted until 1095.[43]

The number of centres in the early Anglo-Saxon period to which the production of extant manuscripts can safely be attributed is very small – essentially just Canterbury, Lindisfarne, Minster-in-Thanet, Wearmouth-Jarrow and Worcester – but it can easily be tripled by including those places for which documentary or archaeological evidence makes significant book production certain or highly likely – notably Barking, Exeter, Hartlepool, Hexham, Lichfield, London, Malmesbury, Melrose, Nursling, Ripon, Rochester, Whitby, Winchester, York – and then multiplied again if one admits centres on the grounds of archaeological or ecclesiastical importance alone (Bardney, Bradwell-on-Sea, Breedon, Brixworth and so on). A similar exercise may be carried out for the late Anglo-Saxon period and here the list of centres to which extant books and scribal activitiy may reasonably be attributed is fuller: Abingdon, Barking, Bath, Canterbury (Christ Church and St Augustine's Abbey), Cerne, Chester-le-Street, Crowland, Ely, Exeter, Eynsham, Glastonbury, Hereford, London, Malmesbury, Peterborough, Ramsey, Rochester, Shaftesbury, Sherborne, Wells, Winchester (New Minster, Old Minster and Nunnaminster), Winchcombe, Worcester and York. In both cases, these rough and ready procedures would result in a total of between about fifty and one hundred named and nameable centres – though there is the important distinction that in the earlier period they are scattered across the whole country, while in the later one they are focused in the south.

42 Gameson 1992d, 1995a and 2000b.

43 Gameson 1996a and 2005.

Neither list in its fullest state could have any pretension to completeness. The accident of knowing that the master scribe Ultán wrote, and the poet Ædiluulf composed, at an unnamed dependency of Lindisfarne (perhaps Bywell or Crayke, bordering the Vale of Pickering[44]), and the high density of writing implements found at Flixborough, a centre unnoticed in the documentary record, remind us how haphazard and lacunose are the sources at our disposal. Conversely, the message of the examples considered above is that scriptoria, even of the grandest foundations, were not continuously productive. Monks and canons did not just write books as a matter of course: on the contrary, the dynamic of a centre was dependent upon its circumstances and personalities at a given time. Our notional map of the principal scriptoria, generally located in major religious houses, must, therefore, be conceived as slowly but surely evolving as individual centres waxed and waned following political and ecclesiastical changes, according to the presence or otherwise of house authors, talented calligraphers, bibliophile superiors, and in response to the particular needs of the day. Even in the heyday of production, first in the eighth century then in the century before the Norman Conquest, it is unlikely that more than half of our nameable scriptoria were energetically active in any given generation.

Scribal work

Aldred's note, quoted earlier, that he wrote in a tent far from home – a rare glimpse of the practicalities of such activities – provides a useful reminder that the physical circumstances in which scribal work might be accomplished were potentially quite diverse. The first relatively clear reference to a scriptorium in the sense of a communal writing-room relates to the generation after the Conquest and the special circumstances of the professional scribes hired (thanks to lay sponsorship) by Abbot Paul of St Albans;[45] even if the document accurately records the situation in the late eleventh century (as opposed to the mid twelfth century when it was reputedly drawn up, or the mid thirteenth century when the version that has come down to us was actually penned), it reflects the particular situation of a group of hired lay professionals for whom, assuming they were not to be installed within the heart of the monastic complex, inevitably disrupting the seclusion and tranquillity of Regular life, a special space had to be constructed. Certainly it would be a mistake to generalise

44 Favoured by Howlett 1975, pp. 122–4, and Lapidge 1996, pp. 394–8, respectively.
45 See n. 22 above.

from this one late case when we have no evidence for similar facilities prior to the Conquest. Nor, given the paucity of evidence for pre-Conquest cloisters and the number of our scriptoria that were associated with non-enclosed regimes, should we imagine the cloister as the setting for much scribal work. On the contrary, we should probably envisage most British books being written, singly or severally, not in a designated writing-room but rather in chambers, halls or other places – wherever the light and space were suitable – and then possibly decorated, and almost certainly bound, elsewhere. One ninth-century Irish scribe famously claimed (in verse) to have been writing in the open air amongst the trees, listening to bird song.[46] However much credence can be given to this lyrical claim (which is not easily reconcilable with the grand size of the manuscript in which it appears), the different stages of book production were doubtless spread around an ecclesiastical complex as was ergonomically most practical.

The extant material reveals divers patterns of collaboration in the task of writing a book. Some volumes are holographs – entirely written by a single scribe. The Lindisfarne Gospels and the Benedictional of St Æthelwold, famous cases of such from either end of our period, both bear inscriptions naming their single scribes, who are thereby identified as Eadfrith and Godeman respectively.[47] The former is generally believed also to have been the decorator of his volume; whether the equivalent was true of the latter is an open question. If a disproportionately high percentage of the very finest manuscripts are holograph – doubtless reflecting the wish to ensure maximum regularity of appearance throughout, or the related decision to entrust the project to the single most talented scribe available – the same is also true of plenty of less exalted volumes. As 'workaday' examples one may cite the tenth-century Worcester Paschasius signed by Sistan, the Malmesbury Old English Gospels signed by Wulfwig, and a couple of Ælfric or Ælfrician homiliaries.[48] Some very low-quality books were also the work of a single scribe (and here the phenomenon might reflect a lack of human resources: there was no one to share the task); however, the lack of stability that characterises extremely poor writing can make it difficult to decide whether one or more hands were involved in a given case. The unruly and idiosyncratic writing, punctuated with equally crude and disorderly decorated initials, of a late eleventh -century copy of the *Vita Wilfridi*, is a case in point.[49]

46 St Gallen, Stiftsbibliothek, 904: Carney 1967, no. IX.
47 BL, Cotton Nero D.iv; Add. 49598.
48 BL, Royal 8 B.xi; Cotton Otho C.i; CCCC, 188; and CCCC, 162.
49 BL, Cotton Vespasian D.vi, part ii.

Then there are books which were mainly written by one scribe with a small contribution from one or more others. In one copy of Ælfric's *Grammar*, for instance, the second hand contributed a mere three and a half lines in the middle of the text; while in the fine late tenth-century Winchester Benedictional in Rouen the second scribe wrote but one page.[50] Circumstances similar to this last example also obtained in the Besançon, Copenhagen and York Gospels, where single scribes wrote most of the main text but a different hand was responsible for a small number of pages, generally very prominent ones, often allied to major decoration.[51] The precise details, and hence the possible rationales, differ from case to case; however, in high-grade books some such distinct leaves, designed to receive artwork, may have been done as a discrete phase of production while, as particularly important pages, they may have been reserved for a senior practitioner.

In scribally more 'populous' manuscripts both the number of hands and the ways in which the stints are apportioned vary enormously. The pattern of collaboration can occasionally be linked to the major divisions of the text: the Old English gospel-book from Bath, in which each of the four gospels was the work of a different scribe, is a case in point.[52] Elsewhere it may be closely allied to the physical structure of the book. Thus in one Old English Bede manuscript, the first thirteen quires were by one hand, and the remaining eighteen by another; while in an eight-quire verse collection, hand 1 essentially wrote quire I, hand 2 wrote quires II, IV and V, hand 3 wrote quire III, hand 4 wrote quire VI, and hand 5 probably did quires VII and VIII.[53] In the first instance, the nature of the 'join' between the stints suggests that the collaborating scribes were working simultaneously; while the orderly apportionment of labour in the second implies a well-organised scriptorium – in this case Christ Church, Canterbury. A celebrated case that combines both these aspects is the monumental pandect, the Codex Amiatinus, that was made at Wearmouth-Jarrow.[54] Its 130 or so quires were apportioned between seven scribes, all but one of whom were responsible for a stint of about twenty quires based around a group (or groups) of biblical books – clearly the carefully calculated product of a well-managed scriptorium.

50 DCL, B.III.32, part 2; second hand on 62v (not the final leaf of a quire). It is not impossible that 71–81 are by a different hand again, though this is probably the main scribe writing in a more compressed manner. Rouen, BM, Y.7, fol. 22v (the verso of the decorated initial page for the blessing for Easter Sunday).

51 Besançon, BM, 14; Copenhagen, KB, G. K. S. 10 (2°); York Minster, Add. 1 (cf. Heslop 1990, pp. 188–95).

52 CCCC, 140.

53 CCCC, 41; TCC, O.2.31.

54 Florence, Bibliotheca Medicea-Laurenziana, Amiatino 1.

The late tenth-century Christ Church Smaragdus, on which six or seven scribes collaborated in a regulated manner, raises a further issue.[55] Here quires I, II and IV were shared in different ways between two or more scribes, while quire III, quires V+VI, quires VII+VIII, quire IX and quires X+XI were each the stint of a different hand. The evidence of spacing within the individual stints implies that the scribes were trying to pace their work according to, and hence were independently working from, the quires of a disbound exemplar. However, in the most intriguing of the shared quires – IV (fols. 25–32), in which the outermost and innermost bifolia (25+32 and 28+29) were by one hand, the second bifolium (26+31) by another, and the third (27+30) by yet another – there is no evidence of cramping or expanding at the end of any of the stints, and words are sometimes split across contributions (31v, for example, ends 'intelle-' and 32r begins '-gere'); thus, unless these scribes all had a preternatural ability to follow the exemplar line by line without having to resort to any of the usual expedients to keep their work on course, this quire would seem to have been copied sequentially from a bound gathering rather than simultaneously from separate sheets. We might, then, deduce that, although the quires of the exemplar were separate, their leaves were not; and we might further suspect that the motive for apportioning the work in this way, and hence including so many scribes in the project, was not simply the wish to expedite the task. This manuscript, from the pioneering phase of the adoption of Caroline Minuscule script at Christ Church, is a copy of the *Diadema monachorum*, a florilegium of readings designed to inspire good practice in the activities of monastic life. Collaboration on such a work would be an effective way to symbolise a new phase in the life of the scriptorium, apotheosising the work of scribes with reformed hands, perhaps responding to a new ethos under the monastic reformer, St Dunstan (archbishop 959–88). The fact that the collection ends with the colophon, 'He finishes saying "Every scribe who writes has fun"', adds to the plausibility of this interpretation.[56]

In other cases, where changes come thick and fast – mid-page, mid-line, even mid-word – as in various late eleventh-century Salisbury manuscripts or an early twelfth-century *Moralia* of Llanthony provenance[57] – speed may indeed have been the prime motivation (though the different rhythms of life in a community of canons – which both these houses were – as opposed to

55 CUL, Ff.4.43: Bishop 1971, no. 8.

56 '[F]init dicendo ludit Quicumque scriptor scribit.' A longer version of the colophon appears in the slightly older CCCC, 206: Gameson 2002d, no. 13. Compare Arras, Médiathèque, 723: Gameson 2006b, pp. 53–7.

57 E.g. Salisbury CL, 10, 63, 168, 179; Oxford, Trinity College, 39 (Qq. I–III).

a monastery, may also have played a part here). Orderic Vitalis describes one type of circumstance that might on occasion have motivated such practices, namely access to a rare exemplar for a strictly limited period of time.[58] On other occasions the phenomenon may reflect a training exercise for debutant scribes.[59] Certainly, the role of the master scribe in instructing the younger generation is articulated in one the colloquies of Ælfric Bata: 'The man who wrote all this was a good scribe and had a fine hand ... Our brothers say that when he was strong in body he taught a lot of boys, youths and young men to write. Some of these good scribes are still alive – others are dead – and are scribes of this monastery.'[60] In the case of Wulfstan the Homilist's 'Lawbook', 'Letterbook' and 'Handbook', by contrast, the irregular structure of the manuscripts, the assorted content, and the various blanks, corrections and annotations, all suggest that it was their nature as compilations that determined their scribal diversity: different hands were put to work as and when literary material was chosen or became available, and time permitted.[61]

The rationale for many of the other patterns of collaboration that are observable in the manuscripts is, however, elusive. Why, for instance, one page and nine lines, two-thirds of the way through a single large quire devoted to the *Passio Edmundi*, were entrusted to a second, inferior scribe is obscure; as is the reason why the principal scribe of the early tenth-century Tanner Bede, having written over 100 folios of the book by himself, then first admitted a colleague (with whom he shared some fifteen folios) and finally gave up altogether, the work being pursued by two further, qualitatively poorer scribes.[62] In both cases, the interweaving of the stints at the 'joins' indicates that the work was all broadly contemporary. In the latter case, the older character of the principal scribe's hand – in comparison to the newer aspects of those of his colleagues – may invite various (morbid) hypotheses as to why he might have relinquished the task; however, there is no way of testing them. Conversely, one possible scenario that could account for similar end results is alluded to, indeed almost advocated, by Anselm who, writing from Bec to the monk Maurice in England,

58 Orderic Vitalis, *Historia ecclesiastica*, bk 6, ch. 3: Chibnall 1969–80, III, p. 218.

59 Muir 1988, esp. pp. xiii and xvi–xvii, suggests this for the prayerbook, BL Cotton Galba A.xiv + Nero A.ii, fols. 3–13. The colophon in BSB, Clm 19456 (Tegernsee, s. x–xi) states: 'Ego Froumundus coepi hunc libellum scribere sed pueri nostri quos docui meo iuvamine perscripserunt' ('I, Froumund, began to write this little book, but our boys whom I taught brought it to completion with my help'): *Colophons*, no. 4571; I have not seen this manuscript. Cf. Cohen-Mushlin 1990.

60 No. 24: Gwara and Porter 1997, p. 134.

61 BL, Cotton Nero A.I: facs.: Loyn 1971; Cotton Vesp. A.xiv (Mann 2004); Copenhagen, KB, G. K. S. 1595 (4°) (facs.: Cross and Tunberg 1993).

62 Lambeth Palace 362, part I; BodL., Tanner 10.

instructs the latter that if he returns to Bec in the near future, he should bring with him whatever he had managed to copy of one particular text, trusting that the transcription – and eventual dispatch – of the remainder would be organised by another colleague in England.[63] In extreme cases, therefore, the scribes whose work would ultimately be bound together as proximate sections of a single text may never have met.

In certain shared books the first scribe is manifestly the best,[64] and so, it might be hypothesised, represents a senior figure in the scriptorium defining the *mise en page*, or the wish to have the start of the volume looking particularly elegant; however, this is by no means invariably the case. In the aforementioned shared Smaragdus from Christ Church, for example, the first stint was in fact contributed by one of the weakest hands represented therein.[65] Again, while in some books the collaborating scribes have broadly similar hands, and, it might reasonably be suspected, were either deliberately selected as co-workers on those very grounds, or endeavoured to assimilate their styles, in order to ensure the visual consistency of the final product, frequently this is not the case. That disparate hands ended up being juxtaposed in a couple of the manuscripts compiled, perhaps in a piecemeal fashion, for the personal use of Wulfstan the Homilist is unsurprising,[66] and that it should prove to be a regular occurrence in the aftermath of the Conquest, as scribes from different racial traditions laboured side by side, was equally inevitable; but the variant styles that regularly co-exist in the books from many centres throughout our period advertise the fact that strict visual homogeneity was not, in general, a high priority.[67] Indeed, in circumstances where people of different generations inevitably worked side by side, sometimes with individuals from other places and traditions amongst them, it could hardly be otherwise.

Other more general factors doubtless also lie behind the different patterns of collaboration to be observed in our manuscripts. In relation to the scriptorium itself, its location, size, nature and endowment, the need (or otherwise) to train the young, the importance and urgency of a project, and the sudden arrival or imminent departure of a particular exemplar could all affect

63 Schmitt 1946–61, ep. 43. Cf. the sources which document an institution possessing part, or an incomplete copy, of a particular work and trying to secure an exemplar for the rest (e.g. from the ninth century, Lupus of Ferrières' letter to Alsigius of York and Pope Benedict III (relating to a Jerome) and from the tenth, Froumundus of Tegernsee's letter to monk ,'R' (about a Horace)): Levillain 1927–35, II, pp. 80 and 122; also I, p. 240.

64 E.g. BodL., Auct. F.3.6 (Prudentius); first stint 1r–v.

65 CUL, Ff.4.43, fols 3r–4r, 5v–10v/15 word 2; 12r/lines 1–16.

66 Copenhagen, KB, G. K. S. 1595 (4°); BL, Cotton Vespasian A..xiv.

67 E.g. the *s.* viii Cambridge–London (CCCC, 197B + BL, Cotton Otho C.v + Royal 7 C.xii, fols. 2–3) and Barberini Gospels (BAV, Barb. Lat. 570), as also arguably DCL, A.II.16.

the deployment of scribal resources, as could the other duties – not to mention the age and health – of particular scribes. (Colophons such as 'Three fingers write but the whole body labours' and 'Just as the port is welcome to the sailor, so is the last line to the scribe', although topoi, underline the point that writing was a physically demanding and time-consuming task.[68]) Then, external to the scriptorium, climatic conditions – poor light, a sudden cold spell, the onset of winter – which enforced short- or long-term cessation of labour will regularly have affected progress and organisation. The extent to which environmental conditions could cause difficulties is advertised by a letter of 763/4 from Cuthbert, abbot of Wearmouth-Jarrow, to Lull of Mainz, apologising for the delay in providing material: 'And if I could have done more, I would gladly have done so. For the conditions of the past winter oppressed the island of our race very horribly with cold and ice and long and widespread storms of wind and rain, so that the hand of the scribe was hindered from producing a great number of books.'[69] Finally, a whole range of further forces, such as famine, pestilence and war, could have had an intermittent but more devastating effect, eliminating personnel, eradicating resources, disrupting supply chains and necessitating changes in plans and priorities. In the second half of the eighth century no less a figure than Æthelberht, archbishop of York (sedit 766/7–779/80), lamented his inability to secure scribes to copy cosmographical works for himself and for Lull of Mainz.[70] If the high quality of the Christ Church books produced in the first half of the eleventh century shows that an exceptional centre could recover relatively rapidly from a hostile onslaught (the overrunning of Canterbury by the Danes in 1011), the discontinuity between this work and the earlier output nevertheless suggests that the event was a watershed in the history of the scriptorium.[71] To sum up: many of the factors that affected the day-to-day work of a scriptorium – including the precise deployment of labour and resources – and hence determined the appearance of its books cannot be identified from the clear yet mute traces they will have left on the pages in question.

The overarching concern of any scriptorium was, naturally, for accuracy in transcription. Alcuin's well-known poem on scribes stresses the point: 'May their hands not make mistakes through foolishness ... Let them zealously

68 Gameson 2002d, nos. 5 and 6 (BnF, lat. 9561; BAV, Pal. lat. 68).

69 Tangl 1916, no. 116; trans. Whitelock 1979, no. 185. Compare Orderic Vitalis, *Historia ecclesiastica*, bk IV, end and bk VI, ch. 3: Chibnall 1968–80, II, p. 360 and III, p. 218.

70 Tangl 1916, no. 124; Haddan and Stubbs 1869–78, III, pp. 436–7. Whether this reflects a temporary or a more general shortage of scribes at York around this time is a moot point. See also chapter 32 below.

71 Gameson 2000b and Chapter 10 in this volume.

strive to produce emended texts and may their pens fly along and follow the correct path. May they distinguish the proper meanings by colons and commas / and put each point in the place where it belongs.'[72] Ælfric subsequently articulated the same concerns in a shriller way in the Prefaces to his two sets of *Sermones catholici*, flagging the importance of correcting every copy against the exemplar:

> Now I desire and beseech in God's name, if anyone wishes to transcribe this book that he carefully correct it by the exemplar lest we be blamed through careless scribes. Great evil does he who writes false, unless he correct it; it is as though he turn true doctrine to false error; therefore should everyone rectify what he formerly mangled, if he wishes to be untainted at God's judgement.[73]

And when urging on a brother who was copying texts for him in England, Anselm declared that he would prefer to have part of a rare work faithfully copied than the whole of it corrupted by errors.[74]

The extensive activity of correcting hands in manuscripts of every sort, from the deluxe eighth-century Codex Aureus to the functional early eleventh-century copy of Gregory's *Dialogi* at Canterbury, attests both to the attention with which they were re-read – and to the need to carry out such remedial work. If the many carefully contrived corrections in the former were necessitated by the unusually demanding, non-sequential way in which the text had to be transcribed, those required in the latter seem to betoken inattention, indeed negligence, on the part of the original scribe.[75] Effective correcting – preserving the purity of a religious text – could be celebrated as a mark of spirituality. Thus Dunstan's first biographer immortalised the fact that 'when [the saint] could see the first light of daybreak [he would] correct faulty books, erasing the errors of the scribes', and a handful of extant manuscripts would seem to preserve his activities in this respect.[76] Sometimes it can be deduced that a faulty or difficult-to-read exemplar had caused problems (as the many minor errors in the Moore manuscript of Bede's *Historia ecclesiastica* were to do for generations of scribes who copied its descendants on the Continent[77]); and on a couple of occasions our scribes explicitly stated that this was the case.

72 Godman 1985, no. 11, pp. 138–9.
73 Clemoes 1997, p. 177; Godden 1979, p. 2. On the general fidelity of early copyists of Ælfric's works: Scragg 2006.
74 Schmitt 1946–61, ep. 60.
75 Stockholm, KB, A.135 (Gameson 2001–2, I, esp. pp. 59–62); Canterbury CL, Add. 32 (Gameson 2008, no. 6).
76 *Vita Dunstani auctore B*, ch. 37: Stubbs 1874, p. 49. For the hand: Hunt 1961; Bishop 1968.
77 CUL, Kk.5.16. Facs. Hunter Blair 1959, and see comment on pp. 34–6; Colgrave and Mynors 1969, pp. lxii–lxiv.

The scribe of one florilegium, for example, begged the reader to deign to correct part of his work, explaining, 'scarcely was the scribe able to write this thus because he was not able to get his hands on a reliable exemplar'.[78]

In his highly inventive *Life* of the seventh-century Mildred of Thanet composed at the end of the eleventh century, the hagiographer Goscelin has his plucky young heroine, in the face of torment, 'writing a little psalter with her maidenly hand, with a neatness and skill which she was sure would make it pleasing to her mother, Domneva [first abbess of Thanet]'.[79] The eighth-century Ultán, it will be remembered, was celebrated in the ninth century for the beauty of his script; and in the eleventh century, one of the monastic colloquies of Ælfric Bata immortalised the 'good scribe with a fine hand'.[80] If quality be judged primarily or partly by external appearance – as clearly it sometimes was – then the very finest works are, unsurprisingly, great gospel-books, psalters and other biblica and liturgica. The Uncial of the Codex Amiatinus, the two Wearmouth-Jarrow gospel-books and the Canterbury Codex Aureus, the Insular Half-Uncial of the Lindisfarne and Durham Gospels, the Insular Set Minuscule of the Echternach Gospels, the Square Minuscule of the Sherborne Pontifical and the Bosworth Psalter, the Caroline Minuscule of the Benedictional of Æthelwold and the Ramsey and Eadwig Psalters are all exceptionally fine, highly calligraphic examples of their respective script-types.[81] Yet such 'general principles' were also, of course, subject to variables such as the scale and resources of particular scriptoria, not to mention the ambient quality of handwriting at the time in question.

A plenitude of skilled scribes in a generally supportive context could result in handsome copies of other texts. The number of well-trained calligraphers working under the aegis of a bibliophile bishop provided the context for the fine copy of Alfred's Old English translation of Gregory's *Regula pastoralis* that was made at Exeter in the third quarter of the eleventh century.[82] General scriptorium discipline and momentum lay behind the visual homogeneity and general attractiveness of many of the Latin manuscripts made at St Augustine's Abbey during the middle third of the tenth century and at Christ Church during the last third. The disparity between the resources of the centres in question doubtless helps to explain why a mid-eleventh-century

78 CCCC, 448, supplement: Gameson 2002d, no. 24.

79 *Vita Deo dilectae virginis Mildrethae*, ch. xiv: Rollason 1982, p. 126.

80 No. xxiv: Gwara and Porter 1997, p. 134.

81 Florence, Biblioteca Medicea-Laurenziana, Amiatino 1; DCL, A.II.17, fols. 103–11; Utrecht, UB, 32, fols. 94–105; Stockholm, KB, A.135; BL, Cotton Nero, D.iv; DCL, A.II.17; BnF, lat. 9389; lat. 943; BL, Add. 37517; Add. 49598; Harley 2904; Arundel 155.

82 CUL, Ii.2.4: Robinson 1988, II, ill. 21 (which does scant justice to the beauty of the original).

Ælfrician homiliary from Christ Church is more elegant than fair copies of the *Sermones catholici* that were certainly or probably made at the author's own scriptorium during his lifetime.[83] Correspondingly, a well-equipped centre must be presumed to have been responsible for the once grand and very fine, if now sadly fragmentary, eleventh-century Old English gospel-book, Bodleian Library, Eng. bib.2; unfortunately, in the absence of any indication of medieval provenance, it is impossible to be more specific.[84]

Conversely, when English book production was in the doldrums in the late ninth and early tenth century, no manuscript, whatever its text, wherever it was written, was going to be particularly handsome – and the script and ornament of the one extant Latin gospel-book from this period are indeed qualitatively modest.[85] Equally, even during what might be regarded as the 'golden ages' of scribal achievement, first in the eighth century and then in the generations around the millennium, the finest work of secondary centres was likely to be inferior to that of the major ones, a phenomenon that the Hereford Gospels and the Barking Gospels would seem to embody respectively for the two periods in question.[86] And even the master scribe of a major centre, like Eadwig Basan of Christ Church, whose extant projects all seem to have been high-status ones, could have 'off-days', not to mention waning years – as is apparent from the comparative weakness of his stint in the great Harley 603 Psalter.[87]

On the whole, such visually execrable manuscripts as have come down to us (and the processes of transmission militated against the survival of such books) are of unknown origin. A scrappy vernacular medical collection and a curiously written grammatical anthology are cases in point.[88] One might reasonably hypothesise, according to content, that such manuscripts represent the work of minor centres, of debutant or waning scribes, or were personal compilations or school books, hence informally or economically produced. In the absence of specific information about the circumstances of their manufacture, such theories, though plausible, can generally be no more than that. Occasionally, however, more contextual data are available. As we have seen, the scrappy appearance of some of the manuscripts associated with Wulfstan

83 TCC, B.15.34: Keynes 1992, plate XXIIa and b. BL, Royal 7 C.xii, fols. 4–218 (facs. Eliason and Clemoes 1966) which is itself more handsome than CUL, Gg.3.28 (Godden 1979, frontispiece). Might this in turn reflect the difference between Cerne and Eynsham?

84 It is first recorded at Flixton Hall, Suffolk, reused as a cover of a court book. If its post-medieval location was not too distant from its medieval home, and if one further (daringly) supposes that this was not far from its pre-Conquest place of origin, one might look to Bury or perhaps Ely.

85 Boulogne, BM, 10: Gameson 2009.

86 Hereford CL, P.I.2; BodL., Bodley 155.

87 BL, Harley 603, fols. 28–49.

88 BL, Harley 585 (de Vriend 1984, pp. xxiii–xxviii with plate III) and Cotton Cleopatra A.vi.

the Homilist doubtless reflects the fact that 'working books' and ad hoc compilations, even if made for important individuals associated with major centres, would by their very nature be altogether less formal than 'library' books that were copied wholesale from pre-existing exemplars. The modest physical quality of the many 'library' books made at Salisbury in the late eleventh century, by contrast, reflects the fact that these volumes were written at some speed by the busy canons of a new centre where the rapid accumulation of a wide range of (then rare) texts, not the external appearance of the copies, was the priority.

As a coda to this, it is worth remembering that the process of attributing early medieval manuscripts to particular scriptoria, which relies on grouping books of similar appearance around those of known or presumed origin – and regular and well-disciplined hands are easier to recognise than variable, ill-disciplined ones – inevitably favours homogeneity over heterogeneity. Many of the books we can localise will, almost by definition, form groups that are fairly regular in appearance. The only available corrective is late Anglo-Saxon Worcester, to which a number of books can be attributed independently of their appearance: significantly, they are more striking for their physical divergences than their similarities. Some of the many unattributable late Anglo-Saxon manuscripts may have been written in very minor centres; others doubtless come from more major ones where a greater degree of variation was permitted or unavoidable. The general homogeneity allied to a distinctive 'house style' that we see in the library books made at Canterbury in the later tenth century was doubtless always the exception rather than the norm.

Rationale

Having stressed the many variables that affected the nature, location, output and dynamic – the very existence indeed – of scriptoria, it is appropriate to conclude by drawing together material touched on above to outline the main reasons why Anglo-Saxon scribes wrote books. Many volumes were, of course, made to be used by the community that produced them. Well-documented examples are two of the three pandects produced under the aegis of Ceolfrith of Wearmouth-Jarrow which, we are told, were destined for the churches of the twin community as permanent reference copies.[89] If medieval shelf-marks show that plentiful Anglo-Saxon books continued to belong throughout the Middle Ages to the community that had made them, annotations and

89 *Vita Ceolfridi abbatis auctore anonymo*, ch. 20: Plummer 1896, p. 395.

additions indicate that some such works could be a long-term investment with a very lengthy 'working life'. The *Romanum* text of the Arundel 155 Psalter, for instance, beautifully copied in the early eleventh century by the Christ Church scribe Eadwig Basan, was laboriously corrected to the Gallican version shortly after the Conquest to suit it for continuing use in a new era; it received a substantial supplement comprising canticles, litany, collects and hymns in the mid twelfth century; while much later inscriptions show that it was still a valued possession on the eve of the Reformation.

Second, books could be written for another community or individual, as a gift or in response to a specific request; rather than loaning an exemplar for transcription, one might offer a new copy. The Stonyhurst Gospel of St John, written at Wearmouth-Jarrow but sooner or later enclosed by the Lindisfarne community within the coffin of St Cuthbert, may be proposed as one such case; the late tenth-century Canterbury grammatical collection whose medieval (and modern) provenance was Worcester as another; the Grimbald Gospels, made at Christ Church but subsequently in Winchester, and the York Gospels, a Christ Church book that was soon in the hands of Wulfstan the Homilist and came to rest at York, are yet others.[90] Ceolfrith's third pandect is documented to have been prepared (or at least selected) as a gift for the papacy; the letters of SS Boniface and Lull provide unequivocal evidence for the way in which Anglo-Saxon scriptoria supplied the needs of the mission field in Germany during the eighth century; while the correspondence of Anselm and of Herbert Losinga offer glimpses of the bibliographical exchange that operated between England and Normandy in the immediate aftermath of the Norman Conquest.[91] If amongst the great religious houses such transcription might be undertaken in the knowledge that sooner or later one might oneself benefit from someone else's pen, when by contrast major scriptoria supplied minor churches, gratitude and prayer may have been the only return. Thus if Ceolfrith's third pandect might be seen as a magnificent thank offering for the wealth of Roman books that had enriched Wearmouth-Jarrow and as an advertisement of the good use to which they had been put, the missionaries in Germany offered little recompense to the scriptoria in the Anglo-Saxon homelands that laboured on their behalf – beyond the promise of ultimate spiritual reward for helping to promulgate and support the faith. Yet the value of this should not be underestimated. St Boniface was ready to stress the point, on one occasion telling Abbess Eadburh of Minster-in-Thanet that, because of the

90 BL, Loan 74; Worcester CL, Q.5; Add. 34890; York Minster Add. 1.
91 See further Part II in this volume on the circulation of books.

books she supplied, God would make her joyful in heaven, and on another that he was praying 'Almighty God the requiter and rewarder of all good works that he may grant [her] in the celestial mansions and the eternal tabernacles and in the heavenly court of the holy angels, an eternal reward'.[92]

A couple of times Ælfric specified the books a priest ought ideally to own, namely a psalter, an epistolary, a gospel-book and a mass-book, a service-book, a 'handbook' (?for confession), a computus, the *Regula pastoralis*, a penitential and lectionaries, along with a passional.[93] Very few parish churches will have had the means to meet this need themselves. The economically conceived eighth-century Royal 1 B.vii Gospels is the sort of copy, now rare but once far more common, that is likely to have been produced by a major centre (in this case perhaps Lindisfarne) to supply the needs of a minor one.[94] Around the millennium Ælfric's bid to supply orthodox preaching material for the church as a whole rested implicitly on the belief that the scriptoria of major foundations would make multiple copies to put the work into circulation – as Canterbury would seem to have done in the case of the *Sermones catholici*.[95] A well-documented example of a similar phenomenon from the late ninth century is Alfred's attempts to distribute his Old English translation of the *Regula pastoralis*. Manuscripts produced by Alfred's scribes were to be sent to every bishopric, where further copies, for wider 'altruistic' distribution, were to be made.[96]

This leads on to our next class, which is production at the behest of secular individuals. While King Alfred, Judith of Flanders and presumably Eldorman Æthelweard certainly or probably had in their own household scribes who made books for them (Old English translations, fine gospel-books, and a Latin version of the *Anglo-Saxon Chronicle* respectively), equally they and other potentates will no doubt have sought volumes from ecclesiastical scriptoria. The copy of the first series of *Sermones catholici* and the translation of Genesis requested by the same Æthelweard, and the *Lives of the Saints* that he and his son, Æthelmær, commissioned from Ælfric, along with the works for Sigeweard, were doubtless copied for them at Cerne and Eynsham, just as the Old English version of the *Rule of St Benedict* that King Edgar commissioned from Æthelwold would presumably have been transcribed at Old or New Minster, Winchester.[97] On the whole, books for a private collection or

92 Tangl 1916, nos. 30 and 35; trans. of latter from Whitelock 1979, p. 811.
93 Fehr 1966, pp. 13–14, 51–2, 126–7. 94 Gameson 1994.
95 Clemoes 1997, pp. 134–68, esp. 162–3.
96 Preface and Epilogue to the *Pastoral Care*: Whitelock 1967, no. II; Dobbie 1942, pp. 110–12.
97 'King Edgar's establishment of monasteries': Whitelock *et al.* 1981, I, no. 33, pp. 150–1.

chapel are far more likely to have been commissioned from a geographically convenient major scriptorium than to have been made by an isolated chaplain-secretary. Moreover, it is in this connection that we can make best sense of the statement in one of the colloquies of Ælfric Bata that a monk might write many books for considerable financial profit.[98] Indeed, King Edgar and Queen Ælfthryth are recorded to have 'paid' Æthelwold with the grant of an estate for translating the *Rule of St Benedict*.[99] Local aristocracy might, on their own initiative or in response to petitions from parish clergy, have shouldered some of the financial responsibility for the literary provisioning of churches in their gift; and purchasing or commissioning the relevant volumes from monastic scriptoria was presumably the easiest way to achieve this. Correspondingly, offering fine books to powerful lay folk could be one way of currying favour with them, as the master scribe Earnwine of Peterborough is reported to have believed when offering a fine psalter and a sacramentary to King Cnut and Queen Emma.[100]

Yet if some volumes were paid for, and a few were produced as diplomatic gifts, the primary motive for writing most books was spiritual. As many of the colophons of our period underline, transcribing was first and foremost an act of devotion, undertaken for celestial rewards. Scribes sought heavenly help for and blessings on their labour; they begged their readers to pray for them; and they hoped their work would help them to achieve salvation.[101] The philosophy implicit in the Anglo-Saxon examples is made explicit in the pictorial and poetic frontispiece of an early eleventh-century manuscript from Saint-Vaast, Arras, in which every aspect of the making of a book is enumerated and seen to attract spiritual blessings. The scribe tells us that the patron saint of the community

> looks down from ... heaven and notes how many letters I trace with my pens, with how many lines the page is furrowed and with how many sharp points the folio is wounded on this side and on that. And then, looking favourably on our work and on our labour, he says: 'As many as are the letters, as many as are the lines and finally as many as are the prickings in this book, so many sins I now remit for you / Christ grants that I have this eternal power.'[102]

Moreover, the benefit is enjoyed not only by the scribe himself, but also by any he should care to nominate. Whether or not money changed hands, irrespective of whether the books were destined for internal or external use, copying

98 Gwara and Porter 1997, p. 134. 99 *Liber Eliensis*, II, 37: Blake 1962, p. 111.
100 William of Malmesbury, *Vita Wulfstani*, I, 1: Darlington 1928, p. 5.
101 Gameson 2002d.
102 Arras, Médiathèque, 860: Gameson 2006b, pp. 59–61, 72–3, no. 11.

Christian texts was vital spiritual work (as Cassiodorus had declared centuries before, every word written by a monastic scribe inflicted a wound on Satan[103]) and it would be rewarded as such. Aldred of Chester-le-Street explained that his work glossing John in the Lindisfarne Gospels was 'so that through the grace of God [he might] gain acceptance into heaven, happiness and peace, and through the merits of St Cuthbert, advancement and honour, wisdom and sagacity on earth'.[104] Writing books was a devotional act which in itself benefited the scribe. The resulting volumes were more than just reading matter, they embodied spirituality in a physical way; and some, such as the Lindisfarne Gospels, were made as spiritual treasures, pieces of heaven on earth. Vehicles of culture and communication, scribes and scriptoria were, to a considerable extent and in a very tangible way, the spiritual engines of Anglo-Saxon England, as of the early medieval West as a whole. The inspired Ultán, with whom we began, was indeed a model worth celebrating.[105]

103 Cassiodorus, *Institutiones*, I, 30: Mynors 1937, p. 75.
104 Kendrick *et al.* 1956–60, pp. 5–16 and bk ii, pp. 5–11.
105 Qui scripsit vivat et qui legat letetur.

4
Writing in the Insular world

MICHELLE P. BROWN

Historical and historiographical context

The term 'Insular' can be taken to refer specifically to the history and culture of the Celtic, post Romano-British and Anglo-Saxon peoples of Britain and Ireland in the period between the retraction of the Roman Empire in the early fifth century and the advent of Viking raiders and settlers during the ninth. One of the major achievements of this era was the construction of a series of successor states in northern Europe, underpinned by the zeal for Christianity of the newly converted and a stability of administrative and social structure ensured by the effective collaboration of church and state. Essential to this process was the dissemination and reception of the Word of God, with its emphasis upon the law, social reform and teaching by example. A prerequisite of this was the reintroduction of literacy to those parts of post-Roman Britain that had lost the art (although some ecclesiastical centres such as Llandaff and Llantwit Major in Wales helped to perpetuate it), and its introduction into those Celtic and Germanic societies which had previously experienced only limited contact with writing, or had eschewed its use in favour of pre-existing oral processes for the preservation of collective memory. Such orality could be highly structured and schooled, preserving sophisticated literary, religious and legal knowledge, as in the case of the Celtic druidic classes. Celtic ogham and Germanic runes both represent proto-literate writing systems, inspired by contact with Roman scripts but used only for short commemorative or talismanic inscriptions. Even if full written literacy had formerly been eschewed in favour of oral mnemonic discipline, there was an existing predisposition towards civil and religious social structures and towards the preservation and transmission of bodies of learning, and this translated with comparative ease into a literate Christian society. The books made by Insular monks and nuns during this age stand as monument to their contribution to the transmission of scripture, to the preservation of elements of the cultures of northern

European prehistory and of the Graeco-Roman world, and to the transition from late Antiquity to the Middle Ages.

The earliest labours of St Augustine, who arrived in Canterbury in 597 at the head of a mission sent by Pope Gregory the Great, were to begin converting the Kentish court and to commit its Germanic law-code to the 'safe-keeping' of writing by phonetically transliterating Old English using Roman characters, and thereby beginning a process of integration of the church into an existing social and land-owning structure.[1] Augustine's followers, and those of Irish missionaries such as Columbanus, Columba, Aidan and Fursey, of Britons such as Patrick, Ninian and Samson, and of Anglo-Saxons such as Cuthbert, Wilfrid, Willibrord, Boniface and his kinswoman, Leoba, spread the processes of conversion and reform to the courts and countryside of Britain, Ireland and Continental Europe, through a plethora of monastic foundations.[2] The role models provided by such committed individuals – publicly acclaimed as saints during their own lifetimes – set new levels of social and spiritual aspiration.

Britain had received literacy and the Christian teaching under Rome's rule, perhaps as early as the first century and certainly during the third, when Christianity achieved popularity amongst merchants and the military along with the 'mystery' cults of Mithras and Isis. In 306 Constantine, the first emperor to embrace Christianity and to enable its ultimate adoption as the state religion, was proclaimed emperor by his troops in York. By the time those troops officially withdrew, a process formalised by the Honorian Rescript of 410, Britain possessed an organised diocesan structure, was sending bishops to attend major church councils in Gaul, and had spawned one of the most erudite heresies of the day – Pelagianism. Although not absorbed by the Roman Empire, Ireland was not isolated, and as early as the 430s the pope dispatched Palladius as bishop to those in southern Ireland who already believed in Christ, and later in the century missionary endeavour was extended by the British bishop, Patrick, to the northern parts of Ireland.

During the fifth century Germanic mercenaries who had served, successively, Rome in Britain and the native Romano-British remnants of its regime began seizing power and land on their own behalf. Despite valiant British resistance, a series of pagan kingdoms had been carved out by the end of the

1 For an overview of the conversion period in England see Mayr-Harting 1977, Gameson 1999 and M. P. Brown 2006b.

2 Notable foundations included Whithorn, Armagh, Bangor, Durrow, Derry, Iona, Melrose, Lindisfarne, Lastingham, Lichfield, Peterborough, Monkwearmouth-Jarrow, Ripon, St David's, Llantwit, Llandaff, Llandeilo Fawr, Bodmin, Sherborne, Wimborne, Minster-in-Thanet, Péronne, Luxeuil, St Gallen, Bobbio, Dol, Landévennec, Echternach, Utrecht, Tauberbischofsheim and Fulda.

sixth century by a migrant miscellany of Germanic peoples who have come to be known as the Anglo-Saxons. The contribution and continuity of the British church during this period is only now beginning to be adequately acknowledged. Wales, Cornwall and parts of Scotland, as well as progressively isolated British kingdoms such as Catterick and Elmet and pockets of native British Christians throughout England, kept the flame of Christianity and literacy alive and carried it to Brittany. Yet the British churches do not appear to have made concerted attempts to convert their warlike Germanic overlords, although evidence is accumulating to indicate a greater level of interaction than previously supposed. The process of conversion therefore largely fell, during the later sixth and seventh centuries, to representatives of the Roman church, notably Augustine and his followers from Rome, and Agilbert and Felix from Gaul, or of the Irish church, such as Columba, Aidan and Fursey.

The earliest surviving Insular manuscripts contain scripture and patristic texts and are from Ireland, dating to the end of the sixth or, more probably, the beginning of the seventh century.[3] They include the earliest extant Insular gospel-book, Codex Usserianus Primus, which contains an 'Old Latin' text and is reminiscent, palaeographically and stylistically, of an early gospel-book from St Columbanus' Irish foundation at Bobbio.[4] Likewise of early date are the Springmount Bog Tablets, a set of wax tablets inscribed with verses from the psalms.[5] These are an unusual survival, given the climatic conditions of northern Europe, for they owe their preservation to loss in a peat bog. They convey graphically the obligation of the priest to be 'psalteratus' – to have memorised and be able to recite the psalms – and recall exhortations to ordinands to spend whatever time possible learning them, even when travelling (as the person studying these extracts may have been when he lost them to the bog). The Cathach of Columcille contains Jerome's Romanum version of the psalter and is the first Insular book in which decoration begins to assume a significant role in articulating the text, with its decorated initials (their crosses and fish perhaps influenced by manuscripts associated with production in Rome under Pope Gregory the Great, combined with native Celtic ornament) and the diminuendo effect of the following letters linking them to the actual text script.[6]

3 For an overview of the study of Insular manuscripts and their palaeography, see Brown 2004. On the earliest Irish manuscripts, see Schaumann, 1978–9, Brown 1982 and 1984 and Dumville 1999.

4 TCD, 55; Milan, Biblioteca Ambrosiana I.61 sup.; this contains a 'mixed' text and, interestingly, the Irish Half-Uncial script is written over a palimpsest of Ulfilas in Gothic.

5 National Museum of Ireland, Dublin, S.A. 1914:2; Schaumann 1978–9.

6 RIA, s.n. The Cathach was long thought to be the actual copy made by St Columba (Columcille) of a psalter owned by St Finian of Moville which occasioned a charge of plagiarism that precipitated tribal conflict and contributed to Columba's departure on *peregrinatio* – voluntary exile for Christ.

The Cathach is the first in a series of high-quality psalters from an Insular milieu. A later Irish example, which is written in Half-Uncial script with illuminated initials and probably dates to the late eighth century, was recently found – complete with binding, satchel and a mat to conceal it – in a peat bog on Faddan More, Co. Tipperary.[7] Others include the Salaberga Psalter and the Blickling Psalter, both probably made in England during the mid eighth century, and the Kentish Vespasian Psalter.[8] The last of these is a particularly impressive volume, written in a fine Uncial script emulating that practised in Rome and decorated with initials and display panels marking the textual divisions of the 'Three Fifties' (Psalms 1, 51 and 101) and a liturgical division of the psalms that serves to commemorate their role in the public prayer life of the church, as well as the mainstay of private devotion. Its imposing miniature depicting King David and his scribes, musicians and dancers shows the psalmist as a contemporary Anglo-Saxon ruler, playing a lyre that corresponds in its detail to one excavated in the famous early seventh-century ship burial at Sutton Hoo. The figure style is reminiscent of Italo-Byzantine forms, while the surrounding arcade is decorated with Germanic animal ornament and Celtic spiralwork and flanked by sprigs of exotic 'Byzantine blossom'. Like the decoration of the Lindisfarne Gospels it combines different cultural ingredients in a visual statement of the international contacts and heritage of the Insular church, albeit in a less intellectually and artistically synthesised and harmonised fashion than that achieved in 'Hiberno-Saxon' masterpieces such as the Book of Durrow and the Lindisfarne Gospels. It also contains the earliest examples of historiated (story-telling) initials, one of many Insular contributions to the integration of word and image. It is thought to have been made in Kent around 720–30, either at Canterbury or perhaps even by the nuns of Minster-in-Thanet, a house known from Boniface's correspondence with its abbess, Eadburh, to have been supplying the mission to the Germanic homelands with impressively penned and sumptuously gilded copies of scriptural texts at this time.[9] In England, as in Frankish centres such as Chelles, Faremoutiers-en-Brie and Corbie, women could also dedicate themselves to the production of books to fill the needs of their own and other, even episcopal, churches.[10]

7 Meehan 2007.

8 Berlin, SB Preussischer Kulturbesitz, Hamilton 553, in Alexander 1978b, no. 14; PML, M 776; BL, Cotton Vespasian A.i (see further Chapter 8 in this volume). There are also four later psalters of conservative Insular fashion from tenth- to twelfth-century Ireland and Wales: Alexander 1978b, nos. 73–5 and 78.

9 Wright 1967a; Brown 2001a.

10 Brown 2001a; McKitterick 1989c.

The earliest extant books which may have been made in England or Scotland (such as DCL A.II.10 and the Book of Durrow)[11] are strongly influenced by those used by the missions of Columba and/or Augustine and made in Ireland, Italy or Gaul. One such is the famous St Augustine Gospels, a late sixth-century Italian gospel-book which has long been thought to have perhaps accompanied Augustine and which certainly reached England during the Insular period.[12] However, differences in approach and practice between the Roman and Irish traditions, notably divergence in the dating of Easter, occasioned an important synod at Whitby in 664 at which the king of Northumbria, Oswy, ordered adherence to the ways of Rome – a significant decision to become an effective part of the European mainstream (ecclesiastically, politically and commercially). The process of reconciliation and integration of the two traditions was accomplished by figures such as St Cuthbert of Lindisfarne, Bishop Ecgbert (an Englishman who was active in Ireland and Scotland) and Abbot Adomnán of Iona. Meanwhile, a new relationship with the ecclesiastical cultures of Italy and Gaul was defined by Theodore of Tarsus, Wilfrid, Benedict Biscop and Ceolfrith. The influential churches they constructed are an eloquent testimony of the impact that the early Christian edifices of Rome made upon them. Biscop and Ceolfrith commissioned masons and glaziers from Gaul to construct their twin monasteries of Monkwearmouth and Jarrow 'Romanorum more' – constructed of stone in Roman fashion – and furnished them with images from Italy and Gaul and with one of the greatest libraries of the age, filled with books obtained on their travels.[13] Another great romanophile was Wilfrid, archbishop of York, who undertook similar building campaigns at Hexham and Ripon where, after his death in 709/10, a purple codex, probably acquired on the Continent, formed the focus of his shrine.

In 716 Ceolfrith left to retire to Rome, taking with him as a gift for the pope one of three great single-volume bibles he had caused to be made in the Wearmouth–Jarrow scriptorium. Ceolfrith died en route in Gaul but his gift, the Codex Amiatinus,[14] was taken on to Rome by his companions; his successor, Abbot Hwætberht, duly received papal acknowledgement of the communities' degree of *romanitas*.[15] Ceolfrith's dedication inscription was erased and his name replaced with that of a local saint, and it was not until the 1880s that it was recognised as the work of English rather than Italo-Byzantine scribes and artists, so 'Roman' are its Uncial lettering, diagrams, miniatures and Vulgate

11 TCD, 57. 12 CCCC, 286. See Marsden 1999 and Ganz 2002.
13 See Chapter 31 in this volume. 14 Florence, Biblioteca Medicea-Laurenziana, Amiatino 1.
15 Wood 1995 and Brown 2003b, p. 63.

text.[16] Yet this was no slavish emulation of Italian exemplars, but the complex work of a dedicated editorial team at Wearmouth-Jarrow, led by the greatest scholar of his day – Bede. In 716, as the most traditional of the Irish foundations, Columban Iona, finally acknowledged conformity to the practices of Rome, Ceolfrith's pandect served as the ambassador of the Insular world, proclaiming its Catholic orthodoxy to St Peter's heir. The Apostolic age had come to fruition. The Word had been carried to the farthest edges of the known world and the distinctive and vital contribution of those far-flung isles was reflected back to the 'Mediterranean' centre – by the medium of its books.

The historical context summarised here is a necessary backdrop to a discussion of Insular palaeography. It has often been said that the distinctive script solutions adopted in the region during this time were born in lonely isolation, the umbilical cord to the post-Roman world of Continental Europe and the eastern Mediterranean severed. Yet no other region was so truly heir to the multi-tiered script system of the Roman world, in which form, function and intent could be balanced and signalled.

The 'Roman system of scripts', developed during the first to the fourth centuries AD, comprised a hierarchy of scripts distinguished by their letter-forms and ductus: Square Capitals; Rustic Capitals; Uncials; Half-Uncials; cursive Half-Uncials, also sometimes known as 'literary cursive' or 'Quarter-Uncials'; Old Roman cursive/New Roman cursive. All of these informed the Insular system at various stages in its development. In each case it evolved its own distinctive practices, some giving rise to what are in effect new script categories. The 'Insular system of scripts' comprises: display script, which may incorporate Square Capitals, distinctive angular or lacertine forms, and Uncial elements; Uncials; Insular Half-Uncials; 'hybrid', set, cursive and current minuscules, distinguished by the degree of formality and speed of execution and resultant variations in ductus. Square Capitals, per se, are also encountered in an Insular epigraphic context, notably the dedication inscription of St Paul's Church, Jarrow. Rustic Capitals were also known, but were not really employed epigraphically, unlike the 'scriptura actuaria' of Roman epigraphy, and only seldom appear in Insular books, although they were used for titles and rubrics by the Wearmouth-Jarrow and Kentish scriptoria which favoured the use of Uncial as a high-grade text script in volumes such as the St Cuthbert Gospel,[17] the Ceolfrith Bibles,[18] and the Vespasian Psalter.[19]

16 De Rossi 1888. 17 BL, Loan 74.

18 Florence, Biblioteca Medicea-Laurenziana, Amiatino 1; BL, Add. 45025 (Middleton leaves), Add. 37777 (Greenwell leaf) and Loan 81 (Banke's leaf).

19 BL, Cotton Vespasian A.i; Wright 1967a.

The impact of literacy, of learning Latin as a foreign language, and an appreciation of the distinction between oration and silent reading seems to have inspired Insular scribes to explore means of enhancing legibility and of clarifying sense and *sententia* through devices such as the introduction of word separation, as distinct from the *scriptura continua* of Antiquity, and of a punctuation system based on *distinctiones*, in which the rising value of a pause was indicated by a rising number of points and the height of their placing in relation to the writing line. These, along with the initiation of the use of decorated letters, line-fillers and run-over symbols in order to aid the navigation and articulation of the text, were major contributions to the history of writing. [20]

This absorption in the art of writing and its adjuncts soon led Insular authors and scribes to experiment with committing texts in their own languages to writing, making Old Irish and Old English the most precocious written western vernaculars.[21] Augustine's alleged translation of the law-code of King Æthelberht of Kent only survives in a twelfth-century copy, the Codex Roffensis,[22] but Bede also refers to the English hymns composed by Cædmon of Whitby during the mid seventh century and his biographers relate that Bede was himself engaged in translating John's Gospel into English on his deathbed in 735. Topographical features are named in English in Anglo-Saxon charters and Old English names occur on funerary sculptures, such as the pillow-stones of Holy Island and Hartlepool, and in other epigraphic contexts. Longer vernacular inscriptions also occur on artistic monuments such as the whalebone Franks Casket,[23] and the Bewcastle and Ruthwell Crosses (the latter carrying verses that later came to form part of the famous poem *The Dream of the Rood*), all carved by Northumbrian sculptors and denoting English political and ecclesiastical influence, extending into British territory in southern Scotland. Written Old English introduced certain runic letters into the Roman alphabet, to denote those sounds that were alien to the Latin tongue. Inscriptions carved entirely in runes are also to be found on memorials and to indicate ownership and talismanic protection on jewellery and weaponry and were scratched through wax onto the carved bone tablets from Blythburgh, perhaps to record the names of those recalled in prayer. The earliest example of a piece of Old English prose surviving in its original manuscript context, however, is the prefatory exhortation to prayer in an early ninth-century Mercian prayerbook, the Book of Cerne,[24] probably made for Bishop Æthelwald of Lichfield (818–30), which also contains an early interlinear Old

20 Parkes 1992 and 1987. 21 Brown 2005.
22 Rochester, CL, A.35; Webster and Brown 1997, pp. 219–20; extracts in Whitelock 1979, no. 29.
23 British Museum and the Bargello, Florence. 24 CUL, Ll.1.10.

English gloss to a Latin prayer originally composed in Ireland, the Lorica of Loding or Laidcenn.[25] Glossaries, in which word lists drawn from Latin texts were glossed in English, also survive (such as the Corpus and Épinal glossaries) and were used in teaching in schools such as that founded in late seventh-century Canterbury by Archbishop Theodore of Tarsus and his North African colleague, Abbot Hadrian, where some Greek was also taught, its syllabus inspiring the poetry (some of it in English) and prose of Aldhelm.[26]

Another important aspect of writing was pragmatic literacy – charters, letters, notes and the like. The earliest dated example of English handwriting is a charter of 679 issued by King Hlothere of Kent.[27] The earliest Anglo-Saxon documents were penned not in a local variant of the New Roman cursive script bequeathed by the Roman bureaucracy to other parts of Europe (regional versions of which, such as Merovingian and Ravenna chancery scripts, at their most cursive can resemble the wanderings of a demented spider), but in clear, stately Uncials. Perceptions of the authority of writing in a biblical and liturgical context evidently exerted a powerful influence upon the rulers of nascent states wishing to identify themselves as heirs to the *dignitas* and *auctoritas* of Rome. British territories, notably Wales, of course continued to perpetuate aspects of Roman law and property tenure and carried on producing documents, such as the Llandaff charters. By the eighth century English charters were regularly written in minuscule scripts more suited for a documentary context. Often dated and localisable (with charters generally being drawn up in cathedral scriptoria on behalf of their recipients), charter hands can provide a valuable point of reference for more anonymous book hands.[28]

Insular display scripts

Display scripts are a striking feature of Insular book production. They consist of enlarged, upgraded or decorated letters, introduced by a major initial or monogram, which formally introduce a text and bridge the gap in scale from its larger opening letter to the main body of the text script. As encountered in Insular manuscripts, display scripts fully integrate the functions of script and ornament. Their elevation to a major component of book manufacture is an Insular initiative, which was to prove extremely influential in the development of the medieval book.[29]

25 Brown 1996. 26 Lapidge 1986b and 1988b.

27 BL, Cotton Augustus II.2; Webster and Backhouse 1991, no. 27; Webster and Brown 1997, pp. 221–1; Sawyer 1968, no. 8.

28 For the application of this methodology, see Brown 1986 and 1996.

29 See further Brown 2003b.

Display lettering and initials fulfil an essential function in the articulation of the text: they serve to draw the reader's attention to significant breaks, be they the openings of books, chapters, verses or liturgical lections. In Antiquity something of this role was addressed by the nature of the scroll itself, which could only contain a relatively short quantity of text, forming one section ('book' or *volumen*) of a longer work, and would be labelled with a colophon stating its content. The codex could contain a longer, continuous text incorporating several 'books' and required something more to assist the reader to navigate its texts. Thus the enlarged initial letter and the rubric entered into the design of early codices (for example, the Codex Augusteus which, unusually, employs Roman Square Capitals – *littera capitalis* – for the body of its text),[30] along with some rudimentary ornament inherited from colophon decoration, often consisting merely of stippling, *virgulae*, minimal curlicues or *hedera* (ivy leaves) in text ink or red (the use of which in such a context and in titles gave rise to the term 'rubric' from the Latin, *rubrica*). The use of colophon decoration to highlight significant elements may be seen, for example, in an early sixth-century copy of Augustine, *De Genesi ad Litteram*, where it marks the explicit.[31] In an Insular context it may be observed in the Codex Usserianus Primus, a gospel-book generally thought to have originated in Ireland during the late sixth or early seventh century.[32] Here it marks the transition from the Gospel of Luke to that of Mark, signalled by a Chi-rho and Alpha and Omega symbols contained, along with the explicit and incipit rubrics, within a box composed of colophon decoration (fol. 149v). In the Rome of Pope Gregory the Great and in Merovingian Gaul rudimentary elements of decoration including crosses, fish and birds were added to the enlarged initial.[33] The origins of this phenomenon have commonly been ascribed to scribes in Gregory's service around 600, but the practice of composing initials partly of zoomorphic forms may be seen to have had an earlier background in sixth-century Italian book production.[34] This may have been an indigenous development, or may have been indebted

30 Berlin, SB Preussischer Kulturbesitz, lat. fol. 416 and Vatican City, BAV, Vat. lat. 3256: *CLA*, I, no. 13. Roberts and Skeat 1987; Brown 1984.

31 Rome, Bibl. Nazionale Centrale Vittorio Emanuele II, Sess. 13.

32 TCD, 55; see Alexander, 1978, no. 1. For a stimulating discussion of the dating of this and other of the earliest extant Insular manuscripts, see Dumville, 1999. His arguments would tend to push the chronology of these manuscripts prior to the seventh century, but the evidence advanced in support of a fifth-century dating and a Continental origin for Usserianus Primus is extremely slight. Recognition that the historical context does not preclude the origins of the 'Insular system of scripts' stemming from the fifth century does not mean of itself that the extant manuscripts need to be strung across the intervening centuries to fill the vacuum.

33 Eg. Gregory's *Regula pastoralis*, Troyes, BM, 504. Petrucci 1971; Zimmermann 1916; Grabar and Nordenfalk 1957.

34 See *CLA*, III, no. 298; III, no. 347; IV, no. 496; XI, no. 646.

to earlier Byzantine or Ravennate elements of which evidence has not survived amongst the few extant illuminated books of the early Christian era. In early Christian Ireland this principle was also warmly embraced. Motifs from indigenous Celtic La Tène art were applied as structural components of the initial and the process of calligraphic embellishment was extended to produce continuation lettering following the initial which diminished in size down to that of the text script, a phenomenon termed 'diminuendo' which may be seen in its boldest early form in the Cathach of Columcille.[35] Whether this volume was made in the sixth or early seventh century, the practice is likely to have had an earlier background and its appearance is perhaps best seen as part of the experiments with word separation and punctuation which took place in Ireland in response to the challenges of book production, of reading patterns geared primarily towards comprehension rather than oration, and of learning Latin as a foreign language.[36] The mnemonic advantages of decoration as an aid to learning passages of text were to be acknowledged and exploited by the schoolmen of twelfth- and thirteenth-century France and they may also have occurred to the teachers of early monastic Ireland, with their ancient legacy of disciplined mnemonic oral tradition and of symbolic use of ornament.[37] The psalms, for example, would have presented a particularly appropriate vehicle for such articulation assisted by ornament. Their verse form and sequential arrangement called for extra care and clarity in layout, and certain of them warranted special note for liturgical usage, such as the 'three fifties', Psalms 1, 51 and 101, the incipits of which were singled out for particularly elaborate decoration in later Insular psalters, as on occasion were other liturgical psalms.[38] The psalms were also the lengthiest Christian text, which needed to be committed to memory by the aspiring religious. The visual layout of the words on the page and the decorated script, which marked the key divisions, may have played an essential part in such a process.

Irish manuscripts used, and in some cases penned, at Columbanus' monastery of Bobbio during the late sixth and early seventh centuries also exhibit signs of experimentation with the use of display script. The Milan Orosius opens with an enlarged ribbon-like initial, drawn in outline as a skeletal or versal form, followed by a line of smaller but similarly drawn continuation lettering, before descending into the text script for its second line.[39] Another

35 RIA, s.n. 36 Parkes 1987, pp. 15–30, and 1992.

37 Hugh of St Victor, while advocating the mnemonic uses of manuscript decoration, saw it as an elementary or 'puerile' necessity and ascribed to it an origin in the schoolrooms of Antiquity. Clanchy 1998, pp. 173–6.

38 Henry 1960; McNamara 1973; Brown 1996.

39 Milan, Biblioteca Ambrosiana, D.23. sup., fol. 2.

Bobbio book, a copy of Jerome's *Commentary on Isaiah*, uses gradation of hierarchy of script and of scale to mark its incipit, where a large initial 'N', featuring a cross-bar composed of two curvaceous fish, is followed by a slight diminuendo of the text script and is introduced by a titling rubric in enlarged Rustic Capitals followed by some colophon decoration.[40] The effect is reminiscent of the titling of antique texts and also of the epigraphic tradition. In Roman monumental inscriptions the first line or lines would often be carved in a larger scale than succeeding ones, and on more portable items, such as the early Christian ampullae from Palestine, differing scales of inscriptions featured in the decorative scheme. In late antique books and painted inscriptions, such as those used as advertisements on the walls of Pompeii, hierarchies of scale of lettering and of grades of script articulate the openings of texts.

A distinctive feature of the Insular system is the ability to match form to function within a hierarchical approach to script.[41] At the summit of the Insular hierarchy in its developed form during the late seventh to ninth centuries was display lettering. This might take the form of the high-grade Square and Rustic Capitals of Antiquity, used for rubrics or as the basis of ornamental display capitals, or to isolate sections of text (such as the prefatory matter penned in Rustic Capitals that precedes the body of the Vespasian Psalter).[42] The Uncial, Half-Uncial and minuscule scripts used to write Insular books might also be elevated to display status by virtuosity of penmanship or the inclusion of additional calligraphic details to highlight passages of text, such as the display or capitular Uncial used for the *capitulae* of the Codex Amiatinus, the display Half-Uncial used in the prefatory matter of the Book of Kells or the flamboyantly calligraphic cursive minuscule with which Ferdomnach, one of the scribes responsible for the Book of Armagh, opened his major sections of text.[43]

The illuminated incipit page reached its zenith in the great Insular gospelbooks, wherein it formed an essential part of the programme of decoration.[44] Why should major initials and display lettering here have transcended their usual function to assume the role of works of art in their own right? The key lies in the nature of the text and its use. The promulgation of the gospels, the most sacred of the texts of Christianity, is the core function of the church and was of paramount importance in the evangelising climate of the early Middle

40 Milan, Biblioteca Ambrosiana, S.45. sup., p. 2.

41 Brown 1990; Brown 1982, I, pp. 101–19; see also Dumville 1999, for a distinctive and consciously contentious overview.

42 *CLA*, II, no. 193; Alexander 1978, no. 29; Wright 1967a.

43 Florence, Biblioteca Medicea-Laurenziana, Amiatino 1; TCD, 58; TCD, 52.

44 For an overview, see Alexander 1978b, Nordenfalk 1977, Henry 1965 and Henderson 1987.

Ages. Boniface's correspondence with Abbess Eadburh of Minster-in-Thanet during the 730s, in which he asks her to send him a copy of the Epistles of St Peter written in gold to impress the natives, indicates that the visual power of the written word, the visible manifestation of the Christian faith, was still fully appreciated and if the expense of penning volumes in chyrsography was seldom undertaken in Insular scriptoria, decorated initials and incipit pages served similarly to enhance the visual impact of the written word.[45] It is likely earlier to have made a similar impression upon the newly converted of the Celtic peoples and upon the Anglo-Saxons. Both Celtic and Anglo-Saxon societies possessed sophisticated pre-literate cultures, and their proto-writing systems (ogham and runes) suggest that they were already susceptible to the potency and potential of writing. They were also used to signalling status and power through visible ornament, notably metalwork, and to embedding symbolism, much of it religious, therein. What could be more natural then, than to apply such a repertoire of decoration to the new medium of the book and to place it at the service of the Word of God. Whatever the intermediate stages of experimentation – obscured in part by the fragmentary nature of the early evidence – it had become the practice by the late seventh century to adorn the opening of each of the gospels with a decorative suite consisting of depictions of the evangelists, as portraits and/or in symbolic guise, perhaps accompanied by carpet pages, and of decorated incipits composed of initials and display script. Nowhere is the programme more harmoniously sustained than in the Lindisfarne Gospels.[46] Here the incipits of each gospel, along with the 'Chi-rho' introducing the Nativity at Matthew 1.18, are introduced by decorated initials or monograms which occupy about a quarter of the page and are followed by four to six lines of ornate display capitals contained within ruled horizontal lines and decorated bands in diminishing scale. The rectilinear nature of the *mise en page* and the overall effect is further enhanced by the script being contained within partial bar borders which extend around the sides of the page which are not already occupied by the initial, and serve, with it, to frame the composition completely. The intricate ornament – combining Celtic La Tène motifs and Germanic or late antique interlace, key and step patterns and zoomorphic elements, along with the bold display capitals with their coloured infills and stippled grounds – produces a strikingly opulent effect which links the incipit pages as seamless artistic diptychs with the facing cross-carpet pages. These openings thereby assume an iconic status, and I have

45 Whitelock 1979, no. 172.
46 BL, Cotton Nero D.iv; Alexander 1978, no. 9; Kendrick *et al.* 1956–60; Brown 2003b.

suggested elsewhere that, along with the preceding evangelist miniatures, they form a sequential meditation upon the nature of Christ, as variously conveyed by each of the gospels and the symbolic portrayal of their authors which serve to express the different character of each gospel and its encapsulation of the complementary aspects of Christ's divinity and incarnation.[47] Thus the sacred nature of the gospel text is celebrated artistically and elevated in status to an object of contemplation in its own right. It is the Word made word, as much an image of the Godhead as are the accompanying cross-carpet pages and the symbolic evangelist images, or as would be a figural image of the Crucifixion or Christ in Majesty. While other monotheistic societies grappled with the implications of the anti-idolatrous third commandment (contributing to the rise of iconoclasm in Byzantium and to the similar response of sacred calligraphy in Islam), the church of the West took its cue from Gregory the Great's dictum that in images the illiterate read. Image and text thus complemented and mutually validated one another, and nowhere is this symbiosis more effectively achieved than in the display openings of the Insular gospel-books. The process of integration is carried one stage further in the Insular invention of the historiated initial, in which a letter contains an image germane to the text, the earliest extant examples of which occur in the Vespasian Psalter, a Kentish product of the 720s–730s.[48] Here the surviving historiated initials introduce Psalms 26 and 52 with images of David and Jonathan, and David as a shepherd respectively. This is part of an eightfold liturgical division of the psalter, emphasised by panels of display script.[49] Another early historiated initial depicting Pope Gregory opens Book II in the St Petersburg copy of Bede's *Historia ecclesiastica* made at Wearmouth-Jarrow in the mid eighth century.[50]

That the roots of the contained display panels encountered both in gospel-books of the Irish–Northumbrian (or 'Hiberno-Saxon') tradition and in the more overtly romanising works of Kent and of Wearmouth-Jarrow are to be found within epigraphic tradition is illustrated in the Trier Gospels, an Echternach product of the second quarter of the eighth century, where the archangels Michael and Gabriel, depicted in a manner reminiscent of classical winged victories, hold a plaque set upon a column.[51] The plaque is inscribed

47 See Brown 1996, pp. 88–9, 103–15 and Brown 2003b.

48 See n. 14, above. NB the two initials depicting a man spearing a beast in Cambrai, BM, 470, which Lowe dates to the first half of the eighth century and ascribes to an Anglo-Saxon centre on the Continent; see *CLA*, VI, no. 740.

49 Psalms 26, 38, 52, 68, 80, 97, 109 and 118, plus the anomalous Psalm 17 which is also marked here and in the Salaberga Psalter.

50 St Petersburg, Public Library, Q.v.I.18; Alexander 1978b, no. 19; Wright 1967a, p. 91; Pächt 1962, p. 55; Dumville 2007.

51 Trier, Domschatz 61, fol. 10r; Netzer 1994a.

with the incipit rubric of the Gospel of St Matthew, arranged in ruled bands like an antique monumental inscription or diploma. Such a classicising rectilinear panelled approach to display lettering is most clearly reflected in eighth-century manuscripts of the Southumbrian 'Tiberius' group, notably the Vespasian Psalter, the Stockholm Codex Aureus, the Blickling Psalter and the Codex Bigotianus.[52] Here Square Capitals and some Uncial letter-forms, either gilded or in colours, are often set against rigid panels with geometric parti-coloured grounds reminiscent of the *opus sectile* and coloured wall plaster of the late antique world, or of coloured window glass. Some physical remains of this sort have been excavated, for example at Jarrow, the scriptorium of which employed a similar approach to its display script, as can be seen in the St Petersburg Bede.[53]

The exuberantly decorated incipit pages of the Lindisfarne Gospels (see Plates 4.1 and 4.2) combine this romanising approach to panels featuring display capitals with a more calligraphic approach to letter-forms and overall design. Another relevant aspect is the display captioning of the evangelist portraits, the angular capitals and syllabic layout of which are reminiscent – as are the figural forms – of the frescoes and icons of Rome and Byzantium. The influence of more overtly romanising scriptoria such as Wearmouth-Jarrow is probably an element here, but the exuberant ornamental openings are very different from the restrained classicism of any of the books thought to have been penned at Biscop's twin foundations, even those possible products which are not so overtly romanising.[54] Lindisfarne's display capitals are drawn versal or skeletal forms. They adopt either a fluid, calligraphic form with zoomorphic, and in one case (fol. 211) anthropomorphic, terminals and interlaced or other metalwork-like infills, or are drawn as angular black capitals. These have been said to incorporate runic forms. This is not strictly speaking the case – genuine runic letters are rare in Insular display script[55] – but what the manuscript capitals do absorb is the pronounced angularity of their forms, clearly seen in the treatment of letters such as 'S', 'O' and 'M'. There is an Insular tradition of mixing Roman capitals and runic letter-forms in epigraphic inscriptions, seen, for example, on the name-stones from Lindisfarne and Hartlepool and on the Ruthwell and Bewcastle Crosses and the Franks Casket, where the scripts are

52 BL, Cotton Vespasian A.i; Stockholm, KB, A.135; PML, M 776; Paris, BnF, lat. 281 and 298.

53 For the use of similar gilded capitals, in a more restrained context, at Wearmouth-Jarrow, see the gospel-book fragments of similar date to the Ceolfrith Bibles, now in Utrecht, UB, 32. For the Jarrow excavations, see Webster and Backhouse, 1991, no. 105 and Cramp, 1969, 1975, 1990 and 2005.

54 E.g. the Durham Cassiodorus (DCL, B.II.30) and DCL, A.II.16: see Brown 2003a.

55 Actual runic letter-forms do feature in the display script of the Lichfield Gospels, Lichfield CL, 1.

used in parallel.[56] The Osgyth Stone from Lindisfarne exhibits a similar angularity in its treatment of its Roman lettering, placed beneath the angular runes, as that seen in the display script of the Lindisfarne Gospels, and so does that on the coffin of St Cuthbert. Page has pointed to an interest, especially manifest at Lindisfarne, in the use of runes as a secondary 'learned' or 'esoteric' script and states that their use there confirms 'the general impression that the coffin runes are learned letters, deriving perhaps from manuscript sources'.[57] Such an approach is consistent with the visual reference to runic script style in the Lindisfarne Gospels display capitals. Greek characters also make an appearance in the display capital repertoire of the Lindisfarne Gospels, and in two subsequent eighth-century gospel-books, the Cambridge–London Gospels and the Royal 1 B.vii Gospels.[58] In the latter the designer has outwitted himself, replacing the Greek 'rho' in 'Christi' on f. 15v with a 'pi', thereby making a nonsense of his display panel.[59] Given the prominent nature of display lettering it is salutary to note how often mistakes seem to have been made: 'In principio eret [sic] verbum', proclaims the Cambridge–London Gospels, while in the Cutbercht Gospels several lines of text have been omitted.[60]

The type of display capitals contained within decorated rectilinear frames, seen in the Lindisfarne Gospels, proved influential in subsequent Insular gospel-book production, appearing in the Lichfield, St Petersburg, Hereford, Rawlinson, St Gallen, Rushworth, St Gatien and McDurnan Gospels, the Book of Kells, the Garland of Howth and the Book of Deer.[61] Its use also extended to other texts, such as the Cologne *Collectio canonum*, the Stowe Missal and some later Irish psalters.[62]

Yet there is another form of display lettering which enjoyed popularity throughout the history of Insular book production. This consists of an initial or monogram followed by a few lines of calligraphic display lettering, or even by angular display capitals of the Lindisfarne Gospels type, unframed and occupying only part of the page. Such treatment serves to illustrate how the calligraphic diminuendo lettering of the Cathach of Columcille evolved into the monumental display openings of the great Insular gospel-books. An early

56 Page 1995, pp. 315–25. 57 Page 1995, pp. 316–17, 321.

58 CCCC, 197B+BL, Cotton Otho C.v and BL, Royal 1. B.vii. See Brown 2003a.

59 See Webster and Brown, 1997, pp. 245–6. On the knowledge of Greek in Anglo-Saxon England, see Berschin 1980, Bodden 1988 and Lapidge 1988b.

60 CCCC, 197B, fol. 2; Vienna, ÖNB Cod. 1224, fol. 22.

61 Lichfield CL, 1; St Petersburg Russian National Library, F.v.I.8; Hereford CL, P.I.2; Bodl., Rawlinson G.167; St Gallen, SB, 51; Bodl., Auct. D.2.19; TCD, 58; TCD, 56; BnF, n.a.l. 1587; Lambeth Palace, 1370; CUL, Ii.6.32.

62 Cologne, DB, 213; RIA, D.II.3; TCD, 50; BL, Cotton Vitellius F.xi; Cambridge, St John's College, C.9.

stage in the process may be observed in Durham A.II.10, where Mark's Gospel opens with a large 'INI' monogram with stylised zoomorphic terminals to its cross-stroke, followed by a line of calligraphically drawn ribbon lettering which exhibits diminuendo. In the Book of Durrow and the Echternach Gospels the initials expand to occupy a quarter to a third of the page and become more elaborate in their decoration.[63] They are followed by three to six lines of display lettering in a mixture of calligraphic forms, emulating in drawn form the fluidity of the pen, along with the more static angular display capitals. Red colophon decoration is also used to emphasise the ground against which the lettering is placed and in Durrow this assumes a stippled form, giving the impression of formal bands. This heightens the rectilinearity and formality, which is further enhanced in the Durham Gospels by its large angular black display capitals.[64] In the Lindisfarne Gospels these trends are refined and systematised. The stippled red grounds incorporate complex interlace and zoomorphic forms, even more reminiscent of the use of the stippling technique of Insular metalwork,[65] or the romanising geometric bands already mentioned in the context of Kentish and Wearmouth-Jarrow production.[66] Thus a technique that may have owed its manuscript origins to the importation of colophon decoration into late antique books seems to have received a new impetus and interpretation under the stimulus of an indigenous form of decoration in another medium.[67]

It is tempting to view the developments in display layout as indicative of a progressive evolution with implications for relative chronology. Indeed, the growth in scale of the areas occupied by display lettering has been used traditionally to bolster the idea of a sequential development, which places the Book of Durrow early in the 'Hiberno-Saxon' group, in the seventh century. This may be the case, but it cannot be argued just from the display context, for the march towards full-page framed incipits was not an inevitable one. Smaller-scale initials with unframed continuation lettering continue to be encountered throughout the eighth century in works such as the Augsburg (Maihingen), Trier, Gotha and Cutbercht Gospels.[68] It should be noted, however, that these examples were all produced under Insular influence on the Continent, where it is likely that features introduced in the late seventh and

63 TCD, 57; BnF, lat. 9389. 64 DCL, A.II.17; Verey 1980.

65 E.g. the background to the inscriptions on the Ardagh Chalice and on the bowls from the St Ninian's Isle treasure.

66 For these and other relevant metalwork analogies, see Ryan 1983, and Youngs 1989.

67 See Brown 1984.

68 Augsburg, UB, Cod. I.2.4°.2; Trier, Domshatz, 61; Gotha, Forschungsbibliothek, Cod. Memb. I.18; Vienna, ÖNB, 1224.

early eighth century through works such as the Echternach Gospels continued to be utilised. Generally, however, such features are perhaps still likely to indicate a comparatively early stage (and often date) within the development of Insular book production.

Insular and Continental influences came together and fused within certain European scriptoria and this has a further bearing upon a discussion of one more major category of display scripts, namely the intertwined lettering linked by biting beast heads and interspersed with other zoomorphic motifs which is characteristic of the Southumbrian 'Tiberius' group of manuscripts of the eighth and first half of the ninth century. Merovingian initials are characterised by their incorporation of bird and fish elements and, as already mentioned, there was a sixth-century Italian tradition for such. Its use was embraced in centres with early Insular connections, notably Luxeuil and subsequently Corbie, Laon and various German scriptoria.[69] Their most evolved forms, however, do not occur until the second half of the eighth century, culminating in the multi-coloured outline capitals interspersed with animals and droleries as line-fillers and abbreviation strokes seen in the Gelasian Sacramentary, the Sacramentary of Gellone and a copy of Augustine, *Quaestiones in Heptateuchum*.[70] Such whimsical motifs make an earlier appearance around 730 in the Kentish Vespasian Psalter. It may be that this was a southern English development, in keeping with the rise of the independent 'Anglian' beast motifs popular in Mercian art, as opposed to the interlaced zoomorphic forms favoured in the Hiberno-Saxon tradition, coupled with some influence from the use of animal figures in Merovingian and Lombardic illumination. The mid-eighth-century Stuttgart Psalter, probably made at Echternach, exhibits a synthesis of Merovingian and Insular components of book production.[71] Its initials feature the characteristic Continental birds and fish, while its panelled bands of display script incorporate zoomorphic heads, foliate extensions and nascent intertwined letters and monograms.[72] Later in the century the Cutbercht Gospels develops the blend further. The introduction of beast heads as linking terminals to letters may once again have been an Insular invention introduced to the Continent, for it occurs in display lettering in the Lindisfarne Gospels.

69 E.g. *CLA*, IV, no. 497; V, no. 692; VI, no. 765; VI, no. 766; VII, no. 852, VII, no. 949; VIII, no. 1208; X, no. 1518; XI, no. 1616; XI, no. 1627

70 Vatican City, BAV, Reg. lat. 316; Paris, BnF, lat. 12048 and lat. 12168. For colour reproductions of relevant folios from the Gelasian Sacramentary and the Sacramentary of Gellone, see Versone 1967, pp. 148 and 187.

71 Stuttgart, Württembergische LB, Cod. Bibl. 2°.12.

72 Webster and Backhouse, 1991, no. 128; Netzer 1995.

The divide between the 'Hiberno-Saxon' approaches to display script and those of their Continental counterparts is effectively bridged by the Barberini Gospels, in its exuberant use of a style of display script associated with the Southumbrian 'Tiberius group'.[73] Here the independent bird, beast, fish and anthropomorphic motifs which are interspersed in the bar panels of the Vespasian and Blickling Psalters are absorbed into lacertine display lettering set upon banded grounds following enlarged initials and monograms which, like their Hiberno-Saxon counterparts, grow to occupy half or more of the page. The gilding of the Kentish works gives way to a prominent use of purple as a panel ground, similarly redolent of imperial, Mediterranean connotations. Barberini has been variously claimed as a Southumbrian, Northumbrian and Continental product, with York sometimes being favoured as an appropriate compromise location, precisely because it merges so many varied political and cultural influences, but its stylistic analogies with sculpture and metalwork, its merging of diverse palaeographical influences and the identity of the 'Wigbald' mentioned in its colophon, who may be the member of the community of the important Mercian royal foundation of Medeshamstede (Peterborough) mentioned in charters of around 800, point to early ninth-century Peterborough as its probable place of origin.[74] Its use of display scripts is certainly closely related to that of the early Tiberius group manuscripts and seems fundamentally to have influenced that of the group's later members. Prominent amongst these is the Tiberius Bede, from which the group takes its name.[75] Here the independent beast motifs seen earlier in the group appear within the initials, but the rectilinear bar panels sprout foliate or zoomorphic motifs at their corners and are filled with the sinuous lacertine display lettering, linked by biting beast heads, seen in Barberini. Such features may also be observed in another, Mercian, member of the group, the Book of Cerne which dates to the third or fourth decades of the ninth century.[76] The lacertine zoomorphic display panels of the Tiberius group are also paralleled in the Book of Kells, where they merge seamlessly with a baroque, flamboyant interpretation of the Hiberno-Saxon

73 Vatican City, BAV, Barb. lat. 570; Webster and Backhouse, 1991, no. 160; Brown 2001b; Brown 2007a.

74 For this possible identification see Brown 2007a.

75 BL, Cotton Tiberius C.ii; Webster and Backhouse 1991, no. 170; M. P. Brown 1996, pp. 169–78, where it is discussed as a probable Canterbury product from the second quarter of the ninth century.

76 CUL, Ll.1.10; Webster and Backhouse 1991, no. 165; Brown 1996. This volume also employs angular red display capitals, reminiscent of those found in the evangelist miniatures of the Lindisfarne Gospels, to provide inscriptions as part of its own complex evangelist images. Like those in Lindisfarne, the Cerne evangelist inscriptions are redolent of the fresco and icon design of the Mediterranean world.

display opening.[77] Another important aspect of Kells here is its extension of the practice of employing display script to highlight an increasing number of text breaks, grading them by virtue of the scale of the decorative display. The Lindisfarne Gospels had also used something of a display hierarchy, the incipits of its prefaces being less elaborate than the actual gospel incipits. This practice is extended in Kells to a greater range of passages, which have been identified as liturgical lection incipits, some of which attract a full-page decorative treatment.[78] Here display scripts play a crucial role in the articulation of the text, recollecting the liturgical use of the gospel-book within a public context. In Kells the use of ornament as an essential component of both private *ruminatio* and impressive display to a wider community can be seen in its fully developed form.

One further Insular manuscript remains to be discussed: the latest member of the Tiberius group, the Royal Bible, a Canterbury book written around 820–40, the same period as the Book of Cerne.[79] In the single remaining gospel incipit page the characteristic Tiberius group bar panels with lacertine script and accompanying major initial introduce the Gospel of St Luke, but are executed in silver and gold upon a purple ground and set beneath an arcade. Other surviving purple pages carry monumental inscriptions contained within carefully ruled lines. These are in alternate lines of silver and gold and recall the epigraphic inscriptions of Antiquity. Such gilded capitals on purple grounds, with their Early Christian allusions, had a tradition of use in Anglo-Saxon England.[80] They occur in the Stockholm Codex Aureus and may have been used in lost works, such as the purple codex commissioned for Ripon by Bishop Wilfrid in the late seventh century.[81] Nevertheless, their use in the Royal Bible is likely to have been directly influenced, as are other aspects of the book, by works made in Charlemagne's Court School.[82]

Insular display script, which had pioneered its own distinctive approach of integrated script and ornament in response to an early Christian, Mediterranean impetus, has here assumed the confidence and experience to achieve in its

77 Kells also features the zoomorphic line-fillers and abbreviation symbols encountered in the late eighth- to early ninth-century members of the southern English Tiberius group. Unless it is to be seen as an isolated earlier manifestation of such features, it would seem logical to view Kells as a product of similar date. See Brown 1994a, pp. 333–43; also Henry 1974 and Fox 1990.

78 See Farr 1997. For the textual basis, see McGurk, 1961. On the use of decoration as textual articulation, see also Brown 1996, pp. 68–128. See also O' Carragain 1994, pp. 398–436.

79 BL, Royal 1 E.vi; Webster and Backhouse 1991, no. 171; Brown 1996; Budny 1985.

80 For their use in Early Christian manuscripts see, e.g., the Codex Palatinus, *CLA*, IV, no. 437, and the Codex Brixianus, *CLA*, III, no. 281.

81 Eddius Stephanus, *Life of Wilfrid*: Farmer 1983, pp. 105–84; Whitelock 1979, no. 154.

82 E.g. the Harley Golden Gospels (BL, Harley 2788) and the Lorsch Gospels (Bucharest, National Library, Filliale Biblioteca Batthyáneum Alba Iulia, R.II.1 + BAV, Pal. Lat. 50.

final stages a harmonious synthesis of visual references to Antiquity and the evolved Insular decorative, calligraphic form. Insular book production did not end with a whimper, in chronic decline – it went out with a bang.

Insular Uncial scripts

The term Uncial is ascribed, probably apocryphally, to St Jerome who, in his preface to the Book of Job, is said to have criticised its ostentatious character and use in expensive purple and golden tomes where its luxuriant rotundity gave the impression of being an improbable 'inch high' (Latin *uncia*, inch).[83] The letters to which he refers could equally as well be capitals, as in the Codex Augusteus, but certainly the earliest major codices containing the sacred texts of the newly sanctioned Christian religion, the fourth-century Codex Sinaiticus and the fifth-century Codex Alexandrinus, are penned in stately Greek Uncials.[84]

The rounded forms of Uncial, so suited to the movement of the reed pen, evolved during the second to fourth centuries AD.[85] They were essentially a mixture of capital letter-forms and Old Roman cursive – the latter often representing a rapider version of the former, written with fewer strokes and thereby assuming 'abbreviated' characters, to the extent of becoming independent forms. A successive fusion of Uncials and New Roman cursive would similarly give rise to fully developed half-Uncial as a more economical solution to the need for a legible, prestigious book script. Literary cursive,[86] the hand of the educated person of late Antiquity, often used for notes and semi-formal purposes, also served to influence these developments and was, according to Julian Brown, the point of reference for the earliest Insular scripts.[87] At the highest levels of production, Uncial competed for favour in the eyes of late antique bibliophiles and publishers with Rustic Capitals and, to a lesser extent, their Square Capital counterparts.[88] These resource-consuming parents of the Roman

83 *PL*, XXVIII 1142A: 'Habeant qui volunt veteres libros, vel in membranis purpureis auro argentoque descriptos, vel uncialibus, ut vulgo aiunt, litteris, onera magis exarata, quam codices, dummodo mihi meisque permittant pauperes habere schedulas, et non tam pulchros codices, quam emendatos.'

84 BL, Add. 43725 and Royal 1 D.v–viii. For early Greek Uncial, see Thompson 1912, pp. 119–217, and pp. 284–97 on Latin Uncial; see also Bischoff 1990, pp. 66–71.

85 Brown 1999, pp. 14–31, esp. pp. 24–5; Brown and Lovett 1999, pp. 39–50.

86 This was wryly termed 'Quarter-Uncial' by E. A. Lowe (1972, I, p. 152, referring to Traube), and still sometimes referred to as such, although 'cursive Half-Uncial' is generally the preferred term.

87 Brown, 1990, pp.14–35, esp. pp. 28–9. Brown 1982 and 1984.

88 As seen in the Virgilius Vaticanus, Virgilius Romanus and Codex Augusteus. For Square and Rustic Capitals, see Brown 1990, pp. 16–19; Brown and Lovett 1999, pp. 21–38; Thompson 1912, pp. 272–84; Bischoff 1990, pp. 55–60.

system of scripts would, like Uncial, survive Antiquity to enjoy a life embedded in display scripts, as initials and in titles and rubrics, but unlike Uncial they would seldom be used for complete texts, save in remarkable feats of emulation of the world of late Antiquity, notably the Utrecht Psalter, that influential Carolingian essay in *romanitas* produced at Hautvillers in the 820s–30s.[89]

It is to the bishops and clerics who inherited the mantle of the Roman bureaucracy, its secretaries and its professional publishers, that we owe the survival of Uncial. The administrative hand of the late Roman Empire, New Roman cursive, would continue to inspire the chanceries of Byzantium, including its western bridgehead, Ravenna, and of the Merovingians to ever greater heights of illegibility, but it was not deemed a suitable vehicle for the transmission of sacred texts. These were generally inscribed in Uncials which increasingly exhibited local variants in details of letter-forms, such as the Merovingian hooked t. Lowe tentatively arranged specimens of Uncial into Frankish, Spanish, African, Byzantine and Italian groups, with some local subdivisions, dating from the Roman and post-Roman periods.[90] The most important and influential patron of Latin Uncials was, of course, Pope Gregory the Great. Around 600 Gregory's Rome was serving as a publishing house for the works of scripture and of patristic commentary, including works by Gregory himself, which were to equip the rapidly expanding church of the West. Such essential tools were designed to impress, especially in a missionary context, and the stately Uncials were the favoured medium.[91] Letters marking the major textual openings were adorned tentatively with Christian symbols such as the cross and the fish. Palaeographers have remarked upon the absence of Uncial script from Irish book production, signalling, obliquely or otherwise, an Irish resistance to Roman influence.[92] This is perhaps to overstress the case, for although this script is not employed in a consistent fashion, Uncial letter-forms do occur sporadically in early Irish manuscripts (the Cathach, for example), and they occasionally occur in Ireland in an epigraphic context, as do other symptoms of Roman influence. However, it does appear to be the case that Irish scribes did not emulate Roman book production as did, on occasion, their Anglo-Saxon neighbours.

It is to those centres consciously committed to cultural *romanitas* that one must look for the most sustained Insular use of Uncial script: the romanophile

89 Utrecht, UB 32; see van der Horst *et al.* 1996.

90 The fundamental discussion of English Uncial, with an invaluable collection of plates, is Lowe 1960. See also Gameson 2001–2.

91 For a discussion of Uncial in the Rome of Gregory the Great, see Petrucci 1971.

92 Lowe 1960, p. 6.

Benedict Biscop's twin foundations of Monkwearmouth and Jarrow, and St Augustine's base at Canterbury. The incredibly numerous leaves (in excess of 3,000) which would have constituted the three pandects commissioned by Abbot Ceolfrith from the Wearmouth-Jarrow scriptoria, prior to his departure for Rome in 716, carry imposing twin columns of formal Uncial script, with decoration limited to the occasional enlarged initial letter or modest ivy-leaf (*hedera*) ornament to mark the end of a major text.[93] Such a restrained *mise en page* is worthy of the Codex Alexandrinus and is truly in keeping with the spirit of late antique book production. The same may be said of the illusionistic, painterly form of the extant miniatures. Notwithstanding tell-tale signs of Insular production, the methods adopted were the best emulations of Mediterranean practice available to the Insular world and were in keeping with Amiatinus' text, which is the earliest, best-surviving witness of the Vulgate.[94] The gift of the pandect occasioned a thankyou letter to Ceolfrith's successor, Hwætberht, in which Monkwearmouth and Jarrow (in the person of Ceolfrith) were praised for their outward and visible signs of an internal, spiritual *romanitas* and were effectively welcomed into the *comitatus* of St Peter, with all the cultural and political benefits which that entailed.[95]

The Ceolfrith Bibles are written in a flat pen Uncial – that is to say, with the nib trimmed and held in such a way that it is parallel to the writing line, with a 0° angle.[96] Writing with a flat pen requires a great deal of pen manipulation and is very time-consuming. It is, therefore, an expensive commodity in terms of human and physical resources. The breadth of characters and the attention to details such as head-strokes and serifs likewise contribute to this. Merovingian examples of Uncial generally adopt a rather fluid approach to ductus, with irregularities in the height of letters and a curvature to many strokes, notably to descenders and to the head of 't'.[97]

93 The surviving representatives of Ceolfrith's bibles are: the volume he took with him on his journey to Rome, the Codex Amiatinus (Florence, Biblioteca Medicea-Laurenziana, Amiatino 1); and fragments of one of the other two volumes (one each for Monkwearmouth and Jarrow), which may have been obtained by King Offa and presented to Worcester, leaves of which (used as binders' waste) are now BL, Add. 37777, 45025 and Loan 81; see Alexander 1978b, no. 7 and Webster and Backhouse 1991, nos. 87–8; for a discussion and bibliography of the process of demonstrating that Amiatinus was an Anglo-Saxon work, see Lowe 1960, pp. 8–13.

94 There is some debate as to whether the text of Amiatinus essentially represents the emended 'authorised version', as edited by Cassiodorus in the Novem Codices, or a Northumbrian edition which utilised the Old Roman version of Cassiodorus' Codex Grandior along with other texts such as the *Novem codices* and a Neapolitan gospel-book to distil a 'Vulgate' text. For a review of the arguments, see Marsden, 1995a and 1995b; for a useful summary of the conventional view, see van der Horst *et al.* 1996, pp. 30–2.

95 Marsden 1995b and Wood 1995, esp. p. 18. For the passages referring to Amiatinus having reached Pope Gregory II and his letter to Hwætberht, see *Vita Ceolfridi*, chs. 37–9: Plummer 1896; trans. Whitelock 1979, pp. 769–70.

96 Brown and Lovett 1999, pp. 41–4.

97 Brown 1990, pp. 38–9.

An English example of the use of this distinctive feature is to be found as an Uncial intrusion into the half-Uncial script of the Barberini Gospels.[98] Its Scribe A consistently uses hooked Uncial 'T' and employs a full Uncial for the titles to the opening Canon Table (fol. 1r) and upgrades his script completely to Uncial for three lines at the end of fol. 111v. His influence, or that of a shared training, can be detected in the hand of the principal scribe and scriptorium master, Scribe C.[99] Ceolfrith's scribes, however, were at pains to preserve a strict regularity of height, verticality and either flat headline serifs or concave wedges (to the heads of S, T and E, for example).[100] Thus, while the Merovingian 't' already resembles the lower-case, minuscule letter-form, those in the Ceolfrith Bibles remain closer to their Square Capital progenitors. These features, along with the elegant layout, *per cola et commata*, are highly reminiscent of Italian Uncial volumes of the sixth century. One of the immediate exemplars is likely to have been a bible (either the lost 'Codex Grandior', the *Novem codices* or perhaps both) from Cassiodorus' monastery of the Vivarium, as indicated in the famous miniature in the Codex Amiatinus of Ezra the Scribe, who is seated before an *armarium* containing the *Novem codices*, Cassiodorus' nine-volume edition of the Bible.[101] Another of Amiatinus' models may have been a Neapolitan gospel-book, a Wearmouth-Jarrow copy of which probably served as the textual exemplar for the Lindisfarne Gospels.[102] The faithful, accurate copying of books was, of course, one of the tenets expounded in Cassiodorus' educational programme, as outlined in his *Institutiones*, composed around 562.[103] The remnants of Cassiodorus' library are now thought to have found their way to Rome, and it may be thence that such a bible and gospel-book were obtained by Biscop for the Wearmouth-Jarrow libraries.[104] The world which such exemplars embodied must have seemed tantalisingly close to the monks who studied them – the sort of proximity that we might feel to

98 Vatican City, BAV, Barb. Lat. 570; Brown 2007a.

99 Scribe C may be the Wigbald for whom prayers are beseeched in the colophon. He occasionally intrudes the hooked 'T' into his script. This distinctive letter-form, which is usually found in Meroviangian Uncial, is also encountered in the display script of BL, Royal 1 B.vii. Frankish participation in the evangelisation of eastern England and/or the availability of Merovingian exemplars may have exerted an influence on the Peterborough scriptorium and other centres in eastern England.

100 Brown and Lovett, 1999, p. 41.

101 Fol. v; Henderson 1993; for an overview of the iconographical issues, along with a distinctive view of the relationship to the Cassiodoran material, see Micheli 1999.

102 Another Wearmouth-Jarrow copy of this gospel-book, written in Uncial, survives as fragments now appended to the Utrecht Psalter. This arrangement is likely to have occurred during Sir Robert Cotton's ownership: see van der Horst *et al.* 1996, pp 30–2; see also Lowe 1960, plates XI–XII.

103 See Reynolds and Wilson 1968, pp. 71–2.

104 *Ibid.*, p. 72.

the England of Dickens when reading a nineteenth-century edition of his works, but with the added frisson of faith.

Some extant examples of Uncial volumes written in Italy during the sixth century are known to have been available in Northumbria: a fragment of Maccabees, and the Burchard Gospels which was restored in Uncial of Wearmouth-Jarrow type during the late seventh century.[105] Instruction by masters such as John the Archcantor, who is known to have deposited writings in the Wearmouth-Jarrow libraries, may also have played a part in the Northumbrian mastery of Uncial script. The Ceolfrith Bibles, in their careful observance of their Mediterranean sources can be said to represent a truly antiquarian evocation of sixth-century Italy on Northumbrian soil. Lowe, however, trounced once and for all the suggestion that Amiatinus was actually written by Italian scribes working in England, pointing to the distinctive nature of the Monkwearmouth-Jarrow types of Uncial and highlighting Insular features in areas such as abbreviations and orthography.[106] The Ceolfrith Bibles remain the greatest physical essay in *romanitas* to have been undertaken in early medieval England in its capacity as an heir to Rome and as a 'client', in this context, of the ultimate heir to Rome's might in the West – the earthly representative of St Peter.[107]

Another example of Wearmouth-Jarrow's Uncial books is the little Gospel of St John, found in St Cuthbert's coffin and probably used at the obsequies surrounding either his burial in 687 or the translation of his relics in 698.[108] Although it conveys an elegance and authority akin to that of the Ceolfrith Bibles, the St Cuthbert (or Stonyhurst) Gospel is a less formal affair. Written with a slanted or angled pen, it would have been easier and quicker to produce. This script is also used for the *capitula* in the Ceolfrith Bibles and has therefore been termed 'capitular Uncial'.[109] The effect is more rhythmic, with fewer serifs and more natural, angled wedges and several of the letter-forms, notably the 'e' with its closed bow and the 't' with its curved head and foot, are effectively Half-Uncials. Here something of the interaction between Uncial and Half-Uncial, as seen in the near-contemporaneous Durham and Lindisfarne Gospels from Lindisfarne (or in the case of the former, perhaps another Cuthbertine house such as Melrose), may be observed.[110] The regularity and breadth of Lindisfarne's 'reformed' or 'Phase II' Half-Uncial, along with its

105 DCL, B.IV.6, fol. 169*; Würzburg, UB M.P.Th.F.68; Lowe 1960, pp. 6–7.
106 Lowe 1960, pp. 8–15; on John the Archcantor, see Bede, *Historia abbatum*, ch. 6.
107 See Webster and Brown 1997, pp. 235 and 247.
108 BL, Loan 74; Brown 1969.
109 Lowe 1960, pp. 9–13; Brown and Lovett 1999, pp. 47–9.
110 DCL, A.II.17 and BL., Cotton Nero D.iv.

Uncial lemmata, have for some time been thought to betoken the influence of Uncial exemplars, either from Italy or via Wearmouth-Jarrow, and in the St Cuthbert Gospel we can begin to see that the route of influences was probably a two-way street.[111] Elsewhere I have discussed the pitfalls of an over-rigid scholarly perception of what constitutes house style in the scriptorium and have indicated that the production of Uncials, as seen at Wearmouth-Jarrow and at Canterbury, is one distinctive but non-exclusive strand of their scribal endeavours, and one which, when it was employed, was probably consciously intended to invoke a cultural *romanitas* as a matter of policy.[112] Thus, the scriptoria of Wearmouth and Jarrow, and those in their orbit, might use Half-Uncial and minuscule scripts for other projects, such as the publication of the works of their most famous son, Bede, and, arguably, the Durham Cassiodorus.[113]

Looking southwards to the heart of Roman influence in Britain, Augustine's Canterbury, we have as a possible model the Uncial script of the St Augustine Gospels, a sixth-century Italian volume which has often been advanced as one of the books which accompanied St Augustine in 597, or which was imported soon afterwords.[114] It was certainly being corrected by an English hand employing Uncial during the eighth century.[115] The oldest-surviving representatives of Kentish Uncial are in fact charters. This is, in itself, noteworthy. One might have expected early documentary production in England to have been influenced by that of the papal or Merovingian chanceries, but instead a high-grade book script was favoured. This probably had much to do with early perceptions of the authority of the written word in a religious context, as enshrined in formal Uncial volumes containing scriptural, patristic and liturgical texts, and probably helped to frame Anglo-Saxon approaches to writing in the pragmatic sphere and to the value of written instruments at law.[116] The earliest dated example of English handwriting occurs in one of these Uncial charters, a grant by King Hlothere of Kent to Abbot Berhtwald of Reculver of land in the Isle of Thanet, dated 679.[117] Such charters were usually commissioned by the recipient and it is likely that this document was written at Reculver which also boasts the remains

111 For a discussion of Lindisfarne Half-Uncial, see Brown in Kendrick 1956–60; Brown 1989; Dumville 1999; Brown 2003b.

112 Brown 2003a.

113 DCL, B.II.30. This manuscript has sometimes been ascribed to Wearmouth-Jarrow, but Budny has suggested that it may have originated in the same centre as BL, Royal 1 E. vi, namely St Augustine's, Canterbury, while Bailey has suggested an origin in southern Scotland; other centres such as those houses in the Vale of Pickering with associations with Wearmouth-Jarrow, however, also furnish promising soil for the cultivation of such influence. Budny 1985, pp. 773–4; Bailey 1978; Brown forthcoming.

114 CCCC, 286; Wormald 1984, pp. 13–35.

115 Lowe 1960, p. 7. plate IIa.

116 Webster and Brown 1997, pp. 211–12, 220–1; Brown 1986.

117 See n. 27, above.

of one of the masterpieces of seventh-century architecture built 'Romanorum more', as well as one of the most classicising pieces of English sculpture, the Reculver Cross. The next Uncial charter is a grant of Œthelred of Essex of 686–8, conveying lands at Dagenham to Abbess Æthelburh of Barking and presumably copied either at St Paul's, London, the seat of Bishop Eorcenwald who is thought to have drafted this grant in accordance with Italian legal formulae, or at Barking, in which case it may be in the hand of a nun.[118] The third is a charter of King Æthelbald of Mercia, dated 736 and relating to land in the Stour Valley in north Worcestershire.[119] This was probably written at Worcester. It is therefore relevant that the oldest Mediterranean Uncial manuscript known to have been circulating in England, a fifth-century copy of Jerome, *In Ecclesiasten*, was subscribed with the name of Abbess Cuthswitha of Inkberrow in the vicinity of Worcester around 700.[120] Worcester and its environs are likely to have produced manuscripts written in Uncial, and an Uncial *Rule of St Benedict* with an eleventh-century Worcester provenance is probably an example of its work during the late eighth century, along with a manuscript of *Paterius* and perhaps even the Codex Bigotianus.[121] Moreover, one of Ceolfrith's three great pandects was probably presented to Worcester by King Offa.[122]

The reign of Offa (757–96), although of great political importance, is poorly represented physically by manuscript material. Offa's role as a patron is signalled by a reference in a copy of an alleged charter of 780 to a *magnam Bibliam cum duabus armillis ex auro*, which he donated to Worcester.[123] Subsequent traditions equated this with a bible which Offa had caused to be copied from an exemplar in San Paolo fuori le Mura in Rome; however, as noted above, it has been suggested that his gift was one of the Ceolfrith Bibles.[124] The copy allegedly obtained by Offa is represented by fragments.[125] The evidence is not conclusive, but it is possible that it was obtained by Offa, presented to

118 BL, Cotton Augustus II.29; Webster and Backhouse 1991, no. 28; Sawyer 1968, no. 1171. References in later medieval booklists of St Paul's Cathedral to a psalter owned by Bishop Eorcenwald are intriguing; had it survived, it would probably have been written in Uncials in London, Essex or Kent during the late seventh century.

119 BL, Cotton Augustus II.3; Webster and Backhouse 1991, no. 152; Sawyer 1968, no. 89.

120 Würzburg, UB, M.p.th.q.2; Lowe 1960, plate, I; Sims-Williams 1990.

121 Bodl., Hatton 48; Worcester CL, Add. 4; BnF, lat. 281 and 298. Brown 1996, pp. 166–7.

122 Turner 1916b, pp. xli–xlii; Webster and Backhouse 1991, no. 87.

123 Wharton 1691, p. 470. 124 See n. 122.

125 BL, Add. 45025 (Middleton leaves), Add. 37777 (Greenwell leaf) and Loan 81 (Banke's leaf), all of which had been used as waste for bindings or estate document wrappers by the Willoughby family of Yorkshire. With the Middleton leaves were found fragments of an early eleventh-century Worcester cartulary, of unusually large format, corresponding to the measurements of the bible leaves. A passage in Hemming's Cartulary (BL, Cotton Tiberius A.xiii) records that St Wulfstan ordered copies of Worcester charters to be written into the bible in Worcester Cathedral and these leaves may all once have formed part of this tome. Turner 1916b, pp. xli–xlii; Ker 1948; Brown 2003a.

Worcester, and later interpreted as having a connection with Rome due to its romanising style. The gift of such an important Uncial manuscript to Worcester would certainly have been appropriate, given its scriptorium's interest in the production of prestigious Uncial charters and manuscripts from an early date. Worcester should therefore probably join Canterbury and/or Minster-in-Thanet and Wearmouth-Jarrow as a major Insular centre of high-class, romanising Uncial manuscript production.

The major Southumbrian place of production for Uncials was, however, Kent. The Vespasian Psalter (Plate 4.3) is commonly attributed to Canterbury *c.* 730. Even if the possibility that it might have been made at Minster-in-Thanet is allowed, its medieval provenance lies in Canterbury, which – perhaps significantly in this context – annexed Minster's property following the Viking raids.[126] It was penned in Uncials of a consummate artistry and, like that of the Ceolfrith Bibles, the script was executed with a flat pen wielded with time-consuming and disciplined detail, yet retaining a calligraphic verve.[127] A strict adherence to head and base lines is observed and serifs stress the horizontality of heads and feet. However, the concave wedges of its Northumbrian counterpart are absent and letter-forms differ, most notably the G, which at Canterbury assumes the Rustic Capital form of a spiral without a tail-stroke. This may also be observed in the highest display contexts of Northumbrian Uncial, as seen in the title piece to the Uncial gospel fragments attached to the Utrecht Psalter.[128] Such variants in a display context suggest that there was a perception of grading, suiting form to function, in the English approach to Uncial: display Uncial, text Uncial and capitular Uncial. It is interesting that the high-grade display form is the norm, however, in the Kentish text Uncial, perhaps owing something to the influence of the Rustic Capitals which were used for the prefatory matter in the Vespasian Psalter.[129] The Codex Bigotianus – perhaps from Worcester – similarly incorporates Rustic Capital prefaces, but does not borrow from its letter-forms for its Uncial text script in the way that Vespasian does.[130] Such features are, however, to be found again in what was probably the next major landmark of Kentish production during the mid eighth century – the Stockholm Codex Aureus.[131] This sumptuous

126 Wright 1967a; Webster and Backhouse 1991, no. 153.

127 Brown and Lovett 1999, pp. 42–7.

128 Lowe 1960, plates XI–XII; Van der Horst 1984, pp. 30–2. These were ascribed by Lowe to Ceolfrith's scriptoria, which is probably correct. On Canterbury manuscripts see also Gameson 1999b and 2001–2.

129 Lowe 1960, plates XXVI–XXVII; Wright 1967a.

130 Lowe 1960, plates XXX–XXXI; Webster and Backhouse 1991, no. 155.

131 Stockholm, KB, A.135: Gameson 2001–2.

gospel-book, with its purple pages adorned with Uncials in gold and silver and framed by crosses, resembles the Vespasian Psalter in many details of its script, as well as its illumination. It too is usually attributed to Canterbury but has also sometimes been ascribed to Minster-in-Thanet, which supplied Boniface with visually stunning books for his mission.[132] Works such as the Codex Aureus would certainly have fitted the bill when it came to instilling a sense of awe and wonder.

The influence of English Uncial on the Continent was signalled by Lowe,[133] as seen in the Stuttgart Psalter, an impressive work from the Echternach scriptorium of the mid eighth century which was probably reflecting Northumbrian influence in this particular script and combining it with Merovingian ornament in its zoomorphic initials.[134] Lowe and Bischoff were even of the opinion that the Carolingian revival of Uncial and Rustic was inspired, in part, by Anglo-Saxon influence.[135] In England they also enjoyed use as what Lowe termed 'islands' in a sea of Anglo-Saxon minuscules or majuscules (i.e. Half-Uncials), serving to highlight titles and rubrics in patristic writings and in the works of Bede throughout the Insular period.[136] If their life as a book-hand in England ended with the Insular period, they were to reappear – doubtless under Carolingian influence – as a display script in the later Anglo-Saxon age. There is a certain irony in the fact that Canterbury, the place that first embraced them as a book-hand, was rather slower than other centres, such as Winchester, to readopt them in this way.

Insular Half-Uncial script

The archetypal form of regular Insular Half-Uncial script, as encountered in the Lindisfarne Gospels and the Book of Kells, belongs to a type that Lowe called 'Insular majuscule', but which Julian Brown termed 'reformed Phase II Insular Half-Uncial'.[137] Brown argued that, following their conversion to Christianity from the fifth century onwards, the Irish received a script known as cursive Half-Uncial that was used for annotation by the educated reader of late Antiquity, rather than by professional scribes.[138] Working from this basis they upgraded the script to produce a Half-Uncial similar to that of the late

132 Whitelock 1979, no. 172. See also his letter to Daniel, bishop of Winchester, pleading that, as his eyesight failed, a book of the Prophets be sent to him, written clearly with 'distinct and detached letters' (*ibid.*, no. 175).

133 Lowe 1934–72.

134 Stuttgart, LB, Bibl. 2°.12: Webster and Backhouse 1991, no. 128; Netzer 1995.

135 Lowe 1960, p. 14 n. 3.

136 *Ibid.*, p. 15, plates XXXVIII–XL.

137 T. J. Brown 1982; M. P. Brown 2003b, pp. 253–71.

138 Brown 1982.

Roman script system, and downgraded it as a working minuscule for more general purposes. What are thought to be the oldest extant Irish manuscripts (such as the Cathach) employ cursive Half-Uncial, giving way to a minuscule which is written more quickly but features some higher-grade letter-forms (sometimes termed 'hybrid minuscule'). The script of the Book of Durrow is more settled and approaches what might properly be called Insular Half-Uncial, the most developed and regular form of which occurs in the Lindisfarne Gospels. Brown saw this development, or 'reform', of earlier Insular Half-Uncial as being primarly influenced by the Uncial script of Wearmouth-Jarrow and its Italian exemplars, the impact of which he detected in the hands of both the artist–scribe of the Lindisfarne Gospels and those seen in the Durham and Echternach Gospels, which were duly ascribed to one hand – the 'Durham–Echternach Calligrapher'.[139] Brown considered the latter to be an older member of the Lindisfarne scriptorium but, influenced by Bruce-Mitford's views on ornament, argued that he wrote Durham and Echternach after the Lindisfarne Gospels but in an older script style.

To my mind this is a contorted view of a more gradual, organic process. There are certainly points in the history of script when thoroughgoing reforms have been undertaken and promulgated within a short timespan, usually as part of a political and/or ecclesiastical imperative, such as the dissemination of Caroline Minuscule as part of a textual and religious programme of reform within the Carolingian Empire under Charlemagne,[140] Although during the early eighth century Wearmouth-Jarrow was apparently circulating gospel-books written in its distinctive Uncial script as a means of disseminating what it considered to be more reliable forms of Jerome's Vulgate text, this did not amount to a formal publication programme.[141] Brown's useful categorisation of the development of Insular script into two major phases can stand without the need to envision the introduction of a conceptual reform of script devised by one influential centre, be it Lindisfarne or Wearmouth-Jarrow – although the interaction of these centres and their traditions may have helped stimulate wider change.

The evolution of Insular Half-Uncial throughout the seventh century is characterised by a progressive introduction of greater consistency and regularity, traceable throughout the pages of the Cathach, DCL, A.II.10, the Book of Durrow, and the Durham and Echternach Gospels. If any doubt be raised that an already well-developed Half-Uncial script was practised in a Columban

139 Kendrick *et al.* 1956–60; Verey 1980.
140 See, e.g., Ganz 1990; McKitterick 1989b.
141 Brown 2003b, pp. 253–71; Meyvaert 2005, appendix.

milieu, consideration should be given to the 'in nomine' inscription with its rounded Half-Uncial characters carved on a pebble (for votive purposes, or perhaps as a trial-piece) and excavated at the royal Dalriadan fort of Dunadd in Argyllshire, the regal power-base for the Columban mission.[142]

For Julian Brown, Phase II of this development was signalled by the adoption in the Durham and Lindisfarne Gospels of a version of the script that exhibited the normalising influence and stately rounded aspect of Italian Uncial of the style practised in Rome. He observed the influence of this 'reformed' script in the hands of later volumes such as the Lichfield Gospels and the Book of Kells, which he was inclined to date early in order to bring them closer to the 'absolute' finishing date of 698 for Lindisfarne's production. Similarly, he outlined the corresponding development of minuscule scripts, in their 'current', 'cursive', 'set' and 'hybrid' forms, throughout Britain and Ireland, again postulating a 'Phase II' which assumed several different forms according to region. Dumville has gone further:[143] while allegedly debunking the idea of a Lindisfarne scriptorium, he has suggested that Wearmouth-Jarrow was responsible for the wholesale 'Phase II' reform of the Insular system and that, as its distinctive Phase II minuscule seems to have evolved as part of a publishing campaign to circulate the works of Bede in the mid eighth century,[144] the reform of Insular Half-Uncial (of which the production of the Lindisfarne Gospels was an essential part) is likely to have occurred there at the same time, since such developments are, he would suggest, unlikely to have been protracted. How then is one to account for the time lapse between its reform of high-grade book script by the introduction of Italianate Uncial around 700 and its completion of the process by a reform of Half-Uncial and minuscule around 740–60? It remains equally likely that the campaign of book production employing minuscule script at Wearmouth-Jarrow, rather than the Uncial which it reserved for sacred texts, was itself influenced by the earlier tradition of cursive minuscule scripts which are found in an Insular milieu from areas as diverse as seventh- to eighth-century Ireland, Continental mission centres such as Willbrord's Echternach and Columbanus' St Gallen, the Canterbury school of Theodore and Hadrian, Boniface's south-western England and the Frisian mission-field, and is to be seen as part of the evolution of the genre into 'Phase II'.[145] Did Wearmouth-Jarrow need Half-Uncial when it had its

142 Brown 2003b, p. 255, fig. 103; Campbell and Lane 1993.

143 Dumville 1999, which suggests many innovative and valuable ways of viewing the earlier stages of development of the Insular system of scripts but which becomes over-dogmatic in the process of its critical analysis of previous work when discussing 'Phase II'.

144 Parkes 1982.

145 Brown 1982.

own uncial for higher purposes and minuscule for others? If it did, there are better candidates (such as the Durham Cassiodorus) for examples of what this may have looked like than the Lindisfarne Gospels which displays little affinity with its codicological and artistic traditions.

There was undoubtedly an earlier Insular tradition of Half-Uncial. Well-represented within books associated with the Columban *parochia*, it was evolving towards a more formal, regular type throughout the seventh century, and had achieved maturity by the time that the Durham Gospels was written, probably in the generation prior to the Lindisfarne Gospels.[146] If, as I have proposed, the Lindisfarne Gospels was made later, during the second decade of the eighth century on Holy Island, then 'Phase II' had already been achieved and Bishop Eadfrith's distinctively overt response to the influence of Uncial script should be seen as a further, rather exotic, development which was a little aside from the mainstream and which exerted limited influence, other than promoting the generic regularity of 'Phase II' Half-Uncial.[147] Its direct palaeographical influence may, however, be manifest in other important books from the Columban federation such as the Book of Kells. In other areas Half-Uncial script gradually evolved along similar stylistic lines or, in some Irish scriptoria, remained staunchly within 'Phase I'.[148] The Lichfield, MacRegol and Rawlinson Gospels, the Lincoln College Luke fragment,[149] one of the scribes of the Cambridge–London Gospels and two of the scribes of the Barberini Gospels all favour a broad, regular Half-Uncial of mature 'Phase II' character. The artists of the Lichfield and Macregol Gospels were also particularly influenced by the decorated incipits and carpet pages of the Lindisfarne Gospels, the former to such an extent as to suggest direct consultation.[150]

Other books exhibit variations of Phase II Half-Uncial, characterised by lateral compression and a less regular aspect with letters of differing heights and more fractured, angular strokes (rather then the generous curves of the Lindisfarne and Durham Gospels). These include Royal 1 B.vii, the Gotha Gospels, the St Petersburg Gospels, the Half-Uncial hand of DCL, A.II.16, the Durham Cassiodorus, Egerton 1046, and other scattered fragments of

146 Verey 1980. Departing from the views expressed in Kendrick *et al.* 1956–60, attributing both volumes to a putative Lindisfarne scribe ('the Durham–Echternach Calligrapher'), I have suggested that the Durham Gospels may have been made either at Lindisfarne or Melrose and that the Echternach Gospels also belongs to this earlier generation and was probably written in Echternach itself by scribes trained in the Irish tradition: Brown 2003b, pp. 253–71.

147 Brown 2003b, pp. 253–71. 148 Brown 1989.

149 Oxford, Lincoln College, 92. The similarity of the script of this volume was noted by Julian Brown in Kendrick *et al.* 1956–60, p. 89.

150 Brown 2007b.

probable Northumbrian gospel-books.[151] Several of these volumes – Royal 1 B.vii, the Gotha and St Petersburg Gospels, which have been ascribed both to Northumbria and Mercia – exhibit features associated with the Wearmouth-Jarrow scriptorium (such as a dedication cross at the top of each page and the marking of lections with a cross formed of points) and were all copied from the same textual archetype as the Lindisfarne Gospels which was circulating from Wearmouth-Jarrow.[152] If Wearmouth-Jarrow did practise a Half-Uncial, it is therefore more likely to have been of this second variety. The closest analogies for the more laborious, stately form encountered in the Durham Gospels, and, in an even more grandiose form, in the Lindisfarne Gospels, lie within books associated within an eighth-century Irish or Columban orbit – the context in which it was first developed.

Brown's 'Phase II' retains its validity but should be seen as the culmination of a process of growth and maturing in book production, stimulated by the increasing availability of earlier textual exemplars. These were brought to these islands by Roman and Frankish missionaries, by subsequent romanophiles such as Theodore and Hadrian, Wilfrid, Benedict Biscop, Ceolfrith and Acca, or shared between communities belonging to extended monastic families with houses on the Continent (such as Luxeuil, St Gallen, Bobbio, Echternach, Utrecht, Salzburg and Fulda).[153] Such stimuli were coupled with an increasing confidence and evolution of earlier indigenous styles of script, decoration and codicological preparation. 'Phase II' would consist of the normalisation of high-grade Uncials and Half-Uncials (with some regional variation) and, more importantly, of experimentation with a range of minuscule scripts of varying degrees of formality (current, cursive, set and perhaps hybrid) which were appropriate for a wide variety of purposes and which, by around 800, had achieved such status that they were even considered an appropriate vehicle for the scriptures. Wearmouth-Jarrow's Phase II minuscule was one such experiment, but other equally successful ones were under way in Ireland, Mercia and Wessex and on the Continent, where, in the circle of Charlemagne and Alcuin of York, they would culminate in the promotion of the multi-purpose Caroline Minuscule.

This level of maturity which marks Phase II was being achieved by Insular scribes during the late seventh century and extended, to varying degrees

151 CUL, Kk.1.24 + BL, Cotton Tiberius B.v, fols. 74 and 76 + Sloane 1044, fol. 2; and BL, Cotton Tiberius. B.v, fol. 75.

152 The dedication crosses are probably derived from Italian exemplars, such as a sixth-century northern Italian gospel-book, Milan, Biblioteca Ambrosiana, C.39 inf., which features prominent Latin crosses in the top left of each folio.

153 Ganz 2002.

depending on the historical circumstances of individual centres, throughout the eighth. It was surely not the invention of any single scriptorium or individual. The Lindisfarne Gospels, embodying a conscious classicism ostensibly as 'romanising' as the higher-grade Uncial scripts of Wearmouth-Jarrow and Kent yet acknowledging and celebrating its indigenous palaeographical roots and the 'Celtic' contribution, is an outstanding example of the mature Insular style of book production which has also fully absorbed and assimilated Mediterranean textual, scribal and artistic influences.[154] As such it is a precocious pinnacle within the development of 'Phase II' rather than its genesis, and represents a somewhat exotic exception rather than the norm as a high-grade Insular book script. This 'reformed' script, with its stately aspect, the determined regularity and adherence to uniform head and base lines, the high frequency of Uncial features and the layout *per cola et commata*, all redolent of the influence of Italian and Wearmouth-Jarrow practices, stands aside from any evolutionary line.

Any such 'evolutionary' interpretation should also be tempered by an acknowledgement that it is applied with the benefit of palaeographical hindsight and is unlikely to have been formalised and uniformly followed by contemporary scribes. Celtic scribes in particular seem to exhibit a healthy lack of concern for phases and categories. In Ireland features of both Phases I and II may be mixed or may occur side by side throughout the eighth and ninth centuries. This renders a primarily stylistic arrangement of examples extremely dangerous. A book such as Durrow, which might appear to represent a less highly evolved form of script and ornament, need not *necessarily* be considered earlier in date on the basis of such considerations alone.

The script of the Lindisfarne Gospels and its immediate associates did continue to exert a more direct influence, however. The Cambridge–London Gospels contain a scribal hand which is reminiscent of that of the Echternach Gospels and of an Irish-trained member of the Echternach scriptorium, Laurentius.[155] However, it also contains a hand strongly exhibiting the palaeographical influence of the Lindisfarne Gospels, reinforcing the art-historical similarities which its evangelist symbols and decorated incipits share with both the Echternach and Lindisfarne Gospels.[156]

The Lichfield Gospels contains a rather artificial, angular Phase II Half-Uncial by one main hand.[157] Its display Half-Uncial, including ductus, as well

154 Brown 2003b.
155 CCCC, 197B and the badly damaged BL, Cotton Otho. C.v. Ó Croinín 1989b.
156 Ó Croinín 1984, 1989b; Webster and Backhouse 1991, no. 83; Netzer 1994a; Verey 1999; Brown 2003b.
157 Webster and Backhouse 1991, no. 90.

as the form of the letters with their distorted bows, finds its closest parallel in the Book of Kells. Lichfield's decoration was directly modelled, in places, on the Lindisfarne Gospels and was also influenced by other works from the Columban *parochia*, such as the Durham Gospels. It would appear, in respect of its decoration, to occupy a developmental place which falls somewhere between the Cambridge–London Gospels and the Book of Kells. The use of actual runic letters in its display script would also argue strongly in favour of an English origin rather than a Welsh, for it is hard to imagine a self-respecting Welsh scribe electing to use them at a time when Anglo-Saxon political and cultural expansion was being actively resisted. It was probably made for a centre closely associated with Lindisfarne, as Lichfield was.[158]

It is likely that eighth-century Mercian production was greatly influenced by that of Northumbria. The Barberini Gospels may offer some tangible evidence for this. It is the work of four scribes (termed A–D in accordance with their occurrence in the manuscript), two of whom write a respectable Phase II Half-Uncial of Lindisfarne type. The master-scribe, Wigbald (Scribe C), is commemorated in the colophon beseeching a prayer on his behalf (fol. 153, *ora pro uuigbaldo*).[159] The hand of scribe A is similar to Wigbald's, but the two remaining scribes produce rather different variants of his Half-Uncial. Scribe D displays a tendency towards hybrid forms and calligraphic mannerisms and inserts playful line-fillers and letter terminals with zoomorphic and anthropomorphic components, somewhat reminiscent of those of Cerne and the Book of Kells. His script finds its closest parallel in the Mercian script seen in an Offa charter of 793×796.[160] Scribe B produces an idiosyncratic but extremely elegant half-Uncial with a strict adherence to head and base lines, small bows and elegantly extended descenders. This script has no direct parallel within the known Insular corpus, but, in the absence of contradictory evidence, it too may be a Mercian hand. This collaboration between Northumbrians and at least one Mercian scribe (D) taken in conjunction with the somewhat inexpert, if imaginative, nature of the latter's work, is suggestive of a teaching role on the part of the northerners. The Northumbrians may have been working in Mercia, or the Mercian in Northumbria, or all of them may have been

158 The volume was in Wales during the mid ninth century, when it was presented to the altar of St Teilo at Llandeilo Fawr, but I have argued in favour of an earlier association with Lichfield on the basis of the stylistic relationships between the Gospels, the Book of Cerne (an early ninth-century prayerbook associated with Bishop Æthelwald of Lichfield) and a painted sculpture of an angel dating to *c.* 800 which probably formed part of the shrine of St Chad: Brown 2007b.

159 Webster and Backhouse 1991, no. 160; Brown 1996, pp. 120–5, 167–78; Gameson 2002d; Brown 2007a.

160 BL, Add. Charter 19790: Sawyer 1968, 139.

working together in an unidentified centre. Stylistic affinities with sculptures at Peterborough, Castor and Fletton, with metalwork and the tentative identification of Wigbald as a member of the Peterborough community would suggest that this was where the Barberini Gospels was made.[161]

Arguably the closest analogy to the Lindisfarne Gospels' stately rounded script and to its more calligraphic display Half-Uncial, however, is to be found in the Book of Kells, in both the main text script and the calligraphic display variants of its prefaces.[162] The similarities are so persuasive that Julian Brown argued that the two volumes were closer in terms of regional and chronological production than most scholars would accept, leading him to suggest the production of Kells in an unspecified monastery in Scotland during the mid eighth century, a view which has not achieved currency, although recent excavations at Tarbat have yielded intriguing evidence of a possible scriptorium, and sculptures that fuse Irish, Pictish and Northumbrian influences.[163] Both books are likely to have been made as major cult items, widely renowned, of key houses within what started as the Columban *parochia*: it is perhaps not so surprising therefore that, although not produced in the same scriptorium in a single developmental phase, they should exhibit affinities. If the Lindisfarne Gospels was made at Lindisfarne, an important house hosting its own major cult and which continued to celebrate its Columban roots alongside its newer ecumenical affiliations, and it was completed in the early 720s, this would in any case narrow the chronological and ideological gap between these two great monuments.[164] Their mutual stylistic relationship to a third, the Book of Durrow, which has been shown to be closely related in its prefatory texts to the Book of Kells,[165] is also explicable in that it is another focal point within the cult of St Columba and was also made in a Columban house. This may have been the same scriptorium that produced the Book of Kells (in which case Durrow is likely to have been the earlier of the two), or one that had access to the same textual exemplar with unusual prefatory matter as that used in the making of Kells. The Lindisfarne Gospels does not relate closely to either of these two great Columban books textually, but enjoys a palaeographical and art-historical relationship with both. The conclusion suggested is of a shared Columban heritage which the artist–scribe of the Lindisfarne Gospels – probably Bishop Eadfrith – was not afraid to integrate freely with other major influences, notably that of Wearmouth-Jarrow.

161 Brown 2007a. 162 Fox 1990.
163 Brown 1971; Carver and Hooper, 2000.
164 Brown 2003b. 165 McGurk 1990.

Insular Minuscule scripts

Some of the earliest extant examples of Insular writing employ minuscule (or lower case) letters. Irish scribes had certainly mastered less formal cursive scripts by the time that the Springmount Bog Tablets were lost to the peat during the early seventh century, and books containing patristic commentary and scholarly library works such as Isidore's *Etymologiae* and Paulinus of Nola's *Carmen natalitia* were written in minuscule scripts in Insular scriptoria during the later seventh and eighth centuries. Cursive minuscule was also the main script employed in charters and for recording the proceedings of councils and synods. There seems always to have been a correlation between form and function, with minuscules being considered appropriate for less formal books and pragmatic literacy, and Half-Uncials or Uncials for sacred text and other formal works. Occasionally, however, this distinction could become blurred, as with the use of Uncials for the earliest southern English charters and with the use of a more formally penned minuscule termed by Julian Brown 'hybrid minuscule', as seen in the Royal Bible which was probably made at Canterbury *c.* 820–40 and was subject to some Carolingian influence.[166] The promotion of the multi-purpose Caroline Minuscule throughout Carolingian territories had significantly challenged the concept of a hierarchy of scripts. In future, variations on a Caroline Minuscule theme would characterise the history of formal medieval book-hands.

Julian Brown subdivided Lowe's 'minuscule' into four categories, distinguished by the amount of speed and formality applied during the act of writing: 'hybrid minuscule', 'set minuscule', 'cursive minuscule' and 'current minuscule'. Within this system the more formal scripts were written with a straight pen, its nib cut at an oblique angle to the shaft so as to compensate for the natural slant at which the pen was held during writing and thereby producing flat heads to minims, while the minuscules were written with a slanted pen, the nib cut at right angles to the shaft and producing slanted tops to minims. Brown's 'hybrid minuscule' was a slanted pen script, with sloping heads to letter-strokes, but was written with the maximum degree of care and formality, with frequent lifts of the pen from the page and with minimal use of ligatures and other linking strokes, and featuring some letter-forms proper to Half-Uncial, such as round 's', Uncial 'R' and 'N' and, for Brown the clinching factor, Insular Half-Uncial 'oc' shaped 'a'. Doyle has questioned the validity of this category, and there is little, apart from the the 'oc' form of

166 BL, Royal 1 E.vi. Budny 1985; Brown 1996; Story 2003.

'a', to distinguish it from Brown's 'set minuscule' (*cursiva formata*), other than what Brown considered to be the scribal intention of emulating Half-Uncial, as used in many of the great Insular gospel-books, without devoting so much time and effort.[167] His 'cursive minuscule' (*cursiva media* or *cursiva media formata*, when at its most formally written) was distinguished by the use of lower-case letter-forms, with the use of ligatures, loops and reversal of ductus on certain letter-strokes in order to heighten the speed of writing. Insular cursive minuscules can, nonetheless, be very carefully and calligraphically written and can assume a heightened degree of formality, transcending their place in the hierarchy. When cursive script was written most rapidly and with least care and formality, this was, for Brown, usefully termed 'current minuscule' (*cursiva currens*). In introducing these shades of grey, Brown was significantly influenced by Lieftinck's terminology for the complex relationships between the many variations of Gothic scripts.[168]

Brown perceived three categories of Phase I minuscule. The first, Phase Ia, was that practised by Irish and Northumbrian scribes in works such as the Book of Mulling,[169] and is characterised by loops, ligatures and reversals of the ductus of certain letters, reflecting some late Roman or post-Roman cursive influence. In Northumbria this was supplanted by the introduction of a highly elegant, efficient and legible Phase II cursive minuscule, best represented by the earliest surviving copies of Bede's *Historia ecclesiastica* written at Wearmouth-Jarrow in the mid eighth century. Phase Ib was that practised in south-west England, as characterised by the surviving autograph annotations added by St Boniface to a Half-Uncial copy of the Apocalypse during the early eighth century.[170] This early West Saxon cursive minuscule is notable for its retention of a number of New Roman cursive features, such as its characteristic reversed ductus 'g', which resembles a long 'z', and other labour-saving tricks, which can be found as late as the ninth century.[171] It may owe something of its origins to the continued activity of the British church in south-west England, leading to the perpetuation of a provincial Roman secretary hand which in turn influenced the more mainstream Insular Minuscule introduced to the region. Brown also acknowledged the presence of other varieties prevalent in southern England, which are best characterised in the early stages by a letter addressed by Wealdhere, bishop of London, to Berhtwald, archbishop of Canterbury, in 704 or 705.[172] The application of chronological phases should

167 Doyle 1992. 168 Bischoff, *et al.* 1954. 169 TCD, 60.
170 Bodl., Douce 140. 171 Crick 1987 and 1997.
172 Crick 1987 and 1997; Dumville 1999, pp. 104–5.

not be over-rigorous, however, and it should be remembered that Irish scribes, such as the flamboyant Ferdomnach who signed the colophon of the Book of Armagh around 807, often continued to employ their traditional minuscule (Brown's Phase Ia) throughout the Insular period and beyond.

Parkes identified a distinctive cursive minuscule developed in the Wearmouth-Jarrow scriptoria which he dated to the 740s as part of a publishing campaign in response to demands for the works of Bede, but which Dumville has placed later in the century.[173] This style, represented primarily by the Moore and St Petersburg copies of the *Historia ecclesiastica* (see Plate 4.4), was seen by Brown as part of Phase II, and the result of a period of indigenous rapprochement with the scribal practices of Rome. In his rejection of Julian Brown's views concerning the Lindisfarne scriptorium, Dumville has gone so far as to propose a direct association between the Lindisfarne Gospels and the Wearmouth-Jarrow Bedan manuscripts, assigning them all a mid-eighth-century origin within Benedict Biscop's romanising foundations, seeing the development in both minuscule and Half-Uncial as part of a wholesale reform of Northumbrian script. A more organic process of development and a more fluid system ordered by palaeographical perception seems preferable to ascribing such change to the will of a reforming scriptorium master.[174]

The use of minuscule scripts also characterises the later members of the Southumbrian Tiberius group of manuscripts such as the Royal Prayerbook, the Book of Nunnaminster and the Book of Cerne.[175] As with the study of Phase Ic minuscule, the evidence of charters has proven of value in assessing the palaeography, relative chronology and regional spread of these distinctive grades of minuscule script. The documents suggest that they were not confined to a particular centre but were current throughout a wider 'Mercian script-province' and that the members of the Tiberius group were made in a variety of scriptoria extending throughout the region.[176]

The use of minuscule scripts for complete texts was certainly not a new development in the ninth century.[177] Northumbrian scribes employed them

173 Parkes 1982, Dumville 2007. The Moore Bede (CUL, Kk.5.16) is considered, following Parkes, to post-date the St Petersburg Bede of *c.* 746. Given recent work by Bill Schipper on the layout of English vernacular manuscripts (Schipper 2003), I wonder whether it might not, however, be closer to the original authorial layout of the text. It is laid out in single columns of long lines, like many later Anglo-Saxon vernacular compositions, but unlike the St Petersburg Bede and BL, Cotton Tiberius A.xiv and Tiberius C.ii, the other pre-Alfredian English copies of the *Historia ecclesiastica*, which are written in more formal cursive minuscule scripts arranged in two columns, more suited to presentation copies or a planned layout for wider dissemination.

174 Brown 2003b, pp. 253–71.

175 BL, Royal 2 A.xx; BL, Harley 2965; CUL, Ll.1.10.

176 Brown 1986, 1996 and 2001b, and 2005.

177 Brown 1996, and 2001b.

during the late seventh and eighth centuries for non-liturgical texts, such as Bede *In Proverbia Salomonis*[178] and the *Carmina* of Paulinus of Nola,[179] and for at least one deluxe liturgical volume – the Echternach Gospels where set minuscule was used to expedite production.[180] The uses of Irish Minuscule, from the seventh to the ninth century, for the pocket gospel-books and other works may also be relevant, as may near-contemporary developments in Caroline Minuscule on the Continent. A characteristic feature of ninth-century southern English manuscript production is experimentation with minuscule forms. There is a tendency to mix and imitate scripts in pursuit of an overall, often calligraphic, effect and high-quality cursive scripts are generally used for works other than complete gospel-books and bibles (although, as we have seen, at the very end of the Insular age the scribes of the Kentish Royal Bible went so far as to employ an elegant hybrid minuscule, perhaps influenced by the use of Caroline in the Touronian Bibles).[181]

There was equally in Southumbria a willingness to mix, imitate and upgrade scripts in order to impart a more imposing appearance to sections of text within minuscule books. This predilection for high-grade, elaborate minuscule scripts of 'mixed parentage' may owe something to developments within the field of charter production.

There is considerable evidence for the growing importance of written evidence in litigation during the early ninth century,[182] and it is likely that recognition of the importance of the written document – reinforced by perceptions of the authority of liturgical manuscripts – may have led to attempts to improve its appearance and thereby increase its authority.[183] The diplomatic field was an appropriate area of scribal innovation and experimentation in the formation of high-class scripts during the late eighth century and the first half of the ninth century.[184]

Ninth-century charters from Christ Church, Canterbury, adumbrate the development of Southumbrian cursive scripts. Kentish documents, other than those connected with Christ Church during the archiepiscopate of Wulfred (805–32), tend to employ a rounded minuscule of even aspect, with modest

178 Bodl., Bodley 819.
179 Vatican, BAV, Pal. lat. 235; St Petersburg, Public Library, Q.v.XIV.1.
180 BnF., lat. 9389. 181 BL, Royal 1 E.vi.
182 Brown 1986; Wormald 1986. 183 Brown 1986.
184 A similar phenomenon may be found in the rediscovery of western cursive scripts within the sphere of charter production during the late twelfth and thirteenth centuries, and the extension of these scripts into use as book-hands from the end of the thirteenth century: Brown 1990a, pp. 92–3.

ascenders and descenders.[185] The transition to more pointed forms and the tentative introduction of calligraphic variants may be observed in charters of the first decade of the ninth century.[186] Their frequency increases steadily to produce a fully developed, highly calligraphic 'mannered minuscule' during the second and third decades of the ninth century.[187] It is interesting that the Royal Bible should reveal a similar preoccupation at St Augustine's (?), Canterbury, where hybrid minuscule was increasingly adopting Uncial, capital and minuscule variant letter-forms and decorative elements to form a distinctive formal script.

From the mid 820s the characteristic and somewhat baroque mannerisms found in charter scripts begin to decline,[188] although the pointed aspect and ductus are retained. This produces more legible forms and a script characterised by its clarity and often elegant simplicity. The best examples of this script date from the mid-820s to the early 840s.[189]

The Christ Church archive presents a rare survival of a comparatively representative section of material for the period in question. We are less fortunate in the case of other major archives. It is important, however, to remember that Kent was, for much of the eighth and ninth centuries, part of the Mercian hegemony.[190] There may have been less of a cultural divide than is generally assumed between Kent and Mercia proper. The concept of a Mercian script-province capable of encompassing the political components of greater Mercia, Kent and Wessex during the second half of the eighth century and the first half of the ninth century, rather as the Irish script-province embraced much of Northumbria during the seventh and early eighth centuries, is not untenable.[191] There were sophisticated patterns of interaction between the Mercian royal house and the Kentish churches during the period.[192] Conflict concerning the primacy of Canterbury and the establishment and relegation of its rival, Lichfield, looms large in these relations, as does the dispute concerning proprietary houses.[193] Even out of this picture emerges some idea of cultural overlap. The formidable Archbishop Wulfred, champion of the rights

185 This may be seen in BL, Cotton Ch. viii.34 (Sawyer 1968, p. 35; Bond 1873–8, II.4), dated 778, in BL, Stowe Charter 7 (Sawyer 1968, 155; Sanders 1878–84, III.7), dated 799, and in BL, Cotton Augustus ii.55 (Sawyer 1968, 1259; Bond 1873–8, I.13), dated 805. It also recurs sporadically, as in BL, Cotton Augustus ii.47 (Sawyer 1968, 1246; Bond 1873–8, II.11), dated 811. Brown 1986.

186 E.g. Sawyer 1968, p. 161.

187 Seen in Sawyer 1968, pp. 169, 177, 178, 186 and 187.

188 Sawyer 1968, pp. 1434 and 1436.

189 Seen in BL, Cotton Augustus ii.94 (Sawyer 1968, 188; Bond 1873–8, II.20), dated 831.

190 Brooks 1984, pp. 111–54.

191 T. J. Brown 1982 and 1984; M. P. Brown 1996 and 2001b; Bischoff 1990.

192 Brooks 1984; see also Cubitt 1995.

193 Brooks 1984, pp. 111–54.

of the church in general, and of Canterbury in particular, was himself of Mercian or Middle Saxon stock.[194] Another important Mercian, Cwoenthryth, daughter and heir of King Coenwulf, was simultaneously abbess of Minster-in-Thanet, an important Kentish house, and of Winchcombe, a major proprietary house of the Mercian royalty.[195] The probable exchange of influences and personnel between these foundations may have entailed some homogeneity, even in scriptorial practices. Brooks has even suggested that Christ Church scribes may have been responsible for drawing up documents for retention by the Mercian royal house.[196] However, those few charters of this period that do survive from centres other than Christ Church, Canterbury, do not display the same range of features, even if they do reveal similar trends and preoccupations.[197]

It may be that earlier Mercian scripts played a significant role in the development of the Canterbury cursives. Both Northumbrian and Southumbrian (Bonifatian) Phase II minuscules have also clearly left their mark, and the Mercian scripts themselves would have sprung from a union of such influences.[198] While it is difficult to define the Mercian system of scripts during the eighth century, charters are once again a vital witness.

Some impression of minuscule scripts during the reign of King Offa of Mercia (757–96) may be gleaned from the few surviving charters issued by him. These tend to employ two scripts. One is a rounded and somewhat inelegant minuscule of the type found in a charter of 764 which features a distinctive round 'd', an open-headed 'a', a 't' with an extended head and a compressed 'er' ligature.[199] The other is a minuscule which displays elaborate hybrid letter-forms and incipient mannerisms of the type later developed so successfully in Canterbury 'mannered minuscule'.[200] The advantages of a calligraphic minuscule for purposes of prestige were readily perceived and exploited at Canterbury, but in Mercia itself there are some early signs of a move towards simplification.[201] This resulted in the elegant and balanced script of the Book

194 *Ibid.*, p. 132. 195 *Ibid.*, pp. 182–5.

196 *Ibid.*, p. 168. BL, Stowe Charter 15 (Sawyer 1968, p. 1436) certainly refers to privileges being stored and consulted at Winchcombe.

197 It has been suggested that Heahberht, bishop of Worcester, like Wulfred at Canterbury, was concerned with the reform of proprietary houses within his diocese, upon Carolingian lines. This contributed to a similar rise in litigation and charter production to that found at Canterbury. Brown 1986 and 1996.

198 Brown 1982. 199 BL, Cotton Augustus ii.26 (Sawyer 1968, 106; Bond 1873–8, I.9).

200 BL, Add. Charter 19790 (Sawyer 1968, 139; Bond 1873–8, II.5), an earlier document of 793×796 which also concerns the Westbury-on-Trym dispute of Sawyer 1968, p. 59.

201 This may be seen in BL, Cotton Augustus ii.4, which is dated 779 but the script of which suggests that it may be significantly later (Brown 1987, n. 54), and Cotton Augustus ii.27 (Sawyer 1968, 106; Bond 1873–8, I.9), the endorsement by Pilheard, written in 799–802.

of Cerne. Following its baroque 'mannered minuscule', the script of Christ Church, Canterbury, may therefore have settled into this more uniform Mercian trend.

There are sufficient divergences in detail to allow the proposal of regional groupings for manuscripts within the Tiberius group. The Harleian Prayerbook, the Royal Prayerbook and the Book of Nunnaminster appear to be the earliest members. They employ hybrid and cursive minuscules which find their closest parallels in charters of King Offa, especially those dating to the 790s,[202] and which may be distinguished from the rounded minuscule of contemporary Kentish documents and from Wulfred's Christ Church minuscule. The stylistic relationships of these manuscripts with the charters and a datable manuscript of saints' lives in Paris (of *c.* 810–25),[203] along with developments in the prayerbook texts, would suggest a chronology of late eighth to early ninth century for the Harleian Prayerbook, and the first quarter of the ninth century for the Royal Prayerbook and the Book of Nunnaminster. All three contain textual and provenance evidence pointing to female production and use, suggesting that the initial development of this thematic devotional genre, and the formal, highly legible minuscule scripts used for it, are likely to have owed a great deal to female spirituality and scribal skills.[204] They were probably made in western Mercia.

The elegant clarity of the pointed minuscule found in the Book of Cerne (see Plate 4.5) finds its closest parallel, within this sequence, in charters dating from the 820s to the 840s.[205] In general stylistic terms Cerne accords with this phase of clarification and simplification, but there is sufficient divergence in detail to suggest that Cerne stands a little aside from the series and was probably not produced in the same centres as these charters. In this respect it differs from a related manuscript, the saints' lives in Paris, which is so close in detail to charters representative of the 'mannered minuscule' phase of *c.* 805 – *c.* 825 as to suggest that it may be intimately related to the Christ Church scriptorium.[206] The decoration of the Paris manuscript places it within the Tiberius group and its decoration and script are strongly suggestive of an earlier phase of development than that represented by the Book of Cerne. Charter evidence favouring a date of *c.* 805 – *c.* 825 for lat. 10861 therefore also indicates a slightly later date for Cerne,[207] reinforced by its similarity to charter hands of the 820s–840s.

202 Sawyer 1968, pp. 139 and 106.
203 BnF, lat. 10861. 204 See Brown 2001a.
205 BnF, lat. 10861; see Sawyer 1968, pp.1434, 1436, 188 and 1438; but it also bears a closer similarity to 59.
206 Brown 1986. 207 Brown 1986, 1996 and 2001b.

The charter which most closely resembles the cursive script of the Book of Cerne has been identified by Wormald as an early ninth-century Worcester forgery of a document supposedly issued in 770, relating to a dispute between Worcester and Berkeley concerning lands at Westbury-on-Trym and Stoke.[208] Although reminiscent of the simplified Canterbury script of the late 820s, this charter is far closer in detail to the Book of Cerne and such stylistic affinity serves to reinforce this book's Mercian origin. Other possible Worcester products, such as Worcester Cathedral Library, Add. 1, may also be seen as forerunners of the hybrid minuscule script found in the Royal Bible and of the cursive minuscule of Cerne and its associates.

Other Mercian works include Salisbury Cathedral Library, 117 (etc.) and Hatton 93 which resemble one another sufficiently to permit an attribution to the same scriptorium. Although it lacks the elegance, if not the assurance, of the Book of Cerne, Hatton 93 resembles it so closely in script (with the pointed aspect, reversed ductus, angular bows, pen-held terminals, ligatures and many corresponding letter-forms), abbreviations, textual apparatus, decoration, palette and codicology (including their shared use of quire numeration by letter) that it is very likely to have been produced in the same Lichfield scriptorium. It even closely resembles Cerne in its unusual use of a line of imitation Half-Uncials (produced with a slanted, rather than a straight pen) as part of its script gradation (fol. 2r) to introduce texts. Hatton 93's whole approach to script gradation is extremely similar to that embodied in Cerne. Features such as a tendency to rounded forms and the frequency of round 'd' indicate a slightly earlier date than Cerne, but it is not impossible that Hatton 93 represents an earlier stage in the development of the same scribe. The *Primum in Ordine* exposition of the mass contained in Hatton 93 has been assumed to give the manuscript a *terminus post quem* of 789 when the text was promulgated within Carolingian territory.[209] While this is not a secure argument, there was certainly Carolingian interest in the piece (used, for example, by Hrabanus Maurus) and, given other evidence for Carolingian influence upon the later members of the Tiberius group,[210] it should not be totally ruled out in this instance.

208 Worcester CL, Add. MS in safe (Sawyer 1968, p. 59; Sanders 1878–84, II pl. Worcester; Brown 1986; Wormald 1986). I am inclined to associate BL, Cotton Augustus ii.4 (Sawyer 1968, 114; Bond 1873–8, I.10), dated 779 but perhaps a later 'forgery', with Sawyer 59 on palaeographical grounds (the former perhaps representing a precursor of Sawyer 59's script), but it should be noted that there are no apparent diplomatic grounds for questioning this document's authenticity.

209 Morrish 1982, 1986 and 1988; *PL*, CXXXVIII, cols. 1173–86. However, this anonymous and undated text seems to have been indebted to earlier work, notably that of Isidore of Seville, and may have enjoyed currency in some form prior to this; the Carolingian link cannot therefore be used to provide a dating. Brown 1996.

210 See, e.g., Brown 1991b.

Salisbury, 117 is not by the same scribe or scribes as Cerne and Hatton 93, although it may also be from the Lichfield scriptorium. It displays a more rounded aspect and employs a smaller, heavier cursive minuscule with a slight slant towards the left. It uses shorter ascenders and descenders and does not favour upward flourishes of head-strokes or linking of words. It does, however, exhibit pen-held terminals, slightly forked descenders, low-slung 'l' and open bows. In general it resembles the 'lapsed' hand found in certain places in Cerne (such as its Old English introduction) more than its main text hand. Interestingly, like Cerne, it contains a number of spelling errors and a weakness in Latinity, perhaps suggesting that this was a feature of the Lichfield scriptorium. Furthermore, all three manuscripts contain elements which suggest that Continental, as well as Insular, exemplars were available there.

Another hand that incorporates many features found in Cerne, especially the 'lapsed' sections, was that responsible for copying a series of episcopal lists.[211] This hand has been ascribed to Mercia and dated 805×814.[212] Its distinctive *litterae notabiliores*, ligatures and use of a Tironian symbol resembling a 7 are also very reminiscent of Cerne. Another cursive Mercian hand updated these lists around 833, his additions including Bishop Æthelwald of Lichfield (818–30), for whom Cerne was probably made.

The cursive minuscules of the Tiberius group also find a number of associates in manuscripts which Lowe dated to the turn of the eighth–ninth centuries and ascribed to Insular centres on the Continent.[213] The possibility of continuing recruitment of new Insular, and especially Southumbrian, personnel to the mission fields has, until recently, been dismissed upon grounds of historical improbability, but this picture is beginning to be modified in the light of new evidence.[214] More work needs to be undertaken in this area, but the possibility of an up-to-date familiarity on the Continent with developments in Insular manuscript production during the late eighth and early ninth centuries has, increasingly, to be admitted.

It may also be possible to identify a West Saxon branch of the group. A Philippus, *Expositio in Job*,[215] may be dated to the mid ninth century and placed in Wessex, probably at Winchester or Sherborne, on the basis of the stylistic

211 BL, Cotton Vespasian B.vi (fols. 104–9).
212 Dumville 1976, pp. 24–5 (following Page).
213 On the evidence of the relationship of its script to charters and to Cerne, a biblical fragment now in the Takamiya Collection in Tokyo should be considered in relation to the group. Other fragments of the same manuscript occur as Düsseldorf UB, A.19 and have a medieval provenance of Werden, diocese of Cologne. Barker-Benfield 1991; Brown 2001b.
214 McKitterick 1989a. 215 Bodl., Bodley 426.

affinity of its script with two West Saxon charters,[216] the scribe of the later of which (dated 847) has been associated by Chaplais with the bishops of Winchester or Sherborne.[217] A copy of Felix, *Vita S. Guthlaci*,[218] was likewise assumed by Lowe to be associated with Winchester, largely on the basis of the similarity of its script to the above.[219] These manuscripts and charters employ a pointed minuscule which accords generally with the simplified minuscule of the rest of the group, but which exhibits a somewhat erratic ductus and a predilection for reversal, perhaps influenced by that prevalent in earlier Bonifatian minuscule, including regular use of a distinctive reversed 'g', resembling a 'z', which occurs earlier in the Insular corpus and which, interestingly, is preserved in later representatives of Irish Phase I minuscule such as the Book of Armagh.[220] This style of minuscule script, even if of ultimately West Saxon origin, may have enjoyed broader geographical currency in the wake of the expansionism of the kings of Wessex from the second quarter of the ninth century onwards, even affecting some Canterbury hands.

Several works may be attributed to Canterbury: the collection of saints' lives in Paris has been identified as a probable Christ Church product of *c.* 810–25,[221] and the Royal Bible as a St Augustine's manuscript of *c.* 815–45.[222] The Tiberius Bede has also been claimed as the work of one of the scribes of the Royal Bible.[223] Its pointed minuscule accords well with the post-mannered-minuscule phase of the Christ Church charters and differs from that of Cerne in many respects, generally lacking its reversed ductus, loops and pen-held terminals, and exhibiting far greater use of round 'd' and short 'r' and a distinctive *et* ligature, with a detached head-stroke to the 't', and a 'g' with a pronounced angularity to its bow. Copies of Gregory, *Homiliae in Evangelia*,[224] Sedulius, *Carmen paschale*[225] and the Corpus Glossary[226] have also been proposed by Lowe as Kentish, possibly Canterbury, works.

From the mid ninth century onwards the extant Christ Church documents exhibit a decline in the standard of cursive script, accompanied, so Brooks maintains, by diplomatic degeneracy and deterioration in Latinity.[227] A

216 BL, Cotton Augustus ii.37 (Sawyer 1968, p. 1438, manuscript 3), dated 838, the text of which could just as well suggest a Christ Church, Canterbury, origin, and Cotton Charter viii.36 (Sawyer 1968, p. 298), dated 847.

217 Chaplais 1973a, pp. 37–9. 218 BL, Royal 4 A. XIV. 219 Ker 1957, pp. 321–2.

220 These features also appear in London, Wilfred Merton Collection, 42 (Bede, *Expositio in Lucae Evangelium*) and in BL, Egerton 1046 (*Liber sapientiae, Ecclesiasticus*), traditionally associated by Lowe with the centre which produced the Durham Cassiodorus. On the origins of this sort of script and its continued use on the Continent, see McKitterick 1989a.

221 BnF, lat. 10861: Brown 1986. 222 Budny 1985.

223 Cotton Tiberius C.ii: Budny 1985, pp. 784–5.

224 CCCC, 69. 225 CCCC, 173. 226 CCCC, 144.

227 Brooks 1984, pp. 155–74.

growing dependence upon the formulaic at the expense of the grammatically correct has been suggested. Attempts have, however, been made to modify this picture of decay.[228]

From the 880s, when Alfred the Great of Wessex had retrieved the military situation sufficiently to retake London from the Danes, to negotiate a partition treaty with their leader, Guthrum, and to turn his attention to addressing the spiritual and educational shortfall to which the leaders of the English increasingly attributed their misfortunes, he assembled a scholarly team, along Carolingian court lines, drawn not only from the Continent (such as Grimbald of Saint-Bertin), but also from Celtic Britain (Asser of St David's in Wales) and from 'free Mercia' (including his own tutor, Bishop Wærferth of Worcester). They and their scribes looked both to the texts of exhortation of the Early Christian era, such as Orosius's *History Against the Pagans* and Gregory the Great's *Pastoral Care*, to Carolingian historiography and biography (such as Einhard's *Life of Charlemagne*), to inspire writings such as Asser's biography of King Alfred, and to the indigenous Insular past to inform works such as Alfred's law-code, the *Anglo-Saxon Chronicle* and the Old English translation of Bede's *Ecclesiastical History*. The script they employed was a minuscule, perhaps inspired in its multi-purpose character by Caroline Minuscule but indebted in its form to the Insular pointed minuscules of the earlier ninth century. Tiberius group manuscripts, such as the Book of Nunnaminster and the Book of Cerne, came as Mercian refugees into Wessex, where their elegant scripts and lively beast heads spawned a new generation of Alfredian successors. Thus Bishop Wærferth's late ninth-century copy of Aldhelm's *In Praise of Virginity*[229] is visibly the heir of such earlier ninth-century works – although his beasties are now given exotic bunches of antique acanthus leaves, imported from Carolingia, upon which to munch contentedly as they ponder the beneficial moral impact that the words from which they sprout will have upon the life and fortunes of the English nation as it moves into the tenth century and the later Anglo-Saxon age.

228 Morrish 1982, 1986 and 1988; Dumville 1983; Brown 1996 and 2001b.
229 BL, Royal 5 F.iii.

5

Script in Wales, Scotland and Cornwall

HELEN MCKEE

It is difficult to present an accurate picture of book production in pre-Conquest Wales, Cornwall and Scotland. This is because so little identifiable material written in these regions has survived – fewer than twenty manuscripts and fragments of manuscripts pre-dating the twelfth century, compared with more than fifty from Ireland and hundreds from England. Very few of our surviving pre-1100 manuscripts written in Wales or Cornwall appear actually to have been preserved in those regions: they travelled to England, or further afield, at an early date.[1] Scotland is in an even worse position, as not one manuscript written earlier than the twelfth century can with certainty be attributed to this region. The unfortunate end result is that our impression of Insular manuscript production tends inevitably to concentrate on Ireland and Anglo-Saxon England.

The earliest manuscript securely identifiable as a product of Celtic Britain was written in the early ninth century.[2] This makes it two hundred or more years later than the earliest products of Ireland and England. For the long period before this date, when books must have been produced but no longer exist, we are forced to rely partly on guesswork. We do know that – as part of the Roman Empire – Wales, Cornwall and the southern part of Scotland would have been introduced to literacy in Latin. They would have been exposed to a range of Roman scripts, including high-grade book scripts such as Rustic Capital and Uncial, as well as Half-Uncial (from the fifth century) and the various cursive scripts used for common purposes. Over time, and certainly by the seventh century, hands from the more informal end of this spectrum had evolved in Britain into Insular script.

In the absence of early manuscript evidence from Celtic Britain, we are fortunate to have epigraphic evidence in the form of inscribed stone

1 On Welsh and Cornish script, see Lindsay 1912b; Huws 2000.
2 BodL., Auct. F.4.32, fols. 19–36 (*Liber Commonei*): Hunt 1961.

monuments: those from Wales and Cornwall provide an almost continuous record of letter-forms from the end of the Roman period onwards.[3] The earliest are in Roman capitals – increasingly debased as time passes – but a major change comes around the sixth or seventh century, when we see capitals giving way to more rounded forms, reminiscent of Insular Half-Uncial or Minuscule. It is probably significant that this is the same time from which the earliest Insular-script manuscripts survive; indeed, the script of the later inscriptions was once termed 'Half-Uncial', and assumed to be influenced by manuscript writing. However, the untidy and monoline forms on the stones have little in common with Insular Half-Uncial as written by scribes. It is now thought that the masons responsible for these inscriptions were borrowing letter-forms not from manuscripts so much as from a more low-grade (and more easily accessible) source: the uninflected cursive script used on wax tablets. The inscriptions cannot be used as a reliable guide to the career of Half-Uncial in Wales and Cornwall.

The earliest manuscript for which a Welsh origin has been hypothesised is the Lichfield Gospels, a magnificently decorated eighth-century gospel-book[4] (see Plate 5.1). The case for a Welsh origin here is based on the fact that the book was at Llandeilo Fawr in the early ninth century, long before it reached Lichfield. However, the Lichfield Gospels is written in Insular Half-Uncial of exceptional quality, and if indeed Welsh would be the only deluxe Welsh manuscript of our period now surviving. The similarities of its script and decoration to those of contemporary Northumbrian manuscripts have encouraged scholars to doubt that it could have been written in Wales – Welsh scriptoria having been poorer and more provincial than those of England, and presumably less likely to produce such a magnificent book – but its textual and art-historical parallels with Irish manuscripts mean that the matter remains unresolved. A second gospel-book for which a Welsh origin has been proposed is the Hereford Gospels (Plate 9.1).[5] This manuscript was copied in Insular Minuscule (albeit quite formal in appearance), on poor-quality parchment, and with little decoration – and, as such, has proven less controversial as a proposed product of Wales than has the Lichfield Gospels.

Our first definitely Welsh book comes from the early ninth century: *Liber Commonei* (so called because its scribal colophon suggests that it was written for a person called Commoneus).[6] It is a compilation of liturgical and

3 Redknap, Lewis and Edwards 2007.
4 Lichfield CL, 1: Jenkins and Owen 1983.
5 Hereford CL, P.I.2: Gameson 2002c.
6 BodL., Auct. F.4.32, fols 19–36: Hunt 1961.

computistical material, the latter including an Easter table for AD 817×835 which suggests that the manuscript was written either during or immediately before this period (outside the bounds of which it would not have been of use). Most of the manuscript is written in a highly competent and calligraphic version of Insular Minuscule. Remarkably, the liturgical material includes lections and canticles in Greek; some of these were written in Greek majuscule (executed with surprising confidence by a scribe who did not understand Greek), though those that would actually have been in liturgical use at the time of writing have been transliterated into Insular Minuscule.

After *Liber Commonei*, most of our earliest Welsh manuscripts fit into a period from the middle of the ninth century until the middle of the tenth. After this there is an apparent gap in the evidence, and then a clutch of survivals from around the year 1100. In most cases these manuscripts have been identified as Welsh because they contain additions in Old Welsh, rather than because their script looks distinctively Welsh. In fact, it is remarkable how dissimilar their scripts can be, not just from manuscript to manuscript but even within an individual manuscript. The Corpus Martianus Capella[7] and the Cambridge Juvencus[8] contain veritable repertories of scribal hands, ranging from flat-topped to rounded to pointed – the Martianus Capella even includes an attempt at Caroline Minuscule, which was the contemporary Continental script, but which had not yet penetrated English scriptoria. The most commonly found variety of Welsh script is a somewhat flattened minuscule, characterised by squarish **a** and **d** with the ascender pulled down: this features, for example, in the Martianus Capella, as well as in glossing hands from the Juvencus. However, in general there appears to have been little pressure towards standardised handwriting in some Welsh scriptoria. It is also probable that almost every extant Welsh manuscript is the sole surviving product of its centre of learning. Regrettably, for most of our period, it is impossible to identify where the centres in question were located.

From the end of the eleventh century, however, we possess two manuscripts which are associable with a single, identifiable centre: the church of Llanbadarn Fawr, near Aberystwyth. Exceptionally, they are also associable with a single family: that of Sulien, who was bishop of St David's on two separate occasions in the second half of the century. The Psalter and Martyrology of Rhygyfarch[9] was copied for Sulien's eldest son, while its decoration was provided by his youngest son, Ieuan; Ieuan also wrote and illuminated a copy of St Augustine's

7 CCCC, 153: Bishop 1964–8a. 8 CUL, Ff.4.42: McKee 2000b.
9 TCD, 50: Lawlor 1914.

De Trinitate.[10] The script of these manuscripts is a highly distinctive version of the flat-topped minuscule found at an earlier period, incorporating mannered features such as decorative subscript letters and exaggerated wedging at the tops of letters. Two more products of Llanbadarn Fawr have been identified from the beginning of the twelfth century, but these indicate that after the Conquest script of Norman type had superseded Insular Minuscule in the Llanbadarn scriptorium.[11]

It is likely that script in Cornwall until the middle of the tenth century followed a similar route to that in Wales. Two manuscripts of the late ninth or early tenth century for which a Cornish origin may be conjectured preserve several contrasting styles of minuscule, a heterogeneity reminiscent of Welsh books: cramped and slanting in the Bern Gospels;[12] variously angular, flat-topped and flourishing in the Leiden Leechbook.[13] However, unlike Wales, Cornwall became absorbed into the Anglo-Saxon kingdom, and this is reflected in the palaeographical record. *Codex Oxoniensis Posterior* – a codex made up of four originally separate manuscripts, of which at least three seem to be Cornish – is the major surviving witness for script in pre-Conquest Cornwall.[14] It shows us Cornish scribes abandoning Insular Minuscule in favour of the Caroline Minuscule used in Anglo-Saxon writing houses, albeit a Caroline with Insular reminiscences in its abbreviations and letter-forms. (The earliest datable examples of Cornish Caroline come from the 940s, in the form of documentary additions to the Bodmin Gospels.)[15] Other scribes in Cornwall retained their native script, however: one such is Bledian, who wrote part of *Codex Oxoniensis Posterior* in an Insular Minuscule which would not seem out of place in Wales.

The limited evidence from pre-Conquest Wales and Cornwall means that any statements about book production there must be tentative. However, a few general trends may be perceived. One of the clearest is a connection with Irish culture. Welsh, Cornish and Irish manuscripts share a distinctive group of abbreviations, introduced about the middle of the ninth century, which appear only rarely elsewhere (and that where there is evidence of Celtic cultural contact). These abbreviations (known as 'Late Celtic') include innovations from Continental script as well as new, elegantly curving versions of pre-existing Insular forms.

10 CCCC, 199.
11 BL, Cotton Faustina C.i, and NLW, Peniarth 540: Peden 1981 and Huws 2000, ch 7.
12 Bern, Burgerbibliothek, 671.
13 Leiden, Universiteitsbibliotheek, Voss. lat. F.96A: Falileyev and Owen 2005.
14 BodL., Bodley 572, fols. 1–50.
15 BL, Add. 9381.

Sometimes the indications of Irish influence in Welsh manuscripts are more overt. The Cambridge Juvencus contains a significant proportion of words in Old Irish among its Old Welsh additions, as well as a poem (in Latin) about an Irishman: moreoever, its main text was copied by a scribe with an Irish name, Núadu (though the colophon in which he names himself was written in Welsh!). Moving forward to the eleventh century, Sulien is known to have founded his school of learning at Llanbadarn after ten years in Ireland. It is not surprising that the Psalter and Martyrology of Rhygyfarch (Sulien's eldest son) commemorates several Irish saints, or that Irish saints feature regularly in Rhygyfarch's *Life of St David*. A related symptom may be that the illumination of the extant Llanbadarn manuscripts has clear affinities with that of contemporary Irish books; however, similarities too with the (limited) illumination in earlier Welsh manuscripts suggest that in this case we are dealing with a decorative idiom common to both Ireland and Wales.

We might expect to see Anglo-Saxon influence in Welsh scriptoria, especially those near the border with England. However, English influence on Welsh script appears mainly confined to the (very) occasional use of the Anglo-Saxon letter thorn, not in surviving manuscripts themselves, but apparently in the manuscripts from which they were copied: for instance, *papep* for *papeth* (Welsh 'what thing') in the Cambridge Juvencus suggests that the scribe saw a thorn in his exemplar but did not recognise it. There were undoubtedly palaeographical links between England and Wales – English Square Minuscule script developed in the late ninth century partly under Welsh influence – but at present the effects on Welsh handwriting are difficult to assess. The influence of the Anglo-Saxon presence in Cornwall is easier to identify, thanks to our several specimens of Cornish Caroline Minuscule.

Scotland is in the unenviable position of having fewer surviving manuscripts from the pre-Conquest period than any other region of the British Isles. In fact, not a single manuscript can with certainty be attributed to Scotland until the twelfth century. There is also a problem with terminology: 'Scotland' as such did not exist for much of our period. The Romans knew the regions north of the Antonine Wall as the home of a people they referred to as *Picti*. In the sixth century, Argyll and the western islands were colonised by Irish invaders (*Scotti*), after which we can make a distinction between the inhabitants of Dál Riata in the west and Pictland in the east. The country was finally united in the middle of the ninth century under Kenneth MacAlpine, and by the end of the century the Picts had been politically, culturally and linguistically eclipsed by their Gaelic-speaking neighbours. One result is that the affinities of the surviving Scottish manuscripts are all with Irish rather than Welsh book production.

In spite of the lack of surviving manuscripts, we know that there were scribes at work in Pictland. Christianity first reached Picts in the sixth century, and by AD 700 there were monasteries (which followed the Rule of St Columba) throughout Pictland. The church required quantities of written material (biblical texts, service books and so on) in order to function, and much of this would have been locally produced. Surviving inscriptions on stone and metal from Pictland display knowledge of the same range of Insular scripts as practised elsewhere (for example, both Insular Half-Uncial and Insular Minuscule are represented on a silver chape from St Ninian's Isle, Shetland).[16]

There are just three pre-Conquest manuscripts for which a Pictish or Scottish origin has been posited. Paradoxically, one of these is one of the best-known Insular manuscripts in the world: the Book of Kells.[17] Written perhaps in the second half of the eighth century, it was preserved at the monastery of Kells, Co. Meath. However, its probable date of production means that it is unlikely to have been written at Kells, since the monastery there was not constructed until the early ninth century (it was built as a new headquarters for the Columban community from Iona). In addition, the monumental Half-Uncial of the codex's script has much in common with Northumbrian manuscripts. The scholarly consensus has been that the Book of Kells was produced in a Columban monastery outside Ireland – whether Iona, Northumbria or eastern Scotland – and that it travelled to Kells when the new monastery there had been constructed. Meanwhile, the somewhat earlier Book of Durrow has clear textual links with the Book of Kells, and has plausibly been suggested as a product of the same place.[18]

The other pre-Conquest manuscript that might be considered Scottish is the Book of Deer,[19] a small gospel-book which was at Deer (Aberdeenshire) in the eleventh century, but was probably written a century earlier. Its Scottish provenance does not necessarily mean that it was written in Scotland, but it is at least a manuscript for which a Scottish origin may be plausibly proposed. It belongs to the Irish tradition of 'pocket gospel' manuscripts (small, easily portable copies of the gospels), its Insular Minuscule is Irish in type, and it contains the 'Late Celtic' abbreviations found in manuscripts from Ireland, Wales and Cornwall. This would all harmonise with an origin in Scotland,

16 T. J. Brown 1993, ch. 10. 17 TCD, 58: Alton and Meyer 1950–1.
18 TCD, 57. 19 CUL, Ii.6.32.

since by the tenth century we know that Ireland and Scotland were culturally very close, but the possibility of an Irish origin cannot be dismissed.

It is impossible to know just how far our picture of book production in pre-Conquest Wales, Scotland and Cornwall has been skewed by the vagaries of manuscript survival. We may presume that Scottish manuscripts were not really such rare beasts as the (lack of) evidence would appear to suggest, but it may have been the case that Scottish scriptoria were less numerous or prolific than those in other parts of Britain. Meanwhile, the majority of our extant Welsh and Cornish books are relatively low-grade – their script merely workmanlike, and their decoration minimal. However, the accomplished Insular Minuscule and Greek majuscule of *Liber Commonei*, not to mention the magnificent productions of late eleventh-century Llanbadarn, should warn us not to expect too little from the Brittonic scribe.

6
English vernacular script

JULIA CRICK

In Tudor England access to the written word was constrained not simply by an individual's acquisition of letters, by his (or her) linguistic knowledge, but by mastery of script and print types. Those who could read print could not necessarily construe script, while black-letter literacy 'was a more basic skill than roman-type literacy'.[1] When readers in eleventh-century England were faced with a similar visual distinction in the presentation of the written word, their levels of literacy were tested more absolutely. Caroline Minuscule, the script of Charlemagne's court and of the universalising aspirations of the reformed church on the Continent, conveyed Latin text; Insular Minuscule, the indigenous product practised only by the English, which employed letter-forms in use in Britain and Ireland for at least three centuries, served as the medium for the vernacular. The visual separation of languages in the three generations before the Norman Conquest constitutes a central and immovable fact in early English cultural history. By 1000, the foreign script, with its imported letter-forms and technical challenges for writers and, no doubt, novice readers, signalled the presence of Latin. English, meanwhile, remained within a familiar and instantly recognisable domestic tradition: the language written by scribes and scholars in their ordinary script. Insular Minuscule proliferated as writing in the vernacular took off on a scale unprecedented within the limits of former Roman Europe. The nature of this vernacular boom is now relatively well understood: it emerged from the radical programme of the later Anglo-Saxon church – the saving of souls through moral correction in the vernacular, spoken and written, itself the product of Alfredian and later Benedictine reform. Less well understood is its vehicle, Vernacular (or Insular) Minuscule and, in particular, the widespread observance of an apparently voluntary cultural partition, in which Latin and the vernacular are represented on the page

The author is grateful to Professors David Dumville, Donald Scragg and Elaine Treharne for helpful comments on an earlier draft.

1 Thomas 1986, pp. 99–100.

in different script types. The implications of this partition in late Anglo-Saxon England, no less than that which operated in the sixteenth century, touch the acquisition and reach of the written word.

In the regions to the north and west of the former Roman Empire, writing in the vernacular developed by a process of subordination to Latin. On the margins of former Roman authority in Britain, Ireland and Germany (and later beyond them when Christianity reached Scandinavia), the imprint of Roman structures was fading or absent altogether and there was no functioning Latinity, or none apparently accessible to the ruling elite; here churchmen faced the immense practical difficulties of crossing both cultural and linguistic boundaries in communicating Christianity to the native population, not least in educating native adherents to continue the task in the next generation.[2] In all these situations written vernaculars emerged as an adjunct to Christianisation – a mechanism for teaching and learning Latin and for schooling the general population in the precepts of the imported religion. Latin allowed the mother tongue to be reduced to the page by supplying mechanisms – an alphabet, notions of grammar and syntax, and script – in order to render intelligible to the eye sounds which had hitherto been received only by the ear. The Gaels had already pioneered the experiment, acquiring written Latin and then a written vernacular by a process of careful cultivation.[3] German began to be written before 800, within a few generations of Christianisation and the acquisition of Latinity, but it faltered in the tenth and eleventh centuries.[4] Meanwhile, in the group of polities lying between the two (the Anglo-Saxon kingdoms), English was written by the seventh century in the form of glosses to imported Latin texts, name-forms within native Latin productions and, if the testimony of Bede is to be believed, written law.[5]

Common features are to be expected in this extended West European neo-Latinate zone: personnel, expertise, texts and knowledge passed in both directions across the Irish and the North Seas in the seventh, eighth and ninth centuries.[6] What distinguishes Old English from emerging vernaculars further east is the degree to which it escaped the shadow of the host language. By the eleventh century written English had begun to colonise areas of communication which, in other times and in other places, might normally have been reserved for Latin. It served as the vehicle for prescriptive and salvatory texts (law, penitentials, prayers), much translated from Latin, and its use for rendering the Bible – a development unparalleled in

2 Law 2003, pp. 125–6. 3 Orchard 2003b.
4 Green 1994. 5 Bede, *HE*, II, 5.
6 See Law 1982a, Orchard 2003b.

other European vernaculars in the early Middle Ages, even Irish – attests the extraordinary authority attached to it.[7] Simultaneously, the proportion of vernacular texts copied soared relative to those in Latin.[8] The fact that by AD 1000 English vernacular writings were visually distinct from their Latin counterparts, written in a script effectively reserved for the vernacular, signals the autonomy and dignity of the emerging language and distinguishes the development of English from that of other contemporary vernaculars in the former Roman West.

The extraordinary efflorescence of written English in the generations either side of the year 1000 conceals a series of enigmas – largely invisible processes of some complexity. The first is simply mechanical and has already been mentioned. The reduction of a spoken language to a written one, the rendering of the aural as visual meant in effect the subordination of the mother tongue to the alphabet and forms of a learned and indeed imported language, Latin. As with other European vernaculars, Latin letter-forms were adopted and Latin script types used. Indeed, during most of the six centuries for which samples survive in their original form, written Old English looked much like Latin, except for the tendency to import letter-forms designed to express specifically Germanic sounds (æsc, eth, thorn, wyn). We may identify as a second fundamental process the linguistic refinement involved in the creation of a written vernacular. First, Old English developed as the dominant vernacular in a linguistic zone which was certainly multi-lingual; second, at the height of the production and multiplication of Old English texts, a dialect spoken by a socially and politically restricted element of the population came to dominate the written language – Standard Old English (West Saxon) – to the near exclusion of dialectal variants.[9] The details lie beyond the scope of the present discussion, but the creation of Standard West Saxon bears on a third process inherent in the formation of vernacular script: the interface of written Old English with Latin, and the interaction between written Old English and the spoken language.

The shape that English writing took naturally reflects its origins and history. Across the Western European zone outlined above, a series of symbolic systems had developed for representing vernacular languages: runic writing in the Germanic-speaking regions and ogham in some Celtic-speaking areas. Runes served as a system of encryption and were well adapted for name-forms (moneyers rendering their names in runic legends on seventh- and

7 On Irish see Dumville 1992, p. 128. 8 Dumville 1992, p. 132.
9 Gneuss 1972, Hogg 1992, Gretsch 2001.

eighth-century coins, for example) but there is little sign that either Anglo-Saxon or Norse runes were exploited as carriers of complex meaning before Christianisation.[10] Instead it was Latin, the learned language, which provided effective mechanisms for writing the vernaculars – an alphabet, notions of grammar and syntax, and a script. Latin was the language of written communication and commentators agree that at least in the early Anglo-Saxon centuries Latin remained the dominant language of literacy, as it was again in the century after the Norman Conquest, before Middle English began to operate as an effective written language.[11] Writing in the vernacular developed in English-speaking Britain alongside Latin relatively early, in the seventh and eighth centuries, initially unobtrusively to record English personal and place-names in Latin texts, and in the form of glosses to key texts to assist novice readers of Latin, and to expose the full spiritual significance of the text.[12] Written German, Irish, Welsh and other Brittonic vernaculars began as mutations of Latin writing, the fruits of the same 'cultural loan'.[13]

Just as the early history of written Old English is embedded in the history of Latinity, so is its palaeography implicit in the discussion of early Insular palaeography as a whole. Until the tenth century Old English merges, chameleon-like, into the palaeography of Insular Latin (for which see Chapter 4 in this volume) and is exemplified in the full range of Insular script. English name-forms are written in Uncial in early charters.[14] Abbess Cuthswith's ownership of a copy of Jerome was signalled in an English inscription written in Latin letter-forms in calligraphic Insular Hybrid Minuscule, *c.* 700.[15] Copies of the Épinal-Erfurt Glossary made in the Continental mission-field in Germany during the eighth century include Old English glosses scattered among the Latin, using the same stock of minuscule letter-forms (including **uu** and **th**) with only modest augmentation.[16] Even when, in the early ninth century, the vernacular had developed as a vehicle for free-standing written texts, Old English remained within the Latin tradition as a script that skilled scribes could write interchangeably with Latin, using the same set of letter-forms and

10 Page 1999, pp. 212–25, Parsons 2004. On the use of runes after Christianisation, see Parsons 1994, pp. 208–11.
11 For a revision of the extent of its dominance see Treharne 2008.
12 Toon 1992; Gneuss 1990; Green 1994; G. Brown 1995; Parkes 1997, pp. 10–13.
13 The term is borrowed from Green 1994, p. 36.
14 BL, Cotton Augustus, II.2, II.3, II.29.
15 Würzburg, UB, M.p.th.q. 2, fol. 1.
16 **Ð** and **þ** occur sometimes but not wyn: Épinal, BM, 72, fos 94–107; Erfurt, Wissenschaftliche Bibliothek, Codex Amplonianus, 2°. 42.

ligatures augmented by æsc and wyn, a technique mastered by scribes at Christ Church Canterbury.[17]

By Alfred's time written English had co-existed with Latin for at least 200 years. When, spurred by military emergency, he turned to the pastoral needs of his people, he looked to the recent past: 'When I remembered how the knowledge of the Latin language had previously decayed throughout England, *and yet many could read things written in English*, I began in the midst of the other various and manifold cares of the kingdom to turn into English the book which is called in Latin *Pastoralis* and in English "shepherd-book".'[18] The English version of Gregory the Great's *Pastoral Care* to which he prefaced these remarks bears witness to the stability of the vernacular as a written language, not just in the articulation of the sounds of the mother tongue but in conventions for its copying. The scribes charged with multiplying copies for dispatch to dioceses employed their habitual script, Insular Minuscule, lightly modified to accommodate Old English sounds, just as scribes had done in preceding generations at Canterbury in the service of successive archbishops.[19] Alfred also stands at the beginning of a new era, however. In the final two Anglo-Saxon centuries the picture changed: the written vernacular was precipitated out of its subordination to Latin and, as the written language grew more ambitious and wide-ranging, a visual distinction began to be observed between Latin and vernacular writing. By the eleventh century, Latin had parted company from Old English in visual terms. Just as in the nineteenth century Gothic font was reserved for German and Roman for Latin, so in the eleventh the vernacular remained in the native script whose roots are traceable to pre-Alfredian times, while the imported Continental script, Caroline Minuscule, signalled the presence of Latin.

By the eleventh century, moreover, Latin was increasingly overtaken by the vernacular in sheer volume of production. Vernacular book production boomed, at least to judge from the volume of Old English manuscripts, the variety of texts produced, and the effective multiplication and dissemination of the works of Ælfric and Wulfstan. The vernacular simultaneously acquired a new importance in government, the Latin diploma being overtaken by the Old English writ by the second quarter of the century.[20] The force, suddenness and apparent disorder of this riot of vernacular activity have acted to defeat ready synthesis. Examples of vernacular script present themselves to palaeographers

17 For example, Stockholm, KB, A.135, fol. 11r, BL, Cotton Augustus II.64. Brooks' Scribe 4: Brooks 1984, pp. 360–1.

18 Alfred, *Cura pastoralis*, preface: Sweet 1871–2, pp. 6–7, Whitelock 1979, p. 889.

19 Bodl., Hatton 20.

20 Sharpe 2003.

as a sort of uneven but universal deposit, resistant to categorisation or ordering of any but the most rudimentary kind, difficult to assign to centres, often ugly and uncalligraphic.[21] In the ordinariness, variety and sheer volume of examples of Insular Minuscule lies a clear cultural message, however: their lack of order in itself constitutes a phenomenon worth probing. The high period of vernacular script leaves an impression of deregulation and improvisation – a number of idiosyncratic autograph hands and named scribes, a lack of identifiable scriptoria in general, an apparent lack of professionalism in all but a few cases. In this period many vernacular texts appear to have been produced and multiplied outside the confines of disciplined scriptoria where house styles are evident. In those rare cases where a specific subtype of script can be identified, it functions as an adjunct to well-recognised innovation in Latin writing (see below), that is, the development of a late standard Anglo-Caroline.[22]

Meanwhile, major questions remain outstanding. How did vernacular literacy relate to Latin literacy? If Latin was copied in relatively few centres, as has been argued, how widely was English written: were there centres at which Vernacular Minuscule was written but not Latin? Was Vernacular Minuscule written as an autograph script as well as a textual script – a script of amateurs as well as professional scribes? What proportion of texts in the vernacular could be described as acoustic: that is, destined for performance to an assembled audience? To what extent did the readers of Vernacular Minuscule read for their own consumption? Why was the separation of scripts observed so apparently universally? While Neil Ker's masterly comments offer general guidance for the dating of vernacular script,[23] and studies of individual centres and manuscripts offer some purchase in isolated areas, the general territory remains uncharted, and for good reason. We can identify at least one centre producing a distinctive type of script, and several signs of reformed script, two linked with the reform of Caroline Minuscule. Both kinds of development – reform and, more especially, apparent disorder – suggest that vernacular script came to fruition in institutional and intellectual circumstances markedly different from those of previous centuries.

The beginnings of Vernacular Minuscule

At first, continuities are more apparent than differences. The Alfredian project to translate 'books which may be most necessary for all men to know'[24] and

21 E.g. the various contributions to BL, Cotton Galba A.xiv. Dr Peter Stokes, of the University of Cambridge, is undertaking a major study of the script: see Stokes 2006.

22 Dumville 1993b termed this 'Style IV'. See Chapter 7 in the present volume.

23 Ker 1957, pp. xxv–xxxiii.

24 Sweet 1871–2, pp. 6–7, Whitelock 1979, p. 889.

the growing autonomy of Old English did not at first bring radical change to the appearance of texts. The Insular tradition of language-blindness in the copying of text continued (but was challenged) in the tenth century: just as in Irish manuscripts Latin and Old Irish were not distinguished palaeographically so, when large-scale books came to be written in Old English, the script employed was as for Latin.[25] Fundamental Insular scribal habits also persisted. Square and Vernacular Minuscule were created in the tenth and eleventh centuries as set forms of script by means of the upgrading and the rendering calligraphic of essentially lowly grades of script, a process which had produced the higher grades of Insular Minuscule in the seventh and eighth centuries. Square Minuscule displayed its Insular Minuscule origins in letter-forms and ligatures, and a number of these features were retained after its metamorphosis into Vernacular Minuscule.[26]

The break with the past, when it came, was associated not with Square and Vernacular Minuscule at all, but with a new arrival. Two generations after Alfred, in the central years of the tenth century, well after the liberation of the vernacular had got underway, militant Benedictine reform brought not just interchange of personnel and importation of texts but the introduction of a specifically Continental script type, Caroline Minuscule, practised in a restricted number of centres. Scribes in elite institutions capable of mastering the new script realised its potential. The acquisition of a non-native script reserved for Latin created possibilities for visual distinctions to be drawn along linguistic lines, with Old English being represented in the ordinary native script. Thus as early as the third quarter of the tenth century royal diplomas copied in the new Caroline Minuscule carried vernacular boundary clauses picked out in relatively diminutive Square Minuscule.[27]

Within half a century, those English scribes who wrote Latin at all wrote it in Caroline Minuscule, leaving Insular Minuscule as the undisputed script of the vernacular, the carrier for a burgeoning literature of moral correction, legal prescription, erudition of all sorts, memoranda and wills, and of course a medium for the capturing of oral performance, poetic and otherwise.[28] The separation of scripts by *c.* 1010 created a visually distinct vernacular realm or rather cordoned off a separate Latin enclave. The symbolic division between

25 E.g. the Old English Hexateuch, BL, Cotton Claudius B.iv.

26 Forms of **e**-ligature, occasional archaisms like the curling tongue of final **e** or the use of majuscule **N**. For Square Minuscule see Chapter 7 in this volume.

27 E.g. Edgar's grant to the abbey of Abingdon of AD 961 (BL, Cotton Augustus II.39). Archbishop Oswald's lease to Cynelm of 984 exemplifies the spread of the practice to non-royal documents (BL, Add. Ch. 19794). On the use of the two scripts see Dumville 1988a, p. 53.

28 Listed by Cameron 1973. On the end of Square Minuscule see Dumville 1988a.

Latin and vernacular, this 'alphabetic apartheid' as it has been called,[29] is unique to Anglo-Saxon England and, potentially at least, it has important implications. Copyists of Latin are likely to have acquired dual competence: bilingualism is a marked feature of calligraphic accomplishment in this era – many masters of Latin script could practise equally stylish Vernacular Minuscule – and so we can imagine practitioners of Caroline Minuscule as an elite group among the writers of Vernacular Minuscule. Users, however, may sometimes have lacked parallel sets of skills, and the existence of two visually distinct zones may have assisted, or indeed impeded, their access to one or other language. The remainder of this discussion takes the form of a series of observations on the consumption and production of Vernacular Minuscule.

Consumption: aural reception

Early signs of the mutation of Square Minuscule into Vernacular Minuscule issue from a very distinctive quarter: reformist circles in the generation after the adoption of Caroline Minuscule, and, more precisely, among the pupils of masters who had espoused Caroline. Evidence comes from the production and duplication of vernacular homilies. Manuscripts of the homilies of the reformers Ælfric and Wulfstan are recognised as innovatory because they imported into the vernacular a system of punctuation developed in Latin to assist oral delivery of liturgical texts, namely by the use of *positurae* to indicate the cadences of the speaker: the comma, the colon, the *punctus versus* and the *punctus interrogativus*.[30] Equally, they mark a departure from the past in the employment of a large and open form of Insular script which would have been easy to read. Comparably heavy, monumental, rounded characters were used in the late phases of Square Minuscule for the copying of liturgical texts, and thus ultimately for acoustic use.[31] Æthelwold's pupil, Ælfric the homilist, wrote the script himself and his collaborators, copyists of his works, in effect developed its use in the circulation of his homilies. It can be seen in the earliest manuscript of the Catholic Homilies, datable to 990, and in the subsequent circulation of the text, occasionally alongside the work of Ælfric's contemporary and fellow reformer, Wulfstan.[32] This system was extended to the pointing of Old English verse and it is striking that the earliest example of this, the Exeter Book, was copied in a monumental Vernacular Minuscule directly comparable with that used in the homiletic tradition.[33]

29 Dumville 1993b, p. 19. 30 Clemoes 1952, Parkes 1992. 31 Dumville 1993b, pp. 146–7.
32 BL, Royal 7 C.xii; CCCC, 162, BodL., Bodley 340 and 342; CCCC, 419, 421.
33 Exeter CL, 3501. O'Brien O'Keeffe 1990.

The conjunction of new script and imported *positurae* in these vernacular manuscripts is a phenomenon of considerable interest. Reformers preached in the vernacular, presumably in order to reach the ears of listeners unskilled in Latin; the use of liturgical punctuation to assist oral delivery within a monumental script of liturgical proportions suggests the production of manuscripts deliberately designed to assist the delivery of acoustic texts. Here comparison with Germany offers elucidation. Dennis Green has laid bare the connection between vernacular culture and reformed Benedictine monasticism in Germany, where vernacular writing followed the same pattern of development from glossing to free-standing translation to independent text, and where the corpus of literature produced bears remarkable similarities to that of England. His study has many resonances for students of English vernacular culture. He has argued that in Germany the drive to the vernacular gained its urgency from the need to save souls, a fact reflected in the volume of material for religious worship and instruction. Indeed, 'Orality is as unavoidable here [in catechetical literature] as the vernacular: together they represent the only way for *illiterati* to gain knowledge of salvation.'[34]

Consumption: readers

There is evidence, then, that the new Vernacular Minuscule provided a suitable vehicle for acoustic texts, and for the transmission and performance of texts, notably homilies and poetry, to an unlettered or partially lettered audience. A separate question is its readership. To what extent did Vernacular Minuscule constitute the bridge to the written word for readers unskilled or unconfident in Latin? Was it the primary script that the English read and wrote? What was the primary language of literacy in later Anglo-Saxon England? Let us begin with scribes. In the tenth century Square Minuscule was arguably the point of entry for a trainee before graduating to the difficulties of Caroline script and the Latin text which it invariably carried.[35] It would be natural to suppose that, after the separation of scripts that occurred in the early eleventh century, this progression was reinforced. Indeed, all the evidence suggests that Vernacular Minuscule was the native script of scribes and scholars in the eleventh century. It was the script in which Ælfric and Wulfstan annotated their works, it was the script used by one Coleman to record his thoughts in the margins of a variety of Old English texts;[36] many scribes who wrote Caroline Minuscule also wrote

34 Green 1994, p. 97. 35 Dumville 1993b, pp. 21–8.
36 BodL., Hatton 113, fol. 78v: Ker 1949; Ker 1971.

the vernacular in Insular Minuscule and there is evidence of residual Insular practice in the work of some scribes of Caroline.[37] Most scribes probably never learned to write Caroline Minuscule at all, as it was a foreign script difficult to master, and, it has been argued, one practised in relatively few centres.[38] These arguments may be extended. Did comparably general patterns of progression apply to readers? Were inexperienced readers able to cope with two sets of letter-forms and to construe Caroline and Insular letter-forms equally well? The Caroline/Vernacular Minuscule distinction demarcated more than a cosmetic divide.

If, as seems likely, Vernacular and Caroline Minuscule denote two registers of expertise, with adherents (whether as readers or writers) needing to pass through one in order to gain access to the other, this raises some difficult questions. Commentators agree that in the first Anglo-Saxon centuries literacy in Latin was primary. Novice readers were introduced to the use of the written word through knowledge of the psalter, and the vernacular was used as a crutch to assist knowledge of Latin (just as in the thirteenth and fourteenth centuries, it has been suggested, Latin was the primary language of instruction and, perhaps, the language of autograph annotation).[39] Some have suggested that in the period after Alfred the teaching of literacy took a new form: instruction in the vernacular.[40] Alfred's vision was different: 'all the youth now in England ... may be devoted to learning as long as they cannot be of use in any other employment, until such time as they can read well what is written in English. One may then teach further in the Latin language those whom one wishes to teach further and to bring to holy orders.'[41] We cannot know to what extent his vision remained utopian, but the notion of a two-stage educational process certainly maps on to the palaeographical evidence where the two registers of script operated as a visual code: first acquaintance with a realm of vernacular texts in Insular Minuscule before graduation to Caroline script and Latin texts. It has been argued that laymen had access to Old English texts not simply as owners of documents, hearers of sermons and even, as Alfred suggests, readers, but as active participants

37 Dumville 1993b, p. 24.

38 Bishop 1971. In the course of work on a new database at the University of Manchester's Centre of Anglo-Saxon Studies, known as MANCASS C11, Professor Donald Scragg and his collaborators have identified more than 500 different scribes writing English in the eleventh century; he has further suggested in private correspondence that perhaps as many scribes again were involved in the copying of occasional glosses, a category beyond the remit of the database (personal communication, 4 August 2004).

39 Gneuss 1990, O'Brien O' Keeffe 1990, Brown 1995, Catto 2003.

40 Bullough 1972, Brown 1995, Godden 2003a.

41 Whitelock 1979, p. 889.

capable of recording as well.[42] If so, members of the laity would have participated fully in English culture in the eleventh century within the cultural zone demarcated by Insular Minuscule; furthermore, the survival of a full-length Latin *Chronicon* written by the ealdorman of the western provinces, Æthelweard, indicates that individuals at least could step outside it into Latinity.

Production: scribes and scriptoria

It is now time to look beyond the reception of Vernacular Minuscule to its practitioners. Grouping manuscripts by centre is, with a few exceptions, not possible.[43] In the hands of expert scribes, however, the script could be rendered calligraphic and distinctive and thus attract imitation. A scribe well known for his distinctive interpretation of English Caroline Minuscule at Canterbury, the so-called Eadwig Basan 'the Fat', developed in his documentary work an interpretation of Vernacular Minuscule which was no less influential.[44] It has already been noted that the Canterbury version of Caroline Minuscule was imitated at Exeter during the campaign to restock the library undertaken there in the third quarter of the century, but the same connection would also account for the distinctive form of Vernacular Minuscule practised there whose characteristics might be described as a subtle variation on that associated with the name of Eadwig.[45] The products of one other centre may perhaps be identified using palaeographical criteria, namely Worcester from the mid eleventh century.[46] Examples of vernacular script written at Worcester sometimes exhibit particular characteristics,[47] but diverse script-forms occur in manuscripts associated with Worcester and it is difficult to avoid the conclusion that the close-knit scriptorium of Exeter was an exceptional phenomenon explained by particular institutional circumstances.

42 Keynes 1990.

43 Ker 1948, p. 50; Ker 1957, pp. lvi–lx, also Dumville 1994b, pp. 186–8.

44 It is characterised by deeply forked ascenders, leftward-turning descenders, the confinement of **d** within the minim-space in contrast to **ð** which was written with an exceptionally long ascender: for example, BL, Royal 1 D.ix, fol. 44v. On Eadwig see Dumville 1993b, pp. 111–40 and Chapter 7 in this volume.

45 On Exeter see Bishop 1971, p. xxiii, Drage 1978, p. 184, Treharne 2003; on its script see Ker 1957, p. lviii, Drage 1978, p. 174. The forms of **d, s, t, y** are regularly the same as those associated with Eadwig; the treatment of **e, ð, g** often diverges.

46 Ker 1957, pp. lvii–lviii; e.g. BodL., Junius 121: Ker 1957, p. 417.

47 Clubbed or tagged rather than split ascenders, a form of **ð** whose ascender ends in a downward tick, a compendium in which **a** nests above the loop of preceding **g**, an old-fashioned form of **e** in ligature in which the **e** does not bisect the top of **t** but returns to the left in a closed loop. See, for example, CCCC, 265 and 322; CUL, Kk.3.18.

The script observable in the majority of eleventh-century vernacular manuscripts, even those produced at a single centre, obeys few rules. Indeed, in this diversity and apparent lack of order, we may see something new. Many, but not all, vernacular books which contain localising evidence hail from episcopal centres (Canterbury, Durham, Exeter, Rochester, Winchester, Worcester, York), not a surprising fact given the pastoral impetus behind the vernacular revolution.[48] But this was also the era of episcopal empires, when bishops holding sees in succession or plurality are likely to have created connections and moved personnel in their progression between major churches: the see of Worcester alone was governed at points in plurality with York, with Crediton and Cornwall, and with Hereford, by bishops who were significant political figures. New possibilities for mobility of ideas and people would thereby have been created and we should perhaps not be surprised at the jumble of influences evident in the written output of the centres under the direction of such men.

The end of Vernacular Minuscule

Vernacular Minuscule survived for over a generation after the Norman Conquest in a number of monasteries. In or shortly after 1099 a scribe at Winchester New Minster attempted to reproduce the script, managing shaky execution of Insular letter-forms but failing to alter his script to Caroline forms when writing Latin.[49] As late as 1107, however, the scribe of a bilingual writ issued in the name of Henry I preserved a clear visual distinction between Latin and Old English.[50] Gradually, however, scribes ceased to observe a distinction between vernacular and Latin script, and writing in Old English returned to its former position as Latin script customised to accommodate English phonology. By the mid twelfth century, English was still being copied and written quite widely, and arguably functioned as a medium for education.[51] Nevertheless, it was now written in Protogothic Minuscule, adapted by the importation of a diminishing number of special letter-forms.[52]

The history of Old English vernacular script proper, therefore, only begins in the century before the Conquest. At this time English flourished as a written language and the written word reached the eyes and the ears of a wider range of the population than at any earlier phase of English history. The

48 See further Treharne 2003, pp. 168–9. 49 BL, Arundel 60, fol. 149.

50 BL, Campbell Charter xxix.5, employing **æ**, **ð**, **þ** and **7** and differentiating the forms of **a**, **f**, **g**, **h**, **r**, **s**.

51 As argued by Treharne 2008. 52 On their diminution see Ker 1962, p. xv.

Conquest brought recognition of the idiosyncrasy and insularity of this tradition, as Norman (and then Anglo-Norman) churchmen were repelled by the 'barbarity' of the language, its traditions, and, no doubt, the alien script in which both were recorded.[53] As the last native-trained churchmen died out one or more generations after the Conquest, Latin once again subsumed the vernacular tradition. Old English Vernacular Minuscule ceased to exist as a living script, and the language which it had carried found other forms of written expression.

53 Although see Dumville 1994a, pp. 95–6.

7
Latin script in England *c*. 900–1100

a

Square Minuscule

DAVID GANZ

English Square Minuscule is a formalised development of the compressed angular minuscule scripts in use in England in the eighth and ninth centuries.[1] Used throughout the tenth century, it is found in some eighty surviving manuscripts with texts in both Latin and Old English, in some fifty royal and private charters, and for entries (including Old English documents) copied into manuscripts whose main texts are in other scripts. All of these specimens seem to have been written south of a line running from the Thames to the Severn (for examples, see Plates 7a.1–3 at the back of this volume).

In the reign of Alfred multiple copies of vernacular translations were distributed through Wessex and Mercia as part of a programme to use Old English as a medium for instruction.[2] The Latin originals were most probably written in Insular Half-Uncial or in Caroline Minuscule;[3] however, the translations were presumably copied at Alfred's court using the compressed pointed minuscule which had become the standard script for books and documents in Wessex.[4] The morphology of Square Minuscule owes much to the competing influences of all these earlier forms of writing, and to the desire to establish a distinctive

I am grateful to Professor M. B. Parkes, Dr Julia Crick, Michael Gullick and the editor for their comments on an earlier draft. This chapter has benefited from numerous unpublished observations and scribal identifications generously supplied by Michael Gullick; it is not possible to acknowledge them individually.

1 The name was coined by Ker 1957, pp. xxv–xxxiii, and was used to characterise a script type by Bishop 1964–8b. Recent work: Dumville 1987 and 1994c. Discussion of letter-forms: Conner 1993, pp. 51–80 and Lockett 2002.

2 Godden 2003a.

3 Possible exemplar of Gregory's *Regula pastoralis*: BL, Cotton Otho A.i (cf. Keynes 1996a); a ninth-century copy of Boethius, *De consolatione philosophiae* in Caroline Minuscule which was in England in the tenth century is BAV, lat. 3363. I am less convinced than others of the importance of Welsh Minuscule as a model (contrast Dumville 1987, 151).

4 In addition to BodL., Hatton 20 (facs.: Ker 1956b), there are fragments of an Alfredian copy in BL, Cotton Tiberius B.xi and Kassel, LB, Anhang 19. The translation of Orosius, including geographical material from the time of Alfred, and from the same scriptorium as the hand(s) of the annals for 892–924 in ASC A, is BL, Add. 47967 (facs.: Campbell 1953). For the earliest copy of the OE Bede, BodL., Tanner 10 see Bately 1992 and Gameson 1992b and c. Note also the lost fragment of the translation of Boethius once in BodL., Junius 86: Ker 1957, pp. 410–11.

script which did not require undue scribal dexterity, in contrast to the calligraphic minuscules that had been used in Wessex before Alfred's reign.[5]

In the late ninth century there was no obvious model for what a book in Old English should look like. The vernacular had previously been used *in extenso* only to gloss Latin texts, being written to a much smaller gauge between the lines of the latter. When the Alfredian translations were first produced they were written in a small script, close to that of such glosses, using the distinctive insular letter-forms. There is good reason to suppose, however, that the master copy of the Alfredian translation of the *Pastoral Care*, of which a leaf survives in Kassel, was deliberately copied in a large script and generous format (fifteen widely spaced lines to the page) in order to serve as an exemplar for later copyists.[6] Written to a larger gauge, the differences between similarly shaped letters were more prominent. **A** is square with the top stroke slanting slightly upwards; the upper bow of **e** may project above the line of writing; ascenders have a spur on the left side and, in the case of **b**, **h**, and **l**, are topped by serifs. The final stroke of **m** and **n** is turned slightly outwards; the bow of **p** is open at the base; the end of the curve of final **t** is turned downwards; in final position the tongue of **e**, the head of **t**, and the rising end-strokes of **a** and **r** are prolonged.[7] Here the script has the accomplishment of West Saxon Minuscule, in so far as that can be judged from its few surviving examples.[8]

The *Anglo-Saxon Chronicle* was begun in Alfred's reign, and the oldest extant copy (the 'Parker' or 'A' manuscript) is the work of a series of scribes who were almost certainly based at Winchester.[9] Because the entries are dated, it is possible to assign dates to blocks of writing in Square Minuscule.[10] The first scribe copied the annals to 891, the second (who was also responsible for the Old English Orosius and for a correction to the Junius Psalter[11]) those from 891 to 920. The third scribe (who also transcribed Bald's Leechbook and a copy of the Old English Bede[12]) copied the annals from 924 to 946 and year numbers to 955. The fourth scribe copied the annals for 962–4, and the fifth those for 969–1000. Such work and other datable manuscripts (see Plate 22.1),[13] along

5 Crick 1997. In order to distinguish the shapes of individual letters in such scripts, often written to a small gauge, the scribe elaborated the forms of the letters, allowing the strokes to taper to a point.

6 Facs. in Ker 1956b, with comment on pp. 14–15.

7 For a Square Minuscule alphabet copied on the flyleaf of CCCC, 223: Budny 1997, II, plate 104.

8 BodL., Bodley 426 is the best instance.

9 CCCC, 173. Facs.: Flower and Smith 1941.

10 Bately 1986, pp. xxi–xlii; Dumville 1994c, pp. 148 and 153.

11 BL, Add. 47967; BodL., Junius 27.

12 BL, Royal 12 D.xvii; Cotton Otho B. xi: Ker 1957, p. 58.

13 E.g. the copy of Bede's *Vitae Cuthberti* that Athelstan presented to his shrine, 934–5 (CCCC, 183: Budny 1997, II, plates 110–52); a Caesarius made for Dunstan when abbot, 940–56 (BodL.,

with certain notes,[14] and of course single-sheet charters (some by hands which also appear in books) establish a rough chronology for the script.

One must be careful, however, not to push such evidence too far. Understanding of Square Minuscule has been greatly advanced by the work of David Dumville, who, following such indications, assigns the manuscripts to fairly narrow chronological phases. He does not, however, explain clearly which features distinguish the script of his phases. When Dumville groups seven manuscripts, dates them to the early tenth century and characterises them as a distinct phase – different from that of a further seven manuscripts – this is a palaeographer's overview of instances of the script. But unless they were in a highly disciplined scriptorium, the scribes themselves, who may have been familiar with more such instances, not to mention other script types, could have decided to tailor their hands or imitate features for a particular context or project. Dumville also believes that the 'phases' were created and changed in the royal writing office: scribes who copied books imitated the new phases 'because of the status and prestige of what was royal'.[15] However, I cannot find in the manuscripts assigned to his phases enough shared conventions in the shaping of individual letters to link them in a common group, or enough such differences to separate them from manuscripts assigned to other groups.[16]

A charter of Athelstan dating from 928 has an eloquent description of the virgin pen dripping tears of the blackest ink.[17] This reminds us that scribes not scripts are at the heart of this story. Those manuscripts which can be attributed to particular centres may reveal that groups of scribes were trained to form letters in similar ways. But even here the shapes of the letters will have changed slightly over time as scribes taught by the same master were succeeded by younger ones trained under another. While palaeographers, with the advantages of hindsight and knowledge of a wide range of scripts, may choose to group specimens of handwriting and classify it is a particular 'type', such

Hatton 30: Watson 1984, II, ill. 14); the same man's pontifical (BnF, lat. 943); *ASC* B, 977–9 (BL, Cotton Tiberius A.vi).

14 Notably the Athelstan donation inscriptions added between 927 and 939 to BL, Cotton Claudius B.v; Otho B.ix; Tiberius A.ii; Royal 1 A.xviii: Keynes 1985. Chaplais 1973a believed that the scribe of that in the third also wrote charters of Edmund and Eadred between 944 and 949, and this is confirmed by the royal style of the language of the inscription which echoes the terminology of charters.

15 Dumville 1994c, pp. 161. 'From the 930s the phases of change are displayed, indeed for the most part are defined, by the series of documents which can be seen to have issued from the royal chancery' (*ibid.*, 157). My unease is shared by Lockett 2002.

16 'Characteristics of the earlier phases of Square Minuscule reappeared in later phases, after having vanished from the extant manuscripts which were produced in between' (Stokes 2006, p. 129).

17 Sawyer 1968, no. 399 (ascribed to 'Athelstan A'); the formula is repeated in no. 400.

taxonomies have strict limitations. It is far from clear that scribes attempted to write a particular script as such, rather than forming letters as seemed fitting in a particular place at a particular time: that wide variations were tolerated in tenth-century English scriptoria is clearly demonstrated by the occasions on which scribes using Square Minuscule collaborated with colleagues writing Caroline Minuscule.[18] The appearance of the hand may be affected by the type of book that is being copied – liturgical works for bishops, for example, were written with far more stylistic pretension than grammar texts destined for the schoolroom.[19] Furthermore, the practices and the pace of change in a minor centre are likely to have been very different from those at a major one. Since few of the surviving manuscripts in Square Minuscule can be securely localised, it is difficult to take proper account of this for much of our sample; however, brief consideration of the general context for scribal work in tenth-century England indicates its relevance for our topic.

There may have been as many as 200 religious houses in ninth-century England – there are certainly as many in Domesday Book – but during the ninth and much of the tenth century there were few monks living in monasteries which followed the Benedictine Rule.[20] Canons were supposedly equipped with the books to hold church services: Chapter 11 of the Old English version of Chrodegang's Rule assumes that elders will read the scriptures to priests, Chapter 16 that canons will daily read either a chapter of this Rule or sermons, expositions of scripture and other improving matter; Chapter 30 implies that a copy of the canonical rules about penance is available; while in Chapter 32 there is a discussion of community reading in Lent.[21] Yet these communities of canons, who were to be reformed in the last quarter of the tenth century, may have lacked the institutional discipline which characterised monastic scriptoria (indeed, the Old English Rule is as concerned with their drunkenness as with their learning). Even after the reforms of the tenth century, the numbers in a given community were often very small: the *familia* of Worcester around 1010 probably only numbered sixteen monks; Evesham had twelve in 1059,

18 Square and English Caroline: BL, Royal 13 A.xv. Square and Caroline: BR, 8558–63, fols. 80–131; BL, Cotton Domitian i. In later bilingual manuscripts the same scribe may write English Caroline for the Latin and Square Minuscule for the OE: see further Chapter 6 in this volume.

19 Daniel 1973, pp. 4–10 provides a helpful discussion of the problems as they apply to tenth-century St Gallen and Freising manuscripts; her account of different scribal generations is a concrete instance of development.

20 King Alfred's law-code speaks of monks as being in the power of a lord and being entrusted with property which they might alienate: sections 18–19: Whitelock *et al.* 1981, I, pp. 29–30. 'King Edgar's Establishment of Monasteries' (Whitelock *et al.* 1981, I, p. 149) records that in 939 only Glastonbury kept the right Rule.

21 Langefeld 2003.

Gloucester eleven in 1072 and Abingdon twenty-eight in 1100.[22] Communities of such a size may not have had many skilled scribes, let alone the means to create and maintain a 'house style' of script. Nor were they the only members of the 'writing force'. Hemming's Cartulary records a Worcester priest named Goding, granted an estate (probably between 987 and 989) because of his work as a scribe.[23] He was clearly not a monk and may not even have been a member of the Worcester *familia*. Such independent scribes may have been 'freer' in their style of writing than those in regular communities.

A brief survey of notable manuscripts copied in Square Minuscule will suggest something of the evolution of the script, while conveying both the diversity of extant examples and the role of as yet unidentified writing centres in their production.

We begin with a manuscript of the letters of Alcuin which should probably be dated to the start of the tenth century and is written in a very large and rather clumsy Square Minuscule that is consonant with an early stage in the evolution of the forms. Its elaborate (for the time) ornamentation – the opening of each epistle is distinguished by a decorated initial followed by large colour-washed capitals – suggests an important patron, though who this might have been, and where the book was made, are unknown.[24] Probably copied from an exemplar from Tours, the manuscript is a testimony to the early status of Square Minuscule as a national script that was preferred to the putative Caroline Minuscule of its textual model.

Command of the new forms during the first third of the tenth century and their use for a high-status project are demonstrated by a magnificent copy of Hrabanus Maurus, *De laudibus sanctae crucis*.[25] The scribe in question also wrote the second half of a copy of Amalarius, *Liber officialis* (in the abridged version known as *Retractatio prima*), an altogether more modest volume.[26] Neither book is of known origin, though Glastonbury has sometimes been suggested for the former on circumstantial grounds. That Square Minuscule was early perceived as appropriate for volumes of the very highest status is demonstrated by its use for a gospel-book around the same time; the origin of this manuscript, too, is unknown.[27]

Another copy of Amalarius, *Liber officialis* (also the *Retractatio prima*) is the work of a scribe whose Square Minuscule (notable for its use of both round

22 Knowles 1940, pp. 712–13.
23 Robertson 1939, pp. 124–6; Sawyer 1968, no. 1369.
24 Lambeth Palace Library, 218, fols. 131–208: Ganz 1993, pp. 169–71.
25 TCC, B.16.3: Keynes 1992, no. 4.
26 Boulogne, BM, 82.
27 Boulogne, BM, 10; Gameson 2009.

and square **a** and for three forms of **s**) is elegant and accomplished.[28] The same hand appears in several other manuscripts, including a Latin *Regula Benedicti* – which was presumably copied for a Benedictine house.[29] Subsequent indications of provenance would localise this skilful practitioner to St Augustine's Abbey, Canterbury, a centre where, owing to the number of attributable manuscripts, the local development of the script can be perceived.[30]

Datable to the mid tenth century is a copy of Caesarius, *In Apocalypsin* that was written by the scribe of a charter of 955.[31] Moreover, this manuscript bears the inscription 'Dunstan abbas hunc libellum scribere iussit', implying that it was copied at Glastonbury during Dunstan's abbacy (between 940 and 956). The scribe's interpretation of the forms includes a small curved **d**, round and long **s**, and a curl on the end of the crossbar of **t**. Broadly coeval and sometimes attributed to Glastonbury are a glossed psalter and a 'companion' psalter commentary, both copied in a version of the script characterised by an **a** that is closed at the top by a single stroke slanting up to the right, by prominent wedges at the tops of **b** and **l**, and by the use of high **e** except before **a** (Pl. 7a.1).[32] The obvious differences between this interpretation of the forms and that in Dunstan's Caesarius sheds little light on the origin of the pair of books since there is no reason to credit Glastonbury at this time with a single 'house style' of script, and neither is their writing obviously akin to the handful of contemporary exercises that can be certainly localised elsewhere.

Presumptively from Winchester is a vernacular medical collection known as the Leechbook which was written by the scribe responsible for a copy of the Old English Bede and for the annals for 925–55 in the Parker Chronicle – this last providing an approximate date for his activities.[33] If a small elegant copy of Aldhelm's verse *De virginitate* was also from Winchester, it reveals the presence there around the same time of a skilled scribe with a rather different approach to the letter-forms.[34]

A distinctive hand that can reasonably be localised to St Augustine's was responsible for a copy of the Latin *Regula pastoralis* and a volume with Jerome's *Vita Pauli* and Felix's *Vita Guthlaci*.[35] The work is weightier than that of the

28 TCC, B.11.2: Temple 1976, ills. 79–80; Keynes 1992, no. 6.
29 TCC, O.2.30, fols. 129–72: Gretsch 1973, pp. 22–4; Keynes 1992, plate VII. The list of sins on fol. 129v shows a concern with the payment of tithes.
30 Bishop 1954–8 and 1959; Dumville 1994c, pp. 36–43.
31 BodL., Hatton 30: Watson 1984, II, ill. 14. Sawyer 1968, no. 563; Chaplais 1973a, p. 47.
32 BL, Royal 2 B.v and 4 A.xiv: Warner and Gilson 1921, plates 22 and 34; Robinson and Stanley 1991, 19.1.1. Gretsch 1999, pp. 26–33, 264–7, suggests that they might come from Glastonbury or Abingdon. Royal 2 B.v was later at Winchester.
33 BL, Royal 12 D.xvii: facs.: Wright 1955; Ker 1957, p. 58. The OE Bede is BL, Cotton Otho B.xi.
34 BodL., Bodley 49: Ker 1957, no. 299; Temple 1976, ill. 62.
35 Oxford, St John's College, 28: Bishop 1971, no. 5. CCCC, 389: Budny 1997, II, plates 209–21.

earlier St Augustine's scribe considered above, and the heavy serifs, flat-topped **a**, **c**, **o** and Uncial **d** define a very clear head line for the minims, enhancing the impression of regularity. Both the books are adorned with characteristic decorated initials and display script which are further indications of the high standards of the scriptorium of St Augustine's at this time – though this did not extend to imposing a single type of Square Minuscule. An important manuscript for which there is, unfortunately, no explicit evidence of origin or provenance is a copy of Isidore's *Etymologiae* (bks I–X); however, the choice and length of the text and the well-sustained scribal performance surely point to a major centre.[36] Its single decorated initial is a competent specimen of a type generally associated with Canterbury.

The trend to heightened regularity and rectilinearity seen in the *Regula pastoralis* and *Vitae sanctorum* mentioned above was further developed by certain practitioners in the last third of the tenth century – by which time some scribes and scriptoria were embracing Caroline Minuscule. Whether or not this particularly monumental form of Square Minuscule was a conscious reaction to that script, the result was unquestionably elegant. The manuscripts in question include service-books such as the Bosworth and Salisbury Psalters (the former written by the scribe of a Dunstan charter of 962, the latter having calendar cycles for 969–87), the Dunstan (or Sherborne) Pontifical (after 959 and before 992×1001) and the Egbert Pontifical, along with the Exeter Book of Old English Poetry.[37] Such accomplished interpretations of the script 'with excellent forms and proportions [and] a stiff and regimented aspect'[38] were written to a larger gauge than any earlier examples and suggest a new desire to make books fit for public reading and display. The scribe of the Dunstan Pontifical also copied a penitential (see Plate 10.5) and a volume of Hrabanus Maurus *De computo* plus Isidore *De natura rerum* and other computistical texts, which have sometimes been seen, collectively, as a suite of archiepiscopal books.[39] Yet if some of these volumes come from Canterbury and the milieu of Dunstan in particular, others do not: the Salisbury Psalter is from the south-west, as may be the Exeter Book, while the Egbert Pontifical may hail from Worcester or even York.[40]

36 Oxford, Queen's College, 320.

37 BL, Add. 37517 (with Sawyer 1968, no. 702); Salisbury CL 150; BnF, lat. 943, and lat. 10575; Exeter CL, 3501.

38 Bishop 1964–8b, p. 246 on Salisbury CL, 150, and BnF, lat. 943. Pal. Soc., I, plates 188–9; Temple 1976, ills. 57–61.

39 BodL., Bodley 718, and Exeter CL, 3507. The former contains a copy of the Quadripartitus copied from a Breton exemplar: Kerff 1982, pp. 20–4 and 72–3. For the association of BnF, lat. 943 with Christ Church see Rosenthal 1992 and, more generally, Ebersperger 1999, pp. 32–44.

40 Sisam and Sisam 1959. Banting 1989 with Ebersperger 1999, pp. 128–35 and Orchard 2002, pp. 68, 84, 91 and 99–100.

Such trends were by no means universal. One example of an idiosyncratic interpretation of the basic forms which may – on the grounds of provenance – be associated with an otherwise poorly represented centre is a gospel-book from Barking.[41] Probably dating from *c.* 1000 or even later – so a time when Caroline was an insistent presence at the main reformed Benedictine houses – it was copied in a very mannered Square Minuscule influenced by Breton letter-forms (in which connection it is interesting to note that its lection list includes the Breton saints Winwaloci of Landévennec and Samson). Another such case (a copy of Donatus, *Ars maior* plus a parsing grammar) may provide further evidence for the diffusion of Square Minuscule as it was perhaps copied in western England or even Wales.[42] Highly distinctive and unlike any other specimen, this untidy interpretation leans to the left (though **g** has a pronounced swing to the right). Here is an instance of Square Minuscule without calligraphic pretension, clearly copied outside the main centres where the script was used.

One grand Old English specimen dating from the second half of the tenth century has already been mentioned, namely the Exeter Book. Another is the large-format copy of the Old English *Pastoral Care* of Worcester provenance and possible origin.[43] In both these manuscripts the Square Minuscule is large and calligraphic, but there the similarities end: the weight of the letters, the density with which they are applied to the page, and the details of many letter-forms are quite different. The same applies a fortiori to the numerous less formal examples. Moreover, if this Old English *Pastoral Care* was a Worcester book, it advertises a bifurcation of script there according to language, for as this scribe penned his vernacular text in a bold Square Minuscule, colleagues were writing Latin ones in varieties of Caroline Minuscule.

All these examples could be multiplied, but the essential points should now be clear. Widely practised with numerous variations, deployed for all purposes (literary and documentary), for all grades of book, and for texts in both Latin and Old English, Square Minuscule was pioneered and preferred as the basic script of greater Wessex during much of the tenth century. That this should be so despite the availability of exemplars and even practitioners of Caroline Minuscule, sheds a fascinating light on the literary culture of tenth-century Southumbria and the nature of its relations with the Continent. Indeed, at various centres, most obviously Canterbury, Square Minuscule exerted an important influence on early exercises, and coloured the local varieties, of that

41 BodL., Bodley 155: Lenker 1997, pp. 430, 436–7.

42 BL, Cotton Cleopatra A.vi: Dumville 1994c, p. 187.

43 CCCC, 12: Robinson and Stanley 1991, 6.1.2.1, 6.2.1.1 and 6.2.1.2; Budny 1997, II, plate 153.

more universal script when it was finally adopted. If as a book-hand for Latin texts Square Minuscule was largely superseded by the early eleventh century, it endured a generation longer in the context of the vernacular.[44] As, under the influence of Caroline writing, the Old English letter-forms, too, gradually became rounder during the first half of the eleventh century, Square Minuscule finally passed out of currency.[45]

44 After *c.* 1000 it was written in a laterally compressed form with longer ascenders and descenders: Dumville 1988a; Stokes 2006.

45 When used for restorations towards the middle of the eleventh century in CCCC, 57, it was clearly 'revived' as a deliberate archaism to match the original stratum of the book: Ker 1957, pp. 46–7; Budny 1997, II, plates 296–320; Graham 1998; Gretsch 2003.

b

English Caroline Minuscule

REBECCA RUSHFORTH

Caroline Minuscule, 'an almost perfect book script', was developed in Francia in the late eighth and ninth centuries, and takes its modern name from its traditional association with the court of Charlemagne.[1] It represents a clarified approach to writing, tending to reject the use of numerous variant letter-forms and complicated ligatures. Plate 7b.2 demonstrates the representative letters: **a** written in the usual printed form with a curved top part over the body of the letter; **g** with a round top, again as in modern type; **f** and **r** also as the modern printed forms; and **s** written a little like a modern **f**, but with a small hook or shoulder on the left of the letter rather than a cross-stroke.

The clarity and relative simplicity of Caroline Minuscule led to its rapid adoption across a wide area of Continental Europe, replacing a diverse range of pre-Caroline minuscules.[2] However, its introduction to England was considerably slower, despite factors which might seem to have favoured its cause. Serious disruption of intellectual life in England by Viking raids in the third quarter of the ninth century occasioned the revival of learning instituted by Alfred the Great (871–99). Continental scholars and books came to England as part of this movement; thus the opportunity arose, at this time of serious discontinuity of English scribal practice, for the adoption of Caroline Minuscule in England. The opportunity was not, however, taken. Instead, Insular script was revived in a simplified form, leading to the creation of Square Minuscule, the predominant script of the tenth century.

Circumstances had changed in England by the middle of the tenth century. The political situation had been secured by the military efforts, after Alfred, of his children Edward and Æthelflæd and his grandson Athelstan. King Athelstan (924–39) was, like Alfred, famous for his encouragement of learning

For specific advice on this essay and general discussion on the topic I would like to thank David Dumville, David Ganz, Simon Keynes, Peter Kidd, Peter Stokes, and Tessa Webber; and most of all Richard Gameson for being a patient and extremely helpful editor.

1 Bischoff 1990, pp. 112–27. 2 Ganz 1987.

and ecclesiastical life. He built up a large network of cross-Channel alliances by arranging dynastic marriages for his plethora of half-sisters. His court fostered Continental princes and attracted Continental scholars, among them Israel the Grammarian.[3] Two young men in particular spent their formative years in this cosmopolitan environment: Dunstan, later archbishop of Canterbury; and Æthelwold, later bishop of Winchester. They were to go on to become major political and ecclesiastical figures, and were the main movers, with a younger monk called Oswald, in the English Benedictine reform. This movement sought to revive monasticism in England through strict adherence to the Rule of St Benedict; it received patronage from secular figures, most notably King Edgar. Its inspiration came in large part from the Continent, where similar reforms had recently been implemented by Gerhard of Brogne (d. 942) and Odo of Cluny (d. 959).[4] The minds of the reformers were as receptive to the Continental Minuscule as to the Continental ideals, and the script which had been available in England as a model since the time of Alfred at last came into common use. Ideological reasons seem to have played a large part in the adoption of Caroline Minuscule in England: it is particularly associated with Æthelwold, Dunstan and Oswald, and with reformed Benedictine houses; and many of the earliest examples contain texts of Benedictine interest.[5]

Earliest specimens

The earliest dated specimens of English Caroline Minuscule are found in single-sheet charters. The main text of a charter of King Eadwig for the year 956, granting land in Berkshire to his *familiarissimus* Ælfwine, is written in a clear and reasonably competent, though not calligraphic, Caroline Minuscule.[6] As Plate 7b.1 shows, the Caroline forms of **a**, **f**, **r** and **s** were used, as was the Caroline **s+t** ligature, but **g** is almost always found in the Insular form with a flat, rather than round, upper part.[7] Furthermore, the forms of **f**, which sometimes descends a little below the line, and on occasion of **r**, **a** and **d**, show a definite incorporation of characteristics from the Insular tradition, as does the use of tall **e** in ligature with the following letter. In contrast, a charter of Edgar for Abingdon Abbey dated 961 has its dating clause and

3 Lapidge 1993, ch. 3. A donation inscription of Æthelstan in BL, Cotton Tiberius A.ii was written in Caroline Minuscule by a foreign scribe.
4 Bullough 1991, Dauphin 1960.
5 Dumville 1993b, pp. 16–18.
6 BL, Cotton Augustus ii.41; Sawyer 1968, no. 594; Bishop 1957, p. 333.
7 In line 2, *dignatus*, the scribe uses the other form.

witness list written in a very accomplished and correct Caroline Minuscule of round, elegant appearance.[8] This script, which is conceivably the autograph of Oswald himself,[9] uses Caroline forms throughout, including **g** with circular upper body; only the occasional lapse in letter-forms, rather than any sustained influence of Insular characteristics, shows that the scribe was more at home in Insular Minuscule. Already in these two charters can be found much that was to be characteristic of the first generations of Caroline Minuscule in England. Contrasting attitudes to the Insular heritage have produced two different forms of Caroline script. The scribe of the Edgar charter's witness list made a concerted attempt to produce a Caroline Minuscule whose imitation of Continental practices extended beyond the mere use of Caroline forms to the actual aspect and execution of the script; the scribe of the Eadwig charter not only retained the Insular form of **g** but allowed characteristics from the Insular tradition to influence the Caroline Minuscule letter-forms that he used, and to permeate the very way he constructed his script. In his pioneering work on English Caroline Minuscule, T. A. M. Bishop gave the label 'Style I' to script which attempted to reproduce a 'pure' Caroline Minuscule; writing with an admixture of Insular forms, as in the Eadwig charter, he labelled 'Style II'.[10]

Another practice found in both these charters was to become characteristic of the deployment of Caroline Minuscule in England: they each retain Insular script for text in the vernacular, writing the Old English boundary clauses and names in Square Minuscule. The scribe of the witness list in the Edgar charter goes so far as to differentiate between the forms of **g** in the Latin word *ego* and in Old English names like *Eadwig*; this degree of care in switching from Caroline to Insular script became common in Anglo-Saxon charters and in other material containing both Latin and the vernacular.[11] The distinction made between the scripts appropriate for the two languages has been seen as a compromise on the part of the reformers, or as signifying the lower status of English texts; it seems equally likely, however, that it pays tribute to the continuing importance of the English tradition of vernacular teaching.[12]

8 BL Cotton Augustus ii.39; Sawyer 1968, no. 690; Bishop 1971, no. 11; and Bishop 1957, p. 333.

9 Thus Dumville 1993b, pp. 52–3; but Lapidge 1993a, pp. 186–7, thinks it unlikely because of some scribal errors in Latinity.

10 Bishop 1971, pp. xi(–xii) n. 1, xxi–xxii, nos. 1–3 and 11–13; and Bishop 1957, p. 332 n. 1.

11 Ker 1957, pp. xxv–xxxiii; see also Chapter 6 in this volume.

12 Dumville 1993b, pp. 18–19; Dumville 2001, pp. 9 and 13. On Æthelwold's English translation of the Benedictine *Rule* see Gretsch 1973.

Style I Anglo-Caroline

Style I Anglo-Caroline Minuscule reproduced Continental Caroline with all trace of the Insular heritage eradicated, and was frequently written with great discipline. This style often had a 'monumental' appearance, epitomised by the script of the Benedictional of St Æthelwold (Plate 7b.2).[13] It is large, round, and written with a thick pen held at a slant. The contrast between thick and thin parts of letters is achieved by the use of this slanting pen – the wedges on ascenders and minims are very slight or non-existent. It is also quite densely written on the page. This particular type of Style I Anglo-Caroline is so attractive and memorable that it has sometimes been seen as the typically English form of Caroline script, although it is in fact only characteristic of the highest-grade liturgical books.[14] Several of the manuscripts written in this way are associated with Æthelwold, bishop of Winchester: his eponymous Benedictional; Edgar's charter for the New Minster, Winchester; and the oldest surviving manuscript of Æthelwold's bilingual version of the Benedictine Rule.[15]

Similarity between the characteristic aspect of Style I Anglo-Caroline Minuscule and that of late eighth- and ninth-century liturgical manuscripts from Corbie suggests that these may have influenced its origins and development.[16] Caroline Minuscule written at Corbie in the late eighth century, particularly the 'Maurdramnus' type,[17] has a large, round aspect, and Bishop pointed out the close resemblance of ninth-century Corbie script to Style I Anglo-Caroline Minuscule.[18] Æthelwold apparently brought monks to Abingdon from Corbie in the tenth century to teach the English monks their way of singing psalms.[19] Another possible source of influence can be seen in the large, round Caroline Minuscule written at Tours,[20] and in script from Saint-Amand and Fleury.[21]

13 BL, Add. 49598; facs.: Prescott 2002.

14 Bishop 1971, pp. xi(–xii) n. 1.

15 BL, Add. 49598; BL, Cotton Vespasian A. viii (see Watson 1979, II, plate 20); and Oxford, Corpus Christi College, 197 (Ker 1957, plate II).

16 Bischoff 1990, p. 124; Dumville 1992, pp. 146–52.

17 On the early script of Corbie see *CLA* VI, pp. xxiii–xxvi. For an example of the 'Maurdramnus' type see *ibid.*, no. 707; also Ganz 1990, plate 13.

18 Bishop 1971, no. 14; also Homburger 1957, and Samaran and Marichal 1974, p. 269, plate XI (BnF lat. 12050).

19 Stevenson 1858, I, p. 129. The influence of Corbie has also been detected in English liturgical texts: Turner 1962, p. xxvi.

20 See Dumville 1992, p. 149, and *CLA*, VI, no. 837. Cf. *CLA*, VI, pp. xxvii–xxix, and Rand 1929.

21 On Saint-Amand see Bischoff 1990, p. 105, and *CLA*, X, pp. viii–xviii; for a plate see Hedlund 1980, I, p. 11, plate 1 (Stockholm, KB, A.136). On Fleury see Berland 1982; and for a plate Samaran and Marichal 1984, p. 231, plate V (Orléans, Médiathèque, 196 (173)).

Style II Anglo-Caroline

Style II was described by Bishop as 'preserving whatever of the English element would not be objectionable or unintelligible to a Continental reader'.[22] It is particularly associated with Dunstan, primarily because of his so-called Classbook, the frontispiece to which shows the saint prostrate before Christ; this was certainly drawn on Dunstan's orders, and is perhaps his own work.[23] The manuscript now comprises four sections bound together at a later date; three of these contain annotations in a hand which has been identified as that of Dunstan himself. His script is a legible and competent, but not calligraphic, Caroline Minuscule permeated with Insular features. Other early examples of Style II suggest that it probably originated before Style I. A manuscript of Smaragdus' Exposition on the Benedictine Rule shows what is probably one of the earliest surviving attempts at Caroline Minuscule by an English scribe; it probably dates from the middle of the tenth century or perhaps even the second quarter.[24] This manuscript also contains annotations in Dunstan's hand.

Because of the strong association between Style II and Dunstan, discussion of its origins has centred around our knowledge of his career. Dunstan was brought up at Glastonbury; he spent time at the courts of King Athelstan (924–39) and his successor Eadmund (939–46), who appointed him abbot of Glastonbury. He was exiled by King Eadwig in 956–7, but was recalled by Edgar when he became ruler of Mercia in 957. On succeeding to the English kingship in 959, Edgar appointed Dunstan to the archbishopric of Canterbury. Dunstan spent his exile in Flanders under the patronage of Count Arnulf I, and seems to have resided at St Peter's, Ghent; it has been suggested that it was at this point that he became familiar with the principles of Benedictine reform and started to write Caroline script.[25] Alternatively, the formative period for his handwriting has been seen as the ten or more years before his exile when he was abbot of Glastonbury, a time which he is said to have spent in study with Æthelwold.[26] The use of Caroline Minuscule in the Eadwig charter of 956, and probably also in a now-lost single-sheet charter of 949,[27] as well as in the aforementioned Smaragdus manuscript, suggests that Caroline Minuscule

22 Bishop 1966, p. IX.
23 BodL., Auct. F.4.32 (SC 2176); facs.: Hunt 1961. See Bishop 1971, no. 1; Budny 1992.
24 CUL, Ee.2.4 (922); Bishop 1968 and 1971, no. 3; Dumville 1993b, pp. 97–8.
25 Brooks 1992; Dumville 1993b, pp. 143–4.
26 Bishop 1968 and 1971, no. 1; see also Hunt 1961; Dumville 1993b, p. 3.
27 Sawyer 1968, no. 550. Although the original single sheet is lost, an imitative early modern copy suggests that it was written in Caroline script; see Keynes 1991, no. 43.

was being adopted in England before Dunstan's exile and that he could have started writing the script before his sojourn in Flanders.

One remarkable feature of the early examples of Style II (including Dunstan's hand) is the frequent use of a distinctive group of abbreviations. Bishop referred to these as Welsh, but they might more appropriately be called 'Late Celtic', as they seem to have come into use in Ireland and Wales around the middle of the ninth century.[28] These include: a two-shaped symbol for *est*; suspended **a** written in the form of two commas; and a *qui*-abbreviation where the superscript **i** is attached to the top of the bowl of **q**.[29] There are a number of possible ways in which these could have been known to English scribes in general and Dunstan in particular. Dunstan is said to have come into contact with a community of Irish scholars and their books at Glastonbury in his youth, and to have been taught by them.[30] Contacts between Wales and England in the late ninth century are reflected in the strong influence of Welsh Reformed Minuscule on the development of English Square Minuscule, and these contacts continued into the tenth century.[31] Furthermore, political troubles in Brittany had led to the presence of a large number of Breton exiles at the court of King Athelstan.[32] By this point Caroline Minuscule had already been adopted in Brittany in a distinctive manner, offering a model for the adaptation of Caroline script to an Insular aesthetic which might have informed the approach seen in Style II.[33] There was certainly movement of books into England from Celtic areas at this time.[34] Of the three sections of St Dunstan's Classbook that he annotated two came from Wales and one, written in Caroline Minuscule, from Brittany.[35] A copy of Martianus Capella written in Wales, partly in Caroline script, was taken to England during the first half of the tenth century;[36] a Cornish miscellany, including some Insular Caroline script, was probably imported to St Augustine's, Canterbury, in the tenth century;[37] and in the Bodmin Gospels we can see a Breton manuscript of *c.* 900 receiving additions datable to the 940s in Insular Caroline in the

28 Bishop 1971, nos. 3, 4, 6; Bishop 1957, pp. 332–3; Lindsay 1912b; Dumville, personal communication.

29 See Chapter 5 in this volume.

30 Brooks 1992, p. 5; Stubbs 1874, pp. 7–12; Bethell 1971, pp. 116–17; Finberg 1969.

31 See Chapter 7a in this volume; Dumville 1987 and Dumville 1994c. See Lapidge 1993a, pp. 225–77, for Ioruert, a Welsh teacher at Æthelstan's Winchester school.

32 Brett 1991.

33 On Breton Caroline see Bischoff 1990, p. 117; Dumville 1993c. However, it is not entirely clear to what extent the 'Late Celtic' abbreviation system was adopted in Brittany: see Lindsay 1912a.

34 Bishop 1967c.; Chapter 5 in this volume.

35 Hunt 1961; Bishop 1968.

36 CCCC, 153; see Bishop 1967b.

37 BodL. Bodley 572 (SC 2026); see Lindsay 1912b, pp. 26–32.

mixed English and Brittonic milieu of Cornwall.[38] Celtic influence on the introduction and form of Style II seems likely, but whether it came from a particular area or from a combination of places is as yet uncertain.

The compromise between Insular tradition and Continental script found in Style II has been seen to mirror the more flexible attitude of St Dunstan to reform:[39] during his abbacy at Glastonbury there were clerics as well as monks in his community;[40] while Æthelwold, associated with the drastic break from native traditions embodied in pure Style I, drove all the clerics out when he took over the Winchester community, allowing them to remain only if they took monastic orders.[41] Another contrast between the attitudes of these two ecclesiastics can be seen in some late tenth-century liturgical books personally associated with them: Æthelwold's Benedictional is written in a very pure round Caroline, the acme of Style I; while a psalter, penitential and pontifical associated with St Dunstan's archiepiscopate at Canterbury are written in Square Minuscule of an imposing monumental type, an Insular script at least equivalent in grandeur to Style I.[42] Despite these last impressive liturgical manuscripts written in Insular Minuscule, by the end of the tenth century Caroline had replaced Insular script as the type of writing used for Latin texts.[43]

Canterbury scriptoria

Styles I and II, each embodying a different attitude to the script, spread quickly with the political and religious success of the Benedictine reform movement. The relatively small number of surviving manuscripts that can be dated and localised makes it difficult to reconstruct the development of each style. However, Bishop was able to build up two networks of manuscripts, linked by shared scribes, dating from the late tenth and early eleventh centuries: one associated with St Augustine's, Canterbury, written in Square Minuscule and Caroline Minuscule; the other from Christ Church, Canterbury, predominantly in Caroline Minuscule.[44]

38 BL, Add. 9381; see Olson 1989, pp. 66–78.

39 Dumville 1993b, pp. 2, 4, 57(–8) n. 257.

40 Brooks 1992, p. 13.

41 *ASC* A, 964, Plummer and Earle 1892–3, pp. 116, 118; Lapidge and Winterbottom 1991, pp. xlv–xlviii, 32–3.

42 On the Benedictional of St Æthelwold see n. 13 above. On the Bosworth Psalter (BL, Add. 37517), the Penitential of Egbert (BodL., Bodley 718 (SC 2632)), and the Sherborne or Dunstan Pontifical (BnF, lat. 943), see Rosenthal 1992.

43 However, a brief return to the use of Insular script for Latin can be seen in the eleventh century, e.g. in CUL, Ff.1.23 (1156); see Dumville 2001, p. 9.

44 Bishop 1957, 1959, 1963a, 1963b, 1966, pp. XIX–XX, and 1971, pp. xxv–xxvi.

At St Augustine's, Bishop saw signs of an 'active and undisciplined scriptorium'. Here both Square Minuscule and Style II Anglo-Caroline Minuscule (Plate 7b.3) were written, sometimes in the same manuscript. Codicological practices such as the arrangement of the parchment seem to have been left to the whim of the scribe. The Caroline script is a particularly elegant form of Style II, typified in a manuscript of Æthicus Ister's *Cosmographia*.[45] The script is confidently and attractively written, with deliberate and consistent Insular usages. The late Celtic features of early Style II do not appear. If Style II did indeed arise at Glastonbury, as is often presumed, then a possible conduit for its importation to St Augustine's is the appointment of a monk of Glastonbury, Sigeric, to the abbacy there by 975.

The Christ Church group of manuscripts written in Caroline Minuscule, Style II, was seen by Bishop as slightly later, dating from the end of the tenth and the start of the eleventh century. It shows an organised and disciplined scriptorium at work. Parchment was arranged in a consistent manner, with a movement from Insular to Continental practice around the turn of the century, and there is evidence for efficient co-operation between scribes. One particular manuscript, containing texts by Isidore and others, is extremely interesting in this regard.[46] Bishop described it as 'a sound piece of book production ... written by twenty scribes'; he suggested that it 'might have been intended to exercise the powers of the entire scriptorium', which he characterised as containing 'three excellent scribes, five very good, eleven respectable and one ... deplorable'.[47] Some changes of hand in this manuscript coincide with changes in quire, suggesting copying by more than one scribe at once: possibly the manuscript was produced under pressure of time from a disbound exemplar. Another of these Christ Church manuscripts, a Smaragdus, also shows signs that its scribes were copying its exemplar quire by quire, page by page, and even line by line.[48] Equally it has been demonstrated that to facilitate production of the coeval Harley 603 Psalter, its model, the Utrecht Psalter, was disbound.[49] Such sophisticated operations, involving elaborate co-operation between scribes, imply an organised and disciplined scriptorium.

45 Leiden, Universiteitsbibliotheek, Scaliger 69, facs.: Bishop 1966.

46 TCC, B.4.27 (141); Keynes 1992, no. 14.

47 Bishop 1963b, pp. 416–17. Although the size of the community at Christ Church, Canterbury, in the early years of the eleventh century is unknown, this may suggest that a significant proportion of them could write a reasonable hand.

48 CUL, Ff.4.43 (1286).

49 BL, Harley 603, and Utrecht, UB, 32, respectively. See Noel 1995.

Whereas earlier examples of Style II Anglo-Caroline Minuscule have frequent Insular usages, extending to letter-forms and abbreviations, these specimens represent a new type wherein the Insular influence has essentially been reduced to an angularity of aspect. This angularity is produced by bold and slanted pen-strokes, so that minims can look like little daggers stuck in the line. The regularity and discipline found in Style I script has been adopted and the appearance of the script on the page is neat and consistent (see Plate 7b.3). The ecclesiastical and political importance of the archbishop of Canterbury meant that the office-holder was usually translated from some other eminent post: for example, Æthelgar (988–90) had previously been abbot of the New Minster, Winchester; Sigeric (990–5) had been abbot of St Augustine's and bishop of Ramsbury; and Ælfheah (1006–13) bishop of Winchester. It is likely that the influx of personnel with a new archbishop provided an opportunity for cross-fertilisation of script styles at this house.

This harmonious merging of the Style I and Style II traditions can be seen in a number of high-grade manuscripts of the early eleventh century, not only those firmly attributed to Christ Church, Canterbury. Scribal specimens from within the Style I and Style II traditions begin to show an increasingly similar aspect: the Style I Bede at Lincoln Cathedral is written in a smaller, less ostentatious hand than is typical of the grandiose early specimens from Winchester;[50] while the Anderson Pontifical is written in a type of Style II Anglo-Caroline which has gained in consistency and regularity and has dropped many of its Insular characteristics.[51] As well as script from within these two traditions, at the end of the tenth century we see some experimentation with Caroline script in England. Notably, at Worcester a short-lived hesitant and shaky form, with a strong emphasis on the downward diagonal slant, was in use around the year 1000.[52]

Standard Late English Caroline Minuscule

By the second decade of the eleventh century at the latest, a pervasive new type of script seems to have developed from this trend to reconcile Styles I and II, a Standard Late English Caroline Minuscule. Discussion of this script

50 Lincoln CL, 182 (C.2.8); Bishop 1967c.

51 BL, Add. 57337; Dumville 1992, p. 77. The Benedictional of Archbishop Robert (Rouen, BM, Y.7 (369)) may show the same sort of development at Winchester in the early eleventh century; see Gameson 2002b, p. 205 n. 24, and for a different view Dumville 1991, p. 53.

52 Bishop 1957, p. 332 n. 1, mentions a third type of English Caroline Minuscule, 'perhaps to be associated with Ramsey and Worcester'. Dumville 1993b, pp. 68–75, has labelled it Style III in continuation of Bishop's *schema*; Bishop 1971, nos. 19 and 22.

has centred around the work of a particular scribe, who wrote a colophon to one of his manuscripts referring to himself as 'Eaduuius cognomento Basan', or Eadwig Basan.[53] This script has become personally associated with Eadwig, perhaps because we know (or can surmise) a relatively large amount about him;[54] however, precursors of his work can be seen in several high-grade manuscripts of the early eleventh century, as Bishop pointed out.[55] In particular the work of a scribe who was involved in a series of mainly high-grade books, and was designated 'B' by Bishop, anticipates many of the features of Eadwig's script; his hand is highly calligraphic, and he may have worked at Peterborough or perhaps been an older contemporary of Eadwig at Canterbury.[56] Plate 7b.4 demonstrates Eadwig's hand: typical letter-forms are **a** with a thin rectangular compartment; **e** with a small eye; **g** with a little vertical stem between the top bowl and the bowl that forms the tail; **r** with a sharp zigzag for an upper part; and **s** with a heavy shoulder. There is very little difference between strokes written at different pen-angles;[57] however, a high degree of thick–thin contrast is provided by his consistent addition of tapering wedges to the tops of ascenders and bold triangular wedges to the tops of minims. This style of writing spread quite quickly and pervasively through England, so that it has been described as 'generically English' and 'a badge of Englishness'.[58]

If the colophon which names him is to be accepted, Eadwig was a monk.[59] Examination of the surviving specimens of Eadwig's script gives some idea of the context in which he worked. He wrote a charter of Cnut dated 1018

53 Bishop 1971, nos. 24 and 25; Pfaff 1992; Gameson 2002b. The type of English Caroline exemplified by his work has been labelled 'Style IV' by Dumville 1993b, ch. IV, in continuation of Bishop's *schema*.

54 He has a name, a relatively large group of attributed specimens, and even a possible self-portrait in BL, Arundel 155 – on this picture see Gameson 1995b, pp.84–6.

55 Bishop 1963b, pp. 424; Gameson 2002b, pp. 205–6; but cf. Dumville 1993a, p. 124.

56 Bishop 1967a identified further specimens of his work, sometimes in association with the scribe he called 'C'. He associated them both with Peterborough on what he admitted were shaky grounds; previously he had attributed the manuscript under discussion to Winchester (Bishop 1957, pp. 333–4). The Canterbury association is primarily stylistic, although one book in which 'B' wrote was at Canterbury by 1020, the earliest recorded provenance for any of his work. For a possible royal connection see Heslop 1990 and Dumville 1993b, pp. 116–20.

57 This can be paralleled in earlier examples from the Style II tradition, for example in some parts of BL, Royal 5 E.xi (e.g. 12r), and BodL., Auct. D. Inf. 2.9 (SC 2638); see Bishop 1971, no. 7.

58 Bishop 1971, p. xxiii; Dumville 1993b, p. 138.

59 The mangled metrical features pointed out by Dumville (1993b, p. 121), suggesting that a pre-existing text was altered in order to insert Eadwig's name; the layout of the colophon, separated from the main text and with each line in a different colour ink; the use of majuscules to highlight the names, as often seen in charters of this time: these all suggest that the scribe did indeed understand what he was writing (even if he was not metrically proficient). However, on occasion colophons were taken over from an exemplar. On colophons in early English manuscripts see Gameson 2002d.

in favour of Christ Church, Canterbury, and this has prompted the suggestion that he worked in a royal writing office.[60] His two other surviving charters, however, are different in character.[61] One is a writ of Cnut written into a gospel-book; this writ, one of the earliest extant, is addressed to the ecclesiastical and secular officials of Kent from the archbishop downwards, and is in favour of Christ Church, Canterbury. Its survival on a blank page in a gospel-book suggests some sort of institutional context for its copying. The other charter is a single-sheet document, also a grant to Christ Church, which purports to date from the early eighth century, but was probably copied from a now-lost sheet which was one of several forged in the time of Archbishop Wulfred (d. 832).[62] Furthermore, the charter of 1018 shows the influence of Wulfred's documents in that it was written on the sheet in 'portrait' rather than 'landscape' format,[63] which is uncommon in eleventh-century charters but usual in the surviving Wulfred single sheets, suggesting that the scribe's diplomatic context was that of the Christ Church archives rather than that of 'normal' eleventh-century charter production. The 1018 charter was probably issued during the same royal visit to Canterbury as the aforementioned writ. The evidence of his documents therefore links Eadwig rather to Christ Church, Canterbury, than to the royal entourage, and although we cannot tell whether he was acting under royal or archiepiscopal orders when he wrote the 1018 charter, he almost certainly did so at Canterbury itself. All of Eadwig's other surviving work is found in high-grade liturgical books:[64] he wrote the whole of one psalter, two gospel-books, a (now-fragmentary) missal and a lectionary, and added material to two psalters and a gospel-book. The psalter that he wrote in its entirety and one of the psalters to which he added material were at Christ Church throughout the Middle Ages, but the rest of his work seems to have travelled to a variety of different locations very soon after its production, and was probably made for use outside Eadwig's community.[65]

60 Dumville 1993b, pp. 125–7.

61 I exclude the charter copied into BL, Cotton Claudius A.iii, 2r–6r (Sawyer 1968, no. 914), about which doubts have been raised; Dumville 1993b, p. 126 n. 75; Gameson 2002b, pp. 201(–2) n. 4.

62 BL Stowe ch. 2; Sawyer 1968, no. 22; see Brooks 1984, pp.132–42, 289–90.

63 That is, on a sheet taller than it is wide, rather than wider than it is tall.

64 I exclude from his corpus Cambridge, Gonville and Caius College, 734/782a, a fragment of a liturgical book, and the illustration in TCC, B.15.34 (369), a collection of vernacular homilies, neither of which seems to me to be in his hand; on the former see Rushforth 2001, and on the latter Keynes 1992, no. 22. I also exclude the pen-trials in the Utrecht Psalter, which are too indefinite to attribute securely. On the recent discovery of a missal fragment written by Eadwig, see Rankin 2004.

65 See Pfaff 1992; Gameson 2002b, p. 213. BL, Arundel 155, the psalter which was at Christ Church, Canterbury, throughout the Middle Ages, could nonetheless have been a commissioned gift – the picture of the monk presenting the manuscript to Benedict on 133r would fit with a donation made by a wealthy member of the community, perhaps on the occasion of taking monastic vows.

Heslop has suggested that Eadwig, along with scribe B (mentioned above) and others, may have been working for a royal agency producing deluxe books as gifts, and there is certainly evidence for royal and noble book-giving at this time.[66] However, there is no reason why such work should have involved his leaving Christ Church, Canterbury – the Benedictine Rule directs that a monk who is a craftsman should practise his craft and allows that his output might be sold[67] – and therefore Eadwig's script should be viewed in the context of other specimens from Christ Church rather than as a representative of some separate royal writing office. Nor is it necessary to posit a royal chancery position for Eadwig to explain the apparent widespread influence of his script. Although in the tenth century the script of charters and that of books seem to have developed closely together, making tenth-century charters invaluable sources for the script history of the time, a palaeographer approaching the charters of the eleventh century with the same hope is quickly disappointed. One possible explanation for this change can be found in a recent suggestion that the nature of desired and displayed wealth underwent a change in emphasis at this period, away from a simple reliance on large land-holdings and towards more prominence being given to luxury movable objects.[68] High-grade manuscripts, usually psalters, gospel-books and other liturgica, frequently moved through gift-giving between high-status individuals and religious houses.[69] Since these books were at least theoretically read every day in church, they presumably had more opportunity to influence script at a local level than charters, which were kept folded in a chest.[70] This may explain the wide influence of the type of script written by Eadwig, whose work in deluxe books can be shown to have travelled, while there is no evidence that he wrote any documents which left Christ Church.

By whatever means, the characteristic combination of letter-forms and aspect found in Eadwig Basan's script spread throughout Anglo-Saxon England so that by the time of the Norman Conquest its influence can be seen everywhere, in the form of Standard Late English Caroline Minuscule. Although there has been no study of the general history of English Caroline Minuscule at this period, a number of beautiful and roughly datable liturgical books give some idea of developments in script. The letter-forms and aspect are typically those found in Eadwig's hand: the script is bold and round; it

66 Heslop 1990; Lapidge 1996, pp. 37–91.

67 Ch. 57; see Logeman 1888, pp. 94–5 (text from *s.* xi^{med} Canterbury copy, glossed in Old English).

68 Fleming 2000. 69 Heslop 1990.

70 Insley 2002; see Tinti 2002, p. 242, for some evidence for Anglo-Saxon storage of charters.

has strong wedges and sometimes a tendency towards exaggeration (see Plate 7b.5). It can on occasion be clumsily written, and this carelessness can extend to other features of the page such as the ruling and spacing of lines. A few letter-forms appear to be found more frequently in English Caroline of this time than previously: for example, **g** with a small gap between the top and tail; **g** with tail closed by a hairline stroke; and **r** split so that it looks like a narrow **v**. Script is often densely written on the page, and for this reason alternative forms of **d**, **f** and **s** may be used in order to avoid clashes with descenders from the line above.

Around the third quarter of the eleventh century some scribes were writing a script remarkably similar in appearance to that of Eadwig Basan. This is true in particular of a group of scribes working at Exeter for Bishop Leofric (1050–72);[71] that they were not alone in this is shown by a pontifical probably made at Canterbury around the same time.[72] Some script from the second half of the eleventh century is so similar to that of Eadwig that manuscripts have occasionally been anachronistically added to his body of work.[73] At Worcester, St Augustine's Canterbury, and Winchester, we can see an exaggerated form of Standard Late Anglo-Caroline Minuscule, with large round bodies to letters and strong, sometimes 'blobby', wedges on minims.[74] In some manuscripts, in particular two high-grade psalters from East Anglia,[75] there is a hint of the return of the influence of Style I Anglo-Caroline Minuscule, with thick–thin contrast achieved through the use of a thick pen held at a slant rather than through the addition of wedges to a thin-pen script.[76] Some script, as always, remained outside the scribal norms: a little prayerbook, probably written at Leominster between 1029 and 1046, shows a variety of old-fashioned and inept different hands, some even writing Latin in Insular script.[77]

71 Drage 1978. 72 CCCC, 44; see Budny 1997, no. 42.

73 For example, Cambridge, St John's College, C.23 (73); and CCCC, 44.

74 Examples include CCCC, 9 and 267 (for plates see Budny 1997, nos. 41 and 47); BL, Arundel 60 (Watson 1979, II, plate 55).

75 The Crowland Psalter, BodL. Douce 296 (SC 21870), and the Bury St Edmunds Psalter, BAV, Reg. lat. 12: see Rushforth 2008 for the dating of these manuscripts. The Bury Psalter has often been attributed to Christ Church, Canterbury, on the grounds of artistic similarities with Christ Church work; however, its script is paralleled in Bury rather than Christ Church specimens, and it contains a large amount of material local to Bury, making it more likely that it was written at Bury and that its unfinished decoration was the work of a travelled artist. Thomson 1972, p. 623 n. 25.

76 Other specimens also suggest a lingering influence from Style I, e.g. BL, Cotton Tiberius C.i, fol. 202.

77 BL, Cotton Nero A.ii and Galba A.xiv; I am grateful to Julia Crick for discussing this manuscript with me.

Notwithstanding these few exceptions, the reconciliation of Styles I and II in the form of Standard Late Anglo-Caroline Minuscule was the typical English script in the middle years of the eleventh century, with a pervasive influence of both letter-forms and aspect. It remained so until English writing received a new injection of Continental influence after the Norman Conquest.

C

The Norman Conquest and handwriting in England to 1100

TERESA WEBBER

The appointment of Continental monks and clerics to senior positions within English monastic and cathedral communities in the wake of the Norman Conquest provided channels through which scribes came to England in unprecedented numbers. At some houses these scribes participated in sustained programmes of book production stimulated by the ideals of monastic and ecclesiastical reform rapidly gaining currency throughout Western Europe during this period. Their impact upon traditions of handwriting in England was by no means uniform. The total number of Continental scribes involved cannot be calculated, but it may not have been very large. They appear to have been concentrated in certain communities more than others. In some places a distinctive variety of Caroline Minuscule, which had become widespread for Latin texts throughout at least southern England and the midlands during the middle decades of the eleventh century, continued to be fostered, little influenced by the handwriting of Continental scribes. In others, the activity of Continental scribes contributed either to the loss of expertise in this native tradition, or, in a few instances, to the development of new local traditions that drew upon features of their own. The newcomers themselves had not all been trained within a single tradition. Some hands reflect various distinctive local or regional characteristics; others are less disciplined and do not follow any identifiable tradition. By 1100, therefore, the native tradition of handwriting for Latin texts had given way to greater diversity in the treatment of letter-forms and features of style.[1] Diversity is likewise apparent in those scribal practices that reflect a scribe's linguistic (as opposed to graphic) profile: punctuation, abbreviation and orthography,

I am grateful to Professor M. B. Parkes, Dr Julia Crick, Michael Gullick and the editor for their comments on an earlier draft. This chapter has benefited from numerous unpublished observations and scribal identifications generously supplied by Michael Gullick; it is not possible to acknowledge them individually.

1 Ker 1960.

although space does not permit a consideration of these aspects of scribal performance here.[2]

Local case studies, based upon the identification and analysis of the work of individual scribes, are a prerequisite for drawing detailed conclusions about the impact of the Norman Conquest upon handwriting in England.[3] The patterns of survival of books of known origin and the current state of published research have necessitated a focus in this chapter primarily upon centres of manuscript production in which Continental scribes played a central role. But such an emphasis may give a distorted impression of the scale of the impact of the newcomers in England, which may only be redressed when a detailed examination of post-Conquest manuscripts written wholly or in part in English Caroline Minuscule has been completed.

The cathedrals of Christ Church, Canterbury, Durham and Salisbury provide the richest evidence of the impact made by Continental scribes in post-Conquest England. The quantity of surviving books, some containing closely datable specimens of handwriting, and the evidence provided by the patterns of collaboration between scribes, rubricators and artists demonstrate that sustained programmes of manuscript production were well under way before 1100. At all three houses, Continental prelates provided the stimulus for the acquisition of similar texts, and Continental scribes dominated the copying, but the character of the organisation of manuscript production and of the handwriting of the scribes involved was rather different.

Christ Church, Canterbury

In 1070 the Anglo-Saxon archbishop, Stigand, was replaced by Lanfranc, abbot of Saint-Étienne, Caen, previously prior of Bec. He was joined by others, from Bec, Caen and elsewhere in northern France, although more than half of the community at Christ Church remained of English birth. Our knowledge of manuscript production and the character of handwriting at Christ Church in the first decade after Lanfranc's arrival is imperfect. The need for books must have been great, not only to support the spiritual and scholarly interests of

2 Parkes 1994.

3 Few surviving manuscripts can be both dated and localised on the basis of non-palaeographical criteria to the period between 1066 and *c.* 1100. With the exception of manuscripts datable to the episcopacy of Bishop Leofric of Exeter (d. 1072), produced as part of a programme of copying that began some years before the Conquest (Drage, 1978), the published catalogues of dated and datable manuscripts include just three (or possibly four) manuscripts from Worcester, three from Canterbury, and one each from Wells and Bury St Edmunds: Watson 1979, plates 47f, 48, 53b, 54–5; Watson 1984, plates 25–6; Robinson 1988, plates 31a–b, 32, 34.

Lanfranc and his colleagues but also to make good the losses of a disastrous fire in 1067. Letters sent by Anselm from Bec to Lanfranc indicate that during the 1070s Lanfranc looked to his former community to supply some of these needs, although only one book has yet been identified as having reached Christ Church through this route: a copy of the collection of canon law known to scholars as the *Collectio Lanfranci*.[4] By the mid 1080s, however, an organised programme of manuscript production was under way. The books contain the handwriting of scribes trained in both native and Continental traditions, but what is noteworthy is the formative influence upon some of them of the handwriting practised by scribes at Bec and (probably) Caen, and the rapid development by scribes at Christ Church of their own interpretations of such handwriting.

More closely datable specimens of script survive from Christ Church than from any other centre in the decades following the Norman Conquest, among them work by Eadmer.[5] In 1097 Eadmer accompanied Archbishop Anselm into exile; the books and documents that he had already produced, and identifiable scribes, rubricators and artists with whom he collaborated, provide a key to the chronology of copying after the arrival of scribes from the Continent.[6] The earliest products, including a newly identified fragment, can be dated to the mid 1080s. They owe much in their overall appearance (small size of handwriting and generous interlinear space, the characteristics of the capitals employed for the rubrication, the style of the major and minor initials) to contemporary (or slightly earlier) books from Bec, including the manuscript of canon law purchased by Lanfranc. It is highly likely that proficient scribes were among the monks who came to Christ Church from Lanfranc's former communities. Additions supplied at Christ Church to a book containing computistical material include notes in the hands of two scribes writing in the Bec 'tradition' (as well as one 'English' scribe).[7] Another scribe who, in 1085 or 1086, added a letter from Pope Clement to Lanfranc to the Christ Church copy of the *Collectio Lanfranci* after it had arrived in England, wrote a hand very similar to that of the Bec scribe who produced the manuscript.[8] A further scribe, tentatively identified as that of two closely related charters of Saint-Étienne, Caen, one datable to between 1066 and 1077, the other to between 1081 and 1087, copied the second part of a volume containing Ambrose and Augustine, the first part of which was written by Eadmer.[9]

4 TCC, B.16.44. 5 Gullick 1998c.
6 Gullick 1998c; Gullick and Pfaff 2001.
7 Now BL, Cotton Caligula A.xv, fols. 120–53, and Egerton 3314.
8 Ker 1960, plate 5. 9 CUL, Kk.1.23, fols 67–134; Bates 1998, nos. 45 and 54.

The impact of Norman handwriting at Christ Church was rapid. The earliest datable evidence of its influence is to be found in Eadmer's handwriting of the mid 1080s. The letter-forms are small and closely spaced, with a steep pen angle, the overall appearance being somewhat denser than contemporary handwriting in the native tradition. Eadmer rapidly developed his own personal style: elements occasionally present in the hands of his Norman colleagues were deployed as a conscious feature of style: for example, a more or less angled stroke replaced the curved strokes forming the letter **o**, the backs of the letters **c** and **e**, the shaft of **t**, the lower bowl of **g**, and the arch of the **s+t** ligature. The hand as a whole displays a rhythmical alternation of thick and thin strokes depending upon their direction.[10]

Within a very few years, and certainly by the first half of the 1090s, other scribes at Christ Church were also adopting and reinterpreting these elements of style in various ways; their work, in turn, came to influence the handwriting of subsequent scribes well into the first half of the twelfth century.[11] A tendency towards angularity in strokes otherwise traced as curves, and a marked contrast between thick and thin strokes traced in different planes are features common to the hands of several Christ Church scribes. Some scribes also exploited another detail of style: the extension of the vertical strokes forming ascenders in a hairline rising at an acute angle, complemented by the addition of a similar hairline to the base of minim strokes and descenders.[12] What used to be considered a homogenous local tradition, the so-called 'Christ Church prickly style', comprised various interpretations that drew (to a greater or lesser extent) upon common elements of style derived ultimately from the handwriting of some Norman scribes.[13]

Christ Church scribes appear to have been the first in England after the Norman Conquest (and perhaps the only ones within the first generation of scribes trained after the Conquest) to have developed a distinctive local variety of a Continental tradition of handwriting. A combination of factors may have been involved. The scribes active there before the arrival of the newcomers may not have worked within an established tradition of penmanship, whereas, by contrast, the scribes involved in book production from the mid 1080s were operating as part of an organised scriptorium, a product, perhaps, of the renewed emphasis upon monastic discipline within the community in

10 Gullick 1998c, plates I and III; Robinson 1988, II, plates 43, 55–6.
11 See, for example, the work of the scribes of the Dublin Pontifical, TCD, 98: Gullick and Pfaff 2001, pp. 284–94, plates 58–60. For an example from after 1120, see Watson 1979, plate 65.
12 Ker 1960, plate 9b; Webber 1995, plate 14b; Webber 1999, p. 98, fig. 2.
13 Gullick forthcoming.

accordance with the customs compiled by Lanfranc.[14] Also crucial was the role played during the 1080s and 1090s by a small group of Continental scribes who had shared the same training, and whose hands displayed a common repertoire that could be drawn upon by their colleagues and pupils.

The development of a local tradition of handwriting at Christ Church did not, however, preclude the involvement of scribes who wrote differently. A scribe trained in (or strongly influenced by) the native tradition was active during the earliest years of this phase of production: his hand appears in at least six manuscripts, in one of which he supplied a note concerning 1083, presumably in or very shortly after that year.[15] A scribe who wrote a rounded 'English-looking' hand rubricated a large proportion of the manuscripts produced at Christ Church in the late 1080s and early1090s.[16] The production of books was evidently of greater concern than uniformity of handwriting.[17]

Durham

A programme of book production was under way at Durham before 1100, and, as at Christ Church, a small group of Continental scribes played a crucial role in its earliest phase. But these scribes do not appear to have been trained in the same place, nor do their hands reflect a shared tradition of penmanship. Their dominance of manuscript production at Durham in the two decades either side of 1100 did not lead to the rapid development of a distinctive local tradition by the first generation of scribes with whom they collaborated.

Continental prelates had occupied the see of Durham since 1071. Institutional continuity was further disrupted in 1083 when the cathedral community was reformed with the transfer to Durham of the recently restored monastic community at Jarrow. It was not until the 1090s that a programme of book production was initiated at Durham, to supplement the books acquired on the Continent by the second of Durham's post-Conquest Continental bishops, William of Saint-Calais (formerly abbot of Saint-Vincent, Le Mans), during his exile in Normandy, 1088–91. Together,

14 Gullick, 1998c, p. 187; Knowles and Brooke 2002.

15 BL, Cotton Caligula A.xv, fol. 141r. He wrote part of London, BL, Egerton 3314 (originally part of the same composite manuscript as BL, Cotton Caligula A.xv, fols. 120–53), and all or part of TCC, B.3.25 and B.4.26; and BodL., Bodley 827. For his hand, see Webber 1999, p. 98, fig. 3, and Gameson 1999c, plate 14 (reduced); also Gullick 2010. Another distinctively English hand is found in a late eleventh-century copy of a writ of Edward the Confessor (Canterbury Cathedral, Ch. Ant. C 3: Harmer 1938, plate opposite p. 339), but it has not yet been identified in any of the Christ Church books.

16 Gullick 1998c, p. 181; Gullick and Pfaff 2001, p. 291 n. 17.

17 Webber 1995, pp. 145–58.

the imported books and those produced at Durham or elsewhere in England formed a substantial donation of forty-nine volumes given by William to the community at Durham before his death in 1096.[18] William was also responsible for bringing at least three Continental scribes to Durham; they either accompanied him on his return, or arrived very shortly afterwards. More scribes from the Continent may have followed.[19] These men spearheaded the programme of manuscript production that began around 1091 and continued well after William's death. Although at least one scribe trained in the English tradition worked at Durham in the late eleventh century, and the monastic community itself appears to have been composed largely of Englishmen, it is Continental hands that predominate in the books.[20]

Two of the scribes brought to Durham by William of Saint-Calais *c.* 1091 appear to have received their early training in Normandy, but it is not possible to localise them any more closely. From the evidence of a scribal colophon in one of the imported books, it is certain that one scribe, named William, had worked for the bishop during his exile in Normandy.[21] This scribe was at work in Durham in the 1090s.[22] An addition he made to the Durham *Liber vitae* indicates that he was still active there 1099×1109. He may be the William named as precentor in an obit added to the Durham cantor's book. The other 'Norman' scribe brought by the bishop to Durham also appears to have been active there from the early 1090s until the end of the first decade of the twelfth century.[23]

The third of the three scribes brought by William to Durham, to judge from his handwriting, had also received his training in north-western France, though not necessarily Normandy. He has been convincingly identified as Symeon, precentor of Durham in or by 1126, and the probable author of the *Libellus de exordio et procursu istius, hoc est Dunelmensis ecclesie*.[24] He was active at Durham (perhaps not continuously) over a far longer period than his two colleagues (until 1128), contributing to over thirty manuscripts, as well as writing single-sheet documents; during the first quarter of the twelfth century he assumed an important supervisory role. The extent to which Symeon's hand

18 Mynors 1939, pp. 32–45; Ker 1960, pp. 23–5; Gullick 1990, 1994, 1998a, 1998d, and 1999, pp. 88–9.

19 Two further Continental scribes, whose earlier careers are as yet unlocalised, played an important role in this first phase of manuscript production at Durham: Gullick 1998a, p. 15 n. 5, on the first and second scribes of NLS, Advocates 18.4.3. The first is reproduced in Mynors 1939, plate 29.

20 On the 'English' scribe, see Gullick 1994, p. 93 n. 2.

21 Durham CL, B.II.14.

22 He is Scribe B of the Durham cantor's book (Durham CL, B.IV.24): Gullick 1994, p. 95; Gullick 1990, pp. 68–9, and 1998a, pp. 20–1.

23 Scribe C of the Durham cantor's book: Gullick 1994, pp. 95 and 97. For other manuscripts in which his hand is found, see Gullick 1998d, p. 107 n. 7.

24 Gullick 1998a, pp. 14–31, supplementing Gullick 1994, pp. 95–109 (on Scribe A); Rollason 2000.

developed over the course of his earlier activity at Durham might suggest that he was younger than his colleagues. Nothing certain is known of his early career, except what may be inferred from his handwriting. Despite his prominent role in book production at Durham, his formal handwriting is the least fluent of the principal scribes there, and has been aptly described as that of 'a scholar who wrote' rather than 'a scribe who was a scholar'.[25]

The circumstances at Durham surrounding the scribal activity of Symeon and his colleagues were in several respects similar to those at Christ Church. They worked within (or for) a cathedral community following the Benedictine Rule, the basis for their observance being the customs drawn up by Lanfranc for Christ Church.[26] They dominated manuscript production over a couple of decades or more, and their standards of production were generally high. But, by contrast with Christ Church, a shared local tradition of handwriting did not emerge at Durham until somewhat later. The different backgrounds of the principal Continental scribes may well have prevented such a tradition emerging early on. In addition, some of them (and especially Symeon) were prepared to admit a certain amount of informality into some of their work, further increasing the diversity of the appearance of the different hands.[27] This, too, would not have been conducive to the development of a shared local tradition.

Salisbury

More locally produced books have survived from Salisbury from the last decade or so of the eleventh century than from any other English religious house at this date. Around fifty books and fragments have been identified, their common Salisbury origin indicated by the 'homemade' quality of their appearance, and by the recurrence of the hands of a large number of scribes often working in close collaboration.[28] They were produced for a community of secular canons, newly established at Salisbury after permission had been granted to transfer the see of the combined dioceses of Sherborne and Ramsbury in 1075. The community was given formal written recognition in a foundation charter of 1091, but may have been in existence in some form or other from an earlier date. The acquisition of books was one of its priorities. None of the manuscripts is closely datable, but among the group of more

25 Gullick 1998a, p. 23.
26 This text, copied in part by Eadmer, forms one element of the Durham cantor's book: Durham CL, B.IV.24, fols. 47–73.
27 Gullick 1998a, esp. p. 23.
28 Webber 1992, pp. 8–21, 143–57.

than a dozen collaborating scribes at least three had taken part in producing royal administrative records datable to 1086.[29] This evidence accords with William of Malmesbury's account of the stimulus given to book production at Salisbury by Bishop Osmund (1078–99).[30] The order in which the books were produced has not been determined, but the patterns of collaboration, and various signs of haste, suggest rapid production over a comparatively short space of time.[31]

The organisation of manuscript production at Salisbury differed somewhat from that at Christ Church and Durham. Whereas at each of these two houses a small group of scribes were responsible for most of the copying, at Salisbury an unusually large number were involved, coming from a wider range of geographical backgrounds. Of the seventeen scribes whose hands have been identified in at least two or more of the surviving books, six, perhaps seven, appear to have been trained in England, but only two of these played more than a minor role.[32] Of the others, some wrote hands that display characteristics typical of many Norman-trained scribes: generally small in scale, compressed, with a steep pen-angle. They include the scribe who played a prominent role as a corrector and perhaps also as an overall director of production.[33] But at least one had had experience further afield, in north-eastern France or the lower Rhineland. His hand has been found in a manuscript from an unlocalised centre in the northern Rhineland.[34] He is likely to have been trained within or close to that region to judge from the similarities between his hand and those of his collaborators in this manuscript.[35] Other Salisbury scribes may have been trained or worked outside Normandy, but it is impossible to localise their earlier careers. Several Salisbury scribes wrote very informal hands which are even more difficult to localise.

It has not yet proved possible to trace the routes by which scribes came from the Continent to Salisbury. William of Malmesbury's report that Bishop Osmund attracted learned *clerici* from far and wide is disappointingly vague. The large number involved, the quality of their handwriting and the shortness of some of their stints suggest that they were not all full-time scribes, and that

29 Webber 1989.

30 William of Malmesbury: Hamilton 1870, p. 184; Winterbottom 2007, p. 288.

31 Webber 1992, p.16.

32 Group I, Scribes iii and vii: Webber 1992; Ker 1976, plates IIIa, IVb and c (scribe iii: Ker's Scribe A) and plate VIb, lines 5–7 (scribe vii: Ker's scribe B2).

33 Group I, Scribe i: Webber 1992, plate 1a.

34 Group I, Scribe viii: Webber 1992, plate 5. The manuscript is now Utrecht Universiteitsbibliotheek, 86.

35 Such as the form of *punctus elevatus*, in which the virgula (or 'tick') faces to the right: Parkes 1992, p. 43.

some may have been canons or members of Osmund's clerical *familia*. Nothing is known of Osmund's own Continental background.[36] At least one Continental scribe who worked at Salisbury had previously been active at Sherborne, to judge from the addition he made to a pontifical subsequently transferred to Salisbury. The addition includes a form for the benediction of a monk, which refers specifically to the monastery at Sherborne.[37] Continental scribes may therefore have been working in the vicinity before a community had become established at Salisbury, and perhaps even before Osmund's appointment in 1078. His predecessor, Hereman (appointed bishop of Ramsbury in 1045 and jointly bishop of Sherborne in 1058 or 1059), was a Lotharingian appointee of Edward the Confessor, and is known to have attracted at least one foreigner to England – the hagiographer, Goscelin, formerly monk of Saint-Bertin in Flanders.[38] Given the diverse backgrounds of the Salisbury scribes, it is not surprising that a local tradition of penmanship failed to emerge. Here too, as at Christ Church, Canterbury, the distinctive English tradition was soon all but gone. Of the group of scribes who collaborated in a second phase of manuscript production at Salisbury during the first quarter of the twelfth century, the hand of only one exhibits obvious characteristics of that tradition.[39]

The handwriting of the Salisbury scribes differs from that of the scribes active at Durham and Christ Church, not only in its geographical range but also in a wider spectrum of formality and expertise. Most striking is the prominent role played by scribes whose hands include several features of rapid, or more simplified 'economical' handwriting. For example, they permitted the shafts of **f**, **r** and long **s** to extend below the ruled line, and paid scant attention either to maintaining an even height, spacing and alignment of letter-forms and their constituent elements or to the execution of the auxiliary features, such as approach and finishing strokes. Some scribes evidently viewed formal and informal handwriting as different grades of Caroline Minuscule, and reserved the latter for corrections, additions and annotations in books, and for routine administrative purposes.[40] But others, at Salisbury and elsewhere, appear to have lacked the ability, the necessary training, or the experience to write a formal hand with consistency, and wrote in a more simplified or rapid fashion even

36 Kemp 1999, pp. xxxiv–xxxv.

37 Group I, Scribe v: Ker 1959, pp. 268–9 (scribe VIII).

38 Barlow 1992, pp. xlviii–xlix.

39 Group II, Scribe 11: Webber 1992, plate 10. Note the upright stroke forming the right-hand side of **a**, the 'reverse-c' form of the lower part of **g**, and the trailing lower limb of **x**.

40 Group I, Scribe iii (Ker's Scribe A). The informality of his hand in the Wiltshire geld account contrasts with the greater formality of his book-hand: Ker 1976, plate IIIa (Wiltshire geld account) and plate IVb–c (a Salisbury book).

when copying books. Some of them could write with great fluency and even panache,[41] but the hands of others exhibit a clumsiness or rudimentary quality little more expert than the rudimentary handwriting of those who could trace the basic elements of each letter, but could not write at length.

The existence of a spectrum of formality and competence, and the perception that different grades of formality were appropriate in different contexts, were by no means new phenomena. But the English evidence of informal handwriting is more prevalent from the late eleventh century onwards, especially in royal documents that survive in greater numbers from this period.[42] The two surviving circuit returns of the Domesday survey, Little Domesday Book and Exon Domesday, provide numerous examples of scribes, Continental and English, writing such hands.[43] The Salisbury manuscripts are an important witness to the role of such scribes in book production, but they are not exceptional. The hand of the main scribe of Domesday Book, for example, has also been identified in communally owned books.[44] It may only be the accident of survival that has permitted the identification of this scribe and the 'Salisbury' scribes of the Wiltshire geld accounts and of Exon Domesday in non-administrative contexts. One might speculate that some at least of the scribes of Little Domesday Book undertook similar activity, but that the relevant books have not survived.

Norman (or Norman-trained) scribes have been identified in manuscripts produced at a number of other religious houses in England before or around 1100: at Abingdon; St Augustine's, Canterbury; Rochester; at the New Minster, Winchester; and perhaps also at St Albans.[45] Unfortunately it is not yet possible to trace their activity and impact with precision. In the case of Abingdon, the New Minster, and St Albans, too few manuscripts survive to assess the extent of the role played by these scribes or to gauge their influence upon those with whom they collaborated. A copy of the gospels was made by Norman scribes at Abingdon for Abbot Rainald (1087–97) as a gift for his former community at Jumièges,[46] but only one other manuscript survives that

41 For example, Salisbury Group I, Scribe ii: Webber 1992, plate 1b. Despite the variations in the formation of the lower part of **g** and the rough manner in which vertical serifs have been added to ascenders of letters such as **b**, **d**, **h** and **l**, his hand displays a fluency of movement characteristic of the practised scribe.

42 Bishop 1961, pp. 6–7.

43 Rumble 1987; Webber 1989; Robinson 2003, plates 4–6.

44 Gullick 1987, pp. 102, 105.

45 Gullick 1999, pp. 85–9. Continental hands are also found, sometimes in collaboration with English scribes, in manuscripts owned by a number of other religious houses (such as Exeter), but their place of production has not yet been established. On the Exeter manuscripts, see Gameson 1999d; Thomson 2006, pp. 48–54, 101–4.

46 Rouen, BM, A.21 (32).

might possibly have been produced there before 1100.[47] Just one manuscript produced at the New Minster at Winchester during the later eleventh century is known to survive: a psalter datable to 1073, one year after the appointment of a Continental abbot, Riwallon, previously a monk of Mont Saint-Michel, but originally from neighbouring Brittany, to judge from his name.[48] A Norman scribe whose hand has been identified in additions to earlier books from the New Minster supplied a lengthy correction to this manuscript, but the original scribes of the manuscript all wrote firmly within the native English tradition.[49] Additions to the New Minster *Liber vitae* that record the names of new members of the community between the accession of Riwallon in 1072 and Hugh in 1100 are written by scribes trained in both English and Norman traditions.[50] Distinctively English hands, however, are absent from the entries that probably correspond to the later years of Riwallon's abbacy and to the abbacy of Robert Losinga (*c.* 1090–8), and are also largely absent from the post-Conquest additions made to the list of men and women in confraternity with the New Minster.[51] St Albans tradition records that its first Norman abbot, Paul, a nephew of Lanfranc, instituted a major programme of book production, hiring professional scribes and drawing upon exemplars loaned by Lanfranc.[52] Sadly, only a tiny group of late eleventh-century books survives from St Albans (not all of which were necessarily made there) – insufficient to make any detailed assessment of the role or influence of Continental scribes.[53] A Norman scribe who may have worked there (he copied a manuscript rubricated by a scribe found in other St Albans books) was, to judge from the presence of his hand in books from Durham and Exeter, an itinerant who may have stayed only a short while.[54]

Larger numbers of manuscripts dating from before or around 1100 survive from St Augustine's, Canterbury, and from Rochester. They contain the handwriting of both scribes trained in Normandy (at Bec or Caen, Mont Saint-Michel and elsewhere) and scribes writing their own interpretations of such

47 BL, Harley 3061, reproduced in Gameson 1999c, plate 16. According to Abingdon tradition, book production in the post-Conquest period was only organised there on a large scale from the abbacy of Fabricius (1100–17), when additional scribes were hired to undertake the task of copying a quantity of patristic texts: Sharpe *et al.* 1996, pp. 4–7.

48 BL, Arundel 60; Keynes 1996b, p. 115 n. 47.

49 Gullick 1999, p. 89. The hand of the Norman scribe is reproduced in Keynes 1996b, fols. 41r and 59r.

50 BL, Stowe 944.

51 Keynes 1996b, fols. 22r–v, 28v, 29r, plates VIII and IX. For the identity of some of those named, *ibid.* pp. 91–2, 97–8.

52 Riley 1867–9, I, pp. 57–8.

53 Thomson 1985, I, pp. 11–14; Gullick 1998b, p. 20 n. 43.

54 Gullick 1999, p. 89; Gullick 1998b, pp. 7, 20, nn. 42–4.

handwriting.[55] At St Augustine's, these scribes worked alongside others who were still writing what, by the 1090s, was a very conservative variety of the late Anglo-Saxon tradition of Caroline Minuscule.[56]

The presence in England of Continental scribes whose hands reflect training or experience outside Normandy has received very little attention, but they too contributed to the diversity of writing during the late eleventh and early twelfth century. Scribes from north-eastern France or the lower Rhineland have been found at Salisbury, in a charter of 1085 of the Lotharingian bishop of Hereford, Robert (1079–95), and in two manuscripts now associated with Hereford.[57] Two (perhaps the earliest) of a related group of nine late eleventh- or early twelfth-century manuscripts with a Bath provenance (probably locally made) contain pen-drawn initials distinctive of manuscripts from the Meuse region.[58] These initials and the accompanying rubrics are almost certainly the work of the principal scribe of these two books, who therefore probably came from this region.

The majority of scribes working in England between the Conquest and 1100 are likely to have received their formative training in England, some of them before the arrival of significant numbers of Continental scribes, others after. Many late eleventh- or early twelfth-century manuscripts survive that contain the hands of scribes writing in the distinctive late Anglo-Saxon tradition of Caroline Minuscule apparently uninfluenced by Continental handwriting. The native tradition was certainly maintained in the late eleventh century at Worcester,[59] at Bury St Edmunds,[60] and perhaps also at the Old Minster, Winchester.[61] The same may be true of several other religious houses, especially in western England and the Fenlands, to judge from the somewhat meagre survivals. Much work remains to be done on these patchy remains, but it will be a difficult task, both because of the loss of manuscripts and our inability to localise closely many of those that have survived.[62] The hands of other

55 Watson 1979, plate 58 (St Augustine's), plate 60 (Rochester); Waller 1984.

56 For example, the scribe of CCCC, 270, datable 1091×1100: Robinson 1988, II, plate 34.

57 Hereford CL, O.VIII.8 and additions to BL, Cotton Nero C.v : Gullick 2001b.

58 London, BL, Royal 5 B.ii and 6 B.ii; Warner and Gilson 1921, IV, plates 40a and 45c; Gullick 2001b, pp. 107–8.

59 Ker 1985; McIntyre 1978; Gullick 1996; Gameson 1996a; Gameson 2005.

60 Bishop 1949–53, p. 434; Bishop 1954–8, pp. 185–7; Watson 1979, II, plate 54.

61 Very few late eleventh- or early twelfth-century manuscripts of Winchester origin are known to have survived, but the same scribe, writing an 'English' hand, has been identified in three manuscripts (BodL., Bodley 126, Winchester CL, 2, and Winchester College, 5), the last of which was at the cathedral by at least the early fourteenth century.

62 Thomas of Marlborough claimed that Walter, abbot of Evesham (1078–1104), 'libros multos fecit' (Sayers and Watkiss 2003, p. 178); a single fragment survives from this period as part of a twelfth-century Evesham binding (Oxford, Jesus College, 51, fol. 1). An inventory from Ely *c.* 1093 records

scribes, however, while betraying an English background in certain features, display a variety of differences in others, such as the form of individual letters, pen angle, and details of style. Some had ceased to employ the characteristic forms and stylistic features of the native tradition to such an extent that their background may no longer be recognisable from their graphic profile alone. Unfortunately, the paucity of scribes of known English background for whom closely datable specimens survive (whether in books or documents), means that there are few cases where it is possible to chart developments within an individual hand or to trace the various circumstances which contributed to shaping those developments. In most instances the process of development is unclear. For example, the hand of one of the two main scribes at Salisbury whose hands indicate an English training (Group I, Scribe iii), exhibits a number of differences from the distinctive native tradition represented in 'purer' form by the hand of the other 'English' scribe (Group I, Scribe vii). In addition to forming certain letters differently (most notably the letter **a**), he wrote with a steeper pen angle and a broader nib, so that the contrast between thick and thin strokes is more marked. Calligraphic details distinctive of the native tradition (flat-topped serifs on ascenders and near horizontal serifs on the feet of minims), present in the hand of his colleague, are absent from his own. Perhaps he was a younger scribe who had become exposed to different traditions of writing while still in the formative stage of his career. Or perhaps his colleague had been trained in a centre in which there was a strong tradition of penmanship, whereas he had not, but had developed his own personal hand independently. Either suggestion must remain speculative.

Two further general considerations need to be borne in mind. First, an analysis of handwriting that proceeds from the study of locatable and datable manuscripts and the identification of patterns of collaboration between scribes, artists and rubricators is the most secure means of approach. But it may lead us to underestimate the part played in the development of handwriting by itinerant scribes who were attached only briefly to any one place where manuscripts were produced. Itinerant 'professional' scribes may have been more numerous in this period than their presence in surviving records suggests.[63] We know still less about how such scribes were trained, the circumstances that shaped the character of their hands, and the influence they may have exercised upon those with whom they worked.

287 volumes, but few pre-twelfth-century books of known Ely ownership are known to have survived; none dates from the late eleventh century: Sharpe *et al.* 1996, p. 127.

63 Gullick 1998b, pp. 1–24.

Second, the characteristics of the handwriting of scribes active in England in this period should not be assessed solely within the context of the Norman Conquest and its aftermath. The channels provided by foreign ecclesiastics appointed by William I were not the only ones through which scribes (and books) entered England from the Continent. Continental handwriting often acted as a source of inspiration and precedent for English scribes in the centuries before and after the Conquest. Furthermore, new generations of scribes might write differently from their seniors even without the inspiration provided by other traditions of handwriting. A systematic analysis of the scribes and handwriting of the books produced at Worcester during the second half of the eleventh century may offer the best opportunity for discerning such processes at work in a centre in which manuscript production was sustained at a fairly high level over an extended period of time, and where Continental scribes played little role.

English manuscripts survive from the last third of the eleventh century in larger numbers than in any equivalent period dealt with in this volume.[64] Nevertheless our understanding of how and where they were produced, and the factors that shaped the character of their handwriting, is still imperfect. The origin of more than half is still unknown, and the great majority of those whose origin has been established come from just six or seven religious houses: Bury St Edmunds, Christ Church and St Augustine's Canterbury, Durham, Salisbury, Worcester and perhaps Exeter. The losses are, of course, incalculable. While it is always tempting, especially in a survey, to emphasise the positive, we must acknowledge that our attempts to draw palaeographical or other conclusions from what has survived must be based upon as firm a grasp of the gaps in our knowledge as upon what we think we know.

64 Between 184 and 329 manuscripts produced in or imported to England between the Conquest and *c.* 1100 are estimated to have survived (the higher number includes books datable as *s.* xi/xii): Gameson 1999c, p. 5.

8

The design and decoration of Insular gospel-books and other liturgical manuscripts, *c.* 600 – *c.* 900

NANCY NETZER

Gospel-books produced in Ireland, Britain and Insular centres on the Continent between about AD 600 and 900 constitute an important phase in the history of medieval book design. Often elaborately decorated and written in formal script, these impressive witnesses to the sacred and authoritative nature of Christ's words and actions, were essential to every stage of Christian learning (see Plates 8.1–3). They supplied spiritual truth to those who studied them privately as well as to those who listened to a passage read daily from the altar during the service. When carried in church processions, they served as a tangible embodiment of the faith, especially for recent, probably illiterate, converts.

From the fourth to the seventh century a gradual process of conversion to Christianity introduced the peoples of Ireland and Britain to a comprehensive system of literacy and spawned the demand for books required to practise the liturgy. As a result, a large number of gospel-books must have been produced; most do not survive. One indication of how prolific such production might have been in Ireland is found in the Book of Armagh written in 807.[1] Primarily a New Testament, the manuscript also contains a series of notes relating to St Patrick (that may have been displaced from a seventh-century text) including a list of books – among which are copies of the gospels – that Patrick dispersed to a notable fifty new churches. For England, conservative estimates of production may be guided by the number of ecclesiastical foundations – more than 200 by the mid ninth century – each of which would have possessed at least one copy of the gospels. Larger foundations would have had several examples, and some ecclesiastics may have had personal copies.[2] Most of these volumes must have been working copies, like the Royal Gospels, a codex of modest size (about 280 × 220 mm) probably datable to the second quarter

1 TCD, 52. 2 Gameson 1994, pp. 43–5.

of the eighth century.[3] Such functional books were simply ornamented with the goal of facilitating use, aiding readability and marking the most important passages clearly. Rather than being protected and preserved, these copies were pressed into service daily, accounting for their poor rate of survival even though they comprised the vast majority of Insular gospel-books. Thus, the extant sample of Insular liturgical books is probably skewed in favour of the large and resplendent, which, far from the norm, were prized and subject to less use. Although innovative and influential in their design and execution, these ceremonial gospel-books, the focus of the following discussion, were relatively unknown to the populace as a whole.[4]

In this period, the church was structured around monasteries. As centres of economic activity, monasteries undertook to meet the demand for books by importing them from the Continent[5] to serve as exemplars for copying and by establishing scriptoria on their premises and making them themselves. Scribe–artists seem to have had high standing. Although their names appear in annals and colophons,[6] unfortunately this information can rarely be used to assign a manuscript to a specific monastery at a certain date. As a result, there has been much controversy over the dating and localisation of many of these codices.[7]

The group of existing Insular liturgical books from this period comprises over sixty-five examples. The vast majority are gospel-books[8] with the addition of a few psalters, bibles, and a handful of individual books from the Old or New Testament. Some survive only as fragments of a few leaves; others are complete volumes. Several are of large size with elaborate decoration, while nine are smaller portable 'pocket' volumes, ranging in size from 175 × 142 mm to 125 × 112 mm, presumably made for personal use and carried in satchels.[9] These Insular manuscripts display greater variety in their layouts, scripts and decorations than the Mediterranean counterparts which served as their immediate or ultimate exemplars. Moreover, Insular gospel-books introduce several novel features, to be discussed below.

With few literary sources to illuminate the manner in which these manuscripts were made, used and received, theories on such matters rely on the detailed study of the codices themselves. Enquiry into these books began

3 BL, Royal 1 B.vii; see Gameson 1994; and Brown 2003b.
4 Gameson 1994, pp. 48–9, 52.
5 Gameson 1999b, pp. 313–26. CCCC, 286 and BodL., Auct. D.II.14 are extant examples.
6 For discussion and a catalogue of colophons in early English manuscripts see Gameson 2002d.
7 An obstacle compounded by the competition of scholarly nationalism: Netzer 1999a, pp. 315–26, and 2001, pp. 169–77; Withers 2000.
8 See McGurk 1961.
9 Discussed in McGurk 1956, pp. 249–70, esp. 250; 1987, pp. 165–19; Brown 1969.

in earnest in the nineteenth century when their splendour was employed as evidence of the high state of civilisation in the British Isles (and especially in Ireland) in the early Middle Ages and when the most elaborate examples began to play key roles in histories of medieval art in general. As early as the mid nineteenth century distinctive characteristics of the books' decoration – various interlaced, curvilinear, geometric and zoomorphic patterns, some with their roots in indigenous Celtic La Tène designs – were distinguished and matched to contemporary works in stone sculpture and metalwork.[10] In the mid twentieth century, scholars like E. A. Lowe, T. J. Brown and Carl Nordenfalk[11] looked more systematically at the scripts, codicology and decoration of the books to construct a chronological development based on style of script and decoration, and to connect some to specific centres.

Nearly a century of such enquiry has resulted in consensus that the earliest of the extant Insular liturgical manuscripts is the damaged and fragmentary Codex Usserianus Primus.[12] Usually dated to the late sixth or, more probably, early seventh century,[13] the manuscript stands apart from the later Insular gospel-books in both script and text. It was written by two scribes in a Half-Uncial similar to that found in two seventh-century manuscripts[14] from Bobbio (the northern Italian monastery founded by the Irish missionary Columbanus in about 613–14) and two extracts from the psalms written on wooden wax tablets found at Springmount Bog in County Antrim in Ireland.[15] It contains an Old Latin text, the version which circulated in Ireland before Jerome's Vulgate began to replace it in the second half of the seventh century.[16] In this early translation, the evangelists' texts are arranged according to Irenaeus' order: Matthew, John, Luke, Mark. Nonetheless, Usserianus Primus includes a series of chapter lists and divisions (so-called Family I) as well as a list of Hebrew names that become characteristic of later Insular gospel-books.[17] Otherwise, the manuscript is more closely linked to forms of book production in the late antique world and displays few distinctive Insular traits.[18] Its size,

10 Netzer 2001, pp. 169–77.

11 *CLA*, I–XI, plus *Supplement*; Brown 1993; Verey *et al.* 1980; Brown 1969; Kendrick *et al.* 1960; and Nordenfalk 1947, pp. 141–74; and 1977.

12 TCD, 55.

13 Dumville, 1999, esp. pp. 36–40, has proposed on the basis of limited evidence of the fifth-century origins of the Half-Uncial script that this and other of the earliest surviving Insular manuscripts could be as early as the fifth century.

14 Milan, Biblioteca Ambrosiana, C.26. sup and D.23. sup; *CLA*, III, nos. 312 and 328.

15 National Museum of Ireland 4–1914.2. Charles-Edwards 2002, pp. 27–45.

16 De Hamel 2001, pp. 13–39.

17 McGurk 1961, pp. 13, 79.

18 Its adherence to the decoration and layout of gospel-books in the Latin West between about AD 400 and 650 has led to debate about whether the book was made in Ireland or imported there in the seventh century (when it was glossed in dry-point) from Bobbio or another Continental centre; see Dumville 1999, pp. 36–40.

with a written area of about 175 × 120–30 mm, distinguishes it from both the smaller Insular pocket gospels and the considerably larger decorated volumes. The volume's only remaining ornamentation marks the transition between Luke's and Mark's Gospels with a Chi-rho and Alpha and Omega symbols within triple rectangles of alternating brown curved strokes and red dots. Projecting semi-circles on the corners and red dots surrounding the monogram are the only elements that presage later developments in Insular decoration. Lack of word division within the single text block, which would require meaning be extracted from oral recitation,[19] reinforces the belief that these books were read aloud, probably from the altar to an audience during the liturgy. A series of dry-point glosses were added in a seventh-century Irish hand. Several provide alternative readings from a Vulgate edition; others appear to be personal notes, probably used as verbal cues for the glossator in teaching, suggesting that the book was used by this stage for study (as well as preaching) and providing clues to the working process of a biblical scholar in Ireland in the seventh century.[20]

The next 'signpost' among the early Insular liturgical manuscripts – and the earliest of undisputed Irish origin – is a damaged and incomplete Gallican Vulgate version of the psalms (30.10–105.13 remain), each preceded by an interpretative rubric, known as the Cathach of St Columba.[21] Psalters, as separate volumes, became more common in the seventh and eighth centuries. The lengthiest of biblical books, the psalms were memorised by aspiring religious and recited daily in the monastic cycle of prayer. Five other deluxe Insular examples survive: three probably produced in England – the Vespasian,[22] Lothian[23] and Salaberga[24] Psalters – one recently unearthed at Faddan More in Ireland, and one written at the Insular foundation at Echternach, the Stuttgart Psalter.[25] Regarded as a relic of St Columcille or Columba (521/2–97) and, as such, encased in a metal shrine (*cumdach*) in the eleventh century, the *Cathach*, measuring about 200 × 130 mm, is traditionally thought to have been penned by the saint himself, who was celebrated as a prolific scribe. According to Adomnán's account of his life, Columcille's last known act of writing was copying a psalter.[26] If this is the manuscript in question, it would date to the end of the sixth century, rather than the mid seventh century to which it is usually

19 De Hamel 2001, p. 16. 20 Ó'Néill 1998, pp. 8–11.
21 RIA, s.n.; Herity and Breen 2002.
22 BL, Cotton Vespasian A.i; Wright 1967b. 23 PML, M 776.
24 Berlin, SB, Preussischer Kulturbesitz, Hamilton 553; Ó Cróinín 1994, 1995.
25 Stuttgart, Württembergische LB, Bibl. 2°.12; Netzer 1995, pp. 119–25.
26 Herity and Breen 2002, pp. 1–14.

ascribed on the basis of script and decoration.[27] Referred to as the *Cathach* (battler) of St Columba because of its enshrined state, the psalter was carried into battle by its hereditary owners to ensure victory. The book's importance lies in that it preserves the earliest extant experiments in what were to be developed as three of the hallmarks of Insular books: first, a distinctive Half-Uncial script; second, enlarged initials decorated with Celtic La Tène trumpets, spirals and peltae that distort the letter's form; and, third, the gradual diminution in the size of letters at the beginning of a section to that of the script (*diminuendo*). The form of Half-Uncial script introduced in the *Cathach* gradually becomes more consistent, legible and regular in later Insular gospel-books.[28] The latter two Irish innovations, enlarged initials within the text block and *diminuendo*, probably result from challenges in Ireland to the learning of Latin as a foreign language; the decorative devices may have served as aids to finding and learning passages of text.[29] Enlarged initials marking the beginning of each of the 151 psalms, with special elaboration for the openings of those signalling the three main divisions of the text (numbers 1, 51 and 101) becomes the standard in Insular psalters. The earliest examples of these initials in the *Cathach* are conceived as elastic forms whose contours expand and contract and spawn alternating curves and dots (like those in the Codex Usserianus), La Tène motifs and animal heads. They mark the earliest phase of the Insular desire to embellish the text itself. The beginnings of this process are probably Irish, but the evolution takes place throughout the British Isles, making it difficult to localise many of the later manuscripts.

One such book whose origin remains in question is a fragment from a two-column gospel-book (or possibly a New Testament) preserved at Durham.[30] A folio-sized volume measuring 385 × 250 mm with its text set out in two columns, the Durham Fragment is the first extant example attesting to the tendency of Insular gospel-books to be larger than their earlier counterparts from the Mediterranean world. The Insular predilection for books on a grander scale could reflect greater resources and/or more widespread use of the text in public reading.[31] The Durham Fragment is usually assigned to a centre in Northumbria, before the Council of Whitby in 664, which adjudicated the rift between the traditions of the early Irish and Roman churches. However, the manuscript may alternatively have been produced in a Columban house

27 For discussion of date see Dumville 1999, pp. 22–6; Herity and Breen 2002; Brown 1993, p. 223.

28 *Ibid.*, pp. 201–20.

29 Parkes 1987, pp. 15–29, and 1992, pp. 20–9.

30 DCL, A.II.10, fols. 2–5, 338–9; C.III.13, fols 192–5; C.III.20, fols 1–2: *CLA*, II, no. 147; Alexander 1978b, no. 5.

31 De Hamel 2001, p. 31.

in Ireland or Dalriada,[32] especially as its Old Latin text is close to that of Usserianus Primus.[33] Introducing the motif of interlace and multi-coloured pigments (yellow, orange, green and blue), the Durham Fragment's decoration and Half-Uncial script are generally thought to signal a step towards the more elaborately decorated Book of Durrow.[34] Three D-shaped compartments formed by various interlaced frames enclose, from the top down, the explicit of Matthew, the incipit of Mark, and the Lord's Prayer. The Durham Fragment's one remaining gospel text incipit, the Initium for Mark, marks an early phase in the elaboration of initials followed by one or several lines of display lettering that evolved from the type of calligraphic *diminuendo* lettering found in the *Cathach*. These incipits to the gospels grow to fill the page and to develop a typically Insular hierarchical system of variously sized initials identifying text breaks throughout the volume.

A Vulgate edition, considered the oldest of the completely preserved gospel-books, the Book of Durrow, is usually assigned a date in the second half of the seventh century and an origin in Iona, Ireland or Northumbria.[35] Durrow is the earliest extant witness to what becomes a more or less consistent programme in Insular gospel-books of using initials to introduce and signify the relative importance of various components. The practice is further elaborated in a group of luxurious and richly decorated Insular gospel-books of which the Lindisfarne, Durham, Lichfield, and Barberini Gospels and the Book of Kells[36] are the best-known examples. In these manuscripts, the largest decorated initials or monograms followed by display capitals signal each of the gospel incipits, the Chi-rho (the beginning of Matthew's narrative proper), and the *Novum Opus* (Jerome's letter to Pope Damasus explaining his new edition and the use of the canon tables) at the beginning of the book as the most important divisions. Less elaborate initials and display script introduce the other general prologues (including Jerome's preface commenting on the four evangelists beginning *Plures fuisse*, and Eusebius' letter to Carpianus on the concordance of the gospels beginning *Eusebius Carpiano*) and the individual prefaces (*argumenta*), lists of chapter summaries (*capitula lectionum*) and Hebrew names for each gospel. Still smaller initials generally distinguish beginnings of chapters within the gospel text, important lections and Eusebian sections. In addition to the elaboration of the script, full-page decorations are introduced in the most sumptuous examples. Full-page

32 Brown 1993, pp. 190–1, 205–9, 224–5; for criticism see Dumville 1999, pp. 29–31.
33 Verey 1969, pp. 137–242; 1973, pp. 575–9; 1989, pp. 145–6.
34 TCD, 57; Nordenfalk 1977, pp. 14–15.
35 Meehan 1996, pp. 17–22; Netzer 1999a.
36 BL, Cotton Nero D.iv; DCL, A.II.17; Lichfield CL, 1; BAV, Barb. Lat. 570; TCD, 58.

pictures of evangelists, their symbols, or a combination of both, decorated pages based on embedded crosses of various forms (dubbed 'carpet pages' for their resemblance to Romano-British floor mosaics[37]) and cross designs with all four symbols (and in one case Christ[38]), often precede each gospel. The gospel texts are usually preceded by canon tables, a series of lists of concordances devised by Eusebius of Caesarea to help the reader navigate and understand relationships between the gospels. In a few cases, like the Book of Durrow and the Echternach Gospels,[39] the canon tables are arranged within rectilinear frames, but more often they are surrounded by elaborate architectural arcades, sometimes containing evangelist symbols and/or apostles. Other full-page miniatures appearing only in a few of the most sumptuous volumes, like the Book of Kells, include the Virgin and Child, Christ and scenes of his arrest, Temptation, Crucifixion and Ascension, the Last Judgment, archangels and a tetramorph. The images may be read on multiple levels: various meanings were intended to be uncovered to reveal central Christian wisdom. Among this repertoire of decorative features the selection and application differ in each volume. Such variety speaks to some combination of the economics of the conception, the context in which the book was made, the function for which the book was intended, and the latitude given to the preferences and skills of the specific scribe–artist. The individuality of each gospel-book underscores the problems of establishing significant parallels between manuscripts and hence assigning them to specific scriptoria. Decorative motifs in the Book of Durrow comprise a combination of (1) La Tène-style curvilinear ornament (trumpets, spirals and peltae) reflecting the influence of earlier Insular metalwork, especially enamel; (2) rectilinear designs, some of which are based on millefiori;[40] and (3) various patterns of interlace, including the earliest animal interlace in an Insular manuscript. The animal forms find parallels in metalwork of the seventh century discovered at Sutton Hoo in East Anglia, near Lichfield in Staffordshire, at Bamburgh in Northumbria and at Dunadd in Scottish Dalriada.[41]

The twin monastery of Wearmouth-Jarrow in Northumbria possessed one of the few scriptoria to which specific manuscripts may be assigned with reasonable certainty.[42] Three giant full bibles (pandects) – rarities in this

37 Kendrick 1938, pp. 98–9. 38 Trier, Domschatz, 61, fol. 1v.

39 BnF, lat. 9389. 40 Youngs 1995, pp. 37–45.

41 For comparanda see Rupert Bruce-Mitford in Kendrick *et al.* 1956–60, pp. 109–12; Bailey 1992, pp. 31–41; Webster and Backhouse 1991, nos. 44–5; Henderson 1987, pp. 29–55; Henderson 1999, pp. 50–2; Henderson and Henderson 2004, *passim*; Campbell and Lane 1993, pp. 52–63; Lane and Campbell 2000, pp. 152–4.

42 Parkes 1982; Brown 2003b, pp. 57–64.

period – are recorded as having been produced there during the abbacy of Ceolfrith (688–716).[43] One was intended for each of the monastery's two churches; of these, only fragments from one copy remain.[44] Ceolfrith set off to deliver the third bible to the pope in Rome but died en route in 716; this volume of 1,030 folios, known as the Codex Amiatinus, remains intact.[45] Its text was compiled and edited at Wearmouth-Jarrow from various sources, including a southern Italian gospel-book and a sixth-century exemplar written in Cassiodorus' monastery near Naples, obtained in Rome by the founder of the twin monasteries, Benedict Biscop (d. 690). The Codex Amiatinus contains one of the purest examples of what has come to be accepted as Jerome's Vulgate edition. Bede probably played a key role in the complex editorial process of this vast enterprise, which produced what is known as the 'Italo-Northumbrian' text and its lists of chapter summaries, a version found not only in the Ceolfrith bibles but also in the extant gospel-books usually assigned to Wearmouth-Jarrow (the Stonyhurst or Cuthbert Gospel of St John and fragments appended to the Durham and Burchard Gospels and the Utrecht Psalter).[46] The work of nine different hands, the Amiatinus script is a formal Uncial, probably consciously imitating that of its Italian exemplar. Initials and decoration are restrained in the late antique tradition and partake of virtually none of the Insular stylistic vocabulary current at the time. Two full-page miniatures – one at the beginning of the book before the Old Testament, depicting the prophet Ezra writing the Bible from memory after the text was lost by fire during the Babylonian captivity, and the other, before the New Testament, showing Christ in Majesty – are painted in the illusionistic style reminiscent of Italian art of the sixth century. The beginning of the pandect contains several diagrams and a plan of Solomon's Temple copied from Cassiodorus' single-volume bible, the Codex Grandior, in Biscop's collection housed at Wearmouth-Jarrow.[47]

43 Bede, *Historia abbatum auctore Baeda*, ch. 15, and *Historia abbatum auctore anonymo*, ch. 20: Plummer 1896.

44 BL, Add. 37777 and 45025; and BL, Loan 81. This copy seems to have been given to Worcester Cathedral by King Offa of Mercia in the late eighth century: Marsden 1995b, pp. 90–8; Webster and Backhouse 1991, pp. 122–3.

45 Florence, Biblioteca Medicea-Laurenziana, Amiatino 1.

46 BL, Loan 74. The Gospel may have been a gift from Ceolfrith's community to its neighbours at Lindisfarne on the occasion of the translation of St Cuthbert's body from the tomb to the altar in 698. Hidden from view in the tomb, the book would have continued to provide a sacred function. This is the only Insular manuscript with its original leather tooled binding. DCL, A.II.17, fols. 103–11; Würzburg UB, M.p.th.f.68, fols. 10–21, 95–6; Utrecht, UB, 32 (script. eccl. 484), fols. 94–104. See Brown 1969; Marsden 1995b, pp. 76–218; Meyvaert 1996, pp. 827–83; Marsden 1998, pp. 65–86; Brown 2003b, pp. 57–64, 151–61.

47 Meyvaert 1996, pp. 827–70. Nees 1999, pp. 148–74.

The library at Wearmouth-Jarrow was one of the most comprehensive in the Insular world;[48] the influence of its texts has been identified in the most lavishly decorated of Northumbrian manuscripts, the Lindisfarne Gospels (Plates 8.1 and 4.1). A southern Italian gospel-book from the library, or a copy of it produced at Wearmouth-Jarrow, probably served as the primary exemplar for the Lindisfarne text, which is arranged *per cola et commata* in the late antique two-column format.[49] The same exemplar seems to have left its imprint to varying degrees on the texts of the somewhat later Royal, St Petersburg, and Gotha Gospels, volumes whose place of origin remains elusive.[50]

A colophon added to the Lindisfarne Gospels in the mid tenth century reveals that the manuscript was written for God and St Cuthbert by a scribe called Eadfrith, who became bishop of Lindisfarne in 698. This colophon has allowed scholars to localise and date the codex to the scriptorium on Holy Island in Northumbria between the period just before 698, when St Cuthbert's relics were relocated to a shrine near the church's high altar, and Eadfrith's death in 721.[51] The growth of Cuthbert's cult as well as Lindisfarne's noted collaboration with Wearmouth-Jarrow, and specifically with Bede, during the first quarter of the eighth century, as well as the inclusion in the book of Roman liturgical features promoted at Lindisfarne around 715, have recently been seen to favour a date of production between about 710 and 725.[52] Thus, within the study of Insular manuscripts, and Insular art in general, the Lindisfarne Gospels serves as one of the few anchored works around which others may be situated both chronologically and geographically.

Moreover, Lindisfarne is equally unusual as a deluxe gospel-book that survives intact, thereby providing a complete lavish and decorative programme for consideration. Indeed, the internal hierarchy and consistency of the book's decorative scheme, unlike Durrow's before it, reveals the development of a carefully worked out plan designed to aid the reader in navigating the text. Major decorated initials or monograms followed by distinctive display lettering, which blends Roman capitals, some Greek characters and runic angular forms, have now expanded to fill an entire page. Such elaborate treatment is reserved for marking the opening of the book (*Novum Opus*) and introducing each gospel, and, consistent with the Insular tradition, Matthew's narrative

48 Bede *Historia abbatum*, chs. 4, 11, 15 in Plummer 1896; Brown 2003b, pp. 60–2; Chapter 31 in the present volume.

49 Brown 2003b, pp. 153–8.

50 BL, Royal MS 1. B.vii; St Petersburg, Russian National Library, F.v.I.8; Gotha, Forschungsbibliothek, Memb. I.18; see Bruno 2001, pp. 179–90; Brown 2003b, p. 55.

51 On the colophon see Brown 2003b pp. 90–110; Nees 2003; Gameson 2001; Roberts 2006.

52 Brown 2003b, pp. 396–7.

(Chi-rho). Smaller decorated initials, often with zoomorphic flourishes, followed by display script confined to a single column, signal the beginnings of the two other introductory prefaces (*Plures fuisse* and *Eusebius Carpiano*) as well as the *argumenta* and *capitula* to each gospel. The latter initials are conceived as distinct matched decorative pairs for each gospel. Much smaller initials (*litterae notabiliores*) distinguish Eusebian sections, chapters (*capitula*), and lections within the gospels by means of a sophisticated graded system employing coloured infills, red dot outlines, contour lines and calligraphic flourishes. Such a methodical approach to organising and clarifying the text for the reader marks a milestone in the development of medieval books and leaves its imprint on the production of subsequent gospel-books in the Insular world.[53] Lindisfarne also adds several features to the known repertoire of manuscript decoration: spaced interlace and interlaced birds and 'dogs' of the so-called Lindisfarne type. The range of pigments, some clearly acquired at great cost, reveals that no expense was spared.

The *opus Dei* of a single scribe–artist, the Lindisfarne Gospels served as the focus for the cult of St Cuthbert, a shrine of sacred text. Its tenth-century interlinear Anglo-Saxon translation, the earliest extant gospel text in English, attests to the book's continued value and use.[54] Comprising 130 of the highest-quality calf skins, implying that those not meeting the standard would have been rejected, the codex displays the splendour usually associated with royal patronage. The manuscript's spaciously extravagant series of sixteen canon tables are unlike sequences of tables found in later manuscripts that derive from the same textual exemplar, suggesting that Lindisfarne's tables stem from a different source.[55] These tables are reminiscent of the illusionistic late antique 'm n' architectural type that places an embracing arch over smaller arches,[56] signifying that Eadfrith consulted a second Italian exemplar. The scribe–artist's transformation of his model by flattening forms and filling arcades with fret patterns, interlace and interlocking birds may have provided a template for adapting Mediterranean tables that was followed in later Insular gospel-books.[57]

A similar stylised adaptation of illusionistic models to the Insular idiom is revealed in Lindisfarne's four portraits of the evangelists. These seated figures, accompanied by their symbols in the Italo-Byzantine tradition, appear to have been composed by Eadfrith from several sources, one of which was probably the Italian model for the Ezra portrait in the Codex Amiatinus.[58] Lindisfarne's

53 *Ibid.*, pp. 299–304; Farr 1997 pp. 46–8. 54 Brown 2003b, pp. 1–11.
55 *Ibid.*, pp. 300–5. 56 Nordenfalk 1938, pp. 208–18.
57 Brown 2003b, p. 302. 58 *Ibid.*, pp. 346–86.

are the earliest extant representations of the evangelists themselves in the Insular corpus (Durrow and Echternach present only the evangelists' full-length symbols), and the first, as well, to show the evangelists specifically as scribes. It is probable that Eadfrith's portraits do not stem from the Italian exemplar used for its text; similar examples are absent from the later manuscripts deriving from the same archetypal text. Rather, the symbolic imagery used by Eadfrith may betray the stimulus of Bede in an attempt to inspire meditation and exegetical reading. The innovations seen in the Lindisfarne portraits appear to have been widely influential, being echoed not only in the British Isles (e.g. the Lichfield Gospels), but also at Continental Insular foundations like Echternach (e.g. the Trier Gospels) and Salzburg (the Cutbercht Gospels[59]). Moreover, Lindisfarne's inscriptions labelling the individual evangelists in Latin letters following the Greek formula '*Ó Agios*' and the symbols after 'Imago' initiate an inscriptional tradition that was developed and modified in later Insular representations of the evangelists. For example, 'Imago' is taken up as a label on the evangelist illustrations in the Echternach, Trier and Cambridge–London Gospels[60], while the Barberini Gospels, probably written in Mercia in the late eighth century, inscribes illustrations of its evangelist scribes with their names.[61] Lindisfarne's rounder, more regular version of the Irish Half-Uncial script (also found in the Echternach and Durham Gospels,[62] both of which may be slightly earlier productions of the Lindisfarne scriptorium) has a long legacy in manuscripts throughout the Insular world.

One scriptorium that clearly felt the imprint of Lindisfarne's innovations both in script and decoration was that at Echternach. Founded in 697 or 698 by the Northumbrian-born and trained missionary Willibrord (who, Bede tells us, spent twelve years of his adult life at the monastery of Rath Melsigi in Ireland before he was sent to the Continent by its abbot Ecgbert to convert the Frisians in 690[63]), the monastery at Echternach must have had an active scriptorium after about 704. Echternach is one of the few centres to which more than a handful of manuscripts written and decorated in the Insular style may be assigned with certainty in the eighth century. Several actually bear the names of scribes whose names appear on Echternach charters from the first two decades of the eighth century. One of these manuscripts, a deluxe gospel-book now in Augsburg,[64] of more modest size (about 247 × 177 mm)

59 ÖNB, 1224. 60 CCCC, 197B, fols. 1–36 and BL, Cotton Otho C.v; Verey 1998.
61 Brown 2003b, pp. 346–7.
62 The Durham and Lindisfarne Gospels share a correcting hand; see Verey *et al.* 1980, pp. 74–6. Further on the script, see Chapter 4 in the present volume.
63 Bede, *HE*, v, 10; Netzer 1994a, pp. 4–5.
64 Augsburg, UB, I.2.4°2. O'Croinin 1982, 1984, 1988; Netzer 1994a and 1994b.

and decorative scope than the most sumptuous Northumbrian examples, employs scripts, texts and decorative initials that find their closest parallels in Irish manuscripts predating the Lindisfarne Gospels.[65] By contrast, three other gospel-books that through a complex sharing of textual and artistic models may also be shown to have been produced at Echternach (the Maeseyck,[66] Trier and Freiburg Gospels[67]) reveal, to different degrees, the legacy of the Half-Uncial script, figure style, evangelist symbols, canon tables and bird interlace of the Lindisfarne Gospels. These gospel-books also demonstrate to varying degrees the process of multi-cultural exchanges that took place there between scribe-artists of Irish, English and Frankish training, sometimes faced with exemplars from foreign traditions. The Echternach gospel-books do not share a 'house script'. Indeed, the lack of stylistic consistency between the products of this scriptorium indicates that workshop practices differed in Insular scriptoria, probably reflecting varying historical circumstances and economic resources.[68]

The work of Southumbrian scriptoria during the eighth century also bears the imprint of their Northumbrian counterparts as well as the strong influence of liturgical manuscripts imported from the Mediterranean world, and to a lesser extent Gaul, following the arrival in Kent in 597 of the Roman missionary Augustine. Throughout the seventh century, the missionaries must have needed gospel-books and psalters for their disciples, yet not one extant example that seems to have been produced on English membrane in a Kentish centre during this period exists. This is either an accident of survival or an indication that the requisite books were largely imported from the Continent, principally Gaul and Italy.[69] Two Italian gospel-books are known to have been in England at an early date, the Corpus Christi Gospels,[70] preserved during the Middle Ages at St Augustine's Abbey in Canterbury, and the Oxford Gospels,[71] possibly at Lichfield in the eighth and at Bury St Edmunds in the eleventh century. Both codices bear various additions in early English hands attesting to continuing use at least until the eleventh century. Corrections to Corpus Christi's gospel text in the late seventh or eighth century against an Italo-Northumbrian text[72] related to the Codex Amiatinus signal Kentish connections to Northumbrian centres. The codex survives with only two of its

65 Netzer 1994a pp. 4–6, 112–20.
66 Maeseyck, Church of St Catherine Treasury, s.n.
67 Freiburg, UB, 702.
68 Netzer 1994a, esp. pp. 25–7, 34–44, 66, 71, 77, 90–102; Netzer 1999b.
69 Gameson 1999b, pp. 313–24. 70 CCCC, 286.
71 BodL., Auct. D.2.14. 72 Marsden 1999.

original six full-page miniatures.[73] One of the two is a seated author portrait of Luke with his symbol, the ox, in a tympanum above. The portraits from this manuscript bear a long legacy of influence on artists in Kent, including serving as a model for illuminations of two of the most sumptuous large-scale books with purple-dyed pages, the Stockholm Codex Aureus,[74] produced probably at Canterbury but possibly at Minster-in-Thanet in the mid eighth century, and the Royal Bible,[75] written at Canterbury between about 820 and 840. The Corpus Christi Gospels' original decorative programme, including probably seventy-two narrative scenes and a series of architectural canon tables in addition to the portraits, is likely to have been exceptional in the late antique world (the Oxford Gospels, which has no illumination epitomises the norm).[76] As such, it would not be surprising if its missing illuminations exerted equal, albeit undetectable, influence on many other, both extant and lost, Anglo-Saxon illuminations.

Letters from St Boniface, the Anglo-Saxon missionary in Germany, to Abbess Eadburh at Minster-in-Thanet (d. 751) reveal that women were able to supply locally produced, luxury manuscripts 'written in gold' by about 735. The earliest books thought to have been written in Kent, the Oxford Acts of the Apostles,[77] the Vespasian Psalter, and the Stockholm Codex Aureus, were probably written within a generation or so of this date. That the codices share scribal and decorative features as well as Canterbury provenance in the Middle Ages has led scholars to assign them dates and origins in close proximity to one another.

A simply decorated volume of modest size (229 × 176 mm) the Oxford Acts contains supplementary prayers that employ the feminine form as well as an incised ('Eadb') reference to Abbess Eadburh that suggests the book may have been produced at Minster. Careful scrutiny of the manuscript's construction and its relationship to the division of labour between the book's two scribes provides information about the variety of working practices within a single scriptorium: the scribes appear to have worked simultaneously on their own sets of quires which they prepared differently. The Uncial script and the decoration (comprising only a few enlarged initials followed by display script) betray the range of Kent's cultural links in their amalgamation of influences from Italian, Northumbrian and especially Frankish, manuscripts.[78]

73 Offsets indicate the missing illuminations. Gameson 1999b, pp. 318–22; Marsden 1995, ch. 12.
74 Stockholm, KB, A.135; Gameson 2001–2, esp. pp. 69–70.
75 BL, Royal 1 E.vi. 76 Gameson 1999b, pp. 320–3.
77 BodL., Selden Supra 30. 78 Gameson 1999b, pp. 326–30.

In contrast, the Vespasian Psalter, of equally modest size (235 × 180 mm; Pl. 4.3) but more sumptuous decoration, bespeaks a more elegant synthesis of Insular, Italian and Frankish elements. The psalm text is the Roman version (in contrast to the *Cathach* which is Gallican[79]), presumably imported to Kent by St Augustine in an Italian codex. However, the ancillary texts (prefaces, canticles and hymns), including several remarkable in the Anglo-Saxon world, suggest compilation from at least three exemplars, thereby indicating the probable abundance of books available at Canterbury, where the psalter was produced. An interlinear gloss in the Mercian dialect of Old English in a ninth-century hand, the earliest known English translation of the psalms, signals the book's continuous use for at least a hundred years. The psalter was probably also in use at Christ Church, Canterbury, in the early eleventh century when texts were added by one of the foundation's well-known scribes, Eadwig Basan. By the early fifteenth century the manuscript, like several others in the deluxe category as mentioned above, seems to have taken on the role of a venerated relic. In his chronicle of St Augustine's Abbey (*Speculum Augustinianum*, 1414–18), Thomas of Elmham describes it enshrined above the high altar of St Augustine's amidst books that were believed to have been sent to Augustine by Pope Gregory the Great.[80]

Presumably following its principal Italian exemplar, Vespasian's single scribe employs a stately classicising Uncial (akin to one in the Oxford Acts), in a single-column format for the psalms and antique Rustic Capitals for prefaces and the titles (*tituli*) for each psalm. Larger initials (three of which contained narrative scenes making them among the first 'historiated' initials) are followed by panels of display script, seemingly of Frankish inspiration yet inhabited by ornamental and zoomorphic forms matched in contemporary Insular metalwork. They alert the reader to the three major divisions of the text (Psalms 1, 51 and 101) as well as to those psalms recited in the daily office. Initials, written alternately in red and blue within a marginal border of red dots, ease identification of verse separations.[81] A similar marginal device for aiding the reader is adapted to a two-column text format in both the Salaberga and Stuttgart Psalters.[82] Such consistency suggests that individual texts, in this case the psalms, may have influenced specific decorative layouts which, in turn, became standardised within the Insular world.

An offset reveals that a cross-carpet page, hinting at Northumbrian inspiration, originally separated the psalms from the canticles. A full-page author

79 See above pp. 228–9.
80 Cambridge, Trinity Hall, 1, text printed in Hardwick 1858, p. 97.
81 Gameson 1999b, pp. 331–7. 82 Notes 24–25 above.

portrait showing David with a harp composing the psalms, his notaries and musicians busily working around him, preceded the psalms. Like the book as a whole, the portrait is a masterful synthesis of Italo-Byzantine, Frankish and Insular (some expressly Northumbrian) sources that marks the beginning of a distinctive aesthetic associated with Southumbrian manuscripts. While this aesthetic expresses allegiance to Rome, it is more adventurous and creative, and less rigid in its adherence to the decorative restraints of Italian book decoration, than the products of Wearmouth-Jarrow.[83]

One of the crowning achievements of this new aesthetic was a gospel-book of grand and – evoking its late antique counterparts – nearly square proportions (395 × 320 mm), the so-called Codex Aureus now in Stockholm. Reviving a custom from late antique luxury manuscripts, pages empurpled with the exorbitantly expensive dye bestow a regal quality on the book. Unique is the alternation of purple and natural parchment pages throughout the gospel text, requiring the insertion of a single leaf in the centre of each gathering of bifolia, and signalling to the viewer, whether literate or not, the supreme value of the words written thereon. The decoration of the Codex Aureus develops the panels of display letters, illusionistically inspired figures and arched frames found in the Vespasian Psalter, while the alternation of coloured Uncial letters within the gospel text itself (silver and gold inks on purple and black and red inks on natural pages) introduces a new concept of decorative enhancement to the Insular gospel-book. Such patterned text on alternately purple and natural pages may have been inspired by a late antique copy of Porfyrius' *Carmina figurata*, a collection of verses written for the Emperor Constantine, the words of which were laid out in various designs; one such copy is known to have been at Christ Church, Canterbury, in the mid eighth century, where the Codex Aureus could have been written. Dazzling and engaging as they were, epitomising the Insular predilection for decoration, such designs embedded in the text imposed hardship on the reader and writer alike. They required a rectangular text block without word division. Moreover, the scribe was forced continuously to change inks and to adjust the spacing and size of the letters to fall on one side of the pattern or the other.[84]

In its elaborate series of arched canon tables, two remaining evangelist portraits (probably based on the (now-lost) equivalents in the Corpus Christi Gospels), and Chi-rho page (breaking with the Insular tradition, incipits to the gospels are not elaborately decorated), the Codex Aureus artists' visual

83 Gameson 1999b, pp. 334–6, 356; Webster and Backhouse 1991, pp. 197–9.
84 Nordenfalk 1951b; Gameson 1999b, pp. 336–43; Gameson 2001–2.

language bespeaks a unity of faith between Kent and Rome: Anglo-Saxon opulence wedded to the traditions of the Roman book production (Plates 8.2–3). [85]

In the ninth century, Canterbury produced another sumptuous, large-format codex (471 × 348 mm) with some purple pages. The work of at least five scribes (the principal of whom added the interlinear gloss, described above, to the Vespasian Psalter), the Royal Bible[86] is written in a derivative of the formal Insular Half Uncial developed at Lindisfarne. Although the manuscript survives as fragments from the New Testament, it was probably a pandect akin to the three commissioned over a century earlier by Ceolfrith at Wearmouth-Jarrow.[87] Four purple pages with monumental explanatory titles (*tituli*) written in gold and silver reveal that a missing series of full-page miniatures accompanied the surviving illustrations. A series of five imposing canon tables is decorated with exuberant animals and interlace matched in contemporary Anglo-Saxon metalwork of the so-called 'Trewhiddle' style.[88] A majestic incipit to Luke conflates features of evangelist portraits and opening initials in a single illumination: an arcade surmounted by a medallion with Christ pantocrator, indebted to a Carolingian Court School model, surrounds a large decorative *Q* followed by two panels of display capitals (*uoniam quidem*); the tympanum contains Luke's symbol, the ox, closely modelled on that in the single surviving Corpus Christi Gospels' portrait.[89] More speculatively, the Royal Bible's purple pages, inscriptions, unusual canon tables well suited to a large-format book, arcaded initial pages, and lost illustrations are thought to retain many of the elements of a lost large-format two-volume late antique bible. With purple leaves and illustrations, this 'Biblia Gregoriana' was still extant and venerated at St Augustine's Abbey in the early fifteenth century, when Thomas of Elmham described it as being in the library room there.[90]

The climax of the development outlined here is generally acknowledged to be the Book of Kells, the most extravagantly decorated of all extant examples and, despite its unfinished state, elevating the gospel-book to new heights. An estimated 185 animal skins went into this book, attesting to the wealth of the monastery where it was made.[91] Most likely written between 750 and 806 at Iona, the island monastery founded by St Columba in 563, the manuscript was by the early eleventh century described as the great Gospel-Book of

85 See Gameson 1999b, pp. 342–6.
86 BL, Royal 1 E.vi; Canterbury CL, Add. 16 + BodL., Lat. bib. b.2(P). Budny 1985; 1999, pp. 237–48.
87 See n. 43. 88 Wilson 1984, pp. 94–6.
89 Wormald 1954, pp. 8–11, plate II. 90 Budny 1999, pp. 259, 264–75.
91 Meehan and Cains 1990, pp. 183–4.

Columcille (Columba, 521–97). Just as the Lindisfarne Gospels were written to honour Cuthbert and became a venerated relic of his cult, so the Book of Kells probably served for Columba. Confirmation of this association occurs within the genealogy of Christ where a merman grabs 'Iona' (Jonah) the word for dove in Hebrew, which is *columba* in Latin.[92]

Kells' unusual arrangement of prefatory texts and canon tables and its single-column layout speak to its close relationship to Durrow. The two probably share a common venerated Irish model where these texts were compiled. Kells' gospel text was copied carelessly; in one instance a page was written twice.[93] Aesthetic qualities of script and decoration, however, appear to have been of the highest concern to those producing the book. Art historians have traditionally demonstrated the manuscript's stylistic connections to works of art datable to the end of the eighth or the beginning of the ninth century from Northumbria, Ireland and Scotland, as well as to manuscripts produced in Charlemagne's Court School.[94] To complicate the story, more recently significant relationships have been established to the scripts and decoration of Southumbrian manuscripts of the late eighth and ninth century.[95] Many stylistic features, like the snake bosses and figures in the so-called Osiris pose, find parallels on Irish sculptural crosses, especially those at Iona and Kells.

Full-page illuminations are more numerous in Kells than in any of its Insular counterparts. Indeed, they comprise a veritable encyclopaedia of all types found in Insular gospel-books. Moreover, examination of the book's construction suggests additional full-page illustrations were intended.[96] The thirty-three that have come down to us consist of eight decorated architectural canon tables with beast symbols representing the evangelists,[97] two canon tables in grid frames, one carpet page, four four-symbols pages (one before each gospel), twelve decorated incipits to the gospels or other passages singled out for special treatment, two evangelist portraits, a Christ enthroned, a Virgin and Child, and two illustrations of scenes from the text (the Temptation of Christ and the Passion of Christ). Given that the manuscript has been rebound several times and that the portraits, the Virgin and Child, and the carpet page are single leaves with blank versos, their original placement, and therefore their

92 Meyvaert 1989, pp. 6–19. 93 McGurk 1990, pp. 57–8, 61–70.

94 Alexander 1990, pp. 265–89; Friend 1939, pp. 611–40.

95 Brown 1994a, pp. 333–43.

96 Possibly miniatures related to the Crucifixion and Resurrection narratives and one following the end of Luke: see Henry 1974, pp. 172–3; Alexander 1978b, pp. 72–3.

97 On the origin of beast canon tables, see Friend 1939, Henderson 1987, pp. 131–41, McGurk 1990, pp. 52–8, Alexander 1990, pp. 268–73, and Netzer 1992.

relationship to the text, remains unknown. The Temptation and Passion, by contrast, appear on bifolia bearing the appropriate texts (Luke 3.36–8 and Matthew 26.30 respectively). Although they constitute the earliest extant full-page pictures inserted within a Latin gospel text, their details do not follow in all aspects the narrative within which they were placed. Rather, they incorporate features from other sources.[98]

Like the other deluxe gospel-books, Kells is large (330 × 240 mm) and written in a generous, elegant Insular Half-Uncial. The presence of more than 2,000 decorative motifs within the text, however, distinguishes Kells from other Insular gospel-books. Many are minor initials, but a myriad of unusual beasts, birds and humans hover, walk or fly between lines of text in a manner unique within the Insular world. Among its 340 existing folios (originally about 370[99]) only two lack coloured decoration. Unlike many of the earlier deluxe gospel-books such as Lindisfarne and Durrow, Kells results from a collaboration among several scribes and artists; how many, the division of labour, and the sequence and duration of production continue to be debated.[100] Recent scholarship has focused on the meaning of minor initials and interlinear imagery within the context of the full-page decoration, suggesting that all the illumination, at its core, aims to focus the reader on apprehending God and his salvation of mankind.[101] It was only by ruminating (*ruminatio*) on the pages that the medieval reader could hope gradually to penetrate the interrelationship of the complex meanings of text and decoration and, in the process, approach comprehension of the book's embodiment of 'the word'. The degree of understanding achieved would naturally differ between readers, depending on their preconceptions, expectations, life experience, and visual and textual literacy. And no individual's reading is likely to have been either complete or definitive.

So too for modern scholars who continue to expend much effort on studying Kells, as well as the other Insular gospel and liturgical manuscripts. Meditation on aspects of their text, script, decoration, glosses, layout and construction, as well as on the religious, historical and social context in which they were produced, remains key to unlocking the multiple layers of meaning embedded not only in the most complex decorative programmes, but also within the less lavishly embellished examples. So many questions about the meanings, uses and circumstances surrounding the production of these books remain

98 See Farr 1997, pp. 51–139.
99 Some of the prefatory texts are missing and John ends in the middle of ch. 17.
100 See Henry 1974, Meehan 1990, Alexander 1990 and Eisenlohr 1994.
101 Pulliam 2006.

unanswered. So much of the evidence is lost, but continued detailed studies of those that remain should provide new pieces in this puzzle, altering along the way the composite picture that emerges. There can be little doubt that these supremely creative objects will continue to reward the ongoing quest to interpret them.

9

The decoration of the earliest Welsh manuscripts

NANCY EDWARDS

The fact that so few books can be associated with Wales prior to 1100 means that it is extremely difficult to build up a picture of the artistic capabilities of scribes in the region and of the cultural and religious influences on their output. With the exception of Llanbadarn Fawr towards the end of the period, it is also impossible to identify specific scriptoria with the resources for illuminated manuscript production. However, the illuminated manuscripts that do survive prior to 1100 indicate that art in Wales was firmly within the Insular tradition, an impression confirmed by the growing corpus of stone sculpture and ornamental metalwork.

The earliest illuminated manuscripts that have a definite or possible association with Wales are two gospel-books. The first of these is an incomplete, eighth-century, luxury copy known as the Lichfield Gospels or the Book of St Chad.[1] Where it was produced is unknown, but an early ninth-century Latin addition at the end of St Matthew's Gospel records that it was bought by Gelhi, son of Arthudd, who 'gave that Gospel to God on the altar of St Teilo'.[2] The foundation concerned may be identified as Llandeilo Fawr (Carmarthenshire). The beginning of the book, possibly one of two volumes, is missing and it breaks off after Luke 3.9. The main surviving ornament is made up of a Chi-rho page marking the declaration of Christ's birth in St Matthew's Gospel; an evangelist page and decorative text at the beginning of Mark's Gospel; and an evangelist page, a page showing the four winged evangelist symbols grouped around a cross, a cross-carpet page and a page of decorative text at the beginning of Luke's Gospel (respectively pp. 5, 142–3, 218–21). In common with other Insular gospel-books of the period, the emphasis is therefore on the beginning of each gospel. Other minor ornament consists of four pages with decorative frames and simple illuminated initials, some enlarged and ornamented with dots, within the text. The complex ornament – frets, spirals,

1 Lichfield CL, 1. 2 P. 141: Jenkins and Owen 1983, p. 50.

interlace and zoomorphic patterns – and the iconography combine extensive use of elegant drawing in ink with the judicious employment of a limited range of pigments which include two shades of mauvish pink, yellow, a bluish green and pale blue, sometimes applied in layers.

Both evangelist pages are highly stylised, consisting of a haloed evangelist holding a book and seated on a throne, accompanied overhead by his evangelist symbol, all set within a frame of fret ornament. The enthroned evangelist and lion of St Mark recall the symbols of Matthew and Mark in the Echternach Gospels.[3] However, the figure opening St Luke's Gospel is more than an evangelist: the representation is imbued with biblical meaning. By holding both the flowering rod of Aaron (symbol of the priesthood) and the cross (symbol of the Passion and Resurrection), the figure also represents both Christ himself and the gospel story.[4]

Art-historically the Lichfield Gospels may be placed somewhere between the Lindisfarne Gospels and the Book of Kells.[5] Though simpler, the page with the four evangelist symbols may be compared with similar pages in the latter, while the Chi-rho page and the cross-carpet page, with its complex geometry and bird and animal interlace, may be compared with the former. The shape of the cross on the Lichfield carpet page is also echoed on a cross-head and cross-slab from Llandeilo Fawr, demonstrating the influence of the manuscript on the sculptural output of the foundation where it was kept.[6] The highly developed, ornamental geometric capitals on the Chi-rho page and opening Initium and Quoniam pages of the gospels appear highly epigraphic in style and seem to have their origins in geometric forms first evidenced on sixth- and seventh-century inscribed memorial stones in Wales.[7]

Second, the Hereford Gospels is a rare surviving example of a non-luxury gospel-book which primarily functioned as a lectionary.[8] The decoration, as well as other features, suggests that it was produced in a scriptorium, either in Wales or on the borders, during the later eighth or early ninth centuries. The surviving decorative scheme is confined to the opening of the gospels of Matthew, Mark and John (see Plate 9.1).[9] Each framed page is set out on a fairly grand scale consisting of an ornamental monogram comprising three letters followed by decorative geometric capitals which give way to a formal

3 BnF, lat. 9389.
4 Henderson 1987, pp. 122–4; O'Reilly 2003, pp. 177–82.
5 BL, Cotton Nero D.iv; TCD, 58.
6 Edwards 2007, Llandeilo Fawr, nos. 2–3.
7 Charles-Edwards 2002, pp. 39–43, and personal communication.
8 Hereford CL, P.I.2. 9 Fols. 1r, 36r, 102r.

Insular Minuscule script. The decoration – spirals, interlace, frets, rosettes and zoomorphic ornament – is fairly simply but competently executed and colour is limited to yellow, pink and orange. The layout of the Mark and John monograms, which have integrated cross-symbols, has been interpreted as incorporating in miniature elements found in the cross-carpet pages of deluxe gospel-books.[10]

Only a small number of other illuminated manuscripts with Welsh associations have survived prior to the late eleventh century. Their modest ornament is limited to calligraphic initials of Insular type. Chronologically the first two items are both now part of the composite volume associated with Glastonbury known as St Dunstan's Classbook.[11] The *Liber Commonei*, written *c.* 817×835, would seem to be a Welsh product and includes computistic material and an archaic form of the Easter Vigil lections and canticles in both Greek and Latin; it is glossed in Old Welsh. The illuminated initials are infilled with cells of red and/or yellow paint and sometimes (e.g. fol. 22r) enhanced with dots and elegantly executed spiral terminals and occasionally with bird-head terminals or interlace. The other is a late ninth- or early tenth-century copy of Ovid's *Ars amatoria*, also glossed in Old Welsh. It has only two instances of decorated calligraphic initials and no paint has been used. The opening 'SI' (fol. 37r) is quite complex (see Plate 9.2), the strokes of the letters terminating and being bound together by delicately drawn animal heads, some with long lappets or biting jaws, some with feline features; one snaps at a mouse. A third manuscript with Old Welsh glosses in the same hand is the original portion of a textbook, the so-called Corpus Martianus Capella,[12] also datable to the late ninth or early tenth century. The simple calligraphic initials ornamented with loops and triangular fishtails have parallels in a copy of Pseudo-Augustine's *Categoriae*,[13] while examples of stylised animal heads are comparable with those in *Ars amatoria*. These creatures are best paralleled in Southumbrian manuscripts of the late eighth and ninth centuries.[14] Their influence on Welsh manuscripts in the late ninth or early tenth century would be consistent with known intellectual contacts between Wales and Wessex during the reign of Alfred.

Four illuminated manuscripts written in the late eleventh and the first half of the twelfth century may be associated with Llanbadarn Fawr (Ceredigion) and the learned family of Sulien, bishop of St David's (d. 1091), who was educated

10 Gameson 2002c.
11 BodL., Auct. F.4.32, fols 19–36 and 37–47; Hunt 1961.
12 CCCC, 153; Budny 1997, no. 7.
13 Bern, Burgerbibliothek, 219; Lindsay 1912b, plate 12.
14 E.g. BL, Cotton Tiberius C.ii; Harley 2965; BAV, Barb Lat. 570; CUL, Ll.1.10.

in Welsh schools as well as in Scotland and Ireland. The most elaborate volume is the Psalter and Martyrology of Rhygyfarch (Ricemarch Psalter), datable to *c.* 1079, which was owned by Sulien's son Rhygyfarch (d. 1099) and illuminated by another of his sons, Ieuan (d. 1137).[15] Ieuan also transcribed and illuminated St Augustine's *De Trinitate*, which is datable to 1085×1091.[16] The decoration of the two manuscripts is remarkably similar (see Plates 9.3 and 9.4).[17] Elegantly executed calligraphic initials of Insular 'knotted-wire' type form the most characteristic ornament in both. The strands of the knots are formed out of the strokes of the letters which terminate in a variety of animal heads, many with lappets, round ears and biting jaws, triangular fishtails, ring-and-dot, spiral curlicues and paired fleshy foliate tendrils. The letters in the Psalter and Martyrology are infilled with a mosaic of orange-red, lemon-yellow and mid green cells and the initials are frequently outlined with orange-red dots; those in *De Trinitate* are similarly decorated, but pigment is used more extensively on the animals and mid green is confined to the opening pages. In addition *De Trinitate* has a single example of a 'ribbon-animal' initial (fol. 1v), where the animal itself, intertwined with strands of interlace and holding one clawed foot in its jaws, forms the letter D.

The psalms in the Psalter and Martyrology of Rhygyfarch, in common with most Insular psalters, are divided into three parts, each beginning with a page of decorative text. For example, the boldly conceived *Beatus vir* page at the beginning of Psalm 1 (fol. 35r), decorated in orange-red, lemon-yellow, mid green and pinky red, commences with a 'ribbon animal' initial B and continues in display capitals. These are framed by a border which terminates in a lion's head and feet and is ornamented with elongated figure-of-eight animals with lappets and long biting jaws enmeshed in interlace strands.

The form and layout of the decoration in both manuscripts is part of an Insular continuum dating back to the eighth century, though details of the ornament and style were subject to change. The 'knotted wire' and 'ribbon animal' initials are clearly part of this continuum. By the late eleventh century, however, other influences are also apparent, though these have been thoroughly moulded to Insular conventions. Details of the interlace-enmeshed animals appear to draw on features of the Viking Ringerike and Urnes art styles, and the foliate tendrils may also have been influenced by tenth-century Anglo-Saxon or Continental acanthus ornament. The layout and ornament of the two Llanbadarn Fawr manuscripts may have drawn on earlier Welsh material

15 TCD, 50; Lawlor 1914. On Sulien see Chapter 38 in this volume.
16 CCCC, 199; Budny 1997, no. 55. 17 Edwards 1995.

which has not survived, but the strongest perceptible influences seem to come from Ireland as, for example, in the 'knotted wire' initials in the fragmentary late eleventh-century Psalter of St Caimin and an early twelfth-century copy of the *Liber Hymnorum*.[18] The Edinburgh Psalter,[19] an eleventh-century manuscript that was probably written in Ireland, but possibly in Scotland, provides the closest parallel.

A second pair of manuscripts associated with the family of Sulien and Llanbadarn Fawr demonstrate the transition between the Insular and Anglo-Norman manuscript traditions. Both were written in Caroline Minuscule but show some continuation of the earlier style of Insular illumination, though at a very reduced level. The ornament in an early twelfth-century copy of Macrobius' *Commentary* on Cicero's *Dream of Scipio* (which also contains Rhygyfarch's *Lament* on the Anglo-Norman invasion of Ceredigion) is confined to a single animal head (fol. 74v).[20] However, the decoration in a fragment of Bede's *De natura rerum*,[21] dating to the first half of the twelfth century, is more extensive. It consists of five rather clumsy illuminated initials, two decorated with interlace picked out in pale yellow and orange pigment, and three of 'ribbon animal' type enhanced with white paint. The latter may be compared with similar 'ribbon animal' initials in the *Liber Hymnorum* mentioned above.

Finally, there is some tantalising evidence for the continuing use of Insular illuminated exemplars in Wales as late as the mid thirteenth century. The earliest version of the Welsh law book *Llyfr Iorwerth*,[22] which was written in a Cistercian foundation in north-east Wales, includes some heavily cropped drawings in the lower margins of three pages (fols. 159v, 180, 189). These include winged evangelist symbols, which have their origins as far back as those in the Book of Armagh (806×807),[23] though evangelist symbols in a similar drawn style were still being produced in Ireland, probably in Armagh, in the early twelfth-century Harley Gospels.[24] The loss of the models for the illustrations in *Llyfr Iorwerth* can only serve to remind us of how much has perished and of the very fragmentary picture presented by the illuminated manuscripts that have survived.

18 Killiney, Library of the Franciscan House of Celtic Studies, A.1; A.2 (now housed in University College Dublin); Henry and Marsh-Micheli 1962, pp. 117–19, 129–34.
19 Edinburgh, UL, 56; Finlayson 1962.
20 BL, Cotton Faustina C.i; Peden 1981.
21 NLW, Peniarth 540; Huws 2000, pp. 104–22.
22 BL, Cotton Caligula A.iii, fols. 149–98; Huws 2000, pp. 177–92.
23 TCD, 52.
24 BL, Harley 1023; Henry and Marsh-Micheli 1962, pp. 146–8.

10

Book decoration in England, c. 871 – c. 1100

RICHARD GAMESON

The book decoration that was practised in England during the two centuries between the reigns of Alfred the Great and William Rufus ranges from isolated decorated initials in modestly conceived volumes to elaborate full-page miniatures in luxurious ones. The present chapter will outline the main chronological development of this artform, and will then consider aspects of its patronage, production and purpose.

The manuscripts associated with the literary programme of Alfred the Great (reigned 871–99) seem to have been qualitatively very modest – something which in itself lends support to the king's pessimistic view of ninth-century Southumbrian literary skills. The decline that he so eloquently lamented necessitated a new start, and although there are unquestionably links with work done earlier in the century, the manuscript art that rose from the ashes – quite literally in the case of centres that had been ravaged by the Vikings – followed new paths. Royal support notwithstanding, the revival was slow. The young Alfred may have admired fine initials (as his biographer, Asser, claimed[1]), but such were beyond the scribes whom he had at his disposal in the 890s: those in the contemporary manuscripts of his Old English translation of Gregory the Great's *Regula pastoralis* are very humble indeed – crude pen-drawn letters elaborated with small and ungainly beast heads, human faces and interlace twists.[2] Nevertheless, these letters stand at the head of a vigorous and lengthy tradition: their robuster descendants – composed of whole or part animals and birds, interwoven with sprigs of foliage (the so-called 'Type I' initials: Plate 7a.2) – were the dominant form of book decoration during the first half of the tenth century, and continued in occasional use into the eleventh.[3] The style, which allied the minor elements of eighth- and earlier ninth-century Anglo-Saxon manuscript art to plant forms of ninth-century Continental ancestry,

1 Asser, *De rebus gestis Ælfredi*, ch. 23: Stevenson 1904, p. 20.

2 BodL., Hatton 20 (facs.: Ker 1956b); Kassel, LB, Anhang 19 (reproduced in Ker 1956b.).

3 Wormald 1945; Gameson 1992b.

was practised at various centres in southern England, being deployed for Latin and Old English texts alike. Moreover, in their heyday such initials were the main – or only – form of adornment in high-status manuscripts including a gospel-book (Plate 10.1), a psalter and the copy of Bede's *Vitae Cuthberti* that was offered to the community of the saint at Chester-le-Street by King Athelstan (d. 939).[4]

During the first half of the tenth century, there was also a modest rebirth of figural art. The five full-page miniatures that were intercalated into the so-called 'Athelstan Psalter' are arguably the earliest examples of the phenomenon: prefixed to the calendar and prefatory prayers were two images of Christ enthroned amidst different choirs of heaven, while depictions of the Nativity, probably the Crucifixion (this page is now lost), and the Ascension were inserted before Psalms 1, 51 and 101.[5] Subsequent witnesses include the historiated initials of the Junius Psalter (now mostly lost), and the frontispiece to the aforementioned *Vitae Cuthberti* – a full-page image showing King Athelstan, his head bent over an open book, standing beside the blessing figure of St Cuthbert.[6] This last manuscript has a manifest connection with the royal court, and the same might be suspected of the others. The pictorial content of these works, limited though their technique and palette may be, nevertheless reveals the creative use of a range of sources: debts to Insular traditions intermingle with responses to Carolingian and even Byzantine art, echoing the steadily widening cultural contacts that characterise the history of the period from Alfred's reign to that of Athelstan.

The importance of Carolingian stimulus in particular is broadcast by a magnificent copy of Hrabanus Maurus' *De laudibus Sanctae Crucis*, which was attentively copied from a ninth-century model, presumably from Fulda.[7] In terms of size, splendour and general quality, not to mention the sophistication with which the paint is handled, this manuscript towers head and shoulders above other English products of the first half of the tenth century. Indeed, although the volume was written by an Anglo-Saxon scribe well known from another context, one commentator has argued that it was decorated by a Fulda artist. As the medieval provenance of the volume is undocumented (it first appears

4 Boulogne, BM, 10 (Gameson 2009); BodL., Junius 27; CCCC, 183 (reproduced: Budny 1997, II, ills. 112–52).

5 BL, Cotton Galba A.xviii + BodL., Rawlinson B.484, fol. 85. The existence of the lost miniature that prefaced Psalm 101 is proven by offsets. Deshman 1997.

6 BodL., Junius 27 (colour plate: Temple 1976, ill. 1); CCCC, 183 (colour plate: Wilson 1984, ill. 203).

7 TCC, B.16.3. Schipper 2007 hypothesises that the art and the Rustic Capitals are Fulda work. The presumed reluctance of Fulda to loan a fine copy of the work that is part of the premise for this hypothesis (p. 48) is irrelevant given that the provenance of one Fulda copy akin to TCC, B.16.3 (namely Amiens, BM, 225) is Corbie in northern France, a centre much closer to England.

in the sixteenth century in the possession of the bishop of Bath and Wells), it is difficult to resolve the question of its origin, let alone the circumstances of its production. What is, however, certain is that the highly talented artist responsible worked alongside an Anglo-Saxon scribe, and that the imagery of *De laudibus* was known and imitated at one centre in England by the mid tenth century. As the number of Anglo-Saxon centres able to have made such a book around the second quarter of the tenth century was strictly limited, and given that Glastonbury is the place that demonstrably had a copy of the work at an early date (since it provided inspiration for the frontispiece to Dunstan's 'Classbook'[8]), it must be the leading contender for the English provenance of this remarkable manuscript, and arguably also for its place of origin.

Glastonbury's connections with the West Saxon monarchy, its role as a seed-bed of monastic reform, and the documented literary and artistic activities of St Dunstan (appointed abbot by King Edmund (reigned 939–46)), make the presence of an active scriptorium there by the mid tenth century a reasonable presumption. If the extremely low survival rate of its books obfuscates the situation, Glastonbury is nevertheless a prime candidate for the centre that produced Athelstan's copy of the *Vitae Cuthberti* as well as the aforementioned majestic Hrabanus (and it is worth noting that the presentation image in the latter is one possible source of inspiration for the pictorial frontispiece of king, saint and book in the former);[9] while the frontispiece to Dunstan's Classbook – the only work from this time that can be securely located at Glastonbury – hints, in both style and iconography, at familiarity with a range of Carolingian art.

Decorated books may have been produced at Abingdon during the abbacy of Dunstan's colleague, Æthelwold (*c.* 954–63); and the latter's enthusiasm for Continental monasticism, his personal tastes (as revealed by his later Benedictional) and the fact that monks were brought in from Corbie in northern France, all encourage the belief that any such work would have been heavily indebted to Continental example. Once again, however, a dearth of evidence prevents us from testing these hypotheses. The only scriptorium to which a run of mid-tenth-century books can be attributed is that of St Augustine's Abbey, Canterbury, and here we perceive something of a dichotomy in artistic terms.[10] The scribe–artists of the decorated initials that

8 BodL., Auct. F.4.32, fol. 1r. Facs.: Hunt 1961. Schipper 2007, pp. 46–7 reviews both other evidence for the presence of a copy at Glastonbury, and the case for identifying it with TCC, B.16.3.

9 The various chains of connections that link CCCC, 183, to Glastonbury are summarised by Gwara 2001, pp.130–40.

10 Compare their 'flirting' with Continental practices of book-making in general at this time: see Chapter 2 in this volume.

adorn the handsome library books that were produced there from the second quarter of the tenth century onwards subordinated native and Continental sources alike to their own house style (the so-called 'Type II' idiom in which letter-shapes are adorned with the heads of birds and beasts, with foliate tufts and with coils of interlace). By contrast, the draughtsmen of the figural images that preface some of the texts made at St Augustine's during the third quarter of the century – the drawings of Christ, of Lady Philosophy and of Aldhelm that introduce copies of Gregory's *Regula pastoralis*, Boethius' *De consolatione Philosophiae* and Aldhelm's prose *De virginitate* respectively – were more overtly indebted to Carolingian art and also share idioms with colleagues working at Glastonbury (Dunstan's Classbook) and Winchester (Æthelwold's Benedictional).[11] Christ and Philosophy are both standing figures, holding a book in one hand; Aldhelm is seated, passing his book to the receptive hands of the first of the veiled women standing beside him (doubtless the female worthies mentioned in his Preface, immediately above the image itself: Plate 10.2). As the provision of pictorial prefaces for 'library' books was to remain the exception rather than the rule, this early cluster of them from St Augustine's is in itself a notable phenomenon. All three of the texts in question were to be much transcribed in late Anglo-Saxon England; the images in these early Canterbury copies might be said to highlight their inspirational – as opposed to 'textbook' – value, and to proclaim the worth of 'library' books in general.

The revival of Benedictine monasticism towards the middle of the tenth century, spearheaded by Dunstan and Æthelwold, fostered further and closer contacts with the Continent and created the preconditions for an expansion in manuscript production as a whole; and following the promotion of the reformers and their cause under Edgar (king north of the Thames from 957, of all England 959–75), the quality and quantity of decorated books increased dramatically. The surviving evidence presents Winchester and Canterbury as the principal centres of production during the generation in question, and this is likely to be broadly accurate.

The primary monuments of Winchester illumination from the heyday of the monastic reform are the New Minster Charter and the Benedictional of St Æthelwold, datable to 966 and 971×84 respectively.[12] The Benedictional

11 Oxford, St John's College, 28 (colour plate: Hanna 2002, plate III); TCC, O.3.7 (Temple 1976, ill. 44); Lambeth Palace, 200, fols. 66–113 (Temple 1976, ill. 132).

12 BL, Cotton Vespasian A.viii, fols. 1–33 (Miller 2001, no. 23, reproducing 29v–33r as plates I–VIII; Rumble 2002); BL, Add. 49598 (facs.: Prescott 2002; detailed comment: Deshman 1995, favouring a date of completion *c.* 973 (p. 261))

was made at Old Minster; the Charter was produced *for* New Minster, though where in Winchester it was actually made is debatable. Unlike most charters (unadorned single-sheet documents), the New Minster Charter takes the form of a luxurious little codex, its text entirely written in gold. Presented on a purple-painted ground within a lavish frame of gold bars and trellis foliage is a pictorial frontispiece which depicts King Edgar (flanked by the Virgin Mary and St Peter) genuflecting in adoration while holding up the charter to the Deity above (who is supported and acclaimed by angels) (Plate 10.3). The image is complemented on the facing page by a couplet that was spaciously set out – the placement of the words corresponding to their pictorial equivalents opposite – and written in golden Uncials, which declares: 'Thus he who established the stars sits on a lofty throne. King Edgar, prostrate, venerates and adores him.'[13] The charter was composed in 966 to celebrate and perpetuate Æthelwold's definitive replacement of secular clergy with Benedictine monks at New Minster – a takeover achieved thanks to material support from Edgar. After casting events into the eternal framework of the fall and salvation of mankind, the lengthy text (probably composed by Æthelwold) justifies Edgar's actions in replacing 'depraved' clerics with model monks as motivated by his wish to do good works, it proclaims the independence of monks, stresses the benefits that the king and the monks derive from each other's support, and declares (ch. 11) that all those who respect and support monastics will find a place with Christ in heaven. The presentation of the document reinforces these grand claims by assimilating the charter to a deluxe liturgical book, thereby projecting its sacrality; while its pictorial frontispiece, which shows the Deity blessing the proffered codex (and hence the deed itself), demonstrates that this controversial act was sanctioned by heaven. At the same time, this image is a strident declaration of Edgar's privileged status (something that is likely to have been all the more welcome, given the questionable circumstances in which he first came to the throne, not to mention his 'weakness' for women): the king enjoys a direct relationship with God (whose representative on earth he is shown to be) and is supported by, and on an equal footing with, the Virgin Mary and St Peter, who are evidently ready to intercede for, and open the kingdom of heaven to him respectively.

The main elements of the art of the frontispiece – namely the exuberant frame, the solid figures with pleated robes, and the heavy use of colour with overpainted highlights which further articulate the draperies – all reappear in

13 Colour plate: Keynes 1996b, plates I–II.

Æthelwold's luxurious Benedictional (Plate 10.4). The text of this volume (its selection of blessings) was probably compiled at Winchester in Æthelwold's day; there is little doubt that the picture cycle which accompanies it was developed there at the same time. Carefully calculated dedicatory verses – presented (in emulation of Carolingian practices) in golden Rustic Capitals – which exactly fill the opening before the first blessing, include the declaration that, 'A bishop, the great Æthelwold, whom the Lord had made patron of Winchester, ordered a certain monk, subject to him, to write the present volume'; and the scribe in question is subsequently named as Godeman (possibly the man of that name whom Æthelwold was to appoint abbot of Thorney).[14] We are also told that Æthelwold 'commanded to be made in this book many frames well adorned and filled with various figures and decorated with numerous beautiful colours and with gold'. This record of Æthelwold's commission thus stresses the frames, the overall decorative effect and the general luxuriousness of the book as much as the figural imagery per se – priorities to which the art of the volume corresponds. Almost all the miniatures in the body of the text are presented within elaborate arched or rectangular frames, constructed from thick gold bars filled with panels of foliage; foliage-adorned bosses, capitals and bases articulate their sides, corners and arches. As the incipits on the facing rectos are written in monumental golden Square Capitals and Uncials and are surrounded by matching frames, the book is punctuated by decorated openings of the utmost opulence.

These borders, which are the hallmark of the Winchester style, combine Franco-Saxon frame types, 'panel-acanthus' of ninth-century Metz ancestry, and trellis foliage of the sort used in southern English art of the earlier tenth century. The Franco-Saxon style, which flourished in northern Francia in the second half of the ninth century, was predominantly aniconic: the elaborate frames (their bars typically filled with panels of regimented interlace) along with the stately, often golden lettering that they contained were the major decorative elements of their books; imagery was rare. The enrichment of such frames with foliage was pioneered in the tenth century at Corvey (Saxony), the great East Frankish daughter-house of Corbie in northern France. Whether such work was known at Winchester in Æthelwold's day is debatable; though the connections between the West Saxon monarchy and their Ottonian cousins in Saxony (above all the marriage of Athelstan's sister, Edith, to Otto the Great), not to mention those between Æthelwold and Corbie, mean that it

14 Fols. 4v+5r; edition: Lapidge 1993a, pp. 143–4. Keynes 1996b, p. 88 rightly urges caution with regard to the often-repeated identification, given that at least two other brothers with the same name were in the community at the right time.

is by no means impossible.[15] Be that as it may, Winchester artists enriched these frame types with foliage of an unprecedented ebullience which, when deployed to surround figural imagery as well as text, dominated the pages in question, creating a new aesthetic. Moreover, the Winchester frames do not simply contain the figures; they are in the same plane as, and interact with them – a phenomenon that was enhanced by the use of a consistent colour scheme across the page as a whole.

The pictorial compositions are themselves dominated by the figures, which are generally set against areas of swirling, abstract colour: there is no attempt to suggest any recessional space, and such 'settings' as appear are evoked by highly stylised architecture and a few props. If in terms of plasticity and volume the figure style is ultimately reminiscent of work from the 'Court School' of Charlemagne ('Ada group') and the iconography of some of the scenes reveals a strong debt to the art of Metz, the general effect is transformed by an overriding interest in surface pattern. While the faces are inexpressive, even ugly, the highlights on the draperies, the flowing hemlines, and the sensuous deployment of colour articulate the picture space in a highly decorative manner, complementing and interacting with the ornate frames. Counterbalanced by the plain golden lettering set against bare parchment within the matching frames on the facing page, the colour and pattern of the pictorial compositions seems all the more vibrant.

The Benedictional starts with a series of full-page miniatures of the choirs of heaven which, echoing in both placement and design the canon tables that introduce gospel-books, form a sort of pictorial litany with ceremonial and eschatological overtones: this is the celestial community that was eternally present at the celebration of mass, the orderly community of the blessed with which Æthelwold joined as he pronounced the blessings in his book, and with which he (and his flock) hoped to be united at the Last Judgement. Indeed the verses recording Æthelwold's patronage of the manuscript, the only text to be entirely written in gold, stand between the last of the choirs and the first blessing, presenting this bishop and his patronage of a luxurious benedictional as a continuation of the cohorts of heaven, most of whom (including all the apostles) are themselves shown holding golden books. Now unfortunately incomplete (only the images of confessors (imperfect), virgins and apostles survive), the cycle of choirs develops an idea that appeared in a more schematic form in two of the miniatures that were added to the 'Athelstan' Psalter half a century

15 Corvey produced books for nunneries closely associated with the Ottonian dynasty and one of its key manuscripts, New York Public Library, MA1, has been associated (on general circumstantial grounds) with Otto the Great himself: Alexander *et al.*, 2005, no. 27.

earlier, which themselves echo the illumination of a sacramentary fragment dating from *c.* 870 that is associated with the circle of the Frankish king, Charles the Bald.[16] Whereas the individual members of the heavenly choirs in these precedents are unidentified, in the Benedictional, by contrast, certain figures are named by inscriptions: particular emphasis is thus given to Saints Gregory, Benedict, Cuthbert, Mary Magdalene and Ætheldreda; and it is probable that Swithun was once similarly distinguished (on the lost page showing further confessors that once faced the present fol. 1r). Gregory, Cuthbert and the Magdelene were widely venerated in England; Ætheldreda, Benedict and Swithun were especially dear to Æthelwold, and all three were also the subject of full-page images in his manuscript.

Twenty lavishly framed full-page miniatures appear within the body of the book, introducing the blessings for selected feasts and depicting the person or event commemorated; the beginning of the text, on the facing page, is presented within a matching frame.[17] A monumental historiated initial and an unframed part-page miniature mark two further feasts. Since the presence of such artwork greatly emphasises the twenty-four feasts in question, the overall effect of this interspersed decoration is further to articulate and personalise the volume. Apart from those feasts that relate to Christ, the Virgin and the great universal saints (Stephen, the two Johns, Peter and Paul, and Michael (lost)), such decoration highlights SS Benedict, Swithun of Winchester, and Ætheldreda of Ely – all reflecting known interests of the patron, owner and user of the book. Æthelwold was a staunch admirer of Benedict and his Rule, (re)imposing it where he could; in 971 he translated the relics of Swithun, a former bishop of Winchester (852–63); and he also promoted the cult of Ætheldreda (d. 679), the founder-abbess of Ely, a community which he refounded in 970.

Equally careful thought lies behind the iconography of the individual images that both individually and collectively – and in parallel to the blessings that comprise the text – develop further themes. There is, for instance, a perceptible emphasis on royalty, something which may well reflect the close connection between Æthelwold and King Edgar in particular and between this king and his monks more generally. The kingship of Christ is explored in several images: the Benedictional includes the first known representation of the Magi crowned as kings, the first of whom, significantly, presents his gift of gold to Christ in the form of three diadems, seemingly symbolising the submission of

16 Respectively BL, Cotton Galba A.xviii; and BnF, lat. 1141 (facs.: Mütherich 1972).

17 Three such openings have been completely or partly lost; these are likely to have included miniatures of the Massacre of the Innocents, the Nativity of the Virgin, and St Michael.

these wise earthly kings to their incarnate Lord. In the Baptism on the facing page, Christ is presented with diadems and sceptres, evoking a secular coronation (and the fact that Edgar was crowned in 973, fourteen years after he became ruler of England but in his thirtieth year – the age at which Christ was baptised – sharpens the likely contemporary relevance of such details).[18] Yet the awesome supremacy of the heavenly king has already been underlined, for in the miniature of the Second Coming a vigorous Christ, accompanied by an army of angels, has inscribed on his thigh the legend 'King of Kings and Lord of Lords', which not only advertises his supreme status, putting earthly kings in their place, but also assimilates him to the fearsome figure of Revelation 19.16 who was to smite the nations, rule them with an iron rod, and mete out the retribution of the sovereign lord.[19]

Further on the theme of royalty, the Benedictional has the earliest known depiction of the Coronation of the Virgin – presented as an element within her Dormition (Plate 10.4).[20] This image of eternal royal reward for the stately, recumbent virgin mother had powerful connotations for female religious (for whose reform Æthelwold was equally concerned) and arguably also for Edgar's queen at the time, Ælfthryth, to whom the care of nuns was committed in the *Regularis concordia* (the harmonising Rule of the reformed communities), and who was the first late Anglo-Saxon queen certainly to have been formally crowned. St Benedict, too, is associated with crowns: the powerful figure who is enthroned under an arch amidst an elaborate architectural setting (perhaps evoking the celestial equivalent of the monastic complex within which the good Benedictine stayed) wears a diadem, supports a book (doubtless his *Rule*) with his right hand, and holds up a crown with his left; he appears to be wearing mass vestments.[21] If, at one level, the crown is presumably the reward for following his Rule, it may simultaneously express the premise that it is model Benedictine priests who confer legitimate royal title.

One can point to iconographic sources for many of the miniatures: a model from Metz (perhaps in the form of an illustrated sacramentary) with scenes similar to those on the late ninth-century Metz casket in Braunschweig was particularly important; a conceptual debt was owed to the early tenth-century Anglo-Saxon miniatures added to the 'Athelstan' Psalter, and there is a clear strain of Byzantine influence (perhaps transmitted by a tenth-century Greek gospel-lectionary). Yet these disparate sources were masterfully harnessed to create a new and coherent cycle which articulated the faith, theology

18 Fols. 24v and 25r respectively.
19 Fol. 9v. 20 Fol. 102v. 21 Fol. 99v.

and politics of Bishop Æthelwold. And while the golden verses at the beginning of the book record his patronage and ownership of the benedictional, the last miniature – showing a contemporary bishop blessing from a golden book upheld by an acolyte – which introduces the text for the dedication of a church, gives an impression of him using it.[22] Where the prefatory verses celebrated Æthelwold's patronage of the manuscript allied to his desire to save his flock, the miniature showed how this was put into practice. Accompanying a benediction which invokes salvation for the faithful, the bishop is portrayed as the means by which the salvific power of the altar and eucharist is transmitted to mortal man. Moreover, this bishop under a baldachino towards the end of the book echoes the similarly presented figure of the annunciate Virgin at the beginning of the main text: as Mary was the vessel of the incarnation that made possible the redemption of humanity, so the bishop is the vehicle for the continuing transmission of salvation to the faithful through the re-enactment of Christ's sacrifice that was embodied in the mass.

Three further, undoubted Winchester works of this generation are a gospel-lectionary fragment in London, a benedictional in Paris, and a benedictional-pontifical in Rouen.[23] The first two books, which were also probably written by Godeman, the scribe of Æthelwold's benedictional, are broadly contemporary with that manuscript; the third, which is intimately linked to it in design and iconography, is slightly later in date. The evidence of the script (which includes a short but high-status passage of 'Godmanesque' Minuscule amidst a more advanced form of Anglo-Caroline) suggests that it was produced around the millennium.[24] The surviving decorated page of the gospel-lectionary – a framed incipit whose initial and borders alike are constructed from golden bars, foliate panels, interlace and beast-head terminals – is a telling advertisement of Winchester's artistic debt to Franco-Saxon models.[25] The general conception is reminiscent, for instance, of the opulent late ninth-century gospel-lectionary that was probably made at Saint-Vaast, Arras, in which parallels for many of the individual details of our manuscript may also be found.[26] The main innovation is the Anglo-Saxon artist's consistent use of foliage (as

22 Fol. 118v.

23 London, College of Arms, Arundel 22, fols. 84–5; BnF, lat. 987; Rouen, BM, Y.7 (Wilson 1903).

24 A manuscript of similar date (*saec.* x^{ex} or x/xi) which might belong alongside these volumes and is broadly affiliated to them by its script, is the gospel-book BnF, lat. 272 (Plate 18.4). Unfortunately, however, every one of its decorated pages has been removed – though a fragment of ornament on the remaining stub from a lost leaf before fol. 19r shows that it once had elaborate gold bar and foliage frames with corner bosses, in the Winchester manner.

25 London, College of Arms, Arundel 22, fol. 84r: colour plate Temple 1976, p. 21; Wormald 1984,frontispiece.

26 Arras, Médiathèque, 1045.

opposed to interlace, or an alternation of foliage and interlace) within the panels of his frame and initial.

The Paris and Rouen Benedictionals were less extensively decorated than Æthelwold's manuscript and they do not bear the stamp of a particular personality in the way that his book does: the former now has nine framed initial pages but no miniatures (though its physical structure suggests that some may have been lost[27]), while the latter had five openings where miniature and incipit in matching frames faced each other, but two of the miniatures have unfortunately been excised.[28] The frames in the Paris benedictional are generally simpler and slenderer than those in Æthelwold's manuscript; more elaborately decorated ones grace the initial pages for the blessings for Palm Sunday, the Ascension and Pentecost, with the most lavish of all marking Easter.[29] The frames in the Rouen Benedictional-Pontifical, by contrast, are more monumental than those in Æthelwold's manuscript, and their foliage more exuberant. The compositions of two of its three surviving miniatures (the Women at the Sepulchre, and the Dormition of the Virgin) have been slightly simplified in relation to the corresponding scenes in the older manuscript (on which they were almost certainly based[30]) and they are set against plain parchment rather than coloured grounds, all of which makes the figural subject matter larger, bolder and more telling – if iconographically less rich. The Rouen version of Pentecost, by contrast, is a 'busier' composition than that in Æthelwold's book and, moreover, is set against a coloured ground rather than the plain parchment that was (uncharacteristically) used for this scene there.[31] Though lacking the two attendant angels that appear in the earlier version, the tongues of flame are more vigorous, the provision of fluttering curtains on the buildings in the spandrels evokes the rushing wind, God's presence is signalled by the hand that now appears in the roundel on the frame-arch, and the addition of a central column and a pair of internal vaults both suggests the 'upstairs room' and evokes the idea of an orderly hierarchical structure with God at its apex, whose spirit inspires man below – almost an allegory for the church.

27 Many of the quires are (now) irregular in structure. It is readily apparent that leaves have or could well have been removed immediately preceding the framed incipit pages on fols. 16r, 26r, 31r, 43r and 68r; such is also possible for those on 41r and 71r; and, though more complicated, is not impossible for those on 63r and 65r. As the manuscript is acephalous, it is impossible to know whether it once had a cycle of the Choirs of Heaven at the start.

28 The manuscript now starts with supplements that were added in Normandy. Although the construction of the first quires is unclear, as the original text starts – after a blank page (4r) – with a list of content, it seems unlikely that a pictorial cycle of the Choirs of Heaven has been lost.

29 Fol. 31r: colour plate Gameson 2000a, ill. 135.

30 Deshman 1995, pp. 267–8.

31 Rouen, BM, Y.7, fol. 29v. Colour plate: Temple 1976, frontispiece.

This image is thus iconographically richer than that in the Benedictional of Æthelwold. In all three cases, therefore, the illuminator of Rouen has worked variations – be they more or less complex – on the visual themes set out in Æthelwold's book.

Considered as a whole, the fine books made at Winchester between *c.* 966 and *c.* 1000 represent a radical departure from the manuscripts that had been produced there (or indeed anywhere in southern England) in the earlier tenth century. They are written in Caroline Minuscule not the native Square Minuscule; they are in Latin not Old English; their display scripts are (following ninth- and tenth-century Continental models) Uncials and Square Capitals not the earlier hybrid English alphabets; extensive use is made of gold, something hitherto virtually unknown; the ornamental vocabulary of foliage and frames is innovative and highly distinctive; and a new wealth of imagery was being deployed. Above all, the manuscripts are outstandingly opulent, including the one late Anglo-Saxon book to be written entirely in gold: Winchester itself was never again to match their quality. Indeed, it is no exaggeration to say that these volumes are more luxurious than almost all the broadly contemporary books produced in Western Europe as a whole, outside a few centres in Ottonian Germany. The fact that the richest manuscripts ever made at Winchester all date from the height of the tenth-century monastic reform underlines the central role played by that movement and by its flamboyant local leader in fostering the necessary conditions for deluxe book production. As at other times and in other places, having 'altar' books of the finest grade was perceived as an expression of spiritual excellence. But in contrast to most other times and places in the early Middle Ages, the volumes in question here were not, for the most part, the widely used gospel-books, gospel-lectionaries and psalters, but rather the altogether rarer benedictionals, the exclusive prerogative of bishops – a fact that underlines the coalescence of episcopal and monastic values that characterises the reform movement in England, above all at Winchester under the direction of the monk–bishop, Æthelwold.

Whereas at Winchester in the 960s there seems to have been a fairly dramatic break with previous English traditions in favour of a new aesthetic that drew heavily upon Continental examples, the scriptoria of contemporary Canterbury appear to have been more conservative: rather than rejecting English traditions of the earlier tenth century, they grafted Continental ideas on to them. Thus if Winchester work proclaimed a rejection of indigenous practices in favour of cosmopolitan ones, Canterbury manuscript art by contrast advertised continuity and the wish to reinvigorate rather than replace local usages. Readily apparent in the case of script – the native Square

Minuscule continued to be used until the end of the century (triumphantly so in the case of some highly prestigious volumes such as the Bosworth Psalter and Sherborne Pontifical: see Plate 10.5), while the early Canterbury Caroline Minuscule that emerged alongside it in the later tenth century was clearly in its debt – this is equally true with regard to decorated initials. The fine library books that St Augustine's Abbey produced from the second quarter of the tenth century onwards were well written in the native Square Minuscule and, as noted earlier, were decorated with pretty pen-work initials constructed from birds, beast and interlace (the 'Type II' style), a few boasting pictorial frontispieces.[32] When, later in the tenth century, Christ Church launched a programme of copying 'library' texts, it adopted aspects of the 'house style' of its near neighbour, including Type II initials and the distinctive coloured display capitals that often accompanied them (Plate 10.5). Indeed one Christ Church book includes a particularly large and complicated decorated letter that was clearly based on the corresponding initial in a St Augustine's copy of the same text.[33] Subjected to minor modifications, such initials and display capitals remained in regular use at Canterbury into the early eleventh century, appearing in many library texts (sometimes in considerable numbers) as well as in a couple of 'altar books'. This continuity is concordant with the fact that, in contrast to Winchester, there seems to have been no sudden change in the nature of the community either at St Augustine's or at Christ Church during the heyday of the Benedictine reform. Although Dunstan, the original leader of the reformers, was archbishop of Canterbury from 959 to 988, he either lacked the personal power and the local political support, or did not see the need, to impose change in the way that Æthelwold had done at the Old and New Minsters. Be that as it may, Canterbury no less than Winchester had access to Continental models of book production and decoration. At Christ Church these included the Flemish (?Liège) gospel-book which Otto I had given to King Athelstan, and the famous fully illustrated ninth-century psalter (now at Utrecht) which was made at Hautvillers in the ambit of Reims probably during the archiepiscopate of Ebbo (816–35, then 840–1).[34] Both Winchester and Canterbury thus possessed volumes decorated in the Franco-Saxon manner; but while Metz models seem to have been particularly influential on the figural art at the former, it was the Reimsian Utrecht Psalter that was determinative in this respect at the latter.

32 Wormald 1945; Gameson 1992b and 1992d.

33 BnF, lat. 6401A, fol. 57v; BodL., Auct. F.1.15, fol. 48v: Gameson 1992d, pp. 195–6, plates 42b, 43a.

34 BL, Cotton Tiberius A.ii (colour plates Puhle 2001, II, pp. 121–1); Utrecht, UB, 32 (facs. Van der Horst and Engelbregt 1984).

Comparison of the fine books of Canterbury and Winchester between *c.* 960 and *c.* 1010 underlines the distinctive characteristics of both (cf. Plates 10.3–4 with Plates 10.5 and 18.1). While Winchester scribes employed lavish frames, even for text, Canterbury ones in general did not; where Winchester used luscious foliate ornament, Canterbury eschewed it; while Winchester images were often fully painted, Canterbury ones were generally rendered in coloured lines alone; whereas Winchester figures tend to be heavy and solid (despite the agitation of their draperies), many Canterbury figures are altogether more vivacious; while Winchester deployed gold for frame bars and display script, Canterbury preferred ordinary colours; whereas Winchester utilised the 'classic' repertoire of Square Capitals and Uncials for display script, Canterbury preferred its own alphabet of hybrid capitals; and while Winchester deployed plain gold or Franco-Saxon-derived major initials, Canterbury employed coloured or 'Type II' ones. Gold is very rare in these Canterbury books, and although it does appear in the Arenberg Gospels of *c.* 1000, even there it was used sparingly.[35] Consequently, the finest Canterbury books of this generation are altogether less luxurious than their counterparts from Winchester.

Many of these Canterbury features are exemplified by the Bosworth Psalter, a physically imposing volume of the later tenth century, perhaps (given its 'new' hymnal and monastic canticles) to be associated with St Dunstan (d. 988) himself.[36] Notwithstanding the grand scale of the book, its decoration is confined to large colourful Type II initials, plus rows of coloured capitals, introducing the four principal divisions of the text; there is no gold. Another such initial (of smaller size, and just rendered in brown with red details) heads the main text in the Sherborne Pontifical, a service-book that was almost certainly made for the same archbishop.[37] A grand penitential which was written by the same scribe as the pontifical and is also adorned with Type II initials and coloured capitals could be another possible candidate for this hypothetical suite of archiepiscopal books (Plate 10.5).[38] The pontifical has in addition to its decorated initial, four full-page, line-drawn prefatory images, which represent the Crucifixion, followed by the persons

35 PML, M 869. Colour plates: Gameson 2000b, plates 6–7.

36 BL, Add. 37517. Colour plate: Gameson 2000b, plate 4.

37 BnF, lat. 943; Rosenthal 1992; Rasmussen 1998, pp. 258–317, plates 9–10. The vigil of the Nativity at the start of the temporale is marked by a large green 'O' plus one line of red capitals.

38 BodL., Bodley 718. A third book by this same scribe, an equally fine Hrabanus, *De computo* and Isidore, *De natura rerum* (Exeter CL, 3507), is not so readily associable with specifically episcopal/pastoral roles. Judging from a photograph, the same scribe would also seem to have written the mass-book fragment, Bloomington, Indiana University, Lilly Library, Poole 41.

of the Trinity.[39] Works of a modest talent, these drawings do not show any response to the art of the Utrecht Psalter – they belong rather to the more stolid tradition of draughtsmanship represented by the frontispieces to St Dunstan's Classbook and the group of library texts from St Augustine's Abbey (Plate 10.2), as well as by the under-drawings of contemporary Winchester miniatures. Whether this was because the style of the Utrecht Psalter had not yet become fashionable, or because the manuscript had not yet reached Canterbury, or more simply because the two artists in question had been trained in and preferred a different tradition, is an open question. The influence of the Reimsian manuscript can, however, be seen in an iconographically similar full-page Crucifixion which prefaces the Arenberg Gospels, a slightly later manuscript, dating from around the millennium.[40] This image is the work of a more skilful artist; nevertheless, the most important stylistic change – a heightened expressionism, especially in relation to gesture and pose – betrays a clear debt to the Utrecht Psalter. The inspiration of the Reimsian psalter is equally if not more manifest in the vivacious drawings that appear above the canon tables of the Arenberg Gospels (forming a multi-part meditation on the nature and significance of Christ: Plate 18.5) and above all in the architectural motifs framing its evangelist portraits (Plate 18.1). The Arenberg Gospels is more elaborately decorated than the earlier Canterbury books we have considered, and, as noted above, its artist makes limited use of gold. Nevertheless the basic aesthetic remains the same: the incipit pages are unframed and consist of large pen-work initials accompanied by lines of monumental hybrid capitals done in different colours (including gold); and although sections of the grounds within the evangelist portraits, canon tables, and Crucifixion frontispiece are filled with colour, and though small parts of the imagery are articulated with gold, the main elements are all drawn in coloured lines – calligraphy and draughtsmanship, not painting, predominate.

The artist of the Arenberg Gospels had clearly studied the Utrecht Psalter closely, and he may well have been one of the contributors to the most ambitious undertaking of this phase of book production at Christ Church – a 'revised' version of it, Harley 603.[41] The Harley 603 Psalter was probably started around the millennium; and the presence of an archiepiscopal figure

39 Leroquais 1937, plates VII–X.

40 PML, M 869, fol. 9v (the current first quire, fols. 1–8, was a later addition); Ohlgren 1992, plates 331–47; comment: Raw 1990, pp.84–5, 111–28.

41 Reproduced Ohlgren 1992, pp. 147–248; colour plates: Gameson 1992d, plates VII–XIV; 2000a, ill. 131; and 2000b, plate 8; comment: Noel 1995.

prostrate beside the cross-nimbed Deity in the initial 'B' to Psalm 1, an early addition, implies that the patron, recipient, or both was – sooner or later – the archbishop. The Utrecht Psalter provided a general template for the layout and specific models for the teeming illustrations of this grand volume; however, whereas the older manuscript had the 'Gallican' text and was written in Rustic Capitals, Harley 603 has the 'Roman' text,[42] the version still preferred at Canterbury, and was written throughout in Caroline Minuscule – changes that added considerably to the complexities of producing the new version. In the earliest stages of the project, four different artists contributed illustrations, working for the most part on separate quires, and seemingly before the text had been written. The number of artists involved, all of them highly skilled, attests to the resources that the scriptorium could call upon at this time (and given the relative poverty of Christ Church pictorial art hitherto, one suspects that some of them were new arrivals, possibly even summoned for this very venture). The page layout of the Utrecht Psalter was imitated, and all four draughtsmen followed closely the design and iconography of its illustrations – though the extent to which they adhered to the details, style, and general aesthetic of the model differed from one to the next. The most striking general change is that, while the ninth-century drawings were monochrome, three of the four Anglo-Saxon artists (conventionally known as A, B and D) worked with coloured lines in the Christ Church manner. This had radical implications for the aesthetic of the images, reducing the illusionism of the model in favour of vibrant surface pattern. Artist D was extraordinarily accurate in reproducing both the overall compositions and the individual details of the relevant illustrations in the Utrecht Psalter, but because he rendered them with coloured lines and, moreover, liked colour contrasts, the general effect was altogether different and more ornamental.[43] This tendency was developed even further by artist A (particularly at the beginning of his stint), who in addition to working in bright colours had a freer approach to the style of the model and treated the elements of the designs more decoratively.[44]

Work on the project soon took a different direction. In this next phase the scribe now wrote first and no longer imitated the layout of the Utrecht Psalter. Correspondingly, the artist of this section (F), unlike his colleagues, did not try to replicate the content of the illustrations of the ninth-century manuscript – something which the difference in the size and placement of the spaces that were available for his contributions would have made difficult – but rather used

42 Except for a short passage exactly coinciding with the stint of one particular scribe (50r–54r).
43 Colour plate of his work: Gameson 1992d, plate XII.
44 Colour plates: Gameson 1992d, plates VII–VIII; 2000a, ill. 131.

its imagery as a starting point for compositions of his own. The edges of his drawings sometimes intruded or were woven into the text-block – as at Psalm 138, where with spectacular appropriateness the beast-mouth Hell which is the setting for an image of the Harrowing physically engulfs verse 21, 'If I ascend into Heaven you are there; if I descend into Hell you are there' (Plate 10.6).[45] Artist F used the pictorial language of the Utrecht Psalter with increasing freedom as his work progressed, and whereas the ninth-century pictures are generally literal illustrations of the psalter text, his illustrations sometimes included more allusive elements. Although technically less accomplished and containing fewer elements, his drawings are thus bolder and iconographically more interesting than those of the other Anglo-Saxon artists. The image for Psalm 127 provides a thought-provoking example.[46] It consists of three main elements: a king and a queen at table, with children serving them; a king giving money to a group of humble hooded figures; and a scene of monastic foot-washing. While the first part is a modified version of a motif from the corresponding illustration in the Utrecht Psalter (referring to verses 1–3), the other elements have no parallel there, nor are they mentioned in the text of the psalm. They seem rather to have been inspired by the Psalm Commentary of Augustine who interpreted the phrase 'your children's children' in the final verse as an allusion to the everlasting life that one would receive in return for giving alms; Artist F has expressed this latter idea via two prominent contemporary practices, namely the Royal Maundy, and the foot-washing which formed an important part of the monastic ritual for Maundy Thursday.

Despite the archiepiscopal connection, the number of contributors, and the radical change in approach to the project embodied in Artist F's section, Harley 603 seems to have been temporarily abandoned when it was, at most, only two-thirds completed. Whether this was the result of internal problems, external factors or a combination of both is a moot point. The work was clearly exceptionally time-consuming and taxing, and given that the foundation already possessed the Utrecht Psalter itself, enthusiasm might have faltered, then flagged – particularly if the patron had died. This leads us to the alternative possibility, namely that the work may have been overtaken by events – in particular those of 1011, when Canterbury was overrun by Vikings and (as the *Anglo-Saxon Chronicle* records) *all* the ecclesiastics were captured; Archbishop Ælfheah was martyred the following year.[47] That this was indeed the context for a forced break in the project is suggested by the fact that the second scribe

45 Fol. 71r: Ohlgren 1992, p. 243.
46 Fol. 66v: Ohlgren 1992, p. 234.
47 *ASC* C: O'Brien O'Keefe 2001, p. 96.

of the original phase is known to have been active before 1011, for he wrote a charter in 1002×3; while the datable work of Eadwig Basan, the scribe who subsequently continued the text (and none of whose pages received illustrations), all comes from the second and third decades of the eleventh century.

The sacking at the hands of the Vikings did not depress Christ Church book production and decoration for long; however, its character seems to have changed somewhat thereafter. While some elements of the earlier 'house style' continued, others were abandoned in favour of features that had been typical of Winchester illumination during the late tenth century: gold now appears in profusion, and more elaborate frames with foliate ornament are used (Plates 10.7 and 10.8). The highest-quality script similarly seems to represent a synthesis of the former Canterbury and Winchester styles. Whether this mirrors a change in the composition – or even nature – of the community of Christ Church is an unanswerable question; however, it undoubtedly reflects the interrelations, and exchange of personnel, between different reformed houses. If a possible early context for the acquisition of Winchester manuscript art had come in 988, when Dunstan was succeeded by Æthelgar, who, prior to his stint as bishop of Selsey (980–8), had been abbot of New Minster (964–80), this is likely to have been limited by the fact that within two years he was dead. A more significant opportunity arose in 1006 with the elevation to the archbishopric of Ælfheah/Ælphege, the man who had been Æthelwold's successor at Winchester and had occupied that see for over twenty years (984–1006). Be that as it may, the more settled conditions that followed the accession of Cnut (1016), a king conspicuous for his generosity to Christ Church, will surely have helped to foster a climate favourable to the production of fine books.

Several of the Christ Church manuscripts in the new style were written by the master scribe Eadwig Basan who recorded his name in the colophon to one of his gospel-books. In a psalter that he wrote at some point between 1012 and 1023, Psalms 1, 51 and 101 are marked by full-page decorated initials conceived in the Anglo-Saxon version of the Franco-Saxon style, and presented within elaborate gold and foliage frames.[48] Yet if the frames are a clear response to Winchester art, the use of coloured not golden capitals for the display script accompanying the initials represents a modest continuity with former Canterbury practices. Between the psalms and the canticles there is a full-page image of St Benedict and the monks of Christ Church.[49] The saint is a majestic, enthroned figure, his identity reinforced by the words on his halo;

48 BL, Arundel 155. Colour plates: Gameson 1992d, plates XV–XVI; and 2000b, plate 9. Further on Eadwig see Chapter 7 in the present volume.

49 Fol. 133r: colour: Backhouse *et al.*, 1984, plate XVIII; Gameson 2000b, plate 9.

the subsidiary status of the monks is shown not only by their smaller size, but also by the fact that they are rendered in lightly tinted outlines and are not, like Benedict, fully painted. The monks are holding up a book which – the writing on it shows – represents the *Rule of St Benedict* itself, and to which the saint is gesturing. The words on Benedict's head-band indicate that, as a model monk, he has the 'Fear of God' always before his eyes. Part of a scroll that is directed towards him by the hand of God above declares, 'He who hears you, hears me' (Luke 10.16; words used twice in Chapter 5 of the Rule, where they support Benedict's stipulation that a monk owed instant obedience to his superiors). Appropriately, the part of the same scroll that hangs down towards the monks instructs them to 'Be obedient to your superior' (echoing Hebrews 13.17). The image is broadly similar to other early medieval depictions of St Benedict with monks and nuns, such as those in the Rule Book of Niedermünster of the second quarter of the eleventh century, and the Martyrology of Monte Cassino of *c.* 1100.[50] Like these, it is a dramatic declaration of the community's commitment to the Rule and of its special relationship with St Benedict; but in contrast to them, the obligations involved in that relationship are defined more fully. Whatever the nature of the Christ Church community in the period from Dunstan to Ælfheah (960–1012), and whatever its degree of monasticisation, this image provides clear evidence for a firm commitment to Benedictine values shortly after the debacle of 1011.

The same artist was responsible for the illumination of the small but exquisite gospel-book in which Eadwig Basan recorded his name (Plate 10.7).[51] The general conception of the decoration in this volume is, like that of the psalter, manifestly indebted to Winchester art, but once again there are idiosyncrasies. The details of the frames of the evangelist portraits, with their heavy gold bars that twist and interlock to form geometrical patterns and their relatively sparse foliage, are quite distinct from known Winchester work; moreover, the gospel incipit on the facing page is neither framed nor even decorated but simply comprises one modest-sized plain gold initial plus a line of coloured capitals, echoing older Canterbury books. One image in the Eadwig Gospels is – like the miniature of St Benedict we have just considered – articulated with inscriptions, namely the portrait of St John. The evangelist is shown crushing under his feet the heretic Arius (d. *c.* 336); John's left toes actually rest on his

50 Berlin SB, Preussischer Kulturbesitz, Theol. lat. qu. 199 (colour plate: Mütherich and Dachs 1987, plate 17); Naples, Biblioteca Nazionale, VIII.C.4 (colour plate: Romano 1993, plate XX).

51 Hanover, Kestner-Museum, W.M.XXIa.36; plates: Ohlgren 1992, pp. 372–92; colour plates: Backhouse *et al.* 1984, plate XVII; Gameson 2000b, plates 10–11; Henke 2005, pp. 65–6; comment: Gameson 2002b.

head. Arius' inverted scroll contains his heretical denial of the co-eternity of Christ ('There was a time when he was not'), which has literally been overturned by St John with his mystical evocation of the Godhead, 'In the beginning was the Word, and the Word was with God, and God was with the Word; thus it was in the beginning' (John 1.1), which appears on his scroll, the end of which hits Arius' head. Whereas John looks out at the beholder and his text is easily read, thus communicating orthodoxy, Arius looks across the picture space and his text is upside-down, thereby containing the heresy. It is an open question whether this unusual image was inspired by a particular event, as opposed to a general wish to proclaim orthodoxy. However, given the extreme rarity of depictions of Arius in earlier medieval art, it is striking that the production of the manuscript broadly coincides with the documented emergence of non-orthodox views (which, whatever the rights and wrongs of the affairs, were brutally suppressed) at Orléans in 1022 and Arras in 1025, centres with which the English church had strong contacts. Interestingly, a second visual condemnation of Arius appears in a Winchester prayerbook of 1023×1031: prefacing the office of the Trinity therein is a formally simple but theologically rich image which shows the three parts of the Trinity, plus the Virgin and Child – thereby evoking Christ's dual nature – all arranged within a celestial sphere, triumphing over a Trinity of evil that comprises the Devil, Judas and our heresiarch, who are squashed and bound below them, the two men already in Hell, the Devil seemingly being driven thither.[52] Although certainly produced at New Minster, some connection with Canterbury is indicated by an unmistakable iconographic debt to three illustrations in the Utrecht Psalter.[53] More generally, this is another witness to the cross-fertilisation of scriptoria which underlies the manuscript art of the earlier eleventh century.

St John is also accorded special treatment in the Grimbald Gospels, another high-grade book that was written by Eadwig Basan – though this time decorated by a different artist.[54] Once again the beginning of John's text is itself an integral part of the design and meaning of the composition, which is simultaneously an elaborate theophany and a schematic presentation of Christian history – from the Word in the beginning, through the Incarnation and the Christian people of the world, to the Last Judgement. The elaborate frames that surround the portrait of the evangelist and the facing incipit are filled not with foliage but with figures. The Trinity, Virgin and Child, and seraphim

52 BL, Cotton Titus D.[xxvi] + xxvii, fol. 75v: Günzel 1993; Keynes 1996b, pp. 111–23.

53 For Psalm 109, the *Gloria*, and the *Credo*: fols. 64v, 89v and 90r.

54 BL, Add. 34890, fols. 114v+115r: Millar 1926, plate 17; colour plate: Backhouse *et al.* 1984, plate XVI.

appear in the upper roundels, accompanied by angels – inviting iconographic comparison with the drawing in the aforementioned Winchester Prayer Book (though where *that* illustrated the penalty for crossing the Godhead, the present imagery advertises the merits of acclaiming it). These are adored by the twenty-four elders of the Apocalypse (who fill the side and lower borders), along with companies of kings, bishops and saints (appearing in the other roundels). In the roundel below St John, two angels hold up naked human souls. This is the only Anglo-Saxon manuscript in which such a frame is devoted to imagery – seemingly a further example of Canterbury adapting the Winchester features it borrowed. The most striking precedents for such an approach are, in fact, supplied by the scriptorium of Saint-Bertin (at Saint-Omer) during the abbacy of Odbert (*c.* 986–1007).[55] The Grimbald Gospels is also unusual for the extensive use that was made of silver (now unfortunately blackened) alongside gold (Plate 10.8); and this is a second feature which is more easily paralleled at Saint-Bertin than in England. These parallels should be set alongside other evidence for artistic and bibliographic exchange with Saint-Bertin which, it is worth remembering, is closer to Canterbury in terms of distance and journey-time than is Winchester.[56]

Whereas in the late tenth century it was Winchester that produced the most opulent volumes, by the second and third decades of the eleventh this distinction belonged instead to Canterbury – and it is interesting to note that the one truly deluxe volume of eleventh-century date to which we can ascribe a Winchester (New Minster) provenance, namely the Grimbald Gospels, was in fact made at Canterbury.[57] Other fine Canterbury books were also 'exported': the Eadwig Gospels, for instance, reached Hersfeld in Germany very soon after it was made; while the Arenberg Gospels was at Deutz, outside Cologne, by the twelfth century, if not before. The Bury Psalter, which dates from after 1032, may be another case.[58] Though certainly written *for* Bury St Edmunds, the relationship of some of its marginal drawings to the imagery of the Utrecht Psalter on the one hand and to seven drawings that were added to the Psalter of Odbert of Saint-Bertin on the other, points to a connection with Canterbury. Even if this manuscript were not itself made there, its artwork presumably draws on that of a lost illustrated psalter which *was* sent from Canterbury to Bury.

55 Surveyed: Gameson 2006b. 56 See chapter 14 in this volume.

57 The principal decorated Winchester books of *s.* xi are BL, Cotton Tiberius C.vi (Psalter); Cotton Titus D.xxvi+xxvii (prayerbook); Cotton Vitellius E.xviii (Psalter); Stowe 2 (Psalter); Stowe 944 (New Minster *Liber vitae*).

58 BAV, Reg. lat. 12. Plates: Ohlgren 1992, pp.249–97.

In point of fact, the number of English centres that were producing fine decorated books seems to have expanded slightly in the early eleventh century – echoing the general upturn in southern English book production as a whole. However, given that formerly localised features – such as gold bar and foliage frames, agitated draperies, along with stylistic and iconographic echoes of the Utrecht Psalter – also became more widespread while the Anglo-Caroline Minuscule practised in divers centres became more uniform, it is difficult if not impossible to use criteria of 'general appearance' to establish the origin of many of the deluxe volumes that were produced after the millennium, particularly since we know that certain scriptoria supplied fine books to other centres, not to mention individuals. The luxurious Sacramentary of Robert of Jumièges, which is ornamented with an extensive cycle of intercalated miniatures and framed initial pages, is a case in point.[59] An inscription reveals that it was given to the abbey of Jumièges in Normandy by Robert while he was bishop of London (1044–51), but where he got it from and – not necessarily the same – where it was made, are matters of debate. Internal evidence indicates a connection, direct or indirect, with one or both of the Fenland houses, Ely and Peterborough (and the fact that the latter had a skilled illuminator at about the right time is established by a documentary reference[60]). Yet it is also affiliated to a group of enigmatic books, mainly of high grade, produced in the first third of the century, which are linked by common scribes but have different artists, and which visually have points of comparison both with Winchester volumes of the late tenth century and with Canterbury ones of the second and third decades of the eleventh (see Plate 18.3).[61] The origin of the sacramentary (like that of the group as a whole) is likely to remain a matter of debate, but the problem is in itself a product of, and a witness to, the increasing range of centres – and circumstances – in which such volumes were now being made.

Arguably typical of these changing patterns is the fact that the finest books of the mid eleventh century are mainly associable with important individuals rather than institutions: whatever role lay patronage may have played earlier in the century, it was clearly an important force by the 1050s and 60s. We know that Earl Ælfgar of Mercia (d. 1062) and his wife, Ælfgifu, commissioned a decorated gospel-book which they presented to the abbey of Saint-Rémi, Reims, in memory of their son who was buried there; while Judith of Flanders, who was only in England from 1052 to 1065, appears to have had a small group of

59 Rouen, BM, Y.6 (Wilson 1896). Colour plates: Backhouse *et al.*, 1984, plate XIV; Wilson 1984, ill. 265; Gameson 2003, plate 15.
60 *Vita Wulfstani*: Darlington (ed.) 1928, p. 5; Winterbottom and Thomson 2002, p. 16.
61 See note 118 below.

Anglo-Saxon scribes and illuminators working in her household (Plates 10.9 and 18.2). Equally, 1057–68, the decade of her residence in England, is the most likely time for Margaret, daughter of Edward the Exile, to have acquired the decorated Anglo-Saxon gospel-lectionary that she subsequently had with her in Scotland (Plate 10.10).[62] Ælfgar and Ælfgifu's gospel-book is decorated in an archetypical late Anglo-Saxon style, the evangelists appearing within gold bar and foliage frames – though, in an interesting departure from convention, their gospel texts actually begin on substantial 'plaques' inscribed in golden capitals within the portraits, not on separate incipit pages.[63] Judith's four fine gospel-books appear to have been produced as a set, having different selections of text, and artwork with complementary styles and emphases.[64] The three that were decorated by English illuminators seem to have been designed to look as different as was possible within the canons of late Anglo-Saxon manuscript art. A further highly significant element of personalisation appears in the form of the female suppliant grasping the bottom of the cross in the frontispiece to one of them (the only one, incidentally, to contain the full text of the gospels), assuming that this is indeed Judith herself – an interpretation which the diminutive scale, lack of halo, and gold-adorned robes of this figure would support (Plate 10.9).[65] The circumstance that she is below the crucified Christ's right hand suggests that she is likely to be numbered among the sheep rather than the goats. Judith certainly appears in the frontispiece to another of her gospel-books (one largely written by an Anglo-Saxon but illuminated by a Fleming) where she is shown standing prayerfully and humbly (though well dressed) beside Christ.[66] The fact that she is here physically linked to the Deity by a book – presumably the one in which the image appears – advertises her lively appreciation of the role of (fine) manuscripts in achieving communion with the divine. The point was spelled out in the inscription on the (now lost) original treasure binding of Ælfgar and Ælfgifu's gospel-book which specifically described that manuscript as 'a book of pardon for the fallen, an embassy for life' and implored St Remigius to be mindful of their son in order that he might remain with the saint in heaven as on earth.[67]

62 BodL., Lat. liturg. f.5: Rushforth 2007.

63 Reims, BM, 9; colour plate: de Lemps and Laslier 1978, plate v. Compare in this respect, e.g., BL, Add. 27926 (?Hildesheim; *s.*xii²).

64 PML, M 708 and M 709; Monte Cassino, Archivio della Badia, 437; Fulda, Hessische LB, Aa.21; plates: Ohlgren 1992, pp. 432–57. Comment: McGurk and Rosenthal 1995; Rosenthal and McGurk 2006.

65 PML, M 709, fol. 1v: colour plate: Temple 1976, ill. 289.

66 Fulda, Hessische LB, Aa.21, fol. 2v; colour plate: Luckhardt and Niehoff 1995, II, ill. 29.

67 The text is known from a *s.* xvii^med transcription by Guillaume Marlot, monk of Saint-Rémi: printed in Hinkle 1970, p. 31 n. 4.

If the Anglo-Saxon illuminations in all these books are essentially essays in idioms pioneered at Winchester a century earlier, stylistic change is nevertheless apparent. The delicacy of contour and shade seen in two of Judith's gospel-books[68] gives way in one of the others (as also in Ælfgar and Ælfgifu's codex) to a firmer treatment of line, to flatter surfaces and to more striated use of colour.[69] This trend, the origins of which can be perceived in earlier eleventh-century volumes such as the Eadwig and Bury Gospels,[70] was taken a stage further during the third quarter of the eleventh century. In the Hereford gospel-lectionary, the Caligula Troper, and the Tiberius and Arundel Psalters (the last two seemingly datable to post-1064 and *c.* 1073 respectively) line is harder still, and colour, when used, more solid and intense (Plate 10.11).[71] Yet while these books manifest broadly comparable stylistic developments, they are otherwise divergent and cannot be considered to form a group. They certainly display a spectrum of approaches to the task of adding illustrations to texts. The main decoration in one of the psalters consists of a pair of highly stylised crucifixions (the work of different hands) preceding Psalms 1 and 51, while the other is prefaced by a lengthy pictorial cycle (comprising a diagrammatic evocation of Creation, a short sequence of the life of David and a long one of that of Christ, followed by images of Pentecost and of Michael slaying the dragon) – an early example of a trend that was to flourish in the twelfth century. And if the gospel-lectionary remains faithful to the late Anglo-Saxon norms for illuminating the gospels (canon tables and four evangelist portraits), the miniatures in the Troper embrace subjects that were hitherto rare or unrepresented in Anglo-Saxon art, notably the release of St Peter from prison, the martyrdom of St Lawrence, the annunciation to Joachim, and Joachim and Anna. The diversity of such work attests to the continuing vigour of English illuminators; the extent to which it may represent the budding of indigenous Romanesque idioms is obscured by the fact that it coincided with the Norman Conquest, a catalyst for altogether more dramatic change.

Distinctively Anglo-Saxon artwork continued to be produced for a generation or so after 1066, co-existing, then intermeshing, with Norman traditions. 'Winchester'-style frames were used for a couple of high-grade volumes,

68 PML, M 709 and Monte Cassino, Archivio della Badia, 437. Colour plates: Wilson 1984, ill. 262; Gameson 2000a, ills. 132–3.

69 PML, M 708 and Reims, BM, 9.

70 Hanover, Kestner-Museum, W.M.xxi.a.36; BL, Harley 76; plates: Ohlgren 1992, pp. 416–30; colour: Wilson 1984, ill. 263.

71 Cambridge, Pembroke College, 302 (Ohlgren 1992, pp. 458–72; Heslop 2007); BL, Cotton Caligula A.xiv, fols. 1–36 (Ohlgren 1986, ills. 38–42); Cotton Tiberius C.vi (Wormald 1962); Arundel 60 (Temple 1976, ill. 312; Kauffmann 1975, ill. 1; comment: Kidd 2000).

but even here change is apparent. The foliage that adorns most of the frames in the Arundel 60 Psalter is a Romanesque vinescroll, not an Anglo-Saxon acanthus;[72] the Exeter Gospels may have been conceived in the mode of a fine late Anglo-Saxon volume, but its harsh lines, flat colours and use of yellow and orange in place of gold represent a significant intensification, under Norman and Flemish influence, of the trends noted above.[73] Fluid line-drawing with sensitive shading continued at various centres, above all St Augustine's Abbey, Canterbury, but its main context was now decorated letters; the individual elements of Anglo-Saxon frames were also being broken up and applied to initials.

The presence of Norman scribes and artists in England during the late eleventh century is demonstrated by their contributions to English books. If scribal stints, initials and display script by Norman hands occasionally appear in the manuscripts of St Augustine's Abbey, such work was more pervasive at contemporary Christ Church, while the books produced at Rochester in the late eleventh century are almost wholly Norman in script and ornament. The Abingdon–Jumièges Gospels is a documented case of the phenomenon, for a contemporary inscription records that it was sent by Rainald, abbot of Abingdon 1084–97, to Jumièges (his alma mater); though apparently made in England, the volume is entirely the work of Norman hands.[74] The decoration comprises a suite of fine decorated, sometimes figural, initials rendered in unadorned red line, accompanied by red, blue and black display capitals; there are no evangelist portraits.

At the same time, under Norman impetus a new range of texts was being acquired: England already had a good number of fine gospel-books; the works of the church Fathers were now the focus of scribal effort, and the opportunities they offered for decoration were quite different. Yet if initials and titles rather than full-page miniatures were what was generally required, the quantity of such work was considerable. An increasing number of scriptoria were producing a rising number of books which, on average, had more pages with some decoration than ever before. The ubiquity of the shift may best be illustrated by the case of Worcester which, with the Anglo-Saxon St Wulfstan at its helm until 1095, was undoubtedly one of the more conservative centres. Nevertheless its scriptorium, too, produced patristic texts articulated with

72 BL, Arundel 60, fols. 13r, 52v, 53r: Millar 1926, plate 31; colour plate: Backhouse 1997, no. 19. The frame on fol. 85r (Herbert 1923, ill. VIII) preserves Anglo-Saxon acanthus-adorned corner roundels and mid-side bosses, but the foliage within the frame bars is more formalised and Romanesque.

73 BnF, lat. 14782: Alexander 1966; Kauffmann 1975, ills. 3–6; colour plate: Avril and Stirnemann 1987, plate C; Alexander 1992, ill. 127.

74 Rouen, BM, A.21 (32): Garand *et al.*, 1984, I, p. 263; II, plate XXIX.

decorated initials composed of beasts and foliage, set against multi-coloured grounds, accompanied by coloured display script; indeed these fine copies were in the vanguard of the practice.[75] But then this 'new' trend had a venerable past: the Worcester artists in question may well have noticed points of similarity between their work and the decoration in the Old English copy of the *Regula pastoralis* that King Alfred had sent to that see two hundred years before.[76]

Who were the patrons of decorated books? Evidence for this theme was scattered through our diachronistic survey of the material and this may now usefully be drawn together. Royalty, in the person of Alfred the Great, played a key role at the very beginning of our period. Moreover, although the copy of the *Regula pastoralis* that was made under his aegis has minimal ornamentation, the king joined to the book a valuable *æstel* whose purpose was in part, no doubt, to make a visually unprepossessing volume seem more impressive; his injunction that book and *æstel* should not be separated was more probably intended to safeguard the humble book by association with the valuable *æstel* than vice versa.[77] No surviving manuscripts, decorated or otherwise, can be associated with Alfred's son, Edward the Elder (though he is recorded to have been a keen student of books in English, especially poetry[78]); however, a significant number of books – several of them decorated – passed through the hands of his grandson, Athelstan (d. 939).[79] While most of these volumes were 'second-hand', one was an original commission and it included illumination: the copy of Bede's *Vitae Cuthberti* that Athelstan presented to the community of St Cuthbert at Chester-le-Street between 934 and 939 was decorated with a run of neat 'Type I' initials and a full-page frontispiece that showed the king, head bowed, reading from an open book which he is doubtless presenting to the saint, who blesses him with one hand while holding a closed book with the other.[80] This pictorial declaration of royal literacy as well as generosity may be interpreted in relation to King Alfred's injunction that reading was a precondition for holding political office:[81] a companion image, which depicted the king offering a book to Cuthbert who was seated on his episcopal throne, was added by an Anglo-Saxon artist to a ninth-century Continental gospel-book that Athelstan also presented to the saint's community. Although this

75 E.g. Cambridge, Clare College, 30; BodL., Hatton 23: Gameson 1999c, plate 3; Gameson 2005, figs. 2 and 5.

76 As n. 2.

77 BodL., Hatton 20. Alfred's prose preface: Sweet, 1871–2, I, pp. 8–9.

78 Asser, *De rebus gestis Ælfredi*, ch. 75: Stevenson 1904, pp. 58–9 – which specifies, incidentally, that particular care was taken over the education of the youngest male, Æthelweard.

79 Keynes 1985.

80 CCCC, 183.

81 Asser, *De rebus gestis Ælfredi*, ch. 106: Stevenson 1904, p. 94.

manuscript was tragically reduced to a handful of charred fragments in 1731, suffering further damage in 1865, early descriptions agree that the depicted Athelstan, crowned and genuflecting, was holding a book in his right hand, a sceptre in his left;[82] his humility was thus underlined alongside his majesty, and his literacy and generosity to the church were prioritised over his earthly rule. In both these images Athelstan was shown to be intellectually, spiritually and morally worthy of the throne.

Alfred and Athelstan apart, late Anglo-Saxon kings and queens do not emerge from the surviving evidence as major sponsors of decorated book production; certainly, there is nothing to set beside the known bibliophile activities and manuscript collections of their contemporaries, Otto II and III, and Henry II and III of Germany.[83] Given the ease with which manuscripts pick up spurious associations with celebrities, the paucity of relevant records (of any date) seems all the more telling. An inventory drawn up after 1143 and preserved in the *Liber Eliensis* does include, 'one text of the four gospels which King Edgar gave to St Ætheldreda ... when confirming the liberties of the church'.[84] However, given that the original record was itself compiled some 170 years after Edgar's death, that it tells us nothing about the book itself (as opposed to its treasure binding), and that, even if the association is correct, we have no way of knowing whether Edgar commissioned it new as opposed to passing on a volume that had come into his possession, nor whether he, as opposed to Ely, was responsible for the binding that is so lovingly described, it is difficult to do more than note such a record.

There are, it is true, a few dramatic depictions of kings (and a queen) in late Anglo-Saxon manuscripts; however, one should be careful to distinguish between books which a king used and those which used the king – the images in question belong to the latter class. Edgar is the central figure in the frontispiece to the New Minster Charter (Plate 10.3); equally, the words 'Eadgar Rex' at the beginning of the text proper are presented in particularly large capitals heading a coloured framed page and forming a pendant to the rumbustious circumlocution for God written in similarly large lettering on the facing page.[85] Yet, although nominally a royal 'document', it is likely that this 'charter' was

82 BL, Cotton Otho B.ix. The fragments of an original incipit reproduced: Backhouse *et al.* 1984, p. 25. Reconstruction from literay sources: Keynes 1985, pp. 170–9, with Smith and Wanley's descriptions of the image printed on p. 175, nn. 153–4.

83 Hoffmann 1986, I, pp. 7–24; Mütherich 1986. One thinks rather of the desultory interaction with books of Otto I and Conrad.

84 Bk III, ch. 50: Blake 1962, pp. 290–1.

85 BL, Cotton Vespasian A.viii; see n. 12. Rumble 2002, pp. 65–97. Colour plates: Keynes 1996b, plates I–IV.

composed, designed and its execution overseen by Bishop Æthelwold, and that it was the work of monastic scribes. The frontispiece was undoubtedly designed to flatter the king, reward him for his support, and smooth his path to heaven; however, the primary function of the document was to guarantee the status of the reformed New Minster – to which the charter belonged, and to whose community it was regularly read[86] – and the image is a visual record of the transaction which defined the new community, whose authority it bolsters by showing images, then highlighting the written names, of the royal grantor and the divine guarantor. The depiction of Edgar in the pictorial frontispiece to a copy of the *Regularis concordia* plays a comparable role.[87] Shown seated between two bishops, doubtless Dunstan and Æthelwold, the king is part of an ideal alliance of secular and spiritual authority promulgating this monastic custumal – a point underlined visually by the fact that all three men hold one and the same scroll, representing the text in question. The prologue of the *Regularis concordia* laments the former decline of monasticism, praises Edgar's spiritual focus and political force in effecting reform, and defines a relationship of mutual support between king, queen, monks and nuns. Preserved only in an eleventh-century Canterbury copy, the imagery may well descend (like the text) from an original of the 970s, and was probably devised (like the text) by Bishop Æthelwold and his entourage. Be that as it may, this copy was certainly made by monks for monks; and although unquestionably favourable to Edgar, the primary role of the image was to demonstrate the authority of the custumal, and hence of reformed monasticism more generally, and to advertise the virtues of a harmonious relationship between monastic church and the state – for the benefit of the church.

The highly complimentary depiction of Cnut and Emma-Ælfgifu that was produced at New Minster, Winchester, in 1031 presents a similar situation for it prefaces that community's *Liber vitae*, a volume that was certainly both made at New Minster and kept there.[88] The frontispiece gives the king and queen a uniquely favoured place in the community's prayer-life and hence on the road to salvation, it demonstrates divine endorsement of their rule, and it perpetuates one of their great donations – significantly, not a book but a golden cross. Yet while this page thus projects a view of the royal couple that would be most acceptable 'at court', the book in which it appears is not in any sense a royal manuscript. On the contrary, it was a monastic communal book

86 *Teste* the heading to ch. 22 (the rest of which is lost): 'Quoties et quare in anni circulo hoc fratribus legatur privilegium'.

87 BL, Cotton Tiberius A.iii, fol. 2v: Temple 1976, ill. 313. Backhouse *et al.*, 1984, p. 49.

88 BL, Stowe 944; facs. Keynes 1996b.

par excellence: if alongside the commemoration of bonds of confraternity and prayer obligations, the manuscript embodied New Minster's 'special relationship' with the West Saxon monarchy, this formed part of a 'portfolio' of its history and rights that celebrated the status of the foundation rather than that of royalty. And in the imagery on the next opening, devoted to exploring the all-important subject of the possible fates of the soul, the key players are angels, St Peter, and a pair of ecclesiastics – one of whom was identified at an early date as 'Ælgarus' (doubtless Æthelgar who, prior to being bishop of Selsey and then archbishop of Canterbury, had been first abbot of the reformed New Minster (964–80)).

Cnut was certainly a donor of fine Anglo-Saxon books; yet whether he was also an active patron of them is debatable – the best source for his activities in the former respect does not suggest that he was. The *Vita Wulfstani* records that Cnut sent a fine sacramentary and psalter to Cologne; however, it also informs us that, far from being a royal commission, these volumes were made and offered to the king (and his queen) by the master scribe Earnwine of Peterborough on his own initiative in the hope of preferment.[89] The same is likely to have been true of the illustrated luxury *Vitae sanctorum* – not an obvious choice for a royal diplomatic gift – that Cnut was reputed to have donated to William II of Aquitaine.[90]

The case of Emma-Ælfgifu may have been different. We know that on at least one occasion she commissioned a literary work, the *Encomium Emmae reginae*, in whose frontispiece she was depicted: majestically enthroned, she is taking with both hands the open book that is held up to her by a kneeling cleric; her receiving of the text is central to the composition.[91] (It ought, however, to be remembered that the *Encomium* was composed, and the single extant copy surely written and decorated, in Flanders, not England.) Whether we should then presume that the psalter she is recorded to have given to her brother Robert and the *textus aureus* that she was believed to have presented to Christ Church were new commissions from Anglo-Saxon scribes and artists is an open question.[92] That other routes were open to queens wishing to acquire fine 'altar' books is underlined by the Abingdon Chronicle, which castigates Queen Edith, wife of Edward the Confessor, for appropriating their most

89 William of Malmesbury, *Vita Wulfstani*, I, 1: Darlington 1928, p. 5; Winterbottom and Thomson 2002, p. 16.

90 *Acta Concilii Lemovicencis* II: PL CXLII, col. 1369.

91 BL, Add. 33241. Campbell 1998. Colour plate: Roesdahl *et al.* 1981, p. 156.

92 Orderic Vitalis, *Historia ecclesiastica*, bk III: Chibnall 1969–80, II, p. 42. Gervase, *Gesta regum*: Stubbs 1880, II, p. 56.

valuable treasures, including 'a gospel-book adorned with gold and gems, of marvellous workmanship'.[93]

A measure of uncertainty also surrounds the last decorated volume that we can associate with Anglo-Saxon royalty: the gospel-lectionary of Queen Margaret of Scotland (daughter of Edward the Ætheling and wife of Malcolm Canmore).[94] Though greatly treasured by her (as her near-contemporary biography reveals), the manuscript is, by late Anglo-Saxon standards, a comparatively modest one and may have been a generation old by the time it came into Margaret's hands (Plate 10.10). Whether the *textus argenteus* she was recorded to have presented to the shrine of St Cuthert at Durham was this manuscript or a different gospel-book is debatable.[95]

In sum, while the scanty surviving evidence undoubtedly gives an inadequate picture of the extent of late Anglo-Saxon royalty's interaction with decorated books which were, after all, an important part of the currency of political power, nevertheless, the paucity of extant manuscripts with royal associations (even spurious ones) and the near-dearth after 939 of illuminated books which were demonstrably royal commissions, suggests that they were not outstanding patrons of them. Indeed, from the late tenth century onwards, members of the high-ranking nobility are more visible as patrons than are royalty. It is inconceivable that Æthelweard (d. *c.* 998), ealdorman of the western shires, the author of a Latin chronicle, who (with his son, Æthelmær) 'sponsored' the work of Ælfric, did not also commission and own books, some of which will doubtless have been decorated; and, as we have seen, Ælfgar and Ælfgifu of Mercia and Judith of Flanders, wife of Tostig Godwinson, certainly did (Plates 10.9 and 18.2). Equally, Harold Godwinson was remembered for having given (while still an earl and not yet king) three large golden gospel-books and five silver-gilt ones to his foundation of Waltham.[96] Correspondingly, there are extant eleventh-century manuscripts for which it has proved tempting to posit a secular destination. The extensively illustrated Old English Hexateuch is one such case; the extraordinary-shaped Paris Psalter (lacking a calendar, organised according to the Roman office rather than following Benedictine use, and with parallel Latin–Old English texts) is another.[97] In the absence of hard evidence, however, such suggestions remain just that.

93 *Chronicon Monasterii de Abingdon*: Stevenson 1858, I, p. 485.

94 BodL., Lat. liturg. f.5. Facs.: Forbes-Leith 1896; comment: Gameson 1997; Rushforth 2007.

95 Reginald of Durham, 'Libellus': Raine 1835, ch. 98. Rushforth 2007, pp. 85–6, argues cogently for this being a different book.

96 Waltham Chronicle, ch. 16: Watkiss and Chibnall 1994, pp. 32–3.

97 BL, Cotton Claudius B.iv; BnF, lat. 8824: facs. Colgrave 1958; Ó'Néill 2001.

The most visible patrons are, of course, ecclesiastics – occasionally individually, more frequently collectively – some of whom were the 'manufacturers' as well as 'consumers' of the volumes in question. The image in the early eleventh-century Arundel 155 Psalter which shows a group of Christ Church monks holding up a copy of the *Rule* to St Benedict himself, while one of their number clutches the saint's feet and brandishes a psalter (presumably this very manuscript), provides a potent visual evocation of a decorated book as a communal possession;[98] so, too, in a subtler way does the group of Winchester monks (the central one holding a book) depicted under arches at the bottom of the frontispiece to the New Minster *Liber vitae*.[99] Many of the volumes surveyed here were doubtless made and used as such. Yet even within communities, particular individuals occasionally stand out as energetic patrons – and, as just noted, one figure is singled out in Arundel 155. The presence of a bibliophile abbot, prior or bishop was crucial for the sponsorship of decorated books, just as talented artists were needed if they were to be produced 'in-house'. Now whoever may be intended by the prone figure depicted in Arundel 155, we know that the master scribe Eadwig Basan played a key role in the production of this and other high-grade books; correspondingly, the figures of Ælfwine, monk, dean, then abbot (1031–57) of New Minster, and of Ælfsige the scribe can be perceived behind the New Minster *Liber vitae* and other coeval Winchester manuscripts.[100]

High-ranking clergy must have possessed their own books, many of which will subsequently have passed into institutional collections. Between 1002 and 1005 Ælfric, archbishop of Canterbury, bequeathed his personal book collection to St Albans (where he had formerly been abbot), while leaving his psalter, doubtless decorated, to Ælfheah/Ælphege, the bishop of Winchester who was to be his successor at Canterbury.[101] Bishop Ælfwold of Crediton bequeathed (997×1012) his three service books to Crediton, but left a Hrabanus and a martyrology to a layman – Ordwulf, son of Ealdorman Ordgar and founder of Tavistock.[102] Æthelwold of Winchester certainly commissioned a magnificent benedictional for his own use, specified the nature of its decoration, and doubtless oversaw many of its details; the other decorated Winchester benedictionals were presumably also made for particular bishops, albeit no longer certainly identifiable. These are very fine books; by contrast, the pontifical that was probably made for St Dunstan and the portiforium which probably

98 BL, Arundel 155, fol. 133r; colour plate: Backhouse, *et al.* 1984, plate XVIII; Gameson 2000b, plate 9.
99 BL, Stowe 944. 100 Keynes 1996b, pp. 66–9.
101 Whitelock *et al.* 1981, I, no. 44, p. 241.
102 *Ibid.*, no. 52, pp. 384–6.

belonged to St Wulfstan of Worcester are rather more modest – service-books, even those designed for episcopal use, were by no means invariably lavish.[103] The small-format but compendious Winchester prayerbook that was effectively the personal property of Ælfwine during his stint as dean of New Minster (and who may, moreover, have been one of its two main scribes) is likewise neat but not lavish; nevertheless, it is punctuated by three full-page drawings, one of which (the Crucifixion) incorporates an inscription that specifically relates the image – along with the devotions that follow – to the owner of the book: 'may this cross consecrate Ælfwine in body and mind, hanging on which [cross] God drew all things to him'.[104]

Another decorated volume that may have been made for an individual churchman is an illustrated herbal: it has an arresting prefatory image of a monk offering the volume to a towering ecclesiastic who, flanked by a soldier, transfixes a lion with a staff (Plate 10.12).[105] While the possibility that the central figure is a representation of one of the authors (Aesculapius or Apuleius) cannot be ruled out,[106] the visual evidence – an unhaloed triumphant churchman holding a closed book and being offered another – hardly supports this interpretation. On the contrary, the iconography, which combines elements of Christ triumphant with echoes of donor portraits and ruler imagery, seems calculated to project the majesty, spirituality and learning of the ecclesiastical figure. This image more than holds its own with the famous depictions of 'episcopal might' that were produced for Ottonian contemporaries, notably Egbert of Trier (977–93) and Sigebert of Minden (1022–36): in England, no less than Germany, bishops and abbots were powerful men, great players on the political as well as the ecclesiastical stage, and they were better placed than secular grandees to recognise and exploit the power of fine books to smooth their paths in both these theatres of action. Equally, the presence of the prostrate archbishop in the initial to Psalm 1 in the Harley 603 Psalter hints that he might have instigated, or at least been the projected recipient of, this ambitious project, even though the (unfinished) book eventually became a communal one. But then, as the wills cited above underline, great ecclesiastical patrons might commission manuscripts on behalf of, or at least with a view to the eventual enriching of, a particular ecclesiastical institution. The book-collecting activities of Bishop Leofric (d. 1072) for Exeter in the third quarter of the eleventh century and those of Bishop William of Saint-Calais/Carilef

103 BnF, lat. 943; CCCC, 391.
104 BL, Cotton Titus D.xxvi+xxvii: Günzel 1993; Keynes 1996b, pp. 111–23.
105 BL, Cotton Vitellius C.iii, fol. 11v; facs.: d'Aronco and Cameron 1998 with colour plate I.
106 Indeed, it is favoured by d'Aronco and Cameron 1998, pp. 27–30.

(d. 1096) for Durham in the final quarter are well-documented cases in point. The situation is exemplified by the two surviving volumes from a three-volume set of Augustine's *Enarrationes in Psalmos* that was made for William. One includes an image of the illuminator (Robert Benjamin) at the feet of the bishop who is shown as a commanding figure directly below a (rather diminutive) bust-figure of the Deity; the other ends with a colophon that names the scribe (also a William) and records the bishop's commissioning of the book while in exile.[107] William of Saint-Calais was clearly the patron, but the volumes were presumably destined for, and rapidly reached, his see of Durham where they were promptly listed among 'the books that Lord William the bishop gave to St Cuthbert'.[108]

Who were the illuminators; where and how did they work? Some may have been 'artists' who worked in a variety of media, a few of whom might have been hired professionals. The last was demonstrably the case for certain book illuminators in twelfth-century England; however, for earlier periods, lacking extant panel and wall paintings and with a dearth of records relating to illuminators as opposed to scribes, hard evidence is elusive. The strongest case, albeit wholly circumstantial, relates to the artist of the frontispiece of the 'Ramsey Psalter', the only really grand book from the circle of St Oswald of Worcester (d. 992); the same person, active around the millennium, was manifestly also responsible for all the major decoration in a deluxe gospel-book that was made and kept at Saint-Bertin in Flanders, for the addition of evangelist figures to another gospel-book that had probably been written somewhere in the same region but ended up in Germany, for a dedication-colophon image in a copy of Gregory *On Ezekiel* that was made at Fleury and stayed there; and for drawings of the constellations in an astronomical compilation that may also have been produced at Fleury.[109] The circumstances that this individual never seems to have worked as a text scribe and that he was clearly peripatetic, able to spend periods of time, some evidently long, at different places in England and on the Continent, added to the fact that his contributions were invariably restricted to the highest-status artwork in the books in question, all favour the suggestion that he was a professional artist rather than a monastic scribe.

Most book decorators, by contrast, were probably also scribes, and the overwhelming majority were doubtless ecclesiastics. A certain Ælfnoth *pictor et sacerdos* appears in tenth place in the *Nomina fratrum novi cenobii* list of the New

107 DCL, B.II.13 and B.II.14: Mynors 1939, nos. 31–2, plates 20–1.

108 Booklist in DCL, A.II.4: reproduced Gullick 1990, fig. 1; New Pal. Soc., 1st series (1903), plate 17.

109 BL, Harley 2904; Boulogne, BM, 11; PML, M 827; Orléans, Médiathèque, 175; BL, Harley 2506. See Gameson 2010.

Minster *Liber vitae*;[110] and that monastic scribes could also be artists is documented in the cases of St Dunstan and Earnwine of Peterborough[111] – indeed work by the former probably survives in the form of the pictorial frontispiece to his so-called 'Classbook'.[112] Equally, when a book is entirely written by one hand and decorated by a single artist, it is obviously possible that the scribe and artist were one and the same; the likelihood increases if the artwork in question is closely woven into the text, and it is further enhanced if the book was seemingly the product of a small scriptorium. A strong candidate on all these fronts is the Salisbury Psalter, the product of a south-western centre, possibly Shaftesbury, whose initials, all by one hand, are closely interwoven into the holograph text.[113] The same is true where well-integrated decoration of a certain style appears within the work of one particular scribe of a shared book but nowhere else – as is the case in the Tanner Bede, whose main run of decorated initials corresponds exactly with the stint of the principal scribe.[114] A similar case can be made for associating the full-page illustrations in the eleventh-century New Minster Prayerbook with its second scribe ('Scribe B'), in whose stints they all appear; and here there is the further possibility that this hand was that of Dean Ælfwine for whom the manuscript was made.[115]

The Benedictional of Æthelwold (Plate 10.4) was written by one scribe (Godeman) and decorated by a single hand, but as this very high-grade book was the product of a large writing centre – Winchester – at the peak of its creativity, more caution is required. Moreover, the decoration of the other fine books that were written by Godeman, though using the same idioms as the benedictional, is not obviously the work of the same artist. Similarly, the Arundel 155 Psalter and the Eadwig Gospels are both written almost entirely by one scribe (Eadwig Basan) and are decorated by the same artist, who, it is therefore very tempting to deduce, may have been one and the same; however, the strength of the deduction is undermined by the fact that other works by the same scribe – including one further holograph book – are decorated by different illuminators.[116] Moreover, as Eadwig did not in fact write the canon tables of his eponymous gospel-book, fourteen out of the eighteen decorated

110 Birch 1892, p. 31.

111 *Vita Dunstani auctore B*, ch. 12: Stubbs 1874, pp. 20–1; *Vita Wulfstani*, I 1: Darlington 1928, p. 5; Winterbottom and Thomson 2002, p. 16.

112 BodL., Auct. F.4.32. Budny 1992 offers a detailed and more reductive view of the extent of Dunstan's contribution to the drawing.

113 Salisbury CL, 150.

114 BodL., Tanner 10 (two decorated initials of a lesser quality accompany the stint of Scribe 4, and were doubtless his work): Gameson 1992b and c.

115 Keynes 1996b, pp. 66–7 and 111–13.

116 BL, Arundel 155; Hanover, Kestner-Museum, W.M.XXIa.36; and BL, Add. 34890; also Florence, Biblioteca Medicea-Laurenziana, Plut. XVII.20, and York Minster, Add. 1.

pages in this key manuscript do not show close collaboration between this scribe and artist, but rather the reverse – something which hardly favours the case for identifying the two.

As these last examples indicate, within a given scriptorium books might be made by teams of scribes and artists in changing combinations. At one extreme is the early tenth-century Boulogne 10 Gospels (Plate 10.1), largely written by a single scribe and decorated by one artist, but including a short stint by a second scribe which, since it appears within the body of the text, was an integral part of the original work.[117] At the other extreme is the altogether more ambitious Harley 603 Psalter whose initial phase involved the collaboration of two scribes and four artists, all exceptionally able. A complementary but more intractable case, dating from the early eleventh century, is the enigmatic group of four deluxe gospel-books plus a fine sacramentary which were written by the same three scribes working in various combinations – one of whom (known as 'B') appears in all of them – but which are decorated by different artists (Plate 18.3).[118] It is a moot point whether this reflects the diverse configurations of personnel that were possible within a short period in one major scriptorium, the 'turnover' of artists at one place over a span of more than a decade, or the exchange of personnel between different centres. After all, a scribe–artist with a career akin to that of St Dunstan – or someone in the entourage of such a man – could have been working alongside people from Glastonbury in 955, from Ghent in 956, with personnel from London and from Worcester in 958, and then in association with Canterbury scribes by 960. Whether such figures would always have had time to complete their projects in a given centre before moving on is another matter. A letter of 1124×34 from the abbot and prior of Westminster to the prior and community of Worcester discussing the fate of a monk from Great Malvern, who had been working on a missal in Worcester but had fled to Westminster, records quite different circumstances with a potentially similar result – this one monk could have contributed to books in three centres within a short period of time, and there was some doubt over whether he would finish his work at Worcester.[119]

Some of our books provide eloquent testimony to the heavy demands and many uncertainties of production, for they are not completed. As we have seen, the Harley 603 Psalter, an exceptionally complicated and time-consuming

117 Boulogne, BM, 10, Scribe 2 writes some twenty lines in Mark's Gospel.

118 BL, Loan 11; Royal 1 D.ix; Copenhagen, KB, G.K.S. 10 (2°); TCC, B.10.4; Rouen, BM, Y.6. The gospel fragment Bodl., Lat. bib.b.1, fols. 73–4 may also belong to the group; Cambridge, Pembroke 301 is sometimes (questionably) joined to it. Dumville 1993b, pp.116–20 with 139; Pfaff 1995a, pp.15–19. See further Chapter. 18 in this volume.

119 Mason 1988, no. 248A, pp. 116–17.

undertaking, was first streamlined (Plate 10.6) and then aborted; subsequent interventions, first in the later eleventh century and then in the second quarter of the twelfth, failed to bring it to completion. Comparable cases – manuscripts with extensive illustrative programmes that remained unfinished – are the Old English Hexateuch, the Junius 11 Codex of Old English Biblical Poetry, the Ashmole Herbal and the Add. 24199 Prudentius.[120] The vast majority of the more than 400 illustrations in the Hexateuch were sketched out (by the same hand) but the degree of completion to which they were brought varies enormously.[121] In Junius 11, thirty-eight illustrations were supplied by one artist (in quires I–VI), a further ten by a second (in quire VII), while around 100 spaces were left unfilled (in quires VIII–XVII).[122] The pictures of plants in the herbal were contributed up to the first space on fol. 36v but not for the remainder of 36v–43. In the Prudentius, the original late tenth-century artist accomplished sixty-one framed drawings in the first three quires, albeit increasingly unfinished in the last few pages;[123] he began one on the first leaf of quire IV (to which further details were added at a later date), and then gave up, leaving about a third of the cycle blank. Subsequently, motifs were supplied in a piecemeal fashion to the spaces in quires IV and V by at least three different hands, one probably active in the third quarter of the eleventh century, another in the twelfth; a few spaces remain wholly or largely empty.

The decoration of plenty of other high-grade manuscripts is also incomplete, albeit less dramatically. One thinks of the Paris Psalter (where small vignettes were inserted in the spaces left by the shorter Latin text within the first quire but not thereafter), the Grimbald Gospels (which lacks only the display script on one of the incipit pages: Plate 10.8); the Bury Psalter (where the space needed for the incipit to Psalm 101 seems to have been miscalculated), the Pembroke 301 Gospels (in which the artwork was designed and partly painted by one hand, then partially redone and continued by a second, less skilled hand, but the portraits of Mark, Luke and John remained unfinished); the Besançon Gospels (whose Mark portrait was only partly done); and the Copenhagen Gospels (whose full programme of decoration has many little details that were not quite finished).[124] In addition, many more modest

120 BL, Cotton Claudius B.iv, facs.: Dodwell and Clemoes 1974; BodL., Junius 11, facs.: Gollancz 1927; BodL., Ashmole 1431; BL, Add. 24199.

121 Dodwell and Clemoes 1974, pp. 61–4, distinguishing five stages between initiation and completion: faint sketch; colouring of grounds; outlining of main pictorial details; completion of faces and supply of frames; finally highlights and finishing touches.

122 The exact number is uncertain owing to the loss of leaves.

123 From fol. 21r.

124 BnF, lat. 8824 (facs.: Colgrave 1958); BL, Add. 34890, Luke (NB the incipit to Mark has been excised so its degree of completion is unknown); BAV, Reg. lat. 12; Cambridge, Pembroke

manuscripts have blank spaces for ornamental initials that were never executed; one of the most extensive runs of such spaces appears in an ambitiously conceived copy of the Old English *Historia ecclesiastica*.[125] The general phenomenon continued in the wake of the Conquest, as the Wadham and the later Bury Gospels, for instance, show.[126] Indeed, the latter is a particularly extreme case: none of the major artwork – for which ample space had been carefully reserved – was ever supplied.

It is generally impossible now to know what led to the abortion, or non-completion, of the original scheme in such cases, and the precise circumstances no doubt differed from book to book. Contributing factors, one might speculate, could have included the death or departure of the patron or artist, the need to work on something else more urgently, a lack of relevant pigments or other materials, dwindling funds for paying a hired 'professional', and the onset of winter, not to mention external pressures such as Danish invasions. In connection with unfinished work, it is worth remembering that according to some then-current 'moral tales' extolling the virtues of scribal work, every element one contributed towards a book – each pricking, each ruling, each word, etc. – brought spiritual benefit, and not merely the completed volume as a whole.[127] While this was not in itself a motive for non-completion, it did mean that leaving a project unfinished to move on to another need not have been perceived as having a negative impact on the artist's spiritual 'balance sheet'. Be that as it may, collectively these manuscripts are an advertisement of the human variables that were integral to manuscript production but which are now generally irrecoverable. At the same time, the fact that texts were very rarely left incomplete, but unfinished artwork is comparatively common, reminds us that decoration was generally the last stage of production, that it was not essential for the comprehension and use of most books, and that talented artists were in shorter supply than competent scribes.

The number of places with which the production of decorated books can be certainly associated during our period is comparatively limited: in addition to Canterbury and Winchester, it includes Barking, Crowland, Exeter, Glastonbury, Peterborough, Worcester and also perhaps Winchcombe. The number of places to which more than one significantly decorated book can

College, 301; Besançon, BM 14 (those for Matthew, Luke and John have seemingly been excised); Copenhagen, KB, G. K. S. 10 (2°).

125 CCCC, 41.

126 Oxford, Wadham College, A.18.3 (Alexander 1970, ills. 31–4; Kauffmann 1975, ills. 17–18); Cambridge, St John's College, C.23 (73).

127 E.g. the prefatory image and poem in Arras, Médiathèque, 860 (Jerome, *In psalmos*; Saint-Vaast, *s.* xi[1]); reproduction and edition in Gameson 2006b, pp. 59–61 and 72–3.

be securely attributed is very small: Canterbury and Winchester, along with the household of Judith of Flanders (Plate 10.9), and (more tentatively) Peterborough. The picture has undoubtedly been distorted by massive and uneven losses of material along with a paucity of evidence for localising a fair percentage of what survives; nevertheless, the general impression that a small number of centres were responsible for a high percentage of the major illuminated manuscripts, while other scriptoria occasionally indulged in decoration on a limited scale, is fundamentally plausible. The point is underlined by Worcester and Exeter, two centres for which we have a reasonable number of attributable manuscripts. We can thus see that Worcester, leisurely in embarking upon book production, did not indulge in decoration until the middle of the eleventh century and then only in a limited way.[128] Exeter, whose scriptorium and 'library' were largely creations of the time (and initiative) of Bishop Leofric (1050–72), seems to have produced only one decorated manuscript at this time – a fully but modestly illuminated gospel-book.[129] Yet if major illuminated volumes were the prerogative of a small number of scriptoria, many were probably distributed thence to other centres (and individuals). If this was already happening in the second quarter of the tenth century (and the copy of Bede's *Vitae Cuthberti* that Athelstan gave to the community of St Cuthbert suggests that it was[130]), Glastonbury is most likely to have fulfilled the role of supplier. Winchester, it is safe to say, did so in the last third of the century; and Christ Church, Canterbury, moved to the fore in this respect during the third and fourth decades of the eleventh century. It would be a mistake to imagine that even these centres were continuously productive: on the contrary, the evidence indicates that their output waxed and waned according to the needs, resources and personalities at a particular time.

The ambiguous evidence of a large number of unattributable or difficult-to-localise volumes dating from the fifty years before the Norman Conquest suggests that there was then an increase in the number of centres practising major book decoration. This is consonant with other indications that scribal culture as a whole was flourishing at this time and had a broader base than hitherto, a phenomenon which is likely to have been helped by the return to greater stability after the long years of Danish assaults and the enhanced prosperity following upon the contingent release from Danegeld payments. Whatever the truth of this last point, there was certainly a proliferation of centres producing books with minor decoration after 1066. The nature of the ornamentation that

128 Gameson 1996a. 129 BnF, lat. 14782; see n. 73.
130 CCCC, 183; see nn. 4 and 9.

was then fashionable, namely decorated initials, was (unlike full-page miniatures within lavish golden frames) within the reach of almost any scriptorium; and with the notable exception of Salisbury, most centres adopted decorated initials as an integral part of scribal activity. Hitherto an essentially southern phenomenon, book decoration had, by the end of our period, spread towards the Humber (Lincoln) and beyond (Durham).[131]

What type of texts received decoration? With regard to 'library' books, the answer is related to when and where they were produced. After 1066, 'reading' books were often adorned with decorated initials wherever they were made (apart from Salisbury). Before the Conquest, by contrast, it was only at Canterbury that such volumes were regularly enhanced with ornamental initials (Plates 10.2, 10.5). The point is underlined by the fact that a copy of Æthicus Ister's *Cosmographia* that was made at Worcester *c.* 1000 does not have decorated initials, whereas the slightly earlier Canterbury manuscript that was probably its exemplar does.[132]

It would also appear at first sight that works in the vernacular were much less likely to have had decoration of any sort than those in Latin. This is certainly true of gospel-books, Latin copies of which were regularly decorated, Old English ones never. Otherwise, however, the matter is less clear-cut, particularly if the Canterbury library books (which are almost all in Latin and, as just noted, are very much the exception within their genre for being ornamented) are removed from the equation. Anglo-Saxon reading books and homiliaries – the majority of the extant material in Old English – were not by and large decorated, but then neither, prior to 1066, were most of their Latin equivalents. The presence of decorated initials in certain Old English texts (as also in the Anglo-Saxon copy of the Old Saxon *Heliand*) shows that the vernacular was in no way a bar to ornament,[133] and pictures duly appear in the Old English versions of the illustrated 'handbooks' *The Marvels of the East* and the *Pharmocopoeia*.[134] Then, in a class of their own are the very extensive narrative cycles that were lavished on the Old English versions of Old Testament books in the Junius 11 poetry collection and the Cotton Claudius B.iv Hexateuch.[135] While the *Pharmocopoeia* and the *Marvels* are texts with illustrations, Junius 11 was conceived to be, and the Hexateuch was realised as, a picture book: for

131 Surveyed by Thomson 1989, and by Mynors 1939 and Lawrence-Mathers 2003 respectively.

132 BL, Cotton Vespasian B.x; Leiden, Universiteitsbibliotheek, Scaliger 69.

133 CCCC, 41 (OE Bede); BL, Cotton Caligula A.vii (Old Saxon *Heliand*); BL, Cotton. Tiberius B.i (*ASC*). BL, Add. 47967 (OE Orosius); BodL., Tanner 10 (OE Bede); BodL., Bodley 340+342 (Homiliary); BodL., Hatton 20 (OE *Regula pastoralis*).

134 BL, Cotton Vitellius A.xv and C.iii.

135 Facs.: Gollancz 1927; Dodwell and Clemoes 1974.

here the amount of space allotted to pictorial matter approaches (in Junius) or even exceeds (in the Hexateuch) that occupied by written text. Outstanding for their iconographic inventiveness as well as for the sheer quantity of their imagery, both volumes, and above all the Hexateuch, betoken considerable investment of time, effort and thought. The intended function of, and audience for, these ambitious projects remains elusive: use in the schoolroom, for the illiterate or semi-literate within monastic communities, or for secular nobility are all possibilities. What is certain, however, is that the alliance of extensive pictorial narrative and vernacular text made them potentially more accessible to a much greater cross-section of society than most other types of book. For if the partnership of word and image in the Hexateuch permits the sophisticated user to contemplate the dialogue between the pictures and the vernacular text (and possibly even the underlying Latin), it affords his simpler counterpart an attractive and intelligible entrée to key events of Old Testament history.

The number of Latin service-books with major decoration is small: five benedictionals/pontificals, four sacramentaries, one missal and one troper. The list includes two of the most opulent manuscripts of our period (the Benedictional of Æthelwold (Plate 10.4) and the Sacramentary of Robert of Jumièges); nevertheless, such books were clearly the exception rather than the rule.[136] It is impossible to offer meaningful statistics in the case of missals and sacramentaries, most of which survive in a highly fragmentary state, but of benedictionals/pontificals (more of which have come down to us reasonably intact) we have twice as many that are undecorated as decorated – which, as it happens, is also true of the very small corpus of tropers (Plate 10.11).[137] Given that the losses of service-books have undoubtedly been particularly high, there can be no doubt that very many more ordinary copies have perished than luxury ones, and hence that undecorated copies once outnumbered decorated ones by a much higher ratio. But then notwithstanding their exalted function, these volumes – unlike most other books – had texts which could go out of date; moreover, consonant with their still fluid content, there were as yet few conventions concerning how to decorate them. The production of a lavishly decorated service-book was thus by definition the result of exceptional circumstances. In the case of the Benedictional of Æthelwold we

136 On the corpora in general: Dumville 1992, ch. 3; Pfaff 1995a.

137 BL, Cotton Caligula A.xiv has illustrations, whereas CCCC, 473, and BodL., Bodley 775, have a modestly decorated initial (Alexander 1970, ill. 30) and a single gold one respectively for the first Introit trope for Advent. CCCC, 473, emphasises the tropes for *Gloria* and the *Agnus* with enlarged plain coloured capitals.

can relate the initiative to an identifiable and charismatic patron; it is regrettable that evidence for the original owners and contexts of other examples is lacking.

There are some sixteen significantly decorated Anglo-Saxon psalters, ranging in date from the early tenth century to around the time of the Conquest (see Plate 21.3). The great variations not only in their degree of luxury but also in the approaches taken to ornamenting them mirror the general diversity in size, quality and presentation of the manuscripts themselves, which in turn reflects the centrality of the text in contemporary spiritual life and the variety of uses to which it was put. While one example has an extended prefatory cycle of narrative scenes from the lives of David and Christ, another boasts literal illustrations preceding each psalm, and yet another has individual illustrative motifs in the margins of the text.[138] Where some have prefatory images of the Crucifixion, others contain intercalated miniatures of the life, sacrifice and triumph of Christ;[139] and while some have decorated or historiated initials, others do not. The most common figural subjects are, as one would expect, King David and Christ.

Yet psalters are not numerically the most common decorated texts: that distinction belongs to the gospels, of which there are some twenty copies – plus five decorated gospel-lectionaries (Plates 10.1, 10.7–10, 18.1–3 and 18.5).[140] Moreover, whereas only a third of the psalters included gold, the metal was used in most of these gospel-books. (The fact, noted above, that no Old English copy of the gospels has significant ornament is thus all the more striking.) Interestingly, only a couple of our gospel-books were produced before *c.* 1000, whereas over twenty date from around or after the millennium, the greatest concentration being in the first third of the eleventh century.[141] Their programmes of decoration are, unsurprisingly, more standardised than those of psalters, generally following the familiar formula of canon tables, evangelist portraits and decorated incipits. Within these parameters, many variations were possible – as we have seen, one artist used the canon tables to explore the nature of the Godhead, while another took advantage of the opening of John's Gospel to make a complex statement about salvation history[142] – but attempts

138 BL, Cotton Tiberius C.vi; Harley 603; BAV, Reg. lat. 12. Further on Anglo-Saxon psalters in general see Chapter 21 below.

139 E.g. BL, Harley 2904; CUL, Ff. 1. 23 respectively.

140 See further Chapter 18 below.

141 This pattern might suggest that older Insular (and other) copies were still seeing active use in *s.* x and beyond, something which annotations and additions from this period sometimes confirm, as e.g. in CUL, Kk.1.24; Hereford CL, P.I.2; Lichfield CL, 1; and BL, Royal 1 B.vii. See also Dumville 1992, pp. 119–27.

142 PML, M 860; BL, Add. 34890.

to expand them are few. Only three artists introduced general frontispieces, though this should be seen in relation to the likelihood that some high-grade copies will have been fronted by imagery as part of their long-lost treasure bindings.[143] Two of the three pictorial frontispieces (prefacing the book as a whole) show the Crucifixion, the other (heading the first gospel) depicts a majestic crowned, blessing Deity holding a cross-inscribed book and pointing to the incipit to Matthew on the facing page, thus advertising the divine authority of the text and seemingly inviting or instructing the reader to enter it (Plate 18.3).[144] The principal theme explored visually within gospel-books is, naturally, the activities of the evangelists (shown at different stages of the physical process of writing), their spirituality (evoked by their symbols), their divine inspiration (indicated by the hand of God, or by their interaction with their symbol[145]), and the relationship between their accounts (illustrated in the canon tables and articulated via the interrelationships between the imagery of the evangelist portraits). The special status of the words of the gospels and psalms as divinely inspired scripture, the centrality of both texts to almost every aspect of spiritual life, along with the fact that there was a much stronger and broader pre-existing tradition for ornamenting them, doubtless accounts for the regularity with which copies were decorated (though such associations were evidently not transferred to Old English gospel-books). Here decoration inspired man and glorified God. In service-books, by contrast, it inspired man and sometimes arguably also glorified man – in the person of the human user. One of the purposes of Æthelwold's Benedictional was surely to project the majesty as well as the piety of its owner (Plate 10.4). The lavish Sacramentary of Robert of Jumièges and the Caligula Troper were doubtless designed to fulfil similar roles, though for whom in particular is unfortunately now unknown (Plate 10.11).

We have here been touching upon the functions of late Anglo-Saxon manuscript art, and it is appropriate to conclude with further general reflections on this theme. The decoration of texts – which, of course, had a long history by the tenth and eleventh centuries – was an outgrowth of, and a means of intensifying, the various roles that books performed. Decoration could help

143 The sixteenth-century inventory of the treasures of Saint-Rémi, Reims, describes the treasure binding of the gospel-book of Ælfgar and Ælfgifu as adorned with depictions of the Crucifixion and God the Father, plus four angels (Hinkle 1970, pp. 24–6).

144 PML, M 869 and M 709; TCC, B.10.4.

145 Notably St Matthew in the Grimbald Gospels (BL, Add. 34890, fol. 10v; colour plate: Temple 1976, ill. 215) and Cambridge, Pembroke College, 301, fol. 10v (colour plate: Rushforth 2007, fig. 26).

a book to present information, expand the range of what it might convey, and assist in making it memorable. Initials subdivided and articulated the text; illustrations aided the reader in visualising its content. A narrative such as the *Psychomachia*, Prudentius' poetic allegory of the struggle for the soul, was more vivid and affective with action-filled pictures; the events of the Old Testament as recounted in the Old English Hexateuch were more intelligible and memorable when accompanied by illustrations. Just as the poetic telling of biblical narrative and eschatological drama, preserved in Junius 11, elevated the tone and presented the stories with an epic grandeur, so the accompanying illustrations might in theory highlight particular incidents and issues by rendering them visible and concrete – though in reality the positioning of the images within the narrative left something to be desired in this case. An image of Dunstan, Edgar and Æthelwold all holding the same document stressed the official status of the *Regularis concordia* (as well as projecting the virtues of a harmonious alliance between church and state),[146] just as the depiction of a venerable author working under divine inspiration underlined the spiritual authority of the words that followed – be it of the gospels or a commentary. In all these cases the artwork added more than just illustration: it articulated the text, it could often be read in its own right, independently of as well as in tandem with the writing, and it added very considerably to the interest, attractiveness, value and potency of the book.

Some artwork could have a metaphysical function. Images of the Divinity raised the mind of the reader from the language on the page to the celestial realms beyond, inviting reflection on the nature of the Deity in particular and on spiritual mysteries in general. At its best, some book illustration was visual theology, offering vivid and memorable glimpses of the mysteries that pass human understanding. Indeed, the iconography of the Benedictional of Æthelwold and the canon tables of the Arenberg Gospels, to take a couple of examples, are as much theological statements as the writings of Berengar of Tours (d. 1088) and Lanfranc of Bec and Canterbury (d. 1089) (Plates. 10.4, 18.5). Anglo-Saxon artists in the generations around the millennium explored central concepts of the Christian faith – the Incarnation, the Crucifixion, the role and status of the Virgin Mary, and perhaps most challenging of all, the Trinity – with determination and flair, producing devotional and inspirational images with a significant theological content.[147] The opening of John's Gospel in the Grimbald Gospels, for instance, is a more powerful and overt exposition

146 BL, Cotton Tiberius A.iii. 147 Raw 1990 and 1997b.

of the Godhead and of its implications for mankind than any tract, yet is still rich in subtleties.

More generally, decoration enhanced the visual appeal and material worth of key books, making them attractive *objets d'art*, resonant status symbols and worthy gifts, thereby better suiting them for a range of practical functions (and let it not be forgotten that the vast majority of tenth- and eleventh-century manuscript art was ornamental as opposed to figural). Æthelwold's golden benedictional and Judith of Flanders' decorated gospel-books advertised the prestige of their owners, as well as serving their spiritual needs (Plates 10.4, 10.9). The beauty of the finest service-books, psalters and gospel-books reflected the honour with which they were regarded; the supreme craftsmanship along with the expensive materials that were lavished on them made them luxurious objects that could command awe and wonder – such that King Malcolm of Scotland, though illiterate, could admire those used by his Anglo-Saxon queen, Margaret, and might further enrich them with precious materials (Plate 10.10).[148] These marvellous treasures – a synthesis of books, *objets d'art*, and sacred relics – were fitting expressions, almost pieces indeed, of heaven. As such, they were all the more effective as tools for interacting with the divine.

There is no doubt that great churchmen like Æthelwold appreciated the kudos and splendour of fine works of art, and prized art's ability to project and immortalise particular values – not to mention the exponents of them. Such aesthetic and material aspirations interlocked, rather than conflicted, with the spiritual functions of the works in question. Æthelwold's highly personalised benedictional simultaneously represented spirituality, devotion and self-aggrandisement: it honoured the user of the book, his bishopric and his other foundations, the relevant patron saints, and above all, God – contributing to winning the favour of heaven. Whoever may or may not not have looked at these luxurious volumes – and we can be sure that they were shown to anyone who mattered – contemporaries knew that God and the saints saw them. Moreover, like the mass (at which it was used) such a book was, through its sublime glory, a potent channel for divine grace, helping mortal man to walk with God. The most explicit form of this idea was to depict a particular human figure actually in the presence of a saint or the Divinity. Images such as Athelstan before St Cuthbert, the community of Christ Church alongside St Benedict, not to mention those of Dunstan, Edgar, Cnut, Emma-Ælfgifu, and Judith of Flanders in the presence of Christ (Plates 10.3 and 10.9) gave

148 *Vita S. Margaretae*, ch. 6: Hinde 1868, p. 241.

the human figures in question the inestimable blessing of a perpetual, direct relationship with heaven. They thus realised the wish of the many prayers and formulae that implored the Deity to remember and protect his loving servants, to join them now and hereafter to the company of heaven, and to bring them metaphysically and physically to his presence.

11

Bookbindings

MICHAEL GULLICK

Among the tenth-century notes added to the end of the Lindisfarne Gospels is one concerning the production of the manuscript:

> Eadfrith ... originally wrote this book ... And Æthilwald ... impressed it on the outside and covered it ... And Billfrith ... forged the ornaments which are on it on the outside and adorned it with gold and with gems and also with gilded-over silver – pure metal.[1]

Whatever the status of this text, the inclusion of the names of a binder and a goldsmith is very unusual among pre-Conquest records of book production. A binder would have covered the 'outside' of a manuscript – the Lindisfarne text does not specify with what, and the meaning of 'impressing' the cover is uncertain – and a goldsmith would have decorated it. However, a binder would usually do more than merely covering the outside, although his other work is mostly invisible when completed. There are four main operations in binding a manuscript: first, sewing the quires together; second, attaching the boards (which may or may not have been made by the binder); third, covering the boards; and, last, decorating the covers.[2] Æthilwald was only attributed the third of these operations in the Lindisfarne text, and Billfrith was credited with the fourth.

Unfortunately, almost nothing is known about pre-Conquest binders and there are so few surviving bindings that very little is known about their work either. Only seven of the principal manuscripts containing Old English are in medieval bindings, or have any part of a medieval binding, of *any* date.[3]

1 BL, Cotton Nero D.iv fol. 259r, translated in Kendrick *et al.* 1956–60, p. 5, and Brown 2003b, pp. 103–4 (with, at pp. 205–6, a speculative account of the earliest binding).

2 For the medieval written evidence for these operations see Vezin 1989.

3 I have not had the opportunity to examine Vercelli, Biblioteca Capitolare, CXVII (*s.* x²) which Ker 1957, p. xli, states has medieval boards. A suggestion that the binding of the 'Cædmon' manuscript of Old English Poetry (BodL., Junius 11) was 'Anglo-Saxon' (Ker 1957, p. 408, wisely had 'medieval') has been shown to be unfounded (Raw 1984).

Several collections with important pre-Conquest manuscripts, such as those of Matthew Parker, Robert Cotton, and Robert and Edward Harley, were assembled at times when collectors systematically rebound their books. Of the old ecclesiastical libraries with pre-Conquest books which were not all alienated at the Dissolution of the Monasteries or later, only Worcester still has some pre-Conquest bindings.[4] A pioneer survey of surviving bindings on pre-Conquest manuscripts of English origin or provenance, published in 1975, listed barely a dozen examples, all of which have been repaired or reworked, mostly in both medieval and modern times.[5] Many of the survivors are in the Bodleian Library at Oxford, and these have been described in minute detail in an exemplary study.[6] Since 1975 four more have been identified elsewhere, although the origin of the binding of one of these is uncertain.[7]

Medieval bindings with wooden boards can be divided into three main types, according to the system employed to attach boards to the sewn quires of a manuscript. These types are termed 'Carolingian' (to which nearly all pre-Conquest bindings of English origin or provenance belong), 'Romanesque' and 'Gothic'. In the history of bookbinding these terms are strictly typological and do not refer to limits of date. The earliest English Carolingian binding is tenth-century (the earliest Continental ones are late eighth), and the earliest English Romanesque bindings are datable to the 1080s (the earliest Continental ones are mid-eleventh). There are a few early European bindings of another type whose origins lie in the eastern Mediteranean and the beginnings of the codex form of book. One, in superb condition, is on the late seventh-century English-made Stonyhurst Gospel, and it is one of the most important European medieval bindings of any date to have survived.

What follows is an account of the Stonyhurst Gospel and its relatives, of English Carolingian and early Romanesque bindings, followed by a discussion of some other kinds of evidence concerning pre- and post-Conquest bindings. Because of the huge losses, other kinds of evidence, written and visual, as well as some Continental bindings, are introduced to supplement the evidence of the English bindings themselves. While this account is a summary of what is known, it is also a reflection of how much is unknown. And it should never be

4 Gullick 2001a, p. xliii.

5 Pollard 1975. BL, Add. 9381, a Breton gospel-book in England by *s.* x^{med} (Pollard 1975, no. 19), has post-Conquest boards.

6 Clarkson 1996b.

7 Copenhagen, KB, G. K. S. 1595 (4°) (*s.* xi^{in}) has early, perhaps contemporary, oak boards whose origin is uncertain (Morrish Tunberg 1993 and Gerritsen 1998b). A fifth binding, PML, M 708 (*s.* xi^{med}), may have contemporary boards, but the evidence is difficult to evaluate (C. Clarkson cited in McGurk and Rosenthal 1995, p. 297). I have not examined the New York bindings.

forgotten that the structural details and appearance of any medieval binding are as characteristic of their time and place as script and decoration.

The earliest English bindings

The Stonyhurst Gospel was written and probably bound at Wearmouth-Jarrow at the end of the seventh century. It was placed in the coffin of Cuthbert (d. 687), perhaps on the occasion of his translation in 698, as this was where it was found in 1104, enclosed in a red satchel or 'budget' (now lost).[8] It is the earliest decorated European binding which is still on the manuscript for which it was made, and, but for a few later minor repairs, appears to be more or less exactly as it was when it left the hands of its first binder.[9]

The Stonyhurst Gospel is a small book and its quires were attached together with thread in what can be termed 'chain-stitch sewing', employing two pairs of 'sewing stations', with the thread passing between each pair of stations in the 'spine-fold' at the centre of each quire. The use of one variety of chain-stitch sewing groups the Stonyhurst Gospel with a small number of other early European manuscripts which also employed this 'primary sewing' technique. It may have been the earliest sewing technique to have been used by European binders for multi-quire codices, and its origin appears to lie in the Near East.[10]

The disposition of the sewing stations in the Stonyhurst Gospel – two pairs close together, one each close to the head and tail of the spine – occurs elsewhere. Recent conservation work on a Continental manuscript of the second half of the seventh century which passed into the hands of Boniface (d. 754), revealed that the original sewing employed two pairs of sewing stations, with evidence that thread once passed between each pair as in the Stonyhurst Gospel.[11] Similar evidence occurs in two eighth-century Northumbrian manuscripts.[12]

In the Stonyhurst Gospel there is evidence to suggest that it was first intended to use three primary sewing stations. The folded quires were pricked, one at a time, with three regularly placed tiny holes a few millimetres from

8 The English Province of the Society of Jesus, Stonyhurst College, 55, on loan to the British Library (Loan 74). For budgets see Waterer 1968, and Sharpe 1985.

9 Powell 1956; Powell and Waters 1969; Clarkson 1996b, pp. 59 and 63–4. For a summary: Szirmai 1999, pp. 95–6.

10 Szirmai 1999, pp. 16–23, 33–4, 46–8, 53–7 and 67–9.

11 Fulda, Hessische LB, Codex Bonifatianus 2. Ritterpusch 1982, p. 49 and plate 4.

12 Worcester CL, Add 3 (fragments) (hitherto unpublished), and Kassel, LB, Theol. Qu. 2. For the latter: van Els, 1972, pp. 9 and 24–5. Unfortunately, its cover was removed in 1968 when the manuscript was unnecessarily rebound; see Scholla 2002, pp. 151–5.

the spine-folds. This technique was employed to 'mark up' the position of stations, and, although it was not universally employed, is now well known in manuscripts of the eighth to twelfth centuries.[13] However, no set of stations was made in the spine-folds of the Stonyhurst Gospel using the pricked guide holes, and the nature of the sewing technique which would have used the stations is unknown.

An eighth-century Northumbrian gospel-book (the Cambridge–London Gospels) has evidence that its first binding had four sewing stations, with sewing thread passing between them all along the centre spine-folds of each quire.[14] This, with the Stonyhurst Gospel evidence, suggests that at least two different sewing techniques were known in eighth-century Northumbria, and probably elsewhere in England. This was certainly true on the Continent, and the evidence of Codex Bonifatianus 2 can be compared to an important ninth-century binding which used chain-stitch sewing employing three sewing stations, and therefore cannot have been sewn in exactly the same manner.[15]

The boards of the Stonyhurst Gospel are birch covered with red goatskin. Both covers are decorated but the 'upper' one was more elaborately treated than the 'lower'. The vertical and horizontal framing elements and the central plant scroll motif were raised by moulding the cover skin over cord or leather attached to the board. The interlace elements were drawn with a pointed tool into the cover skin while it was damp, and filled with yellow or blue colour when dry.[16] The 'lower' cover was also decorated with a central panel of drawn lines, and these were also coloured. It has been proposed that both covers were carefully pre-planned employing geometrical principles to develop the designs.[17] The covers use Insular decorative forms, although the plant scroll motif on the upper has more about it of the Mediterranean than the British Isles. The raising of elements of the design on the upper cover also occurs in some Islamic bindings from the ninth century onwards, pointing to an Eastern origin for the technique.[18]

13 Szirmai 1999, p. 143 and fig. 8.2.

14 CCCC, 197B (fragments). Pickwoad 1994, pp. 114–15 and figs. 13–15, but failing to give positions of the sewing stations in the spine-folds.

15 Karlsruhe, Badische LB, Aug. perg. 233. Szirmai 1999, p. 101 and fig. 7.2, reproducing a photograph made and published in the 1930s as the manuscript was unnecessarily rebound in 1972.

16 Powell and Waters 1969, pp. 52–4. For the technique of drawing into damp leather see Waterer 1968, p. 80. Colour reproductions of the upper cover: Brown 1969, frontispiece, and Webster and Backhouse 1991, p. 121.

17 Stevick 1987, reprinted in Stevick 1994, pp. 26–32.

18 Szirmai 1999, p. 59. For a well-preserved eleventh-century Islamic example, see Miner 1957, no. 43 and plate 13.

If the structural and decorative features of the Stonyhurst Gospel binding appear to owe rather more to the East than the West, the special nature of the book and the absence of any contemporary European bindings with which to compare it, make it a genuinely unique artefact, difficult to evaluate and place within a broad historical context.

The Victor Codex is a sixth-century Italian book which passed into the hands of Boniface. The most spectacular feature of its binding is the survival of twelve of twenty-two pieces of metal 'furniture', some decorated, on the covers. These have been dated to the seventh or eighth century and attributed to Northumbria. Each board originally had four 'corner pieces', two pieces each at the fore and back edges, and one each at the head and tail edges.[19]

The boards are Carolingian,[20] covered with red skin decorated with small blindstamped tools of Carolingian type. Boards and covering are almost certainly no earlier than the ninth century, and could be as late as the eleventh. Therefore, as the earliest possible date is later than Boniface's death and the date of the metal furniture,[21] the boards and the covering cannot be English in origin as the book has been on the Continent since the eighth century.[22] The Victor Codex is likely to have been regarded as an important relic at Fulda after the death of Boniface and the decorated binding may have been a manifestation of this feeling. The metal furniture may either have been taken over from an earlier binding of the Victor Codex, or taken from elsewhere, and not become associated with the manuscript until after the death of Boniface.[23]

English Carolingian bindings

There are fifteen manuscripts with some part of a contemporary or early Carolingian binding. However, two of these, both from Exeter, do not have matching boards, for each has one reused board, taken from other bindings in the fifteenth century.[24] And two manuscripts now only have one of their

19 Fulda, LB, Codex Bonifatianus 1. Wilson 1961. For large reproductions of the covers see Köllner 1976, plates 921–2 (I have not seen this binding).

20 For diagrams of the 'lacing path pattern' of the boards and a reproduction of part of the inner face of the lower board, see Wilson 1961, fig. 4 and plate 37, and Szirmai 1999, fig. 7.8 (where classified as Type I).

21 Wilson 1961, p. 215, concluded that the binding was contemporary with the furniture. For the tools on the lower cover see *ibid.*, fig. 3, and for a later date for the binding see Vezin 1988, pp. 394–5.

22 Wilson 1961, p. 210.

23 In view of the different dates proposed for the binding and the furniture, the relationship between the two deserves to be reinvestigated. I am grateful to Leslie Webster of the British Museum for confirming Wilson's date for the furniture (private communication).

24 CUL, Ii.2.4 (hitherto unpublished) and BodL., Auct. F.1.15 (Clarkson 1996b, no. II).

Carolingian boards.[25] This makes a total of twenty-nine boards from seventeen bindings. The manuscripts with Carolingian boards range from lavishly decorated books, such as the Grimbald Gospels and the Bosworth Psalter, to plain ones, such as a collection of grammatical texts.[26] Few centres are represented among the survivors, for most originate from either Canterbury or Worcester, and the medieval provenance of most of them is either Canterbury, Worcester or Exeter.

Only one of the bindings has survived in virtually pristine condition, a late example which also has Romanesque features, dating from soon after *c.* 1076.[27] Most of the evidence comprises pre-Conquest boards reused by later medieval binders on the books for which they were originally made. This feature prompts the question of how many pre-Conquest bindings survived intact until the Dissolution of the Monasteries. However, given that the survivors come from so few centres, this may be more a reflection of rebinding programmes at these centres than a reflection of universal practice. Unfortunately, little has been published on individual manuscripts,[28] and very little is known about late medieval programmes of rebinding earlier manuscripts at English centres. (Christ Church, Exeter and Worcester are known to have had extensive repair or rebinding campaigns in the late Middle Ages, and there may have been others.)

It is usually impossible to determine why it was considered necessary to resew and rework earlier bindings. Only one, perhaps two, pre-Conquest bindings have their original primary and end-band sewing: one still has contemporary primary and end-band sewing, and the other may have.[29]

All but two of the bindings appear to have been originally sewn on 'supports' of cord. The exceptions are post-Conquest examples sewn on 'straps' or 'bands' of skin, almost invariably used in Romanesque bindings.[30] It appears that most, if not all, had boards made of oak, as were the majority of Continental Carolingian boards.[31]

25 BL, Add. 34890 (Pollard 1975, no. 9), and Worcester CL, Q.21 (Gullick 2001a, fig. 5).

26 BL, Add. 34890 and Add. 37517 (Pollard 1975, no. 8), and Worcester CL, Q.5 (Gullick 2001a, fig. 4).

27 Canterbury CL, Add. 172. Gameson 2008, pp. 147–68.

28 For an exemplary study treating the complicated and confusing evidence concerning the early bindings of DCL, A.II.17 (*s.* vii/viii) see Powell 1980.

29 BodL., Bodley 229 (*s.* xi[1]) and Bodley 331 (*s.* x/xi) (Clarkson 1996b, nos. VII and IV).

30 CUL, Ii.2.4 and Canterbury CL, Add. 172. Skin supports do occur in some Continental Carolingian bindings; see Szirmai 1999, p. 112. Here and throughout I usually use the neutral term 'skin' rather than 'leather' or 'tawed skin' to avoid being precise about the nature of the skin used for sewing supports or covering since there is much uncertainty in the matter. See further Clarkson 1996b, p. 212, and Szirmai 1999, p. 171 n. 6.

31 Szirmai 1999, p. 103.

The boards of Continental Carolingian bindings were attached in different ways to sewn quires, and these attachment methods can be divided into groups. Most English Carolingian boards belong to the commonest Continental group,[32] as well as three which are related to this group. One binding has unusual boards, although there are a few Continental parallels.[33] Concerning the nature of the wood employed and the methods of attachment, there is nothing 'Anglo-Saxon' about the boards that distinguishes them from their Continental contemporaries.

Because nearly all pre-Conquest bindings have been reworked and repaired, only three retain any part of their original covering skin.[34] The most complete of these still has one of two extensions of the cover skin at the ends of the spine ('tabs'), with a 'perimeter sewing' of blue thread, the only English pre-Conquest tab to survive.[35] The same binding also has a contemporary or near-contemporary ink title running down the spine, the only early spine-title to survive.[36]

Only two of the pre-Conquest bindings have evidence of straps to keep their boards closed when their books were not in use. One has a strap anchored with three copper-alloy nails near the centre of the lower board, passing around to a projecting copper-alloy 'side-pin' near the centre of the upper board,[37] an arrangement not found in any Continental bindings. The strap is certainly early, possibly contemporary, but the metal strap-end (which has a hollowed dome to go over the pin to keep it in place) is of uncertain date and almost certainly a replacement. Radiographs of the boards of an earlier binding show that it apparently once had two similarly placed straps, each fixed with three nails, passing to side-pins on the upper board.[38] These contemporary or near-contemporary straps anchored at the centres of the lower boards seem to be a feature unique to these two English Carolingian bindings, for they do not appear on Continental ones. However, the apparent absence of a 'fastening' system on most English bindings is in sharp contrast to Continental bindings, nearly all of which do have evidence of fastening.[39]

32 Four 'board attachment' methods (Types I–IV), have been distinguished, the commonest being Type I. Szirmai 1999, pp. 103–12 and figs. 7.6–7.12.

33 Szirmai 1999, pp. 111–12 and fig 7.12 (Type IV).

34 BodL., Bodley 775 and Hatton 113 (Clarkson 1996b, nos. IX and XIV), and Worcester CL, Q.5. For the nature and character of covering skins used in Continental Carolingian bindings, see Szirmai 1999, pp. 127–8.

35 The tabs of Continental Carolingian bindings have a variety of profiles; see Szirmai 1999, pp. 125–6 and fig. 7.26.

36 Many Continental Carolingian bindings have spine-titles; see Szirmai 1999, pp. 129–30.

37 Worcester CL, Q.5.

38 BodL., Bodley 319 (Clarkson 1996b, no. V, fig. 24).

39 Szirmai 1999, pp. 131–2.

One case study

The Grimbald Gospels, a richly decorated manuscript made *c.* 1020 at Christ Church, Canterbury, was probably sewn and bound soon after it was written.[40] At the end of the eleventh century (by which date it was at Winchester), it may have been resewn and rebound reusing the original boards. This rebinding is suggested by the use of skin supports (unusual in Carolingian bindings) and the presence of an additional quire at the end of the manuscript containing text written by an expert Norman scribe whose hand has been identified in other Winchester books.[41] At the end of the Middle Ages the manuscript was rebound again. One of the boards was retained, extensively reshaped according to the fashion of the time, but the other board – presumably either lost or damaged – was replaced with a new one. It seems unlikely that a manuscript such as this was heavily used, so it is notable that it was considered necessary to rebind it twice over a period of 500 years.

From Carolingian to Romanesque

The change from 'Carolingian' to 'Romanesque' bindings in England was not a sudden one, for there are several bindings of the middle or second half of the eleventh century which have both Carolingian and Romanesque features. One is the Winchester Troper, made *c.* 1050 at the Old Minster, Winchester. This has end-band supports of skin (unusual in Carolingian bindings) laced into the boards in Carolingian fashion, but two primary supports, whose nature is unknown, laced into the boards in Romanesque fashion.[42] Another is a late eleventh-century manuscript made at St Augustine's, Canterbury, with sewing supports of skin but boards with a lacing path that is Carolingian.[43] Finally, two post-Conquest Worcester bindings with skin supports each have peculiar, but different, lacing path patterns in their boards.[44]

It is likely that these features reflect a period of experiment and change as the transition from Carolingian to Romanesque binding structures took place. It is probably significant that the four bindings discussed above were

40 BL, Add. 34890. 41 Bishop 1954–8, pp. 190–1.

42 BodL., Bodley 775 (Clarkson 1996b, no. IX and figs. 41–4).

43 Canterbury CL, Add. 172.

44 BodL., Hatton 23 and Hatton 48 (Clarkson 1996b, no. VIII and figs. 35–40, and no. I and figs. 5–8). Jan Szirmai has kindly drawn my attention to two Continental bindings which have similar peculiar lacing paths to the first of these: St Gallen, Stiftsbibliothek, 97 (*s.* ix, unknown origin) and Würzburg, UB, M.p.th.f.71 (*s.* xi, Amorbach).

made at places (Winchester, St Augustine's and Worcester) where book production appears to have been more or less continuous between the middle and end of the eleventh century, and where an English ethos, especially in matters of script, continued for at least a generation after the Conquest. Even in binding, the old and the new appear to have existed side by side for a period.

English Romanesque bindings

The earliest known Continental examples of Romanesque bindings date to about the middle of the eleventh century.[45] There are some 175 manuscripts of English origin or provenance datable between the Conquest and *c.* 1100 of which not many more than about half a dozen are still in contemporary bindings, the earliest ones datable to the 1080s.[46] The appearance of the earliest English Romanesque bindings coincides with the beginning of extensive post-Conquest programmes of book production at a number of centres, and these probably accelerated the adoption of the new manner of binding.[47]

The earliest bindings come from two cathedral monasteries, Durham and Christ Church, and two secular cathedrals, Hereford and Salisbury. A manuscript of uncertain origin, written between 1081 and 1088 and given to Durham by 1096, has what is probably the earliest datable post-Conquest binding.[48] The sewing, on skin supports, and lacing path pattern in the boards is thoroughly Romanesque. The binding has a thick cover skin, tabs with a squarish profile, and two straps attached to the lower board, passing to side-pins on the upper. (Two recesses were cut at the fore edge of the upper board for straps, but these were never used.) The straps were not anchored in recesses at the fore edge (as would be usual by about 1100), but set a little way back. Later these straps were replaced by a single strap on the upper board passing to a side-pin on the lower, and this in turn was replaced by two straps on the upper board passing to 'clasps' on the lower. This is an unusually complicated history, but the replacement of straps and the use of different fastening systems on one binding over a period of time is quite common.[49]

45 Szirmai 1999, pp. 140–2.

46 The figure of 175 is based upon the list in Gameson 1999c, supplemented by my own observations.

47 Pollard 1962; Clarkson 1993. Two local surveys: Gullick 1993 and 2001b, and Gullick and Hadgraft 2008, pp. 98–103.

48 Cambridge, Peterhouse, 74. For the origin see Gullick 2001b, pp. 102–3, and for the date Philpott 1994, pp. 131–2.

49 For fastening systems see Szirmai 1999, pp. 167–9 and 251–62, also Cockx-Indestege and Hermans 2004, with many illustrations; and Gullick and Hadgraft 2008, pp. 102–3 and 105.

A manuscript made at Christ Church, Canterbury, datable to the 1080s, has what is probably the earliest surviving more or less pure English Romanesque binding.[50] Its features include coloured end-band thread (blue), tabs at the end of the spine faced with textile (now fragmentary) straps anchored on the upper board passing to side-pins on the lower, and evidence that it was once enclosed in a 'chemise' or 'overcover' of skin.[51] The binding of a manuscript written at Hereford, also datable to the 1080s, has similar features to the Christ Church one (blue end-band thread and tabs faced with textile).[52] It also had one unusual feature, two fore-edge pins (now both lost) in the leading edge of the upper board as part of the fastening mechanism.[53]

The general characteristics of these three early Romanesque bindings include the use of two or three primary sewing supports which more or less divide the height of the spine into equal parts, long lacing path patterns in the boards, and end-bands that were worked once.[54] The boards of these bindings, flush with the edges of the leaves (as is usual), are all of oak, the wood commonly used not only in English Carolingian bindings but also, with few exceptions, in English Romanesque bindings. None of the three has a contemporary spine-title for, although not rare, these are not common on English Romanesque bindings. The earliest surviving example is on a Worcester-made binding of the last third of the eleventh century.[55]

It is notable that there is a different fastening system on each of the three bindings discussed above, and some bindings, such as two late eleventh-century bindings from Salisbury and Worcester, do not have one.[56] It appears that the usual English manner of fastening with a strap (or straps) on the upper board to a side-pin (or pins) on the lower was adopted gradually, perhaps at a different rate at different centres, and that there was no uniformity in this matter before 1100.[57]

50 BodL., Bodley 827. (Clarkson 1996b, no. XI and figs. 50–3, where dated between 1080 and 1110.) My date in the 1080s is based upon unpublished research.

51 For a fairly typical Romanesque overcover see Clarkson 1993, fig. 13; also Szirmai 1999, p. 165 and fig. 8.21. Overcovers, which appear to be unknown on Carolingian bindings, can be easily added or replaced.

52 Hereford CL, O.viii.8. Mynors and Thomson 1993, p. 57.

53 For pins set in the leading edge of the boards of some Continental Carolingian bindings, see Szirmai 1999, pp. 131–2 and figs. 7.30–1. Unlike the Hereford binding, the Continental bindings with fore-edge pins have them set into the lower board.

54 'Compound end-bands', with a secondary, usually decorative, sewing, are unknown before 1100.

55 BodL., Hatton 23 (Clarkson 1996b, p. 188 and fig. 38). It is possible that spine-titles were put on overcovers but, as many of these have been lost, any titles they may have had have been lost with them.

56 BodL., Bodley 835 and Hatton 48 (Clarkson 1996b, no. I).

57 Not all *s*. xii English Romanesque bindings had fastenings, and the use of a strap (or straps) on the lower board (rather than the upper) does occur on some *s*. xii bindings.

Two case studies

Hereford Cathedral O.iii.2, a ninth-century French manuscript with a collection of bibliographical texts, was probably imported into England soon after the Conquest. The indistinct impression of a Carolingian lacing path pattern from the lower board visible on the last leaf shows that it was bound soon after it was written. The book was rebound in England, probably either in the late eleventh or early twelfth century, as the nature and disposition of its sewing supports and sewing thread are Romanesque. At Hereford in the 1620s the boards were removed, the Romanesque sewing retained and the manuscript enclosed with pasteboards covered with leather.[58]

Great Domesday Book contains the result of the survey of England ordered by William the Conqueror in late 1085. The manuscript was probably bound in or soon after 1088, and, although it was subsequently rebound at least five times, there is still enough physical evidence to reconstruct something of the first binding. The position of the sewing stations was marked up with tiny holes and the manuscript was sewn on three primary supports plus end-bands. The end-bands were probably sewn with blue thread.[59]

The binding histories of these two manuscripts can only be released from a knowledge of binding structures combined with informed observation, and similar histories can often be made of other rebound manuscripts. In particular the character, relative position and number of primary sewing stations from different sewing campaigns can reveal how often a manuscript has been rebound.[60]

Treasure bindings

Soon after the death of Wilfred, bishop of Hexham and York, in 709, his biographer observed that the bishop

> had ordered, for the good of his soul, the four gospels to be written out in letters of purest gold on purpled parchment and illuminated. He also ordered jewellers to construct for the books a case (*bibliothecam*) all made of the purest gold and set with the most precious gems.[61]

58 Gullick 1993, p. xxix, and Mynors and Thomson 1993, pp. 17–18.

59 London, National Archives, E31/2. Gullick 1987, pp. 107–9 and fig. 15. For a rebinding in 1346 see Ayton 1989.

60 Recent accounts of the binding histories of two pre-Conquest manuscripts: Gullick 2007, pp. 56–7, and Rankin 2007, pp. 4–5.

61 Colgrave 1927, pp. 36–7.

Whether *bibliothecam* refers to a binding or a protective box is uncertain, but there must have been many pre-Conquest bindings covered with precious metals, jewels, and sometimes ivories. These are now only known from descriptions in written sources.[62] William of Malmesbury in his history of Glastonbury related how the abbey's earliest benefactor, Ine, king of Wessex (688–726), gave gold for the covers of gospel-books in the chapel he furnished.[63] King Æthelstan (927–39) gave a richly decorated Continental-made gospel-book to Christ Church, and a contemporary verse inscription recording the gift suggests that the king was responsible for the binding decorated with jewels.[64] A gospel-book with a treasure binding associated with King Edgar (959–75) in a mid-twelfth-century inventory from Ely is another example of a royal gift.[65] Rather later, the biographer of Margaret of Scotland (d. 1093) mentioned that at least on one occasion her husband ordered a goldsmith to decorate one of the queen's books with gold and jewels.[66]

A glimpse into the means by which one religious foundation acquired at least some of the materials for a treasure binding is found in a note that was added in the second half of the eleventh century to a tenth-century Continental gospel-book that had reached England soon after it was made. This states that two laymen, Ælfric and Wulfwine, goldsmiths of Eadgifu, gave gold to make the gold wire used on the binding. The manuscript was at Thorney by about 1100 and it may be that the binding was made at or for the abbey.[67]

At the time of the Conquest important centres may have possessed a large number of treasure bindings. An inventory, probably drawn up in 1093, of the plate, vestments and books at Ely records fourteen gospel-books (large and small) decorated with gold and silver. The inventory also mentions fifty-seven service-books, twenty-two psalters and a little over 200 other books, a total of 291 volumes.[68] This is a rare glimpse into the number of books owned by a large centre in the late eleventh century, but it is notable that only the bindings of the gospel-books are mentioned. In the mid twelfth century another Ely inventory mentions fifteen large and two small gospel-books in treasure bindings (three more in total than listed in the earlier one), and nearly all of them are described. A Crucifixion scene on one or other of the covers was a common scheme.[69] Another record, an inventory drawn up in 1315 at Christ

62 A large number of these can be retrieved from the index in Lehmann-Brockhaus 1955–60; and see Dodwell 1982, pp. 201–3.
63 Scott 1981, p. 96.
64 BL, Cotton Tiberius A.ii. Lapidge 1981, p. 95.
65 Blake 1962, pp. 290–1.
66 Hinde 1868, p. 241.
67 BL, Add. 40,000. Ker 1957, no. 131, prints the note.
68 Blake 1962, p. 233.
69 *Ibid.*, p. 234.

Church, Canterbury, describes a number of treasure bindings, several of which had no book. This suggests that the bindings were old in the fourteenth century, and, to judge by the descriptions of their decoration, some of them were probably earlier than 1200 and a few may even have been pre-Conquest.[70]

Some written references to treasure bindings lament their loss, for the richness of their materials made them vulnerable, in both the pre- and post-Conquest periods, to marauding invaders or cash-strapped abbots and priors. In the late eleventh century the Worcester monk Hemming recorded that earlier in the century, in order to raise tribute for the Danes, the community had to sacrifice a number of treasures from their church, including precious bindings.[71] In the immediate post-Conquest period manuscripts with treasure bindings were appropriated (as were other movable objects) by Continental ecclesiastics appointed to positions of importance in the English church and sent abroad, a tribute of sorts to the quality and reputation of English metalwork.[72]

For an impression of what some early English treasure bindings might have looked like it is necessary to turn to Continental evidence. A pair of eighth-century ivory open-work panels (the Genoels-Elderen diptych) may once have been attached to a binding, and, while they are now thought to be Continental, they have been attributed to England in the past.[73] One panel shows a triumphant Christ holding a book with a decorated cover featuring a cross with splayed arms. An early ninth-century silver-gilt cover, decorated with enamels and precious stones, attributed to a workshop in the southern Rhine, features an identical cross. The general appearance and some of the details of the Rhenish binding clearly owe much to Insular models.[74] In addition, there are a number of Continental bindings with carved ivories set into recesses in their boards. It has been proposed that several extant Anglo-Saxon ivories might once have been on such bindings,[75] and a lavishly decorated early eleventh-century gospel-book was still enclosed in boards with empty recesses in the eighteenth century, probably to house artefacts, possibly including ivories.[76] Finally, two

70 Legge and St John Hope 1902, p. 79.

71 Hearne 1723, I, pp. 248–9.

72 Dodwell 1973, Dodwell 1982, pp. 230–1, and Dumville 1994b.

73 Brussels, Museés Royaux d'Art et d'Histoire, inventory 1474. Beckwith 1972, no. 3 and fig. 14. The origin of the diptych has been reviewed, and an origin in southern Bavaria proposed, by Neuman de Vegvar 1990. See also Webster and Backhouse 1991, no. 141 (with colour plate).

74 New York, PML, M 1. Needham 1979, no. 5 (with colour plate), and Webster and Backhouse 1991, no. 132 (with colour plate of a modern copy). The binding is on a manuscript for which it was not made and incorporates later additions.

75 Beckwith 1972, nos. 38–40.

76 BL, Royal 1 D.ix. Warner and Gilson 1921, I, p. 18 (citing an eighteenth-century description).

of the four mid-eleventh-century English gospel-books made for Judith, later countess of Flanders (d. 1094), still have early silver-gilt treasure bindings.[77] While the metalwork was probably made in Flanders after Judith left England in 1065, these remain valuable for our enquiry, given the similarities that have been observed between English and Flemish artefacts of the period.[78]

Blindstamped bindings

Although a number of Continental Carolingian blindstamped bindings are known, no such English binding has survived, nor are any known to have existed.[79] However, an Anglo-Saxon tool, with a simple decorative pattern, which could have been used to decorate bindings, has survived.[80]

'Limp bindings' or bindings with limp covers

Listed in the ninth-century catalogue of books at St Gallen are thirty *libri scottice scripti*, that is to say manuscripts written by either British or Irish scribes.[81] Eight of them are described as in *quaternio* or in *quaternionibus* and these would have been 'booklets', either without covers or with limp covers of some kind.[82] (Three of the manuscripts are single-quire booklets, and one a two-quire booklet.) An eighth-century Northumbrian manuscript, containing part of Bede's *Historia ecclesiastica*, which was probably at Fulda by the ninth century, had, until quite recently, an early Continental limp cover, and this was probably the kind of manuscript referred to in the St Gallen catalogue.[83] A ninth-century Continental manuscript with a limp cover of skin was at Malmesbury by the late tenth century, and it was still there in the early twelfth when it was used by William of Malmesbury.[84] This, and other such bindings, are not inferior versions of bindings with wooden boards, but practical structures, usually of sound and even sophisticated construction.[85] Although there is no evidence

77 PML, M 708 and M 709. Needham 1979, nos. 8 and 9 with plates (M 708 in colour). For the structural aspects of the bindings (which are difficult to observe and evaluate) see McGurk and Rosenthal 1995, pp. 297–8 and 300–1.

78 Dodwell 1982, p. 201 and n. 136.

79 All the known Continental examples are listed by Vezin 1988.

80 London, British Museum, Department of British and Medieval Antiquities, 1953–11–2, 1. Wilson 1961, p. 214 and plate 38b.

81 Lehmann 1918, p. 71. Reviews of the written evidence: Vezin 1997, Scholla 2002, pp. 39–57, and (mostly later and English material) Gullick 2006, pp. 156–9.

82 For the physical characteristics of booklets, see Robinson 1978.

83 Kassel, LB, Theol. Qu. 2. Van Els 1972, pp. 9 and 24–5.

84 BodL., Marshall 19. Vezin 1982.

85 Szirmai 1999, pp. 285–319, Scholla 2002, pp. 87–195, describes eighty-nine bindings with limp covers of *s.* ix to *s.* xiv.

that manuscripts with limp covers were made in pre-1100 England, it seems almost certain that they once existed.

Visual evidence

Representations of books in manuscripts, sculptures and other artefacts have not been collected systematically, and they have received little attention from binding historians.[86] One of the earliest is in an Italian manuscript that may have been brought to England by Roman missionaries at the end of the sixth century.[87] The book it shows has boards flush with the edges of the leaves, and 'ties' at the leading and tail edges of the boards (ties at the head edge may have been inadvertently omitted by the artist). A book such as this could have served as a model for the earliest bindings made in England.

Most of the books shown in a cupboard in the portrait of Ezra in the early eighth-century Codex Amiatinus (made at Wearmouth-Jarrow but closely based upon a sixth-century Italian model), have decorated covers (one with a cross), spine-titles, and straps or ties to keep them closed.[88] A book in the mid-eighth-century Codex Aureus has a cover with panels (two rectangular and one circular) of an uncertain nature, probably a representation of a treasure binding (Plate 8.2).[89] A cross with splayed arms features on the cover of a book on an eighth-century ivory,[90] and this is more or less contemporary with the more detailed representation of a book on the Genoels-Elderen diptych.[91] Later representations of books (English and Continental) sometimes show covers, often divided with vertical and horizontal lines into discrete areas, decorated with motifs such as dots, circles, squares and so on, and these are probably stylised representations of treasure bindings. (Many examples are found, for example, in the tenth-century Benedictional of St Æthelwold.[92])

One of the earliest representations of a book with tabs at the ends of the spine occurs in the eighth-century Barberini Gospels,[93] and this is several centuries earlier than the only known pre-Conquest binding with tabs.[94] About

86 For an exception see Clarkson 1997.

87 CCCC, 286. Webster and Backhouse 1991, no. 1 and colour plate.

88 Florence, Biblioteca Medicea-Laurenziana, Amiatinus 1. Alexander 1978b, no. 7 and ill. 27. For the spine-titles and a good reproduction of the books in the cupboard see Bruce-Mitford 1968/9, p. 9 and plate 5.

89 Stockholm, KB, A.135. Nordenfalk 1977, plate 36.

90 Munich, Bayerisches Nationalmuseum, inventory MA 158. Beckwith 1972, ill. 21.

91 See n. 73 above.

92 BL, Add. 49598. Deshman 1995, colour plates 1–7, 10, 15, 27–9, 32 and 33, and Prescott 2002 (facs.).

93 BAV, Barb. lat. 570.

94 Worcester CL, Q.5.

the middle of the eleventh century representations of books begin to be quite informative, for example in the Cotton Troper (Plate 10.11),[95] evoking the solid, powerful presence that is one of the most characteristic physical qualities of Carolingian and Romanesque bindings with wooden boards.

During the period to 1100, writing, decorating and binding manuscripts was almost certainly regarded as an integral process, capable of being carried out by one hand. Even when he was a bishop, so William of Malmesbury tells us, Osmund, bishop of Salisbury (1078–99), did not disdain to write or bind manuscripts.[96] Late eleventh-century Salisbury manuscripts are books made for study, and most of the books that Osmund bound were almost certainly rather plain. The explicit linking of writing and binding by William is rarely found in English written sources, but it is unlikely that it would have disturbed either the sensibilities of William's readers or those who made or used books in earlier centuries. Today it is not difficult to see a wide range of the kinds of manuscripts made in pre-1100 England, but it requires considerable imagination to be able to recover and visualise the work of early English binders.

95 BL, Cotton Caligula A.xiv. Gameson 1991, fig. 23.
96 Hamilton 1870, p. 184.

PART II THE CIRCULATION OF BOOKS

12

Exchanges between the British Isles and the Continent, *c.* 450 – *c.* 900

ROSAMOND MCKITTERICK

When the Vindolanda tablets, dating from between AD 90 and 120, were discovered on Hadrian's Wall in the 1970s, they changed dramatically our understanding of the place of Roman Britain in the literate world of the Roman Empire. The range and variety of the texts represented on the hundreds of ink-written wooden tablets included military documents and reports, occasional literary texts and references (to Vergil and Catullus, for instance) and a wealth of personal letters exchanged with people elsewhere in Britain, north-west Gaul and Rome itself. These letters include autographs by individuals, even the wives of the military commanders, as well as professional writers. The several hundred men and women responsible for these remnants of the Vindolanda community were not members of the social and literary elites but were nevertheless people for whom the individual power to generate and control texts was important.[1] The Roman capital and cursive scripts on the tablets, coupled with the evidence of stone inscriptions, are an eloquent witness both to the presence, and possibly the introduction, of writing to the region as a consequence of the Roman army's occupation of Britain, and to the connection between the production of literary texts and of administrative documents.[2] The collection as a whole is a salutary reminder not only of Britain's communication with the rest of the Roman world, but also of the Romano-British population's participation in the literary culture of that world. Further, the Roman script system survived and was in the process of development in western Britain and Ireland before the arrival of the English in the course of the fifth and sixth centuries. Italian and Frankish forms of Roman script were then introduced by the missionaries into the areas of Britain occupied by the English.[3]

Occupation by groups from outside Britain, the consequent introduction of new intellectual influences and the widening of cultural horizons, and the

1 Bowman 1994a. 2 Handley 2003. 3 McKitterick 2006a.

maintenance of links with the known world, remain constant themes in the history of the book in Britain. This chapter, however, will focus on a period when contacts with the Continent and English and Irish contributions to Continental affairs were particularly notable. These can be seen in the contexts of political and ecclesiastical links between the kingdoms of Kent, Wessex and Northumbria and the Franks,[4] the expansion of trade across the North Sea,[5] the work of the Irish and Anglo-Saxon missionaries in Frisia, Hesse, Thuringia, Bavaria and the kingdom of the Franks from the seventh to the tenth centuries,[6] the presence of the Englishman Alcuin at the court of Charlemagne,[7] and the remarkable work in the later ninth century of a number of Irish exiles such as John Scotus Eriugena, Martin of Laon and Sedulius Scotus of Liège, some of whom were associated with King Charles the Bald.[8]

These contacts, furthermore, have to be set against the background of links with the Continent throughout the period of English settlement in sub-Roman Britain. Although valiant attempts to place the Vergilius Romanus codex in late or sub-Roman Britain have been contested,[9] the evidence of inscriptions and visual allusions to literature in mosaics and on decorated metalwork and pottery indicate that literary links with Continental Europe and the rest of the Roman world were maintained to some degree before the fifth century. The clearest remnants of literary links with Rome may be the codicological practices of the earliest surviving Insular books. These appear to preserve some elements of late Roman practices of book production.[10] It is in the context of the spread of Christianity and the Graeco-Roman literary culture in which the Christian religion was embedded, however, that the clearest avenue of cultural influence can be observed. In the writings of St Patrick and of Gildas, for instance, we are presented with men educated within the late Roman tradition and conversant with many texts current elsewhere in the empire.[11] How much of late Roman Christianity,

4 *Annales Bertiniani*, 856, 858, 862: Rau 1972, pp. 92, 96, 108; Wood 1991; Wallace-Hadrill 1965; Story 2003; Stafford 1981; Enright 1979; Nelson 1992; Campbell 1975 and 1980; Bullough 1975; Wormald 1988; Cubitt 1995 and 1997.

5 Johanek 1985.

6 Levison 1946; Schieffer 1954; Clarke and Brennan 1981; Wood 1992; Keynes 1985; van Houts 1992.

7 Bullough 2004; Depreux and Judic 2004.

8 Contreni 1978, 1984, 1992; Löwe 1982; Ní Chatháin and Richter 1984, 1987, 1996, 2002; Sedulius: Simpson 1988; John Scotus Eriugena: Sheldon-Williams 1968, and Jeauneau 1964 and 1972; Hellmann 1906; Schrimpf 1982.

9 BAV, Vat. lat. 3867, *CLA*, I, no. 19: Wright 2001 and Dark 1994.

10 Brown 1984 and Chapter 2 in this volume.

11 Dumville and Abrams 1993; Lapidge and Dumville 1984. See also Thompson 1984. On Patrick see Chapter 27 in this volume.

let alone of late Roman culture, survived into the Anglo-Saxon period can only be guessed, though there is some degree of consensus that it was not negligible.[12]

Even so, it is only with the arrival of Augustine of Canterbury in Kent and then Aidan of Ireland in Northumbria some decades later that we begin to get firmer evidence for England's links with the wider world and how much it drew from both West and East in its intellectual and religious development.[13] Although evidence of artefacts from archaeological excavations has provided crucial indications of the material context for such links,[14] the extant manuscripts from early medieval England, alongside allusions by writers in early Anglo-Saxon England to texts for which there is no longer any contemporary manuscript witness, indicate the complete dependence of the early Anglo-Saxon church on texts brought from elsewhere, especially Frankish Gaul and Rome. These meagre survivals have reinforced assumptions about the kind of basic texts the Christian missionaries would have needed and imported for their evangelising work. The necessary texts are usually supposed to have comprised at least the gospels, if not the entire Bible, the decisions of the early ecumenical councils of the church, liturgical texts for the celebration of the Eucharist, and a calendar for determining the cycle of the Christian year.[15]

Once the work of training English clergy began, more texts would have been needed, with grammars to teach Latin, exegesis to help explicate scripture, computus to aid in calculating the date of Easter, books about Roman law, liturgical chant, and no doubt other books to introduce the new converts to the Roman educational tradition. Bede tells us that Pope Gregory sent books to England with the second batch of missionaries – Mellitus, Justinus, Paulinus and Rufinianus – and it is likely that Augustine brought some books with him as well.[16] Not one of these supposed volumes has survived apart from the sixth-century Italian gospel-book traditionally associated with Augustine, namely the Corpus Gospels, and the possibly seventh-century Bodleian Gospels, in England by the late seventh and the eighth century respectively.[17] A sixth-century Uncial copy of the works of the Italian bishop Ambrose of Milan with eighth-century annotations in Old English may have reached northern France via England.[18] In this respect

12 Meens 1994; Stancliffe 1999; Campbell 1971.
13 Mayr-Harting 1972 and Sims-Williams 1990. For Ireland see Chapters 4 and 8 in this volume.
14 Spearman and Higgitt 1993; Webster and Backhouse 1991.
15 Gneuss 1968; Gameson 1999b.
16 Bede, *HE*, I, 29: Colgrave and Mynors 1969, p. 104.
17 CCCC, 286 and BodL., Auct. D.II.14: *CLA*, II, nos. 126 and 230.
18 Boulogne-sur-Mer, BM, 32: *CLA*, VI, no. 735: see Marsden 1999.

the surviving charters from Kent provide important evidence of the impact of such Christian teaching, for we have Latin charters written in England in Roman-style Uncial script from as early as 679. In addition, the biblical glosses – that is, the explanations and interpretations of difficult words in the biblical books – intended for students and associated with the Greek archbishop Theodore of Canterbury (consecrated 668; in England from 669, d. 690) along with the earliest home-produced books discussed elsewhere in this volume, provide further indications of the number of imported texts in the course of the seventh century and the extent to which they were absorbed into English culture.[19]

All this dependence on outside contact and acquisition needs to be emphasised, for there has been a tendency to assume that the English and Irish were in a strong position to introduce the essentials of Christian and Romano-Greek culture to the areas they visited as evangelists. The reality is a rather more complex process of interaction with the Franks and other peoples west and east of the Rhine and south of the Alps and Pyrenees than is usually imagined. It is the extant manuscripts which provide the principal means of understanding the process. This evidence can be augmented by letters, references in narrative histories, hagiographies and confraternity books,[20] liturgical borrowings (especially of coronation *ordines*[21]), relics, artefacts, artists' sources of inspiration and the like. Furthermore, tenth-century connections and monastic reforms have been suggested by Ute Schwab as the background against which the links between Old English and Old Saxon poetry should be studied.[22]

Past studies have in common their necessary preoccupation with what in the most generous spirit can still only be called scraps of often ambiguous evidence. All would concur with James Campbell when he remarked (apropos England but it has wider application) that when the diversity and in some degree the scale of the relationships which these limited sources indicate are considered, it seems likely that the various regions of the British Isles resembled and were linked with their neighbours 'to a large extent and in more important ways than can categorically be proved'.[23] Aside from the ever-growing quantity of archaeological evidence,[24] the surviving books and texts considered in this chapter constitute the bedrock of evidence.

19 Bischoff and Lapidge 1994; Lapidge 1995.
20 Gerchow 1988; Rollason *et al.* 2004; McKitterick 2004.
21 Schramm 1934; Nelson 1980.
22 Schwab 1986; Hofmann 1959; Haubrichs 1979, 1988.
23 Campbell 1986, pp. 206–7.
24 E.g. Hamerow and MacGregor 2001; Hansen and Wickham 2000; Reynolds 2005; Williams 2005.

Links between the British Isles and the Continent during the seventh century should first be considered within the context provided by Bede in his *Historia ecclesiastica* for England's connections across the North Sea. These were primarily between Neustria (the Seine region and present-day Normandy and Picardy) and Burgundy in the Frankish kingdom and the kingdoms of East Anglia, Kent, Wessex, Mercia and Northumbria. This is clear from the careers of such men as the Anglo-Saxons Wilfrid and Benedict Biscop, and the Franks Agilbert and Leuthere, and the presence of Englishwomen in the Frankish convents of Les Andelys-sur-Seine, Chelles and Faremoutiers.[25] The manuscripts provide further evidence. These include books of English origin but later Continental provenance, or of Frankish origin written in one of the scripts of the Insular (that is, as developed in the British Isles) script system or revealing Insular symptoms such as characteristic abbreviations or codicology.[26] Insular methods of preparing membrane, for example, are apparent in the 'palace' or 'Ada school' group of books associated with the court of Charlemagne and produced in a centre in the Rhine–Moselle region.[27] Furthermore, particular texts, such as the commentary on Job by Philippus, the *Carmina* of Paulinus of Nola, the work of the grammarian Servius, the Latin version of Theodore of Mopsuestia's commentary on Paul's Second Epistle to Timothy, and the writings of a number of classical authors, may owe their preservation as well as their transmission to Insular interest and efforts.[28] They may even have been brought to the Continent by the English and Irish though, equally, it is important to remember the quantities of books taken from Gaul to England by such travellers as the Northumbrian monk Benedict Biscop (d. 689),[29] as well as the links between Gaul and Ireland in the early Middle Ages.[30] In addition, a number of minor works by both English and Irish writers are preserved in early Frankish copies. These include the works of Aileran and Adomnán,[31] the *Life of Pope Gregory the Great* by a nun or monk of Whitby, the anonymous *Life of St Cuthbert*, Alcuin's poem on the bishops, kings and saints of York, the *Miracula Niniae* written by Alcuin's pupils at York, the penitential attributed to Egbert, and Cuthbert's letter on the death of Bede. English grammar books, such as the *Ars Bonifacii* and *Ars Tatuini*, are also recorded in Frankish

25 Bede, *HE*, III, 8 and IV, 23: Colgrave and Mynors 1969, pp. 236–45 and 407.
26 See McKitterick 1989a, 1989c and Brown 1974; also Chapters 2 and 4 in the present volume.
27 McKitterick 2008, pp. 345–63.
28 McKitterick 1989a, pp. 400–2; Law 1979; Brown 1975; Reynolds 1983.
29 Bede:, *Historia abbatum*, chs. 6 and 9: Plummer 1896, pp. 369 and 373.
30 Whitelock *et al.* 1982.
31 Breen 1996; Meehan 1958; Charles-Edwards 2000; e.g. St Gallen, Stiftsbibliothek, 355 (Adomnán, *Vita Columbae*).

Neustria. The transmission of the Irish compilation known as the *Collectio canonum Hibernensis* involved Brittany as well as Francia.[32] Even more significant are the number of Neustrian manuscripts containing the works of such major English authors as Bede and Aldhelm, with the biblical exegesis of Bede and his *De temporum ratione* particularly well attested. Very few West Frankish library lists from the Carolingian period survive, but some that do, from Saint-Wandrille, Saint-Riquier and Saint-Germer-de-Fly, provide a solid testimony to the dissemination of Bede's works in late eighth- and early ninth-century West Francia.[33]

Among surviving manuscripts from the Frankish kingdoms both west and east of the Rhine is a substantial group which displays Insular traits of one kind or another. Such traits comprise letter-forms, abbreviations, indications that they might have been copied from an Insular exemplar, decorative motifs in display capitals, preparation of the membrane, pricking and ruling practices, Old Irish or Old English annotations, annotations in Insular Minuscule, or spelling. These books are concentrated in a few centres, most of which can be established as having Insular connections of some kind. Tours, for example was presided over by the English scholar Alcuin of York (d. 804), but Insular scribes appear to have been active in Tours both before and after Alcuin's incumbency of the abbacy. The cluster of manuscripts with Insular symptoms can also be linked to the constellation of nunneries in the Seine river basin and the plain of Picardy, namely Chelles, Jouarre, Faremoutiers, Rebais, Les Andelys-sur-Seine, the centre producing the script known as 'a-b minuscule', and Laon.[34] Chelles, the most prominent of these convents, had been refounded and endowed by the Englishwoman, Queen Balthild, widow of the Merovingian king Clovis II, and later became a Carolingian royal convent presided over by female members of the Carolingian royal house, not least Charlemagne's sister Gisela. Moreover, Bede, as already mentioned, records that a number of Englishwomen were sent to Brie, Chelles and Les Andelys-sur-Seine; and both Agilbert and Leuthere, the brother and nephew respectively of Abbess Theudlechildis of Jouarre, served as bishops to the West Saxons in England.[35] The books produced in these Frankish centres are mainstream patristic theology and biblical commentary with the works of Augustine, Jerome and Gregory the Great strongly represented. The nuns in these centres

32 Breen 1983; Ó Corraín *et al.* 1984; Kéry 1999.

33 *Gesta abbatum Fontanellensis*: Pradié 1999, pp. 106, 130, 140–2, 162–6, 172; Hariulf: *Chronicon Centulense*: Lot 1894, pp. 69, 89–96; McKitterick 1989b, pp. 169–78.

34 McKitterick 1989c and 1992.

35 Bede, *HE*, IV, 23 and III, 7, 25, 28; IV, 1; V, 19.

also copied a number of mass books, possibly to supply nearby episcopal sees with essential liturgical texts. These books – the Gelasian Sacramentary, the *Missale Francorum*, the *Missale gallicanum vetus* – all played a crucial role in the history of the liturgy.[36] Indeed, a strong argument has been presented that the old Gelasian Sacramentary known to us in the manuscripts produced at Jouarre or Chelles is an Anglo-Saxon modification of an earlier Gallican sacramentary.[37] The centres' strong English connections may indicate a route by which such texts could reach England, though equally the English appear to have contributed to the Frankish liturgy.[38]

Links between Ireland and the Continent were partly independent from those of England. Work on the extent of the Irish presence as well as influence and how it can be identified is in progress; many of the old certainties are being questioned.[39] The career of Columbanus (d. 615) and his establishment of the monasteries of Luxeuil in Burgundy and Bobbio in the Lombard kingdom of northern Italy have long been recognised as potential channels of Irish intellectual and religious traditions on the Continent even if the reality is proving very much more complicated in terms of identifying Irish (as distinct from Breton, Frankish and Lombard) elements with any certainty. The manuscripts of Bobbio in particular, many of them written in Insular script, are proving a fertile ground for investigation.[40] There is still less to be ascertained about the contribution of the settlement of Irish monks at Péronne,[41] the work of Kylian in Franconia and his association with Würzburg,[42] or the possibly direct connections between Salzburg and Irish monasteries of Iona and Clonmacnoise suggested by the names of Irish abbots entered into the Salzburg *Liber vitae* in the eighth century.[43] There is, on the other hand, a clear indication of Irish presence at the monastery of St Gallen in the ninth century, about which more will be said below.

The manuscripts of Echternach are also crucial for any understanding of Insular connections with the Continent. Echternach, founded with Carolingian family support by the Northumbrian cleric Willibrord (d. 739) at the end of the seventh century, appears to have provided a centre where English, Irish

36 Hen 2001. 37 BAV, Reg. lat. 316: *CLA*, I, no. 105; Hen 1997.

38 Hen 2002.

39 The older enthusiasm of Bieler 1963 and Picard 1991 has also been tempered: see Whitelock *et al.* 1982; Ní Chatháin and Richter 1984, 1987, 1996, 2002; Kershaw 2008 and especially Meeder 2009.

40 Zironi 2004 and for later developments Crivello 2001.

41 Traube 1920. 42 St Kilian 1989.

43 McKitterick 2004, pp. 174–85; Forstner 1974; Dopsch and Juffinger 1984; Hennig 1970; Riain-Raendel 1982.

and Frankish interests could combine.[44] The corpus of manuscripts which can be associated with Echternach offers many contrary indications. The books reveal Frankish and Insular scribes working side by side with strong links to nearby Trier and receptive to local and regional traditions of book production.[45] The little clutch of books associated with Willibrord himself, such as the Calendar and Martyrology, record both Insular and Frankish interests in the saints commemorated. The texts of these and other gospel-books associated with Echternach, as well as the scribes working on them, also reflect the joining of Frankish and Insular tradition. This is particularly evident in the Trier Gospels which was the result of collaboration between a Merovingian Frankish scribe and an Insular one called Thomas.[46] Moreover, some of the texts in the many books from Echternach that are written in Insular scripts may have come directly from Ireland; the paschal tables are a case in point.[47]

This interaction between incoming Insular (at least the English and Irish) and local (Frankish) scribal traditions is a feature of all the Insular foundations and centres with Insular connections on the Continent. Brittany appears to have been an important conduit of Insular texts, though an understanding of this is only gradually emerging.[48] Pursuing English or Irish texts and Insular traits in script and book production uncovers a very wide network across Western Europe. This is nowhere more apparent than in connection with the foundations associated with Boniface and his followers, which were quite distinct from the links established by Willibrord in Frisia and the lower Rhine.[49]

From the eighth century onwards the Rhineland and regions further east are the areas where English connections are most substantially to be documented; the Irish evidence is more ambiguous, but both categories require further investigation.[50] The evidence again takes the form of books and texts of English or Irish authorship, most notably those of Bede, transmitted to the Continent, works by others in whose introduction to centres in the Frankish kingdoms the English or Irish may have played a role, and books showing signs of Insular scribal involvement or influence. Distinctively Insular types of script written at the Insular foundations of Fulda, Hersfeld, Würzburg and Werden, for example, have been identified.[51] The peculiarities of Continental Insular hands may in part be attributed to the continuance of links between

44 Wampach 1930; Kiesel and Schroeder 1989; Ferrari *et al.* 1999; Polfer 2000.
45 McKitterick 2000 and 1990.
46 Trier, Domschatz, 61, *CLA*, IX, no. 1364 and Netzer 1995.
47 Ó Croínín 1984, 1990.
48 See, e.g., the material gathered by Deuffic 1985.
49 McKitterick 1991; Wood 2001.
50 Meeder 2009.
51 Spilling 1978; Bischoff and Hofmann 1952; Drögereit 1951.

Ireland, England and the Frankish realms well into the ninth century. Some, indeed, may reflect developments in Insular scripts in the late eighth and first half of the ninth century, a period very poorly documented in books of English and Irish origin.[52]

Let us consider the evidence of the library catalogues, a number of ninth-century examples of which survive from the upper and middle Rhineland and Franconia and come from both English and Frankish foundations. The library catalogue of the monastery of Reichenau on Lake Constance, for example, was probably compiled by Reginbert of Reichenau (d. 847) in 821 or 822, nearly a century after the monastery's foundation. By 822 the community had accumulated an impressive library of over 400 volumes. The books are listed in sections according to their function. That is, there is reading and general wisdom in scripture and theology; practical knowledge (law and medicine); ecclesiastical ritual (liturgical books); ascetic discipline and the religious life (monastic rules and saints' lives); education (grammars and schoolbooks).[53] Within these broad categories, the authors are placed in roughly chronological order.[54] How rough will be appreciated when it is observed that the English author Bede is placed between Cassiodorus and Isidore of Seville. The list of Bede's works, indeed, is selective, for it includes samples of his exegetical work, such as his homilies on the gospels and his commentaries on Luke, Acts, the Apocalypse, Tobit, Esdras and Proverbs, as well as his more technical writings on *computus*, metrics, orthography and the *De natura rerum*.[55] Some of these books appear to have been copied by Reginbert himself. Hunzo, a priest in the time of Abbot Erlenbald (823–38) gave a compendious volume to the library which contained a *Gesta pontificum* (presumably the *Liber pontificalis*, a history of the popes from St Peter to the ninth century, presented as a series of biographies), the sixth-century Frankish author Gregory of Tours' *Histories* and Bede's *Ecclesiastical History of the English People*.[56] At a slightly later stage more of Bede's biblical exegesis was acquired and is listed as follows:

> *Beda super actus apostolorum volumina* VI, *super Thobiam et Ezram* I, *De templo salomonis* I, *De tabernaculo et vasis eius* I, *In proverbia Salomonis* III, *In* VII *canonicas epistolas* I, *De gratia Dei et in cantica canticorum* I, *super genesim* I, *De temporibus volumina* VI, *In Lucam* III, *In Matheum* III, *In Marcum* IIII, *In genesim* I *in quo et Hieronimus super Matheum, Questionum volumen* I.[57]

52 McKitterick 1989c. 53 Lehmann 1918, pp. 240–52.
54 McKitterick 1989b, p. 197. 55 Lehmann 1918, p. 249.
56 *Ibid.*, p. 256. 57 *Ibid.*, p. 264.

Two other authors from Britain represented in the Reichenau catalogue need to be noted. The first of these is Aldhelm of Malmesbury with copies recorded of the *Aenigmata*, *Metrum de laude virginum* and *De pedum regulis*.[58] Further, of great interest among the volumes copied by Reginbert is Adomnán of Iona's *De locis sanctis*. This text, which provided an account of the Frankish bishop Arculf's visit to the Holy Land, was presented to Aldfrith, king of Northumbria, in about 686.[59] All the earliest extant manuscripts of this work are in fact Frankish, and none dates from before the middle of the ninth century.[60] Reginbert's copy may well be one of the earliest witnesses to the *De locis sanctis*, having reached the Lake Constance region in the first half of the ninth century.[61]

At St Gallen an impressive collection of books had been assembled by the middle of the ninth century.[62] St Gallen was another Alemannian foundation of the early eighth century, established on the site of the hermitage of Gallus, a follower of the Irish ascetic Columbanus. This Irish connection is thought to be reflected in some of the books later in the monastery's library, though the links with English foundations in Franconia were possibly even more important.[63] The earliest library catalogue, compiled *c.* 850, for example, preserves an addition made in the same hand as that which wrote the notes on the original catalogue, a substantial record of a group of books *in scottice scripti*, that is, Irish or Insular script. Among them are a number of Old and New Testament books in single volumes – Genesis, Ezekiel, St John's Gospel, Acts (two copies), the Epistles of Paul, the canonical epistles, the Book of Revelation; patristic works and biblical commentaries – Augustine's *Enchiridion*, Bede's commentary on Proverbs, commentaries on the Song of Songs and on the Book of Kings; a missal, Boethius' *De arithmetica*, the poetry of Vergil, Juvencus (two copies), Sedulius, Bede's *De arte metrica*; a group of saints' lives and translations – the *Life* of Hilary, the passion of Marcellinus and Petrus, the discovery of the body of St Stephen, the translation of St Gall, the legend of the Innocents; and two volumes each of prayers and texts concerning the ecclesiastical grades and *ordines*. Given that the hand which made the list is from the later ninth century, it may constitute a crucial record of books either brought by visitors from the British Isles or copied at St Gallen itself from existing exemplars by scribes trained in the Insular tradition, in the course of the ninth century.[64]

58 *Ibid.*, p. 250. 59 *Ibid.*, pp. 257, 261.
60 Bieler 1958. 61 Lehmann 1918, p. 30.
62 St Gallen, Stiftsbibliothek, 728: Lehmann 1918, p. 75; Duft 1983.
63 McKitterick 2002b.
64 I have further work on this list and the St Gallen catalogue in hand.

Further, the original St Gallen catalogue includes a number of Bede's works, comprising his commentaries on Luke, Mark, Acts, the Apocalypse (three copies), the seven canonical epistles, Tobit, Esdras and Nehemiah, the Song of Songs and the Canticle of Habakkuk, as well as his homilies on the gospels and treatise on the temple of Solomon. The St Gallen library also had copies of Bede's ecclesiastical history, his works on computus and time, the *Martyrology* and the *Life of St Cuthbert* (in the same volume as the tract on virginity by Bede's compatriot Aldhelm). The same catalogue inserts Bede's school texts on orthography and metre, Aldhelm's *Riddles* and another copy of Aldhelm's poem in praise of virginity in the section on school books. Adomnán's *Life of Columba* is also listed. Books copied under Abbot Grimalt of St Gallen (841–72) included Bede on the Song of Songs. The books given by Abbot Hartmut (872–83) included Bede's *De natura rerum* and *De temporibus* as well as the *Martyrology*.[65] Script and texts, therefore, indicate Insular connections if not Insular presence at St Gallen, but there are two further sources of evidence, namely the annotations in Old English and Old Irish entered in many St Gallen codices in the ninth century,[66] and the Leiden glossary, written at St Gallen *c.* 800, some of whose entries may well have been drawn from books glossed by scholars who had been taught at Canterbury, though the evidence is problematic.[67]

The catalogue of the Alsatian monastery of Murbach for the third quarter of the ninth century was also well stocked with Bede's commentaries.[68] Twenty-one of the works of Bede, including his biblical exegesis, are listed. On the Old Testament these comprised his commentaries on Kings, Proverbs, Tobit, Esdras and Nehemiah; on the New Testament, Murbach possessed Bede's homilies on the gospels, and the commentaries on Mark, Luke, Acts, the canonical epistles and the Apocalypse. Further, Murbach had copies of the treatises on the tabernacle, the temple of Solomon, and time, Bede's books on metre, the *De natura rerum*, the *Martyrology*, the *Life of Cuthbert*, and the *Historia ecclesiastica*. The long lists of desiderata for which the Murbach library is famous, moreover, had an extensive list of a further twenty-four of Bede's works, knowledge of which had been derived from Bede's own list of his writings supplied at the end of the *Historia ecclesiastica*.[69] These included the *Historia abbatum*, many of the minor works of

65 Lehmann 1918, pp. 84 and 87. 66 Clark 1926; Draak 1957 and 1967.
67 Leiden, Universiteitsbibliotheek, Voss. lat. Q.69: Hessels 1906 and Glogger 1907 for the text; Lapidge 1986b for the Canterbury hypothesis.
68 Milde 1968 and Hummer 2005.
69 Bede, *HE*, v, 24: Colgrave and Mynors 1969, pp. 566–70.

Bede, and his letters, as well as a handful of works of which no trace survives anywhere.

All the catalogues of Lorsch, the immensely wealthy middle-Rhineland monastery founded 762/3 and taken under royal protection soon afterwards, are bound together in the ninth-century codex now in the Palatine collection in the Vatican.[70] The oldest Lorsch booklist is dated *c.* 830. It includes the *In Regum librum* XXX *quaestiones* of Bede among works of Gregory the Great and Eucherius and Adomnán's *De locis sanctis* among the *grammatici* or school books.[71] The second library catalogue is on fols. 44r–66v and is dated between 830 and 840. It lists a large number of Bede's exegetical works as well as the *Historia ecclesiastica* after the works of Gregory the Great.[72] The third of the Lorsch catalogues, occupying fols. 1–34 of the same codex, includes biblical and liturgical books and monastic rules; it was dated by Bernhard Bischoff to the third quarter of the ninth century. It also lists Bede's works after Gregory the Great, in a consistent association that is significant, given Bede's own familiarity with Gregory's writings and the latter's place in the history of the conversion of the English. Bede's *Historia ecclesiastica* is listed at the outset and complemented by many of the works of biblical exegesis, the *De temporibus*, and again the brief Chronicle in the *De temporibus*.[73] In addition, in the section headed *grammatici*, Bede's treatise on metre was in the same volume as Aldhelm's poem in praise of virginity; another volume joined Bede on metre with his poetic version of the *Life of St Cuthbert*.[74] The books of Gerward were added at the end *c.* 860.[75] Gerward, who retired with his personal library to Lorsch after time at the court of the Emperor Louis the Pious (814–40), owned Bede's *De templi aedificatione*, the commentaries on Luke and the Song of Songs and Bede's *Hexameron* (that is, the *Libri* IV *in principium Genesis*).[76] Altogether, Lorsch possessed the solid core of Bede's exegesis that was so striking a feature of the Alemannian monasteries. An interest at Lorsch in the careers of the English missionaries appears to be reflected in the library copies of the *Vitae* of Willibrord and Boniface. Lorsch also possessed the account of Arculf's journey to the Holy Land.

None of the other East Frankish libraries has left quite so many traces of Bede, though this may reflect their closer ties with Wessex and Mercia than with Northumbria.[77] Fulda, founded by the southern English missionary

70 BAV, Pal. lat. 1877. 71 Häse 2002, Katalog A, p. 97 and Ca, p. 165.
72 *Ibid.*, Katalog B, p. 135. 73 *Ibid.*, Katalog Ca, pp. 154–5.
74 *Ibid.*, pp. 164–5.
75 Bischoff 1974 and 1989; Häse 2002, Katalog Cb, pp. 154 and 168.
76 Häse 2002, Katalog Cb, pp. 168 and 331–9.
77 McKitterick 1991.

Boniface in 744, had some volumes of Bede's exegesis on the New Testament and the *De temporum ratione*.[78]

The collection of one major Frankish Rhineland centre, on the other hand, is a further indication of the Frankish reception of Bede's works. Cologne's booklist of 833 represents the energy with which Hildebald, archbishop from 785 to 819, assembled books and encouraged his own and other scriptoria to write them for his cathedral library.[79] The small sample of Bede's works is listed between those of Augustine and Jerome, but among the extant manuscripts from Cologne only the *De natura rerum* and the works on time are to be found.[80] The Épinal-Erfurt Glossary, dated to the first half of the eighth century, provides a strong indication of the Anglo-Saxon glossary tradition. Its links with the Leiden Glossary, moreover, indicate how the two strands, Insular and Continental, were readily intertwined with, and augmented, each other.[81]

The catalogue information can be extended with that derived from extant books. Only four works of Bede can be linked with Echternach, namely a fragment of Bede's commentary on the Apocalypse from the late eighth or early ninth century, his commentaries on the Song of Songs and on Luke, and the *De arte metrica* in a collection of grammatical texts, possibly from Echternach from the middle decades of the ninth century.[82]

From the Carolingian scriptoria of the monasteries of Augsburg, Freising, Tegernsee, Mondsee and Salzburg there survive altogether thirty volumes of the works of Bede.[83] Two-thirds of these are his main exegetical works on books of the New Testament (Mark, Luke, John, Acts, the seven canonical epistles and the Apocalypse/Book of Revelation). Two concern the Old Testament.[84] The only other works with an English link are the Mainz or Fulda copy of Willibald's *Life of Boniface*, which appears to have arrived in Regensburg *c.* 930,[85] and the codex from Eichstätt of the late eighth or early ninth century containing Hugeburc's *Hodoeporicon* of Willibald, and Willibald's *Vita Bonifacii* in Freising's library.[86]

A link between Salzburg, Saint-Amand, and the Insular foundation of Würzburg is suggested by Würzburg, UB, M.p.th.q.46 which shows marks

78 Schrimpf 1996, pp. 29–47. 79 Dekker 1895, pp. 215–16. 80 Jones 1932.

81 Épinal, BM, 72 (*CLA*, VI, no. 760); Sweet 1883; Lindsay and Thomson 1921; Pheifer 1974.

82 BnF, lat. 10400, lat. 9569 (from western Germany), lat. 9571 and lat. 11275. See McKitterick 2000.

83 Bischoff 1974 and 1980.

84 For details on these manuscripts see Bischoff 1974 and 1980 and McKitterick 2002b.

85 Munich, Bayerische Staatsbibliothek, Clm 14708.

86 *Ibid.*, Clm 1086.

of Saint-Amand and Salzburg scribes and was in Würzburg by 976. Traces of Insular exemplars have been discerned in Bede's commentary on Mark and his *De arte metrica*, a south German manuscript from the second half of the ninth century whose provenance is Regensburg. [87] The *De orthographia* in Regensburg's library is part of a miscellany written in West Francia or Brittany in the second half of the ninth century in a script showing Insular influence.[88] In one instance, one of the manuscripts of Bede, the *De ratione metrica*, appears to come from northern Italy.[89] Other books in the libraries of Freising and Regensburg containing Bedan texts came originally from northern France, such as *De temporum ratione* (possibly from Saint-Amand; at Regensburg) and *De schematibus et tropis* (Francia; Freising).[90] These may be attributable to links with Salzburg which enjoyed a close connection with Saint-Amand in northern France in the early ninth century as a result of the early career at St Amand of Arn, who subsequently became bishop, then archbishop, of Salzburg.[91]

Links between Fulda, Mainz and Würzburg account for some of the works of Bede in the Würzburg library in the middle of the ninth century, such as the Martyrology, *De temporum ratione*, and the commentaries on Acts (from Fulda), the seven canonical epistles (though it is not certain that this was ever in Würzburg) and the Apocalypse.[92] From Mainz also came a copy of Boniface's poems and the treatise *De syllabis*.[93] Other books, such as the *De tabernaculo*, the *Historia ecclesiastica*, another copy of the Martyrology, and Aldhelm's *De virginitate*, were all produced at Würzburg in the second third of the ninth century under Bishop Hunbert.[94] They appear to depend on Insular exemplars such as the manuscript of Bede's *De temporum ratione*, of which one small fragment from the late eighth or early ninth century survives.[95] There is also a remnant of Bede's *Historia ecclesiastica* which was produced by the Mainz scriptorium in the ninth century.[96] Recent work on the transmission of early annals further augments our knowledge of creative links between Northumbria and Kent in particular, and the Rhineland and Franconia.[97]

So far I have looked only at the eastward direction of the exchange of texts between England and the Frankish kingdoms. We need now to turn towards

87 *Ibid.*, Clm 14292 and 14420. 88 *Ibid.*, Clm 14387.
89 *Ibid.*, Clm 6435. 90 *Ibid.*, Clm 14725 and 6399.
91 Niederkorn-Bruck and Scharer, 2005.
92 Würzburg, UB, M.p.th.f.50, Fragm. 10, Fragm. 11, M.ch.f.20; BodL., Laud misc. 442; Bischoff and Hofmann, 1952, pp. 47, 51, 55, 104, 116, 117.
93 Würzburg, UB, M.p.th.f.29; Bischoff and Hofmann, 1952, pp. 135–6.
94 Würzburg, UB, M.p.th.f.59, M.p.th.f.118, M.p.th.f.49 and M.p.th.f.21; Bischoff and Hofmann, 1952, pp. 122–5, 127.
95 Würzburg, UB, M.ch.f.206; Bischoff and Hofmann 1952, p. 104, and *CLA*, IX, no. 1398.
96 Ottermann 1998. 97 Story 2005.

the west in order to see what was introduced into England from the Frankish kingdoms. Further, the Carolingian material as a whole needs to be assessed in order to gauge the significance of the contribution from the Frankish regions discussed above.

The relative meagreness of the evidence in Anglo-Saxon England in terms of quantity is immediately striking. For one thing, there are no library catalogues to speak of, but only a handful of brief booklists from the later Anglo-Saxon period.[98] For another, the handlist Helmut Gneuss has prepared, of extant manuscripts written or owned in England before 1100, only rarely yields codices whose precise century, let alone decade or year of entry into Britain, can be pinned down.[99] To anyone used to the abundant evidence for Insular activity on the Continent and the wealth of material relating at least to an interest in the works of Bede, the paucity of manuscripts is disconcerting. Nevertheless, the range of authors and texts is not inconsiderable and many are recorded more than once.[100]

Of the thousand or so manuscripts and fragments Gneuss surveyed for the second edition of his handlist (his final number is 947 but he intercalated numerous 'subnumbers' for extra items), eighty-eight (counting the duplicates) contain Carolingian authors or Frankish liturgical texts. It is possible that composite manuscripts contain additional texts. A closer look, however, establishes that half of the Carolingian authors occur in books written in England in the middle or later half of the eleventh century, and thus cannot conclusively be regarded as having been introduced into England before, rather than after, the Norman Conquest. A further thirty-two manuscripts – that is, almost all the remainder – are extant in English copies of the tenth century and thus presumably reflect the contacts with such centres as Ghent and Fleury in relation to the monastic reforms of the later tenth century.[101]

Continental copies of the ninth or early tenth century of Carolingian authors are as follows:

Adalbert of Metz, *Speculum Gregorii* (epitome of *Moralia in Iob*) (Salisbury CL, 101)
Alan of Farfa, *Homiliarium* (BL, Harley 652)
Alcuin, *Epistolae* (BL, Harley 208) (from Saint-Denis)
Ansegisus, *Capitularium collectio* (extracts: Breton, now BodL., Hatton 42)

98 Lapidge 1985 and 2006. 99 Gneuss 2001.
100 McKitterick 2002b, table II, pp. 147–8.
101 See Chapter 14 below; Cubitt 1997; Foot 2006.

Dunchad (or Martin of Laon?), *Commentarium* on Martianus Capella (CCCC, 330)

Dungal, *Poetae* and *Epistolae* (BL, Harley 208) (from Saint-Denis)

Frankish kinglist (CCCC, 223, and BL, Cotton Vespasian B.vi)

Halitgar of Cambrai, *Poenitentiale* (BodL., Bodley 516)

Hrabanus Maurus, *In epistolas Pauli* (Cambridge, Pembroke College 308) (from Reims)

Hrabanus Maurus, *In Hester*, *In Judith* (Arras, Médiathèque, 764, Part I) (from north-east France)

John Scotus Eriugena, *Carmen* 9 (CCCC, 223) (from Arras)

Remigius of Auxerre, *Commentarium* on Martianus Capella (BL, Royal 15 A.xxxiii) (from Reims).

Some Carolingian authors are to be found in English manuscripts of the tenth century; it is conceivable that these texts reached England during the ninth century:

Abbo of Saint-Germain-des-Prés, *Bella Parisiacae urbis* (BL, Harley 3826)

Adalbert of Metz, *Speculum Gregorii* (TCC, B.4.27)

Adrevald, *Miracula sancti Benedicti* (Cambridge, St John's College, F. 27 (164))

Alcuin, *De orthographia* (BL, Harley 3826)

Alcuin, *De dialectica* (CCCC, 206)

Alcuin, *Epistolae* (BL, Cotton Tiberius A.xv, fols. 1–173)

Amalarius of Metz, *Liber officialis* (TCC, B.11.2 and BL, Cotton Vespasian D.xv)

Dunchad, or Martin of Laon, *Commentarium* on Martianus Capella (and Martianus Capella, *De nuptiis Philologiae et Mercurii*) (CCCC, 153 (produced in Wales)

Dungal, *Monasticha Catonis* (Cambridge, Gonville and Caius College, 144 (194))

Gerbald of Liège, First Episcopal Capitulary (BodL., Bodley 718)

Hrabanus Maurus, *Computus* (Exeter CL, 3507)

Hrabanus Maurus, *Liber sanctae crucis* (TCC, B.16.3) (England, *s.* x or Germany *s.* ix)[102]

John the Deacon, *Vita sancti Gregorii* (BodL., Bodley 381)

Lupus of Ferrières, *De metris Boethii* (TCC, O.3.7)

Musica Enchiriadis (CCCC, 209)

Paschasius Radbertus, *De corpore et sanguine domini* (BL, Royal 8 B.xi)

102 McKitterick, 2005; Schipper 2007.

Remigius of Auxerre, *Commentarium* on Sedulius, *Carmen paschale* (BodL., Lat. th.c.4, and Cambridge, Gonville and Caius College, 144)
Remigius of Auxerre, *scholia* on Martianus Capella and Priscian (Cambridge, Magdalene College, Pepys 2981[5], and BL, Cotton Domitian i)
Smaragdus of St Mihiel, *Expositio in regulam sancti Benedicti* (CUL, Ee.2.4)
Smaragdus of St Mihiel, *Diadema monachorum* (CUL, Ee. 2. 4)
Smaragdus of Saint-Mihiel, *Expositio libri comitis* (Worcester CL, F.91)
Theodulf of Orléans, *Expositio missae* (BL, Royal 8 C.iii)
Theodulf of Orléans, *De ordine baptismi* (BL, Royal 8 C.iii)
Usuard of Saint-Germain-des-Prés, Martyrology (CCCC, 57).

In addition, I simply note here copies of biblical, liturgical and patristic texts, Continental copies of which reached England before the eleventh century:

Psalterium gallicanum, (CCCC, 411) (from Reims)
Jerome, *In Isaiam* lib. VIII–XVIII (Cambridge, Pembroke College, 17) (from Tours)
Jerome, *Tractatus in Psalmos* (Cambridge, Pembroke College, 91) (from northern Francia)
Mass book and antiphonary (Cambridge, Pembroke College, 46, fols. A and B) (from Francia)
Edictum de fide (Cambridge, Pembroke College, 108) (East Francia)
Arator, *Historia apostolica* (TCC, B.14.3, fols. 1–4) (from Nonantola)
Jerome-Gennadius-Isidore, *De viris illustribus* (Hereford CL, O.II.2)
Augustine, *De nuptiis et concupiscentia* (BL, Add. 23944)
Augustine, *Contra Iulianum* (BL, Add. 23944)
Eusebius-Rufinus, *Historia ecclesiastica* (Worcester CL, Q.28)

In three cases, however, we are fortunate to have the Continental exemplar as well as the English copy. The Worcester codex containing Smaragdus' *Expositio libri comitis*, for example, appears to have been copied from a West Frankish manuscript of the second half of the ninth century, now in Oxford.[103] A compilation containing Isidore of Seville's *Quaestiones in Vetus Testamentum*, Adalbert of Metz's *Speculum Gregorii*, and Augustine's *In epistolam*, written in West Francia and now in Salisbury, was the exemplar for a tenth-century copy of all these texts made at Canterbury and now in Cambridge.[104] A Canterbury copy of Amalarius' *De officiis* made in the second quarter of the tenth century may have drawn on a copy of this text from

103 Worcester CL, F.91 and BodL., Barlow 4.
104 Salisbury CL, 101 and TCC, B.4.27. See Brownrigg, 1978.

Landévennec in Brittany of about the same date, which was possibly then available in Canterbury.[105]

Among the 114 Continental manuscripts brought or sent to England at some stage between their production and the end of the eleventh century and still extant, eleven contain the *De temporum ratione*, *Vita Cuthberti* and biblical exegesis by Bede. Indeed Bede's are almost the only works of an English author re-imported. The other is Aldhelm's *Aenigmata* in a late ninth-century manuscript from northern France which had reached Canterbury by the second half of the tenth century.[106] Other imported codices contain a reasonable range of patristic and early medieval authors.

It is striking, moreover, that with only five exceptions from the East Frankish realm, all these Continental manuscripts come from either the northern part of the West Frankish kingdom or (a handful only) from the Loire Valley. Two of these East Frankish exceptions are ninth-century manuscripts and had reached England by the tenth century. One contains the decrees of the Council of Constantinople in 680, and was at the English court by the tenth century.[107] The other, possibly from the Rhineland, is a copy of Gregory's *Moralia in Iob*.[108] The remaining three books, Burchard of Worms' Decretals and two copies of the Romano-German Pontifical, date from the eleventh century.[109] One of the latter appears to have been brought from Cologne to York. Only two East Frankish authors are represented. First of all, Hrabanus Maurus' commentary on the Epistles of Paul, a book originally given by Archbishop Hincmar of Reims to St Mary's Abbey at Reims in the middle of the ninth century, may have reached Ely shortly thereafter.[110] Hrabanus Maurus' Commentary on Judith, written in north-west France, was in England by the tenth century.[111] Other works by Hrabanus, namely the *De clericorum institutione* and *De computo*, survive in England in English copies. The problematic copy of his *Liber de sanctae crucis* might have been written in East Francia in the Fulda region in the ninth century rather than in England in the tenth as is usually supposed, for its strange Caroline-influenced Insular features combined with thoroughly Continental Rustic Capitals indicate a centre with mixed scribal traditions.[112]

Another East Frankish or German author is the anonymous poet of the Old Saxon *Heliand*. One of the manuscripts of this poem was written in southern

105 TCC, B.11.2, and CCCC, 192. 106 BL, Royal 15 A.xvi.
107 BL, Cotton Claudius B.v. 108 BodL., Bodley 310.
109 BL, Cotton Claudius C.vi; Cotton Tiberius C.i, fols. 43–203, and Cotton Vitellius E.xii (from Cologne).
110 Cambridge, Pembroke College, 308. 111 Arras, Médiathèque, 764.
112 TCC, B.16.3: McKitterick 2005 and Schipper 2007. Cf. pp. 250–1 above.

England in the second half of the tenth century by someone who had learnt how to write Insular script.[113] His or her adaptation of some of the word-forms to Old English may indicate an English scribe or that the scribe of an earlier exemplar had been English. It appears, furthermore, that part of the Anglo-Saxon Genesis poem is a translation of the Old Saxon Genesis. The questions of the inspiration or influence between Old Saxon and Old English literature raised by these poems are still being debated. No one has yet been able to account satisfactorily for the copying of the *Heliand* in England.[114] It may stand simply as an indication of far richer cultural connections between England and Saxony than are apparent in the surviving evidence.

This meagre extant evidence in England, especially in the ninth and tenth centuries, might lead us to suppose that there was little connection between England and the West and East Frankish realms, were it not for the substantial nature of the evidence for the dissemination of Bede's works, and for Insular presence on the Continent in the Continental manuscript and textual evidence.[115] The material from both sides of the English Channel and the North Sea, indeed, has important implications as well as raising many questions, to some of which I now turn.

The greater bulk of the evidence from the Bavarian monasteries demonstrates their production of Bede's main works of biblical exegesis 'in-house', and thus the availability of exemplars which for the most part have left no indication that they were from England or in Insular script. This suggests second- or third-generation copies, either from the kind of manuscript also represented in these houses, namely, works of Bede in south German (Bavaria and Alemannia), north German (Hesse, Thuringia, Franconia, Saxony) or West Frankish exemplars, or from older copies made perhaps originally from Insular exemplars. One of the difficulties of this kind of evidence is that the second- or third-generation copies could be either mere months or decades apart and do not allow us to chart any credible precise chronology for the transmission of Bede or any other Insular author on the Continent.[116] It is certainly the case, as we have seen, that the Carolingian library catalogues from east of the Rhine provide us with important evidence for the dissemination of many of Bede's works on the Continent within a century or so after his death. The ninth-century catalogues, indeed, represent the fruits of active book production and acquisition over at least the half-century preceding their compilation, and possibly since the monasteries' foundations.

113 BL, Cotton Caligula A.vii. 114 Priebsch 1925 and Behaghel 1965.
115 McKitterick, 1989b. 116 Whitelock 1960; Rollason, 2001; Hill 1998 and 2006.

Bede's *In proverbia Salomonis* and *De arte metrica* are the only texts from the British Isles among the collection of books *in scottice scripti* recorded at the beginning of the St Gallen booklist.[117] Further, as the term *in scottice scripti* could equally well be applied to Anglo-Saxon Minuscule, it is possible that this famous list may be as much a tribute to St Gallen's connections with Anglo-Saxon foundations in Germany, or even England itself, rather than exclusively with the Irish, as is usually assumed.[118] Although the presence of a few Irishmen at St Gallen in the second half of the ninth century is well attested, there is no clear indication that many, or any, reached there earlier than that.[119] Anglo-Saxons possibly at St Gallen have left traces of their presence in Old English glosses, not least in the Leiden Glossary referred to above and, more convincingly, in two sections of the *Vocabularius Sancti Galli*.[120] In an earlier part of the same book, which is in effect a little theological encyclopaedia, there is an Old English gloss on the names of the animals in Leviticus, ch. 11, explaining which animals are to be found neither *apud nos* nor *in Britannia*.[121] A number of biblical codices and works of Bede also contain Old English glosses.[122] Yet the St Gallen confraternity book, compiled from *c.* 813 onwards, but possibly replacing earlier fragments, does not record that St Gallen was linked by prayer with any of the main Anglo-Saxon foundations on the Continent.[123] Insular presence seems to be, therefore, less a matter of institutional connections than of individuals who joined the community at St Gallen.

The only earlier pieces of information in terms of library contents that can be added as a case study concern Bede's *Ecclesiastical History*, the *De temporum ratione*, and some of the exegetical books. Bede's *History*, of course, was not just a remarkable historical work, full of information about the history of Britannia, the development of the English church, many kings and saints and the crucial role of Pope Gregory, it also contained the list of the author's works – which was drawn on, as noted above, by the Murbach librarian at least for information about books to be acquired. Bede's influence on the historical writing of the Continent has yet to be fully investigated, but I have argued elsewhere that a greater influence in terms of understanding and representation of the past was exerted by his World Chronicle which forms Chapter

117 St Gallen, Stiftsbibliothek, 728, p. 4; Lehmann 1918, p. 71.
118 Duft 1974 and Clark 1926.
119 Duft 1982, Draak 1957 and 1967.
120 St Gallen, Stiftsbibliothek, 913.
121 St Gallen, Stiftsbibliothek, 913, pp. 139–45. Clark 1926, pp. 55–70 at 68–69, and 300; Baesecke 1933.
122 St Gallen, Stiftsbibliothek, 254, p. 253; 295, pp. 96–172; 299, pp. 3–5; 878, p. 321.
123 St Gallen, Stiftsarchiv, C3 B55: Piper 1884, pp. 1–144, and Borgolte *et al.* 1986.

66 of his *De temporum ratione*.[124] Further, his understanding of history more generally was very effectively communicated in his exegesis of scripture,[125] though the impact of this on the Continent has also not been considered.

First of all there is the famous reference to Bede's *Ecclesiastical History* in the library catalogue of Würzburg *c.* 800.[126] Second, there is the presence of the Moore Bede, written at Jarrow-Wearmouth, at the court of Charlemagne by the end of the eighth century.[127] Although the main text is written in the distinctive Jarrow-Wearmouth Phase II Insular Minuscule, a short compilation *De consanguinitate*, derived from Isidore's *Etymologiae* (IX.6, 28–9) and the Roman council of 721, was added at the end of the book in a hand close to that of the Harley Golden Gospels produced in association with the royal court of Charlemagne.[128] It appears to have been from the royal court that many descendants of the Moore Bede were disseminated in West Francia. It is the 'M' family of texts it represents that dominates the Continental tradition of the *Historia ecclesiastica*, whereas a recognisably distinct family, known as that of the 'C' text, had the monopoly in England.[129]

There are, nevertheless, important indications that it was not only the Carolingian royal court that can be credited with the transmission of the *Historia ecclesiastica*. A representative of the 'C' text of the late eighth century and written in Northumbria had reached Fulda shortly afterwards.[130] At the least the *Libellus responsionum* from Book I.27 in the 'C' version had reached southern Alemannia by the tenth century.[131] The recently discovered fragment of a Mainz copy of the *Historia ecclesiastica*, mentioned earlier, contains IV.98.[132] Other early manuscripts now in St Petersburg, Würzburg and Namur, indicate different eighth-century copies of Bede's great work arriving on the Continent.[133] It is particularly interesting that there is a specifically East Frankish or German family of Bede manuscripts. To the Würzburg codex, produced under Bishop Hunbert of Würzburg (832–42) which might be a copy of the *Historia* listed in the catalogue of *c.* 800,[134] can be added another copy of the work now in St Gallen, and later copies of it.[135] There is also the Weissenburg

124 McKitterick, 2006b. 125 Hilliard 2007.
126 BodL., Laud misc. 26, fol. 260r; Lowe 1928.
127 CUL, Kk.5.16; Parkes, 1982 and compare Lowe 1926.
128 Bischoff 1965b; McKitterick 2008, pp. 345–63.
129 Colgrave and Mynors 1969, pp. xlii–lxx.
130 Kassel, Gesamthochschulbibliothek, Theol. Qu.2: *CLA*, VIII, no. 1140.
131 See, further, Meyvaert 1959. 132 Ottermann 1998.
133 St Petersburg, Russian National Library, Q.v.I.18. Würzburg, UB, M.p.th.f.118, and Namur, Bibliothèque Communale, 11, fols. 1–60.
134 Bischoff and Hofmann 1952, p. 144, and Lowe 1926.
135 Compare Allen 1996.

codex of the late eighth century. This is written in an early Caroline Minuscule related to that of the Ada Gospels group from the Moselle and Trier region, appears to have been made from an Insular exemplar, and is decorated with initials in the Insular style. It may also have been associated with the royal court.[136] Further, a group surviving only in twelfth-century copies, all containing Northumbrian annals for the years 732–66, may be descended from yet another early arrival on the Continent from Northumbria.[137] Thus there were at least six distinct copies of Bede's *History* in the Frankish kingdoms by the end of the eighth century.[138]

Just as the transmission of Bede's *Historia ecclesiastica* is predominantly Frankish, so the history of the two strands of transmission of the *De temporibus* and the *De temporum ratione* are also primarily Continental.[139] One family of manuscripts is centred on St Gallen and Reichenau (with a link to Bobbio) and the other connects Auxerre, Fleury, Cologne and Trier in the ninth century, with a link to England again in the eleventh century. If we draw on the indications of the knowledge of Bede's treatises on time reflected in the encyclopaedias on time produced at the Carolingian royal court, then it would appear that someone in northern Francia had knowledge of this part of Bede's work by the 760s.[140] It is important to be circumspect in attributing too much to Bede's influence; it is most likely that the Franks' initial interest in dating according to the year of the Incarnation and the calculations of the date of Easter were derived directly from Dionysius Exiguus and not from Bede. Bede's work, in short, fell on well-prepared ground.[141]

The difficulty remains to determine the means by which Bede's works reached the Continent, let alone other texts from England and Ireland. The third early corpus of evidence about the transmission of Insular work provides one tangible clue. These are the general references in many saints' lives to individuals bringing books back to the Continent from England, as, according to the *Vita Liudgeri*, the Frisian Liudger (d. 809) did when returning from his studies under Alcuin at York.[142] The letters of Boniface, the English missionary from Wessex who became bishop of Mainz (d. 754), and his successor Lull, probably from Mercia (d. 786), however, are more usefully specific.[143] Boniface had asked for the exegetical works of Bede from

136 Wolfenbüttel, Herzog August Bibliothek, Weissenburg 34; Colgrave and Mynors 1969, pp. lxv–lxvii and *CLA*, IX, no. 1385.
137 Colgrave and Mynors 1969, pp. lxvii–lxix.
138 See further Westgard 2006.
139 Jones 1977 and Wallis 1999.
140 Borst 1993.
141 McKitterick 2004, pp. 92–6.
142 Diekamp 1881, p. 17, and Pertz 1829, p. 408.
143 McKitterick 1991.

Wearmouth and Bede's homilies on the gospels and a commentary on proverbs from Archbishop Egbert of York.[144] In 764, Abbot Cuthbert of Jarrow and Wearmouth sent gifts, including Bede's *Life of St Cuthbert of Lindisfarne* in prose and verse, to Bishop Lull of Mainz. He promised, furthermore, to try to send Lull works by Bede of which the latter lacked copies, and apologised that the severity of the winter, 'with cold and ice and long widespread storms of wind and rain, so that the hand of the scribe was hindered from producing a great number of books', has prevented him from sending more.[145] In a later letter, Lull asked for Bede's *De templo*, the commentary on the Song of Songs, and the book of epigrams.[146] Cuthbert's reply, sending him the *De templo*, is still extant.[147] Lull clearly directed requests for books to others in Northumbria, for Archbishop Coena of York replied to a request from Lull asking for books about the earth and tides and other works of cosmography, saying that he had only very difficult books on this subject and so far had not been able to procure any scribes to copy them.[148] In another letter to Coena, Lull asked for Bede's commentaries on Samuel, on Ezra and Nehemiah, and on Mark.[149] York, Jarrow and Wearmouth, therefore, are perceived in Fulda and Mainz at least as potential sources for the works of Bede. Possibly Lull too had learnt of them from Bede's list in one of the early copies of the *Historia ecclesiastica* circulating on the Continent, though some of his other more general requests are more speculative. Jarrow appeared to be better able to supply books than York, and it was at the former that the distinctive minuscule was devised, as Malcolm Parkes has suggested, in order to supply the demand for the texts of their famous alumnus.[150]

This has been a discussion that is arguably dependent on exceptional evidence and authors. By the ninth century, Bede had been accorded a place by Carolingian library compilers and cataloguers alongside Jerome, Augustine and Ambrose, not to mention the chronologically closer Gregory the Great, Isidore of Seville and Cassiodorus. For Bede to be regarded in this manner within a century of his death argues for a very widespread familiarity with his work, but it also raises the question of why he was so elevated. Bede no doubt assisted his own reputation by providing a list of his works. Yet it is one of the ironies of the manuscript distribution that it suggests that Bede's fame, especially for his exegesis and his school texts, was far greater on the Continent than in England in the first two centuries after his death. The richest

144 Boniface, epp. 76 and 91: Tangl 1916, pp. 158–9 and 206–27.
145 *Ibid.*, ep. 116, pp. 250–1.
146 *Ibid.*, ep. 126, pp. 263–4.
147 *Ibid.*, ep. 127, pp. 264–5.
148 *Ibid.*, ep. 124, pp. 261–2.
149 *Ibid.*, ep. 125, pp. 262–3.
150 Parkes 1982.

concentrations of his work, moreover, were in centres not usually regarded by modern scholars as those of strong Insular influence.

There is also the problem of how much 'national' distinctions are relevant in the context of cultural connections. And there is the problem of identification. There is little, apart from palaeographical, decorative and codicological traits, that can mark out one Latin text as fundamentally different in character from another in the early Middle Ages, regardless of where it was written. The recently revived debate about the character of a distinctively Irish approach to biblical exegesis and how much of it can be attributed to the extension of identifiably Irish influence to the Continent is a classic instance of the difficulties modern scholars have encountered.[151] Tracing the transmission of a particular text or work by a particular author, such as the *Canones hibernenses* or the works of Bede, has at least some rationale.[152] But there is little reason to suppose that those reading him had in any way singled out Bede, for example, as an English author. Nor can we necessarily regard the dissemination of works by Bede within the Frankish kingdoms as either typical or unusual unless he is compared with the dissemination of the work of other contemporaries or near contemporaries and with the patterns of transmission of classical and patristic authors more generally. One could chart similarly wide distributions for some of Alcuin's or Hrabanus Maurus' works,[153] as well as for the writings disseminated from the Carolingian royal court, such as the *Annales regni francorum*,[154] the Frankish royal capitularies, especially in the collection made by Ansegisus,[155] the *leges*,[156] the *Collectio Dionysio-Hadriana*,[157] the *Hadrianum* sacramentary[158] or the Homiliary of Paul the Deacon.[159] For other Frankish and English authors, and most likely the Irish ones as well, it would appear that distribution was, on the whole, far more localised.[160]

Here we also come up against the randomness of the survival of our evidence, quite apart from the difficulty of establishing a precise chronology for production and distribution. The answer is not to group the little evidence for connections we do have into already known episodes of contact, as has tended to be done hitherto. The evidence takes us into the unknown, in which

151 Bischoff 1954; Gorman 2002; debate usefully summarised in Tibbetts 2003.
152 Meens 2001; Shannon 2005; Kershaw 2008; Meeder 2009.
153 Bullough 1998; Spilling 1982; Fleckenstein 1982.
154 Kurtz 1895, pp. 9–15; McKitterick 2004, pp. 84–119; Reimitz 2000 and McKitterick 2008, pp. 31–54.
155 McKitterick 1977, p. 21; Schmitz 1996; Mordek 1995.
156 McKitterick, 1993. 157 Mordek 1969.
158 Vogel 1986, pp. 61–102.
159 Grégoire 1980, 423–86 and compare Gatch 1977.
160 Meeder 2009.

political links also provide an important context.[161] As I indicated in 1989 (in relation to links between England and Neustria),[162] the manuscripts bear witness to a far more extensive network of communication, exchange and unity of purpose from either side of the Channel and the North Sea, and a far closer integration of Frankish and English religious enterprise, than historians have been wont to imagine hitherto. Precisely because of the difficulties and uncertainties of dating and transmission, we need to think in terms of the continuous passage, on however small a scale, of individuals across Western Europe. Modern notions of nationality would appear to be anachronistic; it is not yet clear how attitudes to others were defined, though work on the formation and expression of identity and the 'other' in the early Middle Ages is well underway.[163] Peregrinating men and women brought their cultural baggage with them and have left the traces we can still observe and which have been the focus of our attention in this chapter. There is still a great deal of work to be done before we can understand these traces and interpret them correctly.

161 Wood 1991; Story 2003. 162 McKitterick 1989a.
163 See the series *Nationes*, 1975, 1978, 1980, 1983, 1985, 1987, 1989, 1991. See also Pohl and Reimitz 1998 and Corradini *et al.* 2003. I have benefited greatly and gratefully from comments from Michael Gullick and Teresa Webber about some of the manuscripts referred to in this chapter.

13

The circulation of books between England and the Celtic realms

HELEN MCKEE

The Lichfield Gospels, one of the most magnificent surviving manuscripts from the British Isles, has lain quietly in the library at Lichfield Cathedral for hundreds of years (Plate 5.1).[1] At the beginning of the ninth century, however, it was in Wales: a contemporary memorandum records that it was acquired, for the price of an 'excellent horse', by a man called Gelhi, and presented by him to the altar of St Teilo (that is, Llandeilo Fawr in Glamorganshire). We do not know from whom Gelhi acquired the book: indeed, its previous owners may have been raiders, who had plundered it from a religious house (in Wales, or further afield?). The Gospels remained at Llandeilo for some time – long enough to receive numerous additions (some lengthy, some merely memorialisations of the deceased), but by the second half of the tenth century it had come to Lichfield. It is not known how or why.

The career of this manuscript may be used to illustrate some of the certainties, and also the insuperable ambiguities, surrounding the circulation of books between England and its Celtic neighbours – Ireland, Wales, Cornwall, Scotland and Brittany. It is known that books did travel from the Celtic realms to England, but the circumstances behind their journeys are often obscure. Equally, it seems self-evident that books must have travelled in the reverse direction (that the Lichfield Gospels began its life in England, rather than Wales, is assumed by many medievalists) – but confirmation is hard to find.

Books must have circulated between the various regions of the British Isles from a very early period. Missionary activity would have been a particular stimulus to travel (for instance, many Irish manuscripts would have been taken to Northumbria from the 630s onwards). However, physical evidence of this is hard to come by. The problem is the lack of extant manuscripts, especially with regard to the Insular Celtic regions (Ireland, Wales, Cornwall and Scotland), whose manuscripts seem to have been significantly less likely

1 Lichfield CL, 1.

to survive than those of Anglo-Saxon England. For much of the period our sources are second-hand: Anglo-Saxon copies of Celtic texts (such as the *De excidio Britanniae* of Gildas, written in Wales in the fifth century), or Anglo-Saxon manuscripts which were copied from Celtic exemplars (such as Pelagius on the Pauline Epistles).[2]

The situation becomes a little clearer in the tenth century. Book collections in late Anglo-Saxon England appear to have contained an appreciable proportion of Celtic books: we know of several from Ireland, several from Wales, a much smaller number from Cornwall, and a much larger number from Brittany. These books vary considerably in type, from deluxe copies of the gospels to workaday copies of popular school texts. Some were in royal ownership (for example, the MacDurnan Gospels,[3] presented by King Æthelstan to Christ Church Cathedral); others were the property of obscure ecclesiastics and scholars whose names have only survived in booklists or ownership inscriptions. Even the tiny quantity of surviving manuscripts makes it clear that Celtic books were widely available in Anglo-Saxon England – and occasionally Anglo-Saxon manuscripts themselves provide clues to the presence in England of further Celtic books, now lost (abbreviations of Celtic type, for example).

It is easy to forget that this traffic in books need not have been one-way. English manuscripts which were in Welsh ownership are hard to identify, for instance, but this does not mean that such did not exist: we simply do not have the means to distinguish them. In fact, the major evidence for the transmission of English books to the Celtic realms comes from Brittany (many more of whose medieval library holdings have survived), and even that has only recently been recognised.

Sometimes it is possible to point to particular historical events which must have stimulated the passage of books between England and one or more of its Celtic neighbours. One of the most important of these events was the accession of Alfred the Great to the throne of Wessex and the cultural renaissance which he inaugurated. Confronted by declining literacy across his realm, Alfred recruited scholars to make up the deficit, some from Wales (notably his biographer Asser, who was from St David's), and some from Brittany (Asser mentions that there were Bretons at Alfred's court, while Breton churches were among those to which Alfred gave donations).[4] Numerous manuscripts must have come from these (and other) regions to help restock England's

2 Dumville 1993a, essay XIII. 3 London, Lambeth Palace, 1370.
4 Asser, *Life of Alfred*, §§ 76, 102: Stevenson 1904, pp. 60, 89.

depleted libraries, and Celtic exemplars undoubtedly lie behind many of our late ninth- and tenth-century manuscripts in Anglo-Saxon script.

The Breton contribution to English cultural life became even more marked in the early tenth century. Driven from their country by Viking raids in the 910s, Breton ecclesiastics, politicians and scholars escaped eastwards into Francia and north into Southumbria. They must have brought books with them, and although the exiles returned to Brittany when the Viking threat diminished, some of their books must have remained. (Starving Breton exiles in Francia had to sell their books to survive, and it may be that a similarly depressing trade lies behind the presence of many Breton manuscripts in English book collections.) Certainly a substantial number of Breton books are preserved in Anglo-Saxon libraries. These books are generally datable to the turn of the tenth century, when Breton scriptoria were at the height of production, so it is unfortunately not possible to say that the arrival in England of any one book must be due to the reform begun by Alfred rather than the Breton diaspora a few decades later. Their texts tend to the utilitarian, so we find material like the commentary on Sedulius by Remigius of Auxerre, Alcuin's and Bede's works on Latin orthography, Eutyches' study of the Latin verb (owned by the tenth-century reformer St Dunstan), and at least two copies of the canon law collection known as *Collectio canonum Hibernensis*.[5] Such books would all have been of use to the reformers of the late ninth century, but there would still have been a need for them throughout the late Anglo-Saxon period. A booklist from the end of the tenth century tells us of one 'Æthestan', apparently a grammatically inclined monk at St Augustine's, Canterbury, whose collection of books included at least two Breton volumes.[6]

The Welsh contribution to Alfred's reform programme was probably substantial: however, although we know that there were Welshmen at Alfred's court, we cannot identify any manuscripts they might have brought with them. We do know that a reformed version of Insular Minuscule whose origins lie at this time (English Square Minuscule) was based at least in part on Welsh models. However, it is not until the tenth century that we have physical evidence for the presence of Welsh books in Southumbria, beginning with the 'Corpus Martianus Capella'.[7] This copy of Martianus Capella's *De nuptiis Philologiae et Mercurii* (a guide to the seven liberal arts) was written in Wales, but appears to

5 Cambridge, Gonville and Caius College, 144; CCCC, 221; BodL., Auct, F.4.32, fols. 1–9; BL, Cotton Otho E.xiii; BodL., Hatton 42.

6 See the booklist in BL, Cotton Domitian i, fol. 55v: Lapidge 2006, pp. 133–4. The two Breton books are CCCC, 221, and (probably) Cambridge, Gonville and Caius College, 144.

7 CCCC, 153: Bishop 1964–8a.

have been at Canterbury by the 930s, when several missing pages were supplied in a form of Square Minuscule associated with St Augustine's Abbey. (At a slightly later date, it was further supplemented by a commentary on the text.) Interestingly, several tenth-century manuscripts from St Augustine's contain 'Late Celtic' abbreviations (abbreviations characteristic of Insular Celtic manuscripts from *c.* 850 onwards), suggesting that Celtic books were available as models there, and there may even have been Celtic personnel.

Other English centres for which there is particular evidence for a Celtic presence are Glastonbury Abbey and the Old Minster, Winchester. St Patrick was venerated at Glastonbury, which was accordingly a popular focus of Irish pilgrimage. The earliest *Life of St Dunstan* mentions Irish pilgrims at the time that Dunstan was there as a young monk (possibly the 930s), and adds that he 'applied himself attentively to their books, which expounded knowledgeably the pathway of righteous belief'.[8] Although apparently none of these Irish books has survived, Glastonbury is thought to have been the earliest known owner of St Dunstan's Classbook, a composite volume which comprises two Welsh manuscripts bound together with one Breton and one English book, and which was famously annotated by Dunstan himself:[9] it is not surprising that this house, like St Augustine's, produced manuscripts containing 'Late Celtic' abbreviations. Winchester, meanwhile, is known to have been the home in the mid tenth century of a Welsh schoolmaster called 'Ioruet' (Iorwerth) – perhaps just one of several Celtic immigrants, but exceptional because his name has been preserved. So far, no book associable with Ioruet has been recognised, though we can identify a collection of Cornish (and possibly Welsh) manuscripts that had reached the Old Minster by the end of the century, namely *Codex Oxoniensis Posterior*.[10]

Most of the surviving Welsh and Cornish manuscripts from English libraries are as utilitarian as those from Brittany. We have computistical material; theological works by Augustine and Caesarius of Arles; Martianus Capella and Juvencus, who were popular Latin-curriculum authors; and so on (Ovid's *Art of Love*, one of the texts from St Dunstan's Classbook, is a little more surprising, although we may note that its second and third books were expurgated). In some cases these manuscripts had reached England encrusted with glosses in what for the Anglo-Saxons would be incomprehensible languages, but this did not stop them from being used. Missing pages in the Corpus Martianus Capella were supplied after its arrival at St Augustine's, Canterbury, while the

8 *Sancti Dunstani vita auctore B.*, ch. 5: Stubbs 1874, p. 11: Lapidge 1993a, p. 422.
9 BodL., Auct. F.4.32: Hunt 1961. The Welsh components of this codex are fols. 19–35 and 37–46.
10 BodL., Bodley 572.

Cambridge Juvencus – which was already copiously annotated in Welsh, Irish, and Cornish or Breton – received a new layer of Latin glosses from a Worcester scribe.

The majority of Celtic manuscripts from Anglo-Saxon England are Brittonic – whether Welsh, Breton or Cornish. However, there is considerable evidence for the presence of Irishmen in England, ranging from the anonymous pilgrims at Glastonbury Abbey whose books Dunstan studied to named personalities such as the three mariners, Dubsláine, Mac Bethad and Maél Inmuin, who (according to the *Anglo-Saxon Chronicle*) set out in a boat without oars, travelling wherever the wind should take them – they landed in Cornwall in 891 and immediately headed for the court of Alfred[11] – to say nothing of those who had evangelised Northumbria more than two centuries earlier. In view of this it is perhaps surprising that we do not know of more extant Irish manuscripts which were definitely in Anglo-Saxon hands. One possible candidate is a fragmentary gospel-book in Durham, whose earliest provenance is Northumbria, but which is written in a Half-Uncial which looks typically Irish; it may be an Irish import or the work of an Irish expatriate.[12] It would not be the only Irish gospel-book to have come to England, for we know of several others, including pocket gospel manuscripts; one of these is the volume which Athelstan presented to Canterbury Cathedral,[13] but the other Irish pocket gospel-book to reach England has less lofty associations – it bears the name of an otherwise unknown deacon called Edward.[14]

Perhaps relatively few books from Ireland have survived in English collections because Irish scholars tended to use England merely as a staging-point on a longer journey. It seems to have been common for Irish scholars to cross Wales or Cornwall, and then southern England, on their way to the European mainland. For example, we know that some time in the second quarter of the ninth century an Irishman called Dubthach passed through Gwynedd on his way to the Continent: he enjoyed demonstrating a cryptographic code ('Dubthach's Cryptogram') along the way, and various texts composed in it survive in manuscripts from Wales, Brittany and Francia.[15] Another Gael whose name has come down to us is Cathróe, a cleric who travelled to the Continent in the early 940s: he was treated with considerable honour, being summoned to Edmund I's court, and actually conducted thence to his ship

11 *ASC*, 892: Plummer and Earle 1892–9. 12 DCL, A.II.10 (etc.).
13 London, Lambeth Palace, 1370. 14 BL, Add. 40618.
15 See CUL, Ff.4.42; Angers, BM, 477; BR, 9565–6: Derolez 1952.

by the archbishop of Canterbury.[16] The large number of Irish manuscripts preserved on the Continent testifies to the travels of these and many of their compatriots.

Most of this survey has concentrated on the passage of books from the Celtic realms to England, rather than vice versa, and this reflects the bias of the available evidence: we know little enough about the native books in Insular Celtic libraries, let alone what English volumes they may have contained. However, there are a few clues. For example, occasionally Welsh manuscripts have the letter **p** for the sound /θ/ or /ð/ in Welsh words (*pep* for *peth*, *Guipno* for *Gwyddno*), which suggests that a scribe had seen the Anglo-Saxon letter thorn in his exemplar, and did not recognise it. Thorns must have been in use in some Welsh scriptoria at least, and if a letter-form could travel across the border then so could manuscripts.

The clearest evidence for the circulation of books from England to one of the Celtic regions comes from Brittany. After the cataclysm of the early tenth century when so many Bretons and their books were driven out of Brittany (some to refuge in Southumbria), it was in part with English help that the Breton kingdom was re-established in the 930s. And it was also with English help that Breton book production was restarted after the hiatus: recent research has indicated that English exemplars were available to Breton scribes in the mid tenth century.[17]

This chapter began with the Lichfield Gospels. It will end with another Celtic gospel-book now in England: the MacRegol Gospels, also known as the Rushworth Gospels.[18] This is an Irish manuscript, partly written by a scribe called Mac Regol, who has been identified as an early ninth-century abbot of Birr, Co. Offaly. By the tenth century the book had reached Northumbria, where it received Old English glosses, some of them from a Northumbrian who bore the Welsh name Owun, and some of them from a Mercian. The MacRegol Gospels reminds us of the complex chains of communication which the career of a manuscript can never illuminate more than partially. Books did not travel in isolation: without knowing more of the human element we can never have more than half the story.

16 Colgan 1645, pp. 494–507; Anderson 1922, I, pp. 431–3.

17 Dumville 1993a, essay XIV.

18 BodL., Auct. D.2.19.

14

The circulation of books between England and the Continent, *c.* 871 – *c.* 1100

RICHARD GAMESON

At some point around 1020, a high-ranking calligrapher–illuminator at Peterborough called Earnwine presented King Cnut and Queen Emma with a fine sacramentary and a psalter; Cnut subsequently sent the two volumes to Cologne as gifts; in 1054 Bishop Ealdred of Worcester tarried in Cologne 'on the king's business', where he was presented with the very same books, which he then brought back to England. We only learn of the adventures of these volumes because they were then entrusted to (St) Wulfstan, a member (possibly prior) of the community of Worcester who, as it happened, had come into contact with them at Peterborough many years before, and their return to his care was thus celebrated as a miracle by his biographer.[1] Other manuscripts can be seen to have made similar round-trips. A compilation of Old Testament, liturgical and computistical texts that was written in northern France in the third quarter of the ninth century had apparently crossed the Channel by the early tenth century when certain letters were retraced by an Anglo-Saxon hand; artwork added by another Anglo-Saxon implies that it was still in England at the end of the tenth century; however, a series of additions by Norman scribes suggests that it migrated to Normandy during the first half of the eleventh century, and its medieval provenance was Jumièges.[2] A collection of tracts and letters by Jerome written in the second half of the ninth century, probably in the Loire region, had passed into Anglo-Saxon hands by the end of the ninth century, as a short colophon in Insular Minuscule at the bottom of the last page of text reveals; prayers added to the originally blank verso show that it was still in England in the earlier tenth century. At some point thereafter, however, the volume re-crossed the Channel and ended up in Normandy; subsequent additions suggest that it was

1 *The Vita Wulfstani of William of Malmesbury*: Darlington 1928, pp. 5 and 15–16; Winterbottom and Thomson 2002, pp. 16 and 40; *ASC* D, 1054.

2 Rouen, BM, A.292 (Cat. gén. 26) : Hesbert 1954, pp. 25–7, plates IV, V and LXI.

there in the first half of the twelfth century and probably by 1100.[3] Similarly, a copy of Hrabanus Maurus' *In Judith* and *In Hester* written in north-east France at the end of the ninth century had reached England by the millennium, as modest annotations by Anglo-Saxon hands attest; it left these shores around the time of the Conquest with Abbot Sæwold of Bath, being one of the volumes that he offered to the community of Saint-Vaast at Arras – in which town it remains.[4]

Now what is exceptional in these cases is not the fact that the books passed to and fro between England and the Continent, but rather the circumstance that their travels have left clear traces and so are recoverable. Many manuscripts must have crossed the Channel on loan as exemplars at one time or another, yet assuming they were returned, it would only be possible to perceive that they had ever left their homeland if they received substantial additions in the other country – something that was unlikely to happen to a borrowed book without compelling reasons – or if they had singular textual features that would enable direct descendants (if they also happen to survive) to be identified as such. A Prudentius in Paris is a case in point.[5] The whole book is written, and much of it rubricated, in a mid-ninth-century Continental Caroline Minuscule; the *Psychomachia* was supplied with illustrations in an illusionistic style, to which at an uncertain later date, one or more hands made modest additions (firming up some of the outlines and adding details); none of this work looks English. The first three titles were supplied in ninth-century Continental Rustic Capitals;[6] the rest, by contrast, are in a quite different type of Rustics, whose form is most readily paralleled in England. Armed with this insight, one might also interpret the hand that did the tituli on fols. 65v–67v as an eleventh-century English one. Late medieval jottings in the upper margins of 77v and 78r indicate that the manuscript was by then on the Continent once again. The evidence is slender and easily overlooked but is just sufficient to suggest that the book might have been in England in the eleventh century.

Numerous early Continental manuscripts are now, of course, in English repositories, and vice versa; however, without clear evidence both of origin and of early and subsequent provenance, it is difficult to know whether such books reached their adoptive home in the early Middle Ages, the late Middle Ages, or

3 Rouen, BM, A.425 (Cat. gén. 453); provenance: Rouen, Saint-Ouen. The original text stopped on 93r, line 9; a crude ?Continental *s.* ix hand then added a short prayer. At the bottom of the leaf an Insular hand of *s.* ix^{2}–ix/x added, 'Pax poscendi premium a deo scribendi'. Other prayers were added to the verso by at least two different and slightly later (*s.* x^{1}) Anglo-Saxon hands. Fols. 1–3 and 95–8, structurally separate and in Continental hands of *s.* xi/xii–xii^{med}, were attached at an uncertain date; the former includes (2r) an informal note mentioning an abbot of Lyre (Eure).

4 Arras, Médiathèque, 764 (Cat. gén. 739), part 1: fols. 1–93: Gameson 2002a, pp. 166 and 181.

5 BnF, lat. 8085. 6 Fols. 55v and 56r, col. 1.

in more recent times. As *ex libris* inscriptions were the exception not the rule in Anglo-Saxon England, and library shelf-marks unknown, it is only annotation or imitation that can prove early acquisition. Exemplifying the problems is Cambridge, Corpus Christi College, 193, a late eighth-century copy of Ambrose's *Hexæmeron* which, annotations show, was still on the Continent in the tenth and earlier eleventh century; its presence amongst the books of Matthew Parker indicates that it was in England in the sixteenth century and it had most probably come from an English monastic library. Ambrose was collected fairly energetically in England in the generation after the Norman Conquest and this, it might reasonably be presumed, was its most likely time of arrival on these shores. However, there is no evidence that such was actually the case; moreover, the idiosyncratic Merovingian Minuscule in which it was written would not have made it an easy volume to use by that date.[7] A comparable example of the difficulties of tracking transmission in the opposite direction is provided by a copy of Boethius' *De consolatione philosophiae* that is now in Paris.[8] Produced in Canterbury in the late tenth century, this stately volume was supplied with plentiful marginal and interlinear glosses at the time of writing. From the thirteenth century onwards it received further extensive annotation and glossing in France, and its medieval provenance was Saint-Victor's in Paris, as inscriptions on fols. 2r and 2v demonstrate; Saint-Victor's was founded in 1113. Tantalisingly, on five pages there are glosses or jottings by an informal and difficult-to-date but probably eleventh-century Continental-looking hand: which side of the Channel was the book when this scribe used it? The manuscript may have reached the Continent in the eleventh century, but it is impossible to be certain, and its transfer might reflect the cosmopolitan clerical culture of the twelfth or early thirteenth century rather than bibliographical exchange during the period that concerns us here. Such uncertain cases, seductive though they may be, cannot be used for our enquiry. Nor is this the end of our problems, for even when the combined evidence of provenance and annotations shows that a book had migrated to another country at an early point in its history, there remains a degree of ambiguity since the oldest 'foreign' interventions may significantly post-date its arrival in its new home.[9]

7 Another example from many: the four leaves (fols. 1*–4*) from a *s.* ix[1] copy of Alan of Farfa's homiliary that preface BL, Harley 652 (a *s.* xi[ex] volume of Paul the Deacon's homiliary, written at St Augustine's Abbey, Canterbury) clearly served as the paste-down and flyleaves for that manuscript in the later Middle Ages (as the added shelfmark attests); given their date and the nature of the text, it is a reasonable hypothesis that the book which they represent reached England before 1066 – but it can be nothing more than that.

8 BnF, lat. 14380.

9 E.g. the earliest English additions to BL, Egerton 874 (north-east France; *s.* ix[2]), which consist of prayers and part of an office of St Augustine of Canterbury, date from the second half of the

The difficulties that afflict our topic – in addition to the universal problem of large-scale losses – are thus particularly fierce. Nevertheless, by taking the witness of 'foreign' interventions in tandem with documentary, textual and visual evidence for bibliographical exchange, and alongside general historical data, it is possible to sketch the outlines of our subject with some confidence.

Given the wealth of manuscripts produced in the Carolingian Empire during the ninth century, and the dearth of Anglo-Saxon ones from the same period, it is no surprise that the predominant direction in which books flowed during the 100 years following the accession of King Alfred (AD 871) was from the Continent into England. Alfred himself played an important role in promoting this process. Family connections between the West Saxon monarchy and the later Carolingian dynasty are likely to have fostered an awareness of the riches of Continental libraries and led both directly and indirectly to the transmission of at least some of this material to Alfred's court circle. One manuscript which seems to have arrived at this time, fairly shortly after it was written, is the aforementioned collection of Jerome's writings that is now in Rouen[10] – though it must be stressed that it has no demonstrable connection with Alfred. A prime candidate for a text that did reach England under Alfred's aegis is Boethius' *Consolation of Philosophy*, a work which does not appear to have been known in England before that king's time and whose rise to general popularity was essentially a ninth-century phenomenon, yet which Alfred included in his 'programme' of translations – presumably relying on a recently imported manuscript. One Carolingian copy that travelled to England at an early date has come down to us: written in the Loire region in the first half of the ninth century, it was seemingly in British hands by the end of the century and was in England (Glastonbury) by the mid tenth century at the latest – a history which reminds us that a few Carolingian books might have reached England via British intermediaries.[11]

It is safe to assume that Alfred's Continental helpers, Grimbald of Saint-Bertin and John the Old Saxon, will have been conduits for the importation of at least some manuscripts. Echoes of the influence of the latter may perhaps be seen in the circumstance that copies of the Old Saxon *Heliand* and the Old

eleventh century; however, if the manuscript was indeed the exemplar for BodL., Hatton 30 (see n. 22 below), it must have reached England more than a century earlier.

10 Rouen, BM, A.425.

11 BAV, Vat. lat. 3363: Parkes 1991, pp. 259–62 with 1992, plate 71; Godden 2005; Sims-Williams 2005. Against the association that has sometimes been made between this manuscript and Asser: Wittig 1983, esp. pp. 161–2 (n. 20).

Saxon Genesis were produced in late Anglo-Saxon England (though it must be acknowledged that the surviving English manuscripts of these works date from roughly a century after John's arrival).[12] Some of the Carolingian books from north-east France and Flanders that were demonstrably in England by *c.* 900 may have arrived through the agency of Grimbald: one thinks in particular of a 'Flemish' Prudentius whose provenance in the later ninth century appears to have been Saint-Bertin and which was extensively corrected by ?Flemish and early tenth-century Anglo-Saxon hands.[13] Other volumes that had migrated to England by the beginning of the tenth century included a psalter, a missal, a collection of canons, a Fortunatus, the Jerome in Rouen mentioned earlier, and a copy of the same author's *De uiris illustribus* and other texts.[14]

A more intriguing case is the first stratum of the Leofric Missal. The manuscript was clearly in England very soon after it was made (as additions in English hands attest) and a recent thorough study has underlined the English characteristics of the text, highlighting the likelihood of an English patron, probably an archbishop of Canterbury;[15] however, this part of the book is entirely continental (northern French/'Flemish') in script and decoration, not to mention codicology. But then around 900, when English book production was in the doldrums, commissioning such a volume from a thriving Continental scriptorium that specialised in such texts was almost certainly the most reliable way for an important English ecclesiastic to secure a reasonably handsome copy; and if he were based in Canterbury, geographically closer to Flanders than to much of England, such would hardly have been difficult to organise. Whatever the exact circumstances in which it was produced and procured, the volume attests to bibliographical connections between southern England and northern Francia *c.* 900. Another relatively high-status volume that arrived during the first half of the tenth century is the gospel-book into which the *Liber vitae* of Thorney Abbey was eventually inserted. While its precise place of origin (Brittany or western Francia) is debated, the manuscript seems to have been written early in the tenth century. A substantial

12 BL, Cotton Caligula A.vii; BodL., Junius 11.

13 CCCC, 223. The case of Cambridge, Pembroke College, 308 (Hrabanus, *In Epistolas Pauli*, IX–XIX), written at Reims in the time of Archbishop Hincmar (d. 882), is far more ambiguous. While the text is the sort that is more likely to have been imported before as opposed to after 1066, none of the very short early interventions is racially diagnostic (though the dark ink in which they are written might be held to favour England over the Continent). The earliest addition that can, with reasonable certainty, be regarded as English is the formal title on the final verso, dating from *c.* 1100. The late medieval provenance of the book (as shown by an *ex libris*) was Ely.

14 Respectively: BL, Cotton Galba A.xviii; Royal 4 A.xiv; BodL., Hatton 42; BL, Add. 24193; Rouen, BM, A.425; and BL, Cotton Caligula A.xv.

15 BodL., Bodley 579: Orchard 2002.

correction by an Anglo-Saxon hand (30r) plus a group of Old English glosses demonstrate that it soon reached England, where it was also marked up with lection cues for liturgical use. The book was demonstrably at Thorney by *c.* 1100, but there is unfortunately no evidence to identify the English milieu to which it first came.[16]

A milieu that was identifiably a focal point for the importation of manuscripts in the second quarter of the tenth century was the court of King Athelstan, doubtless reflecting the number and diversity of foreign dignitaries who frequented it, not to mention the king's family connections with ruling dynasties in both East and West Francia. The 'foreign' books known to have passed through Athelstan's hands include a magnificent illuminated gospel-book from North Francia or Flanders (which seemingly reached him via the court of his brother-in-law, Otto the Great of Germany) and a copy of the Acts of the Council of Constantinople, along with one Irish and two Breton gospel-books. All these volumes Athelstan donated to English religious houses.[17]

An opportunity for an influx of manuscripts from Flanders in particular was provided by his successor, King Edmund, who in 944 settled at Bath a group of ecclesiastics from Saint-Bertin displaced by the monastic reforms of Gerard of Brogne. It is not impossible that Arras, Médiathèque, 764, part I (Hrabanus Maurus' *In Judith* and *In Hester*) was one of the books they brought with them: as noted above, this volume was written in north-east Francia at the end of the ninth century; it was in England by the late tenth century at the latest (as annotations in Anglo-Saxon hands show), and its provenance was presumably Bath, since it is almost certainly one of the volumes that was subsequently given to Saint-Vaast, Arras, by Abbot Sæwold of that house.[18]

While Edmund offered some Flemish clergy a refuge from the monastic reforms of their homeland, he equally ratified the appointment of St Dunstan as abbot of Glastonbury in the 940s, thereby initiating the first phase of the Benedictine reform movement in England. Henceforth the circle of the monastic reformers was increasingly central to the importation of books. This should not lead us to associate every 'foreign' volume with the reform movement: some may well have gone to the communities of clerics that they vilified, while others can certainly be linked to St Augustine's Abbey, Canterbury, a monastic community that was apparently thriving outside the initial orbit of the reformers. Nevertheless, a fair number of foreign books can be associated

16 BL, Add. 40000: Ker 1957, no. 131; Clark 1985.
17 BL, Cotton Tiberius A.ii; Cotton Claudius B.v; Lambeth Palace Library, 1370; BL, Royal 1 A.xviii; Cotton Otho B.ix: Keynes 1985.
18 See n. 4.

more or less directly with reformed foundations, and the number would doubtless be appreciably greater if the libraries of Glastonbury, Abingdon and Winchester – dynamic axes of the movement – had enjoyed a better survival rate. Annotations in Anglo-Saxon hands show a number of Carolingian volumes to have reached England in or by the mid tenth century. The small, scrappy Alcuin, British Library, Harley 213, is a case in point: written at the end of the ninth century, with continental contributions continuing into the early tenth, the manuscript bears additions by an ill-disciplined hand displaying Insular, Square Minuscule and some Caroline features which is most probably English work of mid-tenth-century date;[19] its medieval provenance was Winchester. Or, if the manuscripts had arrived at a slightly earlier date, they were studied more extensively and attentively from the mid tenth century than hitherto. A rare demonstrable case of such is the mid-ninth-century Continental Fortunatus, British Library, Add. 24193: a couple of notes in an Anglo-Saxon cursive minuscule suggest that the volume had reached England by *c.* 900;[20] however, it was in the second half of the tenth century that the first couple of quires were rewritten by an Anglo-Saxon scribe. The authors represented in this body of books are Alcuin, Aldhelm, Bede, Juvencus and Isidore, along with Caesarius and Augustine.[21] That at least some of these volumes did indeed gravitate into the circle of the reformers is indicated by the fact that they bear annotations in a hand which is probably that of St Dunstan (Plate 14.1).[22]

The number of volumes that can be shown to have been imported between the mid tenth century and the early eleventh is much greater than in the previous generations, and this is probably a fair reflection of reality, echoing the quickening of monastic life in southern England, along with the closer relations to monastic centres on the Continent that this brought. In so far as the origins of the manuscripts in question can be established, the vast majority come from three regions of western Francia: the Loire (effectively Tours and Fleury), the north-east (Reims and its hinterland), and the north (northern France and Flanders) – all major book-producing areas that were geographically fairly

19 On fols. 141v–2r.

20 Fols. 67r and 116v (erased).

21 BL, Harley 213; Lambeth Palace Library, 377, 237; BL, Harley 526; Royal 15 A.xvi; Boulogne, BM, 63; BodL., Rawlinson C.697.

22 Lambeth Palace Library, 237; BodL., Rawlinson C.697. On the annotating hand in question: Hunt 1961; Budny 1992. If BL, Egerton 874 (north-east France; *s.* ix[2]; ?at St Augustine's Abbey, Canterbury by *s.* xi[2]) was indeed the exemplar for BodL., Hatton 30, the copy of Caesarius, *In Apocalypsin* with a contemporary inscription recording that Abbot Dunstan had it written (see Morin 1942), p. 249 n. 21), then this manuscript too must have passed through Glastonbury in his time.

near to southern England and with which Anglo-Saxons had well-established connections. Interaction with Corbie, Fleury and St Peter's in Ghent is particularly clearly documented in written sources, and although the accidents of survival have deprived us of the book collections that would reveal the influence of the first and the last (Abingdon and Glastonbury, along with that of St Peter's, Ghent itself), there is no reason to doubt its likelihood. The texts that were demonstrably imported in this period were still, for the most part, a restricted selection of devotional and practical religious literature, confirming the limited needs and tastes of the English monastic reform movement. A few patristic texts appear, but these were clearly marginal to the main focus of interest which was evidently the writings of the Anglo-Saxon authors Aldhelm, Alcuin and Bede – something which provides striking testimony both to the conservatism of later Anglo-Saxon literary culture and to the extent to which native book collections had indeed been depleted during the ninth century. Alongside the works of these English writers one finds Christian poetry (Fortunatus) and reference (Isidore's *Etymologiae*), church councils, homiliaries, a limited selection of Carolingian commentary, and parts of the Bible (in more or less luxurious forms). Another work which, indirect evidence shows, came to England at this time and reflects exactly the same tastes was a massive hagiographical compilation. The collection in question, whose earliest extant descendant is the so-called Cotton-Corpus legendary, would appear to have been assembled in Flanders in the late ninth or early tenth century but was known to Ælfric by the millennium.[23]

If the range of imported texts was thus restricted, the books in question were clearly used, as is shown by the various additions and glosses in Anglo-Saxon hands, not to mention the English descendants of their texts. Thus a monumental volume of Isidore and other works that had been made in western France in the late ninth century served as the exemplar for a Christ Church copy just over a century later,[24] and this same centre embarked upon an ambitious attempt to produce its own version of the Reimsian Utrecht Psalter, with its extensive cycle of illustrations positively teeming with figures.[25] Elsewhere, Anglo-Saxon use of imported books is variously attested by occasional glosses,[26] by additions and jottings,[27] and sometimes even by extensive glossing: thus a Continental copy of Prosper was (judging by what

23 Jackson and Lapidge 1996.
24 Respectively Salisbury CL, 101, and TCC, B.4.27.
25 Utrecht, UB, 32; BL, Harley 603. See further Chapter 10.
26 E.g. BodL., Lat. class. C.2, fol. 18, etc.
27 E.g. BodL., Bodley 516.

remains) supplied with a nearly continuous gloss in Old English.[28] The most ambitious such exercise appears in the Reimsian Psalter, Cambridge, Corpus Christi College, 272.[29] Written *c.* 883×4 and still on the Continent in the tenth century – as the hand responsible for the final prayers added to fol. 183 shows – it was clearly in England, probably Canterbury, by the earlier eleventh century when the psalter text was supplied throughout with an extensive gloss, the work of at least three contemporary Anglo-Saxon scribes; in order to achieve this so neatly, the manuscript must have been disbound at the time (Plate 14.2). (The same was presumably true of another manuscript from the same region, the Utrecht Psalter, when its illustrations were being copied at Christ Church around the millennium.[30]) Use is equally shown by 'restorations' that varied from replacing isolated pages[31] or a couple of quires[32] to rewriting the greater part of the text. Of the twenty-nine quires that composed the ninth-century Continental Isidore, Bibliothèque nationale de France, lat. 7585, only seven remain intact, with a further three whose inner leaves still represent original work; the extensive restoration that was undertaken in England in the later tenth century included retracing faded letters, supplying the outer sheets of the three quires noted above, and rewriting a total of nineteen quires – all of which had to be achieved so as to interlock exactly with preserved original parts.[33] Most of the restoration was accomplished by two scribes, with very small interventions by two others, and with corrections and glosses by yet others. Quite what happened to the volume is debatable; however, given that some of the surviving original leaves – notably those at either end – are patently damp-stained, and that the replacement leaves appear at the beginning and the end of the volume, extensive water damage seems the most likely explanation. It is a nice question whether the presumed damaged sheets could themselves have served as the exemplars for their replacements or whether a second copy had to be found. Our manuscript was still in England in the first half of the eleventh century when a text in Old English was added to the endleaf, but subsequent additions to the same folio (including the compelling 'Sator arepo...' word-square) along with jottings elsewhere suggest that it may have returned to the Continent by the twelfth century.

Some such cases, where the English scribes were retracing the original letter-forms or supplying leaves to match the original stratum, offer insight into how certain Anglo-Saxons – and those at Canterbury in particular – familiarised

28 BL, Cotton Tiberius A.vii.

29 Robinson 1988, I, no. 149; II, plate 7; Koehler and Mütherich 1999, I, pp. 200–6; II, plates 174–8.

30 See n. 25; Noel 1995.

31 CCCC, 430.

32 BL, Add. 24193.

33 Bishop 1971, no. 6.

themselves with Continental Caroline Minuscule. Many of the original pages preserved in the above-mentioned Isidore (BnF, lat. 7585) were retraced in part, and here (though not, it must be said, in their independent work) the Anglo-Saxon scribes generally followed the original letter-forms very closely. A copy of Job and Ezra made in northern Francia (?Saint-Bertin) in the first half of the ninth century, which was in England by the millennium, is written in a type of script that lies behind the Caroline Minuscule practised at Canterbury in the second half of the tenth century; parts were restored by an Anglo-Saxon scribe who had clearly paid close attention to the proportions and letter-forms of the original.[34] The transformation of southern English script and decoration in the later tenth century (phenomena discussed elsewhere in this volume) pays eloquent tribute to the attentiveness with which Anglo-Saxon scribes studied and imitated Continental manuscripts, particularly from the main centres noted above.

By the second half of the tenth century, if not before, the traffic in books had become a two-way street as England was herself sending significant numbers of manuscripts to the Continent. The evidence suggests that this, too, was intimately linked to the monastic reform movement. Indeed, while a few Anglo-Saxon manuscripts may have been exported in the first half of the tenth century, volumes of such a date with a Continental provenance are more likely to have left the country in the second half of the century. The evidence of early additions points in this direction: both the Anglo-Saxon gospel-book of earlier tenth-century date that came to Saint-Vaast and the early tenth-century Amalarius that migrated to Saint-Bertin were annotated in their Flemish homes around the millennium.[35]

The first area that can be seen to have received significant numbers of Anglo-Saxon books is Flanders (a then-fluid territory comprising parts of modern northern France and Belgium). This, of course, is the part of mainland Europe that is nearest to England and, in consequence, the region through which many travellers to and from the Continent would have passed, whatever their ultimate destination.

An interesting documentary reference seems to show the (illegal) transmission of an Anglo-Saxon manuscript into secular Continental hands, probably Flemish or Norman. A letter from an anonymous bishop of a monastic cathedral (plausibly identified as Æthelwold of Winchester) addressed to a

34 BL, Arundel 125; Gameson 2002a, figs. 3–4. Cf. BL, Add. 24193 – careful retracing of almost every letter on fols. 17v+18r.

35 Boulogne, BM, 10 and 82.

duke or count, probably Arnulf II of Flanders (965–88), implores the latter to return a gospel-book that had been 'stolen' from the monastic church by two 'depraved' clerics, and which he had subsequently bought (from a third party) for three mancuses. It has been hypothesised that the 'reprobates' were some of the secular clerics whom Æthelwold had expelled from Winchester in 964. If, incidentally, the count did as he was asked, then this was one of the many books that would have crossed the Channel twice.[36]

In addition to other direct evidence for the transportation of English books to Flanders (namely Anglo-Saxon manuscripts that were demonstrably in the region at an early date[37]) there is indirect evidence in the form of clear echoes of Anglo-Saxon illumination in local work – though the fact that Anglo-Saxon artists patently served in Flemish scriptoria, above all Saint-Bertin, greatly complicates the task of deploying such evidence for the present enquiry. At least two, possibly three, Anglo-Saxon artists participated personally in the efflorescence of book production at Saint-Bertin during the abbacy of Odbert (*c.* 986 - *c.* 1007), who was himself the principal local illuminator. Yet while many of the Anglo-Saxon elements that appear in Odbert's artistic vocabulary may have been derived directly from the Anglo-Saxons who worked in his scriptorium at one time or another, some of them cannot have done so. Odbert shows familiarity, for example, with Anglo-Saxon initial ornament of a type that flourished in the first half of the tenth century and was not used by any of the Anglo-Saxons who are known to have plied their trade under his direction. It is logical to assume, therefore, that his inspiration for such archaic motifs came from older Anglo-Saxon books; and indeed one such volume dating from the first half of the tenth century, with initials of precisely the type in question, was demonstrably at Saint-Bertin by the millennium.[38]

The manuscript art practised at nearby Saint-Vaast (Arras) in the first half of the eleventh century likewise clearly owed a debt to Anglo-Saxon models. Here there is less evidence for English personnel actually working in the scriptorium,[39] which simplifies the situation in one respect; however, there is the new problem of distinguishing between direct and indirect transmission of Anglo-Saxon motifs: the point is that some of the work in question is likely

36 Stubbs 1874, p. 362. Suggested context: Lapidge 1993a, pp. 126–8 and 190–2 – though the subsequent mention of 'a certain girl captured by your Danes' might point rather to Normandy.

37 Inventoried: Gameson 2002a, pp. 186–8.

38 Boulogne, BM, 82.

39 The only possibly English hand that I have noted in a Saint-Vaast book of this generation appears in Arras, Médiathèque, 343 (Boethius), fols. 4r–v and 17r–18v. Fols. 17, 18 and 19 are all singletons, but as fol. 4 is conjoint with fol. 6, which is part of the stint of an archetypically 'Flemish' hand, this suggests that the Anglo-Saxon (or Anglo-Saxon trained) scribe was indeed working alongside Flemings.

to have been informed by the English-influenced art of Saint-Bertin, a house with which the community at Arras had close connections. Nonetheless, at least some of the foliate frames produced at Saint-Vaast suggest knowledge of Anglo-Saxon originals (as opposed to Saint-Bertin interpretations thereof), while one of the decorated initials in their giant bible is so close to a letter in a Canterbury manuscript that the latter was almost certainly the inspiration for the former; as the known medieval provenance of the Canterbury book was France (Dol(e)), it seems reasonable to conclude that it had indeed reached Arras by the second quarter of the eleventh century.[40] Equally, the evidence of early annotations shows that the one extant Anglo-Saxon gospel-book to have been produced in the first half of the tenth century was in Flanders by the millennium, and its known provenance was Saint-Vaast.[41]

Anglo-Saxon books continued to reach Flanders – and vice versa – throughout the eleventh century. A collection of glossaries, written in England in the early eleventh century, for instance, was there by the middle of the century; a Prudentius produced around the millennium and still in England in the early eleventh century (when it received Old English glosses) had moved to Flanders within a century, being recorded in the Saint-Bertin library catalogue of 1104; and in the aftermath of the Conquest, Abbot Sæwold of Bath enriched Saint-Vaast with a substantial bequest of books, some of which were of English origin.[42] Conversely, when the scholarly monks of Saint-Bertin, Folcard and Goscelin, came to England in the mid eleventh century, it is likely that both groups brought some books with them, and they may subsequently have been conduits for the arrival of more. Some of the texts which we know that Goscelin considered to be particularly important – Augustine's *Confessiones* and *De civitate Dei*, Eusebius' *Historia ecclesiastica*, and the Cassiodoran *Historia tripartita*[43] – were very rare books in eleventh-century England, and it is not unreasonable to suppose that he will have taken measures to import copies if the opportunity presented itself; all were available in contemporary Flanders. Whatever the truth of that point, at least one copy of the *Encomium* that Queen Emma, widow of both Æthelræd and Cnut, commissioned from an ecclesiastic at Saint-Omer must have been brought to England before 1066; indeed, the extant manuscript – the work of two mid-eleventh-century hands, one of which is typically Flemish – is probably the copy in question.[44]

40 BnF, lat. 6401A (echoed in Arras, Médiathèque, 559): Gameson 1998.

41 Boulogne, BM, 10; Gameson 2009.

42 BR, 1828–30. Boulogne, BM, 189 (cf. Becker 1885, no. 77). Saewold's bequest: Lapidge 1985, no. VIII; the extant Anglo-Saxon manuscripts in question are now Arras, Médiathèque, 867 and 1029.

43 *Liber confortatorius*, III, 'mensa scripturarum': Talbot 1955, pp. 80–1.

44 BL, Add. 33241. Scribe 1: Campbell 1998, ills. 3 and 4.

A handful of Anglo-Saxon manuscripts produced in the late tenth century or thereabouts ended up at Saint-Bênoit-sur-Loire (Fleury). Whilst Englishmen were visiting Fleury from the mid tenth century onwards, at first they seem to have been 'borrowers' rather than donors of literary material. Indeed, at some point between 974 and 984 Dunstan was asked to use his influence to engineer the dispatch to Fleury of several volumes that, having been brought over to England, were now needed there again; the books in question were then at Winchester, with the exception of one ('the commentary of Florus') which was in the hands of Abbot Osgar of Abingdon (d. 984) – who, as it happens, had previously been sent to Fleury by Æthelwold.[45] A particularly favourable context for the exchange of books with Fleury around the millennium was the abbacy of Abbo. Schoolmaster of Fleury for some twenty years, then frustrated in a first bid for its abbacy, Abbo had come to England (Ramsey) in 985; he returned to his alma mater a couple of years later when the abbacy became vacant again, holding the post from 988 until his death in 1004. Now, it is logical to presume that this redoubtable scholar would have been accompanied by manuscripts on his journeys to and from England. That he brought his own *Computus* and the *De computo ecclesiastico* of Helperic of Auxerre is apparent from the reflections of them in English material, above all the work of Byrhtferth of Ramsey.[46] At least one of Abbo's own compositions must have travelled in the opposite direction: the *Quaestiones grammaticales*, written for his 'dearest English brothers in Christ' while he was still a 'deacon', was apparently composed at Ramsey, but the two extant copies, both of eleventh-century date and seemingly of Fleury origin or provenance, attest to its transmission to the Loire.[47]

One extant volume which may have travelled between Ramsey and Fleury is a calendar and computistica now in Paris.[48] The calendar, written by an English scribe in the late tenth century, is associable liturgically with Ramsey; while the computistica, which include a version of Helperic associated with Abbo and which continue from and are connected to the end of

45 Stubbs 1874, no. XIV, pp. 376–7; Lapidge 2003a, pp. 220–2, who argues that Dunstan's correspondent ('L') was none other than Lantfred. For the suggestions that two of the books contained Augustine and Ausonius and lie behind the copies of those texts in CUL, Kk.5.34 (*s.* x^{ex}; Winchester) see Carley 1987, esp. 204–12.

46 Baker and Lapidge 1995, pp. xxi–xxii and liii–lix. See also Chapter 36 below.

47 The tract begins: 'Dilectissimis in Christo Angligenis fratribus, maximeque in monasterio sancti patris Benedicti sub scola uirtutum regulariter uitam degentibus, ex Floriacensi coenobio eiusdem patris uernula Abbo, genere Francus, professione monachus, officio diaconus, in essentialiter Bono salutis perpetue munus': Guerreau-Jalabert 1982, p. 209; cf. Baker and Lapidge 1995, p. xxi. Extant manuscripts: BAV, Reg. lat. 596, fols. 10–23; and BL, Add. 10972, fols. 39v–48.

48 BnF, lat. 7299: Barker-Benfield 1976, esp. pp. 152–5; Lapidge 1993a, pp. 395–6.

the calendar, are the work of an English and a Continental scribe writing in alternation. Both the calendar and the computistica were subsequently augmented on the Continent (the additions to the former include an obit for Abbo) and their provenance was Fleury. It is unclear at what stage they were joined to the broadly coeval Macrobius with which they now share an early modern binding: this part of the volume, wholly Continental in appearance, bears no physical traces of a sojourn in England, though it is worth noting that the text was known to Byrhtferth of Ramsey. Another case may be an enigmatic, now composite Boethius manuscript, much of which was written in a rich black typically English ink by a difficult-to-parallel but probably Anglo-Saxon hand dating from around the millennium and which has contemporary artwork in an Anglo-Saxon style, but which travelled abroad almost immediately (as the glosses written in Continental ink in script with Fleury features suggest), and was sooner or later associated with broadly contemporary Continental material, part of it demonstrably connected with Fleury.[49] Be all that as it may, we know that Abbo was the direct cause for the export of one manuscript from England to Fleury, namely a copy of the *Vita Dunstani* by B, which was made at St Augustine's Abbey, since it came with the request that he versify the work – a task which his murder at La Réole in 1004 prevented him from carrying out.[50] That bibliographical relations continued after Abbo's death is confirmed by the biography of his successor, Gauzlin (1004/5–30), which notes that a magnificent benedictional, all of whose incipits were written in gold, was sent to the new abbot from Ramsey.[51]

One of the late tenth-century Anglo-Saxon manuscripts that reached Fleury in the first half of the eleventh century (a fine sacramentary) had travelled there via Mont Saint-Michel, as the list of Montois monks that was added to it

49 BnF, lat. 6401. Avril and Stirnemann 1987, no. 19, colour plate B. Fols. 15r–158r are written in a very black, English-looking ink by a hand which, though not easily paralleled either in England or in 'France', could more easily be placed in the former than the latter. (If perchance the manuscript was made at Ramsey, whose other books have seemingly perished, this might help to explain why the hand is difficult to parallel.) Artwork in an idiosyncratic Anglo-Saxon style appears on 15r and 158v–9r. Fols. 159 ff. are written in *s.* xi Continental hands; fol. 171 bears an epitaph for Abbot Gauzlin of Fleury (d. 1030).

50 St Gallen, Kantonsbibliothek (Vadiana), 337. Colour plate: Bosc-Lauby and Notter 2004, p. 144.

51 *Vita Gauzlini*, ch. 55: Bautier and Labory 1969, p. 94. Since the erroneous suggestion that the manuscript in question was the *s.* x^{2} Winchester benedictional, BnF, lat. 987 (New Pal. Soc., I, plates 83, 84), has recently been revived by Eric Palazzo (in Bosc-Lauby and Notter 2004, p. 146) and by Alexandre and Lanoë 2004, p. 17, it is worth stressing that this cannot have been the case: a major supplement of *s.* xi$^{2/4}$ (datable to after 1023), extensive reworking of many of the original prayers *in rasura* in *s.* xi$^{2/4\text{-med}}$, many interlinear changes and additions of *s.* xi^{med}, and an added prayer (79r) of *s.* xi^{2}, all clearly done by English hands, show that lat. 987 was still in England after Gauzlin's death.

by a known Mont Saint-Michel hand attests.[52] Whatever the precise circumstances behind the wanderings of this manuscript, it is clear that many Anglo-Saxon books entered Normandy during the eleventh century and that, while some of them were acquired (legitimately or otherwise) in the aftermath of the Conquest, a good number had arrived before then. The aforementioned sacramentary, for instance, demonstrably reached Mont Saint-Michel sometime between 991 and 1009; the luxurious benedictional-pontifical in Rouen, almost certainly came to Rouen Cathedral in the period 989×1037; an opulent sacramentary was given to Jumièges by Robert of Jumièges while he was bishop of London (1044–51) and probably earlier rather than later during this period; and a fine gospel-book in Paris had likewise reached Normandy by the mid-eleventh century, as corrections in a Norman hand reveal.[53] But then there had been a close connection between England and Normandy at the highest level for several generations before 1066: Emma, the queen of England from 1002–35, was the daughter of Duke Richard I of Normandy; her son Edward, king of England from 1042 to 1066, had lived in exile in the duchy for a quarter of a century (1016–41) before he came to the throne and maintained close relations with it thereafter – embodied most famously in his promise of the kingdom to Duke William. That, in addition to the political interrelations such connections implied, these individuals might themselves be responsible for the transfer of books from England to Normandy is suggested by a detail recorded by Orderic Vitalis. He notes that a grand psalter which was one of the treasures of the community of Saint-Evroult in his own day, had belonged to Emma of Normandy when she was the wife of Æthelred (i.e. before 1017); she had given it to her brother Robert, archbishop of Rouen 987×9–1037, whose son, William, had subsequently appropriated it for his wife, Hawise; this last eventually offered it to the community of Saint-Evroult, at the prompting of her own son, Robert II de Grandmesnil.[54]

Like the lost psalter of Saint-Evroult which, we are told, was adorned with images, several of the Anglo-Saxon books that were imported into Normandy before the Conquest were extensively decorated. Correspondingly, the influence of Anglo-Saxon manuscript art can be perceived in the output of certain

52 Orléans, Médiathèque, 127: Grémont and Donat 1967; Davril 1995, esp. pp. 22–6. Colour plate: Bosc-Lauby and Notter 2004, p. 145.

53 Orléans, Médiathèque, 127; Rouen, BM, Y.7, and Y.6; and BnF, lat. 272: Gameson 2003.

54 Orderic Vitalis, *Historia ecclesiastica*: Chibnall 1969–80, II, p. 42. The circumstance that Orderic specifically describes Emma as the wife of Æthelræd (rather than the daughter and sister of dukes of Normandy), and the fact that her possession of the manuscript would predate the rise of significant book decoration in Normandy, allied to the nature of the volume itself, strongly suggest that the manuscript in question came from England.

Norman scriptoria, above all those of Fécamp and Mont Saint-Michel, during the eleventh century; and in so far as the Norman work in question is datable, its centre of gravity falls before rather than after 1066. The systematic excision of the decorated pages from the great majority of Fécamp manuscripts prevents a detailed exploration of the influence of Anglo-Saxon illumination there (though the vestiges of acanthus borders that survive in a few books leave no doubt as to its reality). However, the foliate frames that adorn a number of manuscripts made at Mont Saint-Michel – above all a sacramentary – demonstrate that their artists had had the opportunity to contemplate fine Anglo-Saxon codices before the Conquest.[55] The fact that at both Mont Saint-Michel and Fécamp such frames were used to introduce patristic texts as well as 'altar' books, indicates the readiness of their scribes to deploy in new contexts the motifs they found in Anglo-Saxon sources – as well as reflecting the different emphases of the book collections, and hence scribal efforts, in the two countries.[56]

Queen Emma was, like many Normans, of Scandinavian descent, and her second husband, Cnut the Great, was, of course, the ruler of an empire that embraced England, Denmark, Norway and possibly also parts of Sweden. If Cnut provides the most obvious context for Anglo-Saxon involvement in the Christianisation of Scandinavia, the connections between the two churches were longer-lasting and more extensive. Anglo-Saxons were an appreciable force in Denmark throughout the eleventh century – in thinly veiled opposition to the ambitions of the German church (from 1043 Scandinavia was technically part of the ecclesiastical province of Bremen). Shortly after the Norman Conquest we find a couple of English abbots, perhaps refugees, at the court of Sven Estridsen, king of Denmark 1047–74/5; and it was to Evesham that King Erik the Good looked for monks to staff a monastery at Odense around 1095. One of the first and most important 'missionary' kings of Norway, Olaf Tryggvason, had accepted Christianity in England under Æthelred; Olaf Haraldsson, king of Norway from 1015×16 – *c.* 1028 employed 'many bishops and priests from England' (according to a hostile Adam of Bremen) to consolidate the inroads made by his violent programme of Christianisation;[57] equally, the foundation of monasteries at Nidarholm and Selja at the end of the eleventh century is generally associated with English influence; the latter (near Bergen) was dedicated to St Alban. If a lack of narrative sources leaves the

55 Esp. Avranches, BM, 59 and 163; and PML, M 641 (colour plate: Gaborit-Chopin *et al.*, 2005, p. 324).
56 See further Gameson 2003.
57 *Gesta Hammaburgensis Ecclesiae Pontificum*: Schmeidler 1917, pp. 117–18.

activities of such individuals and places shadowy, the witness of manuscript fragments provides eloquent testimony to the extent of English involvement in Scandinavia as a whole.[58] Such evidence is now most exiguous precisely where one would expect it to be strongest: in relation to Denmark; however, this is doubtless merely one of the many tragic side-effects of the great fire of Copenhagen of 1728 which utterly destroyed the contents of the university library, the principal – indeed almost the sole – repository of 'native' medieval manuscripts (and hence of all the early imports too).[59] A group of fragments in Oslo from some ten English liturgical books ranging in date from the tenth century to the end of the eleventh, confiscated at the Reformation (1537) and reused in bindings and wrappers, reflects the export of manuscripts from England to provide for the basic needs of the young church in Norway.[60] A smaller collection of fragments from Anglo-Saxon liturgical books in Stockholm (supported by rather more from the twelfth century) shows that English manuscripts also reached Sweden – though in the absence of adequate historical sources, the precise contexts for this transmission are unclear.[61]

Other regions also exchanged books with late Anglo-Saxon England; however, in contrast to the areas that we have just considered, most of the remaining cases appear to be more isolated – the result of a particular personal contact or of an unwonted visit rather than as illustrative of well-established routes of cultural exchange. The illustrated *Vitae sanctorum* that apparently reached Duke William II of Aquitaine, for instance, seems to have been a one-off gift from Cnut,[62] just as the fine Anglo-Saxon gospel-book at Saint-Rémi, Reims, was an exceptional offering from Ealdorman Ælfgar of Mercia (1057–62) and his wife Ælfgifu, made in memory of their son who happened to have died at Reims en route between England and Rome.[63] The compact Anglo-Saxon gospel-book whose subsequent provenance was the abbey of Saint-Claude in

58 Also relevant is the small *s.* xi wooden lid of Anglo-Saxon workmanship bearing the remains of an inscription which included the name 'Leofwine' that was found in Lund, if, as is possible, it was from a pen case: Graham-Campbell 1980, no. 317; Okasha 1984.

59 Valiant attempts have been made to identify routes whereby the Wulfstanian compilation, Copenhagen, KB, G. K. S. 1595(4°), could have reached Scandinavia at an early date, Tunberg (in Cross and Tunberg 1993, pp. 59–62) suggesting it may have been sent to Odense on the establishment of that house at the end of *s.* xi, Gerritson 1998 hypothesising that it was specifically made *c.* 1020×2 for presentation to Gerbrand on his consecration as bishop of Roskilde; however, specific evidence is lacking, and the manuscript is first documented in Denmark only in 1784–6.

60 The provisional list in Gneuss 2001, pp. 134–5, is likely to be extended by future work. For discussion of later indirect evidence for the transmission of Anglo-Saxon homiletic texts to Norway see Abram 2004.

61 Stockholm, Riksarkivet, Fr 2070; 2427; 2497; Mi 1; and Mi 134. Colour plates: Abukhanfusa 2004, ills. 17–19. The suggestion (reported *ibid.*, pp. 21–2) that Fr 2070 may have been written in Sweden as opposed to England seems highly dubious.

62 *PL*, CXLIII, col. 1369.

63 Reims, BM, 9: Hinkle 1970.

the Jura would seem to be another such case: the precise circumstances of its travels are undocumented, but it had apparently left England by the second half of the eleventh century, when it was corrected by a Continental hand; it was subsequently 'customised' by two different Continental scribes who added lection lists to the end and the beginning of the book in the first half of the twelfth century and *c.* 1200 respectively.[64] The circumstance that in the 1080s Goscelin of Saint-Bertin directed a lengthy tract from England (where he was then resident) to Angers reflects the fact that his friend Eva of Wilton had recently repaired there – and in this case the title of the work immortalises its journey.[65]

Unsurprisingly, the further one moves from England, the scarcer the evidence becomes. With regard to East Francia (Germany), one can still point to the exchange of a fair number of manuscripts, albeit spread fairly thinly across the country as a whole. The inscription 'King Otto' and 'Matilda the king's mother' in a late Carolingian gospel-book that came into the possession of Athelstan suggests that it reached him via the court of Otto the Great who was, from 929, his brother-in-law.[66] Æthelweard (d. 988) presumably dispatched a copy of his Latin version of the *Anglo-Saxon Chronicle* to Essen whose abbess, his distant cousin Matilda (Otto I's grand-daughter), was its dedicatee, and he records the fact that he had previously sent her other historical matter.[67] She may have reciprocated by sending him the texts or extracts bearing on other parts of their extended family, for which he asked in return.[68] It is inconceivable that Benna, the ecclesiastic from Trier who came to England around 975 and served as priest, painter and possibly tutor to Edith of Wilton (961–84), the daughter of King Edgar, did not arrive with some books in his baggage.[69] The circumstances surrounding the transfer of the one manuscript made at Trier in the late tenth century that did come to England (emerging

64 Besançon, BM, 14.

65 'Incipit confortatorius liber Goscelini monachi ab Anglia ad Evam apud sanctum Laurentium pro Christi nomine inclusam missus Andegavis': BL, Sloane 3103, fol. 1v; Talbot 1955, p. 26. The provenance of the one known copy of the work (Sloane 3103) was Norman: Saint-Sauveur-le-Vicomte (Manche).

66 BL, Cotton Tiberius A.ii: Keynes 1985, plates II–III. Puhle 2001, cat. III.13 with colour plates.

67 Campbell 1962, pp. 1–2, 34; van Houts 1992. No copy of Essen provenance survives or is seemingly recorded.

68 BL, Cotton Cleopatra D.i, part II (Vegetius, *Epitome rei militaris*), written in a late tenth-century Essen type of script but in England (St Augustine's Abbey) in the Middle Ages, has attractively but unprovably been hypothesised to have been a gift from Matilda to Æthelweard (Bodarwé 2000, pp. 113 and 114).

69 Goscelin, *Vita Edithae*, ch. 7: Wilmart 1938, p. 50. The possible identification of Benna with the Master of the Registrum Gregorii, the great itinerant Ottonian artist some of whose work was done for Egbert of Trier, is judiciously discussed and ultimately rejected by Hoffmann 1986, I, pp. 122–6.

in the possession of King Henry VIII) are deeply obscure; the fact that the volume was a supremely luxurious gospel-book, written in gold on purple parchment, heightens the mystery. However, the connections between Trier and the West Saxon royalty that Benna embodies and the fact that Egbert, bishop of Trier 977–93 and an outstanding patron of the arts, was related through his mother, Hildegard, to the house of Wessex, provide one possible – albeit wholly hypothetical – context for the transmission of this magnificent volume.[70] Whatever the history of this book, an early eleventh-century copy of the Old English Orosius had certainly found its way to Trier by the end of that century – when, however, it was recycled.[71] The Eadwig Gospels, written at Christ Church, Canterbury, had reached Germany, seemingly Hersfeld, very soon after it was written and shows signs of having been a specific commission (Plate 10.7);[72] another Christ Church manuscript, the slightly older Arenberg Gospels, was certainly in Deutz outside Cologne by the first half of the twelfth century (Plate 18.1).[73] As we have seen, Cnut personally sent to Cologne two manuscripts (which eventually found their way back to England), while Judith of Flanders brought her Anglo-Saxon gospel-books to Bavaria upon her marriage to Welf IV in 1070×1, and left three of them to the family foundation of Weingarten Abbey (Plate 18.2).[74]

Some texts from Germany evidently reached England in the mid eleventh century. In one case this was fairly soon after composition: one portion of a sprawling collection of Latin verse that was copied in England in the mid eleventh century is the so-called 'Cambridge Songs', an important component of which is of overtly Teutonic interest, seven items dealing with emperors of Germany, others mentioning archbishops of Cologne, Mainz and Trier; one of these items is Wipo's lament upon the death of the Emperor Conrad II, composed after 4 June 1039 – but patently known in England within a couple of decades of this date.[75] By contrast, the Romano-Germanic pontifical, which appears to have reached England around the same time, had been compiled (at Mainz) a century earlier (*c.* 961). The two mid-eleventh-century German copies of the text that are known to have been in England by the third quarter

70 PML, M 23: Lowe 1972, II, pp. 399–416; Ronig 1993, I, no. 17, plates 93–4.
71 BAV, Reg. Lat. 497, fol. 71: Wilmart 1945, pp. 710–19; Ker 1957, no. 391; Bately 1964.
72 Hanover, Kestner-Museum, W. M. XXIa.36; the supporting apparatus was completed by a Hersfeld scribe of *s.* xi$^{2/4}$: Gameson 2002b.
73 PML, M 869. The earliest evidence of its presence in Germany is the addition on 14r of a forged letter purportedly of Gregory VII (1073–85) concerning the sanctity of Heribert of Deutz, archbishop of Cologne 999–1021, written in a *s.* xii^{1} hand; see Rosenthal 2005.
74 PML, M 708 and M 709; Fulda, Hessische Landesbibliothek, Aa.21: McGurk and Rosenthal 1995.
75 CUL, Gg.5.35. Facs.: Breul 1915; the lament is *ibid.*, no. 17 and Ziolkowski 1994, no. 33.

of the eleventh century can plausibly be associated with specific individuals – one with Ealdred, bishop of Worcester, then archbishop of York, who, it will be recalled, had a long sojourn in Cologne in 1054; the other with the Fleming Hereman who was bishop of Ramsbury from 1045 to 1055 and then of Sherborne (1058–78) when the see was transferred there (this manuscript subsequently migrated to Old Sarum when the see moved again).[76]

Ceolfrith, abbot of Wearmouth-Jarrow (d. 716), may have proposed to transport to Rome one of the largest books ever made in England (Codex Amiatinus), but his lead does not seem to have been followed by very many others – even with smaller tomes. Given the number of Anglo-Saxons who visited, or were even resident in, Rome, one might reasonably expect to find a fair scattering of late Anglo-Saxon manuscripts with an Italian medieval provenance; however, such is not the case. Only a couple are presently known; moreover, their early Italian provenance seems likely to have been the result of accident rather than design. The Vercelli Book, completely in Old English, is a most unlikely gift for an Italian dignitary or foundation, and is reasonably conjectured to have been brought south by an Anglo-Saxon for his own use and then left at Vercelli through force of (unknown) circumstances.[77] Equally, the Anglo-Saxon gospel-book at Monte Cassino, one of the volumes made for Judith of Flanders, was probably in fact offered to Empress Agnes of Germany shortly after Judith arrived in *that* country, and then passed on to Monte Cassino by Agnes.[78] While the early history of a Canterbury gospel-lectionary that is now in Florence has yet to be investigated,[79] and although some late Anglo-Saxon books that were once in Italy may have been lost, nevertheless so exiguous is the surviving sample that it seems reasonable to presume that the corpus was never very great. Correspondingly, only one Italian volume (or, more accurately, a small part thereof) dating from after 800 can currently be shown to have been in England before the Conquest: the four folios in question, from a copy of Ambrose's *Expositio de Psalmo CXVIII*, had certainly been recycled as endleaves by the fourteenth century, and the casual jottings which

76 BL, Cotton Vitellius E.xii, fols. 116–60 (see Lapidge 1983); and BL, Cotton Tiberius C.i (Ker 1959).

77 Vercelli, Biblioteca Capitolare, CXVII. Facs.: Foerster 1913 and C. Sisam 1976; see also K. Sisam 1953, pp. 109–18. Cf. note 108 below; also Chapter 26.

78 Monte Cassino, Archivio della Badia, BB 437: Newton 1999, pp. 233–40. The most recent commentator (Fabrizio Crivello in Stiegmann and Wemhoff 2006, II, pp. 302–3), whose criticisms in no way negate Newton's attractive hypothesis, reverts to the older speculation that the volume was given to Monte Cassino by Matilda of Tuscany, who would putatively have acquired it via her (second) marriage in 1089 to Welf V of Bavaria, the son of Judith of Flanders and Welf IV. Either way the manuscript had a staging point in Germany.

79 Florence, Biblioteca Medicea-Laurenziana, Plut.XVII.20.

demonstrate that they were in England by the tenth century hint equally that they may already have been scrap by then.[80] English archbishops and other pilgrims may regularly have visited Rome (and other sites in Italy) and the Holy See may well have been the notional head of the Western church, but from the late eighth century the de facto centre of spiritual gravity had moved north to the heartlands of the Carolingian Empire; and thereafter it was the Carolingian church, geographically far more convenient, that supplied England with authoritative literary resources.[81]

Whatever the Norman Conquest may or may not have achieved in other spheres, it unquestionably affected the circulation of books between England and the Continent. In essence, it accelerated and focused the traffic: more books were crossing the Channel, and a higher percentage of them were passing between England and Normandy. Some Anglo-Saxon refugees to the Continent doubtless took manuscripts with them. Sæwold, abbot of Bath, would seem to have been one such case: he left England around the time of the Conquest, settling at Saint-Vaast, Arras, to which community he bequeathed a collection of books, a couple of which had patently come from England.[82] As one would expect, a good number of Anglo-Saxon manuscripts (of various dates) reached Normandy during the generation after 1066. In the early 1070s Anselm, then prior of Bec, wrote to Lanfranc, now archbishop of Canterbury, requesting copies of a couple of specific texts (the *Rule of St Dunstan* – presumably the *Regularis concordia* – and a *Life* of the same saint) which were unobtainable in Normandy but would obviously be available at Canterbury.[83] Anselm then wrote to the monk Maurice, asking him to encourage two other expatriates, Henry and Gundulf, to look for this same *Rule* and also for Bede's *De temporibus*.[84] He explained that he wanted the latter in order to correct the copy at Bec; the books would be returned in due course. Other letters show that Maurice transcribed medical texts in

80 TCC, B.14.3, fols. 1–4: two bifolia. Glue stains on 1r and the title written at the top of 2r show that these were the paste-down and flyleaves for the main volume (Arator; *s.* x/xi; Christ Church by *s.* xiv). There are casual jottings by two distinct hands on 1v and 3v. The latter (the start of the *Pater noster*), written in black ink in a crude Square Minuscule, shows that the item was in England before the production of the manuscript to which it was subsequently joined – and that it was already subject to casual use. The other addition – the first line of the *Pater noster* followed by the phrase, 'Dominus Eeduuordus bene fit [?for sit]', plus two further words which are rather fainter – is difficult to date.

81 For the intriguing possibility that the new 'Salerno' translation of the *Aphorismi* travelled from Monte Cassino or Salerno to England at the very end of our period, see Gasper and Wallis 2004.

82 Lapidge 1985, no. VIII; the Anglo-Saxon manuscripts in question are Arras, Médiathèque, 867 and 1029.

83 Anselm, ep. 39: Schmitt 1946–61, III, p. 151.

84 Anselm, ep. 42: Schmitt 1946–61, III, p. 154. The latter was not a particularly rare text in northwest Europe.

England for Anselm.[85] Some of the extant Anglo-Saxon reading books that reached Normandy in the late eleventh century may likewise have been targeted acquisitions, designed to plug specific gaps. The late tenth-century Canterbury copy of Gregory's *Dialogi* that reached Jumièges, the coeval Winchester *Vita Swithuni* that came to the same place, and the later eleventh-century Augustine and Alcuin that migrated to Mont Saint-Michel are cases in point.[86] A few older items that had themselves been imported into England might also have been of interest: one thinks of the Carolingian Jerome and the copy of the Wisdom books plus computistica that, after a sojourn in England, moved on to Lyre, then Saint-Ouen, and to Jumièges respectively.[87] However, England was not particularly rich in the sort of library texts that Norman foundations are likely to have wanted, and many of the acquisitions were instead gospel-books and liturgica. Thus an early eleventh-century Winchester benedictional and a coeval Canterbury calendar migrated to Saint-Evroult, where both were supplemented (the former by Orderic Vitalis himself: see Plates 14.3 and 14.4), while a later eleventh-century Winchester missal was transported to Saint-Wandrille, where it was annotated around 1100.[88] Shortly after the Conquest, one tenth-century Anglo-Saxon gospel-book was demonstrably at Notre-Dame du Château (Cherbourg), the foundation of William the Conqueror; while another, probably dating from the second quarter of the eleventh century, came to the *collégiale* of Saint-Evroult at Mortain, the foundation of Robert of Mortain.[89] There is a reasonable chance that both these books were 'requisitioned' rather than bought. Another gospel-book would seem to have been written and decorated by Norman expatriates at Abingdon under Abbot Rainald (1084–97), an alumnus of Jumièges, to send back to his alma mater – as a contemporary inscription at the front declares.[90] Other volumes copied by Normans in England and dispatched to their homeland, but whose circumstance of production were not similarly recorded, would now lurk unrecognisable in Norman *fonds*.

Yet however many manuscripts the Normans begged, bought or borrowed – not to mention appropriated – from England, the number they were

85 Anselm, epp. 43 and 60: Schmitt 1946–61, III, pp. 155 and 174–5. These do seem to have been rare texts at the time.

86 Respectively Rouen, BM, A.337; U.107; Avranches, BM, 81. See further Gameson 2003.

87 Rouen, BM, A.425 and A.292.

88 Alençon, BM, 14; BnF, lat. 10062, fols. 162–3; Le Havre, BM, 330 (Turner 1962).

89 BL, Cotton Tiberius A.xv, fol. 174; Mortain, Collégiale Saint-Évroult, s.n. Another gospel-book or service-book, now lost but represented by the additional pages BAV, Reg. lat. 946, fols. 72–6 (see Gameson 2003, pp. 158–9), would seem to have reached the cathedral of Avranches.

90 Rouen, BM, A.21 (32): Garand *et al.* 1984, I, p. 263; II, plate XXIX.

directly or indirectly responsible for bringing into the newly conquered land was greater. The different conception of what an ecclesiastical book collection should contain that was promoted in the aftermath of the Conquest necessitated the acquisition of many texts, above all the writings of the church Fathers, that were poorly represented – if at all – in England in 1066. The works in question thus had to be imported. Herbert Losinga's letter to Fécamp (his alma mater) asking for a copy of Suetonius, with the explanation that he had been unable to find the text in England, doubtless stands for many similar requests.[91] Some such manuscripts were outright acquisitions; but even when the intention was to make copies locally, exemplars still had to be borrowed from overseas, particularly at first, and the numbers of manuscripts crossing the Channel at the end of the eleventh century must have been formidable. If some of the required volumes were taken from 'existing stock', others were written in Normandy specifically for export to England. The letters of Anselm show, for instance, that he tried – not without problems – to arrange the production of a copy of Gregory's *Moralia* to send to Lanfranc in Canterbury.[92] The case of Durham is particularly well documented. Symeon of Durham's tract on the history of his church, written in the early twelfth century, recorded that Bishop William of Saint-Calais/Carilef took advantage of his exile in Normandy (late 1088 to September 1091) to gather resources for his English see: 'in the third year of the Bishop's expulsion ... the king was pacified and restored to him all his former possessions in England. He did not return empty-handed but took care to dispatch to the church before he came himself many sacred vessels for the altar and diverse ornaments of gold and silver as well as several books'.[93] On fol. 1r of the extant volume of Saint-Calais' two-volume giant bible is a contemporary list of the books which he gave to Durham – a mixture of patristics, post-patristic theology, Rules and service-books – more than twenty of which survive.[94] While some were written in England, others are wholly Norman in script and decoration and were presumably among the books that he commissioned or acquired during his 'exile'. In one such case (a copy of the third and final volume of Augustine, *In Psalmos*) this is effectively confirmed by a contemporary colophon which begins: 'This work Bishop William commanded at the time when he withdrew from his bishopric'.[95]

91 Anstruther 1846, ep. 5.
92 Anselm, epp. 23, 25, 26: Schmitt 1946–61, III, pp. 130, 133, 134.
93 Symeon of Durham, *Libellus de Exordio*: Rollason 2000, pp. 242–4.
94 DCL, A.II.4, fol. 1r: New Pal. Soc., 1st ser., plate 17; Browne 1988.
95 DCL, B.II.14, fol. 200v (note 107 below). See further in general Mynors 1939, Gullick 1990, and Lawrence-Mathers 2003.

A centre that appears to have acquired many of its late eleventh-century books from Normandy is Exeter; moreover, they seem to have come from a variety of locations in the duchy.[96] If Salisbury, by contrast, seems to have produced most of its library books in-house, the unusually wide range of texts that were copied there still implies a highly energetic procuring of Continental exemplars.[97] Most of the manuscripts that swelled the libraries of Christ Church, St Augustine's Abbey, Rochester, and St Albans were likewise made 'in-house' (albeit by members of the community itself in the first three cases, and by hired professionals in the last), and documentary and textual evidence indicates that borrowed exemplars (or their copies) circulated between these communities – doubtless a pattern that was repeated elsewhere (though is now more difficult to perceive). While Christ Church and St Augustine's were next-door neighbours, Rochester and St Albans were linked to Canterbury by personal connections – Bishop Gundulf of Rochester (1077–1108) was a close friend of both Lanfranc and Anselm, while Abbot Paul of St Albans (1077–93) was a relative of Lanfranc and had been a monk in his house at Caen. One of several physical witnesses to the circulation of Norman exemplars among some members of this 'group' is the St Augustine's Abbey copy of Lanfranc's glossed version of the Pauline Epistles, a direct or indirect copy of the (lost) Bec original which, a letter from Anselm at Bec indicates, was sent to Christ Church at Lanfranc's request around 1076.[98] Correspondingly, the *Gesta abbatum S. Albani* records that the exemplars used in the scriptorium of St Albans that was established under Abbot Paul were supplied by Lanfranc.[99]

If many of the manuscripts that were imported to and remained in England at this time came from Normandy, a significant number (over two-fifths of the identifiable total) came from elsewhere, principally northern France and Flanders. Such areas, with which England had traditionally enjoyed close bibliographical relations, were geographically convenient; moreover, as a result of energetic copying campaigns earlier in the eleventh century, their libraries were well stocked with the sort of texts that were now sought by churchmen in England. The French manuscripts of Augustine and Pseudo-Augustine, and of Gregory's Homilies, both dating from *c.* 1000, that reached England

96 Gameson 1999d. The slightly different reading of the evidence in Thomson 2006 (with which I am not in accord) would still require the transmission of numerous exemplars.

97 Webber 1992.

98 Canterbury CL, Add. 172 (Gameson 2008, no. 15); Anselm, ep. 66: Schmitt 1946–61, III, pp. 186–7. Anselm hoped that a copy of some of the works therein – or the manuscript itself – could be sent back in due course.

99 Thomas Walsingham, *Gesta abbatum Monasterii Sancti Albani*: Riley 1867, I, pp. 57–8.

in the later eleventh century are cases in point.[100] Equally, while Lanfranc, Herbert Losinga and Scollandus logically turned for literary resources to the communities they knew best in Normandy (Bec, Caen, Fécamp and Mont Saint-Michel), Baldwin, abbot of Bury 1065–97/8, would naturally have resorted to his alma mater, Saint-Denis – as several Bury acquisitions of this time seem to show. A fairly clear case is the massive, two-volume version of Paul the Deacon's homiliary, certainly of eleventh-century French origin, presumably from Saint-Denis, to the end of one part of which a late eleventh-century Bury scribe added the reading and homily for the Assumption of Mary.[101] It is likely that many older books – Carolingian copies of patristic texts – also entered England at this time. Although it is often difficult to prove that a ninth- or tenth-century book reached England in the late eleventh century rather than either earlier or later, such is occasionally demonstrable. For example, a mid-ninth-century Saint-Denis copy of Bede's *In Evangelium Lucae*, which received a note in Old English around 1100, which was energetically repunctuated and 'aerated' in England in the early twelfth century, and whose medieval provenance was Bury, may plausibly be regarded as another acquisition of Baldwin's day.[102] The late ninth-century bibliographical handbook that came to Salisbury at the end of the eleventh century and the mid-ninth-century Smaragdus that reached Worcester shortly after the Conquest are other cases in point – as, too, may be a tenth-century copy of Augustine's *Epistolae* which was corrected in the later eleventh century in a probably Anglo-Norman hand, and also bears a series of interventions that straddle the twelfth century.[103]

Let us now sum up. If the surviving evidence, fragmentary and ambiguous as it is, permits only a very imperfect glimpse of our field, what we nevertheless see is substantial and impressive: books were manifestly circulating between England and the Continent in significant numbers from the late ninth century, in some quantity from the mid-tenth century, and in very considerable numbers by the end of the eleventh. Correspondingly, many, perhaps most, ecclesiastics who travelled must have done so carrying books – not to mention requests for them.

100 BodL., Bodley 229; Worcester CL, Q.21.

101 Cambridge, Pembroke College, 24 (*s.* xi²); Bury addition, fols. 374v–5v: Gransden 1998, plate LXVIIB; Webber 1998, plate XLVA. The history of the companion volume of the collection (Pembroke College, 23) was presumptively the same.

102 Cambridge, Pembroke College, 83 (Gransden 1998, plate LXVB). Pembroke, 91 (Jerome, *In Psalmos*; *s.* ix¹ᐟ³; northern France: Gransden 1998, plate LXVIA) is another candidate: it bears no interventions from Anglo-Saxon, Norman or Anglo-Norman hands, but appears on the late *s.* xii Bury booklist (CBMLC, B13.4).

103 Hereford CL, O.III.2; BodL., Barlow 4; BL, Add. 23944.

Considered as a whole the phenomenon invites several general reflections. The first arises from the fact that books are heavy and some, such as the Saint-Calais/Carilef Bible, extremely so. Now, as a formal binding represents an appreciable part of the total weight, it seems reasonable to presume that manuscripts will have been transported in a disbound state (within some sort of wrapper), if at all possible – as was often the case in later centuries. High-status volumes prepared for presentation as gifts, particularly 'diplomatic' ones, are more likely to have been offered bound (such may well have been the case for the Abingdon–Jumièges Gospels, for instance, given that the contemporary inscription which commemorates Abbot Rainald's gift lingers over the precious binding[104]) and it is a moot point whether an already-bound book would have been pulled in order to facilitate transportation.[105] Newly written manuscripts, by contrast, particularly if destined for export, would surely have been left as disbound quires. Such a hypothesis would also help to explain the extent and neatness of the annotations which several such volumes received shortly after arrival in a new land and which have been fundamental to our enquiry. The fact that a Hersfeld scribe could insert numbers to the pre-existing canon tables of the Eadwig Gospels, supply correspondences in some of the margins, prefix prefatory matter and append a lection table, all in a neat hand, strongly suggests that the book left England as disbound quires, while the circumstance that the Reimsian Utrecht Psalter seems to have been in bits when it was used by a team of artists at Canterbury around the millennium raises the possibility that it had travelled to England from the Continent in this state.[106]

Second, it is worth remarking the extent to which exported books conform to general patterns of production and collecting in the countries that made and received them respectively. The point here is that the factors that have affected the transmission of medieval books to the present day have differed from one country to the next – in England the Dissolution of the Monasteries and the Reformation in the sixteenth century represented the greatest disruption; in

104 See n. 90.

105 Given the paucity of surviving bindings from this period, it is striking that there is still one example which preserves evidence to suggest that this might have happened, namely the *s.* ix bibliographical handbook from Francia that came to Salisbury at the end of *s.* xi (Hereford CL, O.III.2). The impression of a Carolingian lacing path that can still be seen on the final leaf indicates that the manuscript was bound at an early date, while its sewing supports and threads show that it was rebound shortly after the time it would seem to have reached England. See further Chapter 11.

106 Hanover, Kestner-Museum, W.M.XXIa.36 (Gameson 2002b, esp. pp. 214–22); Utrecht, UB, 32 (Noel 1995, pp. 130–5 – suggesting that it was pulled at an early stage in the production of Harley 603).

France, by contrast, it was the Revolution at the end of the eighteenth century; in Germany the secularisation of monasteries at the beginning of the nineteenth; and so on – with divergent implications for the survival rate of different types of texts. To cite just one obvious case, liturgical books faced much severer perils in England than in France. The quantity of Anglo-Saxon gospel-books, even service-books indeed, that survive on both sides of the Channel indicates that this really was a focus of effort in our period. Equally, given the high rate of survival of late eleventh- and twelfth-century patristic works from English collections, the paucity of earlier examples is likely to reflect a real lacuna. Correspondingly, the fact that a couple of the mere handful of English patristic manuscripts that are of earlier date found their way to Normandy accords with the more precocious rise in interest in such works at selected centres there. Such indications must not be overstated; however, those books that travelled and were preserved abroad do provide some independent confirmation for the 'received' picture of local book culture in the countries in question. In particular, they support the view that Anglo-Saxon institutions were rarely interested in more than liturgical, pedagogical and devotional reading until the later eleventh century.

Third, given that much of our evidence takes the form of anonymous additions and voiceless marks of provenance, it is worth stressing the extent to which personal connections may be presumed, or occasionally (thanks to letters and dedications) shown, to be central to the phenomenon that we are investigating. Individuals generally sent books to, or received them from, people they knew; they acquired them in person while abroad; they dispatched them as targeted gifts. Æthelweard sent his *Chronicle* to his distant cousin, Matilda of Essen; the abbot of Saint Augustine's dispatched the *Vita Dunstani* to Abbo at Fleury; as a newcomer to Germany, Judith of Flanders seems to have presented Empress Agnes with one of her gospel-books; Lanfranc turned to Anselm for bibliographical support, Baldwin of Bury to Saint-Denis; and so on. Knowledge of what was in a particular collection, and the circumstance that personal 'friends' would be predisposed not just to help but to go – literally as well as metaphorically – the second mile explains why bibliographical exchange often echoes networks of personal connections and individual travels. Such cases simultaneously advertise some of the ways in which manuscripts functioned as diplomatic gifts and spiritual currency.

The broader context for this, however, was the fact that the vast majority of English and Continental readers – ecclesiastics – were part of a supranational organisation, all of whose members had, in theory, an urgent moral obligation to help their brothers and sisters in Christ, the length and breadth of Christendom. Overseas travel, be it in the service of church or state, was integral to some ecclesiastical posts; the loan or gift of an urgently needed text was a Christian duty. The letters begging colleagues in other lands (*familiares* indeed) for specific texts, were undoubtedly just the tip of an iceberg of such requests, many of which were doubtless fulfilled. Travel was not only a precondition of giving and receiving bibliographical offerings, it was an opportunity to browse the holdings of the many foundations one would visit along the way, and to make requests. The insistence of these, we might imagine, varied according to the character and status of the individual in question: while a scholar such as Abbo of Fleury may have begged and borrowed, a 'prince-bishop' such as William of Saint-Calais would seem to have made his requests more forcibly, proffering resources – and perhaps other rewards – to ensure that they were carried out. The colophon to one of Saint-Calais' books specifically records that he ordered and paid for it: 'The material and labour for the work are to be credited to him: the material to his expense, but the labour to his command'.[107]

Fourth, it is worth bearing in mind that most books in transit, like the ecclesiastics carrying them, doubtless moved in slow stages from one religious house to the next. How many, one wonders, were admired, solicited and hence lingered somewhere unexpected en route; or ended up in the 'wrong' place simply because of transport or other problems. Equally, given the weight of the commodity, the possibility of exciting new acquisitions – either loan or gift – may have required travellers to leave or deposit volumes which they were carrying. Faced with the (still) rich holdings of Vercelli, which Anglo-Saxon – whether travelling south towards Rome, north towards Francia and England, or even attending the Synod of Vercelli in 1050 (an occasion deemed worthy of notice in the *Anglo-Saxon Chronicle*[108]) – would not have been prepared to sacrifice a dowdy well-used codex of vernacular homilies and poetry in order to be able to carry one such treasure away? In short, some 'exchanges' were doubtless serendipitous, even accidental, while the nature of travel in our period encouraged the forging of bibliographical links.

Now, the closer one looks to 'home', the more frequented were the routes and hence the stronger and more regular were the chains of supply. Our fifth and final point is thus the issue of geographical location. The evidence shows

107 DCL, B.II.14: 'Hoc exegit opus Guillelmus episcopus ... / materies operisque labor reputantur eidem. / Materies sumptu sed labor imperio ...'

108 *ASC* E, 1047. The chronicler's interest was excited by the condemnation of Bishop Ulf of Dorchester. Though the Norman Ulf is unlikely to have treasured this OE book or to have regarded it as a suitable gift (cf Sisam 1976, pp. 44–5, *contra* Herben 1935), he will not have travelled alone, and an Anglo-Saxon in his retinue may have taken it.

unequivocally that the nearer the country to England, the more extensive the exchange of books therewith. The political unification of England and Normandy from 1066 notwithstanding, the most substantial body of bibliographical traffic in our period as a whole was with northern France and Flanders, the area closest to the English coast. Indeed, it is possible that some of the books from elsewhere that ended up in England were also part of this phenomenon, having been transmitted via Flanders: some Breton material, for instance, may have arrived not directly from Brittany but rather from northern France, whither in 926 had retreated the monks of Landévennec. Moreover, it is the scriptoria from these same areas that seem to have exerted the greatest influence on late Anglo-Saxon script and decoration, and in whose work the influence of Anglo-Saxon manuscript art was felt first. The next most important region in terms of intensity of bibliographical exchange was Normandy, a phenomenon which was well established before the enormous boost it received from the Conquest of 1066. Thereafter – a significant way behind – one would rank Scandinavia; and part of the explanation for the dramatic drop in intensity is that this was essentially a one-way traffic, with England supplying a newly Christianised land which had little written matter to offer in return.[109] As one moves further away, the quantity drops further (Germany, with which exchange appears to have been relatively thin, if widely diffused) and then tails off (Italy, with which it seems to have been fairly minimal). In point of fact, of course, the effect of geography in this connection continued within England. In an era when travel by boat could be easier, and was certainly swifter, than by horse or wagon, when the *literati* of Europe shared a common language, and when 'England' was an imperfectly unified polity, it is hardly surprising that more manuscripts circulated between southern England and the littoral of mainland Europe – above all Canterbury and northern Francia – than between the south and the north of England itself. Close attention to such 'micro-regions' straddling national borders has the potential to tell us as much as any study that is rooted in modern political units.

109 The abbacy at Abingdon of Rodulf (1051–2), who seems previously to have been bishop in Norway, then Iceland, has plausibly been identified as the most likely context for a jotting in Scandinavian runes added to a *s.* x² manuscript of Abindgon provenance (CCCC, 57), but this is far from being an imported book.

PART III TYPES OF BOOKS AND THEIR USES

15

The book in Roman Britain

R. S. O. TOMLIN

When Albanus of Verulamium came to the river on his way to martyrdom, its waters parted miraculously, and he was executed on the green hill beyond, the site of the modern cathedral and city of St Albans.[1] The Roman town he left behind was ultimately abandoned, and by the eleventh century its ruins had become a subterranean slum infested by thieves and prostitutes. To abolish this eyesore and to salvage bricks to rebuild their church, the abbots of St Albans started demolition. In one of the buildings, in a wall recess, the workmen found 'along with a number of lesser books and rolls, a strange book-roll which had suffered but little in spite of its great age'. It was written in the language of the ancient Britons, in a peculiar script which only an elderly priest could read; he found it was the *History of St Alban*. When this had been translated into Latin and published, the original crumbled miraculously into dust. But 'the other books' found here and elsewhere, 'in which the inventions of the devil were contained', were discarded and burnt; they contained details of pagan cult.[2]

This moral tale, with its implication that ancient manuscripts when found are always religious, is harder to accept than the eleven witnesses to the discovery and punctual disappearance of the gold tablets of the Book of Mormon. But the setting is circumstantial, and perhaps the monks elaborated an actual discovery of buried Roman manuscripts.[3] However, this is doubtful, and we reach firmer ground in North Wales in the mid nineteenth century:

> The wooden book in question was found by the farm servants as they were cutting turf for fuel, deep in the earth with a thick layer of peat soil covering it. When first found, it was of the form and size of a thick octavo, and consisted of some 10 or 12 leaves joined together with a wire which was entirely corroded. All the leaves except the covers had a narrow raised margin on both sides in

1 Bede, *HE*, 1, 7.
2 *Gesta abbatum monasterii sancti Albani*, 1, 26–7 (translated in Wheeler 1936, pp. 35–7).
3 Wheeler 1936, p. 38.

> order to preserve the impression; they were written upon on both sides, the two covers on the *inside* only.[4]

This 'book' was literally a Roman *codex*, using the word in its earlier sense: a block of wood formed by binding together a series of *stilus* writing-tablets. The Trawsfynydd Codex, if it may be so called, was found in a peat bog, a context which recalls that of Ireland's earliest manuscript, the Springmount Tablets. It was not published at the time, but in 2003 it was brought to the British Museum for identification; by now it was reduced to a single leaf which proved to be the first 'page'. With it came the letter just quoted, written by an eye-witness who thought the Codex was 'probably a relic of the ancient Druids, who may have employed a modification of the Roman alphabet to write their own language'. He was not entirely wrong. The surviving leaf has lost its wax coating, a mixture of beeswax and soot, but it retains a black discoloration in which an arabesque of unstained wood preserves a ghost of the original writing. This is indeed Roman cursive, second-century or perhaps a little earlier, but the language is not Celtic, despite the find-spot; it is Latin – standard formulae from a Roman will: for example, the requirement that the heir enter into his inheritance within a hundred days.[5]

These formulae are quoted by Gaius in the *Institutes*, the only ancient textbook of Roman law to survive entire, and they show that legal handbooks were available in Roman Britain. We hear of two British wills. The chief pilot of the British fleet left his estate to a colleague on trust for his infant son, but the son died before he came of age: did the property pass to the trustee, or to the next of kin, the testator's brother-in-law? The question was decided by a famous first-century jurist, Javolenus Priscus, who was then serving in Britain as deputy-governor for juridisdiction.[6] Some years later, in about 118, the Emperor Hadrian wrote to the governor of Britain about the estate of a legionary who had committed suicide. His right to make a valid will turned on whether he had killed himself to avoid prosecution, or because he was ill and tired of life.[7] Second-century Britain, with its growing cadre of Roman citizens which included a legionary garrison of 15,000 men, would have generated many thousands of Roman wills. This 'page' is the only survivor.

The Roman world was governed by Roman law, and the lives even of the illiterate majority were regulated by written records, but the proportion

4 Condensed from an undated letter by 'M.Ll', arguably the barrister Morgan Lloyd (1820–93) writing in the 1840s.

5 Tomlin 2001. 6 *Digest*, 36.1.48: Mommsen 1870.

7 *Digest*, 28.3.6,7: Mommsen 1870.

which survives is minute. In Britain four or five hundred *stilus* writing-tablets have now been found, but few of them are legible (see Plate 15.1). To call them 'waxed' tablets would be an exaggeration: the wax has almost always perished, and the text must be reconstructed from the scratches left in the wood by the needle-pointed *stilus*. It is usually a palimpsest, unreadable because the tablet was reused. Some business letters have been deciphered, but they are evidence only of utilitarian literacy.[8] More relevant to the history of the book are three legal documents found in recent years, since they imply the presence of law books and other works of reference. The first is a loan-note from Carlisle in standard form dated 7 November 83, in which a legionary of the Twentieth lends money to a colleague.[9] A little later in date is a 'page' from London, the first of three tablets which formed the deed of sale of a Gallic slave girl called Fortunata. It certifies 'that the girl in question is transferred in good health, that she is warranted not to be liable to wander or run away, but that if anyone makes good his claim to the girl in question or any share in her ...' The text breaks off here, within the standard formula when real property (which included slaves and transport animals) was conveyed by *mancipium*. This formula is known from Roman legal writings, as well as from the actual deeds which survive.[10] Again from London, perhaps a little later still, there is the first 'page' of a record of court proceedings dated 14 March 118 (Plate 15.1). It concerns the ownership of five acres of woodland in what is now Kent. The wood is named; also identified are the (now deceased) owners of neigbouring properties.[11] This fragment implies not only court records and legal decisions in Roman London – in other provinces we find such documents being quoted by interested parties in public inscriptions – but also a detailed register of land ownership; this was maintained not as a public service, but as a source of fees for officials and a necessary tool for taxation.

Such tablets imply the existence of handbooks and archives, but no British tablet has yet been found to contain a 'literary' text, even though they were used to catch the passing inspiration: the belletrist Pliny, for example, says that he sometimes went hunting, 'but not without my writing-tablets; so, even if I catch nothing, I bring something back'.[12] It is Pliny who wrote to Neratius Marcellus, governor of Britain in 103, when he is mentioned in the Vindolanda ink tablets (of which more in a moment), recommending the scholar Suetonius for a short-term commission in the British army. Suetonius transferred it to a kinsman, but he may have visited Britain years later, as

8 *RIB*, II.4, 2443.7 and 16; others (unpublished) from Vindolanda.

9 Tomlin 1992.

10 Tomlin 2003.

11 Tomlin 1996a.

12 Pliny, *Letters*, ix, 36.6.

secretary to Hadrian in 122.[13] If so, he is one of the few Roman authors who saw Britain. Books and 'literature' are correspondingly hard to find here, and their existence must be inferred.

It is not that Britain was illiterate. The arrival of literacy can be dated precisely, to 25 September 54 BC. On this day Julius Caesar and Quintus Cicero, the orator's younger brother, wrote to him 'from the nearest shores of Britain' as the invading army prepared to leave the island. Cicero in Rome received their letters (or joint letter) on 24 October.[14] Almost a century later, in AD 43, the Roman army returned. In company with the emperor Claudius was a doctor, Scribonius Largus, who soon afterwards published his extant *Compositiones*. Among these prescriptions is the toothpaste used by the Empress Messalina 'to whiten the teeth', but sadly, nothing at all about Britain.[15]

When the army advanced into Wales and northern Britain, two of its generals acquired literary associations. Most of Wales was conquered by Pliny's friend and patron Sextus Julius Frontinus, governor in 74–7, who subsequently wrote three surviving books: a treatise on land-surveying, an expert account of Rome's aqueducts, and the *Stratagems*, the latter being a military manual, or rather an anthology of literary anecdotes, which surprisingly ignores Britain altogether. In 98 another of Pliny's friends, the historian Tacitus, published a biography of his father-in-law Gnaeus Julius Agricola, sometime governor of Britain (78–84), who led the army into the far north. The *Agricola* commends its hero for introducing the sons of chieftains to higher education: by rating local talent above Gallic erudition, he is said to have made these Celtic speakers aspire to making speeches in Latin.[16] This may have prompted the contemporary joke that British barristers learnt their eloquence from Gaul, and even Thule (a half-legendary island in the far north) was thinking of hiring a teacher of rhetoric.[17] Thus the satirist Juvenal; his friend Martial even claims that his own epigrams were read in Britain.[18] These items are conventional – they invert the persistent topos that Britain is remote and uncultured – and Juvenal's other knowledge of Britain may be 'literary' and second-hand.[19] But there is support from two dedications made at York by Scrib(onius) Demetrius, if we identify him with Demetrius of Tarsus, a Greek teacher of literature who toured Britain shortly before 83/4.[20] By the second century, therefore, we may

13 *Ibid.*, iii, 8; see Birley 1981, pp. 366–8; and, more briefly, Birley 2005, p. 224.

14 Cicero, *Ad Atticum*, iv, 18, 5. For pre-Roman literacy see Williams 2002 and 2007.

15 Scribonius Largus, *Compositiones*, clxiii and lx.

16 Tacitus, *Agricola*, 21, 2. Compare *Annales*, iii, 43; young Gaulish aristocrats were being educated at Autun in AD 21.

17 Juvenal, *Satires*, xv, 111–12.

18 Martial, *Epigrams*, xi, 3.

19 Syme 1984, esp. pp. 126–8.

20 *RIB* 662 + add. and 663.

guess that a literary education was available for the few native-born Britons who could afford it.

Agricola's conquests were short-lived, and by about the time of his biography the northern frontier had receded to the Tyne–Solway isthmus. Here 'the depth, quality and quantity of literacy' has now been revealed by the Vindolanda tablets, hundreds of fragmentary wooden leaves inscribed in ink, discarded as rubbish.[21] Many are scraps of military documentation: accounts and lists relating to the fort and the commandant's household, notes of working-parties, stereotyped applications for leave and reports from sub-units, even a table of the unit's strength on 18 May (the year not stated, but in the mid-90s): 752 men divided between Vindolanda and Corbridge, with detachments at London and elsewhere, and thirty-one men off sick, ten of them 'suffering from inflammation of the eyes'.[22] Important for the history of the book are two 'notebooks' itemising with dates the issue of foodstuffs and the consumption of chickens, made by stitching tablets together end to end in a 'concertina' format; the editors carefully remark that they are not a primitive codex, but nonetheless 'evidence for the format and use of folded wooden writing-material in a period and in a context which is surely of significance for the development of the early codex'.[23] It must be added, however, that there is a superficially similar document from Carlisle, a note of wheat and barley issued to a contemporary cavalry regiment. This was inscribed on a single strip of wood, which was then scored and folded, and secured by means of a loop passed through a hole in one corner. It was not a 'notebook' with separate 'pages', but only the wooden equivalent of a rolled-up strip of papyrus.[24]

These documents are literate, not literary, but there is a tantalising sub-literary scrap, a note of British fighting skills: 'There are very many cavalry. The cavalry do not use swords nor do the wretched Britons mount in order to throw javelins.'[25] It might remind us of the elder Pliny's first book; he was Pliny's uncle, and he was commanding a regiment on the Rhine when he wrote a treatise (now lost) on the subject of throwing the javelin. Many of the Vindolanda tablets are correspondence; these include business letters – Octavius reports large-scale purchases of sinew, corn and hides – and letters by the military – the officer commanding an outpost reports that his men are

21 *Tab. Vindol.* and Bowman and Thomas 2003; quoting Bowman 2006, p. 88 (and see Bowman 1994). Contemporary ink texts have also been found at Carlisle (Tomlin 1998).

22 *Tab. Vindol.*, 154. Soldiers' tombstones record their exact years of service but often estimate the age at death, which implies use of military records.

23 *Tab. Vindol.*, 581; quoting Bowman and Thomas 2003, p. 23.

24 Tomlin 1998, pp. 36–51.

25 *Tab. Vindol.*, 164.

short of beer – but some do have literary quality. The principal 'archive' is that of the commandant Flavius Cerialis, who was probably a Romanised Batavian noble; his correspondence is striking for its 'accumulation of formal literary phrases' which can be paralleled in Pliny's own published letters.[26] Cerialis was undoubtedly well educated, despite his Germanic origin, and it is hardly surprising that several scraps of Vergil have now been found at Vindolanda.[27] One has apparently been annotated, which suggests that Cerialis' children were being taught from a copy of Vergil there.[28] More unexpected is the letter received by their mother from another commandant's wife; Claudia Severa invites her to a birthday party on 11 September: 'I give you a warm invitation to make sure that you come to us, to make the day more enjoyable for me by your arrival.' This is almost certainly the earliest known example of writing in Latin by a woman. Her Latin, it has been noted, is 'elegant, colloquial and syntactically correct'.[29]

Cerialis refers to Pliny's friend Marcellus when he drafts a letter to his own patron Crispinus, wishing him health and success; these good wishes Crispinus has 'earned' throughout his career. It is likely that Crispinus was a Roman senator, a provincial governor or the commander of a legion, and that Cerialis is alluding delicately to favours received; his letter thus attests the network of patronage which linked Rome with the periphery.[30] It may be compared with an elegant British letter of the third century. Tiberius Claudius Paulinus, who governed northern Britain in 220, wrote from his new province to a Gallic notable: 'Unequal though they are to your deserts, I beg you to accept these few tokens of esteem.' The tokens were a special cloak and tunic, a gold brooch set with jewels, two rugs, a British blanket, a sealskin – and the promise of a short-term commission in the legion at York, the salary to be paid in gold. 'The gods and the Emperor's sacred Majesty willing', adds Paulinus, 'you will receive hereafter other things more worthy of your affection.' It emerges that the recipient had recently intervened to save Paulinus from prosecution for misgovernment in his previous post.[31]

This is the only surviving letter by a governor of Britain, but there are some scraps of official correspondence: fragments of three legal decisions by the Emperor Septimius Severus when he was here (208–11); part of a letter from the Emperor Constantine to the governor-general (*vicarius*) in 319; two personal letters from his nephew Julian to Alypius, who was governor-general in

26 Adams 1995, p. 129. 27 Bowman 2006, p. 89.
28 *Tab. Vindol.*, 118. 29 *Tab. Vindol.*, 291; Adams 1995, p. 129.
30 *Tab. Vindol.*, 225 with Tomlin 1996b, p. 462.
31 *CIL*, xiii, 3162.

about 358.[32] Roman rule had lapsed when the Emperor Honorius wrote his famous letter to the communities of Britain.[33]

Among the Vindolanda tablets is a draft petition to 'Your Majesty' (quite likely the governor) from an unnamed 'man from overseas' who has suffered a beating although innocent, and has failed to gain redress from the local authorities.[34] Its tone of despair and righteous indignation recalls a growing class of sub-literary documents found in Britain in recent years, the 'curse tablets' scratched on sheets of lead.[35] This convenient term is misleading: most of them are not really curses, in the sense of spells aimed out of malice at a named person, but petitions addressed to a god – Sulis Minerva at Bath, for example; Mercury in the Cotswolds at Uley – seeking redress, most often in cases of theft. Typically the unknown thief is to suffer ill health until he returns the stolen property. By contrast with the Vindolanda tablets they are later in date (ranging from the second century until the fourth), and they are written in the towns and countryside of southern Britain by civilians, not soldiers, who do not even claim to be Roman citizens. They are quasi-legal in their idiom and their plaintive ideas of justice and retribution, and they repeat the same phrases and ideas. It would be tempting to see them as the work of professional scribes using reference books, but in fact the expertise of their handwriting ranges very widely, and no duplicates, whether in wording or handwriting, have yet been found. So it seems that they were often the petitioners' own work.[36] Their language can be quite sophisticated: at Pagans Hill, for example, a victim is to be 'wearied with every sort of hardships', a phrase used by the historian Livy; and at Bath, Basilia asks that the thief of her silver ring or his accomplice have 'all his intestines quite eaten away' (Plate 15.2), a phrase used later by Gildas but as a Christian image.[37] Some petitioners encipher their texts – in mirror-image letters or by reversing the sequence in various ways – and at Uley a long Latin text is written in Greek letters.

This bilingualism is surprising in the countryside, but is parallelled by an inscribed gold leaf from Norfolk, which invokes the god Abrasax to guard the bearer. This invocation is written in Greek by a Latin speaker, since he slips inadvertently into Latin letters, before identifying the beneficiary in Latin.[38] Another such leaf has been found in a field near Oxford, which invokes names

32 *Digest*, 28.6.2.4; Kaygusuz 1986; *Theodosian Code*, xi, 7.2; Julian, *Letters*, 9 and 10.

33 Zosimus, vi, 10.

34 *Tab. Vindol.*, 344 + add.

35 *RIB* publishes seven identified before 1955, but the present total is approaching 250, principally from Bath (Tomlin 1988) and Uley (Tomlin 1993); for recent surveys see Tomlin 1993 and 2002.

36 Tomlin 1988, esp. pp. 63–74 ('formulae') and 84–94 ('handwriting').

37 Hassall and Tomlin 1984, p. 336, no. 8; *Tab. Sulis*, 97.

38 Tomlin 2004.

of power in Greek to ensure a healthy childbirth.[39] Such amulets are much rarer than 'curse tablets', but like them they contain formulae which can be paralleled outside Britain; perhaps the most remarkable is an unpublished text on pewter, the alloy of tin and lead typical of Britain, which was found in the Thames in London: it quotes a Greek metrical charm against the plague which was circulated in the 160s by a cult centre in Asia Minor.[40]

The texts quoted are manuscript fragments, not books, but they imply works of reference as well as people who could read and write. This is not the place to quantify the 'literacy' of Roman Britain.[41] The impression given by graffiti on personal belongings – mostly pottery – is that even 'literate' people could often only write their own names in laboured capitals. They were like the fictional businessman who might not be educated, but could read 'letters cut on stone'.[42] British stone inscriptions belong mostly to the world of the army and the administration, and to a few towns; they become rare after the mid third century. The *stilus*-written texts on lead and wood afford a wider perspective in time and place.[43] But illiteracy was certainly the norm, only a minority reading books and being capable of literate composition. Their small achievement is now largely lost and cannot be quantified, but evidence remains of classical education and literature in Roman Britain.[44] Some people knew classical authors, Vergil in particular, and mastered the complementary technique of writing verse.

Vergil at Vindolanda has been mentioned already. The first fragment to be identified was a line from a little-read part of the *Aeneid*, Book IX.[45] A much more famous phrase is the tag *conticuere omnes*: 'they all fell silent', at the beginning of Aeneas' narrative in Book II. This cliché (it occurs in graffiti at Pompeii and elsewhere) was inscribed on a tile at Silchester (Plate 15.3).[46] A fragment of wall-painting at the Otford (Kent) villa carries another phrase from the *Aeneid*, *bina manu*, which would have captioned Aeneas or his Italian rival Turnus 'with two (spears) in his hand'.[47] The most exciting of Vergilian souvenirs was found in Somerset when digging a grave for a diseased sheep: the mosaic pavement in the bath-house of the Low Ham villa. In a central octagon there is Aeneas' manipulative mother, a somewhat sinister Venus with two cupids. Grouped

39 Tomlin 2008. 40 Lucian, *Alexander*, 36.

41 Very low, according to Harris 1989, esp. pp. 268–70; but for more positive views see Bowman 2006 and n. 43 below.

42 Petronius, *Satyricon*, 58.

43 Hanson and Conolly 2002; Tomlin 2002; Tomlin 2009.

44 Barrett 1978; Ling 2007. 45 *Tab. Vindol.*, 118.

46 *RIB*, II.5, 2491.148 (*Aeneid*, II, 1).

47 *RIB*, II.4, 2447.9 (*Aeneid* I, 313 or XII, 165); Ling 2007, pp. 76–8.

around it are four rectangular panels of scenes from the *Aeneid*: the Trojan fleet arrives in Africa, and Venus, naked except for a body-chain like the one in the Hoxne Treasure, introduces Aeneas to Queen Dido, both in Book I; then Dido, Aeneas and Ascanius ride out to the hunt, and Aeneas embraces a now-naked Dido in the forest, both in Book IV. A likely date is the mid fourth century.[48] Vergilian imagery had already circulated in late third-century Britain – literally so, since it was used in the locally minted coinage of the usurper Carausius (286–93).[49] Carausius is greeted by a personification of Britain with the words *expectate veni*: 'Come, long-expected one.' This invocation is adapted from Book II of the *Aeneid*, but the echo is not a happy one: they are virtually the words of Aeneas to the ghost of Hector.[50] Carausius also celebrated his seizure of power by striking silver coins of old-fashioned purity with the mint-mark RSR in the exergue. This puzzled numismatists until it was neatly explained as another Vergilian reminiscence by comparing two unique bronze medallions of Carausius, one with the mint-mark RSR, the other with the letters I. N. P. C. D. A. These are the initial letters of the words in two famous lines of Vergil's 'Messianic' Fourth Eclogue: *redeunt Saturnia regna / iam nova progenies caelo demittitur alto*. 'The Golden Age returns; now a new generation is sent down from high heaven.'[51]

The Low Ham mosaic is also puzzling, since the four panels should really be viewed from the outside – but the walls are in the way. Was it really intended for a larger room? Is it a clumsy scrapbook of images taken from an illustrated manuscript of Vergil? A famous example springs to mind, the Vatican *Vergilius Romanus*, but there is no direct connection; only perhaps a distant common ancestor. This manuscript has even been claimed for Roman Britain, but can be dated on stylistic grounds to the later fifth century; its sumptuous quality and superb Rustic Capitals also argue a metropolitan origin, perhaps in Rome itself.[52]

At the Lullingstone (Kent) villa there is a mosaic illustration of the myth of Europa and the bull. Jupiter in disguise abducts another nymph, below the unique metrical caption: 'If jealous Juno had seen the bull's swimming, she would have had better cause to go to the house of Aeolus.'[53] The scene is not Vergilian, but the allusion is: in Book I of the *Aeneid*, Juno asks Aeolus to wreck

48 Toynbee 1964, 241–5; Cosh and Neal 2005, pp. 253–7 (mosaic 207.1).
49 Casey 1994, p. 58.
50 Vergil, *Aeneid*, II, 282–3; see Barrett 1978, 308.
51 Vergil, *Eclogue*, IV, 6–7; see de la Bédoyère 1998, pp. 79–88.
52 Wright 1992. Insular origin is suggested by Henig 1995, pp. 126 and 157, and maintained in Henig 2002, pp. 82 and 121.
53 *RIB*, II.4, 2448.6, with Barrett 1978; Witts 2005, colour plate 3.

the Trojan fleet to prevent Aeneas from reaching Italy. Since the epigram is on the dining-room floor, perhaps it was improvised over dinner by a landowner who knew his classical mythology and Latin poets. His prosody is Ovidian, however, not Virgilian, and anticipates the early modern English schoolboys who composed their Latin verse from the clichés of a handbook called *Gradus ad Parnassum*.

Europa and the bull are also found at the Keynsham villa near Bristol, one of 'that series of varied subjects drawn from classical mythology with which Romano-British town and country dwellers delighted to ornament their floors'.[54] They include four examples of Bellerophon killing the Chimaera, sometimes with Christian symbols, and at least ten of Orpheus charming the beasts.[55] Like their eighteenth-century counterparts who re-created the landscape of the Grand Tour, Romano-British landowners commissioned pictures of their reading. Long before this fourth-century apogee of the mosaic pavement, by coincidence the northern frontier saw a Greek expert in mythology. Aulus Claudius Charax commanded the Second *Augusta* Legion in the early 140s, probably when it spearheaded the reconquest of southern Scotland. He would thus be the officer depicted on the Bridgeness slab from the Antonine Wall, a Roman general despite being a rich and scholarly Greek, the benefactor of the Greek cities which record his career; he wrote forty books of histories, now lost, which were read by Byzantine scholars for the mythical prehistory of the Aegean world.[56]

Vergil's Fourth Eclogue inspired Carausius' moneyer; the Seventh may have prompted a merchant to gild the letters of his metrical dedication to the Mothers if trade were good.[57] Sadly there is no trace of gilding. The inscription was discovered long before 1907, when the *Cambridge History of English Literature* claims the Irish *Hymn of St Sechnall* as 'the earliest piece of Latin verse produced in these islands'.[58] There is quite a scattering of verse in the inscriptions of Roman Britain.[59] Some are epitaphs, the earliest being that of a legionary in the army of invasion who died as Eagle-bearer of the Fourteenth: there is no wine in the Underworld, he reminds us, so live, but decently, while ye may.[60] At York a father 'deceived by empty hopes' reproaches the gods of the Underworld for taking his thirteen-year-old daughter.[61] At Carlisle there is

54 Toynbee 1964, p. 241. See further, Henig 2002; Witts 2005, ch. 3, 'Stories of heroes'.
55 Rainey 1973; Neal and Cosh 2002; Cosh and Neal 2005; Witts 2005.
56 Birley 2005, p. 253, who also makes the identification with *RIB*, 2139; Spawforth 1986.
57 *RIB*, 2059; compare Vergil, *Eclogues*, VII, 35–6.
58 James 1907, p. 65, when the *Hymn* was thought to be fifth-century.
59 For 'Carmina' see the Indexes of *RIB*, I, p. 94, and *RIB*, II, p. 39.
60 *RIB*, 292 + add. (Wroxeter). 61 *RIB*, 684.

the epitaph of a Greek, possibly a Christian, whose soul has been recalled by the Fates after being out on loan.[62] At Brough-under-Stainmore there is even an epitaph in Greek hexameters.[63]

There are also religious dedications, like that to the Mothers already mentioned. The outpost fort of Risingham has produced not only a metrical epitaph, but also the hexameters of 'the wife of Fabius' (probably a commandant's wife with the unmetrical name of Aurelia Eglectiane) who dedicates an altar to the Nymphs.[64] At Carvoran there is a ten-line poem in which the commandant (probably an African) identifies Tanit, the heavenly protectress of Carthage, with the Syrian Goddess.[65] At Cirencester, the provincial governor dedicates a Jupiter column like those he would have known at home near Reims.[66] There are also Greek hexameters, like the pewter amulet and the tombstone already mentioned, inscribed on altars to medical deities by two Greek doctors at Chester, to Astarte and the Tyrian Hercules at Corbridge.[67]

Two tiles from Binchester even carry an obscure erotic fragment: 'Armea has taught me to say goodbye to every other girl.'[68] None of these verses is the fruit of high literary culture. Often they show the influence of spoken language, and are composed by the ear rather than in direct imitation of classical models. At best they are the work of educated men fond of puzzle-solving, like the persons who copied the AREPO word-square at Cirencester and Manchester.[69] This palindrome is unlikely to be a Christian cryptogram, but we do have one piece of Christian Latin verse from Roman Britain, a hexameter incised below the rim of a silver bowl in the Water Newton Treasure: 'Bowed in submission, Lord, I worship Your sacred altar.'[70]

Like the martyrdom of St Alban or the portrait of Christ in the Hinton St Mary mosaic, this was inspired by the most important Roman book ever to reach Britain, the collection of translated Hebrew and Greek texts known as the Bible.[71] No actual fragment has yet been found, but since Christianity was a 'religion of the book', the Bible's presence may be inferred from Christian archaeology.[72] There may even be a written echo from Bath, in a fourth-century 'curse tablet': the thief who has stolen six silver coins is accursed, 'whether pagan or Christian, whether man or woman, whether boy or girl, whether

62 *RIB*, 955; the phrase recurs in *CIL*, iii, 3335, and implies a common work of reference.
63 *RIB*, 758. 64 *RIB*, 1253; 1228 (with *RIB*, 1482).
65 *RIB*, 1791 + add. 66 *RIB*, 103.
67 *RIB*, 461 and Wilson and Wright 1969, p. 235, no. 3 (Chester); *RIB*, 1124 and 1129 (Corbridge).
68 *RIB*, II.5, 2491.146 and 147. 69 *RIB*, II.4, 2447.20; II.6, 2494.98.
70 *RIB*, II.2, 2424.2. 71 Cosh and Neal 2005, 156–60 (mosaic 172.1).
72 Thomas 1981, who justly remarks (p. 54): 'a late Roman British society able to produce a Pelagius must, after all, have had its more interesting side'.

slave or free'. Mutually exclusive clauses like this are found in ancient prayers, and are typical of British 'curse tablets', but this reference to Christianity is unique; perhaps the author was parodying St Paul to the greater glory of the goddess of the sacred spring: 'There is neither bond nor free, there is neither male nor female: for ye are all one in Sulis Minerva.'[73]

During the fourth century Christianity became the Empire's dominant religion, thanks to its conversion of an emperor proclaimed at York; years later, when he recommended himself to the eastern provinces, Constantine dated his reign 'from that Sea beside the Britons and the parts where it is appointed by a superior constraint that the sun should set'.[74] It is not surprising, therefore, that the first British author whose books actually survive was a Christian. This is Pelagius, who tells us nothing about himself; but his enemies concur that he came from Britain.[75]

Here he was educated in literature and rhetoric, and first read the Bible, before leaving for Rome, where he studied law. This he abandoned for Christian theology, in which he became an authority; his reading of the theologians Ambrose, the anonymous 'Ambrosiaster', Jerome and Augustine, whom he quotes in his *Commentary on the Pauline Epistles*, must belong to this period; likewise the Eastern influence which has been detected.[76] This reconstruction depends on identifying him with the nameless 'monk' attacked by Jerome in 394 for his eloquent preaching, for expounding the Bible to female ascetes, for courting the aristocracy – in fact, for doing in Rome what Jerome had done there ten years before.[77] Jerome says that he was ignorant of Cicero and Aristotle, and sarcastically calls him 'a master of eloquence', while himself pointedly quoting Cicero, Vergil, Persius, Juvenal, Terence and Horace, all the standard authors, but this only means that Pelagius did not advertise his own classical education. He came into greater prominence early in the fifth century, when he read Augustine's *Confessiones* and was provoked by the repeated phrase 'Grant what you command, and command what you will' into developing his own doctrine of God's commandment to man.[78]

Pelagius' influential writings and their effect in Britain, both of which are later than the end of Roman rule in 408/11, need not be discussed here.[79] He has intrigued students of Roman Britain as the best-known product of its

73 *Tab. Sulis*, 98, with Galatians 3.28.
74 Eusebius, *Life of Constantine*, II, 28 (trans. Cameron and Hall 1999). For Constantine at York, see Hartley *et al.* 2006.
75 Rees 1988, pp. xii–xiv.
76 Rees 1991, p. 33; Markus 1986.
77 Jerome, *Letter* 50, with Rees 1988, pp. xii–xiv.
78 Augustine, *Confessions*, X, 29.40 (trans. Chadwick 1991).
79 Thomas 1981, pp. 53–60.

system of education. His date of birth is not known, but he was contemporary with his great opponent Augustine (born 354), so he must have 'graduated' from Britain soon after 376, the year when the poet Ausonius prompted his former pupil, the Emperor Gratian, to establish public chairs of rhetoric and literature in the diocesan capitals of the Gallic prefecture. These included London, which gives it a tenuous claim to primacy over universities founded more recently at Oxford and Cambridge.[80] Gratian's directive already implies the presence of private teachers, like Augustine at Carthage and Rome in 376–84, but we do not know that it was carried out; and even if public chairs were indeed founded in London, modern practice was evidently anticipated by not replacing the holders when they retired.

Pelagius' Latin has been characterised as mostly clear and correct, but austere and laboured, as if it were a second language.[81] The preface to his *Letter to Demetrias* (414) conventionally rates content above style, with the engaging image of wholemeal bread rather than white. Classical tags are very rare: the *Aeneid* for the sack of Rome (410), Juvenal for the truism that the penniless traveller has nothing to fear from robbers.[82] The constant classical allusion in Jerome's writings is quite absent; Pelagius associates enthusiasm for literature with worldly ambition.[83] Early education may have given him a power of self-expression, but his studies at Rome made him reject its content; like Augustine, he would have honoured words, those 'precious cups of meaning', while condemning his teachers for the wine of error they served in them.[84] Augustine could not criticise his mother outright, but he conjectured her motives in forcing a literary education upon him; Pelagius likewise adds a significant gloss to the words of St Paul telling fathers not to provoke their children: 'Do not make them learn anger by driving them to worldly studies, but train them in the discipline of the Divine Law. Such parents he commands sons to obey.'[85]

Did Pelagius leave Britain because he quarrelled with his own father? More likely it was ambition that brought him to Rome, like Augustine in 383. Pelagius is justly claimed as the first surviving British author, but he wrote, not in Britain, but in Rome. He was an expatriate, his writings occupying a

80 *Theodosian Code*, xiii, 3.11 (376), as interpreted by M. W. C. Hassall of University College, London, (re)founded in 1825/8.
81 Rees 1991, p. 20. 82 De Plinval 1943, pp. 72–4.
83 Pelagius, *Letter to Demetrias*, 11, 2; but inconsistent with 13 (young minds are more receptive to a literary education).
84 Augustine, *Confessions*, I, 16.26.
85 Pelagius, *Commentary on the Pauline Epistles*; Ephesians 6.4.

place in Romano-British literature analogous to that of Conrad's novels in the literature of Poland.

A nonentity called Silvius Bonus, a Briton who criticised Ausonius' poetry, is the target of some feeble epigrams: a Briton called Bonus ['good'] is a contradiction in terms.[86] This might imply that Continental literature circulated in Britain, but really it is the old topos that Britain was remote and uncultured. Pelagius' critic Jerome, who claims to have heard of British cannibals when he was in Gaul, remarks that even Britain heard of his patron Pammachius' hostel – but three months after Egypt and Persia.[87] It is also disconcerting to find the poet Rutilius Namatianus in 417, some years after the formal end of Roman rule in Britain – not that he realised this – praising a fellow Gaul he met in Tuscany; Victorinus had been a popular governor-general of Britain, and Rutilius comments:

> True, the place is remote, the edge of the world,
> But he governed it as he would have central Rome.
> More credit to him, for seeking the approval
> Of men whose disapproval hardly matters.[88]

But then, if you were a late-Roman intellectual looking at Roman literature, it would be a long time before you thought of Britain.

86 Ausonius, *Epigrams*, 107–12.
87 Jerome, *Against Jovinianus*, II, 7; *Letter*, 77.10.
88 Rutilius Namatianus, *De reditu suo*, 503–6.

16

The use of the book in Wales, *c.* 400–1100

T. M. CHARLES-EDWARDS

The student of the book in early medieval Wales, and also in those other areas that remained British-speaking, labours under a modest handicap: there are no surviving books known to have been written in Wales or Cornwall before the ninth century.[1] From the British-speaking kingdoms of northern Britain there survive no books at all.[2] The history of the British book must, therefore, be written by circuitous processes of reasoning: by inference from texts written by Britons but only surviving in later and non-British manuscripts, from other modes of lettering, notably inscriptions on stone, and, finally, from comparison with Ireland. The comparison with Ireland is justified because it was part of the one Insular cultural province; not only did it have the same scripts, essentially the same orthography for Latin texts, the same methods of constructing a codex, but current practice usually evolved in the same direction and at much the same time.[3] Moreover, in the early part of our period, there were Irish colonies in Britain, including Wales, and British missionaries in Ireland; even in a later period, there is ample evidence of continued scholarly and ecclesiastical links across the Irish Sea.[4]

I am grateful for advice generously given by Gifford Charles-Edwards, Helen McKee and Paul Russell. A concise but helpful survey of the subject is Pryce 1998a, and for more palaeographical and codicological aspects, Huws 1998.

1 As we shall see, Wales and Cornwall were too closely linked up to the tenth century for it to be helpful to consider them apart.

2 For the purposes of this chapter, 'British' will refer to Welsh, Cornish, Breton and Cumbrian (using 'Cumbrian' as a short-hand term for all the Britons of the North).

3 A good example from the ninth century is pointed out by Dumville 1999, pp. 125–6.

4 Charles-Edwards 1999; Grabowski and Dumville 1984, pp. 209–26, on the Irish connections of *Annales Cambriae*; Chadwick 1958, pp. 93–110, on Irish scholars at the court of Merfyn Frych, king of Gwynedd, and their links with other Irish scholars in the Carolingian Empire. In the twelfth century the Anglesey church of Caergybi/Holyhead claimed to have a dependent church in Meath, Cell Mór Mo Chop (Wade-Evans 1944, p. 240, § 13); the form of the name Mo Chop and corroboration in *Corpus Genealogiarum Sanctorum Hiberniae* (Ó Riain 1985) § 722.98, make the claim very plausible, although dating is difficult; Llangrannog in Ceredigion remembered that it had the same founder as Dulane, just to the north of Kells (in the kingdom of Brega), Wade-Evans 1944, p. 146, § 6; there was a 'house of the Britons' at Kells itself: *The Martyrology of Oengus the Culdee*, Stokes 1905, 26 October, Notes, p. 228.

There are two fundamental reasons why the distribution of surviving manuscripts cannot be taken as an indication of the usage of books.[5] First, to stick to a position so closely dependent upon one category of evidence would entail a lack of consideration for other categories of evidence, especially texts and inscriptions. Second, it would be to forget that, in general, pre-Norman Welsh manuscripts survived only if they were taken to England in the tenth century and were there preserved in ecclesiastical libraries.[6] Similarly, it is broadly true that early Irish books survived only if they were taken to Francia or to Italy in the eighth or ninth centuries. English books survived somewhat better because they travelled along both routes to preservation – Francia in the eighth and ninth centuries and into the libraries of reformed English monasteries and cathedrals in the tenth century. There is a well-known chronological horizon for the survival of books, namely the establishment of churches, monasteries or cathedrals, which had a tolerably uninterrupted physical and institutional existence until the early modern or, at best, the French Revolutionary period. In other words, what made books survive was nothing to do with either book production or book use, but rather what happened to the places in which out-of-date texts happened to be preserved through laudable inertia.

These considerations also matter because they explain not just the overall scarcity of books but also the imbalance, both geographical and chronological, in direct manuscript evidence. The libraries that gave hospitality to our surviving pre-Norman Welsh manuscripts were generally those of churches reformed in the tenth century; these, however, were concentrated in Wessex, the lower Severn Valley and the Fenlands. Hence it was predominantly southern British books that survived, those from South Wales and Cornwall.[7] Political and ecclesiastical links were also usually stronger with southern than with central and northern Wales, while Cornwall was incorporated into the English kingdom in the tenth century.[8] It is hardly surprising, therefore, that no early book survives from Cumbria (Strathclyde).

5 Sims-Williams 1998, pp. 18–24.

6 Good examples are the Lichfield Gospels (Lichfield CL, 1) and St Dunstan's Classbook (BodL., Auct. F.4.32).

7 E.g. the Lichfield Gospels from Llandeilo Fawr; the copy of Ovid, *Ars amatoria*, Book I, in St Dunstan's Classbook to be discussed below, shown to be from South Wales by the dialect form *ceintiru*; BodL., Bodley 572, Cornish but with Welsh glosses in one section; for the Juvencus manuscript see McKee 2000b.

8 As illustrated by the career of Asser; by Edward the Elder's ransoming of Cyfeilliog, bishop of Ergyng, *ASC* A, 918 = 914; by Sawyer 1968, no. 913, a grant of land at Over by King Æthelred, 1005, to Dewstow: Ker 1948, pp. 73–4; Finberg 1972, no. 147; Whitelock 1979, p. 352 and nos. 115, 131; Tremerin, who appears as the last name in the Clas Cynidr list (after which 'he departed for Hereford'); Fleuriot 1976–8, pp. 225–6, and in *The Chronicle of John of Worcester*: Darlington and McGurk 1995, *s.a.* 1055, Tremerig, *ASC* C, Tremerin, *ASC* D, 1055.

What we have in the early period, bereft of surviving books,[9] is some central facts about the history of Insular scripts, inscriptions and a very few texts. What saves the day is that we can discern some broad directions in the religious and cultural history of late antique and early medieval Britain.

In its use, as in its scripts and construction, the British book began as a local variety of the late Roman codex, namely the variety predominant in fourth-century Roman Britain, a relatively prosperous 'diocese' of the late Empire. Among the letter-forms available, and which played a part in later developments, were Half-Uncial and New Roman Cursive; Uncial is only visible in the odd letter-form, while *capitalis* was apparently kept for inscriptions.[10] What determined which varieties were to be influential in the development of Insular script was probably not so much any supposed provincial poverty or remoteness of late Roman Britain, but rather which scripts were favoured by the British church in the fifth century.[11] This conclusion is, if not absolutely proved, rendered beyond serious doubt by the resulting situation. The Insular hierarchy of scripts was common to Ireland and Wales, and also to Cornwall and Brittany (Cornwall only up to the mid tenth century, Brittany only up to the ninth century).[12] If we assume that the starting-point was the British church in the century in which Brittany was founded, in which some British kingdoms were ruled by Irish settlers, and in which Irish Christianity was nurtured, predominantly, though not exclusively, by British clerics and monks, we can account without difficulty for the seventh-century situation. Any other hypothesis would require much more improbable historical reconstruction.

It is easy, because of the eloquence of Gildas and a tendency to concentrate on the affairs of the eastern part of the British Isles, to suppose that the conditions in which the British church functioned in the fifth and sixth centuries were entirely governed by war and territorial contraction. War and territorial loss were very real; but, alongside what Gildas called 'the ruin of Britain', there opened up a new mission-field in Ireland. Details of the Latin orthography used by the Irish, as well as the way they pronounced Latin, have confirmed the importance of the British role in their conversion.[13] The mission-field generated a demand for books, a demand likely to have encouraged the development

9 Even if Martin Henig was right about the *Virgilius Romanus* (*CLA*, I, no. 19), it was not the kind of late antique book that was the basis of subsequent developments: Henig 1985, pp. 18–19; Dark 1994, pp. 184–91; Dumville 1999, p. 15.

10 For examples of *capitalis* and New Roman Cursive, see Tomlin 1988, nos. 94–111. Uncial provided alternative Insular forms of **d**, **r** and **s**, and an occasional **a**.

11 *Pace* Brown 1993, pp. 221–2.

12 See Chapters 4 and 5.

13 Jackson 1953, pp. 122–48, modified in important respects by McManus 1983, pp. 21–71. This was not true of the earlier Latin influence in the construction of the ogham alphabet.

of a minuscule script. These were not only liturgical, biblical and patristic texts. The Irish were not Latin speakers but they were now being drawn into the Latin church: they therefore needed grammars and word-lists. This reinforced a trend under way at home. Spoken British Latin survived into the sixth century, but it may have vanished in the seventh. As Ireland and Pictland came into the Latin church, the Britons, former citizens of the Empire, moved away from their past, a past in which bilingualism in Latin and British had been widespread. Britons as well as Irish and Picts arrived at a shared situation: Latin was now a language of the book, a language that some might learn to speak as well as to write, but whose oral life was largely controlled by written texts.

These changes suggest that we should distinguish between two chronological phases: a post-Roman period up to the seventh century and a subsequent, more purely Welsh period. In the first, bilingualism in Latin and British persisted, though always and increasingly to the advantage of British. In parts of Wales, Irish was also spoken for much if not all of this phase.[14] In the later phase, however, Welsh (a daughter language of British) was the sole spoken language. On the one hand we have the Britain of Gildas, on the other the Wales of Asser.

A way to explore the contrast between these two phases is to consider the literate context of books. By using this phrase, 'literate context', I wish to raise the question of how far, in a culture in which the book is present, it is surrounded by other, independent forms of literacy, such as documents. These other forms may be divided between those in which a text is inscribed (by making an indentation on a surface) and those in which they are written by pen and ink. The first includes the stone (and wooden) inscription, and also the wax tablet. The second will include governmental or legal documents and letters. The book itself has links with both techniques of lettering, since, although the principal text was written with pen and ink, glosses were sometimes added by a dry point – in other words by a technique falling under the overall heading of inscribing.[15] We may then draw a contrast between a cultural situation in which the book exists among several other forms of literacy and one in which it stands in isolation.

There are reasons for thinking that sixth-century Britain may not have been entirely without those modes of literacy that secured the downfall of Egidius. Although there are no curse tablets to demonstrate the survival of New Roman

14 Sims-Williams 2002, esp. pp. 22–32.

15 Some dry-point glosses were added to what may be the earliest Irish manuscript, the Codex Usserianus Primus: Ó Néill 1998; on this manuscript see also Dumville 1999, pp. 35–40.

Cursive in Britain after the fourth century, there are two kinds of evidence that render it likely. These do not include the role of New Roman Cursive in the formation of the Insular variety of Half-Uncial, since that influence may have had its effect in the fourth century. The first is the survival, attested by Gildas, of the technical terms of late Roman government, and also of the rhetorical skills required of those who rose to high office.[16] This suggests that, in spite of economic decline, political fragmentation and territorial contraction, the old literate techniques of authority were still required in government. A second piece of evidence comprises the letter-forms that were used as intrusive elements in fifth- and sixth-century inscriptions which have *capitalis* as their base. It has been usual to claim that such forms derive from Insular Half-Uncial or the allied minuscule – in other words that they represent the intrusion of book letter-forms into epigraphy. This is rendered unlikely, however, by the clear contrast between such early intrusive letter-forms and the undoubtedly Half-Uncial inscriptions which may be dated to the ninth, tenth and eleventh centuries. The latter have, for example, the characteristic half-uncial '**oc**' form of **a**, which is not found in the earlier, post-Roman inscriptions. The majority of the intrusive forms in the post-Roman inscriptions are likely to derive from cursive, not from a book script. It may be significant that the epigraphic evidence both attests the survival of cursive in post-Roman Britain and also the survival of spoken Vulgar Latin, and that both seem to fade out in the seventh century.

The break between the post-Roman phase and early medieval British culture is marked in North Wales by the Catamanus inscription, and another nearby inscription, designed by the same man. Both are from south-west Anglesey and both have a unique form of **a**, probably derived from Uncial.[17] So far as its shape is concerned, it could either come from Uncial or from New Roman Cursive (the Uncial **a** is itself a calligraphic version of a cursive letter-form). There is, however, a close parallel in an **a** used in a so-called 'diminuendo' effect in the Cathach traditionally ascribed to St Columba.[18] Since this effect involves the use of larger and sometimes higher-grade letters, the likelihood is that this unusual **a** entered the Insular repertoire from a high-grade script, and therefore from Uncial rather than from Cursive. For one thing, the **a** is relatively large compared with neighbouring letter-forms. A possible explanation is that this **a** had survived as a special letter-form from the fourth century, when Uncial as well as Half-Uncial may well have

16 Lapidge 1984, esp. pp. 48–50. 17 Nash-Williams 1950, nos. 13 and 35.

18 Dublin, Royal Irish Academy, s.n.; an example is on fol. 48, the beginning of Psalm 90, in the first **a** of *Qui habitat*.

been known in Britain. Again, epigraphy can give indirect evidence on book scripts.

The Catamanus inscription, together with its companion, has a further dual importance: on the one hand, it is the first inscription in Gwynedd whose base is not *capitalis*. Instead, it is an example of a very unusual type, the 'mixed' inscription in which no letter-form is employed as the base but rather an eclectic assemblage of letters of different origin. On the other hand, it is also the last Latin inscription for some centuries in the heartland of Gwynedd (the old counties of Anglesey, Caernarvonshire and Merionethshire). It marks the end of a separate set of letter-forms for inscriptions; but it also marks the end, in north-west Wales, of the epigraphic memorial habit – in other words the habit of putting up inscriptions on stone to commemorate the dead. The domination of the book within what was now a more limited field of literate activity came to be more assured in the seventh century. In South Wales, where the epigraphic habit was revived in the ninth century, notably at such centres as Llanilltud Fawr,[19] the letter-forms were now those of book script and the sites at which inscriptions survive were, in general, churches likely to have been active scribal centres. In North Wales, the Tywyn inscription of the ninth century was also in Half-Uncial script and in Welsh; it is, however, a unique survival.[20]

Another technique, apart from inscribing on stone, almost certainly endured throughout the period, even though the evidence is exceedingly limited. When someone learnt to write at this period, he began by using a stylus and a wax tablet. The best, and only direct evidence for the role of the wax tablet in Insular writing is from northern Ireland, the Springmount Bog Tablets.[21] These, however, may well date from the sixth century and thus from a period when relations between Ireland and Celtic Britain were especially close.[22] The first hand (there is more than one) was very competent with the stylus but had not yet learnt how to write a book-hand. This is shown by his attempt to imitate a book-hand serif on an ascender (such serifs were foreign to the type of ascender used on wax tablets, which instead employed approach strokes). He produced his imitation serif but put it on the wrong side of the ascender.[23] The implications of this example are, first, as has been noted, that the inscribing

19 Nash-Williams 1950, nos. 220, 222, 223 (this may be associated, as Nash-Williams suggested, in comment on nos. 220 and 222, with Llanilltud's status as a royal burial church); Royal Commission on Historical Monuments 1976, nos. 911–12, 932–3, 953–4.

20 Sims-Williams 2002, pp. 6–10.

21 *CLA*, Suppl., no. 1684.

22 Dumville 1999, pp. 31–5.

23 I am grateful to Gifford Charles-Edwards for pointing this out to me and for discussing its significance.

technique with the sharp-pointed stylus upon wax produced a partially different set of letter-forms; second, that many may have been competent with a stylus but entirely, or almost entirely, without experience in writing on parchment; and, third, that we can, therefore, grade the literate into three broad categories: those who only read; those who read and inscribed with stylus and wax tablet; and those who read, inscribed with stylus, and wrote with quill on parchment. Wax tablets were used in education (the Springmount Bog Tablets probably belong to this category), in literary composition,[24] and, probably, for letters.[25] The wax tablet was intended to be reused; for this reason it was unlikely to end up in an administrative archive or a library book-cupboard. Its original ubiquity is intimately related to the reason why hardly any examples survive.

Within the early phase up to the seventh century, certain developments occurred that were to be crucial in shaping the functions of the Welsh book until the Norman Conquest and the full impact of the Gregorian reform. In Italy, Gaul and Spain, the old municipal education of Antiquity – with its strong bias towards the arts of verbal persuasion and the word-for-word study of a narrow canon of literary texts – barely survived into the sixth century.[26] In Latin-speaking Europe the church was not committed to a syllabus often seen as too pagan; and it was not dependent on the old syllabus and its teachers, the grammarian and the rhetor, to provide literate priests equipped to celebrate the Latin liturgy.[27] West and south of the Rhineland and north-eastern Gaul, almost everyone who mattered now spoke Latin.[28] In Britain the church had no such comfort: although some spoke Latin as well as British, they were a declining minority; by about 700 they had ceased to exist. The old municipal

24 Adomnán, *De locis sanctis*, Praef. and II.2: Meehan 1958, pp. 36 and 42.

25 Cf. the gloss on the Welsh Ovid, *Ars amatoria*, which explained *tabellas* by *aepistolas* (fol. 42r/22, to l. 385 of the text) but also (fol. 38r/2 to l. 71) by Old Welsh *cloriou* 'surfaces', where *tabellae*, in the context, refers to pictures on the *Porticus Liviae* (in other words, the glossing was not mechanical but sensitive to the particular references of the text). Another good example is the distinction made between 38ᵃ20, where *guaroimaou* (literally 'play-places') glosses *theatris* and 38ᵃ34 where *estid* 'sitting' glosses *theat(h)ro*. In the first case, the glossator understands the Latin word to refer to theatres, places where plays are put on; in the second, which talks of *uela* which hang over the *marmoreo ... theatro* he correctly understands that the 'sails' are awnings over the seating area, not the theatre as a whole.

26 For these schools see Marrou 1956, p. 305; for their demise Riché 1976, pp. 24–38.

27 E.g. Gregory of Tours on his ecclesiastical education, *Vita Patrum*, ii, Pref.: James 1985: 'I have not been polished by the cultivated reading of secular writers; instead the blessed father Avitus, bishop of Clermont, exhorted me to study ecclesiastical works.'

28 E.g. Gogo, the *nutritor* of the child-king Childebert II (Gundlach *et al.* 1892, no. 16), refers to himself, in consciously elaborate Latin, as 'a barbarian writer who has rather learnt from Dodorenus the languages of barbarian tribes than from Parthenius of good memory to master rhetorical composition'. His Latin epistolary style was designed to demonstrate that he had, in fact, learnt both.

system of education was not, therefore, left to wither with the *civitates* and their aristocratic *ordines* or *curiae*, for whom it had existed.

The British church, therefore, retained the schools but reconstructed the syllabus: biblical exegesis was the culmination of study. This can be inferred from several kinds of evidence: from the witness-lists of charters, from odd scraps of evidence offered by Gildas, Bede and the *Life of St Samson*, and from the pattern of education established in Ireland during the period when the British church played the major role in conversion.[29] Most of the Llandaff witness-lists before the eleventh century derived from archives not at Llandaff but at churches in Ergyng (south-west Herefordshire) and Gwent.[30] Of these, many included a *lector* within the clerical section of the list, generally placed immediately after a bishop or abbot and before the ordinary clergy.[31] Other terms for what is likely to be the same office were, in early charters (and also in a very limited revival in the eleventh century), *magister*, and in a small interconnected group of ninth-century charters, *scriptor*.[32] Of these the earlier term, *magister*, recalls the *magister elegans*, 'refined teacher', mentioned by Gildas as having instructed 'almost all Britain' and, in particular, Maglocunus, the future king of Gwynedd and the *magister*, identified as Illtud, said to have been the teacher of St Samson of Dol.[33] Another term, probably for the same office, was *scholasticus*, found in one of the documents added to the Lichfield Gospels when they were at Llandeilo Fawr in Carmarthenshire.[34] In the late eleventh-century *Life of St David* by Rhygyfarch, the saint was said to have been taught by a *scriba*, Paulentus or Paulinus, who instructed him 'in the three parts of *lectio* until he (David) was a *scriba*'.[35] Rhygyfarch's term for a scriptural scholar, *scriba*, was standard in Ireland from the seventh to the ninth century.[36]

29 In the *Vita Prima S. Samsonis*, § 7 (Flobert 1997, p. 156), *philosophia* includes the seven liberal arts and is placed alongside study of the Bible; Charles-Edwards 1998b, pp. 66–8.

30 Probably including Welsh Bicknor/Llangystennin Garth Benni in Ergyng and Llandogo in Gwent: Davies 1978, pp. 151–9.

31 *Liber Landavensis*: Evans and Rhŷs 1893, 161a [= the first charter to begin on p. 161], 161, 162a, 169b, 170, etc. *Lector* is also used in one charter in the Llancarfan collection, *Vitae sanctorum Britanniae et genealogiae*: Wade-Evans 1944, p. 130, § 62, but there Pill *lector* is the last of the clerical witnesses. In the *De raris fabulis*, no. 1 in Stevenson 1929, pp. 1–11, the teacher is *lector* or *doctor*, the pupils *scholastici*.

32 *Magister*: *Liber Landavensis*: Evans and Rhŷs 1893: pp. 127b (highly suspect text); 140, 164, 174b (all seventh- or very early eighth-century); 269, 271, 274 (all late eleventh-century and associated with Lifris of Llancarfan and Bishop Herewald of Llandaff); *scriptor*, 224, 239, 245 (all referring to the same person, and associated with Gower and western Glamorgan).

33 *Vita prima S. Samsonis*: Flobert 1997, p. 156, § 7.

34 No. 5: Evans and Rhys 1893, p. xlvi.

35 *Vitae sanctorum Britanniae et genealogiae*: Wade-Evans 1944, p. 153, § 10.

36 The first example in the Annals of Ulster is *s.a.* 697; obits are frequent from 724; cf. Charles-Edwards 2000, pp. 264–77.

Intimately associated with the importance of a *lector* within major churches, namely those staffed by a clerical community (in some later texts known as a *classis*, Welsh *clas*), was the right of a leading ecclesiastical scholar to be a full member of a synod. This was crucial because, in addition to episcopal authority, both the British and Irish churches were governed by synods.[37] On the evidence of Bede, the British church allowed learning as well as episcopal orders to qualify someone for participation in the supreme decision-making bodies of the church.[38] Yet this would hardly have been conceivable if the syllabus had remained what it had been before the triumph of Christianity, vulnerable to the damning criticisms levelled by St Augustine in his *De Doctrina Christiana* and his *De civitate Dei*. On a grand scale, beyond that of the local synod, Gildas' *De excidio Britanniae* reveals the new Christian scholar in action, able to interrogate scriptural authority as a basis on which to pass judgement on those who had strayed, whether they were adulterous and murderous kings or otherwise holy but heretical monks.

The argumentative strategy employed by Gildas, by which he assembled scriptural texts and *exempla* to pass judgement upon the shortcomings of different orders within a Christian society – kings, bishops and priests – was what underlay the early eighth-century *Collectio canonum Hibernensis*.[39] One of the latter's sources was a collection ascribed to Gildas.[40] It has been proposed that the *Hibernensis* was intended for the British as well as for the Irish church.[41] This seems unlikely, in that the timing of the text's composition seems to be directly related to the adoption by Iona of the Roman Easter; yet the manuscript tradition demonstrates that it was rapidly received in Brittany, while later evidence suggests a fairly early reception in Wales as well.[42] It is, therefore, fair to ask whether the same fundamental conditions that produced the *Hibernensis* in Ireland might have encouraged its reception in Wales. While Irish canon law was a law of the church, it was quite as prepared to lay down rules for kings as it was for bishops and other clergy. Moreover, the *Hibernensis* was compiled for a church which did not use Roman law in the way that was taken for granted in Gaul or Italy. In the later Roman Empire and its successor states, bishops had secular as well as ecclesiastical judicial authority, and therefore employed the

37 For a general survey, see Dumville 1997.

38 Bede, *HE*, II, 2: '*episcopos siue doctores … VII Brettonum episcopi et plures uiri doctissimi*'; on this see Stancliffe 1999, pp. 131–4.

39 The two types of evidence on which the *Hibernensis* depended were texts, *testimonia*, from authoritative sources, and *exempla* from the Bible or the history of the church: Charles-Edwards 1998a; for similar use of *exempla* in Gildas, see *De excidio*, ch. 73.

40 Sharpe 1984, pp. 194–6. 41 Sheehy 1982, pp. 527–8.

42 H. Bradshaw in Wasserschleben 1885a, pp. lxiii–lxxv; Dumville 1994d; Pryce 1986.

law of the Empire alongside the canons of the church.[43] Yet Gildas says that the Britons 'gave only superficial obedience to the edicts of the Romans', while later Welsh law is much more Celtic than Roman.[44] On the other hand, the Llandaff and Llancarfan charters belong to a tradition that, while styled 'the Celtic charter', actually traced its origins to late Roman diplomatic.[45]

A hypothesis to account for these facts is that Roman law never entirely displaced native British law; that the latter triumphed in the secular sphere in the post-Roman period; but that the church developed a legal tradition of its own. Because this ecclesiastical law existed in a society in which Roman law survived only vestigially, it was in a quite different context from that in which 'the canons' had existed under the Empire. In Britain, as in Ireland, it was not possible for the canons to be an ecclesiastical adjunct to the law of an emperor who was the head of the Christian world, who summoned councils and took a strong line with popes. Native British law may never have had the status in ecclesiastical eyes possessed by Roman law; this would be unsurprising if it were, as yet, unwritten. Instead of 'the canons' it was now thought to be necessary to have a fully developed legal system with its own jurisprudential principles: scripture was the highest authority in textual terms; in terms of human authorities, the papacy was the ultimate court of appeal.[46] The authority of scripture was what Gildas proclaimed as much as his Irish imitators, Columbanus and Cummian.[47] The British church was, then, more dependent on biblical scholarship than were its Continental counterparts, while it was increasingly, and soon wholly, dependent on its teachers to provide clergy who were *litterati*. This state of affairs, common to Wales and Ireland, explains why Middle Welsh *yscolheic*, while etymologically meaning 'man trained in a school', actually meant 'cleric', and why a Welsh vernacular term for the pupils in an ecclesiastical school was *meibion llên*, a direct counterpart to Irish *maicc legind*;[48] it also explains why the scholar might be admitted to participate alongside bishops and leading abbots in the synods of the church.

The trend of these developments was to drive clerical and secular society further apart. The church had a law of books backed up by the penitentials; the

43 Gregory of Tours, *Vita Patrum*, VIII, on Nicetius, bishop of Lyons, as a judge; Council of Orléans I (AD 511), ch. 1; *Lex Ribvaria*, § 61.1 (Beyerle and Buchner 1954, I.3, 2, pp. 108–9).

44 Gildas, *De excidio*, ch. 5.

45 Davies 1982a; for a general survey see Broun 1995.

46 Wasserschleben 1885b, XIX (scripture comes first in the *ordo inquisitionis causarum*) and XX.5*b* (with the longer text in Recension B already attested in Cummian, *De controversia paschali*: Walsh and Ó Cróinín 1988, ll. 276–7); Columbanus, ep. V: Walker 1957, pp. 36–57).

47 Winterbottom 1976.

48 *Pedeir keinc y Mabinogi*: Williams 1930, p. 244, n. on 61.17; compare also Irish *scolóc*; Wade-Evans 1909, 114.3, *meibon lleyn yr eglwys*.

latter's textual tradition went back to sixth-century Wales. Lay society lived by a law that was probably still oral; and although, in Ireland, a written ecclesiastical law, a 'lettered law',[49] soon engendered a written secular law, there is no evidence for Welsh law books until the tenth century; and even then the later tradition ascribing a foundational Welsh law book to the authority of Hywel Dda (*d.* 950) is, in the eyes of some scholars, complete fiction,[50] although others would give it some credence.[51]

Yet there was never a complete divide between a clerical order, for whom books were a central element in daily experience, and a secular order in which they were not. Gildas' 'refined teacher' had a future king as his pupil; another of Gildas' wicked kings spent some time under monastic vows.[52] Although there was sometimes conscious opposition between ecclesiastical scholar and professional vernacular poet, the latter was also anxious to display a learning largely derived from Latin sources;[53] and the Latin scholar, for his part, seems sometimes to have taken on something of the magical persona of the druid.[54] The existence of a single standard orthography for Old Welsh, Old Cornish and Old Breton (with some variations) implies a tradition of writing in the vernacular.[55] It is also likely that this tradition included more than merely the proper names, interlinear glosses and marginal verses in which Old Welsh largely survives. It has to be remembered, yet again, that the route to preservation via tenth-century England was open to Latin, not vernacular, manuscripts. The textual tradition of the *Gododdin* implies pre-Norman copies; in the view of some scholars, these copies must have included at least one deriving from the North British kingdom of Allt Clud (Dumbarton), the later Strathclyde or Cumbria.[56]

Surviving manuscripts from the ninth and tenth centuries show that the various dividing lines between clerical and lay, Latin and vernacular, literate and non-literate, did not coincide. Apart from the 'Computus Fragment', they contain Latin texts;[57] the presence of Welsh is marginal or interlinear. Yet we have to ask what this implies. Does it signify that the role of the vernacular within the ecclesiastical community from which the books came was indeed marginal? Or does it suggest, at the other extreme, that Latin texts existed

49 Thurneysen 1927, p. 175, § 1.
50 Davies 1996, 8.
51 Charles-Edwards 1989, pp. 75–86.
52 Gildas, *De excidio*, chs. 28, 36.
53 Haycock 1983–4.
54 Jones 1941–4, pp. 137–8, on the evidence of *Armes Prydein fawr*; Williams 1955, l. 193, and *Vita prima S. Samsonis*, Flobert 1997, §§ 2 and 3 (*librarius* as 'sorcerer').
55 Sims-Williams 1991, pp. 20–86.
56 Koch 1997, pp. lxxx–lxxxiii; for a more sceptical line see Isaac 1999, pp. 55–78.
57 The Computus Fragment, CUL, Add. 4543, a single leaf: Williams 1926–7.

within communities that spoke only Welsh, and thus that Latin books were studied in clerical communities that never spoke Latin?

As we have seen already, spoken British Latin, as a language of the home, was dead, probably by *c.* 700. What we are asking, therefore, is whether ecclesiastical teachers taught their pupils to speak as well as to read Latin; and whether, if Latin was spoken, it was a language customarily used within the school, if not in the ecclesiastical community as a whole. Two categories of evidence offer the possibility of an answer to this and other questions – glossed manuscripts and colloquies designed as aids to the teaching of Latin. Yet although glossing may often bear some relationship to teaching, the evidence needs to be scrutinised.[58] Two rather different examples are the Cambridge Juvencus and the Oxford Ovid.[59] The latter consists of a copy of Ovid, *Ars amatoria*, Book I, on a single quire forming the last section of St Dunstan's Classbook, so-called because the different sections of the manuscript were brought together by St Dunstan before he ceased to be abbot of Glastonbury in 957.[60] The Juvencus is a complete manuscript of fifty-five folios, of which two are missing;[61] the glosses were written by several hands, but the main text was written by a single scribe, who wrote a colophon in which he named himself as Núadu and asked for prayers. The name is Irish, but the request was made in Old Welsh. Similarly, the glosses are mainly in Latin; most of those in the vernacular are in Welsh but a few are in Old Irish.[62] The evidence offered by this manuscript that an ecclesiastical community within Wales might contain Irishmen as well as Welshmen, and probably one Breton, has been challenged, but on insufficient grounds.[63]

In two ways, the manuscripts are quite different. It has been thought that a single scribe wrote the entire quire in St Dunstan's Classbook containing Ovid's *Ars Amatoria*, Book I, apart from the last leaf;[64] this is in an Anglo-Caroline hand which has been identified as that of St Dunstan. Yet it seems

58 The problems are examined by Lapidge 1982 (the Welsh Juvencus manuscript in Cambridge is discussed on pp. 111–13).

59 CUL, Ff.4.42 (*s.* ix² and x¹); facsimile and edition: McKee 2000a; the last section of BodL., Auct. F.4.32 (SC 2176), *s.* x¹; facs.: Hunt 1961.

60 Presumably before he was temporarily exiled in 956.

61 See McKee 2000a and 2000b.

62 The Welsh glosses were edited by Stokes 1860–1; the Irish glosses by Stokes and Strachan 1901–3, II, p. 44.

63 Harvey 1991. For the interpretation of the glossators' backgrounds and activities followed here, see McKee 2000a and 2000b. For a different example, where an Irish glossed text of Priscian's Latin grammar was copied in Brittany with Breton glosses, partly Brittonicised Irish glosses, and also some Welsh glosses, perhaps from a different source, see Lambert 1982.

64 This is asserted without discussion by Budny 1992, p. 115; the only dissentient voice of which I am aware is Conway 1997, p. 15, who distinguishes two scribes, of whom the first is clearly Hand A in my classification.

more likely that three Insular hands contributed: Hand A, an exceptionally accomplished scribe, wrote the text up to fol. 42r, line 18; Hand B from fol. 42r line 19 to the end of fol. 46r; Hand C wrote fol. 46v, while Hand D (St Dunstan) wrote the final page, fol. 47r.[65] Most of the glosses are in the section copied by Hand A (ll. 1–379 of Ovid's text). Once Hand B took over, he added glosses on seven further lines, ll. 383–9; then there was a long gap without any glosses until the last lines of fol. 45r. At that point there are glosses on ll. 623–52 (fol. 45r36–45v26). A possible partial explanation of this last burst of glossing is that, in the exemplar used by Hand B, there was one page of approximately thirty lines towards the end of Book I that contained glosses. In Hand B's copy, the thirty lines were not on a single page even though he wrote thirty-nine lines to a page. The exemplar may have been a smaller manuscript. Hands C and D wrote no glosses at all. In examining the glosses, therefore, we may be looking beyond the existing manuscript to one or more earlier books; the immediate exemplars were still Welsh, since both Hand A and Hand B wrote Welsh as well as Latin glosses to their own sections of the text, and there is no positive evidence that either added glosses beyond what they found before them. The Juvencus is a living text, even though it is a much less elegant production. The number of glossing hands working on a text that they themselves had not written contrasts with the Ovid manuscript, in which Hands A and B glossed text that they themselves had written. Whereas the Ovid manuscript is prodigal of space (the text is written by metrical lines), the Juvencus is not. The Ovid, then, is more likely to have been a patron's book, whereas the Juvencus was a school text.[66] Yet, behind the Ovid, there must have been an exemplar which, in some fundamental ways, was more like the Juvencus, a text in which the interpretation conveyed by the glosses was still being elaborated; and, on the other hand, some of the Juvencus glosses have been shown to have been copied.[67]

These two manuscripts thus suggest a double distinction within Welsh book production: between a patron's book and a school text, and between a text accompanied, as in the Juvencus, by an accumulating interpretation, and a text, such as the Ovid, whose interpretation has been arrested. But the character of the glossing, even when arrested, enables us to look behind the surviving manuscript to earlier books. Many of the glosses in the Ovid manuscript are elementary parsing, identifying cases of nouns and adjectives or identifying

65 Among other points of difference, Hand A and Hand B formed the letter **a** differently, while Hands B and C were much less accomplished scribes than Hand A.

66 Cf. Lapidge 1982, p. 126, who would deny the title 'classbook' to the manuscript as a whole.

67 *Ibid.*, pp. 111–13.

parts of speech. On the first page, but hardly, if at all, later, there are also what have been called 'syntax marks' or 'construe marks', namely marks to indicate syntactical relationships, such as agreement between a noun and adjective or a noun and a verb.[68] Of the lexical glosses most offer straightforward equivalents. When, therefore, these glosses or marks were first written, as opposed to when they were copied into our manuscript, they were of a thoroughly schoolroom character.

The idea that the glosses on the Ovid text derive from an earlier manuscript, or several, is supported by one more surprising example. In line 76, standard editions read:

> cultaque Iudaeo septimo sacra Syro

The last word, *Syro*, appears only in our manuscript, and even then only as a gloss: *deo* is what Hand A wrote in his text. What the exemplar may have had was not so much a gloss as an emendation, something such as *uel Syro*, 'or (rather) *Syro*'. This was then taken to be a gloss on *deo*, 'to the (Syrian) god'.

Indirectly, therefore, one surviving manuscript can tell us something about other manuscripts now lost – about a tradition of copying, of textual explanation and of annotation. The contrast between the Juvencus and the Ovid manuscript in terms of the quality of the penmanship and the relationship of the glossing hands to text hands suggests a corresponding difference in their use. The Juvencus manuscript was a working copy actually studied within a community, while the Ovid manuscript might derive its glosses from such working copies but was itself a grander product, betraying no evidence of current scholarly use, and perhaps belonging to an individual of high rank. In both manuscripts Latin glosses outnumbered Welsh ones, from which it may be inferred that both languages were used in schools, but that Latin had precedence.

Another indication that Latin had priority within pre-Norman Welsh education is the 'scholastic colloquy' entitled *De raris fabulis*, 'On rare expressions', known from Oxford, Bodleian Library, Bodley 572.[69] This is a Cornish manuscript but is itself a collection of distinct sections containing quite different texts.[70] *De raris fabulis* is one of these texts, contained in its own section of the manuscript; it has numerous Welsh as well as a few Cornish and English

68 Draak 1957; for indications of grammatical relationships in Brittonic manuscripts, see Lambert 1987.

69 SC 2026; Stevenson 1929, pp. 1–11; cf. Olson 1989, pp. 60–2; Lewis 1926–7, pp. 1–4; Williams 1929–31. Winterbottom 1968 offers an important discussion of another Insular colloquy (the 'Hisperic Colloquy'), no. II in Stevenson 1929, with connections with the *Hisperica famina*.

70 Lindsay 1912b, pp. 26–32, and plates XIV and XV.

glosses. These glosses are especially frequent on those lists of recondite words that gave the whole work its title. Although the glosses are mainly Welsh, the manuscript is written in a number of hands, partly Insular, but in the case of the *De raris fabulis*, Anglo-Caroline; moreover, the scribe that wrote the Welsh glosses also wrote the text. The likelihood, therefore, is that our portion of the manuscript was written in the second half of the tenth century in Cornwall.[71] Since the glosses were almost all written by the text hand, there is no difficulty in supposing that they were copied from the exemplar; and since the glosses are mainly Welsh, that exemplar is likely to have come from Wales.

The tradition of the colloquy as an aid in teaching a foreign language goes back to Antiquity.[72] The *De raris fabulis*, however, is very much a text of its place of composition, Celtic Britain,[73] and of the centuries between the end of spoken British Latin and the Norman Conquest. It delights in a (probably fictional) defeat of the English at the hands of the Britons, and it assumes that the teaching of Latin takes place within an ecclesiastical community of a distinctly unascetic tone. The terminology used for a church and its personnel is recognisably British.[74] Yet, though the immediate context is British, the individual scholar is assumed to be mobile. For the purposes of the dialogue, the pupil is to imagine himself as a foreigner, a *peregrinus*, who begs for the help of the *princeps*, the head of the church to which he has come. The *princeps* replies, 'Where were you?' To this the pupil answers, 'Till now I was reared or fostered [he is made to use two words to extend the range of vocabulary covered] in Ireland or in Britannia or in Francia.'[75] The relationship between teacher and taught is usually presented as one between two individuals, as analogous to fosterage rather than to simple inclusion within a group over which the teacher presides. Indeed, the connection between teaching and the ubiquitous institution of fosterage is likely to be one of the social foundations of early medieval Welsh (and Irish) culture.[76] Yet, while the primary relationship was a personal one between teacher and pupil, there were physical accoutrements: someone

71 Lindsay, *ibid.*, p. 28, argued against this position, but on grounds that, to my mind, cannot prevail against the combined evidence of the text's association with unquestionably Cornish sections of the manuscript and the Anglo-Caroline script. The latter had some impact in Wales, probably in the south-east, before the Norman Conquest, as shown by CCCC, 153, Martianus Capella: Bishop 1964–8a, whose Hand C, illustrated in Lindsay 1912b, plate IX/1, wrote in hybrid Insular-Caroline.

72 Marrou 1956, pp. 263–4, 268–7.

73 Mention of the *comes* as being in charge of a *civitas* and the *dux* in charge of twelve *civitates* suggests a Frankish link, and that might favour Brittany as the ultimate place of origin, if it were not for mention of the Britons defeating the English, *De raris fabulis*, § 24: Stevenson 1929, p. 9 (these *Saxones* are unlikely to be the Saxons of the Bessin, in spite of Gregory of Tours, *Histories*, x, 9).

74 E.g. 'abbas huius podi uel princeps huius loci': Stevenson 1929, p. 2, § 5 (fol. 42r).

75 *De raris fabulis*: Stevenson 1929, § 14.

76 Kerlouégan 1968–9, pp. 101–46.

might be instructed to look after not merely the teacher's goods, but 'especially the *scola* and the *bibliothicae librorum*',[77] the room in which instruction was given. In that room the book-cupboards were kept, including *libri canonici* (books of the canonical scriptures) and the *liber grammaticus, id est, Donaticus*, 'grammar-book, i.e. book of Donatus'.[78] In this *scola* the pupil would be taught 'the law of Latinity' as well as, later, the exegesis of the Bible. The colloquy was itself part of this instruction in 'the law of Latin', and must have been intended by its author to find a place in the *scola*'s book-cupboard, alongside the *Ars Minor* and *Ars Maior* of Donatus and other works. It shows that the intention remained to instruct the pupil to speak as well as to read and write Latin.

Yet the Latin culture of pre-Norman Wales remained very closely attached to the book. In the *De raris fabulis* the pupil asks to read, *legere*, with his teacher, *lector* 'reader'; what they are engaged in is *lectio*.[79] In a more general sense, *lector* could, occasionally, be used of the pupil himself. What they studied was, in Welsh, *llên*, from Latin *legenda*, 'those things that should be read'. When a teacher, such as the outstanding *magister* mentioned by Gildas, had more than one or two pupils, we must not imagine them all with copies of the text being studied, but rather that the teacher dictated a passage from a book, which he alone possessed, to be copied by each pupil on his wax tablet. Then he could proceed to expound the current portion of text: 'we shall leave nothing doubtful or obscure in it'.[80] The glosses suggest that the main language of exposition was Latin, but with occasional explanations of words by their Welsh equivalents.

This education was still intact at Llanbadarn Fawr in Ceredigion, and at Llancarfan in Morgannwg in the late eleventh century. Llanbadarn was the home of the best-known scholarly family of Wales before the Gregorian reform, in alliance with Anglo-Norman control of the church, introduced fundamental change. This family is known to us principally through a Latin poem by Ieuan ap Sulien, *Carmen Iohannis de vita et familia Sulgeni*.[81] In this poem Ieuan celebrates his native kingdom, Ceredigion, and declares that his father, Sulien, was born at Llanbadarn Fawr 'of a distinguished stock of parents', who were 'always wise'.[82] Here *sapiens* is likely, on Irish evidence, to mean 'scholar' in the sense of someone who had the attainments required to give him high rank through his learning. This was the public recognition that had enabled his

77 *De raris fabulis*, § 4: Stevenson 1929, p. 2.

78 *De raris fabulis*, § 6: Stevensons 1929, p. 3; Middle Welsh *dwned* is a loan from ME, but there may well have been an earlier borrowing directly from Latin, **Dunodig*.

79 *De raris fabulis*, § 6: Stevenson 1929, p. 3. 80 *Ibid.*

81 It is edited and translated by Lapidge 1973–4, at pp. 80–9.

82 *Carmen*, ll. 86–7.

predecessors to appear alongside bishops, anchorites and the greater abbots in synods. Sulien, therefore, came from a family of scholars, but his own learning was not merely home-grown. When, as an *infans* (up to seven years), he learnt his Latin psalter, he was also taught to write it out.[83] He then went to other Welsh schools; and subsequently, although intending to go to study in Ireland, he was blown off course to Scotland, where he studied the traditional seven liberal arts for five years. He subsequently went to Ireland, where he studied the Bible. There is nothing fundamental to distinguish either the curriculum or the mobile pattern of study from the experience of the young Leinsterman, Columbanus, in the third quarter of the sixth century. He went from early studies in Leinster to the school of a teacher called Sinilis, and then finally to Bangor (near Belfast). Stages in education might be punctuated by journeys from one teacher to the next. The education of Sulien also illustrates the enduring connections between those Celtic countries that had been brought closer together by the great missionary campaigns of the fifth and sixth centuries. There were to be signs in the twelfth century that Armagh might have developed a university, but by then Wales, at least for Latin studies, was no longer part of the same cultural province.[84]

The Norman invasion of Dyfed in 1093 was a disaster for the old learned tradition, based as it was on family tradition allied with hereditary church possessions. At least one member of the family would hold an important ecclesiastical office in the new Wales,[85] but the hold of the family on the church of Llanbadarn was at an end. Another poem, by a brother of Ieuan, Rhygyfarch (who also wrote the *Life of St David*), is a lament for a Wales subjected to the Norman yoke:[86]

> Nothing is of any use to me now but the power of giving: neither the law, nor learning, nor great fame, nor the deep-resounding glory of nobility, not honour formerly held, not riches, not wise teaching, not deeds nor arts, not reverence of God, not old age; none of these things retains its station, nor any power. Now the labours of earlier days are despised; the people and the priest are despised by the word, heart and work of the Normans.

83 I thus interpret *edidit*, l. 88.

84 This is suggested by the ruling of the Synod of Clane, recorded in the Annals of Ulster, *s.a.* 1162, that 'no one should be a lector in any church in Ireland unless he were an alumnus of Armagh', and the grant made by Ruaidrí Ua Conchobair, king of Ireland (Annals of Ulster, *s.a.* 1169), 'to the lector of Armagh, in honour of St Patrick, to provide teaching to students from Ireland and Scotland'.

85 Daniel ap Sulien died in 1127 as archdeacon in Powys: Jones 1952, *s.a.*; his son, Cedifor ap Daniel, died in 1163 as archdeacon of Ceredigion (*ibid. s.a.* 1162 = 1163).

86 *Planctus Ricemarch*: Lapidge 1973–4, pp. 88–91, ll. 8–17.

17

The biblical manuscripts of Anglo-Saxon England

RICHARD MARSDEN

Introduction

In the spring of 716 eighty monks, including the ailing Abbot Ceolfrith, left the twin monastery of Wearmouth-Jarrow in Northumbria, travelled down to the south coast and crossed the Channel to begin the long trek through France and over the Alps to Rome. Among the gifts for St Peter's in their baggage was a huge Bible. It weighed about 32 kilos and was 250 mm thick, with 1,030 pages of 505 × 340 mm. On the verso of fol. 1 was a florid dedicatory inscription in Latin metres:

> To the body of the illustrious Peter, justly to be honoured, whom lofty faith consecrates head of the church, I, Ceolfrith, abbot from the farthest ends of England, send tokens of my devoted feeling, desiring for me and mine that we may have for ever a remembered place in the heavens, among the joys of so great a father.[1]

The abbot died in France during the journey, but the bible appears to have reached St Peter's. It survives today in Florence and is known as the Codex Amiatinus, having spent many years at the monastery of San Salvatore at Monte Amiata.[2] As the earliest surviving complete Vulgate Bible anywhere, its importance is inestimable and it is one of the greatest monuments of English book-making.

At almost the same time that the Northumbrian monks were heading for Rome, the Anglo-Saxon missionary Boniface, from Wessex, was beginning forty years of work among the heathen Germans.[3] From time to time he would write home with requests for books, and in one letter he asked Eadburh,

1 For Latin text, see Marsden 1995b, p. 88.

2 Florence, Biblioteca Medicea-Laurenziana, Amiatino 1. *CLA*, III, no. 299; Marsden 1995b, pp. 108–23; Marsden 2008b.

3 Talbot 1954, pp. 25–62.

abbess of Minster-in-Thanet, Kent, to copy out for him, in letters of gold, 'the Epistles of my lord, St Peter, that a reverence and love of the Holy Scriptures may be impressed on the minds of the heathens to whom I preach'.[4] In a subsequent letter to the bishop of Winchester, Boniface, whose eyesight was failing, had a more practical request, for a volume he remembered using in England, 'in which six prophets are to be found together ... written out in full with clear letters'.[5] When Boniface was murdered in Germany by a pagan mob, they found in his boxes many more scriptural volumes which were presumably without physical adornment, for the mob threw them away as worthless. They were said to have been recovered later from fields and marshes, miraculosuly unharmed, and were returned to the monastery of Fulda.[6]

The activities of Ceolfrith and Boniface give us valuable insights into the history of the Anglo-Saxon Bible. First, it is clear that the monasteries of the north and the south of England were able by the eighth century to produce biblical manuscripts of high quality and in numbers exceeding their own requirements. Second, an essential aspect of the transmission of scripture in the early medieval period was the part-bible. As Amiatinus proves, the concept of 'the Bible' as a single volume or pandect containing all the canonical books of the Old and New Testaments, was in fact well known (and had been since at least the sixth century), but in practice such volumes were a comparative rarity until the ninth century. For both economic and practical reasons, the Bible circulated predominantly in separate parts.[7] Third, the biblical volume was often more than merely a vehicle to transmit the sacred texts. The Codex Amiatinus was an iconic gift designed to advertise the achievements of the monastery at the ends of the earth and win status for the giver in the Roman church. Equally, Boniface's 'golden' epistles (assuming his request for them was granted) were to be a symbol of militant Christianity, an artefact whose splendour might make it a potent catalyst of conversion. Fourth, for our knowledge of the Anglo-Saxon Bible we are dependent on the vagaries of manuscript survival and chance report in secondary sources. Were it not, for instance, for the information available from two contemporary chroniclers, one of them Bede, we would have no idea that Amiatinus was only one of three such great volumes made under Ceolfrith; scraps of a second have in fact survived as wrappers for estate documents but there is no trace of the third.[8] None of Boniface's scriptural volumes appears to be extant and we would know nothing of them but for the fact that his correspondence has been preserved. Hundreds of other

4 Tangl 1916, no. 35; Talbot 1954, p. 91. 5 Tangl 1916, no. 63; Talbot 1954, p. 118.
6 Whitelock 1979, no. 158. 7 McGurk 1994, p. 1.
8 Marsden 1995b, pp. 123–9; and see below on Offa's Bible.

biblical manuscripts must have been in use by the Anglo-Saxons of which no fragment survives and on which the record is silent.

I have deliberately started my account with a complete pandect and volumes of New Testament epistles and Old Testament prophets, rather than with the more celebrated Anglo-Saxon gospel-books, in order to emphasise the inclusive nature of the concept of 'the Bible' at this time. Raw statistics can foster a lopsided view: seventy-three of the ninety biblical manuscripts of Anglo-Saxon provenance extant from the period are (or were once part of) gospel-books. There is no doubt that the gospels were indeed the most copied and distributed section of the Bible, but their survival rate is disproportionate. Three-quarters of the extant gospel-books are high-quality, high-status volumes, likely to have been the treasured possessions of churches, cults or even individuals. Great care was taken to preserve them. In general, other part-bibles did not receive such treatment, and their survival was much more precarious. If we extend our view to the whole of Western Christendom, we find that gospel-books constitute a much smaller proportion –40 per cent of some 350 extant biblical manuscripts made before about 800[9] – but that is still likely to be an inflated figure. In this chapter I aim to give fair weight to other part-bibles, from both the Old and New Testaments, as well as to the far less numerous complete bibles.

The story of the Anglo-Saxon Bible is of course inseparable from the story of the establishment of Anglo-Saxon Christianity. It is a truism that Christianity is a religion of the book. Jerome noted in the prologue to his commentary on Isaiah that 'he who does not know the scriptures does not know the power and wisdom of God, and he who is ignorant of the scriptures is ignorant of Christ, for scripture opens the kingdom'.[10] For the missionary, the material presence of the word is essential. For the priest, the tools of the trade are a psalter and service-books which will include a gospel-book or gospel-lectionary, along with further reading books containing other necessary sections of the Bible. For the monk, the conviction that God speaks through scripture is taken to its logical conclusion; the reading aloud of the Bible, and meditation on it, are the framework of everyday life.

The Bible with which we deal here is almost exclusively the Vulgate. But we must remember that to talk of 'the' Vulgate in the earlier medieval period is misleading, for this was an age of fluid textual traditions. Biblical manuscripts may vary considerably in their textual details, often with apparent randomness but sometimes in ways which enable us to identify discrete textual traditions,

9 McGurk 1994, pp. 3–4. 10 Adriaen 1963, p. 1.

associated perhaps with a specific redactor or known copying centre. Pre-Vulgate Latin textual traditions, which are conveniently subsumed under the catch-all heading 'Old Latin', feature only occasionally in our story, notably in connection with the Codex Aureus (discussed below) and with some early Irish manuscripts. The Latin Bible was dominant in England until the Reformation, but the foundations of scripture in English were already being laid during the Anglo-Saxon period, and in a final section I shall deal briefly with the beginnings of the vernacular Bible.

The bibles of the Anglo-Saxons were not the first known in Britain. It is likely that Christianity reached the Roman-occupied territory during the later second century, as a result of individual commercial and military contacts between Britain and Gaul, rather than through missionary activity.[11] The new religion seems to have made steady progress during the third century, though suffering a period of persecution during which St Alban became the first recorded British martyr. By the mid fourth century, following the official acceptance of Christianity by Rome, the British church, though probably always small, was sufficiently organised to be sending bishops to meetings abroad; and the author of a noted heresy, Pelagius, was a Briton, born *c.* 380. Christianity had spread to Ireland by the fifth century and during the latter half of that century, even as the pagan Anglo-Saxons were settling in, and coming to dominate, what we now call England, it was establishing itself in southern Scotland. The British church would continue intact in the Anglo-Saxon period and there is evidence of constructive co-existence between it and the evolving English church.[12] The first biblical volumes will have come from Gaul, Italy or Spain, but it is probable that extra copies and replacements were then made locally. It is unlikely that there were any complete bibles among them, for, as I have noted, they seem to have been a rarity in Christendom before the ninth century and would have required massive resources for their production. From a study of the writings of the sixth-century British historian Gildas, and St Patrick in Ireland, we can even deduce something of the textual character of the biblical material being used – a mix of Old Latin and Vulgate versions, it would seem, a situation confirmed in rare fragments of bibles survivng from early medieval Ireland.[13] There is no reason to think that the British church's books – arguably the earliest British books of all – were not in the conventional form of the parchment codex. However, none of them

11 Deanesly 1963, pp. 1–40; Thomas 1981, pp. 79–83; Frend 2003.
12 Mayr-Harting 1972, pp. 118–20.
13 Burkitt 1934; Bieler 1947; Doyle 1976; McNamara 1987, pp. 33–9.

Table 17.1 *Biblical manuscripts from pre-Conquest England, by type*

Complete bibles	6 (including 4 fragments)
Part-bibles (OT):	
Prophets	2 (both fragments)
Maccabees	1 (fragment)
Pentateuch	2 (both fragments)
Wisdom	1
Part-bibles (NT):	
Gospel-books	73 (including 17 fragments)
Acts	2
Pauline Epistles	2 (one a fragment)

survives, even fragmentarily, and so our story must begin from the conversion of the Anglo-Saxons.

The evidence

The physical evidence for the history of the Bible in England before the Norman Conquest is a corpus of ninety manuscripts ranging from complete volumes to single scraps of parchment. This evidence, which includes books imported into England, as well as those copied there, is summarised in Table 17.1 Excluded from this list are several complete bibles produced around the close of the eleventh century, because they are more appropriately thought of as early Norman than Anglo-Saxon. As I note below, one was certainly copied in Normandy and the texts of the others show the clear influence of newly imported exemplars from the Continent.

The judgement as to whether a manuscript fragment derives from a complete bible or a part-bible has been made on the basis of page size. The more substantial body of Continental survivals confirms what the Anglo-Saxon evidence suggests, namely that there is a direct correlation between size and form. Complete bibles have larger pages than part-bibles, for more material is to be contained within a single volume; part-bibles can have smaller pages and are as a consequence more manageable.[14] The two complete Anglo-Saxon bibles, and the four manuscripts identified as coming originally from such bibles, are between 470 and 560 mm high and 335 and 365 mm wide. The

14 A significant anomaly in the Continental record is provided by the pandects made under the direction of Theodulf at Orléans at the turn of the eighth century; these measure only about 320 × 240 mm. Marsden 1995b, pp. 19–22.

manuscripts which I have identified as deriving from Old Testament part-bibles are between 250 and 350 mm high and 180 and 260 mm wide. In broad terms, the dimensions of gospel-books are similar: height ranges from 225 to 350 mm, and width from 165 to 275 mm.[15]

The above corpus of evidence, as indicated already, cannot be considered to give us a balanced view of the Anglo-Saxon bible. What have survived disproportionately are the most precious and elaborate volumes; this applies of course to the Codex Amiatinus but more especially and consistently to the gospel-books. That the picture supplied by our group of survivors is woefully incomplete may be deduced from a comparison of texts. Even competent scribes make errors and sometimes deliberate emendations, so that each copy differs from its exemplar; the differences are then transmitted when that copy serves in turn as an exemplar for more copies, when some errors or emendations may be corrected but new ones will be introduced. Representative manuscripts copied in such a chain are quite easily identifiable, and, if there are enough of them, can even be placed in their proper order of copying. However, with only a few exceptions (such as the series of 'Judith' gospel-books discussed below), our earlier Anglo-Saxon biblical monuments do not show any such intimate connection with others in the corpus. This suggests that several, and often many, copying generations – and thus many lost copies – separate our various biblical manuscripts from each other. Part of the explanation may also be that many more exemplars from abroad were being used, with their own idiosyncrasies of text, than is evident from the surviving corpus. The textual history of the early medieval Vulgate, of which our Anglo-Saxon material is a part, is a three-dimensional jigsaw puzzle, from which most of the pieces are now missing.

We shall consider our material in two broad chronological groups. The first, from the Gregorian mission of 597 to *c.* 850, encompasses the conversions, the school of Theodore and Hadrian at Canterbury and the Northumbrian 'golden age' centred round Bede in the early eighth century, and it draws to a close in the early ninth century in an extended period of ecclesiastical, monastic and political decline consequent at least in part on the depredations of Viking raiders.[16] The later period begins with the renaissance of learning instigated by King Alfred (d. 899) and encompasses the crucial monastic reform and expansion of the second half of the tenth century, in which learning and literature revived, and it ends with the coming of the Normans in 1066. Like all such

15 Exceptional are two gospel-books discussed below: the Stonyhurst Gospel of John (135 × 93 mm) and the Codex Aureus (395 × 320 mm).

16 Gneuss 1986, pp. 673–6; Morrish 1986, pp. 97–9.

divisions of complex historical processes, this one is over-simple. There is good evidence, for instance, that the kingdom of Mercia (with Worcester as its most important centre) was subject to no disastrous decline in its monasteries, and thus in learning, during the ninth century.[17] Indeed, the Alfredian renaissance in Wessex was to an important extent underpinned by the efforts of Mercian scholars (and at least one from further west, in Wales) and Mercian literary traditions. And a significant biblical manuscript to which I have already alluded – a sister pandect to the Codex Amiatinus, made in Northumbria around 700 – helps to prove continuity of a sort. It was in Worcester by about 800 and seems to have been used for copying there, for its very distinctive text of Tobit is found in a manuscript produced in the south-west, probably Cornwall, in the late ninth or earlier tenth century.[18] Further evidence of continued scholarly activity in westerly parts of the country is furnished by a gospel-book now in Bern, which was copied in the late eighth or early ninth century, probably in the south-west but possibly in Wales.[19]

The manuscripts 597 – *c.* 850

From the earlier period there is evidence for three complete bibles (two of them represented only by fragments), six Old Testament part-bibles (five of them fragmentary), thirty-nine gospel-books (seventeen fragmentary, several others incomplete), and four other New Testament part-bibles (one fragmentary), two containing Acts and two the epistles of Paul.

The conversion of Anglo-Saxon England was effected by missions originating in both Ireland (via Iona) and Italy, and these countries were sources for the earliest biblical manuscripts to reach the Anglo-Saxons. Surviving Irish evidence, however, is very slim, probably because the less formal nature of the manuscripts and the less 'mainline' character of their texts meant that they were less likely to be preserved. Most of the imported manuscripts came from Italy, and the earliest is a small gospel-book long associated with St Augustine's mission to Kent in 597. The 'St Augustine's Gospels', as it is still known, had been copied in Italy in the sixth century and originally contained several pages of illustrations, though only two survive.[20] The volume is a suitably portable one, measuring only 245 × 180 mm, and it would be nice to be able to affirm that it had indeed been in the luggage of the saint when he landed in 597, but there is no proof. It could instead have been among the other manuscripts

17 Lapidge 1996, p. 425. 18 Marsden 1994.
19 Bern, Burgerbibliothek, 671. Ker 1957, no. 6.
20 CCCC, 286. *CLA*, II, no. 126; Gameson 1999b, pp. 318–22; Marsden 1999.

which, according to Bede, Gregory was soon sending to Kent.[21] Emendations made to its text confirm only that it had arrived in England by the eighth century. But even if this gospel-book were indeed St Augustine's, it was probably not the first known to the southern English. The Kentish king, Æthelberht, though a pagan, had married Bertha, daughter of King Charibert of Paris and granddaughter of Clovis, some ten to fifteen years before Augustine's arrival. A Christian, she was accompanied by Bishop Liudhard as her personal chaplain, and he will have needed service-books, a psalter, and probably a copy of the gospels for use at his church of St Martin's in Canterbury.[22]

We do not know how soon after Augustine's arrival at Canterbury books were being copied there, or elsewhere in the south. As the mission progressed, the demand for biblical and liturgical volumes must have been pressing and could not for long have been met simply by imports. Certainly before the end of the seventh century charters, at least, were being written in Uncial in Kent, as well as in Mercia and Essex.[23] From the 630s, or earlier, Canterbury had been the site of a remarkable school which would win renown for the range of its erudition in both secular and sacred learning and be highly praised by Bede.[24] In its heyday in the latter part of the century, it was run by the newly appointed archbishop (667–90), the Greek expatriate Theodore, and his assistant Hadrian, an African.[25] There can be little doubt that Hadrian and Theodore brought books with them from Rome, probably including biblical volumes. None survives, but exegetical comments on the Bible derived directly from notes taken in the Canterbury classroom do, and the textual form of Vulgate citations in these notes offers some evidence that Italian manuscripts different from those available more or less contemporaneously in the north – and so presumably imported independently – were in use at Canterbury.[26]

Documentary sources add further information. A gospel-book is mentioned by Bede in connection with Theodore's duties at the Synod of Hatfield in 679, for instance,[27] and the correspondence of Boniface provides clear evidence that the monasteries of southern England had books of scripture for export.[28] Less reliable, though probably with some basis in fact, is an account by the early twelfth-century historian, William of Malmesbury (who died *c.* 1143), of how a complete bible was acquired by Aldhelm, bishop of Sherborne, an alumnus

21 Colgrave and Mynors 1969, p. 104.
22 Hunter Blair 1990, pp. 215–16; Brooks 1984, pp. 5–6.
23 Sawyer 1968, no. 8; Webster and Backhouse 1991, no. 27.
24 Colgrave and Mynors 1969, pp. 332–4.
25 Lapidge 1986b, pp. 45–72.
26 Marsden 1995c; Bischoff and Lapidge 1994.
27 Marsden 1995b, p. 62 and n. 7.
28 Boniface obtained books directly from Northumbria also.

of Theodore's Canterbury school.[29] When walking one day near Dover, he was offered the bible by some sailors from Gaul, but their price was too high. They put back to sea but a storm blew up and only Aldhelm's prayerful intervention saved them. Now the sailors were happy to sell him the bible at a more reasonable price, and it was still to be seen at Malmesbury in the twelfth century, according to William.

The earliest identifiable biblical manuscript produced south of the Humber is a copy of Acts, written by two scribes in a Kentish form of Uncial.[30] Its medieval provenance was St Augustine's Abbey, Canterbury, but it was conceivably copied under the aegis of St Boniface's correspondent, Abbess Eadburh, at Minster-in-Thanet. A few years after this, the Vespasian Psalter, the first known witness to the Romanum text of the psalms, was made at St Augustine's,[31] and towards the middle of the eighth century came the Codex Aureus, the most luxurious of all Anglo-Saxon gospel-books, and the largest at 395 x 320 mm (Plates 4.3 and 8.2–3).[32] The book was at Christ Church, Canterbury,by the second half of the ninth century but may equally have been made at St Augustine's or, less likely, Minster-in-Thanet. One of the many remarkable features of this gospel-book is its text, which is in places a hybrid of Old Latin and Vulgate readings without direct parallel in other known copies. Three other gospel-books, two surviving only fragmentarily but both approaching the Codex Aureus in size, while the other (the Codex Bigotianus) is a little smaller, bear witness to the production of further fine manuscripts in Kent in the eighth century.[33] That this tradition continued into the ninth century is shown by the surviving remnants of a complete bible.[34] Only seventy-nine leaves carrying the gospels and part of Acts, written in Half-Uncials and hybrid minuscule script, are extant, but they are enough to show what a sumptuous volume it was, with its elaborate decoration in gold and silver and its purple pages; originally it contained a full programme of illustrative miniatures. Some scholars, on the basis of a fourteenth-century library inscription from St Augustine's, have identified this book with the so-called *Biblia Gregoriana*, supposedly directly associated with the great pope, but this is unlikely.[35]

29 Hamilton 1870, pp. 377–8.

30 BodL., Selden Supra 30 (3418). *CLA*, II, no. 257; Gameson 1999b, pp. 327–30.

31 BL, Cotton Vespasian A.i. *CLA*, II, no. 193; Gameson 1999b, pp. 330–6. See also Chapter 8 in the present volume.

32 Stockholm, KB, A.135. *CLA*, XI, no. 1642; Gameson 2001–2.

33 BL, Add. 37518, fols. 116–17; St Petersburg, Russian National Library, O.v.I.1 + Avranches, BM, 48, fols. i and iii, 68, fols. i–ii and 71, fols. A–B; and BnF, lat. 281. *CLA*, II, no. 176, VI, no. 730, and V, no. 526; Gameson 1999b, pp. 346–56.

34 BL, Royal 1 E.vi + Canterbury CL, Add. 16 + BodL., Lat. bib. b.2 (P) (2202). *CLA*, II, nos. 214, 244; Webster and Backhouse 1991, no. 171; Budny 1985.

35 Budny 1999, pp. 254–8.

Evidence of the production of biblical manuscripts in the south outside Kent is rare, but one such may be an Old Testament part-bible, perhaps a Pentateuch or Heptateuch, of which four leaves survive in three separate locations.[36] Written in a set minuscule, possibly in Mercia, at the close of the eighth or the beginning of the ninth century, the fragments carry parts of Numbers and Deuteronomy. The text of the lattter includes the canticle *Audite caeli* and the fact that this is marked by two elaborate snake-heads might suggest that this book (which is not simply a lectionary) was used liturgically.

Whatever the activities in Southumbria, the bulk of the early evidence for the Anglo-Saxon bible derives from the north. Some of the manuscripts used there initially certainly came from Ireland in the wake of Aidan's mission, but we have only indirect evidence of this. A gospel-book made in Northumbria in the mid seventh century, for instance, was copied from an Irish exemplar, to judge from its text,[37] and the version of the psalms used in the Codex Amiatinus (Jerome's final revision from the Hebrew) appears to be of Irish origin also.[38] Irish influence is especially visible in the style of decoration of Northumbrian gospel-books.

The evidence for manuscripts of Italian origin, on the other hand, is abundant. A leaf from a codex copied in Italy in the sixth century, which reached England in the second half of the seventh century, survives in the library of Durham Cathedral; it has text from Maccabees and was used as an exemplar in the making of Ceolfrith's three pandects.[39] An Italian manuscript containing Acts in Latin and Greek, dating from the sixth or seventh century, was in Northumbria by the time of Bede, who may have used it.[40] Both of these codices – part-bibles, to judge by their size – may have been brought to England by Benedict Biscop, avid book collector and founder of the twin monasteries of Wearmouth-Jarrow. In a rare description of the mechanics of importing books into Anglo-Saxon England, we learn from Bede that Benedict made five visits to Rome, returning with books as well as relics, paintings and other sacred objects. In 671, for instance, he brought back 'a large number of books on all aspects of sacred knowledge', and two years later 'a great mass of books of every sort'.[41] That these included biblical

36 BodL., Lat. bib. c.8 (P) + Salisbury CL, 117, fols. 163–4 + Tokyo, Toshiyuki Takamiya Collection, 21. *CLA*, II, no. 259; Marsden 1995b, pp. 240–9.

37 A dozen leaves are preserved in DCL, A.II.10, fols. 2–5, 338–9 + C.III.13, fols. 192–5 + C.III.20, fols. 1–2. *CLA*, II, no. 147; Alexander 1978b, no. 5; Verey 1989, pp. 145–6.

38 Marsden 1995b, p. 141.

39 DCL, B.IV.6. Marsden 1995b, pp. 83–5.

40 BodL., Laud gr. 35 (1119). *CLA*, II, no. 251; Laistner 1957, pp. 157–9.

41 Plummer 1896, pp. 369 and 391.

volumes is not in doubt, and one of them is specifically mentioned, a pandect with a text in the Old Latin tradition.[42] It has been argued persuasively that this was originally one of the bibles used by the civil servant turned scholar, Cassiodorus, at Vivarium in Italy in the late sixth century.[43] But Biscop was not the only ecclesiastic indulging his passion for collecting books, using the wealth with which the church of this period was well endowed by royal or noble patrons. Wilfrid, bishop of Hexham (died 709), spent time in both Italy and Gaul and introduced relics and treasures into the churches under his control, and his successor, Acca, was praised by Bede for a 'very large and most noble library', which included passions and other ecclesiastical books.[44] One of Wilfrid's treasures was a gospel-book commissioned (perhaps on the Continent) for the new church at Ripon and written, so Stephen of Ripon tells us, 'in purest gold on purpled parchment, and illustrated'.[45] The manuscript was considered important enough to be included in Wilfrid's epitaph, but it has not survived.[46] There must have been substantial libraries also at Lindisfarne, Ripon and Hexham; and that at York, built up by the founder of the school there, Ælberht, is known from an account of it in a poem by Alcuin, to whom it was beqeathed.[47]

In sum, it would seem that by the closing decades of the seventh century Northumbria's monastic and ecclesiastical libraries were well stocked with imported manuscripts of Italian and, to an uncertain extent, Irish origin, while home scriptoria were now producing volumes of their own, using the imported books as exemplars. We know most about production in the scriptorium – or perhaps scriptoria – of Wearmouth-Jarrow.[48] Abbot Ceolfrith, who had become head of the twin house after Benedict's death in 688, decided to have three pandects made.[49] The first two were to be placed in the two home churches of St Peter at Wearmouth and St Paul at Jarrow, for the convenience of the monks; the Codex Amiatinus, which was completed by 716, was destined for Rome, to be presented to St Peter's. The production of the three pandects shows us plainly what massive financial resources were available to Ceolfrith: more than 1,500 calf skins were required for the three books.[50] The Codex Amiatinus (like its two sister pandects, as far as we can tell) carries the complete Vulgate text of both testaments, written in a consistently excellent Uncial script which had been developed by the native scribes

42 *Ibid.*, p. 379. 43 Marsden 1995b, pp. 116–23.
44 Colgrave and Mynors 1969, p. 530. 45 Colgrave 1927, p. 36.
46 Colgrave and Mynors 1969, pp. 528–30.
47 Gneuss 1986; Godman 1982, pp. lxii–lxxv and 120–6. 48 Parkes 1982.
49 Plummer 1896, pp. 379 and 395; Marsden 1995b, pp. 85–106.
50 Gameson 1992a; Parkes 1982.

of Northumbria on the basis of Italian models. There are three magnificent painted miniatures: a two-page depiction of the tabernacle, a full-page Christ in Majesty, and the so-called 'Ezra miniature'.[51] In the foreground of this last, a scholar in the vestments of a high priest is at work with his pen in an open volume, presumably of scripture. On the shelves of the large cupboard behind him are the nine volumes of a bible, their titles – no longer easy to read – on the spines. A Latin epigraph to the picture reveals that, ostensibly at least, the scholar is the prophet Ezra, famed for the part he played in the survival of the Jewish nation during the Babylonian capitivity by preserving the scriptures. The miniature was probably copied into Amiatinus from a version in the Old Latin pandect which Benedict Biscop had brought to Wearmouth-Jarrow from Italy and which may have belonged to Cassiodorus. If this is so, it is possible that the 'Ezra' figure represented Cassiodorus himself, though this has been disputed.[52] Whatever the case, the miniature implicitly endorses and sanctifies the work of the monastic scriptorium in the propagation of the written word.

One of the two pandects placed in the churches at Wearmouth and Jarrow subsequently disappeared without trace, perhaps destroyed during Viking attacks in the 790s. The other found its way to Worcester towards the end of the eighth century, where it can be identified with the bible known as 'Offa's Bible', given by the celebrated eighth-century king of Mercia to the cathedral priory there. As to how Offa came by the book, one theory is that it was stolen by the Vikings and that Offa paid a ransom for it; another is that it was a gift from the king of Northumbria, made on the occasion of Offa's marriage to the king's daughter in 792. Offa's Bible seems to have survived intact at Worcester until the Reformation, when it was broken up and some of the leaves used as document binders in the estate office of an English man of property. By great good fortune a dozen of these leaves turned up in three separate locations during the twentieth century.[53]

A number of Uncial gospel-book leaves now bound with other books were probably also copied at Wearmouth-Jarrow.[54] The best-known complete book from there is the Stonyhurst Gospel of John, but this is in what has come to be known as 'capitular Uncial', a smaller form of the trademark house script, developed initially for copying non-scriptural items in the great pandects.

51 Bruce-Mitford 1968, pp. 9–14; Marsden 1995a, pp. 3–15, plate 6.

52 Marsden 1995b, pp. 116–23; Meyvaert 1996.

53 BL, Add. 37777 + Add. 45025 + Loan 81. *CLA*, II, no. 177; Webster and Backhouse 1991, no. 87a–c; and Marsden 1995b, pp. 90–8 and plate II.

54 Parkes 1982, p. 4.

Such a script was appropriate for a volume measuring only 135 × 90 mm.[55] The Stonyhurst John, which is still in its original binding, was found in the coffin of St Cuthbert, the greatest of the northern saints (*c.* 635–87), when his relics were transferred in 1104 to the sanctuary of the newly built Durham Cathedral. It had perhaps been presented by the Wearmouth-Jarrow community to Lindisfarne on the occasion of the exhumation and elevation of Cuthbert in 698. By the mid 740s, Wearmouth-Jarrow had followed other Northumbrian houses in developing an Insular minuscule script, but no biblical manuscripts in a minuscule, or intermediate, script seem to have been produced there.

A dazzling series of decorated gospel-books proves that other Northumbrian centres rivalled Wearmouth-Jarrow in the quality, if probably not in the quantity, of their output. In some cases there is uncertainty about which side of the Irish Sea specific works were copied, and this reminds us of the vital debt of Northumbria to Ireland. The Lindisfarne Gospels, made at the monastery on Lindisfarne (or Holy Island), neatly encapsulates the meeting of Celtic and Roman Christianity, for, while much of its decorative vocabulary is of Irish ancestry, its evangelist portraits and above all its text were copied from Italian exemplars (Plates 4.1 and 8.1).[56] No expense seems to have been spared in its production, for it was created especially to adorn the shrine of St Cuthbert, who had been bishop of Lindisfarne and was buried there. When the monks of Lindisfarne abandoned their island in 875 under Viking threat, the gospel-book, the body of Cuthbert and other relics went with them on an epic seven years of wandering before they found a resting place at Chester-le-Street, where they stayed until their removal to Durham, their final home, in 995. At Chester-le-Street, a complete Old English interlinear gloss was added above the Latin text.

Several other gospel-books of possible Northumbrian origin have been attributed to Lindisfarne also, but our knowledge of the scriptorium there is very limited.[57] The most plausible candidate is the Durham Gospels (see Frontispiece), which is written, like the Lindisfarne Gospels, in formal Half-Uncials.[58] There are close artistic and palaeographical links between Durham and Lindisfarne, but textually there are differences which may suggest an earlier date for the Durham book, and aspects of the prefatory matter are firmly in an Irish tradition.[59] The Echternach Gospels has

55 BL, Loan 74. *CLA*, II, no. 260; McGurk 1961, no. 37; Webster and Backhouse 1991, no. 86; Brown 1969.

56 BL, Cotton Nero D.iv. *CLA*, II, no. 187; McGurk 1961, no. 22; Alexander 1978b, no. 9; Webster and Backhouse 1991, no. 80; Backhouse 1981; Kendrick *et al.* 1956–60 (facsimile). See also Chapters 4 and 8 in the present volume.

57 Brown 1989, pp. 151–63.

58 DCL, A.II.17 + Cambridge, Magdelene College, Pepys 2981 (19). *CLA*, II, no. 149; Verey *et al.* 1980.

59 Verey 1989, p. 146.

been attributed to Lindisfarne also, but with far less certainty. Whatever its origins, it ended up at the monastery after which it has been named (in what is now Luxembourg), founded in 698 by Willibrord, an Irish missionary of Northumbrian birth.[60] Textually it differs from both Lindisfarne and Durham, with an apparent mix of Irish and Italian traditions, and a colophon transmits a claim for descent from a manuscript belonging to Jerome himself; the text was later emended to incorporate more pronounced Irish readings. Echternach may share a scribe with Durham, but this does not prove an origin at Lindisfarne itself. Lindisfarne, Durham and Echternach are characteristic of the complex story of the Northumbrian gospel-book. It involves the conscious adoption of an Italian text (most clearly seen in Lindisfarne itself), but this was then likely to be subject to alterations under the influence of Irish textual traditions; ancillary elements in the Irish tradition were often much in evidence also.

There is a further range of contemporary gospel-books which reveal an altogether different concept, in terms of economy of effort and cost of production, from that which inspired the Lindisfarne Gospels and similar books. One such volume is British Library, Royal 1 B.vii, a gospel-book probably copied in Northumbria some time during the eighth century, but about which little else is known – except that it was still in use in 925, according to a manumission mentioning King Athelstan, entered in a blank space on fol. 15v.[61] It is a competent but calligrapically unambitious work, written in irregular Half-Uncials far smaller and more cramped than those of the great presentation volumes, and it is copied on low-quality parchment; indeed, almost every detail of its realisation sets it apart from the Lindisfarne Gospels.[62] Such comparatively poor quality is hard to find among extant gospel-books, though another example is the Hereford Gospels, which was copied quite late in the eighth century, perhaps in the West Midlands or even Wales, for the hastily writtten hybrid Insular minuscule script shows Celtic influences.[63] The book is not without decoration but this is unambitious (with only two colours used, for instance, in its initial pages: see Plate 9.1).[64] The slim evidence for this sort of non-presentational gospel-book is not surprising but is deceptive. What such books represent is the workaday bible: not the icon but the utilitarian volume, used for reference and study by monk and priest, and perhaps for reading in church services. Indeed, in

60 BnF, lat. 9389. *CLA*, v, no. 578; Alexander 1978b, no. 11; Webster and Backhouse 1991, no. 82; Netzer 1989b.

61 Keynes 1985, pp. 185–6. 62 Gameson 1994. 63 Hereford CL, P.1.2.

64 Gameson 2002c; Webster and Backhouse 1991, no. 91.

connnection with the latter function, the Royal volume has the start of liturgical readings marked thirty-six times in the margin, either by a rubric or by a cross. Volumes such as these, carefully but economically produced in terms of both time and cost, have little to ensure their survival. Yet there can hardly be any doubt that they were the norm for the Anglo-Saxon church and must have outnumbered by far such magnificent artefacts as the Lindisfarne Gospels.

Other part-bibles of this period seem to be utilitarian in concept also, and it is remarkable that they, or in most cases fragments of them, have survived at all.[65] The earliest may be two leaves of Leviticus (from a Pentateuch or Heptateuch, to judge from page size), copied apparently in Northumbria in the opening years of the eighth century; they are written in Half-Uncials, though with little flair.[66] From the end of the eighth century or early in the ninth come a leaf of Daniel, in what is probably a Northumbrian hybrid minuscule, and a leaf with parts of Obadiah and Jonah, in a set minuscule of uncertain origin.[67] The former might derive from a volume of major prophets, the latter from one containing the minor prophets. The most substantial Old Testament witness is the forty-eight-folio Egerton 'wisdom' codex containing Proverbs, Ecclesiastes, Song of Songs, Wisdom and Ecclesiasticus.[68] The text is incomplete in Proverbs and Ecclesiasticus and the codex seems to be a compilation of sections of two originally separate Northumbrian part-bibles, one, in set minuscule, of poor textual quality but reasonable presentation, the other, in hybrid minuscule, abysmal in all respects. An odd feature of this book is numerous textual 'corrections', which as often as not make things even worse than they were. Leaves from two New Testament part-bibles containing some or all of the Pauline Epistles and copied in the first half of the eighth century may be of Northumbrian origin also.[69]

A characteristic feature of the earlier Anglo-Saxon biblical manuscripts is the division of the text *per cola et commata*, that is, into units of sense; usually there are two columns. The system originated in the classical period to facilitate effective public reading. It predominated in biblical manuscripts of the sixth and seventh centuries and was frequently used for those produced in the earlier eighth.[70] In later manuscripts, the text is presented continuously, except sometimes for small gaps between verses, and with varying amounts

65 Marsden 1995b, pp. 236–61. 66 DCL, C.IV.7. *CLA*, II, no. 154.

67 Respectively, Cambridge, Magdalene College, Pepys 2981 (4), and Cambridge, Gonville and Caius College, 820 (h). *CLA*, II, no. 129.

68 BL, Egerton 1046. Marsden 1995b, pp. 262–306.

69 TCC, B.10.5 (216) + BL, Cotton Vitellius C.viii, fols. 85–90, and BnF, lat. 9377, fol. 3. *CLA*, II, no. 133 and *CLA* Suppl., no. 1746.

70 Marsden 1995b, pp. 32–5.

of punctuation; two columns are still normally used but long lines in a single column are an alternative, usually found in smaller manuscripts. Division *per cola et commata* is a feature of all the Anglo-Saxon complete bibles and Old Testament part-bibles from the sixth and seventh centuries (including Amiatinus and the sister pandect), along with the Durham Leviticus (probably first half of the eighth century) and both earlier and later parts of the Egerton wisdom codex (first and second half of the eighth century), but not of the three manuscripts produced in the later eighth or earlier ninth century. The fine early gospel-books, such as Lindisfarne, Echternach and the Codex Aureus, use the older system, too. The abandonment of division *per cola et commata* was clearly connected with the large demand it made on space, a problem reflected also in the evolution of scripts. Uncial, the classic script of the early Italian bibles, was consciously adopted, with modifications, at Wearmouth-Jarrow during the period of Ceolfrith's abbacy as the house script for great display volumes, and continued to be used in its reduced 'capitular' form for the Stonyhurst Gospel of John and other manuscripts. But soon Wearmouth-Jarrow followed other English scriptoria in using scripts which were quicker to write and more economical in space. Half-Uncials are used in most of the fine Northumbrian gospel-books and in the Durham Leviticus, as also in Royal 1 B.vii. In all later mansucripts until the mid tenth century, we see either an intermediate Insular majuscule or one of the several grades of minuscule.

The manuscripts, *c.* 850 – *c.* 1070

From the later Anglo-Saxon period there survive one complete bible, the fragments of two others, and thirty-four gospel-books, all of which are complete or nearly so. There is no direct evidence of other part-bibles but this absence, as we shall see from an indirect source, is a distortion of the record. We are frustratingly ill informed about the transmission of the Bible at this time. None of the writers of extant chronicles and letters thought fit, as their early predecessors did, to record the making or distribution of biblical manuscripts. This may be because the biblical manuscript had long ceased to provoke the wonder it had fostered during the early years of Christianity. Presentational manuscripts, especially gospel-books, were certainly still being made and were highly valued, but they were more likely to be used as diplomatic gifts than for public ostentation. Indeed, there is a sense in which the biblical manuscript had now become a more integral and therefore less remarkable part of the life of church and state.

There is no evidence for continuity of production of biblical manuscripts either in Wessex or the north during the ninth century, though, as was noted above, copying at Mercian centres such as Worcester and other parts of western Britain seems to have continued. There were scriptoria again capable of producing respectable manuscripts in England at least as early as the 930s, but the new biblical manuscripts that we first learn about are imports. They come mostly from (West) Francia, to which the focus of manuscript production had moved from Italy by the end of the seventh century. Their arrival may be seen as an aspect of the regular cultural traffic which had been re-established between the Continent and England during Alfred's lifetime and especially strengthened during the reign of his grandson Athelstan (924/5–39). He was famous as a collector of holy relics and books, which were either procured on his behalf from the Continent or presented to him as gifts, and he in his turn gave generously, donating relics, books and other treasures to religious foundations all over England. One gospel-book, given to Christ Church, Canterbury, may have been copied at Lobbes in Belgium; others seem to have come from Brittany, including one given to St Augustine's, Canterbury, and another to the community of St Cuthbert at Chester-le-Street.[71] The latter was one of three gospel-books presented by Athelstan to that community, and according to a list of donations the other two were 'decorated in gold and silver'.[72] Gospel-books would continue to be imported during the tenth and early eleventh centuries. A further nine extant examples came to England either from Brittany or the Loire region. Interestingly, Ireland, too, now played a part again in supplying England with scriptural manuscripts. Three extant gospel-books seem to have originated there, including the MacDurnan Gospels, a 'pocket gospel-book' probably copied in Armagh late in the ninth century and given by Athelstan to Christ Church, Canterbury.[73]

Continuity in the use of biblical volumes between the earlier and later Anglo-Saxon periods is hard to assess. We have seen that one of the Wearmouth-Jarrow pandects, Offa's Bible, appears to have been still in use in Mercia in the ninth century, and that an undistinguished gospel-book copied in Northumbria in the eighth century was in use at least as late as the reign of Athelstan, when a manumission in Old English was inserted. It would clearly be extreme to conclude that, as the monastic system weakened during the ninth century, all the

71 Respectively, BL, Cotton Tiberius A.ii, Royal 1 A.xviii, and Cotton Otho B.ix. Keynes 1985, pp. 147–53, 165–85.

72 The list survives in an early history of St Cuthbert's cult but was apparently written originally in Otho B.ix, a book largely destroyed by fire in the eighteenth century. Lapidge 1985, p. 50; Keynes 1985, pp. 170–9.

73 London, Lambeth Palace Library, 1370. McGurk 1986, p. 45 and n. 4; Keynes 1985, pp. 153–9.

books associated with it were necessarily destroyed, though they may have been dispersed.[74] There is indirect evidence of the survival of high-grade early manuscripts at York, despite the Viking occupation. As late as the thirteenth century an early (unidentified) Northumbrian gospel-book, probably set out *per cola et commata* and written in Uncial or Half-Uncial script, appears to have been used as one of the exemplars for a bible that was probably copied there.[75] Whatever the survival rate of older manuscripts into the first half of the tenth century, however, we might guess that the rise of Caroline Minuscule in England would soon have made earlier Insular scripts seem outlandish, and that there may therefore have been a natural tendency to replace books in these scripts by more modern, user-friendly, volumes.

The earliest extant biblical manuscript produced in England during the later Anglo-Saxon period is a gospel-book now in the municipal library in Boulogne, copied in the mid tenth century in the south or south-west (Plate 10.1).[76] It is written in an Anglo-Saxon Square Minuscule and thus differs from all subsequent surviving biblical manuscripts, for which Caroline Minuscule was used. From this time onwards, even though some manuscripts continued to be imported, copying at the revived monastic centres in England seems to have proceeded in earnest to meet increasing demand. The extant manuscripts are, as ever, mostly gospel-books. They include the fine Arenberg Gospels (Plate 18.5) and the York Gospels, which were both probably made at Christ Church, Canterbury.[77] Nine more were made in the early years of the eleventh century, including the Royal Gospels, the Eadwig Gospels and the Grimbald Gospels (Plates 10.7–8).[78] Most of these are clearly presentational volumes, commissioned for specific centres, but the question of who the patrons were is a difficult one. There is no proof, by way of inscriptions or other indication in the manuscripts themselves, of royal patronage in the production of any biblical manuscripts. A case has been made for a group of about fifteen lavishly illustrated gospel-books having been commissioned by King Cnut (1016–35) and his queen, Emma, but it is not an overwhelming one.[79] Lay patronage by wealthy individuals is more apparent. Between 1062 and 1065, Earl Ælfgar commissioned an illuminated gospel-book in England in memory of his son

74 On the movement of books during the later Anglo-Saxon period, see Dumville 1992, pp. 96–108, and Chapter 14 in the present volume.

75 Lapidge 1986a, pp. 427–8.

76 Boulogne, BM, 10. Temple 1976, no. 10; Gameson 2009.

77 Respectively, PML, 869, and York Minster Library, Add. 1. McGurk 1986, p. 43; Temple 1976, nos. 56 and 61. See, further, Chapter 18 in this volume.

78 BL, Royal 1 D.ix, Hanover, Kestner-Museum, W.M.xxia.36, and BL, Add. 34890. McGurk 1986, pp. 43–4; Temple 1976, nos. 70, 67 and 68.

79 Heslop 1990; Lapidge 1996, pp. 58–9; cf. Gameson 2002b, p. 207.

Burchard; he gave it to the church of Saint-Rémi, Reims, where his son was buried.[80] A strong argument has been made also for the commissioning activites of Countess Judith of Flanders, who was in England between 1051 and 1064 as the wife of Earl Tostig of Northumbria. Four lavish gospel-books written in English Caroline Minuscule seem to have been commissioned by her and may even have been made in her own household (Plates 10.9 and 18.2).[81] Three were probably bequeathed to the monastery at Weingarten, established by Judith's second husband and their elder son; the fourth reached Monte Cassino.

Such patronage is an important aspect of what has been called the 'commercialisation' of book production during the later Anglo-Saxon period.[82] The forces of supply and demand saw one centre ordering mansucripts from another, as well as individual commissions, and ensured that work of high quality was especially valued. A remarkable scholastic colloquium – an imaginary dialogue in Latin used as a teaching tool – composed by Ælfric Bata in the early eleventh century depicts a professional scribe bartering with a prospective customer, who wants an ecclesiastical book (he lists a psalter, a hymnal, an epistolary and so on) and is prepared to pay handsomely for it.[83] This appears to show that monastic scriptoria sold books for profit. Whatever the commercial forces at work, some at least of the scriptoria attached to the minsters of Anglo-Saxon England seem to have become by the close of the tenth century as productive as those of three hundred years previously.[84]

Notable in this late period – and unknown before – is the habit of using bibles in which to preserve important political documents.[85] The volumes involved were presumably the most precious owned by a particular house and this use tied them intimately to it. A good example is a relatively large, ornamented gospel-book written before 1019 and in the possession of Christ Church Cathedral priory.[86] It contains a note in Old English (on a blank page before the start of Mark's Gospel) confirming the receiving of King Cnut and his brother Harold, along with three other laymen, into confraternity there. In addition there is a deed to the effect that Cnut solemnly confirmed the rights of Christ Church at the request of Lyfing, archbishop of Canterbury (1013–20). As Cnut was obviously there in person, the date must have been

80 Reims, BM, 9. McGurk 1986, p. 44; Temple 1976, no. 105; Hinkle 1970; Lapidge 1996, p. 87.

81 McGurk and Rosenthal 1995; Newton 1999, pp. 233–40. Despite some textual differences, it is likely that the four books were in large part copied from a single exemplar.

82 Gameson 2002b, p. 212.

83 Lapidge 1996, pp. 43–5; for text, see Gwara and Porter 1997, pp. 130–6.

84 Following Blair 2005, pp. 2–4, I employ the term 'minster' to describe any religious establishment with a church, whether a monastery or not.

85 Keynes 1986, p. 81.

86 BL, Royal 1 D.ix. Temple 1976, no. 70; Backhouse *et al.* 1984, no. 52.

between the end of 1016 and the winter of 1019. Another gospel-book, the York Gospels, is closely associated with Cnut also, but in a more overtly political way.[87] About 1020, it was supplemented with a new gathering of four leaves, among whose miscellaneous contents is a letter from Cnut to his people, designed apparently to reassure them and assert his royal authority during his absence in Denmark.[88] He promises security and the punishment of evil-doers, and he instructs his officials to enforce both divine and secular law. The York volume, like gospel-books elsewhere, was in use as an oath-book during the later Middle Ages and it still fulfils that role today at the installation of the archbishop of York and other senior clergy.

The sole extant complete bible produced in the later Anglo-Saxon period is a two-volume work dating from *c.* 1000 and now in the British Library, as Royal 1 E.vii + viii.[89] It is the largest known Anglo-Saxon biblical manuscript, with pages of *c.* 560 × 340 mm. Although its later provenance is Christ Church, Canterbury, there is no conclusive evidence that it was copied there and it may have come from another scriptorium in the south. It is written, with great consistency and accuracy, in what was by now the universal script, English Caroline Minuscule, in a form which suggests a date just before the end of the tenth century (if it were after all copied at Christ Church) or a little later (if made elsewhere). Some leaves at the start of Genesis became lost or damaged and were replaced after the Conquest. A single painted miniature, now fol. 1v, depicts God wielding compasses in the act of creation, but there is otherwise no embellishment.[90] The Royal Bible may be typical of the post-monastic reform period – a high-quality but essentially functional book. Given its 'modern' script and its thorough reliability, it is not surprising that it continued to be used after the Conquest. Not all was well with it, however, in the view of the ecclesiastics of the new Norman dispensation. It was by now certainly at Christ Church, where, soon after the Conquest, a recognised scribe of that house worked meticulously through the whole book, imposing new orthographical conventions and modifying spellings with impressive consistency.[91] He made some textual emendations, too, which presumably brought Royal into line with current Continental, or at least Norman, requirements (see further below).

87 York Minster Library, Add. 1. Barker 1986; Temple 1976, no. 61; Backhouse *et al.* 1984, no. 54.
88 Keynes 1986, pp. 81–3 and 95–6.
89 Marsden 1995b, pp. 321–7. The bible has been in two volumes (of 208 and 203 folios) at least since the thirteenth century, if we are right to identify it with the 'Biblia bipartita ... in duo uoluminibus' noted in a catalogue of the books at Christ Church between 1284 and 1331. See James 1903, p. 51.
90 Heimann 1966, pp. 53–4; Temple 1976, no. 102 and ill. 319.
91 Webber 1995, pp. 155–6; Marsden 1995b, pp. 333–4.

My assumption that Royal 1 E.vii + viii was a characteristic product of the period is strengthened by fragments which appear to be from two other bibles of similar size, format and quality. Each fragment had been used as a binding strip in later books and each happens to come from Old Testament books: parts of three minor prophets (Micah, Nahum and Habbakuk), copied probably a little before the Royal Bible, and part of Numbers 1–2 from the middle of the eleventh century.[92] The evidence of the three manuscripts, and especially the fact that they seem to be of a reliable 'standard' grade, with few special decorative features, suggests that complete bibles were less of a rarity by the end of the Anglo-Saxon period. In this sense, there is continuity with the bibles that were to be produced under the Normans and which therefore, strictly speaking, fall outside our 'Anglo-Saxon' remit. They too are competently produced (with careful corrections to the text, where necessary), functional and largely unremarkable. Such are the Gundulf Bible, made at Rochester for the bishop before the end of the century,[93] the Saint-Calais or Carilef Bible, actually copied in Normandy but in place in Durham by 1096,[94] and the Lincoln Chapter Bible, made in England in or before 1110.[95] In size they are fairly uniform, and somewhat smaller than the Royal Bible.[96] Each is, or was, in two volumes, though in the case of the Carilef Bible, only the second survives; we know from a list on its front flyleaf that the original two volumes were among forty-nine donated by the Norman bishop of Durham, William of Saint-Calais (1081–96), to his cathedral library.[97] The text of the Lincoln Bible seems to have been copied from newly imported (Norman) exemplars, as we might expect, and the influence of the Alcuinian textual tradition is strong. The text of the Carilef Bible, however, often differs from it, and thus it is not possible to speak of a 'standard' Anglo-Norman text, any more than of a standard Anglo-Saxon one. The corrections made to the text of the Royal Bible after the Conquest regularly (but not invariably) match the readings of Lincoln. The Gundulf Bible certainly has the same textual ancestor as Royal, as many shared idiosyncratic readings prove, but there has been an intervening phase of emendation. If there is continuity with the later Anglo-Saxon period among these post-Conquest bibles, it is in the fact

92 Respectively, Columbia, University of Missouri-Columbia, Fragmenta Manuscripta 4; and BL, Sloane 1086, no. 109. Webber 1995, pp. 155–6; Marsden 1995b, pp. 43–4 and 379–94.

93 San Marino, CA, Huntington Library, HM 62. Gameson 1999c, nos. 899 and 900.

94 DCL, A.II.4. Gameson 1999c, no. 200. The extant volume contains Daniel to Maccabees, then Psalms, followed by the New Testament.

95 Lincoln CL, 1 (A.1.2), and TCC, B.10.5 (216). Gameson 1999c, nos. 154 and 328.

96 The Lincoln Bible, for instance, has pages of 495 × 325 mm (text area 375 × 230 mm), compared with the Royal Bible's 560 × 340 mm (460 × 240 mm).

97 Browne 1988.

of their textual diversity – a situation belied by the relative uniformity in orthography and presentation.

It is a quirk of the survival process that no Old or New Testament part-bibles other than gospel-books are extant from the late Anglo-Saxon period. From the purely practical point of view, it would be hard to believe that such volumes did not continue to be essential, for study, for copying and for private reading, alongside complete bibles and gospel-books. Luckily, indirect but reliable evidence that this was indeed the case is provided by booklists in contemporary inventories or records of donation.[98] Bibles or part-bibles occur in eight lists, though a specific identification is not always easy, owing to the brevity of the entries. Gospel-books figure most prominently. One is listed among books donated by Bishop Æthelwold of Winchester (963–84) to the monastery at Peterborough; two are included in an inventory of the service-books owned by the church at Sherburn-in-Elmet, Northumbria, in the mid eleventh century; four are in a list of liturgical books owned by the monastery at Bury St Edmunds in the time of Abbot Leofstan (1044–65); two, described as large and ornamented, are among some fifty books procured by Bishop Leofric for the church of Exeter around 1070; and one is mentioned in a long list of books owned by an unidentified centre (possibly Worcester) at the end of the eleventh century. A copy of Revelation is among the books owned by an unknown schoolmaster called Athelstan in the second half of the tenth century, and a volume of the Pauline Epistles appears to have been in use in the same period by a monastic centre which may have been Peterborough. As for the Old Testament, the list of Bishop Leofric's books offers the main evidence: it includes a volume of the four major prophets (Isaiah, Jeremiah, Ezekiel, Daniel), separate copies of both Ezekiel and Isaiah, one of Song of Songs, and another of Maccabees. A copy of Daniel appears in the list from the unidentified centre noted above, and a Heptateuch is mentioned among books donated around 1070 by Sæwold, sometime abbot of Bath, to the church of Saint-Vaast in Arras, though whether he acquired it in England or on the Continent cannot now be determined.[99] Complete bibles are absent from these lists, probably because they would have a fixed place in a church; they would not need cataloguing and would be less likely to be moved around.

The range of biblical manuscripts suggested by such lists (and confirmed of course for the earlier period by surviving examples) was certainly paralleled on the Continent, where some forty part-bibles (excluding gospel-books), copied

98 Lapidge 1985. Thirteen lists of various kinds are extant.
99 Sæwold's list also includes a gospel-book decorated in silver.

between *c.* 500 and *c.* 1000, are extant.[100] Fourteen of the continental part-bibles consist of, or include, collections of the wisdom books; almost equally popular are codices containing the major or minor prophets (or a combination of both) and others containing the deuterocanonical books, Judith, Esther, Ezra, I–II Maccabees and Tobit, or a selection of three or four of these. Perhaps surprisingly, there is comparatively little Continental evidence for the circulation of the Pentateuch, Heptateuch or Octateuch independently. There are at least three cases, however, where a Pentateuch, a Heptateuch or an Octateuch has been included in a volume with other Old or New Testament books. There seems no reason to doubt that, were the English record fuller, we would see the same comprehensive range of biblical manuscripts as on the Continent.

We know that the books of the Old Testament circulated also in Anglo-Saxon England in manuscripts which were not bibles or part-bibles, or liturgical books, but compilations of miscellaneous items for exegetical, devotional or pedagogical use.[101] There are two examples of complete Old Testament books in such contexts, one from the late period (Proverbs), the other from eighth-century Northumbria (Job). Another manuscript, from the early eleventh century, has a large extract from Sirach. Above we noted a further Insular example, Cornish rather than Anglo-Saxon, in the form of a copy of Tobit (using the Amiatinan text of Offa's Bible), which was probably made in the early tenth century.

The vernacular Bible

The Latin Vulgate remained the official Bible of the English church from the Anglo-Saxon period until the Reformation, but the concept of the part-bible in the contemporary English vernacular was already established by the end of the tenth century.[102] At least as early as the time of Bede, extended passages of scripture had been put into Old English, probably for instructional purposes, and from the ninth century the practice of providing Latin psalters, and then gospel-books, with a continuous Old English interlinear gloss became widespread. There were extensive poetical paraphrases or reworkings, too, of parts of Genesis, Exodus, Daniel and Judith. The first continuous Old English translation of scripture seems to have been a version of the first fifty psalms made by King Alfred (871–99). They survive only in a mid-eleventh-century manuscript, known as the Paris Psalter, and are followed

100 Berger 1893, pp. 374–422; Marsden 1995b, p. 44.
101 Marsden 1995b, pp. 307–20.
102 Shepherd 1990; Marsden 1996.

by a metrical rendering (not by Alfred) of the remaining one hundred psalms; a parallel Latin text has been added, too, though this is not the one used by Alfred, nor that currently used in the monasteries.[103] A uniquely shaped book (its dimensions are 526 × 186 mm), the Paris Psalter was presumably commissioned by a devout lay person.

In the wake of monastic expansion and reform of the mid tenth century, more and more key Latin works were produced in Old English versions, and these encompassed parts of the Bible. A full translation of the four gospels was made in the closing years of the tenth century, though we do not know where or by whom; it was much copied, to judge from the fact that six complete manuscripts and fragments of others have survived.[104] Then, in the early years of the century, a compilation of various Old Testament translations was made, to produce a vernacular Hexateuch in one of its two main manuscript versions and a Heptateuch in the other.[105] The date and place of compilation are unclear, but we do know that Abbot Ælfric of Eynsham was responsible for the first half of Genesis, part of Numbers, and Joshua. From his own writings (including a preface to the Genesis translation) we learn that he translated Genesis and Joshua at the request of his patron, the ealdorman Æthelweard, who with his son was the founder of both the monasteries with which Ælfric was associated, Cerne Abbas and Eynsham.[106] The date of the work was probably between 992 and 1002. It is not known who was responsible for the other translations (more than one person seems to have been involved) and who made the compilation, nor whether the same patron was involved. The Hexateuch manuscript, made apparently in the middle of the eleventh century, must certainly have been commissioned by someone wealthy; it is a handsome book, with the Old Testament narrative fitted between almost 400 coloured paintings. It was at St Augustine's Abbey, Canterbury, at least by the fifteenth century and may have been made there. Sufficient numbers of manuscript witnesses to the Old Testament compilation survive, albeit often in fragments, to prove that, like the translation of the gospels, it was much copied, and in a variety of forms; some copies were being read and annotated well after the Norman Conquest, even as late as the thirteeth century.

103 BnF, lat. 8824. Ó'Néill 2001; Colgrave 1958 (facsimile).

104 Liuzza 1994–2000, I, pp. xvi–xlii.

105 BL, Cotton Claudius B.iv, and BodL., Laud misc. 509. Marsden 2008 (edition based on Laud misc. 509); Dodwell and Clemoes 1974 (facsimile of Cotton Claudius B.iv); Withers 2007 (with CD-ROM of Cotton Claudius B.iv).

106 Marsden 2008, p. lxx.

The Anglo-Saxon vernacular part-bibles are not, however, evidence of a popular movement to provide direct access to scripture for the laity, as the Wycliffite translations of the late fourteenth century would be. Indeed, in the preface to Genesis noted above, Ælfric himself articulated reservations about the very idea of vernacular scripture. Almost everything about the manuscripts that survive, including the corrections and often learned annotations, suggests that they never strayed far from a monastic or ecclesiastical context – though use by especially pious, noble lay people is not excluded. In one manuscript of the Heptateuch, a twelfth-century scribe has carefully entered the Vulgate Latin version above large sections of the text, as though to reassert the primacy of the Latin source.[107] In one copy of the Old English gospels, there are rubrics relating particular passages to the feast-days on which they are to be read, though there is no reason to think that the vernacular text was used in the actual mass.[108] It is likely that Old English translations were used as adjuncts to the Latin, which remained sacrosanct. They may have had a particular role in the education of young monks learning Latin, especially at a time when the monastic system in England was being reformed and expanded.

Assessment

We have seen that the Anglo-Saxon Latin Bible circulated to a limited extent in complete volumes but more often in discrete parts, with gospel-books always numerically dominant. After the conversions in the early seventh century, the required books were initially imported from Italy and Ireland, until monastic scriptoria were established and began home production. The pattern was repeated in the tenth century when, after a period of decline in the monasteries and a relative stagnation in learning, monastic reform and the consequent increase in scholarly activity created a demand for new biblical volumes; this was satisfied at first by importation, mostly from Francia now, until copying in England got under way again. For the earlier period, some documentary evidence about the mechanics of copying and distribution is available, but almost none for the later period.

The question of how many biblical volumes were in circulation in Anglo-Saxon England is an intriguing but very difficult one. Clearly, access to scripture in some form was a fundamental necessity for cleric and monk alike. For a start, the celebration of the mass and the monastic office involved

107 Marsden 2005. 108 Liuzza 1998.

regular scriptural readings, though these seem to have been provided mostly by specific liturgical volumes. A pastoral letter written by Ælfric on behalf of Wulfsige, bishop of Sherborne, probably soon after 992, includes specific instructions to mass-priests about the 'weapons' needed for their spiritual work; these include a psalter, an evangeliary (i.e. a gospel-lectionary with prescribed readings arranged according to the church year), an epistolary (with readings from Acts or the Apocalypse, as well as the epistles), a missal, songbooks, a manual, a computus, a passional, a penitential and a reading book (with items such as saints' lives and homilies).[109] Six gospel-lectionaries used in Anglo-Saxon England and fragments of two others survive,[110] but it is clear that the prescribed gospel passages might often be read from a complete gospel-book. Twenty-three of those extant – from the earlier and later Anglo-Saxon periods – show evidence of such use, in the form either of annotations in the text or of lists of readings. For the night office, substantial parts of the Old Testament were to be read, and a lectionary would presumably have been used here also. A surviving fragment of Lamentations in a liturgical version, which may be of Continental rather than English origin, could be from such a book.[111] The Egerton wisdom codex has lections marked in two places (in Proverbs and Wisdom), though sustained liturgical use seems unlikely.[112] There is no evidence that any of the few surviving, or partly surviving, complete bibles was used systematically for liturgical purposes, though we may note that in the Codex Amiatinus two lections were marked (in Isaiah and John) while the bible was still in Northumbria, and several others were added during its long sojourn in Italy; there also, neumes were inserted in parts of Daniel, Jonah and Lamentations.[113]

Part-bibles other than gospel-books appear to have filled two main roles throughout the Anglo-Saxon period. In the great centres of manuscript production, such as Wearmouth-Jarrow, a range of exemplars for copying was clearly essential; the evidence suggests that the text of Ceolfrith's Vulgate pandects was compiled from various sources, not a single pre-existing bible. But for Bede, and scholars elsewhere in the bigger minsters, part-bibles must have been a necessity for detailed scriptural study, too; a pandect would have been quite impractical for prolonged use. Such was presumably the use made of the part-bibles which feature in the late booklists. Perhaps, too, they were among the volumes from which monks chose one every year for personal reading and

109 Whitelock *et al.* 1981, I, pp. 206–7. 110 Gneuss 1985, pp. 108–9.

111 Columbia, University of Missouri-Columbia, Fragmenta Manuscripta 1. Voigts 1988.

112 Marsden 1995b, pp. 265, 287; and see above, p. 420.

113 Marsden 1995b, pp. 89–90, and Marsden 2011, pp. 230–2.

study. The interesting question of what biblical manuscripts Ælfric had to hand (at Cerne Abbas or Eynsham), when he was producing his great volumes of homilies at the end of the tenth century and the beginning of the eleventh, has never been explored.

Arriving at reasonably accurate figures for the number of potential 'consumers' of biblical material in the minsters of Anglo-Saxon England, large and small, and thus for the numbers of volumes that were copied or imported, is made difficult by the fact that the ecclesiastical and monastic infrastructure is imperfectly documented. A gazetteer of Anglo-Saxon England shows that around 700 churches or religious foundations of some sort had come into existence during the first four centuries of the Christian period, though some of them can be identified now only from archaeological remains; no doubt others have disappeared without any trace.[114] Such an overall figure, however, hides great complexities, both of chronology and definition. The foundations ranged from great minsters with cathedral churches, libraries and important schools, to tiny local places of worship. Many minsters, perhaps 200 or even more, had been founded during the boom period of Anglo-Saxon monasticism in the seventh and earlier eighth century, but some flourished for relatively short periods. On the other hand, a few early minsters were endowed with great wealth and thus had the purchasing power to obtain biblical manuscripts and other books to satisfy more than their basic devotional requirements; Wearmouth-Jarrow is the prime example, with its generous royal support. Other important centres in the north with libraries and scriptoria included Lindisfarne, Ripon and Hexham, as well as York. In the south, Canterbury was perhaps pre-eminent, but Malmesbury, too, is likely to have possessed a substantial library, as is Worcester in the west.

Apart from some minsters in the east of England, most of the early foundations seem to have survived the decline of the ninth century, many of them as colleges of secular canons (that is, not organised according to a strict monastic rule). These sometimes persisted at such a reduced level, however, that they might be occupied only by two or three priests. A number of the monasteries were refounded and expanded during the period of Benedictine reform in the mid tenth century. Forty-nine Benedictine houses for men and ten for women have been identified as flourishing *c.* 1060, along with forty-seven colleges of secular canons (though this figure may be an underestimate).[115] A more centralised ecclesiastical structure is apparent in England from now on, with the supply of books perhaps focused on a limited

114 Hill 1981, pp. 145–53. 115 *Ibid.*, p. 153.

number of communities (to judge, at least, from the evidence of attributable surviving manuscripts). Canterbury, with its two houses, was one of the most important, along with Winchester (also with two houses); Worcester, too, continued to thrive.

As far as the distribution of biblical manuscripts is concerned, the example of Bury suggests that multiple copies were routinely available in the more prominent tenth-century minsters. Private ownership must also be taken into account.[116] Although everything in a monastery was theoretically co-owned, higher-ranking ecclesiastics could own books; we have seen the examples of Ælberht of York and Leofric of Exeter. Outside religious communities, pious and wealthy (often royal) laymen and laywomen owned books, and sometimes commissioned lavish volumes.

A recent estimate of the number of gospel-books required by the 200 or more ecclesiastical foundations of one sort or another established during the first two centuries after the conversion was a cautious 300, allowing that there would be multiple copies at the larger and wealthier sites.[117] To add to these, we may attempt an estimate of the many other varieties of part-bible of which we have clear evidence in this earlier period. It would be reasonable to suppose that the major houses possessed, in addition to their gospel-books, a selection – and perhaps a comprehensive range – of collections of Old Testament scripture, as well as several further New Testament volumes containing Acts, Revelation or selections of epistles. It is thus scarcely credible that our notional figure of 300 for gospel-books would not at least be matched, but in all likelihood far surpassed, by the total for these other books: some 600 such part-bibles might be expected, but 1,000 would not be surprising. Complete bibles will always have been rare, but we have evidence of several, and an original total of forty or fifty is likely. We thus arrive at an overall figure of some 1,000, but perhaps nearer 1,500, biblical volumes (a motley collection, to be sure) in use during the period up until about the middle of the ninth century.

For the later period, the numbers of manuscript survivals are similar, and although we have seen that there are no part-bibles (other than gospel-books) among them, booklist evidence shows conclusively that they were in fact in wide use. As for complete bibles (which could be in two volumes), it is hard to imagine any of the bigger churches being without one; nothing about the Royal Bible, as we have seen, suggests that it was a great rarity (a view confirmed by the fragments surviving from two other similar bibles).

116 Gneuss 1986, pp. 685–7. 117 Gameson 1994, pp. 43–4.

All in all, given what we know of the growing power of the church, and the intensity of learning and manuscript production in the Benedictine monasteries, not to mention a sustained lay, and especially royal, interest in bibles, we may assume that the number of biblical manuscripts in use was at least at the same level as in the earlier period. Thus we may assert with some confidence that more than 1,000 biblical manuscripts of all sorts must have been in use during the later years of Anglo-Saxon England. But how many of these were new, and how many were the same books that had been in use in the earlier centuries? Given the evidence we have seen, a plausible answer might be that, while many of the older manuscripts probably did survive for later use, especially those of higher quality, they were more and more likely, as time wore on, to be replaced by new volumes, written in the script which was now standard for Latin works (and soon for those in the vernacular also) – Caroline Minuscule. Some of these volumes were certainly imported from the Continent, but many were undoubtedly being copied in England itself.

However, there is a yet further complication which renders the above estimates redundant as the Anglo-Saxon period draws to a close. My figures for ecclesiastical foundations have drawn mainly on the evidence of a network of a hundred or more identified minsters. They have not taken account of the many small estate churches, serving the rural population, which emerged as such a prominent feature of the landscape of England during the tenth century. It is out of these churches, financed by lords of the manor and supplied with their own priests, that the parochial system which is so characteristic of post-Conquest England, and familiar to this day, evolved.[118] By the time of the compilation of the Domesday Book in 1086, parish churches numbered several thousands, though there were proportionally fewer in northern and some western parts of the country, where pastoral responsibility for the countryside remained more often with the larger minsters. To cite extreme examples, Lincolnshire alone had 245 churches and Suffolk had 345, and both figures exclude churches in the major towns.[119] The initially ephemeral nature of such foundations makes it unlikely that they would have possessed much in the way of books, at least to begin with (and a question mark hangs over the ability of some priests to read), yet if they functioned at all as places of regular worship, they could only have done so with a modest complement of service-books, along perhaps with psalters and gospel-books; and the

118 Blair 2005, especially chs. 6–8.
119 Godfrey 1962, pp. 321–2; Blair 2005, pp. 399–401.

more prosperous may have been proud to possess complete bibles. Provision of the required volumes in any number must have been a major undertaking, but the full statistics of demand, and the mechanisms of supply, are hidden from us.[120]

120 I am indebted to Julia Barrow, John Blair and Sarah Foot for productive discussions on the history of the Anglo-Saxon church.

18

Anglo-Saxon gospel-books, *c.* 900–1066

PATRICK MCGURK

In this period Anglo-Saxon gospel-books are easily the most numerous of all surviving Latin biblical codices. Twenty volumes and one fragment survive. All save one have been dated to the last seventy years before the Norman Conquest, many of these being attributed to thirty or forty years *c.* 1000–40 (see list A at the end of this chapter). They are among the most luxurious of books with their use of gold, their generous layout, and extensive, innovative illustrations. Some are particularly close to each other, sharing scribes, a similar textual apparatus, and conventions in their 'architecture'. This chapter will consider first their contents, their makeup and layout, their decoration and illustrations before examining where, when and why they were made.

A gospel-book at this period could have different accessory texts. It might open with a varied group of general prefaces and arcaded canon tables (Plate 18.5); each gospel could be introduced by a preface and chapter list; and the book could end with a capitulary or list of gospel readings for the year.[1] Two of the general opening texts, the letter of Jerome to Pope Damasus, usually known by its first words *Nouum opus*, and the letter of Eusebius of Caesarea to Carpianus (*Eusebius Carpiano*), included an explanation of the concordance system, arranged in ten canons and devised by Eusebius for the gospels; these canon tables came at an early date to be enclosed under varied and beautiful arcades (Plate 18.5). The other two general introductory texts, known by their first words as *Plures fuisse* and *Sciendum etiam*, came from Jerome's introduction to his commentary on Matthew, and discussed the four evangelists. The inclusion of these texts, and the order in which they appeared could differentiate the witnesses (see list B at the end of this chapter).

1 Bruyne 1920, pp. 153–8 for general prefaces. Nordenfalk 1938 for canon tables. Regul 1969 for individual gospel prefaces. Bruyne 1914, pp. 240–311 for chapter lists. Frere 1934, pp. 59–214, Klauser 1935, pp. x–lxx, Lenker 1997, pp. 107–14, 413–56 for capitularies.

Here the gospel text is itself often divided into paragraphs corresponding to Eusebian sections and chapter divisions, the first of which are sometimes intermittently, and the second rarely, indicated in the margins.[2] The opening of the whole book and of each gospel could be accented in various ways, by announcing incipits in capitals, and by initial pages, often enclosed in foliate frames. Particular texts within each gospel could also be highlighted. Besides the arcaded canon tables near the beginning of the codex, a portrait of an evangelist in varying poses and with different attributes, and often accompanied by his symbol, could face the opening initial page of a gospel (Plates 18.1–2).

Texts could be further differentiated. Accessory texts like the canon tables, the general preliminary texts or the capitularies would be placed on a separate quire or quires. The preliminary texts for the whole book or for a particular gospel and the capitularies could be further distinguished by being written in a smaller script. Care might be taken to ensure that a gospel began on a new quire. Eusebian divisions and chapter references would be added in the margin next to the appropriate paragraph, or nearest to the pertinent initial in the few cases where the text was laid out in a block. A pair of illuminated evangelist portrait and initial pages at the opening of gospels, which were occasionally placed on a separate bifolium, would be painted after the main part of the gospel text was written. Occasionally leaves meant for painting would be of thicker parchment. Surprisingly little attempt was made to reduce the unsightly effect of ruling on illuminated pages.

Seventeen of our complete survivors are sumptuous productions with an abundance of decoration and illustration, a spacious layout, and often the use of gold in initials and capitals. Two of the three plainer books are written in English Square Minuscule, an inheritance from the Insular past. The first of these, now at Boulogne, is easily the earliest of our survivors, being datable to roughly 930, and is very different in appearance and content from the other nineteen (Plate 10.1).[3] The Insular past is evident in many features besides script. Its gatherings are quinions and have the hair side outside with hair facing flesh. Its Mark, Luke and John chapter lists belong to the 'C' family found earlier only in eighth-century Northumbria and in the Lindisfarne Gospels (with which it shares the description of the Mark lists as 'capitula lectionum').[4] It has also the quasi-capitulary found in the Lindisfarne Luke and John chapter lists.[5] The emphasis given to Matthew 1.18 ('Christi autem generatio') exceeds, as in

2 Bruyne 1914, pp. 500–26 for chapter divisions and Eusebian sections.
3 Boulogne, BM, 10 (2 vols.): Gameson 2009.
4 Bruyne 1914, pp. 270–311 for the 'C' family.
5 Brown 1960, pp. 34–7.

some earlier Insular examples, that given to the opening words of Matthew 1.1 ('Liber generationis'). The second Square Minuscule gospel-book, which was at Barking in the eleventh century, is related by its capitulary and other features to an import from Landévennec.[6]

The remaining seventeen are written in Caroline Minuscule and many bear strong marks of Carolingian influence. The ninth-century gospel-books of the Carolingian Reims school, for instance, lie behind the restrained and plain introduction of prefatory texts which is found in many gospels, such as the Besançon Gospels and the related but now imperfect Paris Gospels. Most books use gold extensively, for illumination and for textual emphasis. Thus a book would open with an incipit and a large B initial (both in gold) for Jerome's greeting to Pope Damasus ('Beato papae Damaso Hieronimus') in his letter *Nouum opus*, and would use gold capitals throughout for incipits and explicits, plain gold initials and lines of Uncials and Rustics to introduce prefaces and chapter lists, gold in the illuminated evangelist and symbol portraits and in the framed initial pages to each gospel, and gold initials for new paragraphs throughout the gospel text. The most developed and ornate of the books are the Trinity Gospels, written by the scribe called B whose work is found in many other gospels, and the Grimbald Gospels, the work of the well-known Christ Church, Canterbury, scribe Eadwig Basan.[7] In them Carolingian influence and Anglo-Saxon splendour combine with dazzling effect, Trinity adding a resplendent Christ in Majesty page before the Matthew portrait (Plate 18.3) and a full incipit page in gold capitals before each gospel, and Grimbald the same incipit pages with golden capitals as well as an extensive programme of illustrations on the John portrait and initial pages.[8] The Arenberg Gospels, which is earlier than these, uses gold sparingly, but opens the book with a Crucifixion, and has an extensive iconographic programme in the canon tables in coloured line-drawing and distinctive architectural arcades above the evangelist and symbol pages (Plates 18.1 and 18.5).[9] Each gospel begins with a large plain initial and lines of display capitals of the kind developed in England in the second half of the tenth century.[10] It is a complex book but stands apart from the apparently linear development found in the gospels of Scribe B.

Many of these books were lavishly and extensively illustrated. From an early date gospel-books could have arcaded canon tables at, or near, the opening of

6 BodL., Bodley 155. 7 TCC, B.10.4. Grimbald: BL, Add. 34890.
8 Temple 1976, ill. 212; Backhouse, Turner and Webster 1984, plate XVI.
9 Ohlgren 1992, ills. 331–47; Rosenthal 1974 and 2005.
10 Ohlgren 1992, ills. 341, 343, 345, 347.

a book, and evangelist picture pages before each gospel. Surviving examples abound from the ninth century onwards, and the illustrations in the Anglo-Saxon books looked back to these precursors. The canon table arcades, which were often historiated, varied from Arenberg's plain arches to Pembroke's round or pointed ones with pediments and enclosed in very varied frames with roundels. Complex iconographic programmes were illustrated above the arcades in some, particularly in Arenberg, Trinity, Pembroke and Bury.[11] Arenberg's are the most inventive (Plate 18.1). They follow immediately upon the representation of the Crucifixion with which the book opens, and illustrate in four pairs of theophanic images the divine plan for man's salvation ranging from the teachings and sacraments of the church to the Last Judgement. Trinity's tympana contain a blessing Christ between Alpha and Omega, and busts of angels, saints, apostles and evangelist symbols with peacocks, lions, eagles, griffins and plant scrolls decorating the spandrels, and these holy images are immediately followed by the magnificent full-page Christ in Majesty which precedes the first gospel (Plate 18.3). Bury's and Pembroke's tympana are as richly adorned.

The poses and attributes of the evangelist portraits are diverse.[12] They had precursors in scores of earlier gospel-books, and it is not always possible to trace a particular influence or model. The evangelists could be within frames, simple with coloured panels in York, or elaborate with foliate infilling and corner medallions, roundels and quatrefoils containing busts in Trinity; or they could be in complex architectural settings as in Arenberg.[13] The evangelists themselves could be seated frontally or in profile, preparing to sharpen a pen, or dipping or holding it up, writing and meditating on their text with a book on a lectern or knee.[14] If accompanied by a symbol, this would normally be above them and smaller, in a tympanum if they were under an arch, or above to their right, holding a scroll or a book, and sometimes in a close physical relationship with the writer (Plate 18.1). Occasionally the symbol would be larger and standing on the ground behind or in front of the evangelist.[15] In the Judith Monte Cassino Gospels the symbol was placed in the tympanum of the arch on the facing initial page.[16] John, sometimes distinguished from the others, could be inspired by a dove speaking into his ear, or by a hand of God above,

11 Ohlgren 1992, ills. 332–9 (Arenberg), ills. 348–62 (Trinity), ills. 458–64 (Pembroke 301), ills. 417–29 (Bury = BL, Harley 76).

12 Alexander 1986, pp. 77–9, Rosenthal and McGurk 2006; Karkov 2007.

13 Temple 1976, ills, 181, 183–4, Ohlgren 1992, ills. 364, 366, 368, 370, 340, 342, 344, 346.

14 For the view that the evangelists were sometimes arranged sequentially in the process of writing, see Alexander 1986, pp. 69–70, and Karkov 2007.

15 Temple 1976, ills. 242, 286.

16 Ohlgren 1992, ills. 451, 453, 455, 457.

and could trample Arius under foot.[17] In the York Gospels the hand of God replaces symbols, and is in direct contact with the evangelists. In the Barking Gospels a standing angel replaces the evangelist.[18]

The transmission of the Word of God is visually represented in these evangelist picture pages. Differences or variations are often significant, the distinguishing features of some John portraits reflecting the contrast between his gospel's concentration on Christ's divinity and the other gospels' recording of his earthly deeds. It has been proposed that the unique iconography of the York Gospels' evangelists pages was tailor-made for the book's first user and probable intended recipient, Wulfstan, since it represents his view that man's contact with God should be direct; and it has been argued that the variations in the iconography of the three Anglo-Saxon sets of Judith evangelist portraits can be explained in terms of distinctions between evangelists and of the particular function of the different books.[19] Grimbald opens John with a double-page portrait and incipit where the frames at the top have images of the Trinity, Virgin and Child flanked by roundels with cherubim, and, at the sides and bottom, kings, clergy, holy men and women, and souls of the dead. The mysteries of the Trinity and Incarnation are adored by the heavenly choirs which illustrate the text written in gold capitals on the opening page.[20]

The range of illustrations to consider would have been wider had not two categories of gospel-book been excluded from this survey: books illustrated on the Continent by Anglo-Saxon artists such as the Saint-Bertin Gospels (Boulogne, BM, 11) and gospel-lectionaries or selective books such as the Getty leaves or the St Margaret Gospels.[21]

Surprisingly, many of these opulent books are unfinished, sometimes apparently through negligence. The capital letters on the Luke initial page of the Grimbald Gospels, for instance, were not inserted, leaving a large decorated Q initial stranded alone on the page in its acanthus frame (Plate 10.8), and in the capitulary alternate initials are omitted. Incipits and explicits and headings, normally among the rubricator's finishing touches in many manuscripts, and initials for paragraphs in the text, are spasmodically forgotten, even though appropriate space has been provided. The insertion of marginal Eusebian and chapter divisions is often incomplete, apparently often inadvertently. In Pembroke 301 three of the evangelist drawings and the text on the Luke

17 *Ibid.*, ills. 448, 346, 391. 18 Temple, ills. 177–8.
19 Heslop 2004, Rosenthal and McGurk 2006.
20 O'Reilly 1992, pp. 179–80; Gameson 1992d, pp. 216–19.
21 Los Angeles, J. Paul Getty Museum, 9; BodL., Lat. lit. f. 5 (Rushforth 2007); Cambridge, Pembroke College, 302 (Karkov 2007).

initial page have been left unfinished.[22] Scribes or artists might sometimes be no longer available, but that is different from the spasmodic rubrication or negligent attention to detail found in many of these luxury manuscripts.

Canon tables and their numerals were a source of error. As concordances those in the Arenberg Gospels were not easily usable, their numerals being imperfectly aligned.[23] There are shared mistakes in canon I in three manuscripts, the Trinity, Pembroke and Bury Gospels, and an error in canon II in the first may have led to glaring omissions in the other two.[24] The sequence of numerals in canon II of the York Gospels is misleading and would have caused difficulties if used.[25] The canon tables in the Reims Ælfgar Gospels are erroneously identified: distributed on ten pages, the headings wrongly assign a canon per page and bear no relation to the erratic text below where the numerals have barely reached canon VII by page 10.

Many books are closely interconnected textually. Many years ago Glunz, in what is still the only study of the gospel text in late Anglo-Saxon England, identified six books with a related text: the Trinity, Grimbald, Bury, Royal and Pembroke Gospels as well as a post-Conquest book from Bury at St John's College, Cambridge, and to these could be added the Kidderminster Gospels.[26] The capitulary in five of these seven – Trinity, Royal, Bury, St John's and Kidderminster – shared a common lacuna in August and September and was derived from a common archetype.[27] The text of the gospel prefaces in four of these books, Trinity, Royal, Kidderminster and Bury, is also closely related, and here they are joined by three of the Judith books.[28] The errors common to the canon tables in Trinity, Pembroke and Kidderminster have just been noted. The chapter lists in Trinity, Kidderminster, Bury, Pembroke and Grimbald belong to the same family, and NPES is the order of the general prefatory texts of the already mentioned group identified by Glunz with the exception of Pembroke which omits them (see list B). The scribe designated B wrote all of Trinity and most of Kidderminster and Royal, and these form a tightly knit group, sharing the order NPES for the introductory prefaces, a similar text for the gospels and individual prefaces, and a capitulary, the first two also having the same set of chapter lists. In contrast the two gospels written by Eadwig Basan, namely Grimbald and Hanover, each has a different text and set of accessories.[29]

22 Ohlgren 1992, ills. 412, 413, 415. 23 McGurk 1993, p. 255 n. 37.
24 *Ibid.*, p. 255. 25 McGurk 1986, pp. 50–1.
26 Glunz 1933, pp. 140–7. Cambridge, St John's College, C.23; BL, Loan 11.
27 Frere 1934, pp. 157–64, Lenker 1997, pp. 442–56.
28 McGurk 1986, pp. 51–2; the Judith Gospels are nos. 6, 14, 15 and 16 in list A.
29 McGurk 1986, pp. 52–3, 55, Gameson 2002b, p. 217.

Nineteen of the surviving books have been dated to the last seventy years before 1066, reflecting the period of church reform and monastic revival and direction. Few can be precisely dated. The latest, the Reims Gospels, can be plausibly identified with the gospels given to Saint-Rémi of Reims by Earl Ælfgar of Mercia between 1062 and 1065.[30] The four books associated with Judith of Flanders were probably made when she was in England (1052–65) and very likely not long before the expulsion of her husband Tostig in 1065.[31] The York Gospels was at York by 1020–3, and the Royal Gospels was probably at Christ Church, Canterbury, by 1018 when Eadwig Basan copied on one of its folios Cnut's writ of 1017 confirming the house's liberties.[32] Tentative dates for the remaining manuscripts depend on comparison with these markers and on palaeographical and art-historical analysis. Perhaps the most famous illuminated manuscript of this period, the Benedictional of Æthelwold, was written in a stately minuscule at Winchester between 971 and 984, and the comparable, though smaller, script in the Besançon and Paris Gospels has been dated a little later to *c.* 1000 (Plate 18.4), though comparanda for the artist's work in Besançon suggest the 1020s at the earliest.[33] Eadwig Basan, who wrote Grimbald and Hanover, and also contributed to the York Gospels, was active in the second and third decades of the eleventh century.[34] Other books may be dated by comparison with Eadwig's. Scribe B's hand looks earlier, as does that of the scribe designated C who wrote the general prefatory matter and capitulary in two of his books, Royal and Kidderminster, and the script of the Pembroke Gospels is contemporary even if it was not his work.[35] The Bury Gospels' distinctive mannered hand appears of the same period as Scribes B and C. The display capitals in the Arenberg Gospels fit best in a Christ Church, Canterbury, context of the end of the tenth century. This leaves two books in Caroline Minuscule: the York and Copenhagen Gospels, which have been dated earlier to *c.* 1000, though it has been argued that their execution was spread over many years. In the York Gospels the prefatory matter is written in Square Minuscule and this suggests a date earlier than that of the fourth scribe, Eadwig Basan, who wrote the verso of the Matthew initial page clearly after the following recto had been written, and it has been assumed that the manuscript was left unfinished for a long period from shortly before 1000 until Eadwig completed it a decade or two later. Recently the case for its being

30 Hinkle 1970. 31 McGurk and Rosenthal 1995, pp. 285–8.
32 Bishop 1971, p. 22; Keynes 1986, pp. 81–3, and Barr 1986, pp. 104–5.
33 Heslop 1990, pp. 171, 188–91.
34 Gameson 2002b, pp. 202–6, Karkov 2006.
35 Dumville 1991, pp. 41–2.

a unitary production has been made forcefully and persuasively, and it could therefore be dated to an early period of Eadwig's scribal activity sometime after the appointment of Wulfstan (for whom the book may have been made) as archbishop of York in 1002.[36] It still remains unique among these gospel-books in combining Insular Square with Caroline Minuscule. The making of the Copenhagen Gospels (which has a Matthew portrait clearly like that in the Lindisfarne Gospels) has also been seen as extending over some years from c. 1000, when the main scribe wrote, to c. 1020 when Scribe B contributed the portrait, initials, opening texts of Mark, Luke and John and the marginal Eusebian numerals. As was the case with the York Gospels, the interval in time between the first scribe and the last need not have been long and the manuscript could have been planned and executed at more or less one go.[37] Details in many books certainly seem to have been left unfinished, but it is unlikely that many were desultory productions spread over several years.

More books are attributed to Canterbury than to any other centre in the late Anglo-Saxon period, and this is true of these gospel-books. Eadwig Basan's two de luxe Gospel-books, Grimbald and Hanover, may quite well have been made there. Grimbald has a capitulary different from that found in many other books, and it is similar to Arenberg's, another probable Canterbury book.[38] Eadwig also contributed to the York Gospels, whose evangelist portraits share features with those in Grimbald and Arenberg. The script of the Besançon and Paris Gospels and the drawings of the first have connections with known Winchester books, and are localised there with good reason. Scribe B was involved in four gospel-books, and a Fenland centre, more particularly Peterborough, has been suggested as his home.[39] The scribe of the Pembroke Gospels' hand is very close to, if not identical with, that of Scribe C who contributed to two of Scribe B's books, and he may also have worked there. Four books were prepared for Judith of Flanders, possibly in her household. None of the remaining books has been firmly associated with a specific centre. Nine out of the twenty are associated with three scribes and at the most three centres. There are no gospel-books associated with many known English centres, such as Abingdon and Worcester, and it might quite well be that a few scriptoria specialised in the making of deluxe books partly for export.

Why were these books made? The Reims Gospels, an opulent book with its now-lost cover, was given to Saint-Rémi by Ælfgar of Mercia in memory of Burchard, his son, who was buried there. The four books associated with

36 Heslop 2004. 37 Heslop 1990, pp. 167–8, 191–5.
38 Lenker 1997, pp. 420–4. 39 Bishop 1967a, pp. 39–41.

Judith of Flanders are a unique surviving example of an early medieval private commission. They have a distinctive package of texts, confining the accessories to the Mark, Luke and John prefaces so that the books open directly with the Gospel of Matthew with its portrait and initial pages. They have no marginal Eusebian or chapter references, and the genealogies of Christ in Matthew and Luke, and the Passion texts are the only ones given emphasis. The scribe who wrote most of the books, being accompanied by a second in one, and a third poor scribe in another, almost certainly used one text exemplar for his books. Three of the books had curiously selective gospel texts. The selections in the Monte Cassino Gospels could represent the readings suitable for private devotion, but it is not easy to interpret the sometimes arbitrary selections in the other two. The books were probably covered with precious bindings at an early date, and in two an illuminated scene in which Judith appears preceded the Matthew portrait; in the first she is shown embracing the foot of the cross in a Crucifixion, in the second (the work of a Low Countries artist) presenting a book to Christ. The four books may have been made for use in Judith's private *capella* in England.[40] The text of the scribe common to all four books was very close to that of the three earlier gospel-books of Scribe B. There is not the same internal or documentary evidence to account for the making of the other deluxe books considered in this chapter. Many travelled from where they were made. Eadwig's Hanover Gospels was completed by a German hand of the second quarter of the eleventh century. His Grimbald book was at the New Minster, Winchester, by *c.* 1100. The York Gospels to which he contributed may have been made for Archbishop Wulfstan, and was certainly at York by 1020–3. The Besançon Gospels was at the abbey of Saint-Claude (Condat) in the Jura by the end of the twelfth century when a capitulary was added. The Copenhagen Gospels had neumes of Germanic aspect added in the late twelfth century. The Arenberg Gospels was at Cologne by the early twelfth century. The Royal Gospels, if made outside Canterbury, had probably reached Christ Church, Canterbury, by 1018. Inference as well as documentary evidence has suggested the occasion and the reasons for the sponsoring of the Reims and Judith books. Lay ownership and donation of books is well documented in the eleventh century. It has been argued that most English deluxe books were commissioned by Cnut and Emma and given as presents to centres here and abroad.[41] Their generosity is well attested, and the hypothesis has much to recommend it. It is true that it is not supported by any internal evidence or confirming statements in the books corresponding to those found in one or

40 McGurk and Rosenthal 1995, pp. 251–308. 41 Heslop 1990.

two of the books given a century earlier by Athelstan, but many of them must have had luxury covers where the donors' wishes might have been recorded. It does, however, compel some of the books to be dated later than might be acceptable, and the association of so many books with the reign of Cnut does not allow the dating criteria for some styles to be moved back, as well as forwards, in time. Most of these deluxe books must have been sponsored, but it is not certain that Cnut and Emma are the only candidates. The reasons for the making of the magnificent Harley 603 Psalter for Archbishop Æthelnoth of Canterbury have been carefully analysed. The interpretation of the iconography of the hand of God which appears in the evangelist portraits of the York Gospels as tailor-made for Archbishop Wulfstan of York might be convincing, but it is still not certain who paid for the making of either of these archiepiscopal books.

It is worth pausing to consider another recorded benefactor of gospels, Godgifu, Edward the Confessor's sister. British Library, Royal 1 D.iii from Rochester is reportedly one of her books and it may have been acquired after 1066 from her manor at Lambeth.[42] Of possible Continental origin, its first scribe may be English. It is scruffy, desultory and unfinished, and contrasts sharply with the other reported benefactions, though like them it may have had a metal cover with precious stones. It is, however, worth remembering that Judith of Flanders seems to have commissioned or acquired a relatively plain gospel-book when she was in the Low Countries after 1065. This book, now at Stuttgart, was also desultory and unfinished, and yet in early thirteenth-century Weingarten, Abbot Berthold thought it worth embellishing with a splendid illuminated bifolium. Its association with Judith and the prestigious metal cover which once adorned it gave it distinction.[43]

The deluxe books were prestigious productions. Their illuminations must have both impressed and instructed many as well as their beneficiaries. On their blank or added leaves writs and grants (the Royal and Fulda Judith Gospels) and, in the York Gospels Wulfstan's 'Sermo lupi' and Cnut's letter from Denmark, were copied in the securest of safe deposits.

Their iconography and painting may have influenced future artists in the centres which kept them. They were certainly taken out for particular services and occasions: the added neumed Blessing of the Paschal candle on Holy Saturday found in the Copenhagen book, the Pentecost lesson added in an early twelfth-century Weingarten hand to the Fulda Judith Gospels and

42 Watson 1996, p. 531; Registrum Roffense: Thorpe 1769, p. 122.
43 Württembergische LB, H.B.II.46. McGurk and Rosenthal 1995, pp. 303–8.

the liturgical notes added later in the Paris Gospels provide such evidence, while the original stress marks and neumes in the Paris Gospels suggest such an intention. They must have been displayed in processions and employed in occasional services. But most were not made for frequent use: the capitularies were often impractical, and the absence of marginal references made locating particular texts difficult. Yet their sumptuousness, their gold and their splendid metal covers made them treasures worthy of their patrons, makers and recipients.

A: Anglo-Saxon gospel-books, 930–1066

1. Besançon, BM, 14. *c.* 1000. Winchester? At the abbey of Saint-Claude (Condat) by the end of the twelfth century.
2. Boulogne, BM, 10 (2 vols.). *c.* 930. Provenance Saint-Vaast, Arras.
3. Cambridge, Pembroke College, 301. Early eleventh century. Peterborough?
4. TCC, B.10.4. Early eleventh century. written by Scribe B. Peterborough? The Trinity Gospels.
5. Copenhagen, KB, G. K. S. 10 (2°). Early eleventh century. Scribe B wrote some pages. Peterborough? In Germany by the twelfth century.
6. Fulda, LB, Aa.21. Third quarter of the eleventh century. Made for Judith of Flanders. Completed in the Low Countries. At Weingarten by 1094.
7. Hanover, Kestner-Museum, W.M.xxia.36. 1010–30. Written by Eadwig Basan. Christ Church, Canterbury. Completed in Germany by the second quarter of the eleventh century.
8. BL, Add. 34890. 1010–30. Written by Eadwig Basan. Christ Church, Canterbury. At New Minster, Winchester, by the fourth quarter of the eleventh century. Known as the Grimbald Gospels.
9. BL, Add 63143. Fragment of one folio. Luke 22.1–19. Early eleventh century.
10. BL, Harley 76. First quarter of the eleventh century. At Bury St Edmunds by the end of the eleventh century. Known as the Bury Gospels.
11. BL, Loan 11. Early eleventh century. Peterborough? Written by Scribe B with opening and concluding accessory texts by Scribe C. At Windsor Castle by fourteenth century. Known as the Kidderminster Gospels.
12. BL, Royal 1 D.iii. Mid eleventh century. Associated with Godgifu, Edward the Confessor's sister. At Rochester Cathedral.
13. BL, Royal 1 D.ix. Early eleventh century. Peterborough? Written by Scribe B with opening and concluding accessory texts by Scribe C. At Christ Church, Canterbury, by 1018.

14. Monte Cassino, Archivio della Badia, BB 437, 439. Third quarter of the eleventh century. Made for Judith of Flanders.
15. PML, M 708. Third quarter of the eleventh century. Made for Judith of Flanders. At Weingarten by 1094.
16. PML, M 709. Third quarter of the eleventh century. Made for Judith of Flanders. At Weingarten by 1094.
17. PML, M 869. *c.* 1000. Christ Church, Canterbury. At Cologne in the early twelfth century. Known as the Arenberg Gospels.
18. BodL., Bodley 155. Early eleventh century. At Barking by the twelfth century.
19. BnF, lat. 272. *c.* 1000. Winchester? In Normandy eleventh century or later.
20. Reims, BM, 9. Third quarter of the eleventh century. Made for Earl Ælfgar in memory of Burchard, his son, 1062–5, and given to Saint-Rémi, Reims.
21. York Minster, Library, Add. 1. Early eleventh century. ?Christ Church, Canterbury. Eadwig Basan wrote in this volume. At York 1020–3. Used by Archbishop Wulfstan.

B: Preliminary texts

1. Order of preliminary matter:
   (Key: N = *Nouum opus*. P = *Plures fuisse*. E = *Eusebius Carpiano*. S = *Sciendum etiam*. Bracketed numerals refer to gospels in list A)
   - NPES: Besançon (1), TCC (4), Royal 1 D.ix (13), Loan 11 (11), Harley 76 (10), Add. 34890 (8).
   - NSEP: Copenhagen (5), York (21).
   - NP: Boulogne (2), Reims (20).
   - P: 869 (17).
2. Number of canon tables:
   - 15: TCC (4), Harl. 76 (10), Pembroke 301 (3).
   - 18: Boulogne (2).
   - 8: York (21).
   - 14: Hanover (7).
   - 10: Reims (20).
3. Chapter lists families:
   (Bruyne 1914, pp. 240–311).
   Mt. Mk. Lk. Jn.
   – I I I: Besançon (1).
   A A A B: TCC (4), Loan 11 (11) lacking Mt., Add. 34890 (8).
   – A A B: Pembroke, 301 (3).

– A P^i P^i: Hanover (7).
A P P^i P^i: York (21).
B C C C: Boulogne (2).

4. No chapter lists: Royal 1 D.ix (13), Harley 76 (10), four Judith books (6, 14–16).
5. Common capitulary: TCC (4), Royal 1 D.ix (13), Loan 11 (11), Harley 76 (10).

19

Liturgical books

RICHARD W. PFAFF

To speak meaningfully of the function of liturgical books in England before AD 1100 requires first a simple distinction between their use as resources for the performance of liturgies and their character as books. Certain Christian liturgies can be conducted without the aid of books, either because they have been committed entirely to memory or because they are improvisatory in nature. Examples of the former would be emergency baptisms, confirmations and the office of compline, while some kinds of blessings (like that of foxhounds in modern times), intercessions for particular new necessities – incursions of Vikings or, later and in eastern Europe, Mongols – and, in the very earliest period, perhaps even the eucharistic prayer, may well have been largely extemporaneous in character.

At the other pole of this basic distinction, the existence of a 'liturgical book' – to be precise, a book that falls more sensibly into the liturgical category than into any other – does not guarantee that it was used liturgically. Sumptuously produced gospel-books are an obvious case here, and indeed loom large throughout our period. But it would be unwarranted to suppose that the liturgical gospel at mass was regularly read from, say, either of two famous gospel-books in earliest England, the Lindisfarne Gospels or the Codex Aureus.[1] So those, and other celebrated books of the same sort, will be treated, largely with respect to their decoration and illumination, in other chapters of the present volume. Similarly with psalters: it certainly cannot be proved, and cannot reasonably be assumed, that the sorts of splendid psalters which acquire art-historical nicknames were employed in the actual performance of the daily office.

Problems caused by the fortuitousness of the survival of manuscripts centre with liturgical books particularly on how typical those which have survived can be thought to be. The problem is intensified by the fact that in liturgical

1 Respectively, BL, Cotton Nero D.iv, and Stockholm, KB, A.135.

studies the word 'typical' has, as well as its everyday meaning, a specialised meaning as being an officially authorised book for worship, like the Pian Missal of 1570 or the Book of Common Prayer of 1549. While the mentality behind this specialised meaning is that of the printed books and the (very likely related) authoritarian mindsets often manifested by post-Reformation ecclesiastics, the notion inevitably carries over into the study of medieval liturgy.

We must therefore be careful not to posit any particular surviving witness as typical of an entire class. Affinities between and among surviving books do exist, of course, and must be traced. But this must be done in full awareness of the fact that the number of extant liturgical books for the period to 1100 is so small that generalisations had best be eschewed in favour of reference to specific codices.

One further preliminary caveat must be uttered: that the evidence for our subject is badly skewed temporally. Of the books we can be reasonably sure were used in the performance of liturgies, nearly all date from the last century and a half of our period. So it is the case not only that books from the early centuries are much rarer in number, but that the kind of information they provide for the present topic is somewhat indirect. This means that, whereas for books dating from about 950 onwards we can approach the subject mainly according to such original owners or such religious houses as can with reasonable confidence be established, for the period from the early seventh to the mid tenth century both extrapolation and conjecture must be employed more extensively than could be wished.

Given that the books used by the Anglo-Saxons in Christian worship must in the first instance have been those brought by the missionary monks who accompanied Augustine of Canterbury in 597 and that Continental liturgical books from the late sixth and even seventh centuries are so scarce as to make inference from them next to impossible, for the earliest period little more can be said than that the service-books brought back by Benedict Biscop and Wilfrid (to name only the most familiar figures) must have included mass-books, texts for psalms and biblical lections, and very likely some *libelli* (in effect, pamphlets) used for occasional services like the visitation of the sick or the consecration of churches. By *c.* 700 fully developed liturgical observance can be confidently supposed at Wearmouth, Jarrow, Ripon, Hexham, Lindisfarne, and maybe a few other northern centres, and at Canterbury (perhaps both the cathedral and the monastic foundation generally known at St Augustine's), Worcester, and a handful of other places in the south.

By this time also the imported books are being complemented, and possibly even outnumbered, by those of Insular production. But, despite the survival of a few celebrated books like the Lindisfarne Gospels or the three splendid psalters written in eighth-century England – the Salaberga, Vespasian and Lothian,[2] the first made probably in Northumbria, the second possibly in Canterbury, the place of origin of the third is disputed – we have only scanty evidence as to the kinds of books actually used in the regular conduct of services in this earliest period.

In theory such regular conduct of services would have required a large complement of liturgical books. For the mass, a sacramentary (mostly for the parts said or sung by the celebrant), chant collection (later to evolve into the gradual), and texts out of which the epistle (with, occasionally, Old Testament readings also) and gospel-lections could be read would be needed. The daily office would have required even more: access to the psalms and hymns (whether in a formal psalter or through combinations of a memorised core and written bits), a repertory of office chants (eventually to emerge as the antiphonal), collectar (the officiant's book at the office), and sources from which the biblical, patristic and hagiographical lessons at the night office could be read. For occasional services officiated by a priest, texts – again, whether memorised or read from a pamphlet or (possibly) a book – for such discrete rites as baptism, visitation of the sick and burial of the dead would have been needed; while for those which required episcopal presidency, ranging from confirmation (very simple) to the dedication of a church (enormously complex), the component parts, in whatever physical forms their rites were originally presented, would eventually be gathered into a pontifical.

Some hint as to the format of a volume out of which the lessons at the night office (later, and normatively, called matins) were read in the eighth century may be obtained from a fragment of an apparently large book, the untrimmed leaf at least 330 × 220 mm. (written space 270 × 160–70), in two columns of probably twenty-seven lines.[3] The contents seem to be appropriate to matins on Christmas Day – somewhat unusual lections from Isaiah and a sermon of Augustine – and it seems likely that there were comparable readings for at least other notable feasts. The text is, however, written *per cola et commata*, which requires a lot of space for a relatively small amount of material; as the letters are generous in height and the lines well spaced, if the bifolium represented by the surviving fragments was part of anything like a complete office lectionary, the book would have been fat indeed, even if divided – as was later practice – into two seasonal volumes.

2 Respectively, Berlin, SB, Hamilton 553; BL, Cotton Vespasian A.i; New York, PML, M 776.

3 Taken from the binding of an incunabulum at Ushaw College, Durham, it has been separately mounted and catalogued as manuscript 44: Doyle 1992.

The mass-book fragments of eighth-century date suggest codices impressive in size, layout and script.[4] These, along with the fragmentary office lectionary, enable us to suppose that at least the advanced centres of book production in England before the Viking incursions had the capacity to supply liturgical books suitable for the use of the officiant at the daily offices and the celebrant at mass. Whether chant-books for either mass or office were written is much more doubtful. If they had been, this would have been earlier than any surviving chant-books from the Continent, and Bede's comments about the teaching of Roman chant by James the Deacon at York and Maban of Hexham (the latter for no fewer than twelve years) say nothing about their leaving a written corpus – something which Bede would almost certainly have mentioned had it been the case.[5] As for the psalmody which forms the meat of the daily office, great psalters like the three of the eighth century, noted above, are too luxurious to have been produced in any numbers. Even though two of the three (Salaberga and Vespasian) have canticles, and the latter has hymns as well – canticles and hymns being features which render discrete copies of the psalms liturgically viable – both seem likelier to have been intended for what might be called liturgical supervision than for liturgical use seven times daily.[6]

A partial office-book known as the Durham Collectar, on the other hand, clearly represents an attempt to supply the distinctive prayers and other formulae needed by the officiant at the daily office.[7] The rudimentary, and quite inadequate, organisation of this material, and the fact that its exemplar seems to have been a Continental book, alike suggest that at least when and where the main part of this composite codex was written – *c.* 900, probably in south-western England – there was a lack of suitable books for the office. The obvious context would therefore seem likely to be that of the Alfredian book programme, and the collectar's editor has suggested Grimbald as a plausible conduit for the Continental exemplar (the manuscript has had added to it, probably in the third quarter of the tenth century, three quires of further, largely liturgical, material, written at Chester-le-Street by Aldred, the celebrated scribe who glossed the Lindisfarne Gospels).

The Continental import that unquestionably sheds light on the making of liturgical books in England is the famous Leofric Missal, although such light

4 Listed in Gneuss 2001, *passim*; a few of the more important are discussed in Pfaff 1995a, pp. 9–10.

5 *HE*, II, 20 and V, 20 respectively.

6 In addition to those three psalters, there are three single-leaf fragments listed by Pulsiano 1995, p. 69; this chapter, pp. 61–85, provides a full conspectus of a number of matters having to do with psalters of the Anglo-Saxon period. See also Chapter 21 in the present volume.

7 DCL, A.IV.19: Corrêa 1992.

is diffuse and controversial.[8] At heart this is a late ninth-century mass-book of the supplemented Gregorian type common in northern Francia by that time; it was brought to England, quite possibly to Canterbury, by, at the latest, the second quarter of the tenth century. The layers of additions it subsequently received, including a calendar that shows strong Glastonbury elements, are too complex even to be summarised here. At least two stages of pontifical material are present, the latter clearly to be connected with Leofric, bishop of Exeter 1050–72, which explains the book's nickname.

Leofric is the figure from pre-1100 England with whom liturgical books can be most extensively connected. His interest in liturgy and in books alike is manifested in three other codices, each of which may very possibly have been made for him: the Leofric Collectar, the Leofric Psalter, and the Exeter Pontifical. It is instructive to note the variety of sizes as well as contents of these books. The collectar is a somewhat complicated codex, thick (256 folios) but handbook size (215 × 135 mm (*c.* 180 × 100 written space)), with twenty-one single lines to a page.[9] It was probably written either for Leofric's personal use or possibly for the use of the (new) secular community at the cathedral. The contents, primarily the capitula and collects for the daily office, would seem to have enabled Leofric to officiate at those 'hour-services' on occasions when he might plausibly have been with his cathedral clergy. Four scribes have been identified, one of whom wrote all save thirty-five of the leaves.

Another of those scribes wrote most of the Leofric Psalter.[10] This is a large book (*c.* 285 × 190 mm, written space mostly *c.* 240 × 140 mm), whose opening initial is an ambitious ten lines high (comparable initials for Psalms 51 and 101 were never executed); the volume was meant to be imposing. A second scribe, who wrote the last seven folios, seems to have been faced with the challenge – which he met most puzzlingly – of laying out daily office material in a way that might provide a kind of template for the 'ordinary season' services; so the book was clearly conceived with an eye to liturgical usefulness as well as being a show piece.[11]

In turn, the main scribe of the Leofric Psalter worked as a secondary scribe on the Exeter Pontifical.[12] This book lacks something (apparently not much)

8 BodL., Bodley 579: Orchard 2002; this supplants the fine edition by Warren 1883. Hartzell 2006, pp. 400–27, gives extensive review of contents and detailed listing of all neumed elements.

9 BL, Harley 2961: Dewick and Frere 1914–21; Watson 1979, no. 718; Drage 1978, pp. 369–70; Corrêa 1995, pp. 51–2; Hartzell 2006, pp. 293–303.

10 BL, Harley 863; Ker 1957, no. 232; Watson 1979, no. 638; Drage 1978, pp. 366–8 (the calendar is a late twelfth-century insertion); Hartzell 2006, pp. 280–5.

11 For the considerable peculiarity of this 'template' section, see Pfaff 1999, pp. 80–2.

12 BL, Add. 28188. The majority of its 170 blesssings seem to be original compositions.

at both beginning and end, which probably deprives us of absolute proof of Leofric's ownership and/or use, but such is overwhelmingly likely. Some dependence for contents, particularly in certain pontifical blessings, on East Anglia (North Elmham?) or the Fens (Ramsey?), as well as on Winchester, has been noted, but evidence of original, probably Exeter, composition is ample.[13] This book is small, *c.* 180 x 120 mm (135 × 85 mm written space), with proportionally small writing; the rubrics are written in both red and orange, and sometimes also in blue and green for an alternating-line effect. There are also some good initials, and some planned but never filled in. It is codicologically possible that the pontifical and benedictional portions were originally separate *libelli*.[14]

These three books, taken in conjunction with the additions Leofric had made to the already supplemented Continental mass-book which comes therefore to be the 'Leofric Missal', are only part of what seems to have been a programme of book production at Exeter under that bishop's stimulation.[15] It seems clear that the supplying of a more or less coherent set of books for the worshipping use of the cathedral community, as well as for the bishop himself, was a high priority.

Though there seem to be no other cases as extensive as Leofric's of the association of liturgical books with a specific person or religious house, there are still enough such instances to flesh out our picture. In houses established in the context of the Benedictine reform, one of the desiderata must have been the provision of liturgical books by which the rich worshipping life of the *Regularis concordia* could be carried out. One such book, dating from quite early in the movement (late 970s?), is the Winchcombe Sacramentary – if, as seems likeliest, the ascription of the manuscript to that house is correct.[16] In contents not differing greatly from many other Gregorian sacramentaries of that period, it includes a strong emphasis on St Kenelm, Winchcombe's supposed founder: he is virtually the sole Anglo-Saxon saint represented in what seems otherwise a largely Frankish complement, and the book was at Fleury by the early eleventh century. But its Kenelm material was pretty clearly copied in the Robert of Jumièges mass book to be considered presently, and the script and decoration are both in the Winchester style (broadly conceived).

No tenth- or early eleventh-century mass-book firmly ascribable to either the Old or New Minsters at Winchester has survived anything like complete,

13 Watson 1979, no. 322; Prescott 1987, p. 130; Lapidge 1991, no. IX.
14 According to the codicological analysis in Drage 1978, p. 358.
15 *Ibid.*, *passim*; Conner 1993.
16 Orléans, Médiathèque, 127: Davril 1995.

but fragments and complementary books enable us to get a reasonably full picture. The Old Minster may have been the source of the large book (290 × 195 mm (210 × 125 mm written space)) of which thirty-two leaves survive, now at Worcester Cathedral (Plate 22.2).[17] The contents are mostly votive masses and forms for ministering to the sick and dead, neither category being specially instructive; but it is noteworthy that chant texts or tags, and occasionally neumes, are provided for some masses, a few of which have epistle and gospel readings as well: so this seems to be close to what is generally termed a *missale plenum*, or a missal as distinct from a sacramentary.

Also from the Old Minster are two celebrated chant-books which between them show the extensiveness of the repertory of mass texts and music there by the turn of the millennium: the so-called Winchester tropers at Oxford and Cambridge.[18] The Oxford manuscript, though written in the mid eleventh century (with later additions), is almost certainly based on a late tenth-century codex. It contains, as well as a sizeable number of the somewhat free, gloss-on-text compositions called tropes, a large selection of chants for the Ordinary of the mass (for example, 107 Alleluias), and in that respect is close to being a gradual. The notion that it was made for the use of the precentor, suggested by its contents, is borne out by its tall and narrow physical form (*c.* 275 × 170 mm, single column with four-line staves). The Cambridge book, probably written *c.* 1025, contains more tropes and fewer mass chants, with in all some 174 bits of polyphony, the earliest extant repertory in Europe. That chant-books could be highly decorative as well as utilitarian is shown by a fragmentary codex called variously the Caligula, Hereford, and London troper; only thirty-six folios of it survive, but these contain no fewer than eleven paintings, of Christological and hagiographical subject matter, that seem intended to illustrate the adjacent tropes (Plate 10.11).[19]

Evidence concerning liturgical books at the other male monastic house in Winchester, the New Minster, exists in both direct (if partial) and indirect witnesses. The former is known as the New Minster missal, which begins only with the Friday after Easter and lacks some material at the end.[20] What survives – mainly, the rest of the temporale and almost all of the sanctorale – is largely in the *missale plenum* format. Its modern editor has suggested that

17 Worcester CL, F.173: Warren 1885; Turner 1916b prints several of its prayers; Hartzell 2006, pp. 635–8.

18 Respectively, BodL., Bodley 775 and CCCC, 473; partial, and composite, edition: Frere 1894; cf. Planchart 1977 and Hartzell 2006, pp. 428–57 and 88–109. Facsimile of CCCC, 473: Rankin 2007. See also Chapter 22 in this volume.

19 BL, Cotton Caligula A.xiv: Teviotdale 1995, pp. 42–3; Hartzell 2006, pp. 238–42.

20 Le Havre, BM, 330: Turner 1962; Hartzell 2006, pp. 193–202.

it might have been, as well as a service-book in its own right, something of a reference copy, and certain textual peculiarities hint that it might reflect post-Conquest changes; if so, they happened fairly early, for the book looks as though it was written in the 1070s.

Indirect, and earlier, evidence for the New Minster comes in the extremely complex book nicknamed, cumbersomely, the Red Book of Darley.[21] The heart of it is a substantial segment of a sacramentary probably written at the New Minster around 1060 (its paschal tables suggest the dating), notably an unusually extensive common of saints, some intriguing votive masses of a strongly monastic character, and masses for Olaf of Norway (martyred 1030) and for St Nicholas. But the calendar (elaborately laid out and decorated) and one of the litanies indicate that the book also spent time at Sherborne Abbey, and it seems somehow to have reached Derbyshire – the book was found at Darley, in the Peak District, in the sixteenth century, hence the nickname – where the best inference is that it was used by a local (parish?) priest. It provided him with material for some of the occasional services, notably baptism, ordeals, visitation of the sick and burial. Some of the contents are rather puzzling, but this Derbyshire priest's liturgical life was potentially enriched by the provision of daily office material for the end of Holy Week and Easter and for the common of saints; furthermore, much of this material is neumed, as though for choral recitation. There are major illustrations at the beginning of the canon of the mass and numerous good initials.[22] In the twelfth century further lections were added, and at that time also the book was joined to a copy of *Solomon and Saturn* to make up the present composite codex.

A pair of codices from the very end of our period are all that can be adduced as direct evidence for liturgical books at the two great Canterbury houses (the calendars in psalters are better seen as indirect evidence: that is, for feasts, and their grading, potentially kept at a particular house). A missal clearly designed for St Augustine's was apparently complete shortly after 1091, but in the twelfth century the book was in many places erased and supplemented with chant texts and lesson tags; nonetheless, its original contents are discernible as being basically conservative but with a considerable element of originality in textual detail as well as a strong local aspect in the saints included.[23] No comparable mass-book survives for Christ Church, but the nucleus of a gradual – which, containing as it does the chants for the mass, is in effect the

21 CCCC, 422. Unedited; see Hohler 1972; Pfaff 1995b, pp. 21–4; Budny 1997, no. 44; Hartzell 2006, pp. 66–88.

22 Robinson 1988, ill. 30; Budny 1997, ill. 606.

23 CCCC, 270; ed. (eccentrically) Rule 1896.

musical parts of a missal – seems to have been copied there as a foundational book for the new monastic house at Durham, established in 1083 (Plate 22.4). This book, the Cosin Gradual, reflects its Canterbury model in including some chants for specifically pontifical occasions like the dedication of a church.[24] Its small size (160 × 110 mm, written space 115 × 70 mm) and careful notation make it plain that this is almost certainly a cantor's book. Only part of the sanctorale survives, and none of the common of saints.

Among books to be associated with specific persons rather than houses at least three are mass-books, one is a miscellany mainly for the daily office, and the majority are, as would be expected, pontificals. The Leofric Missal has been discussed above, along with the collectar, psalter and pontifical probably used by that bishop of Exeter. The early eleventh-century book known as the Missal of Robert of Jumièges is almost certainly the product of a monastic scriptorium, Ely or Peterborough being the likeliest possibilities, and some of its contents would apply only to a religious house.[25] But it is elaborately illustrated and seems to have been designed for a grand user, or at least grand use (the fact that it lacks pontifical blessings prevents us from postulating with certainty that the original owner was a bishop), and by 1044–51 it had come into the possession of Robert Champart, the Norman who was bishop of London during those years and who gave the book to his former abbey at Jumièges. Its contents are at once extremely full and somewhat individual, as though the compiler had been a person of some confidence and, perhaps, authority; but there is no reason to think that this person was Robert, who did not come to England until thirty years or so after the book was written.

Another prelate from the Continent, Giso, bishop of Wells 1061–88, is traditionally associated with a sacramentary which is as yet unedited save for the calendar, the extensive additions to which make it a virtual archaeological site for students of hagiography.[26] As it exists, the codex would have been extremely hard to use, whether by Giso or by anyone else; possibly it, like the New Minster missal, had something of the character of a reference copy.

By contrast, an office miscellany called the Wulstan Portiforium bears signs of having been purpose-written for hard use by Giso's exact contemporary, (St) Wulfstan, bishop of Worcester 1062–95.[27] Its complex contents, mostly having to do with the daily office – 'portiforium' is one of the names

24 Durham UL., Cosin v.v.6: Hartzell 1975, Hartzell 2006, pp. 168–81.

25 Rouen, BM, Y.6 (274): Wilson 1896.

26 BL, Cotton Vitellius A.xviii; calendar edited in Wormald 1934, but without the numerous obits.

27 CCCC, 391; partial edn. Hughes 1958–60; see Corrêa 1995, pp. 57–8; Budny 1997, no. 43; Hartzell 2006, pp. 53–66. 'Wulfstan' is now the preferred spelling, and the earlier nickname, 'Portiforium Oswaldi', is simply incorrect.

by which the full office-book was sometimes known in the Middle Ages – are best explained on the supposition that this was the book that Wulfstan carried with him around his large diocese, especially when visiting its numerous religious houses, in order to preside at the office; but there is also material that would enable a bishop busy but faithful to his spiritual duties at least in part to keep up with the daily office privately: one of the functions of the book broadly called a 'breviary', of which this is certainly a precursor.[28]

The most numerous class of books extant from the late Anglo-Saxon period are the distinctively episcopal books usually called pontificals, though sometimes the section of episcopal blessings at mass, which can be substantial, is separated into a distinct book called the benedictional. Some twenty of these survive (not all complete, and in two cases badly damaged by fire).[29] Here it must suffice to notice two connected with the monastic reformers Æthelwold and Dunstan and two that take us into the final decade of the eleventh century. The Benedictional of St Æthelwold, arguably the best-known late Anglo-Saxon liturgical book, is datable to that prelate's episcopacy at Winchester, 963–84, and probably after 971 (Plate 10.4).[30] The magnificence of its illustrations has until recently tended to overshadow the importance of its contents, the study of which reveals the considerable amount of originality in the composition of the blessings included and their influence on subsequent English collections.[31] The original ownership of the Dunstan Pontifical is not quite as clear, and the fact that it was (subsequently) possessed by Wulfsige, bishop of Sherborne *c.* 992–1002, has given rise to the alternative nickname of the Sherborne Pontifical.[32] The art-historical evidence for Canterbury production,[33] and therefore for Dunstan's ownership, is somewhat stronger than the specifically liturgical, and that this is the earliest English pontifical extant makes assessment of its contents on a comparative basis risky; on balance, Dunstan still seems the likeliest original owner.

A pontifical of probable Canterbury origin written in the early eleventh century shows up at Worcester towards the end of the century; there a good deal of material was added, apparently for the use of Samson, Wulfstan's successor as bishop (1096–1112), hence its nickname of the Samson Pontifical.[34] That Samson was a Norman does not seem to have prevented the reuse of this

28 Pfaff 1999, pp. 82–4.

29 Full list and summary discussion: Nelson and Pfaff 1995; compare Dumville 1992, pp. 66–95.

30 BL, Add. 49598; facs. Warner and Wilson 1910 and Prescott 2002. See Deshman 1995.

31 Prescott 1988.

32 BnF, lat. 943; virtual edition: Rasmussen 1998, pp. 258–317 at 259–61; Hartzell 2006, pp. 520–8.

33 Rosenthal 1992.

34 CCCC, 146; Dumville 1992, p. 72; Budny 1997, no. 31; Hartzell 2006, pp. 28–38.

Anglo-Saxon book as (so far as we can ascertain) a prime tool of his episcopate. Continental influence was coming into episcopal liturgy during the second half of the century; however, its source is not Normandy but Germany, in the so-called Romano-German pontifical (PRG) that had originated around Mainz in, probably, the 950s.[35] Very likely brought to England after a Continental stay by Ealdred, bishop of Worcester 1046–62 and archbishop of York 1061–9, the PRG is apparent in three pontificals used in England: most notably in an originally German book (sometimes called, from its modern shelfmark, the Tiberius Pontifical) which received considerable additions at Sherborne and also at Old Sarum, where it was taken by Bishop Osmund when the see was moved there in 1078.[36] But the subsequent influence of the PRG in England is less great than might have been expected, given these auspices.

Clearly the year 1100 is not a meaningful terminus for the story of liturgical books in England. Nonetheless, the vigour with which such books were evidently produced in England between roughly 960 and the end of the eleventh century is, from the surviving codices alone, undeniably impressive. How many such books were made, or in use, we cannot even guess, despite the existence of several booklists that enumerate liturgical (among other) books in collections owned by individual houses or donated by specific persons.[37] When one tries to extrapolate imaginatively from the small number that have survived to the hundreds, probably thousands, that have not, it is obvious that liturgical codices must have been one of the major categories of book production in late Anglo-Saxon England.

35 Vogel and Elze 1963–72.

36 BL, Cotton Tiberius C.i; on this so-called Tiberius Pontifical, see Ker 1959; Hartzell 2006, pp. 250–6. On the other two books Lapidge 1981 and 1983 with, respectively, Hartzell 2006, pp. 38–42 and 271–4.

37 Lapidge 1985.

20

Anglo-Saxon prayerbooks

BARBARA RAW

The six prayerbooks that have survived from Anglo-Saxon England fall into two groups, the first of which belongs to the late eighth or early ninth century,[1] while the second dates from the eleventh.[2] These are not the only collections of prayers for private use, however. Wulfstan, bishop of Worcester, stated that everyone, lay people as well as religious, should know the *Pater noster* and Creed in English, if not in Latin, and followed this statement with a translation of the two texts.[3] A verse translation of the *Pater noster* occurs in the Exeter Book and translations and expansions of the *Pater noster*, *Gloria*, and Apostles' Creed, are found in Cambridge, Corpus Christi College, 201, and Bodleian Library, Junius 121, the so-called *Benedictine Office*.[4] A group of prayers in Old English, which are generally agreed to be by Ælfric and which include translations of the *Pater noster*, Apostles' Creed and Niceno-Constantinopolitan Creed, were copied in the late tenth or early eleventh century at the end of a manuscript of the Catholic Homilies thought to be close to Ælfric's original copy.[5] These prayers form what is effectively a small prayerbook, possibly intended, like the two sets of Catholic Homilies, for use by Ælfric's patrons at Cerne Abbas. The first seven prayers are translated from texts found in manuscripts such as the Leofric Missal, the Missal of Robert of Jumièges, the Leofric Collectar or the Portiforium of St Wulfstan, and are in the plural form; the final three prayers, on the other hand, are based on biblical texts and are in the singular.[6] Most eleventh-century Anglo-Saxon psalters are followed by sets of prayers which could have acted as private prayerbooks: the

1 BL, Harley 7653 (Harley Prayerbook); BL, Royal 2 A.xx (Royal Prayerbook); BL, Harley 2965 (Book of Nunnaminster) and CUL, Ll.1.10 (Book of Cerne).
2 BL, Cotton Galba A.xiv (Galba Prayerbook) and BL, Cotton Titus D.xxvi + xxvii (Ælfwine Prayerbook).
3 Bethurum 1957, pp. 166–8.
4 Krapp and Dobbie 1936, pp. 223–4; Dobbie 1942, pp. 70–80; Ure 1957.
5 Godden 1979, p. xliii; CUL, Gg.3.28, fols. 261v–2v, printed Thorpe 1844–6, II, pp. 596–600.
6 Bzdyl 1977; BodL., Bodley 579; Rouen, BM, Y.6; BL, Harley 2961; CCCC, 391.

Arundel 155 Psalter, written by the scribe Eadwig Basan between 1012 and 1023, includes a series of forty-four prayers in Latin with an Old English gloss, all in the singular and clearly intended for private use.[7] A gathering added by Eadwig to the eighth-century Vespasian Psalter includes copies of the *Te Deum* and Athanasian Creed, glossed in Old English, and a series of lengthy prayers including seven in honour of the cross and the crucified Christ.[8] Other books containing fairly extensive sets of private prayers are the Portiforium of St Wulfstan, which includes, among other items, an Old English version of the Good Friday veneration of the cross,[9] and a Canterbury manuscript which contains a similar devotion, though in Latin, again for private use, and offices in honour of the Virgin Mary and All Saints.[10]

The earliest of the six separate prayerbooks is the Harley Prayerbook, written in the late eighth or early ninth century and consisting of a single gathering of seven folios, with a text which is incomplete at beginning and end.[11] Next come two manuscripts dating from the second quarter of the ninth century: the Royal Prayerbook[12] and the Book of Nunnaminster [13] The fourth of these early prayerbooks, dating from *c.* 818–30, is the Book of Cerne (Plate 4.5).[14] All four of these early prayerbooks are related palaeographically, and have Mercian connections.[15] The Harley Prayerbook has been annotated by a hand which occurs also in the Royal Prayerbook, a manuscript with a Worcester provenance. The Book of Nunnaminster includes a record of property given to Winchester's Nunnaminster by Alfred's wife, Ealhswith, who came from Mercia and who may have owned the manuscript.[16] The Book of Cerne includes an acrostic poem whose capital letters give the name Aedeluald episcopus, and a breviate psalter with a heading referring to an Oeðelwald episcopus; there is some argument as to whether the bishop in question is Æthilwald of Lindisfarne (721–40) or Æthelwald of Lichfield (818–30), though the latter seems more likely.[17]

These four manuscripts share a number of features. In contrast to the prayers in the Ælfric manuscript, or those in the Arundel 155 Psalter, their

7 Holthausen 1941, pp. 231–54 (fols. 171r–83r) and Campbell 1963, pp. 84–117 (fols. 183r–92v). Further on Eadwig see Chapter 7b in this volume.

8 BL, Cotton Vespasian A.i, fols. 155r–60v; Wright 1967b.

9 Hughes 1958–60, II, pp. 1–24.

10 BL, Cotton Tiberius A.iii, fols. 44r–60v and 107v–15v; Dewick 1902, cols. 19–48; Lapidge and Winterbottom 1991, pp. lxviii–lxxvii.

11 BL, Harley 7653; Warren 1893–95, II, pp. 83–97.

12 BL, Royal 2 A.xx; Warren 1893–5, II, pp. 97–102; Kuypers 1902, pp. 201–25.

13 BL, Harley 2965; Birch 1889.

14 CUL, Ll.1.10; Kuypers 1902.

15 Brown 1996, pp. 162–84.

16 Birch 1889, p. 96.

17 Kuypers 1902, pp. 41 and 174–95; Dumville 1972, pp. 274, 393 and 397–9; Brown 1996, pp. 133, 143–4 and 181–3.

texts are in Latin, though the Royal Prayerbook includes some Old English interlinear glosses to the *Pater noster*, Creed, canticles and some of the prayers, the Book of Cerne has some instructions in Old English on how to pray, together with a few Old English glosses, and there is a single gloss in the Harley Prayerbook. The Harley and Royal Prayerbooks, and the Book of Nunnaminster, also include Greek transliterations of some Latin texts.[18] It seems likely that the Harley and Royal Prayerbooks, and the Book of Nunnaminster, were owned and used by women.[19] The Harley Prayerbook refers to the user as *Dei famula* and prays for protection for *ancillas Dei*, while the litany includes a list of twenty-one female saints[20] The Royal Prayerbook contains several gospel readings referring to healings of women, and its litany includes eleven female saints, in addition to the Virgin Mary.[21] The prayers in the Book of Nunnaminster include two feminine forms, and a prayer of confession added on a flyleaf of the manuscript in the early tenth century includes the words, *ora pro me peccatrice*, again suggesting female ownership.[22]

The Royal Prayerbook, the Book of Nunnaminster and the Book of Cerne follow a similar pattern. All three begin with a series of extracts from the gospels, which would provide a basis for meditation. In Nunnaminster and Cerne the chosen passages are the Passion and Resurrection narratives; in Royal, by contrast, the passages selected for inclusion consist largely of descriptions, taken from St Matthew's Gospel, of Christ curing the sick and possessed, and giving power to his disciples to do likewise, together with the genealogy of Christ (Matt. 1.1–18) and Peter's profession of faith (Matt. 16.13–19); these are followed by passages on the Incarnation and Christ's divine nature taken from the gospels of Luke and John. In the Royal manuscript the gospel passages are followed by a series of prayers, some attributed to named persons, a litany and a group of hymns. The manuscript also includes an alphabetical series of prayers on the life, death and Resurrection of Christ which are closely related to a series of prayers in the contemporary Book of Nunnaminster.[23] The Book of Nunnaminster and the Book of Cerne, like the Royal Prayerbook, include prayers attributed to named authors, for example Augustine, Gregory, Jerome, Hugbald and Laidcenn (Plate 4.5). Unusually, the Book of Cerne includes what seems to be an early example of liturgical drama, dealing with Christ's

18 Brown 1996, p. 152; Bodden 1988, p. 228.
19 Brown 2001, pp. 51–8.
20 Warren 1893–5, II, pp. 83–4 and 86; Lapidge 1991, pp. 75 and 210–11.
21 Lapidge 1991, pp. 75 and 212–13.
22 Birch 1889, pp. 68–9 and 97; Brown 2001a, pp. 54–5.
23 Kuypers 1902, pp. 213–18; Raw 1997a, pp. 151–3.

harrowing of Hell.[24] This manuscript is also distinguished from the other early prayerbooks by its elaborate decoration, in particular the paintings of the four evangelists and their symbols which precede the gospel extracts.[25]

All four early prayerbooks draw on Irish sources as well as Roman ones. The version of the *Te Deum* in the Harley Prayerbook has variants found in Irish texts, while the prayer *Rogo Patrem* occurs also in the Leabhar Breac.[26] The Book of Cerne includes long litany-like prayers of Irish type; like the Book of Nunnaminster it contains the Irish Lorica of Laidcenn, while the Royal Prayerbook includes the Celtic Prayer of Moucan.[27] But the Royal Prayerbook and the Book of Cerne also contain texts taken from the public liturgy of the church. Like the later Ælfwine Prayerbook, which specifies the recitation of the *Benedicite*, *Gloria*, *Credo* and *Pater noster* on waking,[28] the Royal Prayerbook includes copies of the *Pater noster*, Apostles' Creed, *Magnificat*, *Benedictus*, *Benedicite* and *Gloria*, while the Book of Cerne includes the *Te Deum* and *Benedicite*. The Book of Cerne also contains three prayers which combine verses from the psalms or the New Testament with the *Gloria* or *Pater noster* in a way reminiscent of parts of the official office.[29] The influence of the public liturgy of the church can be seen again in some of the shorter prayers in the Book of Nunnaminster and the Book of Cerne, for example the prayers *De epiphania*, the first half of which is taken from the collect for the Feast of Epiphany in several Gelasian sacramentaries,[30] or the *Oratio in Caena Domini*, the opening phrases of which are taken from a collect for Maundy Thursday found in the Sacramentary of Gellone and among the prayers 'pro peccatis' in the Durham Collectar and Leofric Missal.[31] Other prayers in the Book of Nunnaminster which echo phrases from the public liturgy are *De auriculo absciso*, *De inrisione Domini* and *Item de Resurrectione*.[32] None of these prayers occurs in the Royal Prayerbook. In the case of Nunnaminster's *Deus qui humanae substantiae*, the opening words of which correspond to part of a collect for the third mass of the Nativity in the Leofric Missal and a collect for Vespers of the Nativity in the Sacramentary of Gellone,[33] the corresponding prayer in the Royal Prayerbook does not include the phrases taken from the liturgy.[34]

24 Kuypers 1902, pp. 196–8; Dumville 1972.

25 Brown 1996, pp. 68–128.

26 Warren 1893–5, II, pp. 86 and 93–5.

27 Birch 1889, pp. 90–5; Kuypers 1902, pp. 85–8 and 219–21; Howlett 1998a, pp. 57–68.

28 Günzel 1993, p. 143.

29 Kuypers 1902, pp. 99–102.

30 Birch 1889, pp. 64–5; Kuypers 1902, pp. 138–9; Dumas and Deshusses 1981, p. 13; Saint-Roch 1987, p. 7v.

31 Birch 1889, pp. 67–8; Kuypers 1902, p. 139; Dumas and Deshusses 1981, p. 124; Corrêa 1992, p. 167; Orchard 2002, p. 453.

32 Birch 1889, pp. 69, 71 and 79.

33 *Ibid.*, p. 63; Orchard 2002, p. 110; Dumas and Deshusses 1981, p. 5.

34 BL, Royal 2 A.xx, fol. 29r, Kuypers 1902, p. 213; Raw 2004.

The most striking example of the adaptation of liturgical texts comes in the prayer *De tenebris* in the Book of Nunnaminster. Its second part is closely paralleled by the prayer *O unigenitus* in the Royal Prayerbook; the first part is very different, however.[35] In the past it has been compared to a passage in the Old English poem *The Dream of the Rood* (52–6) and considered as something specifically Anglo-Saxon. In fact, the first part is taken word for word from a Preface for the Maundy Thursday reconciliation of penitents, found in three Frankish sacramentaries of the late eighth or early ninth century: the Sacramentary of Gellone, the Sacramentary of Angoulême and the Bobbio Missal.[36]

Many of the prayers in the Book of Cerne are also found in the three earlier prayerbooks, though not always in the same order, and this may imply the use of common sources, possibly in the form of small booklets similar to the Harley Prayerbook. In addition, some of these early prayers continued in use into the tenth and eleventh centuries, in the *Regularis concordia*, the Portiforium of St Wulfstan and the Galba Prayerbook.[37]

Whereas the Book of Nunnaminster had a clear theme (the Passion of Christ) the Galba Prayerbook, which also comes from Winchester's Nunnaminster and which dates from about 1029, has no apparent structure.[38] The entries in it were written by numerous different scribes, some of whom had a rather poor grasp of Latin, and it seems likely that it was originally a series of blank quires in which various items of interest could be entered. The manuscript includes a calendar and computistical material as well as a rather random collection of prayers, together with some Old English translations and texts. In some respects the Galba Prayerbook continues the traditions of the earlier books: it includes some Irish material, several lengthy confessions dealing with all possible kinds of sins, and at least eight prayers which occur in one or more of Royal, Nunnaminster and Cerne. Side by side with these pieces, however, are many items which are found in more official books such as collectars and sacramentaries.[39] One such item is the collect in honour of St Æthelwold possibly composed by Wulfstan, precentor of Winchester.[40] As was the case in the four earlier prayerbooks, some of the prayers contain feminine forms, the most interesting being a prayer beginning *Suscipe sancta Trinitas* and based on the offertory prayer of the mass;[41] the prayer allows the speaker, described as *peccatrix*, not merely to ask for forgiveness of sins in this world and eternal rest in

35 Birch 1889, p. 74; Kuypers 1902, p. 215; Raw 2004.
36 Dumas and Deshusses 1981, p. 80; Saint-Roch 1987, p. 84; Lowe 1991, p. 62.
37 Brown 1996, pp. 141–2. 38 BL, Cotton Nero A.ii + Cotton Galba A.xiv.
39 Muir 1988, pp. xvi–xxxi.
40 *Ibid.*, p. 159; Lapidge and Winterbottom 1991, pp. cxv and cxxi.
41 Muir 1988, p. 31.

the next for all Christian people, but to join in the offering being made by the celebrant as though she were herself playing that role. Further evidence that members of the congregation recited their own prayers during mass, rather than following the words recited by the celebrant, comes from the Ælfwine Prayerbook,[42] which includes a prayer to be said at the beginning of the canon of the mass, during the *Te igitur*.[43] The manuscript also includes a group of three prayers headed *Oratio sacerdotali*, to be said privately by the celebrant before beginning the mass.[44]

The Ælfwine Prayerbook was written for Ælfwine, dean and later abbot of New Minster, Winchester, between 1023 and 1032, and contains several references to him,[45] while obits of six members of his family have been added to the calendar. Like the Galba Prayerbook, the Ælfwine manuscript is a miscellany. It includes a calendar and computistical material, numerous prognostics and a copy of Ælfric's *De temporibus anni*, in addition to a litany, a collectar and a large collection of prayers for private recitation, including short offices in honour of the Trinity, the Virgin Mary and the cross.

The main collection of prayers in the first of the two Ælfwine volumes, Titus D.xxvii, is preceded by a copy of the Passion according to St John and the prayer *Ave alma crux*. After this comes a drawing of the Crucifixion, a long series of prayers in honour of the cross, a prayer to the speaker's guardian angel, a second drawing showing the Trinity with the Virgin Mary, three short offices in honour of the Trinity, the cross and the Virgin Mary, and a group of prayers to the Trinity and various saints.[46] The main series of private prayers in the second volume, Titus D.xxvi, follows the collectar, starting with a devotion based on the penitential psalms. There follows a litany of the saints, possibly for private recitation, and a series of collects and other prayers ending with five prayers to St Nicholas added by a later scribe.[47] A drawing of Ælfwine with St Peter precedes the collectar.[48]

The Ælfwine Prayerbook differs noticeably from the other Anglo-Saxon prayerbooks, including the contemporary Galba Prayerbook. First, the Irish element has disappeared; there is a greater emphasis on a more liturgical kind of prayer, and a preference for devotion to the cross rather than meditation on the events of Christ's life. In place of the long prayers detailing every kind of sin which fill the eighth- and ninth-century manuscripts, there is a series of collects to be said daily for sinners.[49] A prayer in the Royal manuscript which

42 BL, Cotton Titus D.xxvi + xxvii; Günzel 1993.
43 Günzel 1993, p. 194. 44 *Ibid.*, pp. 116–17.
45 *Ibid.*, p. 109, fig. I and p. 187. 46 *Ibid.*, pp. 122–42.
47 *Ibid.*, pp. 175–97. 48 *Ibid.*, fig. III. 49 *Ibid.*, pp. 170–2.

calls on Christ to protect various parts of the body, through the power of his cross, is adapted in Ælfwine's book to ask Christ to be near, within, around, before, after and above the petitioner and to lead him into the heavenly kingdom.[50] Where the Book of Nunnaminster and the Royal Prayerbook include a series of prayers focusing on the details of Christ's Passion, and the Book of Cerne contains a prayer, *Domine Ihesu Christe Adoro te*, which recalls the main events of Christ's life and which appears in abbreviated form in the Good Friday ceremonies of the *Regularis concordia*, the Ælfwine manuscript offers a collection of psalms, collects and other prayers to be said in front of a crucifix, including the elaborate *Kyrie* from the Good Friday liturgy, but not the better-known *Adoro te* prayer.[51] Where the Royal Prayerbook, the Book of Nunnaminster and the Book of Cerne include a small number of prayers in honour of the Trinity or the Virgin Mary, the Ælfwine Prayerbook has three formal offices in honour of the Trinity, the Virgin Mary and the cross, the second of which may preserve one of the supplementary offices introduced at Winchester by St Æthelwold.[52] Similar offices intended for private recitation are found in an eleventh-century manuscript from Christ Church, Canterbury, copied from a Winchester exemplar, and in a tenth-century psalter which had reached Christ Church, Canterbury, by the eleventh century, though it was probably written at Winchester.[53] The second distinctive feature of the Ælfwine Prayerbook is the three drawings accompanying the prayers, which offer a programme of meditation quite independent of the text of the manuscript.[54] The drawing of the Crucifixion includes an inscription drawing attention to Ælfwine's baptism, when he was sealed with the sign of Christ's cross. The drawing of the Trinity with Mary not only stresses Christ's nature as both God and man, and his equality with his Father, but offers a vision of the heavenly kingdom to which Ælfwine aspires. The third drawing, of Ælfwine himself with St Peter, allows the owner of the manuscript to visualise himself having attained his goal, and standing alongside the doorkeeper of heaven. The theological content of these drawings reveals the distance private prayer has come from the lengthy and repetitive confessional prayers or the narrative focus of the prayers concerned with Christ's Passion in the Book of Nunnaminster and the alphabetical series of prayers in the Royal Prayerbook.

50 Kuypers 1902, p. 221; Günzel 1993, p. 126.
51 Kuypers 1902, pp. 114–17; Günzel 1993, pp. 123–8.
52 Lapidge and Winterbottom 1991, pp. lxvii–lxxvii.
53 BL, Cotton Tiberius A.iii and BL, Royal 2 B.v; Dewick 1902, cols. 1–48.
54 Raw 1997b, pp. 176–88.

In different ways, however, all six prayerbooks give some indication of what might lie behind St Benedict's instructions to his monks, 'Gif hwylc hyra eft onsundran diglice gebiddan wille, mid stilnesse anfealdlice he ingange and hine gebidde, na mid hluddre stefne, ac mid teara wope and mid his heartan and ealles geþances gymene' ('If any of them wishes to pray secretly and in private, let him simply go in quietly and pray, not in a loud voice, but with weeping and with his heart and all thankfulness'),[55] or the words of the *Regularis concordia*, 'Ceterum unusquisque secretis oratorii locis, in quantum Sancti Spiritus gratia clementer instigaverit, peculiaribus teste Deo cum bonorum operum vigilantia consulte utatur orationibus' ('For the rest, all shall be free to give themselves voluntarily to private prayer in the secret places of the oratory, with God as their witness, and to be watchful in good works according as the grace of the Holy Ghost in His mercy shall inspire them').[56]

55 Gneuss 1964, p. 81. 56 Symons 1953, p. 4.

21

Psalters

M. JANE TOSWELL

According to the early twelfth-century *Vita* of Christina of Markyate, toads (thought to be both evil and poisonous) invaded the anchorite's cell, squatting everywhere – even on her psalter. She held firmly to her manuscript and refused to give up singing the psalms in honour of Christ; the toads disappeared. Christina used her psalter both as book and as sung text, driving out the devils, the toads, by the dual power of the manuscript she held and the belief she espoused.[1] Similarly, in Felix's *Life of Guthlac*, when disguised fiends attack the future saint, Guthlac vanquishes them with a single sentence, the psalm verse: 'His auditis beatus Guthlac exsurgens psallebat: Convertantur inimici mei retrorsum, et reliqua' ('Let my enemies be put to flight, etc.').[2] A psalm verse, the action of singing a psalm, and a psalter were potent weapons against evil in early medieval Britain and Ireland. The psalter could also quell enemies, a martial quality exemplified by the Cathach of St Columba, supposedly the copy of the Gallican psalter written by Columba in Ireland.[3] 'Cathach' means 'battler', and the Cathach, enclosed in an appropriate reliquary, was carried into battle in the forefront of the Irish clans. In fact, the reliquary itself became so prominent in the national imagination that its purpose, preserving the psalter, was forgotten. In the nineteenth century, back in Ireland after two centuries in France, the reliquary was finally opened and the psalter rediscovered.[4]

While psalter manuscripts and their uses are the focus here, we must first remind ourselves that the Book of Psalms was a living text for the Anglo-Saxons and the Irish. Not only could they speak directly to God the way that Christ did, but they could also use the very language used by Christ to do so. Bede learned two different versions of the psalter by heart, and in his final days chanted the psalms during every available moment as the best preparation for meeting with his God.[5] Earlier, according to Adomnán, Columba of Iona spent

1 Talbot 1959, p. 98. 2 Colgrave 1956, p. 100. 3 RIA, 12.R.33.
4 For other book-shrines see Ryan 1989. 5 Ward 1991; Lapidge 1993b.

his last days copying the psalms, ending at Psalm 34.[6] The psalter served as the meditational focus for several extant Old English poems, both explicitly in the renditions of the metrical psalter and the Kentish Psalm 50, and implicitly in the opening of the *Creation of the World*, a loose translation of Psalm 18. More generally, its cadences and vocabulary underlie much Anglo-Saxon poetry, in both style and structure. For example, both the imprecation at the end of *The Wife's Lament* and the imagery of exile and alienation in *The Wanderer* and *The Seafarer* recall the lament psalms. The psalter was so intrinsic a part of the mental structure of the individual Anglo-Saxon that quoting from it was simply referencing a beloved friend of both parties, something which hardly needed explanation. Thus, the Easter antiphon, taken from Psalm 117.22, appears in the Old English *Menologium* as commentary upon the importance of this, the greatest movable feast in the Christian calendar: *Þis is se dæg ðæne drihten us / wisfæst worhte wera cneorissum / eallum eorðwarum eadigum to blisse* ('This is the day which the wise Lord made for us, for the generations of men, as a joy for all the blessed dwellers on the earth'). The psalms, then, were beloved friends, lyric texts which provided both a history of the inner life of every individual and a hope for salvation through faith and praise.

The psalter was constantly present in the mind of the ordinary Anglo-Saxon; it also imbued the physical surroundings in various ways. For example, Psalm 90.15 – in which Christ treads on the beasts, upon the asp and the basilisk, and upon the lion and the dragon – had a rich independent life in Anglo-Saxon England. It formed part of a charm against black ulcers that ordered them to dry up, to shrink for the individual patient, who like Christ expects to tread confidently upon the beasts which are the ulcers (a somewhat mundane use for the verse, but one no less important for the individual in question).[7] An illustration of the psalm verse similarly appears on the principal face of the Ruthwell Cross, and Christ over the beasts appears at the top of the west face of the shaft of the Bewcastle Cross. Taken out of its Davidic context, this psalm verse served iconographically as a precise image of Christ triumphant over all creatures, living and mythical. Individual psalm verses, then, appeared in contexts as disparate as 20-foot standing crosses from the northern extremities of early Northumbria and medical manuscripts of Wessex copied in the aftermath of the Norman Conquest.

A manuscript copy of the psalter was itself a tangible manifestation of Christian worship, a primer for the recitation of the office, and a set of personal

6 Sharpe 1995, p. 228.

7 From *Lacnunga*, BL, Harley 585, fol. 136r–v. Neither of the other two versions of this charm includes this line.

devotions. A psalter was much more likely to be produced for an individual than any other text of the early church. In the generation after the Norman Conquest, Christina of Markyate is closely associated with the St Albans Psalter, with its texts in both Latin and Old French, and glosses in Old English.[8] Gospels were for public usage; although psalters could likewise be public documents for use in the teaching of Latin, the training of oblates in the offices, and for singing the liturgy, they could also be for the contemplation and devotion of an individual Christian soul. Theologians commonly describe the psalms as a microcosmic version of the whole Bible, the Old Testament text most explicitly linked to its New Testament fulfilment. Psalm 31.6 'Into thy hands, O Lord, I commend my spirit' provides the last words used by Christ on the cross in Luke 23.46. In Manchester Cathedral, this verse is carved, in Latin and in an idiosyncratic script which may be either ninth-century or post-Conquest, into a red sandstone slab forming part of the cathedral fabric in the west face of the north interior wall of the chancel screen. There the verse had a public context, exhorting the faithful to continued faith in God and his works; in the psalm, David's faith is a more private and individual matter, with a wider range of petitions reflecting the individual's anguish and uncertainty, and calling for help against his enemies. The history of Anglo-Saxon psalter manuscripts, then, is a study of texts intended for three purposes: first, public recitation in the fellowship of Christian worship, integral parts of the office, outward and corporate expressions of praise and penitence; second, private meditation, for what has been described as the '*compunctio cordis*, that bright sorrow without which Christianity is merely a religion and a rite';[9] and, third, as a learning text to be memorised by oblates as their first Latin text, and to be contemplated by scholars for its intricacies both of doctrine and of poetic expression.

The psalter, then, has many contexts. It seems only fitting, therefore, that in the early Middle Ages three separate versions of the psalms were in use. The Roman psalter, reputed to be Jerome's first translation of the psalms into Latin, was rejected in Continental Europe in favour of the Gallican Psalter, Jerome's second effort. (His third rendition, the Hebrew Psalter, refers in its title to his return to the Hebrew psalms to check readings and correct his first efforts; this, however, did not gain popular acceptance and generally appears to have been a scholarly text, used for study of the many difficult passages.) In England, rather surprisingly, the Roman Psalter persisted into the eleventh century, and developed an affinity with the vernacular that held into the twelfth. That the eighth-century Vespasian Psalter made in Kent has the Roman text

8 Hildesheim Dombibliothek, St Godehard 1. 9 Ward 1991.

is not surprising (Plate 4.3),[10] but copies of the Roman psalter continued to be produced even long after the adoption of the Gallican Psalter (later the Vulgate) on the Continent during the Carolingian renaissance. The Harley 603 Psalter, a deluxe Canterbury manuscript started around the millennium with an extensive programme of illustration derived from the (Gallican) Utrecht Psalter,[11] has a Roman text, except for one quire, which, curiously, is Gallican.[12] So is the Regius Psalter, a central text in the Winchester psalter tradition.[13] The Roman psalter therefore maintained an unusual popularity in England throughout the Anglo-Saxon period and beyond. The 'Eadwine Psalter', a triple psalter copied at Canterbury in the mid twelfth century, has Old English glosses above the Roman text, Latin commentary from the *Glossa ordinaria* above the Gallican text, and Anglo-Norman glosses above the Hebrew Psalter.[14]

At the same time, this popularity was not hegemony: the majority of extant English-produced psalters, glossed or unglossed, are Gallican. Texts of the psalter copied on the Continent and brought to Anglo-Saxon England are invariably Gallican. Ælfric uses the Gallican psalter in his quotations from the psalms, reflecting the usage of his mentor Æthelwold at Winchester. In short, although the Roman Psalter maintained a surprising currency, especially at Canterbury, by the late tenth century the Gallican version had largely been adopted for Insular usage.

An Anglo-Saxon psalter manuscript could vary in size from the palm of the hand (the Galba or Athelstan Psalter[15]) to over half a metre in height (the Paris Psalter[16]). The decoration could range from a very plain and straightforward presentation of the psalms alone (the Regius Psalter) to a complex set of illuminations, marginal drawings, rubrics and versals (the Bury Psalter).[17] Its repertory and presentation of texts could range from a straightforward closely written copy of the Roman psalter with only canticles, a litany and some prayers for ancillary material (the Laud Psalter[18]), through to a glossed psalter with a Gallican copy of the text, Anglo-Saxon glosses and syntactic markings (the Lambeth Psalter[19]), on to a full-sized interlinear translation in syntactically garbled Old English (the Cambridge Psalter[20]), and even up to a complete facing translation in Old English poetry and prose (the Paris Psalter). Anglo-Saxon usage, however, does not follow the traditional distinction between

10 BL, Cotton Vespasian A.i. 11 Utrecht, UB, 32.
12 BL, Harley 603. The Gallican section corresponds with the stint of one scribe.
13 BL, Royal 2 B.v. 14 TCC, R.17.1.
15 See Deshman 1997. 16 BnF, lat. 8824.
17 BAV, Reg. lat. 12. 18 BodL., Laud lat. 81.
19 London, Lambeth Palace Library, 427.
20 CUL, Ff.1.23 (sometimes called the Winchcombe or the Ramsey Psalter).

the biblical psalter (containing only the psalms as they appear in the Bible) and the ferial psalter, with its psalm divisions, prefatory material, collects, calendars, prayers and other accretions. Save in the Royal Bible, in double psalters designed for study purposes – such as the Psalter of Saint Ouen[21] or the Ricemarch Psalter[22] – and the psalters which survive only in single pages (from which we cannot draw any conclusions about the format of the rest of the manuscript), the biblical psalter does not occur in the surviving Insular corpus.

Psalters could also acquire further accretions of two kinds. In the first place, the person commissioning the manuscript might decide to add some prayers or collects, a litany, some canticles, one of the standard psalter prefaces, and other texts of various kinds (hymnals, computistic material, calendars) to the manuscript. Thus, at the simpler end of the scale, the eleventh-century Stowe Psalter has a set of psalter collects following each psalm, and a set of canticles.[23] At the other extreme is Wulfstan's 'Portiforium', whose Gallican psalter occupies barely 100 of the 360 folia in the codex – which is in essence a portable service-book.[24] Second, after the completed psalter manuscript reached its home – whether in a religious foundation or with an individual – it often became the repository for other important documents. Thus, the earliest original charter of an English king – that of King Hlothere of Kent granting property in the Isle of Thanet to Abbot Berhtwald of Reculver in May 679 – survives because it was bound into a Christ Church, Canterbury, volume containing a ninth-century psalter and eighth-century gospels.[25] Similarly, appended to the Eadwine Psalter is a fascinating set of architectural drawings, presumptively of Christ Church.[26] The Psalter of Count Achadeus, a ninth-century Reimsian manuscript that had reached Canterbury by the eleventh century (Plate 14.2), has on its flyleaves material from Christ Church roll-books.[27] Most famously, perhaps, the Blickling Psalter (Plate 21.1) found use in the late Middle Ages and afterwards as an oath-book in the city of Lincoln.[28]

Some fifty psalters of Insular origin (broadly conceived) survive. Others most certainly existed: indeed, every parish church should have had at least one, while monastic establishments will have had multiple copies. Some, no doubt, wore out; in later centuries others became unrecognisable or devalued. Thus evidence for the survival of one psalter comes from three binding-strips in printed codices now found in libraries as far apart as Cambridge, Haarlem

21 Rouen, BM, A.41 (Cat. gén. 24). 22 TCD, 50 (A.4.20).
23 BL, Stowe 2. 24 CCCC, 391.
25 BL, Cotton Augustus II.2. The leaf was previously bound with the Utrecht Psalter.
26 TCC, R.17.1. 27 CCCC, 272. 28 PML, M 776.

and Sondershausen. Many other psalter manuscripts survive only as single leaves or a gathering in obscure record offices or private libraries which can be difficult to identify; Helmut Gneuss lists seven or so psalter fragments not previously mentioned by the cataloguers of Anglo-Saxon and Irish manuscripts.[29] Only two of these surviving psalters form part of splendid Bible pandects: the Codex Amiatinus, which includes a copy of the scholarly Hebrew Psalter,[30] and the Royal Bible.[31] Others are Continental imports for various purposes. For example, the double psalter now at Salisbury was a learned Continental product, with fully fifteen psalter prefaces before elegant copies of the Hebrew and Gallican Psalters on parallel pages. It has extensive commentary both in the margins and at the end of each psalm, and seems likely to have been principally useful for didactic purposes, though it also has imaginative decorative initials.[32] Similarly, the 'Southampton Psalter' is a small but extensively ornamented Irish copy of the psalms with very extensive Anglo-Saxon additions.[33] The Anglo-Saxons imported copies from different traditions, and incorporated them into their own usage.

The parameters of that use varied considerably. The Harley 603 Psalter, one of the glories of Anglo-Saxon illumination, with elegant and lively line-drawings derived with differing degrees of fidelity from those in the Utrecht Psalter, is a deluxe volume (Plate 10.6); however, its practical use is difficult to determine.[34] It is, unusually, a biblical psalter with none of the additions that would demonstrate liturgical use, though it does have the psalms correctly divided. Now ending abruptly in Psalm 143 and lacking illustrations for thirty-two of its psalms, the manuscript was never finished despite being worked on intermittently for more than a century. The extent of its indebtedness to the Utrecht Psalter changes over the course of time, reflecting different phases of production. The first compiler decided to use Caroline Minuscule rather than Rustic Capitals, a Roman rather than a Gallican text, and multi-coloured lines rather than monochrome ones for the illustrations. However, further changes, probably reflecting differing priorities in the scriptorium, ensued. In some quires the illustrator is in charge, and the text fits around the newly reconceived drawings, which may even have preceded the Latin onto the page. In others, the scribe dictates the production, and the text has priority. Unfortunately, at some point the impetus for this grand project disappeared, so that it was never

29 Gneuss 2001.
30 Florence, Biblioteca Medicea-Laurenziana, Amiatino 1.
31 BL, Royal 1 E.vii+viii. See further Chapter 17 in this volume.
32 Salisbury CL, 180. 33 Cambridge, St John's College, C.9 (59).
34 Noel 1995.

completed. The use for which the manuscript was intended remains something of a conundrum. Against liturgical use at Christ Church, Canterbury, is the circumstance that the text is largely Roman, though the greater part of five of the longer psalms is Gallican; there are no corrections either to the Roman or the Gallican passages, so there was no attempt to impose uniformity for use in the office. Nor could the manuscript have functioned as a teaching text. Similarly, although the drawings are engaging interpretations of the psalter text, they are in the first place incomplete, and in the second place their combination of motifs and images is sufficiently complex that they would provide a very uncertain guide to a reader trying to use the illustrations to interpret the text. As mnemonic devices, or foci for meditation, they might well function for the devout Christian since they do provide predominantly literal renditions of the psalms. The manuscript seems best interpreted, therefore, as a private reading text for someone well versed in the psalms; given the time lavished on it and the intelligent beauty of the layout, text and illustrations, that person must have been influential and important.

Other surviving psalter manuscripts are more obviously practical and less ornamental, such as a small, neat book copied at St Augustine's, Canterbury, at the end of the eleventh century.[35] Missing the opening folia, the text of the Gallican Psalter begins at Psalm 9.8, and following the psalter is a set of canticles, a litany, prayers and a hymnal with canticles. Although much of the original decoration is lost, a display initial with a gold-leaved first line ornaments Psalm 109. Also gold and purple initials mark the eightfold liturgical division of the psalter (at Psalms 1, 26, 38, 52, 68, 80, 97, and the aforementioned 109). Missing are what were probably elegant decorated openings for Psalms 1, 51 and 101, reflecting the ancient Irish but by this time very common threefold division of the psalms. The manuscript is elegant and functional, with each Latin verse written across the full page, the script and letter spacing sized so that many of the lines are justified. Each psalm begins with a two-line gold initial, each verse with a one-line versal alternately blue, red or green in the left-hand margin. The punctuation is similarly effective and unobtrusive, with a *punctus elevatus* after the membrum (the first half of the psalm verse) and a lower *distinctio* (to the modern eye a full stop) at the end of the verse. This was not a manuscript for public display; thus, although the psalm headings or rubrics are in gold, they are written in the same Caroline Minuscule as the rest of the text, not in any form of display script. The psalm divisions used for recitation during the offices are clearly marked, and the very few Latin glosses

35 Rouen, BM, A.44 (231).

that appear are not contemporary with the manuscript, having been added for comprehension by later generations of users. Immediately following the psalter are three short penitential prayers, requesting the help of God for the *famulus tuus* and hoping that the psalms might do the singer some heavenly benefit. The manuscript, with its ordered, neat and accurate copy of the psalter, and the additions typical of a ferial psalter, was designed for individual use by someone well acquainted with the monastic office – most likely a high-born cleric.

This psalter, the product of a monastic scriptorium in the aftermath of the Conquest for an educated and highly literate Christian, received only a few sporadic Latin glosses, reminders of allegorical interpretations or explications of difficult words. Glossing was, however, one of the most interesting of the Anglo-Saxon responses to the psalter. Almost from the earliest of times, the Anglo-Saxons glossed the psalter in the vernacular. Also from the earliest of times, these vernacular glosses developed from the sporadic to the comprehensive, from unexpected additions between the ruled lines in a small bookhand to being planned for in the production of the manuscript. The glosses themselves suggest a developing pattern of sophistication in the vocabulary and syntactic choices of the glossators. Traditionally, the psalter glosses have been divided into two groups, named for their earliest and most coherent exempla: the A tradition, from the Vespasian Psalter; and the D tradition, from the Regius or Royal Psalter.[36] While the distinction is a useful one, the study of the Anglo-Saxon glossed psalters is a field rich with cross-influences and complications: Gallican glosses in a Roman psalter, double glosses, brief passages of commentary interspersed in the margins, and occasional shifts from one gloss tradition to the other. The A tradition is generally defined as pragmatic and fairly simple. The implication is that perhaps this was the earliest round of psalter-glossing, and consistency and accuracy were the only real considerations. The Regius Psalter, a careful and coherent product of Winchester during the Benedictine reform, provides a scholarly and thoughtful set of glosses which appear to have become a new standard of excellence in late Anglo-Saxon England.[37] The Regius Psalter itself is scrupulous in ways that its copies are not: never are the *nomina sacra* glossed, and most proper names are not anglicised, the majority not even glossed. However, a simplistic interpretation that suggests that the A tradition of the Vespasian Psalter, housed at Canterbury, gave way in later Anglo-Saxon England to the D tradition based at Winchester would be utterly mistaken.

36 Sisam and Sisam 1959. 37 Gretsch 1999, pp. 261–331.

The Blickling Psalter, an eighth-century copy of uncertain provenance, is sometimes placed at Canterbury because the Latin is a Roman psalter with close connections to the Roman text of the Vespasian Psalter, but the manuscript also has ties to Northumbria. Its script and layout resemble volumes associated with Lindisfarne (Plate 21.1). Written *per cola et commata*, each psalm verse occupies an average of two lines, with the versal in the left margin surrounded by red dots. There are some indications that the Latin text was ruled and written first. The tituli, the rubrication, and the decoration of the psalm initials fit into spaces left by the manuscript designer and the scribe. Given that at the foot of each page there is evidence of compression in the text, it is possible that the scribe was following the exemplar page for page. Like the Lindisfarne Gospels, the manuscript was not originally intended for glossing. The heavily decorated initials are very elaborate at the beginning of the manuscript, and they do not always balance or fit properly in the space available, which suggests that the illustrator was having some difficulty. In the last third of the manuscript, the initials follow standard models of interlace and geometric designs with bird or snake heads. As a result, they are less original, less elaborate, and less eye-catching.[38]

After the completion of the planned codex, many layers of accretion followed. In the late eighth or early ninth century, a single hand – possibly even the rubricator – scrawled in red ink some fifty Old English glosses of hard words. A neat hand of the late tenth century glossed more difficult words (verbs, nouns and especially proper nouns) into the vernacular, occasionally adding Latin allegorical interpretations. This layer of glossing sometimes looks like a teaching exercise – a way of moving students quickly through learning both Latin and the psalter at the same time. Once, an entire verse receives a complete translation in the right-hand margin. Another layer of glosses of similar date is mainly concentrated in one opening of the manuscript, with very sporadic appearances elsewhere. Beside each verse, mostly in the right-hand margin, is a sentence or two from the standard commentaries (Jerome and Cassiodorus were preferred in Anglo-Saxon England) explicating the psalm. The next layers of additions are mostly musical: a rubricator marked many antiphonal psalm divisions and all the diapsalma (the equivalent to the Hebrew *selah*, a musical direction), and various kinds of musical notation also appear – letters over the Latin words to indicate pitch, neumes especially in the first lines of several psalms, and musical cues. In the fifteenth century a calendar was attached to

38 The pages marking the threefold division of the psalms are unfortunately missing. They could provide more information as to the originality of the decoration.

the beginning of the psalter, perhaps replacing an outdated earlier one. In the later Middle Ages, then, despite its antique script and the superseded Roman text, this manuscript was still being used in an ecclesiastical foundation. In the Renaissance, the manuscript continued in use, though in a different context. A page at the end of the codex received gospel passages (those often used for oath-swearing) and the flyleaves – and occasionally the text – acquired many signatures of assorted dignitaries from Lincoln. The largest and perhaps most appealing of these is George Davye, who signs 'on this day of the month 1605' on a flyleaf, and provides his name in several other places.[39] The manuscript had become a civic talisman. The Blickling Psalter thus demonstrably has had a long and varied history from its inception to the early seventeenth century, when it became an object for antiquarian study. Other Anglo-Saxon psalters experienced similar fates.

Dating from the first half of the eleventh century, the Lambeth Psalter (Plate 21.2) (a Gallican text) is a much later and, in its conception, a more sophisticated and learned product. The manuscript is something of a bravura performance, including canticles, prayers, a set of lunar prognostications and tables, and even a prayer in Old English. Perhaps the best example of a teaching psalter from Insular sources, it has very extensive glossing, often two and sometimes three vernacular equivalents to each Latin *lemma*. The manuscript was ruled only for the Latin psalter, and the rubrics or *tituli* were clearly added after the main text of the psalms since at times they run down the side of the page. However, as the illustration of Psalm 149 demonstrates, this manuscript has elegance and clarity, and if it does not achieve the level of professionalism of the Regius Psalter it comes very close to it. The origin of the manuscript remains obscure. Rejecting, whether consciously or not, both the A and D traditions of psalter-glossing, Lambeth includes nearly 50 per cent more glosses than any other version, offering double glosses and interpretations of many difficult words: it thereby reflects a reconception of the whole premise of using a glossed psalter to teach both Christianity and Latin. The script of the glosses is a neat book-hand, the work of someone used to gauging space available, with or without dry-point ruling to help, and fitting the text in crisply. Though not a display manuscript in any respect, the Lambeth Psalter bears witness to heavy contemporary usage, since there are numerous alterations and additions to the gloss, possibly by the same scribe going back over the work, but not necessarily. The syntactic markings below the Latin psalter are

39 In the Blickling Homilies manuscript (Princeton University Library, W. H. Scheide Collection, 71), also at Lincoln for some time, he proudly signs himself, 'George Davye, Macebearer'.

particularly intriguing, as they very simply, using a selection of dots and commas, lead the reader through the syntax of the sacred original. Also, a prayer is added in one space on fols. 141–2, and fifteen lines of alliterative verse from the second half of the eleventh century were added to fol. 183v. No musical annotation appears, and the manuscript does not appear to have been in the 'public domain'. Added pages at the beginning of the manuscript bear psalter prefaces and a prayer. There is less evidence in the Lambeth Psalter for usage in later eras, though the litany in the manuscript dates from the fifteenth century and may replace an earlier one, and a lost leaf after fol. 77 was supplied, probably in the late fifteenth or early sixteenth century.

The Cambridge Psalter (also occasionally known as the Winchcombe Psalter), is often classed as a glossed psalter, sometimes as having an 'alternate line gloss',[40] but the manuscript is perhaps best thought of as an alternate line translation (Plate 21.3). The very peculiar presentation of texts makes it clear that the Old English has equivalent, if not greater, importance than the Latin text of the Roman Psalter. The scribe's Latinity was dismal indeed. The Old English, a literal set of glosses to the psalms in the tradition of that appearing in the Vespasian Psalter, was written in bright red (now faded), the Latin in a slightly watery brown, and the psalm headings or *tituli* are green. The effect is colourful but unexpected, given that rubrics are generally red (reflecting the term 'rubric') and texts in brown or black ink, with green used only as a versal or for decoration. Opinions differ as to where this idiosyncratic manuscript was written. The Latin psalm verse sprawls across the page for most of the manuscript, since in the first quire, when the Latin text was written more normally with six or so words to the line, the Old English was continually running into the gutter. The solution the scribe adopted in the next quire was to stretch out the Latin text to 4–5 words per line. There is, unusually, no punctuation whatsoever in the Old English text, though the copy of the A gloss is a coherent and intelligent one. However, in the absence of punctuation, a reader would have difficulty construing the text – another odd feature of this odd manuscript. It even seems possible that the Old English was written first for most of the manuscript, with Latin accommodated to its layout. The set of canticles is a standard one, and the litany and prayers are largely unexceptional. There is, however, a carelessness of presentation throughout: rarely do the canticles have titles or headings; the line spacing, both vertically and horizontally, is uneven throughout because of inaccurate ruling; and the parchment is dark, oily to the touch, and of relatively poor quality, to the extent that

40 First noted in Ker 1957, no. 13, pp. 11–12.

the folio with the opening miniature for Psalm 1, the *Beatus vir*, even has holes. The illustration of the opening of Psalm 149, fol. 249v, demonstrates the awkwardness of the manuscript layout. The Old English text, which some think a direct copy of the Vespasian Psalter gloss, is of the A tradition, with literal and practical interpretations of the Latin original. The Old English is the most coherent component of this otherwise rather scruffy manuscript; here, perhaps, the vernacular achieves an unusual priority. Whether this means that the manuscript was intended for use by a member of the laity, perhaps someone attending some monastic offices but not wholly versed in the sacred language, is an open question.

Finally, having considered the use of the psalter in the vernacular as an aid to learning Latin, let us examine the substantial evidence for scholarly study of the psalms in Insular centres. Here the story begins, unsurprisingly, in Ireland where the Springmount Bog Tablets, with verses from the psalms written as learning exercises, inaugurate a long tradition of psalter study.[41] These wax tablets (the layer of wax being applied over yew) survive only because they were lost in a peat bog in the seventh century; they record verses from Psalms 30–2 and reflect the fundamental need to be adept in the psalter – *psalteratus*.[42] The Irish knew the psalter at a level far above basic memory work, however: the division of the psalter into three quinquagenes, the 'three fifties', is an Irish development of the early Middle Ages, and evidence for extensive Irish psalter commentary survives. In fact, from Ireland and Anglo-Saxon England survives most of the evidence for the lost psalter commentary of Theodore of Mopsuestia, a late fourth-century exegete interested in literal, literary and historical approaches to the psalter as well as other books of the Bible. He was condemned and superseded in the early church by the more traditional four fold exegesis focusing on allegorical and anagogical interpretations.[43] More conventional commentaries on the psalms, including Augustine, Cassiodorus and Jerome, were also in use. At Winchester during the Benedictine reform study of the psalter reached new heights of codification and organisation, such that the Regius Psalter, with its careful and scholarly glosses, was complemented by a set of companion volumes: one volume from an original four-volume Jerome commentary on the psalms, with some tabs for reference purposes, survives.[44] Written in the same hand as the Regius Psalter, it is

41 Dublin, National Museum of Ireland, S.A. 1914. More recently, in July 2006, another peat bog in Faddan More, Co. Tipperary, produced twenty folios of an eighth- or ninth-century psalter, wrapped in vellum rather than bound.

42 Webster and Backhouse 1991, no. 64.

43 Ó'Néill 2001, pp. 37–44.

44 BL, Royal 4 A.xiv.

clearly a scholarly tome for advanced study and exegesis. Psalter scholarship in the British Isles was idiosyncratic, with its Theodorean influences as expanded through centuries of Irish scholarship and its further development of literal approaches even in psalm illustration, but it also had its conventional aspects, using psalter prefaces and commentaries from the more orthodox traditions of early medieval exegesis.

Psalters are idiosyncratic books, and the surviving Insular copies before *c.* 1100 reflect that individual nature. Their uses overlap, so that some were used for teaching Latin and learning the psalms and also for reciting or singing the office, while others combined monastic usage with private devotion. The larger and grander copies provided the occasion for extensive illustration, and the presence of the Utrecht Psalter at Canterbury in the early eleventh century enabled it to be used as an exemplar both for programmes of psalter illustration and for a particular style of line-drawing. Most strikingly, the decision to follow the Utrecht Psalter's programme of literal illustration suggests that Insular artists and scribes focused on literal rather than allegorical interpretations of the psalter. In the psalter armies battle, David prays to an unseen God, farmers plough their fields, and children play. The Gallican Psalter, with its freight of Latin allegorical commentary, had achieved parity – and perhaps more – with the Roman Psalter, but the Christological focus of the psalms was not the only structure of interpretation available to the individual Anglo-Saxon.

Having started with the devotional activities of that independent spirit of early Norman England, Christina of Markyate, we should conclude with three well-known Insular men embedded in the political and ecclesiastical hierarchies of their day. According to Adomnán of Iona, Columba sang the psalms in church with the brethren so clearly and sweetly, uplifted above all the other voices, that every word could be heard by people more than a mile away – not invariably, but occasionally, as a miracle.[45] Bede was by his own account much taken with the psalter. In the *Historia ecclesiastica*, he recounts how during a plague, when only the abbot Ceolfrith and one young boy were left capable of chanting the psalter, the abbot tried briefly to cut back on the recitation of the whole psalter with antiphons, but was unable to endure the curtailed worship. Many think that the young boy in question was Bede, a child oblate already more than capable of chanting the entire psalter. Bede also created the first abbreviated psalter, intended not only as a mnemonic device for remembering the psalms and their order but also as a devotion in itself.[46] The Book of Cerne,

45 Sharpe 1995. 46 Ward 1991; Lapidge 1993b.

incidentally, has another breviate psalter, perhaps of Irish origin, as part of its complement of Christian prayers and devotions.[47] Finally, King Alfred was especially devoted to the psalter, such that he completed a translation into Old English prose of the first fifty psalms. A century later, Cnut seems to have used grand psalters as gifts to cement alliances, thereby proving the political worth of deluxe manuscripts. His predecessor, the king of Wessex, had a more personal relationship with the psalms. Moreover, if the West Saxon genealogy is to be believed, Alfred was following in the psalmic footsteps of his distant ancestor, King David of Israel. David, no doubt, would have approved, both of the personal and of the political usage.

47 CUL, Ll.1.10.

22

Music books

SUSAN RANKIN

The first music books in Britain

The earliest reference to books of music used in the English church is in Bede's *Ecclesiastical History of the English People*:

> Benedict received this Abbot John and brought him to Britain in order that he might teach the monks of his monastery the mode of chanting throughout the year as it was practised at St Peter's in Rome. Abbot John carried out the pope's instructions and taught the cantors of the monastery the order and manner of singing and reading aloud and also committed to writing all things necessary for the celebration of festal days throughout the whole year; these writings have been preserved to this day in the monastery and copies have now been made by many others elsewhere.[1]

The committal in writing of 'all things necessary for the celebration of festal days', and the making of copies from this central source for use elsewhere, suggests a perceived need to perform the liturgy in a specific way, recognised as being correct: without a written version, 'the order and manner of singing and reading aloud' might not be properly maintained. Within Bede's words a paradox lies hidden, however: what was being recorded in written form might include information about texts to be sung (as incipits or full texts), and texts to be read (ditto), along with rubrics about how the liturgy was to be performed, but it was all in the medium of words alone. For in early eighth-century Britain, there was no practice of writing musical notation and, as in Continental Europe, no concern with a notational system suitable for

1 'Accepit et praefatum Iohannem abbatem Brittaniam perducendum, quatinus in monasterio suo cursum canendi annuum, sicut ad sanctum Petrum Romae agebatur, edoceret; egitque abba Iohannes ut iussionem acceperat pontificis, et ordinem uidelicet ritumque canendi ac legendi uiua uoce praefati monasterii cantores edocendo, et ea quae totius anni circulus in celebratione dierum festorum poscebat etiam litteris mandando, quae hactenus in eodem monasterio seruata et a multis iam sunt circumquaque transcripta.' *HE*, IV, 18: Colgrave and Mynors 1969, pp. 388–9.

recording chant melodies. Those ways of singing taught by John were certainly memorised by him during his training in Rome – Bede had named him as the archcantor of St Peter's – and then taught through some kind of rote practice to the cantors of Wearmouth-Jarrow. Bede's *Ecclesiastical History* is full of stories about singers brought from one place to another to teach proper singing: in particular, his account of the activities of Bishop Acca of Hexham is eloquent about the problems of preserving specific ways of singing:

> Further, he invited a famous singer named Maban, who had been instructed in methods of singing by the successors of the disciples of St Gregory in Kent, to teach him and his people; he kept him for twelve years teaching them such church music as they did not know, while the music they once knew and which had begun to deteriorate by long use or neglect was restored to its original form.[2]

In what sense then can John's writings be described as 'music books'? The answer belongs in the interaction of memory and sight in the act of singing. The practice of singing from exemplars which can only have recorded words is described elsewhere: in an example dating not much later than Bede's *Ecclesiastical History*, the first *Ordo Romanus* (describing the papal mass and transmitted to Gaul before 750), the cantor sings the gradual responsory holding a 'cantatorium'.[3] In this situation the cantor may have used the words written in the cantatorium as a guide by which to search his memory for the melody: for such an elaborate melody as that of a gradual, each single word could become a significant visual symbol.

When the passing on of music from one generation to another depended on a combination of oral and written transmission, any book containing texts intended to be sung should be considered a 'music book'. An account of music books in Britain should therefore begin with one copied before Bede wrote his *Ecclesiastical History*. The Antiphoner of Bangor, consisting of thirty-six leaves, was copied in the late seventh century at Bangor on the southern shore of what is now Belfast Lough.[4] Much of the material in this book was intended for the divine office, with a large complement of hymns, canticles, collects and short antiphons; but it also contains some liturgy for the mass. Its contents

2 'Cantatorem quoque egregium, uocabulo Maban, qui a successoribus discipulorum beati papae Gregorii in Cantia fuerat cantandi sonos edoctus, ad se suosque instituendos accersiit, ac per annos xii tenuit, quatinus et quae illi non nouerant carmina ecclesiastica doceret, et ea quae quondam cognita longo usu uel neglegentia inueterare coeperant, huius doctrina priscum renouarentur in statum.' *HE*, v, 20: Colgrave and Mynors 1969, pp. 530–1.

3 Andrieu 1971, p. 87; Huglo 1988, p. 96, records other examples, including one from a text composed in 487.

4 Milan, Biblioteca Ambrosiana, C.5.inf.: Warren 1893–5; see also Curran 1984.

are so all-embracing that Cabrol argued for its having been made for the abbot himself,[5] a book on the basis of which the liturgy could be managed, rather than one intended for the direct use of the person who organised and led singing in the choir. Other fragments of Irish books of this same period appear to be of the same type: that is, containing a mixture of liturgical materials.[6]

The antiphoner cited in the *Dialogus* associated with Egbert, archbishop of York,[7] may also have been of this inclusive kind, since the writer envisages it as the counterpart of a missal:

> In his antiphonary and missal, St Gregory through [Augustine] his aforementioned legate, intended this feast to be celebrated in the full week of Pentecost by the English Church. Not only do our antiphonaries bear witness, but also those which we had examined with their missals at the churches of Saints Peter and Paul.[8]

Read as indicating books of office liturgy, as a counterpart to missals for the mass, the volumes named 'antiphoners' by this writer would have included prayers and readings as well as chants – as in the case of the Bangor book (which has prayers and chants, but no readings). But there is another way of understanding the juxtaposed references: if 'missal' is taken as indicating not a plenary book, but rather a collection of mass prefaces and prayers – thus what was also known as a sacramentary ('liber sacramentorum')[9] – then the description 'antiphonarius' could indicate the kind of specialised music book which later became the norm in the Carolingian Empire, including only the texts for chants (with, by the end of the ninth century, their melodies also).[10] Alcuin's use of 'de antiphonario' as a rubric in the last section of his devotional florilegium *De laude dei* also depends on this more specialised sense of the word: the texts he cites in this section are demonstrably drawn from the repertory of material sung rather than read in the divine office (and, in a few cases, the mass).[11] Since Alcuin probably composed his *De laude dei* while still at York, we

5 Cabrol 1907–53. 6 See Gamber 1968, nos. 151–63.

7 Bullough 1991, pp. 5–6, and 2004, pp. 230–1, considered this passage to have been part of an interpolation associated with Egbert's successor, Ælberht, and to date from after the mid eighth century.

8 'Hoc autem jejunium idem beatus Gregorius, per praefatum legatum, in Antiphonario suo et Missali, in plena epdomada post Pentecosten Anglorum æcclesiæ celebrandum destinavit. Quod non solum nostra testantur Antiphonaria, sed et ipsa quæ cum Missalibus suis conspeximus apud apostolorum Petri et Pauli limina.' Haddan and Stubbs 1869–78, III, p. 412; trans. from Cubitt 1995, p. 150.

9 On the use in Anglo-Saxon England of the Latin 'missale' and Old English 'mæsse-boc' to indicate a sacramentary see Gneuss 1985, pp. 99–102.

10 On early uses of the term 'antiphoner' see Bullough 2004, p. 194 n. 195.

11 On Alcuin's *De laude dei*, see most recently, Bullough 2004, pp. 193–204, and on the chants Constantinescu 1974 and Rankin 2011.

might surmise that a book exclusively for the use of the cantor was known in Northumbria before 770.

*

The paucity of surviving music books copied in Britain before the late tenth century is striking, especially in the light of evidence which directly associates a concern for correctness in the singing of chant with written exemplars. In this respect the importance of Roman models implied in Bede's account of the work of John at Wearmouth-Jarrow in the years 678–80 is reinforced by the canons of the council held by Archbishop Cuthbert at Clofesho in 747. Here reference is made to a 'written exemplar from the Roman church':

> That in one and the same manner the holy feasts of the Lord's dispensation in the flesh should be celebrated properly in all matters relating to them, that is, in the office of baptism, in the celebration of masses, in the manner of the chant, according to the written exemplar which we have from the Roman church, so that in a cycle of the whole year, the feastdays of the saints are venerated on one and the same day according to the martyrology of the same Roman church with the appropriate psalmody or cantilena.[12]

In a study of the liturgical provisions of this council, Cubitt has shown how the growth of a 'sense of a Roman tradition in English liturgy' which stretched 'back to Gregory himself' was given permanence in the extensive liturgical provisions which 'explained and justified existing customs', while elevating 'Roman practice as an authoritative norm'.[13] As later in Carolingian Europe the focus on Roman liturgical practice underlay the impetus to produce new, correct books for the use of priests and cantors, so surely also in Anglo-Saxon England. And yet, for the eighth and ninth centuries, there is no trace, even in fragmentary form, of either a Roman or an Anglo-Saxon 'music book'. The closest we can come to information about what was sung in England is through Alcuin's excerpts in *De laude dei*. Even the incipits of Proper chants added in the margins of a sacramentary copied for the use of Plegmund, archbishop of Canterbury (890–923), themselves date from the late tenth century.[14]

12 'Ut uno eodemque modo Dominicæ dispensationis in carne sacrosanctæ festivitates, in omnibus ad eas rite competentibus rebus, id est, in Baptismi officio, in Missarum celebratione, in cantilenæ modo celebrantur, juxta exemplar videlicet quod scriptum de Romana habemus Ecclesia. Itemque ut per gyrum totius anni natalitia sanctorum uno eodemque die, juxta martyrologium ejusdem Romanæ Ecclesiæ, cum sua sibi convenienti psalmodio seu cantilena venerentur.' Haddan and Stubbs 1869–78, III, p. 367: trans. in part from Cubitt 1995, pp. 142–3.

13 Cubitt 1995, pp. 150–1.

14 BodL., Bodley 579, the Leofric Missal. For a detailed study of the various layers in this book (although without palaeographical comment on the marginal chant incipits) see Orchard 2002.

This lack of early Anglo-Saxon sources of chant renders the survival of sources securely datable to the tenth century all the more significant, especially since the way in which they lay out chant differs from the manner of presentation in the Bangor Antiphoner. Two sources show the transmission of chant texts in a manner which can be traced back, in Continental sources, at least to the late eighth century. A book given to Chester-le-Street by King Athelstan between 934 and 939 contains Bede's prose and verse *Lives* of Cuthbert, with a mass and office for that saint.[15] Plate 22.1 shows part of fol. 94r with texts of office chants: these are written in a smaller script than the preceding prayers for the mass. Such a distinction of size, commonly observable in sacramentaries, missals and pontificals – thus books whose principal users were priests rather than cantors – is likely to have been introduced for the sake of clarity: the distinction between, on the one hand, prayers, readings and rubrics, and, on the other, texts to be sung, would have helped a priest to know when he should not take the lead. Of course, one of the immediate physical results of using a smaller script was that it left a larger empty space between written lines of text (since ruling distances remained the same); and it was into that space that many early notations were written in books not at first prepared for musical notation. That such space for musical notation was a by-product of the distinction of script sizes, and not vice versa – the script was reduced in size in order to enter musical notation – is easily verified, since in this kind of presentation the chant texts are often abbreviated (much less usual when notation is envisaged) and syllables of words are never spaced for melismatic passages. Both features can be seen in the Chester-le-Street book, where, in addition, the space above the chant texts has often been used for the addition of accent marks.

Another source of office liturgy, a breviary now surviving as six leaves preserved at the front and back of a later book, was copied in Square Minuscule at some time in the second half of the tenth century.[16] Here the layout is identical to that for the Cuthbert office in the Chester-le-Street book, with a freely flowing exchange between larger and smaller scripts, common use of abbreviation in the texts to be sung, and no syllable spacing.

In such sources as these, musical notation was not envisaged. Were it not for the survival, even if in extremely distressed form, of material with musical notation copied in England in the first half of the tenth century, it would be possible to argue for the direct association of notation with the Benedictine

15 CCCC, 183. On this manuscript see esp. Keynes 1985, pp. 180–5. The texts of the Cuthbert office and mass are edited in Hohler 1956.

16 BL, Royal 17 C.xvii, fols. 2–3, 163–6.

revival and reform undertaken in the second half of the tenth century. Two leaves bound at the front of Cambridge, Pembroke College, 46 contain antiphons (fol. B) and part of an Alleluia cycle (fol. A). The state of preservation of these leaves is so bad that much is now illegible. Nevertheless, the spacing of words for notation is easily distinguished,[17] and some passages of text have notation in an ink which appears similar to that of the text-hand, and may thus have been entered when the leaves were first copied.[18] These scraps thus indicate the use of musical notation alongside an Anglo-Saxon text-hand much earlier than the bulk of extant examples of Insular notation – which date from the end of the tenth century, and, above all, the mid eleventh century – revealing as simplistic any hypothesis that credits the Benedictine revival with the introduction of the idea of notation to Anglo-Saxon England. Nonetheless, it remains true that evidence for widespread use of musical notation belongs to a later period; the expectation in scriptoria that could produce high-grade books such as that given to Chester-le-Street with an office for Cuthbert was certainly that music belonged to the art of the cantor, rather than to the activity of the scribe.

Musical literacy

When the breviary of which fragments survive in Royal 17 C.xvii was made, musical notation was simply not envisaged; whereas in the only other extant pre-Conquest Anglo-Saxon breviary (another fragment of five leaves, from Muchelney), probably copied in the second quarter of the eleventh century, the complete integration of musical notation into textual layout, and the use of a nuance-rich and well-written form of notation, can be observed.[19] The time frame for the adoption the concept of musical notation in Anglo-Saxon England, for the development of an Insular form of musical script, and for understanding of the consequences of musical notation in the preparation of books, must be broadly that set by these two sources, from the middle of the tenth century to the 1030s. At the earlier end of this period it is difficult to refine what is no more than a hazy impression, not only because of the lack of sources, but also because many examples of notation were added to texts at a later date. For, during a long period of transition, besides those books

17 This is especially clear for the melismatic Alleluia, on fol. A.

18 The first layer of notation, in 'Breton' neumes, is sporadic; a later layer, in a different ink, uses Insular neume forms.

19 BL, Add. 56488. For information about the contents and date of copying of this source I am indebted to Jesse Billett.

conceived *ab initio* for musical notation, there are many examples of books in which musical notation was not originally envisaged, but has nevertheless been used extensively. Perhaps the most dramatic demonstration of the change away from the 'text as aide-memoire for musical delivery' culture of the tenth century is the survival of six gatherings in a book made in the 1020s or 30s which depend for their *raison d'être* on musical notation: in these gatherings, second voices to accompany chant melodies – whose texts and melodies were already available elsewhere – were notated.[20]

The idea that some aspects of music could be recorded in writing must have been familiar to many Anglo-Saxons in the tenth century: some will have had the chance to see and to handle fully notated books comparable to two graduals made in Laon and in the west of France, the first in the last quarter of the ninth century, the second in the early tenth.[21] In the second half of the tenth century, contact with Continental houses encouraged by the Benedictine reforming bishops would surely have brought to Anglo-Saxon England monastic scribes familiar with forms of musical notation, perhaps even carrying notated music books. In this context, the most conspicuous evidence of musical influence from Continental Europe is the report of Abbot Æthelwold's request to Corbie to send to Abingdon 'highly skilled men' to teach his monks the proper manner of reading and singing.[22] Æthelwold became bishop of Winchester in 963; thus the invitation will have been extended before that date. The report is significant because of the very close relation between notations associated with Corbie and the kind of notation written in sources connected with Winchester from the early eleventh century onwards. Above all, the Antiphoner of Mont-Renaud,[23] copied at Corbie in the mid tenth century, and notated later either at Corbie or somewhere within its direct sphere of influence, shares with the Winchester type of notation both the parallelism of up and down strokes and many neume forms, including cursive looped ways of writing and the disposition of separate strokes in melodic figures composed of multiple neumes.[24] Plate 22.2 shows this type of notation in a mid-eleventh-century missal from the Old Minster.[25]

The Winchester style of Insular notation may have used a type of script developed at Corbie as its immediate model; the wider context of its model(s)

20 CCCC, 473, fols. 135–90; on this polyphonic repertory see Rankin 2007, ch. 9.

21 Laon, BM, 239: facs. in *Paléographie musicale* 10 (1909). Chartres, BM, 47: facs. in *Paléographie musicale* 11 (1912).

22 'viros solertissimos'; see Stevenson 1858, I, p. 129. On Æthelwold's liturgical interests see Lapidge and Winterbottom 1991, pp. LX–LXXXV.

23 The manuscript is in a private collection; facs. in *Paléographie musicale* 16 (1955).

24 For a detailed study of Winchester notation, see Rankin 2007, chs. 4 and 5.

25 Worcester CL, F.173.

was certainly northern French. Another quite different way of writing musical notation, otherwise predominantly found in sources from the west of France (and therefore named 'Breton'), is prominent in a series of early Anglo-Saxon sources, both written on the Continent and brought early to England, and written in England.[26] Thirteen bifolia from a sacramentary recovered from the binding of the Winton Domesday date from the tenth century; these were copied somewhere on the Continent, and have notation of the Breton kind for the Easter Exultet and the Preface which follows.[27] That the sacramentary came to England before *c.* 1000 is implied by the presence of a marginal note in Square Minuscule; but perhaps just as interesting as the textual note is the fact that some passages of Breton notation have been over-written using Insular neume forms. These musical alterations support the implication of later textual annotations that the book *was* used in England, indeed that it continued to be used throughout the eleventh century.

The fragments in Pembroke 46 are the earliest extant source of musical notation written beside an Anglo-Saxon text-hand: here Breton notation seems to have been added when the texts were copied, whereas, for some of the passages which remained unnotated, Insular neumes were added at a different time. This and several late tenth- and early eleventh-century sources prove beyond doubt that Breton notation was not only seen but also written by the Anglo-Saxons. In a fine eighth-century Northumbrian gospel-book, a clumsy hand of the late tenth century has added the responsory *Deum time et mandata eius* with Breton notation in a margin;[28] in a copy of Bede's *Lives* of St Cuthbert probably made at St Augustine's, Canterbury, in the mid-tenth century, a text-hand of the late tenth or early decades of the eleventh century has entered texts for three chants; these are accompanied by Breton notation written by two different hands.[29] Finally, in the Harkness Gospels, made in Brittany in the ninth century, a later addition shows the writing of Breton neumes associated with an Insular text-hand of the mid or later tenth century: whether or not the book itself was ever in England, the neumes can be linked with a scribe trained in England.[30]

26 Huglo 1963 presents a general survey of these notations, with source lists.
27 London, Society of Antiquaries 154*: on which see Wormald 1976; Dumville 1992, p. 80, and Pfaff 1995b, pp. 26–8. The parchment is of a quality well below that associated with books from Anglo-Saxon England.
28 CUL, Kk.1.24, fol. 7r, upper margin.
29 BL, Cotton Vitellius A.xix, fol. 88r; reproduced in Bell 2001, p. 46. Insular neumes are written above the first words ('Sacerdos magnus sanctus Martinus'), but the continuation of this chant and the notation over the two Alleluias which follow is Breton. On fol. 89r of this source, yet another kind of neumatic notation (northern French) appears.
30 New York Public Library, 115; on later entries to this book see Hartzell 1981, pp. 85–97. On the two types of notation in Anglo-Saxon books see also Gullick and Rankin 2009.

One of the most substantial Insular sources to be notated in Breton neumes – which must have been written in England in the early eleventh century – is Bibliothèque nationale de France, lat. 943. As a pontifical combined with a benedictional, this was not intended for the use of a cantor during the performance of the liturgy – when it should be in the hands of the presiding bishop – but it has extensive notation for the rites of consecration of a church.[31] The main part of this book was copied in a fine Square Minuscule, and was probably written at Canterbury for the use of Archbishop Dunstan himself, thus between 959/60 and 988.[32] The layout of the text indicates that musical notation was not at first envisaged, but space was available above the chant texts, which were written smaller than the texts read by the bishop (in black) and the rubrics (in red); here notation was added in a hand as stylish and controlled as that of the main text scribe. On the basis of an antiphon added in the margin on fol. 78r, the notating hand can be directly associated with an Anglo-Saxon (Caroline) text-hand, itself dating from the late tenth or early eleventh century. Since the book was probably taken to Sherborne by Bishop Wulfsige (991×993–1002) in that period, the notation may have been written there.

Although the musical notation in this pontifical may have been written at Sherborne rather than at Canterbury, the evidence from other sources in which Breton notation is used is strongly indicative not only of a link between this notation and Canterbury, but of Canterbury as its principal place of use in England. Marginal additions of the late tenth century made to the earlier layers of the Leofric Missal – probably at that time in Canterbury – have notation of this kind, whereas those in passages copied after the book was taken by Leofric to Exeter use Insular neumes.[33] More significant is the extensive notation in a book containing Bede's prose and verse *Lives* of St Cuthbert, with offices for Cuthbert, Benedict and Guthlac.[34] In his studies of Canterbury hands, Bishop was able to show the two main scribes of this book working at Christ Church in the late tenth and early eleventh century.[35] The text-hand in the chant passages may well be the first of these: certainly it writes the same type and style of Caroline Minuscule, datable to this period. The office for

31 Since it is usually in the pontifical that liturgy for the consecration of a church and associated ceremonies is recorded, it is relatively common to find the chants for that mass notated in such books.

32 Following a summary of previous work on the origin and provenance of BnF, lat. 943, Dumville 1992, pp. 82–4, explains that 'its first intended owner is most unlikely to have been anyone other than Dunstan'.

33 On the Leofric Missal see n. 14 above.

34 BL, Harley 1117.

35 Bishop 1963b, pp. 414–23 and plates 13c, 15.

Cuthbert was also notated in Breton neumes in a book from St Augustine's copied in the same period.[36]

Only the sacramentary fragment from the Winton Domesday could suggest any link between Winchester and Breton notation, and there the notation written before the book came to England was in part replaced by Insular neumes. It is possible, therefore, to suggest quite a simple pattern for the process of adoption and early development of musical scripts in England: an older model, now known principally in western French sources, and adopted at Canterbury and in some centres in the west of England, and a younger, northern French model adopted in Æthelwold's houses. The parallel to the division of Anglo-Saxon text scripts into two types, linked with two establishments – Style I associated with Winchester and Style II with Canterbury – is unavoidable. However, it is difficult to progress beyond the level of noticing the analogy between use of text scripts and music scripts: unlike the story which connects Corbie musicians with Æthelwold's Abingdon, there is no recognised example of notation from Glastonbury or of notation in a book handled by Dunstan. Thus, the attraction of a clean and simple line connecting the use of Breton notation with Glastonbury and then, through Dunstan, Canterbury, has no material support. Indeed, given the demonstrable presence in early tenth-century England of many Breton exiles,[37] there is no reason to limit to one or two locations the situations in which exposure to the possibilities of musical notation, and a specific way of writing it, might have occurred.

The influence of scriptorium discipline on these two notational types is quite noticeable, above all in the high calligraphic quality of most examples – independent of their semiological content (full or otherwise). One of the visually most striking qualities of many Insular notations of the Corbie–Winchester type is an extreme perpendicularity of upward and downward strokes; such notations may be further rendered harmonious through the circular curvature of a stroke turning from an upward to a downward movement (for example in the *clivis*, ͷ). This perpendicularity is already observable in what may be the earliest examples of such notation, in the fragments from a tenth-century antiphoner now traceable in small fragments at Arendal and Rygnestad:[38] in the occasional notations in the Ecgberht Pontifical of unknown origin, made somewhere in England before 1000,[39] and in the Lanalet Pontifical, made

36 BAV, Reg. lat. 204. 37 See Brett 1991.

38 For precise details of these fragments see Gjerløw 1979, pp. 21–3 and plate 1; see also Hartzell 2006, no. 321.

39 BnF, lat. 10575: see, with further bibliography, Dumville 1992, pp. 85–6; two pages with neumes are reproduced in Rankin 1987, as plate XVII a–b. See also n. 54 below.

perhaps at Wells in the first decade of the eleventh century.[40] Of course, the presence of notations in all three sources needs to be qualified, since in none of these cases was the text laid out for musical notation, and, in all three, some passages which could have been notated have not been.

Although a great deal of palaeographical work remains to be done, it is already possible to discern habits of writing which suggest identifiable scriptoria. In books made at Winchester in the second and third quarters of the eleventh century the parallelism of axes remains, but the angle of strokes is often slightly inclined to the right. The circularity of the upper turns remains a noticeable calligraphic aspect of the Winchester notations. In books made (or notated) at Worcester and at Exeter in the third quarter of the century, the angle of strokes returns close to the perpendicular, while the circular shape of upper turns is less prominent, not least because a downwards stroke will tend to be written much closer to the preceding upwards stroke (thus ᑎ becomes ᑎ).[41] At Canterbury, the writing of Breton notation must have been abandoned in the early years of the eleventh century: that at least is the implication of notations written into a fragment of a noted missal of the first quarter of the eleventh century,[42] a pontifical copied at St Augustine's or Christ Church in the mid eleventh century,[43] and an office for St Mellitus in a book from St Augustine's,[44] copied on endleaves in a hand extremely similar to that responsible for the rest of the book, and recognised as working at the end of the eleventh/beginning of the twelfth century.[45] Plate 22.3 shows an example of Insular notation, from an antiphoner copied at Christ Church, Canterbury, in the early decades of the eleventh century.[46]

By the third quarter of the century, English scribes had begun to treat the space between text lines occupied by musical notation in a new way: where previously most neumes were positioned along an imaginary line parallel to the text line (within groups progressing towards the upper right as a result of the movement of the pen between neumes),[47] now they began to move the

40 Rouen, BM, A.27 (368). Reproductions in *Paléographie musicale* 3 (1891/2), plate 178A; Hesbert 1954, plates II–III; and Corbin 1977, plates 30a, 30b.

41 For reproductions of a Worcester notator's work see Hughes 1958–60; on the Exeter notations see Rankin 1984.

42 Canterbury CL, Add. 128/52: on which see Gameson 2008, no. 8.

43 CCCC, 44.

44 CCCC, 267, fols. 2v–3v. The composer of this office clearly revelled in the musical opportunities offered by this saint's name: the first chant opens: '[O] Mellite dulcissime condigne tu nomine pietate mellifice bonitate melliflue et melliger caritate', and the third chant reads '[A]nglis mellifluus Mellitus mellificavit alleluia'.

45 Described by Bishop as 'round' and 'archaic': see Bishop 1959, p. 95 (this manuscript wrongly cited there as 276).

46 Two groups of fragments from this antiphoner survive as BL, Burney 277 (fols. 69–72) and Stowe 1061 (fol. 125); on the correct order of leaves see n. 92 below.

47 On such habits of writing see Rankin 2007, pp. 26ff.

neumes up and down within the space in order to provide some guide to their pitch. A concern with the length of strokes or the placing of neumes to indicate pitch was not absent from earlier Insular notations; the difference is that where in the earlier notations movement up or down in the open area above the text might be used to clarify a specific passage, now every neume was specially placed. In the Cosin Gradual this change in notational practice can be directly associated with contact with Norman music scribes,[48] since the curved strokes of this notation are unlike earlier insular work and, in contrast, typical of Norman notations from the mid-eleventh until the end of the twelfth century (see Plate 22.4). The major part of the Cosin Gradual was copied at Christ Church, Canterbury, in the last years of the century,[49] before being sent to Durham; Hartzell has argued that it could have been presented to Durham when William of Saint-Calais (Carilef) became bishop in 1081.[50]

The neumes in the Cosin Gradual are not yet precisely placed, but it was not long before the practice of writing neumes on dry-point lines appeared in Insular work. In a quire ruled for musical notation with fifty closely set lines per page, a scribe working at St Augustine's, Canterbury in the early twelfth century copied out chants for the office and mass of St Mildred (see Plate 22.5).[51] In these notations, as in the Cosin Gradual, those ways in which the shapes of neumes were altered as a direct result of the new concern with precise pitch notations, are highly visible: what was previously written as a thin stroke (one note), or a stroke turned upwards (two rising notes) or a stroke turned downwards (two descending notes) now developed small note heads; the vertical position of the note heads clarified information about pitch in a more definite fashion.

*

By the early years of the eleventh century, the possibilities offered by musical notation, and knowledge of how to write it, were well established in at least two centres in Anglo-Saxon England (and probably more widely). By the middle of the eleventh century, there were plenty of musically literate scribes spread around the country. Once musical notation had been launched in this way, books intended for the exclusive use of the cantor – graduals, office antiphoners, tropers and sequentiaries – were always planned with its inclusion in

48 Durham University Library, Cosin V.v.6.

49 Hartzell 1975, pp. 134–5, dates the book in the last quarter of the century, while noting the palaeographical views of T. A. M. Bishop and N. Ker on the main text-hand: both dated the work as 'very late-eleventh-century or early-twelfth'.

50 Hartzell 1975, pp. 139–40.

51 BL, Harley 3908, fols. 43–50; on these chants see Sharpe 1991, with a reproduction of fol. 48r.

mind. In other types of liturgical book, however, it took considerably longer for the needs of notation to become part of copying practice.

As an example of the issues which text scribes had to master, and of how long it took for those issues to be resolved, the book-type of the pontifical offers a useful test case. Such volumes are better represented for Anglo-Saxon England than any other kind of liturgical book.[52] A 'pontifical' might be thought rather distant from the activities of a cantor, and others who could read and write notation, but this would ignore the fact that much of the liturgy in a pontifical was quite specific to it and was not usually copied into any other liturgical book. There is little likelihood of the kind of overlap produced by, for example, a plenary missal and a gradual. Indeed, a cantor preparing for consecration ceremonies might need access to the local pontifical, in order to check details of the melodic delivery of processional chants which were not necessarily sung with any regularity. But few of the pontificals made in Anglo-Saxon England in the course of the eleventh century were prepared with notation in mind (although several were later notated). Only in a book made in the last decade of the eleventh century at Christ Church, Canterbury, can the combination of texts spaced for music with musical notation entered be seen,[53] and here the notation is quite distinct from the Insular kind treated above, having the heighting, noteheads and curved neume forms characteristic of Norman work.

Books for the cantor

Booklists

A clause in a penitential copied around the millennium (but dependent on earlier exemplars)[54] includes a list of books required by a priest before he is consecrated by the bishop:

> he who would accept the priestly authority, firstly let him think about God and prepare his weapons before the hand of the bishop touches his head, that

52 Fragments of more missals survive, but it is the pontifical which is preserved in larger numbers as a full text; on Anglo-Saxon pontificals see Dumville 1992, ch. 3, and Nelson and Pfaff 1995.

53 TCD, 98 (B.3.6). Michael Gullick has argued that this notation was added in the early twelfth century, perhaps in the 1110s: see Gullick and Pfaff 2001.

54 BnF, lat. 10575: here material derived from an earlier penitential text is copied as a prologue to a pontifical. The background to this prologue is much disputed: although possibly associated with Egbert of York, there is no extant Anglo-Saxon source dating before lat. 10575. For a summary of the arguments, with bibliography, see Bullough 2004, pp. 233–6, and, on the relation of later booklists to this one, Gatch 1977, pp. 42–4.

> is, the psalter, the lectionary, the antiphoner, the missal, the book for baptisms, the martyrologium.[55]

These 'weapons' include, for the singing of chant, the antiphoner. A list prepared in very much the same spirit by Ælfric of Eynsham differs very little: 'A mass-priest shall have a missal and an epistle-book and a song-book and a lectionary and a psalter and a handbook and a penitential and a computus.'[56] Where, in the Latin list, all liturgical readings would have to be found in the lectionary, Ælfric's list has both an epistle-book and a lectionary; in both lists the missal ('mæsse-boc') is likely to have been what is elsewhere called a sacramentary (thus including just the prayers);[57] for the chants, Ælfric's 'song-book' must be read as the equivalent of 'antiphoner' in the Latin list. Both lists are intended to be comprehensive, and it is therefore likely that the book described by the terms 'antiphoner' and 'song-book' included chants for both mass and office – as, for example, in the antiphoner made in the circle of Charles the Bald in the 870s.[58] But Ælfric's list is here revealed as more prescriptive than descriptive: by the eleventh century, it was much more common for the mass chants to be copied in a different book from those sung in the divine office. For Anglo-Saxon England, this division is upheld in a series of book-lists describing actual libraries. A list of the service-books and ecclesiastical furniture belonging to the church of Sherburn-in-Elmet, copied into the York Gospels in the mid eleventh century, appears to include all those books needed for the maintenance of the liturgy in a church:

> twa Cristes bec ... & .i. aspiciens & .i. ad te levavi & .ii. pistelbec & .i. mæsseboc & .i. ymener & .i. salter[59]

In the office liturgy, *Aspiciens a longe* was the first responsory of the night office for the first Sunday in Advent: in other words, it was where a book of chants for the office might start. Equally, the Introit antiphon for mass on the first Sunday of Advent began *Ad te levavi*, and this was usually the first item in a book of chants for the mass. It had become the practice, in some chant-books copied in the late ninth and tenth centuries, for the first A of each of these chants to be decorated, sometimes occupying a whole page. And from this

55 'qui voluerit sacerdotalem auctoritatem accipere, inprimitus pro Deum cogitet et preparet arma ejus, antequam manus Episcopi tangat caput, id est psalterium, lectionarium, antefonarium, missalem, baptisterium, martyrologium'. Haddan and Stubbs 1869–78, III, p. 417.

56 'Mæsse-preost sceal habban mæsse-bóc and pistel-bóc, and sang-bóc and ræding-bóc and saltere and handbóc, and penitentialem and gerim.' Letter II, § 157: Fehr 1966, pp. 126–7. From Ælfric there are two further booklists of the same kind (one in Latin): Letter I, § 52: see Fehr 1966, p. 13; Letter 2, § 137: Fehr 1966, p. 51.

57 See p. 484 and n. 9 above. 58 BnF, lat. 17436. 59 Lapidge 1985, pp. 56–7.

the habit developed in Anglo-Saxon England of naming the two books in this way.[60] Other Anglo-Saxon lists, from Bury, Exeter and possibly Worcester, use the same terminology.[61]

Besides the two main books of mass and office chants, these booklists name three other categories of music book: the 'mæsse-boc' or 'missale' (missal), which, if fuller than a sacramentary, could include chant texts; the 'ymener' (hymn book), notably absent from the prescriptive lists made by Egbert and Ælfric, but a standard element when groups of liturgical books appear in booklists; and the tropere/troparium (troper). Of these three, the first two categories were often copied without musical notation: only the troper was bound to be notated. Indeed, in the *Monasteriales Indicia*, a mid-eleventh-century text in Old English explaining monastic sign language, the entry for a troper reads: 'When you want a troper, then move your right hand and turn with your right index finger over your chest in front, as if you were notating.'[62]

One last category of book is not well represented in the booklists: the office-book equivalent to the missal, containing prayers, psalms, readings and chants, known later as a breviary. Such books were not in wide use anywhere before the twelfth century: Gneuss points out that no Old English term occurs in the booklists.[63] Nevertheless, like the book-type 'missal' which survives in a variety of forms, books of office liturgy made before the twelfth century are of varying kinds. The list of Leofric's donations to Exeter includes both a 'nihtsang' and a 'forealdodne (worn-out) nihtsang'.[64] Both must refer to books used in the night office.[65] In this list, the 'nihtsang' is preceded by a 'collectaneum' and followed by an 'adtelevavi', encouraging Gneuss' deduction that antiphoners for the night office were indicated.[66] But it is at least possible that something closer to the later book-type of 'breviary' was meant: at least that category of book is not as absent from Anglo-Saxon survivals as Gneuss then implied.[67]

Surviving books: music for the mass

Of the three categories of 'full music books' in Anglo-Saxon England – the gradual containing Proper and Ordinary chants of the mass, the troper, with additional mass compositions, and the antiphoner, with the office chants – many remnants survive. But the vast majority of these remnants exist now

60 Gneuss 1985, pp. 102–3 and 116–18.

61 Lapidge 1985, pp. 57, 74 (Bury), 65 (Exeter), 69 (Worcester).

62 'Đonne þu tropere haban wille þonne wege þu þine swiran hand. and tyrn mid þinum swiþran scyte fingre ofer þine breost fore weard swilce þu notian wille.' Banham 1991, no. 11.

63 Gneuss 1985, p. 112. 64 Lapidge 1985, pp. 64–9.

65 That is, the office commonly (but misleadingly) known as 'matins'.

66 Gneuss 1985, p. 117. 67 Gneuss 1985, pp. 110–11.

only in the form of small fragments, and the pattern of survival can hardly reflect the number of music books made and used in Anglo-Saxon England. The only category for which more than one complete codex remains extant is the troper; three of these form the basis for almost all modern knowledge of Anglo-Saxon musical practice and composition. Only one gradual – copied close to 1100 – survives as a book, and even this has large sections missing;[68] there is no antiphoner of which more than a few fragments remain. Inevitably, therefore, any developed sense of how many books were made, and where, is severely limited by the disappearance of most Anglo-Saxon examples, and the difficulties inherent in working with fragments.[69] Even for the category of troper, no surviving exemplar matches the relevant entries in booklists for libraries at Bury and Exeter.

The reason for this generic loss of Anglo-Saxon music books is surely that they quickly fell into disuse. For the ways of writing and reading musical notation adopted in late Anglo-Saxon books were virtually obsolete by the second quarter of the twelfth century, even earlier in the more progressive centres such as Canterbury. Once new attitudes to musical transmission and new techniques for its notation had been introduced by the Normans, the writing of neumes in the open space above the text, without precise techniques of heighting to indicate pitch, was no longer really functional:[70] the musical culture had altered to expect information of different kinds to be recorded in writing, with less dependence on memory and oral transmission for melodic pitch patterns. The older graduals and antiphoners, in which nothing other than chant texts with neumatic notation were recorded, would have seemed valueless, and in need of replacement with up-to-date copies.

Those fragments of graduals which survive are therefore very precious indeed. The earliest fragments copied in Anglo-Saxon England containing mass chants are the two folios bound into Pembroke 46 which date from the first half of the tenth century. Folio A has part of a cycle of Alleluias, probably starting with Advent and continuing into the Sundays after Easter.[71] The next trace of a gradual is the supposed model for parts of Oxford, Bodleian Library,

68 Durham UL, Cosin V.v.6; the main loss is the greater part of the sanctorale. On this manuscript see p. 493 and nn. 48–50 above.

69 Lists of surviving liturgical books and fragments can be compiled from Gneuss 2001; in addition, details of books and fragments containing musical notation written in England up to 1200 can be found in Hartzell 2006.

70 See above, p. 493.

71 The pages are bound upside-down, thus reversing the order of recto and verso. For the content see now Hartzell 2006, no. 48.

Bodley 775, itself copied at Winchester in the mid eleventh century.[72] Parts of this composite book, specifically the cycle of Proper chants (represented by incipits of the Introits, Graduals, Offertories and Communions, with the Gradual verses written out in full within this cycle), appear to depend directly on an exemplar of *c.* 980. The hypothesis of a tenth-century exemplar for this layer of Bodley 775 is interesting, since the type of book represented by that model is very old indeed: lists of incipits of Proper chants, presented feast by feast, can be dated to the earliest period of production of chant-books, with well-known ninth-century examples from Saint-Amand and Senlis.[73] Besides its cycle of Proper chant incipits arranged by feast, Bodley 775 also includes (separately) individual cycles of Alleluias, Tracts and Offertory verses.

The gradual represented by two leaves bound into Harley 110 is of a different kind, with full Proper chants written out feast by feast, without Alleluias, but including Offertory verses.[74] Although the host book, a copy of Prosper's *Epigrammata* and Isidore's *Synonyma*, was made at Christ Church, Canterbury, in the late tenth century, both text and music scripts of the gradual fragments suggest that this book was copied at Winchester in the second quarter of the eleventh century; the notating hand may even be the same as that responsible for most of Bodley 775.[75] Again, it is the exemplar for this book which has particular significance, for the rubrics naming feast days also include capitular numbers, in the same manner as early sacramentaries and some graduals, such as that copied at Corbie in 853.[76]

Small fragments of six further eleventh-century graduals are known,[77] but the most substantial example of this book-type (albeit with compact dimensions) from late Anglo-Saxon England is the Cosin Gradual, copied at Christ Church, Canterbury, in the late eleventh century.[78] Whether sent as early as 1081 or not, it certainly reached Durham soon after the main parts of the book

72 The hypothesis that BodL., Bodley 775 is an anachronistic manuscript, reflecting 'a prototype from the last quarter of the tenth century', was first proposed in Holschneider 1968, pp. 24–7, and supported by Planchart 1977, pp. 40–3. For a qualification of their views, see Rankin 2005.

73 BnF, lat. 2291, and Paris, Bibliothèque Sainte-Geneviève 111; on such lists see Palazzo 1993, p. 94.

74 BL, Harley 110, fols. 1, 56: Hiley 1993, plate 4 (fol. 56r), and Bell 2001, p. 21 (fol. 1v).

75 Hiley 1993, p. 413.

76 BnF, lat. 12050. The gradual text is edited in Hesbert 1935 as source K (Corbiensis).

77 BL, Royal 5 E.vii (fol. i), copied *s.* xi^{in}; TCD, 371 (pp. i/ii, 149/50), from a fine book, copied *s.* xi^{1}; Oslo, Riksarkivet 214, 2–3 (Gr 2), copied *s.* xi^{2}; Stockholm, KB, A.128 (fols. 1–6); CUL, Inc.5.B.3.97, both copied *s.* xi^{ex}; and Oslo, Riksarkivet 244, 1–2 (Gr 15), copied *s.* xi^{ex}/*s.* xii^{in}. The origin of Oslo, Riksarkivet 226, 3–9 (Gr 1b) is uncertain; it may have been copied in Norway. The Scandinavian designations by type of liturgical book ('Gr 00') do not represent shelfmarks, and do not transfer from one library to another: Oslo Gr 1 would not be the same source as Stockholm Gr 1.

78 See above, p. 493 and n. 49.

had been copied, and was then customised for use there. The main category of material added to Cosin V.v.6 in the north was sequences (also known as proses), compositions in verse and music, delivered mainly with one syllable per note. Such compositions post-date the establishment of the Gregorian Proper chants, the earliest examples (as melodies alone) being traceable to the mid ninth century in Carolingian Europe. In these new liturgical songs local saints could be venerated – in the case of the Cosin Gradual, Aidan, Cuthbert and Oswald – and the building up of an appropriate repertory of sequences represented an important task for the local cantor. This was also characteristic of repertories of tropes, another new kind of composition, in which new phrases were interpolated into Gregorian Proper chants (the Introit, Offertory and Communion antiphons), allowing the elucidation and elaboration of the older text, or simply a heightened level of praise. Such new compositions allowed and encouraged communities to make the Roman chant heritage more directly their own.

Repertories of tropes and sequences had become highly developed in several Continental centres during the tenth century; they were first simply assembled in large numbers, but were later sorted, so that the repertories were liturgically organised, and only the precise number of tropes and sequences required for any one liturgical feast included. This move towards more prescriptive books can be read, at least in part, as the direct outcome of an increasing understanding of such books as expressive of local achievement in liturgical practice – practice which would serve the local community well in petitioning God, Christ and their patron saints.

Three books from Anglo-Saxon England contain trope and sequence repertories. The earliest, Cambridge, Corpus Christi College 473, was made at Winchester in the 1020s or 30s and can be divided into three main parts: a cycle of tropes for the temporale and then the sanctorale (fols. 10–70), cycles of untexted and then texted sequences for the liturgical year (fols. 81–134), and a cycle of *organa* (second voices to accompany chant, thus 'polyphony'; fols. 135–90).[79] Bodley 775, also made at Winchester, but in the mid eleventh century, is closely linked to Corpus 473 through its trope and sequence repertories; however, it is a different kind of book, having much more of the material included in a gradual, although not arranged in the manner that was standard on the Continent by this date.[80] The third example, made in an unidentified

79 See n. 20 above.

80 On these two books and their repertories of tropes, sequences and polyphony, see Frere 1894; Holschneider 1968; Planchart 1977; and Rankin 2007. On the relation of the two books, see Rankin 2005.

scriptorium in the second half of the eleventh century, contains, besides most of the proper tropes copied in the two earlier books, a substantial number of unique tropes.[81] In its current state this manuscript breaks off 'in medias res', leaving open the question as to whether it once included sequences and proses.

In their different ways, all three of these books uphold the hypothesis that their contents were perceived as special and in some way different from that of volumes containing the Gregorian Proper chants. Of course, they were of a different type, and less likely than graduals to be limited by older exemplars and traditions of copying, but there is a more fundamental difference of conception. Entirely unusual rubrics, such as 'Ecce pulchri tropi' and 'Incipiunt sancti modulamina dulciter hymni, quem cecinere chori Christo nascente superni', can be found in the two Winchester books.[82] In size Corpus Christi College 473 is tiny (though fat), and in many diverse ways indicates its purpose as a book made substantially by and for one individual – a person trained to the highest levels of musical technique (both in singing and in writing), with the main responsibility for the conduct of festive liturgy, and an interest in composing for it. The later Winchester book, although also likely to have been used mainly by the cantor of the Old Minster, could be better described as a backwards-looking record: its concern with full cycles of several genres of chant, old as well as new, indicates its more conservative nature. The Cotton Troper includes, embedded between tropes for different feasts, eleven large miniatures 'of Christological and hagiographical subject matter', surrounded by newly composed Latin hexameter inscriptions (Plate 10.11). It is more likely to have been made for a highly placed patron than for a cantor's immediate use: candidates for whom strong arguments have been made include two bishops of Worcester, Wulfstan (1062–95) and his immediate predecessor, Ealdred (bishop of Hereford and Worcester, 1056–60).[83] All three books, however diverse in type, reveal the perception of these new repertories as of considerable artistic and spiritual value.

The dimensions of these books containing mass chants is remarkably consistent: the larger size of book is represented by the gradual–troper Bodley 775 (written space 200 × 100 mm), the gradual fragments in Harley 110 (195 × at least 90 mm, probably 100 mm with the missing portion restored), and the gradual fragment in Royal 5 E.vii (at least 182 × 110 mm). A smaller

81 BL, Cotton Caligula A.xiv. On this book see Teviotdale 1991; on all three tropers see Teviotdale 1995; on the unique tropes in the Cotton Troper see Jonsson 1993.

82 CCCC, 473, fol. 42r and BodL., Bodley 775, fol. 64r.

83 Teviotdale 1995, p. 42 (suggesting Wulfstan), and Heslop 2007 (suggesting Ealdred).

size is represented by the troper Corpus 473 (written space 115 × 62 mm) and the Cosin Gradual (114 × 64 mm). Both the latter have sixteen written lines, but the number of lines in the larger books varies (Bodley 775: 16; Harley 110: 20; Royal 5 E.vii: 19); evidently the relation between size of written space and number of lines was not a simple formula dependent on content. The Cotton Troper sits between these two sizes, with a written space of 161–3 × 72–4 mm.

One last category of books for the mass in which musical notation was often provided was the *missale plenum*. Such books are represented for the late tenth and the early, mid and late eleventh century by several groups of fragments in Stockholm and Oslo:[84] for the mid eleventh century by a substantial fragment from the Old Minster at Winchester (Plate 22.2),[85] another probably from Worcester,[86] two folios in the Cathedral Library at Canterbury,[87] and for the second half of the eleventh century by a book from the New Minster at Winchester (missing the portion of the temporale from Advent to Easter),[88] and a series of fragments (now in several libraries) from a book associated with Exeter during Leofric's episcopate.[89] There are numerous other small fragments whose origin has not been identified. There are also other kinds of missal, not intended to include the full chants; a fragment copied by Eadwig Basan, thus probably at Canterbury in the early decades of the eleventh century, represents a kind of missal in which some chants were to be notated and others not.[90] The Missal of St Augustine's, a fine book copied at that abbey at the end of the eleventh century, has the incipits of Introit antiphons before each set of prayers and Proper prefaces, evidently intended to help a priest to know that he had the book open at the right page (since the mass began with the Introit antiphon), and having nothing to do with those who would sing the chants.[91]

84 Oslo, Riksarkivet, 206 + 209, 1–5 + 239, 6–7 (Mi 2); 207, 1–4 + 208, 1–8 + 210, 1–3 + Copenhagen, Rigsarkivet, 3084 + 3085 (Mi 70); 227, 1–23 (Mi 11); 228, 1–21 (Mi 14); 274, 1 (Mi 101); 876, 1–2 + 905, 1–7 + 1016c (Mi 25); Stockholm, KB, Isl. perg. 8°, no. 8; Stockholm, Riksarkivet, Fr.26449–51 + Göteborg, UB, Friherre August Vilhelm Stiernstedts Samling, no 3 (Mi 134), and Fr. 2427. It is unlikely that any of Oslo, Riksarkivet, 202, 1–2 (Mi 3); 204a, 1–4, 9–10 (Mi 5); 230, 1 (Mi 15); Stockholm, Riksarkivet, Fr.25916–20, etc. (Mi 1: nineteen sets of fragments now in various libraries, listed in Gneuss 2001 as no. 936 and Hartzell 2006, as no. 340), were copied in England.

85 Worcester CL, F.173. See Pfaff 1995b, pp. 25–6; and Thomson 2001, p. 116.

86 BL, Royal 5 A.xii: Hartzell 1989, pp. 45–97.

87 Add 128/52. See n. 42 above.

88 Le Havre, BM, 330: Turner 1962.

89 London, Westminster Abbey 36, nos. 17–19, etc. (dispersed fragments listed in full in Gneuss 2001, as no. 524, and Hartzell 2006, as no. 203); a contemporary missal fragment listed under Stonyhurst (Gneuss 2001, no. 756.5) is now BL, Add. 79528.

90 BodL., Lat. liturg. D.3, fols. 4–5: see Rankin 2004.

91 CCCC, 270: Rule 1896.

Surviving books: music for the office

Anglo-Saxon office antiphoners have survived only as fragments, alongside a series of *sui generis* books of office liturgy including notated chants. But the book-type was an important one, as is demonstrated by the quality of fragments representing three high-grade music books. The earliest of these was probably copied at Christ Church, Canterbury, in the first decades of the eleventh century.[92] It includes part of the office for the translation of St Benedict on 11 July, but the proposal to connect it with Canterbury also rests on the closeness of the text-hand to that of Eadwig Basan. If the Canterbury identification is correct, this source provides the earliest indications of how Insular, as opposed to Breton, notation was being written at Canterbury in the early decades of the eleventh century (Plate 22.3). Another group of fragments come from an antiphoner probably copied at Winchester in the mid eleventh century.[93] Its written space is a little larger than that of the contemporary mass-book Bodley 775 (213 × 117 mm), and virtually identical to that of the earlier Canterbury book (211 × 117 mm). Another antiphoner, whose place of origin is difficult to determine, was unusually wide (written space 219/216 × 150 mm) for a chant-book.[94] Although probably post-Conquest, this text-hand appears to imitate the monumental style of Style I Anglo-Caroline. The content of the surviving leaves deserves study, since they contain parts of offices for the Invention of St Stephen, for Oswald (of Northumbria), for St Machutus and for St Iustus.[95] Six leaves from a late eleventh-century antiphoner preserved in Dublin come from a book of less high quality than these three earlier ones.[96]

Other kinds of books for the office liturgy, in which more categories of material than the chants are represented, survive in greater numbers and mostly as books rather than fragments. Some may be loosely grouped under

92 Now BL, Burney 277 (fols. 69–72) and Stowe 1061 (fol. 125). The correct order of the folios and parts of folios preserved in Burney 277 is 71, 72, 70, 69. The leaf preserved in Stowe 1061 was cut from what is now Burney 277, fol. 69: placed together, the two parts form the entire folio.

93 Lincoln CL, 298C (2 folios) and BL, Harley 3405 (fol. 4). The second of the two Lincoln folios once sat immediately beside that preserved in the Harley manuscript.

94 BL Royal 12 F.xiv (fols. 1–2, 135); BodL., Selden Supra 36 (fols. 73–4); and BodL., Selden Supra 36* (fol. 1).

95 The office for St Stephen was composed in the early tenth century by Stephen of Liège: for a study and edition see Jonsson 1968. In Royal 12 F.xiv, passages with notation are those drawn from Stephen of Liège's composition, whereas those passages without notation have been added to that office. The Oswald office in this fragment is more obscure, being entirely different from those two offices already edited, one composed in England, the other in southern Germany.

96 TCD, 370a. Besides the Arendal fragment of an antiphoner mentioned above there are fragments of two Anglo-Saxon antiphoners in Oslo: Riksarkivet, 223, 1–2 (Ant 6); 226, 1–2 (Ant 2). On these see Gjerløw 1979, pp. 23–5. The origin of 225, 1–2 (Ant 3) is uncertain, and it may represent a book made in Norway.

the heading 'breviary', although such a title cannot, in this period, denote a specific set of contents; others are more clearly described as a 'collectar' or a psalter, with extra material. Unlike the tenth-century office-book represented by fragments in Royal 17 C.xvii, these later books all use musical notation when chant texts are present.[97] They include the mid-eleventh-century Muchelney Breviary of which parts of eight folios survive;[98] the Leofric Collectar,[99] made at Exeter between 1050 and 1072, and notated by the same music scribe as a psalter with canticles and offices, also made at Exeter under Leofric;[100] the so-called Portiforium of St Wulstan, made at Worcester in the second half of the eleventh century, including collects with chants, a psalter, hymnary and other material;[101] and the Red Book of Darley, in which specific offices, but no complete cycles are copied, and where musical notation is only infrequent.[102]

The diversity of these various books of office liturgy indicates that it would be false to draw a parallel between them and the mass-book in which different kinds of material were eventually brought together (missal); the various surviving examples of missals fall more easily into groups than the office-books, for which grouping is hardly possible. In Anglo-Saxon England there seems to have been no standard way to make a book of office liturgy (apart from the antiphoner), each manuscript representing a set of choices made in a particular institution by those responsible for making it. In this, the difference between the office and the mass as liturgy, and the history of their celebration in Anglo-Saxon England, must have some place. For the celebration of the eight daily offices involved a series of choices about the number and order of psalms sung at each, and the ways in which chants would be linked to them, quite apart from the readings; for the latter, houses which followed different monastic or canonical rules would need different numbers and arrangements. It is entirely possible that, as a result of the Benedictine reform, the establishment of a suitable office liturgy for any individual monastic community involved much re-working: the diversity of the book-types may be a direct result of many separate attempts to prepare a suitable liturgy.[103]

In relation to office liturgy one other kind of book held considerable significance. Collections of material related to one specific saint often included,

97 On Royal 17 C.xvii see above, p. 486; for a general as well as specific presentation of office-books, see especially Corrêa 1995.
98 BL, Add. 56488. See n. 19 above.
99 BL Harley 2961: Dewick and Frere 1914–21.
100 BL Harley 863. On the Exeter notator see Rankin 1984, p. 111.
101 CCCC, 391: Hughes 1958–60.
102 CCCC, 422. On this, the oddest of the books listed here, see especially Hohler 1972.
103 On the efforts made towards and problems encountered in building the office liturgy, see Billett 2010.

besides a *Vita*, material especially composed for liturgical celebration. The earliest Anglo-Saxon example of such a book (as well as the earliest example of a saint's office composed in Anglo-Saxon England) is, of course, Corpus Christi College 183, with Bede's two *Lives* of Cuthbert, and liturgy for his mass and office.[104] An assemblage of materials relating to Cuthbert, Benedict and Guthlac, including offices for all three, was made at Christ Church, Canterbury, around the millennium.[105] Books from Bury St Edmunds and St Albans, each copied in the second half of the eleventh century, present materials for celebrating their patron saints.[106] As and when such offices were composed, they were frequently recorded in other more or less relevant situations, sometimes simply wherever enough blank parchment could be found. This was the case for offices in honour of Augustine (of Canterbury), Guthlac, Katherine, Julian, Mellitus, Nicolas and Stephen (Invention); some of these offices were certainly composed in England, while others were introduced through Norman influence in the later eleventh century.[107] One of the most interesting dedicated collections is that for St Mildred, whose relics rested at St Augustine's, Canterbury; a book containing her *Vita*, twelve lessons for the night office, and a cycle of chants for the office probably composed by Goscelin, followed by a sequence for the mass, was made there in the early years of the twelfth century.[108]

Other kinds of music books

Two other kinds of music books survive from Anglo-Saxon England: those in which songs are collected, to which musical notation was sometimes added, and books of music theory. Of instrumental music there is no representation in notation, merely descriptions in words and in pictures.

Song-books

Several classical or late antique texts included songs: in Anglo-Saxon England, the most widely circulated of these were Boethius' *De consolatione philosophiae* and Prudentius' *Cathemerinon*. In such books, musical notation was commonly added (although it was almost never copied at the same time as the original text, and thus not transmitted with it). Copies of the *De consolatione philosophiae* used

104 See above, p. 486. 105 BL, Harley 1117.

106 Copenhagen, KB, G. K. S. 1588 (4°) (with Abbo's *Vita* of Edmund, followed by the office); PML, M. 926, with an office for St Alban, within a collection of liturgical and hagiographical texts. This collection also includes an office for St Birinus.

107 On the composition of saint's offices in England see Hughes 1993 and Hiley 2001.

108 See above, p. 493.

in Anglo-Saxon England often have notation. One made in Canterbury around the millennium is by far the most heavily notated;[109] this notation is possibly pre-Conquest, since the neumes are Insular, and Canterbury appears to have switched to Norman neume forms well before the end of the century. Another Canterbury book has notation over ten metra by several hands;[110] most are likely to have been written in Canterbury, although three can be linked with Exeter (where the book was taken by Leofric).[111] For Prudentius' *Cathemerinon* no survey of the notations has yet been undertaken: some of those passages notated in Oxford, Bodleian Library, Auct. F.3.6, another of the books given to Exeter by Leofric, are in the hand of that same Exeter scribe identified in the Boethius book and in several liturgical sources.[112]

Songs from the *De consolatione philosophiae* could be copied with other songs in anthologies: such books are rare, but one of the most important early medieval examples was made at St Augustine's, Canterbury, in the mid eleventh century, its model brought from the lower Rhine area.[113] The presence here, as in the Boethius manuscripts, of several different (Insular) notating hands, reveals the interest over long periods in using the book to record a particular way of singing a song.

Books of music theory

Texts concerned with the teaching of music in circulation in the early Middle Ages either belonged to one of two traditions of thought or attempted to combine them:[114] texts which deal with music as a liberal art date from late Antiquity, while the theory of modes, used to ensure the correct singing of Gregorian chant, was formulated in the late eighth century. Theoretical texts composed in the late ninth and early tenth centuries incorporate material from both traditions, as well as new ideas about musical practice. On the side of the liberal arts, Martianus Capella's *De nuptiis Philologiae et Mercurii* is well represented in Anglo-Saxon England, but never in association with other musical material. Rather it is Boethius' *De institutione musica* which sits in a codex beside the *Musica* and *Scolica Enchiriadis*, texts probably composed in northern France in the second half of the ninth century, and the *Commemoratio brevis*, a useful

109 Private collection; olim Geneva, Bibliotheca Bodmeriana, 175.

110 BodL., Auct. F.1.15.

111 Rankin 1984, p. 111. Other Anglo-Saxon sources of the *De consolatione philosophiae* with notation include TCC, O.3.7; El Escorial, Real Biblioteca, E.II.1; BnF, lat. 14380; and BAV, Vat. lat. 3363.

112 Rankin 1984. Notated sources of the *Cathemerinon* listed in Hartzell 2006 include also CCCC, 223; DCL, B.IV.9; and BL, Cotton Cleopatra C.viii.

113 CUL, Gg.5.35. For reproductions of the pages containing songs see Breul 1915; Page 1981; and Ziolkowski 1994, with bibliography.

114 For useful recent surveys see Huglo 2000 and Bower 2002.

guide to psalm-singing composed in the early tenth century.[115] Made at Christ Church, Canterbury, in the late tenth century, this volume shows how the study of music theory in this period could bring together antique knowledge of the numbers underlying musical sounds with technical rules about how to sing music well. It is worth noting that the two *Enchiriadis* treatises included instructions on how to compose a second, polyphonic, voice to accompany an already existing melody; the manner of formulation of the *organa* notated in the Winchester Troper is directly based on the rules for improvisation set out in the two *Enchiriadis* treatises. These polyphonic voices can also be linked with techniques described in the *Micrologus* of Guido d'Arezzo. No copy of this survives from Anglo-Saxon England, only an extract in a late eleventh-century Norman book taken to Durham.[116] One other ninth-century treatise, the *De harmonica institutione* by Hucbald of Saint-Amand, was copied as an addition to the large Canterbury compilation which ended with songs.[117]

Evidence of the study of music theory other than at Canterbury is hard to come by. But, in a study of music books which has to contend with their overwhelming loss, it seems fitting to end with traces of a lost book. A 'Breviloquium super musicam', composed by Wulfstan, monk, priest and cantor of the Old Minster at Winchester in the late tenth century, was used by a later commentator on Boethius' *De institutione musica*.[118] From his extracts we can infer that Wulfstan's book was itself close to Boethius' text – perhaps an extended commentary on it. The rediscovery of Wulfstan's lost book on music would be of enormous interest.

115 CCCC, 260: on which see Bishop 1963b, p. 415.
116 DCL, B.II.11.
117 CUL, Gg.5.35 (fols. 263r–72v).
118 On this lost book see Lapidge and Winterbottom 1991, pp. xvi–xvii. The later commentary is edited: Hochadel 2002.

23
Anglo-Saxon schoolbooks

SCOTT GWARA

Pedagogy

Anglo-Saxon schoolbooks might be defined as the books read, taught or potentially available in an Anglo-Saxon monastic or cathedral school.[1] Yet immediate – and in many cases unresolvable – objections arise from this position. One might say, in fact, that the evidence can embrace contrary hypotheses: either the Anglo-Saxons had rigorous book-centred schooling that progressed from grammatical instruction to advanced reading, or they had just enough education to manage ecclesiastical duties, meditative, liturgical or administrative. Most argue a position of brilliance and ubiquity.[2] But the truth is, our account of Anglo-Saxon pedagogy derives from late Roman and provincial precedents (of Gaul, mainly), extant booklists or books (native and otherwise, annotated or not, Latin and vernacular), and descriptions of monastic routines, both English and Continental. None of this evidence can be appraised without equivocation, especially because the existence of books never guarantees their use in a classroom.

However defined, the schoolbooks were nearly always written in Latin, an *acquired* language indispensable to the transmission of Christian culture. Determining whether and how a book was taught in the pre-Conquest period therefore means assessing bilingual competence. An Anglo-Saxon had almost no native linguistic cognates, let alone a comparable syntax (apart from inflections), for decoding Latin, which second-language practitioners of diverse

1 Parochial schools and court academies did not exist in Anglo-Saxon England; lay and cloth attended either a monastic or a cathedral school. Because cathedral schools were generally proximate to monasteries (if indeed they were not monastic themselves), and because bishops and archbishops often professed as monks, the school curriculum may not have differed significantly in most large centres. This article does not identify the curriculum of secular canons, which in the tenth and eleventh centuries was likely to be a lean version of the monastic one, with emphasis on the *Rule of Chrodegang* (cf. Langefeld 1996).

2 E.g. Lendinara 1991; Gretsch 1999.

ability taught to learners also of diverse ability. Furthermore, we must acknowledge passive and active competencies, reading versus writing, with the presumption that the proficiency of a brilliant native *author* may not reflect that of *any* native reader.[3] One must likewise consider the context of medieval learning: *all* engaged in physical and ecclesiastical duties (the *opus Dei* above all), which gave little time for learning and which was mentally fatiguing.

The Roman model[4]

In a Roman school a boy would learn both language arts and arithmetical calculation in the elementary curriculum. On the linguistic side he would tackle speaking, writing and reading letters (phonemes), syllables, words and sentences. Accurate pronunciation, morphology and basic metrical scansion would be taught in the early years. The student employed a tablet smeared with beeswax, on which was incised a practice assignment (sometimes delivered by dictation), to be copied and recited. Students frequently committed vocabulary lists to memory and are known to have chanted lessons in aid of memorisation. They would memorise verses drawn (for example) from Menander's plays, Pseudo-Cato's *Distichs* and the fables of Aesop and Avianus, or else pithy anecdotes from Valerius Maximus' *Factorum et dictorum memorabilium libri novem* (i.e. 'Memorable Deeds and Sayings') and other such compendia. In so far as the Roman school handled 'moral education', it was often embodied in these elementary readings.

The 'poets' were studied next: Homer for Greek epic; Aeschylus, Sophocles and Euripides for tragedy; Vergil for Latin epic; Ennius and Pacuvius for Roman tragedy. Prose was left for a later stage of study under a 'rhetor'. Details of language were scrutinised, enunciation practised (in the absence of punctuation and word-division) for appropriate delivery. The lessons, almost wholly descriptive, followed the stages of *praelectio* ('preliminary reading'), for which the master would recite and comment on linguistic and metrical issues. Parts of the *praelectio* blurred into *enarratio*, the exposition of expressive language: types of metaphor, metonymy, synecdoche, simile, etc. The reflective stage of *iudicium* ('evaluation') appraised the ethical content of one's reading, whether (for example) a man acted righteously, and why.

Once the preliminary education had been completed, the *grammaticus* ('grammar school teacher') passed his students on to the *rhetor* or 'rhetoric master'.

3 In fact, much Latin verse (especially in the early period) was confected from borrowed centos (cf. Orchard 1992); and even the prolific Aldhelm had a highly unorthodox method of poetic composition (cf. Lapidge 1979).

4 The best guides to Roman education include Bonner 1977 and Marrou 1956.

The *rhetor* would augment their early training with advanced instruction in *oral* delivery, basically linguistic manipulation. In fact, this component of Roman education, which has no correlate in the Anglo-Saxon schools, focused expressly on *production*. By contrast, elementary studies generally emphasised memorisation, recitation and rote 'analysis' over original composition.

Pedagogical emphases in the Anglo-Saxon monastic school

Monastic Christian education was 'vocational', emphasising the training needed to perform the liturgy and devotions as well as other ecclesiastical duties, if necessary.[5] Outlines of Roman pedagogy seem to have been retained, with the substitution of Christian texts for pagan ones. One universal difference stands out: the earliest stage of preparation demanded *acoustic* memorisation of the psalter. Oblates and novices had to participate in chanting the psalter, regardless of their comprehension.

Significant evidence of Anglo-Saxon monastic pedagogy derives from dialogues ('colloquies') authored by Ælfric Bata *c.* 1000.[6] Bata depicts a daily routine punctuated by services, refection, play (and truancy!), hygiene and travel. He describes a classroom of youths led by an older assistant but directed by a master, who tests the boys' skills and administers punishment (a rebuke, a slap, the lash). Boys of diverse ages and talents *memorised* and *recited* set texts (*accepti loci*), probably copied from one or more shared books. Emphasis lay on rote memorisation rather than original production, and 'writing' often meant nothing more than copying. Practical arithmetic consisted of counting (reciting the ordinal and cardinal numbers) and estimating relative monetary values. As part of their schooling the boys were drilled in liturgical procedure.

The elementary curriculum of the Anglo-Saxon monastery

Speaking Latin

Evidence exists for *instruction* in spoken Latin during the Anglo-Saxon period. Differences between spoken and written Latin are identifiable, above all in syntax, but pronunciation in both registers probably observed no classical standard.[7] In the seventh-century Canterbury school of Archbishop Theodore

5 Jones 1976.

6 Gwara and Porter 1997. For descriptions of the early medieval school see Riché 1976; Baker and Lapidge 1995, pp. lxxix–lxxxvi; Lapidge 1982.

7 Pyles 1943.

(d. 690) and Abbot Hadrian (d. 709),[8] Vulgar Latin traits, such as loss of final nasals with subsequent confusions of case and gender, crop up in lecture notes delivered orally.[9] Features of spoken Latin may have been written in 'correct' orthography.

Theodore's famous school employed the *Hermeneumata pseudodositheana* or 'Interpretations of Pseudo-Dositheus', an anonymous teaching dossier which included multiple colloquies for practising oral fluency.[10] Dialogues from the *Hermeneumata* model conversations between master and student or between student and *paedagogus*, a slave responsible for a young boy's behaviour. Later recensions disclose how such dialogues were formatted in graduated linguistic complexity.

For the post-Viking period, David Porter has revealed how multiple derivatives of a text inspired by the *Hermeneumata* called 'De raris fabulis' disclose the pedagogy of spoken Latin. A student rehearsed basic conversations by reference to a menu of lexical choices, available in accompanying glossaries, as the following selection from Ælfric Bata's *Colloquia* (*c.* 1000) highlights: 'Faciam, domine mi, sicut mihi precepisti uel iussisti' ('I will do, sir, just as you ordered or commanded me'). Here one may choose between verbs of different conjugations, *praecipere* or *iudicare*. Porter has shown how formulations can be deployed in Bata's paradigms.

> Quid quaeris, puer mi, aut quid vis, aut quid aspicis, aut quid cogitas, aut quo properas, uel quid loqueris, quid agis, quid dicis, aut quae est necessitas tua uel pro qua causa huc venisti?
>
> (What do you seek, my boy? Or what do you want? Or what are you looking for? Or what are you thinking about? Or where are you going? Or what do you have to say? Or what are you doing? Or what do you say? Or what do you need? Or for what reason have you come here?)

He explains: 'There are nine second-person present-tense sentences, one third-person present-tense question with the copula, and one second-person question in the perfect ... [There are] eight accusatives, one locative, one nominative and one ablative.' The syntactic complexity associated with these locutions (especially subordination) only reflects the stylistic choices built into the phrasing. Other books apparently available for oral practice in Latin included Isidore's *Synonyma*, which served as boilerplate for the production of multiple locutions differing in emphasis: 'O mors, quam dulcis es miseris! O mors, quam suavis es amare viventibus! Quam iucunda es, o mors, tristibus

8 Bischoff and Lapidge 1994. 9 Gwara 1995. 10 Dionisotti 1982.

atque moerentibus' ('Death, how kindly thou art to the wretched, how sweet to those living in bitterness, how delightful to the despondent and the sorrowful'). Ælfric Bata cites extensive sections.[11]

Rhetoric

Anglo-Saxon monks imitated a specialised Christian (or monastic) lexicon and phraseology, in speaking as in writing. Classical rhetoric had no place in the Anglo-Saxon curriculum, although Gabriele Knappe has observed that 'rhetorical manuals were known': the anonymous *Ad Herennium*, Isidore's *Etymologiae* Book II,[12] Martianus Capella's *De nuptiis Philologiae et Mercurii*, Priscian's *Praeexercitamina*, Donatus' *Ars maior*, book III.[13] With the exception of the *Ad Herennium* and the Priscian, these were wholly diagnostic, not trained on production but on analysis. Thus Isidore defines without demonstration of variety or context: 'species causarum ... quinque: honestum, admirabile, humile, anceps, obscurum' (*Etym.* II.viii.1: 'five kinds of argument: honest, admiring, humble, doubled-sided and vague'). One can imagine the *application* in reading scripture, say (or, better still, certain Fathers), but in producing speeches the relevance cannot be demonstrated.

Knappe endorses instruction in 'grammatical rhetoric', especially figures and tropes, topoi, *inventio* (finding a theme) and *dispositio* (arranging it), all of which concern *reading* first and writing second. The proposed model of Cassiodorus' *Expositio psalmorum* actually covers a kind of *enarratio*, best called 'explication' or 'interpretation' rather than 'rhetoric', as in Psalm 1.1 (Beatus vir qui non abiit ... non sedit): 'nota quam pulchre singula uerba rebus singulis dedit, id est *abiit*, *stetit* et *sedit*. Quae figura dicitur hypozeuxis, quando diversa verba singulis apta clausulis apponuntur.'[14] Isidore defines hypozeuxis (e.g. 'veni, vidi, vici') in his Book I on grammar (*Etym.* I.xxxvi.4).

While theoretical manuals may have been in short supply, Gildas' *De excidio et conquestu Britanniae* could be invoked, if reluctantly, for the early period, as Gildas had been trained in forensic oratory.[15] Early or late, one may propose Aldhelm's 'hermeneutic' *Prosa de virginitate* as a model of Latin discourse. Declamations in Ælfric Bata's *Colloquia difficiliora* imply that 'elevated' words and collocations like *dindima* ('secrets'), *supernus arbiter* ('heavenly judge') and

11 *PL*, LXXXIII, col. 832; cf. Gwara 1997.

12 References to Isidore's *Etymologiae* (= *Etym.*) derive from Lindsay 1911.

13 Knappe 1998.

14 Adriaen 1958, p. 31; 'Notice how elegantly [the Psalmist] gave single words to each concept: "he departed, stepped, sat". The rhetorical figure is called hypozeuxis whenever diverse words suitable for a single clause are so deployed.'

15 Lapidge 1984.

medullitus ('to the marrow') could be deployed in conversation, perhaps in the manner of the so-called 'Colloquium hispericum'.[16] This kind of dense Latin replete with archaisms, Graecisms, neologisms, distributive numerals and obscure or learned vocabulary has often been called 'hermeneutic' and takes inspiration largely from Aldhelm's treatise.[17] It appears chiefly in writing, such that the implicit rhetoric of the *Colloquia difficiliora* is unique in the period.

Reading Latin: grammar

A booklist from the second half of the tenth century arguably enumerates texts once owned by a teacher and may therefore document one Insular curriculum:[18] Isidore's *De natura rerum*, Persius' *Satires*, Donatus' *Ars maior* and *Ars minor*, glosses on Pseudo-Cato's *Distichs* (probably by Remigius of Auxerre), Sedulius' *Carmen paschale*, 'dialogues' (probably colloquies like those mentioned above), glosses on Donatus (a commentary by any number of authors), a parsing grammar beginning 'Terra que pars', a work by Alcuin (probably *De orthographia* or *De grammatica* but possibly *De virtutibus et vitiis*), the biblical Apocalypse, a computus (or elementary mathematical/astronomical book). I propose to follow the course of instruction implied in this booklist, which plausibly covers two stages of preparation: elementary and advanced. At its core lies Latin grammar.

Grammar texts available in the early Insular period were based almost wholly on the works of Roman grammarians epitomised in fourth-century treatises which imparted the salient grammatical features but allowed for individualised embellishment.[19] Donatus, whose *Ars minor* and *Ars maior* covered elementary and advanced subjects respectively, was extensively imitated.[20] Donatus' pagan treatise was aestheticised with the substitution of Christian vocabulary and quotations, and the anonymous tracts circulating in the Anglo-Saxon period have been gathered by Vivien Law under the title of 'the Christian grammarians', emphasising the 'Ars Asporii'.

Almost two dozen classical grammarians were known to the Anglo-Saxons, not to mention a few Christian grammarians represented principally by Asporius.[21] Pre-Viking age teachers venerated Donatus (fl. *c.* 350), but his books – intended for native speakers – do not preserve full paradigms useful for non-natives. For the Anglo-Saxons the deficiency was ameliorated by 'parsing grammars' (such as 'Terra que pars' mentioned above), by anonymous tables

16 Gwara 1996, pp. 100–10. The style of Persius' *Satires* may also be relevant here.
17 Lapidge 1975. 18 Lapidge 1985, pp. 50–2 (no. III).
19 Law 1982, p. 13. 20 *Ibid.*, pp. 14–16. For an edition see Holtz 1981.
21 Law 1982a, pp. 11–41.

of nominal declensions (called *Declinationes nominum*), and by what Law has called 'elementary grammars'. Native productions of Aldhelm, Bede, Tatwine and Boniface, the elementary grammars offered exposure to full paradigms, as Law reports: 'Insular elementary grammars are characterised by their concern with the inflecting parts of speech.'[22] Taking Boniface's 'de nomine' from the *Ars grammatica* as an example, one finds gender, number, composition, termination and desinence neatly organised.[23] To be distinguished from the elementary grammars are the 'exegetical grammars', which cover more theoretical topics related to pronunciation, morphology and accidence.[24]

By the mid tenth century, Priscian's *Institutiones grammaticae* had become the leading grammar textbook. Its significant offshoot is Ælfric's *Grammar*, written in Old English for Latin instruction.[25] The *Excerptiones de Prisciano*, on which Ælfric based his *Grammar*, perfectly exemplifies a tenth-century grammar curriculum. One learns, for example, parts of speech, like the verb: 'It is the distinguishing characteristic of the verb to signify action or receiving action, or both, via mood, form and tense (and without case).'[26] Declensions earn treatment *in extenso*: 'Because gerunds and the supine/participle forms neither distinguish grammatical person nor have tenses (elements which verbs cannot exist without) they also take on cases.'[27] The *Excerptiones* (which had limited circulation) reflect an abridgement of Priscian's vast *Institutiones grammaticae*, but Ælfric's *Grammar* cuts even more radically. As Porter remarks, 'For inflected parts of speech ... missing forms are supplied so that full paradigms appear in place of partial ones, and new concepts are also without exception accompanied by definition and examples.'[28] Ælfric translated his more or less complete paradigms into Old English.

Etymology

Etymology formed a related component of grammar and could be found widely deployed in 'literary', biblical, liturgical and even scientific domains (as, for example, Bede's *De temporum ratione*: 'nox dicta quod noceat aspectibus uel negotiis humanis'; 'night is so called because it harms human observations or transactions', *Etym.* VII, 1, p. 295). It was felt that, as an apparatus of creative reflection, etymology could betray the essence of a thing, bringing one closer to objective understanding.[29] Isidore's *Etymologiae* was the primary source of Latin derivations for Anglo-Saxon readers, although few manuscripts of

22 *Ibid.*, p. 54. 23 Gebauer and Löfstedt 1980, pp. 15–32.
24 Law 1982a, pp. 81–97. 25 Zupitza 1880.
26 Porter 2002, p. 59. 27 *Ibid.*, p. 197.
28 *Ibid.*, p. 31. 29 Amsler 1989.

the entire work actually survive from this period; epitomes and excerpts are known, however. Many of Isidore's derivations are fanciful, but their occurrence in texts and glosses may reveal a linguistic precision covered in grammatical study. Yet etymologies may also have functioned to help readers remember rare Latin terms ('venabula dicta quasi venatui abilia': 'boar-spears named as if "appropriate for hunting"', *Etym.* XVIII, 7, 4).

Elementary readings

As explained above, oblates as young as six or seven were obliged to participate in divine services, which in the monastery consisted almost wholly of recitation of the psalms. The entire psalter had to be memorised, and the youths would have chanted Latin they failed to grasp. The phenomenon may explain the astonishing numbers of surviving psalters glossed in Old English.[30] In addition to the Bible and their chant, with all its intricate liturgical apparatus, the boys almost certainly tackled some 'elementary' Latin texts, as the schoolmaster's booklist suggests. Instruction in Christian ethics was paramount. Because the master's booklist names Remigius' gloss to the *Distichs* of Pseudo-Cato, the *Distichs* itself may have been prominent.[31] A fulcrum of moral learning, it comprised versified sayings like 'Think not that evil-doers surely win; / Tho' hidden for a while, time shows their sin.'[32] Similarly gnomic (but of uneven challenge) were Isidore's *Sententiae*, Defensor's *Liber scintillarum*,[33] Alcuin's *Liber de virtutibus et vitiis*, the fables of Aesop or Avianus or biblical proverbs. The *Sententiae* consist of prose maxims arranged topically. About gluttony one may read how 'the fire of desire rises with the fuel of food' (42.7) or that 'food induces drinking, drinking induces drunkenness' (43.1).[34] These lessons encouraged moral awareness as well as facility in reading Latin verse or prose.

A separate colloquy collection by Ælfric Bata confirms maxims as teaching texts. Young students beg a 'transmarine' monk to impart his doctrine, consisting entirely of maxims:

> As much as the humble are pleasing to God, so are the proud displeasing to him. God more quickly hears one prayer of a humble man than a hundred prayers of a proud man. Out of sight, out of mind. Better a stick that bends than one that

30 Pulsiano 1999; see also Chapter 21 in this volume.

31 This seems to be true only in the later period, inasmuch as Aldhelm and Bede do not show familiarity with the *Distichs*.

32 II, 8: Chase 1922, p. 25: 'Nolo putes prauos homines peccata lucrari: / Tempore si peccata latent, et tempore parent'.

33 Getty 1969. 34 Cazier 1998.

breaks. The humble ascend to the kingdom of God and the proud fall down into the pit of punishment.[35]

The vocabulary of these 'teachings' could even presume advanced learning. Bata's colloquies also cite from biblical proverbs and Alcuin's 'Praecepta vivendi'.[36] If the witness of Oxford, Bodleian Library, Rawlinson G.57 is any evidence, these 'elementary' works may have circulated in anthologies. The Rawlinson volume preserves the *Distichs* of Cato, the fables of Avianus and Aesop, and the Latin *Iliad*. The contents suggest that we should not overemphasise the Christian content of monastic learning. A second teaching anthology may be British Library, Cotton Vespasian D.vi, from Canterbury, which preserves the *Distichs*, the Book of Proverbs, Alcuin's *De virtutibus et vitiis* and minor Old English texts. The first two of these works are exactly those cited in Bata's colloquies.

Moral instruction apparently centred on two areas: virtues acquired by precept, as from the Psalter, the Book of Proverbs, the *Distichs*, and related texts like Smaragdus' *Diadema monachorum* or Cassiodorus's *Expositio psalmorum*; and social behaviorus derived from the Benedictine *Rule* and commentaries such as Smaragdus' *Commentaria in Regulam sancti Benedicti*.[37] The *Diadema*, a vehicle of tenth-century reformed Benedictinism, illustrates with biblical precedent the practices and consequent attitudes of a monk, such as 'how a monk ought to collect treasure in heaven': 'ubi hostem et expugnatorem non timemus ... ubi non timemus occultum furem, neque violentum raptorem' ('by not fearing our enemy or opponent ... by fearing neither the hidden burglar nor the violent mugger').[38] Cassiodorus' *Expositio* served as an inspired illumination of the psalter, verse by verse, often word by word: '*Beatus* ergo *uir* dicitur ... quasi bene aptus, cui omnia desiderata succedunt' ('a man is called "blessed" as if "well prepared", to whom all desired things accrue').[39]

Christian moral character would also have been moulded in the context of the saint's life, either delivered orally in the refectory or read in a passional,[40] or of the homily, whether heard in church or school, or studied informally later. The saint's life has parallels in multiple works like Jerome's *De viris illustribus*, Isidore's *De ortu et obitu patrum* or Pseudo-Bede's *Liber de ortu et obitu patriarcharum*. More important in this context, however, is the sermon, for which a number of vernacular models survive, the most important by Ælfric.[41] In fact,

35 Gwara and Porter 1997, p. 189. 36 Gwara 1996, p. 74.
37 Hill 1992. 38 *PL*, CII, col. 644.
39 Adriaen 1958, pp. 29–30. 40 Such as those by Ælfric: Skeat 1881–1900.
41 Godden 2000; Pope 1967. Other collections are the Vercelli Homilies (Scragg 1992) and the Blickling Homilies (Kelly 2003).

a sermon on the good Christian and the Ten Commandments concludes Bata's *Colloquia*:

> One who loves chastity, who often flees drunkenness, who hates pride, who shuns envy, who does not steal, who bears no false witness, who neither lies nor perjures, who does not commit adultery, who often comes to church to pray, who honours his elders – a man like this is called and *is* a true Christian.[42]

It seems possible that the homily and the sermon (if I may discriminate) were the primary sources of patristic learning for the period, in which Bede alone seems to have excelled. The important figures were Augustine, Jerome and Gregory, some of whose works were pre-digested in homiliaries, especially that by Paulus Diaconus.

Vernacular language study and bilingualism

Far less is known about instruction in Old English, although the emergence of a standard lexicon centred on Winchester almost certainly highlights the function of a prominent school.[43] Translation in the period brought Latin and Old English into very close contact, and presumably a suitable native terminology was needed for Latin vocables, especially when those words might be loan-translations or other Latin derivatives and learned abstractions. One thinks here of loan-translations like *anhyrn* ('one-horn') for *unicornis* ('unicorn') and *þreones* ('three-ness') for *Trinitas* ('the Trinity'),[44] or of echoic terms like OE *meregrota* 'sea-pebble', a gloss to Latin *margareta* 'pearl', and OE *carcern* 'prison' + 'house' (='ærn') coined from Latin *carcer* 'prison'.[45]

It seems possible that bilingual glossaries contributed to the emergence of standard and learned Old English vocabularies. In addition to being a glossary itself, Ælfric's *Grammar* (mentioned above) incorporated a brief *Glossary* that circulated widely in ever expanding recensions. Ælfric compiled a 'class-glossary' in which Latin words were arranged by subject and defined by a single Old English interpretation: body parts, social ranks, birds, tools, etc. Such class-glossaries were essential elements of elementary language instruction, but they may have contributed to lexical simplification and subsequent 'standardisation' as well as artificial coinages.

King Alfred's educational plan (of the late ninth century) popularised vernacular renderings of Gregory the Great's *Cura pastoralis* and *Dialogi*, St Augustine's *Soliloquia*, Boethius' *Consolatio philosophiae*, Orosius' *Historia*

42 Gwara and Porter 1997.

43 Hofstetter 1987. A Canterbury school vocabulary has been proposed as well: Pulsiano 1994b; see also Gneuss 1972.

44 Gneuss 1955.

45 Meritt 1941.

adversus paganos, and Bede's *Historia ecclesiastica*. At least some of these translations might be said to have made texts of an 'advanced' curriculum accessible to those without sufficient facility in Latin to read them.

A multitude of translations from the tenth century suggest that Old English may have been taught at the time.[46] It is impossible to know if these translations were ever deemed 'schoolbooks' in the way their Latin originals may have been, as much as they attest to Old English learning. In fact, Ælfric's preface to his translation of Genesis expresses a deep anxiety about the context of biblical reading necessary for interpretation and suggests that non-ecclesiasts had vernacular reading skills: 'ic ondræde, gif sum dysig man þas boc ræt oððe rædan gehyrþ, þæt he wille wenan, þæt he mote lybban nu ... swa swa þa ealdan fæderas leofodon' ('I fear if a naive man should read the book [Genesis] or hear it read, that he will expect that he can live now ... as the patriarchs did').[47]

In British Library, Cotton Tiberius A.iii the post-Conquest attribution to 'elurici bate' (Ælfric Bata) of an Old English gloss to the *Regularis concordia* suggests that this famous teacher may have relied on vernacular glossing in the classroom.[48] The *Regularis concordia* was a comprehensive manual of monastic liturgy.[49] The manuscript contains some works that were probably studied in the elementary curriculum: the Benedictine *Rule* glossed in Old English,[50] Ælfric's *Colloquy*,[51] computistical prognostics and prayers. In fact, the Canterbury library catalogue recording the manuscript's contents calls the *Rule* 'Batte super Regulam beati Benedicti' or 'Bata's [book] on the blessed Benedict's *Rule*'. A second entry called 'Batte secundus' or 'Bata's second [book]' may describe an anthology (now lost) that included Priscian with an Old English gloss (?Ælfric's *Grammar*), dialogues ('locutio latina glosata Anglice ad instruendos pueros'), a glossed Benedictine *Rule*, a collection of homilies and sermons, and possibly a copy of the *Regularis concordia* glossed in Old English. The contents contain many 'elementary' school texts outlined above.

Science

Science in the Anglo-Saxon classroom took the form of computus (calculation of ecclesiastical and other dates by astronomical means) and natural history. The grammarian's booklist includes Isidore's *De natura rerum*, an elementary work suited to introducing astronomy and 'science', since it defines the major

46 Stanton 2002. 47 Crawford 1922, p. 76. 48 James 1903, p. 50.
49 Symons 1953. 50 Gretsch 1973. 51 Garmonsway 1947.

concepts: years, months, weeks, hours, courses of the sun and moon, equinox and solstice, eclipses, rains, thunder and lightning, snow, wind, plague, oceans, rivers, land masses, etc. About wind, for example, it is said 'est aer commotus et agitatus' ('wind is air commingled and stirred up').[52] Better known than Isidore's tract is Bede's *De natura rerum*, a distillation of Pliny's *Historia naturalis* and Isidore.[53] Bede's astronomical subjects could be said to cover essential questions relevant to the Bible, especially Genesis, although they may explicate literary works as well. Perhaps the most widely known, if rather compendious, source of natural history for the Anglo-Saxons was Isidore's *Etymologiae*, an encyclopaedia of classical and post-classical learning. For example, Chapters 13–20 cover the elements, water, wind; lands, seas and mountains; cities, fields, agrarian measurements; gems and precious stones, glass, and metals; plants; instruments of war; ships and their outfits, clothes, tools; foods and transportation. Elementary computus belongs in the Anglo-Saxon curriculum and may be best represented in Bede's *De temporum ratione* or *De temporibus*.[54] *De temporum ratione*, for example, details in Chapter III 'the smallest measurements of time': 'Recipit autem hora .iv. punctos, .x. minuta, .xv. partes, .xl. momenta ... non enim hae divisiones temporum naturales, sed uidentur esse condictiuae' ('an hour has 4 points, 10 minutes, 15 parts, and 40 moments, yet these divisions are not natural and appear to be stipulated').[55] Measurements are shown to be artificial by any number of calculations. A letter of *c.* 670×675 by the Anglo-Saxon Aldhelm proves that computus, astronomy and arithmetic were taught at a very advanced level prior to Bede's time but probably without a 'textbook' as useful as *De temporum ratione*.[56] After the Viking age the enterprising Byrhtferth taught computus at Ramsey Abbey, mostly with reference to Bede's tracts. Mathematical computation and arithmology (as in, say, Macrobius' *In somnium Scipionis*) may have been taught as well, but probably only at a basic level, unless we consider chant (i.e. music) to have been taught with a theoretical dimension.

The advanced curriculum

Having progressed from the preliminary texts, one encounters the advanced reading of the hypothetical curriculum. My use of the term 'advanced' is deliberately tendentious, for few Anglo-Saxons plausibly had skill or leisure for

52 *PL*, LXXXIII, col. 1006B. 53 Jones 1975.
54 Jones 1977. Ælfric also wrote an elementary *De temporibus anni*; see Blake 2009.
55 Jones 1977, p. 277. 56 Lapidge and Herren 1979, pp. 8, 153.

reading verse, distinguished by a highly artificial lexicon, syntax and prosody. Admittedly, my vade mecum, the grammarian's booklist, includes such works as Persius' *Satires* and Sedulius' *Carmen paschale*, yet these poetic works are problematically associated with monastic *education* in the period.[57]

Wieland and Rigg described Cambridge University Library, Gg.5.35 as a schoolbook, implying that the texts it preserves were studied in a classroom.[58] Wieland subsequently suggested that from annotations in this manuscript 'we can draw certain conclusions as to the teaching techniques employed in the Anglo-Saxon classroom'.[59] He frequently interpreted the glosses as the spontaneous reactions of native teachers. In response, Michael Lapidge observed that texts often called schoolbooks might simply be 'library books', one of which comprised part of an established curriculum.[60] Many volumes are pristine, have little or no glossing, or else the glossing, rather than being native and spontaneous, derives from Carolingian commentaries. Wieland conceded these points, but established criteria for identifying schoolbooks:

> The manuscript must be glossed, and glossed consistently ... the glosses must cover the five areas which one would expect a teacher to comment on: prosody (or more generally stress), lexicon, grammar and syntax and content ... the manuscript must contain such glosses as the accentual marks, the construe marks and the q: or *quare hoc* [why this?] glosses (but not necessarily all three at the same time) ... These three conditions are usually fulfilled only in manuscripts containing texts which can otherwise be shown to be schooltexts.[61]

Although I shall return to glossing in the context of education, these sophisticated and well-conceived criteria still do not supply evidence of classroom use. Except for the *quare hoc* glosses, which might signal the reader to question an author's motive (why would he write this?), nothing proves that these glosses were not used mostly or exclusively for private study.

Latin poetry

The advanced curriculum in the Anglo-Saxon monastery may have included a significant amount of Latin verse. Manuscripts of the following classical texts survive: Vergil (*Aeneid*, with the commentary of Servius; *Eclogues*, *Georgics*), plays of Terence, Ovid's *Ars amatoria*, Statius' *Thebais* and *Achilleis*, Juvenal's *Satires*, Persius' *Satires*, Macrobius' *Saturnalia*. Christian texts were more visible. Prosper's *Epigrammata* may be thought of as superseding Cato's *Distichs*,

57 On Persius see Pulsiano 2001. 58 Rigg and Wieland 1975.
59 Wieland 1983, pp. 2–3. 60 Lapidge 1982, pp. 126–7.
61 Wieland 1985.

a thoroughly pagan work. The versified gospel epitomes – Juvencus' *Historia evangeliorum libri quattuor* and, above all, Sedulius' *Carmen paschale* – enjoyed immense prestige, if manuscript survival and quotation are any guide. Other popular works include Arator's *De actibus apostolorum*, Lactantius' allegorical *De ave phoenice*, Paulinus of Nola's *Carmina*, Venantius Fortunatus' *Carmina*, Aldhelm's *Carmen de virginitate*, and Bede's metrical *Life of St Cuthbert*. In the post-Viking period Prudentius (*Psychomachia*, *Cathemerinon*, *Peristephanon*, *Dittochaeon*) and Boethius (*Consolatio philosophiae*) were popular not only for their philosophy but also for reasons of metrical style. In prose one encounters Gildas in the early period (*De excidio et conquestu Britanniae*), Aldhelm (*Prosa de virginitate*; *Epistola ad Heahfridum*) and Bede (*Historia ecclesiastica*). Schoolmen honoured these native sons for opposite reasons: Aldhelm for his learned style, Bede for his content. For prose writings Orosius' *Historia adversus paganos* stands out in the later period.

Some of these works may have been joined in 'anthologies', such as Gg.5.35 mentioned above. This impressive codex contains major works of Juvencus, Sedulius, Arator, Prosper, Prudentius, Lactantius, Boethius, Hrabanus Maurus (*De laudibus sanctae crucis*), Aldhelm and Milo (*De laude pudicitiae*) alongside an extensive assortment of minor verse: epigrams, hymns, prayers, *enigmata* (or riddles). It cannot yet be known whether Gg.5.35 reflects a curriculum standard, or whether it belonged to a teacher like Ælfric Bata, who would have consulted it only for selections – or, indeed, for amusement. A second such advanced compendium might be identified in Oxford, Bodleian Library, Auct. F.2.14, from mid-eleventh-century Sherborne. The manuscript comprises poems by Wulfstan of Winchester, Theodulus and Lactantius, the anonymous Latin *Iliad*, Avianus's *Fabulae*, the grammar of Phocas and Old English translations of terms from Aldhelm's *Carmen de virginitate*. One observes a combined 'classical' and Christian focus.

We are tempted to call these works 'school texts', even though little evidence confirms them as such. For example, a booklist in Alcuin's *Bishops, Kings and Saints of York* and Alcuin's own verbal borrowings led Peter Godman to conclude that 'Alcuin referred to, and knew well, a "school canon" of late Antique and early Medieval Latin poetry' that included Sedulius' *Carmen paschale*.[62] The Fontes Anglo-Saxonici project records nine authors quoting the *Carmen* 157 times.[63] This figure ultimately accounts for 120 loci distributed throughout the five books. When one observes that Sedulius is cited by Alcuin once, Felix once, Asser once, two anonymous charters once each, Lull once,

62 Godman 1982, p. lxxii. 63 See http://fontes.english.ox.ac.uk/.

Ælfric once, Bede eight times, and Aldhelm 142 times, one begins to question in what sense Sedulius could be called a 'school author'. This pattern typifies citations of other alleged curriculum authors.

One would imagine that Vergil's *Aeneid*, a bulwark of the Roman school, had been sedulously studied in the Anglo-Saxon period. Nevertheless, only one complete and three or four fragmentary *Aeneid* manuscripts are known from the pre-Conquest period.[64] Michael Lapidge describes the Vatican *Aeneid* as 'crisp and clean' and without glossing.[65] This pristine condition belies the presumed consciousness of Vergil in the period. Citations tell a similar story. The Fontes Anglo-Saxonici project lists some 200 loci in 243 citations of the *Aeneid* by twelve authors. Goscelin of Canterbury (ten citations), Abbo of Fleury (three) and Frithegod of Winchester (three) must be removed from this list as authors trained on the Continent. Aldhelm accounts for 162 citations, Wulfstan of Winchester for twenty-four, Bede for nineteen, Felix for thirteen and Byrhtferth for three. An additional five references are found uniquely in Boniface, Lull, Alfred and in two charters. These data could suggest that Aldhelm, Bede, Felix and Wulfstan knew the *Aeneid* well, but I would prefer to say that while Aldhelm shows comfortable familiarity with the entire text, the other Insular authors cite heavily from the first half alone:

Wulfstan: book **1** (4×), **2** (4×), **3** (6×), **4** (3×), **8** (2×), **9** (1×), **12** (4×)
Bede: book **1** (5×), **2** (6×), **3** (1×), **4** (1×), **6** (2×), **8** (1×), **10** (2×), **12** (1×)
Felix: book **1** (4×), **2** (4×), **4** (2×), **5** (1×), **11** (1×), **12** (1×)
Byrhtferth: book **2** (1×), **4** (1×), **9** (1×)

Abbo taught Byrhtferth, but because Frithegod departed for Brioude (*c.* 958) before Wulfstan was born, we must seek another literary influence on Wulfstan, perhaps Lantfred of Fleury.[66] Citations of Vergil in the native authors I name could therefore be traced directly to these Frankish proponents. This evidence suggest that certain books of the *Aeneid* may have been independently studied by those few interested in writing verse but that the *Aeneid* should not without reflection be considered a staple 'schoolbook'.

History and geography

Anglo-Saxon monks may have studied historiography at an advanced stage of preparation.[67] Production of the *Anglo-Saxon Chronicle* and the translations of Bede's *Historia ecclesiastica* and Orosius' *Historia adversus paganos* suggest the

64 The complete text is BAV, Reg. lat. 1671. On the various fragments, see Lapidge 1982, p. 129 n. 17.
65 *Ibid.*, p. 101. 66 Lapidge and Winterbottom 1991, p. l. 67 Parkes 1976b.

prominence of the subject. A fourth relevant text detailing church history include Eusebius' (Rufinus') *Historia ecclesiastica*. More 'geographical' in focus are Isidore's *Etymologiae*, the *Historia Alexandri* and other texts of comparable oriental focus.[68]

Glosses and glossography

Wieland theorised that the variety and extent of glosses indicated a text's adoption as a schoolbook, the idea being that annotations aided a teacher's or student's reading. Glosses were largely Latin and Old English, and Wieland has classified the Latin glosses by function: prosody, lexical, grammatical, syntactic and commentary. A gloss on metre might indicate a syllable length, short or long, whereas a lexical gloss might specifically be a *differentiae* gloss, discriminating between (near-)homonyms, e.g. *pignus*: *pignus pignoris filium*, *pignus pigneris uestium* ('a pledge, of a pledge: concerning brothers; a pledge, of a pledge: concerning clothes'). Lexical glosses primarily explain one word by another.[69] Grammatical glosses describe cases, pronoun referents, tenses, person, etc. A special case is a 'suppletive' gloss, which supplies an unstated or formerly stated reference, such as a verb's understood subject or object. Syntactic glosses consist of symbols used to navigate Latin syntax, which differs significantly from Germanic syntax familiar to speakers of Old English.[70] Finally, commentary glosses 'interpret' by decoding metaphors, providing etymologies, summarising content or giving sources.

Sometimes these functions do not describe the ways in which the text could be negotiated. For example, it seems that books belonging to the 'elementary' curriculum boast a large proportion of 'simple' glosses suitable for beginners. The copy of Pseudo-Cato's *Distichs* in Cambridge, Trinity College, O.2.31 (Christ Church, *s*. x/xi) boasts a profusion of suppletive glosses such as: MVLTI] homines, CVNCTIS] hominibus, NVLLI] homini, BONIS] hominibus, MVLTIS] hominibus, MVLTORVM] hominum. Even the commentary glosses betray a similarly simplistic approach, as II.xi reveals:

> Aduersum notum noli contendere uerbis;
> Lis rebus minimis interdum maxima sunt.
>
> (Do not quibble in words with a friend (or: a famous man); sometimes a great lawsuit develops from trifling things.)

'Adversum notum' is glossed 'contra amicum', even though 'notus' could mean any acquaintance or man of importance. The glossator has reached

68 Howe 2008. 69 Wieland 1983, pp. 44–5. 70 Robinson 1973.

for the commonest rendering of the Latin. If these glosses were indeed the work of a *magister scholarum*, we might be able to excuse mistakes as comparable simplifications. For example, the gloss 'per uerba nimia peruenit ad lites' ('with great words one causes lawsuits') above 'minimis interdum maxima' reverses the sense of the epigram, since trifling words spoken to big men cause strife. Can we see, however, an attempt to read trifling words as evidence of grandiosity?

Glosses generally simplify or explain. Aldhelm's *Prosa de virginitate* has similarly easy annotations, but other interpretations also render Aldhelm's unfamiliar diction, sometimes wrongly. Consider the following selection:[71]

> Siluester, qui apud Romam pontificalis cathedrae suscepit sacerdotium, per omnes Europae prouincias et florentis Ausoniae parrochias, quam glaciales Alpium saltus praeruptis scopulorum cautibus cingunt.
>
> (Silvester, who received the office of the pontifical throne at Rome, throughout all the provinces of Europe and the parishes of blossoming Italy, which is bounded by icy passes of the Alps with their craggy cliffs of outcrops.)

The following Latin glosses are found (I omit the Old English ones and combine glosses from multiple sources):[72]

> SILVESTER] papa; APVD ROMAM] cum romanis; PONTIFICALIS] summi sacerdotii; CATHEDRAE] sedis; SVSCEPIT] tenuit; SACERDOTIVM] gradum; OMNES] cunctas; FLORENTIS] crescentis; AVSONIAE] italie; PARROCHIAS] regiones; GLACIALES] frigidas; ALPIVM] montium; SALTVS] gelata aqua; PRAERVPTIS] fractis; SCOPVLORVM] saxorum eminentium; CAVTIBVS] saxis, petris, rupibus; CINGVNT] ambiunt, circumdant.

Using the glosses, one could translate: 'Pope Silvester, who held the title of the highest priesthood of the chair among the Romans, throughout all the provinces of Europe and the parishes of growing Italy, which is surrounded by the cold frozen water of mountains with broken rocks of high cliffs'. Quite clearly, some of these words (*sedis*, *crescentis*, *fractis*) could be deemed non-contextual. Nearly all, however, translate subordinate terms (e.g. 'house-sparrow') with basic terms (e.g. 'sparrow'), or basic terms with superordinate ones (e.g. 'bird'). For example, *alpium* (basic: 'of the Alps') is translated by *montium* (superordinate: 'of the mountains'). Second Language Acquisition 'Prototype Theory' explains this phenomenon of Lexical Simplification – a

71 Gwara 2001, pp. 301–3. 72 *Ibid.*, pp. 300–2.

process by which translation reduces linguistic complexity – a common practice of foreign-language learners.

Other kinds of glossing exist. Of course, vernacular glosses abound, often supplying grammatical translations – even at the expense of one-for-one lexical correspondences. A substantial proportion of the Old English glosses consist of just a few letters that translate word components: roots, affixes or inflections. A gloss to the word *subrogare* ('to substitute') in Bede's *Historia ecclesiastica* reads *under* ('under'), obviously translating only the Latin element 'sub'.[73] This gloss and others like it may mean that students were taught Latin roots (e.g. *rogare*: 'to ask') and common affixes, from which they may have been expected to extrapolate the sense. Literal renderings like *cwyldbærlice* ('lethally') to *pestifere* may disclose rather more comprehensively the practice of semantic parsing: *cwyld* ('death') = *pestis* ('plague') + *bær* ('carry') = *fer* ('carry') + *-lice* (adverbial termination) = *-e* (adverbial termination).[74] Some Old English was invented as Latin nonce translations, perhaps even as mnemonic aids. This may be true of echoic renderings, such as APOFORETA] *æppelfatu*.[75]

Glossaries

If glosses do signal the function of a book as a school text, glossaries may also have belonged to a school. Quite different from a modern dictionary, the glossary is frequently compiled from marginal or interlinear interpretations culled from specific works, and when found unalphabetised these groups are called *glossae collectae*. The translated word, called a 'lemma', is rendered by Latin or Old English (or mixed) *interpretamenta*, and the glosses may be roughly alphabetised by first letter or letters. We know that one glossary from seventh-century Canterbury fathered dozens of congeners, the most famous of which are the Épinal-Erfurt, Leiden and Corpus Glossaries.[76] Other glossaries had more specific focuses, such as a grammarian's glossary in British Library, Harley 3826,[77] or a glossary that accompanied Abbo of Saint-Germain-des-Prés' *Bella parisiacae urbis*,[78] or a list of the winds.[79] For the later period the Cotton Cleopatra A.iii and Harley 3376 glossaries stand out.[80] While we know that such glossaries were plundered for advanced writing in Latin and for practising vocabulary flexibility in the colloquies, we cannot be sure how they were employed in a school, except as handy reference.

73 Meritt 1945, p. 8. 74 From the *Liber scintillarum*: Getty 1969, 8.25.
75 From glosses to Abbo of Saint-Germain-des-Prés *Bella parisiacae urbis*: Zupitza 1887.
76 For Épinal-Erfurt: Pheifer 1974; for Leiden: Holthausen 1916–17; for Corpus: Hessels 1890. On their common origin and relationship: Lapidge 1986b; Pheifer 1987.
77 Gneuss 1994. 78 Lendinara 1990. 79 Pulsiano 1994a.
80 For Cleopatra: Quinn 1956; Stryker 1951; Kindschi 1955. For Harley: Oliphant 1966.

24
Law books

PATRICK WORMALD

There is, properly speaking, no such thing as an Anglo-Saxon law book. There are books, imported and home-grown, of ecclesiastical ('canon') law. Several important collections of secular legislation from before 1066 were assembled in the post-Conquest period. But the only volumes written in pre-Conquest England which contain the laws of lay society are devoted for the most part to non-legal texts. All the same, it would be precipitate to draw conclusions about what once circulated from what now survives. A useful comparison may be drawn with 'charters'. These title deeds were originally written on single pieces of parchment. Though more than 100 survive, single sheets are scarce in all but a few archives, because they were copied into comprehensive cartularies. There was even less reason to keep individual copies of codes once they were assumed into collections like those of the twelfth century. We can no more conclude that laws were available only in such forms than that charters were kept only in cartularies. For that very reason, an account of pre-Conquest law books should begin by asking what can be learned about the law books of the Old English period from those that were made after it came to an end.

In the first place, we may consider the very latest pre-modern copy of a legal text in Old English to survive (no. **15** in the appendix at the end of the chapter). The first thing to note about it is that it is the second part of a composite manuscript, the first being the utterly different no. **4**. This is one example, nos. **7** and **11** being another, of the way that this exercise is complicated by the determination of early modern antiquarians to convert our material into what suited their bibliographical purposes. That aside, **15** is in a class of its own, because it alone of the entire series is the sort of book that one can easily imagine being carried round by judicial officials. Though on the large side, it is a self-contained quire, i.e. a pamphlet, made of decidedly down-market parchment, and containing an uncalligraphic copy of Cnut's code. All that is odd about it – and this *is* odd – is its date: up to a century after law books in Old English should have ceased to be of any use to the French- or Latin-speaking authorities. Nevertheless, we are at liberty to suppose that this is what a 'normal' Anglo-Saxon law book would have looked like.

We may turn, second, to a numerous and important class of post-Conquest law book: those that might be characterised as 'legal encyclopedias'. With the exception of **11**, which dates from either side of the Conquest, these are of the first quarter of the twelfth century. What is at once obvious from the list is that they contain many more legal texts than any of our other witnesses. Furthermore, unlike most others, they contain *nothing but* law texts, a few extraneous items like the 'shipmen' in no. **12** aside. It is to these collections that we owe most of what we know about pre-Conquest law. This is in itself an important clue to why they were made. Nos. **12**, **13** and **14** (**13** being the Latin translation known as *Quadripartitus* (1106×18), itself extant in six copies from the two centuries after its composition, but helpfully regarded here as a single manuscript in its own right, as it was in the first instance a compilation like others of this date) each show signs of having gone out of their way to assemble materials from repositories other than their 'home' library. It is, for instance, possible to demonstrate that a leaf was added to **14** so as to incorporate the anonymous texts known as *Be Blaserum* and *Forfang*, which its editor took to be extra clauses of the Alfred-Ine *domboc* (law-code). When we note that the same series of texts recurs in **12** and **13** too, it becomes clear that Rochester's scribe expanded his original text of Alfred-Ine after examining one like those available to his contemporaries.

Given the individual efforts invested in assembling these several codices, it is striking how similar they nonetheless turn out. Each has texts that do not appear in others: for example, the unique early Kentish codes in **14**. But what is found in one tends to be found in the rest. By 1100, it was evidently difficult, however hard one tried, to unearth what was not generally available. Even if the category of fragmentary or lost manuscripts contains two books (**16**, **18**) with unique codes of Æthelred (and these may in fact be variant versions of otherwise extant texts), the remainder offer the standard materials. It seems to follow that such losses of pre-Conquest legislation as there may have been are not, for once, to be blamed on Norman-French indifference to Old English ways.

Of particular interest is the form in which materials reached twelfth-century editors. The point is most clearly made by the treatment of *Be Blaserum* and *Forfang* in **12**. The first begins on the next line after the end of 'Alfred-Ine', just as if it were one of that code's clauses. The second follows in the same fashion. These two texts must have been attached to Alfred-Ine sometime back in the transmission, because the pattern recurs not only in the revised **14** but also in **13**. After *Forfang*, **12** launches into the *Hundred Ordinance* as if it too were part of the same text, and again the conjunction reappears in **13**. Alfred's *domboc* had acquired extra clauses on arson, murder, cattle-theft and hundredal organisation, with little done to distinguish these from the main text. This is only a particularly blatant example of a tendency evident throughout twelfth-century collections. Comparison suggests the prior existence of a series of 'mini-collections' which had already gathered together some of the texts. Why else, for instance, should two of Edmund's codes, but not the third, always follow Edward's two? In **12** and **13**, these pairs are accompanied by tracts on oaths, marriage and feud; while neigbouring items in **12** and **14** are a charm to recover stolen cattle and a formulary. Though cattle-theft was one of Anglo-Saxon law's main concerns, the charm is of course out of place and the rubricator of **12** put a red line through it. It may have been that the collector of **13** was quicker on the uptake, which enabled him to drop charm and formulary altogether. The Alfred-Guthrum treaty turns up among this sequence of texts in **12** too, despite having appeared earlier in the book. We may conclude that a mini-collection comprising Edward and Edmund codes, Alfred-Guthrum and the other tracts, charm included, was available to the makers of **12**, **13** and **14**. One could then hypothesise several groups of the same sort.

The kind of mini-collection we are envisaging is in fact extant in no. **11**, the first (though later) part of British Library, Cotton Nero A.i. Here, Cnut's code is backed up by those of Edgar and Alfred, but tracts on Peter's Pence and judgement are inserted between Alfred's rubrics and text. The date of that collection, *c.* 1066, raises the possibility that it was itself an early example of the urge to compile that the Conquest engendered. We may get a further idea of how mini-collections circulated in their 'raw' state by looking more closely at their distribution in twelfth-century manuscripts. In **13**, the tracts form a sequence after II Edmund, but in **12** they are interrupted by Alfred-Guthrum. Alfred-Guthrum is not in **14** at all, while Edward-Guthrum has *Wergeld* as an indistinguishable appendix, a unique instance of **14** reproducing its exemplar as automatically as did **12**. This implies that groups of texts were at one point transmitted in such a way that they could be reshuffled as they went. The best guess is that each had its own sheet(s) or gathering among sets of loose leaves within a temporary cover (whether folder or roll), so that more and less 'official' pronouncements easily became mixed up.

Post-Conquest volumes therefore provide suggestive clues to the way that law-codes were disseminated in the Old English kingdom. But since they afford no proof, it is all the more important to contemplate the way in which law *is* found in pre-Conquest books. If it can be shown that there is a logic in the arrangements they have, that might seem to put the burden of proof on those wishing to argue that any hypothetical alternatives were at all common. Such logic is in fact detectable in *every* case. An immediate indicator is the very fact that parts of otherwise independent manuscripts behave in much the same way. In the case of the first pair, this is no surprise, because there is little doubt that **2** was in the first instance copied from **1**. Even here, however, it will emerge that the later volume amplifies the themes of the earlier. Nearly all the rest, moreover, are examples of what Archbishop Wulfstan of York and Worcester (1002–23) – or his scribes – did with law-codes; and the fact that none of these pairs was directly copied one from another shows that their resemblances must have been intended by their compilers.

Since so many surviving law books are associated in one way or another with Wulfstan, it is best to take them first – even if this means continuing to chart a chronologically reversed course through the evidence. One pairing brings us to codices of church law. The two in question (**9**, **10**) are essentially versions of what scholars have liked to call 'Archbishop Wulfstan's commonplace book', but which is better recognised as his 'canon collection'. Another version of it constitutes what is now the second part of **7**, a manuscript which features the archbishop's own hand. In each case, Wulfstan's scribes copied a set of canonical and penitential texts alongside a series of much shorter excerpts from the Bible and conciliar decrees (a selection itself known unhelpfully as the 'Excerptiones Ecgberti', after the eighth-century archbishop of York, to which some of its clauses were falsely attributed). The most notable feature of **9** and **10** compared with books confined to secular law is their more elegant presentation. Some use is made of display scripts, initials are multi-coloured and clauses clearly demarcated. The same goes, on the whole, for books of this type imported from the Continent (for example, Bodleian Library, Hatton 42) or books evidently copied from such imports (like Bodleian Library, Bodley 718); these, significantly, were demonstrably volumes quarried by Wulfstan for his own collection. In amongst the canon law materials come related secular codes: IV Edgar (**9**), because this is first of all a code about tithe payment; and a set of status tracts including one on compensation for society's various secular and clerical ranks (**10**), because, in a part of the book that seems systematically to give vernacular equivalents of Wulfstan's 'canon collection', they balance Latin works on priestly rank.

Meanwhile, the first part of no. **7** forms another pair with **8**. On closer examination, the former turns out to consist of a series of more or less disarticulated 'booklets', differing in scribe, layout and type of marginalia yet repetitious in content, so leaving a distinct impression that they had rather different medieval histories. Since, however, they are similar in design and overall aspect, they probably came off the same 'production line'. In other words, Wulfstan's scriptorium was issuing a series of books of this type. The relevant part of no. **8** gives every appearance of having been copied from one of them. These volumes are devoted to a variety of programmes of Christian living. Wulfstan's *Institutes of Polity* gives each segment of a Christian society its role and standards. His homilies adjure its members to live up to them. His laws lend them the force of governmental authority. In point of fact, though, it is not easy to tell the difference between one genre of text and another, whether in presentation or indeed content. They do not even have distinctive titles. Æthelred's codes are labelled '*Be Angolwitena gerednesse* (on the decrees of the English wise men)', or '*Be cyricgriðe* (on church-peace)', just like homilies or sections of the *Institutes*. The rubrics of each type of text are in small black capitals with a red wash, separate 'clauses' being marked by smaller colour-washed initials. The same goes, *mutatis mutandis*, for the equivalent part of **8**, from a generation later. That the various contents of these manuscripts were presented in so similar a way argues that they were meant to serve a similar purpose.

Something of that purpose may be guessed from considering the sizes of the volumes. Nos. **7** and **11** are much the smallest of those under consideration. In the case of **11** (like the contemporary and conceivably similar fragment, **17**), this may reflect the fact that post-Conquest law books anyway tend to be smaller than Old English products (as with **12**). No. **7** itself was evidently a pocket book, intended for carrying around. Preachers, however, would have found it more immediately useful than judges. Its codes are concerned with the church. Its common themes are far more obviously moral than legal. Yet, in the circumstances, that is probably a false distinction. What concerned Wulfstan was that the English should be holy enough to merit God's favour. The particular medium adopted to convey that message was unimportant compared with its urgency. As for **8**, it was not itself the output of a Wulfstan scriptorium, though its Wulfstanian nucleus probably derived from York. The book as a whole apparently came from Winchester's New Minster; and the way in which the exhortatory core was set amidst the *Regularis concordia*, confessional texts, a list of the 'Resting-Places of English Saints', and narratives of beneficent and malign administration in Pharaonic Egypt (*Joseph*) or the Hellenistic Levant (*Apollonius*), inclines one to wonder whether it was not a sort of coaching manual for the New Minster nursery of monk-bishops, future servants of God and king alike.

A related pattern recurs in no. **6**. This introduces a third pairing, that of laws in 'holy books', inasmuch as Cnut's 1020 letter to the English is found among addenda to a decorated gospel-book from York. But here again, the 'Wulfstan hand' appears. Once more, a legal text is laid out in very much the same way as the Wulfstan homilies that keep it company. The prose of each is broken down by initials shaded in red ink, meaning that Cnut's letter and Wulfstan's tracts both read as sets of clauses. As with 7 and 8, modern editorial convention is really all there is to distinguish 'law' from 'homily'. The other manuscript of this pair, no. 5, raises a rather different set of issues. It is a pontifical which, in yet another early modern antiquarian intervention, was mixed up with two others. The legal texts come on what were originally its opening leaves: first, the Latin text of a code known as 'VI Æthelred' (a substantially variant version of 'V', the code of 1008 which is found twice in 7 and also in 8); and then, in another and conceivably slightly later hand, a vernacular paraphrase and amplification of it. But whereas the parchment of the Latin is perceptibly the same as in the rest of the volume, that of the Old English consists of a set of half-sheets of poorer quality. In other words, the codicology is consistent with the hypothesis that extra space was created to add the vernacular version to the Latin. The Latin's final clause is entered on the first half-sheet and may thus itself be an addition. It records how an at first unnamed archbishop of York had committed to writing 'these legal statutes or decrees ... issued at our synodical assembly' by an at first unnamed king. It was Wulfstan's own hand that identified the king as Æthelred and himself as the archbishop: this is one more Wulfstan book.

But this pontifical would not have been of much use to him as archbishop of York. It does not contain the rite for consecrating bishops, an archbishop's special responsibility, which appears in the other main pontificals of the time; and in some other respects it seems outdated compared with books compiled for the leading prelates of the early eleventh century. The 'Thureth' recorded in a verse inscription on its opening folio to have 'bedecked [the volume] with fair ornament' and 'many treasures' might then most plausibly be identified with a known Fenland magnate who had Peterborough connections, and who could have given the book to Wulfstan (probably another Fenlander) when he became bishop of London in 996. What that would mean is that the pontifical was not in current use when legal texts were added to it. There is a case that both the Latin and Old English texts were *drafts* of envisaged codes, and that the Old English at least was made with a view to Cnut's legislation; that would explain the wariness in naming Æthelred as their original author. If so, we could guess that this elaborately adorned volume was kept in a cathedral treasury, as the York Gospels were. It would have received and enshrined texts whose solemnity was comparable with that of God's own word, in that they too were intended to dictate the way of life for his own people. To return for a moment to charters: these were sometimes preserved with '*haligdom*, relics', or in sacred books. Their proems and sanctions reinforced their instructions with the blessings or curses of God. They were to that extent holy documents. The same could be said of Wulfstan's laws.

A similar scenario might be envisaged for our fourth pairing, one again involving Wulfstan, albeit comprising codes that were admired but not composed by him. Nos. **3** and **4** are actually sets of loose leaves. They would have had little chance of surviving the Middle Ages as they stand, unless as part of a binding (as was clearly the case with **17**); nor, given the inclination of twelfth- and sixteenth-century collectors to keep or put laws together, are they at all likely to have come originally from volumes containing other legal texts. Among signs that these were from grander books – of the same sort as **5** or **6** – is that their parchment is finer than one would expect in books meant for ordinary circulation. They are also too big to have been conveniently carried in a satchel around law courts: one is the largest pre-1066 'law book', and the other's size is otherwise exceeded only by a fragment (**16**) from what was arguably a high-status liturgical volume itself. Indeed, **3** almost demonstrably began life in a service-book. The first recto of its two leaves carries a slightly later and unfinished liturgical text which, unlike the following Edgar code, observes the two columns for which they were originally ruled. As they stand now, moreover, they are part of a huge and mainly hagiographical collection from Worcester, whose *pre*-Cotton foliation shows that it was once more comprehensively jumbled than it can have been by the most cack-handed antiquarian. Among the constituents of this potpourri were leaves from a Worcester cartulary that had been inserted into one of the two great sister bibles of the Codex Amiatinus, which Worcester believed that it had been given by King Offa. They may therefore have been slotted into the bible/cartulary when the recto scribe removed them from his liturgically dictated way. That would then explain how they came through the Middle Ages.

The indications with regard to **4** are more ambiguous. Medical texts like those on its opening pages are sometimes found in school books. A schoolroom provenance is further suggested here by scribal doodles: 'Ælfmær Pattafox, you want to flog young Ælfric.' Yet property memoranda like the collection's third item were often inserted in more solemn contexts such as **6** (which, in point of fact, contains a record of the recovery of lands lamented as lost in **4**). Allowing for the possible exception of this case, the message of all pre-Conquest pairs so far examined is the consistent integration of Anglo-Saxon secular law-making with the yet more binding law of God in various manifestations. That this was the dominant motif of the career of Archbishop Wulfstan, the Old English kingdom's most articulate legal mind, makes it the more likely that the conjunction was deliberate.

The position with our last (if earliest) pairing was perhaps only ostensibly different. In no. **1**, the famous 'Parker' codex of the *Anglo-Saxon Chronicle*, Alfred's *domboc* was intentionally juxtaposed with the *Chronicle* at an early date, and not impossibly written to accompany it. This was done either at one of Winchester's minsters or in the royal court itself, at a time when the West Saxon dynasty's spokesmen were seeking to persuade all Anglo-Saxon peoples of its claims to rule them. When the book was transferred to Canterbury, apparently as Ælfheah of Winchester became archbishop, it was copied for his Winchester successor (**2**). But this was no mere mechanical exercise. The most important of Æthelstan's codes was inserted on to blank leaves preceding Alfred-Ine. More particularly, the whole collection was tacked on to a copy of the vernacular version of Bede's *History*. The *Chronicle* was first and foremost a record of the West Saxons' military achievement, and was perhaps juxtaposed with their law-code to produce a West Saxon equivalent to the Book of Exodus, wherein another people's wanderings reach a triumphant conclusion as they are given God's law. Bede's, however, was a history of the *whole* English people, one evidently written with an eye to their special destiny. Not only was the volume given this extra scope at the outset. Added after the *domboc* were: (a) another set of medical recipes, whose historical resonance is implied by the fact that the medical encyclopaedia from which they most probably derived had been copied by the same scribe as wrote a block of annals in **1** and the *Bede* in **2**; (b) a text of the Burghal Hidage, the administrative blueprint for Wessex's defence in the late ninth century, when its very survival was threatened by the Danes; and (c) a poem on 'Seasons of Fasting' that was at pains to justify the particular liturgical heritage of the English, as bequeathed to them by their apostle, Pope Gregory. In other words, the volume as a whole became a memorial of English identity at a time when the English were once more under Scandinavian attack. The preface of Alfred's code put Anglo-Saxon law beside God's. His *domboc* spelled out the terms of God's covenant with a new elect. That makes admirable sense of the regular juxtaposition of English and divine law thereafter.

Little can constructively be said about the fragmentary or lost manuscripts at the end of the list. But we have already noted that **16** was probably like **3–6**, and that **17** was, for what the point is worth, of similar dimensions and date to **11**. The remains of **18–20** offer not even a basis for guesswork. But it may be observed that the scope of the pages **20** lost since Nowell and Lambarde seem to have used them for the *editio princeps* of the Anglo-Saxon laws (1568) was quite like that of **3–4**; while there are grounds for wondering whether the original form of **19**, transmitted only by an early nineteenth-century transcript, was not rather like that of **15**.

All in all, extant pre-Conquest law books represent a distillation of the new kingdom's formative ideology. We have seen that this is no reason to think that such was the only kind of law book circulating in pre-Conquest England. But the survival of so many books of a similarly explicable type affords a compelling indication of *one* reason, perhaps even the *main* reason, why early English secular law was put into writing. Two instructive comparisons may be made here: in the first place, books of church law were, as already said (**9**, **10**), self-contained and well presented. Second, law books from the Frankish Empire, and still more those from its Italian constituent, often do meet the sort of expectations that the modern mind has of a law book. We have clearly written, logically organised and effectively portable legal manuscripts (along with more than a few seemingly designed as presentation volumes) from during and after the reign of Charlemagne (768–814); and in the case of the Italian (Lombard) and Spanish (Visigothic) codes, we have such books from near the date of their composition. What survives from Anglo-Saxon England may thus be some measure at least of the prevailing level of its literate and legal culture: one beholden less to any sort of secular legal profession and more to the priorities and horizons of bishops.

Appendix: Summary inventory of Anglo-Saxon law books

KEY:
Bold: legal or quasi-legal texts
[ ]: extraneous matter
– : linked texts in manuscript
...: gap in manuscript
//: break in manuscript

1. CCCC, 173: provenance ?Winchester; Christ Church, Canterbury (*s*. x^{med})
- *Anglo-Saxon Chronicle*, **Alfred-Ine**, papal and episcopal lists.

2. BL, Cotton Otho B.xi: origin ?Winchester (1001×1015)
- OE Bede, *Anglo-Saxon Chronicle*, papal and episcopal lists, **II Æthelstan**, **Alfred-Ine**, Burghal Hidage, 'Seasons of Fasting', medical recipes

3. BL, Cotton Nero E.i: provenance Worcester (*s*. x/xi)
- ['Passionary', Worcester cartulary], liturgical text, **IV Edgar**

4. BL, Harley 55(A): provenance Worcester (*s.* xi¹)
   - Medical recipes, **II–III Edgar**, Property memorandum
5. BL, Cotton Claudius A.iii: provenance ?Worcester?/??York (*s.* x/xi–xi¹)
   - **VI Æthelred (Latin/OE)**, Pontifical
6. York Minster, Add.1: provenance York (1020×1023)
   - Gospel-book, property memoranda, Wulfstan homilies, **Cnut 1020**
7. BL, Cotton Nero A.i(B): provenance ?Worcester/??York (*s.* xi¹)
   - Wulfstan Homilies, *Institutes of Polity*, **I Æthelstan, I Edmund, II–III Edgar, V Æthelred, VIII Æthelred** (pt.), **Grið** // *Polity*, Wulfstan Homilies, **V Æthelred**
8. CCCC, 201: provenance New Minster Winchester (*s.* xi^med^)
   - *Regularis concordia* frag. // Wulfstan Homilies, *Polity*, etc., **VIIa Æthelred, Northumbrian Priests' Law, II–III Edgar, V Æthelred, I Æthelstan, VIII Æthelred, I Edmund, Geþyncðu – Norðleoda laga – Mircna laga – Að – Hadbot, Cnut 1018**, *Apollonius of Tyre* // Saints' resting-places // OE Genesis (Joseph) // Penance formulae
9. CCCC, 265 : origin Worcester (*s.* xi^med^)
   - Wulfstan 'Canon Collection', excommunication and penance formulae, **IV Edgar**, penance formulae, Ælfric letter to Eynsham, etc.
10. CCCC, 190: origin Worcester/Exeter (*s.* xi¹/xi^med^)
    - Wulfstan 'Canon Collection', Ælfric 'Pastoral Letters' (OE), penitential texts, **Mircna laga – Að – Hadbot**
11. BL, Cotton Nero A.i(A): origin ??Christ Church, Canterbury?? (*s.* xi^med^)
    - **I–II Cnut, II–III Edgar, Romscot, Iudex, Alfred-Ine**
12. CCCC, 383: origin St Paul's (*s.* xi/xii)
    - **Alfred-Ine – Be Blaserum – Forfang – Hundred – I Æthelred, Alfred-Guthrum, Edward-Guthrum, II Æthelstan … I-II Cnut, I–II Edward, I-II Edmund, Swerian, Alfred-Guthrum, Wifmannes Beweddung, Wergeld**, charm, **Hit Becwæð, II Æthelred, Dunsæte, Rectitudines – Gerefa**, shipmen, West Saxon genealogical king list.
13. *Quadripartitus*: (compiled 1106×18); six manuscripts or groups of manuscripts:
    - (i) BL, Cotton Domitian viii, fols. 96r–110v [Dm]; *s.* xii²/⁴: origin ?West Midlands.
    - (ii) Manchester, John Rylands University Library, Lat 420 [M]; *s.* xii^med^; origin and provenance unknown until ?in Library of Sir Henry Sidney *c.* 1580; later studied by Spelman.
    - (iii) BL, Royal 11.B.ii, fols. 103r–166v [R]; *s.* xii³/⁴; prov. Worcester.

(iv) BL, Add. 49366 [Hk]; *s.* xii3/4; origin and provenance unknown until in hands of Archbishop Parker, thence in those of Sir Edward Coke and his descendants at Holkham Hall.

(v) BL, Cotton Titus A.xxvii, fols. 89r–174v [T]; *s.* xii/xiii; provenance St Augustine's, Canterbury.

(via) Manchester, John Rylands University Library, Lat. 155 (+ BL, Add. 14252) [Rs]; *s.* xiii[in]; provenance London Guildhall.

(vib) BL, Cotton Claudius D.ii [K2]; *s* xiv[1]; used by Andrew Horn when finalising the texts in vic, vid, bequeathed by him to Guildhall.

(vic) CCCC, 70+258 [Co]; *s* xiv[1]; Horn's 'working copy', also given to Guildhall.

(vid) Oxford, Oriel College, MS 46 [Or]; *s.* xiv[1]; also probably Horn's work, also given to Guildhall.

I–II Cnut, Alfred-Ine – Be Blaserum – Forfang – Hundred, I Æthelstan – Æthelstan Alms – II Æthelstan – Norðleoda laga – Mircna laga – Að – Hadbot, III Æthelstan, IV Æthelstan, V Æthelstan, VI Æthelstan, Ordal, Alfred-Guthrum, Alfred-Guthrum Appendix, Edward-Guthrum, I–II Edward, I–II Edmund, Swerian, Wifmannes Beweddung, Wergeld, I Æthelred, III Æthelred – Pax – Walreaf – IV Æthelred, II Æthelred, Dunsæte, VII Æthelred, Iudex, II–III Edgar, III Edmund, William ladung, [William Articles], Geþyncðu, Rectitudines, Henry I Coronation, Henry I Courts

14. *Textus Roffensis*: origin and provenance Rochester (1123×5)
    - **Æthelberht, Hlothere, Wihtred, Hadbot,** West Saxon genealogical king list, **Alfred-Ine** – *Be Blaserum – Forfang*, **Ordal, Walreaf, II Æthelstan, V(–IV) Æthelstan, Pax, Swerian, Að, Mircna laga, Edward-Guthrum, I–II Edward, I–II Edmund, I Æthelred, William ladung, III Æthelred,** ordeal rituals, **Instituta Cnuti, William Articles,** papal decretals, **VI Æthelstan, Geþyncðu – Norðleoda laga, Wifmannes Beweddung,** charm, **Hit Becwæð, Henry I Coronation, excommunication formulae,** papal, patriarchal and episcopal lists, royal genealogies; Rochester cartulary, etc.

15. BL Harley 55(B): origin and provenance unknown (*s.* xii[med])
    - **I–II Cnut.**

16. BAV, Reg. lat. 946, fol. 75v: provenance (in *s.* xii[1]) Avranches (*s.* xi[1])
    - **'X' Æthelred.**

17. BL, Burney 277: origin and provenance unknown (*s.* xi[2])
    - **Alfred-Ine.**

18. BL, Cotton Otho A.x: origin ???Malmesbury (? *s.* xi[1])
    - **'IX' Æthelred.**

19. BodL., Vet. A.3c.196: origin and provenance unknown, transcript of 1811 from Norwich
    - **II–III Edgar.**
20. BL, Add. 43703 [Nw2] (1560s)
    - **(?Alfred-Ine), II Æthelstan, V Æthelstan, Iudex.**

25

Manuscripts of the *Anglo-Saxon Chronicle*

SIMON KEYNES

The systematic analysis of manuscripts containing versions of the text known as the *Anglo-Saxon Chronicle* originated during the reign of Queen Elizabeth I, as part of an attempt to assemble and organise information about the available sources for English history. In 1565 (or thereabouts) John Joscelyn, chaplain and Latin secretary to Matthew Parker, archbishop of Canterbury, constructed a list of six manuscripts each designated 'Chronica Saxonica'. He arranged his list in an order determined by the point at which each chronicle ended (977, [1001], 1006, 1066, 1080, 1148), numbering them accordingly (1–6), indicating in each but one case the manuscript's apparent or supposed place of origin, and identifying its current owner. All six of the manuscripts listed by Joscelyn survive to the present day, though one must add to his list one manuscript which he had overlooked, and a twelfth-century leaf from a manuscript now lost. The seven manuscripts, and one fragment, have been known since 1848 by letters of the alphabet (A–H), symbolising the continued recognition of their collective identity as a group of related texts. (Further details of each manuscript are given in the appendix at the end of this chapter, pp. 551–2.)

The fact that these manuscripts are known collectively as the *Anglo-Saxon Chronicle* creates the impression (for the unwary) that they constitute a single continuous narrative: official in status, consistent in nature and uniform in authority. It is an impression which might be compounded by a cursory reading of the annals themselves: laconic, impersonal, seemingly objective, driven only by the changing pace of events, with little sense of direction or deeper purpose. Of course the truth was quite different. The compilation of the original 'common stock' lies clearly enough in the reign of King Alfred the Great (871–99), though scholars differ in their views of the precise extent of the original work (whether it continued to 890, 891 or 892). The common stock must itself be distinguished from the work of a multiplicity of later chroniclers, writing at different times and places, for purposes of their own, and between them covering the years from the Alfredian point of departure to the middle of the twelfth century. Each of the extant manuscripts began its life as the end-product of a particular process of transmission, with distinctive features peculiar to itself, and thus its own story to tell. Four of them show further scribal activity after the initial act of copying, representing the process of continuation in the tenth and eleventh centuries (manuscript A), in the second half of the eleventh century (manuscripts C and D), or in the twelfth century (manuscript E). One has to bear in mind, however, that physical evidence of precisely this kind was lost each time the process, at any earlier stage, had involved an act of copying, concealing much from our view. Nor can one assume that the manuscripts which have chanced to survive necessarily provide an adequate basis upon which to reconstruct the process of transmission across a period of 250 years. The difficulty resides in penetrating the complexities which lie behind the transmitted text in each manuscript, in working out the relationships between all of the manuscripts, in taking account of manuscripts now lost, and in distinguishing between the separate elements which in various combinations make up the 'whole'. There are bound to be differences of opinion in all matters of detail, and only the general pattern is clear.

On its first appearance, in the early 890s, the *Anglo-Saxon Chronicle* represented a most significant development in Anglo-Saxon perceptions of the past. From his vantage point at Jarrow in Northumbria, Bede had responded to what he regarded as the abuses prevalent in his own day, to the intended advantage of posterity. In his *Historia abbatum*, written in the 720s, he presented an idealised account of the history of his own house; and in his *Historia ecclesiastica gentis Anglorum*, completed in 731, he took up his cause on a larger stage, affirming the need to respect the authority of the church of Canterbury and indeed of the church of Rome. In the late 740s, south of the Humber, Æthelbald, king of the Mercians, and Cuthbert, archbishop of Canterbury, responded to the same abuses in a rather different way, by circulating a collection of improving texts, comprising some admonitory letters, the canons of the Council of Clofesho (747), a charter, and a digest of Pope Gregory's *Pastoral Care*. There could be no question that Bede's approach was the more compelling. At one level, he wrote of 'East Angles', 'West Saxons', 'Mercians', 'Northumbrians', and all the rest, acknowledging the differences between them; and at another level he wrote of the 'English people', as if he were conscious at the same time of their larger collective identity. Yet the first word in Bede's *Ecclesiastical History* is *Brittania*; and it was 'Britain', as a concept inherited from the Roman past, which provided the political context in which his kings and their peoples moved. The wide range of Bede's terminology remained part of common usage in the later eighth and ninth centuries, and finds reflection, for example, in charters, in the letters of Boniface and Alcuin, and in an early ninth-century compendium of useful information which incorporates a collection of Anglo-Saxon royal genealogies and episcopal lists. Learned men would have been conscious of the notion of the 'English' people (*gens Anglorum* or *Angelcynn*); but distinctions between 'Angles', 'Saxons' and other peoples were still respected.

The *Anglo-Saxon Chronicle* took shape as a conversion of Bede's *Ecclesiastical History* into a different literary form (suggested by his chronological summary, in Book v, chapter 24), and as an extension of his story into the eighth and ninth centuries. Yet while Bede's concern had been with the abuses which prevailed in his own day, the Alfredian chronicler was more concerned with the struggle against the Viking invaders. There can have been nothing like a common enemy, or threat, to make people conscious more of the similarities than of the differences between them, and to make their leaders more inclined to exploit such feelings to a political or military advantage. The arrival of a 'great heathen army' in 865 led to the conquest of the ancient Anglian kingdoms of East Anglia, Mercia and Northumbria, and in Wessex to a struggle which lasted throughout the 870s. King Alfred rose to the challenge; and in the years following his victory at the battle of Edington, in 878, he embarked upon the extraordinary programme of reform and regeneration which lends such distinction to the latter part of his reign, and which determined his legacy to the English people. Among his initiatives was the provision of translations of several 'improving' texts, notably Pope Gregory's *Pastoral Care*, St Augustine's *Soliloquies*, Boethius' *Consolation of Philosophy* and the psalter. The Old English translations of Orosius' *World History*, and of Bede's *Ecclesiastical History of the English People*, seem to have formed part of the same plan. The 'common stock' of the *Anglo-Saxon Chronicle* was once regarded as a 'private' compilation, by an ealdorman in the south-west; but the more natural presumption, not least in view of the scale of the undertaking, is that Alfred's plan extended also to the production of a chronicle, which in complementing the works of Orosius and Bede would serve to provide the English not only with a sense of their common past, but also with a clear indication of their shared interest in putting aside former differences in order to withstand the threat which faced them all. The compilers of the *Chronicle* worked hard under difficult circumstances to bring together material drawn from a variety of written sources, including Bede's *Ecclesiastical History*, a collection of royal genealogies and episcopal lists, and (one assumes) whatever earlier sets of annals had come to hand; no doubt they also made use of material which had to be processed from oral into written form, and assigned its appropriate or approximate place in the annalistic framework. In so doing, the compilers were reflecting the aspirations of those in King Alfred's circle who in the 880s saw themselves as part of an emerging political order, in which Alfred himself was cast not simply or exclusively as 'king of the West Saxons' but, in a formulation calculated to be inclusive of a wider combination of peoples, as 'king of the Anglo-Saxons'.

In no way had the victory at Edington secured peace in Alfred's time, let alone for the more distant future. In 880 an army which had assembled at Fulham, on the Thames, decided to turn its attention towards the Continent. We need not doubt that Alfred and his advisors remained keenly interested in the activities of this army throughout the 880s; and it seems likely that it was the return of the 'great Danish army' to England in 892 that precipitated a sense of renewed crisis in Alfred's reign and prompted the decision to 'publish'. Although there is no hard evidence that multiple copies of the *Chronicle* were distributed in the early 890s, there is reason to think that such was the case. The king is known to have had a network of scribes whom he could call his own. The evidence of the Old English *Pastoral Care* shows how copies of that work were multiplied and distributed. There are indications of a significant break in the text of the *Chronicle* after the annal for 892. Moreover, the copies of the *Chronicle* which lie behind the so-called 'Annals of St Neots', and behind Æthelweard's Latin *Chronicon*, were closer to the lost original than the copies used by Asser, writing his *Life of King Alfred* in 893, and by the first scribe in the 'Parker Chronicle' (manuscript A), who was active *c.* 900. It seems likely, therefore, that copies of the *Chronicle* were multiplied and distributed in 892–3, in much the same way as copies of the Old English *Pastoral Care*.

The multiplication of copies of the *Chronicle* in the late ninth century implies that the Alfredian common stock was distributed in order to meet a demand, or to suit a particular purpose. Whether this had any useful effect is another matter; but Asser moved fast to use it as a basis for his own portrayal of the king, probably for the intended benefit of a readership in Wales, and it is striking how he elevates the narrative to a struggle of 'Christians' against 'pagans', and how he projects Alfred as 'King of the Anglo-Saxons', yet does not shrink from criticism, exposing certain matters which the West Saxon chronicler had left well hidden. The question is what became of the multiple copies of the *Chronicle* in the late ninth century and thereafter. A chronicle of this kind was not a closed book, whose textual integrity had to be respected. Its voice was seemingly impersonal, and its scope was 'national', conveying no overt signs of association with a particular author or religious house. Moreover, the annalistic format gave it an instantly recognisable structure, which had a natural beginning but which had no inevitable or natural end. In other words, a chronicle of this nature extended an open invitation to be improved, whether by making additions or alterations in the existing body of text, or by act of continuation. We can but guess what might have prompted anyone to pull a copy of the *Chronicle* from the shelf and to start making changes: perhaps when another set of annals, or indeed another copy of the *Chronicle*, came to hand; perhaps when an event took place which was of local or personal interest, and which was deemed worthy of remembrance; or perhaps when the turn of events gave cause for reflection, in order to explain what had come to pass. The fact is that there were no rules, nor even any conventions. The 'continuation' of the *Chronicle* in the late ninth, tenth and eleventh centuries was a matter left to private or personal initiative, and thus in effect to chance; and the challenge is to identify, by subject matter, outlook, literary style, or textual history, those annals, or sets of annals, which might be regarded as constituting its separate parts. The accompanying diagram (Fig. 25.1) necessarily involves the simplification of complex evidence, but is intended to convey at least some sense of the development from the Alfredian common stock, by way of various intermediate stages, to each of the extant manuscripts.

While some manuscripts of the common stock were doubtless left untouched, others began sooner or later to 'grow', whether by the addition of original entries, or by the addition of particular blocks of annals received from elsewhere. The oldest extant manuscript of the *Chronicle* (manuscript A), was written in the late ninth or early tenth century. The chronicle is preceded in this manuscript by a genealogical regnal list, establishing the 'West Saxon' and specifically Alfredian context of all that follows, although it need not have been part of the original conception. The common stock is taken in one hand to the end of the annal for 891, at the bottom of a page; and it seems to have been some time before any continuations were added. The first three of the identifiable continuations of the common stock were generated by further stages in the struggle against the Danes. The annals for 893–6 are clearly distinct from what precedes or follows them, and read like an account of the activities of the Viking army during the three years from 892 to 895, prompted by the relief occasioned by its dispersal in the summer of 896, although not written until after some further engagements with elements of the dispersed army later in the same year. They were composed by someone singularly well informed about the campaigns of these years, whose view of events was more obviously from the centre than from a particular locality. The next identifiable continuation, comprising a set of annals from 897 to 914, covers Alfred's death and the early stages of Edward the Elder's campaign against the Danes who had previously settled in the east midlands, reaching a climax with the submission of Earl Thurcetel to Edward at Buckingham. A third set of annals takes the narrative

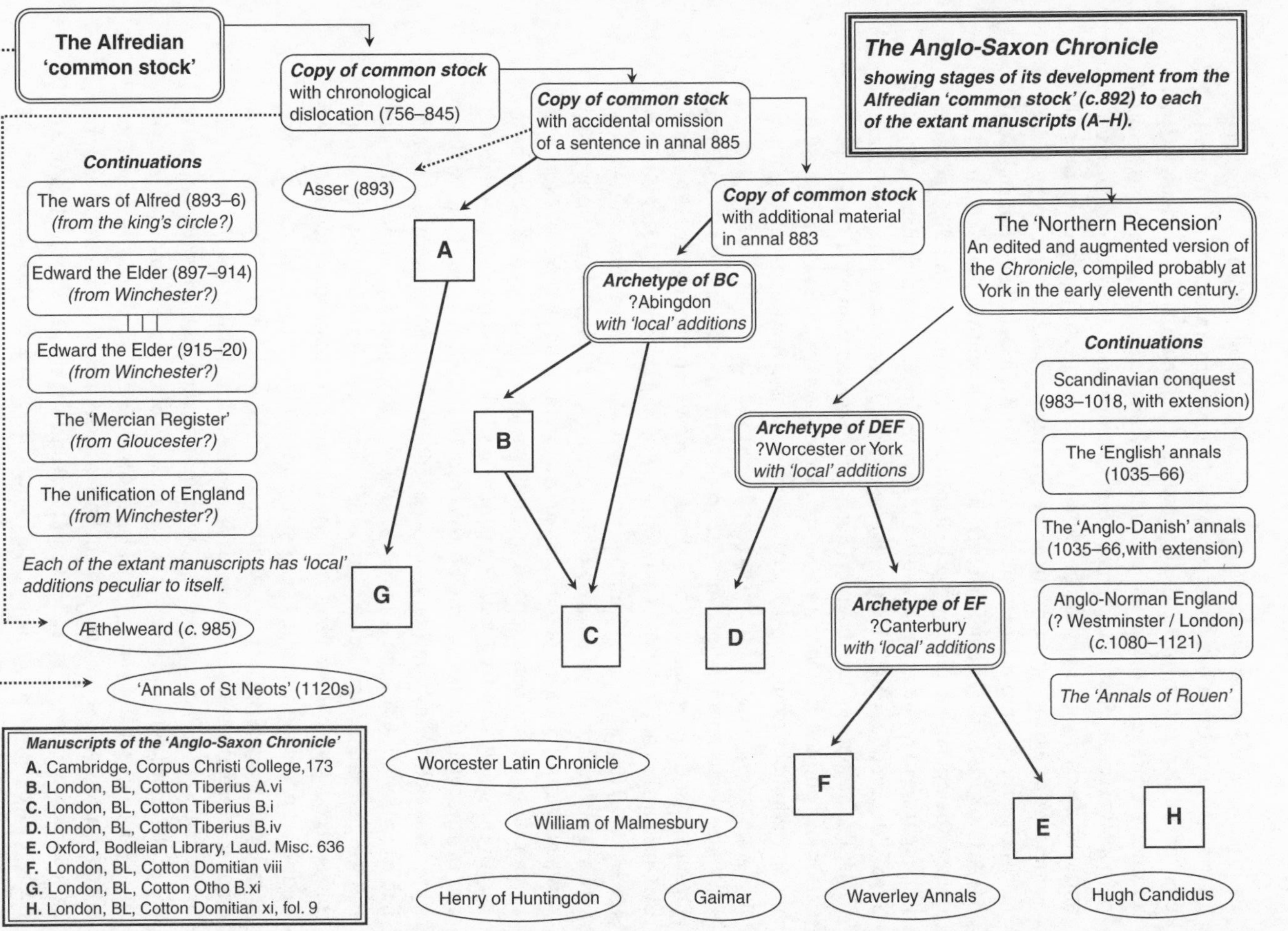
The Anglo-Saxon Chronicle
showing stages of its development from the Alfredian 'common stock' (c.892) to each of the extant manuscripts (A–H).
The Alfredian 'common stock'
Copy of common stock with chronological dislocation (756–845)
Copy of common stock with accidental omission of a sentence in annal 885
Copy of common stock with additional material in annal 883
The 'Northern Recension' An edited and augmented version of the Chronicle, compiled probably at York in the early eleventh century.
Continuations
The wars of Alfred (893–6) (from the king's circle?)
Edward the Elder (897–914) (from Winchester?)
Edward the Elder (915–20) (from Winchester?)
The 'Mercian Register' (from Gloucester?)
The unification of England (from Winchester?)
Each of the extant manuscripts has 'local' additions peculiar to itself.
Asser (893)
Æthelweard (c. 985)
'Annals of St Neots' (1120s)
A
Archetype of BC ?Abingdon with 'local' additions
B
C
G
Archetype of DEF ?Worcester or York with 'local' additions
D
Archetype of EF ?Canterbury with 'local' additions
F
E
H
Continuations
Scandinavian conquest (983–1018, with extension)
The 'English' annals (1035–66)
The 'Anglo-Danish' annals (1035–66,with extension)
Anglo-Norman England (? Westminster / London) (c.1080–1121)
The 'Annals of Rouen'
Worcester Latin Chronicle
William of Malmesbury
Henry of Huntingdon
Gaimar
Waverley Annals
Hugh Candidus
Manuscripts of the 'Anglo-Saxon Chronicle'
A. Cambridge, Corpus Christi College,173
B. London, BL, Cotton Tiberius A.vi
C. London, BL, Cotton Tiberius B.i
D. London, BL, Cotton Tiberius B.iv
E. Oxford, Bodleian Library, Laud. Misc. 636
F. London, BL, Cotton Domitian viii
G. London, BL, Cotton Otho B.xi
H. London, BL, Cotton Domitian xi, fol. 9

25.1 *The Anglo-Saxon Chronicle*

forward from 915 to 920, culminating this time with the submission to Edward of the Scots, Northumbrians and Strathclyde Welsh. The second and third sets of annals have much in common, and it seems likely that both represent the view of an observer from the centre of King Edward's operations; but of course they tell only part of the story. All three of these sets of annals were copied into manuscript A, probably by a single scribe in more than one stint, probably in the second quarter of the tenth century, probably at Winchester; and at about the same time a copy of the law-code of King Alfred (with the appended laws of Ine) was added to the manuscript, suggesting that it was intended to be seen as a consolidated record of the achievements of Alfred and Edward, father and son. The first and second sets of annals, but not the third, found their way into the archetype of manuscripts BC. Elsewhere, another chronicler kept a brief record of the activities of Æthelflæd, lady of the Mercians, during the first quarter of the tenth century, which has come to be known to modern scholarship as the 'Mercian Register'. This found its way, as a separate block of annals retaining its own identity, into the archetype of manuscripts BC, and goes some way towards redressing the bias of the more obviously West Saxon record.

Given what is known of the major political, social, ecclesiastical and administrative developments which took place in the tenth century, between the accession of King Æthelstan (924) and the death of King Edgar (975), it has to be admitted that the entries in the *Anglo-Saxon Chronicle* for the central decades of the tenth century are somewhat disappointing. The evidence of charters, law-codes and coins, of hagiography, book production, and much else besides, takes us a long way beyond the bare record of events supplied in the *Chronicle*; and one can see that various aspects of the period were simply not well suited to the conventions of the genre, and could not have been reduced to the requirements of an annalistic framework. Annals for the years between 934 and 975, recording events which could in retrospect be recognised as forming part of the political unification of England, were copied (in more than one stage) into manuscript A, at Winchester, and (perhaps as a set) into the archetype of manuscripts BC, probably at Abingdon. The triumphantly jingoistic poem on the battle of Brunanburh, marking King Æthelstan's victory over a confederation of the Hiberno-Norse and the Scots, formed the annal for 937, and was complemented by a shorter poem, on King Edmund's redemption of the 'Five Boroughs' (Leicester, Lincoln, Nottingham, Stamford and Derby) from Norse control, which formed the annal for 942. More restrained attention was given to further stages of Edmund and Eadred's dealings with the Northumbrians and the Scots, in the annals for the 940s. For the reign of Eadwig no attention was paid to the division of the kingdom in 957; and, for Edgar, the annals start with his accession in 959, leave aside the 960s, and fasten thereafter on the death of the ætheling Edmund in 971. As if to match the beginning, the set of annals culminates with two more poetical entries, covering the coronation of King Edgar in 973, and his death in 975, ending with an allusion to the troubles during the reign of Edward the Martyr, the appearance of a comet, and a manifestation of divine punishment, in the form of a mercifully short-lived famine (976). In manuscript A, at Winchester, these annals were combined with some strictly 'local' annals for the 960s, and in the archetype of manuscripts BC, probably at Abingdon, they were combined in much the same way with other material, including a text of the 'Mercian Register' (entered after the annal for 914) and 'local' annals of a different kind (including an acknowledgement of the division of the kingdom in 957). In the late 970s, during the reign of Edward the Martyr (975–8), a new manuscript of the *Chronicle* was produced at Abingdon, perhaps reflecting a wish to consolidate the record at what might have seemed to be a reasonably propitious moment. Interestingly, the scribe of manuscript B chose to end his work with a copy of the genealogical regnal list for the West Saxon dynasty, found also in manuscript A, extending it by the addition of the names of Alfred's successors in the tenth century, and in this process providing important information on the exact lengths of their reigns.

The reign of King Æthelred the Unready (978–1016) witnessed the renewal of Viking raids in England, escalating to invasions in the early eleventh century. Learned and religious men seem to have begun to search for inspiration in the struggles of the past, and to seek divine assistance by cultivating a new generation of saints; certainly, there was much activity in these times of trouble. In the mid-980s, manuscript A of the *Chronicle* was enhanced by the addition of a set of papal and episcopal lists. At about the same time, Æthelweard, ealdorman of the western provinces, used a manuscript of the common stock, to 892, as the basis for his own Latin *Chronicle*, in which he sought to inform his distant cousin Matilda of Essen about the deeds of their common ancestors. The impact of renewed Viking activity began to be felt more severely in the 990s, and finds due reflection in Ælfric's *Lives of the Saints*. It may be no coincidence that the earliest *Lives* of Dunstan, Æthelwold and Oswald were written during the same period, and that Byrhtferth of Ramsey, author of the *Vita S. Oswaldi*, produced other historical works, including his 'Historical Miscellany', and (it seems) a set of 'local' annals covering the early history of Ramsey Abbey. In the early years of the eleventh century, a new manuscript of the *Chronicle* was produced at Winchester, as part of another significant exercise. In a natural extension of what had been done before, a scribe seems to have taken from the shelf a mid-tenth-century manuscript of the Old English Bede, and appended to it a fair copy of manuscript A (with continuations to 1001), including the episcopal lists, and the law-code of King Alfred, in what thus became manuscript G. Henceforth manuscript G remained at Winchester, and a few years later, *c.* 1012, its episcopal lists were updated. For its part, manuscript A seems to have been taken to Canterbury, conceivably by Ælfheah, bishop of Winchester since 984, on his appointment as archbishop in 1006, although it was some time before any more annals were added.

Perhaps the most ambitious work produced during this period was the so-called 'Northern Recension' of the *Anglo-Saxon Chronicle*. It would appear that a manuscript of the Alfredian common stock, without any of the later continuations, was taken north at some indeterminate point in the tenth or early eleventh century, where it served as the basis for the production of a more ambitious version of the *Chronicle*, in which (among other modifications) the rather limited amount of information about northern England, found in the original, was augmented by the addition of material drawn from at least two sets of 'northern' annals, providing coverage of events in the eighth, late ninth and tenth centuries. For the purposes of the 'Northern Recension', these annals were rendered into the vernacular. The most striking feature of the compilation is the occurrence of an extended reflection on the reign of King Edgar in the annal for 959, and of a shorter one on the troubles occasioned by Edgar's death under 975. As has long been recognised, both passages are written in the distinctive style of Wulfstan, archbishop of York 1002–23. It would seem to follow that Wulfstan himself was at work on the 'Northern Recension' in the early eleventh century, at a time when the Vikings were oppressing the English as never before; and it may be that he was looking to the past not only for inspiration but also for an explanation of the present difficulties.

The 'main' account of King Æthelred's struggle against the Viking invaders, and of the conquest of England by Sven Forkbeard and Cnut, reflects the dismay and desperation of a defeated people, and was evidently put together soon after the end of Æthelred's reign. The annals extended probably into the early 1020s, and may or may not have received further additions, into the early 1030s, before finding their way as a set into the archetype of manuscript C, probably at Abingdon, and into the archetype of manuscript DEF, at Worcester or York. It remains uncertain where the annals originated. They were long regarded as the work of an 'Abingdon' chronicler; but it is unlikely that the 'Abingdon' elements are integral to the narrative. Other suggestions include Canterbury, Ramsey and London. In producing this record of a long and troubled period, the chronicler must have been able to draw on earlier material, supplying miscellaneous information (including obits and appointments) as well as information about the Viking raids and invasions. The fact remains, however, that he would appear to have constructed his own narrative with a view to a particular end, holding it together with recurrent turns of phrase and spicing it up with expressions of his own views and feelings. Famously, the chronicler was not afraid to criticise the conduct of affairs, or indeed to apportion blame; but whether it is good history is a different matter. The account can be set beside some 'local' annals for the early 980s, incorporated in the archetype of manuscript C, and beside 'local' annals for the years 991 and 1001, entered in manuscript A. The comparison serves as an object lesson in some of the basic principles of source criticism, which can be taken much further if the comparison is extended to include other forms of evidence.

The annals which cover the reign of Cnut offer little more than a register of the king's absences abroad on other business, and, as in the cases of Æthelstan and Edgar, one feels that Cnut's activities in England were of a kind which escaped or defied reduction to annalistic form. Yet the political faction which had originated with the rise of Earl Godwine, in the early 1020s, broke surface immediately after Cnut's death in 1035, and became still more acute after the accession of Edward the Confessor in 1042. Domestic affairs were animated as never before, and there was fresh cause for taking the *Chronicle* down from the shelf. A new manuscript, known to modern scholarship as manuscript C, was produced apparently at Abingdon in the mid-1040s. The scribe began his book with a text of the Old English calendar-poem, or *Menologium*, and a series of gnomic verses, and then set about the construction of a chronicle from the material to hand. His main source was the manuscript containing the common stock, with various tenth-century continuations, which in the late 970s had been used by the compiler of manuscript B; to which (it seems) had been added some more 'local' annals, a copy of the separate set of annals describing the Scandinavian conquest of England (extending into the 1020s or early 1030s), and perhaps the beginnings of a new set of annals for the later 1030s and early 1040s. As entered in manuscript C, the annals express horror at Earl Godwine's treatment of the ætheling Alfred in 1036, disapproval of the Anglo-Danish regime, and (in 1042) pointed recognition of Edward's right to the throne. Further annals were added from 1045 in short stints, apparently still at Abingdon. Although this chronicle is regarded as hostile to Earl Godwine, there is little sense of triumph at his fall from power in 1051, or indeed of dismay on his restoration in 1052; and one suspects that many were wary of a turn of events which had briefly favoured Edward's Norman friends, and relieved when it all came to nought. There are no annals for 1057–64, though coverage is provided for 1065–6, as if to record the inglorious ending to a once glorious tale. Unfortunately the last leaf of the manuscript was removed or lost; and, as a result, the annal for 1066 breaks off mid-sentence at the foot of a page, just before reaching the events of October.

Another new manuscript of the *Chronicle* was produced apparently at Worcester or York in the mid or later 1040s. It was based on a copy of the 'Northern Recension' which had been augmented during the second quarter of the eleventh century with more 'local' material, and into which had also been entered a copy of the account of the Scandinavian conquest of England. The new manuscript, known to modern scholarship as manuscript D, certainly extended beyond the end of Æthelred's reign, and might have reached into the 1030s or 1040s; but the part of the manuscript covering this period was rewritten at a later stage, possibly in the 1050s or perhaps as late as the 1070s, presumably to tidy up the text or to make particular changes. One can imagine that the sensitivity of certain issues, and the rapidly changing course of events, would have complicated any chronicler's task in the central decades of the eleventh century; and that whenever new information came to hand, it might well have been necessary to make certain alterations. At the risk of over-simplification, annals for a period from 1035 onwards, which we can read in manuscript C in what would appear to be their 'original' form, occur in an edited form in manuscript D, combined with information drawn from other sources and with 'local' additions. Some of C's antagonism towards Earl Godwine was toned down, as if to avoid giving offence. Yet in the annal for 1051, the D-chronicler provides a compelling analysis of Godwine's fall from power, ending with a crucial reference to Duke William's visit to England soon afterwards. It is manuscript D which goes on to provide the fullest coverage of the events of 1066, sharing some material with manuscript C and some with the archetype of manuscript E; and since manuscript D was clearly 'interested' in Ealdred, bishop of Worcester 1046–62 and archbishop of York 1061–9, it is appropriately this manuscript which explains Ealdred's role in the submission to Duke William at Berkhamsted and in the coronation of William at Westminster. The peroration in manuscript D recalls Archbishop Wulfstan's turn of phrase in the annal for 975, and the tenor of the account of the Scandinavian conquest: 'And always after that it grew much worse. May the end be good when God wills!'

Another copy of the 'Northern Recension', with additional material, was brought south apparently in the second quarter of the eleventh century. It found its way to St Augustine's, Canterbury, and served later, at Christ Church, as the archetype of manuscripts EF. Those responsible for keeping up the chronicle at Canterbury seem to have been in touch with their counterparts elsewhere, at least to judge from the occurrence of material for the

1040s shared with manuscript C, and from the occurrence of material for the 1050s, 1060s and 1070s shared with manuscript D. Of course the 'Canterbury' chronicle also developed a line of its own. It became, in a sense, a chronicle of the Anglo-Danish political establishment: instinctively defensive of Earl Godwine's actions in 1035; deafeningly silent on the treatment of the ætheling Alfred in 1036; optimistic for Edward in the early 1040s; dismayed by the turn of events in 1051; delighted by Godwine's restoration, and by the expulsion of the Normans, in 1052; unmoved by the return of Edward the Exile in 1057; and firmly committed to the notion of Harold, as Edward's intended successor, in 1066. There is no wailing, however, about the lot of the English: the Conquest happened, and after William's consecration 'people paid taxes to him, and gave him hostages, and afterwards bought their lands'.

The *Anglo-Saxon Chronicle* survived the Norman Conquest, and indeed continued to flourish. The annals in manuscript D extend to 1079, persisting in their 'northern' interests and in their instinctive commitment to the 'English' cause, with particular attention paid to Edgar the Ætheling, and to his sister Margaret of Scotland, as surviving members of the English royal dynasty. From 1068 to 1076, manuscript D also shares material with the archetype of manuscripts EF, some of which seems 'English' and some 'Norman' in outlook; but after 1079 manuscript D came to an end. The annals in the archetype of manuscripts EF continued, covering the years from 1080 to 1121, providing a major source of information for the reigns of William I, William Rufus and Henry I. It is surprisingly difficult to discern a particular local interest; and as well as the famous passages – for example, the slaughter of the monks at Glastonbury (1083), the inception of the Domesday survey (1085) and the portrayal of King William (1087) – one finds interest taken in the king's itinerary, in royal appointments, and in all kinds of natural phenomena. In his account of King William, the chronicler remarks that he had 'once lived at his court'; and the overall impression is of a set of annals maintained with remarkable steadiness over a period of about forty years, never far from centres of royal power. The archetype was used at Canterbury, *c.* 1100, in the production of manuscript F, in which each annal is followed directly by a version in Latin. Thereafter, in the early 1120s, the archetype was made available for copying by a Peterborough scribe. It is interesting to see how in this process a 'national' chronicle was converted into a 'local' or 'house' chronicle, by the addition of material on matters of local interest at particular points throughout the narrative. The new manuscript (E) was maintained at Peterborough initially by the original scribe, making entries in short stints from 1122 to 1131. His successor provided a retrospective account of the reign of King Stephen (1135–54), when it was said that 'Christ and his saints were asleep'. The account is cast in the form of annals, but was probably given that form in the mid 1150s, when it was copied into the manuscript. The single leaf designated manuscript H contains the closing words of an annal for 1113, followed by the greater part of an annal for 1114, written in short stints, reporting on the king's movements and also providing a detailed register of mainly ecclesiastical appointments. It is by no means certain that the leaf ever formed part of a once complete manuscript of the *Chronicle*; for, given the nature of its content, it may have originated as a form of bulletin, intended to serve as a source of basic information.

The *Anglo-Saxon Chronicle* was a living and developing text for over 250 years, from the 890s to the 1150s. In the late eleventh and twelfth centuries, it also helped to ensure that the 'Anglo-Saxon' view of the Anglo-Saxon past would survive the Norman Conquest, and would contribute to the formation of an English historical tradition. For many reasons it was found expedient, after the Conquest, not to break with the past, but instead to respect and even to cultivate it. Attention was directed towards a community's accumulation of charters, relics, treasures, lands and sources of revenue; and, as members of religious houses realised how much they had to gain from the assertion of royal foundation, or from the investigation of ancient rights, the need was also felt for more accessible forms of historical writing in which to set down a particular or coherent view of the past. Wulfstan, bishop of Worcester 1062–95, is known to have instructed his monk Hemming to put the Worcester muniments in order, and at much the same time he instigated work on the construction of the Latin chronicle formerly known as the chronicle of Florence of Worcester (who had worked on it before his death in 1118), but now as that of John of Worcester (who was working on it in the early 1120s). As might be expected, the Worcester monks had access to a manuscript closely related to manuscript D (if not necessarily to D itself); more remarkably, they also had access to the annals for 915–20, found only in manuscript A, to some of the later tenth-century annals found only in manuscript C, and, for the eleventh century, to material in manuscripts C and D, and even to the late eleventh- and twelfth-century annals in manuscript E. Perhaps they had at least one chronicle from each of the three main branches of the textual tradition; or perhaps they had collected material for their purposes from various religious houses. At Christ Church, Canterbury, the monks had manuscripts A and B, as well as the archetype of manuscripts EF, and much else besides; and it was there, in the first decade of the twelfth century, that a member of the community, well known from his interventions in manuscript A, set about the production of manuscript F as a bilingual exercise, for a particular purpose, with a strongly local dimension. For his *Gesta regum*

Anglorum, William of Malmesbury (d. 1142) used a copy of a chronicle related to the archetype of manuscripts EF, as the basis for his own rather more discursive account of the Anglo-Saxon past. At about the same time Henry, archdeacon of Huntingdon, was at work on his *Historia Anglorum*. He would have been able to rummage through the libraries of several of the ancient religious houses of eastern England; and as well as a chronicle related to the archetype of manuscripts EF, he seems also to have made use of something akin to manuscript C. Symeon of Durham derived much of the material for his *Historia regum* from his Latin sources, and there is little that reflects direct use of a manuscript of the *Chronicle*; the fact remains, however, that the mid-twelfth-century catalogue of the library at Durham Cathedral registers the existence, among a group of nine *Libri Anglici*, of 'Cronica duo Anglica', suggesting that at least two such chronicles had found their way to the far north of England, and may lie somewhere behind his work. Another item in the same group of *Libri Anglici*, identified as 'Elfledes Boc', has been regarded as a copy of the 'Mercian Register', which is a pleasant but entirely wishful thought. At Bury St Edmunds, in the 1120s or 1130s, a manuscript of the *Chronicle*, apparently without the chronological dislocation in annals 756–845, and seemingly not extending beyond 912, was used as a basis for a Latin chronicle which has come to be known as the 'Annals of St Neots'. In the late 1130s, the clerk Geffrei Gaimar used a 'Northern Recension' of the *Chronicle* for his *Estoire des Engleis*; interestingly, he seems to have regarded the *Chronicle* as a work associated in some way with Winchester and King Alfred. Manuscript E of the *Chronicle* was used at Peterborough, probably in the 1160s, as the basis for a Latin house-chronicle by Hugh Candidus; and a manuscript closely related to its archetype lies behind the annals for the period from 1000 to 1118 found in a Latin chronicle compiled at Waverley, a Cistercian house near Farnham in Surrey, in the late twelfth or early thirteenth century.

It is a truism to say that we should think in terms of the 'Anglo-Saxon Chronicles' in the plural, rather than in terms of a single chronicle; and we should do so not simply because the extant manuscripts provide so much variation from the original common stock, but because there must once have been so many more copies of the text, in various stages of its transmission, dispersed quite widely among religious houses throughout England. In addition to the extant manuscripts, their respective archetypes, and whatever lies behind the various works in Latin, we can but wonder whether there were other copies of the *Chronicle* which have left no trace, at houses such as Shaftesbury, Glastonbury, Ely, St Albans, Burton and Eynsham. Its wide distribution ensured that the *Chronicle* helped to maintain an awareness of the Anglo-Saxon past, in ways which might have informed the house-histories, house-chronicles and chronicle-cartularies which began to proliferate in the twelfth century. Of course the *Chronicle* continues to exert its influence, still to some extent through the eyes of the Anglo-Norman historians and their successors, but also more directly. It is well understood by modern scholarship that the annals speak with many voices, from different places, reflecting a variety of interests; and that they have to be approached by historians with all due circumspection. In the late 1830s, John Mitchell Kemble discovered the 'chronological dislocation' in a long section of the common stock, and chose instead to put his faith in charters. Since then, it has come to be more widely recognised that historians of Anglo-Saxon England must deconstruct the text, look beneath the surface of recorded events, and take account of a wider range of evidence if they are ever to escape from the pervasive influence of what will always remain, nonetheless, by far their most important source.

Appendix: Manuscripts, facsimiles and editions

Understanding of the *Anglo-Saxon Chronicle*, whether as a work of Old English literature or as a primary source for our knowledge of the Anglo-Saxon past, is obscured by the difficulty of distinguishing between the component parts of the extant versions of an imaginary whole. The two earliest editions of the vernacular text were published in the seventeenth century: Abraham Whelock's edition of manuscript G (1644), and Edmund Gibson's edition of manuscript E (1692), both furnished with translations into Latin. All five of the editions of the *Chronicle* published in the nineteenth century took better advantage of the surviving manuscripts, in ways satisfying some purposes but not others. In 1823 James Ingram created a composite text which could be read as a continuous narrative, furnishing it with a translation into modern English. Richard Price aimed for much the same effect in a more disciplined way; and the publication of his edition in Henry Petrie's *Monumenta Historica Britannica* (1848) lent grandeur as well as authority to the text. In 1861 Benjamin Thorpe produced an edition, for the Rolls Series, in which the several versions were set out in parallel columns, to the reader's advantage. In 1865 John Earle published an edition, prepared in the 1850s, in which he accorded precedence on facing pages to the earliest and latest manuscripts (A and E), with material from other manuscripts displayed in a subordinate position. Charles Plummer adopted the same principle for his edition, published in 1892, complemented by a second volume with an introduction and detailed notes (1899).

For all this scholarly endeavour, it cannot be said that the *Anglo-Saxon Chronicle* has yet been 'edited'. In recent years several volumes of a collaborative work have appeared, comprising semi-diplomatic editions of the texts transmitted in each of the surviving manuscripts, as listed below. This represented the necessary first stage; and the next will be to establish a clean text of the original (Alfredian) 'Common Stock', comprising annals from the Roman conquest of Britain to 892, so that it can be read as its compilers had intended, and judged on terms of its own. The serious complications arise thereafter; and it remains an even greater editorial challenge to distinguish between the separate annals, or sets of annals, which make up the various continuations from 893 onwards, to identify the circumstances which from time to time prompted the production of a new copy or recension of the extended whole, whether at Glastonbury, Abingdon, Canterbury or elsewhere, and to understand the processes whereby particular sets of annals were written, taken or sent from one place to another, edited, and augmented (Fig. 25.1). The replacement of Plummer's introduction and notes would be a further challenge, equally necessary and no less worthwhile.

The most authoritative and accessible translation of the 'Common Stock', and of its various continuations to 1042, is to be found in Whitelock's *English Historical Documents* (1979). The annals for the last years of the Anglo-Saxon period, and thereafter, are to be found in the second volume of the same series.

Manuscript A (Cambridge, Corpus Christi College, 173). Description: Ker 1957, no. 39. Facsimile: Flower and Smith 1941. Edition: Bately 1986.

Manuscript B (London, British Library, Cotton Tiberius A.vi). Description: Ker 1957, no. 188. Edition: Taylor 1983.

Manuscript C (London, British Library, Cotton Tiberius B.i). Description: Ker 1957, no. 191. Edition: O'Brien O'Keeffe 2001.

Manuscript D (London, British Library, Cotton Tiberius B.iv). Description: Ker 1957, no. 192. Edition: Cubbin 1996.

Manuscript E (Oxford, Bodleian Library, Laud Misc. 636). Description: Ker 1957, no. 346. Facsimile: Whitelock 1954. Edition: Irvine 2004.

Manuscript F (London, British Library, Cotton Domitian viii). Description: Ker 1957, no. 148. Facsimile: Dumville 1995c. Edition: Baker 2000.

Manuscript G (London, British Library, Cotton Otho B.xi). Description: Ker 1957, no. 180. Edition: Lutz 1981.

Manuscript H (London, British Library, Cotton Domitian ix, fol. 9). Description: Ker 1957, no. 150. Edition: Plummer and Earle 1892–9, pp. 244–5.

26

Old English homiliaries and poetic manuscripts

DONALD SCRAGG

Apart from scraps of English as marginalia in Latin manuscripts or occasional sentences in documents, the history of the book in English begins in the ninth century, most of the material from that period dating from the last decade of the century and being related to the literary activities of King Alfred and his intellectual circle.[1] As the tenth century proceeds, increasing numbers of manuscripts survive, but it is from the eleventh that the greatest number dates. Here we find a use of the vernacular unparalleled in any other Western European language until the later Middle Ages. Well over 200 manuscripts and documents written in English by more than 500 scribes survive from this century. If one adds the large number of English and Latin manuscripts with occasional glosses and marginalia by other hands, we have an extraordinary number of people writing English – probably more than a thousand.

It is usually assumed that the most important survivals from the period are books containing poetry. There is occasional verse in a variety of manuscript contexts during the tenth and eleventh centuries, but most of the poems that we consider important occur in four large volumes. Two date from the 970s, the other two from the end of the century or the beginning of the eleventh. The earlier two, the Exeter and Vercelli Books, are named for the towns in which they now rest.[2] The former is a large anthology of secular and religious verse given to Exeter by Leofric, bishop of Devon and Cornwall 1046–72, as part of a bequest of over fifty books (many of which can still be identified). This was some hundred years after it was written and we know nothing of where Leofric had found the book. Leofric moved his see from Crediton to Exeter in 1050 and he clearly attempted to build a substantial library in the new episcopal base. The Exeter Book is large in scale and written in a bold

1 See Chapters 25 and 34.
2 Exeter CL, 3501, fols. 8–130; Vercelli, Biblioteca Capitolare, CXVII. Facs.: Chambers, Förster and Flower 1933; Sisam 1976.

clear hand; though undecorated, it is a handsome volume.[3] A few of its poems are long (up to 900 lines), amongst these being *Christ's Ascension* and *The Passion of St Juliana*, each signed with a runic acrostic by a poet called Cynewulf.[4] But the majority are short (including the so-called elegies such as *The Wanderer* and *The Seafarer*), some, such as its many riddles, consisting of only a few lines. Although the majority of the poems are homiletic or moralising, many of the riddles have obscene double entendres, and in *The Husband's Message*, *The Wife's Lament* and *Wulf and Eadwacer* we have the closest that Old English verse comes to love poetry. It has been argued that the book was written at Exeter, but this is inherently unlikely. Linguistically there are signs that it was copied continuously from an earlier book. Again, it has been argued that it was not designed as one book but comprises three 'booklets', the first of which (quires 1–6) was written last. There is no unambiguous support for this theory; indeed, it appears to contradict the linguistic evidence.[5]

The Vercelli Book offers an interesting contrast – all the more so given that there are relatively few other survivals from the era in which the two manuscripts were written. It too is an anthology, but its contents are entirely religious, mainly homilies and saints' lives. The largest part of the book (twenty-three of its twenty-nine items) is in prose. Its six poems (including two more with Cynewulf's runic acrostic) appear in three groups, suggesting perhaps that its compiler saw little distinction between verse and prose and was more interested in content. Again, the book is large-scale; the written area is larger and there are more lines in the last five quires than in the first fourteen.[6] The writing, although almost certainly that of one man, varies slightly in appearance because of the change of size. It is likely that the manuscript was written over an extended period of time; certainly, in contrast to the Exeter Book, it was not copied continuously from an existing volume but was compiled from a variety of sources, as occasional spaces between items indicate. The last leaf of the third quire, for example, has been removed: it was probably blank since half the preceding page is also blank, following the end of an item. A new item begins at the head of the next quire; presumably this had already been written before what is now the third quire was completed. Confirmation that the scribe was not copying an existing collection

3 320 × 220 mm, with a writing space of 240 × 160 mm and 23 lines per page.

4 See Chapter 33.

5 On linguistic uniformity see Sisam 1953, pp. 97–108. The 'booklets' theory is advanced by Conner 1993; a detailed response can be found in the introduction to Muir 1994. Conner also suggested Exeter as its origin; for a full response see Gameson 1996b.

6 Quires 1–14: writing area 220 × 143 mm, usually in 24 lines. Quires 15–19: writing space 230 × 152 mm, with 31–3 lines per page.

comes from changes in language from item to item, and from some repetition of material. The writing of the Vercelli Book is less beautiful than that of the Exeter Book; the manuscript has a few decorated initials but their hesitant aspect and the circumstance that they only appear in certain items are concordant with the picture of compilation from different sources at different times suggested by other evidence. The poems include *The Dream of the Rood*, perhaps the most famous Old English religious poem. The manuscript's origin is in the south-east, the scribe drawing intermittently on the resources of a major library, presumably one of those at Canterbury, while not necessarily himself working there. The circumstances whereby it reached Vercelli, a town in northern Italy some 80 kilometres east of Turin, are unknown. Marginalia suggest two things: that it was not made for export, for other copies of parts of it are indicated by pen-trials by scribes other than the main hand, and that it was in Italy by the end of the eleventh century (an eleventh- or early twelfth-century entry in an Italian hand appears in a blank space). Since Vercelli was an important stopping-point on the road to Rome, the likelihood is that it crossed the Alps in the baggage of the entourage of an eleventh-century prelate or important pilgrim, and was left there to provide pious reading for a sick cleric.[7]

The two later poetic codices again provide a marked contrast with one another, one an ambitious volume, the other much more workaday. The Junius manuscript (named for the seventeenth-century Dutch theologian who presented it to the Bodleian Library) contains a long verse paraphrase of the Old Testament book of Genesis, and medium-length poems based on central chapters of Exodus, and on the opening of the book of Daniel, the last ending imperfectly.[8] Some decades after the creation of the book an additional quire was added, containing a series of shorter poems on New Testament themes known collectively as *Christ and Satan*. This was inserted into the outer leaf of the last quire of the original book, the rest of that quire being lost (hence Daniel ends imperfectly). The Old Testament verse is generously illustrated with line drawings for the first 88 of the surviving 212 pages, the work of two artists, the first using brown ink, the second also making use of red and green. The drawings end at page 88, the rest of the text being left with blank spaces, which show that the illustrations were drawn after the text was written. It was envisaged on an expansive and expensive scale, its pages having a modest writing and drawing area relative to the general dimensions.[9] The contents

7 Cf. Chapter 14. 8 BodL., Junius 11. Facs.: Gollancz 1927.
9 Writing area 225 × 120 mm in the original part of the manuscript within a page size of 324 × 196 mm.

of the book accord so precisely with the verse that Bede tells us that the seventh-century poet Cædmon composed, that the book has been known since Junius' day as the Cædmon manuscript, but the poems are now accepted as being of different authorship. It has been argued that the volume was made at Malmesbury on the basis of the association of the second artist with the so-called Corpus Prudentius,[10] a manuscript whose later provenance was Malmesbury, and because of the relationship of the artwork to architectural styles there; however, Canterbury seems more likely since that was where the Prudentius probably originated.[11]

The last of the poetic codices is arguably the most important. The *Beowulf* manuscript suffered badly in the Cotton Library fire, and its singed and crumbling pages are now bound in paper frames.[12] It contains, before its most famous item, three prose pieces, a *Life of St Christopher* (lacking its opening), *The Marvels of the East* (heavily illustrated) and *The Letter of Alexander to Aristotle*. Following *Beowulf* is another poem, now fragmentary, based on the Old Testament book of Judith. While manuscripts normally have a rationale, it is not easy to establish one for this collection. Even commonplace books are built around the interests of the compiler, and were we to suppose that the scribe or anthologist of this collection had access to only a limited library resource, he would surely still have made his selection on the basis of some principle. But a credible common theme in the items of the *Beowulf* manuscript has so far eluded scholars. A book of monster tales has for long been the most popular but nonetheless unsatisfactory explanation, but other possibilities, such as a series of treatises on pride (again not entirely convincing) or on royal responsibilities, are currently being advanced.[13] The point is an important one, for the combination of damage to the manuscript and a lack of recognisable context for its best-known item means that we have no sure means of understanding its creation or early ownership. However, since three of the four items other than *Beowulf* deal with religious or moral issues, it is probable that the book was – like almost all other survivals from the period – of ecclesiastical origin and intended to provide readers with material for moral contemplation. Although it is difficult to establish the full dimensions of the book because of the damage, the writing space is much smaller than that of the other poetic codices.[14] The illustrations to *Marvels* (which were made by the scribe rather

10 CCCC, 23.

11 For Malmesbury see Lucas 1981; for Christ Church, Canterbury, see Temple 1976. For speculation about a Winchester origin see Ohlgren 1975.

12 BL, Cotton Vitellius A.xv, fols. 94–209. Facs.: Malone 1963.

13 Sisam 1953; Orchard 1995b; Powell 2006.

14 195 × 130 mm.

than by a separate artist) appear crude by comparison with those in a later copy of the same text.[15] The book is written by two scribes, with the change of hand occurring in mid-sentence in *Beowulf*. There has been an attempt to prove that the second scribe is the author of the poem, but the argument has not found favour.[16] The opening of *Judith* is lost, and there are signs of wear on the last leaf of *Beowulf*, so that it is possible that the two have not always been together. The whole book was bound up with a twelfth-century manuscript in the seventeenth century, presumably by Robert Cotton.

Important as the poetry seems to us, its recording on expensive parchment was of less significance to contemporaries than was the copying of prose, to judge from the number of surviving manuscripts, for verse only accounts for around 6 per cent of extant Old English. Within the prose, by far the most important genre is homiletic literature, sermons and saints' lives, which are found in over sixty manuscripts. Whereas almost all of the poems occur in unique copies, the homilies are often found in multiple copies whose dates range over a century and more, and this gives us the opportunity to analyse manuscript relations, copying techniques and, with more difficulty, audience expectations. The earliest manuscript containing sermon literature in English is the Vercelli Book already mentioned, which is some fifteen or twenty years older than any other book of homilies. It is not, however, a preaching book or homiliary, but rather a collection of pious reading. Eleven of the twenty-three prose pieces in the manuscript are unique, and it is therefore a valuable early window into homiletic literature. It is uncertain when its pieces were composed, but it is likely that most if not all were products of the later tenth century.

The most prolific and accomplished writer of homiletic prose of the period is known to us by name: Ælfric, monk and mass-priest as he calls himself, who was educated at Winchester but who composed most of his extensive writings at the monastery of Cerne Abbas in Dorset.[17] Around 150 homilies and saints' lives by Ælfric survive. The best known are in two series of forty known as the Catholic Homilies, written between 989 and 992/5 and consisting of preaching material for Sundays and feast days throughout the church year. They were commissioned by Sigeric, archbishop of Canterbury 990–4, to whom the prefaces of both series were dedicated. Two copies survive which are thought to have been written in Ælfric's own scriptorium at Cerne Abbas. There is little doubt about the first, which contains the first

15 BL, Cotton Tiberius B.v, vol. I. Facs.: McGurk *et al.* 1983.
16 Kiernan 1981. For the rebuttals see Gerritson 1998a.
17 See Chapter 35.

series only, without its prefaces.[18] Two folios have deletion of text, with notes in the margin explaining them. The content of these notes shows them to be the work of the author himself. The same hand made a large number of other minor changes throughout the manuscript. This then, the earliest surviving copy of the first series of the Catholic Homilies, would seem to be a fair copy made by skilled scribes, presumably from the author's draft on wax tablets, to which he then made changes; accordingly, it can be dated to around 990. It offers a fascinating glimpse of the way in which the homilies were composed. The second manuscript, written during the 990s, is the earliest containing the full text of both series, and is likely to be either another product of the Cerne Abbas scriptorium or to be a close copy of one.[19] Thirty-six other manuscripts or manuscript fragments have copies of all or part of the Catholic Homilies. From this wealth of material, we can deduce that the author continued to revise the homilies, probably throughout his life (he died around 1010). Six textual traditions of the first series have been identified. We have evidence, for example, of the version of both series which was sent to Sigeric, with an explicit statement from the author that the two might be merged into one. Sigeric appears to have done just that, and many copies survive of this single chronological arrangement of items from the two series, augmented with a few pieces that are not by Ælfric.[20] Most of them were either written in one of the Canterbury houses (Christ Church or St Augustine's),[21] or can be shown to be copies of this Canterbury tradition though made elsewhere.[22] Some of the manuscripts in this tradition are so closely associated with one another that we can trace alterations or marginal additions copied from one to another,[23] although not necessarily directly since other copies might have intervened. This practice suggests that certain libraries had multiple copies of the same text, and that occasionally they were collated.

Books containing homiliaries survive in a variety of forms and sizes. The majority of Ælfric homilies are in large-scale codices with bold handwriting, clearly designed for public reading. A few, however, occur in smaller books more easily carried by a preacher from place to place. A collection which includes three homilies for the dedication of a church is obviously a book for a bishop, which he would need to have with him and is therefore of smaller

18 BL, Royal 7 C.xii. Facs.: Eliason and Clemoes 1966.
19 CUL, Gg.3.28.
20 The earliest and fullest is BodL., Bodley 340+342.
21 BodL., Bodley 340+342 itself and CCCC, 162.
22 CCCC, 198 (Worcester) and 303 (Rochester).
23 Cf. CCCC, 162 and 303; also CCCC, 178 and BodL., Hatton 114.

format.[24] Similarly small in scale is a two-volume homiliary containing only a small number of items and written in a large hand; presumably this is a book for use in preaching – perhaps again by a bishop – but compact enough for carrying about.[25] Even more portable were single quires, not initially bound into a book. We have evidence of a number of these which, because they have a prominent crease across the page, were folded to put into a pocket.[26] Such a folded booklet is the quire containing *Christ and Satan* that was inserted into the Junius manuscript. Other homilies were preserved in contexts which suggest that their copyists had limited access to expensive parchment; for example, six are written in the margins and blank spaces of a copy of the Old English translation of Bede's *Historia ecclesiastica*.[27] These were entered at different times, alongside – and in one case around – other vernacular material, one homily being written before and after a charm which must have been in place before copying of the homily was begun.

In addition to those by Ælfric there survive approximately 140 homilies by anonymous authors, and at least twenty-two ascribed to a slightly younger contemporary of Ælfric, Wulfstan, archbishop of York and bishop of Worcester. In addition to homilies, a range of other material such as law-codes and administrative writings is attributed to Wulfstan. He appears to have been directly responsible for the production of some surviving books, and his handwriting has been identified in marginalia and annotations in ten manuscripts, including material in both Latin and Old English.[28] Like Ælfric, he is often at pains to correct the work of his scribes or to indicate changes of heart in material that he had written. But whereas Ælfric's changes are mostly concerned with content rather than style, in Wulfstan's case it is the opposite. The force of Wulfstan's prose style comes from the use of repeated, often empty, rhetorical phrases and alliterating or rhymed near-synonyms. In his alterations to his work we can see him adding more of these. One manuscript annotated by Wulfstan is clearly a working collection, sometimes known as his commonplace book.[29] It contains a selection of his homilies and laws, but its principal item is a series of accounts of the conditions of men of different social status and vocation known as the *Institutes of Polity*. Two other manuscripts preserve different full versions of *Polity*:[30] in the commonplace book we have a version of the earlier

24 London, Lambeth Palace, 489; written space 167 × 85 mm.

25 CCCC, 419 and 421; written space 170 × 80 mm.

26 E.g. what is now the twentieth quire of BodL., Hatton 115, originally independent but bound with the present manuscript at an early date, probably before the thirteenth century.

27 CCCC, 41. 28 Ker 1971; see also Chapter 37.

29 BL, Cotton Nero A.i, fols. 70–177. Facs.: Loyn 1971.

30 CCCC, 201, pp. 1–178, and BodL., Junius 121.

with changes that take it in the direction of the later – in other words, it is a book that shows the archbishop's current thoughts. Appropriately, it is constructed on a very different scale from books for preachers, being a small codex with wide outer margins, perhaps to allow for annotation.[31]

The corpus of homiletic and related manuscripts, then, includes two books that were effectively working documents in the hands of the best-known homilists of the time. Other owners of books before the Norman Conquest are hard to trace. Archbishop Sigeric, as has been shown, owned copies of Ælfric's two series of Catholic Homilies but these manuscripts have not survived. Ælfric composed his *Lives of Saints* for Æthelweard, ealdorman of the western shires, and his son Æthelmær, but we have no record of the books actually sent to them. Leofric of Exeter's book-collecting activities were noted above in relation to the Exeter Book; among his many manuscripts are some that contain homiletic texts: the copy of Bede's *Historia ecclesiastica* with homilies in the margins,[32] and the two-volume portable homiliary,[33] both referred to above.

Manuscripts were compiled in different ways. Most books considered in this chapter were copied by a single scribe throughout (like the Vercelli Book), although some had extra items added by other scribes, either soon after the original scribe had completed his work or many decades later. Other books, however, were copied by more than one scribe, with no obvious logic to the apportionment of the work. One such is the Blickling manuscript (a collection of early sermons comparable to the Vercelli Book) which is for the most part copied by one scribe but which has another hand intervening occasionally. In part, the work of the second scribe is explicable because he copied just the beginning of items, presumably to indicate to the principal scribe what should be copied next; but his intervention in the middle of items, often to copy only a few lines, is hard to explain. Even more difficult is understanding the nature of the recording of an additional homiletic item in a Worcester manuscript. It is largely copied by one scribe but two others intervene at four intervals, each writing no more than a page or so, and sometimes only fifteen or sixteen lines.[34] In some manuscripts there is evidence of careful pre-planning. They are copied by a small team of scribes, each responsible for one or more blocks of quires.[35] We can see the pre-planning in the way in which the ends of the scribal stints are 'tailored', the script being compressed or expanded to allow the copyist to end at his appointed place in the text and at the same time fill

31 Page size: 165 × 105 mm, with written space a mere 135 × 60 mm.
32 CCCC, 41. 33 CCCC, 419 and 421.
34 BodL., Junius 121, item 78.
35 This is evident in CCCC, 198, part I (fols. 1–287): see Scragg 1985.

his quire. With scribes working simultaneously in such a way, books might be produced more quickly. Such a production method could work only for the reproduction of existing collections, and not for those such as the Vercelli Book or the Blickling manuscript which are compiled from a number of different source volumes.

It is well-nigh impossible to establish the place of origin of the vast majority of pre-Conquest vernacular books, and nearly as difficult to show their early provenance. We do have some knowledge of a few centres of production at particular periods. There are a number of homiliaries associated with Canterbury which were discussed above in relation to the dissemination of the work of Ælfric, but whether the surviving books were made at Christ Church or St Augustine's, or even at the neighbouring house at Rochester, is not clear. Scribes at Exeter were particularly productive in the third quarter of the eleventh century, producing copies of homilies as well as other religious material. Worcester, with which a significant number of manuscripts can be associated, is particularly important for the preservation of books associated with Wulfstan, bishop there from 1002 to 1016, and this includes his homilies. Ælfric's homilies also survive in Worcester copies; and a single homiliary, largely by Ælfric, has been identified as having been written at Winchester.[36] Nevertheless this leaves huge gaps in our knowledge. We have no homiletic texts from the important centres of London (where Wulfstan was bishop from 996 to 1002), Glastonbury, Malmesbury or Sherborne, which is not to say that such places did not possess them, since at least twelve major homiliaries and books of saints' lives (legendaries) survive of whose medieval history we know nothing. Even when we have evidence for the origin of a text, such as the Canterbury version of the Catholic Homilies, the movement of scribes and of books means that we cannot be certain that a particular copy was made in the south-east. Indeed, one copy of this version is annotated by the so-called 'Tremulous Hand', a scribe who is known to have worked at Worcester.[37] Thus either the book – or part of it – was written at Canterbury and then carried to Worcester, or it is a Worcester copy of such a volume.

36 Bishop 1971; Godden 1975.   37 CCCC, 198.

PART IV COLLECTIONS OF BOOKS

27

Patrick, apostle of the Irish

DAVID HOWLETT

Two authentic works have survived to the modern era, an *Epistola ad milites Corotici*, 'Letter to the Soldiers of Coroticus', in which Patrick excommunicates a post-Roman British tyrant who had murdered some Christian catechumens and sold others into slavery, and a *Confessio*, 'Confession', in which Patrick explains himself to those whom he had converted in Ireland and justifies his mission to those who had opposed it in Britain.[1] The letters survive in eight manuscripts: the earliest giving an abridged text copied at the beginning of the ninth century in Armagh; a second during the tenth century, perhaps in the diocese of Soissons; a third about the year 1000 at Worcester; a fourth during the eleventh century, owned if not written at Jumièges; three during the twelfth century in northern France and in England; and one during the seventeenth century.[2] As among these eight manuscripts seven are independent of each other, the text of the letters is fairly secure. In these compositions Patrick describes his fatherland as *Brittanniae* 'the Britains' and neighbouring regions as *Galliae* 'the Gauls', and he refers incidentally to coinage, *solidi* and *scriptulae*, implying that he was born while Roman administration still functioned in a Britain divided into several provinces, perhaps about AD 390, certainly before 410. He states that he was born into a family of landowners, slaveholders, civil servants and churchmen. His grandfather Potitus (whose name means 'empowered man') was a priest, and his father Calpornius (whose name, associated with the Roman plebeian gens Calpurnius and the name of Julius Caesar's wife Calpurnia, derived from καλπη + *urna* + *-ius*, designating one who bears a 'pitcher' or 'urn' in religious ceremonies) was a deacon and a decurion, a member of a municipal senate, an official responsible for the rendering of taxes. Patrick's own name (derived from *pater* + *-icius*, meaning 'like a father') designates 'a man noble in rank'. Because of the meaning of his name and the status of his family Patrick explicitly claimed *nobilitatem*, 'nobility', for himself.

1 Bieler 1993; Howlett 1994b. 2 Gwynn 1913, 1937.

Around 405, as a fifteen-year-old *adolescens*, he was captured on a family estate near Bannavem Taburniae, presumably Banna Venta Berniae, 'market town at the promontory of Bernia', perhaps Sabrinae 'of the Severn' or Berneich 'land of the Bernicians', but more likely in a southern civilian zone than in a northern military one. As Patrick contrasts the behaviour of Coroticus (a name related to Old Welsh Ceredigion, modern Cardigan) with that of Romano-Gaulish Christians dealing with pagan Franks, his mission probably preceded the conversion of the Franks, perhaps in 496 and certainly before 511. This is consistent with dates of the Annals of Ulster, which record Patrick's arrival as a missionary in Ireland in 432, his foundation of Armagh in 444, and his death in 461, when he would have fulfilled the biblical span of seventy years (alternatively in 491, when he would have been about 100).

After capture, Patrick was enslaved near the Forest of Foclut in Ireland for six years, during which the nominal religion of his boyhood intensified into the beginning of a series of seven dreams that informed his career. Having learned in the first that he would escape to his fatherland, he journeyed 200 Roman miles (188 modern ones), presumably from north-west to south-east across Ireland, whence he sailed for three days. On landing, his company wandered for twenty-eight days through wilderness, nearly starving until they discovered food after Patrick's prayer for help. There followed a great temptation by Satan in a second dream, escape from perils which lasted one month, an account of a later dream which foretold accurately a captivity of two months, then return to his family in Britain, and a fourth dream *in iuuentute*, 'in youth' (22–42), in which a man named Victoricius (sometimes identified with Victricius, bishop of Rouen, *c.* 330 – *c.* 407), bore a letter with the *Vox Hiberionacum*, 'the voice of the Irish', summoning him to evangelise them. In the fifth dream Christ spoke within him. In the sixth he saw and heard the Holy Spirit praying inside his body, *super me, hoc est super interiorem hominem*, 'above me, that is above my inner man'. In the triumphant seventh vision, following his degradation, Patrick was joined to the Trinity as closely as to the pupil of an eye.

After the raid by Coroticus, Patrick sent a letter seeking redress with a priest *quem ego ex infantia docui*, 'whom I have taught from infancy', implying, since infancy ended at seven and ordination to the priesthood occurred at thirty, that he had been in Ireland more than twenty-three years. Rejection of that letter elicited the letter of excommunication we know as the *Epistola*. As Patrick states in it *Non usurpo*, 'I am not claiming too much', one infers that his critics believed he was exceeding the limits of his authority. His attempt to excommunicate from Ireland a tyrant in Britain may have provoked the attack, which he relates at the thematic crux of the *Confessio*, an attack on his status as bishop when he was at least fifty-one, in his *senectus*, 'old age', (which began after forty-two) by ecclesiastical *seniores*, 'elders', in Britain who tried him during his absence. They charged him with a sin, committed when he was fourteen, confessed at least seven years later, after escaping from Ireland, before becoming a deacon. The sin was revealed by the *amicissimus*, 'dearest friend', to whom he had confessed it, the man whose statement *Ecce dandus es tu ad gradum episcopatus*, 'Behold, you are bound to be appointed to the grade of bishop', stands at the symmetrical centre of the *Confessio*.

Although modern scholars have supposed that Patrick was poorly educated, a barely literate rustic who struggled to express himself in a language he could not master, his two extant letters are, not according to a Ciceronian model but certainly by biblical standards, masterpieces. Though Patrick's writings may contain quotations from hymns, liturgical texts or a creed, the originals have been lost, preventing recognition of any source but one. If Patrick was a *homo unius libri*, 'a man of one book', that book was the Latin Bible, which he quoted both economically and brilliantly, using its phrases to claim identity of his vocation and mission with those of the lawgiver Moses and the Apostle Paul, relying upon readers' knowledge of the unquoted contexts of his quotations and allusions to clarify his explicit meanings, to suggest implicit overtones and undertones, and to attack his critics. Uniquely in the paragraph of the *Confessio* in which, addressing *domini cati rethorici* ('lords, skilled rhetoricians'), he appears to proclaim his ignorance, Patrick composed in Ciceronian clausular rhythms, arranged in patterns by type – thereby establishing his literary credentials. Elsewhere he composed in cursus rhythms which, like his biblical orthography, diction and syntax, are faultless. His prose, arranged *per cola et commata*, 'by clauses and phrases', exhibits varied forms of complex word play. Every paragraph is both internally coherent and bound in larger patterns within comprehensively architectonic compositions, in which every line, every word, every letter has been arithmetically fixed. His prose consistently evokes biblical typology, an effective means of linking the events of his personal life with sacred and universal history.

Patrick nowhere states that he brought any ecclesiastical assistants with him from Britain, but he affirms repeatedly that he is a bishop in Ireland, referring often to those converted, baptised, confirmed, ordained as clerics, and admitted to the religious life as both monks and nuns in Ireland. He never describes his education, nor does he name any authoritative teacher or ecclesiastical patron or ordaining bishop. In stating at the beginning of the *Epistola* that he is *indoctus* he does not lament that he is 'unlearned'; rather he proclaims that he is 'untaught' by men, and he continues directly: *Hiberione constitutus episcopum me esse fateor. Certissime reor a Deo accepi id quod sum* – 'established in Ireland I confess myself to be a bishop. Most certainly I think I have received from God what I am.' He mentions his dealings with Irish kings (*praemia dabam regibus*, 'I habitually gave rewards to kings'), with the sons of kings in his retinue (*dabam mercedem filiis ipsorum qui mecum ambulant*, 'I habitually gave a fee to the sons of the same [kings] who walk with me'), with the lawyers or brehons (*qui iudicabant* 'who customarily judged'), to whom he distributed *non minimum quam pretium quindecim hominum* ('not less than the price of fifteen men'), with noble women (*una benedicta Scotta genetiua nobilis pulcherrima adulta erat quam ego baptizaui*, 'there was one blessed Irish woman, born noble, very beautiful, an adult whom I baptised'), and with others (*quae mihi ultronea munuscula donabant et super altare iactabant ex ornamentis suis, et iterum reddebam illis* 'who habitually gave to me voluntary little gifts and hurled them upon the altar from among their own ornaments, and I habitually gave them back again to them').

Though Patrick mentions no absolute date, he makes it abundantly clear in internally consistent chronology that the milieu in which he lived and worked was late Roman and post-Roman Britain and Ireland of the fifth century. From at least the sixth century onward Patrick has been revered as the effective founder of the church in Ireland, celebrated in the panegyric 'St Sechnall's Hymn', *Audite omnes amantes Deum*, composed probably during the fourth quarter of the sixth century and quoted during the seventh. Patrick is cited as *papa noster*, 'our father', in Cummian's letter about the Paschal controversy written in the year 633 to Ségéne, abbot of Iona, and Béccán the Hermit. There are references to three lost *Lives* of Patrick written by Bishop Columba of Iona, Bishop Ultán moccu Conchobuir of Ardbraccan, and Ailerán the Wise, lector of Clonard, by the middle of the seventh century. From the end of the seventh century a hagiographic dossier in support of the metropolitan claims of the church at Armagh includes memoranda, *Collectanea* by Tírechán, a pupil of Bishop Ultán, and a *Vita* by Muirchú moccu Macthéni, a pupil of Cogitosus of Kildare. By the end of the eleventh century or the beginning of the twelfth there were four additional *Vitae*.[3]

The *Synodus Episcoporum* or 'First Synod of St Patrick', extant in a single manuscript copied from an Insular exemplar and written at the end of the ninth century or the beginning of the tenth in a scriptorium under the influence of Tours, may have issued from a synod between 447 and 459 by the missionaries Palladius, Auxilius and Isserninus, the first sent in 431 by Pope Celestine

3 Bieler 1952–3, 1971, 1979; Orchard 1993; Howlett 1995, pp. 138–52, 342–6.

ad Scotos in χριstum credentes, 'to the Scots [i.e. Irish] believing in Christ'. The text was attracted to the Patrician dossier by propagandists at Armagh late in the seventh century.[4]

Patrick's works remain the oldest extant literary texts written by a native of these islands, in these islands, for inhabitants of these islands. As attempts to make articulate sense of his turbulent life they bear comparison with works of Augustine, Boethius and Peter Abelard. They afford clear indications of the forms of thought and the levels of literacy in both author and audience in both Britain and Ireland during the fifth century.[5]

4 Bieler 1975b; Howlett 1998b.
5 Bury 1905; Bieler 1949; Carney 1961; Mohrmann 1961; Binchy 1962; Bieler 1968; Hanson 1968; Dumville *et al.* 1993.

28

The library of Iona at the time of Adomnán

THOMAS O'LOUGHLIN

Introduction

The monastery of Iona,[1] situated just off the north-west coast of Britain, was founded by Columba (521 – 9 June 597) sometime in the latter half of the sixth century. However, most of our knowledge about the monastery comes from the end of the seventh century, during the abbacy of Adomnán (679–704). From Adomnán's pen we have two works, the *Vita sancti Columbae* and the *De locis sanctis* (both, as internal evidence shows, written while he was abbot), and these constitute the principal sources of our information about Iona. Our third source is Bede, whose information in his abbreviation of Adomnán's *De locis sanctis* (probably written early in the eighth century), and in the fifth book of his *Historia ecclesiastica gentis Anglorum* (finished in 731), relates to the same period, Adomnán's abbacy.[2] Since no library list from Iona has survived, and the only extant manuscript that can be linked with certainty to the island is a copy of the *Vita sancti Columbae*,[3] it is on the basis of the texts quoted in Adomnán's two books (Bede's information about the island and Adomnán adds nothing here) that we must reconstruct the contents of the island's library. Over the years several famous illuminated biblical manuscripts have been linked with Iona, usually on the basis of their decorative style; but even if there were conclusive proof of their connection with Iona, this would add nothing to our knowledge of its *library* resources, as it is obvious that the community possessed copies of the New Testament in Latin. A stronger, albeit still circumstantial case, can be made for the fragmentary psalter known as the 'Cathach' which later traditions link with Columba and which, on palaeographical grounds, has been

1 *Í* or *Io* in Irish was rendered in Latin as *Ioua insula* (Adomnán) and *Hii insula* (Bede); Iona is a late medieval misreading of Ioua.

2 The relationship of Bede to Adomnán can be seen as one of disciple to master; the topic is examined in detail in O'Loughlin 2007, pp. 188–98.

3 Schaffhausen, Stadtbibliothek, Generalia 1.

dated to *c.* 600.[4] Since this psalter contains interesting *tituli* for the psalms, it has been argued that it provides evidence about the library of the place where the manuscript was made. However, such assertions rely on a confusion between the manuscript and its text. This psalter's text originated in a place where there was significant study of the psalms along with the resources for that study, but we have no evidence that the place in question was also the location in which the Cathach was written. It might be that the manuscript was written where that work was done, or it may simply be a copy/descendant of a scholarly exemplar/original that was drawn up elsewhere. Hence, the Cathach cannot be used as evidence for the library of Iona; and even if that manuscript's link with Iona were certain, it would merely show that there was one psalter intended for study use on Iona, a fact that is not in doubt.

The evidence from the *De locis sanctis*

The *De locis sanctis* is usually seen as a record of a pilgrimage to Palestine made by a 'Gaulish bishop' named Arculf sometime in the late seventh century.[5] Exactly how much of its information is derived from his experience cannot be ascertained with certainty, but Adomnán tells us that what Arculf related in no way differed from what was already known on Iona from books contained in the library,[6] and Adomnán refers on other occasions to books about Palestine in his possession.[7] An examination of the content reveals that the work has a far more sophisticated purpose than simply a 'virtual tour' through a pilgrim's recollections.[8] In chapter after chapter, specific problems in biblical exegesis, many of which had been flagged in the writings of Jerome and Augustine, are addressed and resolved by reference to what can be seen at the actual geographical sites that are mentioned in the scriptures. The most elaborate attempt to reconcile contradictory biblical details concerns the location of the places mentioned in the neighbourhood of Jerusalem in the days before the Crucifixion of Jesus, which in turn would solve the chronological differences between the evangelists.[9] Adomnán, while using Augustine's *De consensu evangelistarum* (without acknowledgement), produced a very different solution to the famous knot based on combining details regarding times and distances

4 RIA, s.n. CD-ROM facs. in Herity and Breen 2002.

5 Prooemium. 6 Bk I, ch. 1, §2 and bk II, ch. 30, §21.

7 For example, Bk II, ch. 1, §5 and bk II, ch. 27, §6.

8 What is said here is a summary of the research presented in O'Loughlin 2007.

9 Bk I, ch. 25.

from the various gospels. The reader is then invited to assume that the solution can be confirmed from Arculf's experience. This whole approach puts one immediately in mind of Augustine's desire, expressed in *De doctrina christiana*, that there should be a geographical manual for such problems.[10] While Adomnán does not quote the *De doctrina christiana*, the content and method of the *De locis sanctis* suggest that he was attempting to produce the manual Augustine desired, and certainly medieval users of the *De locis sanctis*, from Bede onwards, saw the work as just such a handbook. So, what texts can be found quoted in *De locis sanctis?*

Although Adomnán only cites the authors of the works he used on two occasions, Jerome at 2, 11, 3 and Juvencus at 1, 17, 1, it is clear that his reading went well beyond this. Adomnán uses two of the major writers of the Latin Christian tradition: Augustine and Jerome. We know with certainty that he had Augustine's *De civitate Dei* and his *De consensu evangelistarum*, and most probably the *De doctrina christiana*. Adomnán used at least six works by Jerome: the *De situ et nominibus locorum Hebraicorum*;[11] the *Liber quaestionum hebraicarum in Genesim*; the *Commentarii in evangelium Mathaei*; the *Commentarii in Naum*; the *Commentarii in Osee*; and the *Commentarii in Hiezechielem*; and Denis Meehan, who prepared the 1958 edition of the text, argued that there was evidence for a further four or five. The presence of this range of works from one major exegetical figure in the Latin tradition suggests that there may have been sizeable holdings of several other important patristic authorities. Since these are major works (both intellectually and in physical size), comprehension of which required their readers to be fully integrated within a tradition of Christian learning and debate, their presence negates two assumptions that have dogged much writing on early Christian Ireland: first, that it was intellectually remote from the standard books of the Latin West – if these works were accessible then there is no reason why the same could not have been true of any work of Augustine then in circulation; and, second, the notion that, while full of holy monks and austere ascetics, Irish monasteries had little interest in the discipline of theology as such. These are not 'works of piety': all assume the study of Christian beliefs in a formal way; while the *De consensu*, in particular, presupposes the setting of a teacher working through the sacred texts with students.

When we move to 'second-rank' authors we see the range of writers available on Iona. It is not surprising that Adomnán had access to Gregory the Great's *Dialogi*, which was from the start a monastic favourite, nor that he had

10 Bk II, ch. 29, §45.

11 This is Jerome's Latin translation of the *Onomasticon* of Eusebius of Caesarea; on this work see Freeman-Grenville, Chapman, and Taylor 2003; and Notley and Safrai 2005.

a copy of Cassiodorus on the psalms, for it too was written with a monastic audience in mind. If the fame of Cassiodorus had spread to Iona, there is no reason why it should not have possessed his *Institutiones* that not only provided guidance on exegesis but supplied a list of *desiderata* for the ideal monastery. As noted already, Adomnán refers to having several books relating to the Holy Land; however, only one work explicitly devoted to describing places has so far been identified: the *De situ Hierusolyma* by Eucherius of Lyons.[12] In addition he was able to gather much geographical information from two works by Isidore: the *Etymologiae* and the *De natura rerum*. Written earlier in the seventh century, these texts were just beginning a long career as standard repositories of information on the natural world. Adomnán drew upon four other works: the *Historia evangelica* by Juvencus; the Latin translation of Josephus in which Adomnán describes his source *de tertio Iudaicae captivitatis libro* (from the third book on the Jewish captivity) (2, 20, 5), and which we usually refer to as 'Hegesippus'; the *Chronicon* of Sulpicius Severus; and, last, Paulinus of Nola's *Epistola XXXI* (*ad Severum*), the source for a miracle attributed to the Holy Cross whereby a dead youth was raised to life.[13]

Over the years scholars have detected 'influences' of classical writers such as Vergil and Pliny in the work, but on no occasion is there sufficient evidence to prove that Adomnán had seen the text, while the presence of scraps of information derived from ancient sources (such as Pliny's *Naturalis historia*) can be explained by their use in Isidore whose presence on Iona is otherwise attested. It is clear that not all of Adomnán's sources in *De locis sanctis* have yet been identified: the language or the level of detail in certain passages indicates reliance on unknown, elusive, or possibly no longer extant written sources. Filling out a list with entries such as 'anon.', 'On St George' or 'anon.', 'On Constantinople' tells us little about the library – except to remind us that it was certainly larger than we can reconstruct.

The evidence from the *Vita Columbae*

The *Vita* was written to serve a very different purpose: it demonstrates, using a pattern derived from the *Dialogi* of Gregory the Great, that Columba was capable of prophetic revelations, divine miracles and angelic visitations (second preface), and that he still presides over the community of Iona and

12 For an examination of the question of the authorship of this work, see O'Loughlin 2007, pp. 214–22; moreover, since he had this work by Eucherius, there is no reason why he should not have had access to Eucherius' two widely used textbooks: the *Formulae* and the *Liber instructionum*.

13 Bk I, ch. 11, §2.

those associated with it as their heavenly intercessor. Adomnán makes clear that his sources for the *Vita* are the records – written and oral – preserved among his brethren, and research yields further knowledge of what books were being read there. Several works used for the *De locis sanctis* are also found in the *Vita*; here I shall only mention works that have not already been noted.

Hagiography, by its nature, relies on the subject of each *Vita* being perceived as fitting into a pattern, for it is conformity to the established models of holiness in other *Vitae* that established the sanctity of the particular saint being written about. So what evidence have we that Adomnán adopted materials from other *Vitae* for Columba? One of the basic texts establishing the genre is the *Vita Antonii* by Athanasius as translated by Evagrius of Antioch. He also used the key text written in Latin that shaped the genre: the *Vita Martini* by Sulpicius Severus. In this reliance on Athanasius and Sulpicius, we can see that Adomnán was in line with the larger Latin tradition. But if the major *Vitae* were available to him, so were relatively minor lives. The *Vita Germani* by Constantius can be identified from the *Vita Columbae*, along with the anonymous *Actus Silvestri*.[14] The use of these works can be taken as an indication of the fairly wide hagiographic holdings at Iona. Moreover, the use of the *Actus Silvestri* shows us that alongside hagiographic material there were possibly other works relating parts of the history (or more accurately the pseudo-history) of the church. Closer in time and place than these widely disseminated *Vitae*, an earlier member of the community had written down materials relating to the life and miracles of Columba. Adomnán tells us he used this earlier *Vita*, and indeed we can reconstruct that work in part. It is plausible, but not certain, that the writer of this earlier *Vita Columbae* was Cumméne who was abbot from 657 to 669. Last, there is evidence for Jerome's *De viris inlustribus*. While this is not hagiography in the strict sense, it does list those who 'had given wise words to the people ... [who] were the glory of their own times and left a name'.[15] For our purposes its presence on Iona has another significance because this work played an important role in identifying the '*auctoritates*' within the tradition, and acted as a guide to the early Christian writers whose books any medieval library would have been glad to possess. Incidentally, through Bede's words of praise for the learning displayed in the *De locis sanctis*, Adomnán himself was included in the later updates of the *De viris inlustribus*.

The monastic life was, in essence, life according to a rule, and so legal texts had a place of special importance. Several scholars have noted the influence

14 Cf. Dekkers, 1995, item 2235. 15 Sirach 44.4–8. Dekkers 1995, item 616.

of Benedict's *Regula* in their studies of the *Vita*; however, given the overlaps that occur between various early monastic *regulae*, the precision of this identification needs further study. The basic point is that there was at least one *regula* of Continental origin on Iona, and there is every possibility that there were several. The fact that any *regula* from the Continent was being used on Iona presents serious problems for those who argue that its monasticism was isolated, idiosyncratic and out of step with Latin monasticism elsewhere. Another text with a bearing on monasticism is Dionysius Exiguus' *Epistola I*. Dionysius, a Scythian monk, lived and worked in Rome in the first half of the sixth century where he was dubbed *exiguus* ('the little one') by Cassiodorus on account of his humility. Dionysius was the first great collector of canon law in Latin, and if Iona had one work by him, then equally it could have had several of his writings. Dionysius' collection was an important source for the great Irish work of this period, the *Collectio canonum Hibernensis*, whose main claim to fame is that it replaced Dionysius' chronological arrangement of material with a systematic one.

Four other works by Christian writers can be identified: two sermons by Leo the Great (XII and L); and the *Dialogi* and second *Epistola* of Sulpicius. The two sermons may reflect the presence of a larger homily collection for use not only in study, but the liturgy. The use of one letter by Sulpicius may indicate the community had access to all three of them, implying that they had all his extant, authentic writings. Scholars have advanced arguments for the influence of Vergil on certain passages in the *Vita*, but as with the *De locis sanctis* the similarities are too distant to make such a claim with any certainty; and I, for one, would reject the suggestion: the words are similar, but in different cases, and without any hint in the context that one is to recognise an allusion; nor is it the case that Adomnán is adopting Vergilian phrases unconsciously. Last, in the account of the saint's final days (*Vita* 3, 23) there is the story of the monastery's horse crying at the thought of Columba's approaching death. This is a variant of the 'prophetic horse' tale found both before (Xanthos foretelling the death of Achilles[16]) and after (in saints' lives) the time of Adomnán, but it does not point to the presence of any particular work on Iona.

Other evidence

One other piece of textual evidence that is directly relevant to Iona's library appears in the seventh-century Irish poem *Amra Choluimb Chille* in praise of

16 *Iliad*, bk XIX, lines 404–23.

Columba. It includes the phrase, 'the books loved by Cassian' (*libuir ut car Cassion*). These are undoubtedly the *Conlationes* and the *De institutis coenobiorum* which were basic texts for all Western monks because they translated the ideas of the first monks of Egypt and Palestine to a European context. Even without this reference we could assume their presence, as many of the disciplines and monastic structures that can be established for Iona and other early insular monasteries – for instance, their penitential system – are based directly on John Cassian.

More problematic is the evidence for books based on the Latin poem *Altus prosator* that is traditionally ascribed to Columba and is certainly very early. Several images in the poem have been taken as indicating the presence of non-canonical works such as 1 Enoch or the Gospel of Nicodemus, or of patristic commentaries. However, while it is most likely that there were several works on Iona that would fall into the category of 'apocrypha' as later defined, the allusions are too generic for them to be used as pointers to specific works.[17] The value of these allusions is that they demonstrate, once again, that the literary culture of Iona was far broader than the library list we can establish.

Two other categories of works were definitely present on Iona but, regrettably, we cannot specify particular texts. The first category is Latin grammatical treatises. These would have been necessary not only for teaching Latin for the liturgy and for study, but also in order to instruct teachers how to write and how to train others in the language. We may find Adomnán's writing style 'sinewy' (Bede described it as *laciniosus*), but he does have a genuine and individual style. The second category is liturgy which includes not only the obvious books for the Eucharist and the office, but also calendar materials of various kinds. Clearly, computistical works for establishing the liturgical cycle were an important matter for we know from several sources that calculating the date of Easter was a matter of dispute both on the island and between the island and elsewhere. But linking Iona with any particular pre-Bedan computus is going beyond the evidence: all we can say is that there must have been several works relating to the topic available for advancing the argument for and against different reckoning methods. That Iona made contributions to another form of liturgical book, the martyrology, is witnessed by strata in later Irish martyrologies.[18] In all probability it was a version of the *Martyrologium hieronymianum* that was used on Iona; then, as was the way with such works, the community added their saints to its cycle before their form of the text became the basis of another place's usage.

17 See O'Loughlin 2007, pp. 229–33. 18 See Ó Riain 2006, pp. 57–74.

The question of the presence of *Vetus Latina* texts on Iona

Much speculation has been devoted to 'the form of the biblical text' on Iona which, in turn, has focused on the presence of non-Vulgate lemmata in Adomnán's works. This speculation wraps together two separate questions: first, the question of the form of the Vulgate used on Iona, assuming (as did the nineteenth-century editors) that there are well-defined regional text-forms; and, second, the question of whether there were biblical texts on Iona – as distinct from pre-Vulgate echoes retained in the liturgy – that did not belong to the Vulgate (i.e. what are generally described as *Vetus Latina*). It is best to begin by clearing up the second question: in every case that a distinctly non-Vulgate reading occurs in either work, its presence can be explained by the fact that Adomnán is at that point using a known patristic work and follows the scriptural text he found embedded in that source. There is no evidence that any *Vetus Latina* version, as such, was being used on Iona. When, then, we study the biblical text exhibited directly by Adomnán we find that there are no significant variants that would allow us to relate it to any particular family of Vulgate texts. This is particularly frustrating for any scholar who might wish to anchor a specific biblical manuscript to Iona on the basis that it shares variants with Adomnán.

Conclusion

Monasteries were places that valued the acquisition of literacy, Latinity and doctrine. Accordingly, they valued the technical skills this literacy demanded in preparing writing materials (skins, inks, wax tablets), in the labour of transcription[19] and in checking the copy against its exemplar[20] along with the work of decorator and binder. Thus when Adomnán portrays Columba retiring to his cell on the day of his death to spend his last hours writing a psalter, he is not just retelling an anecdote, but showing the saint as engaged in a work suitable to monks until the very last moment.[21]

Interest in producing books can be found in the earliest monastic documents. 'Antony so closely listened to what he heard read that he missed nothing and remembered everything; because of this memory he had no need of books.'[22] Implicit in this is that every monk less holy than Antony did need

19 See *Vita*, bk I, chs. 19, 23; bk II, ch. 16. 20 See *Vita*, bk III, ch. 23.
21 *Ibid.* 22 Athanasius, *Vita Antonii*, 3.

Table 28.1 *List of texts*

Author	Text	A	B
anon.	*Actus Silvestri*	•	
Athanasius	*Vita Antonii*	•	
Augustine	*De civitate Dei*	•	
	De consensu evangelistarum	•	
	De doctrina christiana		•
[?] Benedict	*Regula*	•	
Cassiodorus	*Expositio psalmorum*	•	
	Institutiones		•
Constantius	*Vita Germani*	•	
[?] Cumméne	*Vita Columbae*	•	
Dionysius Exiguus	*Epistola* I	•	
Eucherius	*De situ Hierusolyma*	•	
	Formulae spiritalis intellegentiae		•
	Liber instructionum		•
Gregory the Great	*Dialogi*	•	
'Hegesippus' / Josephus	*Historiae*	•	
Isidore	*Etymologiae*	•	
	De natura rerum	•	
Jerome	*De situ et locorum*	•	
	De viris inlustribus	•	
	Liber quaestionum hebraicarum in Genesim	•	
	Commentarii in evangelium Mathaei	•	
	Commentarii in Naum	•	
	Commentarii in Osee	•	
	Commentarii in Hiezechielem	•	
	Liber interpretationis hebraicorum nominum		•
	Epistola 46		•
	Epistola 108		•
Pseudo-Jerome	*Martyrologium* [*Hieronymianum*]	•	
John Cassian	*Conlationes*	•	
	De institutis coenobiorum	•	
Juvencus	*Historia evangelica*	•	
Leo the Great	*Sermo* XII	•	
	Sermo L	•	
Paulinus of Nola	*Epistola* XXXI	•	
Sulpicius Severus	*Chronicon*	•	
	Vita Martini	•	
	Dialogi	•	
	Epistola II	•	

A = Text certainly present on Iona, as cited, quoted or referred to in some other way.
B = Text probably present on the basis of the general content of works produced on Iona.

books. The liturgy apart, monastic identity was generated from rules, maxims and the material on the monastic heroes (lives, conferences, admonitions), and even in unscholarly houses these were read as basic routine.[23] The monastery as 'a school of holiness' was, of necessity, a school of literacy, and so needed a library. Readily visible in those medieval foundations whose books or library lists have been preserved, this trait was present from the start: the Nag Hammadi library belonged to a Pachomian-type community in Egypt; while the fourth-century 'Codex Sinaiticus' was found in St Catherine's Monastery in Sinai.[24] Such attention to writings demanded an equal attention to their acquisition and reproduction. It is against that background we should view what we can learn about the monastery of Iona in Adomnán's time, and against which we should also view his picture of Columba – Columba the scribe who produced books throughout his life, who was called to check a book made by another monk for errors, who was interrupted while working, made psalters and hymnals for the office, and who continued working with books until his death.[25]

23 Benedict, *Regula*, 42. 24 Cf. Elliott 2000, pp. 43–5.
25 *Vita*, bk I, ch. 23; bk II, chs. 29, 8–9.

29

Literacy in Anglo-Saxon England

M. R. GODDEN

In trying to define the extent of literacy in Anglo-Saxon England, we have to face the fact that there is virtually no explicit evidence on the subject from the period; comments on the subject are extremely rare, and the few we have are more rhetorical than informative. We have to try to assess the situation from the evidence of the forms of written text that were produced, who they appear to have been produced for, and how representative various literate or illiterate individuals or groups may have been.

Literacy in Latin

There were two languages in extensive use for writing and reading in England – Latin and English – and it is convenient to distinguish at the outset between literacy in Latin and literacy in English. At the time of the conversion, Latin was an entirely foreign language to the English, who had had relatively little contact with the Roman Empire or with Latin-speaking Britons. The language had to be learned at school, and however much pupils were taught to converse in Latin, especially in monastic schools, it was always primarily a written language in England. Those who could speak Latin or comprehend it when spoken or read aloud could almost certainly read it in a book, and many were no doubt more comfortable with written Latin than the spoken or recited form.

Competence and indeed skill in reading and writing Latin came remarkably quickly to the English after conversion. Within seventy years Aldhelm was composing highly sophisticated Latin verse and prose, and was soon followed by a series of imitators including Tatwine (d. 734), Boniface (d. 754) and Æthilwald (fl. 700). Contemporary readers of his tortuous and esoteric style evidently included the nuns for whom he wrote the *De virginitate*, and his work functioned as a school text throughout the Anglo-Saxon period. Bede reported that students from the school of Theodore and Hadrian 'know Latin and Greek just as well as their native tongue'.[1] Bede's own output in Latin was enormous, and widely read on the Continent. Alcuin's scholarship brought him to the attention of Charlemagne and he played a key role in the revival of learning on the Continent. If the tenth-century reform movement in England produced no one of the calibre of such figures, at least in relation to Latin, it nevertheless produced some very competent users of the language, in the form of Ælfric, Byrhtferth and Wulfstan Cantor. A sequence of Insular grammars of Latin, and later colloquies, testify to the centrality in English education of learning to read, write and speak Latin.[2]

How far that competence in Latin spread through the population is an important question. Bede refers to the fluency in Latin and Greek that was achieved by the pupils of Hadrian and Theodore as something already exceptional by his own time.[3] Latin was the only language of the liturgy and in principle all clerics should have been competent in it. Persistent evidence suggests that this was far from the case, and perhaps not always expected. In a letter of 734 to Egbert, archbishop of York, Bede urges that the archbishop should:

> endeavour to impress deeply on the memory of all under your rule the Apostles' Creed and the *Pater noster*; those who know Latin will have learnt them well, but you should make the ignorant people – that is those who are acquainted with no language but their own – say them in their own language and repeat them assiduously. This ought to be done not only in the case of laymen ... but also of those clerics or monks who are ignorant of the Latin language ... I have often given to many ignorant priests both of these texts, translated into the English language.[4]

If by the final remark he means that he gave the priests written copies of the *Pater noster* and the Creed in English for their use, then it would seem that they could at least read the vernacular. Possibly they could also read Latin texts without understanding them, and thus have participated in, or even conducted, liturgical services by a combination of reading aloud and memorising from books consulted earlier. Bede seems to take for granted this level of ignorance, and makes no proposals for remedying it beyond providing translations. Egbert's own *Dialogue* mentions 'a grasp of letters' as a necessary requirement for the ordination of a priest ('si adsecutus est litteras'), but only at the end of a long list of quite different requirements or disabilities, and he does not say whether this should embrace an understanding of Latin.[5] A few years later,

1 *HE*, IV, 2: Colgrave and Mynors 1969, p. 335.
2 Law 1982a; Gwara and Porter 1997.
3 *HE*, IV, 2: Colgrave and Mynors 1969, p. 335.
4 Whitelock 1979, p. 800.
5 Haddon and Stubbs 1869–78, III, p. 410.

at the Council of Clovesho in 747, it was decreed that all priests should learn how to perform their office properly, and also how to interpret and expound in their own language the Creed and the words that were spoken in the mass and the office of baptism, if they did not know them.[6] The implication is presumably that the priests could recite the Latin liturgy, from memory or reading or a combination of the two, but did not know what it meant and so could not explain it to others. King Alfred, in the 890s, describes the situation in his own time where few (he presumably means few priests) could understand their services, at least outside Northumbria, or translate a letter from Latin; and the clergy in general could make little use of Latin books because they did not know the language.[7] He presents this as a fearsome decline from earlier states of educational richness in England, but it may be that what was different was not the ignorance of the general clergy which he so emphasises but the absence of a smaller elite of learned figures equal to Bede or Alcuin, or at least Ælfric or Wulfstan Cantor (of Winchester). It is certainly striking that he had to import scholars from Wales and overseas to support his programme of education and translation, and that the one Anglo-Saxon 'scholar' in his team whose work we know, Wærferth, bishop of Worcester, though highly praised by Asser, produced a rendering of Gregory the Great's *Dialogues* that testifies to a worryingly poor grasp of both Latin and history.[8] In the preface to the translation of Gregory's *Regula pastoralis* Alfred remarks flatteringly on the learned bishops available to him, but it is nevertheless a translation designed in the first instance for the use of bishops, and the verse preface claims that not all English bishops could manage the Latin text. One extant copy is addressed to Wærferth, who would seem to be in that category.

No more than Bede or the Council of Clovesho did the king propose a campaign to restore Latin literacy among the clergy. His primary concern seems to have been to inculcate an ability to read English and to make texts available in the vernacular. Of Latin he says only, 'let Latin be taught to those to whom one wishes to teach it, and whom one wishes to raise to a higher rank (*to hirran hade*)', and although this has often been translated as 'to holy orders' there seems in fact to be no evidence in support of this interpretation. The needs of the secular clergy are indeed a striking absence from the educational programme; and given the king's acknowledgement that not all the bishops in his kingdom could themselves understand Latin it is perhaps hardly surprising that he made no proposals for training the clergy in general in Latin, since the training would inevitably have been a task for the bishops

6 *Ibid.*, p. 366. 7 Sweet 1871–2, p. 3. 8 Godden 1997.

to administer. When Ælfric wrote the preface to his *Grammar* towards the end of the next century he claimed that knowledge of Latin had continued in a low state until the monastic reform of the mid-century led by Dunstan and Æthelwold and the consequent revival of learning. Whether this reform extended to the secular clergy is again doubtful. His words are, perhaps deliberately, ambiguous:

> It is therefore necessary now for God's ministers and monks to take care that holy learning does not cool off or decline in our times, as it did in England a few years ago, so that no English cleric knew how to compose or interpret a letter in Latin, until Archbishop Dunstan and Bishop Æthelwold again restored learning in the monastic life.[9]

The ignorance is firmly attributed to the clerics and the restoration of learning to the monasteries, albeit with a veiled implication that it had declined there too. If the implication is that the restoration of Latin learning in the monasteries may have ended the total ignorance of the clergy in general he does not quite say that it did, or how far the improvement went. And in his preface to Genesis written around the same time he refers to unlearned clerics in his own time who might only partially understand Latin. He wrote pastoral letters in the vernacular on behalf of bishops Wulfsige and Wulfstan, for them to read out to their assembled clergy, because the clerics could neither read Latin nor comprehend it; and his two collections of vernacular homilies were apparently intended primarily for the use of priests who could read them out in church to their congregations, presumably because they were not able to work directly from the Latin homiliaries drawn on by Ælfric. His almost invariable habit in these homilies of translating the gospel reading for the day before expounding it suggests that he felt unable to count on the clergy's ability to do even that. Wulfstan in his so-called *Canons of Edgar* warns educated clerics not to mock their half-educated brethren, but to try to improve them if they know how to, and he finds it necessary to instruct priests not to conduct the mass without using a book, and to invite them to look at it during the service 'if they wish'.[10] Byrhtferth of Ramsey wrote his *Enchiridion*, a miscellany of computistical, theological and rhetorical learning, in alternating Latin and English to suit the differing capacities of his readers, as he explains; on the one hand there are the young monks, who can handle Latin and complex ideas, on the other the clerics, who need the explanations in English and at a simpler level (the older monks are presumably assumed to

9 Wilcox 1994, pp. 115–16; Zupitza 1880, p. 3. 10 Fowler 1972, pp. 4, 8.

know the material and not to need instruction). Byrhtferth seems to suggest that it might be among the duties of the young monks to go on to instruct the old clerics in such matters.[11]

A recurrent theme throughout the period is indeed this distinction between the monks who might be expected to know Latin and the secular clergy who often did not. The great Latinists were mostly monks (Aldhelm, Bede, Boniface, Ælfric, Byrhtferth, though apparently not Alcuin, even though he ended his life as abbot of Tours), to which we might add the anonymous authors of early *Lives* of Gregory the Great and Cuthbert, and Felix (author of the early *Life* of Guthlac); and the great schools were mainly at monasteries or monastic cathedrals. Ælfric's vernacular works are explicitly addressed to the laity or the secular clergy, while his Latin writings are for monks (the *Life of Æthelwold*, the *Letter to the Monks of Eynsham*). And Byrhtferth makes the distinction explicit in his *Enchiridion*. But this was probably far from an absolute rule, and there may have been an element of wishful thinking, or church politics, in such claims or implications. Bede mentions monks and clerics as being often ignorant of Latin, and does not imply that these are novice monks. Æthelwold's translation of the Benedictine *Rule* into English may have been undertaken for the benefit of novice monks recruited from the laity and the secular clergy in the first generation of the reform movement, but the currency of the translation from the late tenth century onwards, in both male and female houses, suggests that it continued to have a use in monastic establishments.[12] One might note too that the standard document of the reform movement on monastic liturgy and practice, the *Regularis concordia*, survives in only one copy in Latin but there are two separate translations into English. Although Ælfric never acknowledges that any of his vernacular works were written for monks, except perhaps the *Grammar* which he insists is only for the boys in the monastic school, some of them have an obvious interest for a monastic readership (the *Lives of Saints* collection, some parts of the Catholic Homilies) and most survive mainly in manuscripts from monastic libraries. His reference to the decline of Latinity in the past, and its revival under Dunstan and Æthelwold, cited above, seems to imply a decline among monks as well (or perhaps a decline in monastic practice generally) while resolutely avoiding saying so. At least in the later Anglo-Saxon period, scholarship, and especially Latinity, was a very important aspect of the monastic claim to be superior to the secular clergy, but evidence of actual reading and the contents of texts suggests it may not always have been valid.

11 Baker and Lapidge 1995, p. 120. 12 Jayatilaka 2003.

Alongside the monks, nuns and clerics, there were also at least some laymen who could supposedly read and write Latin. Aldfrith, king of Northumbria (686–705), studied in Ireland in his youth and had a reputation for great learning; Aldhelm addressed a lengthy Latin treatise on numerology and metrics to him. King Alfred is supposed to have learnt to read Latin at the age of thirty-nine, according to Asser, and to have personally translated Latin texts into English, and his reference to the learned men who once flourished in England, 'both from the religious order and the worldly', suggests that he at least thought that knowledge of Latin had been a feature of the laity in the past. Asser also claims that Alfred had his youngest son, Æthelweard, educated at a school with 'all the nobly born children of virtually the entire area, and a good many of lesser birth as well',[13] and that pupils at this school studied both Latin and English books, and also learnt to write. According to later records this Æthelweard had two sons who died at the battle of Brunanburh, so presumably there was no question of him being educated for the church. As noted above, Alfred's reference, in his introductory letter on the state of learning, to teaching Latin to those destined for higher rank may well refer to positions of secular authority as well as clerical. Whether Alfred really did know Latin well enough to translate texts like Augustine's *Soliloquies* (and to write an additional third book for it) must be doubted, but there seems at least to be a conviction, in his own time and later, that lay Latinity was not an eccentric notion. A century later another Æthelweard, the ealdorman for the south-west (died not later than 1001), appears as the apparent author of a Chronicle written in an elaborate and highly stylised form of Latin, based on the *Anglo-Saxon Chronicle* and the Old English Bede, all done amid his many other responsibilities as administrator and military leader. Since the same Æthelweard is found frequently entreating Ælfric to translate Latin texts into English for him there must be some doubt whether he wrote, rather than commissioned, the Latin Chronicle; however, the fact that such a man would present himself as a master of ornate Latin prose is significant. Perhaps the strongest circumstantial evidence for a modest lay competence in Latin is the large number of Anglo-Saxon charters written in Latin that survive, many of them recording the ownership of estates by laymen. There is clear evidence that lay landowners attached considerable importance to such documents, which enshrined the results of transactions that were presided over and witnessed by secular and religious leaders alike. The continued use of Latin for such texts long after many other kinds of documents had shifted to the vernacular suggests that they were not

13 Keynes and Lapidge 1983, p. 90.

entirely a closed book to their owners: their Latin is very formulaic and repetitive, though also often learned and esoteric, and the crucial boundaries of the estates are often in the vernacular. There is at least one piece of positive evidence: an ealdorman, Æthelwulf, in a case dated around 897, could read and understand the Latin charters of Coenwulf king of Mercia 796–821.[14]

Literacy in the vernacular

Anyone living in England who could read a Latin text could obviously also read a text in English, with the possible exception of the occasional ecclesiastic of Continental origin. The process of translating English texts into Latin, for a distinct set of readers unfamiliar with English, is generally a post-Conquest phenomenon, and the occasional earlier examples are probably for readers outside England, such as Æthelweard's version of the Chronicle, written for a Continental kinswoman, and Asser's use of material from the Chronicle in his *Life* of King Alfred, apparently composed for a Welsh public. But there would appear to have been a substantial proportion of the population who could read in English but not in Latin.

Texts written down in English were in use throughout the period, though perhaps increasingly in the last two centuries. The production of documents in the vernacular seems to have begun very soon after the conversion and remained a regular feature of the legal world. Bede reports that Æthelberht of Kent, the king whom Augustine had converted, 'established a code of laws in the manner of the Romans ... written in the English language'. These laws, presumably set down some time before the king's death in 616, survive only in a twelfth-century copy, but were known to Alfred and Wulfstan as well as Bede. The laws of Ine, king of Wessex (688–726), also survive in English, as an appendage to the laws of King Alfred, compiled in the 890s, and indeed English seems to have been the usual language for law-codes. Charters also survive from the reign of Æthelberht onwards, at first in Latin, but English is used as well from at least the late eighth century.[15] Fifty-three of the fifty-eight surviving wills are in English, the earliest probably that of Abba, a minor Kentish landowner, *c.* 832–40. Over one hundred leases survive, in Latin or English.

The use of English in education is indicated by the appearance of English words glossing Latin in a group of early glossaries which seem to reflect the studies of the later seventh century.[16] The writing, and presumably reading, of

14 Morrish 1986, p. 96. 15 Sawyer 1968, p. 35. 16 Pheifer 1974.

religious texts in English is indicated by Bede's claim to have furnished copies of the Creed and *Pater noster* in English to ignorant priests, and by the report that at the time of his death he was producing a translation of the Gospel of St John. Books of the Bible with a continuous gloss in English are evident from the middle of the ninth century, with the Vespasian Psalter (Plate 4.3), and become very common thereafter, especially for psalters. By the tenth century they are joined by glossed texts of other religious works, such as the *Rule of St Benedict* and hymns, and of Aldhelm. Vernacular poetry was also committed to writing from at least the ninth century. When Bede tells his story of Cædmon, the first known religious poet using English, he describes the monks of Whitby (perhaps around AD 670) listening avidly to his poems on the whole sweep of Christian history from the Creation to the Last Judgement, but says nothing to suggest that his poems were committed to writing and there is no evidence that they were. The one piece of Cædmonian verse that does survive, his nine-line hymn, was paraphrased in Latin by Bede without the English original, but the latter was soon added in the margins and flyleaves of copies of the *Ecclesiastical History*, presumably as part of the record of a miracle. But when the *History* was itself translated into English, probably towards the end of the ninth century, the anonymous translator reports that the monks both listened to the poems and wrote them down – presumably reflecting not so much genuine knowledge that this is what happened but an assumption that it would have happened because it had become normal by his time for vernacular poetry to be written and read as well as performed and heard. The best evidence that this was so is Asser's story of how King Alfred's mother, when he was a young boy, owned a book of English poems, apparently decorated, and gave it to her youngest son as a prize for learning to read it or perhaps memorising it.[17] According to Asser again, both Alfred and his children learned English poems, by implication from books, and Alfred himself is credited with producing a substantial body of English verse in written form, if he is indeed responsible for the verse parts of the English adaptation of Boethius' *De consolatione philosophiae*. Further evidence for the writing down of poetry in English by Alfred's time and probably earlier is the work of Cynewulf, which survives only in manuscripts of about the year 1000 but is usually dated to the ninth century; Cynewulf's learned use of Latin sources makes it virtually certain that he was himself literate and indeed learned, and his use of runic acrostics to weave his own name into the epilogues of his four surviving poems suggests that he expected his poems to be read on the page as well as recited,

17 Keynes and Lapidge 1983, p. 75.

since the runic letters are visible in manuscript but would not be recognisable in performance. Literacy in this case would extend to the runic alphabet. Manuscripts containing poetry in English survive only from the tenth and eleventh centuries, and then in small numbers, but the existence of the Exeter Book, a large manuscript devoted exclusively to English verse, shows that the book was by the late tenth century a natural form for such texts.

Alfred himself claimed that no books had been translated from Latin into English before his own initiative around 890, which supposedly prompted versions of the works of Gregory the Great, Boethius, Augustine, Orosius and the psalms. It is true that whereas there is ample evidence for vernacular documents, glosses in or to Latin texts and books of poetry in English before his time, we cannot demonstrate with certainty the existence of substantial texts in English prose at earlier times. There are, though, a number of probable candidates from the ninth century, including the translation of Bede's *Ecclesiastical History* and the collection of brief accounts of saints and Christian festivals known as the *Old English Martyrology*, and perhaps Bald's *Leechbook*; and the report of Bede's work on a translation of St John's Gospel, if it was not just a gloss, suggests that there may have been a much earlier tradition of translation. And certainly from Alfred's time onwards the vernacular is in regular use for books of Bible translations, homilies, saints' lives, history, computus, medicine and much else.

The key question is: who was reading these books and documents, and what are the implications for literacy? As we have already seen, a fair number were explicitly produced for the use of clerics who had no Latin: clear examples are Alfred's version of the *Regula pastoralis*, designed in the first instance for the use of bishops, Ælfric's Catholic Homilies and pastoral letters, and the vernacular parts of Byrhtferth's *Enchiridion*. Others by their very nature seem targeted at the clergy (including monks in some cases): the two versions of the *Rule of St Benedict*, the English version of the *Rule of Chrodegang*, the collections of ecclesiastical laws and rulings associated with Wulfstan, the various penitential collections. But even books such as these seem sometimes to have had additional readers amongst the laity. Ælfric's preface records that Ealdorman Æthelweard was to have a copy of the Catholic Homilies, and that he and his son Æthelmær had commissioned and received in advance many of the saints' lives in his *Lives of Saints* collection (even though, as Ælfric notes, the saints in question were largely those celebrated by the monks and not the laity). Wulfstan's so-called 'pastoral letter' begins, in one manuscript, with an address to 'thegns in this nation, both cleric and lay' and was presumably circulated in written form to leading laymen as well as to clerics. While Alfred insists that there were no books for people to read in the vernacular, he nevertheless acknowledges that many could read English and does not appear to be meaning exclusively clerics. Certainly his programme of education was to focus on teaching the laity to read English and to make books available to them. According to Asser, the king's ealdormen, reeves and thegns were illiterate until Alfred pressurised them into learning to read, and insisted that those who could not manage it should get a relative or servant to read to them; it is perhaps striking that Asser does not even hint that an ealdorman in such straits might need to have recourse to a chaplain or other cleric to read to him. By the late tenth century it seems to be taken for granted that well-off laymen would deal with written texts, even if we cannot be certain that they themselves could read them. In addition to the examples noted above, we might note that Ælfric's translations of the Books of Genesis and Joshua were done at the request of the ealdorman Æthelweard, that other works of the same type were sought from him by a layman called Sigeweard of Eastholon (probably Asthall in Oxfordshire), and that he addressed writings on religious subjects to at least two other laymen, Sigefyrth and Wulfgeat of Ylmandun.

Documents, too, seem to have been part of the life of the landowning laity. Some 1,500 charters survive, stretching over the whole of the period, and although the earliest examples are concerned primarily with ecclesiastical estates, from the eighth century onwards there are charters naming laymen as beneficiaries, with no clear evidence of ecclesiastical interest, and by the late Anglo-Saxon period laymen predominate. The evidence that laymen placed considerable importance on written texts as guarantees of ownership does not of course necessarily mean that they could always read those texts: most charters are in Latin (and not always easy Latin), though often with the boundaries of the estate in English, and possession of the physical charter seems to have been more important than its contents (boundaries apart). Perhaps the most important example of lay use of written documents is the Fonthill Letter. Written in the early decades of the tenth century, this is an account by a layman, probably the ealdorman Ordlaf, of his understanding of an extremely complicated sequence of events involving the ownership of some estates and the criminality of a protégé. It is significant in itself that it uses the letter form rather than oral testimony; but if, as has been argued, the surviving copy, apparently an original, was actually written by Ordlaf himself, it is very useful evidence of the standards of literacy amongst the upper-class laity.[18] Although law books existed, apparently from an early period, Wormald has argued that

18 Gretsch 1994.

they are never invoked in the course of any of the legal cases that are reported and we cannot be certain that an ability to read them was a necessary part of legal expertise.[19] But Alfred at least expected his judges to read, and Keynes has emphasised the abundance of evidence for the importance of legal and administrative documents in the later Anglo-Saxon period, and argues, against Wormald, that written laws played a considerable part in the business of justice.[20] The implication is that a fair proportion of lay administrators were comfortable with the written word.

Many of the texts that we are dealing with here would naturally be read aloud to a group as part of their function – charters in cases of dispute, royal writs, legal pronouncements, sermons, pastoral letters, and of course poetry – and many others could have been. In a world where reading aloud and memorisation played very important roles, the distinction between being able to read a text to oneself and having assistants at hand to read texts aloud may have been comparatively unimportant. As Keynes argues, in the administrative world oral enactments and commands would have remained important, and probably more important, however common written texts were. Certainly the evidence available tells us only about the proliferation of texts of different kinds, and never offers conclusive proof that any individual, apart from a few well-known scholars, or particular class of people could or could not read. The difficulty of making sense of Asser's various remarks about Alfred's literacy, and still more of fitting them to what we otherwise know of Alfred, is a reminder of the complexity of the question. But in the spectrum that runs from oral culture to literate, laymen who recognised the authority of royal writs and charters and wills and laws, who commissioned written biblical translations and saints' lives, and who owned books, belong to the world of literacy and the written word, even if not all of them could decipher the letters or still more write. Listening to a document or text that was composed and circulated in written form is probably closer to the world of literacy than to the earlier world of oral culture suggested by Bede's story of Cædmon. Given the limited familiarity with Latin in all classes and at all periods, the increasing use of the vernacular offered greatly extended access to written texts, for both readers and listeners, and for both clerics and laity.

19 Wormald 1999, p. 143; and see Chapter 24 in this volume.
20 Keynes 1990.

30
Aldhelm's library

ANDY ORCHARD

When, in the course of his magisterial but not always wholly trustworthy history of early England, *Historia ecclesiastica gentis Anglorum*, the Venerable Bede (who died in 735) depicted his elder contemporary Aldhelm, abbot Malmesbury, then bishop of Sherborne (who was born in 639/40 and died in 709/10) as 'vir undecunque doctissimus' ('a man most learned in every way'),[1] such a description, given Aldhelm's extraordinary output and extensive influence, seems entirely appropriate even from so learned an authority.[2] In deploying such a well-used phrase Bede would likely have realised that he was echoing the acclaim that Terentianus Maurus gave Varro, as reported by Augustine in the *De civitate Dei*; but he would also surely have spotted the fact that he himself had used the same words of King Aldfrith of Northumbria (686–705) only a few chapters previously.[3] The association of Aldhelm with, on the one hand, a learned Roman widely celebrated in Continental sources and, on the other, a well-born Anglo-Saxon with exemplary Celtic connections, seems entirely appropriate; and in attempting to assess the extent of Aldhelm's library it is important to remember not only his two-stage education at the hands of teachers from very different backgrounds, but also the extent to which Aldhelm himself decried and attempted to mask the one in exalting and promoting the other. Aldhelm's library is undoubtedly a hybrid one, and his favoured authors clearly changed over time, but in his sheer exuberance, and in his extraordinary keenness to name and claim as influences a range of texts and authors all but unrivalled in Anglo-Saxon England (and indeed elsewhere), Aldhelm remains a striking index of how in his time the kingdom of Wessex (from whose royal

1 *HE*, v, 18: Colgrave and Mynors 1969, p. 514.

2 The standard edition of Aldhelm remains Ehwald 1919. Many of Aldhelm's works have been translated by Lapidge and Herren 1979 (the prose works) and Lapidge and Rosier 1985 (the poetic works).

3 *HE*, v, 12; Fox 2005, p. 225.

family he himself descended) was far from isolated, and in intellectual terms cast frequent glances both East and West.

Indeed, in giving Aldhelm such an estimable pedigree of praise, it is perhaps odd that Bede does not mention him directly as one of the esteemed alumni of the school of Theodore and Hadrian at Canterbury,[4] since it is within just such a lineage that Aldhelm seems to have situated himself, and odder still that when quoting eight lines extracted from the beginning and end of a versified epitaph for Theodore, Bede does not name the author, who may well have been Aldhelm.[5] Although he seems to have spent only a few years at the Canterbury school at some point during the period 670×680 (when indeed his time there was interrupted), and while such a patchy link may explain Bede's reticence, there is no doubt about Aldhelm's wholesale change of allegiance: he quotes Jerome, saying, 'I who thought myself learned, have I begun to be a student again?'[6]

With regard to the education that Aldhelm had at Canterbury, we have the testimony of Bede (who if he fails to mention Aldhelm as an *alumnus*, nonetheless speaks highly of the school (*HE*, IV, 2)), the witness of Aldhelm himself, and further traces from biblical commentaries that seem to be the authentic record of classroom teaching,[7] glossaries[8] and other sources. Two early Anglo-Saxon glossaries in particular stand out in this respect, namely the so-called Leiden and Épinal-Erfurt Glossaries.[9] The evidence of the Leiden Glossary, which shares with Aldhelm a detailed knowledge of the works of Rufinus, specifically of the *Historia ecclesiastica*, is particularly interesting in this regard: it has been argued that the so-called 'third Rufinus glossator', who contributed no fewer than 306 glosses, is to be identified with Aldhelm, and indeed the glossed works tally nicely with what can be deduced elsewhere of Aldhelm's reading, including works by Athanasius, Cassian, Donatus, Gildas,[10] Gregory, Isidore, Jerome, Orosius, Phocas and Sulpicius Severus, as well as Pseudo-Rufinus, *Passio S. Eugeniae*, and Pseudo-Clementine *Recognitiones* (as translated by Rufinus).[11]

In general, Bede's silence with regard to Aldhelm's association with the famed school at Canterbury is all the more striking in that Bede does

4 See further Lapidge 1986b, and the updated version in Lapidge 1996, pp. 141–68; Bischoff and Lapidge 1994; and Lapidge 1995.

5 Orchard 1994, pp. 277–80.

6 Ehwald 1919, ep. I, p. 477, lines 15–16: 'qui mihi uidebar sciolus, coepi esse discipulus?'

7 Bischoff and Lapidge 1994, esp. pp. 266–74.

8 Lapidge 1986b; Lapidge 1996, pp. 141–68; see also Pheifer 1987.

9 See now Lapidge 2010.

10 On Gildas, see Wright 1995a.

11 Lapidge 2007b, pp. 34–48.

highlight the earlier period of Aldhelm's apparently Irish-inspired education at Malmesbury,[12] an intellectual association that conversely Aldhelm himself seems deliberately to have downplayed in later life, comparing Irish teaching unfavourably with that to be had at Canterbury in two letters chiding students who, if we are to believe Aldhelm, had been lured away to Ireland by a dubious combination of spurious learning, pagan classical mythology and loose women.[13] Bede, by contrast, speaks quite favourably of Irish educational opportunities at around the same time, noting that flocks of well-born and less well-born Anglo-Saxons went west to Ireland for their education during the time of Bishop Finán and Bishop Colmán, which can be dated to the period 651–4:[14]

> There were in that place [Ireland] at that time many of the nobility as well as of the lower ranks of the English, who in the time of Bishops Finán and Colmán, had left their native island and retired there either for the sake of sacred reading or a stricter way of life. Some indeed soon bound themselves faithfully to the monastic way of life, but others rather gladly paid attention to reading, wandering about the cells of teachers; and the Irish very freely entertained all these, and took pains to offer them daily sustenance for free, books to read, and teaching without fee.[15]

Such indeed is the situation which seems to underlie the extraordinary and perplexing collection of texts known as the *Hisperica famina*, apparently Hiberno-Latin compositions of the late seventh century that depict just such groups of wandering scholars, parading their arcane knowledge in opaque, allusive and playful language.[16]

Aldhelm's caustic antipathy towards Irish education, as expressed in his own letters, is all the more extraordinary, since his own Irish connections are clear: not only was Malmesbury an Irish foundation, and (according to Bede) Aldhelm's teacher clearly Irish, but we have the evidence of a letter to

12 *HE*, v, 18; Colgrave and Mynors 1969, 514.

13 The letters in question are to Wihtfrith (no. III) and Heahfrith (no. V) repectively: Ehwald 1919, pp. 479–80 and 486–94; Lapidge and Herren 1979, pp. 154–5 and 160–4. Aldhelm's student, Æthilwald, also wrote about Wihtfrith's Irish trip: see Orchard 1994, pp. 23–4. On the background, see now Howlett 1994a; Howlett 1996.

14 *HE*, III, 27: Colgrave and Mynors 1969, p. 312. On the importance of this passage, see further Herren 1974, pp. 33–4.

15 Erant ibidem eodem tempore multi nobilium simul et mediocrium de gente Anglorum, qui tempore Finani et Colmani episcoporum, relicta insula patria, uel diuinae lectionis, uel continentioris uitae gratia illo secesserant. Et quidam quidem mox se monasticae conuersationi fideliter mancipauerunt, alii magis circumeundo per cellas magistrorum, lectioni operam dare gaudebant: quos omnes Scotti libentissime suscipientes uictum eis quotidianum sine pretio libros quoque ad legendum, et magisterium gratuitum praebere curabant.

16 See further Orchard 2000; Carey 2003–4.

Aldhelm from an unknown and anonymous Irishman (*Scottus ignoti nominis*), who salutes Aldhelm for his erudition precisely 'because you have been a visitor in Rome and above all because you were nourished by a certain holy man from our nation';[17] it has even been suggested that the 'holy man' in question was not Maeldúb, the Irishman named by Bede, but the celebrated Adomnán himself. Fragments of two further letters, an exchange between Aldhelm and the Irish Cellanus of Péronne, have also been seen as part of a 'literary war between Aldhelm and Irish scholars towards the end of the seventh century'.[18] Likewise, Aldhelm certainly had close connections with Aldfrith of Northumbria, to whom indeed he seems to have been related, and whose own Irish connections are clear.

The implications of the notion that Aldhelm was the son of King Centwine of Wessex (676–85), a suggestion documented by William of Malmesbury on the authority of the now-lost *handboc* of King Alfred, who succeeded to the crown of Wessex two centuries later, have been explored recently.[19] Such a regional and regal connection may of itself explain Alfred's apparent devotion to Aldhelm and his works, an interest also documented by William, who notes that 'nor did he neglect the composition of poetry in his native language, to such an extent that, according to the witness of the book of Alfred [*i.e.* the *handboc*] which I mentioned earlier, there was no one who was his equal in any age'.[20] Aldhelm's royal lineage, as implied by William, would make Aldhelm the grandson of a Christian convert, since Centwine's own father, King Cynegils (611–42), was baptised by Birinus in 635; as the third and youngest son of Cynegils, Centwine may well have had little hope of succession, and indeed only came to the throne some thirty-five years after his father's death, with his brother Cenwealh, his brother's widow Seaxburh, and a distant cousin Æscwine all intervening. Centwine himself was evidently a pious man, abdicating the throne after nine years to retire to a monastery,[21] perhaps the Irish foundation at Malmesbury, where Bede says Aldhelm was educated.

It has been argued that Aldhelm may have been fostered with the Northumbrian royal family, and at that period may have been educated by

17 Ehwald 1919, p. 494: 'quia tu Romae advena fuisti, insuper quod a quodam sancto viro de nostro genere nutritus es' (Letter VI).

18 Lapidge and Herren 1979, p. 149. The letters in question are nos. IX and X: Ehwald 1919, pp. 498–9; Lapidge and Herren 1979, p. 167.

19 Lapidge 2007b.

20 *Gesta pontificum*, V, 190: 'natiuae quoque linguae non negligebat carmina; adeo ut, teste libro Elfredi, de quo superius dixi, nulla umquam aetate par ei fuerit quisquam'; Winterbottom 2007, p. 506.

21 On the phenomenon, see Stancliffe 1983, esp. pp. 154–5 and 170.

Adomnán in Iona.[22] Certainly, Aldhelm's connections with the Northumbian royal house are strong: King Oswald of Northumbria (634–42) had stood sponsor to Aldhelm's grandfather at baptism and then married Aldhelm's aunt; Oswald and his brother Oswiu both spent time in exile on Iona among the Irish of Dál Riata prior to Oswald's accession, and Oswiu fathered King Aldfrith of Northumbria on an Irish woman called Fín, presumably during the same period. Aldfrith himself spent a significant amount of time on Iona, where he spoke Irish and seems to have sat at the feet of the great and holy Adomnán. On his own testimony, and perhaps as payback for Oswald's sponsorship of his own grandfather, Aldhelm had stood sponsor to Aldfrith at a ceremony of episcopal confirmation some twenty years before he sent his *Epistola ad Acircium* to the then king,[23] so pushing the date of confirmation back to some time before 666. Whatever the combined impact of Aldhelm's putative association with Adomnán and Iona and his documented relationship with Aldfrith, Aldhelm's Celtic connections are clear.

Against this background, it is scarcely surprising that echoes have been traced in Aldhelm's writings of a number of Hiberno-Latin works that seem to have been part of his Celtic education, namely Virgilius Maro Grammaticus and the 'Altus prosator', attributed to Adomnán;[24] further parallels that fall short of direct borrowing in one direction or the other have been detected with the anonymous *Hisperica famina*, mentioned above.[25] In each case, it may be important to note that the texts (or in the case of Virgilius the portions of the texts) in question have a distinctly 'poetic' flavour, albeit that none of them is metrical, since Aldhelm's use of such texts in contexts that contrast Irish learning unfavourably with that of the Canterbury school seems pointedly to highlight his evident pride at the metrical education he received from Hadrian at Canterbury.[26] In further letters, by contrast, especially that to his so-called *patronus* ('patron'), a term which may apply either to Leuthere, bishop of the West Saxons (670–6), or to his successor Haeddi (676–705/6), Aldhelm describes the Canterbury curriculum he had himself followed in some detail, giving a glimpse of the range of topics he studied, including astronomy, computus and, above all, metrical verse.[27] This last topic seems to have become something of an obsession for Aldhelm, and it is striking to note how many of

22 Lapidge 2007b, pp. 27–30. 23 *Ibid.*, pp. 22–6.

24 On Virgilius, and Aldhelm's knowledge of him, see Law 1982a, pp. 42–52, and Law 1995; on Aldhelm and the 'Altus prosator', see Orchard 1994, pp. 54–60, and Stevenson 1999.

25 Orchard 2000. 26 Howlett 1994a.

27 Ehwald 1919, pp. 475–8; Lapidge and Herren 1979, pp. 152–3.

Aldhelm's extant works can be described as 'poetic' in form or style, including those written in prose.[28]

In short, of the two main phases of Aldhelm's intellectual training, which might broadly be characterised as 'Celtic' on the one hand and 'Continental' on the other, it is striking that Bede highlights the first and ignores the second, and Aldhelm himself focuses resolutely on the second, and effectively dismisses the first.[29] Further evidence of Aldhelm's preference for the Mediterranean world of learning over that of the Irish is further alluded to in the letter of an anonymous Irishman mentioned earlier,[30] which speaks of Aldhelm having visited Rome, perhaps in the retinue of the West Saxon King Ceadwalla (685–8), who, like Centwine, abdicated the throne, going to Rome to be baptised and dying there on 20 April 689.[31] Certainly, Aldhelm shows detailed knowledge of epigraphical verse that he may have seen in Rome in situ, and while it is possible that he may have come across such poetry in a number of manuscript collections of such versified inscriptions (so-called *syllogae*) then circulating, it is tempting, given his own composition of similar inscriptional verse (namely his *carmina ecclesiastica*),[32] to associate him more directly with the collecting of inscriptions in Rome itself, and to give him a role in the creation of certain *syllogae*.[33]

Like most authors, Aldhelm appears to have had access to a diverse library that changed over time, but which comprised some texts that were regularly consulted and others that fulfilled a specific purpose for a strictly delimited period. So, for example, of some sixty named authors thus far identified as having been known to Aldhelm, and listed by Michael Lapidge,[34] it is remarkable that two dozen are attested only in what seem to have been his earliest extant works, namely the two metrical treatises *De metris* ('on metres')[35] and *De pedum regulis* ('on the rules governing metrical feet'),[36] and his *Enigmata* ('riddles' or 'mysteries').[37] These three texts, which were composed over an indeterminate period, were collected together as the composite text now known as the *Epistola ad Acircium*, evidently compiled for, and addressed to, King Aldfrith of Northumbria.[38] The *Epistola ad Acircium* closes with a brief

28 On Aldhelm's style in general, see Winterbottom 1977 (for prose); Orchard 1994, pp. 73–125.
29 For an account of the various historical phases of Aldhelm's life, see Lapidge 2007, pp. 66–9.
30 See n. 17 above. 31 Lapidge 2007b, pp. 52–64; cf. Sharpe 2005a.
32 See n. 52 below.
33 Compare Orchard 1994, pp. 203–12, Sharpe 2005a and Lapidge 2007b, pp. 52–64.
34 Lapidge 2006, pp. 178–91.
35 Ehwald 1919, pp. 61–96; Lapidge and Herren 1979, pp. 31–54.
36 Ehwald 1919, pp. 150–201; cf. Lapidge and Rosier 1985, pp. 212–19.
37 Ehwald 1919, pp. 75–149; Lapidge and Rosier 1985, pp. 70–94 and 183–211.
38 Ehwald 1919, pp. 33–204; Lapidge and Herren 1979, pp. 12–13 and 31–46.

Allocutio excusativa,[39] in the course of which Aldhelm compares himself to Vergil in a heavily alliterative passage, stating that 'No one born of our race and nourished in the cradles of the Germanic people has laboured so greatly in this kind of pastime before our humble self',[40] citing as parallel the similar claims of Vergil with regard to his introduction of the Greek genre of didactic verse on agricultural topics into Latin literature.[41] To emphasise his point, Aldhelm actually quotes *Georgics* III, 11–13 and 292–3:[42]

> For I do not reckon that in putting this forth I should be wounded by the dreadful arrows of the proud, nor am I worried that I have been pierced by the most awful shaft of swollen conceit, if for a short while, relying on the lord, I should glory concerning the freely given grace of a divine gift, which is bestowed on individuals not according to the prerogative of pre-existing merits, but through the generosity of heavenly bounty, since indeed that illustrious one, who said 'I first of all, so long as life lasts, returning to my homeland will draw down the Muses from the Aonian peak; first of all to you, Mantua, will I bring back the Idumaean palms' (and the same poet a little further follows up: 'It is a pleasure', he says 'to wander on the heights where the trace of no one earlier leads down to Castalia') I think in saying that he intended to mean that no one of the Latin-speaking peoples before him had written about georgic matters for the descendants of Romulus, even though Hesiod and Homer and other Greeks, relying on the skill of their eloquence and endowed with gift of Argive elegance, had brought forth a fourfold work on agriculture in the Pelasgian tongue.

Apart from the customarily florid language here, and the glancing allusion to Vergil as simply 'that illustrious one' (*illustris ille*), as well as to Hesiod and Homer, the last as an agrarian poet(!), the desire to equal the greatest names of classical verse is breathtakingly clear: where Vergil speaks of 'the Aonian peak' and 'the Idumaean palms', Aldhelm talks of 'Argive eloquence' and 'the Pelasgian tongue', both phrases with clear roots in hexameter verse, to the

39 Ehwald 1919, pp. 201–4; Lapidge and Herren 1979, pp. 45–7.

40 Ehwald 1919, p. 202, lines 5–6: 'Neminem nostrae stirpis genitum et Germanicae gentis cunabulis confotum in huiuscemodi negotio ante nostram mediocritatem tantopere desudasse'.

41 Thornbury 2007, pp. 71–2.

42 Ehwald 1919, p. 202, lines 10–24: 'Non enim hoc proferendo horrendis superciliorum iaculis me vulnerandum arbitror neque dirissima elationis turgidae falarica confixum perhorresco, si paulisper de gratuita divini muneris gratia, quae singulis quibusque non meritorum praecurrentium praerogativa, sed caelestis beneficii munificentia confertur, fretus domino glorier, siquidem illustris ille, qui dicebat: Primus ego in patriam mecum, modo vita supersit, / Aonio rediens deducam vertice Musas; / Primus Idumaeas referam tibi, Mantua, palmas, (et longiuscule idem poeta et infra prosequitur: iuvat, inquit, ire iugis, qua nulla priorum / Castaliam molli devertitur orbita clivo) hoc, inquam, ille versificans significari voluit, nullum ante se Latinorum georgica Romulidis scripsisse, quamvis Hesiodus et Homerus et ceteri Graeci disertitudinis facundia freti et Argolicae urbanitatis privilegio praediti quadrifariam agriculturam lingua Pelasga deprompserint.'

extent that both 'Pelasga' and 'Argolicae' appear in Aldhelm's own verse, albeit only in his *Enigmata* (at XXXV, 6 and XL, 10; and XCV, 2 respectively). Whether one ultimately traces such usages to Vergil's *Aeneid* (II, 252 and IX, 154 (*Pelasga*)), Ovid's *Metamorphoses* (I, 726 and IV, 609 (*Argolicae*); XIII, 268 (*Pelasga*)), or Statius's *Thebaid* (III, 489, VII, 688, VIII, 744, X, 65, XI, 49 and XI, 156 (*Argolicae*)), with all of which texts he can be connected,[43] Aldhelm's affinity with classical verse is here made clear,[44] and offers a striking contrast to Bede, who famously eschews such associations.[45]

Elsewhere in the composite text of the *Epistola ad Acircium* Aldhelm gestures towards a strikingly eclectic selection of authors (namely Andreas Orator, Audax, Cicero, Donatus, Ennius, Junilius, Lactantius, Mallius Theodorus, Orosius, Paulus Quaestor, Phocas, Pliny the Elder, Pompeius, Priscian, Proba, Sallust, Seneca, Sergius, Servius, Sisebut, Solinus, Terence, Valerius Probus and Victorinus). While it might be argued that many of these writers (or at least those who were not themselves grammarians) might have been available to Aldhelm second-hand through a grammatical tradition that if not by any means mainstream was at least identifiable as such, and widely cited in early Anglo-Saxon England,[46] the very fact that Aldhelm chose to parade his learning in this regard says much for his intentions. Another author on whom Aldhelm seems to have relied, particularly in the earlier part of his career, but whose influence lived on, is the apparently North African poet 'Symphosius' (whose name means '[drinking-]party-animal'), whose collection of one hundred three-line *Aenigmata* is mentioned by Aldhelm as the inspiration for his own century of *Aenigmata*. Presumably the North African Hadrian imported the works of 'Symphosius', as well as the collection of verses from the so-called *Anthologia Latina* ('Latin anthology'), a version of which was certainly circulating in North Africa at the time; in such ways, as in the curious combination of metrical terminology (thus far unsourced) that Aldhelm mentions as part of the Canterbury curriculum, it is possible to come closer to hearing Hadrian at work.[47]

Juvenal likewise appears to have supplied some verses as examples for the three texts combined in the *Epistola ad Acircium*, but also to have been remembered and recycled in both the (apparently later) *Carmina ecclesiastica* and the

43 Lapidge 2006, pp. 183 and 187–90.

44 There is a further parallel with the so-called *Versus cuiusdam Scotti de alfabeto* ('Verses of a certain Irishman on the Alphabet' (Glorie 1968, pp. 729–40), the second line of which has several parallels with Aldhelm's own verse.

45 Hunter Blair 1976; Wright 1981–2.

46 Law 1982; Law 1983; Law 1995.

47 Compare the reasoning of Law 1983, p. 51, with regard to the sources of Aldhelm's metrical knowledge.

Carmen de virginitate, and while if the evidence for Aldhelm's knowledge of Ovid's *Metamorphoses* is overwhelmingly skewed towards the *Enigmata*, it is important to note that reminiscences of other odd verses from that text resurface later in his career too. By contrast, for example, almost all of the echoes of Paulinus of Nola or Alcimus Avitus detected to date come in the later *Carmen de virginitate*.[48] For John Cassian, as one might expect, the only parallels are to be found in the prose and verse versions of the *De virginitate*, with an interesting preponderance towards the latter.

Several other authors appear to have been consulted by Aldhelm only in composing the prose *De virginitate*, including Athanasius (as translated by Evagrius), Cyprian of Carthage, Gildas, Paulinus of Milan and Pelagius; most of the material from Jerome used by Aldhelm comes into the same category, while of the books of the Bible, it is clear from his many quotations from them that of the books of the Old Testament, the Books of Genesis, Psalms and (perhaps more surprisingly) Daniel were particular favourites, whereas in the New Testament it was to Matthew among the evangelists that Aldhelm turned most frequently, with Acts and the Apocalypse also well represented. In composing both the prose and verse parts of his *De virginitate*, Aldhelm drew heavily on many saints' *Lives*. although often it is hard to identify precisely which have been used.[49]

Aldhelm's predilection for poetry in terms of language, syntax and genre is exhibited throughout his works, whether through the many references and citations found in his letters, as already noted, or in his glee at producing metrical treatises and illustrative *Aenigmata* collected together and sent to Aldfrith, or in his decision to supplement his prose *De virginitate* with a later, expanded, and in many ways very different poetic *Carmen de virginitate*,[50] so forming a 'twinned work' (*opus geminatum*) after the model of Caelius Sedulius,[51] or in producing the eclectic collection of inscriptional and dedicatory verses designed for individual churches and altars that Ehwald simply describes as 'ecclesiastical poems' (*carmina ecclesisatica*),[52] or even in echoing and surpassing the Hiberno-Latin mode of verse composition in rhythmical octosyllables in his wonderfully vivid account of a storm-tossed trip through Devon and

48 For Paulinus, see especially Wright 1985; Wright 1986.

49 See Lapidge and Herren 1979, pp. 176–8, for a 'Check-List of Sources of Aldhelm's Exemplary Virgins'.

50 The prose *De virginitate* is Ehwald 1919, pp. 213–323; the *Carmen de virginitate* is Ehwald 1919, pp. 327–471. For further discussion and translation of each, see Lapidge and Herren 1979, pp. 51–132 and Lapidge and Rosier 1985, pp. 97–167.

51 As Bede notes (*HE*, v, 18), though he has the relative order of composition wrong: Colgrave and Mynors 1969, 541; Godman 1981.

52 Ehwald 1919, pp. 1–32; Lapidge and Rosier 1985, pp. 10 and 35–58.

Cornwall;[53] in each case Aldhelm underlines the fact that his preferred mode of expression is the heightened and more ornate one of verse.

Given such a developed poetic sensibility, it is unsurprising that so many direct quotations and echoes of an astonishing range of poetry (a range unrivalled by any extant Anglo-Saxon author) should have been identified thus far. In certain cases, we can even guess that Aldhelm's close knowledge of such verses spanned both the Celtic and Continental aspects of his education. Vergil, for example, may well have been a constant companion, and seems to have been a particular favourite of Aldhelm, who echoes him freely, adopting and adapting many aspects of Vergilian diction from across the whole range of the *Aeneid*, the *Georgics* and even the *Eclogues*.[54] Within the Vergilian corpus, and to judge from the reflexes of it thus far identified, Books I, IV, VI (especially), and X of the *Aeneid* seem to have contributed most to Aldhelm's remembered reading, while of Christian-Latin poets the usual triad of Juvencus, Caelius Sedulius and Arator seems to have informed Aldhelm's poetic education,[55] with Venantius Fortunatus, another less commonly read poet, also frequently remembered and recycled.[56] Sedulius is echoed especially freely, with a particular concentration on Books I and IV of the *Carmen paschale*, and indeed a startling focus on the first 100 lines of the work. Given the evidence elsewhere that the Irish demonstrated close knowledge of Sedulius, and that both Vergil and Sedulius are the only verse sources thus far identified for the *Hisperica famina*,[57] it may be that both poets were familiar to Aldhelm from the earliest part of his education, and accompanied him closely in later life. More surprising, perhaps, is Aldhelm's apparent knowledge of poets such as Corippus, Cyprianus Gallus, Damasus, Dracontius, Horace and Statius, none of whose works seem to have circulated widely before the Carolingian period (and indeed, in the case of some, like Corippus, not even then).[58] Slight evidence exists for Aldhelm's first-hand knowledge of Lucretius, and still slighter for Ausonius, Claudius Marius Victor, Eugenius of Toledo, Paulinus of Pella, and Sidonius Apollinaris, though it is hard to be certain. Among the rarities quoted by Aldhelm are Lucan's lost poem *Orpheus*, as well as verses by such obscure authors as Paulus Quaestor and Andreas Orator, who survive as little more than names.

Unlike Bede, who is sometimes silent about the sources he uses, Aldhelm had no qualms at all about mentioning the names of those whose works he

53 Ehwald 1919, pp. 523–8; Lapidge and Herren 1979, pp. 16–18; Lapidge and Rosier 1985, pp. 171–9. See too Orchard 1994, pp. 19–72, and Miles 2004.

54 Orchard 1994; Patterson 2007.

55 Orchard 1994, pp. 161–7; McBrine 2008.

56 Lapidge 1979b; Orchard 1994, pp. 191–5.

57 See Wright 1982; Knappe 1994.

58 Lapidge 2006, pp. 116–19.

had read, or claimed to have read, or remembered, and who influenced his own. Indeed, it was such ostentation in both style and citation, by comparison with Bede's apparent restraint, that led Charles Plummer (in his edition of Bede, naturally enough) to decry Aldhelm's 'puerile pomposity'.[59] Admirers of Aldhelm might well prefer to speak of his engaging enthusiasm, which certainly seems to have been infectious: whatever the size and scope of Aldhelm's own library, we can be sure that he became required reading for generations of Anglo-Saxons to come.[60]

As a mark of Aldhelm's method, as well as the problems facing source-hunters hoping to home in on the contents of Aldhelm's library, we might examine two chapters at the beginning of Aldhelm's *De metris*, in the first of which he quotes extensively from an impressive range of poets, and in the second of which he alludes (equally impressively) to a wide variety of prose authorities. In the course of Chapter 9 of *De metris*,[61] the first in which he is obliged to offer illustrative examples, Aldhelm cites Persius, Juvenal (twice), Lucan (twice), Paulus Quaestor, Prosper of Aquitaine, the anonymous *Versus sibyllae de iudicio*, Phocas, Sisebut, Vergil (twice), Cyprianus Gallus, the Pseudo-Vergilian *Paedagogus*, Arator (twice), and Andreas Orator, a total of twenty-five complete or partial verses, all selected to illustrate different aspects of elision, a feature that Aldhelm himself notably avoids in his own verse.[62] It is impossible to argue that all these verses from such an astonishing range of sources are essential to his argument: the effect (and, one suspects, the likely intention) is simply to dazzle.

It is in the immediately following chapter that Aldhelm announces that he intends to present part of this treatise on metre in dialogue form between an imaginary teacher and his pupil (*De metris*, 10):[63]

> So, in order that the threefold regulations of the heroic hexameter can be more certainly spotted, I shall attempt to set them out snappily and summarily, just

59 Plummer 1896, I, p. liv.

60 See, for example, Orchard 1992; Orchard 1994, pp. 239–92.

61 Ehwald 1919, pp. 78–81.

62 Orchard 1994, pp. 79–84.

63 Ehwald 1919, p. 81, line 9 to p. 82, line 1: 'Igitur, tripertita heroici exametri perpendicula ut certius cognosci queant, strictim summatimque expedire conabor, sicut prisca veterum auctoritas tradidisse monstratur. Videor itaque mihi hoc planius et apertius posse patefacere, si per interrogationem et responsionem pauxillulum reciprocis vicibus stilus varietur, quemadmodum beatus Augustinus per multa librorum corpora hoc est soliloquiorum et de libero arbitrio et eo, quem de magistro praetitulavit, et sex libris de musica fecisse comprobatur, vel Isidorus duobus voluminibus, quae sinonima vel polionima praetitulantur; quod genus dictandi ab undecima appellativorum nominum specie translatum reor. Hoc itidem Iunillius, instituta regularia, quae a Paulo Persa Sirorum scolis naviter instructo didicerat, Primasio, sedis apostolicae pontifici, scribens "ne aliqua, inquit, confusio per antiquariorum, ut adsolet, neglegentiam proveniret, magistro M graecam litteram, discipulis D praeposui, ut ex peregrinis caracteribus et quibus Latina scriptura non utitur, error omnis penitus auferatur".'

as the old authority of the ancients can be shown to have handed them down. I reckon that I can explain more plainly and clearly, if for a brief interval I vary my style in a back-and-forth manner through question and answer, just as St Augustine did in the texts of many books, namely the *Soliloquies*, *On Free Will*, the one he called *On the Teacher*, and the six books *On Music*, or as Isidore did in the two volumes entitled *Synonyma* or *Polyonyma* (I think that this kind of composition was drawn from the eleventh class of common nouns). In the very same way Junilius, dedicating to Primasius, bishop of the Apostolic See, the *Regular Institutes* which he had learned from Paul the Persian, a man well instructed in the schools of the Syrians, wrote 'so that no confusion should arise, as often, through neglect of ancient things, I have assigned to the *magister* ['master'] the Greek letter M and to the *discipulus* ['pupil'] the Greek letter Δ, in order that by these foreign letters, which are not used in writing Latin, all error can be utterly removed'.

The passage is wholly in keeping with Aldhelm's ornate style, beginning as it does with some flamboyant examples of alliteration (*certius cognosci queant*; *strictim summatimque*; *planius et apertius posse patefacere*), especially of doublets (*strictim summatimque*; *planius et apertius*),[64] as well as hyberbaton (*tripertita heroici exametri perpendicula*; *prisca veterum auctoritas*; *multa librorum corpora*; *undecima appellativorum nominum specie*). Yet anyone wishing to reconstruct Aldhelm's library would be well advised to treat the equally flamboyant trailing of alleged models with some caution: despite the confidence with which Aldhelm dances lightly through the relevant works of Augustine (here *Soliloquia*, *De libero arbitrio*, *De magistro* and *De musica*), as well as quoting directly from the Preface to the *Instituta regularia diuinae legis* of Junilius Africanus, no further knowledge of any of these texts has been detected elsewhere among Aldhelm's writings. In sharp contrast to Bede, who was evidently fully familiar with a great range of Augustine's works,[65] Aldhelm was only acquainted (according to the evidence discovered to date) with a handful of other writings of Augustine beyond this list.[66]

The equally breezy reference to Isidore's *Synonyma* in this passage might at first glance seem rooted in more direct knowledge, involving as it does both a variant version of the title and some grammatical analysis,[67] but it is the latter that in fact gives the game away: the whole passage referring to Isidore is

64 The alliterating doublet *strictim summatimque* (and its variant, *strictim et summatim*) is something of an Aldhelmian favourite, appearing five times in total in his works (Ehwald 1919, pp. 75, L. 20; 81, L. 19; 153, L. 26; 162, L. 20; 286, L. 4).

65 See Chapter 31 in this volume; Lapidge 2006, pp. 196–204.

66 Lapidge 2006, p. 179.

67 On the use and knowledge of Isidore's *Synonyma* in Anglo-Saxon England, see now Di Sciacca 2008.

drawn from the *Ars maior* of Donatus.[68] Indeed, despite the impressive roll-call of texts and authors cited by Aldhelm here as models for the pedagogical technique employed in the *De metris*, it can be shown that for much of the text that follows Aldhelm closely echoes Audax, *De Scauri et Palladii libris excerpta per interrogationem et responsionem*. Indeed, so closely does Aldhelm follow Audax that one can narrow down the precise text to a version found in a single manuscript, Munich, Bayerische Staatsbibliothek, Clm 6434, with the relevant section having been copied at Friesing at the end of the eighth century from an Insular exemplar.[69]

As Vivien Law's careful and thorough analysis of Aldhelm's grammatical sources in general amply shows, earlier scholars were wont to overestimate his direct knowledge of such texts, although again Aldhelm can plausibly be identified as a conduit for the transmission of a passage from the treatise *De hexametro versu sive heroico* of Victorinus Maximus in what looks like a later reworking of his *De metris* by Aldhelm himself, a version that later influenced Boniface. This last point is important, since it seems a mark of Aldhelm's intellectual development that he was constantly adopting new texts and ideas, and some sources appear only at certain points in his career, to be cast aside when new authors, works and ideas come along. Such an explanation would account for the fact that in his *De pedum regulis* Aldhelm made little use of the same texts as he had in *De metris*, turning instead to a much wider range of authorities. Rather than drawing on Donatus directly, Aldhelm cites instead from Pompeius, *Commentarius in artem Donati*; for the etymologies of the names of metrical feet, instead of using Audax or even Isidore's *Etymologiae*, Aldhelm instead follows an anonymous text known as the *Epistula S. Hieronymi de nominibus pedum* (perhaps believing that the ascription gave the text greater authority). In his *De metris* Aldhelm had made sparse use of Phocas, *Ars de nomine et verbo*, but in his *De pedum regulis* the work is more centrally applied, along with texts that appear nowhere in *De metris*, notably Priscian, *Institutio de nomine et pronomine et verbo* and (especially) *Institutiones grammaticae*, Sergius, *Commentarius de littera, de syllaba, de pedibus, de accentibus, de distinctione*, and Solinus, *Collectanea rerum memorabilium*. *De pedum regulis* also contains traces of other grammatical works now lost, but with reflexes elsewhere in the works of later authors such as Peter of Pisa, Paulus Diaconus and Julian of Toledo.

Alas, however, having demonstrated that Aldhelm's explicit reference to Isidore's *Synonyma* noted above derives (like so much of his learning) from a

68 Law 1983, p. 48.
69 *Ibid.*, where Law notes that 'Discrepancies between this manuscript and that used by Aldhelm are so minor that Clm 6434 could easily be a direct descendant of Aldhelm's lost copy' (n. 19).

close study of grammatical works, it would be quite wrong to conclude that the *Synonyma* were therefore unknown to him. In fact, Aldhelm is the earliest witness to the so-called *ubi sunt* ('where are they now?') topos that ultimately derives from Isidore's work, and which circulates widely in Anglo-Saxon literature in both Old English and in Latin.[70] Moreover, Aldhelm chooses a highly rhetorically embellished passage derived from Isidore's *Synonyma* on this very theme to form the closing words of his *Epistola ad Acircium* (alliteration is highlighted here in bold, rhyme by underlining, and the biblical quotation in italics):[71]

> Quae est enim labentis mundi prosperitas aut fallentis vitae felicitas? Nonne simillima collatione ut somnium evanescit, ut fumus fatescit, ut spuma marcescit? *Divitiae*, inquit ps*almigrafus, si adfuerint, nolite cor apponere!*
>
> Utinam nobis praesentium rerum possessio non sit futurarum remuneratio! Utinam caducarum copia secutarum non sit inopia! Utinam lenocinantis mundi oblectamenta aeternae beatudinis non gignant detrimenta!
>
> Quin potius transacto fragilis vitae intervallo succedant suffragante Christo perpetua praemia meritorum! Quod ipse praestare dignetur, qui pro nobis in patibulo pependit, cum aeterno patre vivens ac regnans una cum spiritu sancto per infinita semper saecula saeculorum! AMEN.
>
> [For what is the wealth of a transitory world, or the happiness of a failing life? Does it not, by a most apt comparison, vanish like a dream, disperse like smoke, fade like foam? 'If', says the psalmist [Psalm 61.11], 'riches abound, set not your heart upon them.' Would that for us the possession of present goods were not a substitute for those of the future! Would that a wealth of transitory possessions did not prove a dearth of those to come! Would that the blandishments of the fading world did not produce risks to eternal blessedness! Much rather, when the brief span of fragile life is passed, should, with Christ's help, the perpetual prizes of just deserts appear! And may He himself deign to grant this, He who hung for us on the Cross, who lives and reigns with the eternal Father, together with the Holy Spirit for ever and ever, age upon age, amen.]

Aldhelm has moved far from his source here, though its parallelism of phrasing and general tenor mark the following passage clearly as such (Isidore, *Synonyma*, II, 91):[72]

> Breuis est huius mundi felicitas, modica est huius saeculi gloria, caduca est et fragilis temporalis potentia. Dic ubi sunt reges? Ubi principes? Ubi imperatores?

70 Cf. Cross 1956; Orchard 1995a, pp. 456–8; Di Sciacca 2008, pp. 105–48 and 151–4.
71 Ehwald 1919, p. 204, lines 1–9.
72 Compare Di Sciacca 2008, pp. 106 and 150–1.

Ubi locupletes rerum? Ubi potentes saeculi? Ubi diuities mundi? Quasi umbra transierunt, uelut somnium euanuerunt.

[Brief is the happiness of this world, limited is the glory of this age, fleeting and fragile is temporal might. Tell me: where are the kings? Where the princes? Where the emperors? Where are the wealthy? Where are the mighty of this age. Like a shadow they have passed, like a dream they have vanished.]

In adapting this passage from the *Synonyma*, Aldhelm has made it characteristically his own, so much so that when Boniface employs the same topos in his letters, we can be sure that he is imitating Aldhelm, not Isidore.[73] In such ways do echoes of Aldhelm's learning (and his library) linger on.

Aldhelm's royal lineage, and in particular his specific access to the Celtic-based learning of the north and north-west, as well as to the continentally based learning of the south, seems to have given him a unique and highly privileged position within the wider story of English learning, and of Anglo-Saxon libraries in general. In justifying his praise of Aldhelm as (another) 'vir undecunque doctissimus', Bede goes on to describe him as 'both sparkling in style and, as I have said, wonderfully well versed as much in literary as in ecclesiastical works'.[74] When we consider the roots of Aldhelm's extraordinary erudition, it becomes clear that Bede was right: Aldhelm is indeed a 'vir undecunque doctissimus'. But in assessing the extent of Aldhelm's library it is important to recognise the grammatical precision of Bede's words, albeit that they are not originally his own: Aldhelm is not only a man who was taught very much, but one who had his considerable learning from many different places.

73 *Ibid.*, pp. 151–5.
74 *HE*, v, 18: Colgrave and Mynors 1969, p. 514: 'et sermone nitidus, et scripturarum ... tam liberalium quam ecclesiasticarum erat eruditione mirandus'.

31
The library of the Venerable Bede

ROSALIND LOVE

In a letter written as the preface to his commentary on Genesis, addressed to Acca, bishop of Hexham (709–31), Bede listed the authors who had preceded him in commenting on the first book of the Old Testament – Basil, Ambrose, Augustine – and he observed of their writings:

> But because these are so copious and lengthy that such a number of volumes may scarcely be acquired except by the very wealthy, and so profound that they may scarcely be understood fully except by the very learned, it has pleased your holiness to assign to me the task of gathering from all these, as if from the loveliest meadows of a widely blossoming paradise, such things as should seem to meet the needs of the weak.[1]

In these words we can glimpse not only Bede's idea of his own calling – as one of the very learned, with the skill to assimilate difficult and diffuse material and pass on its import to those less fortunate – but also his sense of privilege as a beneficiary of the wealth that brought so many books his way, creating a scholar's paradise, as he saw it. Closer examination of his commentary on Genesis shows that the works mentioned in that letter to Acca were known to Bede not merely by reputation, but that copies of them lay open before him. Basil's commentary in the translation from the Greek by Eustathius, Ambrose's *Hexaemeron*, and several relevant works by Augustine (primarily his *De Genesi ad litteram* but also *De Genesi contra Manichaeos*, his *Confessiones*, and the treatise *Contra adversarium legis et prophetarum*) are just the authors and books which Bede himself named in describing his sources. Once we begin to read his commentary, we can quickly fill Bede's desk with the other works which he was able to use: writings by Jerome, Gregory, Isidore, Pseudo-Clement, Josephus,

1 Jones 1967, p. 1 ('Verum quia haec tam copiosa tam sunt alta ut uix nisi a locupletioribus tot uolumina adquiri, uix tam profunda nisi ab eruditioribus ualeant perscrutari, placuit uestrae sanctitati id nobis officii iniungere ut de omnibus his, uelut de amoenissimis late florentis paradisi campis, quae infirmorum uiderentur necessitati sufficere decerperemus'). My translation; but cf. now Kendall 2008, p. 66.

Orosius, Pliny and Vergil, as well as a relatively new work, an anonymous treatise on the order of creation (*De ordine creaturarum*), thought to have been composed in seventh-century Ireland.[2] That is already an impressive list. To consider, then, that the commentary on Genesis was just one of over forty works which Bede wrote (counting only those which survive and can be attributed to him with certainty), suggests the importance of assessing the extent of the library used by the man who was arguably the most productive of all known authors active in Anglo-Saxon England.[3]

Moreover, placed as he was in a part of England first (and still relatively recently) Christianised with the help of Irish missionaries, but in a monastic community whose founder, Benedict Biscop, brought both inspiration and actual books from Rome, Bede stands at a crossroads between two distinct influences informing England's literary culture. In that regard he is similar to his earlier contemporary Aldhelm of Malmesbury, whose education combined elements of both Irish and continental learning.[4] Another point worth emphasising is that Bede and his community at Wearmouth-Jarrow had a widespread network of contacts. In the preface to his *Historia ecclesiastica* he alludes to the assistance that he received from Nothelm in London and Albinus at Canterbury; and it may be legitimate to infer some degree of bibliographical exchange – in other words, that the library to which Bede had access could in some senses be shared around, be it by lending or by the production of fresh copies.[5] Wearmouth-Jarrow had an active scriptorium which in its heyday, during Bede's own lifetime, was able to produce high-status books both for its own use, and also (in the case of the massive bible known as the Codex Amiatinus) for export, even though subsequently, when Bede's works became popular, the community seems at times to have been pushed to the limits of its capability in the effort to meet requests for copies.[6] The eighth-century correspondence of the Anglo-Saxon missionaries to Germany contains striking examples of such requests, testifying to the forces which acted to disseminate texts more widely.

2 Jones marked many of these debts in the apparatus of his edition, with verbatim quotation italicised in the main text; I have been able to extend the list of such quotations, and sources recorded as the entries on the Fontes Anglo-Saxonici database can give a swift overview of Bede's preparatory reading: Love 2000a. See now also Kendall 2008, pp. 355–9.

3 Alcuin of York may well have written more, on word count alone, and perhaps had a wider range of interests, but he produced a fair proportion of his work on the Continent, which means that to use the sources of his known writings as an index of the books known in Anglo-Saxon England muddies the waters a little. See further Chapter 32 in this volume.

4 See in particular the recent reassessment of Aldhelm's engagement with Irish learning, including a hypothetical sojourn on Iona, in Lapidge 2007; also Chapter 30 above.

5 On Wearmouth-Jarrow as an important point of transmission for texts brought from Rome, see Ganz 2002.

6 Such a crisis is described by Parkes 1982, pp. 15–16.

To consider just one example, Boniface wrote from the German mission field to Hwætberht, abbot of Wearmouth-Jarrow, in about 746, asking him to 'copy and send us some of the treatises of that keenest investigator of the scriptures, the monk Bede'.[7] Although, as already noted, one of Bede's aims in his commentaries was to digest and render more widely accessible the wisdom of the Fathers, one imagines that such activity did not preclude the possibility that his sources themselves could be spread out along his network of contacts. In other words, identifying the books that he had is not simply to gain a snapshot of one very richly endowed and quite possibly unrepresentative collection in late seventh-century northern England, but also to see which books were there that could have been put into wider circulation.

The present essay started life as an attempt to bring up to date a much-cited article on Bede's library first published by M. L. W. Laistner in 1935, in view of the fact that the seventy years since he wrote have seen a stream of editions of Bede's works in the Corpus Christianorum series, as well as translations into English, not to mention the arrival of new scholarly tools, in the form of various CD-ROMs and online concordances to Latin texts.[8] Theoretically, then, it should prove possible to refine significantly the list of Bede's reading which Laistner placed at the conclusion of his essay. A detailed list showing which works Bede cited, where and how he cited them (that is, whether verbatim, only as a reminiscence, or simply by naming a work) is not the remit of the present chapter; and in any case, anyone who wishes to see an updated version of Laistner's list of Bede's reading can now find it conveniently set out in alphabetical order of source-author in one of the appendices to Michael Lapidge's masterly volume, *The Anglo-Saxon Library*.[9] Our aims here are rather to rehearse briefly the means by which Bede's library must have been assembled, and to consider the tools available to us for reconstructing its contents, noting their limitations, and using some specific cases to illustrate the problems.

The story of how the monasteries of Wearmouth and Jarrow accumulated their resources after their respective foundations in 674 and 682 has been told many times before, but may usefully be reviewed here.[10] In his *Historia*

7 Tangl 1916, letter 76, trans. Emerton 2000, pp. 111–12.

8 Laistner 1935.

9 Lapidge 2006, pp. 193–228. I hope eventually to publish my own fully annotated list of Bede's sources, originally intended to form part of the present article; it is based on a thorough review of all the sources cited in the *apparatus fontium* of the editions of Bede's works, and aims to provide some indication of how Bede customarily referred to the works he drew upon: that is, whether he acknowledged his source, how he named it, whether he quoted it verbatim or only paraphrased from it.

10 For example Meyvaert 1979; Fletcher 1981; Neuman de Vegvar 1987, pp. 112–15, 129–30; Marsden 1995b, pp. 79–83, on Benedict Biscop; Wood 1995, on Ceolfrith; Lapidge 2006, pp. 34–5.

abbatum Bede himself supplied crucial information about the gradual acquisition of books, exclaiming over the contents of Benedict Biscop's luggage on his return from successive trips to the Continent and to Rome. So in Chapter IV, he states that Benedict, 'completed his third [actually fourth] journey from Britain to Rome with his usual good fortune and brought back no small number of books covering every aspect of divine learning which he had either bought at a good price, or had been given by friends. On the return journey, when he came to Vienne, he collected those which he had purchased and had left with friends.'[11] Of the fifth trip, Bede reported, 'he came back laden with a good return of spiritual wares yet more plentiful than before: first of all insofar as he brought countless wealth of books of every kind'; and of the sixth, that among his luggage 'there was indeed a great wealth of holy books'.[12]

Bede went on in the *Historia abbatum* to give some hint of Benedict's attitude towards the library he had so painstakingly assembled: 'He gave orders that the most splendid and copious library which he had conveyed from Rome, for the much-needed edification of the church, should be carefully kept intact, and not spoilt by carelessness, or scattered hither and yon.'[13] It is interesting to note, however, that this care not to 'scatter' the books did not preclude using them as portable – and cashable – goods. Bede credits Ceolfrith with seeing through a transaction, first negotiated by Benedict, that land should be purchased for Jarrow from King Aldfrith of Northumbria in exchange for 'a book of the Cosmographers, of marvellous workmanship, which Benedict had bought at Rome'.[14] It is remarkable that this is almost the only book from among Benedict's acquisitions to which Bede makes explicit reference (the other being the large bible discussed below).[15] Strikingly, just before this anecdote, Bede stated, probably with some rhetorical licence, that Ceolfrith 'doubled' the libraries of both monasteries – certainly not by selling books to buy land, but presumably in part

11 Plummer 1896, I, p. 367: 'tertium de Brittania Romam iter arripiens solita prosperitate conpleuit librosque omnis diuinae eruditionis non paucos uel placito praetio emptos, uel amicorum dono largitos retulit. Rediens autem ubi Viennam peruenit, empticios ibi quos apud amicos commendauerat, recepit'.

12 Chs. 6 and 9: Plummer 1896, I, pp. 369 and 373 ('multipliciore quam prius spiritualium mercium fenore cumulatus rediit. Primo quod innumerabilem librorum omnis generis copiam adportauit' and 'magna quidem copia uoluminum sacrorum').

13 Ch. 11: *ibid.*, I, p. 375 ('Bibliothecam quam de Roma nobilissimam copiosissimamque aduexerat, ad instructionem aecclesiae necessariam, sollicite seruari integram, nec per incuriam fedari, aut passim dissipari praecepit').

14 Ch. 15: *ibid.*, I, p. 380 ('dato quoque Cosmographiorum codice mirandi operis').

15 For a conjectured identity for this now-lost book, as the *Topographia Christiana* of Cosmas Indicopleustes, see Bischoff and Lapidge 1994, pp. 209–10, and on its possible later presence at York, Ganz 2002, p. 623.

by overseeing tireless work in the two scriptoria.[16] This observation highlights the fact that Jarrow and Wearmouth must each have had their own book collection, to both of which Bede would have had access: so we should properly speak of Bede's 'libraries', though some would say that we might be better off abandoning the anachronistic notion of a 'library' altogether.[17]

More general conclusions can be drawn from Bede's narrative about the likely sources for the books in those two libraries – not only Rome, but also Gaul: Benedict received the tonsure and studied for two years at Lérins and probably formed lasting connections there; his continuing link with southern Gaul is suggested by Bede's reference to his picking up books left with friends at Vienne. Nearer to home, we may also include Canterbury, where Benedict Biscop was for two years abbot of St Peter and St Paul (later St Augustine's) before founding Wearmouth. This provides a link between Bede and Theodore, archbishop of Canterbury (602–90), who, with Hadrian (Benedict's successor as abbot of St Peter and St Paul, Canterbury), established a school whose curriculum was by all accounts extraordinarily wide.[18] That curriculum was surely served by an appropriate book collection and, via Benedict Biscop, copies or loans from it may well have made their way northwards. The *glossae collectae* preserved in the early ninth-century St Gallen manuscript Leiden, Universiteitsbibliotheek, Voss. Lat. Q.69 (fols. 7r–42r) have been seen as representative of glosses made at the Canterbury school, and of the (roughly) twenty-three texts from which those glosses derive, only four are absent from the list of Bede's reading.[19] The relatively exotic presence of Theodore and Hadrian has been seen as a means by which some more unusual books – for example those containing Greek – may have reached England, and there is no reason why such materials could not have passed northwards.[20]

There can be little doubt that some of the books at Wearmouth-Jarrow came from Ireland. In his *Ecclesiastical History* Bede described how young Englishmen of an earlier generation had flocked to Ireland to be educated, noting in particular that the reasons for going were 'either to study the scriptures or to lead a life of stricter discipline'.[21] He added that the Irish teachers

16 Ch. 15: Plummer 1896, I, p. 380.

17 Meyvaert, 1996, p. 834, and cf. Marsden 1995b, p. 103. On the concept of a 'library' in Bede's time, see Dumville 1994b, pp. 188–91.

18 On the school of Theodore and Hadrian, see Lapidge 1996, pp. 141–68.

19 These are Cassian's *De institutis coenobiorum*, Sulpicius Severus' *Dialogi*, Phocas' *Ars de nomine et uerbo*, and an anonymous *Passio S. Eugeniae*. The contents of the Leiden glossary have been listed by Lapidge 1986b, pp. 54–5, with the argument that these glosses relate to the Canterbury school on pp. 57–9.

20 Bischoff and Lapidge 1994, pp. 155–67.

21 *HE*, III, 27. Bede says that they went for the sake of 'diuinae lectionis', literally 'divine study', which I take to mean Bible study.

were most hospitable in providing 'daily sustenance, books for study and free instruction'. Some of these books surely made their way back to England and it is hard to imagine that Bede, in his thirst for information, would have passed up the chance to sample specimens of scholarship which had acquired such a reputation, whatever we may suppose his attitude was towards the Irish.[22] Missionaries coming to Northumbria primarily from Iona in the 630s almost certainly will have brought books with them, some of which may have made their way to Wearmouth-Jarrow. That was certainly not the end of contact with Columba's community: an Irish work which Bede most certainly knew is the treatise on the holy places (*De locis sanctis*) composed by Adomnán, ninth abbot of Iona, in the 680s.[23] Bede reworked and abbreviated this text to produce his own *De locis sanctis*, and is the sole witness to the means by which Adomnán's work reached Northumbria, brought as a gift by the author himself, to King Aldfrith in about 688.[24] Bede notes that Aldfrith had copies made 'for lesser persons to read', one of which was clearly in his own library, and it is not unreasonable to suppose that other books could likewise have reached Wearmouth-Jarrow from Iona's fairly well-stocked library (judging from Adomnán's own reading).

Yet we should undoubtedly envisage other routes for the passage of books and ideas from Ireland too: Irish origins have been convincingly demonstrated in the case of the computistical material Bede used, material which may have reached him indirectly by means of the south-west of England.[25] He also appears, for example, to have known two treatises composed in Ireland less than a century previously, namely *De ordine creaturarum* and *De mirabilibus sacrae scripturae*, as well as a similarly anonymous commentary on the seven Catholic epistles, which travelled under the name of Hilary of Poitiers, and which was, it has been argued, written in Ireland in the 670s.[26] As well as sharing Bede's enthusiasm for biblical exegesis, the Irish teachers to whom he refers also extended their curiosity to Latin grammar.[27] One of the most remarkable exponents of this discipline was Virgil the Grammarian (Virgilius Maro Grammaticus), whose twin works, his *Epistolae* and *Epitomae*, push well beyond the boundaries of what one would normally expect to find in a grammar book, either for satirical purposes or following some other

22 For contrasting analyses, see Thacker 1996 and Richter 1999, pp. 89–108.

23 Picard 2005, pp. 46–51.

24 An event which Bede records in *HE*, v, 15.

25 Ó Cróinín 1983 and Wallis 1999, pp. xxiii–xxv.

26 Bede's debt to *De ordine creaturarum* and the Pseudo-Hilary commentary is discussed with some detailed textual comparison by Picard 2005, pp. 51–5 and 57–60; on the *De mirabilibus sacrae scripturae* see Smyth 1996.

27 Law 1982a, pp. 85–92.

hidden agenda.[28] It has recently been suggested that Virgil's *Epitomae* came into Bede's hands, and provided some of the material for his handbook on spelling and other matters, *De orthographia*.[29]

Ireland may well have served as the conduit for books from Spain and North Africa, accounting for some aspects of Bede's identifiable reading.[30] He certainly knew a good range of the works of Isidore of Seville (d. 636), for the swift transmission of which Ireland seems to have been crucial – the *Etymologiae* (otherwise known as *Origines*), as well as his *Sententiae*, *De natura rerum*, *De ortu et obitu patrum*, *De ecclesiasticis officiis* and his *Chronica maiora*. Some scholars have suggested that Bede also had copies of two works by Julian of Toledo (d. 690), which would have been even newer at that time than those of Isidore – as we shall see below, the cases for both works offer a good example of the problems to be faced in reconstructing Bede's library.[31] One example of a North African work which looks likely to have reached Bede via Spain and Ireland is the fifth-century commentary on Donatus' *Ars* by Pompeius, whom Bede mentions by name in his *De arte metrica*, even if only to contradict him.[32]

In a discussion of a set of panel paintings which Benedict Biscop brought from Rome to adorn his newly founded monasteries, Paul Meyvaert estimated the sheer weight of some of the contents of the abbot's luggage, neatly emphasising in a very concrete way the extraordinary efforts that went into amassing the storehouse of learning upon which Bede was able to draw.[33] The tangible re-creation of Bede's library will continue to be a theme here, and clearly, then, surviving books themselves should be the starting-point. The available material of this class, however, is extremely disappointing, for precious few extant manuscripts can be identified securely as having been there in Bede's time, and almost nothing of the many books that were brought there from elsewhere. What we do have is a fragment containing some verses from 1 Maccabees, now at Durham, but written in sixth-century Italy.[34] Sad remnant though this scrap of vellum might seem, it neverthless embodies perfectly the story

28 Herren 1995 argues for Virgil's Irish identity, whereas Law 1995, pp. 2–3, takes a more cautious view.

29 Picard 2005, pp. 56–7; cf. the suggestion that the *Epitomae* were an indirect influence upon etymologies which Bede provides in his *De temporum ratione*, in Bracken 2006.

30 On Spain and Ireland, and Bede's knowledge of Spanish works, see the case developed across a sequence of articles by Hillgarth 1961, 1962 and 1984.

31 See p. 622 below.

32 Bede, *De arte metrica*, I, 41 ('Falsoque definiuit Pompeius S non posse liquescere'): Kendall 1975, p. 90. On the transmission of Pompeius' work see Holtz 1971 and Hillgarth 1984.

33 Meyvaert 1979, p. 75, calculates that the works of Gregory the Great alone would have weighed over 45 kilos.

34 DCL, B.IV.6, fol. 169*: *CLA*, II, no. 157; Marsden 1995b, pp. 83–5.

of the Wearmouth-Jarrow library. Richard Marsden has shown, on the basis of the likely size of the complete page from which the fragment comes, that it belonged to a part-bible, containing just a few books of the Old Testament, which must have been exactly the kind of manuscript that was being brought into England in quantity.[35] Textual evidence, as well as layout on the page, suggests that this fragment came from one of the exemplars used to create the three great pandects written at Ceolfrith's behest. Its origins in Italy match up exactly with the book-collecting activity of Benedict Biscop and with the stream of books which followed in the wake of Augustine and his fellow missionaries, represented most famously by the Gospels of St Augustine, produced in sixth-century Italy.[36]

We can add to the Maccabees fragment the surviving books known to have been produced in the Wearmouth-Jarrow scriptorium in Bede's lifetime.[37] The most famous of these is the massive bible mentioned above, the Codex Amiatinus, and its two sisters, together making up the 'three pandects in the new translation' (that is, Jerome's Vulgate), the production of which his anonymous biographer included among Ceolfrith's achievements. Scholars continue to debate the sources of inspiration for the production of these pandects, but one thing seems certain, namely that the idea of creating a volume containing the whole of both Old and New Testaments under one cover, in large format, was prompted by one of the books which Ceolfrith brought from Rome. Although the monks of Wearmouth-Jarrow, Bede included (at least to begin with), seem to have had no idea of the origin of that pandect – that it was one of the bibles made in the sixth century for the use of his monastic community at Vivarium by Cassiodorus Senator, who referred to it as his 'Codex Grandior' ('bigger' to distinguish it from the other bibles he had commissioned) – it must have exuded a powerful mystique, not least if it was anywhere near the dimensions of the Codex Amiatinus.[38] The other books which can be assigned to Wearmouth-Jarrow on the basis of script are liturgical books – gospels, psalters – and copies of Bede's own writings, and then finally a fragment of Gregory the Great's *Moralia in Job*, written in a hand very similar to that of the Codex Amiatinus.[39] Bede's writings betray his profound familiarity with Gregory's works and he can be found citing the *Moralia*, often extensively, in

35 Marsden 1995b, pp. 43–5.
36 CCCC, 286. On the likelihood of a connection with Augustine, see Marsden 1999.
37 Described by Parkes 1982.
38 On Bede's detective work in eventually realising that the Codex Grandior had at least belonged to Cassiodorus, see Meyvaert 1996, restated in Meyvaert 2005, pp. 1100–1.
39 New Haven, Yale University, Beinecke Library, 516: Bischoff and Brown 1985, no. 1849; Lutz 1973.

at least fourteen of his own works. Whether this fragment represents a copy of the *Moralia* produced at Wearmouth-Jarrow for use there or for sending elsewhere, in its dimensions and Uncial hand it can nevertheless give us some impression of a book which was frequently to be found at Bede's elbow.

One further survivor is worthy of consideration, namely a manuscript of relatively small format containing a small selection of the *Carmina natalicia*, hymns composed in the early fifth century by Paulinus for the annual feast of St Felix of Nola – material that very likely reflects the interests of Hadrian, who had come to England after a time presiding as abbot over a monastery in Campania.[40] Vatican City, Biblioteca Apostolica Vaticana, Pal. Lat. 235 dated to the early eighth century, contains six of these hymns, and was copied (from an Insular exemplar) somewhere in Northumbria, either Lindisfarne or Wearmouth-Jarrow.[41] The same six hymns, in the same order, are likewise preserved in a sister manuscript, dated to the first half of the eighth century and also identifiably Northumbrian in origin.[42] Bede used these same hymns to compose his own *Vita* of Felix, as well as to provide specimens of verse in his *De arte metrica*, and Thomas Mackay has shown that his copy belonged to the same branch in the textual transmission of Paulinus' hymns as the two eighth-century Insular manuscripts, albeit that Bede seems to have had a 'better' text.[43] The Vatican copy may well come very near to providing an impression of Bede's own.

Among the surviving liturgical books connected with the Wearmouth-Jarrow scriptorium is the so-called Stonyhurst Gospel of St John, thought to have been sent as a gift to Lindisfarne, and it has been tentatively suggested that other books which a later medieval Durham librarian marked implausibly as 'from Bede's hand' ('de manu Bedae') might have come from the same source.[44] One of these manuscripts may serve as an example of the hazards of trying to match up Bede's reading with surviving books. Durham Cathedral Library B.II.30 contains an eighth-century abridgement of Cassiodorus' *Expositio psalmorum*, and the later inscription, 'de manu Bedae' raises the question of whether this book represents the version of that work which Bede had.[45] The truth is that Bede knew Cassiodorus' commentary and quotes it extensively, including portions which were omitted from the Durham epitome, so that whatever copy he was using was the full three-volume version;

40 Mackay 1976, pp. 78–9.
41 *CLA*, I, no. 87; Brown and Mackay 1988. The hymns in question are nos. 15, 16, 18, 28, 27, 17.
42 St Petersburg, Russian National Library Q.v.XIV.1: *CLA*, XI, no. 1622.
43 Brown and Mackay 1988, pp. 41–50.
44 Brown 1989, p. 153; TCC, B.10.5, DCL, A.II.16 and B.II.30.
45 Mynors 1939, pp. 21–2.

but whether that entirely discounts any connection between B.II.30 and Wearmouth-Jarrow is hard to say.[46]

More speculatively, we might attempt to summon the ghosts of Bede's books by considering other manuscripts sometimes hesitantly assigned to seventh- and eighth-century Northumbria. One such is the fragment of Rufinus' translation and continuation of Eusebius' *Ecclesiastical History* written in Irish Half-Uncial.[47] Opinions have varied as to whether the book from which this fragment comes was made in Ireland or Northumbria, or at a house on the Continent with Irish connections, possibly Bobbio in Italy.[48] This is a work with which Bede was definitely familiar, and regardless of whether we are willing to contemplate the possibility that this last surviving bifolium was ever in Northumbria or not, we may still permit ourselves to use it in order to imagine the probable size and format of Bede's copy.[49] We shall consider other candidates in due course. Yet more distant echoes of the lost books of Wearmouth-Jarrow can arguably be found in books surviving from the Continent which have features suggestive of an exemplar written in England, particularly Northumbria, or in Ireland, and also in the story of the textual transmission of works believed to have been in England.[50] This evidence at the very least can be used to establish or confirm that a work apparently cited by Bede was likely to have been available to him.

There is no surviving library catalogue from Wearmouth-Jarrow. Though we are grateful enough that he did place a list of his own writings at the end of his *Historia ecclesiastica*, Bede did not leave us anything comparable to the famous versified booklist which Alcuin, writing in the 780s, included in his poem on the bishops, kings and saints of York.[51] So the one last resource available to us for building up a picture of the books to which Bede had access, is to identify the sources which he quoted, or alluded to, in his own writings (as Laistner did in the essay already cited).

Before proceeding further, it is essential to emphasise that in attempting to reconstruct Bede's library in this way, we should approach the evidence of identifiable quotations with caution. Laistner observed that Bede may have

46 Bailey 1983.

47 In the Wormsley Library (Collection of Sir John Paul Getty); Bischoff and Brown 1985, pp. 348–9 (no. 1864); Fletcher 1999, pp. 2–3.

48 Breen 1987 arguing for Ireland; Hammond Bammel 1993 suggesting the Continent.

49 For the conjecture that the scribe of this fragment followed the layout of his sixth-century exemplar very faithfully, see Hammond Bammel 1993, pp. 510–11.

50 An example of the first approach is the list of eighth-century manuscripts from the area of the Anglo-Saxon mission in Germany provided by Lapidge 2006, appendix C, and of the second Dumville 1995a.

51 For Alcuin's poem, see Godman 1982; also Chapter 32 below. Bede's bio-bibliography occurs in *HE*, V, 24.

gained access to some works by the same kind of inter-library loan which I have already mentioned as working in the other direction – that is, that he may have taken notes from books only temporarily available to him.[52] The procedure for data-collection which Bede himself described in the preface to the *Historia ecclesiastica*, namely Nothelm's researches at Rome, suggests that we can never be absolutely certain of precisely which works Bede had in 'his' library. If notes could be brought back to Wearmouth-Jarrow about papal correspondence, there seems no reason why Bede could not have had a scrapbook of notes on other subjects: one can easily imagine a request such as 'copy down for me everything you can find at Canterbury about the Book of Revelation, dear Albinus' or the like. We can gain the distinct impression that Bede had a keen interest to know which books were in the possession of others – and that he quite possibly arranged to borrow them – from a stray reference in his work known as *On Eight Questions*, a collection of answers to the queries of others. There Bede referred to a book with illustrations which has been variously interpreted as a copy of Arator's versification of the Acts of the Apostles, or an account of the Passions of the martyrs, imported from Rome, and he referred to details of its pictures in such a way as to imply that he must have seen it.[53] Bede sought to explain why St Paul said that he had received thirty-nine lashes on five occasions by reference to a picture showing the torturer with a four-thonged whip:

> the fact that it should be understood in this way, and was thus understood by the ancients, is attested by a picture in the same book, which the most venerable and learned Cuthwine, bishop of the East Angles [bishop of Dunwich, sometime between 716 and 731], coming from Rome, brought with him to Britain, in which book almost all the sufferings or labours of that apostle were depicted in the appropriate places.[54]

This illustrated volume was seemingly not the only desirable book in Cuthwine's library, since a ninth-century copy of Caelius Sedulius' *Carmen paschale*, now in Antwerp, was made from an exemplar which included a subscription recording Cuthwine's ownership.[55] At any rate, there can be no

52 Laistner 1957, pp. 118–19.

53 Foley and Holder 1999, p. 151, suggest Arator's *Historia Apostolica*, following earlier commentators cited in their note, and Lapidge 2006, p. 27, proposes a *Passio S. Pauli*.

54 *PL*, xciii, col. 456 B–C; 'Quod ita intelligendum, ab antiquis ita intellectum, testatur etiam pictura eiusdem libri, quam reuerendissimus ac doctissimus Cudum Orientalium Anglorum antistes, ueniens a Roma secum in Britanniam detulit, in quo uidelicet libro omnes pene ipsius apostoli passiones sive labores per loca opportuna erant depictae.' See Foley and Holder 1999, p. 151, for the suggestion that this illustrated volume was loaned to Jarrow.

55 Museum Plantin-Moretus, M.17.4: Alexander 1978b, no. 65; Dumville 1995b, p. 104.

mistaking that Bede had seen one of Cuthwine's books; yet we cannot safely conclude that it was ever part of his library.

In the context of reconstructing another now-lost library, that of York, it has been observed that we should not necessarily take absence of citations from a text to mean that an author did not possess a copy of that work.[56] Yet an argument from silence is not of the strongest kind, and a good example of the treacherous territory that must be negotiated here is the debate about whether Bede's library could have contained Cicero's handbook on rhetoric, *De inventione*, despite a conspicuous lack of quotations from it (or even allusions to it) in his writings, at least at the present state of our knowledge. Roger Ray made a case for Bede's deployment of the rhetorical strategies recommended by Cicero, arguing that he was familiar with antique theory in a way only explicable by direct access to *De inventione*.[57] As support for the notion of that work being read in England relatively early we might look to the fragment of a late ninth-century copy said by the scholar who first discovered it to show signs (characteristic abbreviations and letter confusions) of having been copied at Würzburg from an Insular exemplar.[58] But both of these propositions have been put aside as flimsy evidence in the most thorough investigation of classical rhetoric in Anglo-Saxon England to date.[59] As we have seen, perhaps the most impressive book brought to Wearmouth-Jarrow was Cassiodorus' massive pandect, his 'Codex Grandior': in the same influential work in which Cassiodorus referred to the making of that bible, his *Institutiones divinarum et saecularium litterarum*, he alluded also to the copy in 'his' library (*bibliotheca mea*) of Cicero's *De inventione* along with the fourth-century commentary on it by Marius Victorinus, and to the fact that he had made up for the monks at Vivarium a readily portable copy of *De inventione* bound up with Quintilian's *Institutio oratoria*.[60] If we were for a moment to imagine Ceolfrith confronted by the choice of spending his precious resources on one or other of these books – the 'Codex Grandior' or a small-format book on Roman rhetoric – it is not difficult to see where his money would go.

There is a similar peril in filling the silence of Bede's failure to quote from a given work by the assumption that he must surely have known the text in question. There can be no mistaking the high regard Bede had for Gregory the Great and his writings, of which he seems to have known the majority.[61] Yet it

56 See Godman 1982, p. lxvii on the library at York. Also Chapter 32 in this volume.
57 Ray 1987, pp. 14–15; he has restated his case more recently in brief in Ray 2006, pp. 27–8.
58 Würzburg, UB, M.p.th.f.185; Thurn 1977.
59 Knappe 1996, pp. 113 and 151–6. For an English summary of her findings, see Knappe 1998.
60 On Cassiodorus' *Institutiones*, see Halporn 2002, especially p. 54 on *De inventione*.
61 Meyvaert 1964; DeGregorio 2010.

is very striking that when Bede came to compose a commentary on the Song of Songs, though he felt drawn towards Gregory's views on it – to the extent that the final book of his commentary consists of a compilation of the fifty-three places in Gregory's works (the homilies on Ezekiel and on the gospels, the *Moralia in Job* and the *Regula pastoralis*) where the pope discusses a passage from the Song – at no point does he mention the existence of Gregory's own homilies on the Song of Songs, nor does he quote from them. It is difficult to believe, then, that he possessed a copy.[62]

Whatever our view of arguments from silence, we certainly cannot restrict our list of Bede's reading to those authors and works which he named explicitly as his sources. It is well known that Bede had devised a system of abbreviated source-marks for his principal authorities, which he explained in the preface to his commentary on the Gospel of Luke as useful because it was tiresome to have to write out the full names Ambrose, Augustine, Gregory and Jerome every time he cited their work, but important lest he be accused of stealing their words.[63] Aside from this handy reference system, Bede did very often name his source as introduction to a quotation, but by no means in a systematic way; the nature of his style, particularly in his biblical commentaries, means that sometimes quotations were worked seamlessly into the texture – that is, their source was not always explicitly acknowledged. It is not without its own interest to note which authors Bede almost always named when he cited them, and those whom he tended to pass over silently. Just to consider one contrasting pair, he names the Jewish historian Josephus nearly one hundred times – in phrases such as 'Josephus reports' ('refert iosephus') – whereas, although he can be seen making extensive use of various works by Isidore of Seville, he chose to name the Spaniard just three times, and always, perhaps significantly, in order to contradict or correct him.[64]

Hence the other stumbling-block in the path of anybody wishing to use Bede's reading to reconstruct his library is the fact that, despite the appearance of new editions since Laistner's essay, we are still far from achieving a definitive catalogue of works cited by Bede. Such citations are customarily recorded in the *apparatus fontium*, but it has often been precisely that part of the modern editions of Bede's works that has elicited the strongest criticism, because while some of them are thorough and careful, others have

62 This is the view of Holder 1999, p. 372, thus dismissing the source identifications offered in Hurst 1983; he likewise expresses doubt (pp. 370–1) that Bede could have known Origen's commentary in the Latin translation by Rufinus.

63 Hurst 1960, p. 7 (lines 105–15); the practice is discussed by Laistner 1933, and more recently Stansbury 1999.

64 See Wallis 1999, pp. lxxx–lxxxii, for a discussion of Bede's use of, and attitude towards, Isidore.

hardly proved adequate in 'answering to the demands of modern scholarship', to echo Laistner's words.[65] Admittedly in these balmy days when computer-assisted searching begins to take the place of reading texts and knowing them well, it is all too easy to feel superior; nevertheless some of the source identifications offered in the annotations to these editions are too vague or simply misleading.[66] My own work on the sources for Bede's commentary on Genesis, and more recently on Bede's knowledge of John Chrysostom's writings, has suggested that a very great deal still remains to be discovered about his reading, by a painstaking process of interrogating every single paragraph he wrote, a lifetime's task.[67]

The ideal way of proceeding is to take any list of Bede's likely reading derived from identifiable citations, and think of it in terms of that which is tangible, in other words, in terms of *actual* books. Such a method would, for example, seek to correlate the works cited with what is known of later copies and their transmission, with an eye to typical groupings of works in surviving manuscripts or to the question of whether longer texts tend to circulate as a whole, or in subsections (that is, only Books 1–5 of a given work). Examples of the benefit brought by this kind of approach will emerge from the account that follows.

Bede concluded his *Historia ecclesiastica gentis Anglorum* with a brief autobiography and a list of his writings, including this summary of his vocation:

> I have spent all the remainder of my life in this monastery and devoted myself entirely to the study of the scriptures. And while I have observed the regular discipline and sung the offices daily in church, my chief delight has always been in study, teaching, and writing … From the time I became a priest until the fifty-ninth year of my life, I have made it my business, for my own benefit and that of my brothers, to make brief extracts from the works of the venerable fathers on the holy scriptures, or to add notes of my own to clarify their sense and interpretation.[68]

Here we gain an insight into Bede's scholarly priorities and can begin to imagine the kind of materials that he would have needed to fulfil his calling – books which he would have deemed essential, and those which might have been on his wish-list for acquisition at Wearmouth-Jarrow. It is, of course,

65 Lapidge 2006, p. 35; Laistner 1957, p. 118. Cf. the comments of Dolbeau 1996, p. 106 n. 5.

66 For example, see the well-founded criticisms made by Löfstedt 1987 and 1988; Dolbeau 1996, p. 106 n. 5 and p. 120; Holder 1999, pp. 370–1; and Brown 2005, pp. 85–7.

67 Jones' edition of the commentary on Genesis was of high quality and the source identifications mostly accurate and well founded, but it was still possible to add to them for some thirty passages in the first two books.

68 *HE*, v, 24.

another matter to assume that his concerns matched those of the men who had worked to establish the libraries at Wearmouth-Jarrow. Gerald Bonner has commented, 'Benedict Biscop and Ceolfrith had not faced laborious and dangerous journeys to Rome to build up a classical institute. As a result, Bede's is a theological library, designed for a monastery inspired by the spirit of the Benedictine Rule.'[69] He goes on to suggest that there would have been a utilitarianism about the building-up of resources for the two new communities.[70] Yet Bonner's observations come within an article that has a dangerous circularity about it: he notes the pioneering nature of Laistner's article on Bede's library based on citations in his writings, and then continues, 'from this list it appears that the authors used by Bede are predominantly ecclesiastical, with the writings of the greater Latin Fathers being most abundant'.[71] A page or so later, Bonner states: 'the monastic and utilitarian character of the library available to Bede explains the character of his work'.[72] The circularity of this may be crystallised as follows. Question: how do we know what books he had access to? Answer: almost exclusively from citations in his predominantly ecclesiastical works. Question: why did he write the things he did in the way that he did? Answer: because he had a predominantly ecclesiastical library. With little other evidence to use for our reconstruction of that library apart from that which Bede wrote we may struggle in vain to evade the clutches of this 'trap'. In considering whether Bede knew the work of Cicero we have already imagined Ceolfrith making a choice between the sacred and the secular. Yet one wonders whether it is wholly accurate to suppose that he and Benedict Biscop had only utilitarian and spiritually motivated aims when they went on book-buying expeditions. Can there have been other cultural aspirations too? Ian Wood suggested that Biscop and Ceolfrith may have had a slightly different idea of utility from ours, with aspirations to attain the high cultural benchmark of everything that Rome stood for.[73] One might legitimately ask whether their gaze can have passed beyond papal Christian Rome to the more distant pagan antique Rome and its literary culture. There is a sense in which the use of elevated Latin, not merely as a means of communication but with the degree of elegance and sophistication that can be found in some of Bede's prose and certainly in his verse, suggests a desire, even if half-conscious, to be part of a larger continuum than that of the apostles of Rome, St Peter and St Paul.[74]

69 Bonner 1973, p. 80. 70 *Ibid.*, p. 81. 71 *Ibid.*, p. 80.
72 *Ibid.*, p. 82. 73 Wood 1995, p. 15.
74 On Bede's metrical excellence see Lapidge 1993b, and for an exploration of his prose style, Sharpe 2005b and Shanzer 2007.

At any rate, Bede's own stated enthusiasms were to study, to teach and to illuminate the scriptures. The capacity to study and the first beginnings of teaching lie with a knowledge of Latin, for which grammatical texts would be required. Unlike his countrymen of a later generation Bede does not seem to have composed his own elementary grammar book, but we can gain access to his reading in this area through his three treatises *De arte metrica* and *De schematibus et tropis* aimed at a higher level of study, and especially from *De orthographia*, intended perhaps as a handbook for use in the scriptorium.[75] The task of establishing the sources for these works has proved complex, however, not least because books on grammar are necessarily likely to say similar things, and the processes by which such works developed was cumulative and frequently imitative. Thus the source identifications in the twentieth-century editions of these works offer an often bewildering array of alternative possibilities for any given passage, and the well-informed but non-specialist reader might be hard-pressed to work out whether what Bede says in his *De orthographia* about the Latin verb 'to remember' ('memini') derives from the early fourth-century six-book *Ars grammatica* by Marius Victorinus, or the one in five books by Charisius from later in the same century, or the roughly contemporary three-volume work by Diomedes, or from the fifth-century *Ars* by Phocas or from that by Cledonius, or Pompeius' fifth-century commentary on the grammar book of Donatus, or even the earlier commentary by Servius.[76] It seems unlikely that Bede consulted all of these books to compose his short entry on 'memini'; indeed we might well wonder whether he actually had access to them all, and scholars have suggested various ways of coming to a clearer (and perhaps more cautious) view of which ones he did have.[77] If the list for this category of text still seems to suggest a large pile of tomes – Lapidge includes some twenty-five grammatical texts, treatises on orthography and verse works in his list – it is helpful to come back to a mental image of the books themselves, and to the question of how many individual works would in reality be found within one volume.[78] One example will suffice here, namely the small-format compilation made in Northumbria possibly during Bede's lifetime, containing three commentaries on Donatus, those of Pompeius (extracts) and Sergius, and the very recently composed (*c.* 700) *Expossitio Latinitatis* by the so-called 'Anonymus ad Cuimnanum'. These three works may well have started life separately, as they are certainly written by different hands, but were probably put together

75 The purpose of *De orthographia* is explored by Dionisotti 1982b, pp. 121–2.
76 Jones 1975, p. 34, lines 680–3.
77 See, for example, Dionisotti 1982b, and Irvine 1986.
78 A point made by Holtz 2005, p. 17.

relatively early on. The book had reached Murbach by about 800, and is now at St Paul in Carinthia.[79] Interestingly, two parts of the codex were at some point folded lengthways, suggesting that they may have been carried in a pocket: we cannot determine when that happened, but the idea offers a fascinating glimpse of the day-to-day use of this kind of text.

A consideration of the identifiable sources for Bede's treatise on rhetorical figures, *De schematibus et tropis*, offers a good example of the difficulties confronting us. The Corpus Christianorum editor, Calvin Kendall, suggested Julian of Toledo's *Ars grammatica* among the sources for a good many passages in the text.[80] At the time Bede was writing, Julian's would have been a relatively new work, composed only in the 680s. As we have seen, books from Spain do seem to have made their way to Northumbria with remarkable speed, and this work would certainly be a case in point. Yet older research had already shown that all the passages in Bede's work supposedly indebted to Julian can better be accounted for by a source common to them both, a version of the third part of Donatus' *Ars maior*, the so-called 'Christian *ars*', composed in the fifth or early sixth century, possibly in Italy, and now lost completely.[81] As an aside it should be noted that another work of Julian's, the one for which he was probably best known, namely his *Prognosticon futuri saeculi*, should probably also be excluded from our catalogue of Bede's library. Charles Jones suggested a passage from the *Prognosticon* as a parallel for Bede's statement in his *Letter to Plegwine* that Christ became man during the course of the Sixth Age, but that the exact duration of that Age would remain known only to the Almighty.[82] There is indeed a comparable statement at the beginning of the third book of Julian's *Prognosticon*, but a similar observation, and one that is rather closer to Bede's words, can also be found in Isidore's *Etymologiae* (v, xxxix), significantly at the conclusion of an enumeration of the events which mark each of the Six Ages in the form of a mini-chronicle, concluding with the statement 'The time that remains of the Sixth Age is known to God alone' ('residuum sextae aetatis tempus Deo soli est cognitum'). Bede most assuredly knew this section of Isidore's work well, because he had used it to create his own lesser chronicle, placed at the end of his first handbook on chronology, *De temporibus*. More recently it has been proposed that the

79 Stiftsbibliothek, 2.1: *CLA*, x, no. 1451–3; on the significance of this compilation of works see Irvine 1994, pp. 280–2.

80 The case for Bede's use of Julian's work was argued by Beeson 1924.

81 Schindel 1968, elaborated in Schindel 1975, pp. 72–6, 95, and supported by Knappe 1994, pp. 237–8. An English account of Schindel's findings can be found in Franklin 2002, pp. 65–6.

82 Jones 1980, p. 625 ('cursum uero saeculi nullo nobis certo annorum numero definitum, ipsius solum Iudicis cognitum esse scientiae').

Prognosticon was known both to Bede and to Wynfrith (Boniface), on the grounds that their ideas about the otherworld are similar to Julian's, but the evidence does not seem compelling.[83]

Moving on from grammar to the centre of Bede's life, the scriptures, it is obvious that his 'library' must have included biblical texts in various formats, including, as we have noted, a remarkable pandect in the 'old translation', namely the Codex Grandior. In a monastic community whose living fibre was worship and prayer, the scriptures would have been in daily use in the church, and one can hardly speak of gospel-books, psalters or other kinds of liturgical books as part of a 'library'.[84] Yet there is a point worth making here, that Bede's work as a student and interpreter of the scriptures led him inevitably to an interest in seeing more than one version of them, for the purposes of comparison and the attainment of the 'truth'. A fascinating example is the difference in Bede's understanding of the original Greek of the Acts of the Apostles between his first attempt at a commentary on that work and his subsequent supplement to – and correction of – it, in his so-called *Retraction on Acts*. The difference in understanding has been linked to a surviving manuscript, a bilingual Greek/Latin copy of Acts from sixth- or seventh-century Sardinia, which seems to have come into Bede's hands.[85] We can no longer establish for certain, however, whether the Greek text of Acts became accessible to Bede in the period which intervened between the composition of his two commentaries because of the book's arrival at Wearmouth-Jarrow, or simply because with time's passage painstaking study had 'opened' a volume that had been there all the while.[86]

In order to shed light on the scriptures, Bede will have required the copious volumes to which he referred in the quotation from his commentary on Genesis with which we began. Such work, aiming to unpack both the allegorical and spiritual significance and the broadly historical context of the Holy Word would depend not only upon the commentaries of the Fathers, both Latin and Greek in Latin translations, upon sermons and theological works, but also on other scholarly tools, such as handbooks of onomastics, topographies of the Holy Land, books on natural history, even medical textbooks (Bede quotes at

83 Kabir 2001, pp. 93–5.

84 This is a distinction made by Lapidge 2006, who excludes liturgical books from his discussion.

85 BodL., Laud Gr. 35: *CLA*, II, no. 251. On Bede's versions of Acts see Laistner 1937, and on his knowledge of Greek Dionisotti 1982b (with a note on the bilingual copy of Acts, p. 128 n. 4).

86 Scholars have in the past imagined that Laud Gr. 35 was one of the books to arrive with Archbishop Theodore, but a note of caution is sounded by Bischoff and Lapidge 1994, p. 170 n. 156, on the basis of evidence suggesting that the book was still in Sardinia in the second half of the seventh century.

length from Cassius Felix' *De medicina* to explain the nature of the dysentery which St Paul cured in Acts 28.8), as well as accounts of the early church. We have already had occasion to mention one surviving Northumbrian book from this category of text, the fragment of Gregory's *Moralia in Job* at Yale. Another which will give some idea of the way texts tended to be grouped together is Kassel, Gesamthochschulbibliothek, Theol. fol. 21, a manuscript produced in eighth-century Northumbria (it is not known where) and later used at Fulda.[87] It contains Ambrose's *De apologia prophetae David* and two works by Jerome, one being his commentary on Ecclesiastes, which Bede cited on a number of occasions. This codex is of small format, its dimensions (340mm × 265 mm) closely similar to those of the Durham Maccabees, the Wormsley Eusebius (extrapolating from its fragmentary state), and the grammar book mentioned above, all presumably intended to be practical, relatively portable books.

Much has already been done to identify the sources for Bede's biblical exegesis, that is to shed light upon the books which Bede had in this category, but there is plenty of ground left to cover. Lapidge mentions well over one hundred separate relevant works in his list of Bede's reading, including nearly fifty by Augustine alone (not including individual sermons and letters). There are, however, notes of caution to be sounded here.

Among the works which Bede mentioned in the list of his own writings (in *HE*, v, 24), is a compilation of references to St Paul in the writings of Augustine, which has not yet been edited but which provides a rare insight into Bede's working methods, as well as a lesson for source-hunters.[88] Bede described the work, which has come to be known as the *Collectio in Apostolum*, thus: 'in apostolum quaecumque in opusculis sancti Augustini exposita inueni, cuncta per ordinem transcribere curaui' ('everything I have found on the subject of the apostle [Paul] in the works of St Augustine, I have taken care to transcribe in order'). This compilation of Augustine's observations on Paul, plucked from a broad swathe of his writings, was clearly a notebook similar in its purpose to the final book of Bede's commentary on the Song of Songs, in which excerpts from Gregory the Great are strung together for convenience. One might assume that such a compilation stood to add quite significantly to the number of Augustinian texts which we can envisage in Bede's library.[89] Closer analysis of the work has, however, had the reverse effect, principally once it was realised that Bede had drawn some part of the material in

87 *CLA*, VIII, no. 1134.

88 The compilation has never been printed; for a translation, see Hurst 1999.

89 Wilmart 1926, p. 48; a fuller account of Bede's *Collectio* was subsequently printed by Fransen 1961.

the *Collectio* directly from the vast *Excerpta* of Augustine's works made in late fifth-century Naples by Eugippius.[90] This debt seems beyond doubt because there are cases in which Bede's excerpts do not extend beyond those offered by Eugippius or share some peculiarity with his *Excerpta*, such as a textual error or misattribution.[91] Lapidge estimates that Bede's debt to Eugippius could reduce the number of Augustine's works which we think he knew at first hand from forty-eight to as few as eighteen.[92] Still to be established is Bede's wider use of Eugippius' compilation, a task that requires the pursuing of isolated and sparing citations of Augustine in his other writings in order to check for matches with the intermediate source.[93] We can hazard a guess at the means by which Eugippius' *Excerpta* came to be at Wearmouth-Jarrow: an obvious conduit, given the work's origins at Naples, would be Hadrian, with his Campanian connections.[94]

An acknowledgement of this debt to Eugippius detracts somewhat from our sense of Bede's *Collectio* as a treasure-trove of evidence about his library, and also highlights the very obvious dangers of a dependence on identifiable citations alone as an index of first-hand reading. How many other such collections of *excerpta* or florilegia have thus far escaped our attention which might crisply snatch other volumes from Bede's book-chests? Elsewhere I have shown that the extent of Bede's familiarity with the voluminous writings of the Greek Father, John Chrysostom (alias John of Constantinople), can be readily accounted for by the circulation in England of a single volume, containing a collection of thirty-eight Latin homilies purporting to be by 'Iohannes episcopus Constantipolitanus', but mostly in reality anonymous and some of them not even translations from Greek at all, probably bound up with two or three treatises genuinely by John and translated into Latin.[95] Every occasion upon which Bede names John explicitly as a source or authority can be thus accounted for, but what is also worth noting is that material from the collection of thirty-eight homilies can, furthermore, be identified as the source for a number of passages in Bede's exegesis which had not previously been suspected to be quotations from elsewhere.[96]

90 The evidence is set out by Fransen 1987.

91 See *ibid.*, p. 192 for a list of these.

92 Lapidge 2006, p. 36.

93 Details of this dependence are supplied by Fransen 1987.

94 Cf. the suggestion that Hadrian could have consulted Eugippius' library at Naples in Lapidge 2006, p. 20.

95 Love 2007; on the homily collection see Wilmart 1918, Wenk 1988 and Hall and Norris 2011.

96 Love 2007, p. 84. Lapidge's list of the contents of Bede's library includes for John Chrysostom only a *Homilia in diem natalem*, cited as source for a short section of his commentary on Luke; as I have shown in the article just cited, the passage in question derives rather from an anonymous treatise on the birthdates of Christ and John the Baptist, which Bede also used in *De temporum*

A feature of Bede's reading in earlier works of exegesis and preaching that is perhaps worthy of mention in passing is the extent to which his own works offer precious testimony to texts which have otherwise all but perished. We may with justification share Lapidge's sense that reconstructing vanished libraries 'is a very depressing business', since with the loss of Bede's library went books which may well already have been quite rare. For example, Bede used two works of Julian of Eclanum, *De amore* and *De bono constantiae*, to comment on the Song of Songs, and his extensive quotations from them are the only surviving fragments of both texts.[97] Relatively recently it has also come to light that Bede's works provide testimony to the text of certain sermons of Augustine otherwise only transmitted in one surviving manuscript, and in some cases to sermons otherwise now entirely lost.[98]

Whatever our view of the kind of monastic rule under which Bede must have lived out his days, there is some sign that he had a copy of the *Rule* of Benedict, in evidence here and there in his commentaries and homilies.[99] He also cites from the *Conferences* of John Cassian on a number of occasions, though not his *Institutes*, which regulate the monastic institution rather than the spiritual life of the monk. One other work that was a staple of monastic reading and that can also safely be included in Bede's library is Evagrius' Latin translation of Athanasius' *Life of St Antony*, the founding father of the eremitic life.

Next we come to Bede's interest in time-reckoning, and more generally in the recording of Christian history. As already mentioned, some of his computistical materials are thought to have come ultimately from Ireland. Faith Wallis has shown that the core texts on this subject travelled in a computus anthology, gathering to themselves other scientific materials broadly relevant to the central subject matter, and that Bede had before him just such a compilation in preparing his two treatises on time-reckoning, *De temporibus* and *De temporum ratione*.[100] As regards other scientific and technical works in the book collection at Wearmouth-Jarrow, Bede's reading suggests only the short translation of Greek medical lore by Cassius Felix, already mentioned, and some but clearly not all of the thirty-seven books of Pliny the Elder's *Natural History*. For the latter, we have an early eighth-century large-format

ratione. At the present state of our knowledge, then, the works of John (translated into Latin) which Bede certainly knew are the treatise *Quod nemo laeditur*, and two homilies (both included in the collection of thirty-eight homilies), *De proditione Iudae* and *De cruce et latrone*.

97 Bruckner 1910, pp. 9 n. 5, 72 n. 5, 74–5, 107–8.

98 Dolbeau 1996.

99 Van der Walt 1986 supplemented by DeGregorio 2005 and 2008.

100 Wallis 1999, p. xxii, and for a detailed list of Bede's computistical sources, pp. lxxii–lxxix.

manuscript from Northumbria, which contains only Books 2–6, and not all of those now.[101] Finally Bede used a book which at first glance seems an unlikely item for a monastic library, the *Epitome rei militaris* by the late fourth- or early fifth-century author Publius Flavius Vegetius Renatus, which provides not only a detailed account of the equipment and organisation of the Roman army, but also discusses atmospheric conditions and tides.[102] Here and there among the editions of Bede's works the epic poem *De natura rerum*, by the Roman philosopher Lucretius, is cited as a possible source for scientific information. For Bede to have had a copy of this remarkable account of Epicurean philosophy through an investigation of matter would be striking indeed, but none of the three cases where it is suggested as a source is in the least convincing, and to admit Lucretius to the Wearmouth-Jarrow library we would need compelling evidence of other kinds.[103]

It is in the area of historiography that scholars have been the most inclined to pass comment on the inadequacies of Bede's library: its historical collection has been described as 'serviceable, though not specially remarkable' and 'not an ideal library for a great historian'.[104] To some extent our view of that inadequacy may depend on what we suppose Bede's 'needs' to have been. His focus will have been first of all on the explication of the scriptures: here he depended heavily on invaluable sources such as the translations of Josephus' *Jewish Antiquities* and his *Jewish War* (by Cassiodorus and Hegesippus respectively), on Eusebius' *Ecclesiastical History* and *Chronicle*, the former translated and reworked by Rufinus, the latter by Jerome, and on the continuation of Eusebius' work by Prosper of Aquitaine and by the sixth-century Byzantine chronicler Marcellinus Comes. We have already had fleeting sight of Bede's well-thumbed copy of Eusebius (page 615 above); another surviving manuscript, although not known to have been connected with Northumbria, may fairly be said to offer a reasonable approximation to his copy of the *Jewish War*. A sixth-century Italian manuscript of this text had reached England by the eighth century, was perhaps at Nursling in Hampshire, and then made its way to Fulda in Germany, to judge by annotations, some of them in the hand which has been identified as that of Boniface.[105] It has been noted that Bede

101 Leiden, Universiteitsbibliotheek, Voss. Lat. F.4, fos. 4–33: *CLA*, x, no. 1578.

102 Jones 1932.

103 Cf. the views of Wallis 1999, p. 14 n. 19. On the case for an Insular dimension to the transmission of Lucretius, see Dumville 1995a, pp. 220–2.

104 Laistner 1957, p. 100; Ogilvy 1968, p. 5.

105 Kassel, Gesamthochschulbibliothek Theol. Fol. 65: *CLA*, viii, no. 1139; see Ker 1957, p. 157, on scratched glosses in Anglo-Saxon Minuscule; and Lapidge 2006, p. 40, for the suggestion that the book was in the library at Nursling.

did not have access to the other widely used account of the Eastern church, the *Historia tripartita*, translated at Cassiodorus' behest by Epiphanius from the histories of Socrates, Sozomen and Theodoret.[106] This hastily prepared work has often been criticised for its many errors, and we may well wonder whether Bede's quick eye would have been very impressed by it.[107] The world chronicle which Bede included as Chapter 66 of *De temporum ratione* shows that in addition to these sources he also had a compendium of Roman history in the form of Eutropius' *Breviarium*, as well as Orosius' *History against the Pagans*, and that he also had Isidore's *Chronica maiora*. For the biographies of individuals, he used Jerome's *De viris inlustribus* and its supplement by Gennadius, and for news of Rome's bishops and the popes also the *Liber pontificalis*.[108] Several of these same works underpin the earlier sections of Bede's history of his own people – at their head Eusebius-Rufinus as the defining inspiration and stylistic model.[109] To them we can probably add the *Historia Francorum* by Gregory of Tours (which may partly have given Bede the idea to conclude the *Historia ecclesiastica* with a literary autobiography), and certainly also Gildas' *De excidio Britanniae*, not, some would say, strictly a work of historiography, but for Bede nevertheless a vital source of information as well as of moral tone.[110]

Moving on now through his intellectual interests, Bede also wrote Latin verse to an accomplished standard and looked to advise others on how to read and compose it, so he will have needed handbooks on metrics and prosody, and examples of earlier Latin poetry. For this he need have looked no further back than the group of Christian Latin poets who from the fourth century onwards produced hundreds of lines of verse, paraphrasing the scriptures, treating of spiritual matters, or celebrating the saints: Avitus of Vienne, Caelius Sedulius, Cyprianus Gallus, Dracontius, Juvencus, Prudentius, Paulinus of Nola, Venantius Fortunatus, not to mention his own countryman Aldhelm, whose *Carmen de virginitate* and poem-riddles or *Enigmata* Bede knew. I have already quoted Bonner's view that the founders of Wearmouth-Jarrow were not looking to spend their precious resources setting up an institute for classical studies, but recent analyses of Bede's identifiable reading suggest that he had access to more classical Latin verse than we might have expected.[111] Poetry does, on the whole, present particular difficulties with regard to the safety of drawing too many conclusions from a single parallel or reminiscence in one

106 Levison 1935, p. 133. 107 O'Donnell 1979, pp. 215–17.

108 A glance at the index of sources for the translation of *De temporum ratione* gives a good indication of the extent of Bede's debt to them, Wallis 1999, pp. 449–64.

109 On Rufinus as the model for Bede's style in the *Historia ecclesiastica*, see Shanzer 2007.

110 Levison 1935, p. 132, suggests Gregory's influence on Bede.

111 Lapidge 2006 includes Horace, Juvenal, Lucan, Martial, Persius and Claudian.

line of Bede's total poetic output. As was skilfully demonstrated by Andy Orchard in his study of Aldhelm's habits, Anglo-Latin poets tended to rely heavily on the recycling of verses, and upon remembered reading of the works of earlier poets. He noted in particular Bede's tendency to mask borrowed poetic phrases by substituting metrically equivalent synonyms into them.[112]

An extra problem comes with the acknowledgement that grammarians and those who wrote on metrics tended to offer snippets of verse as examples, thus potentially introducing the reader to a great variety of poets indirectly. Here lies a cautionary tale within a cautionary tale. In an article written to commemorate the thirteenth centenary of Bede's birth, Peter Hunter Blair sought, perhaps rather ungraciously in the context, to deny Bede his copy of Vergil by suggesting that every citation he made from that poet's work can be traced to an intermediate source in a grammar book or the like: in other words that his knowledge of Vergil was entirely second-hand.[113] Hunter Blair shored up his argument by pointing to divergences from the received Vergilian text which Bede took over from his intermediary sources, and to particular collocations of groups of lines within such sources. In theory this is exactly the sort of caution with which we should approach using isolated quotations to make any generalisation about an author's reading. Yet, as Neil Wright subsequently showed, Hunter Blair had not taken account of the quotations and reminiscences of Vergil's lines in Bede's longest poem, the hexameter *Life of Cuthbert*.[114] The textual evidence adduced by Wright to show Bede's direct use of Vergil's works for his own epic poem is convincing on its own, quite apart from the other weaknesses that he identifies in Hunter Blair's argument. While acknowledging Bede's undeniably direct dependence upon earlier grammarians, he shows that there are several more Vergilian quotations than previously realised, which cannot be accounted for in this fashion.[115] It seems highly likely, then, that there was a copy of the *Aeneid* as well as Vergil's *Bucolica* and *Georgica* at Wearmouth-Jarrow. In this context it is also perhaps worth noting Lapidge's recent suggestion that Vergil was being studied on Iona in the earlier seventh century, and that Aldhelm may have been one of those who benefited from that study: one might, then, consider the possibility that Bede's own copy of Vergil came from this quarter.[116] The case is thus quite different from that of Horace, for example, from whose verse just four stray lines are identifiable in Bede's works: there is one each in his *De*

112 Orchard 1994, p. 260.
113 Hunter Blair 1976, especially pp. 244–7.
114 Wright 1981, especially p. 363.
115 Wright 1981, pp. 372–4. For further reinforcement of the point, see also Irvine 1994, pp. 277–9.
116 On the study of Vergil at Iona, see Lapidge 2007, pp. 29–30; cf. Chapter 28 above.

arte metrica and *De orthographia* from Horace's *Ars poetica* and *Sermones*, in both cases clearly lifted within longer passages drawn from an intermediate source, Servius' *De finalibus* (where Bede incorporates Servius' variant reading of the line in question) and Charisius' *Ars grammatica* respectively.[117] It is Charisius, incidentally, who provided Bede with his two citations – evidence for the gender of the word *menda* ('spot, blemish') – from that most unlikely of texts for a Northumbrian monk's library, Ovid's *Art of Love*.[118] Then in his *Commentary on Proverbs* (II, xi), Bede has a proverbial utterance from Horace's *Epistulae*, I, 2 ('semper auarus eget') which he used again in Homily II, 4.[119] Rather than supposing that he had a copy of the *Epistulae*, it is more convincing to envisage that he read that tag in Isidore's *Etymologies* (X, 9), or perhaps in Jerome's exegesis of Isaiah (I, ii, 7) or Ecclesiastes (V, ix, 127), both of which he knew and used extensively.[120] Elsewhere in the same commentary on Proverbs (II, xxii) a further two lines from the *Epistulae* can be traced to Augustine's *City of God*, I, 3.[121] The more one studies Bede's working habits, the clearer it becomes that he was an alert reader who by some means or other squirrelled away useful scraps of text for redeployment in a different context later on.[122]

There is one final genre of literature to mention, and that is hagiography. As well as his twin *Lives* of Cuthbert, his reworkings of *Lives* of Felix of Nola and Athanasius, Bede also composed a so-called historical martyrology, which does not survive in its original form, but only within later expanded martyrologies. Nevertheless, a core of Bedan entries can be identified.[123] His stated aim was to note not only the date and place, but also a few details about the circumstances of the martyr's death, details which he seems to have drawn from written accounts of their *Lives*. It is a fascinating task to match the thumbnail sketches he provided in the martyrology with the very many source texts – *Vitae* and *Passiones* – he used, almost watching his eye scan down the page for the same few themes and phrases: brothel, branding-irons, cudgels, beheaded.[124] Bede clearly had a large number of individual hagiographical texts (almost fifty distinct items lie behind the martyrology in total) and one wonders in what form he had them. We are brought again here to the question of actual books, since there is no surviving evidence for

117 Jones *et al.* 1975, p. 101, line 38, and p. 55, line 1188.
118 In *De orthographia*, lines 708–9; Jones *et al.* 1975, p. 35. There is some evidence, however, that Bede had access to Ovid's *Metamorphoses*: Lapidge 2006, p. 221.
119 Hurst and Hudson 1983, p. 72, line 117, and Hurst and Fraipont 1955, p. 211, line 151.
120 Adriaen 1963, p. 32, and Lagarde *et al.* 1959, p. 295.
121 Hurst and Hudson 1983, p. 113, lines 66–7; Dombart and Kalb 1955, p. 3, lines 9–11.
122 See Love 2007, p. 86.
123 See Quentin 1908 and Dubois and Renaud 1976.
124 For a catalogue of the sources for his martyrology see Love 2000b.

large compilations of saints' *Lives*, so-called passionals or legendaries, before the mid eighth century, the earliest surviving example from the Continent being the so-called 'Codex Velseri', written possibly at Soissons and containing twenty-four martyr narratives.[125] It is only from the early ninth century that we find anything comparable surviving for England, namely Paris, BnF lat. 10861, a collection of eighteen *passiones* copied at Canterbury.[126] More research is required into the possible exemplar or sources for that compilation, and whether it reflects materials that had been in circulation in England for some time. For example, one detail about its contents to catch the attention is the fact that it includes a distinctive version of the *Passio* of St Felix of Thibiuca which matches the version known to Aldhelm, Bede and the *Old English Martyrology*.[127] At any rate, I find it on the whole more convincing to envisage a book or books of this kind at Wearmouth-Jarrow than sheaves of lives in the form of individual pamphlets or *libelli*.[128] Bede did, however, observe that Acca at Hexham was an avid collector of the hagiographical texts which might serve to support the great number of saints' relics he had assembled (*HE*, v, 20, referring to *historias passionis eorum*, 'the narratives of their suffering'). This may hint at a profusion of scattered texts assembled from various quarters.[129]

Altogether the breadth of Bede's reading is undeniably impressive, and Lapidge concludes his analysis with the observation that Wearmouth-Jarrow 'was the largest library ever assembled in Anglo-Saxon England'.[130] His own list of books cited runs to just over three hundred items (not including separate letters or homilies, but including the separate *passiones* just mentioned). As has already been suggested, the number of codices accommodating this great range of texts would be significantly fewer, and here and there I have also pointed to individual items which should perhaps on closer consideration be omitted from a list of the contents of Bede's library. We might nevertheless be looking at a remarkable collection of just under two hundred books, of diverse origins and ages. Yet in his Jarrow Lecture George Hardin Brown has warned against getting things out of proportion, and reminds us to allow Bede some real gaps in his knowledge.[131] To be sure, comparison with the extraordinarily wide reading of Aldhelm highlights the limitations of Wearmouth-Jarrow's collection, principally with regard to Latin verse and perhaps also grammatical

125 BSB, Clm. 3514; see Philippart 1977, p. 31.

126 Brown 1986. 127 *Ibid.* p. 125.

128 For the suggestion that Bede had a passional, see Love 1996, p. xv.

129 See Lapidge 2005 on Asser's composition of a now-lost martyrology using the *passiones* he had collected.

130 Lapidge 2006, p. 37. 131 Brown 1996, p. 3.

texts.[132] Scholars have noted other areas of weakness, for example in historiography, as we have already seen, and also in philosophy, though one might well wonder whether this last is as much a reflection of the topics on which Bede chose to write, or perhaps felt himself called to write, as it is a consequence of deficiencies in the materials to hand.[133] Here again a wise observation from Brown's Jarrow lecture offers a helpful corrective: that Bede's educational agenda was monastic rather than scholastic, moralistic rather than abstractly speculative; and Lapidge has noted more recently that at base Anglo-Saxon libraries were functional and assembled in a carefully directed fashion.[134] Also speaking at Jarrow nearly twenty years before Brown, J. D. A. Ogilvy observed, with some irony, 'better a Bede at Jarrow than a dunce in the British Museum'.[135] Bede did indeed have much of what he needed in the books that were around him, and with great intelligence and practical common sense he made the best possible use of them; it is undeniably a sadness that his book collection has disappeared almost completely, but his own prodigious writings do allow us to discern its outlines.

132 Orchard 1994, pp. 219–21, lists verse known to Aldhelm; and cf. the list of his reading assembled in Lapidge 2006, pp. 178–91.
133 Bonner 1973, pp. 88–9.
134 Brown 1996, p. 6, and Lapidge 2006, pp. 128–9.
135 Ogilvy 1968, p. 6.

32

The library of Alcuin's York

MARY GARRISON

Where books are kept
Small roofs hold the gifts of heavenly wisdom;
Reader, learn them, rejoicing with a devout heart.
The Wisdom of the Lord is better than any treasures
For the one who pursues it now will have the pathway of light. [1]

York's remarkable eighth-century library supported a school of European renown.[2] By the third quarter of the ninth century, the school had long since faded from prominence, and the books that had not been dispersed were probably destroyed during struggles with Danish invaders. The library's floruit had spanned a mere few decades – the careers of two teachers. The evidence for the accumulation, contents and character of the books collected at York differs significantly from the evidence available for the libraries of Canterbury and Wearmouth-Jarrow: vivid *obiter dicta* from letters and a handful of poems that lend themselves more easily to sketching a portrait in a landscape – albeit one in chiaroscuro – than to reconstructing a precise catalogue. Yet the evidence for York Minster's library might just as aptly be compared to a long beam of light as to materials for a portrait, for it illuminates not just library history, but early medieval intellectual history and the social world of a unique book collection and of learning more generally – and this, almost entirely from the distinctive perspective of a single individual, Alcuin of York (d. 804).

1 Alcuin, *Carmen*, 105, i: Dümmler 1881, p. 332; see Bullough 2004, p. 322 n. 24 and p. 326 n. 36. Line 3 requires emendation; Dümmler proposes 'mundi' for 'donis' and Bullough, 'patris'. I thank Francis Newton for sharing his translation (which has improved my own) and suggesting the emendation 'domni' for 'donis', which I have adopted. Note that the poem was probably not intended for York.

2 For accounts of the York library, see Barr 1977, pp. 487–539; Lapidge 2006, pp. 40–2 and, for a full list of the conjectured contents of York's library, pp. 228–33; Lapidge 1985, pp. 33–89 at 45–9; Bullough 2004, pp. 256–74; Holtz 1997, pp. 45–60; Hunter Blair 1976, pp. 239–60. I would want to acknowledge particular debts to Lapidge, Bullough, Gneuss and Holtz: the accounts of Bullough and Lapidge should be consulted for full detail about individual works and manuscripts connected with York.

Alcuin would be remembered as 'the most learned man anywhere to be found' or as 'a man most learned in every field'.[3] His learning drew students to the school of York from Ireland, and even from the Continent.[4] It also led the great Frankish ruler Charlemagne to enlist him as an advisor. And so Alcuin spent the second half of his life in Francia, first at Charlemagne's court and later at Tours, where from 796 he served as abbot and continued to teach. Alcuin often emphasised his intellectual debt to his own teacher, Ælberht of York, who had travelled to the Continent in search of new books and new subjects of study.[5] As a result of these expeditions, the breadth of instruction at the school of York surpassed that of Bede's Jarrow.[6] And whereas Bede had had no students of his stature able to carry on his tradition by teaching or writing at his level, Alcuin's tenure at the school of York marks the first time one can trace clear intellectual genealogies across several generations in the early Middle Ages.[7] Alcuin's departure from York means that it is not in Northumbria but on the Continent where his intellectual progeny can be traced; it was there that he wrote the vast majority of his works, and there, too, that he exported at least some part of the remarkable library that had been the foundation of his, and York's, eighth-century intellectual eminence. In short, the intellectual harvest of the eighth-century York library and school came to fruition on the Continent: this gives the library European, rather than merely Insular, significance and also underlies the difficulties in ascertaining its contents.

3 Einhard, *Vita Karoli Magni*: Holder-Egger 1913, ch. 25, p. 30; on the phrase and its origins, see Wallach 1959, pp. 2–3; Fox 2005, p. 215; Garrison 1997, p. 99.

4 Altfrid, *Vita Liutgeri*: Diekamp 1881, chs. 10–11; trans. Whitelock 1979, no.160, pp. 787–8.

5 Alcuin, *The Bishops, Kings, and Saints of York*: Godman 1982, lines 1455–7, pp. 114–15 (hereafter this work will be referred to in abbreviated form as 'Alcuin: York poem': Godman 1982). Godman's translations will be used unless otherwise noted; Holtz 1997 should be consulted for suggestions for repunctuation of some crucial passages. On William of Malmesbury's erroneous attribution of the library to Ecgbert, see Barr 1977, p. 488, and William of Malmesbury, *Gesta Regum Anglorum* I: Mynors *et al.* 1998, i.65.3, pp. 96–7 and William of Malmesbury, *Gesta Pontificum*: Hamilton 1870, p. 246.

6 On York Minster's school superseding the status of Jarrow in the age of Bede: Levison, 1946, p. 153; Hunter Blair 1976, pp. 254–5. Bede's own learning was vast, but it is not clear that he offered or oversaw systematic instruction in all disciplines. In contrast, scribal discipline and organisation at Wearmouth-Jarrow after Bede reached a level apparently without parallel due to the demand for Bede's works, as Parkes 1992 has shown.

7 The contrast may reflect the difference between a monastic school and a cathedral school able to enrol extra-mural students who came to study because of the renown of the school rather than because they had been given to the religious community. Alcuin was remembered as the teacher of a generation of scholars, bishops and abbots; Notker, *Gesta Karoli*: Haefele 1959, I, 2 and 8, pp. 3 and 11; Berschin 1988, see the *grammaticorum* διαδοχή, pp. 123–5 – which makes Alcuin the student of Hrabanus, and Smaragdus the student of Alcuin. Bede's student's name is forgotten but may have been transformed into Simplicius, teacher of Hrabanus. The list is very muddled, but the essential contrast between Alcuin's clear place in a continuous intellectual genealogy and the confusion about a successor for Bede is telling.

Because the books had been collected on the Continent, and because Alcuin spent the second half of his career there, the task of reconstructing York's eighth-century library is bedevilled by significant obstacles. Extant manuscripts from the remains of a lost library that had been obtained chiefly from diverse sources (rather than copied in situ) would not be identifiable by palaeographical evidence: fewer than half a dozen books have been conjecturally identified as having been copied at York in the second half of the eighth century[8] and York does not appear to have been organised for systematic book production at the time.[9] Quotations and allusions in Alcuin's prolific Continental prose writings cannot, for the most part, be treated as straightforward evidence for works he had read in York. There was apparently no catalogue of the collection. But even if Alcuin had not moved to the Continent, whatever remained of York's eighth-century library would surely have shared the fate of other early medieval Northumbrian centres – destruction during the ravaging by the Great Heathen Army (AD 866–7) which afflicted churches and monasteries across Northumbria as far north as the Tyne. The devastation that occurred in York was exceptionally severe: within one year it endured violent capture by the Vikings and a still more violent but unsuccessful attempt at recapture by two ousted Anglo-Saxon kings; a year later it was again attacked by the Danes 'with their accustomed cruelty'.[10]

Counterbalancing the shortcomings in the manuscript evidence, there are testimonies about York's remarkable eighth-century library scattered through various contemporary writings, especially letters, but also poems, one of which is a uniquely illuminating source: Alcuin's versified account of the history of York. In this, his longest poem (known by its editorial title, 'The Bishops, Kings and Saints of York') written for his York Minster colleagues and former students,[11] Alcuin included detailed and affectionate reminiscences of Ælberht's activities as a teacher and book collector. Alcuin named forty-one authors, though without mentioning which of their works were available. Thanks to this account and to scattered references in Alcuin's other

8 For fuller discussion, see below. Lapidge, 2006, pp. 41–2; compare Alcuin, York poem: Godman 1982, pp. 122–7 (apparatus); Bullough 2004, pp. 260–74; Hunter Blair 1976.

9 For evidence that Ælberht had trouble arranging for copying, see Koaena (Ælberht), ep. 125: Tangl 1916, pp. 261–2.

10 Simeon of Durham, *Libellus de exordio*: Rollason 2000, II, 6 (pp. 94–9, 'solita crudelitas' at pp. 98–9); Lapidge 2006, pp. 44–6 on the fate of Anglo-Saxon libraries in the ninth century.

11 The apostrophe to the youth of York at line 1409 establishes York as the primary intended audience. The poem was nonetheless transmitted on the Continent. For an important alternative view of the intended audience, see Riché 1976, p. 383.

writings, it is possible to glimpse the cultural world of the library – how and why the collection was gathered and transmitted, how exceptionally it was valued, and the range of studies it sustained – and to estimate its size: about a hundred volumes.[12]

The Minster would of course have had books before Ælberht's collecting began. The works necessary for ecclesiastical life at a cathedral engaged at first in missionary work and then pastoral care must have been gathered from the start – individual books of the Bible, gospel-books, psalters and liturgical books, calendars, eventually penitentials and canon law. The volumes that served a cathedral's needs would have been institutional property and would have been stored separately from the books used for teaching.[13] Just as the evidence for the teaching library is closely associated with personal initiative, so too the scattered testimonies about the earliest Minster books are also connected to known individuals. Thus Wilfrid was believed to have donated a splendid copy of the gospels in two volumes,[14] and an 'antiphonary and missal' thought to have belonged to Gregory the Great came to York, either through Wilfrid or perhaps earlier, with the first missionaries, Paulinus and James the Deacon, who would in any case have brought essential books.[15] In 735 under Ecgberht, the Minster was elevated from a bishopric to an archbishopric. His pontifical (a liturgical book containing the rites performed by a bishop) survives in a later copy, the earliest extant from Anglo-Saxon England.[16] With the elevation of York to archiepiscopal status, Ecgberht will have had to extend the educational programme and so it is reasonable to suspect that he will have played some role in the genesis of the teaching collection.[17] Indeed William of Malmesbury would later (erroneously) celebrate Ecgberht as the prime mover behind the school and library.[18] Yet contemporary evidence for both school and library points entirely to Ælberht and Alcuin.[19] To their role in gathering and using what one might call York's 'teaching library', and to the curriculum that it supported, we now turn.

12 The combined testimony of the York poem, Alcuin's devotional florilegium *De laude Dei* and a small number of other writings associated with eighth-century York, including the *Miracula Nyniae* and Egberht's *Succinctus dialogus ecclesiasticae institutionis*, can illuminate the works available: Lapidge 2006, p. 41 and 228–33, esp. 231–3. Bullough 2004, pp. 135, 177–80; For the *Miracula Nyniae* written at York: Lapidge 1990, reprinted 1996; Vollmer 1905, pp. xiii and following; Orchard 1992, pp. 114–16; Levison 1940; on *De laude Dei*: Constantinescu 1974.

13 Lapidge 2006, pp. 60–2, 127; Lehmann 1957, pp. 2–5; Gameson 2006a, pp. 13–16.

14 Barr 1977, p. 487. 15 *Ibid.* 16 *Ibid.*; BnF, lat. 10575.

17 Barr 1977, p. 488, Bede, *Epistola ad Ecgberhtum*: Plummer 1896, I, pp. 405–23, at 405–6.

18 William of Malmesbury, *Gesta Regum Anglorum*, I: Mynors *et al.* 1998, I, 65, 3, pp. 96–7, and his *Gesta Pontificum*: Hamilton 1870, p. 246.

19 Barr 1977, p. 488.

Collecting the library and the range of subjects studied

The range of subjects that Ælberht taught had included not only the seven liberal arts – the trivium of grammar, rhetoric and dialectic and the quadrivium of astronomy, arithmetic, geometry and music – but also natural history, history,[20] chant, verse composition, computus and of course biblical exegesis. This scheme of learning far exceeded what was necessary for the basic pursuit of the Christian life.[21] There is no such direct evidence for an equivalent breadth of study anywhere else at the time. The range of the curriculum is all the more remarkable when contrasted with the minimal expectations for clerical learning prescribed in the provisions of eighth-century church councils, both Anglo-Saxon and Frankish.[22] The books that made this wide-ranging programme possible were, according to Alcuin, entirely the result of Ælberht's initiative and his great devotion to the pursuit of wisdom.

> More than once, [Ælberht] took the pilgrim's route to foreign lands
> with joy, led by love of holy wisdom and hope of
> finding new books and studies there
> to bring back with him.
> He travelled devoutly to the city of Rome,
> rich in love of God, visiting holy places far and wide.[23]

20 Not in the subject list but implied by the booklist, Alcuin, York poem: Godman 1982, line 1549, pp. 124–5.

21 On the range of study, see Holtz 1997, pp. 47–51; Bullough 2004, pp. 252–326; Fox 2005; Riché, 1976, pp. 395–6: for the minimal learning required for basic ecclesiastical life, compare the provisions of the Council of Clovesho of 747, which stipulated that clergy should only be able to preach, baptise and assign penance, with no requirement to know Latin (Haddan and Stubbs 1869–78, III, p. 363, ch. 6) and alluded to the recitation of the psalms by those ignorant of Latin (*ibid.*, III, p. 366, ch. 10); and compare also the minimal standard required by Charlemagne's capitularies, even those thought to have been drafted by Alcuin: Holtz 1997, pp. 50–3, esp. p. 53, for the contrast between, on the one hand, the limited 'grammatical apprenticeship' required to ensure the correctness of language and accuracy in holy books and, on the other, the range of study, of the liberal arts and beyond, pursued at court. Bullough 2004, p. 252, on an Irish fourfold scheme of ecclesiastical learning: divine canon, history, number, grammar.

22 Council of Clofesho: Haddan and Stubbs 1869–78, III, pp. 360–75, esp. §7 and §10; *Capitularia*: Boretius 1883, see: *epistola generalis*, no. 30, pp. 80–1; *admonitio*, no. 22, pp. 59–60, §70, §72; *de litteris colendis*, no. 29, pp. 78–9. Holtz 1997, pp. 51–4; Fox 2005, pp. 217–19.

23
> Non semel externas peregrino tramite terras
> iam peragravit ovans, sophiae deductus amore,
> si quid forte novi librorum seu studiorum,
> quod secum ferret terris reperiret in illis.
> Hic quoque Romuleam venit devotus ad urbem,
> dives amore Dei, late loca sancta peragrans.
>
> Alcuin, York poem: Godman 1982,
> lines 1454–9, pp. 114–15.

Alcuin himself had accompanied Ælberht on at least one of these book-collecting pilgrimages.

That the books of Ælberht's library were the essential (and hard won) basis for study and for the transmission not just of learning but also of wisdom, was evident to Alcuin. The point sounds obvious, but it is not: medieval writers had many ways to talk about learning without emphasising its material embodiment in books. Thus Aldhelm described the subjects he studied at Canterbury – at some length – entirely by referring to their content and in pedantic amplified circumlocutions such as 'the hidden ornaments of metrical art are grouped according to letters, words, feet, poetic figures, verses, accents, and rhythms'.[24] By contrast, in his short appreciation of Bede, Alcuin mentioned the latter's devotion to books as the first remarkable trait of Bede's boyhood, even before recounting Bede's entrance to Jarrow and love of sacred studies.[25] And he referred to Ælberht's own education in terms of progress in *book* learning,[26] characterising Ælberht's teaching in the various arts as accomplished through 'holy volumes'.[27] It is particularly striking that the phrase 'holy volumes' clearly denotes works of instruction in the secular liberal arts rather than patristic or exegetical works: in didactic works composed on the Continent, Alcuin would affirm that the seven liberal arts were not merely the pillars of religious learning, necessary as a means to an end, for the study of scripture, but also that they had an intrinsic value as part of divine wisdom itself.[28] Just as he used the lofty word *sophia* (rather than Latin *sapientia*) to designate wisdom in the York poem and in the epitaphs that he wrote for Ælberht and for himself – characterising both his teacher and himself as lovers of wisdom,[29] – so too he used a Greek (ultimately Persian) word for treasure to evoke the great preciousness of the books: they were *caras super omnia gazas*: 'treasures precious above all things'.[30] On the Continent in the ninth century, in wills and inventories, books would come to be categorised as treasures, and liturgical books were regularly regarded as part of a church's treasury,[31] but Alcuin's acute sense of the extraordinary preciousness of books because of the wisdom they transmitted remains idiosyncratic, unparalleled, and as distinctive as his

24 Compare, for example, Aldhelm's ep. 1 (to Leuthere) and ep. 5 (to Heahfrith): Ehwald 1919, pp. 475–78 and pp. 488–93; trans. Lapidge and Herren (1979), pp. 152–3 and pp. 160–3. Quotation from ep. 1, trans. Lapidge and Herren 1979, p. 152. Compare Alcuin, ep. 34 (AD 793–5): Dümmler 1895, p. 75, on dwelling in the seven-columned house of Sapientia.

25 Alcuin, York poem: Godman 1982, lines 1291–2, pp. 102–3.

26 Alcuin, York poem: Godman 1982, lines 1420–1, pp. 110–11.

27 'sacra volumina': Alcuin, York poem: Godman 1982, line 1452, pp. 114–15.

28 Alcuin, *De grammatica*, prologue: *PL*, CI, col. 853; d'Alverny 1946, pp. 245–7.

29 Alcuin, *Carmen*, 2, line 4, 'qui semper sophiam magnus amator erat', and *Carmen*, 123, line 23, 'Alchuine nomen erat sophiam mihi semper amanti': Dümmler, pp. 206–7 and pp. 350–1.

30 Alcuin, York poem; Godman 1982, line 1526, pp. 120–1.

31 McKitterick 1989b, pp. 158–9.

celebration of *sophia* and *sapientia*, which to him could mean the learning that unlocked the mysteries of scripture and creation or the God-given capacity to learn. *Sapientia* was also an alternative name for the Greek σοφία – Old Testament wisdom reinterpreted by Christians as the Logos, Christ himself.[32] The very first line of the York poem invoked Christ as the Wisdom of God in these terms:

> Christ divine, Strength and Wisdom of the Father Almighty.[33]

Holy Wisdom (Alma Sophia) was the unusual dedication of the splendid new church that Ælberht had built, with the close cooperation of Alcuin and Eanbald. It was also the subject of a votive mass composed by Alcuin which included the wish that God prepare a 'worthy dwelling' for Holy Wisdom in the believer's heart.[34] It is impossible not to see a connection between devotion to Christ as wisdom and the unusual pursuit of wisdom through wide-ranging book learning at the school of York.[35]

Ownership, transmission and dissolution of the library

Ælberht's peerless treasures were private, not institutional property. York Minster was served by a religious community, but it was not a Benedictine monastery; ownership of property was permitted. Ælberht would have purchased the books with his own wealth; shortly before his death in 780, Ælberht assigned his library to Alcuin, while passing on his role as archbishop and his other land and wealth to another former student, Eanbald.[36] When Alcuin recounted the story of Ælberht's parallel bequests, he described Ælberht's books and learning in high-flown language to evoke their preciousness, even perhaps to indicate that their importance was on a level with land, wealth and episcopal rank. Alcuin also movingly evoked his own filial devotion:

> Father-like, he [Ælberht] entrusted his books, treasures he valued above
> all, to his other son [i.e. Alcuin], who was constantly at his side
> And whose thirst for learning Ælberht would satisfy.
> (If you wish to know this man's name

32 Newman 1990, p. 114. There is no similar quantity of such a discourse about the books of either Canterbury or Wearmouth-Jarrow. On wisdom and Alcuin's thought, d'Alverny 1946; on medieval wisdom theology more generally, Newman 1990, Law 1995.

33 Alcuin, York poem: Godman 1982, line 1, pp. 2–3: 'Christe deus, summi virtus sapientia patris' (I have changed the capitalisation of the English translation).

34 Bullough 2004, p. 326.

35 *Ibid*. on possible connections between the Alma Sophia church, the school, the library and the votive mass *De sapientia*, composed by Alcuin.

36 Alcuin, York poem: Godman 1982, line 1526 and following, pp. 120–1.

the beginning of the poem will reveal it immediately.)
He divided his wealth in different ways, granting to the one
government of the church, treasure, lands, and money, and
to the other his choice learning, his [teaching] chair and collection of
books, which that famous teacher had collected everywhere,
storing these priceless treasures under one roof.[37]

Even without directly mentioning his own name, Alcuin called attention to his inheritance of the books, 'exceptional treasures', gathered from afar, and their presence together under a single *culmen*.[38]

In 796, a decade and a half after Alcuin had inherited the books (and then left them behind after his departure for the Continent), a new archbishop of York – also named Eanbald – succeeded Eanbald I. Alcuin wrote to congratulate and advise Eanbald II, who was, to his delight, one of his own former students. It is remarkable, even unparalleled, that, amid all the instructions traditionally proffered in letters for such occasions, the special value of the books, the integrity of the collection, and Alcuin's ownership of it are mentioned so prominently, immediately after the opening congratulations at the very start of the letter, and before any advice or admonition:

Praise and glory to the almighty Lord God, who has preserved my days in good health so that I could rejoice in the elevation of my dearest son, and so

37 Alcuin, York poem: Godman 1982, lines 1526–35, pp. 120–1; content in brackets added.

Tradidit ast alio caras super omnia gazas
librorum gnato, patri qui semper adhaesit,
doctrinae sitiens haurire fluenta suetus.
(Cuius si curas proprium cognoscere nomen,
fronte sua statim praesentia carmina prodent.)
His divisit opes diversis sortibus: illi
ecclesiae regimen, thesauros, rura, talenta;
huic sophiae specimen, studium sedemque librosque,
undique quos clarus collegerat ante magister
egregias condens uno sub culmine gazas.

38 It is unclear whether this means the roof of one building, or rather under the pointed pediment of a bookcase like the one depicted in the Ezra miniature in the Codex Amiatinus, or even under the gable of some other sort of book press, chest or case. There are no extant material remains of Anglo-Saxon book chests or cases; the consensus based on a few exiguous references in Latin and Old English has been that chests rather than presses were used; and that *armaria* like the one depicted in the Ezra miniature held few books. On bookcases in Anglo-Saxon England, see Lapidge 2006, pp. 60–2; Gameson 2006a, pp. 14–15; and Ganz 2006, pp. 91–2. On terminology, Teeuwen 2003, pp. 155–6 and pp. 31–2. It is scarcely conceivable that Ælberht's collection, used regularly, located at a prosperous centre and owned by a man with considerable wealth of his own, would have been stored without corresponding care and attention. Alcuin and Ælberht could certainly have seen how books were stored in the Continental and Italian foundations they visited. In an inscription composed for a library (probably not York) (Alcuin, *Carmen*, 105, i: Dümmler 1881, p. 332, on which see n. 1 above), Alcuin referred to books held beneath small roofs – 'parvula tecta tenent caelestis dona sophiae' – which seems to denote cases; his ep. 309 mentions an 'armarium imperiale' at Charlemagne's court: Dümmler 1895, p. 474. If there were indeed as many as a hundred volumes at York, *culmen* here seems most likely to refer to their location in one room.

> that with Him, who is the giver of all good things, bestowing grace, I, the last servant of the church, could have educated one of my sons so that he should be deemed worthy to be the dispenser of the mysteries of Christ and to work in my place in the church where I was raised and educated; and to preside over the treasures of wisdom to which my own master, the beloved Ælberht, archbishop, made me heir.[39]

Was Alcuin implying that he might, in turn, eventually bequeath the books to Eanbald II, or was he stressing his own continued possession of them?[40] The two possibilities are not necessarily mutually exclusive. The familiar Alcuinian library themes here – the preciousness of wisdom and the transfer of ownership of the library by Ælberht's bequest to Alcuin – would both be repeated in another letter, sent within a year, in order to arrange for the removal of some of the York books to the Continent, a venture that would require Charlemagne's support.

> But I, your servant, am partly lacking some of the more choice booklets of scholarly learning which I had in my homeland through the good and most devoted industry of my teacher and also by some toil of my very own.[41]

This characterisation stands apart from Alcuin's other evocations of the library. To Charlemagne, Alcuin first emphasised school learning (*eruditio scolastica*) rather than lofty wisdom; only later in the letter did he elaborate by referring to the biblical commands to pursue wisdom, its importance for salvation, the moral life and good rulership.[42] And in contrast to all his other testimonies about the collection, he here stressed his *own* effort as much as Ælberht's in establishing the library – perhaps to make his request for help more persuasive and authoritative. The full implications of this letter for the possible fate of the collection will concern us later; now it will be useful to look more closely at the depiction of the library and its contents in the available sources.

39 'Laus et gloria domino deo omnipotenti, qui dies meos in prosperitate bona conservavit; ut in filii mei karissimi exaltatione gauderem, et aliquem, ego ultimus aecclesiae vernaculus – eius donante gratia, qui est omnium bonorum largitor – erudirem ex filiis meis, qui dignus haberetur dispensator esse misteriorum Christi et laborare vice mea in aecclesia, ubi ego nutritus et eruditus fueram; et praeesse thesauris sapientiae, in quibus me magister meus dilectus Ælberhtus archiepiscopus heredem reliquit.' From Alcuin, ep. 114: Dümmler 1895, p. 167, lines 3–9.

40 It was Jaffé who thought that Alcuin was expressing an intention to give the books to Eanbald in due course; Alcuin was also expressing the wish that Eanbald II would outlive him despite some illness: see Alcuin, ep. 114: Dümmler 1895, p. 167, lines 12–13 and apparatus n. 5: 'Non enim filii patribus sed patres filiis hereditare debent.'

41 Alcuin, ep. 121: Dümmler 1895, p. 177. Compare Boniface, ep. 63: Tangl 1916, p. 131, where Boniface asked Bishop Daniel of Winchester to obtain from Nursling a large and legible copy of the prophets that had been in Wynberht's possession: another example of a *peregrinus* arranging for a book he had known in his home institution (and which had belonged to his teacher) to be shipped to him; discussed by Lapidge 2006, p. 39.

42 Alcuin, ep. 121: Dümmler 1895, p. 177, lines 18–28.

The first external glimpse of York's reputation as a place where rare books might be obtained dates from the archiepiscopacies of Ecgberht (732 [archbishop 735]–766) and Ælberht (767–80) and comes from the correspondence of the Anglo-Saxon missionaries Boniface (d. 754) and Lull (Boniface's Malmesbury-trained disciple and successor as archbishop of Mainz). Barely more than a decade after Bede's death, Boniface wrote to Ecgberht sending him some of Pope Gregory's letters that he had had transcribed in the *scrinium* in Rome.[43] Boniface explained that he did not believe that these particular letters had reached Britain and that, if Ecgberht wished, he could send more, since he had got many others. In exchange, he asked Ecgberht to make copies for him of some shorter works by Bede, phrasing the request in terms that seem to suggest that no works by Bede had yet reached him.[44] At roughly the same time, he also asked Hwætberht, abbot of Wearmouth, for some works of Bede, again without specifying titles.[45] Slightly later Boniface wrote again to Ecgberht thanking him for a gift of books (*libelli*: the titles are not specified) and entreating him for some works of Bede that he knew of by hearsay and that he thought would be most useful for preaching – *Homiliae* and *In Proverbia*.[46] The direct implications of the gift and the requests for items from York's teaching library are unclear. Although York had a school under Ecgberht, the range of studies and books is entirely undocumented and may not yet have been particularly distinguished: Ælberht himself had acquired his learning elsewhere, in the unnamed monastery where he had been educated.[47] Gregory's writings figure in Alcuin's list of authorities studied at York, and Alcuin would often recommend the *Regula pastoralis* to ecclesiastical colleagues[48] but it is more likely that those of Gregory's letters chosen by one archbishop for another would have been housed with other books pertaining to the archbishop's duties rather than with the school collection.

Boniface's successor at Mainz, Lull, wrote at least twice to Ecgberht's successor Ælberht, seeking books.[49] One of his requests provides the first clear evidence that York (or Ælberht) had attained a reputation for unusual

43 Boniface, ep. 75 (AD 746–7): Tangl 1916, pp. 157–8, lines 13–16. See Bullough 2004, pp. 228–30; Parkes 1982, reprinted 1994, p. 15.

44 Boniface, ep. 75: Tangl 1916, pp. 157–8, lines 8–12.

45 Boniface, ep. 76 to Hwætberht (AD 746–7): Tangl 1916, pp. 158–9.

46 Boniface, ep. 91 (AD 747–54): Tangl 1916, pp. 206–7: *libellos*, p. 207, line 4; the works of Bede: lines 21–4. *Homiliae*: Hurst 1955, *In Proverbia*: Hurst 1983; Bullough 2004, pp. 228–9 n. 301.

47 Alcuin, York poem: Godman 1982, line 1417, pp. 110–11.

48 For Alcuin recommending Gregory's *Regula Pastoralis*, see epp. 39, 113, 116 (to Eanbald II at York), 124, 209: Dümmler 1895.

49 Lull's first letter of request does not survive, but its contents can be inferred from the reply of Koaena (Ælberht) of York, ep. 124: Tangl 1916, pp. 261–2, lines 26–31. Lull's second letter is ep. 125: Tangl 1916, pp. 262–3.

learning: Lull asked for books about a tidal phenomenon and about cosmography – subjects outside the traditional scope of the seven liberal arts, though part of the range of studies that Ælberht had sponsored.[50] Although Ælberht's reply (the only letter extant of the first exchange) does not reveal how Lull had worded his request, it appears from it that Lull had sought a work which treated 'ocean currents bearing land' (perhaps floating islands? silting?)[51] as well as a book by a named cosmographer. Ælberht knew which work was intended in the second case. He declared that he was unable to fulfil either request: for the first, the works either did not exist or were false;[52] for the second, he had not yet been able to obtain sound copies of the work in question or to employ copyists. The terms of Ælberht's refusal seem to show that he had been actively seeking cosmographies[53] himself (and had been able to acquire only works with corrupted text and illustrations), that he would not send his own copy, that he was unfamiliar with any notion about ocean currents carrying land (we cannot say whose – and Ælberht appears to have disapproved of the idea in any case), and perhaps that York was not at that time equipped for regular book production.[54] In short, this is the response of a connoisseur and collector with specialised interests, intent on reliable knowledge and quality.

There is no extant reply to another request – acknowledged as a heavy one – that Lull addressed to Ælberht asking for the gift of several volumes of Bede's exegesis: *Commentarius in primam partem Samuhelis*,[55] *Commentarius in Ezram et*

50 For Boniface's endorsement of the seven liberal arts, see Boniface, ep. 9: Tangl 1916, pp. 4–7 at 5, lines 25–31; Roger 1905, pp. 310–13. On the range of studies at York, see Holtz 1997. On the advisability of the study of geography, see Cassiorodus, *Institutiones*, I, xxv, 'cosmographos legendos a monachis': Mynors 1937, p. 66.

51 'marinis aestibus terram advectantibus', ep. 124: Tangl 1916, p. 261, line 26. On floating islands, see Van Duzer 2004. I thank Francis Newton for correspondence about this passage and the suggestion that floating islands or silting may be the basis of Lull's question, and Maja Kominko for alerting me to Van Duzer.

52 What work had Lull heard of on this subject? Boniface's famous opposition to Virgil of Salzburg's teachings about antipodean peoples (ep. 80: Tangl 1916, p. 179, lines 1–3, on which see Carey 1989) does not seem relevant to the question; could the work have been Aethicus Ister's *Cosmographia*? The *Topographia Christiana* of Cosmas Indicopleustes? (For the suggestion that this letter refers to Cosmas see James 1927, p. 339; this view has not won assent in later literature.) The whale-island in the *Navigatio Sancti Brendani*? Bede's discoveries about tides in *De temporum ratione* and *De temporibus* (on which see Cartwright, 2001, pp. 8 and 13–14; Wallis 2005) do not seem to match. The number of apposite references to floating islands in Pliny's *Historia naturalis* (enumeratred in Van Duzer 1994, p. 264) makes this a likely candidate.

53 The story that King Aldfrith had exchanged an estate of eight hides for a *Topographia Christiania* acquired by Benedict Biscop in Rome (Bede, *Historia Abbatum*: Plummer (ed.) 1896, I, p. 380) shows how precious a fine, rare foreign book could be. Note that Orosius, *Historiae*, bk. 1 could also be considered a work of cosmography (Gneuss 2001, index s.v. Geography, p. 165).

54 James 1927, p. 339, interpreted this as arising from the challenge of copying Greek.

55 Lull refers to the work using a title almost identical to that given by Bede in his own list of works: *HE*, v, 24: Colgrave and Mynors 1969, p. 568, line 2. Bede: *Commentarius in primam partem Samuhelis*: Hurst 1962.

Neemiam[56] and *Commentarius in Marcum*.[57] Lull seems to have learned of these titles from Bede's list of his writings in the *Historia ecclesiastica* whose wording his request matches; during the same decade he also corresponded with Abbot Gutberct[58] of Wearmouth-Jarrow to obtain copies of other works by Bede.[59] That his request to Ælberht accompanied a list of the names of dead friends and brothers implies an ongoing relationship of reciprocal prayer between Mainz and York, and thus perhaps additional lost epistolary exchange which would provide the social context for Lull's imposing demand.[60] It may be significant that Lull asked Ælberht to acquire these books for him, not have them copied: this might corroborate the impression that York in the time of Ælberht was not a centre for the regular production of books. In all, Ælberht's correspondence with Lull seems to illustrate the fame of York as a centre for learning and books, along with the breadth of studies, and suggests that its books were chiefly collected from elsewhere rather than produced in-house.

Since there is no further correspondence extant between Lull and Ælberht (and no books of secure York origin with the relevant later provenance), it is not possible to say whether any gift-books from York found their way to Mainz or Fulda in the eighth century.[61] Under Alcuin's aegis, however, we know of a number of books from York that found their way to the Continent as gifts – an instance of York's library sending shoots of learning abroad even before Alcuin's departure. The Frisian Liudger (d. 809) came from the diocese of Utrecht to study at York with Alcuin on two separate occasions, the second time for three and a half years.[62] He left at short notice (*c.* 773), 'well educated and with an abundance of books', when the threat of violence from a feud caused a hasty exodus of Frisians from the city.[63] An Irish pupil,

56 Lull, ep. 125: Tangl 1916, pp. 262–3 (AD 767–78): Bede, *Commentarius in Ezram et Neemiam*: Hurst 1969; this is the only case where the title Lull uses (*In Esdram et Nehemiam libros tres*) does not closely match Bede's in *HE*, v, 24, p. 568.

57 Lull, ep. 125: Tangl 1916, pp. 262–3; trans. in Whitelock 1979, no. 188, pp. 834–5. Bede, *Commentarius in Marcum*: Hurst 1960, pp. 431–648; Lull's request matches the wording in *HE*, v, 24, p. 568.

58 On the correct form of the name, Gutberct rather than Cuthbert, see Bullough 2004, p. 228 n. 300.

59 Bede, *HE*, v, 25: Colgrave and Mynors 1969, p. 568. Lull, epp. 116, 126, 127: Tangl 1916. Parkes 1982, pp. 15–16.

60 Levison 1946, p. 102.

61 Excepting the *libelli* sent by Ecgberht to Boniface. But see, e.g., Gneuss 2001, no .818, Darmstadt, Hessisches Landes- und Hochschulbibliothek 4262, Bede, *De temporum ratione*, *s.* viii[1], Wearmouth-Jarrow; *CLA*, Suppl., no 1822, Bischoff and Brown 1985. Also Gneuss 2001, nos. 832, 834, 791.

62 Altfrid, *Vita Liudgeri*: Diekamp 1881, chs. 10–12, pp. 15–17; trans. Whitelock 1979, no. 160, pp. 787–9.

63 Altfrid, *Vita Liudgeri*: Diekamp 1881, chs. 11–12, pp. 16–17; ch. 12, p. 17, 'habens secum copiam librorum'; trans. Whitelock 1979, no. 160, pp. 788–9.

Joseph Scottus, also left York for the Continent, remaining in contact with both Liudger and Alcuin; surely he too will have brought books from York.[64] Joseph Scottus' eventual location is unknown – possibilities as distant as Passau and Monte Cassino[65] have been suggested and no books of putative York origin have yet been associated with him. In contrast, Liudger's later career and perhaps even his books are traceable. Some thirty years later, he founded the monastery of Werden which would become a centre of Anglo-Saxon books and learning. It is likely that some of the books that Liudger had brought from York became the property of his monastery; various candidates have been proposed over the years. Since Liudger's departure was hasty and unplanned, one might assume that the books he took were given to him for the occasion rather than prepared. One recent review considered a list of twenty-six volumes or fragments with Werden provenance, Insular origin and palaeographical dating of no later than the early ninth century.[66] Of these, perhaps four out of the eleven certainly Insular manuscripts or fragments of eighth-century date might be deemed likely to have been brought from York by Liudger.[67] The list includes an eighth-century mixed Gelasian sacramentary from Northumbria,[68] a leaf of Cassiodorus's *Expositio psalmorum* (in the abbreviated form which Alcuin knew),[69] binding fragments of Chrysostom's *De reparatione lapsi*, *De compunctione cordis* and the *Pastor Hermae*,[70] and works of Isidore (*Etymologiae* and *De ortu et obitu patrum*[71]), Orosius (*Historiae*

64 Garrison 2004, pp. 715–16; Bischoff, 1981, pp. 164 and 221; p. 164 n. 66 states that Joseph's acrostics show the first evidence for the use, north of the Alps, of material from the Codex Salmasianus.

65 Bischoff 1981, p. 221.

66 Gerchow 1999, pp. 55–7, bringing together items proposed by E. A. Lowe, Bernhard Bischoff, Julian Brown, Bruce Barker-Benfield and Eckhard Freise, superseding Drögereit 1951, pp. 66–82 at pp. 66–71, on which Bischoff 1952, pp. 7–12 at p. 8. For a useful overview of manuscript exchange between Anglo-Saxon England and Continental mission areas in the eighth century, see Lapidge 2006, pp. 81–2 and 148–66; Zeckiel-Eckes 2002 and 2003.

67 Gerchow 1999, pp. 55–6 and 57. I thank Anton Scharer for calling my attention to this. Gerchow suggests eleven candidates for eighth-century books brought from Anglo-Saxon England or Ireland, four from York (Lathcen, Sacramentary, Cassiodorus, Chrysostom); Barker-Benfield 1991, p. 53 (four from Northumbria: the Cassiodorus, Chrysostom, Orosius and Isidore); Bischoff 1952, p. 8, criticizes Drögereit's selection of four candidates for York exports as too recent (Drögereit 1951, p. 75). For another assessment see Zeckiel-Eckes 2003.

68 Münster in Westfalen, UB, Frag. IV.8. Gneuss 2001, no. 856.3, a fragmentary mixed Gelasian Sacramentary, *s.* viii^{i}, Northumbria, provenance Werden.

69 Düsseldorf, UB, Fragm. K16.Z.3/1: *CLA*, Suppl., no. 1786; Gneuss 2001, no. 822; Bullough 2004, p. 256. The leaf was formerly in the Werden Abbey archives and according to Bullough 2004, p. 256, was 'textually- and palaeographically-related' to the Durham Cassiodorus (DCL, B.II.30, *CLA*, II, no. 152) and so might derive from a book Liudger had brought from York.

70 Düsseldorf, UB, Fragm. K1.B215, K2.C118 and K15.009: Gneuss 2001, no. 819, *CLA*, VIII, no. 1187; a mid-eighth-century Northumbrian hand; seven leaves; Bullough 2004, p. 260 emphasising that the notion of this as a York import has 'no worthwhile evidence to support it'.

71 Düsseldorf, UB, Fragm. K15.017 and K19.Z8/7b: Gneuss 2001, no. 821, *CLA*, VIII, no. 1189: Gneuss 2001, no. 818.5, *CLA*, VIII, no. 1184. Düsseldorf, UB, Fragm. K1:B210.

adversus paganos),[72] Jerome (*In epistolam Pauli ad Galatas*),[73] Bede (*Historia ecclesiastica*)[74] and a collection of saints' lives.[75] A lavish sixth-century copy of the Goth Wulfila's translation of the gospels, written in silver on purple parchment, the famous Codex Argenteus, has also been mooted as a book brought by Liudger from York.[76] Another of the conjectured York-export volumes is the *Egloga de Moralibus in Iob*, the Irishman Lathcen's abridgement of Gregory's *Moralia in Job*, copied in an eighth-century Irish hand.[77] It is tempting to associate this item with Liudger's Irish friend, Joseph Scottus: the two had studied together at York and both moved to the Continent at different times where they remained in affectionate contact, exchanging poems and tokens of friendship.[78] No other books of Irish origin are associated with Werden and there is no later regular connection between Werden and the Irish. Did Joseph give Liudger the book on the occasion of his flight or does it represent the ongoing gift exchange of their Continental friendship? The apostolic symbolism of Joseph's request for the gift of a 'polished staff' (whether a walking stick or pastoral staff) in exchange for a poem would be well complemented by a convenient abbreviation of a work by Gregory, the apostle of the English.

What does the gift-provision of books to Liudger reveal about the school and library under Alcuin? The notional York–Werden export books have not been used as evidence for the practices of a York scriptorium and thus might seem to reinforce the surmise that York was chiefly a place where books were gathered, even if it must have had some capacity to produce them. Yet the Ælberht–Alcuin library was sufficiently well stocked to equip a fleeing missionary churchman generously – with *copia librorum*. Presumably the books in question were available, rather than copied for the occasion (hence volumes from elsewhere and of earlier date, but which had fetched up at York, might have been among Liudger's exports). Alcuin's generous gift and his practical

72 Düsseldorf, Nordrhein-Westfalisches Hauptstaatsarchiv, Z11/1: Gneuss 2001, no. 820, *CLA*, Suppl., 1689, *s.* viii², probably Northumbria; Bullough 2004, p. 268 n. 46.

73 Gerleve, Abteibibliothek, s.n.: Gneuss, 2001, no. 892.2, *CLA*, Suppl.,1826.

74 Münster in Westphalen, UB, Frag. I.3: *CLA*, Suppl.,1848; not in Gneuss.

75 Berlin, SB, Theol. Lat. Fol. 355 *CLA*, VIII, no.1068; Gneuss 2001, no. 791.3.

76 Uppsala UB, DG1; Gerchow 1999, p. 57, citing Eckhard Freise in favour; Bischoff 1965a reprinted, 1981, pp. 155 and 168, contra, proposing a court library route from Ravenna. Barker-Benfield 1991, p. 53 n. 40 signals the lack of evidence for a Werden provenance before the sixteenth century.

77 *Egloga de Moralibus in Iob*; *CLA*, VIII, no. 1185. Düsseldorf Landes- und Stadtbibliothek, B.212 + Staatsarchiv s.n. and New York, Columbia University, Plimpton 54.

78 Josephus Scottus: Manitius 1911, pp. 547–9; Garrison 2004, pp. 715–16; Bischoff 1981, pp. 220–1; 1994, p. 101. Joseph, *Carmen*, 1: Dümmler 1881, pp. 150–1 and in Altfrid, *Vita Liudgeri*: Diekamp, ch. 19, pp. 22–4.

concern to ensure Liudger's safety (by sending his follower Putul to accompany him) reinforce the impression of the school under Alcuin as a place of familial warmth, practical know-how and commitment to the spread of Christian learning, with an abundance of books.

Despite the praise lavished on Liudger's learning by his hagiographer, the books that he could have brought from York are without exception works suitable for a missionary and pastor, not for a teacher of the liberal arts. There is a notable lacuna in the list of Werden's early books with Insular connections[79] – no extant fragment of any work on Latin grammar. Yet it is a reasonable assumption that grammar books would have been among the works deemed essential by a well-educated deacon active in any recently evangelised region with a Germanic vernacular.

Indeed, grammar books (by Priscian and Phocas) were the gift that Alcuin sent to his Insular compatriot, Samuel (Beornræd), archbishop of Sens and abbot of Echternach.[80] It is likely that these were works the latter had requested, supplied by Alcuin after meeting Samuel in 780.[81] It is tempting to associate a group of late eighth-century fragments of Priscian's *De nomine, pronomine et verbo*, now in Karlsruhe, and probably of late eighth-century Northumbrian origin, if not with this precise donation, then at least with the well-attested Insular emphasis on grammatical study and with the books that came to the Continent through the eighth-century networks that linked both Northumbrian and Southumbrian missionaries to their homeland.[82] The messenger who conveyed the books to Samuel stopped with other hosts along the way (all are named in Alcuin's poetic account of the journey), but the poem records no other gifts of books, not even to Lull of Mainz, whose learning and devotion to *sophia* Alcuin praised in terms that recall his epitaphs for Ælberht and himself.[83]

Some two dozen manuscripts of eighth-century Northumbrian origin now or formerly housed on the Continent are included in Gneuss' *Handlist*

79 Gerchow 1999, pp. 55–7; Zeckiel-Eckes 2003.

80 Alcuin, *Carmen*, 4: Dümmler 1881, pp. 220–3, line 34, p. 221; on Priscian's *Institutiones*, Law 1994, reprinted 1997, pp. 136–7; O'Donnell 1976; Lapidge 2006, pp. 80–1.

81 Alcuin, *Carmen*, 4: Dümmler 1881, p. 221, line 34: 'tali quia munere gaudet'.

82 Priscian *Institutio de nomine, pronomine et verbo*: Gneuss 2001, no. 831.7, *s.* viii^{ex}, probably Northumbria; *CLA*, VIII, no. 1009; Karlsruhe, Badische Landesbibliothek, Frag. Aug. 122 + Zurich, Staatsarchiv A.G. 19, no. xiii, fols. 26–7; Lapidge 2006, pp. 158–9 and 326. This fragment came from Reichenau. On the distribution of Priscian manuscripts in the late eighth and early ninth century, and Alcuin's probable role in the diffusion of the longer *Institutiones*, see Law 1985, reprinted 1997, pp. 83 and 87 n. 8.

83 Alcuin, *Carmen*, 4: Dümmler 1881, p. 222, lines 53–5: 'doctor ... Ecclesiae specimen, sophiae qui splendor habetur, / Moribus et vita tanto condignus honore'; compare the epitaphs, Alcuin, *Carmina*, 2 and 123: Dümmler 1881, pp. 206–7 and pp. 350–1.

of Anglo-Saxon Manuscripts.[84] A small number of them have been conjecturally associated with York, either on the basis of a match between their contents and works implied by Alcuin's author list, or because of their later provenance, or, in a few cases, because of slightly more compelling suggestions of possible affiliation.[85] That the five most likely volumes represent the distinctive intellectual breadth of the York library and school is a nice coincidence.

First, there is the Moore Bede. One of the earliest copies of Bede's *Historia ecclesiastica*, the manuscript was written in evident haste[86] in Northumbria (perhaps at Wearmouth-Jarrow) and appears to have spent time at Charlemagne's court since the early Caroline Minuscule script of the additions on the final leaf resembles the hand in another book known to have been at the court.[87] The chronology of the additions matches the era of Alcuin's activity: circumstantial evidence of a book brought from York by Alcuin or one of his students?[88] Of the Moore Bede's seven ninth-century copies, four were either written in, or owned by, foundations in the Loire Valley, with the earliest two copies associated with Fleury and Tours[89]: a further indication of some connection with Alcuin or one of his circle.

Second is the Durham Cassiodorus, a copy of Cassiodorus' *Expositio psalmorum* which transmits a distinctive abbreviated text.[90] The same abridgement

84 Gneuss 2001, nos. 791 (N), 818 (W-J), 819 (N?), 821 (N?), 822 (N?), 831.6 (N?), 831.7 (N?), 832 (N), 835 (N), 836 (N), 836.5 (N?), 838 (N), 840.5 (N?), 840.6 (N?), 841 (N? or Southern England), 846 (W-J) 847 (N, Lindisfarne?), 848.4 (N), 853 (N), 856.3 (N), 855.5 (N? or Continent), 885 (N?), 898.5 (N, W-J?), 907 (N? or Mercia), 909 (N), 911.5 (?), 933 (Holtz 1971, p. 53 says northern English), 940 (W-J), 943.8 (N). (I have added 'N' for those which Gneuss records as Northumbrian and 'N?' for those possibly Northumbrian, 'W-J' for those assigned to Wearmouth-Jarrow.) The difficulty of distinguishing manuscripts produced in Anglo-Saxon England from those written on the Continent by Anglo-Saxon scribes or under their direction remains acute. On some inconsistencies in Gneuss' categorisation of Insular manuscripts, and on the advisability of excluding ten of its items, see Lapidge 2006, p. 79. For Lapidge's more stringent list of non-biblical and liturgical manuscripts from the area of Anglo-Saxon mission activity on the Continent, which is not limited to items of Northumbrian origin, see Lapidge 2006, appendix C, pp. 155–66: the list comprises 112 items.

85 Lapidge 2006, pp. 41–2, allows the Moore Bede, the Durham Cassiodorus and the Justinus fragment; Bullough 2004, pp. 255–60, allows the Durham Cassiodorus, the Werden Cassiodorus fragment, the Werden Chrysostom fragments, and rejects the Justinus fragment; Alcuin, York poem: Godman 1982, pp. 122–7, adopts a maximal view, listing in the apparatus to the relevant passage of the York poem a total of eight manuscripts or fragments, though without making explicit claims for York affiliation.

86 Bede, *HE*: Colgrave and Mynors 1969, pp. xliii–iv and lxi–lxii.

87 CUL, Kk.5.16, *CLA*, II, no. 139; Gneuss 2001, no. 25; Wearmouth-Jarrow or Northumbria, *c.* or post-737, provenance Aachen. Lapidge 2006, p. 41. Bischoff 1981, pp. 160–1, linking the addition hand with the early Caroline of London, BL, Harley 2788; Parkes 1982, pp. 26–7, n. 35; Bede, *HE*: Colgrave and Mynors 1969, pp. xliii–xliv and lxi–lxii.

88 Bischoff 1981, pp. 160–1; Parkes 1982, pp. 26–7, n. 35.

89 Bede, *HE*: Colgrave and Mynors 1969, p. lxii.

90 DCL, B.II.30; *CLA*, II, no. 152, *s.* viii$^{2/4}$; provenance Durham. For full discussion of Alcuin's use of the abbreviated version (the one transmitted in this manuscript), its six scribes, its affiliation with the Werden fragment, and divergent views on its origin – Lindisfarne, Wearmouth-Jarrow or even

seems to have been used by Alcuin on the Continent.[91] It is also represented in the Werden leaf, which, as we have seen, may have been brought from York by Liudger.[92] And it was demonstrably *not* this abbreviated version that was available to Bede.[93] Did Alcuin read and excerpt the Durham Cassiodorus (or a close relation) while at York?[94] Was the Durham Cassiodorus perhaps even written at York?[95] These are tantalising but unprovable possibilities. However, if the link between the manuscript itself and York must remain conjectural, nonetheless the technique that it represents – namely, making voluminous patristic exegesis more accessible by producing excerpted texts – is characteristic of Alcuin and his students (including Joseph Scottus).[96] The impulse to excerpt and abbreviate can be seen as reflecting a shared commitment to diffusing learning rather than as an indication of the lowering of standards.

In the author list in the York poem, Alcuin departed from the pattern of citing several authorities for each discipline when he came to the expanded quadrivium; instead he listed one for each discipline. The token historian is Pompeius, and Pliny is the natural historian.[97] Fragments of the works of these two represent the third and fourth conjectures for surviving York books.

Pompeius can be assumed from his place in the list to stand for the Roman historian Pompeius Trogus.[98] His forty-four-book world history, *Historiae Philippicae*, survives only in the *Epitome* of Justinus, of which the earliest witnesses are two mid-eighth-century Northumbrian fragments, one now in London, the other (now lost) formerly in Germany, both apparently from the same volume.[99] When the evidence of the fragments' date and script is

York – see Bullough 2004, pp. 255–8. The volume would not, of course, have to have been written in York to have been used there by Alcuin; Bullough raises the possibility of a York origin without pressing the case at p. 256, and discusses the abbreviation and the inadequacies of the most recent printed edition of the full work for resolving textual questions at p. 258.

91 Bullough 2004, pp. 257–8.

92 See above, p. 645; for a possible additional witness to the breviate text now in Halle, see Bullough 2004, p. 257, n. 21.

93 *Ibid.*, citing Bailey 1983.

94 Bullough 2004, p. 258.

95 Bullough, *ibid.*, raises the possibility without defending it.

96 Fox 2005, p. 224; on Joseph Scottus, Manitius 1911, pp. 547–9. Garrison 2004.

97 Alcuin, York poem: Godman 1982, line 1548, pp. 124–5; Holtz 1997, p. 49; cf. Lapidge 2006, p. 230, no. 18, and p. 324.

98 Alcuin, York poem: Godman 1982, line 1549. Note that the ninth-century will of Gerward, librarian of Louis the Pious, also designates Justinus as Pompeius (Crick 1987, p. 190).

99 Crick 1987, p. 182; Alcuin, York poem: Godman 1982, p. 125, apparatus to line 1549; Holtz 1997, p. 49 n. 12, suggesting a correction to the punctuation in Alcuin, York poem; Bullough 2004, pp. 259–60 and 283; Lapidge 2006, 41–2, pp. 129–30 and 318. The fragments are: BL, Harley 5915, fol. 10 (the 'Bagford fragment') (*s.* viii^{med}, Northumbria) + Weinheim Sammlung E. Fischer s.n. (lost) (Gneuss 2001, no. 441.1; *CLA*, IX, no. 1370, *s.* viii, Northumbria; obelised).

combined with the fact that Alcuin mentioned the work (while no other Anglo-Saxon appears to know it until Asser[100]), and then it is mentioned again in the will of Gerward, the librarian of Louis the Pious, in the ninth century,[101] the Northumbria–Continent–Carolingian court nexus seems again to point to an origin in York's library and to Alcuin as the agent of transmission.[102]

The evidence for item four, the Elder Pliny's *Historia naturalis*, is more tenuous. Besides naming Pliny in his list of *auctores*, Alcuin knew and used his work, but so did Aldhelm and Bede before him, and Wulfstan and Byrhtferth afterwards.[103] The earliest extant Pliny manuscript with Anglo-Saxon connections, now in Leiden, is an incomplete Northumbrian work of the first third of the eighth century; copied from an ancient exemplar, it is also the earliest extant witness made north of the Alps.[104] It shares some distinctive decorative motifs with the Durham Cassiodorus and also has the same ruled area and number of lines per page;[105] the Cassiodorus, as we have seen, is linked in some way to Alcuin. There is also an illustrated excerpt text of the *Historia naturalis* which was formerly thought to be from York, but is now assigned to the Carolingian court in the early ninth century.[106] The Leiden leaves may not have been copied in York and the book they came from may not have been exported from York, but the possibility of a connection remains open and tantalising – at the very least it illustrates how the distinctive breadth of interests evinced by Ælberht, Alcuin and their library would come to flourish on the Continent in places associated with Alcuin despite the much narrower programme of learning enjoined in Charlemagne's capitularies.[107]

100 Lapidge 2006, p. 239.
101 Crick 1987, pp. 190–2.
102 Crick 1987 concluded that textual differences meant that the fragments could not stand behind the subsequent northern European stemma; Bullough adduces more recent scholarship to support the possibility that the Northumbrian fragments are the *fons* of the 'entire later northwestern-European tradition' (2004, p. 259).
103 Lapidge 2006, pp. 184, 220–3, 246, 272; and pp. 130, 325.
104 York poem: Godman 1982, line 1549, pp. 124–5 and apparatus; Gneuss 2001, no. 838; Leiden Universiteitsbibliotheek, Voss. Lat. F.4 fols. 4–33, Pliny, *Historia naturalis*, bks. ii–iv; *s.* viii$^{1/3}$ Northumbria, *CLA*, x, no.1578; Reynolds 1983, pp. 309; Lapidge 2006, pp. 130, 170, 184, 222–3, 246, 272, 325. Bullough 2004, pp. 260, 283. Though currently acephalous and marred by gaps, codicological evidence suggests that this was once a substantially complete text of books I–VI.
105 Lowe comments on 'the curious device of using the hind legs of an animal as a finial', *CLA*, x, no.1578. This device can also be found in DCL, B.II.30 and another eighth-century book sometimes associated with York, the canon law collection in Cologne Dombibliothek, 213, fol. 2v. I thank David Ganz for reminding me of the importance of this manuscript.
106 Bullough 2004, pp. 283–5; Reynolds 1983, p. 310.
107 For letters of Alcuin and Dungal that mention Pliny, see Alcuin, epp. 155 and 170 and Dungal, ep. 1: Dümmler 1895, pp. 250, 280, 577.

Finally, in fifth place there is an eighth-century manuscript of Tiberius Claudius Donatus' *Interpretationes Virgilianae* which was produced by a remarkable collaboration between an Anglo-Saxon scribe (who wrote the first fifty-six leaves in Phase II Northumbrian Minuscule) and another writer who used early Caroline.[108] The palaeographical and textual links to Touronian work have led to the assumption that it was produced at Tours under Alcuin; it is equally possible to imagine it being copied at York by the pupils whom Alcuin had sent to retrieve part of his library.[109]

For none of these five is it possible to venture beyond possibility into certainty. However such scattered, fragmentary and uncertain manuscript evidence is absolutely typical of eighth-century Northumbria: as Michael Lapidge has stressed, not even a single library book has been securely associated with any of the contemporary smaller Northumbrian foundations, namely Hexham, Ripon, Lindisfarne, Hartlepool and Whitby.[110] Then, too, the circulation networks for missionaries' books had other sources, supply lines and Continental depots – some, such as Willibrord and Echternach, linked to Northumbria and others not.[111] Since York's teaching library had been built up by Ælberht's acquisitions abroad (much as Benedict Biscop had established Wearmouth-Jarrow's library), it would have had a substantial proportion of books in Continental script, probably late antique Italian manuscripts for the most part. If such books were subsequently re-exported to the Continent it would be difficult to identify any York phase of their history; indeed, even annotations in Insular script could have been done by Anglo-Saxons abroad. Equally, if Carolingian copies were made of the exemplars originally taken across the Alps on Ælberht's collecting trips, it would be impossible to identify the York phase of their transmission history. Hence, in the absence of more than half a dozen manuscripts even conjecturally associated with the York library, Alcuin's account of the subjects studied at York and his list of forty-one authors have signal importance.

108 Alcuin, York poem: Godman 1982, line 1556, p. 126; *CLA*, III, no. 297 a+b; Florence, Biblioteca Medicea-Laurenziana, XLV.15, which has textual affinities with the Tours book BAV, Reg. lat. 1484. For another example of Anglo-Saxon–Touronian collaboration, see BL, Egerton 2831 (*CLA*, II, no. 196), usually thought to date from before Alcuin's arrival.

109 The attractive suggestion is in Hunter Blair 1976, pp. 251–2; Alcuin, York poem: Godman 1982, p. 126 notes to line 1556. That the parchment is not prepared in the Insular manner need not exclude the hypothesis – the pricking, however, is Insular, as are the omission marks, and it is easy to imagine that Alcuin's helpers would have brought Continental parchment with them to York. Hunter Blair's suggestion has not been pursued by Bullough (2004) or Lapidge (2006).

110 Lapidge 2006, pp. 42–3. (The Lindisfarne Gospels and others in its orbit are excepted because they are not library books.)

111 Ó Cróinín 1984.

The York poem

Alcuin's poem about York illuminates the library in several ways. First, as we have seen, there are reminiscences about Ælbert's book collecting and his bequest of the library to Alcuin: the human story of the accumulation and transfer of the library. Then there is the account of the subjects included in Ælbert's teaching programme and also the list of forty-one authors. Finally, the diction of the poem itself reveals some of Alcuin's own remembered reading.[112]

The poem's date and intended readership bear on the interpretation of its educational and bibliographical reminiscences.[113] It is an account of teaching and books destined in the first instance for others who shared memories of Ælberht and his teaching, as well as those at York who might not. Alcuin clearly imagines York readers known to him, contemporaries and former students, as the poem's audience.[114] He addresses them directly to ask their indulgence before an extended biographical excursus about Ælberht's life;[115] indulgence is necessary because the account, comprising over 150 lines (or almost one tenth of the 1,658-line poem), seems to be a gratuitous amplification of the initial concise, non-biographical encomium of Ælberht.[116] It is this account that provides the context for the description of the teaching programme (lines 1433–53) and the list of the *auctores* (1536–57).

Even as he addressed the York Minster *familia* directly, Alcuin also seemed to imagine a future audience who would not know his name; this, he assumed, would stand at the head of his poem where he directed curious readers, ignorant of his identity, to look.[117] The poem has been seen as a model account of a school intended to inspire 'Carolingian men of

112 Alcuin, York poem: Godman 1982, pp. 141–54, 'Index of Quotations and Allusions', which should be qualified by the conclusions of Lapidge 2006, pp. 228–33; Orchard 1992.

113 For Godman's account of the date and character of the poem see Alcuin, York poem: Godman 1982, pp. xxxix and following; those views will be slightly qualified here.

114 Alcuin, York poem: Godman 1982, lines 1409–11 at pp. 110–11. Cf. Riché 1976, p. 383: 'this work, written in 781–2, was primarily intended to encourage Carolingian men of letters … the poem, it seems to me, represents less Alcuin's remembrances than it does a model for a school – thus, this source must be exploited prudently'.

115 Alcuin, York poem: Godman 1982, pp. 110–11, lines 1409–11:

De quo versifico paulo plus pergere gressu	(I ask you, please, to walk a little farther with me,
Euboricae mecum libeat tibi, quaeso, iuventus	keeping step with my poem, young men of York,
hic quia saepe tuos perfudit nectare sensus	for [Ælberht] often steeped your senses in nectar.)

116 Alcuin, York poem: Godman 1982, lines 1395–1408.

117 Hence his modesty in refusing to name himself in the account of Ælberht's bequests, instead referring the reader to the start of the poem: York poem, lines 1529–30. *Frons* is the Latin word for the outside of a volume. But see Curtius 1953, pp. 515–16, on literary conventions associated with the suppression and mention of authors' names: the convention means

letters'.[118] However, Alcuin would expound his views about teaching, reading, education and the religious life with great clarity in numerous letters, treatises, prologues and even Carolingian legislation, so it may not be necessary to read a memoir suffused with such affection, and with such a schematic and incomplete list of authors, as a programmatic statement. Ælberht's death in 780 gives a *terminus post quem* for the composition of the York poem: no events after that date are recorded. Whether the poem was written soon thereafter, or started then and completed later, perhaps in connection with one of Alcuin's return visits (in either 786 or 790×793) cannot be ascertained with certainty.[119] Since Alcuin clearly assumes that the books are still in situ for a reader to browse,[120] his decision to bring some of the library to the Continent (in late 796 or early 797) is a clear *terminus ante quem* – though the Viking attack on Lindisfarne in 793 might be defended as an earlier outer limit. Whatever view one adopts of its date or purpose, the poem is a historical and memorial account which, when it treats the people and events of Alcuin's own lifetime, is directed in the first instance to others with the same first-hand acquaintance. Thus, although the accounts of the curriculum and books are in some respects allusive or incomplete, they nonetheless constitute familiar reminiscences subject to the check of the first, York, audience's memory rather than an invented ideal programme or covert directions.

Reminiscences evoke a shared social and intellectual world – they do not catalogue it. The account of Ælberht's curriculum (lines 1434–49) is a purple passage which uses figurative description, synecdoche and amplification to list the disciplines of Ælberht's curriculum in vivid and personal, if not always concrete, terms. Ælberht's instruction is characterised as 'diverse streams of learning and the varied dew of knowledge' which waters 'parched hearts'.[121] Subjects are evoked rather than named (rhetoric is 'a flood or rhetorical eloquence', and dialectic a 'polishing with the whetstone of true speech').[122] The quadrivial arts are described at greater length than

that it was also deemed appropriate not to mention one's name in a work even to a familiar audience.

118 Riché 1976, p. 383.

119 Holtz observes that the poem ends with a lament on 'la mort d'Aelberht, ressentie comme toute récente': Holtz 1997, p. 51 n. 17; in his introduction to Alcuin, York poem: Godman 1982, pp. xlii–lxiii, Godman put a case for a later date, suggesting composition after 781/2, perhaps during a return visit to York in 786 or even as late as 793; Bullough 2004, p. xxii, would put Alcuin's departure from York in 786.

120 Alcuin, York poem: Godman 1982, lines 1536 and 1558; Alcuin, ep. 121: Dümmler 1895.

121 Alcuin, York poem: Godman 1982, lines 1432 and following; Holtz 1997, pp. 47–51, is indispensable.

122 Alcuin, York poem: Godman 1982, lines 1435–6, pp. 112–13. Compare Fortunatus, *Vita Martini*: Leo 1881, I, 31, p. 296.

the subjects of the trivium. Yet, for all its high style, the account is nonetheless systematic.[123] The trivium and quadrivium occur in order, followed by computus, with the study of scripture as the culmination of the programme. Two additional subjects are interpolated between the quadrivial arts of astronomy and arithmetic, namely natural sciences and the study of living things.[124] Thus the sequence is as follows (subjects not traditionally part of the seven liberal arts are enclosed in brackets): Grammar, Rhetoric, Dialectic[125]; Music (including chant and hymnody),[126] Astronomy [natural science and the study of animals, or natural history] Arithmetic, Geometry [computus], Scripture.

That the quadrivial studies have eleven lines devoted to them as against three for the trivium suggests that the sciences were Ælberht's area of greatest interest and expertise.[127] In this connection, Lull's request for works about the tides and cosmography takes on fresh significance: it is an indication of Lull's knowledge of Ælberht's interests and book-collecting aims. The request was not a random or opportunist one, but reflected prior dialogue or even acquaintance, whether by letter or *viva voce*. In the early ninth century, the *Naturales quaestiones* of Seneca first surface as excerpts (some three centuries before the earliest manuscripts) in a manuscript linked to the circle of Alcuin;[128] it is tantalising to consider that this evidence of Continental study of natural history may have its ultimate roots in the interests of Ælberht.

The list of the forty-one authors to be found in Ælberht and Alcuin's library (lines 1536–60) closes the Ælberht excursus; it occurs after the description of his retirement, allusion to his death, and account of the double bequest of his archbishopric, lands and other property to Eanbald and the books to Alcuin, but precedes Alcuin's tearful account of Ælberht's death. The role of the list is akin to a property inventory in a will, yet stops short of resembling that genre, for Alcuin presents the list of names as an address to the reader, introduced by a description of Ælberht gathering the books 'under one roof'.[129] 'There you will find…' says Alcuin twice – at the beginning and end of the

123 Holtz 1997; Bullough 2004, p. 253.

124 Bischoff 1958, for an alternative sevenfold quadrivial scheme.

125 iuridica versus veridica: see Alcuin, York poem: Godman 1982, apparatus to line 36, p. 112; Bullough 2004, p. 254; Orchard 1992 on the propensity for minor changes in quoted verse.

126 Alcuin, York poem: Godman 1982, lines 1437–9 and apparatus, pp. 112–13. Godman's interpretation depends on glosses in one manuscript. Poetic composition, usually subsumed into grammar, may also be intended.

127 Holtz 1997, p. 47.

128 Lapidge 2006, p. 68 n. 15 citing Hine 1992 (which adduces new evidence superseding Hine in Reynolds 1983, pp. 376–8).

129 Alcuin, York poem: Godman 1982, lines 1534–5.

list – evoking the library's continued and undispersed presence in a single location.[130]

Alcuin makes it clear that the list is incomplete because the full roster of names would exceed appropriate poetic usage.[131] Of course some names will have been excluded as incompatible with the requirements of the Latin hexameter; nonetheless, the refusal to name all effectively evokes the ample size of the collection. The list is couched in simple and direct language with minimal descriptive additions to fill out the hexameters: most of the names do not have epithets and those that do are qualified by single adjectives: Father Jerome, Bishop Ambrose, astute Orosius.[132] A bequest of books did not have to specify titles: Charlemagne's will famously did not, though other later wills did.[133]

The passage does not follow the conventions of nearly contemporary booklists which include titles and sometimes incipits and are likely to be ordered according to a similar but not identical scheme.[134] Library lists seem to have been an eighth-century innovation of the Anglo-Saxons on the Continent[135] and so it is intriguing to consider whether Alcuin would have brought a list of his books to the Continent with him or even whether Ælberht would have listed the works in a will or a booklist.[136] In short, to regard the list of authors in Alcuin's poem as an inventory manqué is to miss the richness of the poem and its author's complex intentions. Literary verse models and analogues provide a more apposite context for appreciating the distinctness of Alcuin's endeavour. Catalogue poetry was a recognised literary activity, but a list of authors is an entirely different exercise from, say, an ekphrasis listing the fish to be found in the Moselle.[137]

Alcuin's versified list of authors has three important analogues in compositions by Isidore, Venantius Fortunatus and Theodulf, which also name authors; however, none of their lists occurs in a poem that resembles the genre or purpose of Alcuin's, and the number and range of authorities listed by Alcuin is significantly longer than the others (naming forty-one authors as against Isidore's eighteen, Fortunatus' seven Christian–Latin poets and Theodulf's

130 Alcuin, York poem: Godman 1982, line 1536: 'Illic invenies' and line 1558: 'Invenies alios perplures, lector, ibidem'. These phrases indicate that the poem must predate Alcuin's ep. 121 (of late 796 or early 797).

131 Alcuin, York poem: Godman 1982, lines 1560–3, pp. 126–7.

132 Alcuin, York poem: Godman 1982, lines 1541–3 and following, pp. 122–3.

133 Charlemagne's will: Einhart, *Vita Karoli*: Holder-Egger 1911, ch. 33, pp. 37–41; Bischoff 1981, pp. 149–69. The bequest of Gerward, librarian for Louis the Pious, to Lorsch (BAV, Pal. lat 1877, *s.* ix^{med}): Lehmann 1932, pp. 207–13; Crick 1987, p. 190; McKitterick 1989b, p. 186.

134 Gorman 2004; Lapidge 2006, pp. 53–62 and 133–54; McKitterick 1989b, pp. 169–210.

135 Lapidge 2006, p. 148.

136 McKitterick 1989b, p. 199–200.

137 Ausonius, *Mosella*, lines 75–149: Evelyn White 1919–21, I, pp. 230–4.

nineteen authors). Yet all share one essential feature which sets them apart from the eighth-century inventories and library catalogues closely contemporary with Alcuin's poem: they list authors' names, rather than the titles of their works.

In the first book of his *Vita Sancti Martini*, the sixth-century poet Venantius Fortunatus (one of Alcuin's most important poetic models) had named seven Christian Latin poetic predecessors and characterised their works, crowning the list with a modesty topos describing his meagre faculties and explaining his decision to compose a verse *Life* of St Martin all the same.[138] The purpose of these lines was to sketch a Christian literary genealogy while announcing the author's unworthiness, not to give an indication of a programme of study or the contents of a library in a particular place. Alcuin had read these lines; some reminiscences of them can be detected in his account of Ælberht's teaching programme, but not in the booklist.[139] Isidore's *Versus in bibliotheca* were originally destined to be inscriptions, most likely for the walls of a library,[140] perhaps below frescoes with the relevant book containers adjacent, though other locations associated with book chests, or even placement inside codices, have been suggested.[141] They have been characterised as a kind of versified, illustrated version of *De viris illustribus*[142] perhaps modelled on similar compositions from two papal libraries.[143] Isidore's library *tituli* make no mention of classical prose authors and those that mention the pagan poets do so to warn readers of their danger – the intention was to decorate, rather than to describe or catalogue.[144] Their distinct original context, purpose and contents mean that Isidore's *Versus in bibliotheca* cannot be regarded as a close analogue to Alcuin's list of authors, except in one respect: that both have a deictic, or pointing function: 'here you will find'. Yet the scheme of Isidore's verses and the subjects treated, and their order, do not evoke a wide-ranging programme of liberal studies.[145]

138 Venantius Fortunatus, *Vita Martini*: Leo, 1881, pp. 295–6, lines 15–26. Glauche 1970, pp. 5–6; Glauche characterises the authors as Fortunatus' *Gewährsmänner* and points to the possible school use of the *Vita Martini*.

139 Alcuin, York poem: Godman 1982: see, for example, the apparatus to lines 1435–6, pp. 112–13.

140 Fontaine 1959, p. 738.

141 Beeson 1913, pp. 153–5; Fontaine 1959, p. 738.

142 Fontaine 1959, p. 741.

143 Beeson 1913, on earlier library epigrams, pp. 150–2; Fontaine 1959, pp. 738–44; on the transmission of some of the *versus* from Agapitus' library in the Einsiedeln Sylloge, see *ibid.*, p. 739 n. 4; on Gregory, *ibid.*, p. 740. Glauche 1970, p. 7.

144 Fontaine 1959, p. 741; Beeson 1913, pp. 154–5, on Isidore's *praeteritio* concerning classical prose authors, despite his library's good stock of them; see epigram no. x, p. 161.

145 Glauche 1970, p. 7: if the printed verse order corresponds to the layout: scripture, patristics, Christian poets, church historians, contemporary ecclesiastical writers, jurists.

Theodulf's verses 'On the books I used to read and how the fables of the poets can be mystically reinterpreted' names some nineteen authors – patristic writers followed by Christian poets, grammarians and two classical poets – and gives a snapshot of learning. However, the purpose is not to depict a particular library or educational programme,[146] but rather to show how the falsities of the classical poets can be redeemed;[147] and it has even been seen as a kind of disapproving rejoinder to Alcuin.[148] The distinctive features of Alcuin's evidence for the York library in his poem on York – the personal affectionate memoir that evokes the richness and range of the studies and library without either prescribing a programme or offering a catalogue – stand out even more strongly when contrasted with Theodulf, Isidore and Fortunatus.[149]

Table 32.1 shows which of the authors mentioned by Alcuin in his York poem are also named in the aforementioned verses of Venantius Fortunatus, Isidore and Theodulf.[150] Also included are the sources employed by Alcuin in his devotional florilegium *De laude Dei*.[151] For this work, probably compiled during a return visit to York in 790–3, Alcuin excerpted a range of prose and verse writings to create prayers. It thus provides important evidence not only for his library and other books available at York, but sometimes also for the recensions of those works present in York. The final rows of the table show which authors not named in the York poem were laid under contribution for *De laude Dei*, or named by Isidore and Theodulf. This presentation makes the breadth of Alcuin's chosen *auctoritates* immediately apparent, while the number of florilegium works not cited in the York poem highlights the selectiveness, and shaping, of the York poem's list.

As we have seen, Alcuin's list cannot be easily aligned with either nearly contemporary book catalogues or book verses, yet it does have some of the functions of each. It constitutes a clear statement of ownership. When

146 Theodulf, *Carmen*, 45: Dümmler 1881, pp. 543–4; Nees 1991, pp. 65, 119.

147 *Ibid.*

148 Nees 1991, p. 119 n. 42, but see Alcuin, York poem: Godman 1982, pp. lxx–lxxv and notes to lines 1551–3.

149 Contreni 1989, reprinted 1992.

150 For the editions used for each, see notes to the foregoing discussion. For identifications of works, see Lapidge 2006, pp. 228–31. For school reading, Glauche 1970. Note that the table follows the order of Alcuin's poem and that the subject categories follow the interpretations of Holtz 1997, pp. 47–9, rather than those of Godman for the cases where the subject represented by an author's name is disputable.

151 See Constantinescu 1974; Bullough 2004, pp. 177–80, 186–7, 193–204 and additional references in the index; Lapidge 2006, pp. 232–3 for a full list of authors and works. For the accompanying *Miracula Nyniae* probably written by Alcuin's students at York, Vollmer 1905, pp. xiii–xxvi; Levison 1940; Strecker 1964, pp. 943–62; Orchard 1992.

Table 32.1 *Names mentioned in Alcuin's York Poem and Florilegium*

Authors named in Alcuin's York poem	Alcuin, *De laude Dei*	Venantius Fortunatus	Isidore	Theodulf
Patristic				
Jerome			✓	✓
Hilary			✓	✓
Ambrose			✓	✓
Augustine	✓		✓	✓
Athanasius				
Orosius			✓	
Gregory	✓			
Leo				✓
Basil				
Fulgentius				
Cassiodorus				
Chrysostom			✓	✓
Aldhelm	✓			
Bede	✓			
Philosophers				
Victorinus				
Boethius				
History and natural history				
Pompeius (Trogus) (i.e. Justinus)				
Pliny				
Rhetoric and dialectic				
Aristotle				
Cicero				
Christian poets				
Caelius Sedulius	✓	✓	✓	✓
Iuvencus	✓	✓	✓	
Alcimus			✓	✓
Clemens (i.e. Prudentius)		✓	✓	✓
Prosper of Aquitaine				
Paulinus of Périgueux		✓		✓
Arator		✓		✓
Venantius Fortunatus	✓			✓
Lactantius				
Classical poets				
Vergil				
Statius				
Lucan				
Grammarians				
Probus				
Phocas				
(Aelius) Donatus				✓
Priscian				

Table 32.1 (*cont.*)

Authors named in Alcuin's York poem	**Alcuin, *De laude Dei***	**Venantius Fortunatus**	**Isidore**	**Theodulf**
Servius				
Eutyches				
Pompeius				✓
Cominianus				
Authors and works not named in the York poem	Dracontius, Eusebius of Caesarea (in Rufinus' translation), Isidore Anonymous works: *Adhortationes sanctorum patrum* *Passiones martyrum*: Agatha, Agnes, Cosmas and Damian, Juliana, Mary and Martha, (includes Valentine), Polochronius, (includes Abdo and Sennen), *Passio Laurentii*	Authors named by Fortunatus not mentioned by Alcuin: Orientius	Authors named by Isidore not mentioned by Alcuin: Origen, Cyprian, Eusebius, Leander, Theodosius, Paulus, Gaius, Horatius Flaccus, Ovidius Naso, Persius	Cyprian

Alcuin wrote the poem, he could assume that the books (his books) were still all together in one place.[152] And it evokes an ideal image of the *auctores*, the authoritative guarantors of knowledge. His intention seems to be to create a picture of the breadth and authority of the collection; he proceeds, as expected, from patristic works through other subjects to classical poets and late antique grammarians. The aspiration to authoritative and complete knowledge is evident with the opening statement:

> There you will find the legacy of the ancient fathers:
> all the Roman possessed in the Latin world,

152 Alcuin, York poem: Godman 1982, lines 1536 and 1558, pp. 122 and 126.

Whatever famous Greece has transmitted to the Latins,
draughts of the Hebrew race from Heaven's showers,
and what Africa has spread abroad in streams of light[153]

and this is reinforced, rather than diminished, by Alcuin's refusal to name all: *praeteritio*, a standard feature in catalogue verse.[154]

Since only names rather than titles of works are included, inferring the library holdings depends on external evidence such as Alcuin's reading and juxtaposition with the hierarchy of studies outlined in the curriculum description.[155] It is also important to consider how extensive and heterogeneous a collection made up of the volumes represented by forty-odd names could be. Except for extremely long works which could fill several volumes, most medieval codices do not contain a single work by a single author, but are composite; shorter works would almost invariably be bound with others – if they were bound at all. (For example, when Alcuin later recalled some letters about the soul exchanged by Jerome and Augustine, used by him in York, he called the work which contained them both a *liber* and a *libellus*.[156]) Thus the York poem list of authors can hardly be regarded as indicating a collection of individual codices for each name. The name list, then, invites one to imagine a roll-call of authorities,[157] rather than some forty-one codices, one per name, in cases or chests. (Miscellanies covering the language arts of the trivium, such as Berlin, Staatsbibliothek, Diez B. Sant 66, and Paris, BnF, lat. 7530, or, more closely associated with the quadrivium, dialectic, and the legacy of Alcuin, the 'Munich Passages'[158] show how heterogeneous scholarly compilations might be – at the end of the eighth century we glimpse the most vibrant scholarship and study in such works of excerpting and compilation: the zeal for improved corrected editions gains full strength only in the following generation.) In this connection, Alcuin's letter to Charlemagne, written shortly after he had abandoned all hope of returning to England, is worth a closer look. The letter could be interpreted as Alcuin's wish to move his York library to Tours, but it is likely that he intended something rather different and more selective:

153 Alcuin, York poem: Godman 1982, lines 1536–40, pp. 122–3.
154 Alcuin, York poem: Godman 1982, lines 1561–2, pp. 126–7.
155 Holtz 1997, pp. 47–51.
156 Alcuin, ep. 309: Dümmler 1895, p. 474, lines 21–4 – i.e. Alcuin, *De animae ratione*: Curry 1966, pp. 58–9 and *PL*, CI, col. 645; for discussion and conjectural identification of the texts in question: Bullough 2004, pp. 264–6.
157 Glauche 1970, pp. 5–6.
158 Marenbon 1981, pp. 32–56 and 151–66.

I, your Flaccus, according to your exhortation and encouragement, am occupied in supplying to some under the roof of Saint Martin the honey of the sacred scriptures; am eager to inebriate others with the old wine of ancient learning; begin to nourish others on the fruits of grammatical subtlety; long to illumine some with the order of the stars ...

But I, your servant, miss to some extent the rarer books (*exquisitiores libelli*) of scholastic learning which I had in my own country through the excellent and devoted zeal of my master and also through some toil (*sudor*) of my own. I tell these things to your Excellency, in case it may perchance be agreeable to your counsel, which is most eager for the whole of knowledge, that I may send some of our pupils to choose[159] there what we need and to bring into France the flowers of Britain; that not in York only there may be a 'garden enclosed', but in Tours the 'plants of Paradise with the fruit of the orchard', that the south wind may come and blow through the gardens by the river Loire, and the aromatical spices thereof may flow.'[160]

The books are called *libelli*,[161] booklets or short works, owed to the industry and toil of Ælberht and Alcuin – perhaps even compilations that they had made themselves. The items are to be selected, or perhaps even *excerpted*, by some of Alcuin's students from Tours.[162] Whether they were to make copies or simply to select and transport some of the rarer books, there is no suggestion whatever of the wholesale transfer of the library. Alcuin wanted only the works that he had had in York and that were unavailable to him on the Continent. Presumably the remainder of the collection would have stayed in York, and

159 The verb is 'excipio': Latham and Howlett 1975–, fasc. III, s.v.: 1, 'take out, select' and b, 'mark or single out'; 2, 'excerpt'.

160 Alcuin, ep. 121: Dümmler 1895, pp. 175–8 at p. 177, lines 4–17 (AD 796–7); trans. Whitelock 1979, no. 201, pp. 853–4. Cf. Allott 1974, no. 8, pp. 11–13 at p. 12, which removes the ambiguity by rendering 'excipiant' as 'get'. A relevant extract from this letter was included by William of Malmesbury, *Gesta Regum Anglorum*: Mynors *et al.* (ed.) 1998, i.65.3, pp. 96–7 (the translators render 'excipiant' with 'extract').

> Sed ex parte desunt mihi, servulo vestro, exquisitiores eruditionis scolasticae libelli, quos habui in patria per bonam et devotissimam magistri mei industriam vel etiam mei ipsius qualemcumque sudorem. Ideo haec vestrae excellentiae dico, ne forte vestro placeat totius sapientiae desiderantissimo consilio, ut aliquos ex pueris nostris remittam, qui *excipiant* inde nobis necessaria quaeque et revehant in Frantiam flores Britanniae; ut non sit tantummodo in Euborica hortus conclusus, sed in Turonica emissiones paradisi cum pomorum fructibus, ut veniens Auster perflaret hortos ligeri fluminis et fluant aromata illius et novissime fiat quod sequitur in cantico, unde hoc adsumpsi paradigma: 'Veniat dilectus meus in hortum suum' ...
>
> Haec sunt, quae vestra nobilissima intentio non ignorat – quomodo per omnes sanctae scripturae paginas exhortamur ad sapientiam discendam. [Emphasis added.]

161 Latham and Howlett 1975–, fasc. V, s.v. *libellus*: a small book or part of a book.

162 'Excerpt' is not attested as a meaning for 'excipio' in Lewis and Short 1879/1880, s.v.; however, an exceptor is a scribe or amanuensis. 'Excerpt' as a meaning for 'excipio' is attested (by Aldhelm and William of Malmesbury) in Latham and Howlett 1975–, fasc. III, s.v. *excipio*, 2.

perhaps been bequeathed to Eanbald II. The wholesale loss of a library would have been devastating to a school, as Alcuin would certainly have realised. That there was some continuity of learning in ninth-century Yorkshire is evident from Ædiluulf's poem *De abbatibus*, perhaps about a foundation at Crayke.[163] It seems, then, that if Charlemagne responded favourably to Alcuin's request, Alcuin will either have imported only a small portion of the library or else had some volumes copied or even excerpted.[164] (Corroboration for this might perhaps be inferred from Alcuin's reference, in the early ninth century, to a booklet that he had had in York being possibly available in the imperial *armarium*.[165]) This scenario could explain why so few books can even be conjecturally adduced as Alcuin's exports from York. If this hypothesis is accepted, then the earliest evidence for texts and subjects known to have been reintroduced by Alcuin, and for rare items (*libelli exquisitiores*) – such as materials associated with the revival of the study of logic,[166] the works of Boethius, perhaps the *Compendiosa Doctrina* of Nonius Marcellus,[167] even the forged letters of Seneca and Paul or Alexander and Dindimus[168] and the acrostics of Publilius Optatianus Porphyrius[169] – deserves the closest possible scrutiny for clues of transmission from York to Tours. Of course, while he was on the Continent, Alcuin must have discovered and discussed works that he had not had at York (a case in point would be the poetry of Tibullus),[170] but he could not have gained his reputation for extraordinary learning, and he would not have wanted to bring material from York, if the collection there had not been truly exceptional by European standards.

163 Æthelwulf, *De Abbatibus*: Campbell 1967; Lapidge 1990; Orchard 1992.

164 See above nn. 108–9 about Tiberius Claudius Donatus, *Interpretationes Vergilianae* (*CLA*, III, no. 297 a+b; Florence, Biblioteca Medicea-Laurenziana XLV.15) copied in Insular and Caroline Minuscule.

165 In other words, the imagined scenario if Alcuin had had the work copied or brought from York, but left his own copy with the court library – see Alcuin, ep. 309: Dümmler 1895, p. 474, lines 21–30 at line 30; Alcuin, *De animae ratione*: Curry 1966, pp. 58–9, and *PL*, CI, col. 645.

166 Marenbon 1981: on Alcuin reintroducing *De decem categoriae*, p. 31 and pp. 144–70. Bullough 2004, pp. 376–7; Alcuin, *Carmen*, 73: Dummler 1881, p. 295.

167 Lapidge 2006, pp. 104–5. Reynolds 1983, pp. 248–52 at pp. 249–50. Note that the lack of traces of Insular symptoms in the fine early ninth-century Tours manuscript, which is probably of Alcuin's era (Leiden, Universiteitsbibliotheek, Voss. Lat. F.73), could be explained by an archetype brought from the Continent to York, thence back to the Continent. Reynolds (p. 251) observes that Tours played an important role in the work's diffusion.

168 Levison 1946, p. 148. For editions, Barlow 1938 and Kübler 1888; Alcuin's poem of dedication, presenting both works to Charlemagne, is his *Carmen*, 81: Dümmler 1881, p. 300. Bullough 2004, p. 378; Bischoff 1981, p. 158, n. 44.

169 Schaller 1995: the collaboration of Alcuin, Joseph Scottus and Theodulf in composing acrostic verse inspired by the works of Porphyrius (with whose exercises in the genre they are transmitted in Bern, Burgerbibliothek, 212) points to Alcuin as the initiator of the venture. Reynolds 1983, p. xxi. Note though, that Porphyrius was also known to the circle of Boniface.

170 Garrison 2005.

The library in the ninth century

What of the library after Alcuin? There is scant evidence about books and learning in York in the ninth century; what there is points to continuity, even if at a lower level.[171] Whether the collection had been substantially exported by Alcuin or not, it is reasonable to assume that the books necessary for the school would have been acquired or copied in order to maintain instruction at some level. In the middle of the century, Lupus, abbot of Ferrières, wrote to the archbishop of York to renew the bonds of goodwill and reciprocal prayer that, he said, had lapsed, and to ask that any favour he requested might be granted.[172] At the same time, he requested a number of rare books – not from the archbishop, but from the abbot.[173] This may, but does not necessarily, imply a change in the institutional basis of the library, and perhaps also of the Minster community, from regular canons to monks. If the Minster community had become monastic, books would no longer have been owned privately. The books Lupus sought were exegetical and rhetorical; in two cases, he named the works of exegesis using titles which do not correspond closely to extant works or authorial lists, suggesting that the works were unfamiliar to him.[174] The works he sought were Jerome's *Questions on the Old and New Testaments*,[175] Bede's *Questions on Both Testaments* (*sic*), the second volume of Jerome's *Questions on Jeremiah* (*Commentarius in Ieremiam prophetam*?), and all twelve books of Quintilian's *Institutio oratoria*. It is impossible to say whether Lupus expected these volumes to be available at York on the basis of traditions derived from Alcuin (Lupus had been a pupil of two of Alcuin's pupils, Sigewulf and Hrabanus), or because of the (otherwise unattested) renown of York in the mid ninth century, but the imprecise titles might suggest the latter. It is a sign of the new Carolingian culture of book production that Lupus (unlike Lull) requested the volumes in question as exemplars for copying (and even explained where they would be copied and by whom), rather than as gifts outright. His request appears to have been at least partially unsuccessful, for a few years later he would seek two of the same volumes (Jerome and Quintilian) from the pope.[176]

171 Lapidge 1990; Orchard 1992; Æthelwulf, *De abbatibus*: Campbell 1967; see also p. 691 below.

172 Lupus of Ferrières, ep. 61: Marshall 1984, p. 67 (AD 849? AD 852?); trans. Whitelock 1979, no. 215, pp. 876–7.

173 Lupus of Ferrières, ep. 62: Marshall 1984, p. 68 (AD 849? AD 852?); trans. Whitelock 1979, no. 216, pp. 877–8.

174 Cassiodorus, *Institutiones*: Mynors 1937, I.xxi, pp. 59–60; trans. Halporn 2004, pp. 152–3 at p. 153, identifying the work referred to as Jerome, ep. 53; Bede, *HE*, V, 24: Colgrave and Mynors 1969, pp. 567–71.

175 Lupus of Ferrières, ep. 62: Marshall 1984, p. 68, line 14.

176 Lupus of Ferrières, ep. 103: Marshall 1984, pp. 100–1.

We have grown accustomed to grasping some aspects of the world of the medieval book by calculating the speed of the scribe or the number of hides necessary for a volume. Important though these may be to know, they are also the quantifications that speak most to our age and its values. The portrait of York's library is shadowy and obscure when we look closely or press for specifics; its value to Alcuin as a hard-won store of wisdom always associated with the teacher to whom he was devoted, and its fruits on the Continent – whether the *copia librorum* that accompanied Liudger or the tantalising traces at the Carolingian court and in the Loire Valley – cannot easily be pinned down to actual volumes, but the effort and devotion that made them possible can be glimpsed through the poems and letters in a way scarcely possible for the other vanished libraries of early Britain.

33
The library of Cynewulf

FIONA GAMESON

The singular circumstance of being able to give a name to the author of not one but four Anglo-Saxon works of literature has afforded the poet Cynewulf a significance arguably greater than the literary merits of his oeuvre warrant. Be that as it may, the four Old English poems bearing Cynewulf's runic signature provide a unique opportunity to assess the reading of one named poet, based on a corpus of 2,600 lines and embracing the genres of 'catalogue', hagiography and epic. A name, however, is one thing; the issues of who that author might have been, and when and where he may have worked are quite different matters. Informed speculation on these questions – as well as on that of whether he composed works other than those in which his runic signature appears – has led to various conclusions. Currently the most widely held view is that he was an ecclesiastic, active in the early ninth century, and based in Mercia.[1]

The single most important source detectable behind the oeuvre of Cynewulf is, unsurprisingly, the Bible, echoes of various parts of which are scattered throughout three of his four poems. If this was to be expected, it is nevertheless worth remarking that, in an era when the circulation of biblical books other than the gospels and the psalter was restricted, Cynewulf clearly knew and drew upon Job, Proverbs, Chronicles, Maccabees, and various of the prophets from the Old Testament, and upon Acts, the Pauline Epistles, the Letters of Peter and John, and the Apocalypse from the New. The obvious deduction is that he had access to a complete Bible or pandect.

Although the Bible naturally formed the bedrock upon which the Anglo-Saxon church was founded, the examples of the lives and deaths of the members of the early church, the saints and martyrs, provided essential material for reading and preaching, and no fewer than three major forms of hagiographical material are reflected in the poems of Cynewulf. *Juliana* is a *passio*,

1 Sisam 1953, pp. 1–28; see also Fulk 2001; Orchard 2003a. Conner 2001 takes a contrary position.

concentrating upon the torments and death of the saint; *Elene* is a *Vita*, detailing the acts of the eponymous lady (particularly her finding of the True Cross); while *Fates of the Apostles* is akin to a martyrology, with brief entries giving salient facts about the life and death of each saint. Although the exact nature of the sources that Cynewulf drew upon for these works is a matter of debate, certain facts are clear. Cynewulf's version of the *Passio of St Juliana* is nearest in all particulars to that which appears in an early ninth-century collection of Latin saints' lives now in Paris: this – or a close relative of it – would seem to have been his source and the date of the manuscript does not rule out the former possibility.[2] Although its medieval provenance was northern France (Beauvais), the book is believed to have been written at Canterbury.[3] In the case of *Elene*, it is clear that Cynewulf cannot have used the extant manuscript which best parallels his version – an eighth-century volume from St Gallen.[4] In point of fact, although there are striking correlations (even extending to minute details) between the version of events in *Elene* and those found in this copy of the *Acta Cyriaci*, it was obviously not Cynewulf's actual exemplar; this is a text of which there are numerous recensions.[5] Moreover many of the details found in *Elene* also feature in other texts, notably the *Inventio crucis*, perhaps dating from the fifth century, several versions of which circulated in Anglo-Saxon England, and Cynewulf may have drawn upon one or more of these to supplement the copy of the *Acta Cyriaci* that he used.[6]

The role of the Anglo-Saxon poet as editor and arranger, rather than as simple translator of his Latin material, is nowhere more clearly demonstrated than in Cynewulf's handling of his sources for *Fates of the Apostles*. It was long thought that the ultimate sources for this poem were the *Martyrology* of Bede and the *Breviarium Apostolorum*,[7] though at least one commentator has pointed out that it shares more details with the greatly enlarged *Martyrology* of Usuardus produced in the later ninth century.[8] An alternative and more persuasive view, however, is that, rather than using a martyrology, Cynewulf turned to something like a passional which included fuller lives of the apostles, that he then abbreviated himself; while the order of his reworked material may have been inspired by litanies.[9] At the same time, Cynewulf's inclusion in his lines on Thomas of the rarely recorded episode of the raising of Gad[10] suggests either that his passional was particularly comprehensive or that he also

2 BnF, lat. 10861; Lapidge 2003a. 3 Brown 1986.
4 St Gallen, Stiftsbibliothek, 225: *CLA*, VII, no. 928.
5 Gradon 1977, pp. 15–22; Calder and Allen 1976, pp. 59–60.
6 Napier 1894; also Bodden 1987. 7 Krapp 1906, esp. pp. xxx–xxxii.
8 Conner 2001. 9 McCulloh 2000.
10 *Fates of the Apostles*, ll. 54–7.

had access to more unusual material from a different source. Not found in the martyrologies, this event may have been gleaned from the apocryphal Acts of Thomas,[11] or from some other source like the now-lost vernacular poem about that saint to which Ælfric refers when, in his *Excusatio dictantis*, he justifies not providing a version of the *Life* of Thomas.[12] At the very beginning of *Fates of the Apostles*, Cynewulf says that he had gathered his material widely ('samnode wide', 2b): in this case such a claim would seem to have been not poetic licence but a true reflection of an eclectic approach to the available material.

If three of his poems reveal a debt to hagiography, the fourth, *Christ II* (The Ascension), signals Cynewulf's knowledge of certain writings of the Fathers of the church. Although the basic narrative of the Ascension appears in Acts 1. 1–11, Cynewulf's exposition of its significance is drawn from Gregory the Great's homily on the subject.[13] Indeed, the extent to which the poet borrowed from this particular text suggests that he knew it intimately and may even have had a copy of it beside him as he composed. Cynewulf also makes passing use of another sermon by Gregory, this time from his series commenting upon Ezekiel.[14] In addition to the works of Gregory, those of Bede were apparently known to Cynewulf, though his use of them is more sparing – he is indebted to two of Bede's texts concerning the Ascension[15] as well as to the quasi-topographical *De locis sanctis*.[16] That Cynewulf had access to works by Bede, the highly regarded native scholar, and Gregory – who was particularly revered in Anglo-Saxon England and seems to have been comparatively well represented in early English book collections – is not especially surprising. More remarkable, perhaps, is the other patristic author with whom he seems to have been familiar – Ambrose, two of whose works on the psalms may underpin a lengthy passage in Cynewulf's personal epilogue to *Elene*.[17] Although many of the ideas here expressed are found scattered through the works of the Fathers, it is in Ambrose that are found the closest verbal parallels to this part of Cynewulf's poem. As we might expect of a well-educated ecclesiastic, our poet is very familiar with the images and rhetoric of the Last Judgment – eschatological references appear at length in three of his four epilogues[18] – but

11 Elliott 1993, pp. 439–511 esp. 456. 12 Godden 1979, pp. 297–8.

13 Gregory the Great, *Homiliae in euangelia*, xxix: Étaix 1999, pp. 244–54. Identifications in Fontes Anglo-Saxonici.

14 Gregory the Great, *Homiliae in Ezekielem*, II, I, 10: Adriaen 1971, pp. 216–17 and 417–18.

15 Bede, *Homilia*, 2, 15, and *Hymn* 6: Hurst and Fraipont 1955, pp. 280–9.

16 The odd fact that Christ ascends through the open roof of a temple is not in Acts but corresponds to the description of the spot in Bede, *De locis sanctis*, VI, 1: Geyer *et al.* 1965, p. 262.

17 *Elene*, ll. 1286b–1314. Ambrose, *Explanatio super psalmos* xii, § 56, 3–13: Petschenig 1919, p. 47; and *Expositio de psalmo cxviii*, 3, 16: Petschenig 1913, p. 49.

18 Although in *Fates of the Apostles* Cynewulf dwells upon his death and journeying to an afterlife, it is not the usual picture of judgement, fire and answering for sins.

as such themes are widespread in the writings of the Fathers, identifying the exact sources he may have drawn upon is problematic.[19]

In sum Cynewulf's corpus shows not only that he could handle the forms of vernacular poetry, but also that he was a competent translator and editor of the Latin texts he had read. He was well versed in the Bible, and had access to selected works by Gregory, Ambrose and Bede, along with a fairly extensive range of hagiographic writings. This variety of material would seem to imply that the poet was based at a major ecclesiastical centre; if we believe that he was working in ninth-century Mercia, the foundations at Worcester, Hereford and Lichfield come most readily to mind.[20] Further support for a possible Worcester connection might be found in the fact, already noted, that he appears to have had access to a full Bible, something that was a comparative rarity in earlier Anglo-Saxon England, but may well have been available at Worcester in the form of the 'Offa Bible'.[21]

What is also notable about this oeuvre is that it proclaims itself as the product of a poet who was highly conscious of being literate. Not only was Cynewulf a man to whom books and their store of information from the past were of primary importance, he was also someone who, by his use of runic letters to incorporate his name in his poems – unique in the extant corpus – presupposed a written context for their transmission. The difficulty of interpreting the passages within which his 'signatures' are embedded when the rune names are supplied suggests that, though an audience of listeners might have been able to understand these cryptic clues, the primary value of each rune was as a letter to spell out Cynewulf's name to someone reading the text in a manuscript. This could also explain why the runic letters are used quite differently in *Juliana*, where they appear in groups, possibly spelling words, rather than as individual letters.[22]

In addition it is worth noting that, just as in his own works he continually drew upon written sources, so in all his poems except *Juliana* Cynewulf makes mention of books and writings. If predictably there are references to scripture, in such phrases as 'on godes bocum' or 'þurh halige bec',[23] the term he particularly favours is the more general 'fyrngewritu' ('ancient writings').[24]

19 A case in point is the question of the immediate source for *Elene*, ll. 1281b–6a: since this is an idea found in several homiletic texts, is he more likely to be relying upon a text from Caesarius of Arles or informed by native tradition? See Wright 1990.

20 Cartographic presentation of the foundations in the relevant area: Sims-Williams 1990, pp. xiv–xv.

21 Turner 1916b, app. I; see also Chapter 17 in this volume.

22 Page 1999, pp. 191–7.

23 *Elene*, ll. 204b, 290a and 273b.

24 *Elene*, ll. 155a, 373b, 431a, 560b.

Thus in *Elene*, a poem of 1,321 lines, there are sixteen references to books and writing, while in the 426 lines of *Christ II*, there are six.[25] While Cynewulf is by no means unique amongst Anglo-Saxon poets in referring to books, the frequency of such allusions in *Elene* and *Christ II* is proportionately higher than in almost any other work from the Old English poetic corpus. Moreover, in every other poem that is notable for its references to writing and/or books (*Daniel*, *The Phoenix* and *Solomon and Saturn*)[26] there is a readily apparent explanation for the phenomenon. The first of these has at its heart the episode of the 'writing on the wall'; the second is, like the works of Cynewulf, deeply dependent upon Latin sources and may indeed have been influenced by our poet's style;[27] while the third – the richest in allusions to books – is concerned with ancient lore, arcane mysteries, and the posing and solving of riddles.[28] In fact these works, along with the poems of Cynewulf, could be said to belong to a genre of compositions that are dependent upon written texts, which, though expressed in the predominantly oral formulaic mode of Old English poetry, are yet closely linked to a pre-existing written exemplar. In this context Cynewulf's oeuvre stands out by dint of bearing a personal stamp – his signature. Like the scribe who inserted a colophon with his name into a manuscript, begging for the remembrance and prayers of the reader, so Cynewulf spelt out his name in order that the reader, not the hearer, might recognise, remember and pray for him. This supremely literate poet was not alone in turning to books from the past to provide him with the substance of his works, but he seems to have been unique in using them to ensure that he would be remembered by name in the future among literate book-owning communities.

25 *Elene*, ll. 155a, 204b, 290a, 364b, 373b, 387b, 431a, 560b, 654b, 658b, 670b, 674b, 825b–6, 852b, 1211a, 1254b–6a; and *Christ*, ll. 453b, 547b, 673a, 701b, 785b, 793a.

26 *Daniel*: 764 lines, 6 references; *The Phoenix*: 677 lines, 6 references; *Solomon and Saturn* (highly fragmentary): 506 lines, 10 references.

27 Blake 1990, pp. 22–3.

28 This poem also contains runes as part of the text, though not standing by themselves as in Cynewulf's signature passages: Page 1999, pp. 187–8.

34
King Alfred and his circle

ROHINI JAYATILAKA

The author of the preface to the Old English translation of Gregory the Great's *Regula pastoralis*, writing during the reign of King Alfred (871–99), laments the destruction of the books that were once in abundance in England: 'I recollected how – before everything was ransacked and burned – the churches throughout England stood filled with treasures and books.'[1] Only a couple of hundred from the probably thousands of pre-Alfredian books have come down to us, and unfortunately the extant Anglo-Saxon booklists do little to supplement the surviving manuscripts.[2] Given that the evidence that remains is inevitably fragmentary, we shall probably never know how many books were in existence in England in Alfred's day, but the texts that are thought to have been produced during his reign, and possibly under his patronage, suggest that a significant number of volumes were still available to the Anglo-Saxons. The specific works that make up the Alfredian canon have changed over the years[3] and the most recent scholarship on the subject has questioned whether Alfred himself was responsible for writing anything.[4] For the purpose of reconstructing the books available to Alfred and his circle, therefore, I shall consider the collective body of writings associated with the ninth-century court of Alfred.[5] These include the Old English versions of Gregory the Great's *Regula pastoralis* and *Dialogi*, Boethius' *De consolatione philosophiae*, St Augustine's *Soliloquia*, Orosius' *Historiae adversum paganos*, Bede's *Historia ecclesiastica gentis Anglorum*, the prose version of the first fifty psalms of the psalter, the *Anglo-Saxon Chronicle*, the laws of Alfred, and Asser's *Vita Ælfredi*

1 From Gregory's *Pastoral Care*, trans. Keynes and Lapidge 1983, p. 125.
2 Gneuss 1986, esp. p. 645.
3 For general discussions of the Alfredian canon, see esp. Whitelock 1966; Bately 1980a, 1988, 1990, 2003; and Frantzen 1986.
4 Godden 2007.
5 I exclude the *Old English Martyrology* and Bald's *Leechbook*, both of which have only very tenuous connections to Alfred's circle.

regis. What, then, do these Anglo-Saxon writings tell us of the range of texts that were available to Alfred and his circle?

Three of these texts, the *Pastoral Care*, the *Dialogues* and the *Ecclesiastical History*, are fairly close translations of the original works, all of which were well known in earlier Anglo-Saxon England. Much of Bede's original text was omitted from the vernacular version, and a few details are added to it and to the *Pastoral Care*, where reference is very occasionally made to books of the Bible. In sharp contrast to these three compilations are the Old English versions of the first fifty psalms of the psalter, St Augustine's *Soliloquia*, Boethius' *De consolatione philosophiae*, and Orosius' *Historiae adversum paganos*, all of which diverge from the original Latin texts in varying degrees. As a result, they tell us a great deal about the range of books that may have been available to the Alfredian circle.

The most recent editor of the Old English prose version of the first fifty psalms of the psalter observes that this text combines literal translation with paraphrase, explanation and interpretation.[6] The Old English version is based primarily on the Roman version of the psalter, which was current in Anglo-Saxon England in the period before the mid-tenth-century Benedictine reform, but also includes some readings from other versions: the *Gallicanum* and, to a lesser extent, the *Hebraicum* and the *Vetus Latina*. The translator probably knew these various versions directly, though it is also possible that he drew on psalter commentaries based on the *Romanum* and the *Vetus Latina* for some variant readings and interpretations. In addition, each psalm, except the first, is preceded by an introduction, providing a three- or fourfold scheme of interpretative directions based primarily on the Latin commentary known as the Pseudo-Bede *Argumenta*. The translator also drew very occasionally on the historical books of the Old Testament, and quite heavily on various exegetical commentaries, including those by Cassiodorus, Jerome and, indirectly, Theodore of Mopsuestia.

The Old English prose translation of the psalter shows the influence of two types of early medieval biblical exegesis, the allegorical and the literal-historical. The allegorical commentaries which may have been drawn upon by the translator include: Cassiodorus' *Expositio psalmorum*; Jerome's *Commentarioli* and *Tractatus* (which may have been used directly or transmitted through another source, the Pseudo-Jerome *Breviarium in psalmos*, a conflation of Jerome's commentaries and other allegorical commentaries); another Latin commentary,

6 Ó'Néill 2001; for the discussion of the translation of the psalms that follows I have drawn heavily upon Ó'Néill's introduction, esp. pp. 23–96.

known as the *Glosa Psalmorum ex traditione seniorum*, which has recently been shown to have been the source of the Pseudo-Jerome *Breviarium*; and, to a lesser extent, Augustine's *Enarrationes in psalmos*. The literal and historical commentaries the translator appears to have known include: Theodore of Mopsuestia's Greek exposition of the psalms, as it survives in the fifth-century Latin translation of Julian of Eclanum, and in a later anonymous *Epitome* of Julian's work; and another anonymous psalter commentary known as the *Expositio psalmorum*.[7] In addition to these exegetical commentaries, the translator may have been influenced by a Hiberno-Latin work, Adomnán of Iona's *De locis sanctis*. Of these texts, the translator drew most heavily on the commentaries of Julian and the subsequent *Epitome* of his work, the *Expositio psalmorum*, and the Pseudo-Bede *Argumenta*. This is a long and impressive list of texts; however, as Patrick Ó'Néill argues, it is possible that some, even all, of them were known to the translator only in the form of short extracts entered as glosses or marginalia in a particular manuscript – perhaps as Ó'Néill suggests a heavily glossed (*Gallicanum*) psalter of Hiberno-Latin origin.[8]

Augustine of Hippo wrote his two books of the *Soliloquia* in the late fourth century AD. The work remained unfinished and, in his *Retractiones*, Augustine comments that he continued the subject of his second book of the *Soliloquia* in another work known as *De immortalitate animae*. The Old English version comprises a lengthy preface (with no parallel in the Latin), a rewriting of the first two books of Augustine, and an additional third book, intended to complete Augustine's unfinished work. The rewriting and continuation shows familiarity with a range of sources.[9] The first book is a free rendering of *Soliloquia*, Book I, including a translation of an additional passage from Augustine's *Retractiones* which often appears as a prologue to manuscripts of the *Soliloquia*; and for at least one point, the translator may have drawn on Isidore's *Etymologiae*.[10] The second book draws on chapters 1, 2 and 36 of Augustine's Book II, but the remainder is independent and does not use its chapters 3 to 35. Alfred's third book does not use the *Soliloquia* at all; rather he probably drew on the following texts to compile it: Augustine's *De videndo Deo* (ep. 147) and *De civitate Dei*, Gregory the Great's *Dialogi* and homily 40 of his *Homiliae in evangelia*, Julian of Toledo's *Prognosticon*, and Bede's *De natura rerum* and *De temporum ratione*. In addition, occasional parallels in Books I and II of the Old English *Soliloquies* with Boethius' *De consolatione philosophiae* suggest the use of either the Latin

7 This commentary was identified and an edition printed privately by Lucas De Coninck in 1989; cited by Ó'Néill 2001, p. 39 n. 33.

8 Ó'Néill 2001, p. 44.

9 Godden 2001 and 2003c.

10 Godden 2001.

or the Old English Boethius, while a few details were added from books of the Bible. Manuscript copies of most of these texts survive from the Anglo-Saxon period, though many post-date the Alfredian age.

There is so far no evidence that anyone in Anglo-Saxon England had read Augustine's *Soliloquia* before the Alfredian period (though a passing reference by Aldhelm shows awareness of it) and the only two surviving manuscripts of the *Soliloquia* are tenth-century copies: one produced on the Continent was known to be in England by the eleventh century, and the other was produced in England in the first half of the tenth century.[11] Thus the vernacular version is our primary witness to knowledge of the work before the tenth century.

The main source for the Old English Boethius was the early sixth-century text of Boethius' *De consolatione philosophiae*, but it has long been recognised that the Old English version is by no means a literal translation of the Latin, but an adaptation using additional material from a variety of patristic and classical texts. The Alfredian version is the earliest evidence for the knowledge of the *Consolatio* in England. The earliest manuscript of English provenance is a copy made in France in the first half of the ninth century, heavily glossed in Latin at the end of the ninth century in an Insular hand which is generally agreed to have characteristics of south-west Britain, then further glossed by St Dunstan and others at Glastonbury in the mid tenth century, and subsequently feeding into later tenth-century glossed manuscripts of Boethius produced in England.[12]

The possibility that the Alfredian circle drew on a commentary on the Latin Boethius has been much discussed. Though the commentary material preserved in the numerous Boethius manuscripts of the ninth to the eleventh centuries has been thought to derive from two hypothetical early commentaries, attributed to Remigius of Auxerre and the 'Anonymous of St Gallen' respectively, such strict classifications can no longer be sustained.[13] Recent research on these manuscripts has revealed that there is a whole spectrum of

11 Salisbury CL, 173, and BR, 8558–63 (2498).

12 BAV, Vat. lat. 3363. For a description see Parkes 1981; for the most recent views on its provenance see Godden 2005 and Sims-Williams 2005.

13 Though Courcelle 1939 and 1967 are impressive, his classification of the commentary material into specific categories, such as 'Remigian', 'Anonymous of St Gallen' and 'Anonymous of Einsiedeln', has somewhat muddied the waters, and many subsequent scholars simply accepted these classifications (see esp. Bolton 1977, Beaumont 1981, Wittig 1983, and Gibson *et al.* 1995). Courcelle had constructed these distinct categories by analysing a selection of glosses on certain sections of the Boethius text in a few random manuscripts, rather than from full transcriptions or collations of the various extant manuscripts. Work by the Alfredian Boethius Project based at Oxford University has revealed the complexity of the manuscript transmission; for the most recent discussions of this material, which elucidates the problems and issues related to these so-called 'distinct' commentary traditions, see Godden 2003b and Godden and Irvine 2009.

glosses and manuscript groupings, and most manuscripts show a variety of types of glosses and associations with other manuscripts, suggesting that the transmission was far more fluid and complicated. Although the influence of the commentary material on the Old English adaptation had been challenged, it is now clear that the author made extensive use of the kind of material that clustered around the text in contemporary manuscripts.[14] Even so, much of the additional material testifies to wider reading and familiarity in particular with classical legend and science, though it is difficult to pin down precise sources. He certainly knew and used one or more of the various anonymous *Vitae*, which appear either appended to many of the Latin manuscripts of the *Consolatio*, or as glosses to the text; the Bible; Alcuin's *De animae ratione*; and Augustine's *Soliloquia*. For the expansion of classical allusions an enormous range of possible sources has been cited.[15] If we narrow the focus to those which could not have been derived from the commentary, or at least do not appear in any Latin Boethius manuscript of the period, the range is much more limited. It is clear even so that the author had a fair knowledge of classical tradition and was able to supplement the meagre information in his Latin text with a range of detail that is far from dependent on the Latin commentary. The striking point, though, is that it is not possible to identify any particular texts as likely sources for this supplementary information. Parallels can be found with Orosius' *Historiae*, and a fragment of a late ninth-century copy of a commentary on its first two books;[16] Ovid's *Metamorphoses* or the *Fabulae* of Hyginus for additional information on Ulysses and Circe; and the *Breviarium* of Eutropius or some similar epitome of classical history. For some of the additional information about classical history and legend, the author clearly had access to genuine classical traditions, but no plausible source can be identified that would have provided all of it. It may be a case of drawing on a good education and experience of wide reading rather than consulting specific sources for the purposes of the translation. For his detailed information about the elements and other aspects of natural history parallels can be seen with Bede's

14 If an extensive study of the available commentary material on one section of the text (Book III, metre xii, or the Orpheus metre) could conclude that the adaptor of Boethius did not use a commentary at all (Wittig 1983), Malcolm Godden has pointed to much very persuasive evidence elsewhere in the text which confirms that the Old English adaptor did use commentary material (Godden 2006, and Godden and Irvine 2009).

15 For the most recent work on the sources of the Old English Boethius, see Godden and Irvine 2009; for earlier work on the sources see esp. Bately 1990, Brinegar 2000 and Discenza 2001.

16 BAV, Reg. lat. 1650, fols. 1–10. Though this commentary fragment is written in a Continental Minuscule script, characteristic of the type used at Reims, Paul Lehmann has suggested that it was copied from an Insular (probably Irish) exemplar (see Lehmann 1959–62, II, pp. 29–37, esp. pp. 30–1).

De natura rerum; Isidore's *De natura rerum*; Ambrose's *Hexameron*; and Pliny's *Historia naturalis*, but there are few close verbal parallels, and the way in which the author uses the material suggests that it was based on a good education in natural science rather than a specific consultation of particular passages in any of these authors for the purposes of the translation.

The main source of the Old English Orosius is the fifth-century Latin text of Paulus Orosius, entitled *Historiae adversum paganos libri septem*. Despite its great popularity in the Middle Ages and the existence of hundreds of manuscripts, only a handful survive from Anglo-Saxon England, of which a single fragment predates Alfred's period.[17] Like the translator of Bede's *Historia*, the compiler of the Old English Orosius omits much of the original Latin text, reducing Orosius' seven books to six. Unlike the Bede, however, and more like the adaptation of the Boethius, the author of the Old English Orosius adds much detail that is not explicitly in the Latin text (particularly geographical details, identifications of people, and explanations of events or allusions that may not have been familiar to his audience). Some of this may reflect contextual guesses or speculation; some may be based on oral sources, most evidently the account of the voyages of Othhere and Wulfstan;[18] while other details may have been drawn from a map. But much of the additional detail – commonplace in a number of texts – could in theory have come from a wide variety of classical, patristic and later Latin works.[19] Which, if any, of these were directly consulted is difficult to say, since in most cases there is insufficient detail to pinpoint one text as opposed to another, and in many cases information from more than one source may have been conflated. Again like the Old English Boethius, some of the detail may have come by way of glosses in the translator's copy of the Latin original, or perhaps by way of a Latin commentary, and there are a few parallels with existing glosses and the commentary on Orosius' first two books. Glosses and comments on the surviving copies of the *Historia* are rare, but, though it may not have been as extensive as the glossing tradition on the Boethius text, the surviving commentary on Orosius suggests that there probably once was a tradition of glossing and commenting on the text: the commentary is written in double columns and laid out on the page as if it is a single continuous text, but in fact it is no more than a compilation of lemmata and glosses (perhaps drawn from interlinear and marginal comments), separate from the full Latin text. Of these many possibilities, those that seem particularly likely to have contributed material

17 Düsseldorf, Nordrhein-Westfälisches Hauptstaatsarchiv, Z 11/1 (formerly Z.4, Nr 2).
18 Bately 1980b, esp. pp. lxxi–lxxii.
19 For the sources of Orosius, see esp. Bately 1980b, pp. lv–lxxii and Jayatilaka 2001.

to the Old English Orosius, directly or indirectly, include Justinus' *Epitoma*, Isidore's *Etymologiae*, Augustine's *De civitate Dei*, Jerome's *Chronicon*, Bede's *Chronica maiora*, and Livy's *Ab urbe condita*.

Three further texts associated with King Alfred's court, the *Anglo-Saxon Chronicle*, Alfred's law-code and Asser's *Vita Ælfredi regis*, are of a slightly different nature, in that they do not draw primarily on a pre-existing text. The annals known as the *Anglo-Saxon Chronicle* are thought first to have been compiled in King Alfred's circle during the last decade of the ninth century. This original compilation, the so-called 'common stock', extends from the earliest annal (for 60 BC) to that for 892. Thereafter, the annals were added to by numerous chroniclers in a variety of circumstances. The first continuation of this 'common stock', which occurred in Alfred's lifetime and was probably done in his circle, is represented by the annals from 893 to 896, the second by those from 897 to 914. This early material was drawn from a variety of identifiable sources, including: Bede's *Historia ecclesiastica* and *Chronica maiora*; the Bible or biblical commentaries; Isidore of Seville's *Chronicon*; Jerome's *Liber de viris inlustribus*; Rufinus' translation of Eusebius' *Chronicle*; annals relating to Kentish, South Saxon, Mercian and West Saxon history; and the *abrégé félicien* version of the *Liber pontificalis*.[20]

The body of laws issued by King Alfred drew heavily upon the earlier law-codes of Ine, Offa and Æthelbert. But it is in his extensive preface to this law-code, where he sets out his concepts of law and lawgiving, that we see that he was influenced by a variety of other documentary sources which he knew directly or indirectly.[21] Thus in relation to the scriptural passages, primarily from the Book of Exodus, it is possible that Alfred was influenced by the eighth-century Irish *Liber ex lege Moysi*, which was known in England in his time and which contains similar extracts from Exodus. Other sources that may have influenced Alfred were various writings of Hincmar of Reims; a *Collatio legum Romanarum et Mosaicarum*; the letter of Fulco, archbishop of Reims to King Alfred, written about 886; and the *capitulare* of 786 incorporated in the report by the papal legates to Pope Hadrian.

Asser based much of his *Vita Ælfredi regis* on a version of the *Anglo-Saxon Chronicle* which has not survived.[22] The other sources on which he drew include: Aldhelm's prose *De virginitate*; Bede's *Historia ecclesiastica* and possibly his commentaries on Luke and Mark; the Bible; Caelius Sedulius' *Carmen paschale*; Einhard's *Vita Karoli Magni*; Gregory the Great's *Regula*

20 Bately 1979a and 1979b; see also Chapter 25 in this volume.
21 Wormald 1999, esp. pp. 106–7, 416–29.
22 Stevenson 1904, pp. lxxxv–lxxxviii.

pastoralis and probably his *Moralia in Iob*; Thegan's *Gesta Hludowici imperatoris*; and the anonymous *Historia Brittonum* and *Vita Alcuini*.[23] However, which of these he had read in Wales and which he had at his fingertips in Wessex is debatable.

The lament over lost libraries and linguistic ignorance in the Alfredian preface to the *Pastoral Care* has perhaps coloured too much our estimate of the resources available to the Alfredian authors. Together they show familiarity with an impressive range of knowledge, in classical history and legend, natural history, biblical interpretation, and theological and philosophical ideas, and their interest in texts such as the *Soliloquies* of Augustine and the *Consolation of Philosophy* of Boethius testify to contact with works that had never been in the mainstream of English scholarship in the past. The range of works available is perhaps underlined by the relatively little overlap in the sources that they used; even when the Orosius and Boethius are dealing with the same episodes of classical history and legend they seem to draw on different traditions.[24] Yet it remains difficult to pin down the precise works used by these authors, and the task is not helped by the fact that so few pre-tenth-century manuscripts have survived – a couple of hundred as opposed to the 900 or so from the subsequent two centuries of the Anglo-Saxon period. Alfredian authors were not given to citing their sources, and their use of the vernacular and free methods of translation deprive us of the evidence we use for Bede or Aldhelm or Ælfric. Several further points make it difficult to speak of a 'library' in this context. Material used to supplement the basic sources for the psalms, Boethius, the *Soliloquies*, and Orosius may have come from marginal commentary rather than separate books (or, in the case of the geography of the Old English Orosius, a detailed map) and therefore testify to the learning of others rather than the Alfredian authors. Or it may have been supplied by foreign scholars such as Grimbald and Asser who carried knowledge in their heads from their Continental education. And when we speak of 'Alfredian authors' we may be referring to a number of distinct authors who resided in different parts of England and at different times and had no connection with each other. A straw in the wind suggesting that the books themselves were available to the authors is the fact that the huge mass of commentary found in Boethius manuscripts, while undoubtedly making some contribution to the Old English version, still fails to account for a great deal of additional material, and it is unlikely that we have lost much of this commentary material. The

23 See Scharer 1996; and for the most recent work on the sources of Asser's *Vita*, see Hewitt 2003.
24 Bately 1990, p. 65.

confidence shown by authors in rewriting their main sources perhaps hints that they were not relying on titbits fed by their foreign mentors. And the fact that even their main sources do not survive in copies of English provenance before the Alfredian period underlines the point that much was available of which there is now no trace.

35

Ælfric's library

M. R. GODDEN

Ælfric of Eynsham, also known in the past as Ælfric Grammaticus, was a pupil of St Æthelwold and educated at Winchester, where he apparently remained until the age of thirty or so, with access to the no doubt extensive resources of the Old Minster and other centres there. But it was only after he left Winchester around 987 and moved to the newly founded (or refounded) monastery at Cerne Abbas that he began his prolific writing programme, and for this he was presumably mainly reliant on the much more limited collection of books available to him at the new foundation and subsequently at Eynsham, another newly founded monastery to which he moved as abbot in 1005. He identifies his sources, at least by author, quite frequently, and the often close verbal parallels between his vernacular wording and that of numerous Latin texts suggests that he was not simply relying on memory. No record survives of him requesting books from other places or visiting other places to consult them, though he evidently was travelling a good deal, at least later in life, and could have had the opportunity to consult books at Winchester. But the fact that Wulfstan, bishop of Worcester and archbishop of York, consulted him on matters of canon law around 1002 suggests that he was not thought to be cut off from the kinds of resources that large cathedrals could boast.

The nature of his writings, concentrated on vernacular homilies, saints' lives, biblical paraphrase and pastoral letters, strictly limits the range of works that he can be shown to have known.[1] Given his education at Winchester it is inconceivable that he did not know a range of classical and later Latin poetry of the kind drawn on by other writers of the time,[2] but there is not a hint in

1 The known sources for his works are listed in detail in the Fontes Anglo-Saxonici database (at http://fontes.english.ox.ac.uk./; the relevant entries were created by Godden, Jayatilaka and others) and for his Catholic Homilies in Godden 2000. A useful list of his Latin sources culled from Fontes has been printed in Lapidge 2006, pp. 250–66, though this needs to be used with care since it combines probable sources with merely possible ones and excerpts, and full details should still be sought from the database itself.

2 Cf Lapidge and Winterbottom 1991, p. cxi, on Wulfstan the Cantor.

his writings (unless we accept the recent argument that he himself was the author of the *Excerptiones de Prisciano*, which formed the basis of his own vernacular *Grammar* of Latin, and which contains numerous quotations from the classical poets).[3] He knew Bede's metrical *Life of St Cuthbert*, and his readiness to use it rather than relying on the two prose *Lives* suggests that he was perfectly comfortable with Latin verse, but the only other poem he can be shown to have used is a passage of Sedulius which he found quoted in a homily by Bede. Of earlier Anglo-Saxon Latin writers there is extensive borrowing from Bede but only the faintest echo of Aldhelm, which may reflect his distaste for the artificially mannered and esoteric style of writing (the so-called 'hermeneutic style') which was largely created by Aldhelm and became the dominant fashion among Ælfric's teachers and contemporaries. Vernacular writings he knew well – most of the Alfredian corpus, and probably a range of anonymous homiletic and hagiographic writing (again, a body of writing for which he had no liking). His stylistic experiments show a familiarity with vernacular poetry, but the only such work he refers to is a lost poem on St Thomas the apostle.

One important question about the nature of the resources available to him in Cerne or Eynsham is to what extent he relied on collections of excerpts or abridgements, whether compiled earlier by others or extracted by himself on visits to other libraries for his own future use, and did not have access to the full texts in his own library. Many possible cases have been adduced but none has quite proved convincing yet. He evidently made use of two Latin abridgements, of Julian of Toledo's *Prognosticon* and Alcuin's *De animae ratione*, which appear in a manuscript containing texts associated with him.[4] The so-called 'Excerpts' from Julian of Toledo are in fact a Latin sermon, very probably by Ælfric himself, drawing largely on the *Prognosticon* but using material from other sources as well, and freely adapted at times; the Latin rubric suggests that it was intended for the use of others, not just for his own purposes. There are distinct parallels with some of his vernacular homilies and he may have used it as a source for them, but since he also used the *Prognosticon* itself he clearly had the whole text available. The adaptation of Alcuin is similarly a Latin sermon containing other material as well, some of it indeed drawn from Ælfric's vernacular work (and some from the Old English version of Boethius), and not a collection of source material, though there are signs that Ælfric used it for some of his homilies. Again, a collection of excerpts from Latin hagiographic material surviving in a later manuscript now in Paris may, as has been argued, be

3 For the argument see Porter 2002.
4 See Raynes 1957, Gatch 1966, Godden 2000. The manuscript is Boulogne, BM, 63.

a copy of one created by him for use in his vernacular homilies and saints' lives, but the match is far from exact.[5] The suggestion that a lost Chartres adaptation of an abridgement of Priscian's grammatical works, known only from catalogue entries, may have been made by Ælfric as a basis for his subsequent Old English *Grammar* can be no more than a speculation.[6] The much earlier notion, that his pastoral letters made heavy use of a collection of excerpts from church canons known as the *Excerptiones Pseudo-Egberti*, has now been replaced by the view that the collection was itself a late Anglo-Saxon compilation which drew on Ælfric's work rather than vice versa. It is not implausible in principle that Ælfric did use collections of excerpts as a substitute for full texts, but none of the instances adduced so far seem to fit that hypothesis.

For his homilies and saints' lives he relied heavily on two substantial collections of relevant Latin texts. Foremost of these was the vast homiliary compiled by Paul the Deacon. Paul (720 – *c.* 799) was a monk of Monte Cassino who spent some time at the court of Charlemagne and compiled his homiliary apparently at the latter's direction, for reading in the course of the monastic offices.[7] In its original form it contained some 244 sermons and homilies written by, or attributed to, a variety of patristic authors, especially Augustine, Gregory the Great, Bede, Maximus, Leo and St John Chrysostom, and organised according to the church year. Some of them were extracted from commentaries and other longer works, but as far as we can now tell Paul did not rewrite or adapt any of the material. Its contents were continually revised, and especially expanded, over succeeding centuries; the later version printed by Migne in *Patrologia Latina* XCV has some 298 items. A number of copies survive from late Anglo-Saxon England, and its importance as a source-book for Ælfric has been convincingly demonstrated.[8] Ælfric used a number of texts that appear in later versions but not in the original, and it is likely, therefore, that he was using an expanded and revised version, but its precise contents cannot be known. Altogether he used just about a hundred items from the collection in compiling the Catholic Homilies and later homiletic collections, choosing mainly work by (or attributed to) Augustine (14–18 items), Gregory (33) and Bede (33). His frequent reference to those authors by name, when drawing on the homiliary, indicates that his version included attributions, in the text or margins; this presumably explains why he did not mention Paul the Deacon as an authority in the preface, but instead specified the original authors. The sermons attributed to Leo and Maximus are (with one possible

5 Lapidge and Winterbottom 1991, pp. cxlviii–ix. See Godden 2000, p. 415. 6 Law 1987.
7 See esp. Smetana 1959, Clayton 1985, Smetana 1978. 8 Smetana 1959.

exception) not used; possibly they had been eliminated from the copy Ælfric knew.[9] Some ten copies of the homiliary, or adaptations of it, survive from late Anglo-Saxon England, though all probably somewhat later in date than Ælfric himself.[10]

Second only to Paul the Deacon in importance to Ælfric was the anonymous collection of hagiographic material known as the Cotton-Corpus legendary. The legendary is, or was before additions were made, a collection of 165 mainly anonymous saints' lives and other hagiographic narratives, running from January to December. It survives only in manuscripts of English provenance, but is thought to have been originally compiled in northern France or Flanders, in the late ninth or early tenth century.[11] Its importance as a source-book for Ælfric's homilies for saints' days and his *Lives of Saints* collection was demonstrated comprehensively by Patrick Zettel.[12] The texts all survive in other manuscripts and in printed form, but Zettel showed that the manuscripts of this particular legendary not only contained virtually all the hagiographic sources used by Ælfric but also frequently showed the particular variant readings that he must have found in his sources and the particular selection of texts on a particular saint that he employed. It is clear from his evidence that Ælfric must have used a version of this legendary; twenty-four of the items from it were used as sources in the Catholic Homilies, and a further twenty for the *Lives of Saints*.

Two other substantial Carolingian homiletic collections helped to transmit the tradition of patristic commentary, those of Haymo and Smaragdus, both explicitly mentioned by Ælfric in his preface to the Catholic Homilies. The collection of mainly brief expositions of the epistles and pericopes for the year written by Smaragdus, abbot of Saint-Mihiel (died 819), is so derivative from the patristic writings that filled Paul the Deacon's homiliary and were directly used by Ælfric that it is hard to pin down more than the very occasional use. Despite valiant attempts to assert his importance,[13] it is unlikely that Smaragdus was much used by Ælfric, though he may have been a useful name to cite. Haymo was much more adventurous in his collection of homilies on the gospels, and Ælfric often drew on his collection to supplement material gathered from the texts in Paul the Deacon. Beyond these four collections he evidently knew and had access to further works by the major patristic writers.

9 Cf. *ibid*, p. 203. 10 Clayton 1985

11 See Jackson and Lapidge 1996, pp. 133–4.

12 In his Oxford DPhil thesis, 1979. The thesis has never been published, but the essence of the argument, and some detailed examples, are to be found in Zettel 1982.

13 Hill 1992.

Of Augustine he seems to have known at first hand a collection of his sermons, as well as a range of other texts including *De bono coniugali*, *De catechizandis rudibus*, *De diversis quaestionibus ad simplicianum*, *In Iohannis Evangelium tractatus* CXXIV, and *De sancta virginitate*. Jerome is much cited in his work, but mainly for works no longer attributed to him (the *Ecclesiastical History* of Eusebius-Rufinus, the treatise on the Assumption of the Virgin by Paschasius Radbertus) and Ælfric may not have known much at first hand; and there is little trace of Ambrose. He knew Gregory's *Dialogi* and the *Moralia* well. Of other writers on doctrine, he knew and used Julian of Toledo's *Prognosticon* and Martin of Braga's *De correctione rusticorum*. The Carolingian works he used include Alcuin's *De animae ratione*, *Interrogationes et responsiones in Genesim* and *De virtutibus et vitiis*, Ratramnus on the Eucharist and Paschasius on the Assumption, but very little of Hrabanus Maurus except perhaps his *Commentaria in libros Machabaeorum*. His knowledge of history was based on the ecclesiastical histories of Eusebius-Rufinus and Bede; there is no evidence that he knew Orosius, though it would be surprising if he did not, but he does show knowledge of the *Anglo-Saxon Chronicle*. He seems not to have known Gregory of Tours (the only parallels are with excerpts incorporated into the Cotton-Corpus legendary). For science and computus he used Bede's *De natura rerum* and *De temporum ratione* as well as Isidore's *De natura rerum*. For grammar he claims to have relied mainly on the book from which he was taught at Winchester, which has been identified as the *Excerptiones de Prisciano*. In church canons he was an acknowledged authority and the pastoral letters which he wrote at the request of, and in the name of, contemporary bishops and archbishops show familiarity with a range of canonical collections.

All these are texts which Ælfric evidently had at his elbow when he composed his own works at Cerne and Eynsham: the verbal parallels are too close and extensive to depend simply on a well-stocked memory. Whether these represent the bulk of the library available to him or the tip of the iceberg is hard to say: he was not one to show off his learning and we know what books he could access only from those he chose to use for the particular vein of mainly vernacular writing to which he devoted his career. Certainly he never hints at texts he would like to acquire but cannot. The absence of classical literature and philosophy from the list may be as much due to his general distaste for it (evidenced, for instance, in his adaptation of the *Excerptiones de Prisciano* for his *Grammar*, his negative references to philosophers and perhaps his failure to identify Boethius as the source of extensive passages in his own writings on free will) as its unavailability. Still less can we extrapolate from his own resources to those of other rural centres of the (apparently small) size of Cerne. With the support of Winchester and the patronage of Ealdorman Æthelweard and his son the thegn Æthelmær, who founded Cerne, Ælfric may well have been able to bring copies of the texts that he knew he would need in a new foundation, and to acquire others later. We can at least say that, in the right conditions, a scholar at even the smallest and newest foundations in late Anglo-Saxon England could find the resources to produce a large and learned output, outdoing all his contemporaries in larger centres.

36

The library of Byrhtferth

MICHAEL LAPIDGE

The fenland abbey of Ramsey was founded in 966. From the outset it was richly endowed by its two founders, Æthelwine, ealdorman of East Anglia (d. 992), whose residence lay adjacent to the land on which the monastery was built, and Oswald, bishop of Worcester (961–92), who, with the support of King Edgar, provided funds for the construction of the monastic buildings and staffed the monastery with monks from his earlier foundation of Westbury-on-Trym (in modern Bristol). The ample endowment of the original foundation continued to grow through legacies (especially from Æthelwine's family) through the following century, so that by the time of the Domesday surveys (1086), Ramsey was the tenth-richest abbey in England. This wealth was probably employed, inter alia, in the acquisition of books for the monastic library. As an entirely new foundation, Ramsey will have had no books at all in 966; yet a mere fifty years later its most famous native son, the monk Byrhtferth (*c.* 970 – *c.* 1020), was able to draw on the resources of a library containing slightly in excess of 100 titles, bound presumably in somewhat fewer volumes.[1] From these beginnings, the library at Ramsey continued to grow in the period after the Norman Conquest, as a number of late medieval inventories demonstrate.[2]

We would gladly know the ways and means by which the pre-Conquest library of Ramsey was assembled during the first fifty years of its existence. Unfortunately, evidence for this process of acquisition is almost wholly lacking. There is no surviving pre-Conquest inventory of books from Ramsey. Although it must undoubtedly have had its own scriptorium, no identifiable 'house style' of script has ever been recognised, and no library book certainly written at Ramsey has ever been identified. (Unlike at Fleury, on whose model the abbey was founded, the Ramsey monks did not write *ex libris* inscriptions in their books.[3]) In default of evidence such as this, our search for books

1 Lapidge 2006, pp. 266–74. 2 Sharpe *et al.* 1996, pp. 327–419.

3 See the convenient selection of illustrations of them in Alexandre and Lanoë 2004, ills. 146–75.

belonging to the early phases of Ramsey's library is thrown back on to the (quite substantial) corpus of writings, in Latin and Old English, by Byrhtferth. These include computistical writings (a Latin *Computus*, only partly available in print, and the *Enchiridion*, an introduction, in Latin and Old English, to the same *Computus*),[4] hagiography (*Vita S. Oswaldi* and *Vita S. Ecgwini*),[5] and history (*Historia regum*, preserved as part of a longer work of the same name by Symeon of Durham),[6] as well as a vast *collectaneum* of excerpts, classical, patristic and Carolingian, assembled to illustrate two treatises of Bede (*De natura rerum* and *De temporum ratione*), and known as the *Glossae Bridferti in Bedam*.[7] It is fortunate for our enquiry that Byrhtferth was much given to verbatim quotation, for his quotations often allow conclusions to be drawn concerning the books which he had at his disposal.

One may suspect, a priori, that Ramsey acquired books from several identifiable sources: from Abbo of Fleury, who spent two years teaching there (985–7), and who undoubtedly brought books to Ramsey for this purpose (and may have left some of them behind on his return to Fleury); from Worcester, through the agency of Bishop Oswald, Ramsey's co-founder (and also, in theory at least, from York, after Oswald's elevation to its archbishopric in 971); from Winchcombe, after the suppression of that house in 975, when the entire Winchcombe community was moved to the safety of East Anglia and housed en masse at Ramsey; and from other English monasteries with which Ramsey was in intellectual contact. I examine each of these sources in turn.

First, Abbo. Abbo came to Ramsey from Fleury, one of the richest abbeys in France. Fleury housed what was probably the largest library in Europe at that time.[8] Abbo will have known that Ramsey, as a recent foundation, can scarcely have had a comparable library, or even one sufficient to support his teaching; he may also have known that the educational tradition in England was strikingly different from that of continental schools such as Fleury and Reims, where Abbo had studied with Gerbert of Aurillac (later to become Pope Silvester II). In particular, Continental schools from the ninth century onwards devoted their energies to the study of the scientific subjects of the quadrivium (geometry, arithmetic, astronomy and musical harmony).[9] Furthermore, Abbo had

4 Baker and Lapidge 1995 (with the reconstructed *Computus* at pp. 373–427).
5 Lapidge 2008.
6 Arnold 1882–5, II, pp. 3–91; on the attribution of the work to Byrhtferth, see Lapidge 1993a, pp. 317–42.
7 *PL*, XC, cols. 187–278 and 297–548; on the validity of the attribution to Byrhtferth, see Gorman 1996 and Lapidge 2007a.
8 Mostert 1989 (who lists some 1,540 surviving manuscripts which once belonged to Fleury).
9 Glauche 1970, pp. 62–75, and Jeauneau 1975.

distinguished himself in the field of logic (classifiable as a subdivision of dialectic, one of the subjects, with grammar and rhetoric, of the trivium).[10] There is no evidence that any of these subjects had ever been taught in Anglo-Saxon schools, which seem to have been devoted primarily to the study of grammar, as it could be learned from close attention to a graded sequence of curriculum texts.[11] The books which underpinned the study of the quadrivium were Martianus Capella, *De nuptiis Philologiae et Mercurii* and Macrobius, *Commentarium in Somnium Scipionis* and, for logic, the translations and commentaries of Boethius on Aristotle and on Porphyry's *Eisagoge* ('Introduction') to the same. Accordingly, if Abbo was to teach these subjects at Ramsey, he will have had to bring with him copies of Martianus, Macrobius and Boethius. The writings of Byrhtferth help us to qualify this supposition. There is no evidence, for example, that Byrhtferth was interested in logic in any way, and his writings contain no quotation from the logical writings of Boethius. But astronomy was evidently a different matter. In the case of Martianus Capella, Byrhtferth includes several extensive quotations from Book VIII (*De astronomia*) of *De nuptiis* in the *Glossae Bridferti in Bedam*.[12] Even more extensive are the excerpts in that compilation from Macrobius, *Commentarium in Somnium Scipionis*; once again, all of Byrhtferth's quotations from Macrobius, including several in the *Vita S. Oswaldi*, are concerned with astronomy.[13] So this is a subject which Byrhtferth learned at the feet of Abbo. None of the surviving Anglo-Saxon manuscripts of Martianus Capella (most of which contain excerpts only, and rarely from Book VIII) can be identified with that used by Byrhtferth, and hence none can be assigned to the Ramsey library. In the case of Macrobius, however, the very manuscript brought by Abbo to Ramsey appears to survive as BnF, lat. 7299. This is a composite manuscript consisting of three parts (which were arguably combined from very early on), of which parts II (fols. 12*bis*–27; *computistica*, including Helperic, *De computo*) and III (fols. 28–71; Macrobius) are written in the distinctive Caroline Minuscule of Fleury and date from the late tenth century.[14] The text of Helperic in part II contains, in its Chapter 24, a calculation relating to an *annus praesens* of AD 978, and scholars have long associated this redaction of Helperic with Abbo.[15] To these two parts was prefixed a liturgical calendar (now fols. 1–12) which, to judge from its script and its commemorations of Anglo-Saxon saints, was written in England; the fact that it contains three commemorations of St Benedict suggests that it was intended for use at a church dedicated to that saint. At the

10 See Engelen 1993 and esp. Schupp 1997. 11 Lapidge 1996, pp. 455–98.
12 Lapidge 2006, p. 272. 13 *Ibid.*
14 Lapidge 1993a, pp. 395–6. 15 Van de Vyver 1935, pp. 148–9.

time the calendar was written (the end of the tenth century), Ramsey was the only English monastery dedicated to St Benedict. However, the obit of Abbo himself (who was murdered at La Réole in Aquitaine on 13 November 1004) is added to the calendar in a script characteristic once again of Fleury. These facts can all be accounted for by supposing that parts II and III of BnF, lat. 7299 were brought to Ramsey by Abbo in 985, where a liturgical calendar representing Ramsey use was prefixed to the two existing parts; the composite manuscript was then taken back to Fleury by Abbo on his return in 987 (this would explain why the calendar contains a commemoration of St Kenelm, patron saint of the community of Winchcombe which was housed at Ramsey after 975, but not of St Oswald, who died in 992). Before it was taken away, however, Byrhtferth was able to copy from it the lengthy excerpts from Macrobius preserved in the *Glossae Bridferti in Bedam*. A copy was also made of Helperic's *De computo* because, although there is no pre-Conquest English manuscript of the work, several twelfth-century copies carry the *annus praesens* calculation of AD 978, and must, therefore, derive from the (hypothetical) Ramsey copy, even though that copy itself has apparently perished.[16]

Another astronomical text which was apparently brought to Ramsey by Abbo and which is quoted on several occasions by Byrhtferth (both in the *Vita S. Oswaldi* and the *Glossae in Bedam*) is the *Astronomica* of Hyginus.[17] Interestingly, a copy of this text, alongside excerpts from Macrobius and Martianus Capella and astronomical notes by Abbo, is preserved in BL, Harley 2506, a manuscript written at Fleury in the late tenth century (and decorated there by the unknown Anglo-Saxon artist who also decorated the famous psalter BL, Harley 2904, a book which has been recognised as Bishop Oswald's personal psalter, and which was still at Ramsey in the fourteenth century).[18] That Harley 2506 was in England by the early eleventh century is established by a number of annotations in Anglo-Caroline script. Byrhtferth's quotations of Hyginus are too brief to enable us to confirm that he was in fact quoting from this manuscript, but other links with Fleury suggest that it was brought from Fleury to Ramsey in the late tenth century, presumptively by Abbo. Unlike BnF, lat. 7299, it apparently remained there.

Byrhtferth's writings throw light on other astronomical texts which were brought to Ramsey at this time. In the *Epilogus* to his *Vita S. Ecgwini*, for example, he refers explicitly to a treatise known as the *Liber Nemroth*, a work probably of Syrian origin which began to circulate in the West in Latin

16 McGurk 1974. 17 Lapidge 2006, p. 271.
18 Lapidge 1993a, pp. 398–403; see also p. 281 above.

translation during the tenth century.[19] No Anglo-Saxon manuscript of the work survives, and Byrhtferth is the only pre-Conquest author to refer to it. The fact that elsewhere (e.g. in an eleventh-century computistical manuscript from Saint-Denis, now BAV, Reg. lat. 309) excerpts from the *Liber Nemroth* circulate with excerpts from Macrobius and from Abbo himself, suggests once again that it was Abbo who brought this work – or the excerpts from it used by Byrhtferth – to Ramsey. Similarly, at one point in his *Vita S. Oswaldi* Byrhtferth signals his intention to return to an earlier topic of discussion with the words, 'Vtendum puto "anabibazon" uerbo, quod significat "sursum scandens"' (III, 13). It is striking that the only occurrence of the Greek word *anabibazon* together with the gloss *sursum scandens* recorded in electronic databases is in a sermon by the late twelfth-century Cistercian author Warner of Rochefort, sometime bishop of Langres (d. 1199). It is inconceivable that Warner could have known Byrhtferth's *Vita S. Oswaldi*; but since Warner's sermon is primarily concerned with astronomy (the terms *anabibazon* and *catabibazon* are used to describe planetary motion), it is likely that both he and Byrhtferth were drawing independently on a lost and hitherto unidentified astronomical treatise: another work arguably brought by Abbo to Ramsey to sustain his teaching activities there.[20]

But Abbo taught subjects other than astronomy at Ramsey. His *Quaestiones grammaticales*, which is dedicated to the monks of Ramsey, is wholly concerned with Latin metre, especially matters of prosody and scansion.[21] In order to teach metre Abbo will no doubt have had recourse to what then was the standard handbook on the subject, namely Bede's *De arte metrica*. Byrhtferth quotes extensively from Bede's treatise, both in his *Enchiridion* and in the *Vita S. Oswaldi*.[22] What is particularly striking is that, alongside the text of Bede, Byrhtferth also quotes the commentary to it by the industrious Carolingian commentator, Remigius of Auxerre (d. 908), indicating that Byrhtferth had at his disposal a manuscript in which Bede's text was accompanied by Remigius' commentary, perhaps in the form of marginal or interlinear gloss.[23] Unfortunately the manuscript in question does not survive, but it was evidently another Carolingian manuscript brought to Ramsey by Abbo.

Before leaving Abbo's contribution to the Ramsey library, it is worth noting that in both the *Vita S. Oswaldi* and the *Vita S. Ecgwini* Byrhtferth quotes from the *Historia translationis S. Benedicti* of Adrevald of Fleury.[24] No other

19 Livesey and Rouse 1981.
20 For details, see Lapidge 2008, p. 207 n. 10.
21 Guerreau-Jalabert 1982.
22 Lapidge 2006, p. 268.
23 Lapidge 1998, pp. 26–9.
24 *BHL*, 1117.

Anglo-Saxon author appears to have known this work. Given that Ramsey, like Fleury, was dedicated to St Benedict, it is hardly surprising that copies of Adrevald's work – the standard account of how Fleury came into possession of the saint's relics – should have been available at both monasteries. It is interesting, therefore, that Adrevald's *Historia* is preserved in a single manuscript of Anglo-Saxon provenance (and probably origin: the script has never been the subject of detailed study) and tenth-century date, now Cambridge, St John's College, F.27 (164). Although the manuscript later came into the possession of St Augustine's, Canterbury (to judge from the rhymed offices for St Augustine of Canterbury and Abbot Hadrian added in the eleventh century), it is not known where it was written. On the evidence of Byrhtferth's citations of Adrevald, a Ramsey origin would make a reasonable working hypothesis; indeed an attempt to identify the style of Anglo-Caroline script written at Ramsey would plausibly begin with an analysis of this manuscript, together with part I of BnF, lat. 7299, and the Anglo-Caroline annotations in BL, Harley 2506.

Although not represented by a large number of surviving manuscripts, Abbo's contribution to the library at Ramsey was clearly decisive. It is reasonable to suppose, too, that Oswald, Ramsey's co-founder and bishop of Worcester, also contributed books (as well as financial support) to the library there. It is difficult to prove this supposition, but suggestive evidence is supplied once again by the writings of Byrhtferth. At two points of his *Vita S. Oswaldi*, Byrhtferth uses the very rare phrase *probatus in pulsatorio*, 'tested in the penitentiary' (II, 5, III, 7), to describe the rigorous discipline of St Oswald. According to the electronic databases, there is only one occurrence of this phrase in a work earlier than Byrhtferth, namely in a famous capitulary of Charlemagne, the so-called 'Admonitio generalis' of 23 March 789. Although this capitulary enjoyed very limited circulation in its own right, it was widely known because it was largely incorporated in the *Collectio capitularium* of Ansegis of Fontenelle (d. 833), a work wholly compiled from earlier Carolingian capitularies.[25] All surviving manuscripts of Ansegis' compilation are of Continental origin and provenance, with one exception: BodL., Hatton 42, fols. 188–204, a manuscript written in northern France in the first half of the ninth century, but owned in England by the tenth. By the early eleventh century at the latest it had come into the possession of Worcester, where it received annotations by Archbishop Wulfstan (d. 1023);[26] furthermore, excerpts from Ansegis (including passages from the 'Admonitio generalis')

25 Schmitz 1996, p. 468. 26 Ker 1971, pp. 315–16 and 328–30.

were incorporated in two commonplace books compiled for Wulfstan's use.[27] Could Byrhtferth have seen Hatton 42 through the offices of one of Wulfstan's predecessors, Oswald? Or did Oswald provide a copy of Hatton 42 for the library at Ramsey?

In 971 Oswald was elevated to the archbishopric of York (which he held in plurality with Worcester until his death in 992). In his *Vita S. Oswaldi* Byrhtferth provides us with a vivid description of at least one visit by Oswald to his church in York (v, 3). There is no evidence (archaeological or otherwise) to indicate where in York the Anglo-Saxon cathedral was located; and a fortiori no evidence to indicate whether, after the Danish settlements of the ninth century, and nearly two centuries of neglect, any books were to be found in the cathedral library. Nevertheless it is striking that Byrhtferth inserted into his *Historia regum* a copy of a set of annals for the years 732 to 802 which were evidently compiled at York.[28] These 'York Annals' do not survive independently of Byrhtferth, but it is worth asking how he acquired a copy, if not from York itself. By the same token, a poet at Ramsey contemporary with Byrhtferth – and conceivably Byrhtferth himself – composed the 'Metrical Calendar of Ramsey' on the basis of an earlier work of the same kind, the so-called 'Metrical Calendar of York', which was composed at York during the years 754×766.[29] How did a copy of the 'Metrical Calendar of York' get from York to Ramsey, if not through the agency of Archbishop Oswald? In any case, copies of these two works from York – the 'York Annals' and the 'Metrical Calendar of York' – somehow managed to survive the depredations of the ninth century.[30] It is intriguing to think that these copies, and perhaps copies of other works, were still preserved at York when Oswald became archbishop there in 971.

Another potential source of books for the Ramsey library was the monastery of Winchcombe, which was suppressed by Ealdorman Ælfhere of Mercia following the death of King Edgar in July 975. The Winchcombe monks were obliged to flee from Mercia. Their abbot, Oswald's friend Germanus, went in the first instance into exile at Fleury, where he had studied (with Oswald) during the 950s; but the remainder of the community went to Ramsey, at Oswald's invitation (Oswald remained titular abbot of Ramsey until his death), where they were housed under the same roof as the Ramsey monks and where, under the protection of Ealdorman Æthelwine (who lived a few miles away), they were safe from further persecution by Ælfhere. After two years at Fleury, Abbot Germanus rejoined his community at Ramsey, and lived

27 CCCC, 265 and Rouen, BM, 1382 (U.109), fols. 173–98.
28 Hunter Blair 1964, pp. 86–99, and Lapidge 1993a, pp. 318–19.
29 Lapidge 1993a, pp. 343–86.
30 Lapidge, 1996, pp. 429–31.

there until Æthelwine's death in 992 (when he was moved to a vacant abbacy at Cholsey). When the community of monks fled from Winchcombe, they presumably took with them anything portable, including church furniture and books. This statement can be no more than surmise, however, since, as far as we know, no books from a library at Winchcombe itself survive: the so-called 'Winchcombe Sacramentary'[31] was written, for example, not at Winchcombe but at Ramsey, for use by the community of Winchcombe monks domiciled there.[32] Byrhtferth was certainly familiar with this sacramentary (or with its antecedent, presumptively a book from Winchcombe itself). For example, some of the wording in his description of the funeral service of St Oswald derives verbatim from a prayer in the service for the dead in the 'Winchcombe Sacramentary' (cf. *Vita S. Oswaldi* v, 19: 'uixit in carne Christo; uiuit, deposito carnis onere, Domino', and the wording of the 'Winchcombe Sacramentary': 'Deus apud quem mortuorum spiritus uiuunt, et in quo electorum animae deposito carnis onere plena felicitate laetantur').[33] This example demonstrates that the Winchcombe community, whether housed in Mercia or at Ramsey, had their own books. Since the community did not leave Ramsey during Byrhtferth's lifetime (no successor to Germanus as abbot of Winchcombe is recorded until the 1040s), such books as they owned probably found their way into the Ramsey library as the original community of 975 died out.

A new foundation such as Ramsey must have attempted to acquire books from any possible source, but above all by borrowing exemplars for copying from neighbouring monasteries. Although there is nothing from later Anglo-Saxon England to compare with the correspondence of Lupus of Ferrières a century earlier in revealing networks of borrowing and copying between Continental monasteries, contacts of some sort evidently existed between English houses. Byrhtferth's *Vita S. Oswaldi* helps to throw some light on these contacts. It is certain, for example, that Ramsey had acquired from Winchester a copy of Lantfred's *Translatio et miracula S. Swithuni* (composed *c.* 975), for Byrhtferth quotes from it in his *Vita S. Oswaldi* (I, 7). Ramsey had also acquired from Winchester a copy of Wulfstan's *Vita S. Æthelwoldi*, published in 996, since Byrhtferth refers explicitly to this text as well (III, 11); what is astonishing in this case is the rapidity with which the Winchester text became available to Byrhtferth, composing his *Vita S. Oswaldi* at Ramsey during the years 997×1002. But Winchester was not the only source of contemporary hagiography. Byrhtferth quotes at length in his *Vita S. Oswaldi* (V, 6–7) from the

31 Davril 1995: Orléans, Médiathèque, 127 (105).
32 Davril 1995, pp. 22–6; Lapidge 1993a, pp. 391–4.
33 Davril 1995, p. 268, no. 1859.

Vita S. Dunstani by the secular cleric who gives his name only as B. The *Vita S. Dunstani* was dedicated to Ælfric, archbishop of Canterbury (995–1005), and it was presumably from Canterbury that Byrhtferth acquired his copy of B's work. Furthermore, Byrhtferth's quotations are not taken from the first recension of the *Vita S. Dunstani*,[34] but from a later recension of the work made apparently at Canterbury in the attempt to eliminate some of B's most pompous and obscure language.[35] This revised version of the *Vita S. Dunstani* is preserved uniquely in BL, Cotton Cleopatra, B.xiii, fols. 59–90 (St Augustine's, Canterbury, early tenth century). The date of Byrhtferth's *Vita S. Oswaldi* (composed between 997 and 1002) helps to fix the date of this revised version of the *Vita S. Dunstani* (indeed of the *Vita S. Dunstani* itself), and provides another illustration of the rapidity with which hagiographical texts were circulated in late Anglo-Saxon England.

Altogether in the substantial corpus of his writings Byrhtferth quotes from approximately 100 Latin writings. (This figure may seem small by comparison with modern libraries, and even with Carolingian libraries such as Bobbio and Fleury, but by comparison with contemporary Anglo-Saxon libraries it was one of the largest, its holdings being matched only by the library at the Old Minster, Winchester, which sustained the scholarship of Ælfric and Wulfstan Cantor.) In the case of only a small proportion of these (perhaps 10 per cent) is it possible to identify the means by which copies of these writings were acquired by the Ramsey library. Fewer still are represented by surviving manuscripts. It is unlikely that further research (involving, for example, collation of works quoted by Byrhtferth against surviving manuscripts) will alter this picture drastically, given the relatively small number of manuscripts which have survived from Anglo-Saxon England. For example, Byrhtferth's writings contain several verbatim quotations from the *Epistulae* of Jerome; but there is no surviving Anglo-Saxon manuscript dating from (say) the tenth or early eleventh century (English copies of Jerome's *Epistulae* are either eighth-century Northumbrian ones which had long since passed to the Continent, or manuscripts dating from *c.* 1100 which are presumably copies of exemplars reimported into England in the wake of the Norman Conquest).[36] The sad conclusion is that Byrhtferth's library, like all Anglo-Saxon libraries, has vanished, save for a few scattered remnants.

34 Preserved in St Gallen, Kantonsbibliothek (Vadiana) 337.
35 Winterbottom 2000. 36 Lapidge 2006, pp. 271 and 315.

37

The library of Wulfstan of York

ANDY ORCHARD

Wulfstan of York was by any measure a central figure in late Anglo-Saxon England.[1] His political importance as one who not only managed to survive but to thrive during the reigns of both the Anglo-Saxon King Æthelred II (who ruled 978–1013 and again 1014–16) and the Danish King Cnut (who ruled 1016–35), for both of whom he wrote laws,[2] is matched by his contemporary literary impact as a reader, writer and reviser of an impressive range of works in both Latin and Old English, and a source used freely and echoed often by others.[3] The exact extent of Wulfstan's corpus is still a matter of debate, although great strides have been made in the past century or so, largely through closer appreciation of his idiosyncratic style:[4] he has been identified as the author of a range of sermons (often surviving in variant versions),[5] of sundry law-codes, of the prose sections of the *Benedictine Office*,[6] of the so-called *Canons of Edgar*,[7] directed at the secular clergy, of the *Institutes of Polity* (again surviving in variant versions),[8] which outlines the political and social roles of church and state, of two treatises (now called *Gerefa* and *Rectitudines*) that give advice on managing a large estate, and perhaps of two rhythmical passages found on the one hand in the D and E versions of the *Anglo-Saxon Chronicle* under the year 959, and on the other in the D version for 975.[9]

1 See, in general, Whitelock 1942; Bethurum 1957, pp. 54–87; Bethurum 1966; Whitelock 1965; Townend 2004.

2 The codes in question are V–IX Æthelred, Cnut 1018, and I–II Cnut. See further Liebermann 1903–16; Lawson 1994; Whitelock 1941, 1948, 1955; Kennedy 1983; Wormald 1999; Wormald 2004.

3 See now Orchard 2007. On various 'Wulfstan imitators', and the difficulty of distinguishing their work from his, see especially Wilcox 1992 and Scragg 1998.

4 Useful studies include McIntosh 1949; Orchard 1992b, 1997; Dance 2004; Pons-Sanz 2007, pp. 7–31.

5 Still central to any consideration of Wulfstan's homiletic works are Napier 1967 and Jost 1950; a useful set of facsimiles of some of the most important manuscripts is to be found in Wilcox 2000c; see too Loyn 1971.

6 Ure 1957. 7 Fowler 1972. 8 Jost 1959.

9 See Cubbin 1996 (for *ASC* D); Irvine 2004 (for *ASC* E).

Various Latin texts and compilations have also been attributed to Wulfstan on topics and in manuscripts that for one reason or another can be associated with his name.[10] The combined output thus far identified is impressive, and was evidently produced over a sustained period of literary activity that was necessarily combined with heavy political and ecclesiastical duties, albeit both precise dating of individual items and an agreed comparative chronology are still some way off.[11]

While Ælfric, Wulfstan's still more prolific contemporary, has benefited from the close and highly profitable attention of modern editors and source-hunters,[12] Wulfstan's works, in so far as they have been identified at all, have been relatively neglected.[13] New editions to modern standards are sorely needed of almost the entirety of Wulfstan's burgeoning corpus,[14] and such editions will doubtless cast new light on Wulfstan's sources,[15] of whom Ælfric was himself clearly one of the most important.[16] The disparity between the state of source studies for Ælfric and Wulfstan lies in part in the fact that unlike Ælfric, who often signals his sources, Wulfstan hardly ever uses direct quotations, even when his source is in Old English, and in part in the fact that even when echoing the work of others, he always seems to take pains to alter the words, taking the sense and making it his own by overlaying it with his idiosyncratic style. Where Ælfric adopts, Wulfstan adapts, sometimes drifting dramatically away from his source, so that what he said can be far indeed in language and structure and sense from what he originally read. Still, clues to Wulfstan's range of reading can be gleaned from several different kinds of evidence, namely those books he annotated, those books he compiled, and those he echoed in his own works.

10 The identification of such Latin texts is still relatively undeveloped. See now Hall 2004; for the kind of source study such Latin texts require, see too Cross 1989.

11 Attempts have been made to put Wulfstan's vernacular works at least into some kind of sequence, most recently by Wormald 2004, pp. 26–7, and Pons-Sanz 2007, p. 25. Even the date of the *Sermo Lupi ad Anglos*, perhaps Wulfstan's most famous work, and one which appears in three different versions in five separate manuscripts, is at issue: the manuscript witnesses give both 1009 and 1014 as the date, but the text was clearly revised over time. See further, e.g., Wilcox 2004 and Keynes 2007, pp. 203–13.

12 See Chapter 29 in this volume; Lapidge 2006, pp. 250–66.

13 For an overview, largely based on Bethurum 1957, see Hollis 1992–6.

14 Cf. Orchard 2003c, 2004. The standard edition for Wulfstan's sermons remains Bethurum 1957, despite its many defects (on Bethurum as an accurate reporter of manuscript readings, see, for example, McDougall 1995). Given Wulfstan's habit of rewriting and reusing his own material, it may be that electronic editions and transcripts would be particularly helpful; two such electronic editions exist to date: Melissa Bernstein's electronic edition of the *Sermo Lupi ad Anglos* (http://english3.fsu.edu/~wulfstan/) and Joyce Lionarons' electronic edition of Wulfstan's eschatological homilies (http://webpages.ursinus.edu/jlionarons/wulfstan/).

15 For an example of how a single (in this case Latin) text can bear sustained modern source analysis, see Cross 1991.

16 Godden 2004, esp. pp. 362–72; Orchard 2007, pp. 334–41.

Among the books that we can be sure that Wulfstan read are those which, it has been argued, contain corrections and additions in his own hand. These alterations have been described by Neil Ker (who first suggested the attribution)[17] as being essentially of three kinds: the corrections of an overseer emending the errors of other scribes, the 'improvements' of a zealous reader tinkering with received texts, as well as some more substantial changes, generally to the works of Wulfstan, that seem more like those of an author revising his own writings. Several of the manuscripts in question contain a specific selection and combination of texts of particular interest to a bishop, as Mary Bateson identified long ago,[18] and which Dorothy Bethurum first further suggested were part of a 'commonplace book' (a better term might be 'handbook') that could be specifically attached to Wulfstan's name.[19] Such manuscripts, whether they were produced for or annotated by Wulfstan, or were compiled under his supervision, or (as in some cases) seem to reflect earlier such compilations, are naturally of primary importance in attempting to reconstruct Wulfstan's library. No fewer than eighteen such manuscripts survive, as follows (those containing Wulfstan's own hand marked by an '*'; those reflecting the so-called 'commonplace book' by a '†'):

1. †Brussels, Bibliothèque Royale, 8558–63 (2498), fols. 80–131 and 132–53, (*s.* xi[1] and xii, written in England);[20]
2. †Cambridge, Corpus Christi College, 190, pt 1 (*s.* xi[1]), pp. iii–xii and 1–294;[21]
3. †Cambridge, Corpus Christi College, 265 (*s.* xi[med], Worcester);[22]
4. *†Copenhagen, Kongelige Bibliotek, G. K. S. 1595 (4°) (Worcester or York, *s.* xi[1]), Wulfstan's hand on fols. 48r, 65v–6v, and 81r;[23]
5. *London, British Library, Add. 38651 (*s.* xi[in]), Wulfstan's hand on fols. 57–8;[24]
6. *London, British Library, Cotton Claudius A.iii (*s.* x/xi[1]), Wulfstan's hand on fols. 31–86 and 106–50;[25]

17 Ker 1971; see too Cross and Brown 1993, pp. 73–5, and Cross and Tunberg 1993, pp. 44–7.
18 Bateson 1895b.
19 Bethurum 1942. See now Cross 1992 and (especially) Sauer 2000; for additional commentary, see Hill 2004, pp. 320–2.
20 Ker 1957, no. 10; Gneuss 2001, no. 808.
21 Ker 1957, no. 45; Gneuss 2001, no. 59. See further James 1912, I, pp. 452–63.
22 Ker 1957, no. 53; Gneuss 2001, no. 73. See further James 1912, II, pp. 14–21.
23 Ker 1957, no. 99; Gneuss 2001, no. 814. Facsimile: Cross and Tunberg 1993.
24 Ker 1957, no. 130; Gneuss 2001, no. 295.
25 Ker 1957, no. 141; Gneuss 2001, no. 314.

7. *†London, British Library, Cotton Nero A.i (Worcester or York, *s.* xi^{in}), fols. 70–177;[26]
8. *London, British Library, Cotton Tiberius A.xiii (Worcester, *s.* xi^{1}–xi^{ex}), fols. 1–118;[27]
9. *†London, British Library, Cotton Vespasian A.xiv (Worcester or York, *s.* xi^{1}), fols. 114–79;[28]
10. *London, British Library, Harley 55 (*s.* xi^{1}), fols. 1–4;[29]
11. †Oxford, Bodleian Library, Barlow 37 (SC 6464) (*s.* xii/xiii);
12. †Oxford, Bodleian Library, Bodley 718 (SC 2632) (written in England, *s.* xi^{1});[30]
13. *Oxford, Bodleian Library, Hatton 20 (SC 4113) (890–97);[31]
14. *Oxford, Bodleian Library, Hatton 42 (SC 4117) (Brittany, *s.* ix^{2}; France, *s.* x);[32]
15. †Oxford, Bodleian Library, Junius 121 (SC 5232), fols. 9–110 (Worcester, *s.* xi$^{3/4}$);[33]
16. †Paris, Bibliothèque nationale de France, lat. 3182 (Brittany, *s.* xi^{1} or xi^{2});
17. †Rouen, Bibliothèque municipale 1382 (U.109), Wulfstan's hand on fols. 173r–98v;[34]
18. *York, Minster Library, Add. 1 (*s.* xi^{1} – *s.* xi^{2}).[35]

Together, these manuscripts provide an invaluable witness to what Wulfstan read and chose to be transmitted; several also contain substantial extracts from Wulfstan's own works. Space precludes thorough examination here of the contents of each, although detailed studies exist relating precisely how individual manuscripts of this group can cast light on Wulfstan's habits of reading and annotation.[36]

In broad terms, these manuscripts contain a range of material, from collections of canon law, penitential texts, liturgical material, sermons and homilies,

26 Ker 1957, no. 146; Gneuss 2001, no. 341. Facsimile: Loyn 1971.
27 Ker 1957, no. 190; Gneuss 2001, no. 366.
28 Ker 1957, no. 204; Gneuss 2001, no. 383. See further Chase 1975, pp. 8–12.
29 Ker 1957, no. 226; Gneuss 2001, no. 412.
30 Gneuss 2001, no. 592. See too Bateson 1895a; Cross 1992.
31 Ker 1957, no. 324; Gneuss 2001, no. 626. For reproduction see Franzen 1998, with her description at pp. 10–14.
32 Gneuss 2001, no. 629.
33 Ker 1957, no. 338; Gneuss 2001, no. 644. For reproduction see Franzen 1998, with her description at pp. 56–67. See too Pope 1967–8, I, pp. 70–7.
34 Gneuss 2001, no. 925.
35 Ker 1957, no. 402; Gneuss 2001, no. 774. Facsimile: Barker 1986; see too Keynes 1986.
36 The best example is perhaps Sauer 2000, pp. 343–67 (on CCCC, 265 and BodL., Barlow 37); see too Cross 1992 (on Rouen, BM, U.109 (1382)). Each of the facsimiles noted above also has detailed descriptions of the contents.

and letters, together with the occasional poem. Of those texts that Wulfstan seems to have assembled for his own use, there stands out an impressive accumulation of canon-collections of church councils, of precisely the kind that a bishop and archbishop might be expected to consult, including the Councils of Nicaea, Ancyra and Neocaesarea, as well as the second Council of Constantinople, and the Council of Chalcedon, a collection that runs from the fourth century to the eighth. Carolingian compilations are also witnessed, including those of the Council of Aachen (which took place in 816) and part of the collection of canons put forth by Charlemagne and Louis the Pious that was made in 827 by Ansegisus; specifically English texts that are part of the same remit include the canons of the Council of Hertford (672 or 673), the *acta* of the Synod of Chelsea, and the so-called *Constitutions of Oda* (942–6). More widely circulating florilegia, such as Defensor's *Liber scintillarum*, the Hiberno-Latin *Collectio canonum Hibernensis*, and Pirmin of Reichenau's *Scarapsus* are also witnessed, as well as a number of the sermons of Caesarius of Arles, which were themselves often excerpted. From close comparison of the available compilations, a canon collection specific to Wulfstan has been identified.[37] One manuscript of this group, London, British Library, Cotton Vespasian A.xiv, contains not only annotations in Wulfstan's hand but also poetry in his praise (and also in his hand), as well as a large selection of letters by Alcuin, one of which is copied in his own hand, and several of which are reflected in Wulfstan's vernacular works.[38]

It is clear that such a 'commonplace book' would have been an extremely useful handbook for a working prelate, and it is likewise evident from his assiduous annotation that Wulfstan made good use of the materials at his disposal. Special mention should also be made of the collection formerly known as the *Excerptiones Ecgberhti*,[39] which itself quotes the so-called *Quadripartitus* once attributed to Halitgar of Cambrai, as well as a brief collection of canons apparently composed by Gerbald of Liège, alongside various works (especially sermons) by Caesarius of Arles (as already noted), Abbo of Saint-Germain-des-Prés,[40] and Atto of Vercelli.[41] A number of pentitential texts, witnessed in whole or in part, also appear scattered throughout these manuscripts, and obviously were the focus of considerable interest on Wulfstan's part.[42]

Indeed, aside from the sources witnessed by the eighteen manuscripts listed above, it is striking how few other sources and parallels, including extended

37 Cross and Hamer 1999. 38 See now Mann 2004.
39 See now Cross and Hamer 1999. Still extremely useful is Aronstam 1974.
40 Cross and Brown 1989, 1993. 41 See further Cross 1993.
42 In general, see Frantzen 1983; see too Charles-Edwards 1995.

versions of texts represented here, can be deduced from Wulfstan's own works. Many of these were simply the staple of ecclesiastical life, including the Bible (particularly the Old Testament prophets of doom) and liturgical texts,[43] as well as a good number of Ælfric's works, drawn not only from direct correspondence, but also apparently from manuscript collections.[44] In several other cases, it has been deduced that certain Latin texts, themselves often compilations, that appear in these manuscripts, are Wulfstan's own 'working' notes, later to be elaborated in his own distinctive style in Old English. Such is the assumption underlying Dorothy Bethurum's decision to print as Wulfstan's own the composite Latin text *De Anticristo et eius signis*,[45] which draws on both Isidore's *Sententiae* and Adso's *Epistola de Anticristo*, since the Latin text seems to underlie the Old English sermon *De Anticristo* that indeed immediately follows it in two manuscripts.[46] Given that the earliest manuscript containing the complete text of Adso's *Epistola* is Cambridge, Corpus Christi College, 190, discussed above,[47] it seems possible to witness here Wulfstan at work, just as in the so-called *De baptismo*[48] we find an order of ritual for baptism as presented in Jesse of Amiens' *Epistola de baptismo* combined with phrases from the *De ecclesiasticis officiis* of Amalarius of Metz and Theodulf of Orléans' *De ordine baptismi*.[49] This Latin compilation provides the basis for most of Wulfstan's vernacular sermon *Dominica IIII[a], uel quando uolueris* and part of his Old English *Sermo de baptismate*,[50] just as Wulfstan follows closely the Latin wording of Boniface's letter to Archbishop Cuthbert on the duties of the clergy in a Latin tract, which was reworked and expanded in Old English.[51]

Such reorganisation, repetition and recycling of the material at his disposal seems to have been the hallmark of all Wulfstan's work, perhaps best exemplified by his most celebrated composition, the *Sermo Lupi ad Anglos*:[52] if it seems to have drawn (at least in its longest version) on a letter from Alcuin to Archbishop Æthelhard that is found in no fewer than four manuscripts of the 'commonplace book',[53] and if it may have taken its literary impetus either from the *Sermo ad milites* of Abbo of Saint-Germain-des-Prés or from

43 Jones 2004.

44 For some useful examples, see Godden 2004, esp. pp. 362–72; Orchard 2007, pp. 334–41. For a general view of the differences between the two authors, see Stanley 2004.

45 Bethurum 1957, pp. 113–15: Ia.

46 *Ibid.*, pp. 116–18: Ib.

47 Adso's *Epistola* is at pp. 281–91.

48 Bethurum 1957, pp. 169–71: VIIIa.

49 See Cross 1989.

50 Bethurum 1957, pp. 172–4 (VIIIb) and 175–84 (VIIIc).

51 Respectively *ibid.*, pp. 239 (XVIa) and 240–1 (XVIb).

52 Whitelock 1963; Hollis 1977; Wilcox 2000a.

53 CCCC, 190, p. 173; CCCC, 265, p. 7; BL, Cotton Vespasian A.xiv, fol. 146r; BodL., Barlow 37, p. 34. In the Vespasian manuscript the relevant passage is underlined, perhaps by Wulfstan himself: see further Chase 1975, p. 74, lines 109–13; Mann 2004, pp. 245–6; Orchard 2003c, pp. 324–6.

the anonymous text entitled *De tribulationibus* (or from both),[54] he made the resulting Old English text very much his own, to be multiply reworked and excerpted. As is often the case with Wulfstan, whose works were evidently considered important enough to be copied into the twelfth century,[55] one is left with the impression of a busy and deeply engaged man of the world, weighed down with affairs of state, but blessed with a good network of contacts and assistants, supremely confident of his own ability to re-package and re-present the material (whether originally in Latin or Old English) in his own not quite inimitable style.[56]

As a prelate keenly aware of his own status, then, Wulfstan seems to have been far more concerned with product than with process, and as such is a less promising candidate for the precise assessment of his library than (say) Bede or Alcuin or Ælfric or even Aldhelm, each of whom evidently loved learning for learning's sake, and was happy to drop the names of their supposed sources, and to take their place in an unfolding narrative of scholarly and literary endeavour. But Wulfstan, who idiosyncratically made the words and thoughts of others his own, clothed in a self-conscious style that tended to obliterate or at least obscure the books and texts on which he doubtless drew, was evidently a man more than happy to speak for himself, but happy too to have others do his serious reading for him.[57]

54 See further Cross and Brown 1989; Keynes 2007, pp. 172–9 and 203–13, who points out that both of these texts, as well as the relevant Alcuin letter, all appear in close proximity in CCCC, 190.

55 See Cross 1991; Wilcox 2000a.

56 See in particular Wilcox 1992 and Scragg 1998.

57 In composing this brief account, I am indebted to a much longer and unpublished description of Wulfstan's sources passed on to me more than a decade ago by the late Jimmy Cross, whose scholarship and energy remain much missed.

38

Rhygyfarch ap Sulien and Ieuan ap Sulien

DAVID HOWLETT

Sulgenus Sapiens, Sulien the Wise of Llanbadarn Fawr in Ceredigion (1011–91), was twice bishop of St David's, once 1072/3–78 and again 1080–5. Sulien, whose name means 'born on a Sunday', may be responsible for the introduction of the *Vita Sancti Maedoc* into Wales, if he did not himself compose it. The first of his sons, named Ricemarchus or Rhygyfarch, derived from Old Welsh *ri* + *cyfarch* 'salutation of the king (of heaven)' (1056/7–99), composed five extant works: in Latin the prose *Vita Sancti Dauid* (1081), three poems, *De psalterio* 'On the Psalter' (?1079), *De messe infelici* 'On an Unhappy Harvest', and *Planctus Ricemarch*, 'Rhygyfarch's Lament' for the Norman Conquest of Wales (post-1093); and in Welsh perhaps at least part of the Four Branches of the Mabinogi. The fourth son, named after the fourth evangelist Iohannes or Ieuan (d. 1137), also composed five extant works: in Latin the prose *Vita Sancti Paterni* (1081), three poems, *Inuocatio Iohannis* 'Ieuan's Invocation', *Carmen de vita et familia Sulgeni* 'Song about the Life and Family of Sulien' (post-1080), *Disticha Iohannis* 'Ieuan's Distichs'; and in Welsh an englyn on the episcopal staff of St Padarn.[1]

From the family library at Llanbadarn Fawr two manuscripts survive. One contains the *Martyrologium Hieronymianum*, a *Psalterium iuxta Hebraeos Hieronymi*, and on folio 158v in Rhygyfarch's autograph his verses *De psalterio*, in which he names himself the son of Sulien as author, Ithael as scribe of the manuscript, and his brother Ieuan as illuminator (see Plate 9.4).[2] Another contains a copy of Augustine *De Trinitate*, written at his father's request, with all Ieuan's Latin and Welsh verses in his autograph.[3] A third manuscript contains Cicero's *Somnium Scipionis* and Macrobius' *Commentarium* on Cicero with Rhygyfarch's *Planctus* and *De messe infelici*, written by a twelfth-century Norman

1 Wade-Evans 1944; Lapidge 1973–4; Howlett 1995, pp. 233–42, 338–42; Howlett 1998a, pp. 103–18; Thomas and Howlett 2003; Evans and Wooding 2007.

2 TCD, 50 (A.4.20). 3 CCCC, 199.

scribe – perhaps a copy of a manuscript written by Rhygyfarch himself.[4] In addition, the Welsh *Brut y Tywysogion*, though originally compiled at St David's, was from some time late in the eleventh century kept at Llanbadarn Fawr – probably, one infers from the obituaries, by a member of Sulien's family.

Quotations and allusions imply that Rhygyfarch and Ieuan had studied, first in the classical and late Latin tradition, Vergil (*Aeneid*, *Georgics*, *Eclogues*), Ovid (*Metamorphoses*, *Ars amatoria*, *Epistulae ex Ponto* certainly, and probably *Fasti*), Lucan, Juvencus, Prudentius (*Peristephanon*, *Apotheosis*, *Cathemerinon*), Martianus Capella, Caelius Sedulius (*Carmen paschale*), Boethius (*De consolatione philosophiae*), and possibly Statius (*Thebaid*), Horace (*Carmen saeculare*) and Juvenal. They had also studied intently the Latin Bible.

Second, the prose *Lives* imply that Rhygyfarch and Ieuan had studied the works of the primary Cambro-Latin author, Gildas: *De excidio Brittanniae* (published in AD 540), *Epistolae*, and *Penitential*. Rhygyfarch certainly knew the *acta* of synods of the British church, specifically those of the *Synodus Luci Victoriae*, the *Synodus Aquilonalis Brittanniae* held at Llanddewi Breui, and probably the *Excerpta quaedam de libro Dauid*. Both brothers probably knew the *Orationes Moucani*, nine rhyming rhythmical Cambro-Latin prayers, their author identified with the namesake of what Rhygyfarch describes as *Maucanni monasterium* and *monasterium Depositi* 'Maugan's monastery, the monastery of the Deposit', itself identified now with the *Ecclesia maritima* in Ieuan's *Vita Sancti Paterni*.

In the third place, both brothers knew the earliest and most important Armorico-Latin hagiographic text, the eighth-century *Vita Sancti Samsonis*. Rhygyfarch probably knew Wrmonoc's *Vita Sancti Pauli Aureliani* (884), and Ieuan probably knew *Lives* of St Paternus of Vannes in Brittany and St Paternus of Avranches in Normandy, both of whom he identified with St Paternus of Llanbadarn Fawr in his *Vita Sancti Paterni*.

Fourth, clusters of details and biblical typology and the etymologies of place-names and personal names suggest that Rhygyfarch knew from the Hiberno-Latin tradition Tírechán's account of churches founded by Patrick (*c.* 670), and Muirchú moccu Macthéni's *Vita Sancti Patricii* (AD 700), and the *Liber Angeli*, all composed at Armagh, as well as seven other Hiberno-Latin texts. These are as follows. (1) The *Vita Sancti Albei*: important as the source of information about the greatest pre-Patrician saint of Ireland, the story about the pregnant mother and an aphetic priest, the stories about stones at the sites of David's conception and birth, and the story of attempted poisoning;

4 BL, Cotton Faustina C.i.

it was also important as a model for composition of a narrative in repeated diminution by the same ratio, *hemiolus* or *sesquialter*, 1.5 → 1 or 3 → 2. (2) The *Vita Sancti Maedoc*: probably introduced into Wales, if not actually written by Rhygyfarch's father Sulien, it was important as the source of the story about giving eyes and a nose to a flat-faced man, and the story about a manuscript book left lying open in the rain during an interrupting adventure with oxen and a cart; it was also important as a model for composition of a narrative in repeated diminution by the same ratio. (3) The *Vita Sancti Barre* for a story about crossing the sea. (4) The Martyrology of Oengus the Culdee (*c.* 800) for the story of Modomnoc's introduction of bees into Ireland. (5) Rhygyfarch knew either a *Vita Sancti Brendani* or the *Nauigatio Sancti Brendani* composed early in the ninth century. (6) Rhygyfarch knew the *Ordines Sanctorum*. (7) Both brothers knew the seventh-century *Hisperica famina*.

The fifth tradition that provided sources is Anglo-Latin. Both brothers knew works by the first Anglo-Latin author Aldhelm (d. 709), the *Enigmata* and the *Carmen de virginitate*. Rhygyfarch knew well the oldest Anglo-Latin hagiographic text, the *Vita Sancti Gregorii*, composed at the beginning of the eighth century by an anonymous member of Whitby, and the *Life* of the most important Mercian saint, the *Vita Sancti Guthlaci*, composed early in the eighth century by Felix of Crowland, along with Bede's *Historia ecclesiastica gentis Anglorum*, published in 731.

Both brothers understood the ancient tradition of gematria, in which as every letter of the alphabet in Hebrew, Greek and Latin bears a numerical as well as phonetic value, every proper name and place-name exhibits a number as well as a meaning. Both brothers made names and other words exhibit their numerical values both by their placement and by the intervals between their recurrence. Both brothers understood in addition a related rabbinic tradition by which for exegetical purposes one can elucidate the meaning of a name or word by comparing it with another of equal value. Rhygyfarch used metrical rhythms of clausulae, and both brothers used the stressed rhythms of the cursus, as well as elaborate patterns of rhyme and dense word-play to fix and adorn their prose compositions. Both infixed calendrical dates in their texts, always with comprehensive internal consistency.

The astonishing complexity and density of artifice in these works is a function of their purpose and context and date. One purpose of Muirchú's *Life of Patrick* had been to refute any claim by Wilfrid to be metropolitan archbishop of Ireland by advancing the claim of Patrick *totius Hiberniae episcopi doctorisque* 'bishop and teacher of all of Ireland' and also as superior of the bishop of the Isle of Man and of kings of western Britain from Dumbarton to Anglesey, even of the English to the east; one purpose of the *Life of Samson* had been to present Samson as unequalled among the race of Britons past or future; while the author of the Whitby *Life of Gregory* admitted that he knew of few miracles performed by the saint and asked the readers' indulgence if some of the miracles here related had been performed by other saints, as all share in a common sanctity. Rhygyfarch undertook to present David as the greatest saint ever to have lived and worked in Britain, surpassing the greatest achievements of the Apostle of the Irish, the Apostle of the Bretons, and the Apostle of the English. He detailed an ancestry more exalted than that of any other saint, royal and holy, derived directly from the family of the Virgin Mary. He incorporated antenatal incidents involving Patrick and Gildas, adapted narratives about David's conception and birth and baptism from the *Life of Ailbe*, and transferred a miracle performed by the mature Maedoc to the eight-day-old infant David. Rhygyfarch borrowed from the *Life of Gregory* and the *Life of Samson* stories about the golden-beaked dove, bringing them into play earlier in the *Life of David* and closer to his person than in the sources. In accounts of the saint's learning, his founding of churches, and his performing of miracles, Rhygyfarch made David supersede his predecessors – all introduced by name, either as harbingers or as subordinates. The direction of borrowing is always manifest, and Rhygyfarch often doubles the phenomena borrowed from earlier *Lives* to produce the most accomplished work of recycling and one-upmanship in the entire library of Insular hagiography.

Ieuan's poem in praise of his father records extended periods during which Sulien had studied in Ireland and in Scotland, but it derives from the period after Sulien's second consecration as bishop of St David's, after 1080. Cross-references in the *Lives* of Padarn and David suggest that both were commissioned by Sulien and produced at the same time, to advance the reputations of the two saints most important to him – one the patron of his home, the other the patron of his see – for presentation to William the Conqueror on the occasion of his visit to St David's in 1081, *orationis causa* according to the *Annales Cambriae*, though the *Anglo-Saxon Chronicle* reports the incident as a military adventure: *se cyng lædde fyrde in to Wealan*.

The list of churches founded by David suggests a previously unrecognised purpose of the *Life*. By claiming that David had established *Glastonia* 'Glastonbury' (recorded five years later in the Domesday Book as the richest house in England), *Bathonia* 'Bath' (site of the battle of Mons Badonicus, the greatest victory of the British over the English), *Croulan* 'Crowland' (home of the most prominent Mercian saint, Guthlac, and from 1076 the site of the burial of Waltheof, whom William the Conqueror had personally condemned to death), *Repetun* 'Repton' (where Guthlac had received the tonsure), *Colguan*, 'Colva' and *Glascum* 'Glascwm' (on the Welsh side of Offa's Dyke), and *Leuministre* 'Leominster' (on the English side of Offa's Dyke), Rhygyfarch claimed David's authority over churches in an extensive swathe of territory between the provinces of Canterbury and York and more ancient than either of them. By claiming that David had established Raglan in Gwent and Llangyfelach in Gower and that he had personal relations with King Pepiau in Erging and Boducat and Martrun in the province of Kidwelly, Rhygyfarch claimed authority over churches and men both east and west of Llandaff, a potential rival to the church at St David's, mention of which, along with mention of the saints of south-eastern Wales, he pointedly avoids. Rhygyfarch learned this propagandistic device from the *Liber Angeli*, but made it more important than it had been in his source, and used it to introduce his account of the first fire kindled at St David's, smoke from which irritated the pagan Irish king Baia – as in Muirchú's *Life* smoke from Patrick's first fire had irritated the pagan Irish king Loeguire. By stating that smoke from David's fire circled round the entire island of Britain and also Ireland Rhygyfarch suggested that the see of St David, who had received episcopal orders directly from the Patriarch of Jerusalem, should be the metropolitan archiepiscopal see for the entire archipelago of the British Isles. Ieuan's poem about his father suggests that Sulien would be the appropriate metropolitan archbishop. The failure of the proposal does nothing to diminish the greatness of the enterprise of this single family, which produced the finest manuscripts, the finest prose and the finest verse extant in both Cambro-Latin and Old Welsh.

Within two generations other hagiographers had leapt to the defence of Welsh saints excluded from works produced at Llanbadarn Fawr, often appropriating features directly from works by the sons of Sulien, notably in Lifris of Llancarfan's *Vita Sancti Cadoci*, in Caradog of Llancarfan's revision of the *Vita Sancti Cadoci*, in the *Life* of Cadog's parents Gwynllyw and Gwladys, the *Vita Sancti Gundleii*, in the *Vita Sancti Iltuti*, above all in the colossal forgeries of the *Liber Landauensis*, made to advance the claims of the church at Llandaff. All these works bear witness to the primacy and centrality of the writings of Rhygyfarch and Ieuan, to the extent of their reading, and to the intelligent ways in which they could deploy both.

PART V CODA

39

The study of early British books

RICHARD GAMESON

The present volume stands as the latest contribution to a distinguished tradition of scholarship on the manuscripts of early Britain that stretches back to Matthew Parker (1504–75). In the last fifteen years of his life, Parker not only collected and salvaged manuscripts but studied them, he and his entourage scouring their pages for material that could inform his intellectual concerns and buttress his ecclesiastical standpoints. A range of works that he owned in manuscript can be shown to lie behind his *De antiquitate Britannicae ecclesiae cum 70 Archiepiscopis Cantuariensibus* (1572), for example. Parker's intention may often have been polemical – justifying his views and the Elizabethan church settlement in general by tracing them back to an early English church that had been purer, he could claim, than the Roman Catholic one of his own day – but the material was nevertheless scrutinised and published after a fashion. Indeed, his revealingly named *A Testimonie of Antiquitie shewing the auncient faith in the Church of England touching the sacrament of the body and bloude of the Lord* ... (1566/7) included the first edition of any Old English texts – namely the Lord's Prayer, Creed, Ten Commandments, two Ælfric letters and a homily – printed (by the enterprising John Day) using a typeface specially created for the purpose.

A survey of antiquarian work on early British books would be out of place here; however mention should be made of the contribution of the remarkable palaeographer, Humfrey Wanley (1672–1726). An outstanding figure in many ways, he is chiefly relevant to our subject for his *Librorum Veterum Septentrionalium qui in Angliae Bibliothecis extant ... Catalogus* (published at Oxford in 1705). This provided a conspectus of relevant manuscripts that was not superseded until 1957; moreover, it remains a valuable source of information about volumes that were subsequently damaged (notably some of those in the Cotton collection). Much of the work of the next 300 years may be seen as moving slowly but surely towards a more comprehensive and analytical account of the 'old northern books' than Wanley had been able to provide.

Wanley's work aside, it is fair to say that the foundations of modern knowledge of our subject were mainly laid in the nineteenth century, and particularly its second half. Swathes of manuscript cataloguing rendered more accessible and comprehensible the holdings of major repositories. Moreover, this was done in increasing detail and with steadily improving accuracy, as is underlined by the contrast between H. O. Coxe's account of the volumes belonging to Oxford colleges (1852) and Charles Hardwick and H. R. Luard's of those in the Cambridge University Library (1856–67) on the one hand, and, on the other, the early volumes of Falconer Madan's *Summary Catalogue* of manuscripts in the Bodleian Library, published in the 1890s, and M. R. James's treatment of those at Trinity College, Cambridge, issued in 1900–4. Not only are texts more fully identified and datings more accurate in the publications of Madan and James, but fuller information is provided about the manuscripts as artefacts.

In the meantime, the development of photography and then of the means for printing therefrom had revolutionised the field, providing a crucial resource for palaeographical study. When in 1868 J. O. Westwood issued his pioneering anthology of early illumination (*Facsimiles of the Miniatures and Ornaments of Anglo-Saxon and Irish Manuscripts*) he had himself redrawn the folios in question so that they could be reproduced for his lavish colour plates. Although Westwood had worked, as he himself stressed (p. ix), 'with the most scrupulous care, the majority having been [done] with the assistance of a magnifying glass', and though as examples of colour printing the chromolithography is magnificent, these plates nevertheless show careful nineteenth-century copies rather than the actual pages of early medieval manuscripts. Five years later (in 1873) not only did the Palaeographical Society produce the first of its long run of actual-size plates from photographs accompanied by detailed commentary, but a medieval manuscript was reproduced in full photographic facsimile for the first time. The volume in question, though not a British book, was one that, imported into England, had played a central role in late Anglo-Saxon visual culture – namely the Utrecht Psalter. The following year (1874) H. James and J. T. Gilbert's *Facsimiles of National Manuscripts of Ireland*, vol. I (Southampton: Ordnance Survey) published the first photographs of Insular manuscripts; four years later the same body issued the first of its collections of facsimiles of early charters (devoted to those at Canterbury); and five years thereafter (1883) a relevant manuscript whose interest was primarily textual and philological, the Épinal Glossary, was honoured with a facsimile edition. At the end of the century (1896) the newly discovered gospel-lectionary of Queen Margaret of Scotland was reproduced in full under the editorship of

W. Forbes-Leith; the fact that the evangelist portraits and incipit pages, along with all coloured letters within the text, were redrawn by hand for reproduction (distorting their appearance) advertises the continuing limitations of the technology for printing in colour as opposed to monochrome.

It was also in the second half of the nineteenth century that the work of editing relevant texts blossomed (England lagging more than a generation behind Germany in this respect). The Rolls Series was initiated in 1857, the Early English Text Society seven years later; the Henry Bradshaw Society joined them in 1890. Although the quality with which manuscript evidence was treated in the volumes of such series inevitably varied, they unquestionably made it more readily available. Thus Henry Sweet's 1871 edition of *King Alfred's West-Saxon Version of Gregory's Pastoral Care* (EETS o.s. 45 and 50) listed the most important manuscripts of the work, quoting Wanley's account of them, and offered a description of the handwriting of the oldest; William Stubbs included in his *Memorials of St Dunstan* (RS 63; 1874) a serviceable account of the manuscripts of *Auctor B*'s *Life* of that saint, including those at Arras and St Gallen; while in 1896 Charles Plummer could present a detailed and fundamentally correct account of the transmission of the text of Bede's *Historia ecclesiastica* based on a sample of nearly fifty manuscripts (albeit those geographically most convenient).

The patterns of work initiated in the nineteenth century were pursued with increasing refinement in the early twentieth; and thanks to the labours of Victorian pioneers, the next generation could more easily identify and order particular classes of material. In 1910 and 1912 W. M. Lindsay issued his pathbreaking (and yet to be superseded) handbooks on *Early Irish Minuscule Script* and *Early Welsh Script*, and three years later he reported British scribal practices among his exhaustive descriptions of early patterns of abbreviation, *Notae Latinae*. When the following year (1916) Cuthbert Turner published a superb monograph on the earliest manuscript fragments at Worcester Cathedral, in addition to facsimiles, transcriptions and analyses of the items in question, he included handlists of early Worcester charters and books as a whole. E. A. Lowe likewise appended to his introduction to a selection of plates from the oldest copy of the *Rule of St Benedict* (Oxford, 1929) a list of English manuscripts and charters written in Uncial script – presaging the altogether greater and more comprehensive inventories that were to come from his pen in due course.

Reproductions and discussions of manuscripts, above all illuminated ones, had meanwhile multiplied. In 1905 R. Stettiner included the lengthy pictorial cycles from four late Anglo-Saxon copies of the *Psychomachia* in his anthology, *Die illustrierten Prudentius-Handschriften*, while five years later the Benedictional of Æthelwold, masterpiece of the most distinctive late Anglo-Saxon style of decoration (and then in private hands), was reproduced in full facsimile with a detailed commentary by H. A. Wilson and G. F. Warner. The first of the British Museum's handsome 'Schools of Illumination' portfolios, issued in 1914, was devoted to 'Hiberno-Saxon and Early English Schools AD 700–1100'; as well as monochrome plates it included a couple of good colour ones produced from photographs, advertising the technical progress that had been made in this respect. A considerably more compendious set of reproductions of Insular manuscript art was published in Berlin two years later as part of E. H. Zimmermann's *Vorkarolingische Miniaturen*; and during the 1920s, with his monograph on the Lindisfarne Gospels (1923) and a survey of English illuminated manuscripts from the tenth to the thirteenth century (1926), E. G. Millar provided well-illustrated overviews of much of the relevant material for our period as a whole, setting out the chronological evolution of styles and exploring their visual sources. Then in the second quarter of the century T. D. Kendrick integrated illumination into his two-part survey of Anglo-Saxon art in general; while towards the middle of the century Francis Wormald began to publish the path-breaking analyses – be it of different classes of decoration (such as initials, line-drawing, the 'Winchester school') or of particular manuscripts (the Benedictional of St Æthelwold, the Tiberius Psalter) – that brought new clarity to the book decoration of the late Anglo-Saxon period. This he eventually synthesised in his contribution to the multi-author *Le siècle de l'an mil*, published posthumously in 1973.

If manuscript evidence was less intensively mined and discussed (as opposed to edited) by literary scholars in the earlier twentieth century, there were nevertheless exceptions. For in a series of articles, spread across the second quarter of the century and finally reprinted as a collection in 1953, Kenneth Sisam demonstrated how much could be learned from close examination of Old English texts in their manuscript context about the ways in which they were transmitted and used. The same qualities, based on wide familiarity with the relevant manuscripts, inform the introduction to his and Celia Sisam's Early English Text Society edition of the Salisbury Psalter (1959). F. C. Robinson's important and oft-cited article of 1980, 'Old English literature in its most immediate context', exemplified, advocated and reinvigorated approaches that had been second nature to Sisam.

Meanwhile the crucial work of preparing descriptive catalogues continued. Among treatments of individual collections, G. F. Warner and J. P. Gilson's *Catalogue of Western Manuscripts in the Old Royal and King's Collections* (1921) and Roger Mynors' *Durham Cathedral Manuscripts up to 1200* (1939) hold pride of place for the number of relevant manuscripts that they include, the assurance with which they treat them, and the quantity and quality of plates that they publish. Then, two great thematic surveys presented many of the manuscripts that are at the heart of the present volume: E. A. Lowe's multi-volume *Codices Latini Antiquiores* (Oxford, 1934–72) provided palaeographical descriptions, plus actual-size reproductions, of all extant Latin books and fragments up to *c.* 800 (and the demand for his work on British and Irish collections was sufficiently great, apparently, to justify a second edition of that volume alone); while Neil Ker's *Catalogue of Manuscripts Containing Anglo-Saxon* (Oxford, 1957) described all the volumes containing texts in Old English. The former – which, complemented by Lowe's *English Uncial* (1960), underpinned all subsequent work on Insular script and books – has been described as 'perhaps unequalled in value by any other palaeographical publication of the twentieth century' (*ODNB*, s. v. Lowe). The latter, which informed all subsequent study of Old English texts and manuscripts, was justly characterised as 'perhaps the most important single book in the field of Anglo-Saxon studies in the twentieth century' (R. I. Page).

Concomitantly Neil Ker and others, building on the work of M. R. James, established in *Medieval Libraries of Great Britain* (1941; 2nd edn 1964; Supplement 1987), an invaluable guide to the identifiable provenance of manuscripts that had been in British collections in the Middle Ages. Though generally more informative and useful for periods after, as opposed to before 1100, it did bring significant benefits for the latter. In particular by identifying volumes of the same date with a shared provenance, *Medieval Libraries* facilitated the identification of scriptorium styles and even recurrent scribal hands, the recognition of which elsewhere could lead to the localisation of further volumes on the grounds of their appearance alone. This was work in which T. A. M. (Alan) Bishop excelled, and during the third quarter of the twentieth century his articles and monographs on manuscripts written in English Caroline Minuscule brought new order to the Latin manuscripts of later Anglo-Saxon England. The major advances on the palaeographical front aided, and were complemented by, a triad of new, more comprehensive surveys of relevant illuminated manuscripts (the work of Alexander, Temple, and Kauffmann), published between 1975 and 1978. Whereas the last of these three volumes, dealing with the period from 1066, was necessarily highly selective in the number of manuscripts that it could include, the first two (treating the periods up to *c.* 900, and from *c.* 900 to 1066) were able to be far more comprehensive, and were in effect well-illustrated corpora of their respective fields. Building on the broad foundations of all these works that ordered and described large numbers of relevant manuscripts, recording their provenance and assigning them dates and origins according to intelligible principles, Helmut Gneuss was able in 1981 to publish a 'A preliminary list of manuscripts written or owned in England up to 1100'. An essential precondition for a comprehensive overview of the book and literary culture of early Britain had finally been achieved.

If Gneuss's 'Preliminary list' may be viewed as the culmination of generations of work, it was simultaneously the point of departure for more. Not only did it encourage – solicit indeed – additions and corrections of the preliminary corpus, it facilitated more comprehensive examinations of classes of material of all kinds, be they manuscripts of particular date ranges, the output of individual writing centres, or specific classes of texts. More closely focused work, such as that of Crick and Dumville on particular script types, of Gullick, McKee, Rushforth, Webber and the present writer on various scriptoria, of Marsden on biblical manuscripts, of Dumville (again) on classes of liturgical books, of Budny and Ebersperger on the holdings of two particularly important collections, and of the present writer (again) on the manuscripts of the early Norman period, refined dates and attributions, expounded numerous aspects of scribal practice, and elucidated the characteristics of particular writing centres, clarifying relations between them. These and many other advances were reflected in the revised edition of Gneuss's work published in 2001.

Fuller data concerning the survival of particular texts, and more accurate estimates as to the dates of individual manuscripts had likewise facilitated the labours of scholars such as Clemoes, Cross, Godden, Hill, Pope and Scragg in exploring the sources, circulation and dissemination of Old English texts (above all those of Ælfric and Wulfstan), and of Lapidge and others in relation to Anglo-Latin ones. Correspondingly, the quality of the introductions to editions in such series as the Early English Text Society and Oxford Medieval Texts was transformed with regard to the detail in which the manuscript witnesses were described and assessed. These endeavours in turn clarified relationships between manuscripts, and elucidated the character of the scribes and centres responsible, setting the material in specific cultural contexts. Lapidge in particular was adept at weaving together palaeographical, textual and historical evidence to recover intellectual activities which might be associable with particular people and places, sketching convincing vignettes of cultural history.

For other classes of Latin texts, different resources contributed to the advance of knowledge. The steady publication of early medieval liturgical books in general, as of repertories of their component parts, permitted a sharper appreciation of the relationships between individual examples, British and Continental, illuminating the transmission of exemplars. The gains in question are exemplified, for instance, by Andrew Prescott's 1987 study of 'The structure of English pre-Conquest benedictionals', and in Henry Bradshaw Society editions such as Corrêa's of the Durham Collectar, Günzel's of Ælfwine's Prayerbook and Orchard's of the Leofric Missal. Correspondingly, the massive tables of collations of gospel variants and their manuscript witnesses published by Boniface Fischer between 1988 and 1991 revolutionised the task of exploring the affiliation between the texts of early gospel-books, a resource that was put to effective use in connection with British copies and their relatives by McGurk, Netzer and others.

At the same time, new editions of texts, with ever more accurate *indices fontium*, permitted the literary sources of individual authors, and hence the collections of books to which they had access, to be defined with increasing precision. This was an area that was revolutionised in the late twentieth century thanks to the appearance, then the growth and refinement, of searchable electronic databases of texts. Two ambitious collaborative projects, set up in the 1980s, systematically pursued such source studies from complementary perspectives. 'The Sources of Anglo-Saxon Literary Culture' aimed to establish from the full range of available evidence which texts were demonstrably available in Anglo-Saxon England, while 'Fontes Anglo-Saxonici' inventoried identifiable sources behind the writings of Old English and Anglo-Latin authors. The published results (whether in print or electronic form) are invaluable for particular cases, be they individual texts or authors, but are as yet too incomplete to provide a comprehensive picture. Nevertheless, critical use of all these resources, along with unrivalled knowledge of the field as a whole, underlay the first effective synthesis of the content of Anglo-Saxon libraries, focusing on the age of Bede, which was published by Lapidge in 2006. Invaluable in its own right, *The Anglo-Saxon Library* also probes the methodological problems and potential of such investigations in general, indicating what might, and equally what might not, be added to the picture if and when these projects are brought to completion.

Fostering major advances at all stages of the process outlined above, and central to bibliographical work strictly conceived, were facsimile reproductions and editions. Following the pioneering work of the Palaeographical Society, key manuscripts were reproduced in full or part under the aegis of such bodies as the Early English Text Society, the Roxburghe Club, various 'fine art' publishers and, above all, in the series 'Early English Manuscripts in Facsimile' (1951–2002). Embracing visually unprepossessing manuscripts of considerable textual interest as well as handsomely decorated ones, these publications were invaluable in facilitating long-distance study and permitting the comparison of now-scattered volumes, not to mention in fostering a wider use of manuscript evidence more generally. Moreover, their introductions were sometimes path-breaking monographs in their own right. Examples that were landmarks in the development of the field include Warner and Wilson's edition of the Benedictional of St Æthelwold (1910), Gollancz's of Junius 11 (1927), Chambers, Förster and Flower's of the Exeter Book (1933), that of Brown, Bruce-Mitford and others of the Lindisfarne Gospels (1956–60), Wright and Campbell's of the Vespasian Psalter (1967); Clemoes and Dodwell's of the Old English Illustrated Hexateuch (1974), and the multi-author, multi-fascicule 1986/7 edition of Domesday Book. Technically the finest facsimile of an early British book was the 2002 edition of the Lindisfarne Gospels, the quality of which made it an acceptable substitute for the original for many purposes; unfortunately, however, its elevated price put it beyond the reach of most research libraries. One of the most economical was Flower and Smith's 1941 edition of the Parker Chronicle and Laws; widely owned by individuals as well as institutions, it can be seen to have informed much debate not only about this particular manuscript but also on the Chronicle, its chronology, development, and contexts more generally – notwithstanding the fact that the promised commentary volume never materialised.

This field, too, was changing by the turn of the millennium. Provision of images of Anglo-Saxon manuscripts on a larger scale (but much lower quality) was taken up by the 'Anglo-Saxon Manuscripts in Microfiche Facsimile' project (1994–), bringing representations of the manuscripts in Ker's *Catalogue* within the reach of the individual scholar. However, microfiche, never a convenient medium, was rapidly overtaken by events as increasing numbers of relevant volumes became available in digital reproductions of various forms, some of very high quality. More versatile than conventional printed images (sometimes, for instance, offering the possibility of enlarging particular areas of a given page), these newest arrivals have already gone some way towards removing the hindrance that was imposed on our subject during the fourth quarter of the twentieth century when the punitive reproduction fees levied by certain repositories prevented many scholarly works without a subvention from being adequately illustrated. On the other hand, digital facsimiles remain inferior to conventional printed ones for conveying the nature of medieval manuscripts as books; and the extent to which they are, at the time of writing, sweeping most other reproductions, whatever their merits, before them may give cause for regret – not least because their durability is unclear. Relentless technical advances, not to mention market forces, render older versions of these new media obsolete with ever-increasing rapidity; moreover, their stability and longevity as a whole is unknown. Conversely, the production by the Folio Society in 2001 of a high-quality, full-colour (second) printed facsimile of the Benedictional of St Æthelwold at a relatively modest cost demonstrated how new photographic technology could also revitalise a traditional and highly effective medium: whether or not the digital facsimiles produced in the early twentieth-first century (be they on CD-ROM or the World Wide Web) will still be usable a generation hence, this fine volume (like its many venerable printed predecessors) certainly will be.

This rapid sketch of the history of our subject, highly simplified though it is, nevertheless gives a reasonable indication of the general pattern of development: an ever clearer understanding of the corpus of relevant material, closer scrutiny of individual items or linked groups, and a steady improvement of the resources for doing so, have produced the regular advances in knowledge and understanding that underlie the studies published here. It is appropriate to conclude this volume, therefore, by considering how the subject might progress, and in what directions. Five general points may be made.

In the first place, the processes outlined above are far from worked out. The completion of the various collaborative projects noted earlier, as of other great multi-author enterprises such as the 'Corpus of Medieval British Library Catalogues', will make many key facts more readily available, significantly enhancing knowledge across the field as a whole. The number of early British manuscripts that have received detailed scrutiny is comparatively small. Comprehensive investigation of the codicology, text, script, decoration and history of many others has the potential to prove as revelatory as earlier work in this vein – so long as the temptation to focus on the same books can be avoided. Attention has understandably gravitated towards the most handsome volumes and those with texts in the vernacular. The Lindisfarne Gospels, a calligraphic and artistic masterpiece with an Old English gloss, has been the subject of one partial and two full facsimile editions along with countless studies; there are two printed facsimiles and one digital one of both the *Beowulf* manuscript and the Vercelli Book, and two printed ones plus a couple of well-illustrated monographs on the Benedictional of St Æthelwold; and it was doubtless the presence of Welsh and Irish glosses and the earliest written record of Welsh poetry that motivated the production of a facsimile of the Cambridge Juvencus. The studies that have accompanied each of these ventures have been scholarly milestones: important advances across a broader front may reasonably be anticipated when volumes outside the 'popular canon' receive commensurate scrutiny.

Equally, the investigation of particular texts and their affiliations, of scribal and artistic hands and their connections, and of the evolution of individual writing centres – to mention nothing more – can manifestly be pursued further with the prospect of real gains in knowledge. More attention could usefully be paid to the texts of the copies of patristic writings produced during our period which (particularly those made in the tenth and eleventh centuries) are often unreported in modern editions, yet which have the potential to illuminate patterns of cultural exchange. Correspondingly, parallel work on the books, texts and scribal culture of the other lands with which early Britain enjoyed bibliographical intercourse will unquestionably prove revealing for our subject, not only on account of the direct connections that might be indicated or implied but also for the comparative perspectives that may be opened up. The completion of Bernhard Bischoff's *Katalog der festländischen Handschriften des neunten Jahrhunderts* (1998–), for instance, will be of enormous value in both respects.

That said, the losses and imbalances of the evidence impose strict limits on what can be achieved: in general, future work, even on little-studied items, is likely to shed more and brighter light on subjects about which we are already reasonably well informed, leaving shadowy most of the areas that are currently in darkness. Greater integration of the archaeological find evidence relating to writing – inscriptions, tools for parchment-making, styli and other implements, fittings from bindings and so on – may help to revise the current picture of the geographical distribution of literary activities. Convincing evidence for localising an important manuscript to a currently un- or under-represented writing centre may yet be found, possibly permitting certain others to follow in its wake. Nevertheless, such new data and advances will never fill the lacunae caused by the grievous and uneven losses of manuscripts, the lack of documentation for the origin and provenance of many that remain, and the paucity of direct evidence bearing on many practical issues, such as the ways in which they were used and perceived – and by whom.

The second general point is that new questions may be formulated which permit familiar material to be reinterrogated fruitfully from novel perspectives – just as more sophisticated approaches to the nature of literacy in the early Middle Ages, and an enhanced interest in women as readers and book owners added new dimensions to the work of the past generation. Evidence for patterns of usage, be it in relation to individual items or to particular groups of manuscripts or specific texts, has come in for increasing scrutiny, and this can doubtless be pursued further. Incrementally, as a result of work from many sides, the books of Exeter Cathedral in the time of Bishop Leofric (1050–72) and their ramifications have come ever more clearly into view, for instance. Correspondingly, work on glossed texts has moved from a near-exclusive focus on their lexicographical implications to attempts to deduce how the manuscripts in question were used. This (contentious) seam is far from exhausted: indeed the whole question might usefully be re-examined on a broader front in relation to centres such as Canterbury from which a good number of broadly coeval manuscripts of different types, with and without glosses, survive, and in the light of Malcolm Parkes' recent analysis of the various forms of reading that are likely to have been practised in Anglo-Saxon England. Again, however, many questions about patterns of reading and the audiences for texts that are fundamental to the study of the history of the book in later ages are likely to remain unanswerable in relation to our period, and it is wise to be aware that this is so.

While being receptive to new ideas and approaches, we should at the same time be careful not to litter the field with improbable theories and misleading speculations. It is the nature of early medieval studies, given the limitations of the available evidence, that certainty is frequently elusive. There are often sufficient material and facts to construct a theory but not enough to prove (or disprove) it. If a balance of probabilities is frequently the best that can be achieved, we must endeavour to use all the available evidence for a given enquiry, and build only on those theories that are probable, as opposed to those that are merely possible. The pre-eminent practitioners of past generations, whose work has proved the most durable, have proceeded thus. Conversely, failing to consider all the available evidence and presenting speculation and opinion as fact can traduce the material; 'reading' the evidence from a particular 'critical' or 'theoretical' perspective may mean imposing the present on the past and failing to be sensitive to the latter. Recent sustained interpretations of the imagery, and its relationship to the texts, in Junius 11 and the Old English Hexateuch, for example, engaging though they may be, advertise the potential subjectivity of aspects of such work. The circumstance that our early British books are now conveniently listed, dated and localised means that it has become easier for those who lack the broader skills and experience necessary for the judicious evaluation of manuscripts on their own terms to try their hand in the field. Accordingly, some of the publications of the last generation are likely to be of more interest to future scholars for what they reveal about intellectual fashions in certain circles in the late twentieth and early twenty-first centuries than for the light that they shed on the history of the book in early Britain.

Third, there is the issue of the afterlife of early British books. Although the survival and use of Old English after the Norman Conquest and the contexts in which it appears have recently enjoyed a revival of interest, and while excellent work has been done over the years on the collectors and collections of our volumes in the aftermath of the Dissolution of the Monasteries, the attention paid more generally to the use and status of our early medieval manuscripts in the later Middle Ages could profitably be increased. Annotations, additions, (re)foliations and new content pages, not to mention the witness of later library catalogues and added names, provide plentiful evidence for patterns of use (or neglect) in subsequent centuries that have yet to be fully explored. Only intermittently recorded and currently studied on an ad hoc basis, if at all, such indications deserve more comprehensive treatment: only then will true and potentially revealing patterns – not to mention interesting exceptions – emerge. The range of documented possessors and types of use in the later Middle Ages is considerable. Some volumes – whether they remained at the centres that made them or passed to other communities – were reconditioned in one way or another for continuing service at a later date (as happened, for instance, to Canterbury Cathedral, Lit. A.8, a collection of Augustine's sermons that had been made and kept at St Augustine's Abbey and which was refoliated there in the fourteenth century, all the sermons being renumbered and running titles supplied throughout). Others were effectively turned into relics, as was the eighth-century Vespasian Psalter, described in the early fifteenth century by Thomas of Elmham as kept above the high altar of St Augustine's Abbey and believed (erroneously) to have been among the books that Gregory the Great had sent to Augustine. The monks of Durham in the later Middle Ages optimistically credited several of their Anglo-Saxon books to the hand of Bede himself; however, far from being enshrined in a place of honour, a couple of these volumes were subsequently judged – as notes in one of the community's later medieval library catalogues reveal – to be 'of no value'. Certain other early manuscripts joined the ranks of monastic books that effectively became the private possessions of individual members of the community (as did the Eadwig Psalter, given by William Hadley, sub-prior of Christ Church (d. 1500), to John Waltham, from whom it would seem to have been transferred to another brother, William Ingram). The parallel-text Paris Psalter, by contrast, passed into the collection of one of the greatest bibliophiles and art patrons of the later Middle Ages, Jean duc de Berry (d. 1416), wherein it was appreciatively inventoried and described; while the Blickling Homiliary became an inglorious repository for municipal records of the city of Lincoln.

Fourth, steadily improving technology may yet permit real gains in factual knowledge: the advance from the resources that were available for identifying inks and pigments in the middle of the twentieth century to those at the disposal of researchers at the beginning of the twenty-first encourages the belief that further progress will be made. It seems likely that the means for recovering obliterated or damaged texts, for instance, and for the non-destructive investigation of various other aspects of the material fabric of manuscripts will continue to improve; and it is not impossible that technology for recognising, or at least comparing, scribal hands may also evolve. Certainly, there is every reason to believe that the ever-increasing availability of reproductions, whether printed or digital, facilitating the comparison of scattered volumes, will expedite such tasks as collating texts and identifying scribal hands, and hence will assist with refining datings and attributions, and evaluating relationships between manuscripts, to mention nothing else. This simultaneously alerts us to the important point that, whatever may be the progress of technological aids, the expertise of individual scholars with wide first-hand experience of relevant books should still remain central to the discipline. It would be a tragedy if the enhanced availability of reproductions were to remove from future generations – whether through individual laziness or institutional policy (and at the time of writing the standard position of one great repository is not to issue manuscripts) – the opportunity of scrutinising the originals. For it is upon this that sound bibliographical study relies, and always will.

Fifth and finally, it is eminently likely that the corpus of primary material itself will continue to grow. Against the belief that no major finds remain to be made may be set the case of the Vindolanda writing tablets, the first of which were only discovered in 1973. Not only did they revolutionise the study of script and literacy in Roman Britain but (reverting briefly to a point made in the previous paragraph) those with incised, as opposed to ink, texts were only rendered legible thanks to 'modern' photographic technology (images taken in infrared light). Tablets and writing implements continue to be excavated at Vindolanda, and styli straddling the chronological range of the present volume are regularly found at divers locations. The last relatively complete Anglo-Saxon manuscript to come to light was the Anderson Pontifical (now British Library, Add. 57337), discovered in the stables of Brodie Castle, Morayshire in 1970; while the corpus of Insular manuscripts was enlarged as recently as 2006 with the unearthing (literally) of the remains of a decorated psalter at Faddan More, Co. Tipperary. The regularity with which overlooked leaves and fragments are discovered in drawers, within bindings and even between the covers of books in well-frequented repositories gives one every reason to believe that this will continue for the foreseeable future. And if many of the 'new arrivals' will contain predictable texts (which will nevertheless refine our understanding of their popularity), a few will surely be otherwise unrepresented works (like the strip at Westminster Abbey bearing a composite vernacular homily that was published in 1996). Equally, it is possible that further remnants of Anglo-Saxon binding structures are buried, awaiting discovery, within later bindings; and it seems highly likely that further examples of metal furniture and ivory panels from decorated book-covers will appear in archaeological digs, not to mention sale rooms.

To sum up: while the history of the book per se is a young subject, the manuscript and book culture of early Britain is an area in which much effort has been expended and dramatic progress made during the last century and a half, and this is embodied in the essays assembled in the present volume. It may reasonably be doubted that future discoveries and further work will change understanding of the field to the extent that it has been transformed in the last couple of generations; however, there is every reason to believe that they will add invaluable detail to the contours delineated here. This collection is an important milestone in the recovery, recording and interpretation of the history of the book in early Britain, but like all milestones, it marks but one stage on a journey.

Bibliography

Abram, C. 2004: 'Anglo-Saxon influence in the Old Norwegian Homily Book', *Medieval Scandinavia* 14, 1–34

Abukhanfusa, K. 2004: *Mutilated Books: Wondrous Leaves from Swedish Bibliographical History* (Stockholm)

Adams, J. N. 1995: 'The language of the Vindolanda writing tablets: an interim report', *JRS* 85, 86–134

Adomnán, *De locis sanctis* see Meehan 1958

Vita Columbae see Anderson and Anderson 1991

Adriaen, M. (ed.) 1958: *Magni Aurelii Cassiodori Expositio Psalmorum I–LXX*, CCSL 97 (Turnhout)

(ed.) 1963: *S. Hieronymi Presbyteri Opera* 1, *Opera Exegetica* 2, *Commentarium in Esaiam libri I–XVIII*, 2 vols., CCSL 73–73A (Turnhout)

(ed.) 1971: Gregorius Magnus, *Homiliae in Hiezechielem Prophetam*, CCSL 142 (Turnhout)

Alexander, J. J. G. 1966: 'A little-known gospel book of the later eleventh century from Exeter', *Burlington Magazine* 108, 6–16

1970: *Anglo-Saxon Illumination in Oxford Libraries* (Oxford)

1978a: *The Decorated Letter* (London)

1978b: *Insular Manuscripts 6th – 9th Century*, Survey of Manuscripts Illuminated in the British Isles 1 (London)

1986: 'The illumination of the gospels' in Barker 1986, 65–79

1990: 'The illumination' in Fox 1990, 265–303

1992: *Medieval Illuminators and their Methods of Work* (New Haven and London)

Alexander, J. J. G., Marrow, J. H. and Sandler, L. F. 2005: *The Splendor of the Word: Medieval and Renaissance Illuminated Manuscripts at the New York Public Library* (New York and Turnhout)

Alexander, S. M. 1964–5: 'Medieval recipes describing the use of metals in manuscripts', *Marsyas* 12, 34–51

Alexandre, J.-L. and Lanoë, G. 2004: *Reliures médiévales des bibliothèques de France*, 3: *Médiathèque d'Orléans* (Turnhout)

Alidori, L., Benassai, L. Castaldi, L. *et al.* 2003: *Bibbie miniate della Biblioteca Medicea Laurenziana di Firenze* (Florence)

Allen, M. I. 1996: 'Bede and Frechulf at medieval St Gallen', in *Beda Venerabilis: Historian, Monk and Northumbrian*, ed. L. A. J. R. Houwen and A. A. Macdonald (Groningen), 61–80

Allott, S. 1974: *Alcuin of York* (York)

Alton, E. H. and Meyer, P. (eds.) 1950–1: *Evangeliorum quattuor Codex Cennanensis*, 3 vols. (Bern)

Amsler, M. 1989: *Etymology and Grammatical Discourse in Late Antiquity and the Early Middle Ages* (Amsterdam)

Anderson, A. O. (ed.) 1922: *Early Sources of Scottish History A.D. 500 to 1286*, 2 vols. (Edinburgh)

Anderson, A. O. and Anderson, M. O. (eds.) 1991: Adomnán, *Vita Columbae*, rev. edn M. O. Anderson (Oxford) [original edition: Edinburgh, 1961]

Andrieu, M. 1971: *Les Ordines Romani du haut moyen âge*, II: *Les Textes* (Louvain)

Anstruther, R. (ed.) 1846: *Epistolae Herberti Losinga, Osberti de Clara et Elmeri* (Brussels and London)

Arndt, W. (ed.) 1887: 'Vita Alcuini', MGH Scriptores XV.1 (Hanover), 182–97

Arngart, O. (ed.) 1952: *The Leningrad Bede*, EEMF 2 (Copenhagen)

Arnold, T. (ed.) 1882–5: *Symeonis monachi opera omnia*, 2 vols. (London)

1890–6: *Memorials of St Edmunds Abbey*, 3 vols., RS (London)

Aronstam, R. A. 1974: 'The Latin canonical tradition in late Anglo-Saxon England: the *Excerptiones Egberti*', unpublished PhD dissertation (Columbia University)

Avril, F. and Stirnemann, P. 1987: *Manuscrits enluminés d'origine insulaire, VIIe–XXe siècle* (Paris)

Ayton, A. 1989: 'Domesday Book re-bound', *Notes and Queries* n.s. 36, 298–9

Backhouse, J. 1981: *The Lindisfarne Gospels* (Oxford)

1997: *The Illuminated Page* (London)

Backhouse, J., Turner. D. H. and Webster, L. (eds.) 1984: *The Golden Age of Anglo-Saxon Art, 966–1066* (London)

Baesecke, G. 1933: *Der Vocabularius Sancti Galli in der angelsächsischen Mission* (Halle)

Bailey, R. 1978: *The Durham Cassiodorus*, Jarrow Lecture (Jarrow)

1983: 'Bede's text of Cassiodorus' commentary on the psalms', *JTS* n.s. 34, 189–93

1992: 'Sutton Hoo and seventh-century art', in *Sutton Hoo Fifty Years After*, ed. R. Farrell and C. Neuman de Vegvar (Oxford, OH), 31–41

Baker, P. (ed.) 2000: *The Anglo-Saxon Chronicle, a collaborative edition 8: MS F* (Cambridge)

Baker, P. S. and Lapidge, M. (eds.) 1995: *Byrhtferth's Enchiridion*, EETS s.s. 15 (Oxford)

Banham, D. (ed.) 1991: *Monasteriales indicia* (Pinner)

Banik, G. 1990: 'Green copper pigments and their alteration in manuscripts or works of graphic art' in Guineau 1990, 89–102

Banniard, M. 1995: 'Language and communication in the Carolingian Empire', in *New Cambridge Medieval History*, II: *c. 700 – c.900*, ed. R. McKitterick (Cambridge), 695–708

Banting, H. M. (ed.) 1989: *Two Anglo-Saxon Pontificals: The Egbert and Sidney Sussex Pontificals*, HBS 104 (London)

Barker, N. (ed.) 1986: *The York Gospels*, Roxburghe Club (London)

Barker-Benfield, B. C. 1976: 'A ninth-century manuscript from Fleury: Cato *De senectute cum Macrobio*', in *Medieval Learning and Literature: Essays Presented to Richard William Hunt*, ed. J. J. G. Alexander and M. T. Gibson (Oxford), 145–65

1991: 'The Werden Heptateuch', *ASE* 20, 43–64

Barlow, C. W. 1938: *Epistolae Senecae ad Paulum et Pauli ad Senecam, 'quae vocantur'*, Papers of the American Academy in Rome 10 (Rome)

Barlow, F. (ed.) 1992: *The Life of King Edward Who Rests at Westminster*, 2nd edn (London)

Barr, C. B. L. 1977: 'The Minster library', in *A History of York Minster*, ed. G. E. Aylmer and R. Cant (Oxford), 487–539

1986: 'The history of the volume' in Barker 1986, 101–17

Barrett, A. A. 1978: 'Knowledge of the literary classics in Roman Britain', *Britannia* 9, 307–13

Bat-Yehouda, M. Z. 1983: *Les encres noires au moyen âge jusqu'à 1600* (Paris)

Bately, J. (ed.) 1992: *The Tanner Bede*, EEMF XXIV (Copenhagen)

Bately, J. M. 1964: 'The Vatican fragment of the Old English Orosius', *English Studies* 45, 224–30

1979a: 'Bede and the *Anglo-Saxon Chronicle*', in *Saints, Scholars and Heroes: Studies in Medieval Culture in Honour of Charles W. Jones*, ed. M. H. King and W. M. Stevens (Collegeville, MN), 233–54

1979b: 'World history in the *Anglo-Saxon Chronicle*: its sources and separateness from the Old English Orosius', *ASE* 8, 177–94

1980a: *The Literary Prose of King Alfred's Reign: Translation or Transformation?*, inaugural lecture, King's College, London (London); reprinted as *Old English Newsletter subsidia* 10 (1984)

(ed.) 1980b: *The Old English Orosius*, EETS s.s. 6 (London)

(ed.) 1986: *The Anglo-Saxon Chronicle, A Collaborative Edition*, 3: *MS A* (Cambridge)

1988: 'Old English prose before and during the reign of Alfred', *ASE* 17, 93–138

1990: 'Those books most necessary for all men to know: the classics and late ninth-century England, a reappraisal', in *The Classics in the Middle Ages: Papers of the 20th Anual Conference of the Center for Medieval and Early Renaissance Studies*, ed. A. S. Bernardo and S. Levin (Binghamton, NY), 45–78

2003: 'The Alfredian canon revisited: one hundred years on', in *Alfred the Great: Papers from the Eleventh-Centenary Conference*, ed. T. Reuter (Aldershot), 107–20

Bates, D. (ed.) 1998: *Regesta Regum Anglo-Normannorum: The Acta of William I (1066–1087)* (Oxford)

Bateson, M. 1895a: 'The supposed Latin penitential of Egbert and the missing work of Halitgar of Cambrai', *EHR* 9, 320–6

1895b : 'A Worcester Cathedral book of ecclesiastical collections, made *c.* 1000 AD', *EHR* 10, 712–31

Bautier, R.-H. and Labory, G. (eds.) 1969: *André de Fleury: vie de Gauzlin abbé de Fleury* (Paris)

Beaumont, J. 1981: 'The Latin tradition of the *De consolatione philiosophiae*', in *Boethius: his Life, Thought and Influence*, ed. M. T. Gibson (Oxford), 278–305

Becker, G. 1885: *Catalogi bibliothecarum antiqui* (Bonn)

Beckwith, J. 1972: *Ivory Carvings in Early Medieval England* (London)

Bédoyère, G. de la 1998: 'Carausius and the marks RSR and I.N.P.C.D.A.', *Numismatic Chronicle* 158, 79–88

Beeson, C. H. 1913: *Isidor-Studien*, Quellen und Untersuchungen zur lateinischen Philologie des Mittelalters 4.2 (Munich)

1924: 'The *Ars Grammatica* of Julian of Toldeo', *Studi e Testi* 37, 50–70

Behaghel, O. (ed.) 1965: *Heliand und Genesis*, rev. W. Mitzka (Tübingen)

Bell, N. 2001: *Music in Medieval Manuscripts* (London)

Berger, S. 1893: *Histoire de la Vulgate pendant les premières siècles du moyen âge* (Paris)

Berland, J.-M. 1982: 'L'influence de l'abbaye de Fleury-sur-Loire en Bretagne et dans les îles Britanniques du Xe au XIIe siècle', *Actes du 107e congrès national des sociétés savantes: Section de philologie et d'histoire jusqu'à 1610* (Paris), II, 275–99

Bernard, P. 1996: *Du chant romain au chant grégorien (IVe–XIIIe siècle)* (Paris)

Berschin, W. 1980/1988: *Griechisch-lateinisches Mittelalter: Von Hieronymus zu Nikolaus von Kues* (Bern and Munich); rev. and trans. by J. C. Frakes as *Greek Letters and the Latin Middle Ages* (Washington, DC)

Bethell, D. 1971: 'English monks and Irish reform in the eleventh and twelfth centuries', *Historical Studies* 8, 111–35

Bethurum, D. 1942: 'Archbishop Wulfstan's commonplace book', *Publications of the Modern Language Association* 57, 916–29

(ed.) 1957: *The Homilies of Wulfstan* (Oxford)

1966: 'Wulfstan', in *Continuations and Beginnings*, ed. E. G. Stanley (London), 210–46

Beyerle, F. and Buchner, R. (eds.) 1954: *Lex Ribvaria*, MGH, Leges nationum Germanicarum 3.2 (Hanover)

Biddle, M. (ed.) 1976: *Winchester in the Early Middle Ages: An Edition and Discussion of the Winton Domesday*, Winchester Studies 1 (Oxford)

1990: *Object and Economy in Medieval Winchester* (Oxford)

Bieler, L. 1947: 'Die Bibeltext des heiligen Patrick', *Biblica* 28, 35–58 and 236–63

1949: *The Life and Legend of St Patrick: Problems of Modern Scholarship* (Dublin)

1952–3: 'The hymn of St Secundinus', *Proceedings of the Royal Irish Academy* 55C, 117–27

1958: 'The text tradition', in *Adomnán's De locis sanctis*, ed. D. Meehan, Scriptores Latini Hiberniae 3 (Dublin), 30–4

1962: 'The Celtic hagiographer', *Studia Patristica* 5, 243–65

1963: *Ireland: Harbinger of the Middle Ages* (Oxford)

1971: *Four Latin Lives of St Patrick*, Scriptores Latini Hiberniae 8 (Dublin)

1975a: 'Hagiography and romance in medieval Ireland', *Medievalia et humanistica* 6, 13–24

1975b: *The Irish Penitentials*, Scriptores Latini Hiberniae 5 (Dublin)

1979: *The Patrician Texts in the Book of Armagh*, Scriptores Latini Hiberniae 10 (Dublin)

1986: *Studies of the Life and Legend of St Patrick*, ed. R. Sharpe (London)

1993: *Libri Epistolarum Sancti Patricii Episcopi* (Dublin)

Billett, J. 2010: 'The divine office and the secular clergy in late Anglo-Saxon England', in *England and the Continent in the Tenth Century*, ed. D. Rollason, C. Leyser and H. Williams (Turnhout), 429–71

Binchy, D. A. 1962: 'Patrick and his biographers, ancient and modern', *Studia Hibernica* 2, 7–173

Birch, W. de G. (ed.) 1889: *An Ancient Manuscript of the Eighth or Ninth Century, Formerly Belonging to St Mary's Abbey or Nunnaminster, Winchester*, Hampshire Record Society (London)

(ed.) 1892: *Liber Vitae: Register and Martyrology of the New Minster and Hyde Abbey, Winchester* (Winchester)

Birley, A. R. 1981: *The Fasti of Roman Britain* (Oxford)

2005: *The Roman Government of Britain* (Oxford)

Bischoff, B. 1952: Review of Richard Drögereit, *Werden und der Heliand*, *Anzeiger für Deutsches Altertum* 66.1, 7–12

1954: 'Wendepunkte in der Geschichte der lateinischen Exegese im Frühmittelalter', *Sacris Erudiri* 6, 189–281

1958: 'Eine versschollen Einteilung der Wissenschaften', reprinted in Bischoff 1966–81, I, 273–88

1965a: 'Die Hofbibliothek Karls des Grossen', in *Karl der Grosse: Lebenswerk und Nachleben*, II: *Das geistliche Leben*, ed. B. Bischoff (Düsseldorf), 42–62; revised version in Bischoff 1966–81, III, 149–71; English trans. in Bischoff 1994, 56–75

1965b: 'Panorama der Handschriftenüberlieferung aus der Zeit Karls des Grossen', in *Karl der Grosse: Lebenswerk und Nachleben*, II: *Das geistliche Leben*, ed. B. Bischoff, 233–45; reprinted in Bischoff 1966–81, III, 5–38; English trans. in Bischoff 1994, 20–55

1966: 'Die Kölner Nonnenhandschriften und das Skriptorium von Chelles', revised version in Bischoff 1966–81, I, 16–34

1966–81: *Mittelalterliche Studien*, 3 vols. (Stuttgart)

(ed.) 1967: *Mittelalterliche Schatzverzeichnisse*, I: *Von der Zeit Karls des Grossen bis zur Mitte des 13. Jahrhunderts* (Munich)

1974: *Die südostdeutschen Schreibschulen und Bibliotheken in der Karolingerzeit 1: Die bayrischen Diözesen*, 3rd edn (Wiesbaden and Leipzig)

1980: *Die südostdeutschen Schreibschulen und Bibliotheken in der Karolingerzeit*, 2: *Die Vorwiegend Österreichischen Diözesen* (Wiesbaden)

1989: *Die Abtei Lorsch im Spiegel ihrer Handschriften*, 2nd edn (Lorsch)

1990: *Latin Palaeography: Antiquity and the Middle Ages*, trans. D. Ó'Cróinín and D. Ganz (Cambridge)

1994: *Manuscripts and Libraries in the Age of Charlemagne*, trans. M. Gorman (Cambridge)

1998, 2004: *Katalog der festländischen Handschriften des neunten Jahrhunderts (mit Ausnahme der wisigotischen)*. Teil I: *Aachen-Lambach* (Stuttgart, 1998). Teil II *Laon-Paderborn* (Stuttgart, 2004)

Bischoff, B. and Brown, V. 1985: 'Addenda to *Codices Latini Antiquiores*', *Mediaeval Studies* 47, 317–66

Bischoff, B., Budny, M., Harlow, G. Parkes, M. B., and Pheifer, J. D. (eds.) 1988: *The Épinal, Erfurt, Werden and Corpus Glossaries*, EEMF 22 (Copenhagen)

Bischoff, B. and Hofmann, J. 1952: *Libri sancti Kyliani: Die Würzburger Schreibschule und die Dombibliothek im VIII. und IX. Jahrhundert* (Würzburg)

Bischoff, B. and Lapidge, M. 1994: *Biblical Commentaries from the Canterbury School of Theodore and Hadrian*, CSASE 10 (Cambridge)

Bischoff, B., Lieftinck, G. I. and Battelli, G. 1954: *Nomenclature des écritures livresques du IXe au XVIe siècle* (Paris)

Bishop, T. A. M. 1949–53: 'Notes on Cambridge manuscripts, part I', *TCBS* 1, 432–41

1954–8: 'Notes on Cambridge manuscripts, part II', *TCBS* 2, 185–99, 323–36

1957: 'Notes on Cambridge manuscripts, part IV: MSS connected with St Augustine's, Canterbury', *TCBS* 2, 323–36

1959: 'Notes on Cambridge manuscripts, part V: MSS connected with St Augustine's, Canterbury, continued', *TCBS* 3, 93–5

1961: *Scriptores Regis: Facsimiles to Identify and Illustrate the Hands of Royal Scribes in Original Charters of Henry I, Stephen and Henry II* (Oxford)

1963a: 'Notes on Cambridge manuscripts, part VI', *TCBS* 3, 412–13

1963b: 'Notes on Cambridge manuscripts: part VII: the early minuscule of Christ Church Canterbury', *TCBS* 3, 413–23

1964–8a: 'The corpus Martianus Capella', *TCBS* 4, 257–75

1964–8b: 'An early example of the square minuscule', *TCBS* 4, 246–52

(ed.) 1966: *Aethici Istrici Cosmographia Vergilio Salisburgensi rectius adscripta: Codex Leidensis Scaligeranus 69*, Umbrae Codicum Occidentalium 10 (Amsterdam)

1967a: 'The Copenhagen gospel-book', *Nordisk Tidskrift för Bok- och Biblioteksväsen* 54, 33–41

1967b: 'Lincoln Cathedral MS 182', *Lincolnshire History and Archaeology* 2, 73–6

1968: 'An early example of Insular Caroline', *TCBS* 4.5, 396–400

1971: *English Caroline Minuscule* (Oxford)

Blair, J. 2005: *The Church in Anglo-Saxon Society* (Oxford)

Blake, E. O. (ed.) 1962: *Liber Eliensis*, Camden Soc. 3rd ser. 92 (London)

Blake, M. (ed.) 2009: *Ælfric's De Temporibus Anni* (Cambridge)

Blake, N. F. (ed.) 1990: *The Phoenix*, rev. edn (Exeter; original edn 1964)

Bodarwé, K. 2000: 'Shriftlichkeit und Bildung im ottonischen Essen', in *Herrschaft, Bildung und Gebet: Gründung und Anfänge des Frauenstifts Essen*, ed. G. Berghaus, T. Schilp and M. Schlagheck (Essen), 101–17

Bodden, M.C. (ed.) 1987: *The Old English Finding of the True Cross* (Cambridge)

1988: 'Evidence for the knowledge of Greek in Anglo-Saxon England', *ASE* 17, 217–46

Bolton, D. 1977: 'The study of the *Consolation of Philosophy* in Anglo-Saxon England', *Archives d'histoire doctrinale et littéraire du Moyen Âge* 44, 33–78

Bond, E. A. 1873–8: *Facsimiles of Ancient Charters in the British Museum*, 4 vols. (London)

Bonner, G. 1973: 'Bede and Medieval Civilisation', *ASE* 2, 71–90

(ed.) 1976: *Famulus Christi: Essays in Commemoration of the Thirteenth Centenary of the Birth of the Venerable Bede* (London)

Bonner, G., Rollason, D. and Stancliffe, C. (eds.) 1989: *St Cuthbert: His Cult and his Community to AD 1200* (Woodbridge)

Bonner, S. 1977: *Education in Ancient Rome* (London)

Boretius, A. (ed.) 1883: *Capitularia regum Francorum* 1, MGH Legum Sectio II (Hanover)

Borgolte, M., Geuenich, D. and Schmid, K. (eds.) 1986: *Subsidia Sangallensis I. Materialen und Untersuchungen zu den Verbrüderungsbüchern und zu den älteren Urkunden des Stiftsarchiv St Gallen* (St Gallen)

Borst, A. 1993: 'Alkuin und die Enzyklopädie von 809', in *Science in Western and Eastern Civilisation in Carolingian Times*, ed. P. L. Butzer and D. Lohrmann (Basle, Boston and Berlin), 53–78

Bosc-Lauby, A. and Notter, A. (eds.) 2004: *Lumières de l'an mil en Orléanais: autour du millénaire d'Abbon de Fleury* (Turnhout)

Bosworth, J. and Toller, T. M. (eds.) 1898: *An Anglo-Saxon Dictionary* (Oxford)

Bouet, P. and Dosdat, M. (eds.) 1999: *Manuscrits et enluminures dans le monde normand (xe–xve siècles)* (Caen)

Bourke, C. (ed.) 1995: *From the Isles of the North: Early Medieval Art in Ireland and Britain* (Belfast)

Bower, C. 2002: 'The transmission of ancient music theory into the Middle Ages', in *The Cambridge History of Western Music Theory*, ed. T. Christopherson (Cambridge), 136–67

Bowman, A. K. 1994a: *Life and Letters on the Roman Frontier: Vindolanda and its People* (London)

1994b: 'The Roman imperial army: letters and literacy on the northern frontier', in *Literacy and Power in the Ancient World*, ed. A. Bowman and G. Woolf (Cambridge), 109–25

2006: 'Outposts of empire: Vindolanda, Egypt and the empire of Rome', *Journal of Roman Archaeology* 19, 75–93

Bowman, A. K. and Thomas, J. D. 1994: *The Vindolanda Writing-Tablets: Tabulae Vindolandenses* II (London)

1996: 'New writing-tablets from Vindolanda', *Britannia* 27, 299–328

2003: *The Vindolanda writing-tablets: Tabulae Vindolandenses* III (London)

Bracken, D. 2006: 'Virgil the Grammarian and Bede: a preliminary study', *ASE* 35, 7–21

Bradshaw, H. 1889: *Collected Papers* (Cambridge)

Breen, A. 1983: 'Some seventh-century Hiberno-Latin texts and their relationships', *Peritia* 3, 204–14

1987: 'A New Irish Fragment of the *Continuatio* to Rufinus-Eusebius *Historia Ecclesiastica*', *Scriptorium* 41, 185–204

1992: 'The liturgical materials in MS Oxford, Bodleian Library, Auct. F.4.32', *Archiv für Liturgiewissenschaft* 34, 121–53

(ed.) 1996: Aileran, *Interpretatio mystica et moralis progenitorum domini Iesu Christi* (Dublin)

Brett, C. 1991: 'A Breton pilgrim in England in the reign of King Æthelstan', in *France and the British Isles in the Middle Ages and the Renaissance*, ed. G. Jonsdorf and D. N. Dumville (Woodbridge), 43–70

Breul, K. (ed.) 1915: *The Cambridge Songs: A Goliard's Songbook of the XIth century* (Cambridge)

Brinegar, J. 2000: 'Books most necessary: the literary and cultural contexts of Alfred's Boethius', unpublished PhD dissertation (University of North Carolina, Chapel Hill)

Brooks, N. P. 1984: *The Early History of the Church of Canterbury: Christ Church from 597 to 1066* (Leicester)

1992: 'The career of St Dunstan' in Ramsay *et al.* 1992, 103–42

Broun, D. 1995: *The Charters of Gaelic Scotland and Ireland in the Early and Central Middle Ages*, Quiggin Lecture (Cambridge)

Brown, G. H. 1995: 'The dynamics of literacy in Anglo-Saxon England', *Bulletin of the John Rylands University Library of Manchester* 77.1, 109–42

1996: *Bede the Educator*, Jarrow Lecture (Jarrow)

2005: 'Bede's commentary on I Samuel', in *Biblical Studies in the Early Middle Ages: Proceedings of the Conference on Biblical Studies in the Early Middle Ages*, Università degli Studi di Milano-Società Internazionale per lo Studio del Medioevo Latino, Gargnano on Lake Garda 24–27 June 2001, ed. C. Leonardi and G. Orlandi (Florence), 77–103

Brown, K. L., Brown, M. P. and Jacobs, D. 2003: 'The analysis of the pigments used on the Lindisfarne Gospels' in Brown, 2003b, 430–51

Brown, K. L. and Clark, R. J. H. 2004: 'Analysis of key Anglo-Saxon manuscripts (8th–11th centuries) in the British Library: pigment identification by Raman microscopy', *Journal of Raman Spectroscopy* 35, 181–89

Brown, M. P. 1986: 'Paris, Bibliothèque nationale, lat. 10861 and the scriptorium of Christ Church, Canterbury', *ASE* 15, 119–37

1989: 'The Lindisfarne scriptorium from the late seventh to the early ninth century' in Bonner *et al.* 1989, 151–64

1990a: *A Guide to Western Historical Scripts from Antiquity to 1600* (London and Toronto); 2nd edn 1993

1990b: 'A new fragment of a ninth-century English Bible', *ASE* 18, 33–43

1991a: *Anglo-Saxon Manuscripts* (London)

1991b: 'Continental symptoms in Insular codicology: historical perspectives', in *Pergament*, ed. P. Rück (Sigmaringen), 57–62

1994a: 'Echoes: the Book of Kells and southern English manuscript production' in O'Mahony 1994, 333–43

1994b: *Understanding Illuminated Manuscripts: A Glossary of Technical Terms* (London and Toronto)

1996: *The Book of Cerne: Prayer, Patronage and Power in Ninth-Century England*, British Library Studies in Medieval Culture (London and Toronto)

2001a: 'Female book-ownership and production in Anglo-Saxon England: the evidence of the ninth-century prayerbooks', in *Lexis and Texts in Early English: Papers in Honour of Jane Roberts*, ed. C. Kay and L. Sylvester, Costerus n.s. 133 (Amsterdam), 45–68

2001b: 'Mercian manuscripts? The "Tiberius" group and its historical context', in *Mercia: An Anglo-Saxon Kingdom in Europe*, ed. M. P. Brown and C. A. Farr (Leicester), 278–91

2003a: 'House style in the scriptorium: scribal reality and scholarly myth', in *Anglo-Saxon Styles*, ed. C. E. Karkov and G. H. Brown (New York), 131–50

2003b: *The Lindisfarne Gospels: Society, Spirituality and the Scribe* (Lausanne, London and Toronto), monograph and the commentary volume accompanying *The Lindisfarne Gospels* facsimile (Lausanne)

2004: 'Fifty years of Insular palaeography, 1954–2003: an outline of some landmarks and issues', in *Archiv für Diplomatik 50, Schriftgeschichte Siegel- und Wappenkunde*, ed. W. Koch and T. Kölzer (Vienna), 277–325

2005: 'The Tower of Babel: the architecture of the early western written vernaculars', in *Omnia Disce: Medieval Studies in Memory of Leonard Boyle O.P.*, ed. A. J. Duggan, J. Greatrex and B. Bolton (Aldershot), 109–28

2006a: *How Christianity Came to Britain and Ireland* (Oxford)

(ed.) 2006b: *In the Beginning: Bibles before the Year 1000* (Washington, DC)

2007a: 'The Barberini Gospels: context and intertextuality', in *Text, Image, Interpretation: Studies in Anglo-Saxon Literature and its Insular Context in Honour of Eamonn Ó Carragáin*, ed. A. Minnis and J. Roberts (Turnhout), 89–116

2007b: 'The Lichfield Angel and the manuscript context: Lichfield as a centre of Insular art', *Journal of the British Archaeological Association* 160, 8–19

forthcoming: '"Excavating" Northumbrian manuscripts: what can they tell us?', in *New Directions in Northumbrian Archaeology*, ed. S. Newton *et al.*

Brown, M. P. and Lovett, P. 1999: *The Historical Source Book for Scribes* (London and Toronto)

Brown, T. J. (ed.) 1969a: *The Durham Ritual*, EEMF 16 (Copenhagen)

(ed.) 1969b: *The Stonyhurst Gospel of St John* (Oxford)

1971: *Northumbria and the Book of Kells*, Jarrow Lecture (Jarrow); reprinted in *ASE* 1 (1972), 219–46

1974: 'The distribution and significance of membrane prepared in the Insular manner', in *La paléographie hébraique médiévale*, Colloques internationaux du Centre National de la Recherche Scientifique 547 (Paris), 127–35; reprinted in Brown 1993, 125–40

1975: 'An historical introduction to the use of classical Latin authors in the British Isles from the fifth to the eleventh century', *Settimane* 22, I, 237–99; reprinted in Brown 1993, 141–78

1982: 'The Irish element in the Insular system of scripts to circa AD 850' in Löwe 1982, I, 101–19; reprinted in Brown 1993, 201–20

1984: 'The oldest Irish manuscripts and their late antique background' in Ní Chatháin and Richter 1984, 311–27; reprinted Brown 1993, 221–41

1993: *A Palaeographer's View: Selected Papers of Julian Brown*, ed. J. Bately, M. P. Brown, and J. Roberts (London)

Brown, T. J., Bruce-Mitford, R. L. S., Kendrick, T. *et al.* (eds.), 1956–60: *Codex Lindisfarnensis*, 2 vols. (Olten and Lausanne)

Brown, T. J. and Mackay, T. W. (eds.) 1988: *Codex Vaticanus Palatinus Latinus 235: An Early Insular Manuscript of Paulinus of Nola*, Armarium Codicum Insignium 4 (Turnhout)

Browne, A. C. 1988: 'Bishop William of St Carilef's book donations to Durham Cathedral Priory', *Scriptorium* 42, 140–55

Brownrigg, L. 1978: 'Manuscripts containing English decoration 871–1066, catalogued and illustrated: a review', *ASE* 7, 239–66

Bruce-Mitford, R. L. S. 1968: *The Art of the Codex Amiatinus* Jarrow Lecture (Jarrow); repr. in *Journal of the British Archaeological Association* 3rd ser. 32 (1969), 1–25

Bruckner, A. 1910: *Die vier Bücher Julians von Aeclanum an Turbantius* (Berlin)

Brüning, G. 1917: 'Adamnans Vita Columbae und ihre Ableitungen', *Zeitschrift für Celtische Philologie* 11, 213–304

Bruno, V. 2001: 'The St Petersburg Gospels and the sources of Southumbrian art', in *Pattern and Purpose*, ed. M. Redknap, N. Edwards, S. Youngs *et al.* (Oxford), 179–90

Bruyne, D. de 1914: *Sommaires, divisions et rubriques de la Bible latine* (Namur)

1920: *Préfaces de la Bible latine* (Namur)

Budny, M. O. 1985: 'London, British Library, MS Royal 1.E.vi: the anatomy of an Anglo-Saxon Bible fragment', unpublished PhD thesis (University of London)

1992: '"St Dunstan's Classbook" and its frontispiece: Dunstan's portrait and autograph' in Ramsay *et al.* 1992, 103–42

1997: *Insular, Anglo-Saxon and Early Anglo-Norman Manuscript Art at Corpus Christi College, Cambridge: An Illustrated Catalogue*, 2 vols. (Kalamazoo, MI)

1999: 'The Biblia Gregoriana' in Gameson 1999a, 237–84

Bullough, D. A. 1972: 'The educational tradition in England from Alfred to Ælfric: teaching *utriusque linguae*', *Settimane* 19 (Spoleto), 453–94; reprinted with revisions in Bullough 1991, 297–334

1975: 'The Continental background of the [tenth-century English] reform', in *Tenth-Century Studies: Essays in Commemoration of the Millennium of the Council of Winchester and the 'Regularis Concordia'*, ed. D. Parsons (London and Chichester), 20–31, 210–14; revised, retitled reprint in Bullough 1991, 272–95

1977: 'Roman books and Carolingian *Renovatio*', *Studies in Church History* 14; revised reprinted in Bullough 1991, 1–33

1991: *Carolingian Renewal: Sources and Heritage* (Manchester)

1998: 'Alcuin's cultural influence: the evidence of the manuscripts' in Houwen and MacDonald 1998, 1–26

2004: *Alcuin: Achievement and Reputation, Being Part of the Ford Lectures Delivered in Oxford in the Hilary Term 1980* (Leiden and Boston)

Burkitt, F. C. 1934: 'The Bible of Gildas', *RB* 46, 206–15

Bury, J. B. 1905: *The Life of St Patrick and his Place in History* (London)

Butzer, P. L. and Lohrmann, D. (eds.) 1993: *Science in Western and Eastern Civilisation in Carolingian Times* (Basle, Boston and Berlin)

Bzdyl, D. G. 1977: 'The sources of Ælfric's Prayers in Cambridge University Library MS Gg.3.28', *Notes and Queries* 222, n.s. 24, 98–102

Cabrol, F. 1907–53: 'Bangor (Antiphonaire de)', in *Dictionnaire d'archéologie chrétienne et de liturgie*, ed. F. Cabrol, H. Leclercq and H. Marrou, 30 vols. (Paris), II.1, 183–91

Cains, A. 1990: 'The Vellum', in Fox 1990, 177–81

Calder, D. G. and Allen, M. J. B. (eds.) 1976: *Sources and Analogues of Old English Poetry: The Major Latin Sources in Translation* (Cambridge and Totowa, NJ)

Caley, E. R. 1926: 'The Leyden Papyrus X', *Journal of Chemical Education* 3, 1149–66

Cameron, A. 1973: 'A list of Old English texts', in *A Plan for the Dictionary of Old English*, ed. R. Frank and A. Cameron (Toronto), 25–306

Cameron, A. and Hall, S. G. (trans.) 1999: *Eusebius, Life of Constantine* (Oxford)

Campbell, A. (ed.) 1953: *The Tollemache Orosius (British Museum, Additional Manuscripts 47967)*, EEMF III (Copenhagen)

(ed.) 1962: *The Chronicle of Æthelweard* (London and Edinburgh)

(ed.) 1967: *Æthelwulf, De abbatibus* (Oxford)

(ed.) 1998: *Encomium Emmae Reginae*, reprinted with supplementary introduction by Simon Keynes (Cambridge)

Campbell, E. and Lane, A. 1993: 'Celtic and Germanic interaction in Dalriada: the 7th-century metalworking site at Dunadd' in Spearman and Higgitt 1993, 52–63

Campbell, J. 1971: 'The first century of Christianity in England', *Ampleforth Journal* 76, 19–26; reprinted in Campbell 1986, 49–68

1975: 'Observations on English government from the tenth to the twelfth century', *Transactions of the Royal Historical Society* 5th ser. 25, 39–54; reprinted in Campbell 1986, 155–70

1980: 'The significance of the Anglo-Norman state in the administrative history of western Europe', in *Histoire comparée de l'administration (IVe–XVIIIe siècles)*, Actes du XIV Colloque Historique Franco-Allemand, Tours 1977, ed. K.-F. Werner and W. Paravicini, Beihefte der Francia 9 (Munich), 117–34; reprinted in Campbell 1986, 171–90

1986: *Essays in Anglo-Saxon History* (London)

Campbell, J. J. 1963: 'Prayers from MS Arundel 155', *Anglia* 81, 82–117

Carey, J. 1989: 'Ireland and the Antipodes: the heterodoxy of Virgil of Salzburg', *Speculum* 64, 1–10

2003–4: 'The Obscurantists and the sea-monster: reflections on the *Hisperica famina*', *Peritia* 17–18, 40–60

Carley, J. P. 1987: 'Two pre-Conquest manuscripts from Glastonbury Abbey', *ASE* 16, 197–212

Carney, J. 1961: *The Problem of St Patrick* (Dublin)

1967: *Medieval Irish Lyrics* (Dublin)

Carroll, C. 1999: 'Archbishops and church provinces of Mainz and Cologne during the Carolingian Period, 751–911', unpublished PhD thesis (University of Cambridge)

Cartwright, D. E. 2001: *Tides: A Scientific History* (Cambridge)

Carver, M. and Hooper, E. 2000: *Discovery at Tarbat* (York)

Carver, M. and Spall, C. 2004: 'Excavating a *parchmenerie*: archaeological correlates of making parchment at the Pictish monastery of Portmahomack, Easter Ross', *Proceedings of the Society of Antiquaries of Scotland* 134, 183–200

Casey, P. J. 1994: *Carausius and Allectus: The British Usurpers* (London)

Catto, J. 2003: 'Written English: the making of the language 1370–1400', *Past and Present* 179, 24–59

Cazier, P. (ed.) 1998: *Isidorus Hispalensis, Sententiae*, CCSL 111 (Turnhout)

Chadwick, H. (trans.) 1991: *St Augustine, Confessions* (Oxford)

Chadwick, N. K. 1958: 'Early culture and learning in North Wales', in *Studies in the Early British Church*, ed. N. K. Chadwick (Cambridge), 93–110

Chambers, R. W., Förster, M. and Flower, R. (eds.) 1933: *The Exeter Book of Old English Poetry* (London)

Chaplais, P. 1973a: 'The Anglo-Saxon chancery: from the diploma to the writ', in *Prisca Munimenta: Studies in Archival and Administrative History presented to Dr. A. E. J. Hollaender*, ed. F. Ranger (London), 43–62

1973b: 'The origin and authenticity of the royal Anglo-Saxon diploma', in *Prisca Munimenta*, ed. F. Ranger (London), 28–42

Charles-Edwards, T. M. 1989: *The Welsh Laws* (Cardiff)

1995: 'The penitential of Theodore and the Iudicia Theodori' in Lapidge 1995, 141–74

1998a: 'The construction of the Hibernensis', *Peritia* 12, 209–37

1998b: 'The context and uses of literacy in early Christian Ireland' in Pryce 1998, 62–82

1999: 'Britons in Ireland *c.* 550–800', in *Ildánach ildírech: A Festschrift for Proinsias MacCana*, ed. J. Carey, J. T. Koch and P.Y. Lambert (Andover and Aberystwyth), 15–26

2000: *Early Christian Ireland* (Cambridge)

2002: 'The Springmount Bog Tablets: their implications for Insular epigraphy and palaeography', *Studia Celtica* 36, 27–45

Chase, C. (ed.) 1975: *Two Alcuin Letter-Books* (Toronto)

Chase, W. 1922: *The Distichs of Cato: A Famous Medieval Textbook* (Madison, WI)

Chibnall, M (ed.) 1969–80: *The Ecclesiastical History of Orderic Vitalis*, 6 vols. (Oxford)

Clanchy, M. 1993: *From Memory to Written Record, England 1066–1307*, 2nd edn (Oxford)

Clark, C. 1985: 'British Library Additional MS 40,000, ff. 1v–12r', *Anglo-Norman Studies* 7, 50–68

Clark, J. 1926: *The Abbey of St Gall as a Centre of Literature and Art* (Cambridge, MA)

Clarke, H. and Brennan, M. 1981: *Columbanus and Merovingian Monasticism*, British Archaeological Reports, International Series 113 (Oxford)

Clarke, M. 2001: *The Art of All Colours: Medieval Recipe Books for Painters and Illuminators* (London)

2004: 'Anglo-Saxon manuscript pigments', *Studies in Conservation* 49, 231–44

Clarkson, C. 1993: 'English monastic bookbinding in the twelfth century', in *Ancient and Medieval Book Materials and Techniques*, ed. M. Maniaci and P. F. Munafò, 2 vols., Studi e Testi 357–8 (Vatican City), II, 181–200

1996a: 'Annotated bibliography of works by and about Roger Powell', in *Roger Powell: The Compleat Binder*, ed. J. L. Sharpe, Bibliologia 14 (Turnhout), 57–67

1996b: 'Further studies in Anglo-Saxon and Norman bookbinding: board attachment methods re-examined', in *Roger Powell: The Compleat Binder*, ed. J. L. Sharpe, Bibliologia 14 (Turnhout), 154–214

1997: 'Some representations of the book and bookmaking, from the earliest codex forms to Jost Amman', in *The Bible as Book: The Manuscript Tradition*, ed. K. van Kampen and J. Sharpe (London), 197–203

Clayton, M. 1985: 'Homiliaries and preaching in Anglo-Saxon England', *Peritia* 4, 207–42

Clemoes, P. 1952: *Liturgical Influence on Punctuation in Late Old English and Early Middle English Manuscripts*, Occasional Papers, Department of Anglo-Saxon 1 (Cambridge)
(ed.) 1997: *Ælfric's Catholic Homilies, the First Series*, EETS s.s. 17 (Oxford)
Cockx-Indestege, E. and Hermans, J. M. M. 2004: *Sluitwerk Bijdrage tot de terminologie van der Boekband* (Brussels)
Cohen-Mushlin, A. 1990: 'The twelfth-century scriptorium of Frankenthal', in *Medieval Book Production: Assessing the Evidence*, ed. L. L. Brownrigg (Los Altos, CA), 85–101
Colgan, J. (ed.) 1645: *Acta Sanctorum veteris et maioris Scotiae seu Hiberniae sanctorum insulae* (Leuven)
Colgrave, B. (ed.) 1927: *The Life of Bishop Wilfrid by Eddius Stephanus* (Cambridge)
(ed.) 1956: *Felix's Life of Saint Guthlac* (Cambridge)
(ed.) 1958: *The Paris Psalter (MS Bibliothèque Nationale fonds latin 8824)*, EEMF 8 (Copenhagen)
Colgrave, B. and Mynors, R. A. B. (eds.) 1969: *Bede's Ecclesiastical History of the English People* (Oxford)
Collingwood, R. G. and Wright, R. P. 1990–5: *The Roman Inscriptions of Britain*, vol. II: *Instrumentum domesticum*, ed. S. S. Frere, R. S. O. Tomlin *et al.*, 8 fascicules plus index volume (Gloucester/Stroud)
1995: *The Roman Inscriptions of Britain*, vol. I: *Inscriptions on Stone*, rev. edn with addenda and corrigenda by R. S. O. Tomlin (Stroud)
Conner, P. W. 1993: *Anglo-Saxon Exeter: A Tenth-Century Cultural History* (Woodbridge)
2001: 'On dating Cynewulf', in *The Cynewulf Reader*, ed. R. E. Bjork (New York and London), 23–56
Constantinescu, R. 1974: 'Alcuin et les "libelli precum" de l'époque carolingienne', *Revue de l'histoire de la spiritualité* 50, 17–56
Contreni, J. J. 1978: *The Cathedral School at Laon from 850 to 930* (Munich)
(ed.) 1984: *Codex Laudianus 468: A Ninth-Century Guide to Virgil, Sedulius and the Liberal Arts*, Armarium Codicum Insignium 3 (Turnhout)
1989: 'The Carolingian school: letters from the classroom' reprinted in Contreni 1992 as no. XI.
1992: *Carolingian Learning, Masters and Manuscripts* (Aldershot)
Cooley, A. E. (ed.) 2002: *Becoming Roman, Writing Latin? Literacy and Epigraphy in the Roman West* (Portsmouth, RI)
Conway, G. 1997: 'Towards a cultural context for the eleventh-century Llanbadarn Manuscripts', *Ceredigion* 13.1, 9–28
Cooksey, C. and Withnall, R. 2001: 'Chemical studies on *Nucella lapillus*', *Dyes in History and Archaeology* 16–17, 91–6
Corbin, S. 1977: *Die Neumen*, Palaeographie der Musik I/3 (Cologne)
Corradini, R., Diesenberger, M. and Reimitz, H. (eds.) 2003: *The Construction of Communities in the Early Middle Ages: Texts, Resources and Artefacts*, The Transformation of the Roman World 12 (Leiden)
Corrêa, A. (ed.) 1992: *The Durham Collectar*, HBS 107 (London)
1995: 'Daily office books: collectars and breviaries' in Pfaff 1995a, 45–60
Cosh, S. R. and Neal, D. S. 2005: *Roman Mosaics of Britain* II: *South-West Britain* (London)
Coupry, C. 1999: 'Les pigments utilisés pour l'enluminure à Fécamp aux XIe et XIIe siècles', in Bouet and Dosdat 1999, 69–79

Courcelle, P. 1939: 'Étude critique sur les commentaires de la Consolation de Boèce (IXe–XVe siècles)', *Archives d'histoire doctrinale et littéraire du Moyen Âge* 14, 5–140

1967: *La Consolation de Philosophie dans la tradition littéraire* (Paris)

Cramp, R. J. 1969: 'Excavations at the Saxon monastic sites of Wearmouth and Jarrow: an interim report', *Medieval Archaeology* 13, 24–66

1975: 'Window-glass from the monastic site of Jarrow', *Journal of Glass Studies* 17, 88–96

(ed.) 2005: *Wearmouth and Jarrow Monastic Sites* I (Swindon)

Cramp, R. J. and Cronyn, J. 1990: 'Anglo-Saxon polychrome plaster and other materials from the excavations of Monkwearmouth and Jarrow: an interim report', in *Early Medieval Wall Painting and Painted Sculpture*, ed. S. Cather, D. Park and P. Williamson, British Archaeological Reports, British Ser. 216 (Oxford), 17–30

Crawford, S. (ed.) 1922: *The Old English Version of the Heptateuch*, EETS o.s. 160 (London)

Crick, J. 1987: 'An Anglo-Saxon fragment of Justinus's Epitome', *ASE* 16, 181–96

1997: 'The case for a West Saxon minuscule', *ASE* 26, 63–79

Crivello, F. 2001: *La miniatura a Bobbio tra IX e X secolo e i suoi modelli carolingi* (Turin, London and Venice)

Cross, J. E. 1956: '*Ubi sunt* passages in Old English: sources and relationships', *Vetenskaps-societetens i Lund Årsbok*, 25–44

1989: 'Wulfstan's *Incipit de baptismo* (Bethurum VIIIa): a revision of sources', *Neuphilologische Mitteilungen* 90, 237–42

1991: 'Wulfstan's *De antichristo* in a twelfth-century Worcester manuscript', *ASE* 20, 203–20

1992: 'A newly-identified manuscript of Wulfstan's "commonplace book", Rouen, Bibliothèque municipale 1382 (U.109)', *Journal of Medieval Latin* 2, 68–83

1993: 'Atto of Vercelli, *De pressuris ecclesiasticis*, Archbishop Wulfstan and Wulfstan's "commonplace book"', *Traditio* 48, 237–46

Cross, J. E. and Brown, A. 1989: 'Literary impetus of Wulfstan's *Sermo Lupi*', *Leeds Studies in English* 20, 271–91

1993: 'Wulfstan and Abbo of Saint-German-des-Prés', *Mediaevalia* 15, 71–91

Cross, J. E. and Hamer, A. (eds.) 1999: *Wulfstan's Canon Law Collection*, Anglo-Saxon Texts 1 (Cambridge)

Cross, J. E. and Tunberg, J. M. (eds.) 1993: *The Copenhagen Wulfstan Collection, Copenhagen. Kongelige Bibliotek, Gl. Kgl. Sam. 1595 (4°)*, EEMF 25 (Copenhagen)

Cubbin, G. P. (ed.) 1996: *The Anglo-Saxon Chronicle, a Collaborative Edition*, 6: *MS D* (Cambridge)

Cubitt, C. 1995: *Anglo-Saxon Church Councils c. 650–c. 850*, Studies in the Early History of Britain (Leicester)

1997: 'Review article: the tenth-century Benedictine reform in England', *Early Medieval Europe* 6, 77–94

Curran, M. 1984: *The Antiphonary of Bangor and the Early Irish Monastic Liturgy* (Dublin)

Curry, J. J. M. 1966: [Alcuin] 'De ratione animae: a text with introduction, critical apparatus and translation', unpublished PhD dissertation (Cornell University, NY)

Curtius, E. R. 1948/53: *European Literature and the Latin Middle Ages*, trans. R. W. Trask (Princeton, NJ)

d'Alès, A. 1937: 'Tertullian chez Bède', *Recherches de science religieuse* 27, 620

d'Alverny, M.-T. 1946: 'La Sagesse et ses sept filles: recherches sur les allégories de la philosophie et des arts libéraux du IXe au XIIe siècle', in *Mélanges dédiés à la mémoire de Félix Grat*, 2 vols. (Paris), I, 245–78 d'Aronco, M. A. and Cameron. M. L. (eds.) 1998: *The Old English Illustrated Pharmacopoeia*, EEMF 27 (Copenhagen)

Dance, R. 2004: 'Sound, fury and signifiers, or Wulfstan's language' in Townend 2004, 29–61

Daniel, N. 1973: *Handschriften des zehnten Jahrhunderts aus der Freisinger Dombibliothek* (Munich)

Darby, H. C. 1977: *Domesday England* (Cambridge)

Dark, K. R. 1992: 'Epigraphic, art-historical and historical approaches to the chronology of Class I inscribed stones', in *The Early Church in Wales and the West*, ed. N. Edwards and A. Lane (Oxford), 51–61

1994: *Civitas to Kingdom: British Political Continuity 300–800*, Studies in the Early History of Britain (Leicester)

Darlington, R. R. (ed.) 1928: *The Vita Wulfstani of William of Malmesbury*, Camden Soc. 40 (London)

Darlington, R. R. and McGurk, P. (eds.) 1995: *The Chronicle of John of Worcester*, vol II (Oxford)

Dauphin, H. 1960: 'Le renouveau monastique en Angleterre au xe siècle et ses rapports avec la réforme de Saint Gérard de Brogne', *RB* 70, 177–96

Davies, R. R. 1996: 'The peoples of Britain and Ireland 1100–1400, III: Laws and customs', *Transactions of the Royal Historical Society* 6th ser. 6, 1–23

Davies, W. 1978: *An Early Welsh Microcosm: Studies in the Llandaff Charters* (London)

1979: *The Llandaff Charters* (Aberystwyth)

1982a: 'The Latin charter-tradition in western Britain, Brittany and Ireland in the early medieval period' in Whitelock *et al.* 1982, 258–80

1982b: *Wales in the Early Middle Ages* (Leicester)

Davril, A. (ed.) 1995: *The Winchcombe Sacramentary (Orléans, Bibliothèque municipale 127 [105])*, HBS 109 (London)

De Hamel, C. 2001: *The Book: A History of the Bible* (London)

Deanesly, M. 1963: *The Pre-Conquest Church in England*, 2nd edn (London)

Decker, A. 1895: 'Die Hildbold'sche Manuskriptensammlung des Kölner Domes', in *Festschrift der drei und vierzigsten Versammlung deutscher Philologen und Schulmänner dargeboten von den höheren Lehranstalten Kölns* (Bonn), 217–52

DeGregorio, S. 2005: 'Bede, the monk, as Exegete: Evidence from the Commentary on Ezra-Nehemiah', *Revue Bénédictine*, 115, 343–69

2008: 'Bede and Benedict of Nursia' in *Early Medieval Studies in Memory of Patrick Wormald*, ed. S. Baxter, C. Karkov, J. Nelson and D. Pelteret (Farnham), 149–63

2010: 'The Venerable Bede and Gregory the Great: exegetical connections, spiritual departures', *Early Medieval Europe*, 18, 43–60

Dekkers, A. 1995: *Clavis Patrum Latinorum*, 3rd edn (Steenbrugge-Turnhout)

Depreux, P. and Judic, B. (eds.) 2004: *Alcuin, de York à Tours: écriture, pouvoir et réseaux dans l'Europe du haut Moyen Age*, Annales de Bretagne et des pays de l'ouest 111, no.3 (Rennes)

Derolez, A. 2003: *The Palaeography of Gothic Manuscript Books* (Cambridge)

Derolez, A. and Victor, B. (eds.), *Corpus Catalogorum Belgii: The Medieval Booklists of the Southern Low Countries* I: *Province of West Flanders*, 2nd edn (Brussels)

Derolez, R. 1952: 'Dubtach's cryptogram: some notes in connexion with Brussels MS. 9565–9566', *L'Antiquité classique* 21, 359–75

Deshman, R. 1995: *The Benedictional of Æthelwold* (Princeton, NJ)

1997: 'The Galba Psalter: pictures, texts and context in an early medieval prayerbook', *ASE* 26, 109–38

Deuffic, J.-L. 1985: 'La production manuscrite des scriptoria Bretons (VIIIe–XIe siècle)', in *Landévennec et le monachisme Breton dans le haut moyen âge*. Actes du colloque du 15ème centenaire de la fondation de l'abbaye de Landévennec 25, 26, 27 avril 1985 (Landévennec), 289–321.

Dewick, E. S. (ed.) 1902: *Facsimiles of Horae de Beata Maria Virgine from English Manuscripts of the Eleventh Century*, HBS 21 (London)

Dewick, E. S. and Frere, W. H. 1914–21: *The Leofric Collectar*, 2 vols., HBS 45, 56 (London)

Di Sciacca, C. 2008: *Finding the Right Words: Isidore's 'Synonyma' in Anglo-Saxon England* (Toronto)

Diekamp, W. (ed.) 1881: *Die vitae sancti Liudgeri*, Die Geschichtsquellen des Bistums Münster 4 (Münster)

Dionisotti, A. 1982a: 'From Ausonius' schooldays? A schoolbook and its relatives', *JRS* 72, 83–125

1982b: 'On Bede, grammars and Greek', *RB* 92, 11–41

Discenza, N. 2001: 'The sources of Alfred's version of Boethius's *Consolation of Philosophy* (Cameron B.9.3)', in Fontes Anglo-Saxonici: a register of written sources used by Anglo-Saxon authors, ed. Fontes Anglo-Saxonici Project (Oxford): CD-ROM version 1.1 and http://fontes.english.ox.ac.uk/

Dobbie, E. V. K. (ed.) 1942: *The Anglo-Saxon Minor Poems*, Anglo-Saxon Poetic Records 6 (New York)

Dodwell, C. R. (ed.) 1961: *Theophilus, The Various Arts* (London)

1973: 'Losses of Anglo-Saxon art in the Middle Ages', *Bulletin of the John Rylands University Library of Manchester* 56, 74–92

1982: *Anglo-Saxon Art: A New Perspective* (Manchester)

Dodwell, C. R. and Clemoes, P. (eds.) 1974: *The Old English Illustrated Hexateuch: British Museum Cotton Claudius B.IV*, EEMF 18 (Copenhagen)

Dolbeau, F. 1996: 'Bède, lecteur des sermons d'Augustin', *Filologia mediolatina* 3, 105–33

Dombart, B. and Kalb, A. (eds.) 1955: *Aurelii Augustini Opera* XIV, 1–2: *De civitate Dei*, 2 vols, CCSL 47–8 (Turnhout)

Dopsch, H and Juffinger, R. (eds.) 1984: *Virgil von Salzburg: Missionar und Gelehrter* (Salzburg)

Douie, D. L. and Farmer, D. H. (eds.) 1985: *Magna Vita Sancti Hugonis*, 2 vols. (Oxford)

Doyle, A. I. 1992: 'A fragment of an eighth-century Northumbrian office book', in *Words, Texts and Manuscripts: Studies in Anglo-Saxon Culture Presented to Helmut Gneuss on the Occasion of his Sixty-Fifth Birthday*, ed. M. Korhammer *et al.* (Cambridge), 11–27

Doyle, P. 1976: 'The Latin Bible in Ireland: its origins and growth', in *Biblical Studies: The Medieval Irish Contribution*, ed. M. McNamara, Proceedings of the Irish Biblical Association 1 (Dublin), 30–45

Draak, M. 1957: 'Construe marks in Hiberno-Latin manuscripts', *Mededelingen der Koninklijke Nederlandse Akademie van Wetenschappen* 20, 261–82

1967: 'The higher teaching of Latin grammar in Ireland in the ninth century', *Mededelingen der Koninklijke Nederlandse Akademie van Wetenschappen* 30, 109–44

Drage, E. M. 1978: 'Bishop Leofric and the Exeter Cathedral Chapter 1050–1072: a reassessment of the manuscript evidence', unpublished DPhil thesis (University of Oxford)

Drögereit, R. 1951: *Werden und der Heliand: Studien zur Kulturgeschichte der Abtei Werden und zur Herkunft des Heliand* (Essen)

Drogin, M. 1980: *Medieval Calligraphy, its History and Technique* (Montclair and London)

Dubois, J. and Renaud, G. (eds.) 1976: *Édition pratique des martyrologes de Bède, de l'anonyme Lyonnais, et de Florus* (Paris)

Düchting, R. 1968: *Sedulius Scottus: seine Dichtungen* (Munich)

Duft, J. 1974: 'Irische Einflüsse auf St Gallen und Alemannien', in *Mönchtum, Episkopat und Adel zur Gründungszeit des Klosters Reichenau*, ed. A. Borst, Vorträge und Forschungen 20 (Sigmaringen), 9–35

1982: 'Irische Handschriftenüberlieferung in St Gallen' in Löwe 1982, II, 916–37

1983: 'Die Handschriften-Katalogisierung in der Stiftsbibliothek St Gallen vom 9. bis zum 19. Jahrhundert', in *Die Handschriften der Stiftsbibliothek St Gallen: Beschreibendes Verzeichnis Codices 1726–1984*, ed. B. Matthias von Scarpatetti (St Gallen), 11–18.

Duft, J. and Schnyder, R. 1984: *Die Elfenbein-Einbände der Stiftsbibliothek St. Gallen* (Beuron)

Dumas, A. and Deshusses, J. (eds.) 1981: *Liber Sacramentorum Gellonensis*, CCSL 159 (Turnhout)

Dümmler, E. (ed.) 1881: Alcuin, *Carmina*, in MGH Poetae Latini Aevi Carolini 1 (Munich)

(ed.) 1895: Alcuin, *Epistolae*, in MGH Epistolae IV, Karolini Aevi II (Berlin)

Dumville, D. N. 1972: 'Liturgical drama and panegyric responsory from the eighth century: a re-examination of the origin and contents of the ninth-century section of the Book of Cerne', *JTS* n.s. 23, 374–406

1976: 'The Anglian collection of royal genealogies and regnal Lists', *ASE* 5, 23–50

1983: 'Motes and beams: two Insular computistical manuscripts', *Peritia* 2, 248–56

1985: 'Late seventh- or eighth-century evidence for the British Transmission of Pelagius', *Cambridge Medieval Celtic Studies* 10, 39–52

1987: 'English Square Minuscule script: the background and earliest phases', *ASE* 16, 147–79

1988a: 'Beowulf come lately: some notes on the palaeography of the Nowell Codex', *Archiv für das Studium der neueren Sprachen und Literaturen* 225, 49–63

1988b: 'Early Welsh poetry: problems of historicity', in *Early Welsh Poetry: Studies in the Book of Aneirin*, ed. B. F. Roberts (Aberystwyth), 1–16

1991: 'On the dating of some late Anglo-Saxon liturgical manuscripts', *TCBS* 10, 40–57

1992: *Liturgy and the Ecclesiastical History of Late Anglo-Saxon England: Four Studies*, Studies in Anglo-Saxon History 5 (Woodbridge)

1993a: *Britons and Anglo-Saxons in the Early Middle Ages* (Aldershot)

1993b: *English Caroline Script and Monastic History: Studies in Benedictinism A.D. 950–1030*, Studies in Anglo-Saxon History 6 (Woodbridge)

1993c: 'The English element in tenth-century Breton book-production' in Dumville 1993a, 1–14

1994a: 'Anglo-Saxon books: treasure in Norman hands?', *ANS* 16, 83–99

1994b: 'English libraries before 1066: use and abuse of the manuscript evidence', in *Anglo-Saxon Manuscripts: Basic Readings*, ed. M. P. Richards (London), 169–219 (revised version of article originally published in *Insular Latin Studies: Papers on Latin Texts and Manuscripts of the British Isles 550–1066*, ed. M. W. Herren (Toronto, 1981), 153–78)

1994c: 'English Square Minuscule script: the mid-century phases', *ASE* 23, 133–64

1994d: 'Ireland, Brittany and England: some questions of transmission', in *Irlande et Bretagne: vingt siècles d'histoire*, ed. C. Laurent and H. Davis (Rennes), 85–95

1995a: 'The early medieval Insular churches and the preservation of Roman literature: towards a historical and palaeographical reevaluation', in *Formative Stages of Classical*

Traditions: Latin Texts from Antiquity to the Renaissance, ed. O. Pecere and M. Reeve (Spoleto), 197–237

1995b: 'The importation of Mediterranean manuscripts into Theodore's England' in Lapidge 1995, 96–119

1995c: *Facsimile of MS F: The Domitian Bilingual* (Cambridge)

1997: *Councils and Synods of the Gaelic Early and Central Middle Ages*, Quiggin Pamphlet 3 (Cambridge)

1999: *A Palaeographer's Review: The Insular System of Scripts in the Early Middle Ages*, I, Kansai University Institute of Oriental and Occidental Studies, Sources and Materials Series 20.1 (Osaka)

2001: 'Specimina Codicum Palaeoanglicorum', in *Collection of Essays in Commemoration of the 50th Anniversary of Oriental and Occidental Studies, October 2001* (Suita, Osaka), 1–24

2007: 'The two earliest manuscripts of Bede's Ecclesiastical History?', *Anglo-Saxon* 1, 55–108

Dumville, D. N., Abrams, L., and T. Charle-Edwards 1993: *Saint Patrick, AD 493–1993* (Woodbridge)

Ebersperger, B. 1999: *Die angelsächsischen Handschriften in den Pariser Bibliotheken*, Anglistische Forschungen 261 (Heidelberg)

Edwards, N. 1995: '11th-century Welsh illuminated manuscripts: the nature of the Irish connection' in Bourke 1995, 147–55

2007: *A Corpus of Early Medieval Inscribed Stones and Stone Sculpture in Wales* II: *South-West Wales* (Cardiff)

Ehwald, R. (ed.) 1919: *Aldhelmi Opera*, MGH Auctores Antiquissimi 15 (Munich)

Eisenlohr, E. 1994: 'The puzzle of the scribes: some palaeographical observations' in O'Mahony 1994, 196–208

Eliason, N. and Clemoes, P. (eds.) 1966: *Ælfric's First Series of Catholic Homilies: British Museum, Royal 7 C.xii*, EEMF 13 (Copenhagen)

Elliott, J. K. (ed.) 1993: *The Apocryphal New Testament* (Oxford)

2000: *A Bibliography of Greek New Testament Manuscripts*, 2nd edn (Cambridge)

Els, T. J. M. van 1972: *The Kassel Manuscript of Bede's 'Historia Ecclesiastica Gentis Anglorum' and its Old English Material* (Assen)

Emerton, E. (trans.) 2000: *The Letters of Saint Boniface*; reprinted with Introduction and Bibliography by T. F. X. Noble (New York)

Emms, R. 2004: 'St Augustine's Abbey, Canterbury and the "first books of the whole English Church"', in *The Church and the Book*, ed. R. N. Swanson, Studies in Church History 38 (Oxford), 32–45.

Engelen, E.-M. 1993: *Zeit, Zahl und Bild: Studien zur Verbindung von Philosophie und Wissenschaft bei Abbo von Fleury* (Berlin and New York)

Enright, M. 1979: 'Charles the Bald and Æthelwulf: the alliance of 856 and strategies of royal succession', *Journal of Medieval History* 5, 291–302

Erhart, P. and Zeller, B. (eds.) 2006: *Mensch und Schrift im frühen Mittelalter* (St Gallen)

Étaix, R. (ed.) 1999: Gregorius Magnus, *Homiliae in euangelia*, CCSL 141 (Turnhout)

Evans, J. G. with Rhŷs, J. (eds.) 1893: *The Text of the Book of Llan Dâv* (Oxford)

Evans, J. W. and Wooding, J. M. (eds.) 2007: *St David of Wales: Cult, Church and Nation* (Woodbridge)

Evelyn White, H. G. 1919–21: *Ausonius*, 2 vols. (Cambridge, MA)

Falileyev, A. and Owen, M. E. 2005: *The Leiden Leechbook: A Study of the Earliest Neo-Brittonic Medical Compilation* (Innsbruck)

Farmer, D. H. (ed.) 1983: *The Age of Bede* (Harmondsworth)

Farr, C. 1997: *The Book of Kells: Its Function and Audience* (London and Toronto)

Fehr, B. (ed.) 1966: *Die Hirtenbriefe Ælfrics*, reprinted with supplement by P. Clemoes (Darmstadt)

Feller, R. L. (ed.) 1986: *Artists' Pigments: A Handbook of their History and Characteristics* I (Cambridge)

Ferrari, M. C. 1984: *Sancti Willibrordi venerantes memoriam. Echternacher Schreiber und Schriftsteller von den Angelsachsen bis Johann Bertels. Ein Überblick*, Publications du CLUDEM 6 (Luxembourg)

Ferrari, M. C., Schroeder, J. and Trauffler, H. (ed.) 1999: *Die Abtei Echternach 698–1998*, Publications du CLUDEM 15 (Luxembourg)

Finberg, H. P. R. 1969: 'St Patrick at Glastonbury' in his *West Country Historical Studies* (Newton Abbott), 70–88

1972: *The Early Charters of the West Midlands*, 2nd edn (Leicester)

Finlayson, C. P. (ed.) 1962: *Celtic Psalter: Edinburgh University Library MS 56*, Umbrae Codicum Occidentalium 7 (Amsterdam)

Fischer, B. 1952: 'Die Lesungen der römischen Ostervigil unter Gregor der Grosse', in *Colligere Fragmenta: Festschrift Alban Dold*, ed. B. Fischer and V. Fiala (Beuron), 144–59

Fitzhugh, E. W. 1986: 'Red lead and minium' in Feller 1986, 109–39

Fleckenstein, J. 1982: 'Hrabanus Maurus: Diener seiner Zeit und Vermittler zwischen den Zeiten' in Kottje and Zimmerman 1982, 194–208

Fleming, R. 2000: 'The new wealth, the new rich and the new political style in late Anglo-Saxon England', *ANS* 23, 1–22

Fletcher, E. 1981: *Benedict Biscop*, Jarrow Lecture (Jarrow)

Fletcher, H. G. (ed.) 1999: *The Wormsley Library. A Personal Selection by Sir Paul Getty KBE* (London and New York)

Fleuriot, L. 1976–8: 'Les évêques de la "Clas Kenedyr", évêché disparu de la région de Hereford', *Études celtiques* 15, 225–6

Flieder, F. 1968: 'Mise au point des techniques d'identification des pigments et des liants inclus dans la couche picturale des enluminures de manuscrits', *Studies in Conservation* 13, 49–86

Flobert, P. (ed.) 1997: *La vie ancienne de Saint Samson de Dol* (Paris)

Flower, R. and Smith, H. (eds.) 1941: *The Parker Chronicle, CCCC 173 Part I: Facsimile*, EETS o.s. 208 (Oxford)

Foerster, M. (ed.) 1913: *Il Codice Vercellese con omelie e poesie in lingua anglosassone* (Rome)

Foley, W. T. and Holder, A. G. (trans.) 1999: *Bede, A Biblical Miscellany*, Translated Texts for Historians 28 (Liverpool)

Fontaine, J. 1959: *Isidore de Séville et la culture classique dans l'Espagne wisigothique*, 2 vols. (Paris)

Fontes Anglo-Saxonici: a register of written sources used by Anglo-Saxon authors, CD-ROM version 1.1, ed. M. Godden and R. Jayatilaka with D. Miles (Oxford: English Faculty, Fontes Anglo-Saxonici Project); also available at http://fontes.english.ox.ac.uk/

Foot, S. 2006: *Monastic Life in Anglo-Saxon England c. 600–900* (Cambridge)

Forbes-Leith, W. 1896: *The Gospel Book of St Margaret* (Edinburgh)

Forstner, K. (ed.) 1974: *Das Verbrüderungsbuch von St. Peter in Salzburg. Vollständige Faksimile-Ausgabe im Originalformat der Handschrift A1 aus dem Archiv von St. Peter in Salzburg*, Codices Selecti 51 (Graz)

1984: 'Das Salzburger Skriptorium unter Vergil und das Verbrüderungsbuch von St Peter' in Dopsch and Juffinger 1984, 135–40

Fouracre, P. and Ganz, D. (eds.) 2008: *Frankland. The Franks and their World of the Early Middle Ages: Essays in Honour of Dame Jinty Nelson* (Manchester)

Fowler, R. (ed.) 1972: *Wulfstan's Canons of Edgar*, EETS 266 (Oxford)

Fox, M. 2005: 'Alcuin as exile and educator: vir undecumque doctissimus', in *Latin Learning and English Lore: Studies in Anglo-Saxon Literature for Michael Lapidge*, ed. K. O'Brien O'Keeffe and A. Orchard, 2 vols. (Toronto), I, 215–36

Fox, P. (ed.) 1990: *The Book of Kells: MS 58 Trinity College Library, Dublin*, 2 vols., facsimile and commentary (Lucerne)

Fraipont, J. (ed.) 1961: Bede, *De locis sanctis*, CCSL 125 (Turnhout), 245–80

Franklin, C. V. 2002: 'Grammar and exegesis: Bede's *Liber de schematibus et tropis*', in *Latin Grammar and Rhetoric: From Classical Theory to Medieval Practice*, ed. C. D. Lanham (London and New York), 63–91

Fransen, I. 1961: 'Description de la collection de Bède le Vénérable sur l'Apôtre', *RB* 71, 22–70

Fransen, P.-I. 1987: 'D'Eugippius à Bède le Vénérable: à propos de leurs florilèges augustiniens', *RB* 97, 187–94

Frantzen, A. J. 1983: *The Literature of Penance in Anglo-Saxon England* (New Brunswick, NJ)

1986: *King Alfred* (Boston, MA)

Franzen, C. 1998: *Worcester Manuscripts*, Anglo-Saxon Manuscripts in Microfiche Facsimile 6 (Tempe, AZ)

Freeman-Grenville, G. S. P, Chapman, R. L. and Taylor, J. E. 2003: *The Onomasticon by Eusebius of Caesarea* (Jerusalem)

Frend, W. H. C. 2003: 'Roman Britain, a failed promise?', in *The Cross Goes North: Processes of Conversion in Northern Europe, AD 300–1300*, ed. M. Carver (York), 79–91

Frere, W. H. (ed.) 1894: *The Winchester Troper from Manuscripts of the xth and xith Centuries*, HBS 8 (London)

1934: *Studies in Early Roman Liturgy* II: *The Roman Lectionary*, Alcuin Club Collections 30 (London)

Friend, A. M. 1939: 'The canon tables of the Book of Kells', in *Studies in Memory of Arthur Kingsley Porter*, ed. W. Koehler, 2 vols. (Cambridge, MA), II, 611–41

Fuchs, R. and Oltrogge, D. 1994: 'Colour material and painting technique in the Book of Kells' in O'Mahony 1994, 133–71

Fulk, R. D. 2001: 'Cynewulf: canon, dialect and date', in *The Cynewulf Reader*, ed. R. E. Bjork (New York and London), 3–21

Gaborit-Chopin, D. *et al.* 2005: *La France romane au temps des premiers Capétiens (987–1152)* (Paris)

Gamber, K. 1968: *Codices liturgici latini antiquiores* 1, Spicilegii Friburgensis subsidia (Freiburg i. Sch.)

Gameson, R. G. 1990: 'The Anglo-Saxon artists of the Harley 603 Psalter', *Journal of the British Archaeological Association* 143, 29–48

1991: 'English manuscript art in the mid-eleventh century: the decorative tradition', *Antiquaries Journal* 71, 64–122

1992a: 'The cost of the Codex Amiatinus', *Notes and Queries* 237, 79–91

1992b: 'The decoration of the Tanner Bede', *ASE* 21, 115–59

1992c: 'The fabric of the Tanner Bede', *Bodleian Library Record* 14, 176–206

1992d: 'Manuscript art at Christ Church, Canterbury, in the generation after St Dunstan' in Ramsay *et al.* 1992, 187–220

1994: 'The Royal 1 B. vii Gospels and English book production in the seventh and eighth centuries', in *The Early Medieval Bible: Its Production, Decoration and Use*, ed. R. G. Gameson, Cambridge Studies in Palaeography and Codicology 2 (Cambridge), 24–52

1995a: 'English manuscript art in the late eleventh century: Canterbury and its context', in *Canterbury and the Norman Conquest: Churches, Saints and Scholars 1066–1109*, ed. R. Eales and R. Sharpe (London and Rio Grande, OH), 95–144

1995b: *The Role of Art in the Late Anglo-Saxon Church* (Oxford)

1996a: 'Book production and decoration at Worcester in the tenth and eleventh centuries', in *St Oswald of Worcester, Life and Influence*, ed. N. Brooks and C. Cubitt (London and New York), 194–243

1996b: 'The origin of the Exeter book of Old English poetry', *ASE* 25, 135–85

1997: 'The gospels of Margaret of Scotland and the literacy of an early medieval queen', in *Women and the Book: Assessing the Visual Evidence*, ed. J. H. M. Taylor and L. Smith (London), 148–71

1998: 'La Bible de Saint-Vaast d'Arras et un manuscrit anglo-saxon de Boèce', *Scriptorium* 52, 316–21

(ed.) 1999a: *St Augustine and the Conversion of England* (Stroud)

1999b: 'The earliest books of Christian Kent' in Gameson (ed.) 1999a, 313–73

1999c: *The Manuscripts of Early Norman England (c. 1066–1130)* (Oxford)

1999d: 'Manuscrits normands à Exeter aux XIe et XIIe siècles' in Bouet and Dosdat 1999, 107–27

2000a: 'L'arte nell'Inghilterra meridionale e in Fiandra', in *L'arte dell'anno mille in Europa 950–1050*, ed. L. Castel Franchi Vegas *et al.* (Milan), 161–98

2000b: 'Books, culture and the church in Canterbury around the millennium' in *Vikings, Monks and the Millennium: Canterbury in about 1000 AD*, ed. R. Eales and R. Gameson (Canterbury), 15–39

2001: 'Why did Eadfrith write the Lindisfarne Gospels?', in *Belief and Culture in the Middle Ages: Studies presented to Henry Mayr-Harting*, ed. R. Gameson and H. Leyser (Oxford), 45–58

(ed.) 2001–2 : *Codex Aureus: An Eighth-Century Gospel Book*, 2 vols., EEMF 28–9 (Copenhagen)

2002a: 'L'Angleterre et la Flandre aux Xe et XIe siècle: le témoignage des manuscrits', in *Les échanges culturels au Moyen Âge*, Publications de la Sorbonne, Série histoire ancienne et médiévale 70 (Paris), 165–206

2002b: 'The colophon of the Eadwig Gospels', *ASE* 31, 201–22

2002c: 'The Insular gospel-book at Hereford Cathedral', *Scriptorium* 56, 48–79

2002d: *The Scribe Speaks? Colophons in Early English Manuscripts*, H. M. Chadwick Memorial Lectures 12 (Cambridge)

2003: 'La Normandie et l'Angleterre au XIe siècle : le témoignage des manuscrits', in *La Normandie et l'Angleterre au Moyen Âge*, ed. P. Bouet and V. Gazeau (Caen and Turnhout), 131–72

2005: 'St Wulfstan, the library of Worcester and the spirituality of the medieval book', in *St Wulfstan and his World*, ed. N. Brooks and J. Barrow (London), 59–104

2006a: 'The medieval library (to *c.* 1450)', in *The Cambridge History of Libraries in Britain and Ireland*, I, *To 1640*, ed. E. Leedham-Green and T. Webber (Cambridge), 12–50

2006b: '"Signed" manuscripts from early romanesque Flanders: Saint-Bertin and Saint-Vaast', in *Pen in Hand: Medieval Scribal Portraits, Colophons and Tools*, ed. M. Gullick (Walkern), 31–73

2007: 'The script of the original core', in *The Durham Liber Vitae*, ed. D. and L. Rollason, 3 vols. (London), I, 58–65

2008: *The Earliest Books of Canterbury Cathedral: Manuscripts and Fragments to c. 1200* (London)

2009: 'The last Chi-rho in the West: from Insular to Anglo-Saxon in the Boulogne 10 Gospels', in *Form and Order in the Anglo-Saxon World*, ed. H. Hamerow and L. Webster (Oxford), 89–107

2010: 'An itinerant English master around the millennium', in *England and the Continent in the Tenth Century*, ed. D. Rollason, C. Leyser and H. Williams (Turnhout), 87–134

Ganz, D. 1987: 'The preconditions for Caroline Minuscule', *Viator* 18, 23–44

1990: *Corbie in the Carolingian Renaissance* (Sigmaringen)

1993: 'An Anglo-Saxon fragment of Alcuin's letters in the Newberry Library, Chicago', *ASE* 22, 166–77

2002: 'Roman manuscripts in Francia and Anglo-Saxon England', *Settimane* 49, 607–48

2006: 'Anglo-Saxon libraries', in *The Cambridge History of Libraries in Britain and Ireland*, I, *To 1640*, ed. E. Leedham-Green and T. Webber (Cambridge), 91–108

Garand, M.-C., Grand, G. and Muzerelle, D. 1984: *Catalogue des manuscrits en écriture latine portant des indications de date, de lieu ou de copiste*, VII: *Ouest de la France et Pays de Loire*, 2 vols. (Paris)

Garmonsway, G. (ed.) 1947: *Ælfric's Colloquy*, 2nd edn (London)

Garrison, M. 1997: 'The English and the Irish and the court of Charlemagne', in *Karl der Grosse und sein Nachwirken. 1200 Jahre Kultur und Wissenschaft in Europa*, I: *Wissen und Weltbild*, ed. P. L. Butzer, M. Kerner and B. Oberschelp (Turnhout), 97–124

1998a: 'Letters to a king and biblical exempla: the examples of Cathwulf and Clemens *peregrinus*', in *The Power of the Word: The Influence of the Bible on Early Medieval Politics*, ed. M. de Jong, *Early Medieval Europe* 7, special issue, 305–28

1998b: 'The social world of Alcuin: nicknames at York and at the Carolingian court' in Houwen and MacDonald 1998, 59–79

2004: 'Joseph Scottus', in *Oxford Dictionary of National Biography*, ed. H. C. G. Matthew and B. Harrison (Oxford), XXX, 715–16

2005: 'Alcuin and Tibullus', in *Poesía Latina Medieval (siglos v–xv)*, Actas del IV Congreso del Internationales Mittellateinerkomitee, Santiago de Compostela, 12–15 Septiembre de 2000, ed. M. C. Díaz y Díaz and J. M. Díaz de Bustamante (Florence), 749–59

Gasper, G. E. M. and Wallis, F. 2004: 'Anselm and the Articella', *Traditio* 59, 129–74

Gasquet, F. A. and Bishop, E. 1908: *The Bosworth Psalter* (London)

Gatch, M. M. 1966: 'MS Boulogne-sur-Mer 63 and Ælfric's first series of Catholic homilies', *Journal of English and Germanic Philology* 65, 482–90

1977: *Preaching and Theology in Anglo-Saxon England: Ælfric and Wulfstan* (Toronto)

Gebauer, G. and Löfstedt, B. (eds.) 1980: *Bonifatii (Vynfreth), Ars Grammatica*, CCSL 133B (Turnhout)

Gerchow, J. 1988: *Die Gedenküberlieferung den Angelsachsen*, Arbeiten zur Frühmittelalterforschung. Schriftenreihe des Instituts für Frühmittelalterforschung der Universität Münster 20 (Berlin and New York)

1999: 'Liudger, Weden und die Angelsachsen', in *Kloster, Welt, Werden 799–1803: Das Jahrtausend der Mönche*, ed. J. Gerchow (Essen), 49–58

Gerritson, J. 1998a: '*Beowulf* revisited', *English Studies* 79, 82–6

1998b: 'The Copenhagen Wulfstan manuscript: a codicological study', *English Studies* 79, 501–11

Gettens, R. J., Feller, R. L. and Chase, W. T. 1993: 'Vermilion and cinnabar' in Roy 1993, 159–82

Gettens, R. J. and Fitzhugh, E. W. 1993a: 'Azurite and blue verditer' in Roy 1993, 23–35

1993b: 'Malachite and green verditer' in Roy 1993, 183–202

Gettens, R. J., Kuhn, H. and Chase, W. T. 1993: 'Lead white' in Roy 1993, 67–81

Getty, S. 1969: 'An edition with commentary of the Latin/Anglo-Saxon *Liber scintillarum*' unpublished Ph. D. dissertation (University of Pennsylvania)

Geyer, P., Cuntz, O., Francheschini, R. *et al.* (eds.) 1965: *Itineraria et alia geographica. Itineraria Hierosolymitana. Itineraria Romana. Geographica*, CCSL 175 (Turnhout)

Gibson, M. T. and Smith, L. (eds.) 1995–: *Codices Boethiani: A Conspectus of Manuscripts of the Works of Boethius*, 4 vols. to date (London)

Gjerløw, L. (ed.) 1979: *Antiphonarium Nidrosiensis Ecclesiae*, Libri Liturgici Provinciae Nidrosiensis Medii Aevi 3 (Oslo)

Glauche, G. 1970: *Schullektüre im Mittelalter: Entstehung und Wandlungen des Lektürekanons bis 1200 nach den Quellen dargestellt*, Münchener Beiträge zur Mediävistik und Renaissance-Forschung 5 (Munich)

Glogger, P. (ed.) 1907: *Das Leidener Glossar* (Augsburg)

Glorie, F. (ed.) 1968: *Variae Collectiones Aenigmatum Merovingicae Aetatis*, CCSL 133A (Turnhout)

Glunz, H. H. 1933: *History of the Vulgate in England from Alcuin to Roger Bacon* (Cambridge)

Gneuss, H. 1955: *Lehnbildungen und Lehnbedeutungen im Altenglischen* (Berlin)

(ed.) 1964: *Die angelsächsischen Prosabearbeitungen der Benediktinerregel* (Darmstadt) (2nd rev. edn of A. Schröer, *Bibliothek der angelsächsischen Prosa II*)

1968: *Hymnar und Hymnen im englischen Mittelalter: Studien zur Überlieferung, Glossierung und Übersetzung lateinischer Hymnen in England*, Buchreihe der Anglia 12 (Tübingen)

1972: 'The origin of standard Old English and Æthelwold's school at Winchester', *ASE* 1, 63–83

1981: 'A preliminary list of manuscripts written or owned in England up to 1100', *ASE* 9, 1–60

1985: 'Liturgical books in Anglo-Saxon England and their Old English terminology' in Lapidge and Gneuss 1985, 91–141

1986: 'Anglo-Saxon libraries from the conversion to the Benedictine reform', *Settimane* 32, 643–88

1990: 'The study of language in Anglo-Saxon England' (The Toller Memorial Lecture 1989), *Bulletin of the John Rylands University Library of Manchester* 72, 3–32

1992: '*Anglicae linguae interpretatio*: language contact, lexical borrowing and glossing in Anglo-Saxon England' (Sir Israel Gollancz Memorial Lecture), *PBA* 82, 107–48

1994: 'A grammarian's Greek–Latin glossary in Anglo-Saxon England', in *From Anglo-Saxon to Early Middle English: Studies Presented to E. G. Stanley*, ed. M. Godden, D. Gray and T. Hoad (Oxford), 60–86

2001: *Handlist of Anglo-Saxon Manuscripts: A List of Manuscripts and Manuscript Fragments Written or Owned in England up to 1100* (Tempe, AZ)

Godden, M. 1975: 'Old English composite homilies from Winchester', *ASE* 4, 57–65

(ed.) 1979: *Ælfric's Catholic Homilies, The Second Series*, EETS s.s. 5 (Oxford)
1997: 'Wærferth and King Alfred: the fate of the Old English *Dialogues*', in *Alfred the Wise*, ed. J. Roberts and J. Nelson (Cambridge), 35–51
2000: *Ælfric's Catholic Homilies: Introduction, Commentary and Glossary*, EETS s.s.18 (Oxford)
2001: 'The sources of Alfred's version of Augustine's *Soliloquies* (Cameron B.9.4)', in Fontes Anglo-Saxonici: http://fontes.english.ox.ac.uk
2003a: 'King Alfred's preface and the teaching of Latin in Anglo-Saxon England', *EHR* 117, 596–604
2003b: 'The Latin commentary tradition and the Old English Boethius: the present state of the question', Paper at first annual symposium of the Alfredian Boethius Project, Oxford, July 2003: www.english.ox.ac.uk/boethius/Symposium2003.html/
2003c: 'Text and eschatology in Book III of the Old English *Soliloquies*', *Anglia* 121, 177–209
2004: 'The relations of Ælfric and Wulfstan: a reassessment' in Townend 2004, 353–74
2005: 'Alfred, Asser and Boethius', in *Latin Learning and English Lore: Studies in Anglo-Saxon Literature for Michael Lapidge*, ed. K. O'Brien O'Keefe and A. Orchard, 2 vols. (Toronto), I, 326–48
2006: 'The Latin commentary and the Old English text: authorship and kingship', Paper at 4th Annual Symposium of the Alfredian Boethius Project, Oxford, August 2006: www.english.ox.ac/boethius/Symposium2006.html/
2007: 'Did King Alfred write anything?', *Medium Ævum* 71, 1–23
Godden, M. and Irvine, S. (eds.) 2009: *The Old English Boethius: An Edition of the Old English Version of Boethius' De consolatione Philosophiae*, 2 vols. (Oxford)
Godfrey, C. J. 1962: *The Church in Anglo-Saxon England* (Cambridge)
Godman, P. 1981: 'The Anglo-Latin *opus geminatum* from Aldhelm to Alcuin', *Medium Ævum* 51, 215–29
(ed.) 1982: *Alcuin, the Bishops, Kings and Saints of York* (Oxford)
(ed.) 1985: *Poetry of the Carolingian Renaissance* (London)
Gollancz, I. (ed.) 1927: *The Caedmon Manuscript of Anglo-Saxon Biblical Poetry, Junius XI in the Bodleian Library* (Oxford)
Gorman, M. 1982: 'The manuscript tradition of Eugippius's *Excerpta ex operibus Sancti Augustini*', *RB* 92, 7–32 and 229–65
1996: 'The glosses on Bede's *De temporum ratione* attributed to Byrhtferth of Ramsey', *ASE* 25, 209–32
2002: *Biblical Commentaries from the Early Middle Ages*, Millennio Medievale 32, Reprints 4 (Florence)
2004: 'The oldest lists of Latin books', *Scriptorium* 58, 48–63
Gousset, M.-T. and Stirnemann, P. 1990: 'Indications de couleur dans les manuscrits médiévaux' in Guineau 1990, 189–98
Grabar, A. and Nordenfalk, C. 1957: *Early Medieval Painting From the Fourth to the Eleventh Century* (Lausanne)
Grabowski, K. and Dumville, D. N. 1984: *Chronicles and Annals of Mediaeval Ireland and Wales: The Clonmacnoise-Group Texts* (Woodbridge)
Gradon, P. (ed.) 1977: *Cynewulf's 'Elene'*, rev. edn (Exeter)
Graham, T. 1996: 'A runic entry in an Anglo-Saxon manuscript from Abingdon and the Scandinavian career of Abbot Rodulf (1051–2)', *Nottingham Medieval Studies* 40, 16–24

1998: 'Cambridge, Corpus Christi College 57 and its Anglo-Saxon users', in *Anglo-Saxon Manuscripts and their Heritage*, ed. P. Pulsiano and E. M. Treharne (Aldershot), 21–69

Graham-Campbell, J. 1980: *Viking Artefacts: A Select Catalogue* (London)

Gransden, A. 1998: 'Some manuscripts in Cambridge from Bury St Edmunds Abbey: exhibition catalogue', in *Bury St Edmunds: Medieval Art, Architecture, Archaeology and Economy*, ed. A. Gransden, British Archaeological Association Conference Transactions 20 (London), 228–85

Grant, R. J. S. (ed.) 1982: *The Homilies from Corpus Christi College, Cambridge 41* (Ottawa)

Green, D. H. 1994: *Medieval Listening and Reading: The Primary Reception of German Literature 800–1300* (Cambridge)

Grégoire, R. 1980: *Homéliaires liturgiques médiévaux: analyse de manuscrits*, Biblioteca degli 'Studi Medievali' 12 (Spoleto)

Gregory, C. R. 1907: *Canon and Text of the New Testament* (Edinburgh)

Grémont, D. and Donnat, L. 1967: 'Fleury, le Mont Saint-Michel et l'Angleterre à la fin du xe siècle, à propos du manuscrit d'Orléans n° 127 (105)', in *Millénaire monastique du Mont Saint-Michel*, I: *Histoire et vie monastique*, ed. J. Laporte (Paris), 751–93

Gretsch, M. 1973: *Die Regula Sancti Benedicti in England und ihre altenglische Übersetzung* (Munich)

1994: 'The language of the Fonthill Letter', *ASE* 24, 57–102

1999: *The Intellectual Foundations of the English Benedictine Reform*, CSASE 25 (Cambridge)

2000: 'The Junius Psalter gloss: its historical and cultural context', *ASE* 20, 85–121

2001: 'Winchester vocabulary and standard Old English: the vernacular in late Anglo-Saxon England', *Bulletin of the John Rylands University Library of Manchester* 83, 41–87

2003: 'Cambridge, Corpus Christi College, 57: a witness to the early stage of the Benedictine reform in England?', *ASE* 32, 111–46

Grissom, C. A. 1986: 'Green earth' in Feller 1986, 141–67

Grosjean, P. 1960: 'Virgile de Salzbourg en Irlande', *Analecta Bollandiana* 78, 92–123

Gryson, R. (ed.) 2001: Bede, *Explanatio Apocalypseos*, CCLS 121A (Turnhout)

Guerreau-Jalabert, A. (ed.) 1982: Abbo de Fleury, *Quaestiones Grammaticales* (Paris)

Guineau, B. (ed.) 1990: *Pigments et colorants de l'antiquité et du moyen âge, teinture, peinture, enluminure: études historiques et physico-chimiques* (Paris)

Guineau, B. and Vezin, J. 1992: 'Étude technique des peintures du manuscrit *De laudibus sanctae crucis* conservé à la Bibliothèque municipale d'Amiens (Amiens 223)', *Scriptorium* 46, 224–37

Gullick, M. 1987: 'The great and little Domesday manuscripts', in *Domesday Book Studies*, ed. R. W. H. Erskine and A. Williams (London), 93–112

1990: 'The scribe of the Carilef Bible: a new look at some late eleventh-century Durham Cathedral manuscripts', in *Medieval Book Production: Assessing the Evidence*, ed. L. L. Brownrigg (Los Altos, CA), 61–83

1993: 'The bindings', in *Catalogue of the Manuscripts of Hereford Cathedral Library*, ed. R. A. B. Mynors and R. M. Thomson (Cambridge), xxvi–xxxii

1994: 'The scribes of the Durham Cantor's Book (Durham, Dean and Chapter Library, MS B.IV.24) and the Durham martyrology scribe', in *Anglo-Norman Durham 1093–1193*, ed. D. Rollason, M. Harvey and M. Prestwich (Woodbridge), 93–109

1996: 'The origin and date of Cambridge, Corpus Christi College, MS 163', *TCBS* 11, 89–91

1998a: 'The hand of Symeon of Durham: further observations on the Durham martyrology scribe', in *Symeon of Durham: Historian of Durham and the North*, ed. D. Rollason (Stamford), 14–31, 358–62

1998b: 'Professional scribes in eleventh- and twelfth-century England', *English Manuscript Studies* 7, 1–24

1998c: 'The scribal work of Eadmer of Canterbury to 1109', *Archaeologia Cantiana* 117, 173–89

1998d: 'The two earliest manuscripts of the *Libellus de Exordio*', in *Symeon of Durham: Historian of Durham and the North*, ed. D. Rollason (Stamford), 106–19, 358–62

1999: 'Manuscrits et copistes normands en Angleterre (XIe–XIIe siècles)' in Bouet and Dosdat 1999, 83–93

2001a: 'The bindings' in *A Descriptive Catalogue of the Medieval Manuscripts in Worcester Cathedral Library*, ed. R. M. Thomson (Cambridge), xxxviii–xlvii

2001b: 'The English-owned manuscripts of the *Collectio Lanfranci* (s. xi/xii)', in *The Legacy of M. R. James: Papers from the 1995 Cambridge Symposium*, ed. L. Dennison (Donington), 99–117

2006: 'The binding descriptions in the library catalogue from Leicester Abbey', in *Leicester Abbey: Medieval History, Archaeology and Manuscript Studies*, ed. J. Story, J. Bourne and R. Buckley (Leicester), 147–72

2007: 'The make-up of the Durham *Liber Vitae*', in *The Durham Liber Vitae. London, British Library, MS Cotton Domitian A. vii*, ed. D. and L. Rollason, 3 vols. (London), I, 43–57

2010: 'A Christ Church scribe of the late eleventh century' in *The Medieval Book: Glosses from friends and colleagues of Christopher de Hamel*, ed. J. H. Marrow, R. A. Linenthal and W. Noel (Houten), 2–10

forthcoming: 'The scribes of the Canterbury professions between 1070 and 1138'

Gullick, M. and Hadcraft, N. 2008: 'Bookbindings', in *The Cambridge History of the Book in Britain*, II: *c. 1100–1400*, ed. N. Morgan and R. M. Thomson (Cambridge), 95–109

Gullick, M. and Pfaff, R. W. 2001: 'The Dublin Pontifical (TCD 98 [B.3.6]): St Anselm's?', *Scriptorium* 55, 284–94

Gullick, M. and Rankin, S. 2009: 'Review of Hartzell 2006, *Early Music History* 28, 262–85

Gundlach, W., Dümmler, E. and Arndt, W. (eds.) 1892: *Epistolae Merowingici et Karolini Aevi*, I, MGH Epistolae (Berlin)

Günzel, B. (ed.) 1993: *Ælfwine's Prayerbook (London, British Library, Cotton Titus D. xxvi+xxvii)*, HBS 108 (London)

Gwara, S. 1995: 'His master's voice: late Latin in the Milan glosses', *Glotta* 73, 142–8

1996: *Latin Colloquies from Pre-Conquest Britain* (Toronto)

1997: 'Ælfric Bata's manuscripts', *Revue d'histoire des textes* 27, 239–55

(ed.) 2001: *S. Aldhelmi Malmesbiriensis: Prosa de virginitate cum glosa latina atque anglosaxonica*, 2 vols., CCSL 124 (Turnhout)

Gwara, S. and Porter, D. W. (eds.), 1997: *Anglo-Saxon Conversations: The Colloquies of Ælfric Bata* (Woodbridge)

Gwynn, E. (ed.) 1937: *Book of Armagh: The Patrician Documents* (Dublin)

Gwynn, J. (ed.) 1913: *Liber Ardmachanus: The Book of Armagh* (Dublin)

Haddan, A. W. and Stubbs, W. (eds.) 1869–78: *Councils and Ecclesiastical Documents relating to Great Britain and Ireland*, 3 vols. (Oxford)

Haefele, H. F. (ed.) 1959: *Notker Balbulus, Gesta Karoli Magni Imperatoris*, MGH Scriptores rerum Germanicarum, n.s. XII (Berlin)

Hall, T. N. 2004: 'Wulfstan's Latin Sermons' in Townend 2004, 93–109

Hall, T. N. and Norris, M. 2011: 'The Chrysostom texts in Bodley 516', *JTS*, n.s. 62, 161–75

Halleux, R. 1990: 'Pigments et colorants dans la *Mappae clavicula*', in Guineau 1990, 173–80

Halporn, J. W. 2002: 'After the Schools: grammar and rhetoric in Cassiodorus', in *Latin Grammar and Rhetoric: From Classical Theory to Medieval Practice*, ed. C. D. Lanham (London and New York), 48–62

(trans.) 2004: *Cassiodorus, Institutions of Divine and Secular Learning; On the Soul*, introduction by M. Vessey (Liverpool)

Hamerow, H. and MacGregor, A. (eds.) 2001: *Image and Power in the Archaeology of Early Medieval Britain* (Oxford)

Hamilton, N. E. S. A. (ed.) 1870: William of Malmesbury, *De gestis pontificum Anglorum*, RS 52 (London)

Hammond Bammel, C. P. 1993: 'Das neue Rufinfragment in irischer Schrift und die überlieferung der Rufin'schen Übersetzung der Kirchengeschichte Eusebius', in *Philologia Sacra. Biblische und patristische Studien für Hermann J. Frede und Walter Thiele zu ihrem siebzigsten Geburstag*, ed. R. Gryson, 2 vols. (Freiburg), II, 483–513

Handley, M. 2003: *Death Society and Culture: Inscriptions and Epitaphs in Gaul and Spain AD 300–750*, British Archaeological Reports, International Series 1135 (Oxford)

Hanna, R. 2002: *A Descriptive Catalogue of the Western Manuscripts of St John's College, Oxford* (Oxford)

Hansen, H. L. and Wickham, C. (eds.) 2000: *The Long Eighth Century: Production, Distribution and Demand* (Leiden)

Hanson, R. P. C. 1968: *Saint Patrick: His Origins and Career* (Oxford)

Hanson, W. S. and Conolly, R. 2002: 'Language and literacy in Roman Britain: some archaeological considerations', in *Becoming Roman, Writing Latin?*, ed. A. E. Cooley (Portsmouth, RI), 151–64

Hardwick, C. (ed.) 1858: *Historia monasterii S. Augustini Cantuariensis by Thomas of Elmham* (London)

Hardy, A., Dodd, A. and Keevill, G. D. 2003: *Ælfric's Abbey: Excavations at Eynsham Abbey, Oxfordshire 1989–92* (Oxford)

Harmer, F. 1938: 'Anglo-Saxon charters and the historian', *Bulletin of the John Rylands Library* 22, 339–67

Harris, W. V. 1989: *Ancient Literacy* (Cambridge, MA)

Hartley, E., Hawkes, J., Henig, M. and Mee, F., 2006: *Constantine the Great: York's Roman Emperor* (York)

Hartzell, K. D. 1975: 'An unknown English Benedictine gradual of the eleventh century', *ASE* 4, 131–44

1981: 'The early provenance of the Harkness Gospels', *Bulletin of Research in the Humanities* 84, 85–97

1989: 'An eleventh-century English missal fragment in the British Library', *ASE* 18, 45–97

2006: *Catalogue of Manuscripts Written or Owned in England up to 1200 Containing Music* (Woodbridge)

Harvey, A. 1991: 'The Cambridge Juvencus glosses – evidence of Hiberno-Welsh literary interaction?', in *Language Contact in the British Isles*, ed. P. S. Ureland and G. Broderick (Tübingen), 181–98

1992: 'Latin literacy and the Celtic vernaculars around the year AD 500', in *Celtic Languages and Celtic Peoples: Proceedings of the Second North-American Congress of Celtic Studies, Halifax 1989*, ed. C. J. Byrne, M. Harry and P. Ó Siadhail (Halifax, Nova Scotia), 11–26

Häse, A. (ed.) 2002: *Mittelalterliche Bücherverzeichnise aus Kloster Lorsch. Einleitung, Edition und Kommentar*, Beiträge zum Buch- und Bibliothekswesen 42 (Wiesbaden)

Hassall, M. W. C. and Tomlin, R. S. O. 1984: 'Roman Britain in 1983, II: Inscriptions', *Britannia* 15, 332–56

Haubrichs, W. 1979: *Die Kultur der Abtei Prüm zur Karolingerzeit. Studien zum Heimat des althochdeutschen Georgsliedes*, Rheinisches Archiv 105 (Bonn)

1988: *Geschichte der deutschen Literatur von den Anfängen bis zum Beginn der Neuzeit I: Von den Anfängen zum hohen Mittelalter*, Teil 1: *Die AnfängeVersuche volkssprachiger Schriftlichkeit im frühen Mittelalter (ca. 700–1050/60)* (Frankfurt am Main)

Hawthorne, J. G. and Smith, C. S. (trans.) 1979: *Theophilus, On Divers Arts*, 2nd edn (New York)

Haycock, M. 1983–4: '"Preiddeu Annwn" and the figure of Taliesin', *Studia Celtica* 18/19, 52–78

Hearne, T. (ed.) 1723: *Hemingi Chartularium Ecclesiae Wigorniensis*, 2 vols. (Oxford)

Hedfors, H. (ed.) 1932: *Compositiones uariae: Compositiones ad tingenda musiva* (Uppsala)

Hedlund, M. (ed.) 1980: *Katalog der datierten Handschriften in lateinischer Schrift vor 1600 in Schweden*, 2 vols. (Stockholm)

Heimann, A. 1966: 'Three illustrations from the Bury St Edmunds Psalter and their prototypes: notes on the iconography of some Anglo-Saxon drawings', *Journal of the Warburg and Courtauld Institutes* 29, 39–59

Hellmann, D. 1906: *Sedulius Scottus* (Munich)

Hen, Y. 1997: 'The liturgy of St Willibrord', *ASE* 26, 41–62

2001: *The Royal Patronage of Liturgy in Frankish Gaul to the Death of Charles the Bald (877)*, HBS subsidia 3 (London)

2002: 'Rome, Anglo-Saxon England and the formation of the Frankish liturgy', *RB* 112, 301–22

Henderson, G. 1987: *From Durrow to Kells: The Insular Gospel-Books 650–800* (London)

1993: 'Cassiodorus and Ezra once again' in Spearman and Higgitt, 1993, 82–91

1999: *Vision and Image in Early Christian England* (Cambridge)

Henderson, G. and Henderson, I. 2004: *The Art of the Picts: Sculpture and Metalwork in Early Medieval Scotland* (London)

Henig, M. 1979: 'Late antique book illustration and the Gallic prefecture', in *De rebus bellicis*, ed. M. W. C. Hassall and R. I. Ireland, 2 vols. (Oxford), I, 17–37

1985: 'Graeco-Roman art and Romano-British imagination', *Journal of the British Archaeological Association* 88, 1–22

1995: *The Art of Roman Britain* (London)

2002: *The Heirs of King Verica: Culture and Politics in Roman Britain* (Stroud)

Henke, T. 2005: *Fromme Bilderweltten: mittelalterliche Textilien und Handschriften im Kestner-Museum* (Hanover)

Hennig, J. 1970: '*Scottorum gloria gentis*. Erwähnungen irischer Heiliger in festländischen Liturgietexten des frühen Mittelalters', *Archiv für Kulturgeschichte* 52, 177–91

Henry, F. 1950: 'Les débuts de la miniature irlandaise', *Gazette des Beaux-Arts* 6th ser. 37, 5–34

1960: 'Remarks on the decoration of three Irish psalters', *Proceedings of the Royal Irish Academy* 61, section C, no. 2, 23–40

1965: *Irish Art in the Early Christian Period* (London)
1974: *The Book of Kells* (London)
Henry, F. and Marsh-Micheli, G. 1962: 'A century of Irish illumination', *Proceedings of the Royal Irish Academy* 62, section C, 101–64
Herben, S. J. 1935: 'The Vercelli Book : a new hypothesis', *Speculum* 10, 91–4
Herbert, J. A. 1923: *British Museum Reproductions from Illuminated Manuscripts*, series II, 3rd edn (London)
Herbert, M. 1988: *Iona, Kells and Derry: The History and Hagiography of the Monastic Familia of Columba* (Oxford)
Herity, M. and Breen, A. 2002: *The Cathach of Colum Cille: An Introduction* (Dublin)
Herren, M. W. (ed.) 1974: *Hisperica Famina I: The A-Text* (Toronto)
(ed.) 1988: *The Sacred Nectar of the Greeks: The Study of Greek in the West in the Early Middle Ages* (London)
1995: 'Virgil the Grammarian: a Spanish Jew in Ireland', *Peritia* 9, 51–71
Hesbert, R.-J. 1935: *Antiphonale missarum sextuplex* (Rome)
(ed.) 1954: *Les manuscrits musicaux de Jumièges*, Monumenta musicae sacrae 2 (Mâcon)
Heslop, T. A. 1990: 'The production of *de luxe* manuscripts and the patronage of King Cnut and Queen Emma', *ASE* 19, 151–95
2004: 'Art and the man: Archbishop Wulfstan and the York Gospels', in Townend 2004, 278–308
2007: 'Manuscript illumination at Worcester c. 1055–1065: the origins of the Pembroke Lectionary and the Caligula Troper', in *The Cambridge Illuminations: The Conference Papers*, ed. S. Panayotova (Turnhout), 65–75
Hessels, J. 1890: *An Eighth-Century Latin–Anglo-Saxon Glossary* (Cambridge)
(ed.) 1906: *A Late Eighth-Century Latin–Anglo-Saxon Glossary preserved in the Library of the Leiden University (MS Voss. Q. Lat. no. 69)* (Cambridge)
Hewitt, R. 2003: 'The sources of Asser's *Vita Elfredi Regis* (L. D.2.0)', in Fontes Anglo-Saxonici: http://fontes.english.ox.ac.uk/
Hiley, D. 1993: *Western Plainchant* (Oxford)
2001: 'The music of prose offices in honour of English saints', *Plainsong and Medieval Music* 10, 23–37
Hill, D. 1981: *An Atlas of Anglo-Saxon England* (Oxford)
Hill, J. 1992: 'Ælfric and Smaragdus', *ASE* 21, 203–37
1998: *Bede and the Benedictine Reform* (Jarrow)
2004: 'Archbishop Wulfstan: reformer?' in Townend 2004, 309–24
2006: 'Carolingian perspectives on the authority of Bede', in *Innovation and Tradition in the Writings of the Venerable Bede*, ed. S. de Gregorio (Morgantown, WV), 227–49
Hillgarth, J. N. 1961: 'The East Visigothic Spain and the Irish', in *Studia Patristica* IV, Texte und Untersuchungen 79 (Berlin), 442–56
1962: 'Visigothic Spain and early Christian Ireland', *Proceedings of the Royal Irish Academy* 62C, 167–94
1984: 'Ireland and Spain in the seventh century', *Peritia* 3, 1–16
Hilliard, P. C. 2007: 'Sacred and secular history in the writings of Bede', unpublished PhD dissertation (University of Cambridge)
Hinde, H. (ed.) 1868: *Symeonis Dunelmensis Opera et Collectanea* I, Surtees Society 51 (Durham and London)

Hine, H. M. 1992: 'The manuscript tradition of Seneca's *Naturales Quaestiones*: addenda', *Classical Quarterly* 42, 558–62

Hinkle, W. 1970: 'The gift of an Anglo-Saxon gospel book to Saint-Rémi, Reims', *Journal of the British Archaeological Association* 3rd ser. 23, 21–35

Hochadel, M. (ed.) 2002: *Commentum Oxoniense in Musicam Boethii*, Veröffentlichungen der Musikhistorischen Kommission 16 (Munich)

Hofmann, D. 1959: 'Die altsächsische Bibelepik: ein Ablegen der angelsächsischen geistlichen Epik?', *Zeitschrift für deutschen Altertum und deutsche Literatur* 89, 173–90

Hoffmann, H. 1986: *Buchkunst und Königtum im ottonischen und frühsalischen Reich*, Schriften der MGH 30, 2 vols. (Stuttgart)

Hofstetter, W. 1987: *Winchester und der spätaltenglische Sprachgebrauch* (Munich)

Hogg, R. M. 1992: 'Introduction', in *The Cambridge History of the English Language*, I: *The Beginnings to 1066*, ed. R. M. Hogg (Cambridge), 1–25

Hohler, C. 1956: 'The Durham services in honour of St Cuthbert', in *The Relics of St Cuthbert*, ed. C. F. Battiscombe (Oxford), 155–91

1972: 'The Red Book of Darley', in *Nordist Kollokvium II i latinsk liturgiforskning*. Institutionen för klassika språk vid Stockholms Universitet (Stockholm), 39–47

1980: Review of *CCCC 41: The Loricas and the Missal* by Raymond J. S. Grant, *Medium Ævum* 49, 275–8

Holder, A. G. 1999: 'The patristic sources of Bede's commentary on the Song of Songs', *Studia Patristica* 34, 370–5

Holder-Egger, O. (ed.) 1913: Einhard, *Vita Karoli*, MGH Scriptores rerum germanicarum in usum scholarum 25 (Hanover)

Hollis, S. 1977: 'The thematic structure of the Sermo Lupi', *ASE* 6, 175–97

1992–6: 'The sources of Wulfstan of York', in Fontes Anglo-Saxonici: http://fontes.english.ox.ac.uk/

(ed.) 2004: *Writing the Wilton Women: Goscelin's Legend of Edith and Liber Confortatorius* (Turnhout)

Holschneider, A. 1968: *Die Organa von Winchester* (Hildesheim)

Holthausen, F. 1916–17: 'Die Leidener Glossen', *Englische Studien* 50, 327–40

1941: '*Altenglische interlinearversionen Lateinischer Gebete und Beichten*', *Anglia* 65, 230–54

Holtz, L. 1971: 'Tradition et diffusion de l'œuvre grammaticale de Pompée, commentateur de Donat', *Revue de philologie, littérature et d'histoire ancienne* 45, 48–83

1977: 'À l'école de Donat, de saint Augustin à Bede', *Latomus* 36, 522–38

1981: *Donat et la tradition de l'enseignement grammatical: étude sur l'Ars Donati et sa diffusion (IVe–IXe siècles et édition critique)* (Paris)

1983: 'Les grammairiens hiberno-latins étaient-ils des Anglo-Saxons?', *Peritia* 2, 169–84

1984: 'Les manuscrits à gloses et à commentaires de l'antiquité à l'époque carolingienne', in *Il libro et il testo*, ed. C. Questa and R. Raffaelli (Urbino) 139–67

1997: 'Alcuin et la renaissance des arts libéraux', in *Charlemagne and his Heritage: 1200 Years of Civilisation and Science in Europe*, ed. P. Butzer, M. Kerner and W. Oberschelp (Turnhout), 45–60

2005: 'Bède et la tradition grammaticale latine', in *Bède le Vénérable entre tradition et postérité*, ed. S. Lebecq, M. Perrin and O. Szerwiniack (Lille), 9–18

Homburger, O 1957: 'Eine spätkarolingische Schule von Corbie', *Forschungen zur Kunstgeschichte und christlichen Archäologie* 3, 412–26

Houwen, L. A. J. R. and MacDonald, A. A. (eds.) 1998: *Alcuin of York: Scholar at the Carolingian Court*, Germania Latina 3, Mediaevalia Groningana 22 (Groningen)

Howard, H. 2003: *Pigments of English Medieval Wall Painting* (London)

Howe, N. 2008: *Writing the Map of Anglo-Saxon England: Essays in Cultural Geography* (New Haven, CT)

Howlett, D. R. 1975: 'The provenance, date and structure of *De abbatibus*', *Archaeologia Aeliana* 5th ser. 3, 121–30

1994a: 'Aldhelm and Irish learning', *Bulletin Du Cange* 52, 37–75

(ed.) 1994b: *Liber Epistolarum Sancti Patricii Episcopi: The Book of Letters of Saint Patrick the Bishop* (Dublin)

1995: *The Celtic Latin Tradition of Biblical Style* (Dublin)

1996: 'A possible date from Aldhelm's letter to Heahfrith', *Archivum Latinitatis Medii Aevi* 54, 99–103

1998a: *Cambro-Latin Compositions: Their Competence and Craftsmanship* (Dublin)

1998b: '*Synodus Prima Sancti Patricii*: an exercise in textual reconstruction', *Peritia* 12, 238–53

Hudson, J. (ed.) 2002–8: *Historia ecclesie Abbendonensis: The History of the Church of Abingdon*, 2 vols. (Oxford)

Hughes, A. (ed.) 1958–60: *The Portiforium of Saint Wulstan*, 2 vols., HBS 89–90 (London)

1993: 'British rhymed offices: a catalogue and commentary', in *Music in the Medieval English Liturgy: Plainsong and Mediaeval Music Society Centennial Essays*, ed. S. Rankin and D. Hiley (Oxford), 239–84

Huglo, M. 1963: 'Le domaine de la notation bretonne', *Acta musicologica* 35, 54–84

1988: *Les livres de chant liturgiques*, Typologie des sources du moyen âge occidental 52 (Turnhout)

2000: 'Grundlagen und Ansätze der mittelalterlichen Musiktheorie von der Spätantike bis zur Ottonischen Zeit', in *Die Lehre vom einstimmigen liturgischen Gesang*, Geschichte der Musiktheorie 4 (Darmstadt), 17–102

Hummer, H. 2005: *Politics and Power in Early Medieval Europe: Alsace and the Frankish Realm 600–1000* (Cambridge)

Hunt, R. W. (ed.) 1961: *Saint Dunstan's Classbook from Glastonbury: Codex Biblioth. Oxon. Auct. F. 4. 32*, Umbrae Codicum Occidentalium 4 (Amsterdam)

Hunter Blair, P. (ed.) 1959: *The Moore Bede*, EEMF 9 (Copenhagen)

1964: 'Some observations on the "Historia regum" attributed to Symeon of Durham', in *Celt and Saxon: Studies in the Early British Border*, ed. N. K. Chadwick (Cambridge), 63–118

1976: 'From Bede to Alcuin' in Bonner 1976, 239–60

1990: *The World of Bede*, 2nd edn (Cambridge)

Hurst, D. (ed.) 1955: *Bedae Venerabilis Homiliae Euangelii*, CCSL 122 (Turnhout)

1960: *Bedae Venerabilis Opera exegetica: Commentarius in Ezram et Neemiam*, CCSL 119A (Turnhout)

1962: *Bedae Venerabilis Opera II: Opera Exegetica 2. In primam partem Samuhelis Libri IIII. In Regum Librum XXX quaestiones*, CCSL 119 (Turnhout)

1969: *Bedae Venerabilis Opera II: Opera exegetica 3. In Lucae Evangelium Expositio. In Marci Evangelium Expositio*, CCSL 120 (Turnhout)

1983: *Bedae Venerabilis Opera Exegetica pars II*, CCSL 119B (Turnhout) (trans.) 1999: *Bede the Venerable: Excerpts from the Works of St Augustine on the Letters of the Blessed Apostle Paul*, Cistercian Studies Series 183 (Kalamazoo, MI)

Hurst, D. and Fraipont, J. (eds.) 1955: *Bedae Venerabilis Opera* III–IV. *Opera homiletica. Opera rhythmica*, CCSL 122 (Turnhout)

Hurst, D. and Hudson, J. E. (eds.) 1983: *Bedae Venerabilis Opera* II. *Opera Exegetica 2B. In Tobiam. In Proverbia. In Cantica Canticorum. In Habacuc*, CCSL 119B (Turnhout)

Huws, D. 1987: 'The making of *Liber Landavensis*', *National Library of Wales Journal* 25, 133–60; reprinted in Huws 2000, 123–57

1998: 'The medieval manuscripts', in *A Nation and its Books*, ed. P. H. Jones and E. Rees (Aberystwyth); reprinted in Huws 2000, 1–23

2000: *Medieval Welsh Manuscripts* (Aberystwyth)

Insley, C. 2002: 'Where did all the charters go? Anglo-Saxon charters and the new politics of the eleventh century', *ANS* 24, 109–27

Irvine, M. 1986: 'Bede the Grammarian and the scope of grammatical studies in eighth-century Northumbria', *ASE* 15, 15–44

1994: *The Making of Textual Culture, 'Grammatica' and Literary Theory 350–1100* (Cambridge)

Irvine, S. (ed.) 2004: *The Anglo-Saxon Chronicle, a Collaborative Edition*, 7: *MS E* (Cambridge)

Isaac, G. 1999: 'Readings in the history and transmission of the Goddodin', *CMCS* 37, 55–78

Jackson, K. H. 1953: *Language and History in Early Britain* (Edinburgh)

Jackson, P. and Lapidge, M. 1996: 'The contents of the Cotton-Corpus legendary', in *Holy Men and Holy Women: Old English Prose Saints' Lives and their Contexts*, ed. P. E. Szarmach (Albany, NY), 131–46

James, E. (trans.) 1985: *Gregory of Tours, Life of the Fathers* (Liverpool)

James, M. R. 1903: *The Ancient Libraries of Canterbury and Dover* (Cambridge)

1907: 'Latin writings in England to the time of Alfred', in *The Cambridge History of English Literature*, ed. A. W. Ward and A. R. Waller (Cambridge), 65–87

1912: *A Descriptive Catalogue of the Manuscripts in the Library of Corpus Christi College, Cambridge*, 2 vols. (Cambridge)

1927: 'Greek manuscripts in England before the Renaissance', *The Library* n.s. 7.4, 337–53

Jayatilaka, R. 2001: 'The sources of Orosius's history against the pagans (Cameron B.9.2)', in Fontes Anglo-Saxonici: http://fontes.english.ox.ac.uk

2003: 'The Old English Benedictine Rule: writing for women and men', *ASE* 32, 147–88

Jeauneau, E. (ed.) 1964: *Jean Scot, Homélie sur le Prologue de Jean*, Sources chrétiennes 151 (Paris)

(ed.) 1972: *Jean Scot, Commentaire sur l'évangile de Jean*, Sources chrétiennes 180 (Paris)

1975: 'L'héritage de la philosophie antique durant le haut moyen âge', *Settimane* 22, 15–54

Jenkins, D. and Owen, M. E. 1983: 'The Welsh marginalia in the Lichfield Gospels, part I', *CMCS* 5, 37–66

1984: 'The Welsh marginalia in the Lichfield Gospels, part ii: the "surrexit" memorandum', *CMCS* 7, 91–120

Johanek, P. 1985: 'Der "Aussenhandel" des Frankenreiches der merowingerzeit nach Norden und Osten im Spiegel der Schriftquellen', in *Untersuchungen zu Handel und Verkehr der vor- und frühgeschichtlichen Zeit in Mittel- und Nordeuropa*, III: *Der Handel des frühen Mittelalters*, ed. K. Düwel, H. Jankuhn, H. Siems and D. Timpe, Abhandlungen der Akademie der Wissenschaften in Göttingen, phil.-hist. Klasse, Dr Folge 150 (Göttingen), 214–54

Johnson, R. P. 1939: *Compositiones uariae ... An Introductory Study* (Urbana, IL)

Jones, C. A. 2004: 'Wulfstan's liturgical interests' in Townend 2004, 325–52
Jones, C. W. 1932: 'Bede and Vegetius', *Classical Review* 46, 248–9
(ed.) 1967: *Bedae Venerabilis Opera II: Opera exegetica 1: Libri quatuor in principium Genesis usque ad nativitatem Isaac et eiectionem Ismahelis adnotationum*, CCSL 118A (Turnhout)
(ed.) 1975: 'De orthographia', in *Bedae Venerabilis Opera I: Opera didascalia*, CCSL 123 A (Turnhout), 1–57
1976 : 'Bede's place in medieval schools', in Bonner (ed.) 1976, 261–85
1977: *Bedae Venerabilis Opera V: Opera didascalia 2, De temporum ratione* CCSL 123B (Turnhout)
Jones, C. W., Kendall, C. B., King, M. H. and Lipp, F. (eds.) 1975: *Beda Venerabilis, De orthographia, De arte metrica et de schematibus et tropis, De natura rerum*, CCSL 123A (Turnhout)
Jones, C. W. and Mommsen, T. (eds.) 1980 : *Bedae Venerabilis Opera VI, Opera didascalica 3*, CCSL 123C (Turnhout)
Jones, L. W. 1932: *The Script of Cologne from Hildebald to Hermann* (Cambridge, MA)
Jones, P. H. and Rees, E. (eds.) 1998: *A Nation and its Books* (Aberystwyth)
Jones, T. 1941–4: 'Llyfrawr "librarius"', *Bulletin of the Board of Celtic Studies* 11, 136–8
(trans.) 1952: *Brut y Tywysogion: Peniarth MS. 20 Version* (Cardiff)
Jong, M. de (ed.) 1998: *The Power of the Word: The Influence of the Bible on Early Medieval Politics, Early Medieval Europe* 7, special issue.
2000 : 'The empire as Ecclesia: Hrabanus Maurus and biblical *historia* for rulers', in *The Uses of the Past in the Early Middle Ages*, ed. Y. Hen and M. Innes (Cambridge), 191–226
Jonsson, R. 1968: *Historia: études sur la genèse des offices versifiés* (Stockholm)
1993: 'Unica in the Cotton Caligula Troper', in *Music in the Medieval English Liturgy: Plainsong and Mediaeval Music Society Centennial Essays*, ed. S. Rankin and D. Hiley (Oxford), 11–45
Jost, K. 1950: *Wulfstanstudien*, Swiss Studies in English 23 (Bern)
(ed.) 1959: *Die Institutes of Polity, Civil and Ecclesiastical*, Swiss Studies in English 47 (Bern)
Kabir, A. J. 2001: *Paradise, Death and Doomsday in Anglo-Saxon Literature*, CSASE 32 (Cambridge)
Karkov, C. E. 2006: 'Writing and having written: word and image in the Eadwig Gospels', in *Writing and Texts in Anglo-Saxon England*, ed. A. A. Rumble, Publications of the Manchester Centre for Anglo-Saxon Studies 5 (Cambridge), 44–61
2007: 'Evangelist portraits and book production in late Anglo-Saxon England', in *The Cambridge Illuminations: The Conference Papers*, ed. S. Panayotova (London), 55–63
Kauffmann, C. M. 1975: *Romanesque Manuscripts 1066–1190* (London)
Kaygusuz, I. 1986: 'Neue Inschriften aus Aenus (Enez)', *Epigraphica Anatolica* 8, 65–70
Keefer, S. L. 1996: 'Margin as archive: the liturgical marginalia of a manuscript of the Old English Bede', *Traditio* 51, 147–77
Kelly, R. 2003: *The Blickling Homilies* (New York)
Kelly, S. E. (ed.) 1996: *Charters of Shaftesbury Abbey*, Anglo-Saxon Charters 5 (Oxford)
Kemp, B. R. (ed.) 1999: *Salisbury 1078–1217*, English Episcopal Acta 18 (Oxford)
Kendall, C. B. (trans.) 2008: *Bede, On Genesis*, Translated Texts for Historians 48 (Liverpool)
Kendall, C. B., King, M. and Jones, C. W. (eds.) 1975: *Bedae Venerabilis Opera I, Opera Didascalia 1*, CCSL 123A (Turnhout)

Kendrick, T. D. 1938: *Anglo-Saxon Art to AD 900* (London)
et al. 1956–60 see Brown *et al.* 1956–60
Kennedy, A. G. 1983: 'Cnut's law code of 1018', *ASE* 11, 57–81
Ker, N. R. 1941–9: 'The provenance of the oldest manuscript of the Rule of St Benedict', *Bodleian Library Record* 2, 28–9; reprinted in Ker 1985, 131–2
1948: 'Hemming's Cartulary: a description of the two Worcester cartularies in Cotton Tiberius A. xiii', in *Studies in Medieval History Presented to Frederick Maurice Powicke*, ed. R. W. Hunt, W. A. Pantin and R. W. Southern (Oxford), 49–75; reprinted in Ker 1985, 31–59
1949: 'Old English notes signed "Coleman"', *Medium Ævum* 18, 29–31; reprinted in Ker 1985, 121–30
1956a: 'A palimpsest in the National Library of Scotland', *Edinburgh Bibliographical Society Transactions* 3 part 3, 171–8; reprinted in Ker 1985, 121–30
(ed.) 1956b: *The Pastoral Care: King Alfred's Translation of St Gregory's Regula pastoralis (MS Hatton 20 in the Bodleian Library at Oxford)*, EEMF 6 (Copenhagen)
1957: *Catalogue of Manuscripts Containing Anglo-Saxon* (Oxford) (reissued with supplement 1990)
1959: 'Three Old English texts in a Salisbury pontifical: Cotton Tiberius C. I', in *The Anglo-Saxons: Studies in Some Aspects of their History and Culture Presented to Bruce Dickins*, ed. P. Clemoes (London), 262–79
1960: *English Manuscripts in the Century after the Norman Conquest* (Oxford)
1962: 'Introduction', in *The English Text of the Ancrene Riwle: Ancrene Wisse edited from MS. Corpus Christi College Cambridge 402*, ed. J. R. R. Tolkien, EETS o.s. 249 (Oxford)
1971: 'The handwriting of Archbishop Wulfstan', in *England before the Conquest: Studies in Primary Sources Presented to Dorothy Whitelock*, ed. P. Clemoes and K. Hughes (Cambridge), 315–31; reprinted in Ker 1985, 9–26
1976: 'The beginnings of Salisbury Cathedral library', in *Medieval Learning and Literature: Essays Presented to Richard William Hunt*, ed. J. J. G. Alexander and M. T. Gibson (Oxford), 23–49; reprinted in Ker 1985, 143–73
1985: *Books, Collectors and Libraries: Studies in the Medieval Heritage*, ed. A. G. Watson (London), 131–2
Kerff, N. 1982: *Der Quadripartitus, ein Handbuch der karolingischen Kirchenreform* (Sigmaringen)
Kerlouégan, F. 1968–9: 'Essai sur la mise en nourriture et l'éducation dans les pays celtiques d'après le témoignage des textes hagiographiques latins', *Études celtiques* 12, 101–46
1987: *Le De Excidio Britanniae de Gildas: les destinées de la culture latine dans l'île de Bretagne au VIe siècle* (Paris)
Kershaw, P. 2008: 'English history and Irish readers in the Frankish world', in Fouracre and Ganz 2008, 126–51
Kéry, L. 1999: *Canonical Collections of the Early Middle Ages (ca. 400–1140): A Bibliographical Guide to the Manuscripts and Literature* (Washington, DC), 73–80
Keynes, S. D. 1985: 'King Æthelstan's books' in Lapidge and Gneuss 1985, 143–201
1986: 'The additions in Old English' in Barker 1986, 81–99
1990: 'Royal government and the written word in late Anglo-Saxon England', in *The Uses of Literacy in Early Medieval Europe*, ed. R. McKitterick (Cambridge), 226–57
1991: *Facsimiles of Anglo-Saxon Charters*, Anglo-Saxon Charters, Supplementary Series 1 (London)

1992: *Anglo-Saxon Manuscripts and Other Items of Related Interest in the Library of Trinity College, Cambridge*, Old English Newsletter Subsidia 18 (Binghamton, NY)

1996a: 'The reconstruction of a burnt Cottonian manuscript: the case of Cotton MS Otho A. I', *British Library Journal* 22, 143–201

(ed.) 1996b: *The Liber Vitae of the New Minster and Hyde Abbey Winchester: British Library Stowe 944 together with Leaves from British Library Cotton Vespasian A. viii and British Library, Cotton Titus C. xxvii*, EEMF 26 (Copenhagen)

2007: 'An abbot, an archbishop and the Viking raids of 1006–7 and 1009–12', *ASE* 36, 151–220

Keynes, S. D. and Lapidge, M. 1983: *Alfred the Great: Asser's Life of King Alfred and Other Contemporary Sources* (Harmondsworth)

Kidd, P. 2000: 'A re-examination of the date of an eleventh-century psalter from Winchester (British Library, MS Arundel 60)', in *Studies in the Illustration of the Psalter*, ed. B. Cassidy and R. M. Wright (Stamford), 42–54.

Kiernan, K. S. 1981: *Beowulf and the Beowulf Manuscript* (New Brunswick, NJ)

Kiesel, G. and Schroeder, J. (eds.) 1989: *Willibrord, Apostel der Niederlande. Gründer der Abtei Echternach. Gedenkgabe zum 1250 Todestage des angelsächsischen Missionars* (Luxembourg)

Kindschi, L. 1955: 'The Latin–Old English glossaries in Plantin-Moretus MS. 32 and British Museum MS. Additional 32246', unpublished Ph.D. dissertation (Stanford University, CA)

Kirmeier, J., Schutz, A. and Brockoff, E. 1994: *Schreibkunst: mittelalterliche Buchmalerei aus dem Kloster Seeon* (Augsburg)

Klauser, T. 1935: *Das römische Capitulare Evangeliorum. Texte und Untersuchungen zu seiner ältesten Geschichte*, I: *Typen*, Liturgiegeschichtliche Quellen und Forschungen 28 (Münster)

Knappe, G. 1994: 'On rhetoric and grammar in the *Hisperica famina*', *Journal of Medieval Latin* 4, 130–62

1996: *Traditionen der klassischen Rhetorik im angelsächsischen England* (Heidelberg)

1998: 'Classical rhetoric in Anglo-Saxon England', *ASE* 27, 5–29

Knowles, D. 1940: *The Monastic Order in England* (Cambridge) (2nd edn 1963)

Knowles, D. and Brooke, C. N. L. (eds.) 2002: *The Monastic Constitutions of Lanfranc*, 2nd edn (Oxford)

Koch, J. T. 1985–6: 'When was Welsh literature first written down?', *Studia Celtica* 20–1, 43–66

1997: *The Gododdin of Aneirin: Text and Context from Dark-Age North Britain* (Cardiff)

Koehler, W. and Mütherich, F. 1999: *Die karolingischen Miniaturen*, VI: *Die Schule von Reims* II: *Von der Mitte bis zum Ende des 9. Jahrhunderts*, 2 vols. (Berlin)

Köllner, H. 1976: *Die illuminierten Handschriften der Hessischen Landesbibliothek Fulda I: Handschriften des 6. bis 13. Jahrhunderts. Bildband* (Stuttgart)

Korhammer, P. M. 1973: 'The origin of the Bosworth Psalter', *ASE* 2, 173–87

Kottje, R. 1986: 'Die Lex Baiuvariorum – das Recht der Baiern', in *Überlieferung und Geltung normativer Texte des frühen und hohen Mittelalters*, ed. H. Mordek, Quellen und Forschungen zum Recht im Mittelalter 4 (Sigmaringen), 9–24

1987: 'Zum Geltungsbereich der Lex Alamannorum', in *Die transalpinen Verbindungen der Bayern, Alemannen und Franken bis zum 10. Jahrhundert*, ed. H. Beumann and W. Schröder, Nationen: historische und philologische Untersuchungen zur Entstehung der europäischen Nationen im Mittelalter 6 (Sigmaringen), 359–78

Kottje, R. and Zimmermann, H. (eds.) 1982: *Hrabanus Maurus: Lehrer, Abt und Bischof*, Akademie der Wissenschaften und der Literatur Mainz, Abhandlungen der Geistes- und Sozialwissenschaftlichen Klasse Einzelveröffentlichung 4 (Mainz)

Krapp, G. P. (ed.) 1906: *Andreas and the Fates of the Apostles: Two Anglo-Saxon Narrative Poems* (New York)

Krapp, G. P. and Dobbie, E. V. K. (eds.) 1936: *The Exeter Book*, Anglo-Saxon Poetic Records 3 (New York)

Kübler, B. (ed.) 1888: *Iulius Valerius Polemius, Juli Valeri Alexandri Polemi Res Gestae Alexandri Macedonis ... et epistola Alexandri ad Aristotelem* (Leipzig)

Kuhn, H. 1993: 'Verdigris and copper resinate' in Roy 1993, 131–58

Kuhn, S. M. 1948: 'From Canterbury to Lichfield', *Speculum* 23, 619–27

1957: 'Some early Mercian manuscripts', *Speculum* 32, 355–70

Kurze, F. (ed.) 1895: *Annales regni francorum*, MGH SRG 6 (Hanover)

1903: 'Über die Karolingischen Reichsannalen von 741–829 und ihre Überarbeitung', *Neues Archiv* 19, 295–339 and 28, 619–69

Kuypers, A. B. 1902: *The Prayer-book of Ædeluald the Bishop, Commonly Called the Book of Cerne* (Cambridge)

Lagarde, P. de, Morin, G. and Adriaen, M. (eds.) 1959: *Hieronymi Presbyteri Opera I, Opera exegetica 1: Hebraicae quaestiones in libro Geneseos. Liber interpretationis hebraicorum nominum. Commentarioli in psalmos. Commentarius in Ecclesiasten*, CCSL 72 (Turnhout)

Laistner, M. L. W. 1933: 'Source-marks in Bede manuscripts', *JTS* 34, 350–4

1935: 'The Library of the Venerable Bede', in *Bede, his Life, Times and Writings: Essays in Commemoration of the Twelfth Centenary of the Death*, ed. A. Hamilton Thompson (Oxford), 237–66; reprinted in Laistner 1957, 117–49

1937: 'The Latin versions of Acts known to the Venerable Bede', *Harvard Theological Review* 30, 37–50; reprinted in Laistner 1957, 150–64

1957: *The Intellectual Heritage of the Early Middle Ages: Selected Essays by M. L. W. Laistner*, ed. C. G. Starr (New York)

Lambert, P.-Y. 1982: 'Les gloses du manuscrit BN lat. 10290', *Études Celtiques* 19, 173–213

1984: '"Thirty" and "Sixty" in Brittonic', *CMCS* 8, 29–43

1987: 'Les gloses grammaticales brittoniques', *Études Celtiques* 24, 285–308

2003: 'The Old Welsh glosses on weights and measures', in *Yr hen iaith: Studies in Early Welsh*, ed. P. Russell (Aberystwyth), 103–34

Lane, A. and Campbell, E. 2000: *Dunadd: An Early Dalriadan Capital* (Oxford)

Langefeld, B. 1996: '*Regula canonicorum* or *Regula monasterialis uitae?* The Rule of Chrodegang and Archbishop Wulfred's reforms at Canterbury', *ASE* 25, 21–36

2003: *The Old English Version of the Enlarged Rule of Chrodegang*, Münchener Universitätsschriften 26 (Frankfurt)

Lapidge, M. 1973–4: 'The Welsh-Latin Poetry of Sulien's family', *Studia Celtica* 8–9, 68–106

1975: 'The hermeneutic style in tenth-century Anglo-Latin literature', *ASE* 4, 67–111

1979a: 'Aldhelm's Latin poetry and Old English verse', *Comparative Literature* 31, 209–31

1979b: 'Knowledge of the poems in the earlier period', appendix to R. W. Hunt, 'The Poems of Venantius Fortunatus in late Anglo-Saxon England', *ASE* 8, 279–95

1981: 'Some Latin poems as evidence for the reign of Athelstan', *ASE* 9, 61–98

1982: 'The study of Latin texts in late Anglo-Saxon England [1]: the evidence of Latin glosses', in *Latin and the Vernacular Languages in Early Medieval Britain*, ed. N. Brooks (Leicester), 99–140

1983: 'Ealdred of York and MS Cotton Vitellius E. xii', *Yorkshire Archaeological Journal* 55, 11–25; reprinted in Lapidge 1993a, no. 16

1984: 'Gildas's education and the Latin culture of sub-Roman Britain', in *Gildas: New Approaches*, ed. M. Lapidge and D. N. Dumville, Studies in Celtic History 5 (Woodbridge), 27–50

1985: 'Surviving booklists from Anglo-Saxon England', in *Learning and Literature in Anglo-Saxon England: Studies Presented to Peter Clemoes*, ed. M. Lapidge and H. Gneuss (Cambridge), 33–89

1986a: 'Latin learning in dark-age Wales: some prolegomena', in *Proceedings of the Seventh International Congress of Celtic Studies, Oxford 1983*, ed. D. Ellis Evans, J. G. Griffith and E. M. Jope (Oxford), 91–107

1986b: 'The school of Theodore and Hadrian', *ASE* 15, 45–72

1988a: 'A Frankish scholar in Tenth-Century England: Frithegod of Canterbury/Fredegund of Brioude', *ASE* 17, 45–65; reprinted in Lapidge 1993a, 157–81

1988b: 'The study of Greek at the school of Canterbury in the seventh century' in Herren 1988, 169–94

1990: 'Aediluulf and the school of York', in *Lateinische Kultur im VIII. Jahrhundert. Traube Gedenkschrift*, ed. A. Lehner and W. Berschin (St Ottilien); reprinted in Lapidge 1996, 381–98

(ed.) 1991: *Anglo-Saxon Litanies of the Saints*, HBS 106 (London)

1993a: *Anglo-Latin Literature 900–1066* (London and Rio Grande, OH)

1993b: *Bede the Poet*, Jarrow Lecture (Jarrow)

(ed.) 1995: *Archbishop Theodore: Commemorative Studies on his Life and Influence*, CSASE 11 (Cambridge)

1996: *Anglo-Latin Literature 600–899* (London and Rio Grande, OH)

1998: 'Byrhtferth at work', in *Words and Works: Studies in Medieval Language and Literature in Honour of Fred C. Robinson* (Toronto), 25–43

(ed.) 2003a: *The Cult of St Swithun*, Winchester Studies 4.ii (Oxford)

2003b: 'Cynewulf and the *Passio S. Iulianae*', in *Unlocking the Wordhord: Anglo-Saxon Studies in Memory of Edward B. Irving Jr.*, ed. M. C. Amodio and K. O'Brien O'Keeffe (Toronto), 147–71

2005: 'Acca of Hexham and the origin of the Old English martyrology', *Analecta Bollandiana* 123, 29–78

2006: *The Anglo-Saxon Library* (Oxford)

2007a: 'Byrhtferth of Ramsey and the *Glossae Bridferti in Bedam*', *Journal of Medieval Latin* 17, 384–400

2007b: 'The Career of Aldhelm', *ASE* 36, 15–69

(ed.) 2008: *Byrtferth of Ramsey, The Lives of St Oswald and St Ecgwine* (Oxford)

2010: 'Aldhelm and the Epinal–Erfurt Glossary', in *Aldhelm and Sherborne: Essays to Celebrate the Foundation of the Bishopric*, ed. K. Barker and N. Brooks (Oxford), 129–63.

Lapidge, M. and Dumville, D. N. (eds.) 1984: *Gildas: New Approaches* (Woodbridge)

Lapidge, M. and Gneuss, H. (eds.) 1985: *Learning and Literature in Anglo-Saxon England: Studies Presented to Peter Clemoes on the Occasion of his Sixty-Fifth birthday* (Cambridge)

Lapidge, M. and Herren, M. (trans.) 1979: *Aldhelm, The Prose Works* (Cambridge)

Lapidge, M. and Rosier, J. (trans.) 1985: *Aldhelm, The Poetic Works* (Cambridge)

Lapidge, M. and Sharpe, R. 1985: *A Bibliography of Celtic-Latin Literature 400–1200* (Dublin)

Lapidge, M. and Winterbottom, M. (eds.) 1991: *Wulfstan of Winchester: The Life of St Æthelwold* (Oxford)

Latham, R. (trans.) 1958: *Marco Polo, The Travels* (Harmondsworth)

Latham, R. E. and Howlett, D. R. (eds.) 1975–: *Dictionary of Medieval Latin from British Sources* (Oxford)

Law, V. 1979: 'The Transmission of the *Ars Bonifacii* and the *Ars Tatuini*', *Revue d'histoire des textes* 9, 281–9

1982a: *The Insular Latin Grammarians*, Studies in Celtic History 3 (Woodbridge)

1982b: 'Notes on the dating and attribution of anonymous Latin grammarians of the early Middle Ages', *Peritia* 1, 250–67

1983: 'The study of Latin grammar in eighth-century Southumbria', *ASE* 12, 43–71

1985: 'Linguistics in the earlier Middle Ages: the Insular and Carolingian grammarians', *Transactions of the Philological Society*, 171–93; reprinted in Law 1997, 70–90

1986: 'When is Donatus not Donatus? Versions, variants and new texts', *Peritia* 5, 235–61

1987: 'Ælfric's "Excerptiones de Arte Grammatica Anglice"', *Histoire Épistémologie Langage* 9, 47–71

1994: 'The study of grammar' in McKitterick 1994, 88–110; reprinted in Law 1997, 129–53

1995: *Wisdom, Authority and Grammar in the Seventh Century: Decoding Virgilius Maro Grammaticus* (Cambridge)

1997: *Grammar and Grammarians in the Early Middle Ages* (Harlow)

2003: *The History of Linguistics in Europe from Plato to 1600* (Cambridge)

Lawlor, H. J. (ed.) 1914: *The Psalter and Martyrology of Ricemarch*, 2 vols. HBS 47–8 (London)

Lawrence-Mathers, A. 2003: *Manuscripts in Northumbria in the Eleventh and Twelfth Centuries* (Woodbridge)

Lawson, M. K. 1994: 'Archbishop Wulfstan and the Homiletic Element in the Laws of Æthelred II and Cnut', in *The Reign of Cnut, King of England, Denmark and Norway*, ed. A. Rumble (Leicester), 141–64

Legge, J. W. and St John Hope, W. H. 1902: *Inventories of Christ Church, Canterbury* (London)

Lehmann, E. 1957: *Die Bibliotheksräume der deutschen Klöster im Mittelalter*, Schriften zur Kunstgeschichte 2 (Berlin)

Lehmann, P. 1908: 'Erzbischof Hildebold und die Dombibliothek von Köln', *Zentralblatt für Bibliothekswesen* 25, 153–8

1918: *Mittelalterliche Bibliotekskataloge Deutschlands und der Schweiz*, I: *Die Bistümer Konstanz und Chur* (Munich)

1932: 'Das älteste Bücherverzeichnis der Niederlände', *Het Boek* 12, 207–13

1959: *Cassiodorstudien in Erforschung des Mittelalters* (Stuttgart), 38–108

1959–62: *Erforschung des Mittelalters*, 5 vols. (Stuttgart)

Lehmann-Brockhaus, O. 1955–60: *Lateinische Schriftquellen zur Kunst in England, Wales und Schottland vom Jahre 901 bis zum Jahre 1307*, 5 vols. (Munich)

Lemps, M. de and Laslier, R. 1978: *Trésors de la Bibliothèque municipale de Reims* (Reims)

Lendinara, P. 1990: 'The Abbo Glossary in London, British Library, Cotton Domitian i', *ASE* 19, 133–49

1991: 'The world of Anglo-Saxon learning', in *The Cambridge Companion to Old English Literature*, ed. M. Godden and M. Lapidge (Cambridge), 264–81

2001: 'The glossaries in London, BL Cotton Cleopatra A. iii', in *Mittelalterliche volksprachige Glossen*, ed. R. Bergmann (Heidelberg), 189–215

Lenker, U. 1997: *Die Westsächsische Evangelienversion und die Perikopenordnungen im Angelsächsischen England*, Texte und Untersuchungen zur Englische Philologie 20 (Munich and Frankfurt)

Leo, F. (ed.) 1881: *Venantius Honorius Clementianus Fortunatus, Opera Poetica*, MGH Auctores Antiquissimi 4.1 (Berlin)

Leroquais, V. 1937: *Les pontificaux manuscrits des bibliothèques publiques de France*, 2 vols. (Paris)

Levillain, L. (ed.) 1927–35: *Loup de Ferrières, Correspondance*, 2 vols. (Paris)

Levison, W. (ed.) 1905: *Vitae Sancti Bonifatii archiepiscopi Moguntini*, MGH Scriptores rerum Germanicarum 57 (Hanover and Leipzig), 1–57

1935: 'Bede as historian', in *Bede: His Life, Times and Writings*, ed. A. H. Thompson (Oxford), 111–51

1940: 'An eighth-century poem on St Ninian', *Antiquity* 40, 280–91

1946: *England and the Continent in the Eighth Century* (Oxford)

Lewis, C. T. and Short, C. 1879/1880: *A Latin Dictionary* (Oxford)

Lewis, H. 1926–7: 'Glosau Rhydychen', *Bulletin of the Board of Celtic Studies* 3, 1–4

Leyser, K. 1983: 'Die Ottonen und Wessex', *Frühmittelalterliche Studien* 17, 73–97; English trans. in his *Communication and Power in Medieval Europe: The Carolingian and Ottonian Centuries*, ed. T. Reuter (London and Rio Grande, OH), 73–104

Liebermann, F. (ed.) 1886: 'Gerefa', *Anglia* 9, 251–66

1903–16: *Die Gesetze der Angelsachsen*, 3 vols. (Halle)

Lindsay, W. M. (ed.), 1911: *Isidori Hispalensis Episcopi Etymologiarum sive Originum Libri xx*, 2 vols. (Oxford)

1912a: 'Breton scriptoria: their Latin abbreviation symbols', *Zentralblatt für Bibliothekswesen* 29, 264–72

1912b: *Early Welsh Script*, St Andrews University Publications 10 (Oxford)

1963: *Notae latinae*, reprinted with supplement (Hildesheim)

Lindsay, W. M. and Thomson, H. M. 1921: *Ancient Lore in Medieval Latin Glossaries* (Oxford)

Ling, R. 2007: 'Inscriptions on Romano-British mosaics and wall-paintings', *Britannia* 38, 63–91

Liuzza, R. M. (ed.) 1994–2000: *The Old English Version of the Gospels*, 2 vols. EETS o.s. 304 and 314 (Oxford)

1998: 'Who read the Gospels in Old English', in *Words and Works: Essays for Fred C. Robinson*, ed. P. S. Baker and N. Howe (Toronto), 3–24

Livesey, S. S. and Rouse, R. H. 1981: 'Nimrod the astronomer', *Traditio* 37, 203–66

Lockett, L. 2002: 'An integrated re-examination of the dating of Oxford, Bodleian Library, Junius 11', *ASE* 31, 141–73

Löfstedt, B. 1987: 'Zu Bedas Evangelienkommentaren', *Arctos* 21, 61–72

1988: 'Zu Bedas Predigten', *Arctos* 22, 95–8

Logeman, H. (ed.) 1888: *The Rule of St Benet, Latin and Anglo-Saxon Interlinear Version* EETS o.s. 90 (London)

Lot, F. (ed.) 1894: Hariulf, *Cronicon centulense: Chronique de l'abbaye de St Riquier* (Paris)

Love, R. C. (ed.) 1996: *Three Anglo-Saxon Saints' Lives: Vita S. Birini, Vita et Miracula S. Kenelmi, Vita S. Rumwoldi* (Oxford)

2000a: 'The sources of Bede, *Commentarius in Genesim* (Libri I et II)', in Fontes Anglo-Saxonici: http://fontes.english.ox.ac.uk

2000b: 'The sources of Bede's *Martyrologium*', in Fontes Anglo-Saxonici: http://fontes.english.ox.ac.uk

2007: 'Bede and John Chrysostom', *Journal of Medieval Latin* 17, 72–86

Lowe, E. A. 1917–24: *The Bobbio Missal: A Gallican Mass-Book (MS Paris lat. 13246)*, 3 vols. HBS 53, 58, 61; reprinted as one vol. in 1991 (London)

1926: 'A new manuscript fragment of Bede's *Historia ecclesiastica*', *English Historical Review* 41, 244–6; reprinted in Lowe 1972, I, 221–3

1928: 'An eighth-century list of books in a Bodleian manuscript from Würzburg and its probable relation to the Laudian Acts', *Speculum* 3, 3–15; reprinted in Lowe 1972, I, 239–50

(ed.) 1934–71: *Codices Latini Antiquiores*, 11 vols. plus Supplement (Oxford)

1960: *English Uncial* (Oxford)

1972: *Palaeographical Papers 1907–1965*, ed. L. Bieler, 2 vols. (Oxford)

1991: see Lowe 1917–24

Löwe, H. (ed.) 1982: *Die Iren und Europa im früheren Mittelalter*, 2 vols. (Stuttgart)

Loyn, H. R. (ed.) 1971: *A Wulfstan Manuscript Containing Institutes, Laws and Homilies, British Museum, Cotton Nero A. I*, EEMF 17 (Copenhagen)

Lucas, P. J. 1981: 'MS Junius 11 and Malmesbury', *Scriptorium* 34, 197–220

Luce, A., Bieler L., Meyer P. and Simms, G. O. (eds.) 1960: *Evangeliorum quattuor Codex Durmachensis*, 2 vols. (Lausanne)

Luckhardt, J. and Niehoff, F. (eds.) 1995: *Heinrich der Löwe und seine Zeit*, 3 vols. (Munich)

Lutz, A. (ed.) 1981: *Die Version G der angelsächsischen Chronik* (Munich)

Lutz, C. E. 1973: 'A manuscript fragment from Bede's monastery', *Yale University Library Gazette* 48, 135–8

McBrine, P. 2008: 'The English inheritance of biblical verse', unpublished PhD dissertation (University of Toronto)

McCulloh, J. M 2000: 'Did Cynewulf use a martyrology? Reconsidering the sources of the *Fates of the Apostles*', *ASE* 29, 67–84

McDougall, I. 1995: 'Some remarks on Dorothy Bethurum's treatment of glosses in MS. Bodleian Hatton 113', *American Notes and Queries* 8, 3–4

McGurk, P. 1956: 'The Irish pocket gospel book', *Sacris Erudiri* 8, 249–70

1961: *Latin Gospel Books from AD 400 to AD 800*, Les Publications de *Scriptorium* 5 (Brussels and Paris)

1974: '*Computus Helperici*: its transmission in England in the eleventh and twelfth centuries', *Medium Ævum* 43, 1–5

1986: 'Text' in Barker 1986, 43–63

1987: 'The gospel book in Celtic lands before AD 850' in Ní Chatháin and Richter 1987, 165–89

1990: 'The Text' in Fox 1990, 37–152

1993: 'The disposition of numbers in Latin Eusebian canon tables', in *Philologia Sacra: biblische und patristische Studien für Hermann J. Frede und Walter Thiele zu ihrem siebzigsten Geburtstag*, ed. R. Gryson, Aus der Geschichte der lateinischen Bibel 24/2 (Freiburg), 242–58

1994: 'The oldest manuscripts of the Latin Bible', in *The Early Medieval Bible: Its Production, Decoration and Use*, ed. R. G. Gameson, Cambridge Studies in Palaeography and Codicology 2 (Cambridge), 1–23

McGurk, P., Dumville, D. N. and Godden, M. R. (eds.) 1983: *An Eleventh-Century Illustrated Miscellany, British Library, Cotton Tiberius B. V, part 1*, EEMF 21 (Copenhagen)

McGurk, P. and Rosenthal, J. 1995: 'The Anglo-Saxon gospel books of Judith, countess of Flanders: their text, make-up and function', *ASE* 24, 251–308

McIntosh, A. 1949: 'Wulfstan's prose', *PBA* 35, 109–42

McIntyre, E. A. 1978: 'Early twelfth-century Worcester Cathedral Priory, with special reference to some of the manuscripts written there', unpublished DPhil thesis (Oxford University)

Mackay, T. W. 1976: 'Bede's hagiographical method: his knowledge and use of Paulinus of Nola' in Bonner 1976, 77–92

McKee, H. (ed.) 2000a: *Juvencus: Codex Cantabrigiensis Ff.4.42*, 2 vols.: facsimile; text and commentary (Aberystwyth)

2000b: 'Scribes and glosses from dark age Wales: the Cambridge Juvencus manuscript', *CMCS* 39, 1–22

McKitterick, R. 1977: *The Frankish Church and the Carolingian Reforms 789–895* (London)

1985: 'Knowledge of canon law in the Frankish Kingdoms before 789: the manuscript evidence', *JTS* n.s. 36/1, 97–111; reprinted in McKitterick 1994, ch. II

1989a: 'Anglo-Saxon missionaries in Germany: reflections on the manuscript evidence', *TCBS* 9, 291–329; reprinted in McKitterick 1994, ch. VI

1989b: *The Carolingians and the Written Word* (Cambridge)

1989c: 'The diffusion of Insular culture in Neustria between 650 and 850: the implications of the manuscript evidence', in *La Neustrie: les pays au nord de la Loire de 650 à 850*, ed. H. Atsma, 2 vols, Beihefte der Francia 16, (Sigmaringen), II, 395–432; reprinted in McKitterick 1994, ch. III

1990: 'Frankish Uncial: a new context for the Echternach Scriptorium', in *Willibrord zijn wereld en zijn werk*, ed. A. Wieler and P. Bange (Nijmegen), 374–88; reprinted in McKitterick 1994, ch. V.

1991: *Anglo-Saxon Missionaries in Germany: Personal Connections and Local Influences*, Brixworth Lecture, Vaughan Paper 36 (Leicester); reprinted in McKitterick 1995b as ch. I

1992: 'Nuns' scriptoria in England and Francia in the eighth century', *Francia* 19/1, 1–35; reprinted in McKitterick 1994 as ch. VII

1993: 'Zur Herstellung von Kapitularien: die Arbeit des leges-Skriptoriums', *Mitteilungen des Instituts für Österreichische Geschichtsforschung* 101, 3–16

1994: *Books, Scribes and Learning in the Frankish Kingdoms, 6th–9th Centuries* (Aldershot)

1995a: 'Essai sur les représentations de l'écrit dans les manuscrits carolingiens', *Revue française d'histoire du livre* 86–7, 37–64

1995b: *The Frankish Kings and Culture in the Early Middle Ages* (Aldershot)

2000: 'Le Scriptorium d'Echternach aux huitième et neuvième siècles', in Polfer 2000, 499–522

2002a: 'Buch, Schrift, Urkunden und Schriftlichkeit in der Karolingerzeit', in *Vom Nutzen des Schreibens: soziales Gedächtnis, Herrschaft und Besitz*, ed. W. Pohl and P. Herold, Forschungen zur Geschichte des Mittelalter 5, Osterreichischen Akademie der Wissenschaften, phil.-hist. Klasse, Denkschriften 306 (Vienna), 97–112

2002b: 'Kulturelle Verbindungen zwischen England und den fränkischen Reichen in der Zeit der Karolinger: Kontexte und Implikationen', in *Deutschlands und der Westen Europas im Mittelalter*, ed. J. Ehlers, Vorträge und Forschungen 56 (Stuttgart), 121–48

2004: *History and Memory in the Carolingian World* (Cambridge)

2005: 'Trinity College MS B.16.3', in *The Cambridge Illuminations: One Thousand Years of Book Production in the West*, ed. P. Binski and S. Panayotova (London), 54–6

2006a: 'Insulare Schrift', in *Mensch und Schrift im frühen Mittelalter*, ed. P. Erhart and L. Hollenstein (St Gallen), 89–96

2006b: *Perceptions of the Past in the Early Middle Ages* (Notre Dame, IN)

2007: 'The migration of ideas in the early Middle Ages: ways and means', in *Storehouses of Wholesome Learning: Accumulation and Dissemination of Encyclopaedic Knowledge in the Early Middle Ages*, ed. R. Bremmer, K. Dekkers and P. Lendinara, Mediaevalia Groningana (Leuven, Paris and Stirling), 1–17

2008: *Charlemagne: The Formation of a European Identity* (Cambridge)

McManus, D. 1983: 'The chronology of Latin loan-words', *Ériu* 34, 21–71

McNamara, M. 1973: 'Psalter text and psalter study in the early Irish church (AD 600–1200)', *Proceedings of the Royal Irish Academy* 73, section C, no. 7, 201–98

1987: 'The text of the Latin Bible in the early Irish church: some data and desiderata', in Ní Chatháin and M. Richter 1987, 7–55

1990: *The Psalms in the Early Irish Church* (Sheffield)

Malone, K. (ed.) 1963: *The Nowell Codex, British Museum Cotton Vitellius A. xv, second manuscript*, EEMF 12 (Copenhagen)

Maniaci, M. 1995: 'Ricette di costruzione della pagina nei manoscritti greci e latini', *Scriptorium* 49, 16–41

Manitius, M. 1911: *Geschichte der lateinischen Literatur des Mittelalters, erster Teil: Von Justinian bis zur Mitte des Zehnten Jahrhunderts* (Munich)

Mann, G. 2004: 'The development of Wulfstan's Alcuin manuscript' in Townend 2004, 235–78

Marenbon, J. 1981: *From the Circle of Alcuin to the School of Auxerre: Logic, Theology and Philosophy in the Early Middle Ages* (Cambridge)

Markus, R. A. 1986: 'Pelagianism: Britain and the Continent', *JEH* 37, 191–204

Marrou, H. A. 1956: *A History of Education in Antiquity*, trans. G. Lamb (New York)

Marsden, R. 1994: 'The Survival of Ceolfrith's *Tobit* in a tenth-century Insular manuscript', *JTS* 45, 1–23

1995a: 'Job in his place: the Ezra Miniature in the Codex Amiatinus', *Scriptorium* 49, 3–15

1995b: *The Text of the Old Testament in Anglo-Saxon England*, CSASE 15 (Cambridge)

1995c: 'Theodore's Bible: the Pentateuch' in Lapidge 1995, 236–54

1996: 'Cain's face and other problems: the legacy of the earliest English translations', *Reformation* 1, 29–51

1998: 'Manus Bedae: Bede's contribution to Ceolfrith's Bibles', *ASE* 27, 65–86

1999: 'The Gospels of St Augustine' in Gameson 1999a, 285–312

2005: 'Latin in the ascendant: the interlinear gloss of Laud Misc. 509', in *Latin Learning and English Lore: Studies in Anglo-Saxon Literature for Michael Lapidge*, ed. K. O'Brien O'Keeffe and A. Orchard, 2 vols. (Toronto), I, 132–52

(ed.) 2008: *The Old English Heptateuch and Ælfric's Libellus de ueteri testamento et nouo*, EETS o.s. 330 (Oxford)

2011: 'Amiatinus in Italy: the afterlife of an Anglo-Saxon book' in *Anglo-Saxon England and the Continent*, ed. H. Sauer and J. Story (Tempe, AZ), 217–43

Marshall, P. K. (ed.) 1984: *Servatus Lupus, Epistulae* (Leipzig)

Mason, E. (ed.) 1988: *Westminster Abbey Charters 1066–c.1214*, London Record Society Publications 25 (London)

Mayr-Harting, H. M. R. E. 1972: *The Coming of Christianity to Anglo-Saxon England* (London); 2nd edn 1977; 3rd edn 1991

Meeder, S. 2009: 'The spread and reception of Hiberno-Latin scholarship on the Continent in the eighth and ninth centuries', unpublished PhD thesis (University of Cambridge)

Meehan, B. 1990: 'The script' in Fox 1990, 245–56

1994: *The Book of Kells: An Illustrated Introduction to the Manuscript in Trinity College, Dublin* (London)

1996: *The Book of Durrow: A Medieval Masterpiece at Trinity College, Dublin* (Dublin)

2007: *The Faddan More Psalter* (Dublin)

Meehan, B. and Cains, A. 1990: 'Direction of the spine of the calf' in Fox 1990, 183–4

Meehan, D. (ed.) 1958: Adomnán, *De locis sanctis*, Scriptores Latini Hiberniae 3 (Dublin)

Meens, R. 1994: 'A background to Augustine's mission to Anglo-Saxon England', *ASE* 21, 5–17

2001: 'The oldest manuscript witness of the *Collectio Canonum Hibernensis*', *Peritia* 14, 1–19

Meritt, H. 1941: 'Some minor ways of word-formation in Old English', *Stanford Studies in Language and Literature*, ed. H. Craig (Stanford, CA), 74–80

1945: *Old English Glosses (A Collection)* (New York)

Merrifield, M. P. 1847: *Original Treatises on the Arts of Painting*, 2 vols. (London)

Meyvaert, P. 1959: 'Les responsiones de S. Grégoire le Grand à S. Augustin de Cantorbéry', *Revue d'Histoire Ecclésiastique* 54, 879–94

1964: *Bede and Benedict Biscop*, Jarrow Lecture (Jarrow)

1979: 'Bede and the church paintings at Wearmouth-Jarrow', *ASE* 8, 63–77

1989: 'The Book of Kells and Iona', *Art Bulletin* 71, 6–19

1996: 'Bede, Cassiodorus and the Codex Amiatinus', *Speculum* 71, 827–83

2002: 'Discovering the calendar (*annalis libellus*) attached to Bede's own copy of *De temporum ratione*', *Analecta Bollandiana* 120, 1–159

2005: 'The date of Bede's *In Ezram* and his image of Ezra in the Codex Amiatinus', *Speculum* 80, 1087–1133

Micheli, P. 1999: 'What's in the cupboard? Ezra and Matthew reconsidered', in *Northumbria's Golden Age*, ed. J. Hawkes and S. Mills (Stroud), 345–58

Migne, J.-P. (ed.) 1844–64: *Patrologiae Latinae Cursus Completus*, 221 vols. (Paris)

Milde, W. 1968: *Der Bibliothekskatalog des Klosters Murbach aus dem 9. Jahrhundert. Ausgabe und Untersuchungen von Beziehungen zu Cassiodors 'Institutiones'; Euphorion, Zeitschrift für Literaturgeschichte*, Beiheft 4 (Heidelberg)

Miles, B. 2004: 'The *Carmina Rhythmica* of Athilwald : edition, translation and commentary', *Journal of Medieval Latin* 14, 73–117

Millar, E. G. 1926: *La miniature anglaise du xe au xiiie siècle* (Paris and Brussels)

Miller, S. (ed.) 2001: *Charters of the New Minster, Winchester* (Oxford)

Miner, D. 1957: *The History of Bookbinding 525–1950 AD* (Baltimore, MD)

Mohrmann, C. 1961: *The Latin of Saint Patrick: Four Lectures* (Dublin)

Mommsen, T. (ed.) 1870: *Digesta Iustiniani Augusti* (Berlin)

Mordek, H. 1969: 'Dionysio-Hadriana und Vetus gallica – historisch geordnetes und systematisches Kirchenrecht am Hofe Karls des Grossen', *Zeitschrift der Savigny Stiftung für rechtsgeschichte Kanonistische Abteilung* 55, 39–63

1975: *Kirchenrecht und Reform in Frankenreich: Die Collectio Vetus Gallica, die älteste systematische Kanonensammlung des fränkischen Gallien. Studien und Edition*, Beiträge zur Geschichte und Quellenkunde des Mittelalters 1 (Berlin and New York)

1986: *Überlieferung und Geltung normativer Texte des frühen und hohen Mittelalters* (Sigmaringen)

1995: *Biblioteca capitularium regum francorum manuscripta: Überlieferung und Traditionszusammenhang der fränkischen Herrscherlasse*, MGH Hilfsmittel 15 (Munich)

2000: *Studien zur fränkischen Herrschergesetzgebung: Aufsätze über Kapitularien und Kapitulariensammlungen ausgewält zum 60. Geburtstag* (Frankfurt am Main)

Morin, G. (ed.) 1942: *Sancti Caesarii Arelatensis opera varia* (Paris)

Morrish, J. 1982: 'An examination of literature and learning in the ninth century', unpublished DPhil dissertation (Oxford University)

1986: 'King Alfred's letter as a source on learning in England in the ninth century', in *Studies in Earlier Old English Prose*, ed. P. E. Szarmach (Albany, NY), 87–107

1988: 'Dated and datable manuscripts copied in England during the ninth century: a preliminary list', *Mediaeval Studies* 50, 512–38

Morrish Tunberg, J. 1993: 'The binding', in *The Copenhagen Wulfstan Collection*, ed. J. E. Cross and J. Morrish Tunberg, EEMF 25 (Copenhagen), 50–8

Mostert, M. 1989: *The Library of Fleury: A Provisional List of Manuscripts* (Hilversum)

Muir, B. J. (ed.) 1988: *A Pre-Conquest English Prayer-Book, BL, MSS Cotton Galba A.xiv and Nero A.ii (ff. 3–13)*, HBS 103 (London)

1994: *The Exeter Anthology of Old English Poetry*, 2 vols. (Exeter)

Murphy, G. R. 1992: *The Heliand: The Saxon Gospel* (Oxford)

Mütherich, F. (ed.) 1972: *Sakramentar von Metz* (Graz)

1986: 'The library of Otto III', in *The Role of the Book in Medieval Culture*, ed. P. Ganz, 2 vols., Bibliologia 3–4 (Turnhout), II, 11–25

Mütherich, F. and Dachs, K. 1987: *Regensburger Buchmalerei von frühkarolingischer Zeit bis zum Ausgang des Mittelalters* (Munich)

Muzerelle, D. 1989: 'Normes et recettes de mise en page dans le codex pré-carolingien', in *Les débuts du codex*, ed. A. Blanchard, Bibliologia 9 (Turnhout)

Mynors, R. A. B. (ed.) 1937: *Cassiodori senatoris Institutiones* (Oxford)

1939: *Durham Cathedral Manuscripts to the End of the Twelfth Century* (Oxford)

Mynors, R. A. B. and Thomson, R. M. 1993: *Catalogue of the Manuscripts of Hereford Cathedral Library* (Cambridge)

Mynors, R. A. B, Thomson, R. M. and Winterbottom, M. (eds.) 1998: *William of Malmesbury, Gesta Regum Anglorum* I (Oxford).

Napier, A. S. (ed.) 1894: *The History of the Holy Rood-Tree*, EETS o.s. 103 (London)

1967: *Wulfstan: Sammlung der ihm zugeschriebenen Homilien* (Berlin, 1883), reprinted with appendix by K. Ostheeren (Dublin and Zurich)

Nash-Williams, V. E. 1950: *The Early Christian Monuments of Wales* (Cardiff)

Nationes 1975, 1978, 1980, 1983, 1987 1985, 1989 1991: *Historische und philologische Untersuchungen zur Entstehung der europäischen Nationen im Mittelalter*, vols. 1–8 (Sigmaringen)

Neal, D. S. and Cosh, S. R. 2002: *Roman Mosaics of Britain*, 1: *Northern Britain* (London)

Needham, P. 1979: *Twelve Centuries of Bookbindings 400–1600* (New York)

Nees, L. 1991: *A Tainted Mantle: Hercules and the Classical Tradition at the Carolingian Court* (Philadelphia, PA)

1993: 'Ultán the scribe', *ASE* 22, 127–46

1999: 'Problems of form and function in illuminated bibles of the early medieval West', in *Imaging the Early Medieval Bible*, ed. J. Williams (University Park, PA), 122–77

2003: 'Reading Aldred's Colophon for the Lindisfarne Gospels', *Speculum* 78, 333–77

Nelson, J. L. 1980: 'The earliest Royal Ordo: some liturgical and historical aspects', in *Authority and Power: Studies in Medieval Law and Government Presented to Walter Ullmann*, ed. B. Tierney and P. Linehan (Cambridge), 29–48; reprinted in J. L. Nelson, *Politics and Ritual in Early Medieval Europe* (London, 1986), 341–60

1992: *Charles the Bald* (London)

Nelson, J. L. and Pfaff, R. W. 1995: 'Pontificals and benedictionals' in Pfaff 1995a, 87–98

Netzer, N. 1989a: 'The early scriptorium at Echternach: the state of the question', in *Willibrord: Apostel der Niederlands, Gründer der Abtei Echternach*, ed. G. Kiesel and J. Schroeder (Luxembourg), 127–34 and 312–18

1989b: 'Willibrord's Scriptorium at Echternach and its relationship to Ireland and Lindisfarne' in Bonner *et al.* 1989, 203–12

1994a: *Cultural Interplay in the Eighth Century: The Trier Gospels and the Making of a Scriptorium at Echternach*, Cambridge Studies in Palaeography and Codicology 3 (Cambridge)

1994b: 'The origin of the Beast Canon Tables in the Book of Kells reconsidered' in O'Mahoney 1994, 322–32

1995: 'Cultural amalgamation in the Stuttgart Psalter' in Bourke 1995, 119–26

1999a: 'The Book of Durrow: the Northumbrian connection', in *Northumbria's Golden Age*, ed. J. Hawkes and S. Mills (Stroud), 315–26

1999b: 'Die Arbeitsmethoden der insularen Scriptorien. Zwei Fallstudien: Lindisfarne und Echternach', in *Die Abtei Echternach 698–1998*, ed. J. Schroeder (Luxembourg), 65–83

2001: 'Style: a history of uses and abuses in the study of Insular art', in *Pattern and Purpose in Insular Art*, ed. M. Redknap, N. Edwards, S. Youngs *et al.* (Oxford), 169–78

Neuman de Vegvar, C. L. 1987: *The Northumbrian Renaissance: A Study in the Transmission of Style* (London and Toronto)

1990: 'The origin of the Genoels-Eldern ivories', *Gesta* 29, 8–24

Newman, P. 1990: 'Some medieval theologians and the wisdom tradition', *Downside Review* 108, 111–30

Newton, F. 1999: *The Scriptorium and Library at Monte Cassino 1058–1105* (Cambridge)

Ní Chatháin, P. and Richter, M. (eds.) 1984: *Irland und Europa: die Kirche im Frühmittelalter* (Stuttgart)

(eds.) 1987: *Irland und die Christenheit: Bibelstudien und Mission* (Stuttgart)

(eds.) 1996: *Ireland und Europa im früheren Mittelalter: Bildung und Literatur* (Stuttgart)

(eds.) 2002: *Ireland and Europe in the Early Middle Ages: Texts and Transmission* (Dublin)

Niederkorn-Bruck, M. 2004: 'Das Salzburger historische Martyrolog aus der Arn-Zeit und seine Bedeutung für die Textgeschichte des "Martyrologium Bedae"' in Niederkorn-Bruck and Scharer 2004, 155–71

Niederkorn-Bruck, M. and Scharer, A. (eds.) 2005: *Erzbischof Arn von Salzburg*, Veröffentlichungen des Instituts für Österreichische Geschichtsforschung 40 (Vienna and Munich)

Noel, W. 1995: *The Harley Psalter*, Cambridge Studies in Palaeography and Codicology 4 (Cambridge)

Nordenfalk, C. 1938: *Die spätantiken Kanontafeln*, 2 vols. (Göteborg)

1947: 'Before the Book of Durrow', *Acta Archaeologica* 18, 141–74

1951a: 'The beginning of book decoration', in *Essays in Honor of Georg Swarzenski*, ed. O. Goetz (Chicago–Berlin), 321–36

1951b: 'A note on the Stockholm Codex Aureus', *Nordisk Tidskrift för Bok- och Biblioteksväsen* 38–9, 145–55

1977: *Celtic and Anglo-Saxon Painting* (New York and London)

Notley, R. S. and Safrai, Z. 2005: *Eusebius, Onomasticon: A Triglott Edition with Notes and Commentary* (Leiden)

Oates, J. C. T. 1982: 'Notes on the later history of the oldest manuscript of Welsh poetry: the Cambridge Juvencus', *CMCS* 3, 81–7

O'Brien O'Keeffe, K. 1990: *Visible Song: Transitional Literacy in Old English Verse*, CSASE 4 (Cambridge)

(ed.) 2001: *The Anglo-Saxon Chronicle, A Collaborative Edition*, 5: *MS C* (Cambridge)

O'Carragain, E. O. 1994: '"Traditio Evangeliorum" and "Sustentatio": the relevance of liturgical ceremonies to the Book of Kells' in O'Mahony 1994, 398–436

Ó Corraín, D., Breatnach, L. and Breen, A. 1984: 'The Laws of the Irish', *Peritia* 3, 382–438

Ó Cróinín, D. 1982: 'Pride and prejudice', *Peritia* 1, 352–62

1983: 'The Irish Provenance of Bede's Computus', *Peritia* 2, 238–42.

1984: 'Rath Melsigi, Willibrord and the earliest Echternach manuscripts', *Peritia* 3, 17–42

1988: *Evangeliarium Epternacense, Universitätsbibliothek Augsburg, Cod.I.2.4°2*, Codices Illuminati Medii Aevi 6 (Munich)

1989a: 'Is the Augsburg Gospel Codex a Northumbrian manuscript?' in Bonner *et al.* 1989, 189–201

1989b: 'Early Echternach manuscript fragments with Old Irish glosses', in *Willibrord, Apostel der Niederlande*, ed. G. Kiesel and J. Schroeder (Luxembourg), 135–43 and 319–22

1990: 'Early Echternach fragments with Old Irish glosses' in Weiler and Bange 1990, 134–43

1994: *Psalterium Salabergae: Staatsbibliothek zu Berlin, Preussischer Kulturbesitz, MS Hamilt. 553*, Codices Illuminati Medii Aevi 30 (Munich)

1995a: *Early Medieval Ireland 400–1200* (London and New York)

1995b: 'The Salaberga Psalter', in *From the Isles of the North: Early Medieval Art in Ireland and Britain*, ed. C. Bourke (Belfast), 127–35.

2005: 'Hiberno-Latin literature to 1169', in *New History of Ireland*, ed. F. X. Martin, R. T. W. Moody and F. J. Byrne (Oxford), 371–404

O'Donnell, J. J. 1979: *Cassiodorus* (Berkeley, CA)

O'Donnell, J. R. 1976: 'Alcuin's Priscian', in *Latin Script and Letters AD 400–900: Festschrift Presented to Ludwig Bieler*, ed. J. J. O'Meara and B. Naumann (Leiden), 222–36

Ogilvy, J. D. A. 1968: *The Place of Wearmouth and Jarrow in Western Cultural History*, Jarrow Lecture (Jarrow)

Ohlgren, T. H. 1975: 'Some new light on the Old English *Caedmonian Genesis*', *Studies in Iconography* 1, 38–73

1986: *Insular and Anglo-Saxon Illuminated Manuscripts: An Iconographic Catalogue* (New York and London)

1992: *Anglo-Saxon Textual Illustration* (Kalamazoo, MI)

Okasha, E. 1984: 'An inscribed Anglo-Saxon lid from Lund', *Medieval Archaeology* 28, 181–3

1993: *Corpus of Early Christian Inscribed Stones of South-West Britain* (London)

Oliphant, R. 1966: *The Harley Latin–Old English Glossary* (The Hague)

O'Loughlin, T. 1992: 'The exegetical purpose of Adomnán's *De locis sanctis*', *CMCS* 24, 37–53

1994a: 'The Latin versions of the scriptures in use on Iona in the late seventh century', *Peritia* 8, 18–26

1994b: 'The library of Iona in the late seventh century: the evidence from Adomnán's *De locis sanctis*', *Ériu* 45, 33–52

1995: 'Dating the *De situ Hierusolimae*: the insular evidence', *RB* 105, 9–19

1997: 'Adomnán's *De locis sanctis*: a textual emendation and an additional source identification', *Ériu* 48, 37–40

2001: 'Monasteries and manuscripts: the transmission of Latin learning in early medieval Ireland', in *Information, Media and Power through the Ages*, ed. H. Morgan (Dublin), 46–64

2007: *Adomnán and the Holy Places: The Perceptions of an Insular Monk on the Location of the Biblical Drama* (London)

Olson, L. 1989: *Early Monasteries in Cornwall* (Woodbridge)

O'Mahony, F. (ed.) 1994: *The Book of Kells. Proceedings of a Conference at Trinity College, Dublin, 6–9 September 1992* (Aldershot)

Ó'Néill, P. 1998: 'The earliest drypoint glosses in Codex Usserianus Primus', in *A Miracle of Learning: Studies in Manuscripts and Irish Learning. Essays in Honour of William O'Sullivan*, ed. T. Barnard, D. Ó'Cróinín, and K. Simms (Aldershot), 1–28

(ed.) 2001: *King Alfred's Old English Prose Translation of the First Fifty Psalms*, Medieval Academy Books 104 (Cambridge, MA)

O'Neill, T. 1984: *The Irish Hand: Scribes and their Manuscripts from the Earliest Times to the Seventeenth Century* (Portlaoise)

Orchard, A. 1992a: 'After Aldhelm: the teaching and transmission of the Anglo-Latin Hexameter', *Journal of Medieval Latin* 2, 96–133

1992b: 'Crying wolf: oral style and the Sermones Lupi', *ASE* 21, 239–64

1992–3: 'Sources of Aldhelm's *Carmina ecclesiastica*, *Enigmata* and *Carmen de uirginitate*', in Fontes Anglo-Saxonici: http://fontes.english.ox.ac.uk

1993: '*Audite omnes amantes*: a hymn in Patrick's praise' in Dumville *et al.* 1993, 153–73

1994: *The Poetic Art of Aldhelm*, CSASE 8 (Cambridge)

1995a: 'Artful alliteration in Anglo-Saxon song and story', *Anglia* 113, 429–63

1995b: *Pride and Prodigies: Studies in the Monsters of the Beowulf-Manuscript* (Cambridge)

1997: 'Oral tradition', in *Approaches to Reading Old English Texts*, ed. K. O'Brien O'Keeffe (Cambridge), 101–23

2000: 'The *Hisperica famina* as literature', *Journal of Medieval Latin* 10, 1–45

2001: 'Old sources, new readings: finding the right formula for Boniface', *ASE* 30, 15–38

2003a: 'Both style and substance: the case for Cynewulf', in *Anglo-Saxon Style*, ed. C. E. Karkov and G. H. Brown (Albany, NY), 271–305

2003b: 'Latin and the vernacular languages: the creation of a bilingual textual culture', in *After Rome*, ed. T. Charles-Edwards (Oxford), 191–219

2003c: 'On editing Wulfstan', in *Early Medieval Texts and Interpretations: Studies Presented to Donald G. Scragg*, ed. E. Treharne and S. Rosser (Tempe, AZ), 311–40

2007: 'Wulfstan as reader, writer and re-writer', in *Precedent, Practice and Appropriation: The Old English Homily*, ed. A. J. Kleist, Studies in the Early Midddle Ages 17 (Turnhout), 313–43

Orchard, N. (ed.) 2002: *The Leofric Missal*, 2 vols, HBS 113–14 (London)

O'Reilly, J. 1992: 'St John as a figure of the contemplative life: text and image in the art of the Anglo-Saxon Benedictine Reform' in Ramsey *et al.* 1992, 165–85

O'Reilly, J. M. 2003: 'The art of authority', in *After Rome*, ed. T. Charles-Edwards (Oxford), 140–89

Ó Riain, P. (ed.) 1985: *Corpus Genealogiarum Sanctorum Hiberniae* (Dublin)

2006: *Feastdays of the Saints: A History of Irish Martyrologies* (Brussels)

O'Sullivan, D. 2001: 'Space, silence and shortage on Lindisfarne: the archaeology of asceticism' in Hamerow and MacGregor 2001, 33–52

O'Sullivan, W. 1985: 'Insular calligraphy: current state and problems', *Peritia* 4, 346–59

1994a: 'The Lindisfarne scriptorium: for and against', *Peritia* 8, 80–94

1994b: 'The palaeographical background to the Book of Kells' in O'Mahony 1994, 175–82

Ottermann, A. 1998: 'Das Beda-Fragment in HS frag 1 in der Stadtbibliothek Mainz: ein Beitrag zum Mainzer Skriptorium des 9. Jahrhunderts', *Philobiblon* 42, 301–6

Pächt, O. 1962: *The Rise of Pictorial Narrative in Twelfth-Century England* (Oxford)

Padberg, L. von 1995: *Mission und Christianisierung: Formen und Folgen bei Angelsachsen und Franken im 7. und 8. Jahrhundert* (Stuttgart)

Page, C. 1981: 'The Boethian Metrum "Bellum bis quinis": a new song from Saxon Canterbury', in *Boethius: His Life, Thought and Influence*, ed. M. Gibson (Oxford), 306–11

Page, R. I. 1995: *Runes and Runic Inscriptions* (Woodbridge)

1999: *An Introduction to English Runes*, 2nd edn (Woodbridge)

Palazzo, E. 1993: *Histoire des livres liturgiques: le Moyen Âge, des origines au* XIIIe *siècle* (Paris)

Paléographie musicale 2/3 1891–2: *Le répons 'Iustus ut palma' reproduit en fac-similé d'après plus de deux cents antiphonaires manuscrits d'origines diverses du* IXe *au* XVIIe *siècle* I/II (Solesmes)

Paléographie musicale 10 1909: *Antiphonale missarum sancti Gregorii,* IX–X[e] *siècle, Codex 239 de la Bibliothèque de Laon* (Tournai)

Paléographie musicale 11 1912: *Antiphonale missarum sancti Gregorii, xe siècle, Codex 47 de la Bibliothèque de Chartres* (Tournai)

Paléographie musicale 16 1955: *Le manuscrit de Mont-Renaud, xe siècle. Graduel et antiphonaire de Noyon* (Solesmes)

Parkes, M. B. 1976a: 'The handwriting of St Boniface', *Beiträge zur Geschichte der deutschen Sprache und Literatur* 98, 161–79; reprinted in Parkes 1991, 93–120

1976b: 'The palaeography of the Parker Manuscript of the Chronicle, Laws and Sedulius, and historiography at Winchester in the late ninth and tenth centuries', *ASE* 5, 149–71

1981: 'A note on MS Vatican, Bibl. Apost. Lat. 3363', in *Boethius: His Life, Thought and Influence*, ed. M. T. Gibson (Oxford), 425–7; reprinted in Parkes 1991, 259–62

1982: *The Scriptorium of Wearmouth-Jarrow*, Jarrow Lecture (Jarrow); reprinted in Parkes 1991, 93–120

1987: 'The contribution of Insular scribes of the seventh and eighth centuries to the grammar of legibility', in *Grafia e interpunzione del latino nel medioevo*, ed. A. Maierù (Rome), 15–29

1991: *Scribes, Scripts and Readers: Studies in the Communication, Presentation and Dissemination of Medieval Texts* (London and Rio Grande, OH)

1992: *Pause and Effect: An Introduction to the History of Punctuation in the West* (Aldershot)

1994: 'Latin autograph manuscripts: orthography and punctuation', in *Gli autografi medievali: problemi paleografici e filologici*, ed. P. Chiesa and L. Pinelli, Quaderni di Cultura Mediolatina 5 (Spoleto), 23–36

1997: '*Rædan, areccan, smeagan*: how the Anglo-Saxons read', *ASE* 26, 1–22

Parsons, D. 1994: 'Anglo-Saxon runes in continental manuscripts', in *Runische Schriftkultur in Kontinental-Skandinavischer und -angelsächsischer Wechselbeziehung*, ed. K. Düwel (Berlin), 194–220

2004: 'The inscriptions of Viking-age York', in *Aspects of Anglo-Scandinavian York*, ed. R. A. Hall *et al.*, The Archaeology of York, Anglo-Scandinavian York 8.4 (York), 350–6

Patterson, K. 2007: 'A Christian Virgil: the function of Virgilian references in the writings of Aldhelm', unpublished PhD dissertation (Brown University, Providence, RI)

Peden, A. 1981: 'Science and philosophy in Wales at the time of the Norman Conquest: a Macrobius manuscript from Llanbadarn', *CMCS* 2, 21–46

Pertz, G. H. (ed.) 1829: *Scriptores rerum Sangallensium. Annales, chronica et historiae aevi Carolini*, MGH Scriptores 2 (Berlin)

Petrucci, A. 1971: 'L'Onciale Romana: origini, sviluppo e diffusione di una stilizzazione grafica altomedievale (sec. VI–IX)', *Studi Medievali* 3rd ser. 12, 75–134

Petschenig, M. (ed.) 1913: Ambrose, *Expositio de psalmo* CXVIII, Corpus Scriptorum Ecclesiasticorum Latinorum 62 (Vienna)

1919: Ambrose, *Enarrationes in* XII *Psalmos Davidicos*, Corpus Scriptorum Ecclesiasticorum Latinorum 64 (Vienna)

Petzold, A. 1990: 'Colour notes in English romanesque manuscripts', *British Library Journal* 16/1, 16–25

Pfaff, R. W. 1992: 'Eadui Basan: scriptorium princeps?', in *England in the Eleventh Century: Proceedings of the 1990 Harlaxton Symposium*, ed. C. Hicks (Stamford), 167–83

(ed.) 1995a: *The Liturgical Books of Anglo-Saxon England*, Old English Newsletter, Subsidia 23 (Binghamton, NY)

1995b: 'Massbooks: sacramentaries and missals' in Pfaff 1995a, 7–34

1999: 'The "sample week" in the medieval divine office', in *Continuity and Change in Christian Worship*, ed. R. N. Swanson, *Studies in Church History* 35, special issue, 78–88

Pheifer, J. 1974: *Old English Glosses in the Épinal-Erfurt Glossary* (Oxford)

1987: 'Early Anglo-Saxon glossaries and the School of Canterbury', *ASE* 16, 17–44

Philippart, G. 1977: *Les légendiers latins et autres manuscrits hagiographiques*, Typologie des sources du moyen âge occidental (Turnhout)

Philpott, M. 1994: 'The *De iniusta uexacione Willelmi episcopi primi* and canon law in Anglo-Norman Durham', in *Anglo-Norman Durham 1093–1193*, ed. D. Rollason, M. Harvey and M. Prestwich (Woodbridge), 125–37

Picard, J.-M. 1991: *Ireland and Northern France AD 600–850* (Dublin)

2005: 'Bède et ses sources Irlandaises', in *Bède le Vénérable entre tradition et postérité*, ed. S. Lebecq, M. Perrin and O. Szerwiniack (Lille), 43–61

Pickwoad, N. 1994: 'The Conservation of CCCC MS 197B', in *Conservation and Preservation in Small Libraries*, ed. N. Hadcraft and K. Swift, Parker Library Publications (Cambridge), 114–22

Piper, P. (ed.) 1884: *Libri confraternitatum Sancti Galli, Augiensis, Fabariensis*, MGH Necrologia Germaniae, Supplementum (Hanover)

Planchart, A. E. 1977: *The Repertory of Tropes at Winchester*, 2 vols. (Princeton, NJ)

Plesters, J. 1993: 'Ultramarine blue, natural and artificial', in Roy 1993, 37–65

Plinval, G. de 1943: *Pélage, ses écrits et sa réforme* (Lausanne)

Plummer, C. (ed.) 1896: *Venerabilis Baedae Opera Historica*, 2 vols. (Oxford)

1926: 'On the colophons and marginalia of Irish scribes', *PBA* 12, 11–44

Plummer, C. and Earle, J (eds.) 1892–9: *Two of the Saxon Chronicles Parallel*, 2 vols. (Oxford) rev. edn by D. Whitelock, 1952

Pohl, W. and Diesenberger, M. (eds.) 2002: *Integration und Herrschaft: Ethnische Identitäten und soziale Organisation im Frühmittelalter*, Forschungen zur Geschichte des Mittelalters 3, Österreichische Akademie der Wissenschaften phil.-hist. Klasse Denkschriften 301 (Vienna)

Pohl. W. and Reimitz, H. (eds.) 1998: *Strategies of Distinction: The Construction of Ethnic Communities 300–800*, Transformation of the Roman World 2 (Leiden)

Polfer, M. (ed.) 2000: *L'évangélisation des régions entre Meuse et Moselle et la fondation de l'abbaye d'Echternach (Ve–IXe siècle)* (Luxembourg)

Pollard, G. 1962: 'The construction of English twelfth-century bindings', *The Library*, 5th ser. 17, 1–22

1975: 'Some Anglo-Saxon bookbindings', *The Book Collector* 24, 130–59

Pons-Sanz, S. M. 2007: *Norse-Derived Vocabulary in Late Old English Texts: Wulfstan's Work, A Case Study* (Odense)

Pope, J. C. (ed.) 1967–8: *Homilies of Ælfric: A Supplementary Collection*, 2 vols., EETS 259–60 (London)

Porter, D. W. 1994: 'The Latin syllabus in Anglo-Saxon monastic schools', *Neophililogus* 78, 463–82

2002: *Excerptiones de Prisciano: The Source for Ælfric's Latin–Old English Grammar* (Cambridge)

Powell, K. 2006: 'Meditating on men and monsters: a reconsideration of the thematic unity of the *Beowulf* manuscript', *RES* 57, 1–15

Powell, R. 1956: 'The binding', in *The Relics of St Cuthbert*, ed. C. F. Battiscombe (Oxford), 362–74

1965: 'The Lichfield St Chad's Gospels: repair and rebinding 1961–1962', *The Library* 5th series 20, 259–76

1980: 'Notes on the binding' in Verey *et al.* 1980, 108–11

Powell, R. and Waters, P. 1969: 'Technical description of the binding', in T. J. Brown, 1969, 45–65

Pradié, P. (ed.) 1999: [*Gesta abbatum Fontanellensis*] *Chronique des abbés de Fontenelle (Saint-Wandrille)*, Les Classiques de l'histoire de France au Moyen Âge 40 (Paris)

Pratt, D. 2007a: *The Political Thought of King Alfred the Great* (Cambridge)

2007b: 'Problems of authorship and audience in the writings of King Alfred the Great', in *Lay Intellectuals in the Carolingian World*, ed. P. Wormald and J. L. Nelson (Cambridge), 162–91

Prescott, A. 1987: 'The structure of English pre-Conquest benedictionals', *British Library Journal* 13, 118–58

1988: 'The text of the benedictional of St Æthelwold', in *Bishop Æthelwold*, ed. B. Yorke (Woodbridge), 119–47 (ed.) 2002: *The Benedictional of St Æthelwold: A Masterpiece of Anglo-Saxon Art* (London)

Priebsch, R. 1925: *The Heliand Manuscript Cotton Caligula A. viii in the British Museum: A Study* (Oxford)

Prinz, O. (ed.) 1993: *Die Kosmographie des Aethicus*, MGH, Quellen zur Geistesgeschichte des Mittelalters 14 (Munich)

Pryce, H. 1986: 'Early Irish canons and medieval Welsh law', *Peritia* 5, 107–27

1998a: 'The origins and the medieval period', in *A Nation and its Books*, ed. P. H. Jones and E. Rees (Aberystwyth), 1–7

(ed.) 1998b: *Literacy in Medieval Celtic Societies*, Cambridge Studies in Medieval Literature 33 (Cambridge)

Puhle, M. (ed.) 2001: *Otto der Grosse: Magdeburg und Europa*, 2 vols. (Mainz)

Pulliam, H. 2006: *Word and Image in the Book of Kells* (Dublin)

Pulsiano, P. 1994a: 'The Old English *Nomina Ventorum*', *Studia Neophililogica* 66, 15–26

1994b: 'Additional evidence for an Old English "Canterbury Vocabulary"', *Neuphilologische Mitteilungen* 95, 257–65

1995: 'Psalters' in Pfaff 1995a, 61–85

(ed.) 1999: *Old English Glossed Psalters: Psalms 1–50* (Toronto)

2001: 'Persius's *Satires* in Anglo-Saxon England', *Journal of Medieval Latin* 11 (2001), 142–55

Pyles, T. 1943: 'The pronunciation of Latin learned loan words and foreign words in Old English', *Publications of the Modern Language Association of America* 58, 891–910

Quentin, H. 1908: *Les martyrologes historiques du Moyen Âge* (Paris)

Quinn, J. 1956: 'The Minor Latin–Old English Glossaries in MS. Cotton Cleopatra A. III', unpublished Ph.D. dissertation (Stanford University, CA)

Raine, J. (ed.) 1835: *Reginaldi monachi Dunelmensis de admirandi Beati Cuthberti virtutibus*, Surtees Society 1 (Durham)

Rainey, A. R. 1973: *Mosaics in Roman Britain: A Gazetteer* (Newton Abbot)

Ramsey, N., Sparks, M. and Tatton-Brown, T. (eds.) 1992: *St Dunstan: His Life, Times and Cult* (Woodbridge)

Rand, E. K. 1929: *A Survey of the Manuscripts of Tours*, Studies in the Script of Tours 1 (Cambridge, MA)

1934: *The Earliest Book of Tours*, Studies in the Script of Tours 2 (Cambridge, MA)

Rankin, S. 1984: 'From memory to record: musical notations in manuscripts from Exeter', *ASE* 13, 97–111

1987: 'Neumatic notations in Anglo-Saxon England', in *Musicologie médiévale: Notations et séquences*, ed. M. Huglo (Paris), 129–44

2004: 'An early eleventh-century missal fragment copied by Eadwig Basan: Bodleian Library, MS. lat. liturg. D.3, fols. 4–5', *Bodleian Library Record* 19, 220–52

2005: 'Making the liturgy: Winchester scribes and their books', in *The Liturgy of the Late Anglo-Saxon Church*, ed. H. Gittos and M. Bradford Bedingfield, HBS subsidia series 5 (London)

2007: *The Winchester Troper: Introduction and Facsimile*, Early English Church Music 50 (London)

2011: 'Beyond the boundaries of Roman-Frankish chant: Alcuin's *De laude Dei* and other early medieval sources of office chants', in *City, Chant and the Topography of Early Music*, ed. M. S. Cuthbert, S. Gallagher and C. Wolff (Cambridge, MA)

Rasmussen, N. K. 1998: *Les pontificaux du haut moyen âge: genèse du livre de l'évêque*, ed. M. Haverals, Spicilegium Sacrum Lovaniense, Études et documents 49 (Leuven)

Rau, R. (ed.) 1972: *Annales Bertiniani*, Quellen zur karolingischen Reichsgeschichte (Darmstadt)

Raw, B. 1984: 'The construction of Oxford, Bodleian Library, Junius 11', *ASE* 13, 187–205

1990: *Anglo-Saxon Crucifixion Iconography*, CSASE 1 (Cambridge)

1997a: 'Alfredian piety: the Book of Nunnaminster', in *Alfred the Wise: Studies in Honour of Janet Bately on the Occasion of her Sixty-Fifth Birthday*, ed. J. Roberts and J. Nelson (Cambridge), 145–53

1997b: *Trinity and Incarnation in Anglo-Saxon Art and Thought*, CSASE 21 (Cambridge)

2004: 'A new parallel to the prayer *De tenebris* in the Book of Nunnaminster (British Library, Harley 2965, 28r–v)', *Electronic British Library Journal* 2004, article 1

Ray, R. 1987: 'Bede and Cicero', *ASE* 16, 1–15

2006: 'Who did Bede think he was?', in *Innovation and Tradition in the Writings of the Venerable Bede*, ed. S. DeGregorio (Morgantown, WV), 11–35

Raynes, E. M. 1957: 'MS. Boulogne-sur-Mer 63 and Ælfric', *Medium Ævum* 26, 65–73

Redknap, M., Lewis, J. M. and Edwards, N. M. (eds.) 2007: *A Corpus of Early Medieval Inscribed Stones and Stone Sculpture in Wales*, 3 vols. (Cardiff)

Reed, R. 1975: *The Nature and Making of Parchment* (Leeds)

Rees, B. R. 1988: *Pelagius: A Reluctant Heretic* (Woodbridge)

1991: *The Letters of Pelagius and his Followers* (Woodbridge)

Regul, J. 1969: *Die antimarcionitischen Evangelienprologe*, Aus der Geschichte der lateinischen Bibel 6 (Freiburg)

Reimitz, H. 2000: 'Ein fränkisches Geschichtsbuch aus Saint-Amand und der Codex Vindobonensis palat. 473', in *Text-Schrift-Codex. Quellenkundliche Arbeiten aus dem Institut für Österreichische Geschichtsforschung*, ed. C. Egger and H. Weigl, Mitteilungen des Instituts für Österreichische Geschichtsforschung Ergänzungsband 35 (Vienna and Munich), 34–90

2002: 'Anleitung zur Interpretation: Schrift und Genealogie in der Karolingerzeit', in *Vom Nutzen des Schreibens: Soziales Gedächtnis, Herrschaft und Besitz*, ed. W. Pohl and P. Herold, Österreichische Akademie der Wissenschaften, phil.-hist. Klasse, Denkschriften 306, Forschungen zur Geschichte des Mittelalters 5 (Vienna), 167–81

2004a: 'Der Weg zum Königtum in historiographischen Kompendien der Karolingerzeit', in *Der Dynastiewechsel von 751. Vorgeschichte, Legitimationsstrategien und Erinnerung*, ed. M. Becher and J. Jarnut (Münster), 283–326

2004b: 'Die Konkurrenz der Ursprünge in der fränkischen Historiographie', in *Die Suche nach den Ursprüngen. Von der Bedeutung des frühen Mittelalters*, ed. W. Pohl, Forschungen zur Geschichte des Mittelalters 8 (Vienna), 191–209

Reynolds, A. 2005: 'Review article. On farmers, traders and kings: archaeological reflections of social complexity in early medieval north-western Europe', *Early Medieval Europe* 13, 97–118

Reynolds, L. D. (ed.) 1983: *Texts and Transmission: A Survey of the Latin Classics* (Oxford)

Reynolds, L. D. and Wilson, N. G. 1968: *Scribes and Scholars: A Guide to the Transmission of Greek and Latin Literature* (Oxford)

Riain-Raendel, D. 1982: 'Aspects of the promotion of Irish saints' cults in medieval Germany', *Zeitschrift für celtische Philologie* 39, 1–15

Richards, M. 1973–4: 'The "Lichfield" Gospels (Book of "Saint Chad")', *National Library of Wales Journal* 118, 135–46

Riché, P. 1976: *Education and Culture in the Barbarian West, Sixth through Eighth Centuries*, trans. J. Contreni (Columbia, SC)

Richter, M. 1999: *Ireland and her Neighbours in the Seventh Century* (Dublin)

Rigg, A. and Wieland, G. 1975: 'A Canterbury classbook of the mid-eleventh century (the "Cambridge Songs" manuscript)', *ASE* 4, 113–30

Riley, H. T. (ed.) 1867–9: *Gesta abbatum monasterii Sancti Albani*, RS (London)

Ritterpusch, L. 1982: 'Einbandstudien aus der Sicht des Restaurators: Am Beispiel des Ragyndrudis-Codex', *Maltechnik-Restauro* 88, 48–50

Roberts, C. H. and Skeat, T. C. 1987: *The Birth of the Codex* (London)

Roberts, J. 2005: *Guide to Scripts used in English Writings up to 1500* (London and Toronto)

2006: 'Aldred signs off from glossing the Lindisfarne Gospels', in *Writing and Texts in Anglo-Saxon England*, ed. A. R. Rumble (Cambridge), 28–43

Robertson, A. J. (ed.) 1939: *Anglo-Saxon Charters* (Cambridge)

Robinson, F. 1973: 'Syntactical glosses in Latin manuscripts of Anglo-Saxon provenance', *Speculum* 48, 443–75

Robinson, F. C. and Stanley, E. G. (eds.) 1991: *Old English Verse Texts from Many Sources*, EEMF 23 (Copenhagen)

Robinson, P. R. 1978: 'Self-contained units in composite manuscripts of the Anglo-Saxon period', *ASE* 7, 231–38

1988: *Catalogue of Dated and Datable Manuscripts c. 737–1600 in Cambridge Libraries*, 2 vols. (Cambridge)

Roesdahl, E., Graham-Campbell, J., Connor, P. and Pearson, K. (eds.) 1981: *The Vikings in England* (York)

Roger, M. 1905: *L'enseignement des lettres classiques d'Ausone à Alcuin: introduction à l'histoire des écoles carolingiennes* (Paris)

Roger, P. and Bosc, A. 2008: 'Étude sur les couleurs employées dans des manuscrits datés du VIIIe au XIIe siècle provenant de l'abbaye de Fleury', in *Abbon, un abbé de l'an mil*, ed. A. Dufour and G. Labory (Turnhout), 415–36

Rogers, D. 1991: *The Bodleian Library and its Treasures 1320–1700* (Henley-on-Thames)

Rollason, D. 1982: *The Mildrith Legend: A Study in Early Medieval Hagiography in England* (Leicester)

(ed.) 2000: *Symeon of Durham, Libellus de exordio atque procursu istius hoc est Dunhelmensis Ecclesie* (Oxford)

2001: *Bede and Germany*, Jarrow Lecture (Jarrow)

Rollason, D., Piper, A. J. and Harvey, M. (eds.) 2004: *The Durham Liber Vitae* (Woodbridge)

Romano, F. 1993: *Biblioteca Nazionale Vittorio Emanuele III Napoli* (Florence)

Ronig, F. J. (ed.) 1993: *Egbert, Erzbischof von Trier 977–993*, 2 vols. (Trier)

Roosen-Runge, H. 1967: *Farbgebung und Technik frühmittelalterlicher Buchmalerei: Studien zu den Trakten 'Mappae Clavicula' und 'Heraclius'*, 2 vols. (Munich)

Roosen-Runge, H. and Werner, A. F. A. 1960: 'The pictorial technique of the Lindisfarne Gospels', in T. J. Brown *et al.* 1956–60, 261–77

Rosenthal, J. E. 1974: 'The historiated canon tables of the Arenberg Gospels', unpublished PhD thesis (Columbia University, NY)

1992: 'The Pontifical of St Dunstan' in Ramsey *et al.* 1992, 143–63

2005: 'The peregrinations of a thousand-year-old English gospel book (New York, PML MS M. 869)', in *Between the Picture and the Word: Manuscript Studies from the Index of Christian Art*, ed. C. Hourihane (University Park, PA), 165–79

Rosenthal, J. and McGurk, P. 2006: 'Author, symbol and word: the inspired evangelists in Judith of Flanders's Anglo-Saxon gospel-books', in *Tributes to Jonathan J. G. Alexander*, ed. S. L'Engle and G. B. Guest (London and Turnhout), 185–202

Rossi, G. B. de 1888: *La Bibbia offerta da Ceolfrido Abbate al Sepolcro di S. Pietro, Al Sommo Pontefice Leone XIII in omaggio giubilare della Biblioteca Vaticana* (Vatican City)

Roy, A. (ed.) 1993: *Artists' Pigments: A Handbook of their History and Characteristics* II (New York)

Royal Commission on Historical Monuments 1976: *Monuments in Wales, Glamorgan I, part 3: The Early Christian Period* (Cardiff)

Rule, M. (ed.) 1896: *The Missal of St. Augustine's Abbey, Canterbury, with Excerpts from the Antiphonary and Lectionary of the Same Monastery* (Cambridge)

Rumble, A. R. 1987: 'The Domesday manuscripts: scribes and scriptoria', in *Domesday Studies*, ed. J. C. Holt (Woodbridge), 79–99

2002: *Property and Piety in Early Medieval Winchester* (Oxford)

Rushforth, R. 2001: 'The prodigal fragment: Cambridge, Gonville and Caius College, 734/782a', *ASE* 30, 231–44

2007: *St Margaret's Gospel-Book: The Favourite Book of an Eleventh-Century Queen of Scots* (Oxford)

2008: *Saints in Anglo-Saxon Calendars*, HBS 117 (Woodbridge)

Ryan, M. 1983: *Treasures of Ireland. Irish Art 3000 BC–1500 AD* (Dublin)

1989: 'Church metalwork in the eighth and ninth centuries' in Youngs 1989, 125–69

Saint-Roch, P. (ed.) 1987: *Liber Sacramentorum Engolismensis, MS BN lat. 816. Le Sacramentaire Gélasien d'Angoulême*, CCSL 159C (Turnhout)

Samaran, C. and Marichal, R. (eds.) 1974: *Catalogue des manuscrits en écriture latine portant des indications de date, de lieu, ou de copiste, tome III: Bibliothèque nationale, fonds latin (nos. 8001 à 18613)*, 2 vols. (Paris)

Sanders, W. B. 1878–84: *Facsimiles of Anglo-Saxon Charters*, 3 vols. (Southampton)

Sauer, H. 2000: 'The transmission and structure of Archbishop Wulfstan's "Commonplace Book"', in *Old English Prose: Basic Readings*, ed. P. E. Szarmach (New York), 339–93

Sawyer, P. H. 1968: *Anglo-Saxon Charters: An Annotated List and Bibliography*, Royal Historical Society Guides and Handbooks 8 (London)

Sayers, J. and Watkiss, L. (eds.) 2003: Thomas of Marlborough, *History of the Abbey of Evesham* (Oxford)

Schaller, D. 1995: 'Die karolingischen Figurengedichte des Cod. Bern. 212', in his *Studien zur lateinischen Dichtung des Frühmittelalters*, Quellen und Untersuchungen zur lateinischen Philologie des Mittelalters 11 (Stuttgart), 1–26

Scharer, A. 1996: 'The writing of history at King Alfred's court', *Early Medieval Europe* 5, 177–206

2000: *Herrschaft und Repräsentation. Studien zur Hofkultur Königs Alfreds des Grossen*, Mitteilungen des Instituts für Österreichische Geschichtsforschung Ergänzungsband 36 (Vienna and Munich)

Schaumann, B. T. 1978: 'The Irish script of the MS Milan, Biblioteca Ambrosiana, S.45 sup. (ante ca. 625)', *Scriptorium* 32, 3–18

1978–9: 'Early Irish manuscripts: the art of the scribes', *Expeditio* 21, 33–47

Schieffer, T. 1954: *Winfrid-Bonifatius und die christliche Grundlegung Europas* (Freiburg)

Schilling, J. and Oosthout, H. (eds.) 1999: *Boethius, De arithmetica*, CCCM 94A (Turnhout)

Schindel, U. 1968: 'Die Quellen von Bedas Figurenlehre', *Classica et Mediaevalia* 29, 169–86

1975: *Die lateinischen Figurenlehren des 5. bis 7. Jahrhunderts und Donats Vergilkommentar* (Göttingen)

Schipper, W. 2003: 'Style and layout of Anglo-Saxon manuscripts', in *Anglo-Saxon Styles*, ed. C. E. Karkov and G. H. Brown (New York), 151–68

2007: 'The origin of the Trinity Hrabanus', in *The Cambridge Illuminations: The Conference Papers*, ed. S. Panayotova (London and Turnhout), 45–54

Schlosser, J. V. (ed.) 1892: *Schriftquellen zur Geschichte der karolingischen Kunst* (Vienna)

Schmeidler, B. (ed.) 1917: *Adam von Bremen, Hamburgische Kirchengeschichte: Magistri Adamus Bremensis Gesta Hammaburgensis ecclesiae pontificum*, MGH Scriptores Rerum Germanicarum 2 (Hanover)

Schmitt, F. S. (ed.) 1946–61: *Anselmi Opera Omnia*, 6 vols. (Edinburgh)

Schmitz, G. (ed.) 1996: *Die Kapitulariensammlung des Ansegis*, MGH Cap. Nova ser. I (Hanover)

Schmuki, K., Ochsenbein, P. and Dora, C. 1998: *Cimelia Sangallensia: Hundert Kostbarkeiten aus der Stiftsbibliothek St. Gallen* (St Gallen)

Scholla, A. 2002: '*Libri sine asseribus*. Zur Einbandtechnik: Form und Inhalt mitteleuropäischer Kopert des 8. bis 14 Jahrhunderts', unpublished PhD thesis (University of Leiden)

2003: 'Early Western limp bindings: report on a study', in *Care and Conservation of Manuscripts* 7, ed. G. Fellows-Jensen and P. Springborg, Proceedings of the Seventh International Seminar held at the Royal Library, Copenhagen 18–19 April 2002 (Copenhagen), 132–59

Schramm, P. E. 1934: 'Die Krönung bei den Westfranken und Angelsachsen von 878 bis um 1000', *Zeitschrift der Savigny Stiftung für Rechtsgeschichte, Kanonistische Abteilung* 23, 117–242; reprinted in P. E. Schramm, *Kaiser, Könige und Päpste*, 2 vols. (Stuttgart, 1968–71), I, 140–248

Schrimpf, G. 1982: *Das Werk des Johannes Scottus im Rahmen des Wissenschaftsverständnisses seiner Zeit* (Münster)

(ed.) 1996: *Mittelalterliche Bücherverzeichnisse des Klosters Fulda und andere Beiträge*, Fuldaer Studien 4 (Frankfurt-am-Main)

Schupp, F. (ed.) 1997: Abbo von Fleury, *De syllogismis hypotheticis* (Leiden, New York and Cologne)

Schwab, U. 1986: 'Il rapporto fra letteratura anglo-sassone e sassone antica – la sua ambivalenza culturale', *Settimane* 32, II, 537–46

Schweppe, H. 1997: 'Indigo and woad', in *Artists' Pigments: A Handbook of their History and Characteristics*, III, ed. E. W. Fitzhugh (Oxford), 81–107

Schweppe, H. and Roosen-Runge, H. 1986: 'Carmine-cochineal, carmine and kermes carmine' in Feller 1986, 255–83

Scott, J. (ed.) 1981: *The Early History of Glastonbury: An Edition, Translation and Study of William of Malmesbury's De antiquitate Glastonie ecclesie* (Woodbridge)

Scragg, D. G. 1985: 'The homilies of the Blickling Manuscript' in Lapidge and Gneuss 1985, 299–316

1998: *Dating and Style in Old English Composite Homilies*, H. M. Chadwick Memorial Lectures 9 (Cambridge)

2006: 'Ælfric's scribes', *Leeds Studies in English* n.s. 37, 179–89

Shannon, A. 2005: 'The eighth-century Hiberno-Latin compilation and its effect on English Benedictine Reform of the 10th and 11th centuries', *Viator* 36, 107–18

Shanzer, D. 2007: 'Bede's style: a neglected historiographical model for the style of the *Historia ecclesiastica*', in *Sources of Wisdom: Old English and Early Medieval Latin Studies in Honour of Thomas D. Hill*, ed. C. D. Wright, F. M. Biggs and T. N. Hall (Toronto), 329–52

Sharpe, R. 1984: 'Gildas as a Father of the Church', in Lapidge and Dumville 1984, 193–205

1985: 'Latin and Irish words for "book-satchel"', *Peritia* 4, 152–6

1991: 'Words and music by Goscelin of Canterbury', *Early Music* 19, 94–7

(trans.) 1995: *Adomnán of Iona, Life of St Columba* (Harmondsworth)

2003: 'The use of writs in the eleventh century', *ASE* 32, 247–91

2005a: 'King Ceadwalla's Roman epitaph', in *Latin Learning and English Lore: Studies in Anglo-Saxon Literature for Michael Lapidge*, ed. K. O'Brien O'Keeffe and A. Orchard, 2 vols. (Toronto), I, 171–93

2005b: 'The varieties of Bede's prose', in *Aspects of the Language of Latin Prose*, ed. T. Reinhardt, M. Lapidge and J. N. Adams, *PBA* 129 (Oxford), 339–55

Sharpe, R., Carley, J. P. Thomson, R. and Watson, A. G. (eds.) 1996: *English Benedictine Libraries: The Shorter Catalogues*, Corpus of British Medieval Library Catalogues 4 (London)

Sheehy, M. 1971: 'Influences of ancient Irish law on the *Collectio Canonum Hibernensis*', in *Proceedings of the Third International Congress of Medieval Canon Law, Strasbourg, 3–6 September 1968*, ed. S. Kuttner, Monumenta Iuris Canonici Ser. C, Subsidia 4 (Vatican City), 31–41

1982: 'The *Collectio Canonum Hibernensis*: a Celtic phenomenon' in Löwe 1982, 525–35

1987: 'The Bible and the *Collectio Canonum Hibernensis*', in Ní Chatháin and Richter 1987, 277–83

Sheldon-Williams, I. P. (ed.) 1968: *Iohannis Scotti Eriugenae Periphyseon (De Divisione Naturae) Liber Primus*, Scriptores Latini Hiberniae VII (Dublin)

Shepherd, G. 1990: 'English versions of the scriptures before Wyclif', in his *Poets and Prophets: Essays on Medieval Studies*, ed. T. A. Shippey and J. Pickles (Woodbridge), 59–83

Simpson, D. (ed.) 1988: Sedulius Scottus, *Collectaneum miscellaneum*, CCCM 67 (Turnhout)

Sims-Williams, P. 1982: Review of W. Davies, *Llandaff Charters* and *An Early Welsh Microcosm*, *Journal of Ecclesiastical History* 32, 124–9

1984: 'Gildas and vernacular poetry' in Lapidge and Dumville 1984, 169–92

1990: *Religion and Literature in Western England 600–800*, CSASE 3 (Cambridge)

1991: 'The emergence of Old Welsh, Cornish and Breton orthography 600–800: the evidence of archaic Old Welsh', *Bulletin of the Board of Celtic Studies* 38, 20–86

1998: 'The uses of writing in early medieval Wales', in *Literacy in Medieval Celtic Societies*, ed. H. Pryce (Cambridge), 15–38

2002: 'The five languages of Wales in the pre-Norman inscriptions', *CMCS* 44, 1–36

2005: 'A new Brittonic gloss on Boethius: *ud rocashaas*', *CMCS* 50, 77–86

Sisam, C. (ed.) 1976: *The Vercelli Book (Vercelli, Biblioteca Capitolare,* CXVII*)*, EEMF 19 (Copenhagen)

Sisam, C. and Sisam, K. (eds.) 1959: *The Salisbury Psalter*, EETS o.s. 242 (London)

Sisam, K. 1953: *Studies in the History of Old English Literature* (Oxford)

1957: 'Canterbury, Lichfield and the Vespasian Psalter', *Review of English Studies* n.s. 7, 1–10 and 113–31; and n.s. 8, 372

Skeat, W. W. (ed.) 1881–1900: *Ælfric's Lives of Saints*, 4 vols., EETS o.s. 76, 82, 94, 114 (London)

Smetana, C. L. 1959: 'Ælfric and the early medieval homiliary', *Traditio* 15, 163–204

1978: 'Paul the Deacon's patristic anthology', in *The Old English Homily and its Backgrounds*, ed. P. E. Szarmach and B. F. Huppé (Albany, NY), 75–97

Smith, C. S. and Hawthorne, J. G. 1974: *Mappae clavicula: A Little Key to the World of Medieval Techniques*, Transactions of the American Philosophical Society n.s. 64/4 (Philadelphia)

Smyth, M. 1996: *Understanding the Universe in Seventh-Century Ireland*, Studies in Celtic History 15 (Woodbridge)

Spawforth, A. J. S. 1986: review of O. Andrei, *A. Claudius Charax di Pergamo* (1984), *JRS* 76, 327–8

Speake, G. 1980: *Anglo-Saxon Animal Art* (Oxford)

Spearman, R. M. and Higgitt, J. (eds.) 1993: *The Age of Migrating Ideas: Early Medieval Art in Northern Britain and Ireland* (Edinburgh and Stroud)

Spilling, H. 1978: 'Angelsächische Schrift in Fulda', in *Von der Klosterbibliothek zur Landesbibliothek: Beiträge zum zweihundertjährigen Bestehen der Hessischen Landesbibliothek Fulda*, ed. A. Brall (Stuttgart), 47–98

1982: 'Das Fuldaer Skriptorium zur Zeit Hrabanus Maurus' in Kottje and Zimmermann 1982, 165–81

Stafford, P. 1981: 'The king's wife in Wessex', *Past and Present* 91, 5–27

1983: *Queens, Concubines and Dowagers: The King's Wife in the Early Middle Ages* (Athens, GA)

Stancliffe, C. 1983: 'Kings who opted out', in *Ideal and Reality in Frankish and Anglo-Saxon Society*, ed. P. Wormald with D. Bullough and R. Collins (Oxford), 154–76

1999: 'The British Church and the Mission of St Augustine' in Gameson (ed.) 1999a, 107–51

Stanley, E. G. 2004: 'Wulfstan and Ælfric: "the true difference between the law and the gospel"' in Townend 2004, 429–41

Stansbury, M. 1999: 'Source-marks in Bede's biblical commentaries', in *Northumbria's Golden Age*, ed. J. Hawkes and S. Mills (Stroud), 383–9

Stanton, R. 2002: *The Culture of Translation in Anglo-Saxon England* (Cambridge)

Stevenson, J. (ed.) 1858: *Chronicon Monasterii de Abingdon*, 2 vols., RS (London)

Stevenson, J. 1990: 'Literacy in Ireland: the evidence of the Patrick dossier in the Book of Armagh', in *The Uses of Literacy in Early Medieval Europe*, ed. R. McKitterick (Cambridge), 11–35

1999: 'Altus prosator', *Celtica* 23, 326–68

Stevenson, W. H. (ed.) 1904: *Asser's Life of King Alfred, Together with the Annals of St Neots Erroneously Ascribed to Asser* (Oxford)

(ed.) 1929: *Early Scholastic Colloquies* (Oxford)

Stevick, R. D. 1987: 'The St Cuthbert Gospel binding and Insular design', *Artibus et Historiae* 15, 9–19

1994: *The Earliest Irish and English Book Arts* (Philadelphia, PA)

Stiegmann, C. and Wemhoff, M. (eds.) 2006: *Canossa 1077. Erschütterung der Welt. Geschichte, Kunst und Kultur am Aufgang der Romanik*, 2 vols. (Munich)

Stokes, P. A. 2006: 'English Vernacular Script ca. 990–ca. 1035', unpublished PhD thesis (University of Cambridge)

Stokes, W. 1860–1: 'Cambrica I: The Welsh glosses and verse in the Cambridge Codex of Juvencus', *Transactions of the Philological Society*, 204–32

(ed.) 1905: *The Martyrology of Oengus the Culdee* (London)

Stokes, W. and Strachan, J. 1901–3: *Thesaurus Palaeohibernicus* (Cambridge)

Story, J. 1999: 'Cathwulf, kingship and the royal abbey of Saint Denis', *Speculum* 74, 1–21

2003: *Carolingian Connections: Anglo-Saxon England and Carolingian Francia c. 750–870* (Aldershot)

2005: 'The Frankish Annals of Lindisfarne and Kent', *ASE* 34, 59–110

Stryker, W. 1951: 'The Latin–Old English Glossary in MS. Cotton Cleopatra A. III', unpublished Ph.D. dissertation (Stanford University, CA)

Stubbs, W. (ed.) 1874: *The Memorials of St Dunstan, Archbishop of Canterbury*, RS (London)

(ed.) 1880: *The Historical Works of Gervase of Canterbury*, 2 vols. RS (London)

Sweet, H. (ed.) 1871–2: *King Alfred's West-Saxon Version of Gregory's Pastoral Care*, 2 vols., EETS o.s. 45 and 50 (London)

1883: *The Epinal Glossary, Latin and Old English of the Eighth Century* (London)

Syme, R. 1984: 'The *patria* of Juvenal', in his *Roman Papers*, III (Oxford), 1120–34

Symons, T. (ed.) 1953: *Regularis Concordia Anglicae Nationis Monachorum Sanctimonialumque* (Edinburgh and London)

Szarmach, P. (ed.) 1981: *Vercelli Homilies IX–XXIII* (Toronto)

Szirmai, J. A. 1999: *The Archaeology of Medieval Bookbinding* (Aldershot)

Talbot, C. H. 1954: *The Anglo-Saxon Missionaries in Germany* (New York)

1955: 'The *Liber Confortatorius of Goscelin of Saint-Bertin*', *Studia Anselmiana* 37, 1–117

(ed.) 1959: *The Life of Christina of Markyate* (Oxford)

Tangl, M. (ed.) 1916: *S. Bonifatii et Lulli Epistolae: Die Briefe des Heiligen Bonifatius und Lullus*, MGH Epistulae selectae I (Berlin), 2nd edn 1955

Tangl, M. 1966: *Das Mittelalter in Quellenkunde und Diplomatik, Ausgewählte Schriften*, 1, Forschungen zur mittelalterlichen Geschichte 12 (Berlin)

Taylor, S. (ed.) 1983: *The Anglo-Saxon Chronicle: a Collaborative Edition 4: MS B* (Cambridge)

Teeuwen, M. 2003: *The Vocabulary of Intellectual Life in the Middle Ages* (Turnhout)

Temple, E. 1976: *Anglo-Saxon Manuscripts 900–1066*, A Survey of Manuscripts Illuminated in the British Isles 2 (London)

Teviotdale, E. 1991: 'The Cotton Troper (London, British Library, Cotton MS Caligula A. xiv, ff. 1–36): a study of an illustrated English troper of the eleventh century', unpublished PhD dissertation (University of North Carolina, Chapel Hill)

1995: 'Tropers' in Pfaff 1995a, 39–44

Thacker, A. 1996: 'Bede and the Irish', in *Beda Venerabilis: Historian, Monk and Northumbrian*, ed. L. A. J. R. Houwen and A. A. MacDonald (Groningen), 31–59

Thacker, A. and Sharpe, R. (eds.) 2002: *Local Saints and Local Churches in the Early Medieval West* (Oxford)

Thomas, C. 1981: *Christianity in Roman Britain to AD 500* (London)

Thomas, C. and Howlett, D. 2003: '*Vita Sancti Paterni*: the life of Saint Padarn and the Original Miniu', *Trivium* 33, special issue

Thomas, K. 1986: 'The meaning of literacy in early modern England', in *The Written Word: Literacy in Transition, Wolfson College Lectures 1985*, ed. G. Baumann (Oxford), 97–131

Thompson, A. H. (ed.) 1923: *Liber Vitae Ecclesiae Dunelmensis, A Collotype Facsimile*, Surtees Society 136 (Durham)

Thompson, D. V. 1932: 'The *De clarea* of the so-called "Anonymous Bernensis": MS Berne A. 91.17', *Technical Studies* 1, 9–19 and 69–81.

1936: *The Materials of Medieval Painting* (London)

Thompson, E. A. 1984: *Germanus of Auxerre and the End of Roman Britain* (Woodbridge)

Thompson, E. M. 1912: *An Introduction to Greek and Latin Palaeography* (Oxford)

Thomson, R. M. 1972: 'The library of Bury St Edmunds Abbey in the eleventh and twelfth centuries', *Speculum* 47, 617–45

1985: *Manuscripts from St Albans Abbey 1066–1235*, 2 vols., rev. edn (Woodbridge)

1989: *Catalogue of the Manuscripts of Lincoln Cathedral Chapter Library* (Woodbridge)

2001: *A Descriptive Catalogue of the Medieval Manuscripts in Worcester Cathedral Library* (Woodbridge)

2006: *Books and Learning in Twelfth-Century England: The Ending of 'Alter Orbis'* (Walkern)

Thornbury, E. V. 2007: 'Aldhelm's rejection of the muses and the mechanics of poetic inspiration in early Anglo-Saxon England', *ASE* 37, 71–92

Thorpe, B. (ed.) 1844–6: *The Homilies of the Anglo-Saxon Church*, 2 vols. (London)

Thorpe, J. (ed.) 1769: *Registrum Roffense* (London)

Thurn, H. 1977: 'M.p.th.f.185 der Universitätsbibliothek Würzburg, ein unbearbeiteter karolingischer Textzeuge von Ciceros *De inventione*', *Würzburger Jahrbücher für die Altertumswissenschaft* NF 3, 227–30

Thurneysen, R. 1927: 'Introduction to the Senchas Már', *Zeitschrift für celtische Philologie* 16, 302–70

Tibbetts, T. N. S. 2003: 'Uses of the psalter in Carolingian St Gallen', unpublished PhD dissertation (University of Cambridge)

Tinti, F. 2002: 'From episcopal conception to monastic compilation: Hemming's Cartulary in context', *Early Medieval Europe* 11, 233–61

Tischler, M. 2002: *Einharts Vita Karoli: Studien zur Entstehung. Überlieferung und Rezeption*, MGH Schriften 48 (Hanover)

Tite, M., Bimson, M. and Cowell, M. 1982: 'Technical examination of Egyptian blue', *Archaeological Chemistry* 3, 215–37

Tomlin, R. S. O. 1987: 'Was Ancient British Celtic ever a written language? Two texts from Roman Bath', *Bulletin of the Board of Celtic Studies* 34, 18–25

1988: *Tabellae Sulis: Roman Inscribed Tablets of Tin and Lead from the Sacred Spring at Bath* (Oxford); also published as 'The Curse Tablets', in *The Temple of Sulis Minerva at Bath*, II: *The Finds from the Sacred Spring*, ed. B. Cunliffe (Oxford), 59–277

1992: 'The Twentieth Legion at Wroxeter and Carlisle in the first century: the epigraphic evidence', *Britannia* 23, 141–58

1993: 'The inscribed lead tablets: an interim report', in *The Uley Shrines: Excavations of a Ritual Complex on West Hill, Uley, Gloucestershire 1977–9*, ed. A. Woodward and P. Leach (London), 113–30

1996a: 'A five-acre wood in Roman Kent', in *Interpreting Roman London*, ed. J. Bird, M. Hassall and H. Sheldon (Oxford), 209–15

1996b: 'The Vindolanda tablets', *Britannia* 27, 459–63

1998: 'Roman manuscripts from Carlisle: the ink-written tablets', *Britannia* 29, 31–84

2001: 'A Roman will from North Wales', *Archaeologia Cambrensis* 150, 143–56

2002: 'Writing to the gods in Britain', in *Becoming Roman, Writing Latin? Literacy and Epigraphy in the Roman West*, ed. A. E. Cooley (Portsmouth, RI), 165–79

2003: '"The Girl in Question": a new text from Roman London', *Britannia* 34, 41–51

2004: 'A bilingual Roman charm for health and victory', *Zeitschrift für Papyrologie und Epigraphik* 149, 259–66

2008: 'Special delivery: a Greco-Roman gold amulet for healthy childbirth', *Zeitschrift für Papyrologie und Epigraphik* 167, 219–24

2009: 'Writing and communication', in *Artefacts in Roman Britain: Their Purpose and Use*, ed. L. Allason-Jones (Cambridge), 133–52

Toon, T. E. 1992: 'Old English dialects', in *The Cambridge History of the English Language*, I: *The Beginnings to 1066*, ed. R. M. Hogg (Cambridge), 409–51

Townend, M. (ed.) 2004: *Wulfstan, Archbishop of York*. Proceedings of the Second Alcuin Conference, Studies in the Early Middle Ages 10 (Turnhout)

Toynbee, J. M. C. 1964: *Art in Britain under the Romans* (Oxford)

Traube, L. 1907: *Nomina Sacra* (Oxford)

1920: 'Perrona Scottorum' in L. Traube, *Vorlesungen und Abhandlungen*, 2: *Kleine Schriften* (Munich)

Treharne, E. M. 2003: 'Producing a library in late Anglo-Saxon England: Exeter 1050–1072', *Review of English Studies* 54 (214), 155–72

2008: 'English in the post-Conquest period', in *A Companion to Anglo-Saxon Literature*, ed. P. Pulsiano and E. Treharne, 2nd edn (Oxford), 403–14

Tremp, E. 1991: *Die Überlieferung der Vita Hludowici imperatoris des Astronomus*, MGH Studien und Texte 1 (Hanover)

Tschichold, J. 1965: 'Non-arbitrary proportions of page and type area', in *Calligraphy and Palaeography: Essays Presented to Alfred Fairbank on his 70th Birthday*, ed. A. S. Osley (London), 179–91

Turner, C. H. 1916a: 'The churches at Winchester in the early eleventh century', *JTS* 17, 65–8

1916b: *Early Worcester Manuscripts* (Oxford)

Turner, D. H. (ed.) 1962: *The Missal of the New Minster, Winchester (Le Havre, Bibliothèque Municipale, MS 330)*, HBS 93 (London and Leighton Buzzard)

Tweddle, D., Biddle, M. and Kjølbye-Biddle, B. 1995: *Corpus of Anglo-Saxon Stone Sculpture*, IV: *South-East England* (London)

Ure, J. M. (ed.) 1957: *The Benedictine Office: An Old English Text* (Edinburgh)

Van de Vyver, A. 1935: 'Les œuvres inédites d'Abbon de Fleury', *RB* 47, 123–69

Van der Horst, K. and Engelbregt, J. H. A. (eds.) 1984: *Utrecht Psalter: Vollständige Faksimile-Ausgabe im Originalformat der Handschrift 32 aus dem Besitz der Bibliotheek der Rijksuniversiteit Utrecht*, Codices Selecti 75 (Graz)

Van der Horst, K., Noel, W. and Wüstefeld, W. (eds.) 1996: *The Utrecht Psalter in Medieval Art* (Utrecht)

Van der Walt, A. 1986: 'Reflections of the Benedictine Rule in Bede's Homiliary', *JEH* 37, 367–76

Van Deusen, N. (ed.) 1999: *The Place of the Psalms in the Intellectual Culture of the Middle Ages* (Albany, NY)

Van Duzer, C. 2004: *Floating Island: A Global Bibliography* (Los Altos)

Van Houts, E. 1992: 'Women and the writing of history in the early Middle Ages: the case of Abbess Matilda of Essen and Æthelweard', *Early Medieval Europe* 1, 53–68

1999: *Memory and Gender in Medieval Europe 900–1200* (Basingstoke)

Van Poll-van den Lisdonk, M. L. 1981: *Alcuins de sanctis eboricensis ecclesiae vers 1–604: de bronnen can een carolingisch epos* (Rotterdam)

Verey, C. 1969: 'A collation of the Gospel texts contained in Durham Cathedral MSS A.II.10, A.II.16 and A.II.17', unpublished MA thesis (University of Durham)

1973: 'Some observations on the texts of Durham Cathedral MSS A.II.10 and A.II.17', *Studia Evangelica* 6, 575–9

1989: 'The gospel texts at Lindisfarne at the time of St Cuthbert' in Bonner *et al.* 1989, 143–50

1998: 'A Northumbrian text family', in *The Bible as Book: The Manuscript Tradition*, ed. J. Sharpe and K. van Kampen (London and Newcastle), 105–22

1999: 'Lindisfarne or Rath Maelsigi? The evidence of the texts', in *Northumbria's Golden Age*, ed. J. Hawkes and S. Mills (Stroud), 327–35

Verey, C., Brown, T. J. and Coastworth, E. (eds.) 1980, *The Durham Gospels Together with Fragments of a Gospel Book in Uncial (Durham Cathedral Library, MS A.II.17)*, EEMF 20 (Copenhagen)

Versone, P. 1967: *From Theodoric to Charlemagne*, trans. P. Waley (London)

Vezin, J. 1977: 'Leofnoth: un scribe anglais à Saint-Benoît-sur-Loire', *Codices manuscripti* 3.4, 109–20

1982: 'Une reliure carolingienne de cuir souple (Oxford, Bodleian Library, Marshall 19)', *Revue française d'histoire du livre* n.s. 51, 235–41

1988: 'Les plus anciennes reliures de cuir estampé dans le domaine latin', in *Scire litteras: Forschungen zum mittelalterlichen Geistesleben*, ed. S. Krämer and M. Bernard, Bayerische Akademie der Wissenschaften, philosophisch-historische Klasse, NF 99 (Munich), 393–408

1989: 'Le vocabulaire latin de la reliure au moyen âge', in *Vocabulaire du livre et de l'écriture au moyen âge*, ed. O. Weijers (Turnhout), 56–60

1997: '"Quaderni simul ligati": Recherches sur les manuscrits en cahiers', in *Of the Making of Books: Medieval Manuscripts, Their Scribes and Readers: Essays presented to M. B. Parkes*, ed. P. R. Robinson and R. Zim (Aldershot), 64–7

Vogel, C. 1986: *Medieval Liturgy: An Introduction to the Sources*, rev. edn trans. from 1981 edn by N. K. Rasmussen and W. G. Storey (Washington, DC)

Vogel, C. and Elze, R. (eds.) 1963–72: *Le pontifical romano-germanique du dixième siècle*, 3 vols., Studi e testi 226–7 and 269 (Rome)

Voigts, L. E. 1988: 'A fragment of an Anglo-Saxon liturgical manuscript at the University of Missouri', *ASE* 17, 83–92

Vollmer, F. (ed.) 1905: *Fl. Merobaudis reliquiae. Blossii Aemilii Dracontii Carmina. Eugenii Toletani episcopi Carmina et epistolae*, MGH Auctores Antiquissimi 14 (Berlin)

Vriend, H. J. de (ed.) 1984: *The Old English Herbarium and Medicina de Quadrupedibus*, EETS 286 (Oxford)

Wade-Evans, A. W. 1909: *Welsh Medieval Law* (Oxford)

(ed.) 1944: *Vitae Sanctorum Britanniae et Genealogiae*, Board of Celtic Studies, University of Wales, History and Law Series 9 (Cardiff)

Waitz, G. (ed.) 1883: *Herimani liber de restauracione monasterii Sancti Martini Tornacensis*, MGH Scriptores 14 (Hanover)

Walker, G. S. (ed.) 1957: *Sancti Columbani Opera* (Dublin)

Wallace-Hadrill, J. M. 1965: 'Charlemagne and England', in *Karl der Grosse: Lebenswerk und Nachleben*, 4 vols. ed. W. Braunfels: I. *Personlichkeit und Geschichte*, ed. H. Beumann

(Düsseldorf), 683–98; reprinted in J. M. Wallace-Hadrill, *Early Medieval History* (Oxford, 1975), 155–80

Wallach, E. 1959: *Alcuin and Charlemagne: Studies in Carolingian History and Literature* (Ithaca, NY)

Waller, K. 1984: 'Rochester Cathedral Library: an English book collection on Norman models', in *Les mutations socio-culturelles au tournant des xie–xiie siècles*, ed. R. Foreville (Paris), 237–50.

Wallis, F. (trans.) 1999: *Bede, The Reckoning of Time*, Translated Texts for Historians 29 (Liverpool)

2005: 'Bede', in *Medieval Science, Technology and Medicine, An Encyclopedia*, ed. T. Glick, S. Livesey and F. Wallis (London), 81–3

Walsh, M. and Ó Cróinín, D. (eds.) 1988: *Cummian, De controversia paschali* (Toronto)

Wampach, C. 1930: *Geschichte der Grundherrschaft Echternach im Frühmittelalter. Untersuchungen über die Person des Grunders, über die Kloster- und Wirtschaftsgeschichte auf Grund des Liber Aureus Epternacensis (698–1222)* (Luxembourg)

Ward, B. 1991: *Bede and the Psalter*, Jarrow Lecture (Jarrow)

Warner, G. F. 1910–15: *The Stowe Missal*, 2 vols., HBS 31–2 (London)

Warner, G. F. and Gilson, J. P. 1921: *Catalogue of Western Manuscripts in the Old Royal and King's Collections*, 4 vols. (London)

Warner, G. F. and Wilson, H. A. (eds.) 1910: *The Benedictional of St Aethelwold*, Roxburghe Club (London)

Warren, F. E. (ed.) 1883: *The Leofric Missal, as Used in the Cathedral of Exeter during the Episcopate of its First Bishop A.D. 1050–1072* (Oxford)

1885: 'An Anglo-Saxon missal at Worcester', *The Academy* 28, 394–5

(ed.) 1893–5: *The Antiphonary of Bangor: An Early Irish Manuscript in the Ambrosian Library at Milan*, 2 vols., HBS 4 and 10 (London)

Wasserschleben, H. 1885a: *Die irische Kanonensammlung*, 2nd edn (Leipzig)

Wasserschleben, (F. W.) H. (ed.) 1885b: *Collectio Canonum Hibernensis*, 2nd edn (Leipzig)

Waterer, J. W. 1968: 'Irish book-satchels or budgets', *Medieval Archaeology* 12, 70–82

Watkiss, L. and Chibnall, M. (eds.) 1994: *The Waltham Chronicle* (Oxford)

Watson, A. G. 1979: *Catalogue of Dated and Datable Manuscripts c. 700–1600 in the Department of Manuscripts, the British Library*, 2 vols. (London)

1984: *Catalogue of Dated and Datable Manuscripts c. 435–1600 in Oxford Libraries*, 2 vols. (Oxford)

1996: 'Rochester Cathedral Library' in Sharpe *et al.* 1996, 463–537

Webber, T. 1989: 'Salisbury and the Exon Domesday: some observations concerning the origin of Exeter Cathedral MS 3500', *English Manuscript Studies 1100–1700* 1, 1–18

1992: *Scribes and Scholars at Salisbury Cathedral c. 1075–c. 1125* (Oxford)

1995: 'Script and manuscript production at Christ Church, Canterbury, after the Norman Conquest', in *Canterbury after the Norman Conquest: Churches, Saints and Scholars, 1066–1109*, ed. R. Eales and R. Sharpe (London and Rio Grande, OH), 145–58

1998: 'The provision of books for Bury St Edmunds Abbey in the 11th and 12th centuries', in *Bury St Edmunds: Medieval Art, Architecture and Economy*, ed. A. Gransden, British Archaeological Association Conference Transactions 20 (London), 186–93

1999: 'Les manuscrits de Christ Church (Cantorbéry) et de Salisbury à la fin du XIe siècle' in Bouet and Dosdat 1999, 95–105

Webster, L. and Backhouse, J. (eds.) 1991: *The Making of England: Anglo-Saxon Art and Culture AD 600–900* (London)

Webster, L. and Brown, M. P. (eds.) 1997: *The Transformation of the Roman World* (London)

Weiler, A. and Bange, P. (eds.) 1990: *Willibrord zijn wereld en zijn werk* (Nijmegen)

Weitzmann, K. 1977: *Late Antique and Early Christian Book Illumination* (New York and London)

Wenk, W. 1988: *Zur Sammlung der 38 Homilien des Chrysostomus Latinus*, Wiener Studien Beiheft 10 (Vienna)

Westgard, J. 2006: 'The dissemination and reception of the *Historia ecclesiastica gentis Anglorum* of the Venerable Bede in Germany c. 751–1500', unpublished PhD dissertation (University of North Carolina, Chapel Hill)

Wharton, H. 1691: *Anglia Sacra* I (London)

Wheeler, R. E. M. and Wheeler, T. V. 1936: *Verulamium: A Belgic and Two Roman Cities* (Oxford)

Whitelock, D. 1941: 'Wulfstan and the so-called Laws of Edward and Guthrum', *EHR* 56, 1–21

1942: 'Archbishop Wulfstan, homilist and statesman', *TRHS* 4th ser. 24, 24–45

1948: 'Wulfstan and the laws of Cnut', *EHR* 63, 433–52

1954: *The Peterborough Chronicle*, EEMF 4 (Copenhagen)

1955: 'Wulfstan's authorship of Cnut's laws', *EHR* 70, 72–85

1960: *After Bede*, Jarrow Lecture (Jarrow); reprinted in D. Whitelock, *From Bede to Alfred: Studies in Early Anglo-Saxon Literature and History* (London, 1980), ch. v.

1963: *Sermo Lupi ad Anglos*, 3rd edn (London)

1965: 'Wulfstan at York', in *Franciplegius: Medieval and Linguistic Studies in Honour of Francis Peabody Magoun*, ed. J. B. Bessinger Jr and R. P. Creed (New York), 214–31

1966: 'The prose of Alfred's reign', in *Continuations and Beginnings: Studies in Old English Literature*, ed. E. G. Stanley (London), 67–103

(ed.) 1967: *Sweet's Anglo-Saxon Reader in Prose and Verse* (Oxford)

(ed.) 1979: *English Historical Documents c. 500–1042*, 2nd edn., English Historical Documents I (London)

Whitelock, D., Brett. M. and Brooke, C. N. L. (eds.) 1981: *Councils and Synods with Other Documents Relating to the English Church, i: A.D. 871–1204* (Oxford)

Whitelock, D., McKitterick, R. and Dumville, D. N. (eds.) 1982: *Ireland in Early Medieval Europe* (Cambridge)

Wieland, G. 1983: *The Latin Glosses on Arator and Prudentius in Cambridge University Library, MS Gg.5.35* (Toronto)

1985: 'The glossed manuscript: classbook or library book', *ASE* 14, 153–73

Wilcox, J. 1992: 'The dissemination of Wulfstan's homilies: the Wulfstanian tradition in eleventh-century vernacular preaching', in *England in the Eleventh Century*, ed. C. Hicks, Harlaxton Medieval Studies 2 (Stamford), 199–217

(ed.) 1994: *Ælfric's Prefaces* (Durham)

2000a: 'The wolf on shepherds: Wulfstan, bishops and the context of the *Sermo Lupi ad Anglos*', in *Old English Prose: Basic Readings*, ed. P. E. Szarmach (New York), 395–418

2000b: 'Wulfstan and the twelfth century', in *Re-Writing Old English in the Twelfth Century*, ed. M. Swan and E. M. Treharne, CSASE 30 (Cambridge), 83–97

2000c: *Wulfstan Texts and Other Homiletic Materials*, Anglo-Saxon Manuscripts in Microfiche Facsimile 8 (New York)

2004: 'Wulfstan's *Sermo Lupi ad Anglos* as political performance: 16 February 1014 and beyond' in Townend 2004, 375–96

Williams, H. 2005: 'Review article: rethinking early medieval mortuary archaeology', *Early Medieval Europe* 13, 195–218

Williams, I. 1926–7: 'The Computus fragment', *Bulletin of the Board of Celtic Studies* 3, 245–72

1929–31: 'Glosau Rhydychen: Mesurau a Phwysau', *Bulletin of the Board of Celtic Studies* 5, 226–48

(ed.) 1930: *Pedeir keinc y Mabinogi* (Cardiff)

(ed.) 1955: *Armes Prydein fawr* (Cardiff)

1972: *The Beginnings of Welsh Poetry*, ed. R. Bromwich (Cardiff)

Williams, J. H. C. 2002: 'Pottery stamps, coin designs and writing in late Iron Age Britain' in Cooley 2002, 135–49

2007: 'New light on Latin in pre-Conquest Britain', *Britannia* 38, 1–11

Wilmart, A. 1918: 'La collection des 38 homélies latines de Saint Jean Chrysostome', *JTS* 19, 305–27

1926: 'La collection de Bède le Vénérable sur l'Apôtre', *RB* 38, 16–52

1937: *Codices Reginenses Latini*, I (Vatican City)

(ed.) 1938: 'La légende de Ste Édith en prose et vers par le moine Goscelin', *Analecta Bollandiana* 56, 5–101 and 265–307

1945: *Codices Reginenses Latini*, II (Vatican City)

Wilson, D. M. 1961: 'An Anglo-Saxon bookbinding at Fulda (Codex Bonifatianus 1)', *Antiquaries Journal* 41, 199–217

1984: *Anglo-Saxon Art from the Seventh Century to the Norman Conquest* (London)

Wilson, D. R. and Wright, R. P. 1969: 'Roman Britain in 1968. I. Sites Explored. II. Inscriptions', *Journal of Roman Studies* 59, 198–246

Wilson, H. A. (ed.) 1896: *The Missal of Robert of Jumièges*, HBS 11 (London)

(ed.) 1903: *The Benedictional of Archbishop Robert*, HBS 24 (London)

Winter, J. 1983: 'The characterisation of pigments based on carbon', *Studies in Conservation* 28, 49–66

Winterbottom, M. 1968: 'On the *Hisperica Famina*', *Celtica* 8, 126–39

1976: 'Columbanus and Gildas', *Vigiliae Christianae* 30, 310–17

1977: 'Aldhelm's prose style and its origins', *ASE* 6, 39–76

2000: 'The earliest life of St Dunstan', *Scripta Classica Israelica* 19, 163–79

(ed.) 2007: *William of Malmesbury, Gesta Pontificum Anglorum, I* (Oxford)

Winterbottom, M. and Thomson, R. M. (eds.) 2002: *William of Malmesbury, Saints Lives* (Oxford)

Withers, B. 2000: 'A sense of Englishness: Claudius B. iv, colonialism and the history of Anglo-Saxon art in the mid-twentieth century', in *The Old English Hexateuch: Aspects and Approaches*, ed. R. Barnhouse and B. Withers (Kalamazoo, MI), 317–50

2007: *The Illustrated Old English Heptateuch, Cotton Claudius B.iv: The Frontier of Seeing and Reading in Anglo-Saxon England* (London)

Wittig, J. 1983: 'King Alfred's Boethius and its Latin sources', *ASE* 11, 157–98

Witts, P. 2005: *Mosaics in Roman Britain: Stories in Stone* (Stroud)

Wittstadt, K. (ed.) 1989: *St Kilian. 1300 Jahre Martyrium der Frankenapostel*, Würzburger Diözesan-Geschichtsblätter 51 (Würzburg)

Wood, I. N. 1990: 'Administration, law and culture in Merovingian Gaul', in *The Uses of Literacy in Early Medieval Europe*, ed. R. McKitterick (Cambridge), 63–81

1991: *The Merovingian North Sea* (Alingsås)

1995: *The Most Holy Abbot Ceolfrid*, Jarrow Lecture (Jarrow)

2001: *The Missionary Life: Saints and the Evangelisation of Europe 400–1050* (London)

Wormald, F. (ed.) 1934: *English Calendars before A.D. 1100*, HBS 72 (London)

1945: 'Decorated initials in English manuscripts from AD 900 to 1100', *Archaeologia* 91, 107–35; reprinted in Wormald 1984

1952: *English Drawings of the Tenth and Eleventh Centuries* (London); reprinted in Wormald 1984

1954: *The Miniatures in the Gospels of Saint Augustine* (Cambridge)

1962: 'An eleventh-century English psalter with pictures', *Walpole Society* 38, 1–13; reprinted in Wormald 1984

1976: 'Fragments of a tenth-century sacramentary from the binding of the Winton Domesday' in Biddle 1976, 541–9

1984: *Collected Writings*, I: *Studies in Medieval Art from the Sixth to the Twelfth Centuries*, ed. J. J. G. Alexander, T. J. Brown and J. Gibbs (London)

Wormald, P. 1976: 'Bede and Benedict Biscop' in Bonner 1976, 141–69

1977: 'The uses of literacy in Anglo-Saxon England and its neighbours', *Transactions of the Royal Historical Society* 5th ser. 27, 95–114

1986: 'Charters, law and the settlement of disputes in Anglo-Saxon England', in *The Settlement of Disputes in Early Medieval Europe*, ed. W. Davies and P. Fouracre (Cambridge), 13–35

1988: 'Æthelwold and his continental counterparts: contact, comparison, contrast', in *Bishop Æthelwold: His Career and Influence*, ed. B. Yorke (Woodbridge), 14–32

1999: *The Making of English Law: King Alfred to the Twelfth Century*, I: *Legislation and its Limits* (Oxford)

2004: 'Archbishop Wulfstan: eleventh-century state-builder' in Townend 2004, 9–27

Wright, C. D. 1990: 'The pledge of the soul: a judgement theme in Old English homiletic literature and Cynewulf's *Elene*', *Neuphilologische Mitteilungen* 91, 23–30

Wright, C. E. (ed.) 1955: *Bald's Leechbook. British Museum, Royal MS 12 D. XVII*, EEMF 5 (Copenhagen)

1960: *English Vernacular Hands from the Twelfth to the Fifteenth Centuries* (Oxford)

Wright, D. H. 1967a: 'The Italian stimulus on English art around 700', in *Stil und Überlieferung in der Kunst des Abendlandes: Akten des 21. Internat. Kongress für Kunstgeschichte. Bonn 1964*, I (Bonn), 84–92

(ed.) 1967b: *The Vespasian Psalter (BM Cotton Vespasian A.i)*, EEMF 14 (Copenhagen)

1992: *Codicological Notes on the Vergilius Romanus (Vat. Lat. 3867)*, Studi e Testi 345 (Vatican City)

2001: *The Roman Vergil and the Origins of Medieval Book Design* (London)

Wright, N. 1981: 'Bede and Vergil', *Romanobarbarica* 6, 367–71; reprinted in Wright 1995b, no. XI.

1982: 'The *Hisperica Famina* and Caelius Sedulius', *CMCS* 4, 61–76; reprinted in Wright 1995b, no. VIII

1984: 'Gildas's prose style and its origins' in Lapidge and Dumville 1984, 107–28

1985: 'Imitation of the poems of Paulinus of Nola in early Anglo-Latin verse', *Peritia* 4, 134–51; reprinted in Wright 1995b, no. XII

1986: 'Imitation of the poems of Paulinus of Nola in early Anglo-Latin verse: a postscript', *Peritia* 5, 392–6; reprinted in Wright 1995b, no. XIII

1995a: 'Aldhelm, Gildas and Acircius' in Wright 1995b, no. XIV

1995b: *History and Literature in Late Antiquity and the Early Medieval West* (Aldershot)

Wülker, R. P. (ed.) 1884: *Wright's Anglo-Saxon and Old English Vocabularies*, 2 vols. (London)

Youngs, S. (ed.) 1989: *The Work of Angels: Masterpieces of Celtic Metalwork 6th–9th Centuries AD* (London)

1995: 'Medium and motif: polychrome enamelling and early manuscript decoration in Insular art' in Bourke 1995, 37–47

Zechiel-Eckes, K. 2002: 'Vom armarium in York in den Düsseldorfer Tresor: zur rekonstruktion einer Liudger-Handschrift aus dem mittleren 8. Jahrhundert', *Deutsches Archiv* 58, 193–203

2003: '*Universitäts- und Landesbibliothek Düsseldorf. Katalog der frühmittelalterlichen Fragmente vom beginnenden achten bis zum neunten Jahrhundert* (Wiesbaden)

Zettel, P. H. 1982: 'Saints' lives in Old English: Latin manuscripts and vernacular accounts: Ælfric', *Peritia* 1, 17–37

Zettersten, A. (ed.) 1979: *Waldere* (Manchester)

Zimmermann, E. H. 1916: *Vorkarolingische Miniaturen* (Berlin)

Ziolkowski, J. M. 1994: *The Cambridge Songs (Carmina Cantabrigiensia)* (New York and London)

Zironi, A. 2004: *Il Monastero Longobardo di Bobbio: crocevia di uomini, manoscritti e culture*, Instituzioni e Società 3 (Spoleto)

Zupitza, J. (ed.) 1880: *Ælfrics Grammatik und Glossar*, I: *Text und Varianten* (Berlin)

1887: 'Altenglische Glossen zu Abbos Clericorum Decus', *Zeitschrift für deutsches Altertum und deutsche Literatur* 31, 1–27

Concordance of named manuscripts

Abingdon-Jumièges Gospels: Rouen, Bibliothèque municipale, A.21
Achadeus, Count, Psalter of: Cambridge, Corpus Christi College, 272
Ælfwine Prayerbook: London, British Library, Cotton Titus D.xxvi+xxvii
Anderson Pontifical: London, British Library, Add. 57337
Antiphoner of Bangor: Milan, Biblioteca Ambrosiana, C.5.inf.
Arenberg Gospels: New York, Pierpont Morgan Library, M 869
Armagh, Book of: Dublin, Trinity College, 52
Athelstan Psalter: London, British Library, Cotton Galba A.xviii + Oxford, Bodleian Library, Rawlinson B.484, fol. 85
Augsburg Gospels: Augsburg, Universitätsbibliothek, Cod. I.2.4°.2
Augustine, St, Gospels of: Cambridge, Corpus Christi College, 286

Bald's Leechbook: London, British Library, Royal 12 D.xvii
Barberini Gospels: Vatican City, Biblioteca Apostolica Vaticana, Barb. lat. 570
Benedictional of St Æthelwold: London, British Library, Add. 49598
Beowulf Codex: London, British Library, Cotton Vitellius A.xv
Blickling Homiliary: Princeton University Library, W. H. Scheide Collection, 71
Blickling Psalter: New York, Pierpont Morgan Library, M 776
Bodmin Gospels: London, British Library, Add. 9381
Book of Armagh: Dublin, Trinity College, 52
Book of Cerne: Cambridge University Library, Ll.1.10
Book of Deer: Cambridge University Library, Ii.6.32
Book of Dimma: Dublin, Trinity College, 59
Book of Durrow: Dublin, Trinity College, 57
Book of Kells: Dublin, Trinity College, 58
Book of Mulling: Dublin, Trinity College, 60
Book of Nunnaminster: London, British Library, Harley 2965
Bosworth Psalter: London, British Library, Add. 37517
Burchard Gospels: Würzburg, Universitätsbibliothek, M.p.th.f.68
Bury Gospels: London, British Library, Harley 76
Bury Psalter: Vatican City, Biblioteca Apostolica Vaticana, Reg. lat. 12

Cadmug Gospels: Fulda, Hessische Landesbibliothek, Codex Bonifatianus 3
Cædmon Manuscript: Oxford, Bodleian Library, Junius 11

Caligula Troper: London, British Library, Cotton Caligula A.xiv (fols. 1–36)
Cambridge Juvencus: Cambridge University Library, Ff.4.42
Cambridge–London Gospels: Cambridge, Corpus Christi College, 197B + London, British Library, Cotton Otho C.v. + Royal 7 C.xii, fols. 2–3
Canterbury Codex Aureus: Stockholm, Kungliga Biblioteket, A.135
Cathach of St Columba: Dublin, Royal Irish Academy, s.n.
Cerne, Book of: Cambridge University Library, Ll.1.10
Codex Alexandrinus: London, British Library, Royal 1 D. v–viii
Codex Amiatinus: Florence, Biblioteca Medicea-Laurenziana, Amiatino 1
Codex Argenteus: Uppsala, Universitetsbibliothek, DG1
Codex Augusteus: Vatican City, Biblioteca Apostolica Vaticana, Vat. lat. 3256
Codex Bigotianus: Paris, Bibliothèque nationale de France, lat. 281+298
Codex Oxoniensis Posterior: Oxford, Bodleian Library, Bodley 572 (fols. 1–50)
Codex Roffensis: Rochester Cathedral Library, A.3.5 (deposited at Strood, Rochester-upon-Medway Studies Centre)
Codex Usserianus Primus: Dublin, Trinity College, 55
Columba, Cathach of: Dublin, Royal Irish Academy, s.n.
Corpus Glossary: Cambridge, Corpus Christi College, 144
Corpus Martianus Capella: Cambridge, Corpus Christi College, 153
Cosin Gradual: Durham University Library, Cosin V.v.6
Crowland/Croyland Psalter: Oxford, Bodleian Library, Douce 296
Cutbercht Gospels: Vienna, Österreichische Nationalbibliothek, Cod. 1224
Cuthbert Gospel: London, British Library, Loan 74

Deer, Book of: Cambridge University Library, Ii.6.32
Dimma, Book of: Dublin, Trinity College, 59
Dunstan's Classbook: Oxford, Bodleian Library, Auct. F.4.32
Dunstan's Pontifical: Paris, Bibliothèque nationale de France, lat. 943
Durham Cantor's Book: Durham Cathedral Library, B.IV.24
Durham Cassiodorus: Durham Cathedral Library, B.II.30
Durham Collectar/Ritual: Durham Cathedral Library, A.IV.19
Durham Gospel/New Testament Fragment: Durham Cathedral Library, A.II.10, endleaves + C.III.13 (fols. 192–5) + C.III.20 (fols. 1–2)
Durham Gospels: Durham Cathedral Library, A.II.17 (part I)
Durrow, Book of: Dublin, Trinity College, 57

Eadwig Gospels: Hanover, Kestner-Museum, W.M.XXIa.36
Eadwig Psalter: London, British Library, Arundel 155
Eadwine Psalter: Cambridge, Trinity College, R.17.1
Echternach Gospels: Paris, Bibliothèque nationale de France, lat. 9389
Edinburgh Psalter: Edinburgh University Library, 56
Egbert Pontifical: Paris, Bibliothèque nationale de France, lat. 10575
Épinal Glossary: Épinal, Bibliothèque municipale, 72 (fols. 94–107)
Exeter Book: Exeter Cathedral Library, 3501
Exeter Gospels: Paris, Bibliothèque nationale de France, lat. 14782

Godgifu Gospels: London, British Library, Royal 1 D.iii
Gospels of St Augustine: Cambridge, Corpus Christi College, 286
Gospels/Gospel-Lectionary of Queen (St) Margaret of Scotland: Oxford, Bodleian Library, Lat. liturg. f.5
Gotha Gospels: Gotha Forschungsbibliothek, Cod. Memb. I.18
Greenwell Leaf: London, British Library, Add. 37777
Grimbald Gospels: London, British Library, Add. 34890

Harkness Gospels, New York, Public Library, 115
Harley Golden Gospels: London, British Library, Harley 2788
Hereford Gospels: Hereford Cathedral Library, P.I.2
Hereford Gospel-Lectionary: Cambridge, Pembroke College, 302

Junius Psalter: Oxford, Bodleian Library, Junius 27

Kells, Book of: Dublin, Trinity College, 58

Lanalet Pontifical: Rouen, Bibliothèque municipale, A.27
Leiden Glossary: Leiden, Bibliotheek der Rijksuniversiteit, Voss. lat. Q.69
Leiden Leechbook: Leiden, Bibliotheek der Rijksuniversiteit, Voss. lat. F.96A
Leofric Collactar: London, British Library, Harley 2961
Leofric Missal: Oxford, Bodleian Library, Bodley 579
Liber Commonei: Oxford, Bodleian Library, Auct. F.4.32 (fols. 19–36)
Lichfield Gospels: Lichfield Cathedral Library, 1
Lindisfarne Gospels: London, British Library, Cotton Nero D.iv
Lothian Psalter: New York, Pierpont Morgan Library, M 776

MacDurnan Gospels: London, Lambeth Palace Library, 1370
MacRegol Gospels: Oxford, Bodleian Library, Auct. D.2.19
Maeseyck Gospels: Maeseyck, Church of St Catherine, Treasury, s.n.
Maihingen Gospels: Augsburg, Universitätsbibliothek, Cod. I.2.4°.2
Margaret of Scotland, Gospels/Gospel-Lectionary of: Oxford, Bodleian Library, Lat. liturg. f.5
Moore Bede: Cambridge University Library, Kk.5.16
Muchelney Breviary: London, British Library, Add. 56488
Mulling, Book of: Dublin, Trinity College, 60

New Minster Charter: London, British Library, Cotton Vespasian A.viii (fols. 1–33)
New Minster *Liber Vitae*: London, British Library, Stowe 944
New Minster Prayerbook: London, British Library, Cotton Titus D.xxvi+xxvii
Nunnaminster, Book of: London, British Library, Harley 2965

Old English illustrated Hexateuch: London, British Library, Cotton Claudius B.iv
Oxford Ovid: Oxford, Bodleian Library, Auct. F.4.32 (fols. 37–47)

Paris Psalter: Paris, Bibliothèque nationale de France, lat. 8824
Parker Chronicle: Cambridge, Corpus Christi College, 173 (fols. 1–56)

Peterborough Chronicle: Oxford, Bodleian Library, Laud misc. 636
Portiforium of St Wulfstan: Cambridge, Corpus Christi College, 391
Psalter of St Oswald: London, British Library, Harley 2904

Ramsey Psalter: London, British Library, Harley 2904
Red Book of Darley: Cambridge, Corpus Christi College, 422
Regius Psalter: London, British Library, Royal 2 B.v
Ricemarch/Rhygyfarch Psalter and Martyrology: Dublin, Trinity College, 50
Robert of Jumièges, Sacramentary of: Rouen, Bibliothèque municipale, Y.6
Royal Bible: London, British Library, Royal 1 E. vii+viii
Royal Bible Fragment: London, British Library, Royal 1 E.vi
Royal Prayerbook: London, British Library, Royal 2 A.xx

Sacramentary of Robert of Jumièges: Rouen, Bibliothèque municipale, Y.6
St Petersburg Bede: St Petersburg, Russian National Library, Q.v.I.18
St Petersburg Gospels: St Petersburg, Russian National Library, F.v.I.8
Salaberga Psalter: Berlin, Staatsbibliothek, Preussischer Kulturbesitz, Hamilton 553
Salisbury Psalter: Salisbury Cathedral Library, 150
Samson Pontifical: Cambridge, Corpus Christi College, 146
Sherborne Pontifical: Paris, Bibliothèque nationale de France, lat. 943
Southampton Psalter: Cambridge, St John's College, C.9 (59)
Stonyhurst Gospel: London, British Library, Loan 74
Stowe Missal: Dublin, Royal Irish Academy, D.II.3 (fols. 1–11)
Stuttgart/Echternach Psalter: Stuttgart, Württembergische Landesbibliothek, Cod. Bibl. 2°.12

Tanner Bede: Oxford, Bodleian Library, Tanner 10
Textus Roffensis: Rochester Cathedral Library, A.3.5 (deposited at Strood, Rochester-upon-Medway Studies Centre)
Tiberius Psalter: London, British Library, Cotton Tiberius C.vi
Trier Gospels: Trier Domschatz, 61 (olim 134)

Utrecht Psalter: Utrecht, Universiteitsbibliotheek, 32 (Script. eccl. 484)

Vercelli Book: Vercelli, Biblioteca Capitolare, CXVII
Vergilius Augusteus: Vatican City, Biblioteca Apostolica Vaticana, Vat. lat. 3256
Vergilius Romanus: Vatican City, Biblioteca Apostolica Vaticana, Vat. lat. 3867
Vespasian Psalter: London, British Library, Cotton Vespasian A.i
Victor Codex: Fulda, Hessische Landesbibliothek, Bonifatianus 1

Winchcombe Psalter: Cambridge University Library, Ff.1.23
Winchcombe Sacramentary: Orléans, Médiathèque, 127
Winchester Tropers: Cambridge, Corpus Christi College, 473; Oxford, Bodleian Library, Bodley 775
Wulfstan's Portiforium: Cambridge, Corpus Christi College, 391

York Gospels: York Minster Library, Add. 1

Index of manuscripts

General index

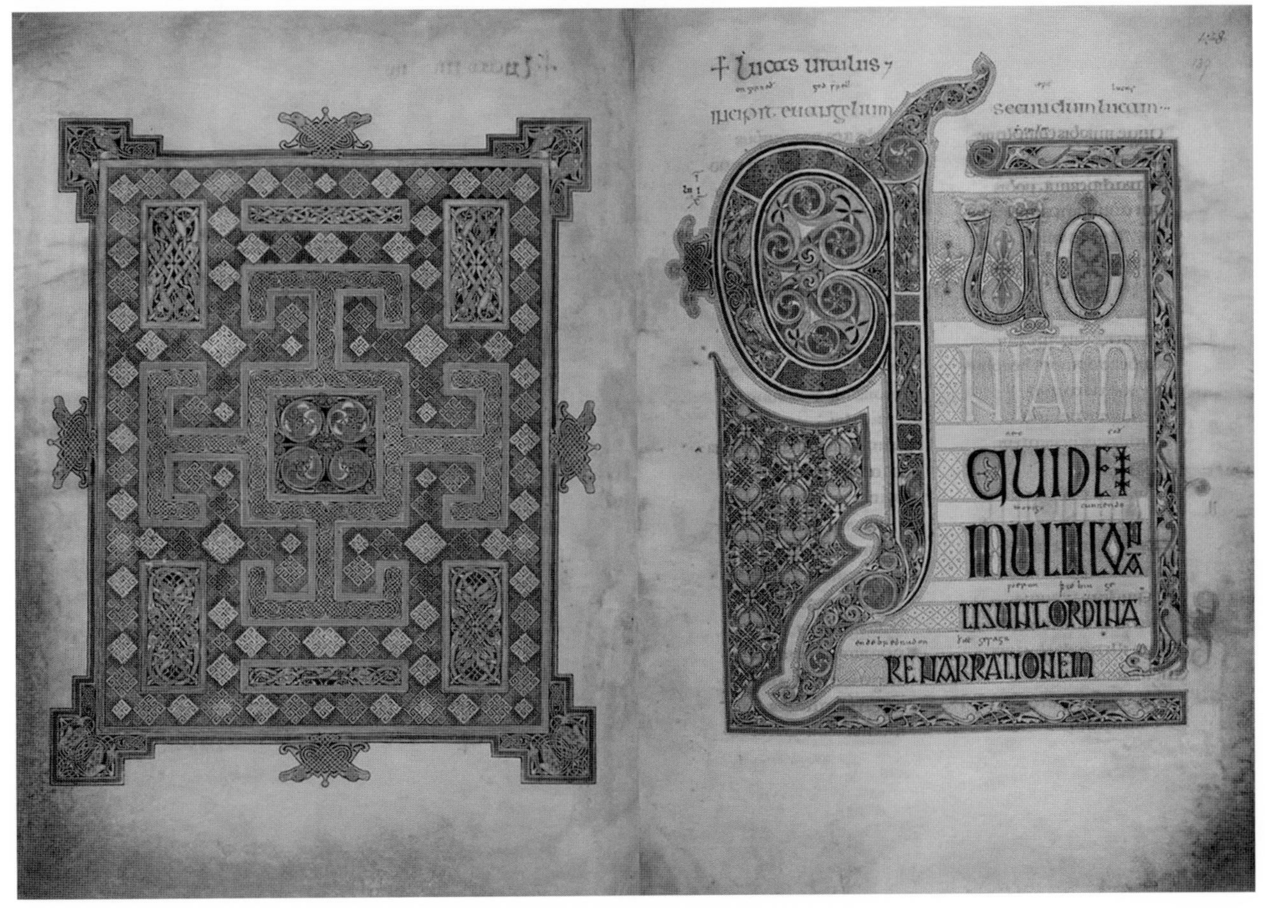

Plate 4.1 The Lindisfarne Gospels (BL, Cotton Nero D.iv, fols. 138v+9r)

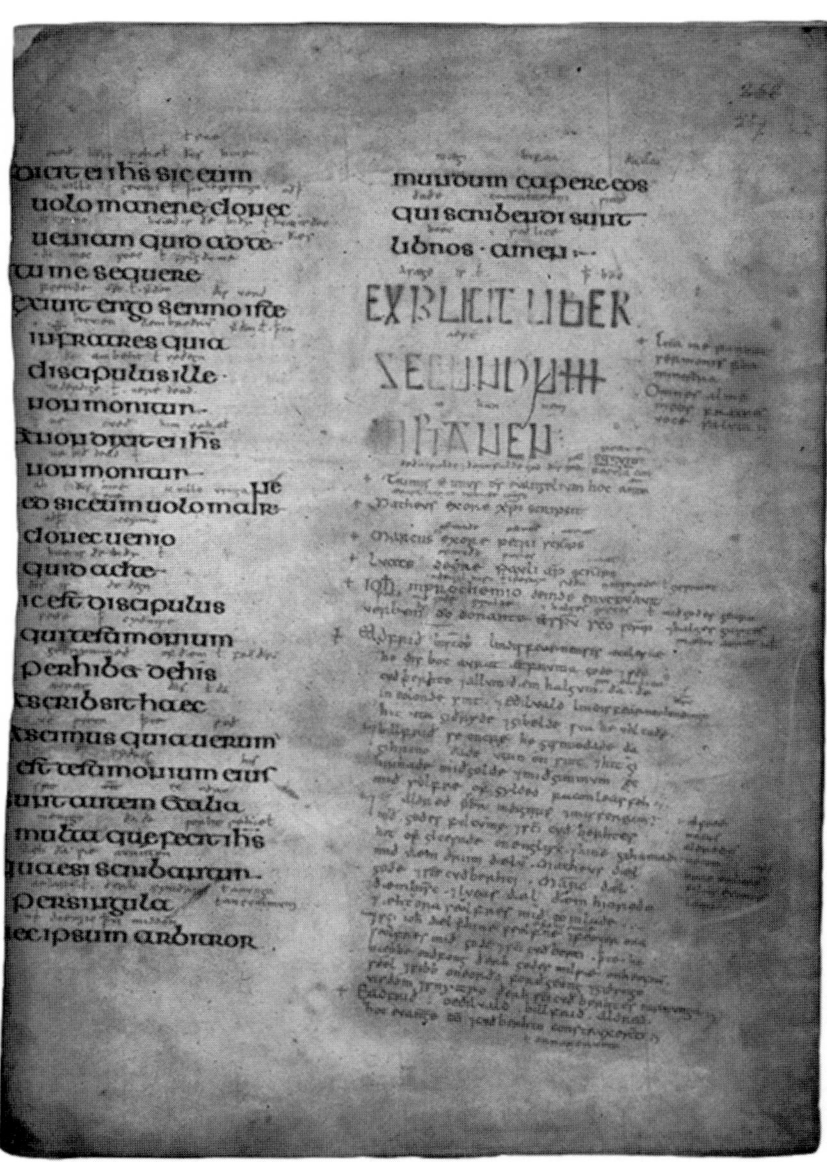

Plate 4.2 The Lindisfarne Gospels (BL, Cotton Nero D.iv, fol. 259r)

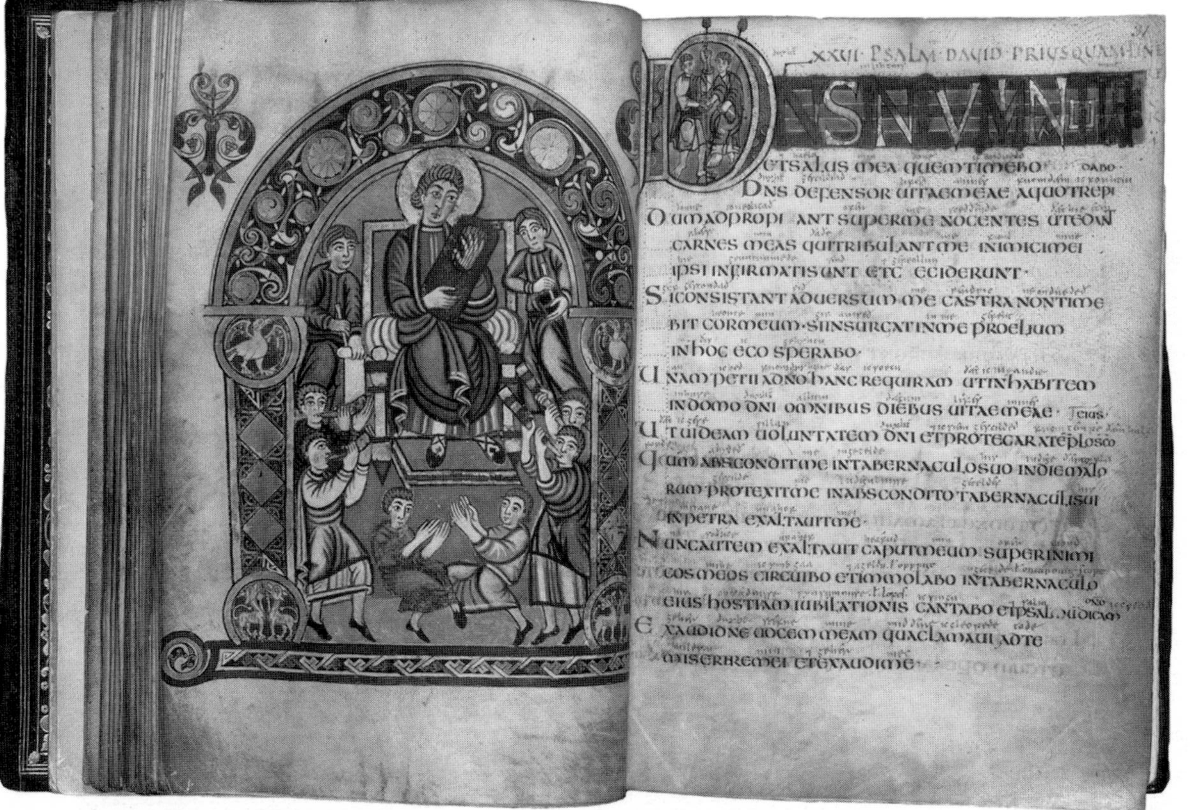

Plate 4.3 The Vespasian Psalter (BL, Cotton Vespasian A.i, fols. 30v+31r)

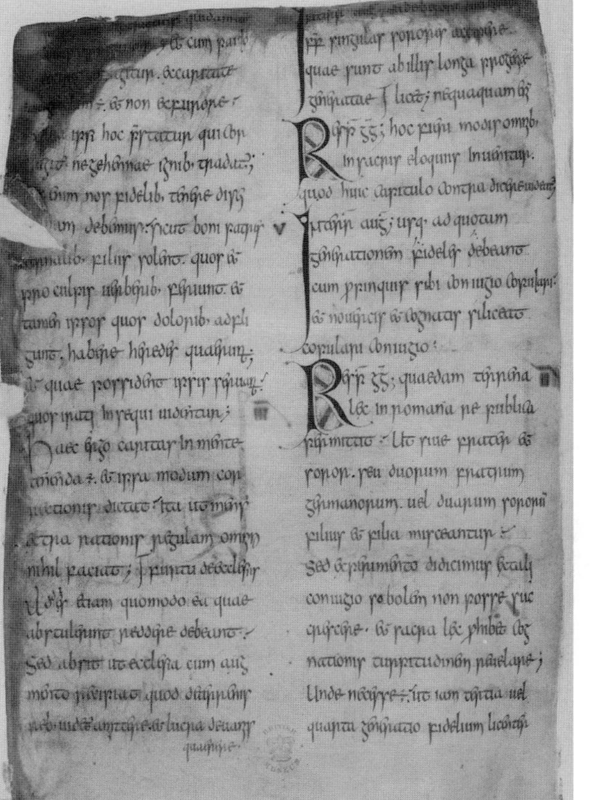

Plate 4.4 Bede, *Historia ecclesiastica* (BL, Cotton Tiberius A.xiv, fol. 26v)

Plate 4.5 The Book of Cerne (CUL, Ll.1.10, fol. 43r)

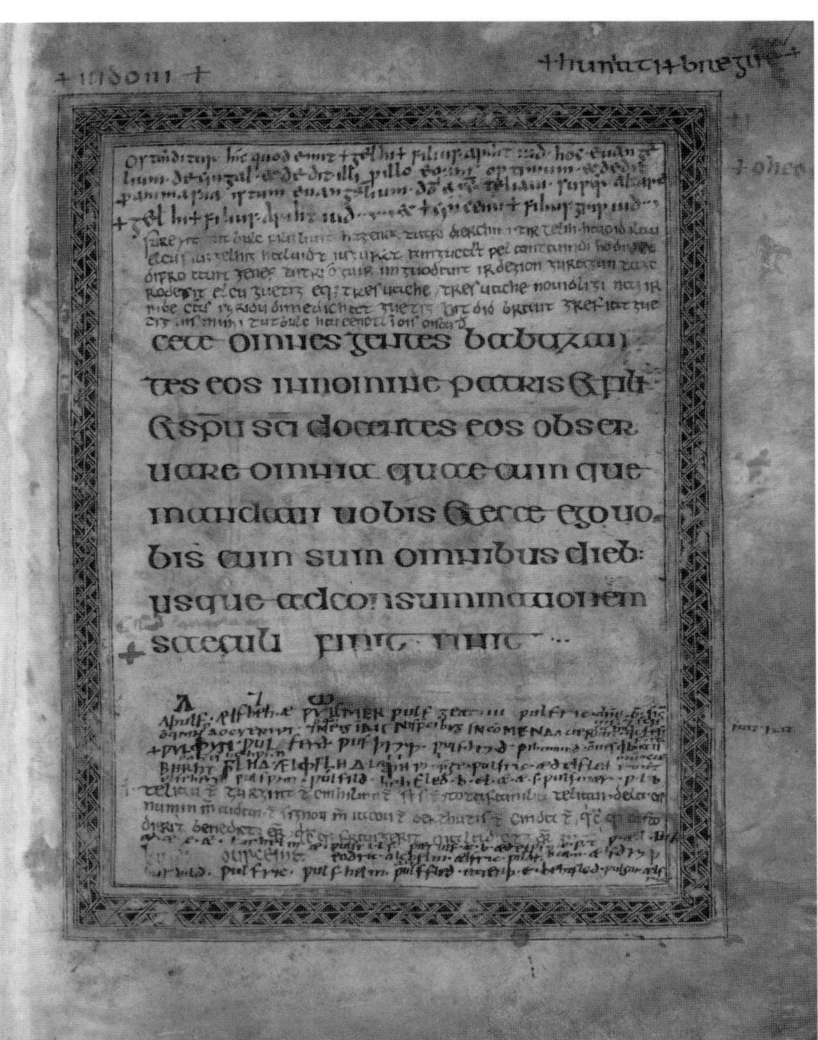

cete omnes gentes babtizan
tes eos innomine patris & fili
& spu sci docentes eos obser
uare omnia quae cum que
mandaui uobis & ecce ego uo
bis cum sum omnibus dieb:
usque adconsummationem
saeculi finit

Plate 5.1 The Lichfield/St Chad Gospels (Lichfield CL, 1, p. 141)

Plate 7a.1 BL, Royal 4 A.xiv

Plate 7a.2 BL, Royal 7 D.xxiv

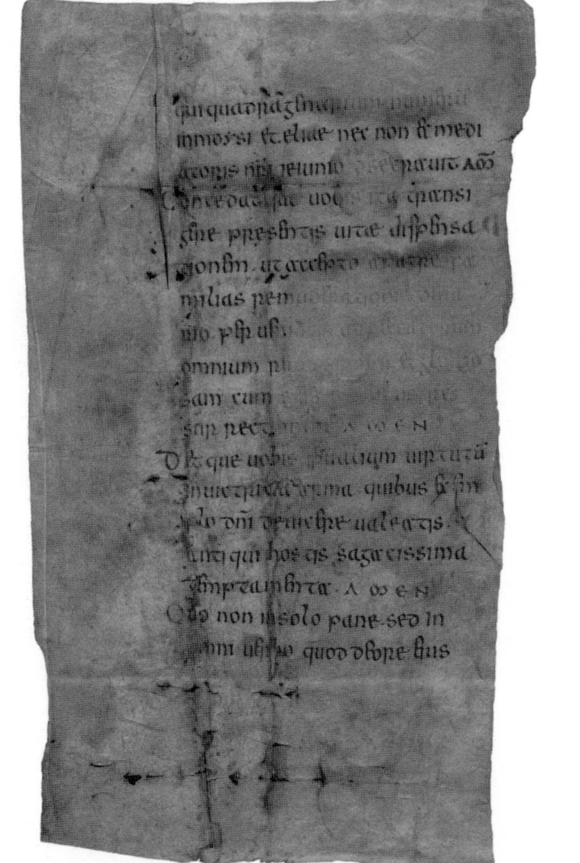

Plate 7a.3a Harvard, Houghton Library, Typ 612, Benedictional (Square Minuscule)

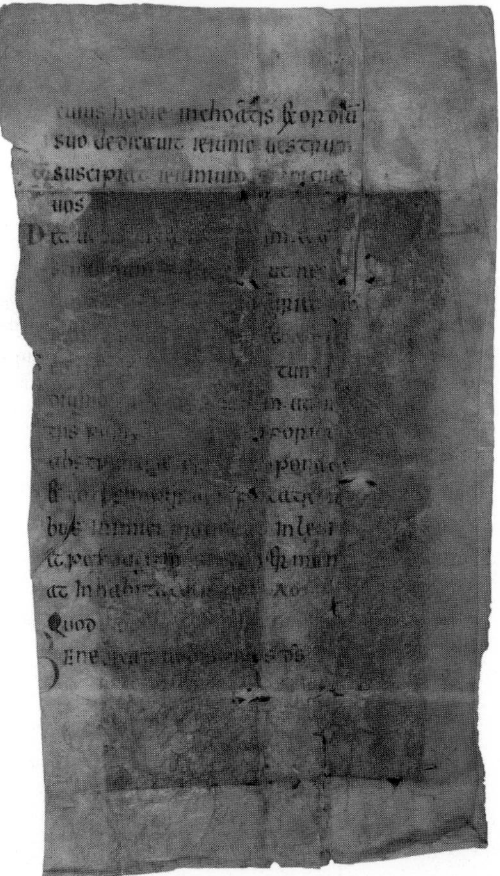

Plate 7a.3b Harvard, Houghton Library, Typ 612, Benedictional

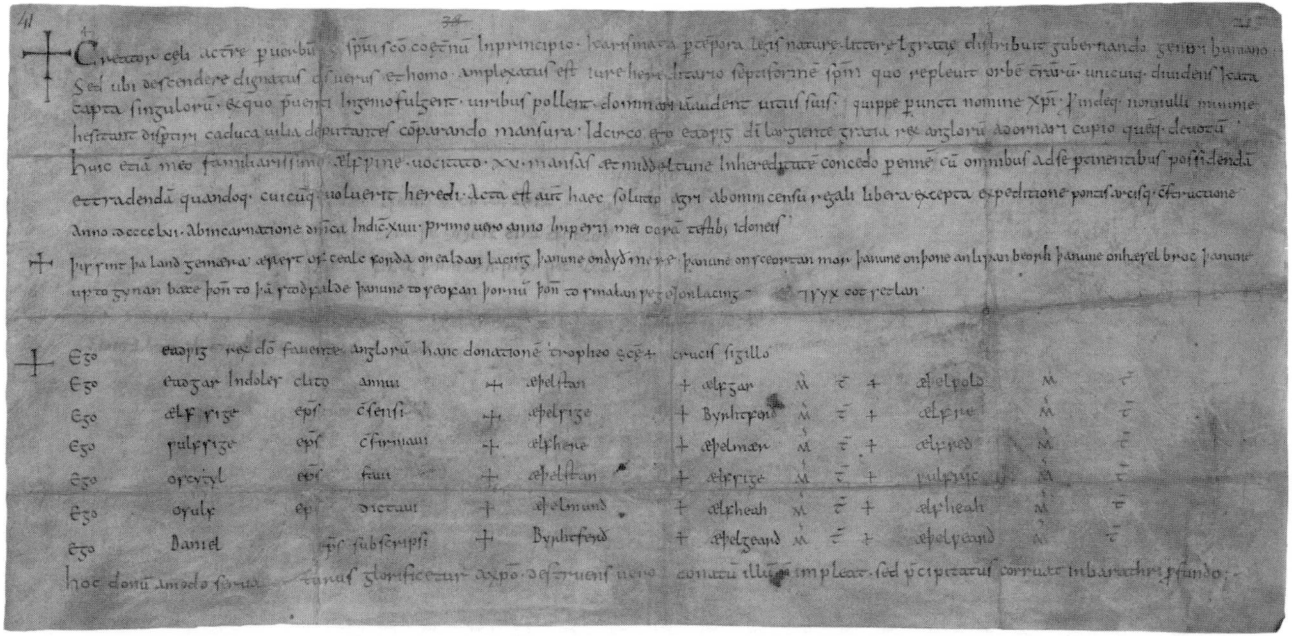

Plate 7b.1 BL, Cotton Augustus ii.41

feritates ita mitiges · ut nihil eorū
iacula tuorum possint generare
dispendia · AMEN
Sed tu pastor bone qui tem& ipsū
nrī causā dedisti propretio . ita
sanguinis tui defende commerciū .
ut & hic te semper sentiant pre
uium . & in aeterna beatitudine
te remunerante mereantur acci
pere praemium · AMEN
Tu ergo omnipotens dnē ihū xpē
benedictionum rore perfunde .
· ut & in presenti uita posita · de
omnibus inimicis te habeant
ereptorem . & hic & in aeternum
semper sentiant protectorē · AMEN
Quod ipse praestare dignetur .
cuius regnum & imperium .
sine fine perman& in saecula

Plate 7b.2 The Benedictional of Æthelwold (BL, Add. 49598, fol. 8v)

149

60

uero dequibus loquimur consuetudo constringit;
Per pende fr̄ car̄. quia omne q̄d inhac mortali
carne patimur exinfirmitate naturæ est. dig
no dī iudicio post culpam ordinatur; Esurire
namque sitire æstuare algere lasescere exin
firmitate naturæ est; Et quid est aliud contra
famem alimenta. contra sitim potum contra æstu
auras. contra frigus uestem. contra lassitudinē
requiem querere. Nisi medicamentum quidem
contra egritudines explorare. femine itaque
& menstruus sui sanguinis fluxus egritudo est.
Si igitur bene præsumpsit. quæ uestimentum
dn̄i inlanguore posita tetigit. quod uni psone
infirmanti conceditur; Cur nonconcedatur
cunctis mulieribus que naturæ suæ uitio infir
mantur; Sc̄e autē communionis misterium in
hisdem diebus pcipe non debet phiberi. si autē
exmagna ueneratione pcipe nonpsumit. lau
danda est. sedsi pcipit non iudicanda; Bonorū
quippe mentium est. et ibi aliquo modo culpas

Plate 7b.3 Penitential, etc. (CCCC, 320, fol. 149r)

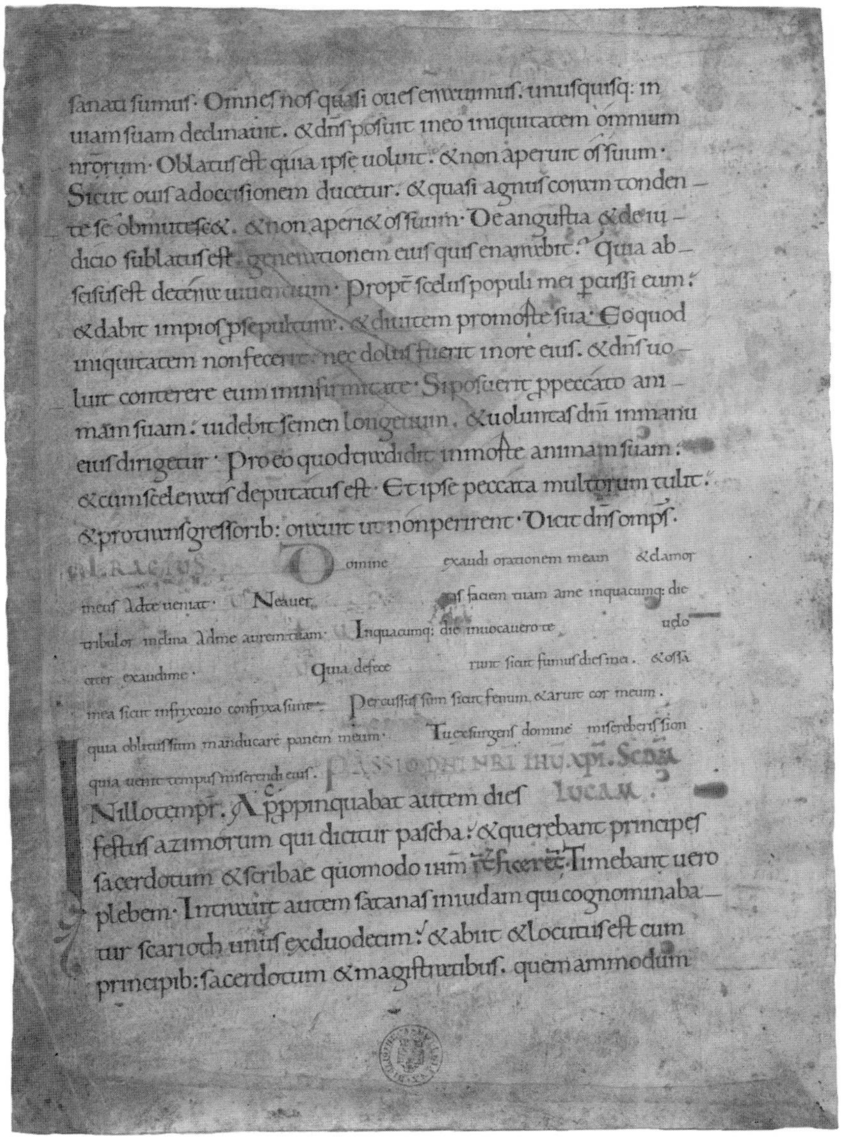
sanati sumus· Omnes nos quasi oves erravimus. unusquisq: in
viam suam declinavit. & dns posuit in eo iniquitatem omnium
nrorum· Oblatus est quia ipse voluit: & non aperuit os suum·
Sicut ovis ad occisionem ducetur: & quasi agnus coram tonden-
te se obmutescet. & non aperiet os suum· De angustia & de iudicio sublatus est. generationem eius quis enarrabit? Quia ab-
scisus est de terra viventium· Propt scelus populi mei percussi eum:
& dabit impios p sepultura. & divitem pro morte sua: Eo quod
iniquitatem non fecerit: nec dolus fuerit in ore eius. & dns voluit conterere eum in infirmitate· Si posuerit p peccato animam suam: videbit semen longevum. & voluntas dni in manu
eius dirigetur· Pro eo quod tradidit in morte animam suam:
& cum sceleratis deputatus est· Et ipse peccata multorum tulit:
& pro transgressorib: oravit ut non perirent· Dicit dns omps.
TRACTUS. Domine exaudi orationem meam & clamor
meus ad te veniat· Ne avertas faciem tuam a me in quacumq: die
tribulor inclina ad me aurem tuam· In quacumq: die invocavero te velo-
citer exaudi me· Quia defecerunt sicut fumus dies mei. & ossa
mea sicut in frixorio confrixa sunt· Percussus sum sicut fenum. & aruit cor meum.
quia oblitus sum manducare panem meum· Tu exsurgens domine misereberis sion
quia venit tempus miserendi eius. PASSIO DNI NRI IHU XPI. SCDM LUCAM.
IN illo tempr. Appropinquabat autem dies
festus azimorum qui dicitur pascha: & querebant principes
sacerdotum & scribae quomodo ihm interficerent. Timebant vero
plebem· Intravit autem satanas in iudam qui cognominaba-
tur scarioth unus ex duodecim: & abiit & locutus est cum
principib: sacerdotum & magistratibus. quemammodum

Plate 7b.4 Missal (BodL., Lat. liturg. d.3, fol. 4r)

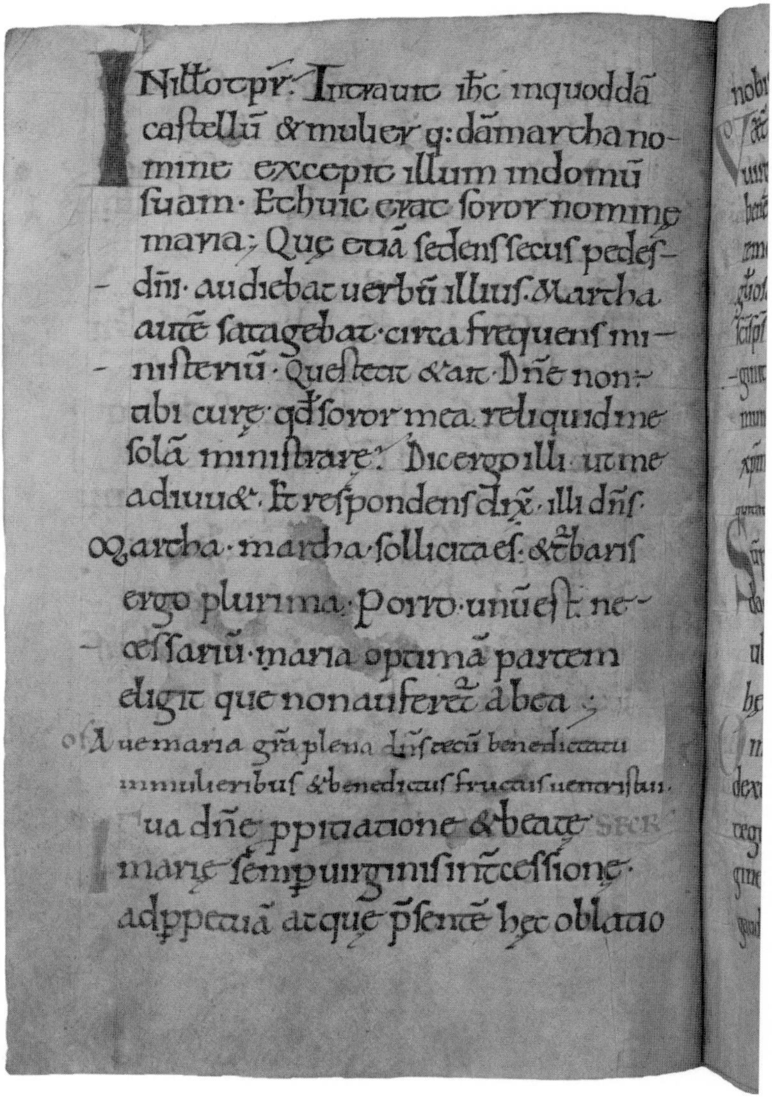
INillo tpr. Intrauit ihc inquoddã
castellũ & mulier q:dã martha nomine excepit illum indomũ
suam. Et huic erat soror nomine
maria; Que etiã sedens secus pedes
dñi. audiebat uerbũ illius. Martha
autẽ satagebat circa frequens mi-
nisteriũ. Questetit & ait. Dñe non
tibi cure qđ soror mea reliquid me
solã ministrare. Dic ergo illi ut me
adiuuet. Et respondens dix. illi dñs.
Martha. martha sollicita es & turbaris
erga plurima. Porro unũ est ne-
cessariũ. maria optimã partem
elegit que non auferetur ab ea ;
Aue maria grã plena dñs tecũ benedicta tu
in mulieribus & benedictus fructus uentris tui.
Tua dñe ppitiatione & beate SECR
marie semp uirginis intercessione
ad ppetuã atque psentẽ hec oblatio

Plate 7b.5 Service-book (CCCC, 422, p. 86)

Plate 8.1 BL, Cotton Nero D.iv, fol. 95r (Lindisfarne Gospels, incipit to Mark)

Plate 8.2 Stockholm, KB, A.135, fol. 9v (Codex Aureus, portrait of Matthew)

Plate 8.3 Stockholm, KB, A.135, fol. 11r (Codex Aureus, Chi-rho page)

Plate 9.1 The Hereford Gospels (Hereford CL, P.I.2, fol. 102r)

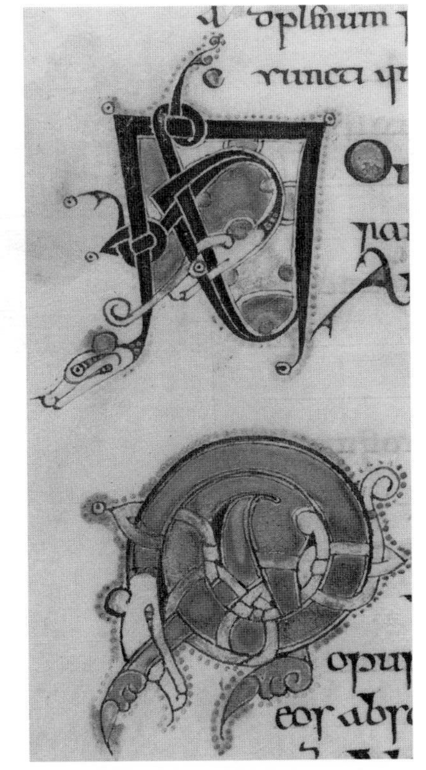

Plate 9.2 Ovid, *Ars amatoria* (BodL., Auct. F.4.32, fol. 37r (detail))

Plate 9.3 Augustine, *De Trinitate* (CCCC, 199, fol. 1v (detail))

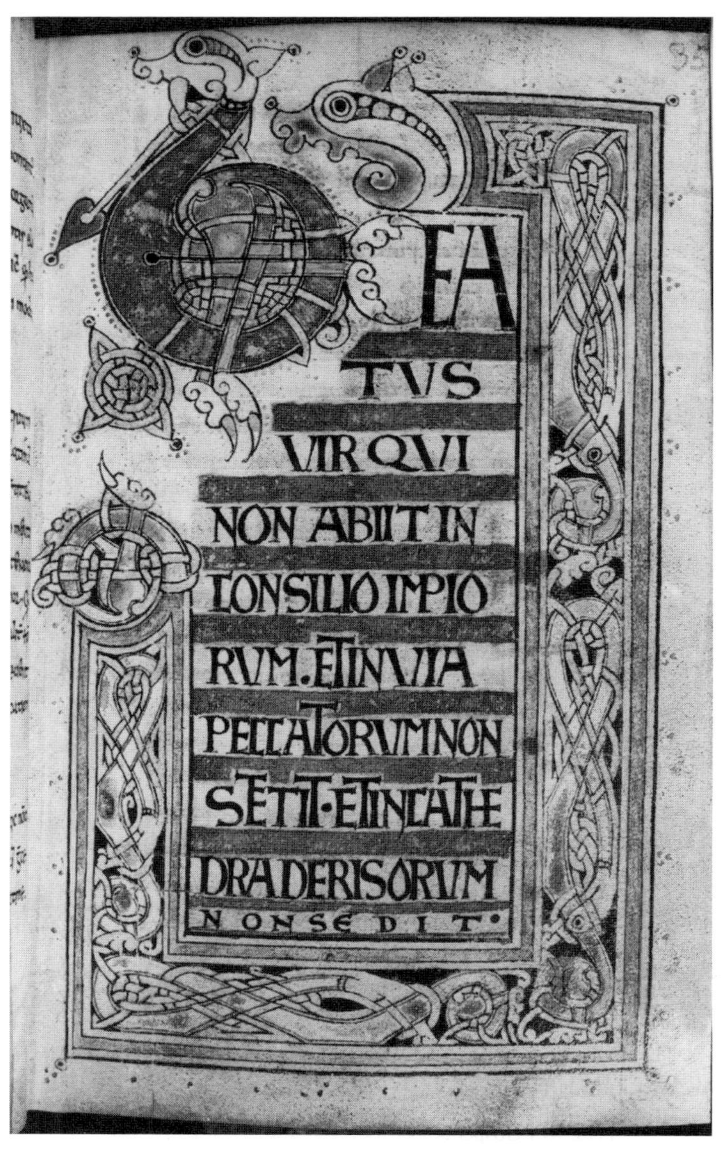

Plate 9.4 Psalter and Martyrology of Rhygyfarch (TCD, 50, fol. 35r)

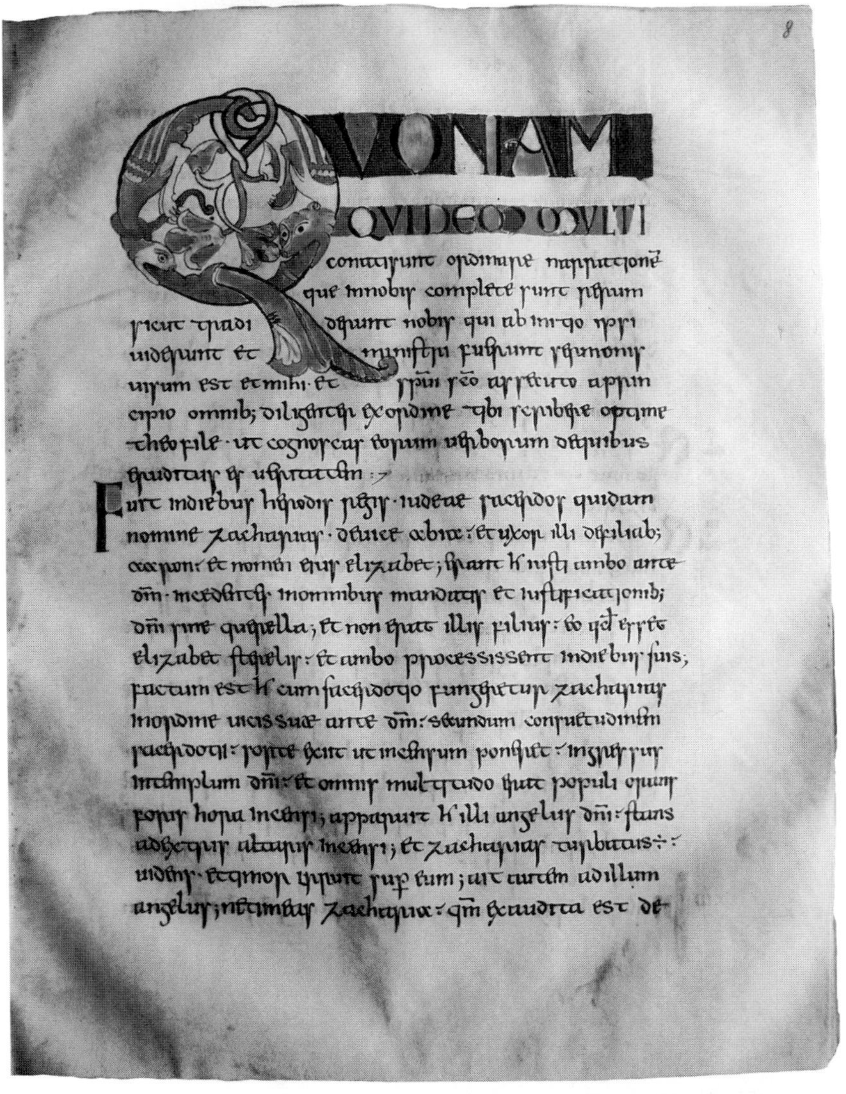

Plate 10.1 Gospel-book (Boulogne, BM, 10, vol. II, fol. 8r)

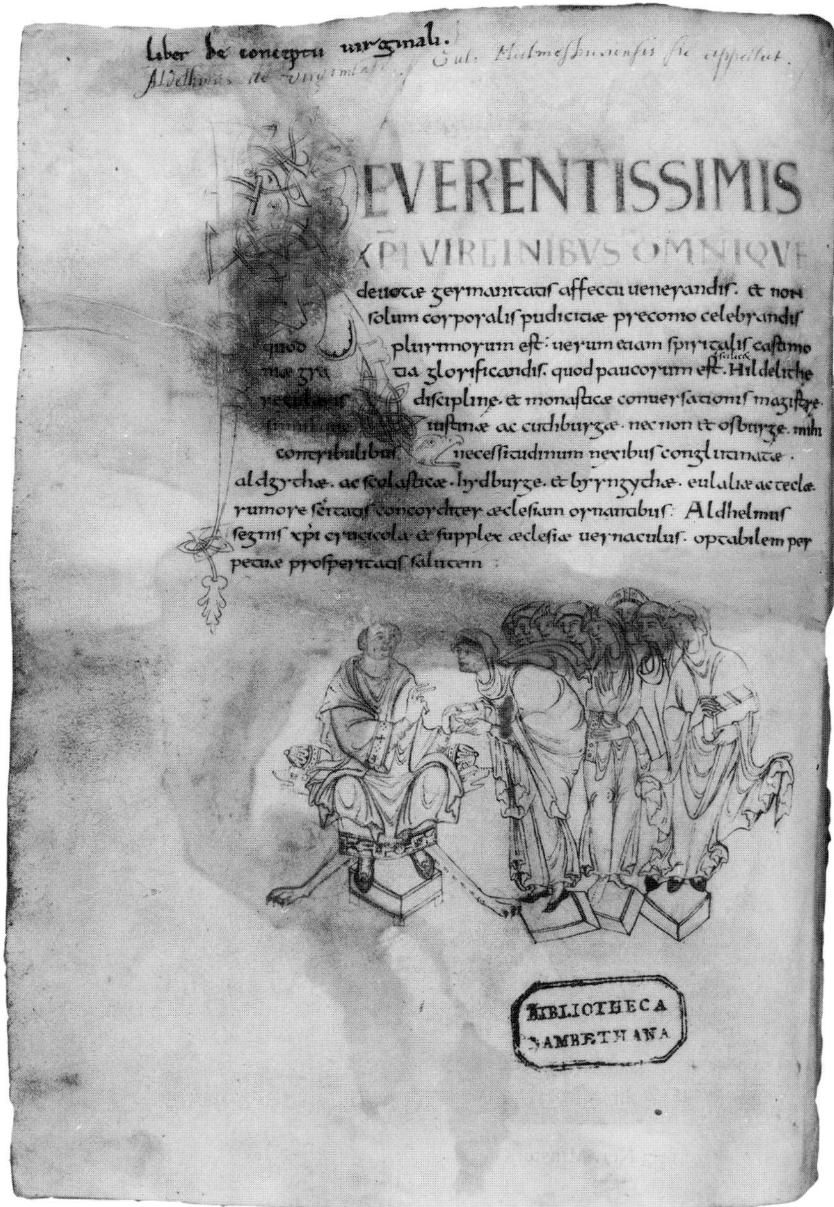

Plate 10.2 Aldhelm, *De virginitate* (Lambeth Palace Library, 200, fol. 68r)

Plate 10.3 New Minster Charter (BL, Cotton Vespasian A.viii, fol. 2v)

Plate 10.4 Benedictional of St Æthelwold (BL, Add. 49598, fol. 102v)

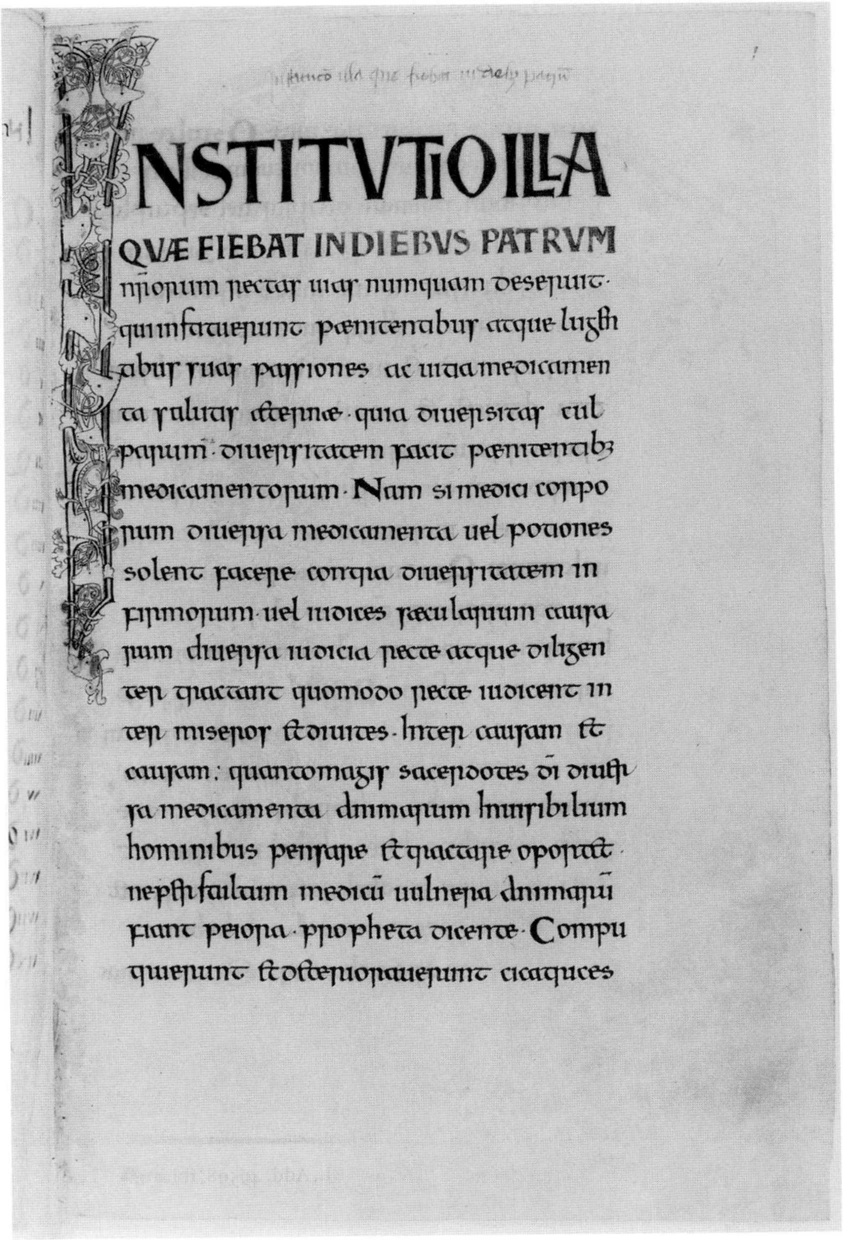

INSTITUTIO ILLA
QUAE FIEBAT IN DIEBUS PATRUM
nriorum rectas uias numquam deseruit·
qui insatiauerunt paenitentibus atque lug
abus suas passiones ac uitia medicamen
ta salutis aeternae· quia diuersitas cul
parum· diuersitatem facit paenitentibus
medicamentorum· Nam si medici corpo
rum diuersa medicamenta uel potiones
solent facere contra diuersitatem in
firmorum· uel iudices saecularium causa
rum diuersa iudicia recte atque diligen
ter tractant quomodo recte iudicent in
ter miseros et diuites· inter causam et
causam; quanto magis sacerdotes dei diuer
sa medicamenta animarum inuisibilium
hominibus pensare et tractare oportet·
ne per stultam scientiam medici uulnera animarum
fiant peiora· propheta dicente· Compu
truerunt et deteriorauerunt cicatrices

Plate 10.5 Penitential (BodL., Bodley 718)

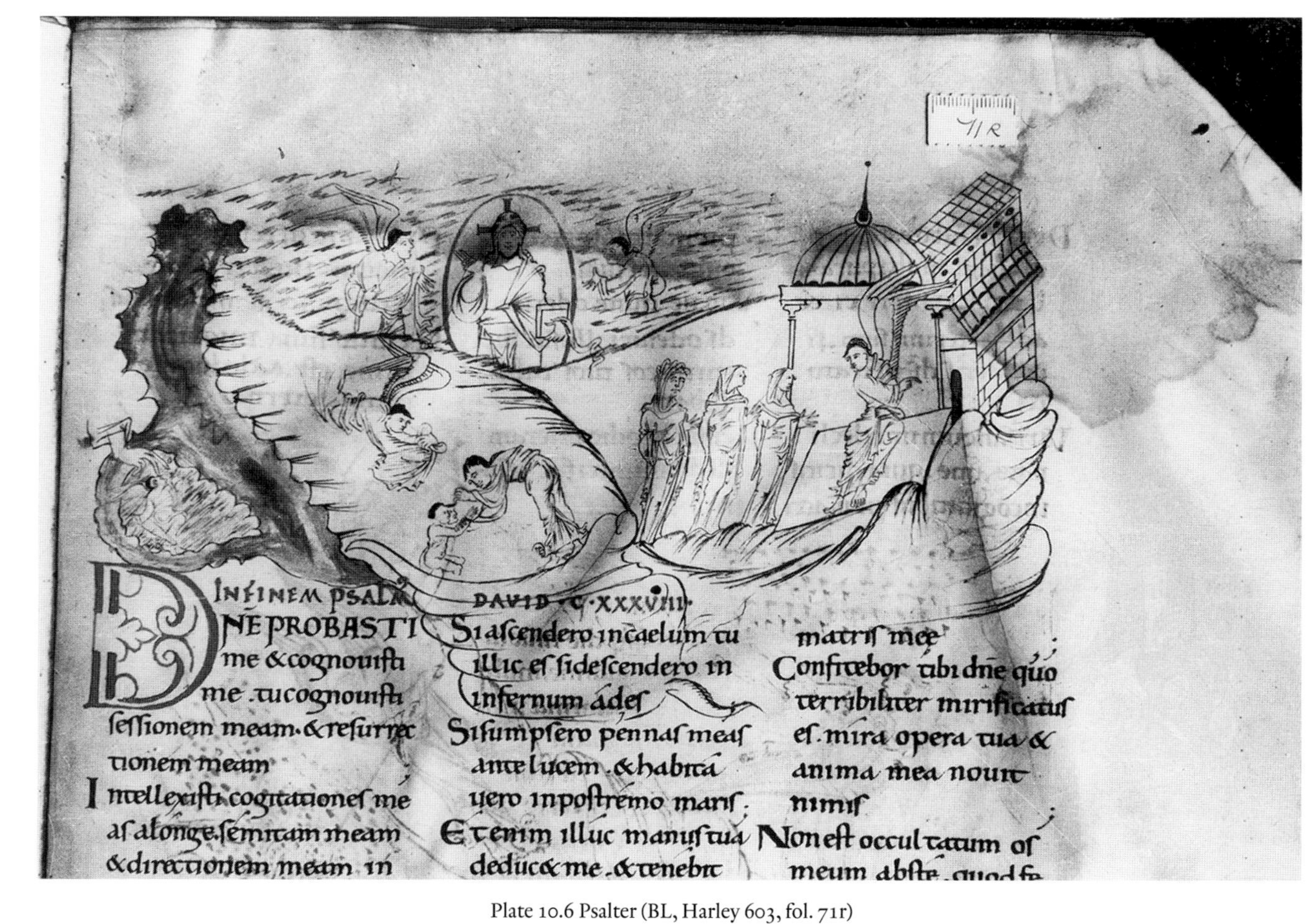

Plate 10.6 Psalter (BL, Harley 603, fol. 71r)

Plate 10.7 Eadwig Gospels (Hanover, Kestner-Museum, W.M.xxia.36, fol. 147v)

Plate 10.8 Grimbald Gospels (BL, Add. 34890, fol. 74r)

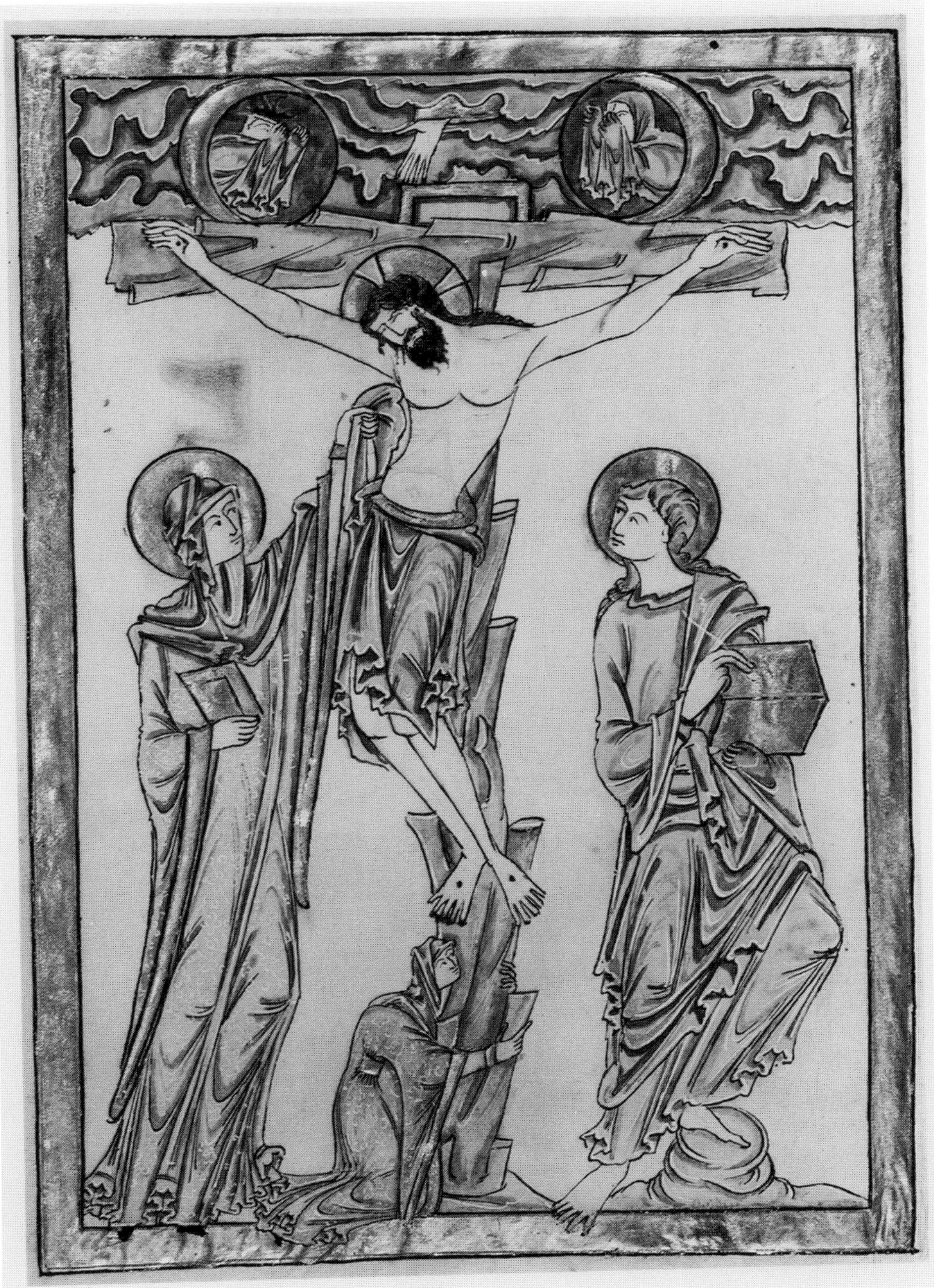

Plate 10.9 Gospels of Judith of Flanders (PML, M 709, fol. 1v)

Plate 10.10 Gospel lectionary of Margaret of Scotland (BodL., Lat. liturg. f.5, fols. 13v+14r)

Plate 10.11 Troper (BL, Cotton Caligula A.xiv, fol. 3v)

Plate 10.12 Herbal and medical texts (BL, Cotton Vitellius C.iii, fol. 11v)

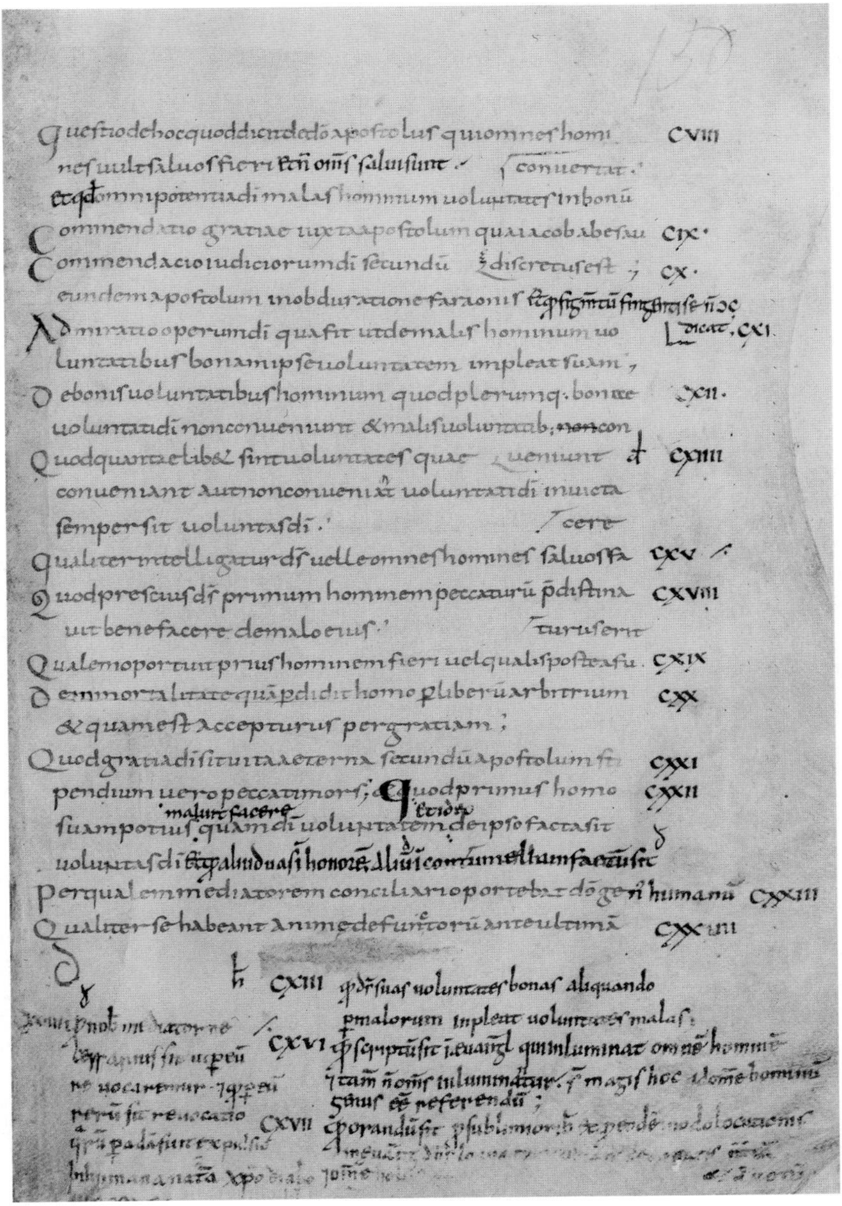

Plate 14.1 Augustine, *Enchiridion*, etc. (Lambeth Palace Library, 237, fol. 150r)

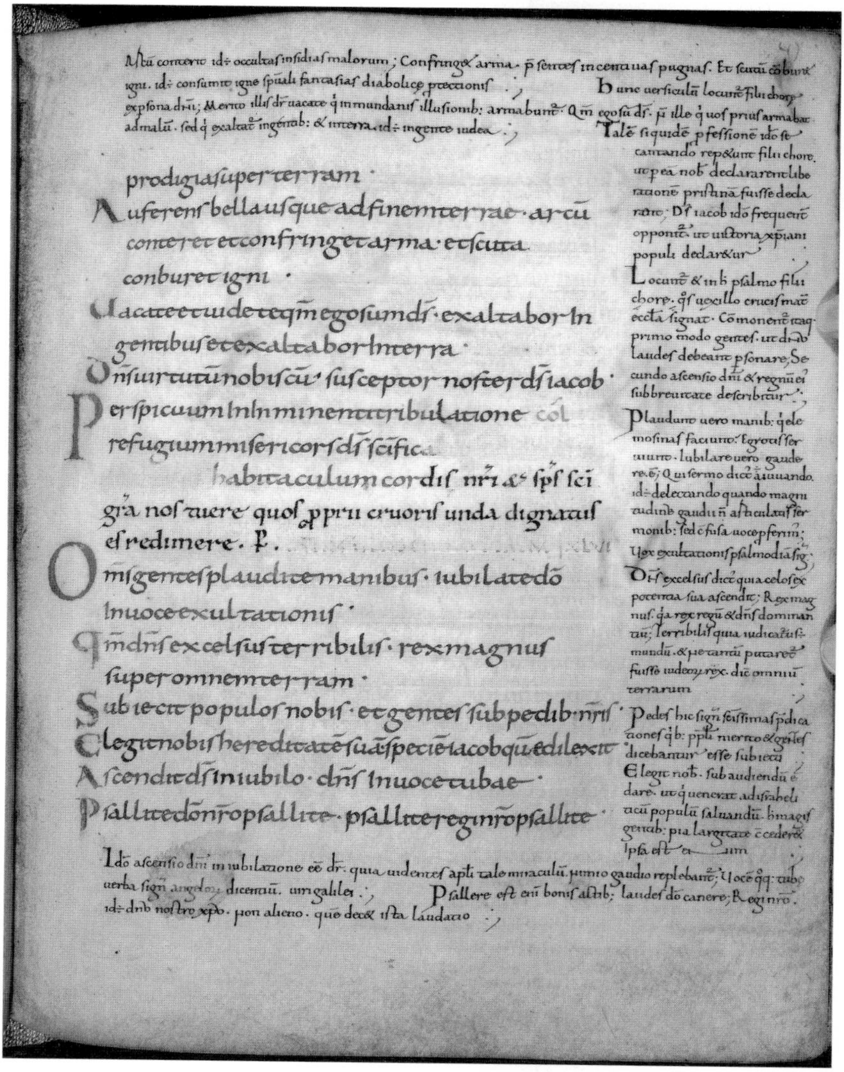

prodigia super terram ·
Auferens bella usque ad finem terrae · arcu
conteret et confringet arma · et scuta
comburet igni ·
Uacate et uidete quoniam ego sum deus · exaltabor in
gentibus et exaltabor in terra ·
Dominus uirtutum nobiscum · susceptor noster deus iacob ·
Perspicuum in inminenti tribulatione
refugium miseris
habitaculum cordis nostri et spiritus sancti
gratia nos tuere quos pretiosi cruoris unda dignatus
es redimere. P.
Omnes gentes plaudite manibus · iubilate deo
in uoce exultationis ·
Quoniam dominus excelsus terribilis · rex magnus
super omnem terram ·
Subiecit populos nobis · et gentes sub pedibus nostris ·
Elegit nobis hereditatem suam speciem iacob quam dilexit
Ascendit deus in iubilo · dominus in uoce tubae ·
Psallite deo nostro psallite · psallite regi nostro psallite ·

Plate 14.2 Psalter (CCCC, 272, fol. 47r)

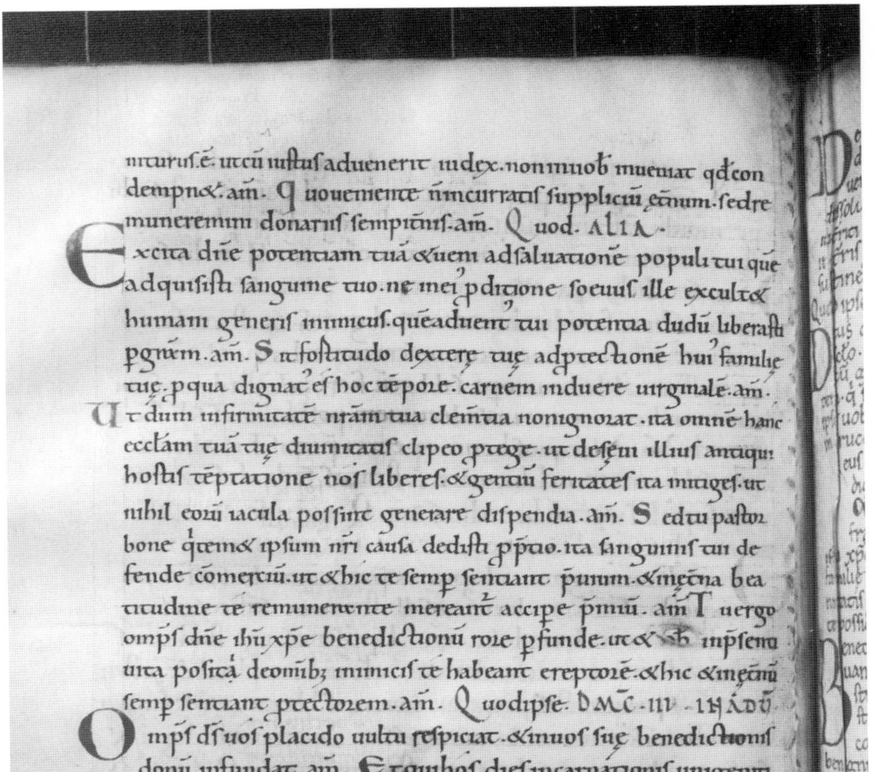

Plate 14.3 Service-book (Alençon, BM, 14, fol. 114v)

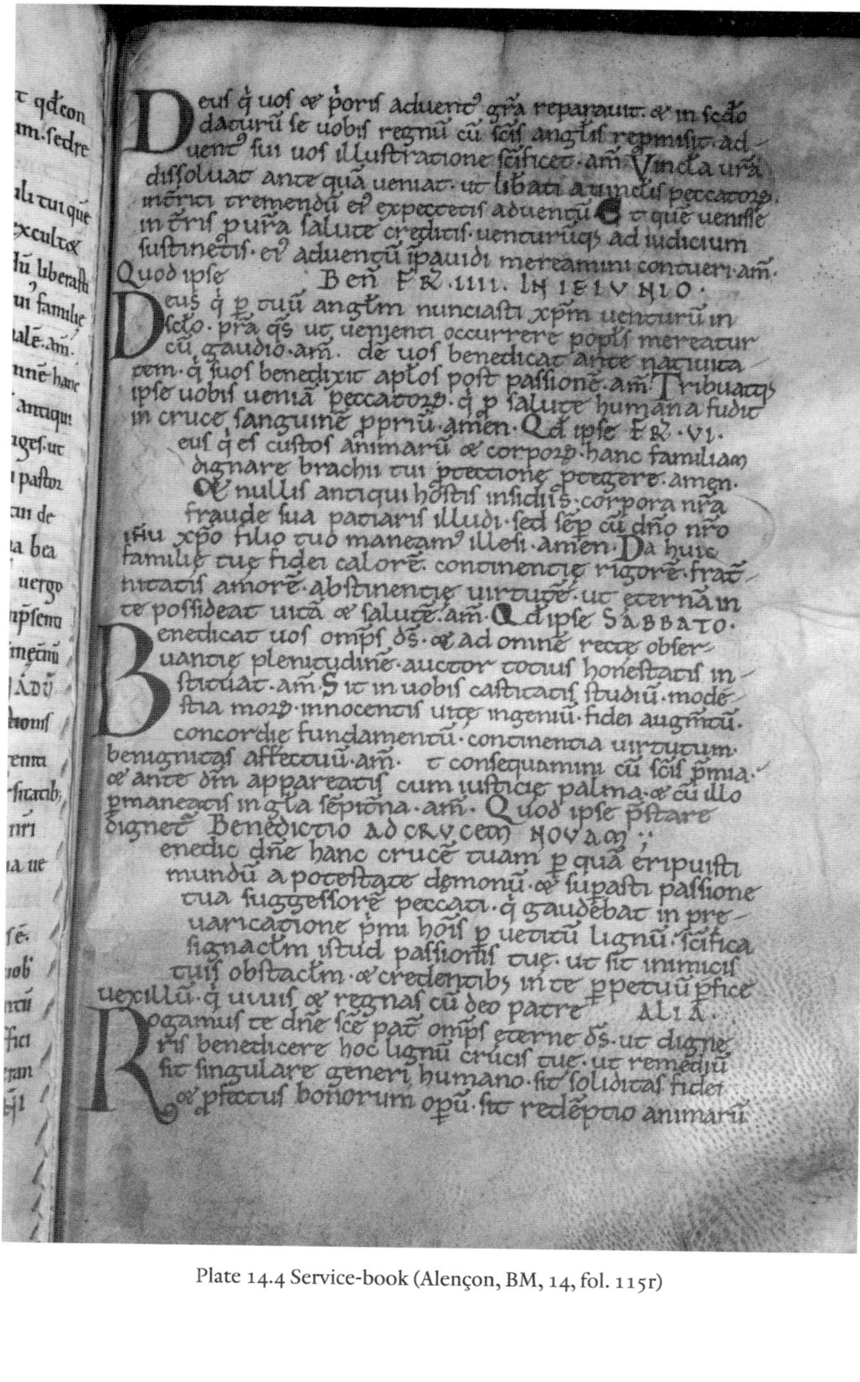

Plate 14.4 Service-book (Alençon, BM, 14, fol. 115r)

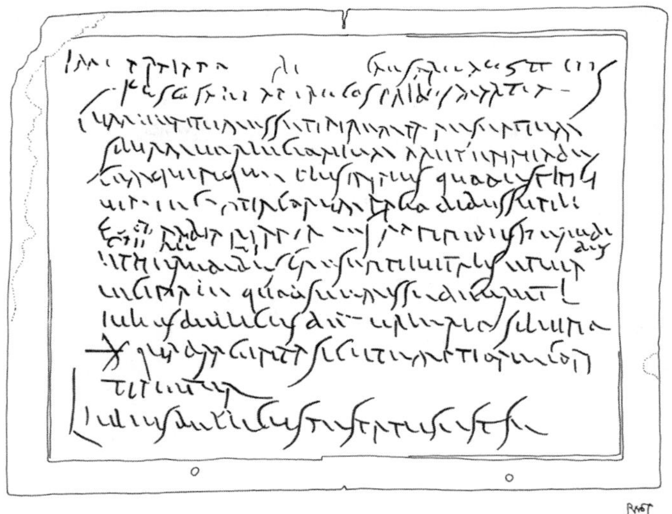

Plate 15.1 London *stilus* tablet, record of court proceedings

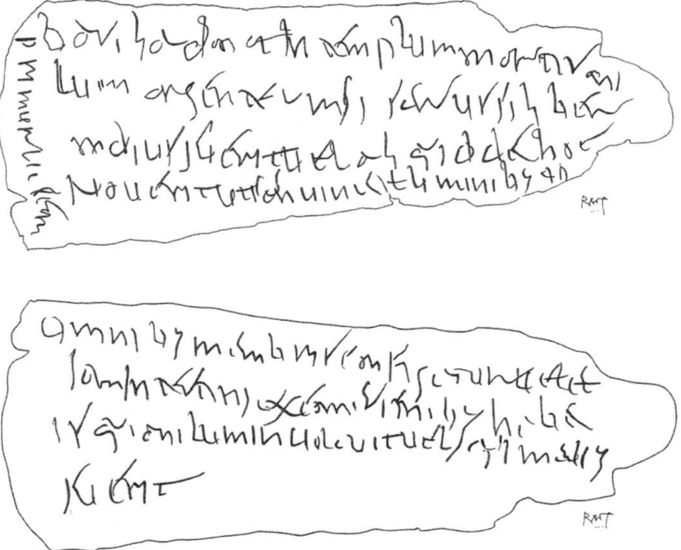

Plate 15.2 Bath 'curse tablet' written by Basilia (*Tab. Sulis* 97)

Plate 15.3 Silchester box tile with graffito *conticuere omnes* (Reading Museum)

Plate 18.1 Arenberg Gospels (PML, M 869, fol. 51v)

Plate 18.2 Gospels of Judith of Flanders (PML, M 709, fol. 2v)

Plate 18.3 Gospel-book (TCC, B.10.4, fol. 17v)

96

mr ccxxxiiii
x

Nouissime recumbentibus illis undecim apparuit. & exprobrauit incredulitatem illorum. & duritiam cordis. Quia his qui uiderant eum resurrexisse non crediderant. Et dixit eis. Euntes in mundum uniuersum. praedicate euangelium omni creaturae. Qui crediderit. & baptizatus fuerit. saluus erit. Qui uero non crediderit. condemnabitur. Signa autem eos qui crediderint. haec sequentur. In nomine meo daemonia eicient. linguis loquentur nouis. serpentes tollent. Et si mortiferum quid biberint. non eis nocebit. Super aegros manus inponent. & bene habebunt. Et dns quidem ihs postquam locutus est eis. assumptus est in caelum. & sedet a dextris di. Illi autem profecti. praedicauerunt ubiq: Dno cooperante. & sermonem confirmante. sequentibus signis.

EXPLICIT EVANGELIUM SECUNDUM MARCUM.

INCIPIUNT CAPITULA.

Zachariae sacerdoti apparuit gabrihel angelus. & annuntiauit ei filium iohannem. & qd iohannes praecederet dnm in spu heliae. & item annuntiauit mariae filium ihm.

Natiuitatem ihu. annuntiat angelus pastoribus. [a]ccepit symeon puerum ihm. & benedixit dm. &

Plate 18.4 Gospel-book (BnF, lat. 272, fol. 96r)

Plate 18.5 Arenberg Gospels (PML, M 869, fol. 11v)

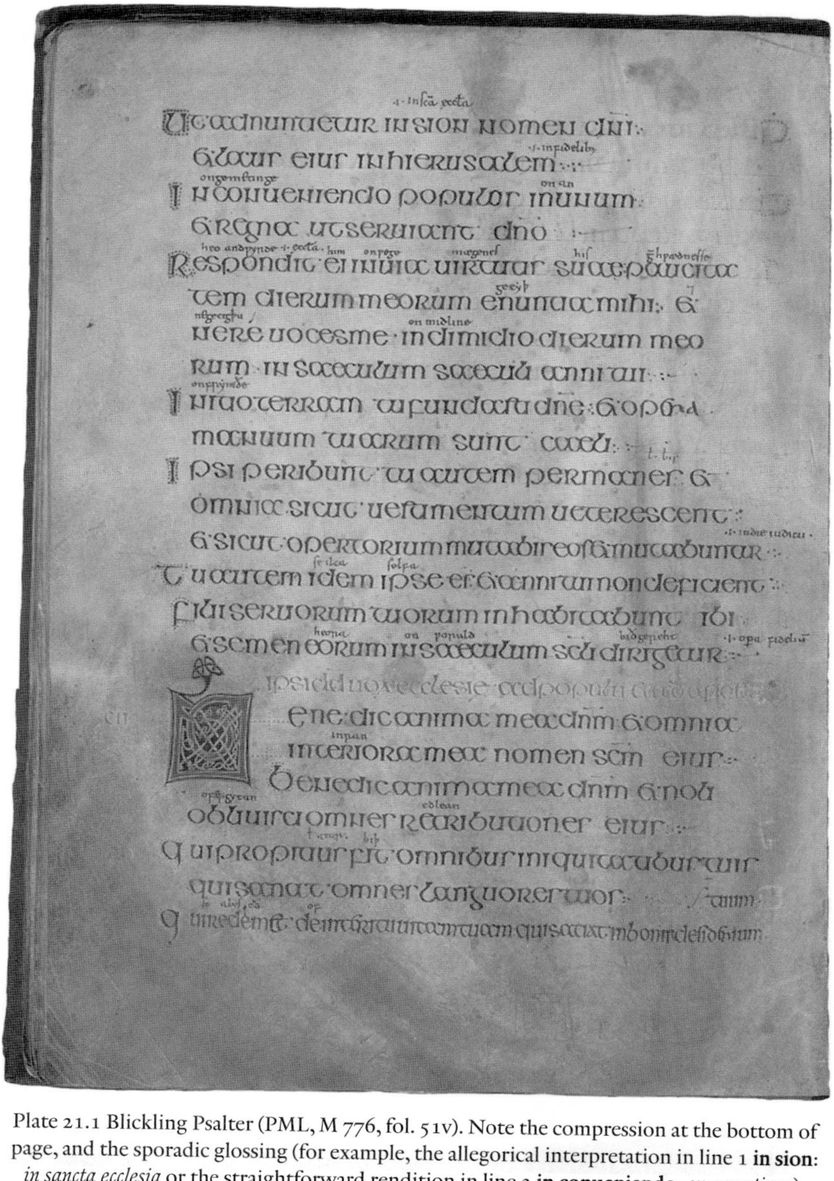

Plate 21.1 Blickling Psalter (PML, M 776, fol. 51v). Note the compression at the bottom of page, and the sporadic glossing (for example, the allegorical interpretation in line 1 **in sion**: *in sancta ecclesia* or the straightforward rendition in line 3 **in conueniendo**: *on gemetinge*).

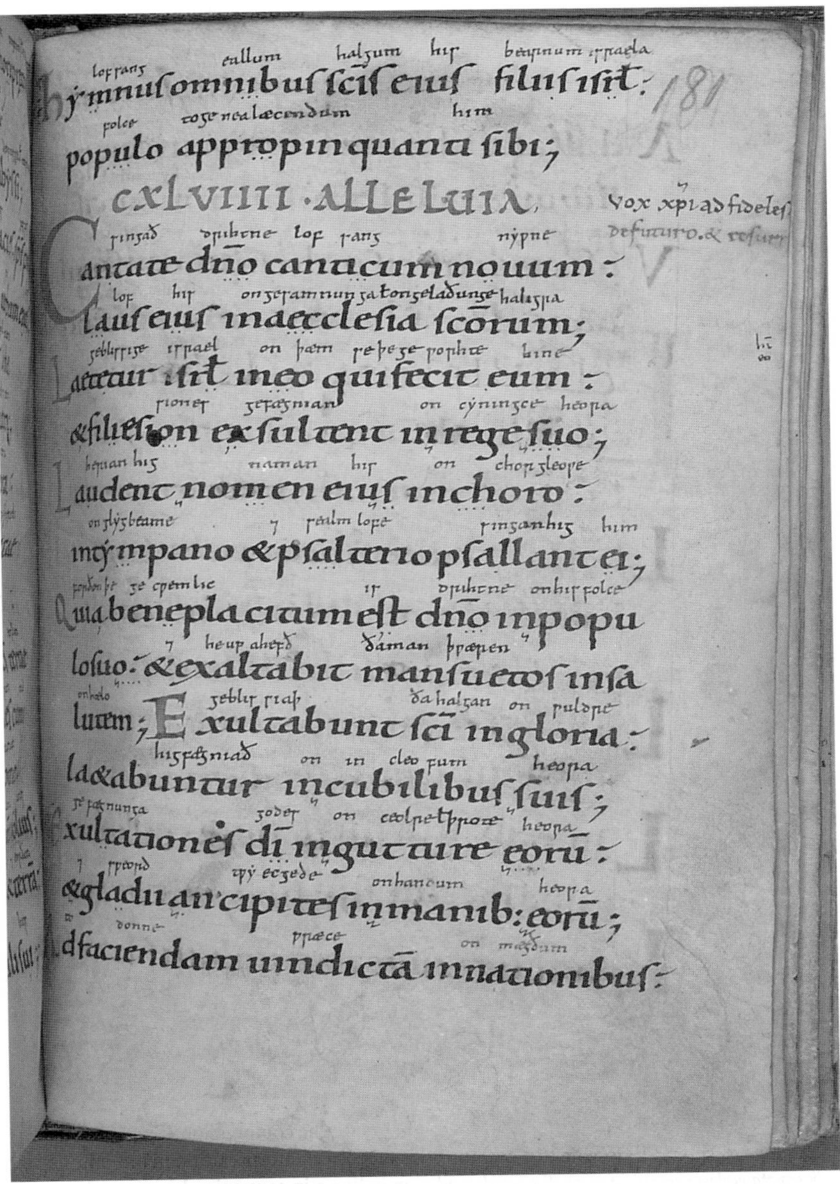
hymnus omnibus scīs eius filiis isrl̄;
populo appropinquanti sibi;
CXLVIIII. ALLELUIA. Vox xpi ad fideles de futuro. & resur
Cantate dn̄o canticum nouum:
laus eius in aecclesia scōrum;
Laetetur isrl̄ in eo qui fecit eum:
& filii sion exsultent in rege suo;
Laudent nomen eius in choro:
in tympano & psalterio psallant ei;
Quia beneplacitum est dn̄o in popu
lo suo: & exaltabit mansuetos in sa
lutem; Exultabunt scī in gloria:
laetabuntur in cubilibus suis;
Exultationes dī in gutture eorū:
& gladii ancipites in manib: eorū;
Ad faciendam uindictā in nationibus:

Plate 21.2 Lambeth Psalter (Lambeth Palace Library, 427, fol. 181r), opening of Psalm 149

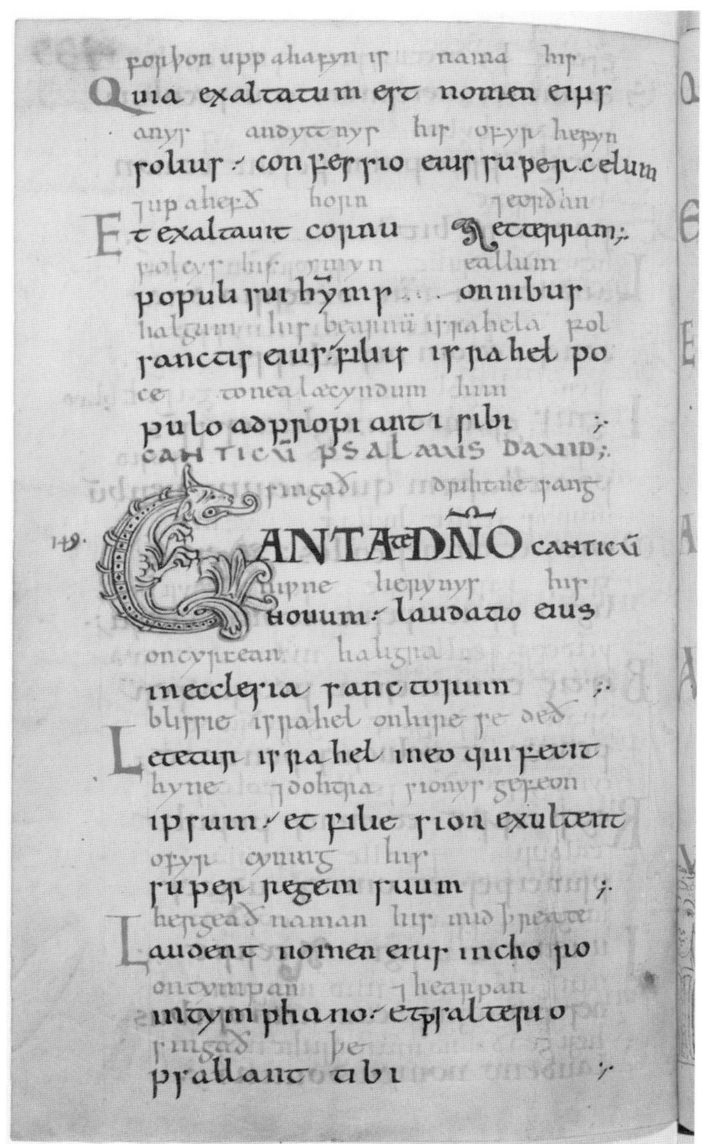

Plate 21.3 Cambridge Psalter (CUL, Ff.1.23, fol. 249v), opening of Psalm 149

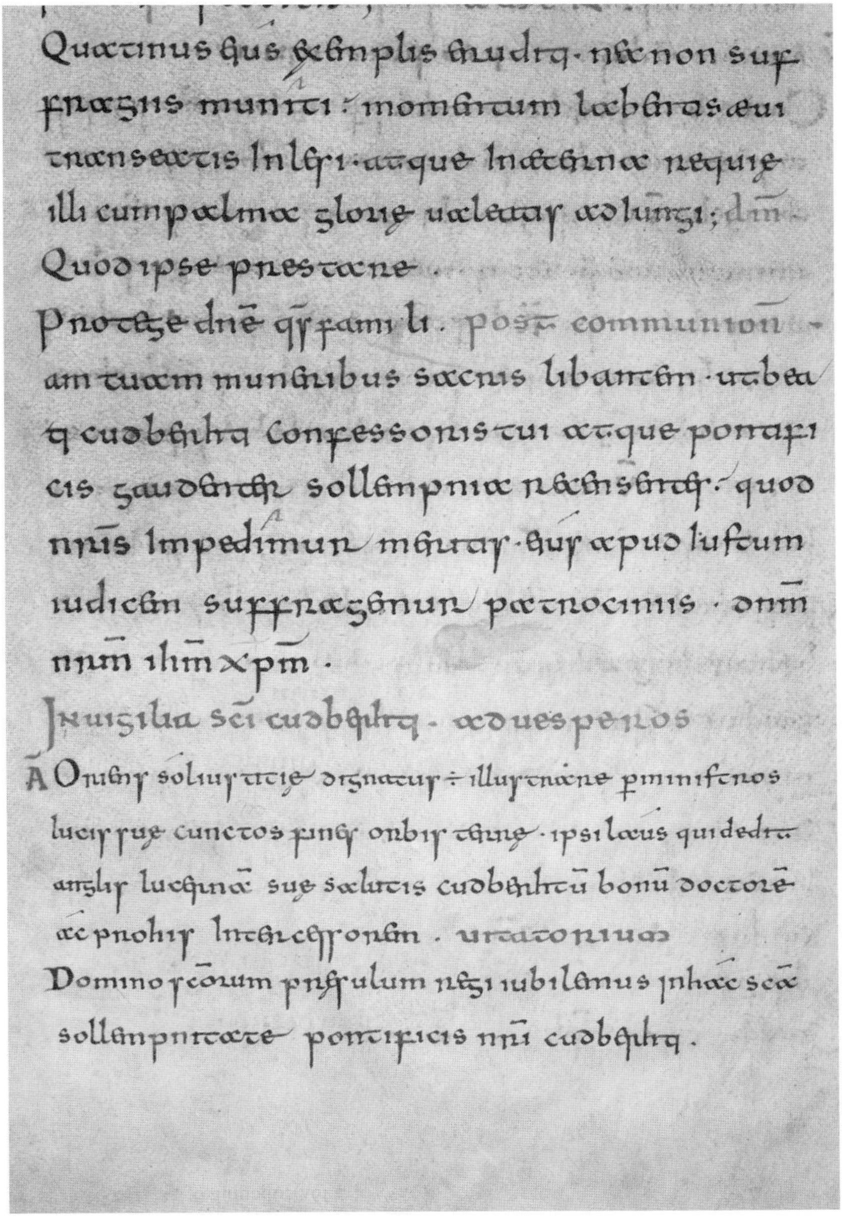
Quatinus eius exemplis eruditi . necnon suf-
fragiis muniti : mortiferas latebras saeculi
transeuntis inlesi . atque incolumes peruenire
illi cum palma glorie ualeatis adiungi ; dm̄
Quod ipse prestare .
Protege dñe quesumus famili . post communion-
am tuam muneribus sacris libantem . ut beati cudbercti confessoris tui atque pontificis gaudentem sollempnia recensentem . quod
nostris impedimur meritis . eius apud iustum
iudicem suffragiorum patrocinus . dnm̄
nrm̄ ihm̄ xpm̄ .
In uigilia sci cudbercti . ad uesperos
A O nimium sollempnitatis dignatur ÷ illustrare primi feros
lucis fue cunctos fines orbis terrae . ipsi laus qui dedit
anglis lucernam sue salutis cudberhtum bonum doctorem
ac pro nobis intercessorem . inuitatorium
Dominum confessorum presulum regi iubilemus in hac sca
sollempnitate pontificis nri cudbercti .

Plate 22.1 Bede, *Vitae Cuthberti* (CCCC, 183, fol. 94r)

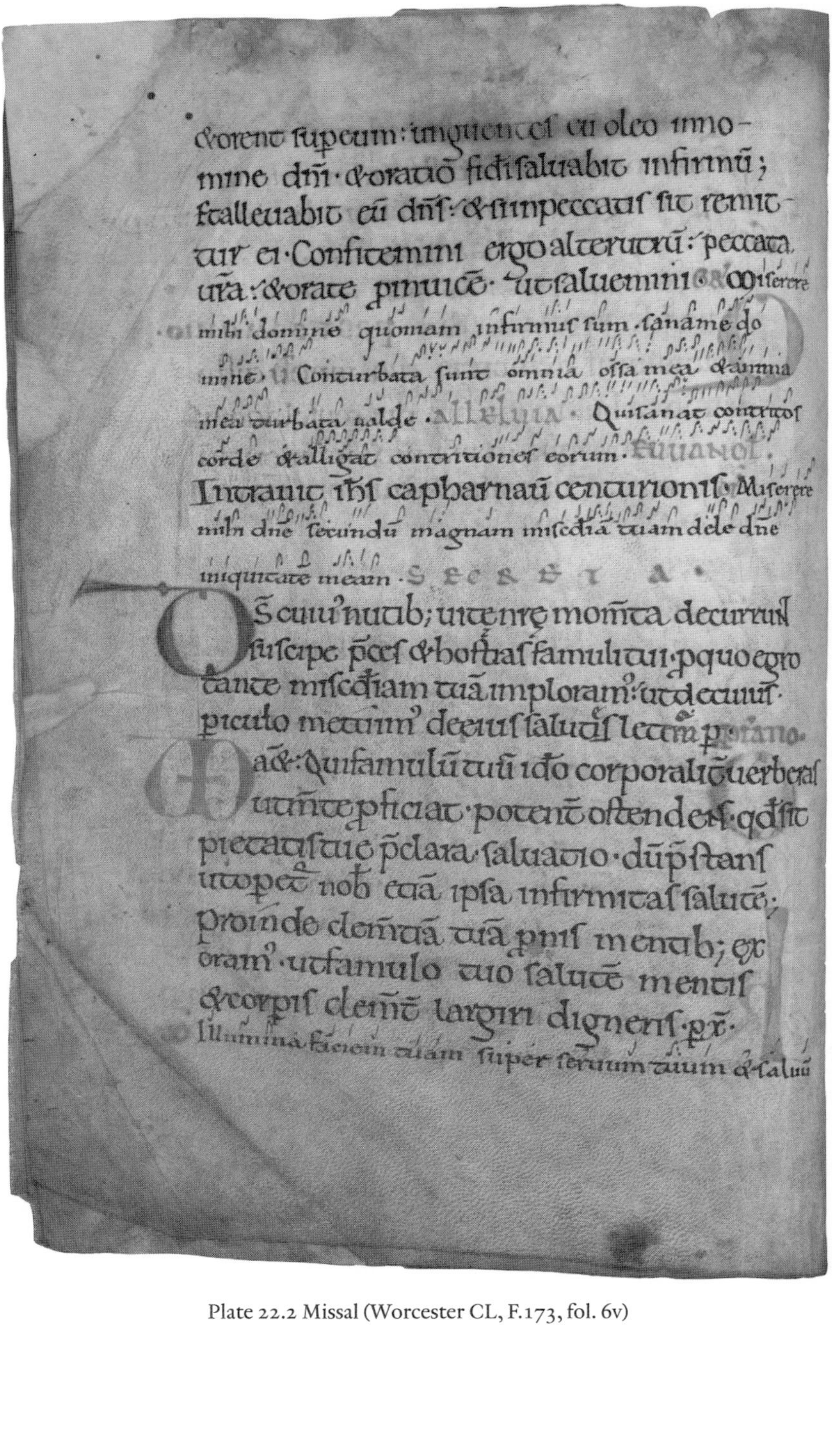

Plate 22.2 Missal (Worcester CL, F.173, fol. 6v)

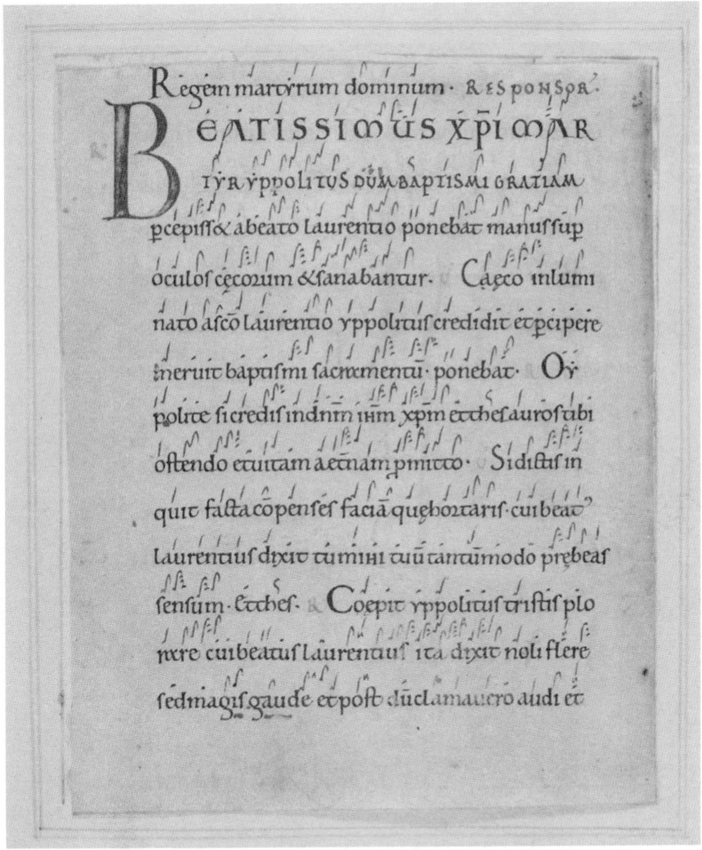

Plate 22.3 Antiphoner (BL, Stowe 1061, fol. 125r)

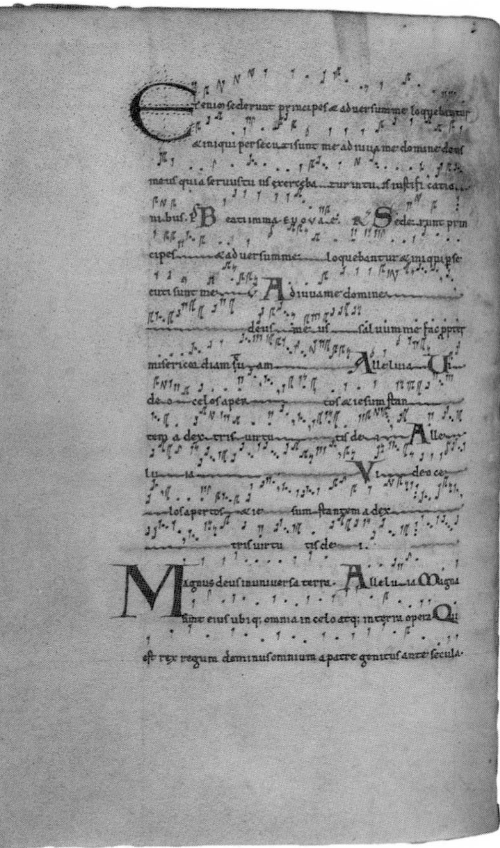

Plate 22.4 Gradual (Durham University Library, Cosin V.v.6, fol. 31v)

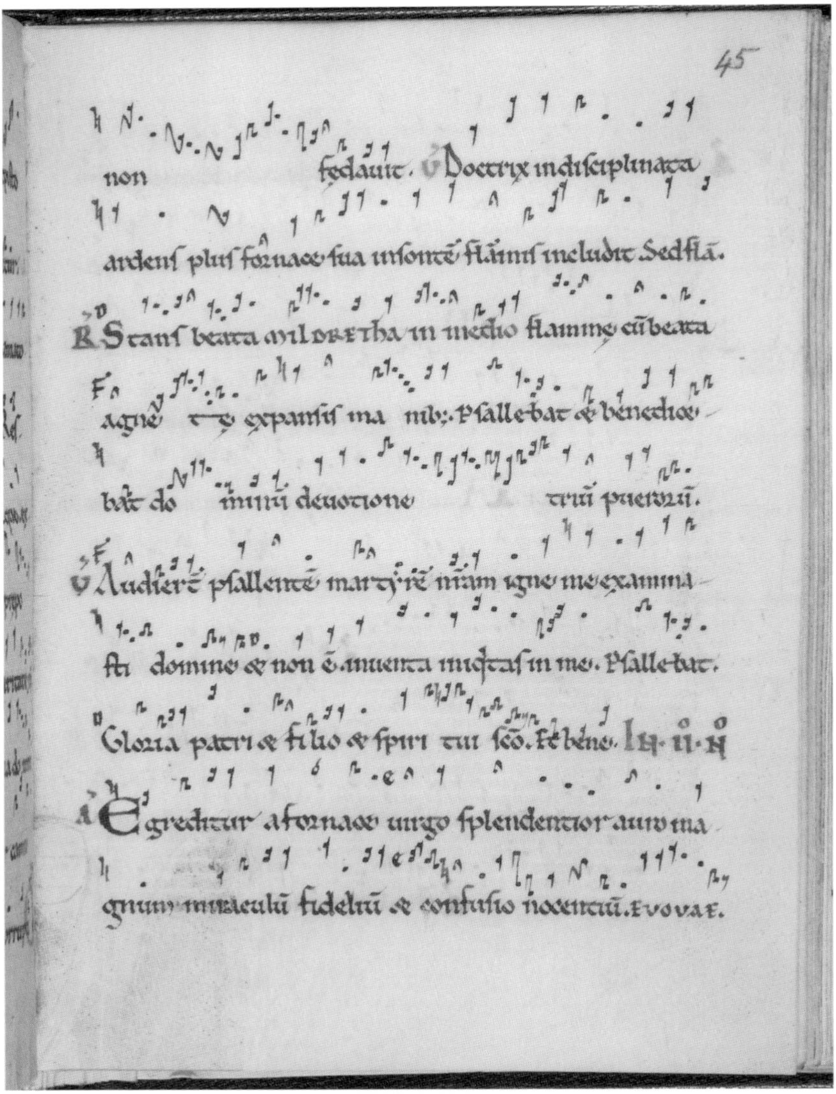

Plate 22.5 Texts for St Mildred (BL, Harley 3908, fol. 45r)